CRIMINAL PROCEDURE
(SCOTLAND) ACT 1995

Other titles in this series:

CRIMINAL PROCEDURE (SCOTLAND) ACT 1995

Sixth Edition

Annotated by:

Iain Bradley

Solicitor Advocate and member of the Crown Office and Procurator Fiscal Service

and

Robert Shiels

Solicitor Advocate and member of the Crown Office and Procurator Fiscal Service

Act of Adjournal (Criminal Procedure Rules) 1996 annotated by

Peter W. Ferguson, Q.C.

First published 1996
Second Edition 1999
Third Edition 2001
Fourth Edition 2005
Fifth Edition 2006

Published in 2007 by W. Green & Son Ltd
21 Alva Street
Edinburgh EH2 4PS

www.wgreen.thomson.com

Printed and bound in Great Britain by
William Clowes Ltd,
Beccles, Suffolk

No natural forests were destroyed to make this product;
only farmed timber was used and replanted

A CIP catalogue record for this book is available from the British Library

ISBN-13   9780 414 01697 2

Annotations © W. Green & Son Ltd 2007

CONTENTS

* * * * * * * *

The content of this book is up-to-date to June 1, 2007.

CRIMINAL PROCEDURE (CONSEQUENTIAL PROVISIONS) (SCOTLAND) ACT 1995

(1995 c. 40)

An Act to make provision for repeals, consequential amendments, transitional and transitory matters and savings in connection with the consolidation of enactments in the Criminal Procedure (Scotland) Act 1995, the Proceeds of Crime (Scotland) Act 1995 and the Criminal Law (Consolidation) (Scotland) Act 1995.

[8th November 1995]

ARRANGEMENT OF SECTIONS

INTRODUCTION AND GENERAL NOTE

[1] The Scots criminal practitioner has had much to think about following recent legislation: the Criminal Justice (Scotland) Act 1995 (c.20) made substantial amendments to the criminal justice system as respects criminal proceedings. Thereafter followed the Criminal Law (Consolidation) (Scotland) 1995 (c.39), the Criminal Procedure (Consequential Provisions) (Scotland) Act 1995 (c.40), the Proceeds of Crime (Scotland) Act 1995 (c.43) and the Criminal Procedure (Scotland) Act 1995 (c.46).

It would be very tempting to ignore the Consequential Provisions Act as being merely "technical law" in that it makes provision for repeals, consequential amendments, transitional and transitory matters and savings in connection with the consolidation of various enactments. However, the Consequential Provisions Act does form part of the series of new Acts, and the greater view can only be obtained by understanding the constituent parts of the change now being brought about.

The Consequential Provisions Act contains seven sections and six Schedules and it is proposed now to outline briefly the nature and effect of each.

Section 1: Interpretation

It is unusual to have the interpretation section at the commencement of an Act. The section provides that the Criminal Procedure (Scotland) Act 1995 is the Principal Act and it, taken with the other new Acts, constitutes the consolidating Acts.

Section 2: Continuity of the law

---

[1] Annotations by Robert S. Shiels, Solicitor in the Supreme Courts of Scotland.

1

The consolidating Acts when taken together do not produce a revolution or a fundamental attack on the criminal justice system of Scotland. An enormous number of individual aspects are, however, changed, sometimes for the effect of the change but often in name to improve the working of the law. Section 2 is statutory confirmation that the change is not intended to affect the continuity of the law. The principle is asserted in subs. (1) and thereafter subss. (2), (3) and (4) underpin the idea that there is or ought to be a smooth progress to the new legislation.

Section 3: Rationalisation of penalties

Criminal offences in statutes are often a reaction to perceived *lacunae* in the options available to prosecutors. The policy decisions prior to such legislation are thus directed at a specific problem. The result is that the statutory criminal law has developed on an *ad hoc* basis with no consistent approach to penalties. The development of sentencing as a coherent and rational subject in itself has required a rationalisation of penalties, hence this section.

Subsection (1) provides that Sched. 1 to the Act shall have effect for the purpose of setting or altering or enabling the Secretary of State to set or alter the various aspects of penalties in statutes.

The *minutiae* of the changes provided for in Sched. 1 reflect the wide variety of statutory provisions to which the rationalising scheme is applied, *e.g.* para. 1 of Sched. 1 deals with amendments relating to penalties and mode of trial for offences made triable only summarily. These offences are made triable only by reason of s.292 of the Principal Act and are specified in Pt. 1 to Sched. 1.

Subsection (2) provides that Sched. 2 to the Act shall have effect for the purpose of amending the enactments specified there.

Schedule 2 is divided into three parts, all of which increase certain penalties. Part 1 concerns offences made triable only summarily. Part II deals with named summary offences and Pt. 3 concerns some summary offences not dealt with in Sched. 1.

Section 4: Transitional, transitory and savings

Section 4 provides that Sched. 3 shall have effect. That Schedule in essence ensures the continuity of the law either by general rules of universal application or specific rules flowing from sections of given Acts.

Practitioners will require to be aware of the possibilities inherent in the changes, *e.g.* para. 2 of Sched. 3 provides that:

> "any document made served or issued after this Act comes into force which contains a reference to any of the repealed enactments shall be construed, except so far as the contrary intention appears, as referring to, as the context may require, including a reference to the corresponding provision of the consolidating Act".

Accordingly, there may be on at least one occasion after April 1, 1996 the service of a certificate of routine evidence in terms of s.26 of and Sched. 1 to the Criminal Justice (Scotland) Act 1980 (c.62) notwithstanding the repeal of that Act of 1980. Paragraph 2 of Sched. 3 operates to provide for an implied reference to s.280 of and Sched. 9 to the Principal Act.

Section 5: Minor and consequential amendments

Section 5 provides that Sched. 4 shall have effect and while many amendments are certainly necessary as a consequence of the repeal of *e.g.* the Criminal Procedure (Scotland) Act 1975 (c.21), not all of the changes are minor. Paragraph 3 so alters the existing law of children to require a register of children found guilty of offences to be kept for every summary court. Again, para. 63 amends the law of legal aid to add to the category of cases with circumstances in which criminal legal aid is available automatically.

Section 6: Repeals

Subsection (1) provides that Sched. 5 shall have effect for the repeals specified in it and it is this authority that ends the life of some old friends, *e.g.* the Summary Jurisdiction (Scotland) Act 1954 (c.48), and a few new ones, *e.g.* the Carrying of Knives etc. (Scotland) Act 1993 (c.13).

Subsection (2) provides that Sched. 6 shall have effect in connection with some sections of the Criminal Procedure (Scotland) Act 1975 specified there. The section provides that the repeal of the specified sections shall not revive any rule of law or practice having effect before the coming into force of the Criminal Procedure (Scotland) Act 1887 (c.35).

Section 7: Commencement

Subsection (2) provides that this Act shall come into force on April 1, 1996.

Abbreviation

The Principal Act: Criminal Procedure (Scotland) Act 1995 (c.46).

Parliamentary Debates

Hansard, H.L. Vol. 565, col. 15; Vol. 566, cols. 385, 582, 894. H.C. Vol. 265, col. 183.

Interpretation

1. In this Act—

"the consolidating Acts" means the Principal Act, the Proceeds of Crime (Scotland) Act 1995, the Criminal Law (Consolidation) (Scotland) Act 1995 and, so far as it reproduces the effect of the repealed enactments, this Act;

"the Principal Act" means the Criminal Procedure (Scotland) Act 1995"; and

"the repealed enactments" means the enactments repealed by this Act.

Continuity of the law

2.—(1) The substitution of the consolidating Acts for the repealed enactments does not affect the continuity of the law.

(2) Anything done or having effect as if done under or for the purposes of a provision of the repealed enactments has effect, if it could have been done under or for the purposes of the corresponding provision of the consolidating Acts, as if done under or for the purposes of that provision.

(3) Any reference, whether express or implied, in any enactment, instrument or document to a provision of the consolidating Acts shall, so far as the context permits, be construed as including, in relation to the times, circumstances and purposes in relation to which the corresponding provision of the repealed enactments has effect, a reference to that corresponding provision.

(4) Any reference, whether express or implied, in any enactment, instrument or document to a provision of the repealed enactments shall be construed, so far as is required for continuing its effect, as including a reference to the corresponding provision of the consolidating Acts.

Rationalisation of penalties

3.—(1) Schedule 1 to this Act shall have effect for the purpose of setting or altering or enabling the Secretary of State to set or alter the penalties or maximum penalties in respect of certain offences or classes or descriptions of offences.

(2) Schedule 2 to this Act shall have effect for the purpose of amending the enactments there specified for the purposes of and in accordance with the provisions of the said Schedule 1.

Transitional, transitory and savings

4. The transitional provisions, transitory modifications and savings contained in Schedule 3 to this Act shall have effect.

Minor and consequential amendments

5. The enactments mentioned in Schedule 4 to this Act shall have effect subject to the amendments there specified being amendments consequential on this Act.

Repeals

6.—(1) The enactments mentioned in Schedule 5 to this Act are hereby repealed to the extent specified in the third column of that Schedule.

(2) Without prejudice to section 16(1)(a) of the Interpretation Act 1978, the repeal by this Act of the provisions of the Criminal Procedure (Scotland) Act 1975 specified in Schedule 6 to this Act shall not revive any rule of law or practice having effect before the coming into force of the Criminal Procedure (Scotland) Act 1887.

Short title, interpretation, commencement and extent

7.—(1) This Act may be cited as the Criminal Procedure (Consequential Provisions) (Scotland) Act 1995.

(2) This Act shall come into force on 1 April 1996.

(3) Subject to subsections (4) and (5) below, this Act extends to Scotland only.

(4) Paragraph 5 of Schedule 3 to this Act and this section also extend to England and Wales and Northern Ireland.

(5) Any amendment contained in Schedule 4 to this Act of any enactment which extends to England and Wales or Northern Ireland shall also so extend.

SCHEDULES

Section 3(1)   SCHEDULE 1

SETTING AND ALTERATION OF CERTAIN PENALTIES

Amendments relating to penalties and mode of trial for offences made triable only summarily

1.—(1) The enactments specified in column 2 of Part I of Schedule 2 to this Act (which relate to the modes of trial of, and the maximum penalties for, the offences which are by section 292 of the Principal Act made triable only summarily) shall continue to have effect subject to the amendments specified in column 3 of that Part.

(2) The said amendments have the effect of altering the maximum penalties available on summary conviction of those offences as well as making alterations consequential on their becoming triable only summarily; and in that Part, column 4 shows the maximum penalties resulting from the amendments.

Penalties on summary conviction for offences triable either summarily or on indictment

2.—(1) Where an offence created by a relevant enactment may be tried either on indictment or summarily, the penalty or maximum penalty on summary conviction shall, to the extent that it included, immediately before the commencement of section 55 of the Criminal Justice Act 1982, a penalty or maximum penalty mentioned in column 1 of the Table below, be amended so as to substitute as a maximum penalty the corresponding penalty set forth in column 2 thereof (unless provision is expressly made by any enactment for a larger penalty or maximum penalty on summary conviction)—

Column 1		Column 2	
Penalty or maximum penalty at commencement of section 55 of Criminal Justice Act 1982		New maximum penalty	
1.	Fine (other than a fine specified in paragraph 3 below, or a fine in respect of each period of a specified length during which a continuing offence is committed).	1.	Fine not exceeding the prescribed sum.
2.	Imprisonment for a period exceeding 3 months.	2.	Imprisonment for a period not exceeding 3 months.

4

	Column 1		Column 2
3.	Fine in respect of a specified quantity or number of things.	3.	Fine not exceeding the prescribed sum in respect of each such quantity or number.
4.	Fine exceeding £100 in respect of each period of a specified length during which a continuing offence is committed.	4.	Fine not exceeding £100 in respect of each such period.

(2) Where by virtue of a relevant enactment, a person summarily convicted of any offence to which sub-paragraph (1) above relates would, apart from this paragraph, be liable to a fine or a maximum fine of one amount in the case of a first conviction and of a different amount in the case of a second or subsequent conviction, sub-paragraph (1) above shall apply irrespective of whether the conviction is a first, second or subsequent one.

(3) Sub-paragraph (1) above is without prejudice to section 5 of the Principal Act (6 months' imprisonment competent for certain offences).

(4) In this paragraph "relevant enactment" means an enactment contained in the Criminal Law Act 1977 or in any other Act (including this Act).

(5) Sub-paragraph (1) of paragraph 7 below shall not affect so much of any enactment as (in whatever words) provides for a person to be made liable, on summary conviction, to a fine or a maximum fine for each period of a specified length during which a continuing offence is committed.

(6) Where an enactment to which sub-paragraph (1) of the said paragraph 7 below applies provides for a person to be made liable to a penalty or a maximum penalty on summary conviction of an offence triable either on indictment or summarily which includes a fine or a maximum fine in respect of a specified quantity or a specified number of things, that sub-paragraph shall apply to that fine or maximum fine.

(7) Sub-paragraph (1) above shall not apply on summary conviction of any of the offences mentioned in sub-paragraph (2) of paragraph 11 below.

Increase of fines for certain summary offences

3.—(1) The enactments specified in column 2 of Part II of Schedule 2 to this Act, which relate to the maximum fines for the offences mentioned (and broadly described) in column I of that Schedule, shall have effect as if the maximum fine that may be imposed on summary conviction of any offence so mentioned were a fine not exceeding the amount specified in column 4 of that Schedule instead of a fine not exceeding the amount specified in column 3 of that Schedule (being the amount of the maximum fine in respect of the offence immediately before the passing of the Criminal Law Act 1977), but this sub-paragraph shall not alter the maximum daily fine, if any, provided for by any of those enactments.

(2) In section 203 of the Local Government (Scotland) Act 1973 (offences against byelaws), except as applied to byelaws made under any provision contained in a local or private Act other than by a local authority, for any reference to £20 there shall be substituted a reference to £50.

(3) Subject to sub-paragraph (4) below, this sub-paragraph applies to any pre-1949 enactment however framed or worded which—

(a) as regards any summary offence makes a person liable on conviction thereof to a fine of, or not exceeding, a specified amount less than £50 which has not been altered since the end of 1948 (and is not altered by this Act); or

(b) confers power by subordinate instrument to make a person, as regards any summary offence (whether or not created by the instrument), liable on conviction thereof to a fine of, or a maximum fine of, less than £50 which has not been altered since the end of 1948 (and is not altered by this Act).

(4) Sub-paragraph (3) above does not apply to any offence to which section 292(2)(b) of the Principal Act applies (offences triable only summarily other than by virtue of express provision).

(5) Every enactment to which sub-paragraph (3) above applies shall have effect as if for the specified amount less than £50 there mentioned there were substituted—

(a) £25 if the specified amount is less than £20; or

(b) £50 if the specified amount is not less that £20.

(6) Where, by virtue of any enactment to which sub-paragraph (3) above applies by virtue of sub-sub-paragraph (a) of that sub-paragraph, a person convicted, of a summary offence would, apart from

this paragraph, be liable to a fine, or maximum fine, of one amount in the case of a first conviction and of a different amount in the case of a second or subsequent conviction, sub-paragraph (5) above shall apply separately in relation to each specified amount less than £50, even if this produces the same instead of different amounts for different convictions.

(7) Sub-paragraph (3) above does not apply to so much of any enactment as in whatever words, makes a person liable or provides for a person to be made liable, on summary conviction, to a fine or a maximum fine for each period of a specified length during which a continuing offence is committed.

(8) Where an enactment to which sub-paragraph (3) above applies provides or confers a power to provide for, on conviction of an offence triable only summarily, a fine or a maximum fine in respect of a specified quantity or a specified number of things, "the specified amount" for the purposes of subsection (5) above is the fine or maximum fine so provided or for which provision may be made.

(9) In sub-paragraph (3) above "pre-1949 enactment" means an enactment passed before 1st January 1949 or an enactment passed on or after that date which whether directly or, through successive re-enactments, indirectly re-enacts with or without modification an enactment passed before that date.

(10) In this paragraph, "enactment" does not include an enactment contained in an order, regulation or other instrument made under an Act.

Penalties for first and subsequent convictions of summary offences to be the same

4.—(1) Subject to sub-paragraphs (2) to (4) and (6) below, this paragraph applies where any enactment—

  (a) makes a person liable on conviction of an offence triable only summarily to a penalty or a maximum penalty; or

  (b) confers a power by subordinate instrument to make a person liable on conviction of an offence triable only summarily (whether or not created by the instrument) to a penalty or a maximum penalty,

which is different in the case of a second or subsequent conviction from the penalty or maximum penalty provided or for which provision may be made in the case of a first conviction.

(2) Where the penalty or maximum penalty for an offence to which section 292(2)(b) of the Principal Act applies has not been altered by any enactment passed or made after 29th July 1977 (the date of the passing of the Criminal Law Act 1977), this paragraph applies as if the amount referred to in sub-paragraph (5)(a) below were the greatest amount to which a person would have been liable on any conviction immediately before that date.

(3) Where any enactment—

  (a) provides or confers a power to provide for a penalty or a maximum penalty which would, but for the operation of paragraph 3(5) above, be different in the case of a second or subsequent conviction from the penalty or maximum penalty provided for or for which provision may be made in the case of a first conviction; and

  (b) otherwise fulfils the conditions of sub-paragraph (1) above;

this paragraph applies to that penalty or maximum penalty as if the amount referred to in sub-paragraph (5)(a) below were the greatest amount to which a person would have been liable or could have been made liable on any conviction immediately before 17th July 1978 (the date of coming into force of section 289C of the Criminal Procedure (Scotland) Act 1975).

(4) This paragraph does not apply to—

  (a) section 5(3) of the Principal Act (imprisonment for certain offences);

  (b) section 78 of the Criminal Justice (Scotland) Act 1980 (vandalism); or

  (c) an enactment mentioned in Part III of Schedule 2 to this Act.

(5) Where this paragraph applies the maximum penalty to which a person is or may be made liable by or under the enactment in the case of any conviction shall be either or both of—

  (a) a fine not exceeding the greatest amount;

  (b) imprisonment for a term not exceeding the longest term (if any),

to which an offender would have been liable or could have been made liable on any conviction (whether the first or a second or subsequent conviction) by or under the enactment immediately before the relevant date.

(6) This paragraph does not affect the penalty which may be imposed in respect of an offence committed before the relevant date.

(7) In sub-paragraphs (5) and (6) above "the relevant date" means—

  (a) in relation to an offence created by or under an Act or, as the case may be, to conviction of such an offence, 11th April 1983; and

  (b) in relation to an offence created under a subordinate instrument or, as the case may be, to conviction of such an offence, 12th October 1988.

Increases of fines for certain summary offences

5.—(1) Subject to sub-paragraphs (3) to (8) and (10) below, this paragraph applies where any Act passed on or before 29th July 1977 (the date of the passing of the Criminal Law Act 1977)—

  (a) makes a person liable on conviction of an offence triable only summarily to a fine or a maximum fine which is less than £1,000; or

  (b) confers a power by subordinate instrument to make a person liable on conviction of an offence triable only summarily (whether or not created by the instrument) to a fine or a maximum fine which is less than £1,000, or a fine or a maximum fine which shall not exceed an amount of less than £1,000,

and the fine or maximum fine which may be imposed or, as the case may be, for which the subordinate instrument may provide has not been altered by any provision mentioned in sub-paragraph (2) below.

(2) The provisions referred to in sub-paragraph (1) above are—

  (a) paragraph 1 above;

  (b) paragraph 3 above (except where paragraph 4(3) above applies);

  (c) section 30(3) of the Criminal Law Act 1977;

  (d) an enactment passed or made after 29th July 1977 and before 11th April 1983.

(3) In the case of an offence to which section 292(2)(b) of the Principal Act applies, sub-paragraphs (2)(a) to (c) above do not apply and the fine or the maximum fine referred to in sub-paragraph (9) below is the fine or the maximum fine for the offence immediately before 29th July 1977 as amended, where applicable, by paragraph 4 above.

(4) This paragraph also applies where any enactment—

  (a) is contained in a consolidation Act passed after 29th July 1977 and before 11th April 1983; and

  (b) otherwise fulfils the conditions of sub-paragraph (1) above as amended by sub-paragraph (3) above where it applies; and

  (c) is a re-enactment (with or without modification) of an enactment passed on or before 29th July 1977.

(5) Subject to sub-paragraph (10) below, where an Act provides or confers a power to provide for, on conviction of an offence triable only summarily, a fine or a maximum fine in respect of a specified quantity or a specified number of things, that fine or maximum fine is the fine or, as the case may be, the maximum fine for the purposes of this paragraph.

(6) Where an Act to which this paragraph applies provides or confers a power to provide different fines or maximum fines in relation to different circumstances or persons of different descriptions, such fines or maximum fines are to be treated separately for the purposes of this paragraph.

(7) This paragraph also applies where the penalties or maximum penalties provided or for which provision may be made by or under an Act on first and on second or subsequent conviction of an offence have been made the same by operation of paragraph 4 above; and in that case the fine or the maximum fine referred to in sub-paragraph (9) below is the maximum fine to which a person is or may be made liable by virtue of that paragraph.

(8) This paragraph does not apply in the case of—

  (a) so much of any Act as (in whatever words) makes a person liable or provides for a person to be made liable to a fine or a maximum fine for each period of a specified length during which a continuing offence is committed;

  (b) section 67(3) of the Transport Act 1962;

  (c) sections 42(1) and 47(1) of the Road Traffic Act 1988;

  (d) an enactment mentioned in Schedule 1 to the British Railways Act 1977 to the extent that the enactment was amended by section 13(1) of that Act;

  (e) an enactment mentioned in Part III of Schedule 2 to this Act or in Schedule 2 to the Criminal Justice Act 1982.

(9) Where this paragraph applies, the fine or, as the case may be, the maximum fine to which a person is or may be made liable by or under the Act shall be increased to the amount shown in column 2 of the Table below opposite the band in column 1 within which the fine or the maximum fine referred to in sub-paragraph (1) above falls.

Column 1	Column 2
Fine or maximum fine	Increased amount
Under £25	£25
Under £50 but not less than £25	£50

Column 1	Column 2
Under £200 but not less than £50	£200
Under £400 but not less than £200	£500
Under £1,000 but not less than £400	£1,000

(10) Where an Act to which this paragraph applies provides or confers a power to provide for, on conviction of an offence triable only summarily, a fine or a maximum fine in respect of a specified quantity or a specified number of things but also provides or confers a power to provide for an alternative fine or maximum fine as regards the offence, sub-paragraph (9) above shall have effect to increase—

    (a) the alternative fine; and

    (b) any amount that the Act provides or confers a power to provide for as the maximum which a fine as regards the offence may not exceed,

as well as the fine or maximum fine which it has effect to increase by virtue of sub-paragraph (5) above.

Standard scale: amendment of enactments

6.—(1) Subject to sub-paragraph (5) below, where—

    (a) an enactment to which sub-paragraph (2) below applies either—

        (i) makes a person liable on conviction of an offence triable only summarily (whether created by that enactment or otherwise) to a fine or a maximum fine; or

        (ii) confers a power by subordinate instrument to make a person liable on conviction of an offence triable only summarily (whether or not created by the instrument) to a fine or a maximum fine; and

    (b) the amount of the fine or the maximum fine is, whether by virtue of that enactment or otherwise, an amount shown in the second column of the standard scale,

for the reference in the enactment to the amount of the fine or maximum fine there shall be substituted a reference to the level on the standard scale shown in the first column thereof as corresponding to the amount in the second column thereof referred to in sub-sub-paragraph (b) above.

(2) This sub-paragraph applies to an enactment in any Act passed before 11th April 1983.

(3) Subject to sub-paragraph (4) below, where an Act provides or confers a power to provide for, on conviction of an offence triable only summarily, a fine or a maximum fine in respect of a specified quantity or a specified number of things, that fine or maximum fine is the fine or, as the case may be, the maximum fine for the purposes of this paragraph.

(4) Where an Act provides or confers a power to provide for, on conviction of an offence triable only summarily, a fine or a maximum fine in respect of a specified quantity or a specified number of things but also provides or confers a power to provide for an alternative fine or maximum fine as regards the offence the fine or the maximum fine for the purposes of this paragraph is—

    (a) the alternative fine; and

    (b) any amount that the Act provides or confers a power to provide for as the maximum which a fine as regards the offence may not exceed.

as well as the fine or maximum fine referred to in sub-paragraph (3) above.

(5) Sub-paragraph (1) above does not apply to so much of any Act as (in whatever words) makes a person liable or provides for a person to be made liable to a fine or a maximum fine for each period of a specified length during which a continuing offence is committed.

(6) Where an enactment to which sub-paragraph (2) above applies confers a power such as is mentioned in sub-paragraph (1)(a)(ii) above, the power shall be construed as a power to make a person liable to a fine or, as the case may be, a maximum fine of the amount corresponding to the level on the standard scale to which the enactment refers by virtue of sub-paragraph (1) above or of a lesser amount.

(7) Subject to sub-paragraph (9) below, where under a relevant subordinate instrument the fine or maximum fine on conviction of a summary offence specified in the instrument is an amount shown in the second column of the standard scale, the reference in the instrument to the amount of the fine or maximum fine shall be construed as a reference to the level in the first column of the standard scale corresponding to that amount.

(8) In sub-paragraph (7) above, "relevant subordinate instrument" means any instrument made by virtue of an enactment after 30th April 1984 and before 12th October 1988 (the date of commencement of section 66 of the Criminal Justice (Scotland) Act 1987).

(9) Sub-paragraph (7) above shall not affect so much of any instrument as (in whatever words) makes a person liable on summary conviction to a fine not exceeding a specified amount for each period of a specified length during which a continuing offence is continued after conviction or the occurrence of any other specified event.

(10) Where there is—

(a) under any enactment (however framed or worded) contained in an Act passed before 12th October 1988,

(b) under any instrument (however framed or worded) made by virtue of such an enactment,

a power to provide by subordinate instrument that a person, as regards any summary offence (whether or not created by the instrument) shall be liable on conviction to a fine, a person may be so made liable to a fine not exceeding a specified level on the standard scale.

(11) Sub-paragraph (10) above has effect in relation to exercises of powers before as well as after 12th October 1988.

Statutory maximum as penalty in respect of summary conviction for offences in subordinate instruments

7.—(1) Where there is, under any enactment (however framed or worded) contained in an Act passed before the relevant date, a power by subordinate instrument to create a criminal offence triable either on indictment or summarily the maximum fine which may, in the exercise of the power, be authorised on summary conviction shall, by virtue of this paragraph, be the statutory maximum (unless some larger maximum fine can be authorised on summary conviction of such an offence by virtue of an enactment other than this sub-paragraph).

(2) Where there is, under any enactment (however framed or worded) contained in an Act passed before the relevant date, a power to create offences triable either on indictment or summarily by subordinate instrument, the maximum fine on summary conviction for such an offence may be expressed as a fine not exceeding the statutory maximum.

(3) Sub-paragraphs (1) and (2) above shall have effect in relation to any exercise of such power before as well as after the relevant date.

(4) Where an offence created by a subordinate instrument made before the relevant date may be tried either on indictment or summarily, the maximum fine which may be imposed on summary conviction shall by virtue of this sub-paragraph be the statutory maximum (unless the offence is one for which by virtue of the instrument a larger maximum fine may be imposed on summary conviction).

(5) Where a person summarily convicted of any offence to which sub-paragraph (4) above relates would, apart from this paragraph, be liable to a fine or to a maximum fine of an amount in the case of a first conviction and of a different amount in the case of a second or subsequent conviction, sub-paragraph (4) above shall apply irrespective of whether the conviction is a first, second or subsequent one.

(6) Sub-paragraph (4) above shall not affect so much of any instrument as (in whatever words) makes a person liable on summary conviction to a fine not exceeding a specified amount for each period of a specified length during which a continuing offence is continued after conviction or the occurrence of any other specified event.

(7) Nothing in this paragraph shall affect the punishment for an offence committed before the relevant date.

(8) In this paragraph "the relevant date" means 12th October 1988 (the date of commencement of section 66 of the Criminal Justice (Scotland) Act 1987).

Fines under secondary subordinate instruments

8.—(1) This paragraph applies to any instrument (however framed or worded) which—

(a) was made before 11th April 1983 (the date of commencement of Part IV of the Criminal Justice Act 1982); and

(b) confers on any authority other than a harbour authority a power by subordinate instrument to make a person, as regards any summary offence (whether or not created by the latter instrument), liable on conviction to a maximum fine of a specified amount not exceeding £1,000,

but does not affect so much of any such instrument as (in whatever words) confers a power by subordinate instrument to make a person liable on conviction to a fine for each period of a specified length during which a continuing offence is continued.

(2) The maximum fine to which a subordinate instrument made by virtue of an instrument to which this paragraph applies may provide that a person shall be liable on conviction of a summary offence is—

(a) if the specified amount is less than £25, level 1 on the standard scale;

(b) if it is £25 or more but less than £50, level 2;

(c) if it is £50 or more but less than £200, level 3;

(d) if it is £200 or more but less than £400, level 4; and

(e) if it is £400 or more, level 5.

(3) Subject to sub-paragraph (5) below, where an instrument to which this paragraph applies

confers a power by subordinate instrument to make a person, as regards a summary offence, liable on conviction to a fine in respect of a specified quantity or a specified number of things, that shall be treated for the purposes of this paragraph as being the maximum fine to which a person may be made liable by virtue of the instrument.

(4) Where an instrument to which this paragraph applies confers a power to provide for different maximum fines in relation to different circumstances or persons of different descriptions, the amount specified as those maximum fines are to be treated separately for the purposes of this paragraph.

(5) Where an instrument to which this paragraph applies confers a power by subordinate instrument to make a person, as regards a summary offence, liable on conviction to a fine in respect of a specified quantity or a specified number of things but also confers a power by subordinate instrument to make a person, as regards such an offence, liable on conviction to an alternative fine, this paragraph shall have effect in relation—

    (a) to the alternative fine; and

    (b) to any amount that the instrument specifies as the maximum fine for which a subordinate instrument made in the exercise of the power conferred by it may provide,

as well as in relation to the fine mentioned in sub-paragraph (3) above.

Fines on summary conviction for offences under subordinate instruments: conversion to references

to levels on scale

9.—(1) Where an instrument which was made under an enactment on or after 11th April 1983 but before 12th October 1988 (the date of commencement of section 54 of the Criminal Justice Act 1988) confers on any authority other than a harbour authority a power by subordinate instrument to make a person liable on summary conviction to a fine of an amount shown in the second column of the standard scale, as that scale had effect when the instrument was made, a reference to the level in the first column of the standard scale which then corresponded to that amount shall be substituted for the reference in the instrument conferring the power to the amount of the fine.

(2) This paragraph shall not affect so much of any instrument as (in whatever words) makes a person liable on summary conviction to a maximum fine not exceeding a specified amount for each period of a specified length during which a continuing offence is continued.

Part III of Schedule 2

10.—(1) The enactments specified in column 1 of Part III of Schedule 2 to this Act, which relate to' the penalties or the maximum penalties for the offences mentioned in those enactments, shall be amended in accordance with the amendments specified in column 2 of that Part, which have the effect of altering the penalties on summary conviction of the said offences and placing the fines on a level on the standard scale; and in that Part column 3 shows the penalties or, as the case may be, maximum penalties resulting from the amendments.

(2) Sub-paragraph (1) above does not affect the penalty which may be imposed in respect of an offence committed before 11th April 1983.

Alteration of penalties on summary conviction of certain offences under the Misuse of Drugs Act

1971

11.—(1) The Misuse of Drugs Act 1971 shall be amended as follows—

    (a) in the entries in Schedule 4 showing the punishment that may be imposed on persons summarily convicted of offences mentioned in sub-paragraph (2)(b) below, for "6 months" there shall be substituted "3 months"; and

    (b) in the entry in Schedule 4 relating to section 5(2)—

        (i) for "6 months" (being the maximum punishment on summary conviction of an offence under that section where a Class B drug was involved) there shall be substituted "3 months", and

        (ii) for "6 months" being the maximum punishment on summary conviction of such an offence where a Class C drug was involved there shall be substituted "3 months".

(2) The offences to which (as provided in paragraph 2(7) above) paragraph 2(1) above does not apply are—

    (a) offences under section 5(2) of the Misuse of Drugs Act 1971 (having possession of a controlled drug) where the controlled drug in relation to which the offence was committed was a Class B or Class C drug;

    (b) offences under the following provisions of that Act, where the controlled drug in relation to which the offence was committed was a Class C drug, namely—

    (i) section 4(2) (production, or being concerned in the production, of a controlled drug);

    (ii) section 4(3) (supplying or offering a controlled drug or being concerned in the doing of either activity by another);

    (iii) section 5(3) (having possession of a controlled drug with intent to supply it to another);

    (iv) section 8 (being the occupier, or concerned in the management, of premises and permitting or suffering certain activities to take place there);

    (v) section 12(6) (contravention of direction prohibiting practitioner etc. from possessing, supplying etc. controlled drugs); or

    (vi) section 13(3) (contravention of direction prohibiting practitioner etc. from prescribing, supplying etc. controlled drugs).

(3) In this paragraph "controlled drug", "Class B drug" and "Class C drug" have the same meaning as in the Misuse of Drugs Act 1971.

Transitional provisions and savings

12.—(1) The following transitional provisions and savings relating to the provisions contained in this Schedule shall have effect.

(2) For the purposes of paragraph 3(2) above, any provision in force at 17th July 1978 (the date of coming into force of subsection (3) of section 289C of the Criminal Procedure (Scotland) Act 1975) which—

    (a) is contained in any byelaw made by virtue of section 203 of the Local Government (Scotland) Act 1973 but not that section as applied to byelaws made under any provision contained in a local or private Act other than by a local authority; and

    (b) specified £20 as the maximum fine which may be imposed on summary conviction in respect of a contravention of, or offence under, any byelaw mentioned in that provision,

shall have effect as if it specified £50 instead, but with no change by virtue of this sub-paragraph in the maximum daily fine, if any, for which it provides.

(3) Paragraph 5 above does not affect the penalty which may be imposed in respect of an offence committed before 11th April 1983.

SCHEDULE 2

Increase in Certain Penalties

Part I

Offences made Triable only Summarily, and Related Amendments

(1) Offence	(2) Enactment	(3) Amendment	(4) Penalties
NIGHT POACHING ACT 1828 (C. 69)	Section 1.	For the words from "such of-fender" onwards substitute "he shall be liable on summary conviction to a fine not exceed-ing level 3 on the standard scale".	Level 3 on the standard scale.
Offences under section 1 (taking or destroying game or rabbits by night or entering land for that purpose).			
PUBLIC MEETING ACT 1908 (C. 66)	Section 1(1).	After "offence" add "shall on summary conviction be liable to imprisonment for a term not exceeding 6 months or to a fine not exceeding level 5 on the standard scale or to both".	6 months or level 5 on the standard scale or both.
Offences under section 1(1) (endeavour to break up a public meeting).			
BETTING, GAMING AND LOTTERIES ACT 1963 (C. 2) Offences under the following provisions — section 7 (restriction of betting on dog racecourses); section 10(5) (advertising licensed betting offices); section 11(6) (person holding bookmaker's or bet-ting agency permit employing a person disqualified from holding such a permit); section 18(2) (making unauthorised charges to bookmakers on licensed track); section 19 (occupiers of licensed tracks not to have any interest in bookmaker thereon); section 21 (betting with young persons); section 22 (betting circulars not to be sent to young persons).	Section 52.	For paragraphs (a) and (b) of subsection (2) (penalties for certain offences) substitute "on summary conviction to a fine not exceeding level 5 on the standard scale or to imprison-ment for a term not exceeding six months or to both".	Level 5 on the standard scale or 6 months or both.

(1) Offence	(2) Enactment	(3) Amendment	(4) Penalties
THEATRES ACT 1968 (C. 54) Offences under section 6 (provocation of breach of the peace by means of public performance of play).	Section 6(2).	For paragraphs (a) and (b) substitute "on summary conviction to a fine not exceeding level 5 on the standard scale or to imprisonment for a term not exceeding six months or to both".	6 months or level 5 on the standard scale or both.

AMENDMENT

Schedule as amended by the Postal Services Act 2000 (Consequential Modifications No. 1) Order 2001 (SI 2001/1149).

PART II

INCREASE OF FINES FOR CERTAIN SUMMARY OFFENCES

(1) Enactment creating offence	(2) Penalty enactment	(3) Old maximum fine	(4) New maximum fine
1...	[...]	[...]	[...]
PUBLIC ORDER ACT 1936 (1 Edw. 8 & 1 Geo. 6) (C. 6) Offences under section 1(1) (wearing uniform signifying association with political organisation).	Section 7(2).	£50	Level 4 on the standard scale.
CHILDREN AND YOUNG PERSONS (SCOTLAND) ACT 1937 (C. 37) Offences under section 46(2) (publication of matters identifying juveniles in court proceedings).	Section 46(2).	£50	Level 4 on the standard scale.
CINEMATOGRAPH FILMS (ANIMALS) ACT 1937 (C. 59) Offences under section 1(1) (prohibition of films in production of which suffering has been caused to animals).	Section 1(3).	£100	Level 4 on the standard scale.
NATIONAL ASSISTANCE ACT 1948 (C. 29) Offences under section 55(2) (obstruction).	Section 55(2) (as amended by Schedule 3 to the Criminal Justice Act 1967).	£10 for a first offence and £20 for a second or subsequent offence.	Level 4 on the standard scale.
AGRICULTURE (SCOTLAND) ACT 1948 (C. 45) Offences under section 50(1) (prohibition of night shooting and use of spring traps).	Section 50(2).	£20 for a first offence and £50 for a second or subsequent offence.	Level 3 on the standard scale.
Offences under section 50A(1) (open trapping of hares and rabbits).	Section 50A(2).	£20 for a first offence and £50 for a second or subsequent offence.	Level 3 on the standard scale.
DOCKING AND NICKING OF HORSES ACT 1949 (C. 70) Offences under section 1(1) (prohibition of docking or nicking horses).	Section 1(3).	£25	Level 3 on the standard scale.
Offences under section 2(3) (offences in connection with importation of docked horses).	Section 2(3).	£25	Level 3 on the standard scale.

(1) Enactment creating offence	(2) Penalty enactment	(3) Old maximum fine	(4) New maximum fine
Offences under section 2(4) (making of false statement).	Section 2(4).	£25	Level 3 on the standard scale.
DOGS (PROTECTION OF LIVESTOCK) ACT 1953 (C. 28) Offences under section 1(1) (owning or keeping a dog which worries livestock).	Section 1(6) (as amended by Schedule 3 to the Criminal Justice Act 1967).	£20 for a first offence and £50 for a second or subsequent offence in respect of the same dog.	Level 3 on the standard scale.
PESTS ACT 1954 (C. 68) Offences under section 12 (spreading of myxomatosis).	Section 12.	£20 for a first offence and £50 for a second or subsequent offence in respect of the same dog.	Level 3 on the standard scale.
ANIMAL (CRUEL POISONS) ACT 1962 (C. 26) Offences under section 1 (offences in connection with use of prohibited poison for destroying animals).	Section 1.	£50	Level 3 on the standard scale.
SEA FISHERIES (SHELLFISH) ACT 1967 (C. 83) Offences under section 7(4) (using prohibited fishing implements etc. in an area of fishery or oyster bed to which section applies).	Section 7(4).	£2 for a first offence, £5 for a second offence and £10 for a third or subsequent offence.	Level 3 on the standard scale.
ABORTION ACT 1967 (C. 87) Offences under section 2(3) (contravening or failing to comply with regulations as to notification).	Section 2(3).	£100	Level 5 on the standard scale.
AGRICULTURE (MISCELLANEOUS PROVISIONS) ACT 1968 (C. 34) Offences under the following provisions— section 1(1) (prevention of unnecessary pain and distress to live- stock); section 2(2) (breach of regulations with respect to welfare of livestock).	Section 7(1).	£100 for a first offence and £200 for a second or subsequent offence.	Level 4 on the standard scale.
SOCIAL WORK (SCOTLAND) ACT 1968 (C. 49) Offences under section 6(5) (obstructing officer in exercise of power under section 6).	Section 6(5).	£10 for a first offence and £50 for a second or subsequent offence.	Level 4 on the standard scale.

(1) Enactment creating offence	(2) Penalty enactment	(3) Old maximum fine	(4) New maximum fine
Offences under section 60(3) (failure to comply with regulations etc. in respect of the control of residential and other establishments).	Section 60(3).	£50	Level 4 on the standard scale.
Offences under section 61(3) (carrying on establishment without registration).	Section 61(3).	£50 for a first offence and £100 for a second or subsequent offence.	Level 4 on the standard scale.
Offences under section 62(6) (failure to comply with a condition of the registration of an establishment).	Section 62(6).	£50 for a first offence and £100 for a second or subsequent offence.	Level 4 on the standard scale.
Offences under section 65(4) (obstructing officer in exercise of power under section 65).	Section 65(4).	£10 for a first offence and £50 for a second or subsequent offence.	Level 4 on the standard scale.
GAMING ACT 1968 (C. 65)			
Offences under section 8(5) (gaming in a street or public place).	Section 8(5).	£50.	Level 4 on the standard scale.
EMPLOYERS' LIABILITY (COMPULSORY INSURANCE ACT 1969 (C. 57)			
Offences under section 4(3) (offences in relation to certificates of insurance).	Section 4(3).	£50.	Level 3 on the standard scale.
Offences under section 5 (employer failing to insure employee).	Section 5.	£200.	Level 4 on the standard scale.
CONSERVATION OF SEALS ACT 1970 (C. 30)			
Any offence under the Act, except an offence under section 11(7).	Section 5(2).	£50 for a first offence and £100 for a second or subsequent offence.	Level 4 on the standard scale.
MISUSE OF DRUGS ACT 1971 (C. 38)			
Offences under section 17(3) (failure to comply with notice requiring information relating to prescribing supply etc. of drugs).	Schedule 4.	£100.	Level 3 on the standard scale.
POISONS ACT 1972 (C. 66)			
Any offence under section 8(1) (contravention of provisions of sections 1 to 7, other than section 6(4), or of the Poisons rules).	Section 8(1).	£50.	Level 4 on the standard scale.

(1) Enactment creating offence	(2) Penalty enactment	(3) Old maximum fine	(4) New maximum fine
Offences under section 6(4) (using title etc. falsely to suggest entitlement to sell poison).	Section 6(4).	£20.	Level 2 on the standard scale.
Offences under section 9(8) (obstructing an inspector etc.).	Section 9(8).	£5.	Level 2 on the standard scale.
HEALTH AND SAFETY AT WORK ETC. ACT 1974 (C. 37)			
Offences under the following provisions— ²section 33(1)(d) ....; section 33(1)(e) (contravening requirement imposed by inspector) where the requirement contravened was imposed under section 20; section 33(1)(f) (prevening etc, any other person from appearing before inspector); section 33(1)(h) (intentionally obstructing an inspector); section 33(1)(n) (falsely pretending to be an inspector).	Section 33(2).	£400.	Level 5 on the standard scale.
SALMON AND FRESHWATER FISHERIES ACT 1975 (C. 51)			
Offences against any provision of the Act not specified in the table in Part I of Schedule 4.	Paragraph 1(2) of Schedule 4.	£50 for a first offence and £100 for a second or subsequent offence.	Level 4 on the standard scale.
Offences under section 1 (fishing with certain instruments for salmon, trout or freshwater fish and possessing certain instruments for fishing for such fish) if not acting with another.	The Table in Part I of Schedule 4.	£50 for a first offence and £100 for a second or subsequent offence.	Level 4 on the standard scale.
Offences under section 19(2) (fishing for salmon during the annual close season or weekly close time).	The said Table.	£100 for a first offence and £200 for a second or subsequent offence.	Level 4 on the standard scale.
Offences under section 19(4) (fishing for trout during the annual close season or weekly close time).	The said Table.	£100 for a first offence and £200 for a second or subsequent offence.	Level 4 on the standard scale.
Offences under section 19(6) (fishing for freshwater fish during the annual close season for freshwater fish and fishing for eels by means of a rod and line during that season).	The said Table.	£100 for a first offence and £200 for a second or subsequent offence.	Level 4 on the standard scale.

17

(1) Enactment creating offence	(2) Penalty enactment	(3) Old maximum fine	(4) New maximum fine
Offences under section 19(7) (fishing for rainbow trout during the annual close season for rainbow trout and fishing for eels by means of a rod and line during that season).	The said Table.	£100 for a first offence and £200 for a second or subsequent offence.	Level 4 on the standard scale.
Offences under section 21 (prohibition on use of certain devices at certain times).	The said Table.	£100 for a first offence and £200 for a second or subsequent offence.	Level 4 on the standard scale.
Offences under section 27 (fishing for fish otherwise than under the authority of a licence and possessing an unlicensed instrument with intent to use it for fishing) if not acting with another.	The said Table.	£50 for a first offence and £100 for a second or subsequent offence.	Level 4 on the standard scale.

AMENDMENTS

[1] Repealed by the Crime and Punishment (Scotland) Act 1997 (c.48) s.62(1) and Sch.1, para.19(2) with effect from August 1, 1997 in terms of SI 1997/1712, para.3.

[2] Repealed by the Lifts Regulations 1997 (SI 1997/831), reg.19, Sch.19, Sch.15, para.1 (effective July 1, 1997).

Sch.2, Part II as amended by the Housing Grants, Construction and Regeneration Act 1996 (c.53), Sch.3.

Sch.2, Part II as amended by the Regulation of Care (Scotland) Act 2001 (asp 8), Sch.4. Brought into force on April 1, 2002 by the Regulation of Care (Scotland) Act 2001 (Commencement No.2 and Transitional Provisions) Order 2002 (SSI 2002/162 (C.8)).

Sch.2, Pt II as amended by the Fire (Scotland) Act 2005 (asp 5), s.89(2) and Sch.4. Brought into force on August 2, 2005 by the Fire (Scotland) Act 2005 (Commencement No. 2) Order 2005 (SSI 2005/392 (C.17)), art.2.

Sch.2, Pt II as amended by the Police, Public Order and Criminal Justice (Scotland) Act 2006 (asp 10), s.101 and Sch.6, para.3. Brought into force on September 1, 2006 by the Police, Public Order and Criminal Justice (Scotland) Act 2006 (Commencement No. 1) Order 2006 (SSI 2006/432 (C.34)), art.2.

PART III

FINES TO BE ALTERED OTHER THAN IN ACCORDANCE WITH PARAGRAPHS 4 AND 5 OF SCHEDULE 1

(1) Enactment	(2) Amendment	(3) New penalty
MILITARY LANDS ACT 1892 (C. 43)		
Section 17(2) (offences against byelaws).	For "five pounds" substitute "level 2 on the standard scale".	Level 2 on the standard scale.
PROTECTION OF ANIMALS (SCOTLAND) ACT 1912 (C. 14)		
Section 7 (selling poisoned grain or placing on any land matter rendered poisonous).	For "ten pounds" substitute "level 4 on the standard scale".	Level 4 on the standard scale.
LAND DRAINAGE (SCOTLAND) ACT 1930 (C. 20)	...	...
¹Section 4 (obstruction of person exercising power of entry).		
LAND DRAINAGE (SCOTLAND) ACT 1941 (C. 13)		
Section 2(2) (obstruction of person exercising power of entry).	For "twenty pounds" substitute "level 3 on the standard scale".	Level 3 on the standard scale.
PUBLIC HEALTH (SCOTLAND) ACT 1945 (C. 15)		
Section 1(5) (contravention of regulations as to treatment and spread of certain deceases).	For "one hundred pounds" substitute "level 5 on the standard scale".	Level 5 on the standard scale and £50 per day during which the offence continues.
...	...	...
LAND DRAINAGE (SCOTLAND) ACT 1958 (C. 24)		
Section 11(4) (obstruction of person exercising power of entry)	For the words from "five pounds" to the end substitute "level 3 on the standard scale".	Level 3 on the standard scale.
BETTING, GAMING AND LOTTERIES ACT 1963 (C. 2)		
Section 28(10) (disclosing information about bookmaker's business).	For "one hundred pounds" substitute "level 4 on the standard scale".	Level 4 on the standard scale.
PLANT VARIETIES AND SEEDS ACT 1964 (C. 14)		
Section 25(9) (obstructing an authorised person)	For "twenty pounds" substitute "level 3 on the standard scale".	Level 3 on the standard scale.
Section 27(1) (tampering with samples).	For "one hundred pounds" substitute "level 5 on the standard scale".	Level 5 on the standard scale or 3 months or both.

(1) Enactment	(2) Amendment	(3) New penalty
AGRICULTURE AND HORTICULTURE ACT 1964 (C. 28)		
Section 20(1) (obstruction, etc. of authorised officer).	For "twenty pounds" substitute "level 3 on the standard scale".	Level 3 on the standard scale.
Section 20(2) (offences under Part III).	For the words from "one hundred pounds" to "two hundred and fifty pounds" substitute "level 5 on the standard scale".	Level 5 on the standard scale or 3 months or both.
INDUSTRIAL AND PROVIDENT SOCIETIES ACT 1965 (C. 12)		
Section 61 (general offences).	For "five pounds" substitute "level 3 on the standard scale".	Level 3 on the standard scale.
RIVERS (PREVENTION OF POLLUTION) (SCOTLAND) ACT 1965 (C. 13)		
Section 11(2) (unauthorised disclosure of information).	For the words from "one hundred pounds" to the end substitute "level 5 on the standard scale".	Level 5 on the standard scale.
FORESTRY ACT 1967 (C. 10)		
Section 24(4) (failure to comply with felling licence).	For "£50" substitute "level 5 on the standard scale".	Level 5 on the standard scale.
Section 46(5) (offences against byelaws).	In paragraph (a) for "£10" substitute "level 2 on the standard scale", and in paragraph (b) for "£5" substitute "level 2 on the standard scale".	Level 2 on the standard scale and 50 pence per day during which the offence continues.
Section 48(3) (obstruction of Forestry Commission officers).	For "£5" substitute "level 3 on the standard scale".	Level 3 on the standard scale.
POLICE (SCOTLAND) ACT 1967 (C. 77)		
Section 43(1) (impersonating a police officer).	For "fifty pounds" substitute "level 4 on the standard scale".	Level 4 on the standard scale or 3 months.
Section 44(5) (offences by constables).	For "ten pounds" substitute "level 3 on the standard scale".	Level 3 on the standard scale or 60 days.
AGRICULTURE (MISCELLANEOUS PROVISIONS) ACT 1968 (C. 34)		
Section 7(2) (obstructing officer authorised to carry out welfare inspections).	For "twenty pounds" substitute "level 3 on the standard scale".	Level 3 on the standard scale.

(1) Enactment	(2) Amendment	(3) New penalty
SALE OF VENISON (SCOTLAND) ACT 1968 (C. 38)		
Section 1(4) (contravention of provisions regarding registration of venison dealers).	For "£20" substitute "level 3 on the standard scale".	Level 3 on the standard scale.
Section 2(4) (failure to keep records, etc.).	For "£20" substitute "level 2 on the standard scale".	Level 2 on the standard scale.
SEWERAGE (SCOTLAND) ACT 1968 (C. 47)		
Section 44 (failure to provide information, etc.).	For "£20" substitute "level 3 on the standard scale".	Level 3 on the standard scale.
Section 48(9) (obstruction of person having right of entry).	For "£20" substitute "level 3 on the standard scale".	Level 3 on the standard scale and £5 per day which the offence continues.
Section 50(3) (unauthorised disclosure of information).	For the words from "£100" to the end substitute "level 5 on the standard scale".	Level 5 on the standard scale.
TRANSPORT ACT 1968 (C. 73)		
Section 97A(1) (tachograph offences).	For "£200" substitute "level 4 on the standard scale".	Level 4 on the standard scale.
Section 97A(2) (failure by employer to secure compliance with section 97A(1)(a)).	For "£200" substitute "level 4 on the standard scale".	Level 4 on the standard scale.
ROAD TRAFFIC (FOREIGN VEHICLES) ACT 1972 (C. 27)		
Section 3(1) (disobeying prohibition on a goods vehicle).	For "£200" substitute "level 5 on the standard scale".	Level 5 on the standard scale.
EDUCATION (SCOTLAND) ACT 1980 (C. 44)		
Section 43(1) (contravention of section 35, 41 or 42).	For the words from "in the case" where first occurring to "£50" where thirdly occurring substitute "to a fine not exceeding level 3 on the standard scale".	Level 3 on the standard scale or 1 month or both.
Section 66(3) (obstruction of inspectors).	For the words from "£20" to "£50" substitute "level 4 on the standard scale".	Level 4 on the standard scale or 3 months or both.
Section 98(2) (failure to register independent school, etc.).	For the words "£20" to "£50" substitute "level 4 on the standard scale".	Level 4 on the standard scale or 3 months or both.

(1) Enactment	(2) Amendment	(3) New penalty
Section 101(2) (using disqualified premises).	For the words from "£20" to "£50" substitute level 4 on the standard scale.	Level 4 on the standard scale or 3 months or both.
Section 101(3) (disqualified person acting as proprietor of independent school, etc.).	For the words from "£20" to "£50" substitute "level 4 on the standard scale".	Level 4 on the standard scale or 3 months or both.
WATER (SCOTLAND) ACT 1980 (C. 45)		
Section 38(7) (obstruction of person exercising power of entry).	For "£25" substitute "level 3 on the standard scale".	Level 3 on the standard scale.
Section 64(2) (failure to provide information, etc.).	For "£25" substitute "level 3 on the standard scale".	Level 3 on the standard scale.
Section 72(3) (penalty which may be provided for contravention of byelaws).	For "the sum of £400" substitute "level 4 on the standard scale".	Level 4 on the standard scale and £50 per day during which the offence continues.
Section 93(7) (failure to provide information, etc.).	For "£200" substitute "level 4 on the standard scale".	Level 4 on the standard scale and £20 per day during which the offence continues.
Paragraph 10(3) of Schedule 4 (offences relating to construction of reservoirs).	For the words from "£50" where first occurring to "continued" substitute "level 3 on the standard scale".	Level 3 on the standard scale.
Paragraph 28 of Schedule 4 (obstruction of person exercising power of entry).	For the words "£25" substitute "level 3 on the standard scale".	Level 3 on the standard scale.

AMENDMENT

[1]Repealed by the Flood Prevention and Land Drainage (Scotland) Act 1997 (c.36), s.8, Sch.

Sch.2, Pt III as amended by the Fire (Scotland) Act 2005 (asp 5), s.89(2) and Sch.4. Brought into force on August 2, 2005 by the Fire (Scotland) Act 2005 (Commencement No. 2) Order 2005 (SSI 2005/392 (C.17)), art.2.

Section 3   SCHEDULE 3

TRANSITIONAL PROVISIONS, TRANSITORY MODIFICATIONS AND SAVINGS

PART I

GENERAL AND MISCELLANEOUS

General saving for old savings

1. The repeal by this Act of an enactment previously repealed subject to savings (whether or not in the repealing enactment) does not affect the continued operation of those savings.

Documents referring to repealed enactments

2. Any document made served or issued after this Act comes into force which contains a reference to any of the repealed enactments shall be construed, except so far as the contrary intention appears, as referring or, as the context may require, including a reference to the corresponding provision of the consolidating Acts.

Provisions relating to the coming into force of other provisions

3.—(1) The repeal by this Act of a provision providing for or relating to the coming into force of a provision reproduced in the consolidating Acts does not affect the operation of the first provision, in so far as it remains capable of having effect, in relation to the enactment reproducing the second provision.

(2) The repeal by this Act of a power to make provision or savings in preparation for or in connection with the coming into force of a provision reproduced in the consolidating Acts does not affect the power, in so far as it remains capable of having effect, in relation to the enactment reproducing the second provision.

PART II

SPECIFIC PROVISIONS

Local government reform

4.—(1) At any time before 1 April 1996 or the coming into force of section 1 of the Local Government etc. (Scotland) Act 1994, whichever is the later, in section 206 of the Principal Act, for subsection (6) there shall be substituted the following subsection—

"(6) In this section the expression "police authority" means a regional or islands council, except that where there is an amalgamation scheme under the Police (Scotland) Act 1967 in force it means a joint police committee."

(2) [Repealed by the Proceeds of Crime Act 2002 (c.29), Sch.12. Brought into force on March 24, 2003 by the Proceeds of Crime Act 2002 (Commencement No.6, Transitional Provisions and Savings) (Scotland) Order 2003 (SSI 2003/210 (C.44)).]

The Principal Reporter

5. Until the coming into force of section 127 of the Local Government etc. (Scotland) Act 1994, for any reference in any provision of the Principal Act to the Principal Reporter there shall be substituted a reference to the reporter of the local authority in whose area any child referred to in that provision resides.

Penalties

6.—(1) The repeal by this Act of any enactment—

    (a) by virtue of which the penalty which may be imposed in respect of any offence is altered; but

    (b) which provides that the penalty in respect of such an offence committed before a particular date shall not be so altered,

shall not affect the penalty which may be imposed in respect of an offence mentioned in paragraph (b) above.

(2) The periods of imprisonment set forth in subsection (2) of section 219 of the Principal Act shall apply to the non-payment of any sum imposed under that section by a court under a statute or order passed or made before 1 June 1909, notwithstanding that that statute or order fixes any other period of imprisonment.

District court procedure

7. The repeal by this Act of section 4 of the District Courts (Scotland) Act 1975 shall not affect the rules of procedure and practice in the district court.

Detention of children in summary proceedings

8. Notwithstanding the repeal by Schedule 2 of the Criminal Justice (Scotland) Act 1987 of section 58A of the Children and Young Persons (Scotland) Act 1937, any child who, before 1 April 1988 (the date of commencement of section 59 of the said Act of 1987), had been ordered to be detained pursuant to the directions of the Secretary of State under section 413 of the Criminal Procedure (Scotland) Act 1975—

    (a) shall, while so detained after such date, continue to be deemed to be in legal custody; and

    (b) may at any time be released conditionally or unconditionally by the Secretary of State, and any such child conditionally released shall be liable to recall on the directions of the Secretary of State and if he fails to comply with any condition of his release he may be apprehended without warrant and taken to the place from which he was released.

Effect of probation and absolute discharge

9. Subsections (1) and (2) of section 246 of the Principal Act shall not affect the operation, in relation to an offender as mentioned in those subsections, of any enactment which was in force as at the commencement of section 9(3)(b) of the Criminal Justice (Scotland) Act 1949 and is expressed to extend to persons dealt with under section 1(1) of the Probation of Offenders Act 1907 as well as to convicted persons.

Restriction on discharge of hospital order

10. Until the coming into force of section 54 of the Criminal Justice (Scotland) Act 1995, in section 59 of the Principal Act for the words "without limit of time" there shall be substituted the words "either without limit of time or during such period as may be specified in the order".

Aiding and abetting

11. Subsection (2) of section 293 of the Principal Act shall not apply in respect of any offence committed before 1 October 1987 (the date of commencement of section 64 of the Criminal Justice (Scotland) Act 1987).

Penal servitude and hard labour

12.—(1) Any enactment which confers power on a court to pass a sentence of penal servitude in any case shall be construed, subject to sub-paragraph (3) below, as conferring power to pass a sentence of imprisonment for a term not exceeding the maximum term of penal servitude for which a sentence could have been passed in that case immediately before 12 June 1950.

(2) Any enactment which confers power on a court to pass a sentence of imprisonment with hard labour in any case shall be construed as conferring power to pass a sentence of imprisonment for a term not exceeding the term for which a sentence of imprisonment with hard labour could have been passed in that case immediately before 12 June 1950.

(3) Nothing in sub-paragraph (1) above shall be construed as empowering a court, other than the High Court, to pass a sentence of imprisonment for a term exceeding five years.

AMENDMENT

Para.12(3) as amended by the Crime and Punishment (Scotland) Act 1997 (c.48), s.13(1). Brought into force on May 1, 2004 by the Crime and Punishment (Scotland) Act 1997 (Commencement No.6 and Savings) Order 2004 (SSI 2004/176 (C.12)), arts 2 and 3.

Supervised attendance orders

13.—(1) In section 235 of the Principal Act, paragraph (b) of subsection (3) shall also apply to an offender where, having been convicted of an offence, he has imposed on him a fine which (or any part or instalment of which) he has failed to pay and the court, prior to 1 April 1991 (the date of commencement of section 62 of the Law Reform (Miscellaneous Provisions) (Scotland) Act 1990), has imposed on him a period of imprisonment under paragraph (a) of subsection (1) of section 219 of the Principal Act but he has not served any of that period of imprisonment.

(2) Where, in respect of an offender, a court makes a supervised attendance order in circumstances where paragraph (b) of the said subsection (3) applies as mentioned in sub-paragraph (1) above, the making of that order shall have the effect of discharging the sentence of imprisonment imposed on the offender.

Hearsay evidence

14. Nothing in the section 259 to 261 of the Principal Act shall apply to—
   (a) proceedings commenced; or
   (b) where the proceedings consist of an application to the sheriff by virtue of section 42(2)(c) of the Social Work (Scotland) Act 1968 or by virtue of Chapter 3 of Part II of the Children (Scotland) Act 1995, an application made,

before sections 17 to 20 of the Criminal Justice (Scotland) Act 1995 came into force; and, for the purposes of paragraph (a) above, solemn proceedings are commenced when the indictment is served.

Confiscation of proceeds of crime, etc.

15.—(1) Where a person is charged with an offence in relation to which provision is made by Part I of the Proceeds of Crime (Scotland) Act 1995, being an offence committed before the coming into force of Chapter I of Part II of the Criminal Justice (Scotland) Act 1995, Part I of the said Proceeds of Crime (Scotland) Act shall not affect the powers of the court in the event of his being convicted of the offence.

(2) Where a person is charged with an offence committed before the coming into force of Part II of the Proceeds of Crime (Scotland) Act 1995, in the event of his being convicted of the offence, the court shall be entitled to exercise the powers conferred by section 223 or section 436 of the Criminal Procedure (Scotland) Act 1975, but not the powers conferred by that Part.

(3) Paragraph (b) of section 2(4) of the Proceeds of Crime (Scotland) Act 1995 shall not apply in the case of an offence committed before the coming into force of Chapter I of Part II of the Criminal Justice (Scotland) Act 1995.

(4) In any case in which, notwithstanding the coming into force of the Bankruptcy (Scotland) Act 1985, the Bankruptcy (Scotland) Act 1913 applies to a sequestration, paragraph 1(2) of Schedule 2 to the Proceeds of Crime (Scotland) Act 1995 shall have effect as if for sub-sub-paragraphs (a) and (b) thereof there were substituted the following paragraphs—

   "(a) property comprised in the whole property of the debtor which vests in the trustee under section 97 of the Bankruptcy (Scotland) Act 1913.
      (b) any income of the bankrupt which has been ordered, under subsection (2) of section 98 of that Act, to be paid to the trustee or any estate which, under subsection (1) of that section, vests in the trustee,".

and paragraph 1(3) of that Schedule shall have effect as if, for the reference in it to the said Act of 1985, there were substituted a reference to the said Act of 1913.

(5) In any case in which a petition in bankruptcy was presented, or a receiving order or adjudication in bankruptcy was made, before 29 December 1986 (the date on which the Insolvency Act 1986 came into force), paragraph 2(2) to (5) of Schedule 2 to the Proceeds of Crime (Scotland) Act 1995 shall have effect with the following modifications—

   (a) for references to the bankrupt's estate for the purposes of Part IX of the said Act of 1986 there are substituted references to the property of the bankrupt for the purposes of the Bankruptcy Act 1914;
   (b) for references to the said Act of 1986 and to sections 280(2)(c), 286, 339, and 423 of that Act there are respectively substituted references to the said Act of 1914 and to sections 26(2), 8, 27 and 42 of that Act;
   (c) the references in subsection (4) to an interim receiver appointed as there mentioned include,

where a receiving order has been made, a reference to the receiver constituted by virtue of section 7 of the said Act of 1914, and

(d) subsection (2)(b) is omitted.

(6) In any case in which a winding up of a company commenced, or is treated as having commenced, before 29 December 1986, paragraph 3(2) to (6) of the said Schedule 2 shall have effect with the substitution for references to the said Act of 1986 of references to the Companies Act 1985.

(7) In any case in which a receiver was appointed as is mentioned in sub-paragraph (1) of paragraph 4 of the said Schedule 2 before 29 December 1986, sub-paragraphs (2) to (4) of that paragraph have effect with the substitution for references to the said Act of 1986 of references to the Companies Act 1985.

Criminal Justice (Scotland) Act 1995 (c. 20)

16.—(1) Any enactment repealed by this Act which has been amended by any provision of the Criminal Justice (Scotland) Act 1995 which has not been brought into force at the commencement of this Act shall, notwithstanding such repeal, continue to have effect until such provision is brought into force as if it had not been so repealed or amended.

(2) Any provision of the consolidating Acts which re-enacts any enactment contained in the said Criminal Justice (Scotland) Act which has not been brought into force at the commencement of this Act shall be of no effect until such enactment is brought into force.

(3) The repeal by this Act of any enactment contained in the Criminal Justice (Scotland) Act 1995 which has not been brought into force shall not have effect until such enactment is brought into force.

Children (Scotland) Act 1995 (c. 36)

17. Any enactment repealed by this Act which has been amended by any provision of the Children (Scotland) Act 1995 which has not been brought into force at the commencement of this Act shall, notwithstanding such repeal, continue to have effect until such provision is brought into force as if it had not been so repealed or amended.

False oaths

18. Where an offence mentioned in section 45(5) of the Criminal Law (Consolidation) (Scotland) Act 1995 is, by any Act passed before 28 June 1933, as originally enacted, made punishable only on summary conviction, it shall remain only so punishable.

SCHEDULE 4

MINOR AND CONSEQUENTIAL AMENDMENTS

Jurors (Scotland) Act 1825 (c. 22)

1. In section 3 of the Jurors (Scotland) Act 1825 (sheriff principal to maintain lists of potential jurors)

(a) the existing provision shall become subsection (1);

(b) in that subsection, for the word "designations" there shall be substituted "addresses"; and

(c) after that subsection there shall be inserted the following subsections—

"(2) For the purpose of maintaining lists of potential jurors under subsection (1) above, a sheriff principal may require any person in the sheriff court district in question who appears to him to be qualified and liable to serve as a juror to provide such information, and in such form, as the Secretary of State may by order prescribe.

(3) A statutory instrument containing an order prescribed by virtue of subsection (2) above shall be subject to annulment pursuant to a resolution of either House of Parliament.

(4) Any person who fails to comply with a requirement under subsection (2) above shall be guilty of an offence and liable on summary conviction to a fine not exceeding level 1 on the standard scale.

(5) In proceedings against a person for an offence under subsection (4) above it is a defence to prove that he had reasonable excuse for the failure."

Bankers' Books Evidence Act 1879 (c. 11)

2. In section 6 of the Bankers' Books Evidence Act 1879 (case in which banker not compellable to

produce book), after the word "1988" there shall be inserted the words "or Schedule 8 to the Criminal Procedure (Scotland) Act 1995".

The Children and Young Persons (Scotland) Act 1937 (c. 37)

3.—(1) The Children and Young Persons (Scotland) Act 1937, shall be amended as follows.

(2) After 62 there shall be inserted the following section—

Register of children found guilty of offences

63. In addition to any other register required by law, a separate register of children found guilty of offences and of children discharged on bond or put on probation shall be kept for every summary court by the chief constable or other person charged with the duty of keeping registers of convictions. The register shall apply to children of such age, and shall include such particulars, as may be directed by the Secretary of State, and it shall be the duty of the keeper of the register, within seven days after any such child has been dealt with by the court, to transmit a copy of the entry relating to the child to the education authority for the area in which the child resides."

(3) Before section 104 there shall be added the following section—

Proof of age a defence

103. Where a person is charged with an offence under this Act in respect of a person apparently under a specified age, it shall be a defence to prove that the person was actually of or over that age."

The Trade Marks Act 1938 (c. 22)

4. In section 58B of the Trade Marks Act 1938 (delivery up of offending goods and material), in subsection (6) for the words "Chapter II of Part II of the Criminal Justice (Scotland) Act 1995" there shall be substituted the words "Part II of the Proceeds of Crime (Scotland) Act 1995."

The Backing of Warrants (Republic of Ireland) Act 1965 (c. 45)

5. In section 8(1)(b) of the Backing of Warrants (Republic of Ireland) Act 1965 (rules of court), for the words "section 457ZA of the Criminal Procedure (Scotland) Act 1975" there shall be substituted the words "section 306 of the Criminal Procedure (Scotland) Act 1995".

Social Work (Scotland) Act 1968 (c. 49)

6.—(1) The Social Work (Scotland) Act 1968 shall be amended as follows.

(2) In subsection (1B) of section 5 (powers of Secretary of State), for paragraph (f) there shall be substituted the following paragraph—

"(f) section 51 of the Criminal Procedure (Scotland) Act 1995;".

(3) In subsection (1) of section 6A (power to hold inquiries) for sub-paragraph (ii) of paragraph (d) there shall be substituted—

"(ii) section 44 or 208 of the Criminal Procedure (Scotland) Act 1995;".

(4)

(a) ...

(b) in paragraph (b)(iii) for the words "the Community Service by Offenders (Scotland) Act 1978" there shall be substituted the words "section 238 of the Criminal Procedure (Scotland) Act 1995";

(c) in paragraph (b)(iv) for the words "section 62 of the Law Reform (Miscellaneous Provisions) (Scotland) Act 1990" there shall be substituted the words "section 235 of the said Act of 1995"; and

(d) ...

AMENDMENT

Para.6(4)(a) and (d) deleted by the Crime and Punishment (Scotland) Act 1997 (c.48) s.62(1) and Sch.1, para.19(3).

Sea Fisheries Act 1968 (c. 77)

7. In section 13(2) of the Sea Fisheries Act 1968 (power to award compensation), for "£400" there shall be substituted the words "level 5 on the standard scale".

European Communities Act 1972 (c. 68)

8. In subsection (1) of section 11 of the European Communities Act 1972 (making a false statement before the European Court) for the words "section 1 of the False Oaths (Scotland) Act 1933" there shall be substituted the words "section 44(1) of the Criminal Law (Consolidation) (Scotland) Act 1995".

Fair Trading Act 1973 (c. 41)

9. In subsection (3) of section 129 of the Fair Trading Act 1973 (time-limit for prosecutions)—
   (a) for the words "section 331 of the Criminal Procedure (Scotland) Act 1975" there shall be substituted the words "section 136 of the Criminal Procedure (Scotland) Act 1995" and
   (b) for the words "subsection (3) of the said section 331" there shall be substituted the words "subsection (3) of the said section 136".

Fatal Accidents and Sudden Deaths Inquiry (Scotland) Act 1976 (c. 14)

10. In section 2(3) of the Fatal Accidents and Sudden Deaths Inquiry (Scotland) Act 1976 for "£25" there shall be substituted the words "level 3 on the standard scale".

Freshwater and Salmon Fisheries (Scotland) Act 1976 (c. 22)

11. [...]

AMENDMENT

Para.11 repealed by the Salmon and Freshwater Fisheries (Consolidation) (Scotland) Act 2003 (asp 15), Sch.4, Part II. Brought into force on April 1, 2005 by the Salmon and Freshwater Fisheries (Consolidation) (Scotland) Act 2003 (Commencement) Order 2005 (SSI 2005/174 (C.8)).

Restrictive Trade Practices Act 1976 (c. 34)

12.—(1) The Restrictive Trade Practices Act 1976 shall be amended as follows.

(2) In subsection (3) of section 39 (time limit for prosecution) the words "section 331 of the Criminal Procedure (Scotland) Act 1975" there shall be substituted the words "section 136 of the Criminal Procedure (Scotland) Act 1995".

(3) In subsection (6) of section 41 (time limit for prosecution of offences relating to disclosure of documents)—
   (a) for the words "section 331 of the Criminal Procedure (Scotland) Act 1975" there shall be substituted the words "section 136 of the Criminal Procedure (Scotland) Act 1995"; and
   (b) for the words "subsection (3) of the said section 331" there shall be substituted the words "subsection (3) of the said section 136".

International Carriage of Perishable Foodstuffs Act 1976 (c. 58)

13. In subsection (2) of section 12 of the International Carriage of Perishable Foodstuffs Act 1976 for the words "section 331 of the Criminal Procedure (Scotland) Act 1975" there shall be substituted the words "section 136 of the Criminal Procedure (Scotland) Act 1995".

Marriage (Scotland) Act 1977 (c. 15)

14. In subsection (3) of section 24 of the Marriage (Scotland) Act 1977 for the words "section 331 of the Criminal Procedure (Scotland) Act 1975 (date of commencement of summary proceedings)" there shall be substituted the words "section 136 of the Criminal Procedure (Scotland) Act 1995 (time limit for certain offences)".

Refuse Disposal (Amenity) Act 1978 (c. 3)

15. In subsection (3) of section 2 of the Refuse Disposal (Amenity) Act 1978 for the words "section 462(1) of the Criminal Procedure (Scotland) Act 1975" there shall be substituted the words "section 307(1) of the Criminal Procedure (Scotland) Act 1995".

16. ...

AMENDMENT

Para.16 deleted by the Crime and Punishment (Scotland) Act 1997 (c.48) s.62(1) and Sch.1, para.19(3).

Interpretation Act 1978 (c. 30)

17. In Schedule 1 to the Interpretation Act 1978—

    (a) in paragraph (b) of the definition of "the standard scale" for the words "section 289G of the Criminal Procedure (Scotland) Act 1975" there shall be substituted the words "section 225(1) of the Criminal Procedure (Scotland) Act 1995"; and

    (b) in paragraph (b) of the definition of "statutory maximum" for the words "section 289B(6) of the Criminal Procedure (Scotland) Act 1975" there shall be substituted the words "section 225(8) of the Criminal Procedure (Scotland) Act 1995".

Customs and Excise Management Act 1979 (c. 2)

18.—(1) The Customs and Excise Management Act 1979 shall be amended as follows.

(2) In subsection (6) of section 118A (duty of revenue traders to keep records), in paragraph (d) for the words "Schedule 3 to the Prisoners and Criminal Evidence (Scotland) Act 1993" there shall be substituted the words "Schedule 8 to the Criminal Procedure (Scotland) Act 1995".

(3) In subsection (3) of section 118C (search warrant) for the words "section 462 of the Criminal Procedure (Scotland) Act 1975" there shall be substituted the words "section 307 of the Criminal Procedure (Scotland) Act 1995".

(4) In subsection (1) of section 118D (order for access to certain information) for the words "section 462 of the Criminal Procedure (Scotland) Act 1975" there shall be substituted the words "section 307 of the Criminal Procedure (Scotland) Act 1995".

(5) In subsection (2) of section 171, in paragraph (b) for the words from "section 289B" to the end of the paragraph there shall be substituted the words "subsection (8) of section 225 of the Criminal Procedure (Scotland) Act 1995 (£5,000 or other sum substituted by order under subsection (4) of that section)".

Customs and Excise Duties (General Reliefs) Act 1979 (c. 3)

19. In subsection (3) of section 15 of the Customs and Excise Duties (General Reliefs) Act 1979, in paragraph (b) for the words from "section 289B" to the end of the paragraph there shall be substituted the words "subsection (8) of section 225 of the Criminal Procedure (Scotland) Act 1995 (£5,000 or other sum substituted by order under subsection (4) of that section)".

Alcoholic Liquor Duties Act 1979 (c. 4)

20. In subsection (1) of section 4 of the Alcoholic Liquor Duties Act 1979, in the definition of "the prescribed sum", in paragraph (b) for the words from "section 289B" to the end of the paragraph there shall be substituted the words "subsection (8) of section 225 of the Criminal Procedure (Scotland) Act 1995 (£5,000 or other sum substituted by order under subsection (4) of that section)".

Hydrocarbon Oil Duties Act 1979 (c. 5)

21. In subsection (1) of section 27 of the Hydrocarbon Oil Duties Act 1979, in the definition of "the prescribed sum", in paragraph (b) for the words from "section 289B" to the end of the paragraph there shall be substituted the words "subsection (8) of section 225 of the Criminal Procedure (Scotland) Act 1995 (£5,000 or other sum substituted by order under subsection (4) of that section)".

Credit Unions Act 1979 (c. 34)

22. In subsection (1) of section 31 of the Credit Unions Act 1979, in the definition of "statutory maximum", in paragraph (b) for the words from "section 289B" to the end of the paragraph there shall be substituted the words "subsection (8) of section 225 of the Criminal Procedure (Scotland) Act 1995".

Estate Agents Act 1979 (c. 38)

23. In subsection (1) of section 33 of the Estate Agents Act 1979, in the definition of "the statutory maximum", in paragraph (b) for the words "section 289B of the Criminal Procedure (Scotland) Act 1975" there shall be substituted the words "subsection (8) of section 225 of the Criminal Procedure (Scotland) Act 1995".

24.—(1) The Ancient Monuments and Archaeological Areas Act 1979 shall be amended as follows.

(2) In section 59, for the words "section 331 of the Criminal Procedure (Scotland) Act 1975" there shall be substituted the words "section 136 of the Criminal Procedure (Scotland) Act 1995".

(3) In subsection (1) of section 61, in the definition of "the statutory maximum" in sub-paragraph (i) of paragraph (b) for the words from "section 289B" to the end of the sub-paragraph there shall be substituted the words "subsection (8) of section 225 of the Criminal Procedure (Scotland) Act 1995 (that is to say £5,000 or another sum fixed by order under subsection (4) of that section for that purpose)".

Isle of Man Act 1979 (c. 58)

25. In subsection (4) of section 5 of the Isle of Man Act 1979, for the words "section 462(1) of the Criminal Procedure (Scotland) Act 1975" there shall be substituted the words "section 307(1) of the Criminal Procedure (Scotland) Act 1995".

Reserve Forces Act 1980 (c. 9)

26. In subsection (2) of section 144 of the Reserve Forces Act 1980, in paragraph (b) for the words "section 289B of the Criminal Procedure (Scotland) Act 1975" there shall be substituted the words "section 225(8) of the Criminal Procedure (Scotland) Act 1995".

Protection of Trading Interests Act 1980 (c. 11)

27. In subsection (5) of section 3 of the Protection of Trading Interests Act 1980, in paragraph (b) for the words "section 289B of the Criminal Procedure (Scotland) Act 1975" there shall be substituted the words "section 225(8) of the Criminal Procedure (Scotland) Act 1995".

Competition Act 1980 (c. 21)

28. In subsection (7) of section 19 of the Competition Act 1980, in paragraph (b) for the words "section 289B of the Criminal Procedure (Scotland) Act 1975" there shall be substituted the words "section 225(8) of the Criminal Procedure (Scotland) Act 1995".

Licensed Premises (Exclusion of Certain Persons) Act 1980 (c. 32)

29. In subsection (2) of section 1 of the Licensed Premises (Exclusion of Certain Persons) Act 1980, in paragraph (c) for the words from "sections" to "1975" there shall be substituted the words "sections 228, 246(2) and (3) and 247 of the Criminal Procedure (Scotland) Act 1995".

Water (Scotland) Act 1980 (c. 45)

30. [Repealed by the Antisocial Behaviour etc. (Scotland) Act 2004 (asp 8), s.144(2) and Sch.5. Brought into force on October 28, 2004 by the Antisocial Behaviour etc. (Scotland) Act 2004 (Commencement and Savings) Order 2004 (SSI 2004/420 (C.31)).]

Solicitors (Scotland) Act 1980 (c. 46)

31. In subsection (1) of section 25A of the Solicitors (Scotland) Act 1980 (rights of audience) for the words from "section 250" to "1975" there shall be substituted the words "section 103(8) of the Criminal Procedure (Scotland) Act 1995 (right of solicitor to appear before single judge)".

Law Reform (Miscellaneous Provisions) (Scotland) Act 1980 (c. 55)

32.—(1) The Law Reform (Miscellaneous Provisions) (Scotland) Act 1980 shall be amended as follows.

(2) After subsection (5) of section 1 (persons excused from jury service for good reason) there shall be inserted the following subsection—

"(5A) Where the clerk of court has, under subsection (5) above, excused a person from jury service in any criminal proceedings he shall, unless he considers there to be exceptional circumstances which make it inappropriate to do so, within one year of the date of that excusal cite that person to attend for jury service in criminal proceedings."

(3) In subsection (6) of that section, for paragraph (c) there shall be substituted the following—

"(c) section 85(8) or 88(7) of the Criminal Procedure (Scotland) Act 1995,".

(4) In Schedule 1 (ineligibility for and disqualification and excusal from jury service)—

   (a) in Part I (persons ineligible), in paragraph (p) of Group B for the words "section 462(1) of the Criminal Procedure (Scotland) Act 1975" there shall be substituted the words "section 307(1) of the Criminal Procedure (Scotland) Act 1995";

   (b) in Part II (persons disqualified from jury service), at the end of paragraph (b) there shall be inserted—

      "(c) in respect of jury service in any criminal proceedings, persons who are on bail in or in connection with criminal proceedings in any part of the United Kingdom.";

      and

   (c) in Part III (persons excusable as of right), at the end of Group D there shall be inserted—

"GROUP DD

Members of certain religious bodies

In respect of jury service in any criminal proceedings, practising members of religious societies or orders the tenets or beliefs of which are incompatible with jury service."

Criminal Justice (Scotland) Act 1980 (c. 62)

33. In subsection (10) of section 80 of the Criminal Justice (Scotland) Act 1980, for the words "section 289B of the 1975 Act" there shall be substituted the words "section 225(8) of the Criminal Procedure (Scotland) Act 1995".

Local Government, Planning and Land Act 1980 (c. 65)

34. In subsection (14) of section 167 of the Local Government, Planning and Land Act 1980, in paragraph (b) of the definition of "the statutory maximum" for the words "section 289B of the Criminal Procedure (Scotland) Act 1975" there shall be substituted the words "section 225(8) of the Criminal Procedure (Scotland) Act 1995".

Animal Health Act 1981 (c. 22)

35. In subsection (2) of section 92 of the Animal Health Act 1981, for the words "section 284 of the Criminal Procedure (Scotland) Act 1975" there shall be substituted the words "section 7(6) of the Criminal Procedure (Scotland) Act 1995".

Contempt of Court Act 1981 (c. 49)

36.—(1) Section 15 of the Contempt of Court Act 1981 (penalties for contempt in Scottish proceedings) shall be amended as follows.

(2) In subsection (2)—

   (a) in paragraph (a) for "£500" there shall be substituted the words "level 4 on the standard scale"; and

   (b) in paragraph (b) for "£200" there shall be substituted the words "level 4 on the standard scale".

(3) For subsection (3) and (4) there shall be substituted the following—

   "(3) The following provisions of the Criminal Procedure (Scotland) Act 1995 shall apply in relation to persons found guilty of contempt of court in Scottish proceedings as they apply in relation to persons convicted of offences—

      (a) in every case, section 207 (restrictions on detention of young offenders);

      (b) in any case to which paragraph (b) of subsection (2) above does not apply, sections 58, 59 and 61 (persons suffering from mental disorder);

   and in any case to which the said paragraph (b) does apply, subsection (5) below shall have effect."

(4) In subsection (5)—

   (a) for the words "section 286 of the Criminal Procedure (Scotland) Act 1975" there shall be substituted the words "section 7(9) and (10) of the Criminal Procedure (Scotland) Act 1995"; and

   (b) for the words "section 376(1)" there shall be substituted the words "section 58(1)".

37. In section 17 of the Matrimonial Homes (Family Protection) (Scotland) Act 1981 (procedure after arrest)—

 (a) in subsection (2) for the words "section 10 of the Bail etc. (Scotland) Act 1980" there shall be substituted the words "section 8 of the Criminal Procedure (Scotland) Act 1995"; and

 (b) in subsection (3) for the words from the beginning to "1980" there shall be substituted the words "Subsections (1) to (3) of section 15 of the said Act of 1995".

Betting and Gaming Duties Act 1981 (c. 63)

38. In subsection (1) of section 33 of the Betting and Gaming Duties Act 1981 in the definition of "the prescribed sum", in paragraph (b) for the words from "section 289B" to the end of the paragraph there shall be substituted the words "subsection (8) of section 225 of the Criminal Procedure (Scotland) Act 1995 (£5,000 or other sum substituted by order under subsection (4) of that section)".

Civil Aviation Act 1982 (c. 16)

39. In subsection (1) of section 105 of the Civil Aviation Act 1982, in the definition of "the statutory maximum" for paragraph (b) there shall be substituted the following—

 "(b) in Scotland, the prescribed sum within the meaning of subsection (8) of section 225 of the Criminal Procedure (Scotland) Act 1995 (that is to say £5,000 or another sum fixed by order under subsection (4) of that section);".

Oil and Gas Enterprise Act 1982 (c. 23)

40. [Repealed by the Petroleum Act 1998 (c.17), Sch.5. Brought into force on February 15, 1999 by the Petroleum Act 1998 (Commencement No.1) Order 1999 (SI 1999/161 (C.5)).

Iron and Steel Act 1982 (c. 25)

41. In subsection (1) of section 37 of the Iron and Steel Act 1982, in the definition of "the statutory maximum" for paragraph (b) there shall be substituted the following—

 "(b) in Scotland, the prescribed sum within the meaning of subsection (8) of section 225 of the Criminal Procedure (Scotland) Act 1995 (that is to say £5,000 or another sum fixed by order under subsection (4) of that section);".

Civil Jurisdiction and Judgments Act 1982 (c. 27)

42. In subsection (4A) of section 18 of the Civil Jurisdiction and Judgments Act 1982 (enforcement of U.K. judgments in other parts of U.K.) for the words from "Part I of the Criminal Justice (Scotland) Act 1987" to the end there shall be substituted the words "the Proceeds of Crime (Scotland) Act 1995".

Aviation Security Act 1982 (c. 36)

43. In subsection (1) of section 38 of the Aviation Security Act 1982, in the definition of "the statutory maximum" for paragraph (b) there shall be substituted the following—

 "(b) in Scotland, the prescribed sum within the meaning of subsection (8) of section 225 of the Criminal Procedure (Scotland) Act 1995 (that is to say £5,000 or another sum fixed by order under subsection (4) of that section);".

Civic Government (Scotland) Act 1982 (c. 45)

44.—(1) The Civic Government (Scotland) Act 1982 shall be amended as follows.

(2) In subsection (8) of section 51, in the definition of "prescribed sum" for the words "section 289B of the Criminal Procedure (Scotland) Act 1975" there shall be substituted the words "section 225(8) of the Criminal Procedure (Scotland) Act 1995".

(3) In subsection (3) of section 52, for the words "section 289B of the Criminal Procedure (Scotland) Act 1975" there shall be substituted the words "section 225(8) of the Criminal Procedure (Scotland) Act 1995".

Insurance Companies Act 1982 (c. 50)

45.—(1) The Insurance Companies Act 1982 shall be amended as follows.

(2) In subsection (3) of section 14, in paragraph (b)(ii) for the words "section 289B of the Criminal Procedure (Scotland) Act 1975" there shall be substituted the words "section 225(8) of the Criminal Procedure (Scotland) Act 1995".

(3) In subsection (2) of section 71, in paragraph (b)(ii) for the words "section 289B of the Criminal Procedure (Scotland) Act 1975" there shall be substituted the words "section 225(8) of the Criminal Procedure (Scotland) Act 1995".

(4) In subsection (1) of section 81, in paragraph (b)(ii) for the words "section 289B of the Criminal Procedure (Scotland) Act 1975" there shall be substituted the words "section 225(8) of the Criminal Procedure (Scotland) Act 1995".

(5) In subsection (4) of section 92, for the words "section 74 of the Criminal Procedure (Scotland) Act 1975" there shall be substituted the words "section 70 of the Criminal Procedure (Scotland) Act 1995".

(6) In subsection (4) of section 94 for the words "section 331 of the Criminal Procedure (Scotland) Act 1975" there shall be substituted the words "section 136 of the Criminal Procedure (Scotland) Act 1995".

(7) In subsection (5) of that section for the words "section 331 of the said Act of 1975" there shall be substituted the words "section 136 of the said Act of 1995".

Industrial Development Act 1982 (c. 52)

46. [...]

AMENDMENT

Para.46 repealed by the Statute Law (Repeals) Act 2004 (c.14), s.1(1), Sch.1, Pt XVI. Brought into force on July 22, 2004 on Royal Assent.

Car Tax Act 1983 (c. 53)

47. [...]

AMENDMENT

Para.47 repealed by the Statute Law (Repeals) Act 2004 (c.14), s.1(1), Sch.1, Pt IX. Brought into force on July 22, 2004 on Royal Assent.

Telecommunications Act 1984 (c. 12)

48. [Repealed by the Wireless Telegraphy Act 2006, s.125 and Sch.9]

AMENDMENT

Para.48(2) and (3) repealed by the Communications Act 2003 (c.21), Sch.19. Brought into force on December 29, 2003 by the Office of Communications Act 2002 (Commencement No.3) and Communications Act 2003 (Commencement No.2) Order 2003 (SI 2003/3142 (C.125))

Para 48 repealed by the Wireless Telegraphy Act 2006, s.125 and Sch.9(effective February 8, 2007)

Road Traffic Regulation Act 1984 (c. 27)

49. In subsection (2) of section 110 of the Road Traffic Regulation Act 1984—
   (a) for the words "section 331 of the Criminal Procedure (Scotland) Act 1975" there shall be substituted the words "section 136 of the Criminal Procedure (Scotland) Act 1995"; and
   (b) for the words "section 331" where they second occur there shall be substituted the words "section 136".

Mental Health (Scotland) Act 1984 (c. 36)

50. [...]

AMENDMENT

Para.50(7)(b) deleted by the Crime and Punishment (Scotland) Act 1997 (c.48), s.62(1) and Sch.1, para.19(3).

Para.50 repealed by the Mental Health (Care and Treatment) (Scotland) Act 2003, Sch.5, Pt I. Brought into force on October 5, 2005 by the Mental Health (Care and Treatment) (Scotland) Act 2003 (Commencement No.4) Order 2005 (SSI 2005/161 (C.6)).

Video Recordings Act 1984 (c. 39)

51. In subsection (1) of section 16C of the Video Recordings Act 1984 (sheriff's jurisdiction), for the words "section 287 of the Criminal Procedure (Scotland) Act 1975" there shall be substituted the words "section 9 of the Criminal Procedure (Scotland) Act 1995".

Repatriation of Prisoners Act 1984 (c. 47)

52. The Schedule to the Repatriation of Prisoners Act 1984 shall be amended as follows—
  (a) in paragraph 4(2) for the words "section 207 or 415 of the Criminal Procedure (Scotland) Act 1975" there shall be substituted the words "section 207 of the Criminal Procedure (Scotland) Act 1995";
  (b) in paragraph 5(3) for "1975" there shall be substituted "1995".

Foster Children (Scotland) Act 1984 (c. 56)

53.—(1) The Foster Children (Scotland) Act 1984 shall be amended as follows.

(2) In section 7, in paragraph (c) of subsection (1) for the words "Criminal Procedure (Scotland) Act 1975" there shall be substituted the words "Criminal Procedure (Scotland) Act 1995".

(3) [...]

AMENDMENT

Para.53(3) deleted by the Crime and Punishment (Scotland) Act 1997 (c.48), s.62(1) and Sch.1, para.19(3).

Rent (Scotland) Act 1984 (c. 58)

54. In subsection (1) of section 115 of the Rent (Scotland) Act 1984, in the definition of—
  (a) "the standard scale" for the words "section 289G of the Criminal Procedure (Scotland) Act 1975" there shall be substituted the words "section 225(1) of the Criminal Procedure (Scotland) Act 1995"; and
  (b) "the statutory maximum" for the words "section 289B(6) of the Criminal Procedure (Scotland) Act 1975" there shall be substituted the words "section 225(8) of the Criminal Procedure (Scotland) Act 1995".

Police and Criminal Evidence Act 1984 (c. 60)

55. In subsection (3) of section 75 of the Police and Criminal Evidence Act 1984—
  (a) for the words "section 392 of the Criminal Procedure (Scotland) Act 1975" there shall be substituted the words "section 247 of the Criminal Procedure (Scotland) Act 1995"; and
  (b) for the words "section 182 or section 183 of the said Act of 1975" there shall be substituted the words "section 228 or section 246(3) of the said Act of 1995".

Companies Act 1985 (c. 6)

56.—(1) The Companies Act 1985 shall be amended as follows.

(2) In section 440, for the words "section 52 of the Criminal Justice (Scotland) Act 1987" there shall be substituted the words "section 28 of the Criminal Law (Consolidation) (Scotland) Act 1995".

(3) In subsection (3) of section 731, for the words "section 331 of the Criminal Procedure (Scotland) Act 1975" there shall be substituted the words "section 136 of the Criminal Procedure (Scotland) Act 1995".

(4) In subsection (4) of section 734, for the words "section 74 of the Criminal Procedure (Scotland) Act 1975" there shall be substituted the words "section 70 of the Criminal Procedure (Scotland) Act 1995".

Surrogacy Arrangements Act 1985 (c. 49)

57. In subsection (6) of section 4 of the Surrogacy Arrangements Act 1985, for the words "section 331(1) of the Criminal Procedure (Scotland) Act 1975" there shall be substituted the words "section 136(1) of the Criminal Procedure (Scotland) Act 1995".

The Bankruptcy (Scotland) Act 1985 (c. 66)

58.—(1) The Bankruptcy (Scotland) Act 1985 shall be amended as follows.

(2) In section 5(4) (meaning of qualified creditor), for the words "or by section 114(1) of the Criminal Justice (Scotland) Act 1995" there shall be substituted the words "or by section 49(1) of the Proceeds of Crime (Scotland) Act 1995".

(3) In section 7(1) (meaning of apparent insolvency), in the definition of "confiscation order", for the words "or by section 114(1) of the Criminal Justice (Scotland) Act 1995" there shall be substituted the words "or by section 49(1) of the Proceeds of Crime (Scotland) Act 1995".

(4) In subsection (2) of section 55 (effect of discharge of bankrupt on certain liabilities), after paragraph (a) there shall be inserted the following paragraphs—

> "(aa) any liability to pay a fine imposed in a district court;
> (ab) any liability under a compensation order within the meaning of section 249 of the Criminal Procedure (Scotland) Act 1995;".

(5) In subsection (2) of section 68, for the words "section 331 of the Criminal Procedure (Scotland) Act 1975" there shall be substituted the words "section 136 of the Criminal Procedure (Scotland) Act 1995".

Animals (Scientific Procedures) Act 1986 (c. 14)

59. In subsection (4) of section 26 of the Animals (Scientific Procedures) Act 1986, for the words "section 331 of the Criminal Procedure (Scotland) Act 1975" there shall be substituted the words "section 136 of the Criminal Procedure (Scotland) Act 1995".

Consumer Safety (Amendment) Act 1986 (c. 29)

60.—(1) The Consumer Safety (Amendment) Act 1986 shall be amended as follows.

(2) In subsection (3) of section 7, for "1975" there shall be substituted "1995".

(3) In section 10 for the words "section 452(4)(a) to (e) of the Criminal Procedure (Scotland) Act 1975" there shall be substituted the words "section 182(5)(a) to (e) of the Criminal Procedure (Scotland) Act 1995".

Insolvency Act 1986 (c. 45)

61. In subsection (3) of section 431 of the Insolvency Act 1986, for the words "section 331 of the Criminal Procedure (Scotland) Act 1975" there shall be substituted the words "section 136 of the Criminal Procedure (Scotland) Act 1995".

Company Directors Disqualification Act 1986 (c. 46)

62. In subsection (1) of section 8 of the Company Directors Disqualification Act 1986, for the words "section 52 of the Criminal Justice (Scotland) Act 1987" there shall be substituted the words "section 28 of the Criminal Law (Consolidation) (Scotland) Act 1995".

Legal Aid (Scotland) Act 1986 (c. 47)

63.—(1) The Legal Aid (Scotland) Act 1986 shall be amended as follows.

(2) In subsection (4) of section 21, for the words "section 462 of the Criminal Procedure (Scotland) Act 1975" there shall be substituted the words "section 307 of the Criminal Procedure (Scotland) Act 1995".

(3) In subsection (1) of section 22 (circumstances in which criminal legal aid automatically available), after paragraph (d) there shall be inserted the following paragraphs—

> "(da) in relation to any proceedings under solemn or summary procedure whereby the court determines (whether or not on a plea by the accused person) whether he is insane so that his trial cannot proceed or continue;
> (db) in relation to an examination of facts held under section 55 of the Criminal Procedure (Scotland) Act 1995 and the disposal of the case following such examination of facts;
> (dc) in relation to any appeal under section 62 or 63 (appeal by, respectively, accused or prosecutor in case involving insanity) of that Act of 1995;"

(4) In subsection (2) of section 23, for the words from "section 41(2)(b)" to the end there shall be substituted the words "section 204(4)(b) of the Criminal Procedure (Scotland) Act 1995".

(5) In subsection (1) of section 25 (legal aid in criminal appeals)—

(a) after the word "sentence" there shall be inserted the words ", other disposal"; and
(b) at the end there shall be inserted the words "other than an appeal in relation to which section 22(1)(dc) of this Act applies".

(6) In subsection (2) of that section—

(a) in paragraph (a) after the word "below," there shall be inserted the words "the Board is satisfied"; and

(b) for paragraph (b) and the preceding "and" there shall be substituted the following paragraphs—

"(b) in the case of an appeal under section 106(1) or 175(2) of the Criminal Procedure (Scotland) Act 1995, leave to appeal is granted; and

(c) in the case of an appeal under any other provision of that Act, where the applicant is the appellant, the Board is satisfied that in all the circumstances of the case it is in the interests of justice that the applicant should receive criminal legal aid."

(7) After the said subsection (2) there shall be inserted the following subsection—

"(2A) Where the Board has refused an application for criminal legal aid on the ground that it is not satisfied as mentioned in subsection (2)(c) above the High Court may, at any time prior to the disposal of an appeal, whether or not on application made to it, notwithstanding such refusal determine that it is in the interests of justice that the applicant should receive criminal legal aid in connection with the appeal, and the Board shall forthwith make such legal aid available to him."

(8) For subsection (5) there shall be substituted the following subsections—

"(5) Subsections (2)(a), (3) and (4) above shall apply to an application for criminal legal aid in connection with consideration under section 107, 180 or 187 of the Criminal Procedure (Scotland) Act 1995 whether to grant leave to appeal as if—

(a) in subsection (2)(a), for the words "of the appeal" there were substituted the words "in connection with consideration whether to grant leave to appeal"; and

(b) in subsection (4), after the word "is" there were inserted the words "subject to leave being granted,".

(6) Subsections (2)(a) and (c) and (2A) to (4) above shall apply to an application for criminal legal aid in connection with a petition to the *nobile officium* of the High Court of Judiciary (whether arising in the course of any proceedings or otherwise) as they apply for the purposes of subsection (1) above.

(7) Subsections (2)(a), (3) and (4) above shall apply to an application for criminal legal aid in connection with a reference by the Secretary of State under section 124 of the Criminal Procedure (Scotland) Act 1995 as they apply for the purposes of subsection (1) above."

(9) In subsection (3) of section 30 (application of section 25 to legal aid in contempt proceedings),—

(a) before the words "Section 25" there shall be inserted the words "Subsections (2)(a) and (c), (2A) to (4) and (6) of";

(b) for the words "it applies" there shall be substituted the words "they apply";

(c) after the word "sentence" there shall be substituted the words ",other disposal";

(d) after the word "application" there shall be inserted the following paragraph—

"(za) in subsection (2a) of that section, the reference to the High Court shall include a reference to the Court of Session;"; and

(e) in paragraph (b) for the word "(5)" there shall be substituted the word "(6)".

(10) In subsection (2) of section 35, for the words "section 331 of the Criminal Procedure (Scotland) Act 1975" there shall be substituted the words "section 136 of the Criminal Procedure (Scotland) Act 1995".

Social Security Act 1986 (c. 50)

64. In subsection (5) of section 56 of the Social Security Act 1986—

(a) for the words "section 331 of the Criminal Procedure (Scotland) Act 1975" there shall be substituted the words "section 136 of the Criminal Procedure (Scotland) Act 1995"; and

(b) for the words "section 331 of the said Act of 1975" there shall be substituted the words "section 136 of the said Act of 1995".

Building Societies Act 1986 (c. 53)

65. In subsection (5) of section 111 of the Building Societies Act 1986, for the words "section 331(3) of the Criminal Procedure (Scotland) Act 1975" there shall be substituted the words "section 136(3) of the Criminal Procedure (Scotland) Act 1995".

Financial Services Act 1986 (c. 60)

66. In subsection (4) of section 203 of the Financial Services Act 1986, for the words "section 74 of the Criminal Procedure (Scotland) Act 1975" there shall be substituted the words "section 70 of the Criminal Procedure (Scotland) Act 1995".

67.—(1) The Banking Act 1987 shall be amended as follows.

(2) In subsection (3) of section 97, for the words "section 331 of the Criminal Procedure (Scotland) Act 1975" there shall be substituted the words "section 136 of the Criminal Procedure (Scotland) Act 1995"

(3) In subsection (4) of section 98, for the words "section 74 of the Criminal Procedure (Scotland) Act 1975" there shall be substituted the words "section 70 of the Criminal Procedure (Scotland) Act 1995".

Consumer Protection Act 1987 (c. 43)

68. In subsection (8) of section 17 of the Consumer Protection Act 1987, for the words from "and section 452(4)(a) to (e)" to the end there shall be substituted the words "and section 182(5)(a) to (e) of the Criminal Procedure (Scotland) Act 1995 shall apply to an appeal under this subsection as it applies to a stated case under Part X of that Act".

The Criminal Justice Act 1988 (c. 33)

69. [Repealed by the Proceeds of Crime Act 2002 (c.29), Sch.12. Brought into force on March 24, 2003 by the Proceeds of Crime Act 2002 (Commencement No.5, Transitional Provisions and Savings and Amendment) Order 2003 (SI 2003/333 (C.20)).]

The Copyright, Designs and Patents Act 1988 (c. 48)

70.—(1) The Copyright, Designs and Patents Act 1988 shall be amended as follows.

(2) In section 108(6) (order for delivery up in criminal proceedings) for the words "Chapter II of Part II of the Criminal Justice (Scotland) Act 1995" there shall be substituted the words "Part II of the Proceeds of Crime (Scotland) Act 1995".

(3) In section 199(6) (order for delivery up in criminal proceedings) for the words "Chapter II of Part II of the Criminal Justice (Scotland) Act 1995" there shall be substituted the words "Part II of the Proceeds of Crime (Scotland) Act 1995".

Road Traffic Offenders Act 1988 (c. 53)

71.—(1) The Road Traffic Offenders Act 1988 shall be amended as follows.

(2) In subsection (5) of section 6 (time limit for commencement of summary proceedings), for the words "section 331 of the Criminal Procedure (Scotland) Act 1975" there shall be substituted the words "section 136 of the Criminal Procedure (Scotland) Act 1995".

(3) In subsection (6) of section 24 (alternative verdicts) for the words "sections 61, 63, 64, 312 and 457A of the Criminal Procedure (Scotland) Act 1975" there shall be substituted the words "sections 295, 138(4), 256 and 293 of and Schedule 3 to the Criminal Procedure (Scotland) Act 1995".

(4) In subsection (2) of section 31 (taking account of endorsation) for the words "section 357(1) of the Criminal Procedure (Scotland) Act 1975" there shall be substituted the words "section 166(1) to (6) of the Criminal Procedure (Scotland) Act 1995".

(5) In subsection (6) of section 32 (extracts of licensing records) for the words "section 357(1) of the Criminal Procedure (Scotland) Act 1975" there shall be substituted the words "section 166(1) to (6) of the Criminal Procedure (Scotland) Act 1995".

(6) After section 33 of the Road Traffic Offenders Act 1988 (fine and imprisonment), there shall be inserted the following section—

"Forfeiture of vehicles: Scotland.

33A.—(1) Where a person commits an offence to which this subsection applies by—

    (a) driving, attempting to drive, or being in charge of a vehicle; or

    (b) failing to comply with a requirement made under section 7 of the Road Traffic Act 1988 (failure to provide specimen for analysis or laboratory test) in the course of an investigation into whether the offender had committed an offence while driving, attempting to drive or being in charge of a vehicle, or

    (c) failing, as the driver of a vehicle, to comply with subsections (2) and (3) of section 170 of the Road Traffic Act 1988 (duty to stop and give information or report accident),

the court may, on an application under this subsection, make an order forfeiting the vehicle concerned, and any vehicle forfeited under this subsection shall be disposed of as the court may direct.

(2) Subsection (1) above applies—

    (a) to an offence under the Road Traffic Act 1988 which is punishable with imprisonment; and

    (b) to an offence of culpable homicide.

(3) An application under subsection (1) above shall be at the instance of the prosecutor made when he moves for sentence (or, if the person has been remitted for sentence under section 195 of the Criminal Procedure (Scotland) Act 1995) made before sentence is pronounced.

(4) Where—

    (a) the court is satisfied, on an application under this subsection by the prosecutor—

        (i) that proceedings have been, or are likely to be, instituted against a person in Scotland for an offence to which subsection (1) above applies allegedly committed in the manner specified in paragraph (a), (b) or (c) of that subsection; and

        (ii) that there is reasonable cause to believe that a vehicle specified in the application is to be found in a place or in premises so specified; and

    (b) it appears to the court that there are reasonable grounds for thinking that in the event of the person being convicted of the offence an order under subsection (1) above might be made in relation to the vehicle,

the court may grant a warrant authorising a person named therein to enter and search the place or premises and seize the vehicle.

(5) Where the court has made an order under subsection (1) above for the forfeiture of a vehicle, the court or any justice may, if satisfied on evidence on oath—

    (a) that there is reasonable cause to believe that the vehicle is to be found in any place or premises; and

    (b) that admission to the place or premises has been refused or that a refusal of such admission is apprehended,

issue a warrant of search which may be executed according to law.

(6) In relation to summary proceedings, the reference in subsection (5) above to a justice includes a reference to the sheriff and to a magistrate.

(7) Part II of the Proceeds of Crime (Scotland) Act 1995 shall not apply in respect of a vehicle in relation to which this section applies.

(8) This section extends to Scotland only."

(7) In subsection (3) of section 46 (combination of disqualification and endorsement with probation etc)—

    (a) in paragraph (b) for the words from "section 182" to the end there shall be substituted the words "section 228 (probation) or 246(2) or (3) (absolute discharge) of the Criminal Procedure (Scotland) Act 1995"; and

    (b) for the words from "section 191" to the end of the subsection there shall be substituted the words "section 247 of that Act shall not apply".

(8) In section 60—

    (a) in subsection (4) for the words "section 315 of the Criminal Procedure (Scotland) Act 1975" there shall be substituted the words "section 140 of the Criminal Procedure (Scotland) Act 1995";

    (b) in subsection (5) for the words "Part II" there shall be substituted the words "Part IX"; and

    (c) in subsection (6)—

        (i) in paragraph (b) for the words "section 312" where they first occur there shall be substituted the words "section 140(4)";

        (ii) in that paragraph for the words "paragraphs (a) to (z) of section 312 of" there shall be substituted the words "section 255 of and Schedule 3 to"; and

        (iii) paragraph (c) shall cease to have effect.

(9) In subsection (7) of section 64 (commencement of proceedings against owner of vehicle) for the words "section 331(1) of the Criminal Procedure (Scotland) Act 1975" there shall be substituted the words "section 136(1) of the Criminal Procedure (Scotland) Act 1995".

(10) In subsection (1) of section 89 (interpretation), in the definition of "court of summary jurisdiction" for the words "section 462(1) of the Criminal Procedure (Scotland) Act 1975" there shall be substituted the words "section 307(1) of the Criminal Procedure (Scotland) Act 1995".

Prevention of Terrorism (Temporary Provisions) Act 1989 (c. 4)

72. [Repealed by the Terrorism Act 2000 (c.11), s.125(2) and Sch.16, Part I. Brought into force on February 19, 2001 by the Terrorism Act 2000 (Commencement No.3) Order 2001 (SI 2001/421).]

Extradition Act 1989 (c. 33)

73. In subsection (13) of section 10 of the Extradition Act 1989 (bail in connection with appeal)—

(a) for the words "section 446(2) of the Criminal Procedure (Scotland) Act 1975" there shall be substituted the words "section 177(2) and (3) of the Criminal Procedure (Scotland) Act 1995"; and

(b) for the words "section 444" there shall be substituted the words "section 176".

Companies Act 1989 (c. 40)

74.—(1) The Companies Act 1989 shall be amended as follows.

(2) In subsection (4) of section 44 (jurisdiction and procedure for offences) for the words "section 74 of the Criminal Procedure (Scotland) Act 1975" there shall be substituted the words "section 70 of the Criminal Procedure (Scotland) Act 1995".

(3) In subsection (4) of section 91 (jurisdiction and procedure for offences) for the words "section 74 of the Criminal Procedure (Scotland) Act 1975" there shall be substituted the words "section 70 of the Criminal Procedure (Scotland) Act 1995".

Prisons (Scotland) Act 1989 (c. 45)

75.—(1) The Prisons (Scotland) Act 1989 shall be amended as follows.

(2) In subsection (1) of section 11 (removal of prisoners for judicial and other purposes), for the words "section 279 of the 1975 Act" there shall be substituted the words "section 132 of the 1995 Act".

(3) In subsection (3) of section 21 (transfer to prison of young offenders) for the words "the 1975 Act" where they first occur there shall be substituted the words "the 1995 Act".

(4) In section 39 (prison rules)—

(a) in subsection (5), for the words "section 279 of the 1975 Act" there shall be substituted the words "section 132 of the 1995 Act"; and

(b) in subsection (7), for the words "section 206 of the 1975 Act" there shall be substituted the words "section 208 of the 1995 Act".

(5) For subsection (3) of section 40 (persons unlawfully at large) there shall be substituted the following subsection—

"(3) In this section—

(a) any reference to a person sentenced to imprisonment shall be construed as including a reference to any person sentenced or ordered to be detained under section 44, 205 or 208 of the 1995 Act;

(b) any reference to a prison shall be construed as including a reference to a place where the person is liable to be detained under the sentence or order; and

(c) any reference to a sentence shall be construed as including a reference to an order under the said section 44."

(6) After section 40 there shall be added the following section—

"Warrants for arrest of escaped prisoners

40A.—(1) On an application being made to a justice alleging that any person is an offender unlawfully at large from a prison or other institution to which this Act or, as the case may be the Prison Act 1952 or the Prison Act (Northern Ireland) 1953 applies in which he is required to be detained after being convicted of an offence, the justice may issue a warrant to arrest him and bring him before any sheriff.

(2) Where a person is brought before a sheriff in pursuance of a warrant for his arrest under this section, the sheriff shall, if satisfied that he is the person named in the warrant and if satisfied that he is an offender unlawfully at large as mentioned in subsection (1) above, order him to be returned to the prison or other institution where he is required or liable to be detained."

(7) In subsection (1) of section 43 (interpretation) for the definition of "the 1975 Act" there shall be substituted the following—

""the 1995 Act" means the Criminal Procedure (Scotland) Act 1995;".

The Criminal Justice (International Co-operation) Act 1990 (c. 5)

76.—(1) The Criminal Justice (International Co-operation) Act 1990 shall be amended as follows.

(2) [...]

(3) In paragraph 2 of Schedule 1, for the words "section 320 of the Criminal Procedure (Scotland)

Act 1975" there shall be substituted the words "section 156 of the Criminal Procedure (Scotland) Act 1995".

AMENDMENTS

Sch.4, para.76(2) repealed by the Serious Organised Crime and Police Act 2005, s.174(2) and Sch.17, Part 2.

Computer Misuse Act 1990 (c. 18)

77. In subsection (7) of section 13 of the Computer Misuse Act 1990, for the words "section 331 of the Criminal Procedure (Scotland) Act 1975" there shall be substituted the words "section 136 of the Criminal Procedure (Scotland) Act 1995".

Law Reform (Miscellaneous Provisions) (Scotland) Act 1990 (c. 40)

78. In subsection (4) of section 20 of the Law Reform (Miscellaneous Provisions) (Scotland) Act 1990 (destination of fine imposed for professional misconduct) for the words "section 203 of the Criminal Procedure (Scotland) Act 1975" there shall be substituted the words "section 211(5) of the Criminal Procedure (Scotland) Act 1995".

The Northern Ireland (Emergency Provisions) Act 1991 (c. 24)

79. [...]

AMENDMENT

Para.79 repealed by the Northern Ireland (Emergency Provisions) Act 1996 (c.22), Sch.7.

Criminal Justice Act 1991 (c. 53)

80.—(1) The Criminal Justice Act 1991 shall be amended as follows.

(2) In subsection (3) of section 24 (deduction of fines from income support)—

(a) in paragraph (a) for the words "section 196(2) of the Criminal Procedure (Scotland) Act 1975" there shall be substituted the words "section 211(4) of the Criminal Procedure (Scotland) Act 1995";

(b) in paragraph (b) for the words "section 66 of the Criminal Justice (Scotland) Act 1980" there shall be substituted the words "section 252 of the Criminal Procedure (Scotland) Act 1995"; and

(c) in paragraph (c) for the words "section 403(1)(a) or (b) of the Criminal Procedure (Scotland) Act 1975" there shall be substituted the words "section 222(1)(a) or (b) of the Criminal Procedure (Scotland) Act 1995".

AMENDMENT

Para.80 as amended by the Powers of Criminal Courts (Sentencing) Act 2000 (c.6), s.165 and Sch.12, Pt I.

Dangerous Dogs Act 1991 (c. 65)

81. In subsection (9) of section 4 of the Dangerous Dogs Act 1991 (destruction and disqualification orders)—

(a) for the words "section 411 of the Criminal Procedure (Scotland) Act 1975" there shall be substituted the words "section 221 of the Criminal Procedure (Scotland) Act 1995"; and

(b) for the words "Part II" there shall be substituted the words "Part XI".

Social Security Administration Act 1992 (c. 5)

82. In subsection (7) of section 116 of the Social Security Administration Act 1992—

(a) for the words "section 331 of the Criminal Procedure (Scotland) Act 1975" there shall be substituted the words "section 136 of the Criminal Procedure (Scotland) Act 1995"; and

(b) for the words "section 331 of the said Act of 1975" there shall be substituted the words "section 136 of the said Act of 1995".

Timeshare Act 1992 (c. 35)

83. In subsection (3) of section 11 of the Timeshare Act 1992 (prosecution time limit), for the

words "section 331 of the Criminal Procedure (Scotland) Act 1975" there shall be substituted the words "section 136 of the Criminal Procedure (Scotland) Act 1995".

Friendly Societies Act 1992 (c. 40)

84. In subsection (5) of section 107 of the Friendly Societies Act 1992 (prosecution time limit), for the words "section 331(1) of the Criminal Procedure (Scotland) Act 1975" there shall be substituted the words "section 136(1) of the Criminal Procedure (Scotland) Act 1995".

Trade Union and Labour Relations (Consolidation) Act 1992 (c. 52)

85. In subsection (6) of section 45A of the Trade Union and Labour Relations (Consolidation) Act 1992 (prosecution time limit), for the words "section 331 of the Criminal Procedure (Scotland) Act 1975" there shall be substituted the words "section 136 of the Criminal Procedure (Scotland) Act 1995".

Prisoners and Criminal Proceedings (Scotland) Act 1993 (c. 9)

86.—(1) The Prisoners and Criminal Proceedings (Scotland) Act 1993 shall be amended as follows.

(2) Subject to any specific amendment under this paragraph, for the words "1975 Act" where they occur there shall be substituted the words "1995 Act".

(3) In subsection (1) of section 5 (fine defaulters) for paragraph (a) there shall be substituted the following paragraph—

> "(a) under section 219 of the 1995 Act (imprisonment for non-payment of fine) or, by virtue of that section, under section 207 of that Act (detention of young offenders);".

(4) Section 6 (application of Part to young offenders etc) shall be amended as follows—

- (a) in paragraph (a) for the words "section 207(2) or 415(2)" there shall be substituted the words "section 207(2)";
- (b) for the words "section 205" there shall be substituted the words "section 205(1) to (3)";
- (c) for the words "section 206" where they occur there shall be substituted the words "section 208"; and
- (d) for the words "section 207(2)" there shall be substituted the words "section 207(2)".

(5) In section 7 (children detained in solemn proceedings) for the words "section 206" where they occur there shall be substituted the words "section 208".

(6) In section 11 (duration of licence)—

- (a) in subsection (3), for the words "section 212A" there shall be substituted the words "section 209"; and
- (b) in paragraph (b) of that subsection, for the words from "the" in the second place where it occurs to the end there shall be substituted—

> "there has elapsed—
>
> > (i) a period (reckoned from the date on which he was ordered to be returned to prison under or by virtue of subsection (2)(a) of that section) equal in length to the period between the date on which the new offence was committed and the date on which he would (but for his release) have served the original sentence in full; or
> >
> > (ii) subject to subsection (4) below, a total period equal in length to the period for which he was so ordered to be returned to prison together with, so far as not concurrent with that period, any term of imprisonment to which he was sentenced in respect of the new offence,
>
> whichever results in the later date.
>
> (4) In subsection (3)(b) above, "the original sentence" and "the new offence" have the same meanings as in section 16 of this Act."

(7) Section 14 (supervised release of short term prisoners) shall be amended as follows—

- (a) in subsection (2)—
  - (i) for the words "section 212A(1)" there shall be substituted the words "section 209(1)"; and
  - (ii) for the words "section 212A(2) to (6)" there shall be substituted the words "section 209(3) to (7)";
- (b) in subsection (3) for the words "section 212A(2)" there shall be substituted the words "section 209(3)"; and
- (c) in subsection (5) for the words "section 212A(5)(b)" there shall be substituted the words "section 209(6)(b)".

(8) In subsection (4) of section 15 (variation of supervised release order) for the words "section 212A(2)(b)" there shall be substituted the words "section 209(3)(b)"

(9) In section 16 (commission of offence by released prisoner)—

    (a) in subsection (6), for the words "section 254(3) or 453C(1)" there shall be substituted the words "section 118(4) or 189(1) and (2)"; and

    (b) for subsection (7) there shall be substituted the following subsection—

      "(7) Where an order under subsection (2) or (4) above is made in respect of a person released on licence—

        (a) the making of the order shall have the effect of revoking the licence; and

        (b) if the sentence comprising—

          (i) the period for which the person is ordered to be returned to prison; and

          (ii) so far as not concurrent with that period, any term of imprisonment to which he is sentenced in respect of the new offence, is six months or more but less than four years, section 1(1) of this Act shall apply in respect of that sentence as if for the word "unconditionally" there were substituted the words "on licence"."

(10) In subsection (1) of section 27 (interpretation of Part I), for the words "section 212A" where they occur there shall be substituted the words "section 209".

(11) In section 46 (interpretation) the definition of "the 1975 Act" shall cease to have effect and at the end there shall be inserted the following definition—

    ""the 1995 Act" means the Criminal Procedure (Scotland) Act 1995".

Agriculture Act 1993 (c. 37)

87. In subsection (5) of section 52 of the Agriculture Act 1993 (prosecution time limit) for the words "section 331 of the Criminal Procedure (Scotland) Act 1975" there shall be substituted the words "section 136 of the Criminal Procedure (Scotland) Act 1995".

Railways Act 1993 (c. 43)

88. In subsection (5) of section 148 of the Railways Act 1993 (prosecution time limit) for the words "section 331 of the Criminal Procedure (Scotland) Act 1975" there shall be substituted the words "section 136 of the Criminal Procedure (Scotland) Act 1995".

Finance Act 1994 (c. 9)

89.—(1) The Finance Act 1994 shall be amended as follows.

(2) In subsection (2) of section 22 (records and rules of evidence), in paragraph (d) for the words "Schedule 3 to the Prisoners and Criminal Proceedings (Scotland) Act 1995" there shall be substituted the words "Schedule 8 to the Criminal Procedure (Scotland) Act 1995".

(3) In subsection (3) of section 25 (order for production of documents), for the words "section 462 of the Criminal Procedure (Scotland) Act 1975" there shall be substituted the words "section 308 of the Criminal Procedure (Scotland) Act 1995".

(4) In Schedule 7 (insurance premium tax)—

    (a) in paragraph 1(6)(d), for the words "Schedule 3 to the Prisoners and Criminal Proceedings (Scotland) Act 1993" there shall be substituted the words "Schedule 8 to the Criminal Procedure (Scotland) Act 1995"; and

    (b) in paragraph 4(2), for the words "section 462 of the Criminal Procedure (Scotland) Act 1975" there shall be substituted the words "section 308 of the Criminal Procedure (Scotland) Act 1995".

Vehicle Excise and Registration Act 1994 (c. 22)

90.—(1) The Vehicle Excise and Registration Act 1994 shall be amended as follows.

(2) In subsection (1) of section 32 (effect of certain orders) for paragraph (b) there shall be substituted the following paragraph—

    "(b) or an order under section 228 of the Criminal Procedure (Scotland) Act 1995 placing him on probation or under 246(3) of that Act discharging him absolutely, or".

(3) In subsection (1) of section 41 (effect of certain orders) for paragraph (b) there shall be substituted the following paragraph—

    "(b) or an order under section 228 of the Criminal Procedure (Scotland) Act 1995 placing him on probation or under 246(2) or (3) of that Act discharging him absolutely, or".

(4) In subsection (4) of section 48 (time limit for proceedings) for the words "section 331 of the Criminal Procedure (Scotland) Act 1975" there shall be substituted the words "section 136 of the Criminal Procedure (Scotland) Act 1995".

91. In Schedule 11 of the Value Added Tax Act 1994—

    (a) in paragraph 10(3) (power of entry and search) for the words "section 462 of the Criminal Procedure (Scotland) Act 1975" there shall be substituted the words "section 308 of the Criminal Procedure (Scotland) Act 1995"; and

    (b) in paragraph 11(1) (access to certain information) for the words "section 462 of the Criminal Procedure (Scotland) Act 1975" there shall be substituted the words "section 308 of the Criminal Procedure (Scotland) Act 1995".

Trade Marks Act 1994 (c. 26)

92.—(1) The Trade Marks Act 1994 shall be amended as follows.

(2) In subsection (1) of section 96 (prosecution time limit) for the words "section 331 of the Criminal Procedure (Scotland) Act 1975" there shall be substituted the words "section 136 of the Criminal Procedure (Scotland) Act 1995".

(3) In section 98 (forfeiture)—

    (a) in subsection (2) for the words "section 310 of the Criminal Procedure (Scotland) Act 1975" there shall be substituted the words "section 134 of the Criminal Procedure (Scotland) Act 1995";

    (b) in subsection (6) for the words "Criminal Procedure (Scotland) Act 1975" there shall be substituted the words "Criminal Procedure (Scotland) Act 1995";

    (c) in subsection (9) for the words "section 452(4)(a) to (e) of the Criminal Procedure (Scotland) Act 1975" there shall be substituted the words "section 182(5)(a) to (c) of the Criminal Procedure (Scotland) Act 1995"; and

    (d) in subsection (11) for the words "Criminal Procedure (Scotland) Act 1975" there shall be substituted the words "Criminal Procedure (Scotland) Act 1995".

Criminal Justice and Public Order Act 1994 (c. 33)

93.—(1) The Criminal Justice and Public Order Act 1994 shall be amended as follows.

(2) In subsection (5) of section 25 (restriction on bail) in the definition of "the relevant enactments", for paragraph (b) there shall be substituted the following paragraph—

    "(b) as respects Scotland, sections 205(1) to (3) and 208 of the Criminal Procedure (Scotland) Act 1995;".

(3) In section 102 (provision of prisoner escorts)—

    (a) in paragraph (b) of subsection (3), for the words "Criminal Procedure (Scotland) Act 1975" there shall be substituted the words "Criminal Procedure (Scotland) Act 1995"; and

    (b) in subsection (6)—

        (i) in the definition of "hospital order", for the words "section 174, 174A, 175, 375A or 376 of the Act of 1975" there shall be substituted the words "section 53, 54 or 58 of the Act of 1995"; and

        (ii) in the definition of "warrant", for the words "Act of 1975" there shall be substituted the words "Act of 1995".

(4) In subsection (4) of section 104 (powers and duties of prison custody officers), for the words "section 395(2) of the Criminal Procedure (Scotland) Act 1975" there shall be substituted the words "section 212 of the Criminal Procedure (Scotland) Act 1995".

(5) In subsection (1) of section 117 (interpretation of Chapter), in the definition of "prisoner" for the words "section 215 or 426 of the Criminal Procedure (Scotland) Act 1975" there shall be substituted the words "section 295 of the Criminal Procedure (Scotland) Act 1995".

(6) In section 138 (which supplements section 137 relating to cross-border powers of arrest)—

    (a) in subsection (2), for the words from "subsections (2) to (7)" to "1993" there shall be substituted the words "subsections (2) to (8) of section 14 (detention and questioning at police station), subsections (1), (2) and (4) to (6) of section 15 (rights of person arrested or detained) and section 18 (prints, samples etc. in criminal investigations) of the Criminal Procedure (Scotland) Act 1995";

    (b) in subsection (6)—

        (i) for the words "sections 2 and 3 of the Criminal Justice (Scotland) Act 1980" there shall be substituted the words "sections 14 and 15 of the said Act of 1995";

        (ii) in paragraph (a), for the words "in section 2" there shall be substituted the words "in section 14" and for the words "in subsections (4) and (7)" there shall be substituted the words "in subsections (6) and (9)": and

(iii) in paragraph (b), for the words "in section 3(1)" there shall be substituted the words "in subsections (1) and (2) of section 15".

The Drug Trafficking Act 1994 (c. 37)

94. [...]

Local Government etc. (Scotland) Act 1994 (c. 39)

95.—(1) The Local Government etc. (Scotland) Act 1994 shall be amended as follows.

(2) In subsection (1) of section 127 (the Principal Reporter), for the words "Criminal Procedure (Scotland) Act 1975" there shall be substituted the words "Criminal Procedure (Scotland) Act 1995".

(3) In each of subsections (3) and (8) of section 128 (Scottish Children's Reporter Administration), for the words "Criminal Procedure (Scotland) Act 1975" there shall be substituted the words "Criminal Procedure (Scotland) Act 1995".

(4) In subsection (1) of section 130 (annual report of Principal Reporter), for the words "Criminal Procedure (Scotland) Act 1975" there shall be substituted the words "Criminal Procedure (Scotland) Act 1995".

Deregulation and Contracting Out Act 1994 (c. 40)

96. In subsection (2) of section 2 of the Deregulation and Contracting Out Act 1994, for paragraph (b) there shall be substituted the following paragraph—

"(b) section 292(6) and (7) of the Criminal Procedure (Scotland) Act 1995,".

Children (Scotland) Act 1995 (c. 36)

97.—(1) The Children (Scotland) Act 1995 shall be amended as follows.

(2) In subsection (2) of section 45 (attendance of child etc. at hearing), in paragraph (a) for the words "Schedule 1 of the Criminal Procedure (Scotland) Act 1975" there shall be substituted the words "Schedule 1 of the Criminal Procedure (Scotland) Act 1995".

(3) In section 50 (treatment of child's case on remission by court)—
  (a) in subsection (1), for the words "section 173, 372 or 373 of the Criminal Procedure (Scotland) Act 1975" there shall be substituted "section 49 of the Criminal Procedure (Scotland) Act 1995"; and
  (b) in subsection (2), for the words "the said section 373" there shall be substituted "subsection (7) of the said section 49".

(4) In subsection (2) of section 52 (children requiring compulsory supervision)—
  (a) in paragraph (d) for the words "Schedule 1 of the Criminal Procedure (Scotland) Act 1975" there shall be substituted the words "Schedule 1 of the Criminal Procedure (Scotland) Act 1995"; and
  (b) in paragraph (g), for the words "sections 2A to 2C of the Sexual Offences (Scotland) Act 1976" there shall be substituted "sections 1 to 3 of the Criminal Law (Consolidation) (Scotland) Act 1995".

(5) In subsection (7) of section 53 (information for Principal Reporter) for the words "section 462 of the Criminal Procedure (Scotland) Act 1975" there shall be substituted the words "section 307 of the Criminal Procedure (Scotland) Act 1995".

(6) In section 63(1) (duty of Principal Reporter where informed by constable of detention of a child) for the words "section 296(3) of the Criminal Procedure (Scotland) Act 1975" there shall be substituted "section 43(5) of the Criminal Procedure (Scotland) Act 1995".

(7) In section 78 (powers of arrest)—
  (a) in subsection (8), for the words "Criminal Procedure (Scotland) Act 1975" there shall be substituted the words "Criminal Procedure (Scotland) Act 1995";
  (b) in subsection (11), for the words "section 10 of the Bail etc. (Scotland) Act 1980" there shall be substituted the words "section 8 of the said Act of 1995"; and
  (c) in subsection (12), for the words "Subsections (1) and (3) of section 3 of the Criminal Justice (Scotland) Act 1980" there shall be substituted the words "Subsections (1), (2) and (4) of section 15 of the said Act of 1995".

98. [...]

AMENDMENT

Para.98 repealed by the Pensions Act 2004 (c.35), s.320 and Sch.13, Pt 1. Brought into force on April 6, 2006 by the Pensions Act 2004 (Commencement No. 9) Order 2006(SI 2006/560 (C.13)).

Note

99. The amendments made by this Schedule to—

(a) the Sea Fisheries Act 1968;

(b) the Fatal Accidents and Sudden Deaths Inquiry (Scotland) Act 1976; and

(c) section 15(2) of the Contempt of Court Act 1981,

are in substitution for amendments made to those enactments by section 56 of and Schedule 7 to the Criminal Justice Act 1988 which are repealed by this Act.

Section 6   SCHEDULE 5

REPEALS

Chapter	Short title	Extent of repeal
11 Geo. 4 & 1 Wm. 4 c. 69	The Court of Session Act 1830	Section 18
50 & 51 Vict. c. 35	The Criminal Procedure (Scotland) Act 1887	The whole Act
4 & 5 Geo. 5 c. 58	The Criminal Justice Administration Act 1914	Section 28(3)
12, 13 & 14 Geo. 6, c. 94	The Criminal Justice (Scotland) Act 1949	The whole Act
1 & 2 Eliz. 2, c. 14	The Prevention of Crime Act 1953	Section 1
2 & 3 Eliz. 2, c. 48	The Summary Jurisdiction (Scotland) Act 1954	The whole Act
1968 c. 49	The Social Work (Scotland) Act 1968	Section 31(1)
1975 c. 20	The District Courts (Scotland) Act 1975	Sections 2 to 4 Section 6 In Schedule 1, paragraph 27
1975 c. 21	The Criminal Procedure (Scotland) Act 1975	The whole Act
1977 c. 45	The Criminal Law Act 1977	In Schedule 6, the entries relating to the Criminal Procedure (Scotland) Act 1975 In Schedule 7, paragraph 2 Schedule 11
1978 c. 29	The National Health Service (Scotland) Act 1978	In Schedule 16, paragraph 41
1978 c. 49	The Community Service by Offenders (Scotland) Act 1978	Sections 1 to 8 Sections 10 to 13 Section 15 In Schedule 2, paragraphs 2 and 3
1979 c. 16	The Criminal Evidence Act 1979	In section 1(1) the words "sections 141 and 346 of the Criminal Procedure (Scotland) Act 1975"

Chapter	Short title	Extent of repeal
1980 c. 4	The Bail (Scotland) Act 1980	The whole Act
1980 c. 62	The Criminal Justice (Scotland) Act 1980	Sections 1 to 3
		Sections 4 to 7
		Sections 9 to 43
		Section 45(1)
		Sections 46 to 50
		Sections 52 to 54
		Sections 58 to 67
		Part V
		Sections 78 and 80
		Schedules 1 to 4
		In Schedule 7, paragraphs 25 to 78
1981 c. 45	The Forgery and Counterfeiting Act 1981	Section 26
1982 c. 48	The Criminal Justice Act 1982	Part IV
		Schedules 6 and 7
1982 c. 49	The Transport Act 1982	In section 40, paragraph (c) of subsection (5)
1984 c. 39	The Video Recordings Act 1984	Section 20
1985 c. 66	The Bankruptcy (Scotland) Act 1985	In section 5(4) the words "by section 1(1) of the Criminal Justice (Scotland) Act 1987"
		In section 7(1) the words "by section 1(1) of the Criminal Justice (Scotland) Act 1987"
1985 c. 73	The Law Reform (Miscellaneous Provisions) (Scotland) Act 1985	Section 21
		Sections 36 and 37
		Section 40
		Section 43
		Section 45
		In Schedule 2, paragraphs 16 to 20 and paragraph 23
		In Schedule 3, paragraphs 1, 3 and 4
1987 c. 41	The Criminal Justice (Scotland) Act 1987	Part I
		Sections 56 to 68
		In Schedule 1, paragraphs 4 to 18
1988 c. 53	The Road Traffic Offenders Act 1988	In section 60, paragraph (c) of subsection (6)
1988 c. 54	The Road Traffic (Consequential Provisions) Act 1988	In Schedule 3, paragraph 34
1990 c. 5	The Criminal Justice (International Co-operation) Act 1990	Section 15
		In Schedule 4, paragraph 5
1990 c. 40	The Law Reform (Miscellaneous Provisions) (Scotland) Act 1990	Sections 56 and 57
		Section 62
		Schedule 6
1991 c. 53	The Criminal Justice Act 1991	In Schedule 3, paragraph 8
1991 c. 62	The Armed Forces Act 1991	In Schedule 2, paragraph 9(2)

Chapter	Short title	Extent of repeal
1993 c. 9	The Prisoners and Criminal Proceedings (Scotland) Act 1993	Section 8 Section 14(1) Sections 28 to 35 Sections 37 to 43 In section 46, the definition of "the 1975 Act" Schedules 3 and 4 In Schedule 5, paragraph 1
1993 c. 13	The Carrying of Knives etc. (Scotland) Act 1993	The whole Act
1993 c. 36	The Criminal Justice Act 1993	Sections 68 and 69 In Schedule 5, paragraph 2
1994 c. 33	The Criminal Justice and Public Order Act 1994	Section 47(4) In section 129, subsections (1) to (3) Section 132 In section 157, subsection (7)
1994 c. 37	The Drug Trafficking Act 1994	In section 37, the words "that Part of" where they occur and in paragraph (a)(ii) of subsection (2) the words "Part I of".
1995 c. 20	The Criminal Justice (Scotland) Act 1995	The whole Act
1995 c. 36	The Children (Scotland) Act 1995.	Section 49 In Schedule 4, paragraphs 24, 27 and 29.

Section 6(2)   SCHEDULE 6

PROVISIONS REPEALED WITH SAVINGS

In section 43, the words from "and it shall not be necessary" to the end.

Section 45.

Section 46.

Section 47.

Section 52.

Section 53.

In section 54 the words from "and it shall not be necessary to specify" to the end.

In section 55, the words "it shall not be necessary to set forth the document or any part of it in such indictment".

Section 56.

Section 57.

In section 109, the words from the beginning to "except that".

In section 111, the words "it shall not be necessary that a new warrant should be granted for the incarceration of the accused, but".

Section 124 (except the proviso).

Section 222.

CRIMINAL PROCEDURE (SCOTLAND) ACT 1995

(1995 c. 46)

An Act to consolidate certain enactments relating to criminal procedure in Scotland.

[8th November 1995]

PART IX

SUMMARY PROCEEDINGS

General

Complaints

Citation

Children

Companies

First diet

Pre-trial procedure

Failure of accused to appear

Non-availability of judge

Trial diet

PART XII

EVIDENCE

Special capacity

PART XIII

MISCELLANEOUS

Lord Advocate

INTRODUCTION AND GENERAL NOTE

[1]It has been said that it takes lawyers five years to change a habit: if that is correct then the memory of the Criminal Procedure (Scotland) Act 1975 will linger on for some time, most probably in the reference to the very familiar sections. The Criminal Procedure (Scotland) Act 1995 is a consolidating provision so that much of the legal landscape remains the same even though the reference to individual parts has changed.

The Criminal Procedure (Scotland) Act 1995 has to be seen as part of a substantial Government policy to consolidate Scots criminal law, evidence and procedure. The Criminal Justice (Scotland) Act 1995 amended some aspects of the law of evidence and procedure and made new provisions in relation to attacking the proceeds of crime.

Once the Criminal Procedure (Scotland) Act 1975 (c.21) had been amended the law was consolidated in the Criminal Procedure (Scotland) Act 1995. The complete package of contemporary legislation must be seen to include also the Criminal Law (Consolidation) (Scotland) Act 1995 (c.39), the Criminal Law (Consequential Provisions) (Scotland) Act 1995 (c.40) and the Proceeds of Crime (Scotland) Act 1995 (c.43). The mechanics of the application of much of the law is to be found in the Act of Adjournal (Criminal Procedure Rules) 1996.

Consideration of the new law is restricted in this note to the Criminal Procedure (Scotland) Act 1995. Comprehensive annotations follow and those should help practitioners round the details of Act but there is benefit in knowing the structure of the Act itself: the parts are set out with general reference to some of the interesting sections.

Part I

Sections 1 to 11 make various provisions in regard to the jurisdiction and powers of the criminal courts of Scotland. There is virtually nothing new in this Part, merely a re-ordering of existing powers.

Part II

Sections 12 to 22 make provision for police functions. The power of the Lord Advocate to issue instructions to a chief constable in regard to the reporting of matters continues to provide an important constitutional safeguard, especially when seen in the context of the proviso to s.17(3) of the Police (Scotland) Act 1967 (c.77). The additional provisions reflect the original provision in law resulting from the Criminal Justice (Scotland) Act 1980 (c.62) as interpreted in subsequent case law.

Part III

Sections 23 to 33 consolidate the law of bail: it is the result of this consolidation that several Acts are no longer required, including the Bail etc. (Scotland) Act 1980 (c.4).

Part IV

Sections 34 to 40 deal with the peculiarly Scottish procedure of judicial examination. Sheriff Gerald Gordon referred to the pre-1980 judicial examination as an "empty ritual": see *The Criminal Justice (Scotland) Act 1980* (1981) (W. Green, Edinburgh) p. xviii. Whether very much more is now achieved is debatable but it is nevertheless the start of criminal proceedings leading for many to trial in a criminal court.

Part V

Sections 41 to 51 are provisions dealing with children and young persons in the capacity of

---

[1] Annotations by Iain Bradley, Solicitor in Scotland and Robert S. Shiels, Solicitor in Scotland.

offenders. Reference might also be made to the Children (Scotland) Act 1995 (c.36) which forms an important additional part of current legislation.

Part VI

Sections 52 to 63 make provision for various aspects of mental disorder. Perhaps the most substantial change in the whole of this Act is the introduction in s.55 of examination of facts. This permits evidence to be led (by either party) in order that the court can determine whether it is satisfied beyond reasonable doubt that the accused did the act or made the omission constituting the offence, and if it is satisfied on the balance of probabilities that there are no grounds for acquitting him. This procedure can only follow where an accused is found to be insane: s.54(1). However, it now allows for an examination of circumstances where hitherto no trial would have taken place.

Part VII

Sections 64 to 102 set out the procedural stages and requirement for trial by jury. By s.12 of and Sch.4 to the Criminal Justice (Scotland) Act 1980 there was abolished the mandatory diet in solemn proceedings and in its place there was established as required the preliminary diet. The new provision includes a first diet for solemn procedure in the sheriff court and a preliminary diet as required for solemn procedure in the High Court of Justiciary. Another change in nomenclature is the demise of the "s.102 letter"; the procedure where the accused desires to plead guilty is now found in s.76.

Part VIII

Sections 103 to 132 deal with appeals from solemn proceedings. Undoubtedly the major reform in this regard is the need to receive the grant of leave to appeal from a single judge in chambers: see s.105. The pressure that this rule puts on getting the ground of appeal stated correctly at the outset cannot be over-emphasised. Carefully thought-out appeals against conviction are unlikely to be weeded out early on, but speculative appeals against summary sentences may be much reduced.

Part IX

Sections 133 to 172 replicate generally the rules for summary prosecutions that apply for solemn prosecutions. In the Criminal Procedure (Scotland) Act 1975 the division between solemn and summary procedure was more marked than under this Act, *e.g.* the various latitudes and implied terms are now contained in Sch.3 and apply equally to indictments and complaints by ss.64(6) and 138(4) respectively.

Part X

Sections 173 to 194 replicate generally the rules for summary appeals that apply for solemn appeals. Those familiar with the work of appellate judges will know that numerically the heaviest burden is, or was until the passing of this Act, the appeals against summary sentences. The single judge shift will undoubtedly affect the volume but the concession that two judges may deal with this class of case will be welcomed: s.173(2).

Part XI

Sections 195 to 254 deal with a wide range of post-conviction issues. On occasions the detail of the sections overwhelms the inherent excitement. However, practitioners may look forward to the implementation of s.197 which requires courts at first instance to have regard to sentencing opinions pronounced on statutory authority. It would be crass merely to offer a percentage discount on sentence for a guilty plea but explicit recognition for an acceptance of responsibilities may have a marked effect on summary business.

Part XII

Sections 255 to 286 make provision for evidential matters. There is no attack on the general requirement for a sufficiency of evidence but it is clear from the wide range of provisions that those advising accused persons will require at the earliest opportunity after receiving instructions to narrow the issues and agree evidence accordingly. That is especially the case for routine evidence of the type covered by certificates in terms of s.281 of and Sch.9 to this Act.

Part XIII

Sections 287 to 303 cover a wide variety of matters. The fixed penalty system, under ss.303 and

304, will probably and properly keep out of court a wide variety of minor infringements at the least serious end of criminal behaviour.

Part XIV

Sections 304 to 310 deal with general points but mention must be made of the establishment of the Criminal Courts Rules Council. It is true that many other bodies take an interest in criminal law but this body has the function of keeping under general review the procedures and practices of the courts exercising criminal jurisdiction in Scotland and that in itself is progress: see s.304(9).

Sch.1

Section 21 and Sch.1 give constables powers to take offenders into custody in relation to the offences against children under the age of 17 years.

Sch.2

Petitions and indictments may be in a form set out in Sch.2: see ss.34(1)(a) and 64(2)(a) respectively. The Schedule sets out examples of indictments. Given that the changes are discretionary in regard to the contents of the Schedule, the real question with a variance from an example is whether a change is relevant, not whether it coincides with such an example. Reference may also be made to Sch.5.

Sch.3

The structure of the 1975 Act was such that identical provisions were made for solemn proceedings and summary proceedings respectively. This duplication was felt to be unnecessary and by ss.64(6) and 138(4) the contents of Sch.3 have effect as regards indictments and complaints. This Schedule will repay careful reading regularly by court practitioners because of the complexity of the provisions that frequently render pleas to the relevancy, for example, unnecessary and assist with more efficient pleading.

Sch.4

The regime of supervision and treatment orders was introduced by s.50 of and Sch.2 to the Criminal Justice (Scotland) Act 1995. The development is simply repeated in this Act.

Sch.5

This Schedule provides forms of change in addition to those in Sch.2. Questions may be raised as to why the Schedules are separate or what benefit is conferred by them in any event. Further, several of the forms are clearly anachronistic, for example by reference to assault "to the great effusion of blood".

Sch.6

By s.231(1), this Schedule has effect in relation to the discharge and amendment of probation orders.

Sch.7

Supervised attendance orders have been developed as an alternative to imprisonment and such orders have been extended by s.235 and Sch.7.

Sch.8

This Schedule makes provision regarding the admissibility in criminal proceedings of copy documents and of evidence contained in business documents. It should be noted that the Schedule has, by para.8, definitions of terms that are not contained in the main interpretation section.

Sch.9

Proof of routine or incontrovertible evidence is tedious and expensive and this Schedule provides for the increased use of certificates as to these matters. The consolidating nature of this legislation is such that this Schedule has a far wider range of subject-matters that may be covered by certificates.

Sch.10

This Schedule must be read in the context of s.292 and the effect is to establish a narrow range of offences triable only summarily.

Abbreviations

The 1975 Act : Criminal Procedure (Scotland) Act 1975 (c.21).

The 1980 Act : Bail (Scotland) Act 1980 (c.4).

The 1984 Act : Mental Health (Scotland) Act 1984 (c.36).

The 1993 Act : Prisoners and Criminal Proceedings (Scotland) Act 1993 (c.9).

The 1995 Act : Criminal Procedure (Scotland) Act 1995 (c. 46).

The 1996 Act of Adjournal : Act of Adjournal (Criminal Procedure Rules) 1996 (S.I. 1996 No. 513).

Parliamentary Debates

Hansard, H.L. Vol. 565, col. 14; Vol. 566, cols. 384, 581, 894. H.C. Vol. 265, col. 181.

PART I

CRIMINAL COURTS

JURISDICTION AND POWERS

The High Court

Judges in the High Court

1.—(1) The Lord President of the Court of Session shall be the Lord Justice General and shall perform his duties as the presiding judge of the High Court.

(2) Every person who is appointed to the office of one of the Senators of the College of Justice in Scotland shall, by virtue of such appointment, be a Lord Commissioner of Justiciary in Scotland.

(3) If any difference arises as to the rotation of judges in the High Court, it shall be determined by the Lord Justice General, whom failing by the Lord Justice Clerk.

(4) Any Lord Commissioner of Justiciary may preside alone at the trial of an accused before the High Court.

(5) Without prejudice to subsection (4) above, in any trial of difficulty or importance it shall be competent for two or more judges in the High Court to preside for the whole or any part of the trial.

DEFINITIONS

"High Court": s.307(1).
"Lord Commissioner of Justiciary": s.307(1).

GENERAL NOTE

With one exception, the origins of this section are probably more a matter of legal history than a concern for practitioners. Section 1(5), reflecting the collegiate nature of Scottish judges, permits in any trial of difficulty or importance that it shall be competent for two or more judges in the High Court of Justiciary to provide for the whole or any part of the trial. Such problems tend to arise at short notice and while judges are on circuit but there are still a number of instances of this happening: see *HM Advocate v Cairns*, 1967 J.C. 37; *HM Advocate v MacKenzie*, 1970 S.L.T. 81; *MacNeil v HM Advocate*, 1986 S.C.C.R. 288 and *Copeland v HM Advocate*, 1987 S.C.C.R. 232.

Subs.(3)

This subsection must now probably be read in the context of ss.1 and 2 of the Senior Judiciary (Vacancies and Incapacity) (Scotland) Act 2006 (asp 9).

Subs.(5)

In *Stevens v HM Advocate*, 2002 S.L.T. 1249 an accused sought a declaration that a specific statutory provision was incompatible with a provision of law of human rights. A minute to that effect was dismissed. In the course of the Opinion of the Court it was observed that the power to convene additional judges under s.1(5) of the 1995 Act was not available in the present case as that power related to the High Court of Justiciary sitting as a trial court. That capacity was not one that could hear or determine disputes relating to the compatibility of legislation with human rights under the European Convention of Human Rights.

Fixing of High Court sittings

2.—(1) The High Court shall sit at such times and places as the Lord Justice General, whom failing the Lord Justice Clerk, may, after consultation with the Lord Advocate, determine.

(2) Without prejudice to subsection (1) above, the High Court shall hold such additional sittings as the Lord Advocate may require.

(3) Where an accused has been cited to, or otherwise required to attend, a diet to be held at any sitting of the High Court, the prosecutor may, at any time before the commencement of the diet or, in the case of a trial diet, the trial, apply to the Court to transfer the case to a diet to be held at a sitting of the Court in another place; and a single judge of the High Court may—

(a) after giving the accused or his counsel an opportunity to be heard; or

(b) on the joint application of all parties,

make an order for the transfer of the case.

(3C) The judge may proceed under subsection (3) above on a joint application of the parties without hearing the parties and, accordingly, he may dispense with any hearing previously appointed for the purpose of considering the application.

(4) Where no diets have been appointed to be held at a sitting of the High Court or if it is no longer expedient that a sitting should take place, it shall not be necessary for the sitting to take place.

(5) If in any case a diet remains appointed to be held at a sitting which does not take place in pursuance of subsection (4) above, subsection (3) above shall apply in relation to the transfer of any other such case to another sitting.

(6) For the purposes of subsection (3) above—

(a) a diet shall be taken to commence when it is called; and

(b) a trial shall be taken to commence when the oath is administered to the jury.

Amendments

Subss.(3), (4) and (5) as amended, and subss.(3C) and (6) inserted, by the Criminal Procedure (Amendment) (Scotland) Act 2004 (asp 5), s.25 and Sch.1, para.2. Brought into force on February 1, 2005 by the Criminal Procedure (Amendment) (Scotland) Act 2004 (Commencement, Transitional Provisions and Savings) Order 2004 (SSI 2004/405 (C.28)), art.2.

Definitions

"diet": s.307(1).
"High Court": s.307(1).
"judge": s.307(1).
"order": s.307(1).
"prosecutor": s.307(1).

General Note

The general power to settle sittings of the High Court for the disposal of business in the ordinary way is now supplemented with more detailed powers as a result of the amendments to the section. These more detailed powers allow for the transfer of a particular case (a diet or a trial) from one place to another: s.2(3). There need not be a hearing where there is a joint application for such a transfer: s.2(3C). The transfer of such business may be for administrative reasons (existing cases over-running) or there may be other compelling needs (the movement of contentious cases from one location to another). The equivalent in relation to solemn business in sheriff courts is to be found in s.83 of the 1995 Act.

Solemn courts: general

Jurisdiction and powers of solemn courts

3.—(1) The jurisdiction and powers of all courts of solemn jurisdiction, except so far as altered or modified by any enactment passed after the commencement of this Act, shall remain as at the commencement of this Act.

(2) Any crime or offence which is triable on indictment may be tried by the High Court sitting at any place in Scotland.

(3) The sheriff shall, without prejudice to any other or wider power conferred by statute, not be entitled, on the conviction on indictment of an accused, to pass a sentence of imprisonment for a term exceeding five years.

(4) Subject to subsection (5) below, where under any enactment passed or made before 1st January 1988 (the date of commencement of section 58 of the Criminal Justice (Scotland) Act 1987) an offence is punishable on conviction on indictment by imprisonment for a term exceeding two years but the enactment either expressly or impliedly restricts the power of the sheriff to impose a sentence of imprisonment for a term exceeding two years, it shall be competent for the sheriff to impose a sentence of imprisonment for a term exceeding two but not exceeding five years.

(4A) Subject to subsection (5) below, where under any enactment passed or made after 1st January 1988 but before the commencement of section 13 of the Crime and Punishment (Scotland) Act 1997 (increase in sentencing powers of sheriff courts) an offence is punishable on conviction on indictment for a term exceeding three years but the enactment either expressly or impliedly restricts the power of the sheriff to impose a sentence of imprisonment for a term exceeding three years, it shall be competent for the sheriff to impose a sentence of imprisonment for a term exceeding three but not exceeding five years.

(5) Nothing in subsections (4) and (4A) above shall authorise the imposition by the sheriff of a sentence in excess of the sentence specified by the enactment as the maximum sentence which may be imposed on conviction of the offence.

(6) Subject to any express exclusion contained in any enactment, it shall be lawful to indict in the sheriff court all crimes except murder, treason, rape and breach of duty by magistrates.

AMENDMENT

Section 3 as amended by the Crime and Punishment (Scotland) Act 1997 (c.48), s.13(1). Brought into force on May 1, 2004 by the Crime and Punishment (Scotland) Act 1997 (Commencement No. 6 and Savings) Order 2004 (SSI 2004/176 (C.12)).

DEFINITIONS

  "crime": s.307(1).
  "offence": s.307(1).
  "sentence": s.307(1).

After conviction on indictment the maximum sentence that a sheriff may competently impose is five years' imprisonment: s.3(3). There is a power to remit a case to the High Court of Justiciary where a sheriff holds that any competent sentence that can be imposed is inadequate: s.195(1). Further, there is a power to remit where a period of imprisonment in default of payment is in contemplation and that period exceeds five years: s.219(8).

Du Plooy v HM Advocate, 2005 J.C. 1 established guidelines with specific regard to discounting sentences for early guilty pleas. In *McGhee v HM Advocate*, 2006 S.C.C.R. 712 a sheriff indicated that he considered the crime admitted by the appellant merited a sentence of six years' imprisonment and discounted it to five years because of the guilty plea. On appeal against the competency of the sentence *held* that the restriction imposed by s.3(3) falls to be applied to the sentence ultimately fixed by the sheriff, that the question of whether sentence is appropriate for the High Court is a matter for the sheriff, just as is the decision as to whether any competent sentence is inadequate, that when the sheriff holds that the sentence he or she can impose is inadequate it necessarily follows that he is holding that the question of sentence is not appropriate for the High Court, that in these circumstances there is no question of a remit, and it is not for the High Court to consider whether the question of sentence was appropriate for it, that the route by which the sentence reaches the ultimate sentence is not restricted by s.195(1), and that the sentence was competent.

The sheriff

Territorial jurisdiction of sheriff

4.—(1) Subject to the provisions of this section, the jurisdiction of the sheriffs, within their respective sheriffdoms shall extend to and include all navigable rivers, ports, harbours, creeks, shores and anchoring grounds in or adjoining such sheriffdoms and includes all criminal maritime causes and proceedings (including those applying to persons furth of Scotland) provided that the accused is, by virtue of any enactment or rule of law, subject to the jurisdiction of the sheriff before whom the case or proceeding is raised.

(2) Where an offence is alleged to have been committed in one district in a sheriffdom, it shall be competent to try that offence in a sheriff court in any other district in that sheriffdom.

(3) It shall not be competent for the sheriff to try any crime committed on the seas which it would not be competent for him to try if the crime had been committed on land.

(4) The sheriff shall have a concurrent jurisdiction with every other court of summary jurisdiction in relation to all offences competent for trial in such courts.

DEFINITIONS

"court of summary jurisdiction": s.307(1).
"crime": s.307(1).
"offence": s.307(1).

Geographical Restrictions on Sheriff's Jurisdiction

GENERAL NOTE

The ancient lineage of this provision has not been tested much in court: however, in *Lewis v Blair* (1858) 3 Irv. 16 the sheriff had jurisdiction to try a foreign sailor for an offence committed by him aboard a foreign vessel lying within the sheriff's territory, upon a seaman engaged on that vessel. *Shields v Donnelly*, 2000 S.L.T. 147; 1999 S.C.C.R. 890 indicates that while papers may be signed outwith his jurisdiction, a sheriff can only deal with any procedural aspects while within the jurisdiction, and not elsewhere.

A more contemporary example is to be found in *Friel v McKendrick*, 1996 G.W.D. 1–8 in which a passenger appeared at Paisley Sheriff Court on a complaint charged with breach of the peace following his misconduct on an aircraft flying between New York and Glasgow. No objection was taken to the competency of the charge.

It was noted previously that the introduction of the provisions contained in the Sexual Offences (Conspiracy and Incitement) Act 1996 (c.29) raised wide jurisdictional issues. If anything this was a sanguine assessment—see the discussion of *McCarron v HM Advocate*, 2001 S.L.T. 866; 2001 S.C.C.R. 419 at A1–32.6 above which emphasises the strictly territorial nature of the sheriff's jurisdiction. Curiously, s.11 below would permit a trial, on indictment and in limited circumstances, in the sheriff court of (to repeat the marginal note) "Certain offences committed outside Scotland". Perhaps the addition of listed sexual offences to s.11 might provide an answer to the problems raised in *McCarron*.

The power (or rather lack of it) of Ministers to direct matters to specific sheriffs for judicial consideration is discussed in *Wright, Petitioner*, 2004 S.L.T. 491; 2004 S.C.C.R. 324 (extradition committal proceedings addressed by Scottish Ministers to the sheriff principal being heard by another sheriff).

The sheriff: summary jurisdiction and powers

5.—(1) The sheriff, sitting as a court of summary jurisdiction, shall continue to have all the jurisdiction and powers exercisable by him at the commencement of this Act.

(2) The sheriff shall, without prejudice to any other or wider powers conferred by statute, have power on convicting any person of a common law offence—

(a) to impose a fine not exceeding the prescribed sum;

(b) to ordain the accused to find caution for good behaviour for any period not exceeding 12 months to an amount not exceeding the prescribed sum either in lieu of or in addition to a fine or in addition to imprisonment;

(c) failing payment of such fine, or on failure to find such caution, to award imprisonment in accordance with section 219 of this Act;

(d) to impose imprisonment, for any period not exceeding three months.

(3) Where a person is convicted by the sheriff of—

(a) a second or subsequent offence inferring dishonest appropriation of property, or attempt thereat; or

(b) a second or subsequent offence inferring personal violence,

he may, without prejudice to any wider powers conferred by statute, be sentenced to imprisonment for any period not exceeding six months.

(4) It shall be competent to prosecute summarily in the sheriff court the following offences—

(a) uttering a forged document;

(b) wilful fire-raising;

(c) robbery; and

(d) assault with intent to rob.

AMENDMENT

Section 5 prospectively amended by the Crime and Punishment (Scotland) Act 1997 (c.48), s.13(2).

DEFINITIONS

"caution": s.307(1).

"court of summary jurisdiction": s.307(1).

"fine": s.307(1).

"offence": s.307(1).

"prescribed sum, the": s.225(8) [i.e. £5,000].

GENERAL NOTE

The enhanced penalty competent on conviction by a sheriff of a second or subsequent offence inferring personal violence has led to challenges as to what is meant by "inferring personal violence". Section 5(3) repeats the terms of s.290 of the 1975 Act against which several appeals were taken.

The appellate judges have construed the term strictly and in favour of appellants so that threats or hints of violence are insufficient: see *Adair v Morton*, 1972 S.L.T. (Notes) 70; *Sharp v Tudhope*, 1986 S.C.C.R. 64; *Hemphill v Donnelly*, 1992 S.C.C.R. 770; and *McMahon v Lees*, 1993 S.L.T. 593 and *Youngson v Higson*, 2000 S.L.T. 1441, a libel of breach of the peace which had contained no suggestion of violence. The test, following *Sproull v McGlennan*, 1999 S.L.T. 402; 1999 S.C.C.R. 63, approved in *Paterson v Webster*, 2002 S.L.T. 1120, is whether violence was offered to, or visited upon, the person of a specified complainer as set out in the libel.

The relevant dates for liability of an accused to the increased maximum sentence are the dates of commission of the offences, rather than the dates of conviction (*Marshall v Stott*, 2002 S.L.T. 1353; 2002 S.C.C.R. 886). In *Marshall* the Appeal Court approved the practice of lodging extracts of earlier convictions inferring personal violence at the time of moving for sentence. As was noted above convictions of breach of the peace might involve such an aggravation which would not be self-evident. (Refer to the discussion of *Riley v HM Advocate*, 1999 J.C. 308; 1999 S.L.T. 1076; 1999 S.C.C.R. 644 at A4–228 below).

In addition to the maximum sentences for common law offences set out in subs.(2) for a first, or subsequent offence inferring personal violence or dishonesty, it will be noted that subs.(2) operates without prejudice to the maximum sentences imposed by other statutes. The most common examples of the operation of subs.(1) are to be found in the Police (Scotland) Act 1967, s.41, and the Misuse of Drugs Act 1971, s.5 which, summarily, permit sentences of up to nine months' and one year's imprisonment respectively. However the summary tariff for a statutory contravention ordinarily has no bearing upon the sentencing powers available to a sheriff sitting in solemn proceedings; in that situation s.3(3) of the 1995 Act provides that a sheriff can impose a sentence of up to three years' imprisonment, unless the statute enacts a different tariff specifically in relation to solemn proceedings (see generally *Howard v HM Advocate*, 1997 S.L.T. 575).

The previous convictions which in effect authorise the enhanced penalty set out in subs.(3), must be libelled by the Crown in the Notice of Previous Convictions and laid before the court: *Sim v Lockhart*, 1994 S.L.T. 1063. *McPhail v Crowe*, 1997 G.W.D. 17–779 is a rare instance of an incompetent sentence, in breach of subs.(2)(d), being imposed on conviction of a first offence of dishonesty. Provided that the statutory maximum period of imprisonment is not exceeded when subs.(3)(a) is invoked, any combination of concurrent or consecutive sentences can be imposed (*Hepburn v Howdle*, 1998 G.W.D. 18–910).

Since Scots law does not require a *nomen juris* to constitute a competent criminal libel, the court has to have regard to the facts proved or admitted, not simply the terms of the libel, to ascertain whether or not it is dealing with an offence inferring personal violence; *Sproull v McGlennan*, 1999 J.C. 105; 1999 S.L.T. 402; 1999 S.C.C.R. 63. See the discussion at A4–343.

Starrs and Chalmers v Ruxton, 1999 S.C.C.R. 1052 settles that a temporary sheriff cannot, in terms of Art.6 of the European Convention of Human Rights, be regarded as an independent and impartial tribunal for the purpose of determining a trial notwithstanding appointment in accordance with the Sheriff Courts (Scotland) Act 1971 (c.58). Note that in *Starrs and Chalmers* the Appeal Court remitted the case back to the presiding temporary sheriff and directed that he discharge the trial and fix a new trial diet to be heard before a permanent sheriff. This judgment serves to confirm first, that it is entirely compatible with Convention rights for temporary judges to deal with procedural matters and preliminary matters, but not with the determination of a trial itself (see also *Gibbs v Ruxton*, 2000 S.L.T. 310); and secondly, that devolution issues should be adjudicated upon within the existing framework of first and preliminary diets in solemn proceedings, or by debate in summary cases.

Stott v Minogue, 2001 S.L.T. (Sh.Ct) 25 provides a rare example of a preliminary challenge by an accused for the trial judge to demonstrate her ability to adjudge issues to his satisfaction. M claimed that it was necessary for him to know whether the judge was impartial and had no affiliations to freemasonry. The sheriff repelled the challenge, citing her judicial oath of impartiality as a sufficient guarantee. See too *Kenny v Howdle*, 2002 S.C.C.R. 814 concerning the powers of an honorary sheriff to deal with procedural appearances, in this case an application for bail after failure to appear for a deferred sentence.

For a rare example of a fine of, but not exceeding, the prescribed sum in terms of s.5(2)(a) see *Higson v El-Hadji Diouf*, 2003 G.W.D. 29–810 (£5,000 fine). For a discussion of the enhanced and combined effect of ss.5 and 27(3) and (5) see *Penman v Bott*, 2006 S.L.T. 495.

District courts

District courts: area, constitution and prosecutor

6.—(1) Each commission area shall be the district of a district court, and the places at which a district court sits and, subject to section 8 of this Act, the days and times when it sits at any given place, shall be determined by the local authority; and in determining where and when a district court should sit, the local authority shall have regard to the desirability of minimising the expense and inconvenience occasioned to those directly involved, whether as parties or witnesses, in the proceedings before the court.

(2) The jurisdiction and powers of the district court shall be exercisable by a stipendiary magistrate or by one or more justices, and no decision of the court shall be questioned on the ground that it was not constituted as required by this subsection unless objection was taken on that ground by or on behalf of a party to the proceedings not later than the time when the proceedings or the alleged irregularity began.

[handwritten margin note: power to appoint stipendiary magistrate]

(3) All prosecutions in a commission area shall proceed at the instance of the procurator fiscal.

(4) The procurator fiscal for an area which includes a commission area shall have all the powers and privileges conferred on a district prosecutor by section 6 of the District Courts (Scotland) Act 1975.

(5) The prosecutions authorised by the said Act of 1975 under complaint by the procurator fiscal shall be without prejudice to complaints at the instance of any other person entitled to make the same.

(6) In this section—

"commission area" means the area of a local authority;

"justice" means a justice of the peace appointed or deemed to have been appointed under section 9 of the said Act of 1975; and

"local authority" means a council constituted under section 2 of the Local Government (Scotland) Act 1994.

DEFINITIONS

"commission area": s.6(6).
"complaint": s.307(1).
"district prosecutor": s.26(1) of the District Courts (Scotland) Act 1975.
"justice": s.6(6).
"local authority": s.6(6).
"procurator fiscal": s.307(1).

GENERAL NOTE

This section is derived from several parts of the District Courts (Scotland) Act 1975 which brought about very substantial change to the existing system of lay courts of summary criminal jurisdiction. The extensive commentary on the District Courts (Scotland) Act 1975 by Dr Enid A. Marshall in *Current Law Statutes Annotated*, encapsulated the details of the then old system which was to replace it. This section consolidates these matters.

In *Shields v Donnelly*, 2000 S.L.T. 147 a conviction was quashed where the District Court had temporarily moved to an adjacent local authority district while the court building was being refurbished. The Appeal Court emphasised that the powers of District Court judges were restricted to the territorial area over which they had jurisdiction and could not be exercised elsewhere unless statute created a specific exception. See also *Clarke v Fraser*, 2002 S.L.T. 745 discussed at A4–327 below.

Parliament could modify that rule, but had not modified that general rule when it enacted s.6(1) which simply gave the local authority the power to determine where and when the district was to sit within its jurisdiction; that since there was no other statutory provision to support the competency of the justice sitting outwith her district the subsequent proceedings were tainted by a fundamental nullity; and the appeal was allowed.

In *Clark v Kelly*, 2000 S.L.T. 1038; 2000 S.C.C.R. 821, where the role of the assessor was challenged (following *Starrs v Ruxton*, 2000 S.L.T. 42; 1999 S.C.C.R 1052), it was held that the assessor was not a member of the court; his function was confined to advising the court on applicable law. The Appeal Court found nothing incompatible with the terms of Art.6(1) of the European Convention on

Human Rights in the common practice of justices and assessors retiring from the court—and being outwith the presence of the accused—during deliberations. The court recognised that issues which arose during those deliberations which might merit further submissions by parties should be made known to the parties for any additional submissions they might then have.

District court: jurisdiction and powers — *Restrictions Ex*

7.—(1) A district court shall continue to have all the jurisdiction and powers exercisable by it at the commencement of this Act.

(2) Where several offences, which if committed in one commission area could be tried under one complaint, are alleged to have been committed in different commission areas, proceedings may be taken for all or any of those offences under one complaint before the district court of any one of such commission areas, and any such offence may be dealt with, heard, tried, determined, adjudged and punished as if the offence had been wholly committed within the jurisdiction of that court.

(3) Except in so far as any enactment (including this Act or an enactment passed after this Act) otherwise provides, it shall be competent for a district court to try any statutory offence which is triable summarily.

(4) It shall be competent, whether or not the accused has been previously convicted of an offence inferring dishonest appropriation of property, for any of the following offences to be tried in the district court—

(a) theft or reset of theft;

(b) falsehood, fraud or wilful imposition;

(c) breach of trust or embezzlement,

where (in any such case) the amount concerned does not exceed level 4 on the standard scale.

(5) A district court when constituted by a stipendiary magistrate shall, in addition to the jurisdiction and powers mentioned in subsection (1) above, have the summary criminal jurisdiction and powers of a sheriff.

(6) The district court shall, without prejudice to any other or wider powers conferred by statute, be entitled on convicting of a common law offence—

(a) to impose imprisonment for any period not exceeding 60 days;

(b) to impose a fine not exceeding level 4 on the standard scale;

(c) to ordain the accused (in lieu of or in addition to such imprisonment or fine) to find caution for good behaviour for any period not exceeding six months and to an amount not exceeding level 4 on the standard scale;

(d) failing payment of such fine or on failure to find such caution, to award imprisonment in accordance with section 219 of this Act,

but in no case shall the total period of imprisonment imposed in pursuance of this subsection exceed 60 days.

(7) Without prejudice to any other or wider power conferred by any enactment, it shall not be competent for a district court, as respects any statutory offence—

(a) to impose a sentence of imprisonment for a period exceeding 60 days;

(b) to impose a fine of an amount exceeding level 4 on the standard scale; or

(c) to ordain an accused person to find caution for any period exceeding six months or to an amount exceeding level 4 on the standard scale.

(8) The district court shall not have jurisdiction to try or to pronounce sentence in the case of any person—

(a) found within its jurisdiction, and brought before it accused or suspected of having committed any offence at any place beyond its jurisdiction; or

(b) brought before it accused or suspected of having committed within its jurisdiction any of the following offences—

Exclusions

Limits to powers of District Court

    (i) murder, culpable homicide, robbery, rape, wilful fire-raising, or attempted wilful fire-raising;

   (ii) theft by housebreaking, or housebreaking with intent to steal;

  (iii) theft or reset, falsehood fraud or wilful imposition, breach of trust or embezzlement, where the value of the property is an amount exceeding level 4 on the standard scale;

  (iv) assault causing the fracture of a limb, assault with intent to ravish, assault to the danger of life, or assault by stabbing;

   (v) uttering forged documents or uttering forged bank or banker's notes, or offences under the Acts relating to coinage.

(9) Without prejudice to subsection (8) above, where either in the preliminary investigation or in the course of the trial of any offence it appears that the offence is one which—

(a) cannot competently be tried in the court before which an accused is brought; or

(b) in the opinion of the court in view of the circumstances of the case, should be dealt with by a higher court,

the court may take cognizance of the offence and commit the accused to prison for examination for any period not exceeding four days.

(10) Where an accused is committed as mentioned in subsection (9) above, the prosecutor in the court which commits the accused shall forthwith give notice of the committal to the procurator fiscal of the district within which the offence was committed or to such other official as is entitled to take cognizance of the offence in order that the accused may be dealt with according to law.

DEFINITIONS

"fine": s.307(1).
"level 4": s.225(2) [*i.e.* £2,500].
"offence": s.307(1).
"procurator fiscal": s.307(1).
"prosecutor": s.307(1).
"sentence": s.307(1).
"standard scale": s.225(1).
"stipendiary magistrate": s.5 of the District Courts (Scotland) Act 1975.

GENERAL NOTE

This section provides for the jurisdictions and powers of the District Court. It is worth asserting that the additional jurisdiction conferred on a stipendiary magistrate by s.7(5) allows for the prosecution of more serious matters in the District Court. The interpretation of subss.(9) and (10) arose in *Wilson v Stott*, 2004 S.C.C.R. 436 where it was held that the district court's power to remit only applied to cases in which imprisonment was competent, and where the maximum sentence for the offence exceeded that court's statutory powers.

The problems peculiar to Glasgow District Court, where both lay and stipendiary magistrates sit, are highlighted in *Graham v Normand*, 1996 S.C.C.R. 371: an accused after being remanded in custody for trial pled guilty before a lay magistrate and had sentence deferred for reports. He next appeared before a stipendiary magistrate, who refused to continue the case further for sentence to be imposed by a lay magistrate, and imposed sentences exceeding those competent to a lay magistrate. On appeal the sentence was upheld as being neither incompetent nor oppressive. Compare the approach however in *Halleron v Vannet*, 2000 S.C.C.R. 50 where the accused's failure to pay a fiscal fine led to a summary complaint being placed before a lay magistrate and, following a plea being tendered and the case continued for reports, three months imprisonment was imposed by a stipendiary magistrate; the Appeal Court regarded the original forum as being a highly relevant factor in the sentencing process and substituted a sentence of 60 days imprisonment. See also *Main v Normand*, 1996 S.C.C.R. 256. *Maclean v City of Glasgow Council*, 1997 G.W.D. 34–1737 resolved that stipendiary magistrates enjoy the same tenure of office as sheriffs, *ad vitam aut culpam*.

In *Will v McDonald*, 1999 J.C. 135 an appeal was refused. A justice had had previous and not wholly happy dealings with an individual who appeared in a district court as an accused. It was held that the justice ought to have allowed these circumstances to be discussed in open court but it could not now be said that justice had not been seen to be done. It was observed that it would be very difficult for justices to carry out their duties if they were unable to deal with members of the local community with whom they had had previous contact.

It has been held not to be oppressive for a district court to hear proceedings initiated by the local education authority, a separate arm of the local authority (*Matts v Cumming*, 2000 S.L.T. 220). It is doubted, in the light of the decision in *Starrs and Chalmers v Ruxton* (1999 S.C.C.R. 1052), that *Matts* now would be upheld. In any event, see now s.11 of the Bail, Judicial Appointments etc. (Scotland) Act 2000 (asp 9).

The whole status of the legal assessor in the District Court was the subject of challenge in a devolution issue: see *Clark v Kelly*, 2000 S.L.T. 1038. It was held that the clerk to the District Court was confined to acting as a legal adviser to the Justices of the Peace who acted as decision-maker and the clerk was therefore not a member of the court. Further, that there was nothing objectionable in the practice of private communications between clerks and Justices of the Peace provided that these were restricted to the provision of legal advice and that they recognised and raised in open court any matter on which the defence or prosecution might wish to make material comment.

Where an accused first tendered a guilty plea before a district court and was later sentenced for that matter by stipendiary magistrate then the 60 day maximum of the district court (by s.7(6)(a) of the 1995 Act) ought to be the maximum applied, and not the three months allowed the stipendiary magistrate: *Halleron v Vannet*, 2000 S.C.C.R. 50.

Sittings of sheriff and district courts

Sittings of sheriff and district courts

8.—(1) Notwithstanding any enactment or rule of law, a sheriff court or a district court—

    (a) shall not be required to sit on any Saturday or Sunday or on a day which by virtue of subsection (2) or (3) below is a court holiday; but

    (b) may sit on any day for the disposal of criminal business.

(2) A sheriff principal may in an order made under section 17(1)(b) of the Sheriff Courts (Scotland) Act 1971 prescribe in respect of criminal business not more than 10 days, other than Saturdays and Sundays, in a calendar year as court holidays in the sheriff courts within his jurisdiction; and may in the like manner prescribe as an additional court holiday any day which has been proclaimed, under section 1(3) of the Banking and Financial Dealings Act 1971, to be a bank holiday either throughout the United Kingdom or in a place or locality in the United Kingdom within his jurisdiction.

(3) Notwithstanding section 6(1) of this Act, a sheriff principal may, after consultation with the appropriate local authority, prescribe not more than 10 days, other than Saturdays and Sundays, in a calendar year as court holidays in the district courts within his jurisdiction; and he may, after such consultation, prescribe as an additional holiday any day which has been proclaimed, under section 1(3) of the said Banking and Financial Dealings Act 1971, to be a bank holiday either throughout the United Kingdom or in a place or locality in the United Kingdom within his jurisdiction.

(4) A sheriff principal may in pursuance of subsection (2) or (3) above prescribe different days as court holidays in relation to different sheriff or district courts.

Territorial jurisdiction: general

Boundaries of jurisdiction

9.—(1) Where an offence is committed in any harbour, river, arm of the sea or other water (tidal or otherwise) which runs between or forms the boundary of the jurisdiction of two or more courts, the offence may be tried by any one of such courts.

(2) Where an offence is committed on the boundary of the jurisdiction of two or more courts, or within the distance of 500 metres of any such boundary, or partly within the jurisdiction of one court and partly within the jurisdiction of another court or courts, the offence may be tried by any one of such courts.

(3) Where an offence is committed against any person or in respect of any property in or on any carriage, cart or vehicle employed in a journey by road or railway, or on board any vessel employed in a river, loch, canal or inland navigation, the offence may be tried by any court through whose jurisdiction the carriage, cart, vehicle or vessel passed in the course of the journey or voyage during which the offence was committed.

(4) Where several offences, which if committed in one sheriff court district could be tried under one indictment or complaint, are alleged to have been committed by any person in different sheriff court districts, the accused may be tried for all or any of those offences under one indictment or complaint before the sheriff of any one of such sheriff court districts.

(5) Where an offence is authorised by this section to be tried by any court, it may be dealt with, heard, tried, determined, adjudged and punished as if the offence had been committed wholly within the jurisdiction of such court.

Definitions

"complaints": s.307(1).
"indictment": s.307(1).
"offence": s.307(1).
"sheriff court districts": s.307(1).

General Note

There seem to have been few modern authorities on the issue of jurisdiction, although the older cases may still provide assistance should doubts arise: see *Lewis v Blair* (1858) 3 Irv. 16; *Witherington* (1881) 4 Couper 475; *Mortensen v Peters* (1906) 5 Adam 121 and *Lipsey v Mackintosh* (1913) 7 Adam 182.

Competence of justice's actings outwith jurisdiction

9A. It is competent for a justice, even if not present within his jurisdiction, to sign any warrant, judgment, interlocutor or other document relating to proceedings within that jurisdiction provided that when he does so he is present within Scotland.

Amendment

Section 9A inserted by Criminal Justice (Scotland) Act 2003 (asp 7), Part 8, s.59. Brought into force on June 27, 2003 by the Criminal Justice (Scotland) Act 2003 (Commencement No.1) Order 2003 (SSI 2003/288 (C.14)).

General Note

The case of *Shields v Donnelly*, 2000 S.L.T. 147; 1999 S.C.C.R. 890 emphasised the distinction between the procedural powers exercisable by a judge by virtue of his office and those powers which could only be executed within a territorial jurisdiction. The practical impact of this distinction was that warrants could only competently be granted by a judge while he was within his territorial jurisdiction. This new provision irons out this anomaly which impacted particularly upon sheriffs, many of whom might not reside within their sheriffdom.

Crimes committed in different districts

10.—(1) Where a person is alleged to have committed in more than one sheriff court district a crime or crimes to which subsection (2) below applies, he may be indicted to the sheriff court of such one of those districts as the Lord Advocate determines.

(2) This subsection applies to—

(a) a crime committed partly in one sheriff court district and partly in another;

(b) crimes connected with each other but committed in different sheriff court districts;

(c) crimes committed in different sheriff court districts in succession which, if they had been committed in one such district, could have been tried under one indictment.

(3) Where, in pursuance of subsection (1) above, a case is tried in the sheriff court of any sheriff court district, the procurator fiscal of that district shall have power to prosecute in that case even if the crime was in whole or in part committed in a different district, and the procurator fiscal shall have the like powers in relation to such case, whether before, during or after the trial, as he has in relation to a case arising out of a crime or crimes committed wholly within his own district.

DEFINITIONS

"crime": s.307(1).
"procurator fiscal": s.307(1).
"sheriff court district": s.307(1).

Certain offences committed outside Scotland

11.—(1) Any British citizen or British subject who in a country outside the United Kingdom does any act or makes any omission which if done or made in Scotland would constitute the crime of murder or of culpable homicide shall be guilty of the same crime and subject to the same punishment as if the act or omission had been done or made in Scotland.

(2) Any British citizen or British subject employed in the service of the Crown who, in a foreign country, when acting or purporting to act in the course of his employment, does any act or makes any omission which if done or made in Scotland would constitute an offence punishable on indictment shall be guilty of the same offence and subject to the same punishment, as if the act or omission had been done or made in Scotland.

(3) A person may be proceeded against, indicted, tried and punished for an offence to which this section applies—

(a) in any sheriff court district in Scotland in which he is apprehended or is in custody; or

(b) in such sheriff court district as the Lord Advocate may determine, as if the offence had been committed in that district, and the offence shall, for all purposes incidental to or consequential on the trial or punishment thereof, be deemed to have been committed in that district.

(4) Any person who—

(a) has in his possession in Scotland property which he has stolen in any other part of the United Kingdom; or

(b) in Scotland receives property stolen in any other part of the United Kingdom, may be dealt with, indicted, tried and punished in Scotland in like manner as if he had stolen it in Scotland.

(5) Where a person in any part of the United Kingdom outside Scotland—

(a) steals or attempts to steal any mail-bag or postal packet in the course of its transmission by post, or any of the contents of such a mail-bag or postal packet; or

(b) in stealing or with intent to steal any such mail-bag or postal packet or any of its contents commits any robbery, attempted robbery or assault with intent to rob,

he is guilty of the offence mentioned in paragraph (a) or (b) as if he had committed it in Scotland and shall be liable to be prosecuted, tried and punished there without proof that the offence was committed there.

(6) Any expression used in subsection (5) and in the Postal Services Act 2000 has the same meaning in that subsection as it has in that Act.

AMENDMENT

Subss. (5) and (6) inserted by the Postal Services Act 2000 (c. 26), s.127(4) and Sched. 8, para. 24. Brought into force by the Postal Services Act 2000 (Commencement No. 1 and Transitional Provisions) Order 2000 (S.I. 2000 No. 2957 (C.88)), art. 2(3) and Sched. 3 (effective March 26, 2001).

DEFINITIONS

"crime": s.307(1).
"offence": s.307(1).
"sheriff court district": s.307(1).

GENERAL NOTE

It should be noted that specific statutory provisions in relation to the commission of "listed sexual offences" abroad by those ordinarily subject to the jurisdiction of the Scottish courts are contained in ss.16A and 16B of the Criminal Law (Consolidation) (Scotland) Act 1995 above.

Conspiracy to commit offences outside the United Kingdom

11A.—(1) This section applies to any act done by a person in Scotland which would amount to conspiracy to commit an offence but for the fact that the criminal purpose is intended to occur in a country or territory outside the United Kingdom.

(2) Where a person does an act to which this section applies, the criminal purpose shall be treated as the offence mentioned in subsection (1) above and he shall, accordingly, be guilty of conspiracy to commit the offence.

(3) A person is guilty of an offence by virtue of this section only if the criminal purpose would involve at some stage—

(a) an act by him or another party to the conspiracy; or

(b) the happening of some other event,

constituting an offence under the law in force in the country or territory where the act or other event was intended to take place; and conduct punishable under the law in force in the country or territory is an offence under that law for the purposes of this section however it is described in that law.

(4) Subject to subsection (6) below, a condition specified in subsection (3) above shall be taken to be satisfied unless, not later than such time as the High Court may, by Act of Adjournal, prescribe, the accused serves on the prosecutor a notice—

(a) stating that, on the facts as alleged with respect to the relevant conduct, the condition is not in his opinion satisfied;

(b) setting out the grounds for his opinion; and

(c) requiring the prosecutor to prove that the condition is satisfied.

(5) In subsection (4) above "the relevant conduct" means the agreement to effect the criminal purpose.

(6) The court may permit the accused to require the prosecutor to prove that the condition mentioned in subsection (4) above is satisfied without the prior service of a notice under that subsection.

(7) In proceedings on indictment, the question whether a condition is satisfied shall be determined by the judge alone.

(8) Nothing in this section—

(a) applies to an act done before the day on which the Criminal Justice (Terrorism and Conspiracy) Act 1998 was passed, or

(b) imposes criminal liability on any person acting on behalf of, or holding office under, the Crown.

GENERAL NOTE

This section was inserted by s.7 of the Criminal Justice (Terrorism and Conspiracy) Act 1998 (c.40). Although it was explained under reference to terrorism during the parliamentary debates, it in fact applies to all offences and all countries the approach originally taken to "sex tourism" cases in s.16A of the Criminal Law (Consolidation) (Scotland) Act 1995 (c.39), which section is now amended so as to restrict its ambit to incitement. Conspiracy in Scotland to commit an offence in a country or territory outside the UK is now dealt with under the present section.

Subs. (1)

Any act. Subsection (8) excludes any act done before the Criminal Justice (Terrorism and Conspiracy) Act 1998 (c.40) was passed.

Which would amount to conspiracy to commit an offence but for the fact that the criminal purpose is intended to occur ... outside the United Kingdom. This subsection states the preconditions for the section as a whole to have effect. The case must be one in which there is conduct which, in Scots law would amount to a conspiracy except for the fact that the agreement is to do or achieve something outside the UK.

The section was not discussed in Parliament in its own right. Rather, it was taken along with ss.5 and 6, which make equivalent provision for England and Wales and Northern Ireland. Lord Williams of Mostyn, speaking for the Government, explained the policy intention as follows: "Conspiracy is dealt with in Clause 5 and subsequent clauses. These provisions are designed to close off a gap which has been recognised for some time in our response to international terrorism and other international crime. In our country it is not always an offence to conspire to commit criminal acts outside this country. This section of the Bill deals with those people who try to use our country as a safe place to plot the commission of terrorist offences or other crimes abroad. Terrorism and other forms of organised crime cannot be contained by a line on a map. Crime in one country is often instigated and planned in another. We think that there should not be a hiding place in our jurisdiction for terrorists, those who traffic in arms, drug smugglers, money launderers or counterfeiters ... Some powers already exist in this field. Extra-territorial jurisdiction is available for some offences such as computer misuse and sexual offences against children. Other offences are covered, but only in relation to certain countries, under the Suppression of Terrorism Act ... Your Lordships will find no prohibition of incitement in this Bill. That is deliberate as we did not wish to interfere with a tradition which remains valid, noble and distinctive to our country; that is, that political dissent is important and should be allowed, even when it is disagreeable; in fact, particularly when it is disagreeable ... We have included safeguards in Clause 5 and subsequent clauses. The principle of dual criminality—in other words, the conspiracy to commit the unlawful act—depends on the act being unlawful in the foreign country and also in our own domestic jurisdiction" (*Hansard*, H.L. Debs, September 3, 1998, Col. 14).

Lord Williams' remark that "In our country it is not always an offence to conspire to commit criminal acts outside this country" was made against the background of the English case of *Board of Trade v. Owen* [1957] A.C. 602, in which Lord Tucker held that, since the purpose of the criminal law is to protect the Queen's peace and maintain order within the realm, conspiracy to do something in another country is not criminal in English law. This was an essentially nineteenth-century view, reflecting the isolationist approach taken by English courts to jurisdiction over crimes with cross-frontier aspects. That approach has been much criticised in the literature (see, for example, Geoff Gilbert, "Crimes Sans Frontiers: Jurisdictional Problems in English Law" (1992) 63 *British Yearbook of International Law* 415 and Matthew Goode, "Two New Decisions on Criminal 'Jurisdiction': The

Appalling Durability of Common Law", 20 *Criminal Law Journal* 267 (1996) (Australia); but for a contrary view, see Peter Alldridge, "Sex Offenders Act 1997—Territoriality Provisions" [1997] Crim.L.R. 655).

The question whether conspiracy in Scotland to commit crime in a foreign jurisdiction is criminal at common law in Scotland seems never to have been judicially considered. The legislation seems simply to assume that the law of Scotland was as isolationist as that of England and Wales. Since the legislation has now been enacted, the accuracy of that assumption is unlikely ever to be determined. It may, however, be commented that there is no particular reason to suppose that the High Court of Justiciary would have been quite so parochial as its counterparts south of the border, especially since there are in any event material differences between the approaches which the two systems take to jurisdiction in general (see P.W. Ferguson, "Jurisdiction and Criminal Law in Scotland and England", in Robert F. Hunter (ed.), *Justice and Crime*, 1993, 96).

Under the Suppression of Terrorism Act 1978 (c.26), jurisdiction already exists in relation to conspiring within the UK to commit crimes in other Council of Europe countries, India and the United States. This reflects the UK's particular treaty relationships.

Subs.(2)

An act to which this section applies.   See subs.(1).

Subs.(3)

This subsection applies a "double" or "dual" criminality test. The acts or events to be carried out in the foreign jurisdiction in pursuance of the criminal purpose which, by subs.(1) must be of a sort which would be criminal in Scotland if carried out here, must also be such as to be criminal by the law of the place where they are intended to take place. There would, for obvious reasons, be difficulties about criminalising in the UK an agreement to do something in a foreign country if that act would be perfectly lawful in the country where it was to be carried out.

The concept of the double criminality test has been developed most fully in relation to extradition law, where in general the conduct for which it is intended to prosecute the fugitive must be criminal in both the state in which he is to be prosecuted and that in which he is found before extradition can take place. The emphasis is always placed on the acts complained of and precise equivalence in the offence creating provisions is not necessary. Nothing in this subsection suggests that a different approach is intended here.

Subs.(4)

A condition specified in subs.(3) above.   That is, the double criminality requirement.

Shall be taken to be satisfied.   There is a rebuttable presumption that the double criminality requirement is satisfied.

Unless, not later than such time as the High Court of Justiciary may ... prescribe.   Notwithstanding this, subs.(6) gives the court a discretion to permit the accused to require the prosecutor to prove that the double criminality requirement is satisfied without service of a notice.

A notice.   By contrast with notices under, for example, s.280(6)(b) of the present Act, the notice contemplated here cannot simply put the Crown to the proof. The notice must not only state that in the opinion of the accused the double criminality requirement is not satisfied and require the prosecutor to prove it; to be effective it must also state the *grounds* for the accused's opinion. This is likely to involve investigation of foreign law.

Subs.(6)

Since the exercise of the discretion given to the court by this subsection will almost certainly involve the leading of evidence as to the content of foreign law, it seems likely that an adjournment will be required. It might therefore be that the court, in deciding whether to exercise that discretion, will have in mind the three interests which, in terms of *Skeen v McLaren*, 1976 S.L.T. (Notes) 14, it should consider in relation to motions to adjourn (namely that of the accused, that of the prosecutor and the possibility of prejudice to the public interest).

Subs.(8)

Speaking for the Government, Lord Dubs explained that the purpose of this subsection is "not to give minor civil servants carte blanche to pursue criminal careers. It applies to actions which might have to be taken in the course of official duty where there is no exemption. There is a range of circumstances in which technical breaches of the new provisions might otherwise arise. For example, if the police or Customs were planning an undercover operation involving infiltration of an organised crime group, a consignment of drugs or weapons might be tracked to a number of different transit countries, each with a different legal system. There would obviously be no question of prosecution here in those circumstances" (*Hansard*, H.L. Debs, September 3, 1998, Col. 91).

PART II

POLICE FUNCTIONS

Lord Advocate's instructions

Instructions by Lord Advocate as to reporting of offences

12. The Lord Advocate may, from time to time, issue instructions to a chief constable with regard to the reporting, for consideration of the question of prosecution, of offences alleged to have been committed within the area of such chief constable, and it shall be the duty of a chief constable to whom any such instruction is issued to secure compliance therewith.

DEFINITION

"offence": s.307(1).

GENERAL NOTE

This section repeats the terms of s.9 of the 1975 Act which, in turn, derived from the Criminal Justice (Scotland) Act 1949 (c.94), s.33. The Lord Advocate's authority to appoint or remove procurators fiscal and delineate their territorial jurisdictions, is found in the Sheriff Courts and Legal Officers (Scotland) Act 1927 (c.35), s.1(2). By s.12 of that Act the Lord Advocate may also after consultation with the Treasury, by Order direct, notwithstanding the terms of any Act of Parliament, that any sheriff court proceedings for contraventions thereof shall proceed at the instance of the procurator fiscal. The Sheriff Courts (Prosecutions for Poaching) Order 1938 is the only instance in which this power has been exercised.

The Lord Advocate's power to amend or rescind policy, or change the instructions or guidance issued by his predecessors in that office is unfettered; see *MacDonald v HM Advocate*, 1997 S.C.C.R. 408 for its discussion of the constitutional standing of that office.

DETENTION *Detention and questioning*

Powers relating to suspects and potential witnesses

13.—(1) Where a constable has reasonable grounds for suspecting that a person has committed or is committing an offence at any place, he may require—

(a) that person, if the constable finds him at that place or at any place where the constable is entitled to be, to give the information mentioned in subsection (1A) below and may ask him for an explanation of the circumstances which have given rise to the constable's suspicion;

(b) any other person whom the constable finds at that place or at any place where the constable is entitled to be and who the constable believes has information relating to the offence, to give the information mentioned in subsection (1A) below.

(1A) That information is—

(a) the person's name;

(b) the person's address;

(c) the person's date of birth;

(d) the person's place of birth (in such detail as the constable considers necessary or expedient for the purpose of establishing the person's identity); and

(e) the person's nationality.

(2) The constable may require the person mentioned in paragraph (a) of subsection (1) above to remain with him while he (either or both)—

(a) subject to subsection (3) below, verifies any information mentioned in subsection (1A) above given by the person;

(b) notes any explanation proffered by the person.

(3) The constable shall exercise his power under paragraph (a) of subsection (2) above only where it appears to him that such verification can be obtained quickly.

(4) A constable may use reasonable force to ensure that the person mentioned in paragraph (a) of subsection (1) above remains with him.

(5) A constable shall inform a person, when making a requirement of that person under—

(a) paragraph (a) of subsection (1) above, of his suspicion and of the general nature of the offence which he suspects that the person has committed or is committing;

(b) paragraph (b) of subsection (1) above, of his suspicion, of the general nature of the offence which he suspects has been or is being committed and that the reason for the requirement is that he believes the person has information relating to the offence;

(c) subsection (2) above, why the person is being required to remain with him;

(d) either of the said subsections, that failure to comply with the requirement may constitute an offence.

(6) A person mentioned in—

(a) paragraph (a) of subsection (1) above who having been required—

    (i) under that subsection to give the information mentioned in subsection (1A) above; or

    (ii) under subsection (2) above to remain with a constable,

fails, without reasonable excuse, to do so, shall be guilty of an offence and liable on summary conviction to a fine not exceeding level 3 on the standard scale;

(b) paragraph (b) of the said subsection (1) who having been required under that subsection to give the information mentioned in subsection (1A) above fails, without reasonable excuse, to do so shall be guilty of an offence and liable on summary conviction to a fine not exceeding level 2 on the standard scale.

(7) A constable may arrest without warrant any person who he has reasonable grounds for suspecting has committed an offence under subsection (6) above.

AMENDMENT

Subss.(1)(a)(b), (2)(a) and (6)(a)(i)(b) as amended, and subs.(1A) inserted, by the Police, Public Order and Criminal Justice (Scotland) Act 2006 (asp 10), s.81(1)–(5). Brought into force on September 1, 2006 by the Police, Public Order and Criminal Justice (Scotland) Act 2006 (Commencement No. 1) Order 2006 (SSI 2006/432 (C.34)), art.2.

Subss.(1B), (1C), (2)(aa), (3A), (5)(ba), (6)(a)(iii) and (8) prospectively inserted, and subss.(2), (5)(d), (6)(a)(i) prospectively amended by the Police, Public Order and Criminal Justice (Scotland) Act 2006 (asp 10), s.82.

DEFINITIONS

"constable": s.307(1) and s.51(1) of the Police (Scotland) Act 1967 (c.77).

"offence": s.307(1).

GENERAL NOTE

The provisions of s.1 of the 1980 Act, after minor re-numbering of subsections, are re-enacted to form s.13. This section deals with the preliminary stages of police enquiries many of which will never develop into criminal proceedings. It gives a general power to police officers, when they have reasonable cause to suspect that an offence either has occurred or is in the course of commission, to demand information from certain members of the public. Two distinct categories of person are affected by these provisions, those who may have committed an offence, and those who are potential witnesses to an offence.

Powers In Relation To Suspects

Subsection (1)(a) relates to any person whom the officer suspects is guilty of such an offence (whether it is an arrestable offence or not), and empowers the constable to demand that person's particulars and an explanation for the conduct which has given rise to suspicion. Note that at this early stage no caution of any sort need be administered and it seems likely that any reply would be admissible subject to the ordinary rules of evidence.

The criteria governing a citizen's right to arrest and search a suspect were discussed by the Appeal Court in *Wightman v McFadyen*, 1999 S.C.C.R. 664 and in the context of drunk driving see the opinion in *Goodson v Higson*, 2002 S.L.T. 202.

If, however, suspicions were sufficiently tangible for the constable to feel a caution to be appropriate, then the s.13 procedure would not be appropriate; the proper approach would be to caution with a view to charging (in the case of non-arrestable offences) or, where the offence could attract a sentence of imprisonment, to consider whether the circumstances would justify the use of the power of detention now specified in s.14 of the Act (the statutory successor to s.2 of the 1980 Act), or arrest.

In the exercise of his power under subs.(1)(a), an officer must first explain the nature of his suspicion and may then require the potential suspect to remain while the veracity of his particulars is established (provided this can be done quickly) and any explanation given may be noted. It will be observed that in terms of subs.(6) failure to provide particulars or to remain while the explanation given is noted by the officer constitutes an offence which attracts arrest without warrant; nonetheless, a suspect is under no more of an obligation to give an explanation than an officer is to note it.

Doubtless a suspect's failure to offer an account may well serve to heighten the constable's existing suspicions. On an equally pragmatic level, an officer's failure to note an explanation given in response to a s.13 requirement would no doubt attract adverse comment in any subsequent proceedings.

Unlike s.14 below (which has re-enacted the provisions of s.2 of the 1980 Act), where strict adherence to the six hour detention period is demanded, no time limit is stipulated in s.13 for the completion of these initial enquiries, except that the procedure for verifying personal particulars must be capable of being completed quickly (see subs.(3)). While a suspect can be caused to remain for that verification to be made rapidly, it must be emphasised that he cannot be restrained under s.13 while his explanation is examined—that is the role of statutory detention. Reasonable force can be used to ensure that a suspect remains at the scene for the limited purposes of subs.(2); see *Hume v HM Advocate*, 2005 G.W.D. 22–411.

What then is the status of the suspect who is required to remain in terms of s.13(2) or, worse, restrained at the scene by a constable using his powers under s.13(4)? It might reasonably be felt, not least by the hapless suspect, that he is not at liberty to go and is in the officer's custody. However, reference to s.295 of the Act suggests that legal custody or detention only occurs when a person is required to be taken, or is held for the purpose of being taken, to a place for the purposes of the Act. It is notable that s.13(2) studiously avoids use of the word "detain" and the meaning of being required "to remain" for the limited purposes of the section must surely be something more dilute than detention. It is submitted that the precise status of the suspect is by no means clearly established.

Powers In Relation To Potential Witnesses

Subsection (1)(b) applies to persons whom the officer has reason to believe may, wittingly or unwittingly, have information to offer about the offence. It seems that this could extend to the circumstances in which the officer exercised his powers in relation to the suspect under subs.(1)(a): for example, the witness could be a bystander at the time when the suspect gave an explanation to the constable, given if he had not witnessed the offence giving rise to the enquiry.

First, however, a general explanation of the nature of the alleged offence being investigated must be given by the officer to the potential witness. The officer is also obliged to inform the other party of the belief that he or she possesses information relevant to that investigation and that failure to provide personal particulars in those circumstances is an offence.

Police powers in pursuit of requirements under subs.(1)(b) are more limited than those applicable to suspects, for subs.(4) allows the use of reasonable force to ensure that a suspect remains until the enquiries specified in subs.(2) are quickly completed or noted as the case may be. No force may be employed to cause a witness to remain at the scene. All that can lawfully be demanded of a witness is that he provides his name and address, albeit failure to give these particulars will render him liable to immediate arrest (subs.(7)).

Restrictions On Use Of Section 13 Powers

Most obviously an officer can only resort to using his powers under s.13 when he has reasonable cause to suspect that an offence has been committed or is ongoing.

The Act does not attempt to define what would constitute "reasonable cause" and nor need it do so. The phrase has been minutely examined by the courts, albeit usually in the context of the Road Traffic Acts. Suffice to say that the suspicions formed by the officer need not rest upon personal ocular observation; they can stem from the observations of other persons, from "information received" or from prior knowledge of the suspect's habits and background, as well as general knowledge of the area being policed.

It will be appreciated that some of the factors giving rise to cause to suspect, may well be inadmissible as evidence, but that would not disentitle the officer from forming his suspicion. The general considerations are discussed in *McNicol v Peters*, 1969 S.L.T. (J.) 261, notably in Lord Wheatley's judgment at pp.265 and 266, from which it can also be seen that even an ill-founded suspicion can still constitute reasonable cause to suspect. Lord Wheatley returned to this topic in *Dryburgh v Galt*, 1981 S.C.C.R. 26 at 29 noting:

> … the fact that the information on which the police officer formed his suspicion turns out to be ill-founded does not in itself necessarily establish that the police officer's suspicion was unfounded. The circumstances known to the police officer at the time he formed his suspicion constitute the criterion, not the facts as subsequently ascertained.

Nonetheless, the Crown will have to establish objectively that the factors which exercised the constable's suspicions would reasonably create a cause to suspect an offence without, at that stage, amounting to sufficient grounds for detention or arrest or charge.

The section is equally silent on the question of defining "any place" or "a place where the constable is entitled to be". The phrases serve to differentiate between the locus of the offence (where the officer can proceed on his enquiries armed with his suspicions) at the time of the offence or later, and elsewhere, in which latter case a right to information may depend upon the legitimacy of the officer's presence there. For example, the constable may be in a public place, or in a private place where access has been gained by warrant, by invitation or for an unrelated legitimate purpose: each of these different situations may subtly impinge upon the ability of the constable to exercise his powers under s.13. It will also be borne in mind that the degree of restraint used to ensure that the suspect remains, must be reasonable.

If it is established that the force employed was unreasonable, i.e. excessive or inappropriate, or both, then that might well nullify any subsequent evidence and constitute a criminal assault upon the suspect.

There is a dearth of case authorities dealing with this section, a fact which serves to underline its preliminary nature in the scale of proceedings.

Detention and questioning at police station

14.—(1) Where a constable has reasonable grounds for suspecting that a person has committed or is committing an offence punishable by imprisonment, the constable may, for the purpose of facilitating the carrying out of investigations—

(a) into the offence; and

(b) as to whether criminal proceedings should be instigated against the person, detain that person and take him as quickly as is reasonably practicable to a police station or other premises and may thereafter for that purpose take him to any other place and, subject to the following provisions of this section, the detention may continue at the police station or, as the case may be, the other premises or place.

(2) Detention under subsection (1) above shall be terminated not more than six hours after it begins or (if earlier)—

After 6 hours have elapsed detainee has to be

(a) when the person is arrested;

(b) when he is detained in pursuance of any other enactment; or

(c) where there are no longer such grounds as are mentioned in the said subsection (1),

and when a person has been detained under subsection (1) above, he shall be informed immediately upon the termination of his detention in accordance with this subsection that his detention has been terminated.

(3) Where a person has been released at the termination of a period of detention under subsection (1) above he shall not thereafter be detained, under that subsection, on the same grounds or on any grounds arising out of the same circumstances.

(4) Subject to subsection (5) below, where a person has previously been detained in pursuance of any other enactment, and is detained under subsection (1) above on the same grounds or on grounds arising from the same circumstances as those which led to his earlier detention, the period of six hours mentioned in subsection (2) above shall be reduced by the length of that earlier detention.

(5) Subsection (4) above shall not apply in relation to detention under section 41(3) of the Prisons (Scotland) Act 1989 (detention in relation to introduction etc. into prison of prohibited article), but where a person was detained under section 41(3) immediately prior to his detention under subsection (1) above the period of six hours mentioned in subsection (2) above shall be reduced by the length of that earlier detention.

(6) At the time when a constable detains a person under subsection (1) above, he shall inform the person of his suspicion, of the general nature of the offence which he suspects has been or is being committed and of the reason for the detention; and there shall be recorded—

Obligation of officer

(a) the place where detention begins and the police station or other premises to which the person is taken;

(b) any other place to which the person is, during the detention, thereafter taken;

(c) the general nature of the suspected offence;

(d) the time when detention under subsection (1) above begins and the time of the person's arrival at the police station or other premises;

(e) the time when the person is informed of his rights in terms of subsection (9) below and of subsection (1)(b) of section 15 of this Act and the identity of the constable so informing him;

(f) where the person requests such intimation to be sent as is specified in section 15(1)(b) of this Act, the time when such request is—

(i) made;

(ii) complied with; and

(g) the time of the person's release from detention or, where instead of being released he is arrested in respect of the alleged offence, the time of such arrest.

(7) Where a person is detained under subsection (1) above, a constable may—

(a) without prejudice to any relevant rule of law as regards the admissibility in evidence of any answer given, put questions to him in relation to the suspected offence;

(b) exercise the same powers of search as are available following an arrest.

(8) A constable may use reasonable force in exercising any power conferred by subsection (1), or by paragraph (b) of subsection (7), above.

P.TO

(9) A person detained under subsection (1) above shall be under no obligation to answer any question other than to give the information mentioned in subsection (10) below, and a constable shall so inform him both on so detaining him and on arrival at the police station or other premises.

(10) That information is—

(a) the person's name;

(b) the person's address;

(c) the person's date of birth;

(d) the person's place of birth (in such detail as a constable considers necessary or expedient for the purpose of establishing the person's identity); and

(e) the person's nationality.

AMENDMENT

Subs.(9) as amended, and subs.(10) inserted, by the Police, Public Order and Criminal Justice (Scotland) Act 2006 (asp 10), s.81(6). Brought into force on September 1, 2006 by the Police, Public Order and Criminal Justice (Scotland) Act 2006 (Commencement No. 1) Order 2006 (SSI 2006/432 (C.34)), art.2.

DEFINITIONS

"constable": s.307 and s.51(1) of the Police (Scotland) Act 1967.
"offence": s.307(1).
"offence punishable by imprisonment": s.307(6).
"prison": s.307(1).

GENERAL NOTE

This section regulates the practice of removing persons to, and detaining persons at, police stations for the purposes of questioning in relation to specified allegations of criminal conduct prior to charge.

The provisions were originally contained in s.2 of the Criminal Justice (Scotland) Act 1980 (c.62) and followed upon the recommendations of the Thomson Committee (II Chap. 3, recs. 3 to 13). A fixed six hour period of detention was then introduced along with a statutory form of caution distinct from the familiar common law caution. The intention was to allow time for further enquiry by the police where there was reasonable cause to suspect the commission of a crime but insufficient evidence immediately available to press charges. Detention was not, and should not be, regarded as a means of delaying arrest and charge; as soon as it is clear that sufficient evidence exists to arrest a suspect, detention has to be terminated. Note that while detention must be terminated at the point when a sufficiency of evidence is obtained, or within six hours (whichever is earlier), neither the 1980 Act nor this Act require that arrest must follow. However, as a safeguard against oppressive use of detention powers, it remains the case that only one period of detention will be permitted on the same or related grounds (see subs.(3)).

One of the benefits of s.2 detention was that it introduced both clarity and flexibility to the previously grey area between voluntary attendance, when (in theory at least) a person being interviewed was free to leave the police station at any time, and arrest. Deprivation of liberty is unlikely to be an individual's preferred option; nonetheless, it should be appreciated that statutory detention in the form provided by s.14 has the merit of establishing a suspect's legal status beyond doubt both in his mind and in the minds of those responsible for his detention.

Lawful Detention

The elements needed to constitute a lawful detention are not presented chronologically in s.14 but for convenience this course has been followed in the discussion below.

Grounds for Detention

Subsection (1) requires that the constable detaining a suspect must have reasonable grounds for suspecting that he has committed, or is in the course of committing, an imprisonable offence (for discussion of the factors underpinning "reasonable cause to suspect" see note to s.13 above), see

Wilson and Nolan v Robertson, 1986 S.C.C.R. 700. *Houston v Carnegie*, 2000 S.L.T. 333 is an example of a situation in which the detaining officer had neither sufficient direct knowledge nor information upon which to form reasonable grounds for suspicion. Compare *Stark v Brown*, 1997 S.C.C.R 382. In contrast to s.13 powers (the right to require personal particulars from suspects and potential witnesses, and an explanation of circumstances from suspects) which can be exercised in relation to any offence, s.14 detention is only permissible when the offence under investigation can attract a term of imprisonment on conviction.

It will be seen that the section is not a preventative one, i.e. detention cannot be used to inquire into an offence which has yet to occur. In reality this distinction may be more apparent than real; often matters may have advanced sufficiently to consider that contemplation has blossomed into preparation and, accordingly, an attempt at the suspected offence can be established.

Secondly, the only valid purpose of the detention is to assist in the investigation of the matter at hand. If those inquiries can be shown objectively to have been capable of completion without the necessity of detaining the suspect, then logically, procedures should be regarded as vitiated—that is a determination which commonsense suggests it would be difficult for a court to reach.

Information To Be Given To A Detainee

Subsection (6) requires the constable to outline to the suspect the grounds for detention, namely the nature of his suspicions and general details of the offence suspected. It is certain that these steps must be taken at the time when the suspect is detained though, in practice, the grounds will undoubtedly be repeated when the place of detention is reached.

Subsection (9) obliges the officer, before undertaking any questioning of the detainee, to administer the statutory form of caution both when initially detaining the suspect and when presenting him at the place of detention. The statutory caution requires a detainee to furnish his name and address; otherwise he is under no obligation to answer any further questions. Note that in *Tonge v HM Advocate*, 1982 S.C.C.R. 313 the Appeal Court stressed the desirability of administering a common law caution prior to interviews conducted during the six hour detention period.

Best practice also dictates that the statutory caution described above should be administered at the earliest opportunity although failure to do so will not inevitably damage a Crown case fatally. In *Scott v Howie*, 1993 S.C.C.R. 81 the appellant was detained under s.2 of the 1980 Act on suspicion of housebreaking and conveyed to a police office. No statutory caution in terms of s.2(7) (the statutory precursor of s.14(9)), was administered but such a caution was given at the office, as was a common law caution, following which the appellant made a statement whose contents the Crown founded upon. The admitted absence of a statutory caution at the time of detention in the street was not fatal in this instance. However, there can be no doubt that any effort to lead evidence of statements made by the detainee between being stopped by the officers and his arrival at the police office would have foundered on the grounds of inadmissibility.

Reasonable force may be used to effect detention and at that time, or later, to search the suspect's person (see subss.(1), (7) and (8)).

From the moment of detention a suspect is to be regarded as being in legal custody (see s.295 below).

Reference should be made to *Ucak v HM Advocate*, 1999 S.L.T. 392, in which the detention of the accused, a Turk who spoke no English, was held to be lawful although an interpreter was not available during the six hour statutory period; the police had done all that they could to comply.

Removal To A Police Office Or Other Premises

Once detained, the objective has to be to ensure the swift removal of the suspect to a police station or other premises (usually detention will be continued at a police station but that is not demanded by s.14(1)). One of the operational limitations of s.2 of the 1980 Act was that the detainee could only be taken to either a police station or other premises and, once there, could not be removed elsewhere. This could create practical difficulties, for example, in organising a swift identification parade or in detaining individuals for an offence which had been investigated by another officer or had occurred in another police division or area.

European Convention on Human Rights

The Appeal Court was sceptical that detention in terms of the section could properly be regarded as being "charged with an offence", the starting point for application of Art.6 (*HM Advocate v Robb*, 1999 G.W.D. 32–1524). The issue of access to a solicitor during the detention period was raised in *Paton v Ritchie*, 2000 S.L.T. 239; 2000 S.C.C.R. 151. Crown reliance on the terms of a police interview in which the accused was not given access to a solicitor was ruled upon in *Murray v United*

P.T.O
Time 6 months

Kingdom (1996) 22 E.H.R.R. 29; note, however, that in the Northern Ireland case an adverse inference could be drawn by the court from an accused's silence, a rule which has no general application in Scots procedure. This point was emphasised in *Dickson v HM Advocate*, 2001 S.L.T. 674 at 688E; 2001 S.C.C.R. 397 by Lord McFadyen in this five-judge decision. It was noted that the police interview continued despite the accused's general refusal to answer questions in the absence of her solicitor. The court held that this did not per se contravene D's Art.6 Convention rights, the issue of fairness of the interview being a matter for the jury after suitable direction. *Dickson* is noteworthy if only because a specially constituted bench of three judges was convened to hear legal argument in the course of the trial.

It will be remembered also that these powers of detention can only be exercised by "a constable", and are not available to other law enforcement agencies whose powers, if any, are derived on the basis of individual statutory provisions.

Section 14(1) incorporates amendments which were made to s.2 of the 1980 Act by the Criminal Justice and Public Order Act 1994 (c.33), s.129(1). These go some way to answering the logistical difficulties mentioned above. It is now permissible to remove a suspect from the establishment where he has originally been detained to another police office, or other place, for the purpose of facilitating the investigation. So a suspect could be moved between police offices or, say, from a local trading standards office once detained, to a police office for photographing and fingerprinting. A valuable degree of flexibility has been created, but it will be borne in mind that a record of the detention procedures and times, sufficient to comply with the provisions of s.15 has to be maintained (see the notes to s.15 below) and all such inquiries are subject to the six-hour time limit stipulated in s.14(2).

Different considerations apply to removal of detainees between jurisdictions in Great Britain and these are examined below.

The requirement to take the accused "as quickly as is reasonably practicable" does not mean that an accused must be conveyed to the closest police station. Operational factors may make detention at a more distant station appropriate. See *Menzies v HM Advocate*, 1995 S.C.C.R. 550 (suspect detained near Airdrie conveyed to Dunfermline).

The Time Factors

Subsection (2) provides that the period of detention shall not exceed six hours. The 1980 Act contained provisions identical to those now found in subss.(a) and (c) but subs.(b), which re-enacts provisions contained in s.129 of the Criminal Justice and Public Order Act 1994, represents a significant alteration to the old six hour rule.

Generally, the period of detention (six hours or less) will end with the suspect being arrested and charged or, alternatively, released without charge at that time if the grounds of suspicion have not been made out in that time. In the latter case, the police or the Crown would not be barred subsequently from preferring charges arising from the grounds of detention: they would in terms of s.14(3) be unable to detain again using the statutory detention to be found in s.14. In *HM Advocate v Mowat*, 2001 S.L.T. 738; 2001 S.C.C.R. 242 the meaning of subs.(3)'s reference to a further period of detention "on the same grounds or on any grounds arising out of the same circumstances" was reviewed in the absence of any direct authority during M's trial for the murder of C who had been found dead on November 4, 1999.

It soon became clear that M had been one of the last people to see C alive. On November 7, 1999 M was detained in relation to an assault upon another man, R, "and other crimes". While so detained he was questioned about the murder, and it was suggested by the defence that the assault upon R itself was attributed to the fact that R had implicated the accused in the murder. Certainly, police enquiries at that stage involved seizure of clothing, fingerprinting and a house search. At the conclusion of his detention M was charged with assaulting R and more than a month later was detained again, but this time for C's murder. It may be that while the offences investigated (and giving rise to detentions) are different, they could properly derive from the same grounds of suspicion. It has to be said that these may be fine distinctions in reality and serve to emphasise the importance of clarity (both in detention records and in the minds of the officers concerned) in the grounds for detention.

It is possible, of course, if unlikely, that at the end of a period of detention the suspect might opt to remain voluntarily to assist enquiries.

The end of the six-hour detention clearly represents a procedural watershed, for at that point (subject to subs.(b) discussed later) the suspect's status must change to that of a prisoner or a citizen free to return to his own affairs. If procedures laid out in s.14 are complied with, then it would seem that evidence collected during that time will be admissible, despite any subsequent want of procedure; see *Grant v HM Advocate*, 1989 S.C.C.R. 618 where arrest did not occur till some 20 minutes after the end of detention and replies made within the six hours were objected to. The Appeal Court held that subsequent laxity in compliance with formal requirements would not in themselves vitiate what had gone before.

It should not be forgotten that the cross-border enforcement provisions contained in Pt X of the Criminal Justice and Public Order Act 1994 introduce in s.138(6)(a) an allowable period of four hours detention calculated from the time of arrival at a police station outside Scotland, in circumstances described in s.137 of that Act, i.e. where a person is detained in England or Wales for an offence previously committed (or attempted) in Scotland.

So far as Northern Ireland is concerned, quite different provisions, found in s.137(7)(d) apply. A suspect found there and detained in connection with an offence in Scotland can either be taken to the nearest convenient police station in Scotland, or to the nearest designated police station in Northern Ireland, as soon as reasonably practicable (on arrest elsewhere in Great Britain in relation to a Scottish crime, the arresting officer's duty is to take the arrested person either to the nearest convenient police station in Scotland or to a police station within the sheriffdom where the offence is being investigated).

When recourse is had to these cross-border provisions, it should be stressed that it is only competent to convey the detainee to a police office, or to police offices; the references in s.14 of the 1995 Act to "other premises" must then be disregarded.

Lastly, it is worthy of note that the powers of cross-border enforcement bear a surprising, and doubtless unintended, resemblance to the doctrine of hot pursuit which operated in the Scottish and English Borders during the times of the reivers.

Section 14 Detention And Other Statutory Powers

As has been mentioned, the inclusion of subs.(b) has substantially affected the previously clear cut operation of s.14. Now detention under the Act may be only a prelude to further statutory periods of detention. The provisions of the Prevention of Terrorism (Temporary Provisions) Act 1989 (c.4) and the Customs and Excise Management Act 1979 (c.2) as augmented by the Criminal Justice (Scotland) Act 1987 (c.41), ss.48 to 50, spring to mind. Indeed, it will be noted that the Customs legislation cited is a refinement of the 1980 Act's detention provisions and is generally directed against drug smuggling offences.

Subsection (4) requires that a period of detention under any other enactment upon the same grounds, shall be deducted from the six-hour period ordinarily available under s.14. A like provision is made specifically in regard to the Prisons (Scotland) Act 1989 (c.45). Section 41(3) of that Act permits temporary detention within a prison for the purpose of investigating the introduction (i.e. smuggling) of forbidden materials by persons into prisons.

Details To Be Recorded

In addition to the obligation upon the detaining officer to disclose the nature of his suspicions and the reason for detention, subs.(6) stipulates other requirements which must be complied with by the officer and other police officers who become involved in the detention process later. It is an absolute requirement that (i) the time and place at which detention began, (ii) the general nature of the suspected offence, (iii) the time of arrival at the police office or other premises used for detention, (iv) the time, or times, at which the detainee was informed of his right to refuse to answer questions except those requiring his personal particulars (pursuant to subs.(9)) and his right to request that his solicitor and another person be advised of the fact of his detention as provided by s.15 of the Act, and the particulars of the officer who intimates this information, (v) the times when the above requests were made by the detainee and fulfilled by the police, and (vi) the time when detention terminated and/or the time of arrest should be recorded. All of these requirements simply echo the provisions contained in s.2(4) of the 1980 Act; it should be noted however that the corollary of the new power in subs.(1) of this Act to remove the detainee from the police office to "any other place", is that subs.(6)(b) demands that the "other place" should be specified in the record if such a power is exercised (although not statutorily required, it would be prudent to record fully the times of removal to that "other place" and return to the police office).

The practice adopted by Scottish police forces is for the detention forms which constitute the record of detention (stipulated now in subs.(6)), to be raised and maintained at police offices from the moment a detainee arrives there. It follows of course that initially the forms raised will necessarily have a retrospective effect since the detention process will have been initiated elsewhere: consequently it is sound practice for the detaining officer to note the time of initiating detention in his notebook.

In *Cummings v HM Advocate*, 1982 S.C.C.R. 108 the only record produced to show that a statutory caution had been administered was contained in the officer's notebook. This was held to constitute a record sufficient for the purposes of s.2(4) of the 1980 Act. Nevertheless, it is sound practice to ensure that the terms of the statutory caution in subs.(9) are repeated at the police office when documentation is raised.

Purpose Of Detention

While s.2(5) of the 1980 Act did broadly specify the avenues of inquiry which could be followed during detention, reference now has to be made to ss.18 and 19 of the 1995 Act to appreciate the wide-ranging powers which can be exercised (see notes to ss.18 and 19 below). Subsection (7) preserves the right to question and search the detainee. The power of search was held in *Skirving v Russell*, 1999 G.W.D. 15–701 to include a search of a woman's handbag as well as any pockets in her clothing. In *McIntyre v HM Advocate*, 2005 S.L.T. 757 it was held on appeal that the use, for forensic comparison of his voice against earlier taped malicious phone calls, of a tape recording of the accused's interview under caution while detained was fairly obtained and admissible as evidence. This was despite the fact that neither the accused nor the interviewing officers were aware of this possibility during the interview itself.

Questioning

The physical or psychological fitness of the accused to be questioned fairly often arises as an Art.6 Convention issue in the course of trial. This may well lead to a trial within a trial (where evidence is heard by the judge alone outwith the presence of the jury). *Platt v HM Advocate*, 2004 S.L.T. 333; 2004 S.C.C.R. 209 clarifies that the judge applies a proof on the balance of probabilities, but must still give appropriate directions to the jury to emphasise the higher standard of proof which must be applied in their own deliberations. No adverse inference can be drawn from a failure to answer questions put or, as in *Larkin v HM Advocate*, 2005 S.L.T. 1087, to respond "No comment" to such questions.

Rights of person arrested or detained

15.—(1) Without prejudice to section 17 of this Act, a person who, not being a person in respect of whose custody or detention subsection (4) below applies—

(a) has been arrested and is in custody in a police station or other premises, shall be entitled to have intimation of his custody and of the place where he is being held sent to a person reasonably named by him;

(b) is being detained under section 14 of this Act and has been taken to a police station or other premises or place, shall be entitled to have intimation of his detention and of the police station or other premises or place sent to a solicitor and to one other person reasonably named by him,

without delay or, where some delay is necessary in the interest of the investigation or the prevention of crime or the apprehension of offenders, with no more delay than is so necessary.

(2) A person shall be informed of his entitlement under subsection (1) above—

(a) on arrival at the police station or other premises; or

(b) where he is not arrested, or as the case may be detained, until after such arrival, on such arrest or detention.

(3) Where the person mentioned in paragraph (a) of subsection (1) above requests such intimation to be sent as is specified in that paragraph there shall be recorded the time when such request is—

(a) made;

(b) complied with.

(4) Without prejudice to the said section 17, a constable shall, where a person who has been arrested and is in such custody as is mentioned in paragraph (a) of subsection (1) above or who is being detained as is mentioned in paragraph (b) of that subsection appears to him to be a child, send without delay such intimation as is mentioned in the said paragraph (a), or as the case may be paragraph (b), to that person's parent if known; and the parent—

(a) in a case where there is reasonable cause to suspect that he has been involved in the alleged offence in respect of which the person has been arrested or detained, may; and

(b) in any other case shall,

be permitted access to the person.

(5) The nature and extent of any access permitted under subsection (4) above

shall be subject to any restriction essential for the furtherance of the investigation or the well-being of the person.

(6) In subsection (4) above—

(a) "child" means a person under 16 years of age; and

(b) "parent" includes guardian and any person who has the care of a child.

AMENDMENT

Subs.(6)(b) substituted by the Crime and Punishment (Scotland) Act 1997 (c.48), s.62(1) and Sch.1, para.21 with effect from August 1, by the Crime and Punishment (Scotland) Act 1997 (Commencement and Transitional Provisions) Order 1997 (SI 1997/1712), art.3.

DEFINITIONS

"child": s.307(1) as restricted by subs. (6) below.

"constable": s.307(1) and Police (Scotland) Act 1967 (c.77), s.51(1).

"parent": subs. (6) below.

GENERAL NOTE

This section specifies the extent to which arrested or detained persons are entitled to have other persons informed of their circumstances and whereabouts. This must be intimated to the subject as soon as he is presented at the station charge bar or at whatever other place he is being lawfully held in custody. Note that the entitlement does not extend to those attending voluntarily. Section 14(6) requires that the procedure be properly documented at the time of arrival at the police station or "other place", not before.

There are some important differences in the obligations the police are placed under by this section when dealing with arrested, as distinct from detained, persons.

Arrested Persons

In the case of arrested persons, subs.(1)(a) only deals with the right to have friends or relatives told this information and, while the arrested person has to be advised of his right to have a named person told of his circumstances, the police can, when there are legitimate grounds for doing so, delay such a notification. Section 17 makes it mandatory for the arrested person to be advised immediately of his right to have a legal representative (whether personally nominated by the person or acting as the duty solicitor under the Legal Aid Scheme) informed of his status and whereabouts. While that section stipulates that the arrested person must be informed of this right immediately on arrest, it does not demand immediate intimation to the solicitor who is named. Nevertheless an unexplained delay in notification would risk an unfavourable interpretation in subsequent proceedings. There is no obligation upon the solicitor to attend the police station (or other named premises) when notification is received from the police.

It should be noted that separate, more extensive, provisions are made in regard to children, and these are discussed below.

Detained Persons

Subsection (1)(b) relates to suspects detained in terms of s.14. Their rights to intimation differ from those applicable to arrested persons. At the time of detention at a police office or other place, the detainee must be informed of his entitlement to have his circumstances made known to a reasonably named person and to a solicitor. This right applies equally to situations where the subject is held at a police office or elsewhere but greater latitude is permitted in delaying the implementation of the detainee's demands. Informing either the detainee's reasonably named person or his solicitor, or both, can be delayed. Normally notifications requested by the suspect must be acted upon swiftly, in order to comply with the spirit of the Act unless, as subs.(1) stipulates, there are plausible grounds relative to the matter under investigation or affecting the prospects of apprehending others or relating to the prevention of crime (this last being an undefined catch-all) which justify a temporary withholding of notification.

There is no automatic right of access to a solicitor either prior to, or during a detention interview, but the admissibility of evidence obtained from the accused during the interview must still meet a general test of fairness. See *Paton v Ritchie*, 2000 S.L.T. 239; 2000 S.C.C.R. 151 (following *H.M. Advocate v Fox*, 1947 J.C. 30) where the accused's appeal was based upon a purported breach of his

Art.6 rights: the Appeal Court accepted that Art.6 could apply even at this early investigative stage in proceedings. Reference should also be made to *R. v Fox*; *Fox v Chief Constable of Gwent* [1985] 1 W.L.R. 1126; [1985] 3 All E.R. 392, a House of Lords judgement which held that an unlawful arrest did not of itself vitiate subsequent breath test procedures: this case was discussed in *Goodson v Higson*, 2002 S.L.T. 202 where the Appeal Court ruled, on the facts, that there had been no arrest.

Section 15 As Applied To Children

These provisions apply to children aged between eight and 16 years since s.41 statutorily repeats the common law concept of nonage: see also *Merrin v S*, 1987 S.L.T. 193 and the general discussion there of the absence of dole in children under eight years.

In the context of s.15 it will be observed that the definition of "child" found in subs.(6) is narrower than that contained in the Interpretation section (s.308), which in turn refers back to the provisions of the Children (Scotland) Act 1995 (c.36). The narrower definition in subs.(6) has the effect of ensuring that identical provisions apply to all those aged 16 years or more. That section apart, the 1995 Act and Pt II of the Children (Scotland) Act 1995, s.93(2)(b) adhere to the definition of a "child" as either a person less than 16 years old, or a person over the age of 16 years and less than 18 years old who is subject to a supervision requirement.

Subsection (4) places a positive onus upon the police when they think that the person in custody is a child, to take active steps to contact the child's parent or guardian and allow access to the child. This is the case even when it is suspected that the parent or guardian was involved in the offence which gave rise to the child's detention in the first place: subs.(5) allows access to the child to be limited (and, arguably, even refused) where this is essential to the further investigation of the offence under scrutiny or for the safety of the parent or guardian, or both. It is submitted that the grounds for any restriction upon, or refusal of, access in these circumstances should be fully noted by the officers involved. Failure to adhere to these requirements arose in the case of *H.M. Advocate v G.B. and D.J.M.*, 1991 S.C.C.R. 533 and a confession obtained by the police was withheld from the jury.

Generally the Act proceeds on the basis that children arrested for offences shall be liberated to appear at court rather than being detained in custody. See s.43 below which sets out the procedures following the arrest of a child.

Observations

Curiously while s.15 demands that the suspect be informed of these rights and (together with s.14(6)(e) and (f)) that a record of the person and solicitor named be kept along with the times of notification, it is not necessary to record when notification is wilfully delayed or the reasons for so doing. It is submitted that where a departure from the usual practice of notification occurs, this should only be done when the following factors are *all* present; (a) the suspect has been informed of his rights of intimation, and (b) has elected names which are deemed unreasonable or as inexpedient (broadly not in the interests of justice for the reasons expressed in subs.(1)) at that time, and (c) has been informed that such intimation will not be made and advised of the grounds for that decision. The suspect cannot simply be left in the dark if the spirit of s.15 is to have any meaning. As was remarked earlier, it would be expedient, with an eye to later proceedings, that the grounds for delaying notification to the suspect's solicitor or friend be recorded along with the other details stipulated in s.14(6)and subs.(3). Failure to comply with the terms of this section would taint any admissions, prints or samples subsequently obtained from the accused. Adapting the *ratio* in *Grant v H.M. Advocate*, 1989 S.C.C.R. 618 (see notes to s.14 above) suggests that evidence obtained from the accused beforehand would still be admissible.

Drunken persons: power to take to designated place

16.—(1) Where a constable has power to arrest a person without a warrant for any offence and the constable has reasonable grounds for suspecting that that person is drunk, the constable may, if he thinks fit, take him to any place designated by the Secretary of State for the purposes of this section as a place suitable for the care of drunken persons.

(2) A person shall not by virtue of this section be liable to be detained in any such place as is mentioned in subsection (1) above, but the exercise in his case of the power conferred by this section shall not preclude his being charged with any offence.

DEFINITIONS

"constable": s.307(1) and s.51(1) of the Police (Scotland) Act 1967.

"offence": s.307(1).

GENERAL NOTE

More in hope than expectation this section repeats the provisions, word for word, of s.5 of the 1980 Act. The original intention of the section was to enable drunken persons to be dealt with other than by criminal prosecution and it gave the police the option of conveying the offender to a designated place for detoxification. The section can only be applied where such designated places exist and to date only pilot schemes have operated.

While a constable may choose to exercise his powers to deliver a drunkard to a designated place, neither he nor the staff there have any power to compel the subject to remain there. It will also be noted that conveyance to a place is entirely without prejudice to any further proceedings arising from the arrest. It is of interest that this section does not require the offence giving rise to arrest to be one specifically of drunkenness, or to have been committed in a public place, only that the offender offended while apparently drunk. That said, the scope of the powers of arrest for common law offences committed by a drunken offender remains hazy: plainly a common law offence witnessed by a constable would qualify, but what is the position when the suspicion of an offence stems from *ex parte* statements?

Certain statutory powers of arrest of drunken persons do exist. For example, the Civic Government (Scotland) Act 1982 (c.45), s.50(1) created an offence of being drunk and incapable, suggesting a more advanced state of intoxication and incapacity than mere drunkenness, while s.50(5) relates to possession of a firearm or crossbow in a public place while drunk.

The Criminal Justice (Scotland) Act 1980 confined itself to dealing with drunkenness: s.69(c) related to drunken persons on public passenger vehicles en route to designated sporting events; s.74 to drunkenness at a designated sports ground during the currency of a designated sporting event. These provisions are now to be found in Pt 2 of the Criminal Law (Consolidation) (Scotland) Act 1995 (c.39). In the absence of local or centrally funded provision of designated places s.16 is destined to be moribund.

Arrest: access to solicitor

Right of accused to have access to solicitor

17.—(1) Where an accused has been arrested on any criminal charge, he shall be entitled immediately upon such arrest—

Co htaie

    (a) to have intimation sent to a solicitor that his professional assistance is required by the accused, and informing the solicitor—

        (i) of the place where the person is being detained;

        (ii) whether the person is to be liberated; and

        (iii) if the person is not to be liberated, the court to which he is to be taken and the date when he is to be so taken; and

    (b) to be told what rights there are under—

        (i) paragraph (a) above;

        (ii) subsection (2) below; and

        (iii) section 35(1) and (2) of this Act.

(2) The accused and the solicitor shall be entitled to have a private interview before the examination or, as the case may be, first appearance.

GENERAL NOTE

It is mandatory that an accused person, following arrest, must be informed (i) of his right to have a solicitor informed of this development and that the solicitor's services are required (ii) of his right to a private interview with his solicitor which is to be accorded to him prior to the first court appearance on the charges and (iii) where applicable, of his right to have a solicitor of his choosing present at judicial examination and, if need be, for that examination to be delayed up to 48 hours to permit the attendance of that solicitor.

There is no obligation upon the solicitor to attend immediately or, indeed, at all but legal advice must be available before the accused's court appearance.

It will be noted that while a request by the accused to have a solicitor informed of his arrest must be acted upon by the police, there is no similar entitlement to have friends or relatives told of his circumstances though this should ordinarily be permitted; see the discussion in Notes to s.15 above regarding "Arrested Persons".

Grounds sufficient to merit arrest can be less than would be needed to prefer charge (*Hay v H.M. Advocate*, 1998 G.W.D. 35–1780). There is no prohibition on interview by the police after arrest (*Johnston v H.M. Advocate*, 1994 S.L.T. 300).

See also *Van Lierop v McLeod*, 2000 S.L.T. 291 in relation to the extent of admissibility of answers to questions after arrest.

Right of person accused of sexual offence to be told about restriction on conduct of defence: arrest

17A.—(1) An accused arrested on a charge of committing a sexual offence to which section 288C of this Act applies by virtue of subsection (2) of that section shall be entitled to be told, immediately upon his arrest—

(za) that, if he is indicted to the High Court in respect of the offence, his case at or for the purposes of the preliminary hearing may be conducted only by a lawyer;

(a) that, if he is tried for the offence charged, his defence and any proof ordered as is mentioned in section 288C(1) of this Act may be conducted only by a lawyer;

(b) that it is, therefore, in his interests to get the professional assistance of a solicitor; and

(c) that if he does not engage a solicitor for the purposes of the conduct of his case at or for the purposes of the preliminary hearing (if he is indicted to the High Court in respect of the offence) or his defence at the trial, the court will do so.

(2) A failure to comply with subsection (1) above does not affect the validity or lawfulness of the arrest of the accused or any other element of any consequent proceedings against him.

AMENDMENT

Section 17A is inserted by the Sexual Offences (Procedure and Evidence) (Scotland) Act 2002 (asp 9), Sch.1, para.2. Brought into force by the Sexual Offences (Procedure and Evidence) (Scotland) Act 2002 (Commencement and Transitional Provisions) Order 2002 (SSI 2002/443 (C.24)), reg.4 (effective from November 1, 2002).

Subs.(1)(a) as amended by Criminal Justice (Scotland) Act 2003 (asp 7), Sch.4, para.3. Brought into force on November 25, 2003 by the Criminal Justice (Scotland) Act 2003 (Commencement No.3 and Revocation) Order 2003 (SSI 2003/475 (C.26)), art.2(1).

Subs.(1) as amended by the Criminal Procedure (Amendment) (Scotland) Act 2004 (asp 5), s.25 and Sch.1, para.3. Brought into force on December 4, 2004 by the Criminal Procedure (Amendment) (Scotland) Act 2004 (Commencement, Transitional Provisions and Savings) Order 2004 (SSI 2004/405 (C.28)), art.2(1).

DEFINITIONS

"High Court": s.307(1).
"preliminary hearing": s.307(1).

GENERAL NOTE

This section provides that a person charged with any of the sexual offences listed in s.288C of the Act should be advised at the time of arrest of the restrictions upon his conduct of his defence; broadly, he is barred from representing himself and, thus, prevented from precognoscing or cross-examining victims or witnesses in those proceedings. Subs.(2) makes it clear that failure to advise the accused of these restrictions at the time of arrest would not nullify subsequent proceedings. The section is advisory, not mandatory, and it will be remembered that there is an obligation upon the Crown to give note to the accused of these restrictions when serving a complaint or indictment which contains a listed sexual offence. Following the development of victim statements and amendments to s.288C (introduced by ss.14 and 15 of the Criminal Justice (Scotland) Act 2003 (asp 7)), the same restrictions apply to preparation or conduct of any proof of victim statements following conviction of a listed sexual offence.

The Criminal Procedure (Amendment) (Scotland) Act 2004 now provides that a person charged with a listed sexual offence (see s.288C below) cannot be responsible for the preparation, or conduct, of a preliminary hearing personally but must engage a lawyer for the purpose. Subs.(1)(c) entitles the court to appoint a solicitor for these purposes if the accused has not engaged one or, perhaps more likely, has dismissed his existing solicitor. Note that subs.(1)(za) refers to "a lawyer" while subs.(1)(c) applies more narrowly to "a solicitor".

Prints and samples

Prints, samples etc. in criminal investigations

18.—(1) This section applies where a person has been arrested and is in custody or is detained under section 14(1) of this Act.

(2) A constable may take from the person, or require the person to provide him with, such relevant physical data as the constable may, having regard to the circumstances of the suspected offence in respect of which the person has been arrested or detained, reasonably consider it appropriate to take from him or require him to provide, and the person so required shall comply with that requirement.

(3) Subject to subsection (4) below, all record of any relevant physical data taken from or provided by a person under subsection (2) above, all samples taken under subsection (6) or (6A) below and all information derived from such samples shall be destroyed as soon as possible following a decision not to institute criminal proceedings against the person or on the conclusion of such proceedings otherwise than with a conviction or an order under section 246(3) of this Act.

(4) The duty under subsection (3) above to destroy samples taken under subsection (6) or (6A) below and information derived from such samples shall not apply—

(a) where the destruction of the sample or the information could have the effect of destroying any sample, or any information derived therefrom, lawfully held in relation to a person other than the person from whom the sample was taken; or

(b) where the record, sample or information in question is of the same kind as a record, a sample or, as the case may be, information lawfully held by or on behalf of any police force in relation to the person.

(5) No sample, or information derived from a sample, retained by virtue of subsection (4) above shall be used—

(a) in evidence against the person from whom the sample was taken; or

(b) for the purposes of the investigation of any offence.

(6) A constable may, with the authority of an officer of a rank no lower than inspector, take from the person—

(a) from the hair of an external part of the body other than pubic hair, by means of cutting, combing or plucking, a sample of hair or other material;

(b) from a fingernail or toenail or from under any such nail, a sample of nail or other material;

(c) from an external part of the body, by means of swabbing or rubbing, a sample of blood or other body fluid, of body tissue or of other material;

(d) [...]

(6A) A constable, or at a constable's direction a police custody and security officer, may take from the inside of the person's mouth, by means of swabbing, a sample of saliva or other material.

(7) [...]

(7A) For the purposes of this section and sections 19 and 20 of this Act "relevant physical data" means any—

(a) fingerprint;

(b) palm print;

(c) print or impression other than those mentioned in paragraph (a) and (b) above, of an external part of the body;

(d) record of a person's skin on an external part of the body created by a device approved by the Secretary of State.

(7B) The Secretary of State by order made by statutory instrument may approve a device for the purpose of creating such records as are mentioned in paragraph (d) of subsection (7A) above.

(8) Nothing in this section shall prejudice—

(a) any power of search;

(b) any power to take possession of evidence where there is imminent danger of its being lost or destroyed; or

(c) any power to take prints, impressions or samples under the authority of a warrant.

AMENDMENTS

Subs.(2) as amended by the Crime and Punishment (Scotland) Act 1997 (c.48), s.47(1)(a) and (b) with effect from August 1, 1997 in terms of the Crime and Punishment (Scotland) Act 1997 (Commencement and Transitional Provisions) Order 1997 (SI 1997/1712), art.3.

Subs.(3) substituted by the Crime and Disorder Act 1998 (c.37), Sch.8, para.117(1) and (2) (effective August 1, 1997: SI 1998/2327).

Subss.(7A) and (7B) inserted by s.47(1)(d) of the 1997 Act with effect from August 1, 1997 in terms of the Order above.

Subs.(7) repealed by the Crime and Punishment (Scotland) Act 1997, s.47(1)(c). Brought into force on November 17, 1997 by the Crime and Punishment (Scotland) Act 1997 (Commencement No.3) Order 1997 (SI 1997/2694 (C.101) (S.170)).

For the purposes of the Terrorism Act 2000 (c.11), s.41 and Sch.7 (where person detained at a police station in Scotland under those provisions), s.18(2) is substituted by Sch.8, para.20 of the 2000 Act.

Subs.(6)(d) repealed, and subs.(6A) inserted, by Criminal Justice (Scotland) Act 2003 (asp 7), Part 8, s.55. Brought into force on June 27, 2003 by the Criminal Justice (Scotland) Act 2003 (Commencement No.1) Order 2003 (SSI 2003/288 (C.14)).

Subss.(3) and (4) as amended by the Police, Public Order and Criminal Justice (Scotland) Act 2006 (asp 10), s.101 and Sch.6, para.4(2). Brought into force on September 1, 2006 by the Police, Public Order and Criminal Justice (Scotland) Act 2006 (Commencement No. 1) Order 2006 (SSI 2006/432 (C.34)), art.2.

Subs.(3) as amended by the Police, Public Order and Criminal Justice (Scotland) Act 2006 (asp 10), s.83(1). Brought in to force on January 01 by the Police, Public Order and Criminal Justice (Scotland) Act 2006 (Commencement No.2) Order (SSI 2006/607) (C.46), art.3.

DEFINITIONS

"constable": s.307(1) and Police (Scotland) Act 1967 (c.77), s.51(1).
"in custody": s.295.
"relevant physical data": s.18(7A) of the 1995 Act.

GENERAL NOTE

This section is derived from the Prisoners and Criminal Proceedings (Scotland) Act 1993 (c.9), s.28, which gave effect to the recommendations of the Scottish Law Commission's *Report on Evidence: Blood Group Tests, DNA Tests and Related Matters*, Paper No.120, 1989. The current provisions were intended to give clearer expression to the extent of police powers (those contained in s.2(5)(c) of the 1980 Act being somewhat indeterminate) and to apply equally to arrested suspects and to those detained under s.14 of the 1995 Act. Section 18 does give more extensive sampling powers to the police in subs.(6) than were previously available under the 1980 Act, but note that these can only be exercised after authorisation by a senior police officer, i.e. an officer of inspector rank or higher. The tenor of the Act might suggest that the authorising officer should not be involved in the investigation but this is not expressly stated.

The section stops short of permitting the procuring of evidence by methods which case law has defined as invasive, for example, internal physical examinations, endoscopic or colonoscopic examinations. It remains the case that such extreme invasions of bodily privacy, which involve entering the suspect's body, still require the authority of a sheriff's warrant which has to be obtained by the procurator fiscal. An application for a warrant of this kind can be made at any time, but the court will take account of the nature of the examination or sampling proposed, the degree of physical invasion involved (when set against the public interest in the detection of crime), the stage which proceedings have reached and whether, at that time, there is a *prima facie* justification for the application. (See *Hay v HM Advocate*, 1968 S.L.T. 334; *HM Advocate v Milford*, 1973 S.L.T. 12; *McGlennan v Kelly*, 1989 S.L.T. 832; *Smith v Cardle*, 1993 S.C.C.R. 609; *Hughes v Normand*, 1993 S.L.T. 113). The extension of this section to entitle the police to recover "relevant physical data" (as defined in subs.(7A)) primarily reflects the technological advances in the field of fingerprinting brought about by electronic "livescan" fingerprinting. "Livescan" is expected to produce higher-definition print quality (improving detection rates) and to deliver an instantaneous comparison of data on file to enable immediate confirmation of an offender's identity on completion of scanning.

Approval for the use of the Digital Biometrics Incorporation (DBI) Tenprinter 1133S, with palmprint option, was given by the Secretary of State with effect from August 8, 1997 by the Electronic Fingerprinting etc. Device Approval Order 1997 (SI 1997/1939 (S.140)).

Subs.(1)

This stipulates that the section applies to all persons arrested or detained by the police.

Subs.(2)

The reference to an "external part of the body" suggests that physical measurement of a suspect (as in *Smith v Cardle*), would be permissible using s.18 powers but the obtaining of dental impressions (as in *Hay v HM Advocate*) would not and would normally demand a sheriff's warrant. However subs.(8)(b) by implication permits urgent steps to be taken in situations where delay would create a real risk of evidence being irretrievably lost; the legitimacy, or otherwise, of such steps would fall to be considered in any subsequent proceedings.

Subss.(3) and (4)

Superficially, subs.(3) re-enacts the terms of s.2(1)(c) of the 1980 Act which provided for the destruction of fingerprint forms in the event either of their being no proceedings against the accused, or his acquittal following such proceedings. It will be noted that a decision not to proceed against an accused person will not always be because there is an insufficiency of evidence: the Crown may in broad terms decide that prosecution would not be in the public interest for a variety of reasons, or might opt to deal with the matter by way of a warning. It is in these situations, especially where proceedings are maintained against other accused, that intractable problems arise now because of the interaction of subss.(3) and (4).

Subsection (3) refers to "all information derived from such samples" and would seem to be more rigorous than the earlier provisions of s.2(1)(c) of the 1980 Act. The later provision suggests that data obtained as a result of such samples, which could arguably have been retained even after the destruction of the sample material under the 1980 Act, must also be destroyed. Yet while subs.(3) might momentarily be viewed as clarifying the law in this grey area, the terms of subs.(4) serve to qualify and obscure the position.

Subsection (4)(a) permits the retention of the samples, or the information derived from them, where to destroy such would itself "destroy" similar information obtained in relation to a person still accused. Presumably then, sample evidence gathered at an early stage in proceedings from suspect A against whom charges are later dropped, could still be preserved for use as evidence against suspect B now to be prosecuted. In such a situation there would be no obligation upon the police to destroy A's samples at all: they would only be precluded from using them as evidence in any other proceedings against A (see subs.(5) below).

Subsection 4(b) also militates against the general requirement to destroy samples when no proceedings are to follow. In this case both samples and the data derived from them could be preserved to update existing data held by the police about the person concerned, albeit these could not be deployed *directly* in evidence or in the investigation of crime. Since the technology now exists to extract DNA from body samples of the sort specified in subs.(6), this is an issue of no small importance.

There has of course been no judicial interpretation as yet of these subsections.

Subs.(5)

The implications of this provision are discussed above in the Notes to subss.(3) and (4). This appears to open the way to the preservation of databanks derived from samples of previously convicted persons.

Subs.(6)

The samples which can be taken by a police officer, are those deemed to be of a non-invasive nature. In practice these are generally obtained by police casualty surgeons and while subs.(7) permits the use of reasonable physical force to recover the necessary samples, it is likely that doctors would assist in the procedures in the absence of the suspect's consent, only when a sheriff's warrant had been obtained by the procurator fiscal.

Subs.(6A)

This new provision enables a constable, or civilian auxiliary acting under his direction, to obtain mouth swab samples from an arrested person. The consent of a senior police officer is now only required by a constable when it is considered that a degree of force will be necessary to obtain relevant samples.

Retention of samples etc.: prosecutions for sexual and violent offences

18A.—(1) This section applies to any sample, or any information derived from a sample, taken under subsection (6) or (6A) of section 18 of this Act, where the condition in subsection (2) below is satisfied.

(2) That condition is that criminal proceedings in respect of a relevant sexual offence or a relevant violent offence were instituted against the person from whom the sample was taken but those proceedings concluded otherwise than with a conviction or an order under section 246(3) of this Act.

(3) Subject to subsections (9) and (10) below, the sample or information shall be destroyed no later than the destruction date.

(4) The destruction date is—

(a) the date of expiry of the period of 3 years following the conclusion of the proceedings; or

(b) such later date as an order under subsection (5) below may specify.

(5) On a summary application made by the relevant chief constable within the period of 3 months before the destruction date the sheriff may, if satisfied that there are reasonable grounds for doing so, make an order amending, or further amending, the destruction date.

(6) An application under subsection (5) above may be made to any sheriff—

(a) in whose sheriffdom the person referred to in subsection (2) above resides;

(b) in whose sheriffdom that person is believed by the applicant to be; or

(c) to whose sheriffdom the person is believed by the applicant to be intending to come.

(7) An order under subsection (5) above shall not specify a destruction date more than 2 years later than the previous destruction date.

(8) The decision of the sheriff on an application under subsection (5) above may be appealed to the sheriff principal within 21 days of the decision; and the sheriff principal's decision on any such appeal is final.

(9) Subsection (3) above does not apply where—

(a) an application under subsection (5) above has been made but has not been determined;

(b) the period within which an appeal may be brought under subsection (8) above against a decision to refuse an application has not elapsed; or

   (c) such an appeal has been brought but has not been withdrawn or finally determined.

   (10) Where—

   (a) the period within which an appeal referred to in subsection (9)(b) above may be brought has elapsed without such an appeal being brought;

   (b) such an appeal is brought and is withdrawn or finally determined against the appellant; or

   (c) n appeal brought under subsection (8) above against a decision to grant an application is determined in favour of the appellant,

the sample or information shall be destroyed as soon as possible thereafter.

   (11) In this section—

"the relevant chief constable" means

     (a) the chief constable of the police force of which the constable who took or directed the taking of the sample was a member;

     (b) the chief constable of the police force in the area of which the person referred to in subsection (2) above resides; or

     (c) a chief constable who believes that that person is or is intending to come to the area of the chief constable's police force; and

"relevant sexual offence" and "relevant violent offence" have the same meanings as in section 19A(6) of this Act and include any attempt, conspiracy or incitement to commit such an offence.

AMENDMENT

Section 18Ainserted by the Police, Public Order and Criminal Justice (Scotland) Act 2006 (asp 10), s.83(2). Brought in to force on January 1, 2007 by the Police, Public Order and Criminal Justice (Scotland) Act 2006 (Commencement No.2) Order 2006 (SSI 2006/607 (C.46)), art 3.

Prints, samples etc. in criminal investigations: supplementary provisions

19.—(1) Without prejudice to any power exercisable under section 19A of this Act, his section applies where a person convicted of an offence—

   (a) has not, since the conviction, had taken from him, or been required to provide, any relevant physical data or had any impression or sample taken from him; or

   (b) has at any time had—

     (i) taken from him or been required (whether under paragraph (a) above or under section 18, 19A or 19AA of this Act or otherwise) to provide any physical data; or

     (ii) any impression or sample taken from him,

which was not suitable for the means of analysis for which the data were taken or required or the impression or sample was taken or, though suitable, was insufficient (either in quantity or in quality) to enable information to be obtained by that means of analysis.

   (2) Where this section applies, a constable may, within the permitted period—

   (a) take from or require the convicted person to provide him with such relevant physical data as he reasonably considers it appropriate to take or, as the case may be, require the provision of;

   (b) with the authority of an officer of a rank no lower than inspector, take from the person any sample mentioned in any of paragraphs (a) to (c) of subsection (6) of section 18 of this Act by the means specified in that paragraph in relation to that sample; and

    (c) take, or direct a police custody and security officer to take, from the person any sample mentioned in subsection (6A) of that section by the means specified in that subsection.

(3) A constable—

(a) may require the convicted person to attend a police station for the purposes of subsection (2) above;

(b) may, where the convicted person is in legal custody by virtue of section 295 of this Act, exercise the powers conferred by subsection (2) above in relation to the person in the place where he is for the time being.

(4) In subsection (2) above, "the permitted period" means—

    (a) in a case to which paragraph (a) of subsection (1) above applies, the period of one month beginning with the date of the conviction;

    (b) in a case to which paragraph (b) of that subsection applies, the period of one month beginning with the date on which a constable of the police force which instructed the analysis receives written intimation that the relevant physical data were or the sample was unsuitable or, as the case may be, insufficient as mentioned in that paragraph.

(5) A requirement under subsection (3)(a) above—

(a) shall give the person at least seven days' notice of the date on which he is required to attend;

(b) may direct him to attend at a specified time of day or between specified times of day.

(6) Any constable may arrest without warrant a person who fails to comply with a requirement under subsection (3)(a) above.

AMENDMENTS

Subss.(1)(a) and (b) as substituted by the Crime and Punishment (Scotland) Act 1997 (c.48), s.47(2)(a) with effect from August 1, 1997 in terms of the Crime and Punishment (Scotland) Act 1997 (Commencement and Transitional Provisions) Order 1997 (SI 1997/1712), art.3.

Sub.(2)(a) as substituted by the above Act s.47(2)(b) with effect from August 1, 1997 as provided by the Order above.

Subs.(4)(b) as amended by the above Act s.47(2)(c) with effect from August 1, 1997 as provided by the Order above.

Subs.(1) as amended by s.48 of the above Act with effect from November 17, 1997 in terms of SI 1997/2694 (C.101) (S.170).

Subs.(2) as amended by Criminal Justice (Scotland) Act 2003 (asp 7), Pt 8, s.55. Brought into force on June 27, 2003 by the Criminal Justice (Scotland) Act 2003 (Commencement No.1) Order 2003 (SSI 2003/288 (C.14)).

Subs.(1)(b)(i) as amended by the Police, Public Order and Criminal Justice (Scotland) Act 2006 (asp 10), s.77(3). Brought into force on September 1, 2006 by the Police, Public Order and Criminal Justice (Scotland) Act 2006 (Commencement No. 1) Order 2006 (SSI 2006/432 (C.34)), art.2.

DEFINITION

"constable": s.307(1) and s.51(1) of the Police (Scotland) Act 1967.

"relevant physical data": s.18(7A) of the 1995 Act.

GENERAL NOTE

This section gives the police a general power in the course of investigations or after the conviction of an accused, within the permitted period of one month specified in subs.(4), to obtain relevant physical data as defined in s.18A. (See the General Note at A4–49 above.) The power can be utilised within that time in two distinct situations; (i) when no such samples have been taken since conviction (subs.(1)(a)) and (ii) when the materials obtained in the course of detention or arrest of the person have been either insufficient or deficient for the purposes of analysis (subs.(1)(b)). This section operates without prejudice to the Crown's own rights to petition the court for relevant physical data by way of Incidental Application or petition warrant.

The previous requirement that police officers had to obtain the consent of a senior police officer before taking mouth swabs from detained or arrested persons has been rescinded. Furthermore the power to take non-invasive samples from such persons has been extended to civilian custody officers. Consent of a senior officer (an inspector or more senior officer) is now only required when it is felt necessary that a degree of force will be needed to procure samples from a suspect or accused person.

The Permitted Period (subs.(4))

The timescale in the event of conviction is unambiguous—one month from the date of that conviction. This would apply equally in the cases of the imposition of a money fine or caution, probation as defined in s.228 below or a deferment of sentence. Subsection (4)(a) provides for an opportunity to correct acts of omission.

Subsection (4)(b), which applies to suspects under investigation and to those convicted of offences, is by its nature much less precise; the one month timescale is effective from the date upon which the police force instructing a forensic or fingerprint examination of samples previously obtained from the suspect, receives written intimation of their unsuitability. Note that a verbal report to the same effect would not start the clock ticking. It should also be appreciated that subs.(4)(b) does not provide a remedy for situations where no samples had been taken from the suspect; the subsection only operates when samples taken are later found to be defective.

Police Powers Under s.19

The police are entitled, within the permitted period, to require that the accused makes himself available for sampling purposes if he is at liberty or to have access to him for those purposes if he is in custody. No notice need be given to a remand or serving prisoner of the police intention to exercise such powers, but subs.(3)(b) curiously makes it clear that the sampling procedures must be executed, "in the place where he is for the time being": this suggests that the sampling must be carried out in the penal establishment in which the accused is serving his sentence.

A person at large is entitled to no less than seven days notice of the requirement that he attend at a specified place and may also be directed to attend on a particular day and time (or days and times).

Failure to attend the nominated police station as demanded under s.19(3) renders the subject liable to arrest without warrant, but the Act does not treat such a failure as an offence. A further issue which is unresolved in the Act is the position when a suspect does attend as required, but samples are not sufficient for analysis or indeed no samples are taken at all. It is submitted that in the former case the whole procedure in subs.(4)(b) could be invoked anew, but in the latter, the suspect would have fulfilled his obligation and could not be subjected to the procedure again. Note also that subs.(5) is peremptory and is not qualified by any reasonableness test.

It will be necessary if the power of arrest in subs.(6) is to be invoked, that the police can demonstrate that notice of the requirement has been lawfully served upon the subject.

Samples etc. from persons convicted of sexual and violent offences.

19A.—(1) This section applies where a person—

(a) is convicted on or after the relevant date of a relevant offence and is sentenced to imprisonment;

(b) was convicted before the relevant date of a relevant offence, was sentenced to imprisonment and is serving that sentence on or after the relevant date;

(c) was convicted before the relevant date of a specified relevant offence, was sentenced to imprisonment, is not serving that sentence on that date or at any time after that date but was serving it at any time during the period of five years ending with the day before that date.

(2) Subject to subsections (3) and (4) below, where this section applies a constable may—

(a) take from the person or require the person to provide him with such relevant physical data as the constable reasonably considers appropriate;

(b) with the authority of an officer of a rank no lower than inspector, take from the person any sample mentioned in any of paragraphs (a) to (c) of subsection (6) of section 18 of this Act by the means specified in that paragraph in relation to that sample; and

(c) take, or direct a police custody and security officer to take, from the person any sample mentioned in subsection (6A) of that section by the means specified in that subsection.

(3) The power conferred by subsection (2) above shall not be exercised where the person has previously had taken from him or been required to provide relevant physical data or any sample under subsection (2) of section 19 of this Act in a case where the power conferred by that subsection was exercised by virtue of subsection (1)(a) of that section, under this section or under section 19AA(3) of this Act unless the data so taken or required have been or, as the case may be, the sample so taken or required has been lost or destroyed.

(4) Where this section applies by virtue of—

(a) paragraph (a) or (b) of subsection (1) above, the powers conferred by subsection (2) above may be exercised at any time when the person is serving his sentence; and

(b) paragraph (c) of the said subsection (1), those powers may only be exercised within a period of three months beginning on the relevant date.

(5) Where a person in respect of whom the power conferred by subsection (2) above may be exercised—

(a) is no longer serving his sentence of imprisonment, subsections (3)(a), (5) and (6);

(b) is serving his sentence of imprisonment, subsection (3)(b),

of section 19 of this Act shall apply for the purposes of subsection (2) above as they apply for the purposes of subsection (2) of that section.

(6) In this section—

"conviction" includes—

(a) an acquittal, by virtue of section 54(6) or 55(3) of this Act, on the ground of the person's insanity at the time at which he committed the act constituting the relevant offence;

(b) a finding under section 55(2) of this Act, and "convicted" shall be construed accordingly;

"relevant date" means the date on which section 48 of the Crime and Punishment (Scotland) Act 1997 is commenced;

"relevant offence" means any relevant sexual offence or any relevant violent offence;

"relevant sexual offence" means any of the following offences—

(a) rape;

(b) clandestine injury to women;

(c) abduction of a woman with intent to rape;

(d) assault with intent to rape or ravish;

(e) indecent assault;

(f) lewd, indecent or libidinous behaviour or practices;

(g) shameless indecency;

(h) sodomy; and

(i) any offence which consists of a contravention of any of the following statutory provisions—

(i) section 52 of the Civic Government (Scotland) Act 1982 (taking and distribution of indecent images of children);

(ii) section 52A of that Act (possession of indecent images of children);

(iii) section 311 of the Mental Health (Care and Treatment) (Scotland) Act 2003 (non consensual sexual acts);

(iv) section 313 of that Act (persons providing care services: sexual offences);

(v) section 1 of the Criminal Law (Consolidation)(Scotland) Act 1995 (incest);

(vi) section 2 of that Act (intercourse with step-child);

(vii) section 3 of that Act (intercourse with child under 16 years by person in position of trust);

(viii) section 5(1) or (2) of that Act (unlawful intercourse with girl under 13 years);

(ix) section 5(3) of that Act (unlawful intercourse with girl aged between 13 and 16 years);

(x) section 6 of that Act (indecent behaviour towards girl between 12 and 16 years);

(xi) section 7 of that Act (procuring);

(xii) section 8 of that Act (abduction and unlawful detention of women and girls);

(xiii) section 9 of that Act (permitting use of premises for unlawful sexual intercourse);

(xiv) section 10 of that Act (liability of parents etc in respect of offences against girls under 16 years);

(xv) section 11(1)(b) of that Act (soliciting for immoral purpose);

(xvi) section 13(5)(b) and (c) of that Act (homosexual offences);

"relevant violent offence" means any of the following offences—

(a) murder or culpable homicide;

(b) uttering a threat to the life of another person;

(c) perverting the course of justice in connection with an offence of murder;

(d) fire raising;

(e) assault;

(f) reckless conduct causing actual injury;

(g) abduction; and

(h) any offence which consists of a contravention of any of the following statutory provisions—

(i) sections 2 (causing explosion likely to endanger life) or 3 (attempting to cause such an explosion) of the Explosive Substances Act 1883;

(ii) section 12 of the Children and Young Persons (Scotland) Act 1937 (cruelty to children);

(iii) sections 16 (possession of firearm with intent to endanger life or cause serious injury), 17 (use of firearm to resist arrest) or 18 (having a firearm for purpose of committing an offence listed in Schedule 2) of the Firearms Act 1968;

(iv) section 6 of the Child Abduction Act 1984 (taking or sending child out of the United Kingdom); and

"sentence of imprisonment" means the sentence imposed in respect of the relevant offence and includes—

(a) a compulsion order, a restriction order, a hospital direction and any order under section 57(2)(a) or (b) of this Act; and

(b) a sentence of detention imposed under section 207 or 208 of this

Act, and "sentenced to imprisonment" shall be construed accordingly; and any reference to a person serving his sentence shall be construed as a reference to the person being detained in a prison, hospital or other place in pursuance of a sentence of imprisonment; and

"specified relevant offence" means —

(a) any relevant sexual offence mentioned in paragraphs (a), (b), (f) and (i)(viii) of the definition of that expression and any such offence as is mentioned in paragraph (h) of that definition where the person against whom the offence was committed did not consent; and

(b) any relevant violent offence mentioned in paragraph (a) or (g) of the definition of that expression and any such offence as is mentioned in paragraph (e) of that definition where the assault is to the victim's severe injury, but, notwithstanding subsection (7) below, does not include— (i) conspiracy or incitement to commit; and (ii) aiding and abetting, counselling or procuring the commission of, any of those offences.

(7) In this section—

(a) any reference to a relevant offence includes a reference to any attempt, conspiracy or incitement to commit such an offence; and

(b) any reference to—

(i) a relevant sexual offence mentioned in paragraph (i); or

(ii) a relevant violent offence mentioned in paragraph (h);

of the definition of those expressions in subsection (6) above includes a reference to aiding and abetting, counselling or procuring the commission of such an offence.

AMENDMENT

Section 19A inserted by the Crime and Punishment (Scotland) Act 1997 (c.48), s.48.

Subs.(2) as amended by the Criminal Justice (Scotland) Act 2003 (asp 7), Pt 8, s.55. Brought into force on June 27, 2003 by the Criminal Justice (Scotland) Act 2003 (Commencement No.1) Order 2003 (SSI 2003/288 (C.14)).

Subs.(6) as amended by the Mental Health (Care and Treatment) (Scotland) Act 2003 (Modification of Enactments) Order 2005 (SSI 2005/465), art.2 and Sch.1, para.27(2) (effective September 27, 2005).

Subs.(3) as amended by the Police, Public Order and Criminal Justice (Scotland) Act 2006 (asp 10), s.77(4). Brought into force on September 1, 2006 by the Police, Public Order and Criminal Justice (Scotland) Act 2006 (Commencement No. 1) Order 2006 (SSI 2006/432 (C.34)), art.2.

Subs.(3) as amended by the Police, Public Order and Criminal Justice (Scotland) Act 2006 (asp 10), s.101 and Sch.6, para.4(3). Brought into force on September 1, 2006 by the Police, Public Order and Criminal Justice (Scotland) Act 2006 (Commencement No. 1) Order 2006 (SSI 2006/432 (C.34)), art.2.

Samples etc. from sex offenders

19AA.—(1) This section applies where a person is subject to—

(a) the notification requirements of Part 2 of the 2003 Act;

(b) an order under section 2 of the Protection of Children and Prevention of Sexual Offences (Scotland) Act 2005 (asp 9) (a risk of sexual harm order); or

(c) an order under section 123 of the 2003 Act (which makes provision for England and Wales and Northern Ireland corresponding to section 2 of that Act of 2005).

(2) This section applies regardless of whether the person became subject to those requirements or that order before or after the commencement of this section.

(3) Subject to subsections (4) to (8) below, where this section applies a constable may—

    (a) take from the person or require the person to provide him with such relevant physical data as the constable considers reasonably appropriate;

    (b) with the authority of an officer of a rank no lower than inspector, take from the person any sample mentioned in any of paragraphs (a) to (c) of subsection (6) of section 18 of this Act by the means specified in that paragraph in relation to that sample;

    (c) take, or direct a police custody and security officer to take, from the person any sample mentioned in subsection (6A) of that section by the means specified in that subsection.

(4) Where this section applies by virtue of subsection (1)(c) above, the power conferred by subsection (3) shall not be exercised unless the constable reasonably believes that the person's sole or main residence is in Scotland.

(5) The power conferred by subsection (3) above shall not be exercised where the person has previously had taken from him or been required to provide relevant physical data or any sample under section 19(2) or 19A(2) of this Act unless the data so taken or required have been or, as the case may be, the sample so taken has been, lost or destroyed.

(6) The power conferred by subsection (3) above shall not be exercised where the person has previously had taken from him or been required to provide relevant physical data or any sample under that subsection unless the data so taken or required or, as the case may be, the sample so taken—

    (a) have or has been lost or destroyed; or

    (b) were or was not suitable for the particular means of analysis or, though suitable, were or was insufficient (either in quantity or quality) to enable information to be obtained by that means of analysis.

(7) The power conferred by subsection (3) above may be exercised only—

    (a) in a police station; or

    (b) where the person is in legal custody by virtue of section 295 of this Act, in the place where the person is for the time being.

(8) The power conferred by subsection (3) above may be exercised in a police station only—

    (a) where the person is present in the police station in pursuance of a requirement made by a constable to attend for the purpose of the exercise of the power; or

    (b) while the person is in custody in the police station following his arrest or detention under section 14(1) of this Act in connection with any offence.

(9) A requirement under subsection (8)(a) above—

    (a) shall give the person at least seven days' notice of the date on which he is required to attend;

    (b) may direct him to attend at a specified time of day or between specified times of day; and

    (c) where this section applies by virtue of subsection (1)(b) or (c) above, shall warn the person that failure, without reasonable excuse, to comply with the requirement or, as the case may be, to allow the taking of or to provide any relevant physical data, or to provide any sample, under the power, constitutes an offence.

(10) A requirement under subsection (8)(a) above in a case where the person has previously had taken from him or been required to provide relevant physical data or any sample under subsection (3) above shall contain intimation that the

relevant physical data were or the sample was unsuitable or, as the case may be, insufficient, as mentioned in subsection (6)(b) above.

(11) Before exercising the power conferred by subsection (3) above in a case to which subsection (8)(b) above applies, a constable shall inform the person of that fact.

(12) Any constable may arrest without warrant a person who fails to comply with a requirement under subsection (8)(a) above.

(13) This section does not prejudice the generality of section 18 of this Act.

(14) In this section, "the 2003 Act" means the Sexual Offences Act 2003 (c.42).

AMENDMENT

Section 19AA inserted by the Police, Public Order and Criminal Justice (Scotland) Act 2006 (asp 10), s.77(2). Brought into force on September 1, 2006 by the Police, Public Order and Criminal Justice (Scotland) Act 2006 (Commencement No. 1) Order 2006 (SSI 2006/432 (C.34)), art.2.

Section 19AA: supplementary provision in risk of sexual harm order cases

19AB.—(1) This section applies where section 19AA of this Act applies by virtue of subsection (1)(b) or (c) of that section.

(2) A person who fails without reasonable excuse—

(a) to comply with a requirement made of him under section 19AA(8)(a) of this Act; or

(b) to allow relevant physical data to be taken from him, to provide relevant physical data, or to allow a sample to be taken from him, under section 19AA(3) of this Act,

shall be guilty of an offence.

(3) A person guilty of an offence under subsection (2) above shall be liable on summary conviction to the following penalties—

(a) a fine not exceeding level 4 on the standard scale;

(b) imprisonment for a period—

(i) where the conviction is in the district court, not exceeding 60 days; or

(ii) where the conviction is in the sheriff court, not exceeding 3 months; or

(c) both such fine and such imprisonment.

(4) Subject to subsection (6) below, all record of any relevant physical data taken from or provided by a person under section 19AA(3) of this Act, all samples taken from a person under that subsection and all information derived from such samples shall be destroyed as soon as possible following the person ceasing to be a person subject to any risk of sexual harm orders.

(5) For the purpose of subsection (4) above, a person does not cease to be subject to a risk of sexual harm order where the person would be subject to such an order but for an order under section 6(2) of the 2005 Act or any corresponding power of a court in England and Wales or in Northern Ireland.

(6) Subsection (4) above does not apply if before the duty to destroy imposed by that subsection would apply, the person—

(a) is convicted of an offence; or

(b) becomes subject to the notification requirements of Part 2 of the 2003 Act.

(7) In this section—

"risk of sexual harm order" means an order under—

(a) section 2 of the 2005 Act; or

(b) section 123 of the 2003 Act;

"the 2005 Act" means the Protection of Children and Prevention of Sexual Offences (Scotland) Act 2005 (asp 9);

"the 2003 Act" has the meaning given by section 19AA(14) of this Act; and

"convicted" shall be construed in accordance with section 19A(6) of this Act.

AMENDMENT

Section 19AB inserted by the Police, Public Order and Criminal Justice (Scotland) Act 2006 (asp 10), s.77(2). Brought into force on September 1, 2006 by the Police, Public Order and Criminal Justice (Scotland) Act 2006 (Commencement No. 1) Order 2006 (SSI 2006/432 (C.34)), art.2.

Power of constable in obtaining relevant physical data etc.

19B.—(1) A constable may use reasonable force in—

(a) taking any relevant physical data from a person or securing a person's compliance with a requirement made under section 18(2), 19(2)(a) or 19A(2)(a) of this Act, or under subsection (3)(a) of section 19AA of this Act where that section applies by virtue of subsection (1)(a) of that section;

(b) exercising any power conferred by section 18(6), 19(2)(b) or 19A(2)(b) of this Act, or under subsection (3)(b) of section 19AA of this Act where that section applies by virtue of subsection (1)(a) of that section.

(2) A constable may, with the authority of an officer of a rank no lower than inspector, use reasonable force in (himself) exercising any power conferred by section 18(6A), 19(2)(c) or 19A(2)(c) of this Act, or under subsection (3)(c) of section 19AA of this Act where that section applies by virtue of subsection (1)(a) of that section.

AMENDMENT

Section 19B inserted by the Crime and Punishment (Scotland) Act (c.48), s.48(2).

Section 19B as amended by the Criminal Justice (Scotland) Act 2003 (asp 7), Pt 8, s.55. Brought into force on June 27, 2003 by the Criminal Justice (Scotland) Act 2003 (Commencement No.1) Order 2003 (SSI 2003/288 (C.14)).

Subss.(1) and (2) as amended by the Police, Public Order and Criminal Justice (Scotland) Act 2006 (asp 10), s.77(5). Brought into force on September 1, 2006 by the Police, Public Order and Criminal Justice (Scotland) Act 2006 (Commencement No. 1) Order 2006 (SSI 2006/432 (C.34)), art.2.

Use of prints, samples etc.

20. Without prejudice to any power to do so apart from this section, relevant physical data, impressions and samples lawfully held by or on behalf of any police force or in connection with or as a result of an investigation of an offence and information derived therefrom may be checked against other such data, impressions, samples and information.

AMENDMENT

Section 20 as amended by the Crime and Punishment (Scotland) Act 1997, s.47(3).

DEFINITION

"relevant physical data": s.18(7A) of the 1995 Act.

GENERAL NOTE

This section preserves the existing rights of the police to collate and compare fingerprint impressions of accused persons and authorises such operations in relation to other samples lawfully obtained by the police (see the notes to s.18(3) and (4) above). In *HM Advocate v Shepherd*, 1997 S.C.C.R. 246 the Court of Appeal upheld the use of a fingerprint form, lawfully obtained from an accused following arrest in regard to a later offence, to prove earlier offences in which no fingerprint form had been obtained before the accused's full committal. The Court noted that carefully framed questions could avoid revealing that the accused had apparently been involved in another offence, and that the formal evidence of the taking of fingerprints had been incorporated into a statement of uncontroversial evidence. It may be that suitably circumspect questioning could validate the use of a fingerprint form lawfully obtained, but predating the offence libelled. Further, following *Lawrie v Muir*, 1950 S.L.T. 37 and *Namyslak v HM Advocate*, 1995 S.L.T. 528 it will be noted that even irregularly or unlawfully obtained fingerprint forms could be admissible as evidence, provided there was no unfairness to the accused. The 1997 Act has extended these rights to the retention and collation of relevant data which has been gathered in the course of investigation of an offence. On one reading this could entitle the police to retain data garnered from persons other than suspects or accused during an investigation.

Testing for Class A drugs

Arrested persons: testing for certain Class A drugs

20A.—(1) Subject to subsection (2) below, where subsection (3) below applies an appropriate officer may—

(a) require a person who has been arrested and is in custody in a police station to provide him with a sample of urine; or

(b) take from the inside of the mouth of such a person, by means of swabbing, a sample of saliva or other material,

which the officer may subject to analysis intended to reveal whether there is any relevant Class A drug in the person's body.

(2) The power conferred by subsection (1) above shall not be exercised where the person has previously been required to provide or had taken from him a sample under that subsection in the same period in custody.

(3) This subsection applies where—

(a) the person is of 16 years of age or more;

(b) the period in custody in the police station has not exceeded 6 hours;

(c) the police station is situated in an area prescribed by order made by statutory instrument by the Scottish Ministers; and

(d) either—

(i) the person's arrest was on suspicion of committing or having committed a relevant offence; or

(ii) a senior police officer who has appropriate grounds has authorised the making of the requirement to provide or the taking of the sample.

(4) Before exercising the power conferred by subsection (1) above, an appropriate officer shall—

(a) warn the person in respect of whom it is to be exercised that failure, without reasonable excuse, to comply with the requirement or, as the case may be, allow the sample to be taken constitutes an offence; and

(b) in a case within subsection (3)(d)(ii) above, inform the person of the giving of the authorisation and the grounds for the suspicion.

(5) Where—

(a) a person has been required to provide or has had taken a sample under subsection (1) above;

(b) any of the following is the case—

(i) the sample was not suitable for the means of analysis to be used to reveal whether there was any relevant Class A drug in the person's body;

(ii) though suitable, the sample was insufficient (either in quantity or quality) to enable information to be obtained by that means of analysis; or

(iii) the sample was destroyed during analysis and the means of analysis failed to produce reliable information; and

(c) the person remains in custody in the police station (whether or not the period of custody has exceeded 6 hours),

an appropriate officer may require the person to provide or as the case may be take another sample of the same kind by the same method.

(6) Before exercising the power conferred by subsection (5) above, an appropriate officer shall warn the person in respect of whom it is to be exercised that failure, without reasonable excuse, to comply with the requirement or, as the case may be, allow the sample to be taken constitutes an offence.

(7) A person who fails without reasonable excuse—

(a) to comply with a requirement made of him under subsection (1)(a) or (5) above; or

(b) to allow a sample to be taken from him under subsection (1)(b) or (5) above,

shall be guilty of an offence.

(8) In this section—

"appropriate grounds" means reasonable grounds for suspecting that the misuse by the person of any relevant Class A drug caused or contributed to the offence on suspicion of which the person was arrested;

"appropriate officer" means—

(a) a constable; or

(b) a police custody and security officer acting on the direction of a constable;

"misuse" has the same meaning as in the Misuse of Drugs Act 1971 (c.38);

"relevant Class A drug" means any of the following substances, preparations and products—

(a) cocaine or its salts;

(b) any preparation or other product containing cocaine or its salts;

(c) diamorphine or its salts;

(d) any preparation or other product containing diamorphine or its salts;

"relevant offence" means any of the following offences—

(a) theft;

(b) assault;

(c) robbery;

(d) fraud;

(e) reset;

(f) uttering a forged document;

(g) embezzlement;

(h) an attempt, conspiracy or incitement to commit an offence mentioned in paragraphs (a) to (g);

(i) an offence under section 4 of the Misuse of Drugs Act 1971 (c.38) (restriction on production and supply of controlled drugs) committed in respect of a relevant Class A drug;

(j) an offence under section 5(2) of that Act of 1971 (possession of controlled drug) committed in respect of a relevant Class A drug;

(k) an offence under section 5(3) of that Act of 1971 (possession of controlled drug with intent to supply) committed in respect of a relevant Class A drug;

"senior police officer" means a police officer of a rank no lower than inspector.

AMENDMENT

Section 20A inserted by the Police, Public Order and Criminal Justice (Scotland) Act 2006 (asp 10), s.84. Brought into force on January 1, 2007 by the Police, Public Order and Criminal Justice (Scotland) Act 2006 (Commencement No.2) Order 2006 (SSI 2006/607 (C.46)), art.3 and Sch. for the purpose of enabling an order under s.20A(3)(c) of the 1995 Act to be made.

DEFINITIONS

"appropriate grounds": s.20A(8).
"appropriate officer": s.20A(8).
"misuse": s.20A(8).
"relevant Class A drug": s.20A(8).
"relevant offence": s.20A(8).
"senior police officer": s.20A(8).

GENERAL NOTE

Section 20A provides that the police may test a person for a relevant Class A drug if he or she has been arrested under suspicion of committing a relevant offence. The relevant offences are listed in s.20A(8). A person who has been arrested under suspicion of committing any other offence, which is not a relevant offence, can also be tested at the discretion of a senior police officer if he or she believes that misuse of a Class A drug caused or contributed to the offence. Section 20A(8) provides that the Class A drugs that will be tested for are cocaine and diamorphine (heroin). Section 20A(2) provides that the police cannot test a person for a relevant Class A drug if that person has already given a sample for testing after they have been brought to a police station. Section 20A(5) sets out that a further sample can be taken if the original is not suitable for analysis, was insufficient or was destroyed during the testing process.

Subs.(3)

Section 20A(3) sets out the conditions, which must be met before a person is tested for a relevant Class A drug. A sample must also be taken or provided within six hours of that person being brought to a police station. To allow for the policy to be rolled out to particular parts of Scotland and in stages, a sample can only be taken if the Scottish Ministers have made an order by statutory instrument which states that mandatory drugs tests can be carried out in the area in which the police station is located. Such an order will be subject to negative procedure of the Parliament.

Subs.(7)

Section 20A(7) makes it an offence for an arrestee to refuse to comply with a drug test under these powers if required to do so. The maximum penalties for committing this offence are set out in s.20B(6). A constable is required to warn a person of this fact under s.20(4). When a person has been arrested for an offence (other than a relevant offence), a constable must also inform that person that a senior police officer has authorised him or her to take a sample, or require that person to provide a sample. A person must also be told of the reasons why a senior police officer suspects that a Class A drug has been taken.

Assessment following positive test

Section 85 of the Police, Public Order and Criminal Justice (Scotland) Act 2006 provides that an individual who has tested positive for a relevant Class A drug in terms of s.20A of the 1995 Act will be required to attend a drugs assessment with a suitably qualified drugs assessor. A person will be required to remain at that assessment for its duration. Section 86 also sets down that the purpose of the drugs assessment is to establish whether or not the person is dependent on or has a propensity to misuse Class A drugs and whether or not they may benefit from assistance or treatment. There are supplementary provisions in ss.86 to 90 of the Police, Public Order and Criminal Justice (Scotland) Act 2006.

Section 20A: supplementary

20B.—(1) Section 20A of this Act does not prejudice the generality of section 18 of this Act.

(2) Each person carrying out a function under section 20A of this Act must have regard to any guidance issued by the Scottish Ministers—

(a) about the carrying out of the function; or

(b) about matters connected to the carrying out of the function.

(3) An order under section 20A(3)(c) shall be subject to annulment in pursuance of a resolution of the Scottish Parliament.

(4) An authorisation for the purposes of section 20A of this Act may be given orally or in writing but, if given orally, the person giving it shall confirm it in writing as soon as is reasonably practicable.

(5) If a sample is provided or taken under section 20A of this Act by virtue of an authorisation, the authorisation and the grounds for the suspicion are to be recorded in writing as soon as is reasonably practicable after the sample is provided or taken.

(6) A person guilty of an offence under section 20A of this Act shall be liable on summary conviction to the following penalties—

(a) a fine not exceeding level 4 on the standard scale;

(b) imprisonment for a period—

(i) where conviction is in the district court, not exceeding 60 days; or

(ii) where conviction is in the sheriff court, not exceeding 3 months; or

(c) both such fine and imprisonment.

(7) Subject to subsection (8) below, a sample provided or taken under section 20A of this Act shall be destroyed as soon as possible following its analysis for the purpose for which it was taken.

(8) Where an analysis of the sample reveals that a relevant Class A drug is present in the person's body, the sample may be retained so that it can be used, and supplied to others, for the purpose of any proceedings against the person for an offence under section 88 of the Police, Public Order and Criminal Justice (Scotland) Act 2006 (asp 10); but—

(a) the sample may not be used, or supplied, for any other purpose; and

(b) the sample shall be destroyed as soon as possible once it is no longer capable of being used for that purpose.

(9) Information derived from a sample provided by or taken from a person under section 20A of this Act may be used and disclosed only for the following purposes—

(a) for the purpose of proceedings against the person for an offence under section 88 of the Police, Public Order and Criminal Justice (Scotland) Act 2006 (asp 10);

(b) for the purpose of informing any decision about granting bail in any criminal proceedings to the person;

(c) for the purpose of informing any decision of a children's hearing arranged to consider the person's case;

(d) where the person is convicted of an offence, for the purpose of informing any decision about the appropriate sentence to be passed by a court and any decision about the person's supervision or release;

(e) for the purpose of ensuring that appropriate advice and treatment is made available to the person.

(10) Subject to subsection (11) below, the Scottish Ministers may by order made by statutory instrument modify section 20A(8) of this Act for either of the following purposes—

(a) for the purpose of adding an offence to or removing an offence from those for the time being listed in the definition of "relevant offence";

(b) for the purpose of adding a substance, preparation or product to or removing a substance, preparation or product from those for the time being listed in the definition of "relevant Class A drug".

(11) An order under subsection (10)(b) may add a substance, preparation or product only if it is a Class A drug (that expression having the same meaning as in the Misuse of Drugs Act 1971 (c.38)).

(12) An order under subsection (10) above shall not be made unless a draft of the statutory instrument containing it has been laid before and approved by resolution of the Scottish Parliament.

AMENDMENT

Section 20B inserted by the Police, Public Order and Criminal Justice (Scotland) Act 2006 (asp 10), s.84. Brought into force on January 1, 2007 by the Police, Public Order and Criminal Justice (Scotland) Act 2006 (Commencement No.2) Order 2006 (SSI 2006/607 (C.46)), art.3 and Sch. for the purpose of enabling an order under s.20A(3)(c) of the 1995 Act to be made.

DEFINITIONS

"appropriate grounds": s.20A(8).
"appropriate officer": s.20A(8).
"misuse": s.20A(8).
"relevant Class A drug": s.20A(8).
"relevant offence": s.20A(8).
"senior police officer": s.20A(8).

GENERAL NOTE

Section 20B supplements s.20A of the 1995 Act.ubsections (4) and (5) set out procedures which must be followed if a senior police officer decides that a person should be tested for a Class A drug. Subsection (7) imposes a requirement to destroy a sample, which has been taken under s.20A. Subsection (8) also sets down what the information gathered through a mandatory drugs test can be used for. Section 20B(9) provides that the Scottish Ministers can add to or vary the list of trigger offences and or relevant Class A drugs. Such an order will be made by statutory instrument and will be subject to affirmative procedure. There are supplementary provisions in ss.86 to 90 of the Police, Public Order and Criminal Justice (Scotland) Act 2006.

Schedule 1 offences

Schedule 1 offences: power of constable to take offender into custody

21.—(1) Without prejudice to any other powers of arrest, a constable may take into custody without warrant—

(a) any person who within his view commits any of the offences mentioned in Schedule 1 to this Act, if the constable does not know and cannot ascertain his name and address;

(b) any person who has committed, or whom he had reason to believe to have committed, any of the offences mentioned in that Schedule, if the constable does not know and cannot ascertain his name and address or has reasonable ground for believing that he will abscond.

(2) Where a person has been arrested under this section, the officer in charge of a police station may—

(a) liberate him upon a written undertaking, signed by him and certified by the said officer, in terms of which that person undertakes to appear at a specified court at a specified time; or

(b) liberate him without any such undertaking; or

(c) refuse to liberate him, and such refusal and the detention of that person until his case is tried in the usual form shall not subject the officer to any claim whatsoever.

(3) A person in breach of an undertaking given by him under subsection (2)(a) above without reasonable excuse shall be guilty of an offence and liable to the following penalties—

(a) a fine not exceeding level 3 on the standard scale; and

(b) imprisonment for a period—

    (i) where conviction is in the district court, not exceeding 60 days; or

    (ii) in any other case, not exceeding 3 months.

(4) The penalties provided for in subsection (3) above may be imposed in addition to any other penalty which it is competent for the court to impose, notwithstanding that the total of penalties imposed may exceed the maximum penalty which it is competent to impose in respect of the original offence.

(5) In any proceedings relating to an offence under this section, a writing, purporting to be such an undertaking as is mentioned in subsection (2)(a) above and bearing to be signed and certified, shall be sufficient evidence of the terms of the undertaking given by the arrested person.

DEFINITION

"constable": s.307(1) and s.51(1) of the Police (Scotland) Act 1967.

GENERAL NOTE

This section repeats the provisions contained in ss.18(1) and 294(1) of the 1975 Act relating to offences against children under the age of 17 years. The relevant offences are found in Sch.1 to the 1995 Act which now reflects the consolidating amendments contained in the Criminal Law (Consolidation) (Scotland) Act 1995 (c.39).

Section 136(2) preserves the six month timebar provision in relation to statutory proceedings which are prosecuted summarily. Powers to liberate persons charged with a Sch.1 offence are vested in the officer in charge of the police station to which the accused has been brought. The powers, and penalties for failure to comply with the terms of any undertaking imposed, are identical to those contained in s.22 below, but note that liberation can be utilised for potentially more serious charges under s.21: liberation under s.22 is only competent if the charges preferred could be tried summarily.

Evidential Provisions

In proceedings for breach of the terms of a written undertaking made under s.21(2)(a) or the more commonplace provision under s.22(1)(a) below, the Act provides that a copy thereof certified and signed by the liberating officer, shall suffice as proof of the facts contained in it. In entering into such an undertaking an accused person is, in effect, placing himself in a special capacity. Once the court is satisfied as to the terms of the undertaking and that the accused failed to obtemper them, the onus of proof then falls upon an accused to make out reasonable grounds on the balance of probabilities for his failure to attend.

Penalties

Ordinarily, the statutory maximum penalties of imprisonment or fine are laid down in s.3 (sheriff solemn), s.5(2) (sheriff summary) and s.7(7) (district courts) and cannot be exceeded *in cumulo*. Exceptions to this generality are provided in ss.21(4) and 22(4) in relation to breach of written undertakings and s.27(5) in regard to breach of bail conditions. In either case the sentence imposed can be added to that imposed for the substantive matter, even if this results in a cumulative sentence or fine higher than that which the Court could normally impose. See *Kelso v Crowe*, 1992 S.C.C.R. 415—sentencing principles where contravention of bail conditions occur.

Police liberation

Liberation by police

22.—(1) Where a person has been arrested and charged with an offence which may be tried summarily, the officer in charge of a police station may—

(a) liberate him upon a written undertaking, signed by him and certified by the officer, in terms of which the person undertakes to appear at a specified court at a specified time; or

(b) liberate him without any such undertaking; or

(c) refuse to liberate him.

(2) A person in breach of an undertaking given by him under subsection (1) above without reasonable excuse shall be guilty of an offence and liable on summary conviction to the following penalties—

(a) a fine not exceeding level 3 on the standard scale; and

(b) imprisonment for a period—

    (i) where conviction is in the district court, not exceeding 60 days; or

    (ii) where conviction is in the sheriff court, not exceeding 3 months.

(3) The refusal of the officer in charge to liberate a person under subsection (1)(c) above and the detention of that person until his case is tried in the usual form shall not subject the officer to any claim whatsoever.

(4) The penalties provided for in subsection (2) above may be imposed in addition to any other penalty which it is competent for the court to impose, notwithstanding that the total of penalties imposed may exceed the maximum penalty which it is competent to impose in respect of the original offence.

(5) In any proceedings relating to an offence under this section, a writing, purporting to be such an undertaking as is mentioned in subsection (1)(a) above and bearing to be signed and certified, shall be sufficient evidence of the terms of the undertaking given by the arrested person.

GENERAL NOTE

This section permits the officer in charge of a police station, at his discretion, to liberate an accused person pending the submission of a report to the procurator fiscal, or to liberate him to appear at a named court on a specified future occasion, or to hold the person in custody for appearance at court on the next lawful day. These powers only apply when the charges preferred are capable of being prosecuted summarily, but the fact that a written undertaking has been entered into in no way commits the Crown to proceed summarily. Since a suspect has to consent to abide by the specified terms of an undertaking, it is equally open to him to refuse them and in that event it would be incompetent to proceed in terms of subs.(1)(a). The accused would either have to be detained in custody or be liberated for report.

Evidential Provisions

These are identical to those contained in s.21. See the notes on "Evidential Provisions" in that section.

Penalties (subs.(4))

The implications of this provision mirror those in s.21. Refer to the notes on "Penalties" in that section.

PART III

BAIL

Consideration of bail on first appearance

22A.—(1) On the first occasion on which—

(a) a person accused on petition is brought before the sheriff prior to committal until liberated in due course of law; or

(b) a person charged on complaint with an offence is brought before a judge having jurisdiction to try the offence,

the sheriff or, as the case may be, the judge shall, after giving that person and the prosecutor an opportunity to be heard and within the period specified in subsection (2) below, either admit or refuse to admit that person to bail.

(2) That period is the period of 24 hours beginning with the time when the person accused or charged is brought before the sheriff or judge.

(3) If, by the end of that period, the sheriff or judge has not admitted or refused to admit the person accused or charged to bail, then that person shall be forthwith liberated.

(4) This section applies whether or not the person accused or charged is in custody when that person is brought before the sheriff or judge.

AMENDMENT

Section 22A inserted by the Bail, Judicial Appointments etc. (Scotland) Act 2000 (asp 9), s.1.

DEFINITIONS

"complaint": s.307(1)
"offence": s.307(1)
"prosecutor": s.307(1)
"bail": s.307(1)

GENERAL NOTE

The contents of the Bail, Judicial Appointments etc. (Scotland) Act 2000 (asp 9) represent a legislative response to problems which arose following the advent of the European Convention on Human Rights into Scots law in the Scotland Act 1998 (c.46).

On the first appearance of a person from custody, whether on complaint or on petition, the court is automatically obliged to consider his admission to bail. Thus it would not be necessary at that stage in proceedings to make a formal application on behalf of the accused until the court had first deliberated on the question. Subsection (2) permits the court to continue its consideration of bail for up to 24 hours but subs.(3) provides that if the question is not settled within that time then the accused must be liberated. That does not, of course, bar a prosecution but there would be no bail domicile for the accused. Subsection (4) applies these provisions whether or not the accused is in custody in respect of a separate matter.

Bail applications

23.—(1) Any person accused on petition of a crime shall be entitled immediately, on any (other than the first) occasion on which he is brought before the sheriff prior to his committal until liberated in due course of law, to apply to the sheriff for bail, and the prosecutor shall be entitled to be heard against any such application.

(2) The sheriff shall be entitled in his discretion to refuse such application before the person accused is committed until liberated in due course of law.

(3) Where an accused is admitted to bail without being committed until liberated in due course of law, it shall not be necessary so to commit him, and it shall be lawful to serve him with an indictment or complaint without his having been previously so committed.

(4) Where bail is refused before committal until liberation in due course of law on an application under subsection (1) above, the application for bail may be renewed after such committal.

(5) Any sheriff having jurisdiction to try the offence or to commit the accused until liberated in due course of law may, at his discretion, on the application of any person who has been committed until liberation in due course of law for any crime or offence, and having given the prosecutor an opportunity to be heard, admit or refuse to admit the person to bail.

(6) Any person charged on complaint with an offence shall, on any (other than

the first) occasion on which he is brought before a judge having jurisdiction to try the offence, be entitled to apply to the judge for bail and the prosecutor shall be entitled to be heard against any such application.

(7) An application under subsection (5) or (6) above shall be disposed of within 24 hours after its presentation to the judge, failing which the accused shall be forthwith liberated.

(8) This section applies whether or not the accused is in custody at the time he appears for disposal of his application.

AMENDMENT

Subss.(1) and (5) as amended by the Bail, Judicial Appointments etc. (Scotland) Act (asp 9), s.12 and Sch., para. 7(1).

Subs.(6) substituted by the Bail, Judicial Appointments etc. (Scotland) Act (asp 9), s.12 and Sch., para.7(1)(c).

DEFINITIONS

"bail": s.307(1).
"complaint": s.307(1).
"judge": s.307(1).
"offence": s.307(1).
"prosecutor": s.307(1).

GENERAL NOTE

Subs. (1)

"On petition": This makes it clear that s.23(1) to (5) applies only to those accused at the outset of solemn procedure.

"A crime which is by law bailable": By s.24(1) all crimes are bailable except murder, treason and any others for which the Lord Advocate or the High Court admit the accused to bail. In *Boyle, Petr,* 1993 S.C.C.R. 251 an accused on a murder charge was admitted to bail.

"On any occasion on which he is brought before the sheriff": This makes it certain that the accused must be present at the time of the application to the sheriff.

"Prior to his committal until liberated in due course of law": An application for bail cannot be made after such committal on this wording.

"The prosecutor shall be entitled to be heard": The Crown attitude is crucial but not conclusive, having regard to s.23(2). For examples, see *H.M. Advocate v Saunders* (1913) 7 Adam 76 and *Mackintosh v McGlinchey,* 1921 J.C. 75.

Subs. (2)

"His discretion": The decision is one for the sheriff although the Crown attitude is crucial. There is no presumption in favour of the Crown on this question. The decision is based on attitude and is not amenable to proof. *Burn, Petr,* 2000 S.L.T. 538 requires the Crown to furnish some information to justify refusal of bail even at the first calling of the petition when moving for committal for further examination. Further, the court indicated that as soon as practicable on the completion of the Crown's further enquiries an accused ought to be brought back before the sheriff.

There are important aspects to which, broadly, the court will have regard when exercising this discretion: (1) the more serious the crime the less willing the court is to allow bail, unless the Crown offers no objection: *Rennie v Dickson* (1907) 5 Adam 372; (2) the previous record of the accused is an important factor: *MacLeod v Wright,* 1969 J.C. 12; (3) the attitude of the Crown; (4) no fixed abode weighs heavily but is not in itself sufficient to determine the question: *H.M. Advocate v Docherty,* 1958 S.L.T. (Notes) 50; (5) breach of earlier bail, which tends to suggest a contempt for earlier judicial fairness; (6) evidence that the accused will intimidate or threaten witnesses if released.

Subs. (3)

Ordinarily, committal for further examination is followed thereafter by committal until liberated in due course of law. This provision makes it clear that the latter need not necessarily follow the former.

Subs. (4)

A single application for bail is not provided for by this section: an application may be made at the stage of committal for further examination and may be renewed later when the accused next appears. Such an appearance may be for committal until liberated in due course of law or it may be for the purpose of such an application by arrangement.

Subs. (5)

"Jurisdiction": This may be territorial or in terms of statutory powers: see ss.4 and 5.

In *Love, Petr*, 1998 S.L.T. 461, L failed to appear for trial while on bail following committal until liberated in due course of law, and was refused bail on arrest. His application for bail had been made by petition to the nobile officium and L appealed the refusal to the High Court. His appeal by that route was held to be incompetent, the Court noting that s.32(1) was the appropriate avenue for such appeals.

Subs. (6)

"On complaint": This extends shrieval discretion referred to in earlier subsections to "any judge having jurisdiction for the offence". For a definition of "judge", see s.308(1).

Subs. (8)

This subsection rehearses the provision in s.28(3) of the 1975 Act.

The extensive modifications to s.65 of the Act which introduce an entitlement to bail (rather than being liberated) if an accused person has not been indicted within 80 days, and grant bail if a person held in custody, on petition, is not brought before a preliminary hearing within 110 days, or to trial within 140 days of full committal (rather than being declared forever free), are reflected in the amendment to this section.

Note should also be taken of the addition as a condition of bail (where bail would otherwise have been refused) of remote, *i.e.* electronic, monitoring in pilot schemes in Glasgow, Kilmarnock and Stirling sheriff courts with effect from April 18, 2005. See the Remote Monitoring Requirements (Prescribed Courts) (Scotland) Regulations 2005. See generally s.24AZ below.

Bail and liberation where person already in custody

23A.—(1) A person may be admitted to bail under section 22A, 23 or 65(8C) of this Act although in custody—

(a) having been refused bail in respect of another crime or offence; or

(b) serving a sentence of imprisonment.

(2) A decision to admit a person to bail by virtue of subsection (1) above does not liberate the person from the custody mentioned in that subsection.

(3) The liberation under section 22A(3) or 23(7) of this Act of a person who may be admitted to bail by virtue of subsection (1) above does not liberate that person from the custody mentioned in that subsection.

(4) In subsection (1) above, "another crime or offence" means a crime or offence other than that giving rise to the consideration of bail under section 22A, 23 or 65(8C) of this Act

AMENDMENT

Section 23A inserted by the Bail, Judicial Appointments etc. (Scotland) Act 2000 (asp 9), s.2.

Subss.(1) and (4) as amended by the Criminal Procedure (Amendment) (Scotland) Act 2004 (asp 5), s.25 and Sch.1, para.4. Brought into force on February 1, 2005 by the Criminal Procedure (Amendment) (Scotland) Act 2004 (Commencement, Transitional Provisions and Savings) Order 2004 (SSI 2004/405 (C.28)), art.2.

DEFINITIONS

"bail": s.307(1).
"crime": s.307(1).
"offence": s.307(1).
"imprisonment": s.307(1).

GENERAL NOTE

The intention of this reform to long-standing legislation governing bail applications is to enable those serving terms of imprisonment, or on remand for other matters, to make formal application for bail. Hitherto the practice has been that bail applications could only be made when the petitioner was in an immediate position to be liberated on bail, otherwise the application had to be dismissed as incompetent. In the future the court will be obliged to consider a bail application even if the grant of bail cannot be given immediate effect.

In *Monterroso v H.M. Advocate*, 2000 S.C.C.R. 974, the Appeal Court applied a purposive interpretation to subs.(1) and rejected the Crown's efforts to read the provision literally. M had been arrested on arrival in the United Kingdom and was remanded in custody on petition charges following a successful Crown bail appeal. Simultaneously the Home Secretary had refused M entry to the country as a result of these criminal allegations, a decision which led to a concurrent remand under the Immigration Act 1971 (c.7). M sought judicial review of this remand, and bail in relation to the criminal charges. The Crown contended that subs.(1) did not competently apply to M's peculiar circumstances. The Appeal Court held it competent to apply for bail but refused bail on the merits. (The civil proceedings are reported as *Monterroso v Secretary of the Home Department*, 2000 G.W.D. 33–1295).

Bail and bail conditions

24.—(1) All crimes and offences are bailable.

(2) Nothing in this Act shall affect the right of the Lord Advocate or the High Court to admit to bail any person charged with any crime or offence.

(3) It shall not be lawful to grant bail or release for a pledge or deposit of money, and—

(a) release on bail may be granted only on conditions which subject to subsection (6) below, shall not include a pledge or deposit of money;

(b) liberation may be granted by the police under section 21, 22 or 43 of this Act.

(4) In granting bail the court or, as the case may be, the Lord Advocate shall impose on the accused—

(a) the standard conditions; and

(b) such further conditions as the court or, as the case may be, the Lord Advocate considers necessary to secure—

(i) that the standard conditions are observed; and

(ii) that the accused makes himself available for the purpose of participating in an identification parade or of enabling any print, impression or sample to be taken from him.

(5) The standard conditions referred to in subsection (4) above are conditions that the accused—

(a) appears at the appointed time at every diet relating to the offence with which he is charged of which he is given due notice or at which he is required by this Act to appear;

(b) does not commit an offence while on bail;

(c) does not interfere with witnesses or otherwise obstruct the course of justice whether in relation to himself or any other person;

(d) makes himself available for the purpose of enabling enquiries or a report to be made to assist the court in dealing with him for the offence with which he is charged; and.

(e) where the (or an) offence in respect of which he is admitted to bail is one to which section 288C of this Act applies, does not seek to obtain, otherwise than by way of a solicitor, any precognition of or statement by the complainer in relation to the subject matter of the offence.

(6) The court or, as the case may be, the Lord Advocate may impose as one of the conditions of release on bail a requirement that the accused or a cautioner on his behalf deposits a sum of money in court, but only where the court or, as the

case may be, the Lord Advocate is satisfied that the imposition of such condition is appropriate to the special circumstances of the case.

(6A) Subsection (6) above does not apply in relation to an accused admitted to bail under section 65(8C) of this Act.

(7) In any enactment, including this Act and any enactment passed after this Act—

(a) any reference to bail shall be construed as a reference to release on conditions in accordance with this Act or to conditions imposed on bail, as the context requires;

(b) any reference to an amount of bail fixed shall be construed as a reference to conditions, including a sum required to be deposited under subsection (6) above;

(c) any reference to finding bail or finding sufficient bail shall be construed as a reference to acceptance of conditions imposed or the finding of a sum required to be deposited under subsection (6) above.

(7A) In subsection (5)(e) above, "complainer" has the same meaning as in section 274 of this Act.

(8) In this section and sections 25 and 27 to 29 of this Act, references to an accused and to appearance at a diet shall include references respectively to an appellant and to appearance at the court on the day fixed for the hearing of an appeal.

AMENDMENT

Subs.(1) as amended by the Bail, Judicial Appointments etc. (Scotland) Act 2000 (asp 9), s.3(1).

Subs.(5) as amended, and subs.(7A) inserted, by the Sexual Offences (Procedure and Evidence) (Scotland) Act 2002 (asp 9), s.5. Brought into force by the Sexual Offences (Procedure and Evidence) (Scotland) Act 2002 (Commencement and Transitional Provisions) Order 2002 (SSI 2002/443 (C.24)), art.4 (effective from November 1, 2002).

Subs.(5)(a) as amended, and subs.(6A) inserted, by the Criminal Procedure (Amendment) (Scotland) Act 2004 (asp 5), s.25 and Sch.1, para.5. Brought into force on February 1, 2005 by the Criminal Procedure (Amendment) (Scotland) Act 2004 (Commencement, Transitional Provisions and Savings) Order 2004 (SSI 2004/405 (C.28)), art.2.

DEFINITIONS

"bail": s.307(1).
"crime": s.307(1).
"diet": s.307(1).
"High Court": s.307(1).
"offences": s.307(1).
"standard conditions, the": s.24(5).

GENERAL NOTE

Until the advent of the Bail, Judicial Appointments etc. (Scotland) Act 2000 (asp 9), bail in murder cases could only be obtained either at the behest of the Lord Advocate (whose refusal to admit to bail could not be challenged) or by petition to the *nobile officium*; otherwise murder was a non-bailable offence (see, for example, *HM Advocate v Renwicks*, 1998 S.C.C.R. 417; 1999 S.L.T. 407). All crimes are now bailable, but it will be noted that the factors which would previously have justified opposition to bail—the risk of absconding, interference with witnesses, danger to public safety, the risk of further offending and the nature or gravity of the offence—remain valid grounds (see *Monterroso v HM Advocate*, 2000 S.C.C.R. 974). The right of the Lord Advocate to admit persons to bail even after it has been refused, or not sought, at earlier points in proceedings, is preserved.

Where an application for bail is unopposed by the Crown, the judge has no power to refuse bail *ex proprio motu*; see *G v Speirs*, 1988 S.C.C.R. 517, *Maxwell v McGlennan*, 1989 S.L.T. 282 and *MAR v Dyer*, 2005 S.C.C.R. 818.

Ordinarily, a bail order granted by the court will echo the terms of subs.(5) but additional conditions can be imposed, including, where circumstances warrant, the imposition of money bail as caution albeit this is unusual (see for example, *Adam v Kirichenko*, 1995 G.W.D. 26–1373). Note, however, that money bail cannot be imposed as a bail condition where an accused, previously in custody, is granted bail pursuant to s.65(8C) below, i.e. where he has not been indicted for trial within 80 days or his custody preliminary diet or trial have not commenced within the 110 and 140 day limits. The standard bail conditions now require an accused to attend at any diet or hearing of which he has been given due notice. Attention is drawn to s.24A of the Act which allows the court to impose a remote monitoring restriction on an accused's movements as a further condition of bail.

European authorities were discussed in *Roque v HM Advocate* (Crown Office circular A2/2001) in which the accused, a Portuguese national charged on petition with contravening s.1 of the Road Traffic Act 1988 and refused bail, contended that the risk of absconding was not itself sufficient reason for refusing bail. The court accepted that any distinction between the accused and a United Kingdom national for bail purposes had to have an objective and reasonable justification and would not, of course, be based simply on grounds of nationality but on the interaction of a number of related factors. In the event the bail conditions imposed were stringent requiring deposit of a substantial money sum, residence in Scotland, surrender of passport and regular attendance at a police office. The issues which may arise when an accused's passport is to be surrendered as a special bail condition are discussed at A4–67 below.

Note that additional conditions apply when an accused has been charged on a complaint or (more likely) a petition, with a sexual offence listed in s.288C of the Act. In that event the accused accepts that he must not seek to precognosce the complainer in respect of that offence. It is submitted that in circumstances where the fiscal's subsequent enquiries disclose that the offence charged involves a substantial sexual element (s.288C(4)), or where listed sexual offences are revealed, there are two options; either issue a superseding complaint or petition or seek a review of the earlier bail conditions as permitted by s.31 of the Act.

s.24(4)(b)

There seems to be no limit (other than those of reason and common sense) to the "further conditions" that may be imposed in terms of s.24(4)(b) of the 1995 Act: for an example see *Stott v Hussain*, 2004 G.W.D. 10–227.

s.24(6)

The deposit of a sum of money in court as a condition of bail is now probably rare. However, such a deposit is competent and may occur: see *Urquhart, Petitioner*, 2003 G.W.D. 26–735 (French citizen required to lodge money in euros).

Bail conditions: remote monitoring of restrictions on movements

24A.—(1) Where a court has refused to admit a person to bail, the court shall, on the application of that person—

(a) consider whether the imposition of a remote monitoring requirement would enable it to admit the person to bail subject to a movement restriction condition; and

(b) if so—

(i) admit the person to bail subject to such a condition (as well as such other conditions required to be imposed under section 24(4) of this Act); and

(ii) impose, as a further condition of bail, a remote monitoring requirement.

(2) Where a court—

(a) grants bail to any person charged with or convicted of murder or rape; and

(b) in doing so, imposes a movement restriction condition,

the court may, at its own hand, impose, as a further condition of bail, a remote monitoring requirement.

(3) Where a court, in granting bail to a person convicted of murder or rape—

(a) imposes a movement restriction condition; but

(b) does not impose a remote monitoring requirement,

the court shall state reasons for not imposing such a requirement.

(4) In deciding whether to grant bail to a person referred to in paragraph (a) of subsection (2) above, the court shall disregard the availability of the power conferred by that subsection.

(5) Where—

(a) a remote monitoring requirement has been imposed under subsection (2) above on a person charged with murder or rape; and

(b) subsequently, the charge against the person is reduced,

the court shall, on the application of the person, revoke the remote monitoring requirement unless it considers that there are exceptional circumstances justifying the continued imposition of the requirement.

(6) An application under subsection (5) above shall be intimated immediately and in writing to the Crown Agent and the court shall, before determining it, give the prosecutor an opportunity to be heard.

(7) Before considering whether to impose a remote monitoring requirement under subsection (1) or (2) above, the court shall give the accused and the prosecutor an opportunity to be heard.

(8) Before imposing a remote monitoring requirement under subsection (1) or (2) above, the court shall explain to the accused in ordinary language—

(a) the effect—

(i) of the requirement; and

(ii) of any requirement to be imposed under section 24D(3) of this Act; and

(b) the consequences which may follow any failure by the accused to comply with—

(i) the movement restriction condition in respect of which the remote monitoring requirement is to be imposed; and

(ii) any such requirement as is referred to in paragraph (a)(ii) above.

(9) The court shall not impose a remote monitoring requirement under subsection (1) or (2) above unless the accused, after the court has explained to him the matters referred to in paragraphs (a) and (b) of subsection (8) above, has confirmed that he understands those matters.

(10) Subsection (11) below applies where the court is proposing—

(a) to impose under subsection (1) or (2) above a remote monitoring requirement where the movement restriction condition in relation to which the requirement is proposed to be imposed will require the accused to remain in a specified place or places; or

(b) to vary the movement restriction condition in relation to which the requirement is imposed so as to specify a different place or different places.

(11) Before imposing the requirement or, as the case may be, varying the condition, the court shall—

(a) obtain and consider a report by an officer of a local authority about—

(i) the place or places proposed to be specified; and

(ii) the attitude of persons likely to be affected by the requirement that the accused remain there; and

(b) if it considers it necessary, hear the officer who prepared the report.

(12) The court may, for the purposes of subsection (11) above, adjourn the proceedings.

(13) Where a court—

(a) imposes a remote monitoring requirement under subsection (1) or (2) above;

(b) revokes such a requirement; or

(c) varies or revokes a movement restriction condition in respect of which such a requirement has been imposed,

the clerk of the court shall cause a copy of the order containing the requirement, revocation or, as the case may be, variation to be sent immediately to the monitor.

(14) Where, in the course of monitoring in pursuance of a remote monitoring requirement imposed under subsection (1) or (2) above a person's compliance with a condition imposed on bail restricting the person's movements, the monitor becomes aware that the person has breached the condition, the monitor shall immediately notify a constable of the breach.

(15) Where a constable arrests a person under section 28(1) of this Act on the ground that the constable suspects the person of having breached a movement restriction condition in respect of which a remote monitoring requirement has been imposed the constable shall, as soon as possible, notify the monitor of the arrest.

(16) Nothing in subsection (1) above affects any right which a person has to appeal against a decision refusing to admit the person to bail.

(17) However, where in a case in which an application has been made under subsection (1) above following a decision of a court to refuse to admit the applicant to bail—

(a) an appeal is taken against the decision; and

(b) the applicant is refused bail under subsection (1) above,

any appeal against the refusal of bail under that subsection shall be conjoined with the appeal referred to in paragraph (a) above.

(18) In this section and sections 24B to 24E of this Act—

(a) "a movement restriction condition" means, in relation to a person admitted to bail, a condition of bail imposed under section 24(4)(b) of this Act restricting the person's movements, including such a condition requiring the person to be, or not to be, in any place or description of place for, or during, any period or periods or at any time;

(b) "a remote monitoring requirement" means, in relation to a movement restriction condition, a requirement that compliance with the condition be remotely monitored; and

(c) references to the "accused" are references to any person in relation to whom a remote monitoring requirement is imposed or to be imposed under subsection (1) or (2) above.

(19) In this section, "monitor" means, in relation to an order under this section, any person who is, or is to be, responsible for the remote monitoring of the compliance of the person in respect of whom the order is made with the condition imposed in the order restricting the person's movements.

AMENDMENT

Section 24A inserted by the Criminal Procedure (Amendment) (Scotland) Act 2004 (asp 5), s.17. Brought into force on October 4, 2004 by the Criminal Procedure (Amendment) (Scotland) Act 2004 (Commencement, Transitional Provisions and Savings) Order 2004 (SSI 2004/405 (C.28)), art.2(1).

DEFINITIONS

"accused": s.24A(18)(c).
"a movement restriction condition": s.24A(18)(a).
"a remote monitoring requirement": s.24A(18)(b).
"bail": s.307(1).
"monitor": s.24A(19).
"prosecutor": s.307(1).

This section enables the court to consider granting an accused person, whose application for bail has previously been refused, bail subject to the imposition of a movement restriction condition (usually equivalent to a curfew but statutorily defined in subs.(18)) and a remote monitoring requirement. Such a grant can occur at the pre-trial stage and extends, as subs.(2) makes clear, to permit those charged with, or convicted of, murder or rape to be admitted to bail; the expectation is that in these grave cases the court should then impose both a movement restriction condition and a monitoring requirement and will be obliged to state explicitly any reasons for not imposing the two together (subs.(3)).

When the court considers imposing the additional condition of a remote monitoring requirement to a bail order (but not apparently a movement restriction condition) the accused and the Crown are entitled to be heard, but note that this right would not appear to extend to co-accused (subss.(5) and (18)(c)). When making a monitoring requirement the court has to follow the strictures set out in subs.(11) by obtaining a report from the local authority, explain to the accused the nature of the requirement, the consequences of any interference with the electronic tagging equipment and the practical effect of the movement restrictions and has to obtain the accused's consent to these measures.

Note, however, the qualification in subs.(4) applying to those charged with murder or rape; in considering whether to admit the accused to bail, the court must consider the application solely upon its merits and must not be influenced by the availability (or presumably the absence) of remote monitoring or movement restrictions.

Subss.(13) and (14) set out the duties of a monitor (as defined in subs.(19)) and particularly his obligation to report any suspected breach of a movement restriction to the police. (Section 24E below makes evidential provisions for proving such a breach). The police are vested with a power of arrest where the accused fails to comply with his movement restriction, it being treated as a breach of a condition of bail, and are obliged to notify the appointed monitor of the arrest.

The accused's right of appeal against refusal of bail is preserved but where issue is taken with refusal to add a remote monitoring requirement, or a restriction on movement, all issues are to be considered at the same hearing.

With effect from April 18, 2005 a pilot scheme to add electronic monitoring or tagging as an additional bail condition was initiated in Glasgow, Kilmarnock and Stirling sheriff courts. See the note to s.23 above.

Regulations as to power to impose remote monitoring requirements under section 24A

24B.—(1) The Scottish Ministers may by regulations prescribe—

(a) which courts, or description or descriptions of courts, may impose remote monitoring requirements under section 24A(1) or (2) of this Act;

(b) what method or methods of monitoring compliance with a movement restriction condition may be specified in any such requirement by any such court; and

(c) the description or descriptions of persons in respect of whom such requirements may be imposed.

(2) Regulations under subsection (1) above may make different provision in relation to the matters mentioned in paragraphs (b) and (c) of that subsection in relation to different courts or descriptions of courts.

(3) Without prejudice to the generality of subsection (1) above, in relation to district courts, regulations under that subsection may make provision as respects such courts by reference to whether the court is constituted by a stipendiary magistrate or by one or more justices.

(4) Regulations under subsection (1) above may make such transitional and consequential provisions, including provision in relation to the continuing effect of any remote monitoring requirements imposed under section 24A(1) or (2) in force when new regulations are made, as the Scottish Ministers consider appropriate.

(5) Regulations under subsection (1) above shall be made by statutory instru-

ment and a statutory instrument containing any such regulations (other than the first such regulations) shall be subject to annulment in pursuance of a resolution of the Scottish Parliament.

(6) The first regulations under subsection (1) above shall not be made unless a draft of the statutory instrument containing the regulations has been laid before, and approved by resolution of, the Parliament.

AMENDMENT

Section 24B inserted by the Criminal Procedure (Amendment) (Scotland) Act 2004 (asp 5), s.17. Brought into force on October 4, 2004 by the Criminal Procedure (Amendment) (Scotland) Act 2004 (Commencement, Transitional Provisions and Savings) Order 2004 (SSI 2004/405 (C.28)), art.2(1).

DEFINITIONS

"accused": s.24A(18)(c).
"a movement restriction condition": s.24A(18)(a).
"a remote monitoring requirement": s.24A(18)(b).
"bail": s.307(1).
"monitor": s.24A(19).
"prosecutor": s.307(1).

GENERAL NOTE

The Scottish Ministers, by statutory instrument, can nominate the courts or categories of courts which will be able to impose remote monitoring requirements upon accused persons as a condition of bail, the form of monitoring and the categories of accused to be considered eligible for remote monitoring.

Monitoring of compliance in pursuance of requirements imposed under section 24A

24C.—(1) Where the Scottish Ministers, in regulations under section 24B(1) of this Act, empower a court or a description of court to impose remote monitoring requirements under section 24A(1) or (2) of this Act they shall notify the court or, as the case may be, each court of that description of the person or description of persons who may be designated by that court for the purpose of monitoring the compliance with any movement restriction condition of the person in respect of whom the requirement is imposed.

(2) A court which imposes a remote monitoring requirement under section 24A(1) or (2) of this Act shall include provisions in the requirement for making a person notified by the Scottish Ministers under subsection (1) above or a description of persons so notified responsible for monitoring the compliance of the person in respect of whom it is imposed with the movement restriction condition in respect of which it is imposed.

(3) Where the Scottish Ministers change the person or description of persons notified by them under subsection (1) above, any court which has imposed a remote monitoring requirement under 24A(1) or (2) of this Act shall, if necessary, vary the requirement accordingly and shall notify the variation to the person in respect of whom the order was made.

AMENDMENT

Section 24C inserted by the Criminal Procedure (Amendment) (Scotland) Act 2004 (asp 5), s.17. Brought into force on October 4, 2004 by the Criminal Procedure (Amendment) (Scotland) Act 2004 (Commencement, Transitional Provisions and Savings) Order 2004 (SSI 2004/405 (C.28)), art.2(1).

DEFINITIONS

"a movement restriction condition": s.24A(18)(a).

"a remote monitoring requirement": s.24A(18)(b).
"monitor": s.24A(19).

GENERAL NOTE

Following upon s.24B, this section entitles the Scottish Ministers (and not the court itself or relevant local authority) to nominate the agent who will provide monitoring services, and subs.(3) further obliges the court to alter the identity of the monitor as directed by the Scottish Ministers and intimate such change to an accused then subject of remote monitoring.

Subs.(2) is a necessary administrative measure, which requires the court involved to notify the monitoring agent of the particulars of each accused in respect of whom a monitoring order has been made.

Remote monitoring

24D.—(1) The Scottish Ministers may make such arrangements, including contractual arrangements, as they consider appropriate with such persons, whether legal or natural, as they think fit for the remote monitoring, in pursuance of remote monitoring requirements imposed under section 24A(1) or (2), of the compliance of persons in respect of whom such requirements are imposed with the movement restriction conditions in respect of which they are imposed.

(2) Different arrangements may be made under subsection (1) above in relation to different areas or different forms of remote monitoring.

(3) A court imposing a remote monitoring requirement under section 24A(1) or (2) of this Act shall include in the requirement, as a further condition of bail, a requirement that the person in respect of whom it is imposed—

(a) shall, either continuously or for such periods as may be specified, wear or carry a device for the purpose of enabling the remote monitoring of his compliance with the movement restriction condition in respect of which it is imposed to be carried out; and

(b) shall not tamper with or intentionally damage the device or knowingly allow it to be tampered with or intentionally damaged.

(4) The Scottish Ministers shall by regulations specify devices which may be used for the purpose of remotely monitoring the compliance of persons in respect of whom remote monitoring requirements have been imposed under section 24A(1) or (2) of this Act with the movement restriction conditions in respect of which they are imposed.

(5) Regulations under subsection (4) above shall be made by statutory instrument and a statutory instrument containing such regulations shall be subject to annulment in pursuance of a resolution of the Scottish Parliament.

AMENDMENT

Section 24D inserted by the Criminal Procedure (Amendment) (Scotland) Act 2004 (asp 5), s.17. Brought into force on October 4, 2004 by the Criminal Procedure (Amendment) (Scotland) Act 2004 (Commencement, Transitional Provisions and Savings) Order 2004 (SSI 2004/405 (C.28)), art.2(1).

DEFINITIONS

"a movement restriction condition": s.24A(18)(a).
"a remote monitoring requirement": s.24A(18)(b).
"bail": s.307(1).
"monitor": s.24A(19).

GENERAL NOTE

This section enables the Scottish Ministers to make contractual arrangements to obtain remote monitoring services as part of the restrictions on movement scheme. Subs.(4) empowers the Ministers to make regulations specifying the technology to be used for electronic monitoring.

Curiously, given the general thrust of the section, subs.(3) sets out the additional bail condition to be added to the standard conditions upon an accused when a remote monitoring condition is imposed so reference needs to be made to s.27(1)(b) for bail offences.

Documentary evidence in proceedings for breach of bail conditions being remotely monitored

24E.—(1) This section applies in proceedings against a person (referred to in this section as "the accused") for an offence under subsection (1)(b) of section 27 of this Act (failure to comply with a condition imposed on bail) where the condition referred to in that subsection is—

> (a) a movement restriction condition in respect of which a remote monitoring requirement has been imposed under section 24A(1) or (2); or

> (b) a requirement imposed under section 24D(3)(b) of this Act.

(2) Evidence of—

(a) in the case referred to in subsection (1)(a) above, the presence or absence of the accused at a particular place at a particular time; or

(b) in the case referred to in subsection (1)(b) above, any tampering with or damage to a device worn or carried by the accused for the purpose of remotely monitoring his whereabouts,

may, subject to subsections (5) and (6) below, be given by the production of the document or documents referred to in subsection (3) below.

(3) That document or those documents is or are a document or documents bearing to be—

> (a) a statement automatically produced by a device specified in regulations made under section 24D(4) of this Act, by which the accused's whereabouts were remotely monitored; and

> (b) a certificate signed by a person nominated for the purpose of this paragraph by the Scottish Ministers that the statement relates to—

>> (i) in the case referred to in subsection (1)(a) above, the whereabouts of the accused at the dates and times shown in the statement; or

>> (ii) in the case referred to in subsection (1)(b) above, any tampering with or damage to the device.

(4) The statement and certificate mentioned in subsection (3) above shall, when produced in the proceedings, be sufficient evidence of the facts set out in them.

(5) Neither the statement nor the certificate mentioned in subsection (3) above shall be admissible in evidence unless a copy of both has been served on the accused prior to the trial.

(6) Without prejudice to subsection (5) above, where it appears to the court that the accused has had insufficient notice of the statement or certificate, it may adjourn the trial or make an order which it thinks appropriate in the circumstances.

AMENDMENT

Section 24E inserted by the Criminal Procedure (Amendment) (Scotland) Act 2004 (asp 5), s.17. Brought into force on October 4, 2004 by the Criminal Procedure (Amendment) (Scotland) Act 2004 (Commencement, Transitional Provisions and Savings) Order 2004 (SSI 2004/405 (C.28)), art.2(1).

DEFINITIONS

"accused": s.24A(18)(c).
"a movement restriction condition": s.24A(18)(a).
"a remote monitoring requirement": s.24A(18)(b).

"bail": s.307(1).
"monitor": s.24A(19).

GENERAL NOTE

This section makes evidential provisions to allow certified documents to be used to prove non-compliance by an accused with the conditions of a remote monitoring requirement. Following a pattern familiar in the Act, the contents of such a certified statement shall be sufficient evidence (but note, not conclusive) only if a copy has been served upon the accused prior to trial. No period of prior notice is required (compare, for example, the 14 day period in advance of trial provided for service of routine evidence in s.280 of the Act) but subs.(6) gives the court a discretion to adjourn a trial or make any order felt appropriate in the circumstances (*quaere* require the leading of parole evidence) if it is felt that the accused has had insufficient notice of the certified evidence.

Bail: extradition proceedings

24F.—(1) In the application of the provisions of this Part by virtue of section 9(2) or 77(2) of the Extradition Act 2003 (judge's powers at extradition hearing), those provisions apply with the modifications that—

(a) references to the prosecutor are to be read as references to a person acting on behalf of the territory to which extradition is sought;

(b) the right of the Lord Advocate mentioned in section 24(2) of this Act applies to a person subject to extradition proceedings as it applies to a person charged with any crime or offence;

(c) the following do not apply—

(i) paragraph (b) of section 24(3); and

(ii) subsection (3) of section 30; and

(d) sections 28(1) and 33 apply to a person subject to extradition proceedings as they apply to an accused.

(2) Section 32 of this Act applies in relation to a refusal of bail, the amount of bail or a decision to allow bail or ordain appearance in proceedings under this Part as the Part applies by virtue of the sections of that Act of 2003 mentioned in subsection (1) above.

(3) The Scottish Ministers may, by order, for the purposes of section 9(2) or 77(2) of the Extradition Act 2003 make such amendments to this Part as they consider necessary or expedient.

(4) The order making power in subsection (3) above shall be exercisable by statutory instrument subject to annulment in pursuance of a resolution of the Scottish Parliament.

AMENDMENT

Section 24F inserted as s.24A by the Extradition Act 2003 (c.41), s.199. Brought into force on January 1, 2004 by the Extradition Act 2003 (Commencement and Savings) Order 2003 (SI 2003/3103 (C.122)), art.2.

Renumbered to s.24F by the Criminal Procedure (Amendment) (Scotland) Act 2004 (Incidental, Supplemental and Consequential Provisions) Order 2005 (SSI 2005/40), art.4(2), with effect from January 31, 2005.

DEFINITION

"prosecutor": s.307(1)

GENERAL NOTE

Imprisonment pending determination of extradition proceedings may now be avoided in appropriate cases by the grant of bail. The references to the prosecutor are to be red as references to a person acting on behalf of the territory to which extradition is sought: s.24A(1)(a). The Lord Advocate retains the right to admit any person subject to extradition proceedings to bail: s.24A(1)(b). A pledge or deposit of money is competent and bail reviews are not subject to any restriction of time: s.24A(1)(c).

Bail conditions: supplementary

25.—(1) The court shall specify in the order granting bail, a copy of which shall be given to the accused—

(a) the conditions imposed; and

(b) an address, within the United Kingdom (being the accused's normal place of residence or such other place as the court may, on cause shown, direct) which, subject to subsection (2) below, shall be his proper domicile of citation.

(2) The court may on application in writing by the accused while he is on bail alter the address specified in the order granting bail, and this new address shall, as from such date as the court may direct, become his proper domicile of citation; and the court shall notify the accused of its decision on any application under this subsection.

(2A) Where an application is made under subsection (2) above—

(a) the application shall be intimated by the accused immediately and in writing to the Crown Agent and for that purpose the application shall be taken to be intimated to the Crown Agent if intimation of it is sent to the procurator fiscal for the sheriff court district in which bail was granted; and

(b) the court shall, before determining the application, give the prosecutor an opportunity to be heard.

(3) In this section "proper domicile of citation" means the address at which the accused may be cited to appear at any diet relating to the offence with which he is charged or an offence charged in the same proceedings as that offence or to which any other intimation or document may be sent; and any citation at or the sending of an intimation or document to the proper domicile of citation shall be presumed to have been duly carried out.

(4) In this section, references to the court (other than in subsection (2A)) shall, in relation to a person who has been admitted to bail by the Lord Advocate, be read as if they were references to the Lord Advocate.

AMENDMENT

Subs.(4) inserted by the Criminal Procedure (Amendment) (Scotland) Act 2004 (asp 5), s.25 and Sch.1, para.6. Brought into force on October 4, 2004 by the Criminal Procedure (Amendment) (Scotland) Act 2004 (Commencement, Transitional Provisions and Savings) Order 2004 (SSI 2004/ 405 (C.28)).

Subs.(2A) inserted by the Criminal Procedure (Amendment) (Scotland) Act 2004 (asp 5), s.18(2). Brought into force on February 1, 2005 by the Criminal Procedure (Amendment) (Scotland) Act 2004 (Commencement, Transitional Provisions and Savings) Order 2004 (SSI 2004/405 (C.28)), art.2.

Subs.(2A)(a) as amended by the Criminal Procedure (Amendment) (Scotland) Act 2004 (Incidental, Supplemental and Consequential Provisions) Order 2005 (SSI 2005/40), art.3.

DEFINITIONS

"bail": s.307(1).
"order": s.307(1).
"proper domicile of citation": s.25(3).

GENERAL NOTE

The importance for the Crown of this provision lies in the terms of s.25(2) which allows service of the citation to appear at any diet on the accused at the "proper domicile of citation". The importance for the accused lies in his release but there is a balancing factor of providing such a domicile of citation: change is possible on application but failure to observe the requirements has serious consequences, or may have: *McMahon v MacPhail*, 1991 S.C.C.R. 470. Further, the evidence of the points in this section is routine evidence under s.280(1) of and Sch.9 to this Act and may thus be embodied in a certificate for service on the accused.

In *H.M. Advocate v W.* (High Court of Justiciary, February 2001, unreported) the Crown petitioned the *nobile officium* to rescind a purported order by the sheriff which had altered the accused's bail domicile from an address in Northern Ireland, to an address in Eire. The bail application had not been opposed by the procurator fiscal but the Crown stance, following subs.(1)(b), was that such a variation was *ultra vires* and thus incapable of consent. The Appeal Court struck out the alteration, and thus reinstated the earlier bail domicile.

A specific condition requiring the accused to surrender his passport should also stipulate that no application should be made either for the issue of a new passport or the issue of a replacement.

Subs.(2A) provides simplified means for an accused to intimate proposed changes to his bail domicile to the Crown Agent rather than to the relevant sheriff clerk or Clerk of Justiciary. It is now permissible to intimate such changes to the local procurator fiscal; see SSI 2005/40, art.3(4).

In the case of an accused admitted to Lord Advocate's bail (see s.24(2) and (6) above) such intimation is to be made to the Lord Advocate.

Failure to accept conditions of bail under section 65(8C): continued detention of accused

25A. An accused who—

(a) is, by virtue of subsection (4) of section 65 of this Act, entitled to be admitted to bail; but

(b) fails to accept any of the conditions imposed by the court on bail under subsection (8C) of that section,

shall continue to be detained under the committal warrant for so long as he fails to accept any of those conditions.

AMENDMENT

Section 25A inserted by the Criminal Procedure (Amendment) (Scotland) Act 2004 (asp 5), s.25 and Sch.1, para.7. Brought into force on February 1, 2005 by the Criminal Procedure (Amendment) (Scotland) Act 2004 (Commencement, Transitional Provisions and Savings) Order 2004 (SSI 2004/405 (C.28)), art.2.

DEFINITIONS

"bail": s.307(1).

GENERAL NOTE

Before describing the operation of this section, some explanation of its context is appropriate.

One of the innovations introduced by the 2004 Act has been the restriction upon the operation of s.65(4) where an accused in custody is not indicted or brought to trial within the requisite 80 and 110 days; hitherto the consequence of a failure on the part of the Crown to meet these timescales was that the accused would have to be liberated from custody in the first case, and be forever free of all other process in the second. In neither case would the accused be required to provide a bail address of any kind even though the Crown would almost inevitably seek extensions of the timebars to keep proceedings alive.

Section 65(8C) of the Act as now amended is less final in its terms; henceforth the consequences of (a) failure to serve an indictment within 80 days of full committal, (b) failure to hold a preliminary diet within 110 days, and (c) failure to commence the trial within 140 days, in High Court cases only, entitles the accused to be admitted to bail.

(Note that the more familiar 80 and 110 day time limits for service of an indictment and bringing it to trial still apply to sheriff solemn proceedings). Thus s.25A provides that once an accused remanded on petition has to be granted bail, it falls to the court to set bail conditions. If the accused declines to accept the conditions, he stays in custody—the existing petition committal warrant remaining in force.

Section 25A operates without prejudice to the rights of the prosecutor to seek an extension of any (or all) of the periods mentioned above, or to the power of a single judge or appellate court to refuse bail to the accused on the merits, subject always to the necessary timebar extensions being granted to the Crown.

Bail: circumstances where not available
26. [...]

AMENDMENT

Deleted by s.4 of the Bail, Judicial Appointments etc. (Scotland) Act 2000 (asp 9).

GENERAL NOTE

This section previously contained an absolute prohibition upon the grant of bail where an accused charged with attempted murder, culpable homicide, rape or attempted rape had a previous conviction for such an offence, or murder or manslaughter. The imperative nature of the section is plainly at odds with an accused's Art.6 rights under the European Convention. Grounds for opposition to bail are discussed at A4–65 above.

Breach of bail conditions: offences
27.—(1) Subject to subsection (7) below, an accused who having been granted bail fails without reasonable excuse—

(a) to appear at the time and place appointed for any diet of which he has been given due notice or at which he is required by this Act to appear; or

(b) to comply with any other condition imposed on bail,

shall, subject to subsection (3) below, be guilty of an offence and liable on conviction to the penalties specified in subsection (2) below.

(2) The penalties mentioned in subsection (1) above are—

(a) a fine not exceeding level 3 on the standard scale; and

(b) imprisonment for a period—

(i) where conviction is in the district court, not exceeding 60 days; or

(ii) in any other case, not exceeding 3 months.

(3) Where, and to the extent that, the failure referred to in subsection (1)(b) above consists in the accused having committed an offence while on bail (in this section referred to as "the subsequent offence"), he shall not be guilty of an offence under that subsection but, subject to subsection (4) below, the court which sentences him for the subsequent offence shall, in determining the appropriate sentence or disposal for that offence, have regard to—

(a) the fact that the offence was committed by him while on bail and the number of bail orders to which he was subject when the offence was committed;

(b) any previous conviction of the accused of an offence under subsection (1)(b) above; and

(c) the extent to which the sentence or disposal in respect of any previous conviction of the accused differed, by virtue of this subsection, from that which the court would have imposed but for this subsection.

(4) The court shall not, under subsection (3) above, have regard to the fact that the subsequent offence was committed while the accused was on bail unless that fact is libelled in the indictment or, as the case may be, specified in the complaint.

(4A) The fact that the subsequent offence was committed while the accused was on bail shall, unless challenged—

(a) in the case of proceedings on indictment, by giving notice of a preliminary objection in accordance with section 71(2) or 72(6)(b)(i) of this Act; or

(b) in summary proceedings, by preliminary objection before his plea is recorded,

be held as admitted.

(5) Where the maximum penalty in respect of the subsequent offence is specified by or by virtue of any enactment, that maximum penalty shall, for the

purposes of the court's determination, by virtue of subsection (3) above, of the appropriate sentence or disposal in respect of that offence, be increased—

    (a) where it is a fine, by the amount for the time being equivalent to level 3 on the standard scale; and

    (b) where it is a period of imprisonment—

        (i) as respects a conviction in the High Court or the sheriff court, by 6 months; and

        (ii) as respects a conviction in the district court, by 60 days,

notwithstanding that the maximum penalty as so increased exceeds the penalty which it would otherwise be competent for the court to impose.

(6) Where the sentence or disposal in respect of the subsequent offence is, by virtue of subsection (3) above, different from that which the court would have imposed but for that subsection, the court shall state the extent of and the reasons for that difference.

(7) An accused who having been granted bail in relation to solemn proceedings fails without reasonable excuse to appear at the time and place appointed for any diet of which he has been given due notice (where such diet is in respect of solemn proceedings) shall be guilty of an offence and liable on conviction on indictment to the following penalties—

    (a) a fine; and

    (b) imprisonment for a period not exceeding two years.

(8) At any time before the trial of an accused under solemn procedure for the original offence, it shall be competent—

    (a) to amend the indictment to include an additional charge of an offence under this section;

    (b) to include in the list of witnesses or productions relating to the original offence, witnesses or productions relating to the offence under this section.

(9) The penalties provided for in subsection (2) above may be imposed in addition to any other penalty which it is competent for the court to impose, notwithstanding that the total of penalties imposed may exceed the maximum penalty which it is competent to impose in respect of the original offence.

(10) A court which finds an accused guilty of an offence under this section may remit the accused for sentence in respect of that offence to any court which is considering the original offence.

(11) In this section "the original offence" means the offence with which the accused was charged when he was granted bail or an offence charged in the same proceedings as that offence.

AMENDMENT

    Subs.(4A) inserted by the Criminal Procedure and Investigations Act 1996 (c.25), s.73(2).

    Subss.(1)(a) and (4A)(a) as amended by the Criminal Procedure (Amendment) (Scotland) Act 2004 (asp 5), s.25 and Sch.1, para.8. Brought into force on February 1, 2005 by the Criminal Procedure (Amendment) (Scotland) Act 2004 (Commencement, Transitional Provisions and Savings) Order 2004 (SSI 2004/405 (C.28)), art.2.

DEFINITIONS

    "bail": s.307(1).
    "indictment": s.307(1).
    "level 3": s.225(2) [i.e. £1,000].
    "offence": s.307(1).
    "original offence, the": s.27(11).
    "sentence": s.307(1).
    "standard scale": s.225(1).

"subsequent offence, the": s.27(3).

GENERAL NOTE

Subss.(1) and (2)

These subsections create the main bail offences and largely repeat the terms of s.3(1) and (2) of the Bail etc. (Scotland) Act 1980 (c.4).

Penalties for offences, as set out in subs.(2), remain surprisingly low given the potential for disruption to court business and inconvenience to witnesses. Subs.(5) does enact slightly more severe penalties where an accused further offends while on bail.

Subs.(1)(a) closes a potential procedural loophole by emphasising that an accused on bail is obliged to attend any mandatory or peremptory diet fixed in the proceedings.

Unsurprisingly, the section's provisions have generated a substantial volume of case law.

Subs.(4)

In *Boyd v HM Advocate*, 2000 S.L.T. 1358 the libelling, as an aggravation of the substantive offence, the fact that it was committed while the accused was already on bail, was submitted to infringe Art.6(1) of the European Convention. *Boyd* contended that this would unfairly colour the jury's consideration of the merits: the court rejected this argument and held that a properly directed jury's impartiality would not be tainted by inclusion of a bail aggravation.

Subs. (4A)

Offending on bail is an aggravation of the substantive offence provided that this capacity is alluded to in the body of any charge which, it is alleged, was committed while the accused was on bail.

Subs.(4A) indicates that being subject to bail conditions is a special capacity (on which, see the discussion at s.255 below) and that any objection to that capacity must be intimated in solemn proceedings at the first, or preliminary diet, or prior to tendering a plea to a summary complaint.

The discussion below sets out the convoluted history of this provision (itself an object of wonder) only because it could still be relevant for long-outstanding proceedings.

Prior to the coming into force of the Criminal Procedure (Scotland) Act 1995 it had been judicially determined that bail was a special capacity and, that in the absence of a timeous challenge to that capacity, the Crown did not require to prove that a bail order was in force (*Aitchison v Tudhope*, 1981 J.C. 65; 1981 S.C.C.R. 1). However, the cumulative effect of subss.(3) and (4) is that offending while subject of an earlier bail order now falls to be disposed of as an aggravation of the substantive offence; an enhanced sentence may only be imposed where the prosecutor has specifically libelled the existence of the bail order in the body of the substantive charge itself. When sentencing upon the substantive offence aggravated by being committed while on bail, the court shall impose one all-embracing sentence and minute (but apparently not pronounce) the element of sentence attributable to the aggravation (*Hill v HM Advocate*, 1997 S.C.C.R. 376). Where separate offences are prosecuted on distinct complaints, and each offence has been aggravated by being committed while on bail, it is perfectly competent to impose consecutive sentences in relation to both the substantive offences and the aggravations (*Connal v Carmichael*, 1996 G.W.D. 30–1807).

An effect of the draftmanship of the 1995 Procedure Act, possibly unintended, was that bail ceased to be a special capacity and would henceforth have to be proved by the Crown. It will be noted that s.73 of the Criminal Procedure and Investigations Act 1996 (c.25) has introduced the provisions now found in subs.(4A) which, by statute, reintroduce bail as a special capacity.

An unintended defect in draftsmanship of the 1995 Act brought about the removal of bail as a special capacity, as it had been since the passing of the Bail etc. (Scotland) Act 1980 (c.4). (See too *Aitchison v Tudhope*, above). This defect was remedied by the amendments to the 1995 Act introduced by the Criminal Procedure and Investigations 1996 (c.25) with effect from July 4, 1996. In those rare cases still extant where the accused was granted bail between March 31, 1996 and July 4, 1996 inclusive, the commission of further offences in breach of such a bail order will be an aggravating feature but the currency of the order itself will have to be proved, and will not be a special capacity.

Being subject of a bail order granted prior to March 31, 1996 (the date upon which the Criminal Justice (Scotland) Act 1995, s.2, the statutory precursor of the 1995 Procedure Act, came into force) falls to be regarded as a special capacity in accordance with case law (*Aitchison v Tudhope*, above) and contraventions of that bail order should be libelled under s.3(1)(b) of the Bail etc. (Scotland) Act 1980 since it was under that legislation that bail was granted.

Different considerations apply where an accused person has been admitted to bail in terms of ss.24 and 25 of the Criminal Procedure (Scotland) Act 1995 after April 1, 1996 (or more rarely, on March 31, 1996 in terms of s.1 of the Criminal Justice (Scotland) Act 1996). In some situations (i.e. where such a bail order is contravened between March 31, 1996 and July 4, 1996) this will be an aggravating feature of the later offence, if the Crown elects to specify the existence of the earlier s.24 bail order in the libel, but will not be a special capacity; however, where there are contraventions of any s.24 bail order libelled as having occurred after July 4, 1996 (the date when the provisions which now appear as s.27(4A) of the 1995 Procedure Act took effect) the existence of that bail order will be both a special capacity and an aggravating factor in sentencing any subsequent substantive offence.

Subs.(5)

The maximum penalty which may be imposed upon a summary complaint which incorporates a bail aggravation will ordinarily be one of nine months in the sheriff court and eight months in the district court. The maximum penalty can increase in the sheriff court when the accused has cognate prior convictions as provided in subs.5(3) of the Act. See *Hamilton v Heywood*, 1998 S.L.T. 133.

For a discussion of the effect of s.27(3) and (5) see *Penman v Bott*, 2006 S.L.T. 495. In particular it was held (at 499F–H) that the increased powers conferred by s.27(5) were for the specific purpose identified, thus they could only be used to reflect the bail aggravation: if less than six months was attributed to the bail aggravation, the balance could not be used to increase the period available to be attributed to the substantive offence; conversely, if the period attributable to the substantive offence was less than the maximum which that offence could attract if there were no bail aggravation, the surplus could not be used to augment the extra six months provided for by s.27(5).

Subs.(6)

The court's minute of the sentence imposed state the total sentence and then specify the period of the sentence attributed to the bail offence (*Cochrane v Heywood*, 1998 G.W.D. 13–662).

Subs.(7)

It is commonplace to libel a contravention of s.27(7) as an additional charge in the indictment, indeed subs.(8) permits such a charge to be added by amendment up until the trial starts. In *Slater v HM Advocate* (High Court of Justiciary, November 22, 2000, unreported) this factor, and the *ratio* in *Boyd* (discussed in the Notes to subs.(4) above), caused the Appeal Court to refuse a motion for separation of the s.27(7) charge from others on the indictment. It remains the case that in order to advance a reasonable excuse for failing to appear, an accused may have to give evidence to explain his earlier absence and thus render himself liable to cross-examination on the substantive charges.

In *Creevy v HM Advocate*, 2005 S.C.C.R. 272 where the accused in the course of his trial plead guilty, in the presence of the jury, to an earlier failure to appear and did not give evidence himself, the Appeal Court declined to rule the terms of the prosecutor's speech to the jury, which suggested that this admitted failure was scarcely the act of an innocent man, to be improper. Nevertheless, it remains debatable whether acceptance by an accused that he had no reasonable excuse for failing to appear at a diet necessarily infers that his absence was spurred by his conciousness of his guilt of all, or any, of the charges libelled against him. Compare the earlier approach in *Smith (CC) v HM Advocate*, 2004 S.C.C.R. 521.

Subs.(8)

It has to be observed, however, that the terms of subs.(4A), as applied to solemn proceedings, obviously cannot operate in circumstances where the Crown makes use of the concession contained in subs.(8) and adds a bail offence to the original libel prior to the jury being sworn unless the amendment is made at least two days prior to the first (or the preliminary) diet. Such timeous amendment will preserve the Crown's right to treat the extant bail order as a fact of special capacity and, equally, afford the defence an opportunity to challenge that capacity by preliminary plea. Later amendment would deny the defence that preliminary plea and compel the Crown to prove the existence of the bail order alleged to have been contravened. (At the risk of complicating matters yet further, for the sake of completeness it has to be stressed that subs.(4A) is of no application to s.27 bail offences committed before July 4, 1996; in such cases the applicability of a bail order will always have to be proved.)

The court minutes must refer to grants of bail; see *MacNeill v Smith*, 1984 S.L.T. (Sh. Ct) 63. Any special conditions imposed by the court must be stipulated expressly on the face of the copy bail order served upon the accused (*HM Advocate v Crawford*, 1985 S.L.T. 242). It is clear that the currency of a bail order is not affected by whether any subsequent proceedings are solemn or summary (*McGinn v HM Advocate*, 1991 S.L.T. 266) while in *Mayo v Neizer*, 1994 S.L.T. 931 it was held that bail orders continue for so long as the accused is at liberty even if, as an appellant, he abandons an appeal against sentence and awaits arrest on a consequent warrant. In *Fitzpatrick v Normand*, 1994 S.L.T. 1263 it was held that recall or modification of a bail order must be the subject of an express decision by the court.

It will be observed that s.31 *infra* entitles the prosecutor to apply for a review of bail or the conditions of bail.

Subs. (9)

It is a general rule where one substantive offence involves contravention of a number of separate bail orders, that sentences for the bail offences should be consecutive to any sentence imposed for the substantive offence but concurrent with each other: *Milligan v Normand*, 1996 G.W.D. 24–1367, *Appleton v Vannet*, 1996 G.W.D. 12–698 and *Stuart v Heywood*, 1997 G.W.D. 31–1563. It is not incompetent to impose consecutive sentences for each bail offence (*Whyte v Normand*, 1988 S.C.C.R. 465) and the onus for proving that such an exercise of judicial discretion was inappropriate seems to rest with the appellant rather than requiring justification by the sentencing judge. See *Nicholson v Lees*, 1996 S.C.C.R. 551 (at 561B) which summarises the general principles governing the imposition of concurrent and consecutive sentences and note also *Connal v Carmichael*, 1996 G.W.D. 30–1807. Generally, backdating of a sentence to take account of time on remand awaiting trial is usual, and the reasons for refusal of backdating should be specified in the minutes. However, in the case of a failure to appear for trial, particularly on indictment, it cannot be presumed that backdating will occur even where an acquittal is obtained on the original substantive charges (*Bowers v HM Advocate*, 1997 G.W.D. 31–1562).

European Convention on Human Rights

The libelling of a contravention of s.27 of the Act against an accused in conjunction with other charges did not breach the fair trial provisions contained in Art.6 of the Convention (*Boyd v HM Advocate*; *Moffat* and *Erasmuson v HM Advocate*, both High Court of Justiciary, October 27, 2000, unreported).

Act of Adjournal

Refer to Ch.5 of the Act of Adjournal (Criminal Procedure Rules) 1996 (SI 1996/2147) in relation to alteration (or opposing the alteration) of the address specified in a bail order.

Breach of bail conditions: arrest of offender, etc.

28.—(1) A constable may arrest without warrant an accused who has been released on bail where the constable has reasonable grounds for suspecting that the accused has broken, is breaking, or is likely to break any condition imposed on his bail.

(2) An accused who is arrested under this section shall wherever practicable be brought before the court to which his application for bail was first made not later than in the course of the first day after his arrest, such day not being, subject to subsection (3) below, a Saturday, a Sunday or a court holiday prescribed for that court under section 8 of this Act.

(3) Nothing in subsection (2) above shall prevent an accused being brought before a court on a Saturday, a Sunday or such a court holiday where the court is, in pursuance of the said section 8, sitting on such day for the disposal of criminal business.

(4) Where an accused is brought before a court under subsection (2) or (3) above, the court, after hearing the parties, may—

(a) recall the order granting bail;

(b) release the accused under the original order granting bail; or

(c) vary the order granting bail so as to contain such conditions as the court thinks it necessary to impose to secure that the accused complies with the requirements of paragraphs (a) to (d) of section 24(5) of this Act.

(4A) In the case of an accused released on bail by virtue of section 65(8C) of this Act—

(a) subsection (2) above shall have effect as if the reference to the court to which his application for bail was first made were a reference to the court or judge which admitted him to bail under that section; and

(b) subsection (4) above shall not apply and subsection (4B) below shall apply instead.

(4B) Where an accused referred to in subsection (4A) above is, under subsection (2) or (3) above, brought before the court or judge which admitted him to bail under section 65(8C)—

(a) the court or judge shall give the prosecutor an opportunity to make an application under section 65(5) of this Act; and

(b) if the prosecutor does not make such an application, or if such an application is made but is refused, the court or judge may—

(i) release the accused under the original order granting bail; or

(ii) vary the order granting bail so as to contain such conditions as the court or judge thinks necessary to impose to secure that the accused complies with the requirements of paragraphs (a) to (d) of section 24(5) of this Act.

(5) The same rights of appeal shall be available against any decision of the court under subsection (4) above as were available against the original order of the court relating to bail.

(6) For the purposes of this section and section 27 of this Act, an extract from the minute of proceedings, containing the order granting bail and bearing to be signed by the clerk of court, shall be sufficient evidence of the making of that order and of its terms and of the acceptance by the accused of the conditions imposed under section 24 of this Act.

AMENDMENT

Subs.(4A) and (4B) inserted by the Criminal Procedure (Amendment) (Scotland) Act 2004 (asp 5), s.25 and Sch.1, para.9. Brought into force on February 1, 2005 by the Criminal Procedure (Amendment) (Scotland) Act 2004 (Commencement, Transitional Provisions and Savings) Order 2004 (SSI 2004/405 (C.28)), art.2(1).

DEFINITION

"bail": s.307(1).

GENERAL NOTE

With the exception of subs.(4A) these provisions are readily understood. Subs.(4A) deals with a narrow range of offenders—those remand prisoners admitted to bail in solemn proceedings following (a) failure of the Crown to indict within 80 days, (b) failure to hold a preliminary diet in High Court proceedings, or a trial diet in sheriff solemn proceedings within 110 days, or (c) failure to proceed to trial in the High Court within 140 days, each of which failures would entitle the accused to apply for bail. Should such an accused be admitted to bail in terms of s.65(8C) and then breach his bail conditions, subs.(4A) would come into operation.

The subsection requires the accused to be brought back, as soon as practicable, before the court or judge which admitted him to bail, permits the Crown to apply to extend these custody timescales of new, and entitles the court or judge to remand in custody, or to continue or vary the bail order as considered appropriate. Note that the court or judge cannot *ex proprio motu* remand; a motion for a custodial remand must first be made by the Crown or, less likely, the accused must have refused to agree to the bail conditions imposed (see s.25A above).

It is submitted that subs.(4A) would not preclude the Crown from initiating fresh proceedings in the accustomed manner libelling an established (but not an anticipated) breach of bail conditions.

Bail: monetary conditions

29.—(1) Without prejudice to section 27 of this Act, where the accused or a cautioner on his behalf has deposited a sum of money in court under section 24(6) of this Act, then—

    (a) if the accused fails to appear at the time and place appointed for any diet of which he has been given due notice, the court may, on the motion of the prosecutor, immediately order forfeiture of the sum deposited;

    (b) if the accused fails to comply with any other condition imposed on bail, the court may, on conviction of an offence under section 27(1)(b) of this Act and on the motion of the prosecutor, order forfeiture of the sum deposited.

(2) If the court is satisfied that it is reasonable in all the circumstances to do so, it may recall an order made under subsection (1)(a) above and direct that the money forfeited shall be refunded, and any decision of the court under this subsection shall be final and not subject to review.

(3) A cautioner, who has deposited a sum of money in court under section 24(6) of this Act, shall be entitled, subject to subsection (4) below, to recover the sum deposited at any diet of the court at which the accused appears personally.

(4) Where the accused has been charged with an offence under section 27(1)(b) of this Act, nothing in subsection (3) above shall entitle a cautioner to recover the sum deposited unless and until—

    (a) the charge is not proceeded with; or

    (b) the accused is acquitted of the charge; or

    (c) on the accused's conviction of the offence, the court has determined not to order forfeiture of the sum deposited.

(5) The references in subsections (1)(b) and (4)(c) above to conviction of an offence shall include references to the making of an order in respect of the offence under section 246(3) of this Act.

Bail review

30.—(1) This section applies where a court has refused to admit a person to bail or, where a court has so admitted a person, the person has failed to accept the conditions imposed or that a sum required to be deposited under section 24(6) of this Act has not been so deposited.

(2) A court shall, on the application of any person mentioned in subsection (1) above, have power to review its decision to admit to bail or its decision as to the conditions imposed and may, on cause shown, admit the person to bail or, as the case may be, fix bail on different conditions.

(2A) Before determining an application under subsection (2) above, the court shall give the prosecutor an opportunity to be heard.

(2B) Subsection (2C) below applies where an application is made under subsection (2) above by a person convicted on indictment pending the determination of—

    (a) his appeal;

    (b) any relevant appeal by the Lord Advocate under section 108 or 108A of this Act; or

    (c) the sentence to be imposed on, or other method of dealing with, him.

(2C) Where this subsection applies the application shall be—

    (a) intimated by the person making it immediately and in writing to the Crown Agent; and

    (b) heard not less than 7 days after the date of that intimation.

(3) An application under this section, where it relates to the original decision of the court, shall not be made before the fifth day after that decision and, where it relates to a subsequent decision, before the fifteenth day thereafter.

(4) Nothing in this section shall affect any right of a person to appeal against the decision of a court in relation to admitting to bail or to the conditions imposed.

AMENDMENT

Subss.(2A)–(2C) inserted by the Criminal Procedure (Amendment) (Scotland) Act 2004 (asp 4), s.18(3). Brought into force on February 1, 2005 by the Criminal Procedure (Amendment) (Scotland) Act 2004 (Commencement, Transitional Provisions and Savings) Order 2004 (SSI 2004/405 (C.28)), art.2.

DEFINITION

"bail": s.307(1).

GENERAL NOTE

This section applies in a number of separate circumstances: *e.g.* the court may have refused to admit a person to bail. For the general guidelines as to the allowance or refusal of bail, see *Smith v M.*, 1982 S.L.T. 421. Alternatively, a court may have so admitted a person but the person has failed to accept the conditions imposed: for a special condition that was challenged see *Brawls v Walkingshaw*, 1994 S.C.C.R. 7. Also, a court may have required the deposit of a sum of money but that has not been done. In any or all of these circumstances, a person may seek to have the original decision reviewed within modest statutory time-limits and yet otherwise appeal the original decision.

In *Ogilvie v H.M. Advocate*, 1998 G.W.D. 9–438, O's petition for review of refusal of bail was rejected by the sift judge considering O's appeal who was unaware that leave to appeal had been granted by the trial judge and had not seen the trial judge's report. At the full hearing the Court held that review was competent given the terms of s.30 but that leave to appeal a conviction did not automatically infer that an application for bail pending appeal should be granted. See also s.112 below.

Subs.(2A) explicitly provides that the prosecutor now has a right to be heard in *any* application by an accused for review of bail either prior to trial or pending any appeal following conviction on indictment. The same entitlement applies where the Crown appeals claiming undue leniency in sentencing or on a point of law. Intimation of an application for bail review has to be made upon the Crown Agent, and the date of that intimation determines the seven day period within which a hearing must occur.

Bail review on prosecutor's application

31.—(1) On an application by the prosecutor at any time after a court has granted bail to a person the court may, where the prosecutor puts before the court material information which was not available to it when it granted bail to that person, review its decision.

(2) On receipt of an application under subsection (1) above the court shall—

(a) intimate the application to the person granted bail;

(b) fix a diet for hearing the application and cite that person to attend the diet; and

(c) where it considers that the interests of justice so require, grant warrant to arrest that person.

(2A) Subsection (2B) below applies to an application under subsection (1) above where the person granted bail—

(a) was convicted on indictment; and

(b) was granted bail pending the determination of—

(i) his appeal;

(ii) any relevant appeal by the Lord Advocate under section 108 or 108A of this Act; or

(iii) the sentence to be imposed on, or other method of dealing with, him.

(2B) Where this subsection applies, the application shall be heard not more than 7 days after the day on which it is made.

(3) On hearing an application under subsection (1) above the court may—

(a) withdraw the grant of bail and remand the person in question in custody; or

(b) grant bail, or continue the grant of bail, either on the same or on different conditions.

(3A) In relation to an accused admitted to bail under section 65(8C) of this Act—

(a) an application may be made under subsection (1) above only in relation to the conditions imposed on bail; and

(b) paragraph (a) of subsection (3) above shall not apply in relation to any such application.

(4) Nothing in the foregoing provisions of this section shall affect any right of appeal against the decision of a court in relation to bail.

AMENDMENT

Subss.(2A)–(2B) inserted by the Criminal Procedure (Amendment) (Scotland) Act 2004 (asp 5), s.18(4), and subs.(3A) inserted by s.25 and Sch.1, para.10 of the 2004 Act. Brought into force on February 1, 2005 by the Criminal Procedure (Amendment) (Scotland) Act 2004 (Commencement, Transitional Provisions and Savings) Order 2004 (SSI 2004/405 (C.28)), art.2.

DEFINITIONS

"bail": s.307(1).
"diet": s.307(1).
"prosecutor": s.307(1).

GENERAL NOTE

This section enables the prosecutor to apply to the court to reconsider a decision to grant bail. Application must be made on the basis of information relevant to the decision to grant bail which was not available to the court when the decision was taken. Subsection (2) describes the procedure to be followed on receipt of an application by a prosecutor. Subsection (3) specifies the options available to the court on hearing the prosecutor's application. In the absence of this provision under the 1980 Act one reported solution was to petition the court for warrant to apprehend the accused; see *Lockhart v Stokes*, 1981 S.L.T. (Sh. Ct) 71 where efforts to serve an indictment foundered because the domicile given had ceased to be a proper domicile of citation.

The prosecutor's right to bail review is now extended to Crown appeals claiming undue leniency in sentencing or on a point of law.

Subs.(3A) deals with situations where the Crown fail to indict an accused, or progress to trial in solemn proceedings within the statutory timescales set out in s.65 of the Act and the accused is then admitted to bail. While the Crown can seek a review of bail in such circumstances this cannot be used as a means to seek withdrawal of that bail, but only to vary or amend the bail conditions previously imposed by the court.

Bail appeal

32.—(1) Where, in any case, bail is refused or where the accused is dissatisfied with the amount of bail fixed, he may appeal to the High Court which may, in its discretion order intimation to the Lord Advocate or, as the case may be, the prosecutor.

(2) Where, in any case, bail is granted, or, in summary proceedings an accused is ordained to appear, the public prosecutor, if dissatisfied—

(a) with the decision allowing bail;

(b) with the amount of bail fixed; or

(c) in summary proceedings, that the accused has been ordained to appear,

may appeal to the High Court, and the accused shall not be liberated, subject to subsection (7) below, until the appeal by the prosecutor is disposed of.

(2A) The public prosecutor may, in relation to an accused admitted to bail under section 65(8C) of this Act, appeal under subsection (2) above only in relation to the conditions imposed on bail.

(3) Written notice of appeal shall be immediately given to the opposite party by a party appealing under this section.

(4) An appeal under this section shall be disposed of by the High Court or any Lord Commissioner of Justiciary in court or in chambers after such inquiry and hearing of parties as shall seem just.

(5) Where an accused in an appeal under this section is under 21 years of age, section 51 of this Act shall apply to the High Court or, as the case may be, the Lord Commissioner of Justiciary when disposing of the appeal as it applies to a court when remanding or committing a person of the accused's age for trial or sentence.

(6) In the event of the appeal of the public prosecutor under this section being refused, the court may award expenses against him.

(7) When an appeal is taken by the public prosecutor either against the grant of bail or against the amount fixed, the accused to whom bail has been granted (other than an accused to whom subsection (7B) below applies) shall, if the bail fixed has been found by him, be liberated after 72 hours from the granting of the bail, whether the appeal has been disposed of or not, unless the High Court grants an order for his further detention in custody.

(7B) Where, in relation to an accused admitted to bail under section 65(8C) of this Act, the public prosecutor appeals against the conditions imposed on bail, the accused—

(a) may continue to be detained under the committal warrant for no more than 72 hours from the granting of bail or for such longer period as High Court may allow; and

(b) on expiry of that period, shall, whether the appeal has been disposed of or not, be released on bail subject to the conditions imposed.

(8) In computing the period mentioned in subsection (7) above, Sundays and public holidays, whether general or court holidays, shall be excluded.

(9) When an appeal is taken under this section by the prosecutor in summary proceedings against the fact that the accused has been ordained to appear, subsections (7) and (8) above shall apply as they apply in the case of an appeal against the granting of bail or the amount fixed.

(10) Notice to the governor of the prison of the issue of an order such as is mentioned in subsection (7) above within the time mentioned in that subsection bearing to be sent by the Clerk of Justiciary or the Crown Agent shall be sufficient warrant for the detention of the accused pending arrival of the order in due course of post.

AMENDMENTS

Subs.(1) as amended by the Bail, Judicial Appointments etc. (Scotland) Act 2000 (asp 9), s.4.

Subss.(2), (5), (7) and (10) as amended by the Bail, Judicial Appointments etc. (Scotland) Act 2000 (asp 9), s.12 and Sch., para.7(2).

Subss.(2A) and (7B) inserted, and (7) as amended, by the Criminal Procedure (Amendment) (Scotland) Act 2004 (asp 5), s.25 and Sch.1, para.11. Brought into force on February 1, 2005 by the Criminal Procedure (Amendment) (Scotland) Act 2004 (Commencement, Transitional Provisions and Savings) Order 2004 (SSI 2004/405 (C.28)), art.2.

DEFINITIONS

"bail": s.307(1).

"Clerk of Justiciary": s.307(1).

"complaint": s.307(1).
"governor": s.307(1).
"High Court": s.307(1).
"Lords Commissioner of Justiciary": s.307(1).
"order": s.307(1).
"prison": s.307(1).
"prosecutor": s.307(1).

GENERAL NOTE

The essence of this section in the most general of terms is that, by subs.(1), the accused may appeal a refusal of bail and by subs.(2) the Crown may appeal the grant of bail. Each party appealing must give written notice to the other side, by subs.(3). Disposal of the appeal may be by the High Court or a single judge in court or in chambers: subs.(4).

Section 32(1) affords the means for an appeal against refusal of bail: see *Love, Petr*, 1998 G.W.D. 11–528, discussed at A4–63 above.

The 2004 Act inserted subss.(2A) and (7B) to deal with the particular circumstances arising from the introduction of s.65(8C). Once the Crown has failed to meet the statutory timescales for solemn proceedings applying to remand prisoners, the court may opt to grant bail to the accused while keeping proceedings alive. Any Crown appeal relating to that bail grant must arise from the conditions imposed—the decision upon the merits of bail cannot be challenged.

(The Act does provide remedies in the event of an accused's failure to adhere to the conditions imposed; see the note to s.28(4A) above).

Subs.(7B) requires that any such Crown appeal must be heard within 72 hours unless the High Court has granted a longer period.

It would seem necessary to intimate at the time of marking any appeal that additional time is required since, ordinarily, the committal warrant only extends for 72 hours after which time the bail order, as granted, comes into force.

Bail: no fees exigible

33. No clerks fees, court fees or other fees or expenses shall be exigible from or awarded against an accused in respect of a decision on bail under section 22A above, an application for bail or of the appeal of such a decision or application to the High Court.

AMENDMENT

Section 33 as amended by the Bail, Judicial Appointments etc. (Scotland) Act 2000 (asp 9), s.12 and Sch., para.7(3)(a) and (b).

DEFINITIONS

"bail": s.307(1).
"High Court": s.307(1).

PART IV

PETITION PROCEDURE

Warrants

Petition for warrant

34.—(1) A petition for warrant to arrest and commit a person suspected of or charged with crime may be in the forms—

(a) set out in Schedule 2 to this Act; or
(b) prescribed by Act of Adjournal,

or as nearly as may be in such form; and Schedule 3 to this Act shall apply to any such petition as it applies to the indictment.

(2) If on the application of the procurator fiscal, a sheriff is satisfied that there is reasonable ground for suspecting that an offence has been or is being committed by a body corporate, the sheriff shall have the like power to grant warrant for the citation of witnesses and the production of documents and articles as he would have if a petition charging an individual with the commission of the offence were presented to him.

GENERAL NOTE

Solemn proceedings are generally initiated by the presentation of a petition to a sheriff in chambers. The petition may be put before the court along with the person accused of the crime, or the Crown may petition for a warrant to arrest the accused: on occasion where several accused are involved the petition may take both forms. In *Hamilton v H.M. Advocate* 1997 S.L.T. 31, a prosecution under the Trades Description Act 1968, it was held that in contrast to England where proceedings were deemed to commence with service of an indictment (an event which would affect calculation of the time-bar on proceedings), in Scotland proceedings commenced with the obtaining of a petition warrant by the prosecutor or by service of an indictment when no initiating petition had been obtained. Offences committed by corporate bodies can in terms of subs.(2) also be initiated by way of the same petition procedure and, when granted by the court, give the same powers to the Crown as would a petition against an individual accused. Prior to the enactment of s.74(7) of the 1975 Act the form of petition used for offences committed by such bodies was derived from the Criminal Justice (Scotland) Act 1949, s.40(7); indeed until the Second World War solemn proceedings against companies or other corporate bodies were unknown.

The crimes charged are narrated in the third person and s.40 of the 1995 Act requires that the principal petition must be signed by the prosecutor (normally a fiscal or a fiscal depute) and by a sheriff, both of whom must have a jurisdiction derived from one or more of the charges libelled. Subsection (1) refers to the forms of indictments set out in Sch.2 to the Act. It will be noted that these charges originated in the Criminal Procedure (Scotland) Act 1887 (c.35) and many are arcane, obsolescent or obsolete (it has to be doubted that the Crown would ever libel a crime euphemistically as an "attempt to ravish" or "ravish" now—the charge would be one of attempted rape or rape).

As a matter of course the warrant granted by the court will authorise (i) the arrest of the accused and require that he be brought before the court for examination, (ii) the search of his abode or other premises for the purpose of such arrest and to gather evidence, (iii) the citation of witnesses and the production to the Crown of documentary and label productions, and (iv) after examination, his committal for further examination or until liberated in due course of law (technically the first-mentioned step is unnecessary in situations where the petition is of even date with the first appearance of the accused or where the accused is a body corporate). In order to fulfil the Crown's obligations under the European Convention on Human Rights, Arts 5 and 6, a fuller narration of the circumstances which the prosecutor alleges justify the charges libelled in the petition is now routinely served on the accused when the Crown moves for committal for further examination. A fuller outline of the Crown case is likely to follow at full committal. It is usual for this additional information to be put in a paper apart, rather than within the body of the petition itself. Either approach would be acceptable (*Brown v Selfridge*, 2000 S.L.T. 437). See also *Hamilton v Vannet*, 1999 G.W.D. 8–406. It is necessary for the sheriff to consider whether the information provided in a statement provides a sufficiency for committal but no more than a broad outline of the available evidence is required; see *Hynd v Ritchie*, 2002 S.L.T. 984; 2002 S.C.C.R. 755. H's bill of suspension was refused.

In the absence of voluntary provision by the accused, or the securing by the police of bodily samples by way of the powers contained in s.18 of the Act, a separate warrant would have to be craved by the prosecutor to obtain blood or other body fluid samples where invasive means were to be used. See *Mellors v Normand*, 1996 G.W.D. 14–817 and the authorities cited in the Notes to s.18 above.

Judicial examination

Judicial examination

35.—(1) The accused's solicitor shall be entitled to be present at the examination.

(2) The sheriff may delay the examination for a period not exceeding 48 hours from and after the time of the accused's arrest, in order to allow time for the attendance of the solicitor.

(3) Where the accused is brought before the sheriff for examination on any charge and he or his solicitor intimates that he does not desire to emit a declaration in regard to such a charge, it shall be unnecessary to take a declaration, and, subject to section 36 of this Act, the accused may be committed for further examination or until liberated in due course of law without a declaration being taken.

(4) Nothing in subsection (3) above shall prejudice the right of the accused subsequently to emit a declaration on intimating to the prosecutor his desire to do so; and that declaration shall be taken in further examination.

(4A) An accused charged with a sexual offence to which section 288C of this Act applies shall, as soon as he is brought before the sheriff for examination on the charge, be told—

(za) that, if he is indicted to the High Court in respect of the offence, his case at or for the purposes of the preliminary hearing may be conducted only by a lawyer;

(a) that, if he is tried for the offence, his defence and any proof ordered as is mentioned in section 288C(1) of this Act may be conducted only by a lawyer;

(b) that it is, therefore, in his interests, if he has not already done so, to get the professional assistance of a solicitor; and

(c) that, if he does not engage a solicitor for the purposes of the conduct of his case at or for the purposes of the preliminary hearing (if he is indicted to the High Court in respect of the offence) or his defence at the trial, the court will do so.

(4B) A failure to comply with subsection (4A) above does not affect the validity or lawfulness of the examination or of any other element of the proceedings against the accused.

(5) Where, subsequent to examination or further examination on any charge, the prosecutor desires to question the accused as regards an extrajudicial confession, whether or not a full admission, allegedly made by him to or in the hearing of a constable, which is relevant to the charge and as regards which he has not previously been examined, the accused may be brought before the sheriff for further examination.

(6) Where the accused is brought before the sheriff for further examination the sheriff may delay that examination for a period not exceeding 24 hours in order to allow time for the attendance of the accused's solicitor.

(7) Any proceedings before the sheriff in examination or further examination shall be conducted in chambers and outwith the presence of any co-accused.

(8) This section applies to procedure on petition, without prejudice to the accused being tried summarily by the sheriff for any offence in respect of which he has been committed until liberated in due course of law.

AMENDMENT

Subss.(4A) and (4B) inserted by the Sexual Offences (Procedure and Evidence) (Scotland) Act 2002 (asp 9), Sch.1, para.3.

Subs.(4A) as amended by Criminal Justice (Scotland) Act 2003 (asp 7), Sch.4, para.3. Brought into force on November 25, 2003 by the Criminal Justice (Scotland) Act 2003 (Commencement No.3 and Revocation) Order 2003 (SSI 2003/475 (C.26)), art.2.

Subs.(4A) as amended by Criminal Procedure (Amendment) (Scotland) Act 2004 (asp 5), s.25, Sch.1, para.12. Brought into force on December 4, 2004 by the Criminal Procedure (Amendment) (Scotland) Act 2004 (Commencement, Transitional Provisions and Savings) Order 2004 (SSI 2004/405 (C.28)).

DEFINITIONS

"constable": s.307(1) and s.51(1) of the Police (Scotland) Act 1967.

"procurator": s.307(1).
"sheriff": s.4(1) and (4).

GENERAL NOTE

The process of judicial examination is often a part of petition procedure and its origins can be found in the Criminal Procedure (Scotland) Act 1887. After the passing of the Criminal Evidence Act 1898 (c.36) the practice of making "no plea; no declaration" became almost universal and while it remains competent for an accused to make a judicial declaration, it is now a rare event.

As with all petition procedure, judicial examination is held in private, outwith the presence of any co-accused or their agents.

The right of an accused person to emit a judicial declaration is preserved by s.35(4) of the 1995 Act and this can be made at any time before service of the indictment. The terms of a previously prepared statement can be declared by an accused provided that the words used are truly his own; it is not permissible for another person, even his solicitor, to edit or style the declaration since this may alter its sense or character (see *Carmichael v Armitage*, 1982 S.C.C.R. 475).

A rare modern example of a declaration being made and not properly recorded either to meet the statutory requirements of s.20B of the 1975 Act or even the common law standards which prevailed prior to the 1980 Act is found in *Robertson v H.M. Advocate*, 1995 S.C.C.R. 152, discussed in the notes to s.37 below.

Subsection (5) affords the prosecutor an opportunity then, or at a later time, to question the accused either about the contents of such a declaration or about any new admission made to, or heard by, a police officer which is deemed relevant to the charge libelled on the petition.

The prosecutor's right to examine upon any new material certainly can be exercised at any time before service of the indictment and arguably, by inference from *Frame v Houston*, 1995 S.C.C.R. 436, up until the trial commences.

Section 17(2) of the 1995 Act stipulates that the accused shall be entitled to a private interview with his solicitor prior to judicial examination or court appearance and s.35(2), in effect, places the court under an obligation to ensure that access to legal advice has been offered. There is no requirement that an accused person must have had such a private interview or be legally represented at his judicial examination, but the court has to draw the accused's attention to his right to such services. Failure to do so may vitiate any admissions made in the course of the declaration by an accused without benefit of legal representation: see *H.M. Advocate v Goodall*, (1888) 2 White 1.

Subsection (6) gives the sheriff a discretion to delay the first examination for a further 24 hours to allow for the attendance of the agent nominated by the accused. Until the first examination has been concluded it is not competent for the accused to apply for bail.

There is no obligation upon the Crown to seek to judicially examine an accused in any petition case; the procedure for conduct of judicial examinations is laid out in s.36 of the Act and ss.37 and 38 specify the form of the record of proceedings. Subs.(4A), most recently amended by the 2004 Act, now directs the sheriff presiding over petition proceedings to inform an accused, who has been charged with a listed sexual offence (this includes offences which appear to contain a substantial sexual element), that he cannot prepare or conduct his defence personally but must be legally represented. See the General Note to s.17A above and note that s.17A(2) makes it plain that a failure to inform the accused of this restriction is not fatal to subsequent proceedings. Additional provisions are found in the Act of Adjournal (Criminal Procedure Rules 1996), Chaps 5 and 25.

Judicial examination: questioning by prosecutor

36.—(1) Subject to the following provisions of this section, an accused on being brought before the sheriff for examination on any charge (whether the first or a further examination) may be questioned by the prosecutor in so far as such questioning is directed towards eliciting any admission, denial, explanation, justification or comment which the accused may have as regards anything to which subsections (2) to (4) below apply.

(2) This subsection applies to matters averred in the charge, and the particular aims of a line of questions under this subsection shall be to determine—

(a) whether any account which the accused can give ostensibly discloses a defence; and

(b) the nature and particulars of that defence.

(3) This subsection applies to the alleged making by the accused, to or in the hearing of a constable, of an extrajudicial confession (whether or not a full admission) relevant to the charge, and questions under this subsection may only be put if the accused has, before the examination, received from the prosecutor or from a constable a written record of the confession allegedly made.

(4) This subsection applies to what is said in any declaration emitted in regard to the charge by the accused at examination.

(5) The prosecutor shall, in framing questions in exercise of his power under subsection (1) above, have regard to the following principles—

(a) the question should not be designed to challenge the truth of anything said by the accused;

(b) there should be no reiteration of a question which the accused has refused to answer at the examination; and

(c) there should be no leading questions,

and the sheriff shall ensure that all questions are fairly put to, and understood by, the accused.

(6) The accused shall be told by the sheriff—

(a) where he is represented by a solicitor at the judicial examination, that he may consult that solicitor before answering any question; and

(b) that if he answers any question put to him at the examination under this section in such a way as to disclose an ostensible defence, the prosecutor shall be under the duty imposed by subsection (10) below.

(7) With the permission of the sheriff, the solicitor for the accused may ask the accused any question the purpose of which is to clarify any ambiguity in an answer given by the accused to the prosecutor at the examination or to give the accused an opportunity to answer any question which he has previously refused to answer.

(8) An accused may decline to answer a question under subsection (1) above; and, where he is subsequently tried on the charge mentioned in that subsection or on any other charge arising out of the circumstances which gave rise to the charge so mentioned, his having so declined may be commented upon by the prosecutor, the judge presiding at the trial, or any co-accused, only where and in so far as the accused (or any witness called on his behalf) in evidence avers something which could have been stated appropriately in answer to that question.

(9) The procedure in relation to examination under this section shall be prescribed by Act of Adjournal.

(10) Without prejudice to any rule of law, on the conclusion of an examination under this section the prosecutor shall secure the investigation, to such extent as is reasonably practicable, of any ostensible defence disclosed in the course of the examination.

(11) The duty imposed by subsection (10) above shall not apply as respects any ostensible defence which is not reasonably capable of being investigated.

DEFINITIONS

"constable": s.307(1) and s.51(1) of the Police (Scotland) Act 1967.
"prosecutor": s.307(1).

GENERAL NOTE

Section 35(7) provides that judicial examination is to be conducted in chambers outwith the presence of any other accused. It is not mandatory that the accused be legally represented at his judicial examination but it is the norm.

In terms of s.39, charges arising from other sheriff court jurisdictions can competently be included in the petition before the sheriff and the accused can be examined upon all charges.

The procedures specified in s.36 are recognisably derived from s.20A of the 1975 Act but the 1995 Act incorporates the amendments introduced by s.10(1) of the Criminal Justice (Scotland) Act 1995 (c.20): in summary these allow more direct questioning of the accused, require the Crown to make reasonable enquiry into any defence tendered by an accused in the course of his examination and, accordingly, oblige the presiding sheriff to impart additional information to the accused in the course of the judicial admonition which must precede any examination.

The prosecutor is not obliged to conduct a judicial examination at either the first or the further examination stage, but if he elects to do so he must adhere to the provisions laid down in s.36.

The role of the defence solicitor is still a reactive one; he may only consult with his client when the accused requests advice or intervene through the sheriff, as provided by subs.(7), to clarify ambiguities or to solicit answers to questions previously unanswered by the accused. Regulation of the proceedings remains the responsibility of the presiding sheriff.

At no time is an oath administered to the accused and nor can he be cross-examined, facts which following *Morrison v HM Advocate*, 1990 S.C.C.R. 235 at 248E, the trial judge should make known to the jury at trial.

Subs. (1)

The revised terms of subs.(1) now make reference to the prosecutor's function to be able to question the accused about the charge with a view to securing any "admission" as well as any "denial, explanation, justification or comment" the accused may offer. On a strict interpretation of the 1980 Act's provisions the Crown could not directly ask an accused whether he admitted the charge in whole or part, only whether he denied the allegations entirely or not. Such a literal reading hardly lent clarity to the proceedings; indeed one means of complying with such a rigourous interpretation was to question the accused using a double negative ("Is there any part of the charge you do not deny?") then relieve the confusion with the obvious question ("Do you admit the charge or any part of it?"). Such circumlocutions should now be unnecessary but the radical nature of this apparently small amendment should not be under-estimated: an accused may now be asked questions which are directly aimed to achieve his self-incrimination, and his failure to answer (as subs.(8) provides) can be commented upon if he leads evidence at trial. Moreover, his position can be still worse if he simply declines to answer any question put at judicial examination and fails to lead evidence at his trial, since s.32 of the Criminal Justice (Scotland) Act 1995, which repealed s.141(1)(b) of the 1975 Act and now effectively entitles the prosecutor to comment upon such a failure.

Subs. (2)

The scope of the prosecutor's questions in relation to the charge itself are restricted to eliciting whether the accused will advance any sort of defence at the examination. A greater (but still limited) latitude is available to the procurator fiscal when the accused is alleged to have uttered an extrajudicial admission: see the discussion relative to subs.(3) below.

It is of note that subs.(2) is explicitly drafted more broadly than was s.20A(1)(a) of the 1975 Act. As well as the generally understood defences of self-defence, alibi, incrimination and consent it could be argued that temporary insanity, certain forms of automatism, lawful authority or coercion could each equally constitute a defence.

Once a possible defence is stated at judicial examination subs.(10) below places a limited obligation upon the Crown to investigate its substance. Note, however, that there is no *compulsitor* upon the Crown, and no timescale specified for the conduct of these enquiries or even a duty to report findings to the court. Nonetheless, it would be imprudent to ignore this provision if only because it would then be open to the accused at his trial to found upon any lack of diligence in investigating the defence tendered. It is submitted that in terms of subs.(2)(b) the fiscal can justifiably question the accused to obtain sufficient information to allow the Crown to fulfil the statutory duty imposed by subs.(10), namely, investigation of the defence revealed by the examination. During the Committee stage of the Bill the Lord Advocate reiterated that if the procurator fiscal discovered evidence at this stage of proceedings which might assist the accused, then it would be the Crown's duty to make the fact known to the defence (*Hansard*, January 12, 1995, Vol. 560, col. 369).

In the absence of a statutory duty to disclose the outcome of an investigation of any stated defence, or any sanction upon the Crown for failing to investigate, the Appeal Court held in *McDermott v HM Advocate*, 2000 S.L.T. 366 that the provisions in subss.(2) and (10) were administrative in character. The obligation upon the Crown to disclose to the defence evidence which is potentially favourable to an accused's case is stated in *McLeod, Petr*, 1998 S.L.T. 233. Refer also to *Sinclair v HM Advocate*, 2005 S.L.T. 553, a judgment of the Judicial Committee of the Privy Council which considers the topic of disclosure in Scots criminal procedure in conjunction with Art.6 obligations under the European Convention for the Protection of Human Rights And Fundamental Freedoms. Broadly, *Sinclair* places the onus upon the Crown to volunteer and disclose material proactively to the defence rather than reacting to requests for disclosure as occurred in *McLeod*. In *McDermott* the trial judge was criticised for reaching the view, in the absence of evidence one way or the other, that the Crown had not complied with s.37, and for leaving the jury to resolve whether the prosecutor's conduct had been prejudicial.

Subs. (3)

In addition to questions about the charge itself and any defence which the accused may then wish to tender as provided by subs.(1) and (2), the fiscal may also examine the accused upon any extrajudicial utterance made by him to, or within earshot of, a police officer. Note that the Crown may choose whether or not to put these alleged words to the accused and may elect not to do so, particularly when the reply is either mixed, self-serving or discloses previous convictions or references to matters not libelled. See *HM Advocate v Cafferty*, 1984 S.C.C.R. 444.

The 1996 Act of Adjournal stipulates that examination about such extrajudicial admissions can only occur if the presiding sheriff has first received a copy of the text of admissions already served on the accused; this does no more than codify the existing practice.

Although the usual procedure is for the procurator fiscal to examine initially upon the charges on the petition and any appropriate defences before questioning about any alleged replies, there is no statutory necessity to follow this chronology; the only requirements are that the "confession", partial or full, must be served upon the accused in written form prior to the examination for questioning to be permitted and the rules of the 1996 Act of Adjournal are obeyed.

Normally the statement of extrajudicial confessions is annexed to the copy petition served on the accused, though this is not a mandatory requirement. It will have to (i) specify the wording averred to have been used by the accused; (ii) identify the police officer in whose hearing the words were uttered and, by inference, the time and place of the event in order to qualify as legitimate material for the purposes of subs.(3). Where the accused has been interviewed on tape by the police this is usually indicated on the statement of extrajudicial admissions. When the accused has made a voluntary statement which is incriminating, it is the practice to annex a copy of it to the petition and question him about its contents and the circumstances in which it was made.

All of this raises the intractable issue of what does, or does not, constitute an extrajudicial confession: this is particularly problematical when the statement made is in part self-serving or is a veiled attack on the complainer's character (see *Morrison v HM Advocate*, 1990 S.C.C.R. 235 discussed in the notes to subs.(8) below).

A re-assessment of the scope of *Morrison* and its rubric that a mixed statement was only admissible when lead by the Crown, or by the defence when the Crown did not object, is being undertaken by the Appeal Court. Matters become more complex still, though this barely seems possible, where the trial involves more than one accused. See *McCutcheon v HM Advocate*, 2001 G.W.D. 1–22.

In *McKenzie v HM Advocate*, 1982 S.C.C.R. 544 objection was taken by the agent at the examination, to a reply attributed to the accused on the grounds that it was not a confession. The sheriff allowed questioning by the fiscal and permitted the agent to clarify at the conclusion of the questioning. It is submitted that there is no *locus* for such an objection by the agent at this stage in proceedings; it is then solely a matter for judicial discretion. The appropriate time for objection is if, or when, either party (or a co-accused) seeks to found upon the transcript of judicial examination at the trial. The fairness and admissibility of the transcript can be properly weighed then and, in any event, such an approach excludes the possibility of the trial judge being called upon to review the earlier decision of the sheriff who presided at the examination. See also *Moran v HM Advocate*, 1990 S.C.C.R. 40; 1990 S.L.T. 756.

Subss. (5), (6) and (7)

Judicial examination is not an opportunity for the Crown to cross-examine the accused. Subsection (5) underlines the role of the sheriff to ensure the fair conduct of proceedings. The accused must be informed by the sheriff (i) of the right to consult the solicitor appearing with him prior to answering questions and (ii) that the Crown will be under an obligation to investigate, so far as practicable, any defence disclosed during the examination. It is submitted that a judicial failure to admonish the accused with due regard to subss.(6), (8) and (10) would render the resultant transcript of proceedings inadmissible.

Note however that the solicitor's role in the examination is reactive; he may not initiate a consultation with his client during questioning by the fiscal and may only ask questions of his client as permitted by subs.(7). While that subsection does not expressly stipulate it, the practice has developed of giving leave to the defence solicitor to question at the conclusion of the fiscal's examination.

The object of judicial examination is to cause the accused at the earliest stage in proceedings to state his defence both as a means of focusing the issues and as a deterrent to the introduction of spurious lines of defence at the trial. While the accused is entitled to keep his own counsel at the examination, this may work to his disadvantage at his trial when other parties can utilise the provisions of subs.(8) to undermine his defence case. However, the 1996 Act of Adjournal, r.5.5(4) imposes possible limits upon the freedom of others to comment upon contrasts in the accused's position at judicial examination and in his evidence at trial. It is now a matter for the trial judge to consider whether such comments can be made to the jury by other parties, or the judge himself, having regard to the terms of the original petition charges and the libel now before the court. To assist in the judge's deliberations, the prosecutor must be able to provide the original petition or a certified copy.

A number of issues flow from this reform; first, it would seem to be good practice for the Crown as a matter of course to include a certified copy of the petition and, by implication, a certified copy of the written record of any extrajudicial admissions referred to during the examination. Secondly the provision suggests that before either the prosecutor or other accused invoke the right to comment under s.36(8), they should seek the authority of the presiding judge to do so. Thirdly, if the judge resolves to comment it would seem sensible, to say the least, to refer to the original petition and canvass the views of the parties, including the co-accused, before hand and outwith the presence of the jury.

Support for this reading can be found in Ch.25 of the 1996 Rules, for r.25.1(3) permits the trial judge to release copies to the jury of any written record of confession (appropriately edited) referred to during judicial examination.

It must be stressed that subs.(8) only comes into play when the accused leads evidence, from himself or other witnesses, at his trial. An accused who has declined to comment at examination and has not led evidence at trial is outwith the subsection's scope. See *Walker v HM Advocate*, 1985 S.C.C.R. 150 and *Dempsey v HM Advocate*, 1995 S.C.C.R. 431.

In *Walker* it was held on appeal that the statutory provisions of the 1975 Act, s.20A(5) were wrongly applied, the accused having maintained silence throughout and left the Crown to prove its case. Even then note, that while it was conceded that the trial judge had misdirected the jury, this did not in the circumstances, constitute a miscarriage of justice. Nonetheless, where the judge does direct the attention of the jury to the operation of subs.(8) this must be done with restraint and without undue emphasis; see *McEwan v HM Advocate*, 1990 S.C.C.R. 401.

It is common for an accused during examination to decline to answer questions and to state that this has been done on the advice of his solicitor. This stock reply does not protect an accused from unfavourable comment should he choose to lead evidence at his trial. Thus the judge's direction in *Gilmour v HM Advocate*, 1982 S.C.C.R. 590 at 604, that such conduct at judicial examination could not be considered as relevant evidence is much too favourable to the accused. See *Alexander v HM Advocate*, 1988 S.C.C.R. 542.

Subsection (8) does not deal with the potentially intractable situation where an accused, at judicial examination, responds to questioning by providing a self-serving account and founds upon it at trial without leading further evidence. Just such a situation arose in *Morrison*, above, a seven judge decision, which deals (it is hoped) definitively with the approach to mixed statements, or qualified admissions, including extrajudicial confessions. The law is stated at 247F to 248E and is discussed fully by Dr D.B. Griffiths, in *Confessions* (Edinburgh 1994) at pp.90 to 97: Dr Griffiths' comment that *Morrison* "is a difficult case and is always going to remain so", defies contradiction. *Morrison* was revisited in *McCutcheon v HM Advocate*, 2002 S.L.T. 27. Here the Appeal Court upheld Crown objections, approved during the trial, that McC, who had declined to give evidence in his defence, could not seek to have his exculpatory utterances put before the court through the medium of another witness whose sole purpose was to repeat those denials.

Prudence dictates that at trial the presiding judge would do well simply to echo and endorse the "Morrison formula" cited above. See *Smith v HM Advocate*, 1994 S.C.C.R. 72; *Pickthall v HM Advocate*, 1998 S.L.T. 117 (conviction quashed), *MacLeod v HM Advocate*, 1995 S.L.T. 145, *Harley v HM Advocate*, 1995 S.C.C.R. 595 *Geddes v HM Advocate*, 1997 S.L.T. 392 (convictions upheld despite failure to follow *Morrison* explicitly). *Hoy v HM Advocate* 1997 S.L.T. 26 in which the trial judge consciously declined to make a *Morrison* direction, authority was granted for a retrial. Opinion has been reserved however as to whether founding upon exculpatory answers given in the course of a judicial examination would be sufficient to meet the burden of proof resting upon an accused in charges under the Prevention of Corruption Act 1906 (c.34) (*Ridler v HM Advocate*, 1995 S.C.C.R. 655).

Section 32 of the Criminal Justice (Scotland) Act 1995 which repealed s.141(1)(b) of the 1975 Act now entitles the prosecutor, but not co-accused, to comment upon the accused's failure to lead evidence. The removal of this long-standing prohibition introduces a much more telling weapon into the prosecutor's armoury than s.36(8) of the 1995 Act allows. The long-recognised right of the trial judge to comment upon the accused's failure to give evidence under oath was upheld in *Handley v HM Advocate*, 1998 S.L.T. 1104. Note that subs.(8) entitles a co-accused, where an accused leads evidence, to comment upon any refusal to answer by the accused at judicial examination. Care is necessary since a co-accused should not comment upon the failure of an accused to lead evidence (see for example *Shevlin v HM Advocate*, 2002 S.L.T. 739).

Subss. (10) and (11)

See the discussion in the notes to subs.(2) above.

Act of Adjournal

Additional provisions are found in the Act of Adjournal (Criminal Procedure Rules) 1996, Chs 5 and 25. See particularly r.5.5.

Judicial examination: record of proceedings

37.—(1) The prosecutor shall provide for a verbatim record to be made by means of shorthand notes or by mechanical means of all questions to and answers and declarations by the accused in examination, or further examination, under sections 35 and 36 of this Act.

(2) A shorthand writer shall—

(a) sign the shorthand notes taken by him of the questions, answers and declarations mentioned in subsection (1) above and certify the notes as being complete and correct; and

(b) retain the notes.

(3) A person recording the questions, answers and declarations mentioned in subsection (1) above by mechanical means shall—

(a) certify that the record is true and complete;

(b) specify in the certificate the proceedings to which the record relates; and

(c) retain the record.

(4) The prosecutor shall require the person who made the record mentioned in subsection (1) above, or such other competent person as he may specify, to make a transcript of the record in legible form; and that person shall—

(a) comply with the requirement;

(b) certify the transcript as being a complete and correct transcript of the record purporting to have been made and certified, and in the case of shorthand notes signed, by the person who made the record; and

(c) send the transcript to the prosecutor.

(5) A transcript certified under subsection (4)(b) above shall, subject to section 38(1) of this Act, be deemed for all purposes to be a complete and correct record of the questions, answers and declarations mentioned in subsection (1) above.

(6) Subject to subsections (7) to (9) below, within 14 days of the date of examination or further examination, the prosecutor shall—

(a) serve a copy of the transcript on the accused examined; and

(b) serve a further such copy on the solicitor (if any) for that accused.

(7) Where at the time of further examination a trial diet is already fixed and the interval between the further examination and that diet is not sufficient to allow of the time limits specified in subsection (6) above and subsection (1) of section 38 of this Act, the sheriff shall (either or both)—

(a) direct that those subsections shall apply in the case with such modifications as to time limits as he shall specify;

(b) subject to subsection (8) below, postpone the trial diet.

(8) Postponement under paragraph (b) of subsection (7) above alone shall only be competent where the sheriff considers that to proceed under paragraph (a) of that subsection alone, or paragraphs (a) and (b) together, would not be practicable.

(9) Any time limit mentioned in subsection (6) above and subsection (1) of section 38 of this Act (including any such time limit as modified by a direction under subsection (7) above) may be extended, in respect of the case, by the High Court; and an application to the High Court for any such extension shall be disposed of by the High Court or any Lord Commissioner of Justiciary in court or in chambers.

(10) A copy of—

(a) a transcript required by paragraph (a) of subsection (6) above to be served on an accused or by paragraph (b) of that subsection to be served on his solicitor; or

(b) a notice required by paragraph (a) of section 38(1) of this Act to be served on an accused or on the prosecutor,

shall be served in such manner as may be prescribed by Act of Adjournal; and a written execution purporting to be signed by the person who served such transcript or notice, together with, where appropriate, the relevant post office receipt shall be sufficient evidence of service of such a copy.

<small>AMENDMENT</small>

Subs. (9) as amended by the Act of Adjournal (Extension of Time Limit for Service of Transcript of Examination) 1998 (S.I. 1998 No. 2635: effective December 1, 1998).

<small>DEFINITION</small>

"prosecutor": s.307(1).

<small>GENERAL NOTE</small>

This section provides that the record of proceedings at any judicial declaration or judicial examination is to be noted in shorthand or mechanically recorded. In either case it then becomes the responsibility of the prosecutor to effect service upon the accused and his agent of a transcript of the proceedings duly certified as complete and accurate by the person appointed to transcribe the record by the prosecutor. Service must be effected within 14 days of the hearing unless as subs. (7) allows, a trial diet occurs within that time or either the prosecutor or the accused have in terms of s.38 sought rectification of the transcript: in either of these events the sheriff has power to modify the timescale laid out in subs. (6) or, alternatively, postpone the trial diet. The High Court can review the sheriff's decision.

The Act of Adjournal (Criminal Procedure Rules) Chap. 5 regulates the use of both shorthand and tape transcription: applications for rectification of transcripts are to be in the form specified in these Rules.

In *Robertson v. H.M. Advocate*, 1994 S.C.C.R. 152 the previous provisions under s.20B of the 1975 Act were considered. The appellant by Minute of Notice took objection to the competency of proceedings following failure by the Crown either to record his declaration or to serve it upon him prior to the trial diet: he alleged that this could prejudice his case and nullified any proceedings.

While it is of note that the charge which had formed the subject matter of the petition had not been libelled in the subsequent indictment, and the likelihood of prejudice would be slim, the Appeal Court considered the much more fundamental issue of whether or not the provisions of the section were obligatory (in which event the Crown's non-compliance must result in a nullity) or directory in character.

The court in a majority decision took the latter view but it has to be said that even then that conclusion was reached with little common agreement on either the approach or terminology to be adopted. The best that can be said is that while some statutory provisions are so fundamental that failure to comply creates a nullity, s.20B (or its statutory successor) s.37 of the 1995 Act are not such provisions.

For completeness, following conviction Robertson persisted with claims before the Appeal Court that his defence had been prejudiced by the unavailability of his declaration at trial. Following remit to the Sheriff Principal to investigate it was concluded that the declaration did not relate to the subject matter of the indictment, was entirely exculpatory in nature, and the matter could have been, but had not been, raised in the course of the trial and accordingly could not appropriately be raised on appeal. See *Robertson v. H.M. Advocate*, 1996 S.C.C.R. 243; 1996 G.W.D. 5–254.

Refer to s.278 below which deals with the principles to be applied to use of judicial examination transcripts at any trial.

Act of Adjournal

See the Act of Adjournal (Criminal Procedure Rules) 1996 r.5.2 and Form 5.2 which deal with the record of proceedings. The form to be used for intimation where a trial diet has been postponed for the purpose of s.37(7) is found at Form 5.8.

Judicial examination: rectification of record of proceedings

38.—(1) Subject to subsections (7) to (9) of section 37 of this Act, where notwithstanding the certification mentioned in subsection (5) of that section the accused or the prosecutor is of the opinion that a transcript served under paragraph (a) of subsection (6) of that section contains an error or is incomplete he may—

(a) within 10 days of service under the said paragraph (a), serve notice of such opinion on the prosecutor or as the case may be the accused; and

(b) within 14 days of service under paragraph (a) of this subsection, apply to the sheriff for the error or incompleteness to be rectified,

and the sheriff shall within 7 days of the application hear the prosecutor and the accused in chambers and may authorise rectification.

(2) Where—

(a) the person on whom notice is served under paragraph (a) of subsection (1) above agrees with the opinion to which that notice relates the sheriff may dispense with such hearing;

(b) the accused neither attends, nor secures that he is represented at, such hearing it shall, subject to paragraph (a) above, nevertheless proceed.

(3) In so far as it is reasonably practicable so to arrange, the sheriff who deals with any application made under subsection (1) above shall be the sheriff before whom the examination or further examination to which the application relates was conducted.

(4) Any decision of the sheriff, as regards rectification under subsection (1) above, shall be final.

Definition

"prosecutor": s.307(1).

General Note

The procedure for the rectification of errors in, or addition of materials omitted from, the transcript of judicial examination or any declaration are found in this section. If the parties concur that such rectification or amendment is required, then no hearing is necessary; otherwise the prosecutor is obliged to be represented at any hearing though an accused or his agent need not attend.

Act of Adjournal

See the Act of Adjournal (Criminal Procedure Rules) 1996 particularly r.5.6 and Forms 5.6–A to 5.6–C.

Judicial examination: charges arising in different districts

39.—(1) An accused against whom there are charges in more than one sheriff court district may be brought before the sheriff of any one such district at the instance of the procurator fiscal of such district for examination on all or any of the charges.

(2) Where an accused is brought for examination as mentioned in subsection (1) above, he may be dealt with in every respect as if all of the charges had arisen in the district where he is examined.

(3) This section is without prejudice to the power of the Lord Advocate under section 10 of this Act to determine the court before which the accused shall be tried on such charges.

DEFINITIONS

"procurator fiscal": s.307(1).
"sheriff court district": s.307(1).

GENERAL NOTE

The Lord Advocate's discretion to select which sheriff court shall exercise jurisdiction over offences arising from more than one jurisdiction is preserved by this section.

Committal

Committal until liberated in due course of law

40.—(1) Every petition shall be signed and no accused shall be committed until liberated in due course of law for any crime or offence without a warrant in writing expressing the particular charge in respect of which he is committed.

(2) Any such warrant for imprisonment which either proceeds on an unsigned petition or does not express the particular charge shall be null and void.

(3) The accused shall immediately be given a true copy of the warrant for imprisonment signed by the constable or person executing the warrant before imprisonment or by the prison officer receiving the warrant.

GENERAL NOTE

The petition should correspond with the forms prescribed in Scheds 2 and 3 of the Act or as near as may be; see s.34 above and the general note thereto.

In *Mellors v. Normand*, 1996 S.C.C.R. 500 a bill of suspension was taken against full committal on a petition which had charged M with attempting to defeat the ends of justice by his failure to provide blood and saliva samples and dental impressions in compliance with an earlier warrant; while the bill was refused on its merits as being premature, it is noted that the Crown did not challenge its competency. There is no doubt that if an essential feature of a petition charge (designation of accused, a charge and sufficient information in support of the petition) is absent then a bill to suspend a committal warrant would be competent. No such deficiencies were evident in M's case.

PART V

CHILDREN AND YOUNG PERSONS

Age of criminal responsibility

41. It shall be conclusively presumed that no child under the age of eight years can be guilty of any offence.

DEFINITION

"child": s.307(1) and s.93(2)(b) of the Children (Scotland) Act 1995.

GENERAL NOTE

This provision repeats the presumption of nonage found in the Children and Young Persons (Scotland) Act 1937 (c.37), s.55. See also Macdonald (5th ed., Edinburgh 1948), p. 271.

Consequently proceedings against a child aged less than eight years are incompetent and should be disposed of by means of a plea in bar of trial at a first diet in sheriff and jury proceedings or a preliminary diet in the High Court (refer to ss.71 to 73 below).

Prosecution of children

42.—(1) No child under the age of 16 years shall be prosecuted for any offence except on the instructions of the Lord Advocate, or at his instance; and no court other than the High Court and the sheriff court shall have jurisdiction over a child under the age of 16 years for an offence.

(2) Where a child is charged with any offence, his parent or guardian may in any case, and shall, if he can be found and resides within a reasonable distance, be required to attend at the court before which the case is heard or determined during all the stages of the proceedings, unless the court is satisfied that it would be unreasonable to require his attendance.

(3) Where the child is arrested, the constable by whom he is arrested or the police officer in charge of the police station to which he is brought shall cause the parent or guardian of the child, if he can be found, to be warned to attend at the court before which the child will appear.

(4) For the purpose of enforcing the attendance of a parent or guardian and enabling him to take part in the proceedings and enabling orders to be made against him, rules may be made under section 305 of this Act, for applying, with the necessary adaptations and modifications, such of the provisions of this Act relating to summary proceedings as appear appropriate for the purpose.

(5) The parent or guardian whose attendance is required under this section is—

(a) the parent who has parental responsibilities or parental rights (within the meaning of sections 1(3) and 2(4) respectively of the Children (Scotland) Act 1995) in relation to the child; or

(b) the guardian having actual possession and control of him.

(6) The attendance of the parent of a child shall not be required under this section in any case where the child was before the institution of the proceedings removed from the care or charge of his parent by an order of a court.

(7) Where a child is to be brought before a court, notification of the day and time when, and the nature of the charge on which, the child is to be so brought shall be sent by the chief constable of the area in which the offence is alleged to have been committed to the local authority for the area in which the court will sit.

(8) Where a local authority receive notification under subsection (7) above they shall make such investigations and submit to the court a report which shall contain such information as to the home surroundings of the child as appear to them will assist the court in the disposal of his case, and the report shall contain information, which the appropriate education authority shall have a duty to supply, as to the school record, health and character of the child.

(9) Any child detained in a police station, or being conveyed to or from any criminal court, or waiting before or after attendance in such court, shall be prevented from associating with an adult (not being a relative) who is charged with any offence other than an offence with which the child is jointly charged.

(10) Any female child shall, while detained, being conveyed or waiting as mentioned in subsection (9) above, be kept under the care of a woman.

DEFINITIONS

"child": s.307(1) and s.93(2)(b) of the Children (Scotland) Act 1995.

"constable": s.307(1) and s.51(1) of the Police (Scotland) Act 1967.

"High Court": s.307(1).

"local authority": s.307(1).

"parent or guardian": s.42(5) below and in relation to "guardian" only, note also s.307(1).

GENERAL NOTE

While it is theoretically the case that reports of criminal offences committed by children will be submitted to the procurator fiscal in the first instance, administrative directions from the Lord Advocate instruct that such reports involving child offenders aged under 16 years will, ordinarily, be referred to the principal reporter for his consideration. Even where there are factors which merit the submission of a report to the procurator fiscal, the police are still required in terms of the Children (Scotland) Act 1995 (c.36) to furnish a copy of the report to the appropriate reporter. Thereafter it is a matter for discussion between the procurator fiscal and the reporter whether the case should be retained for criminal prosecution or dealt with under the previously-mentioned Act.

When the case is retained by the procurator fiscal to initiate a prosecution, it is mandatory in terms of subs.(1) that any proceedings must occur in the sheriff court or a higher court. Rule 6.3 of the 1996 Act of Adjournal enacts that criminal proceedings can only be raised by the procurator fiscal who is, of course, required to comply with the Lord Advocate's directions. The spirit of s.15 of the 1995 Act (which enacts special provisions in regard to the detention of a child, and parental access to a child held in custody) is echoed in s.54: subss.(9) and (10) contain provisions to segregate children from adult offenders while remanded in custody or awaiting trial at court. Oddly, it is not deemed necessary to separate the child entirely from adult accused. Subsection (9) stops short of this and permits detention in custody, or in the court precincts, and transportation to or from court appearances, in the company of adult co-accused or relatives (whether the relatives are, or are not, accused persons).

In a similar spirit, s.142 of the Act stipulates that summary proceedings against a child must be held in private and in different rooms, or on different days, from the criminal courts in which adults appear. The sole exception to this rule is when the child appears on the same complaint or petition as an adult accused; in that event the case has to proceed in the usual "adult" court. The corollary of these provisions so far as an adult co-accused is concerned, is that when charged along with a child on a summary complaint he will necessarily appear in the sheriff, not the district, court.

The scope of s.142 (which replaces s.366(1) of the 1975 Act) extends to appearances from custody, cited diets and trials but it has been held to be directory rather than mandatory in character: failure by the court to obtemper its provisions would not nullify any subsequent conviction; see *Heywood v B*, 1993 S.C.C.R. 554. It is likely that the provisions of s.42 would equally be construed as being directory in nature. Similarly the 1996 Act of Adjournal, Rule 6.8 indicates that steps should be taken by the court to avoid children attending hearings from mixing with each other by appropriate scheduling of cases and providing suitable supervision of waiting facilities.

Subss.(3), (7) and (8)

Subsection (3) instructs the police to notify the parent or guardian of the child of the impending court appearance and, wherever practicable, to require parental attendance at the court on the appropriate date. Unreasonable failure to attend the court by a parent or guardian after receipt of such notice can attract criminal penalties and, accordingly, the police should warn of this fact when giving notice of the court date.

Where the child is already in the care of the local authority or has a guardian as a result of a court order, the police are under no duty to advise the parent (defined in subs.(5)(a)) of the proceedings. The date and time of the child's court appearance, and the nature of charges must also be communicated by the police to the local authority within whose boundaries the court is situated. In the event of a finding of guilt, that authority will be responsible for preparing background reports about the child's circumstances for the court.

Act of Adjournal

Refer to Chap.6 of the Act of Adjournal (Criminal Procedure Rules) 1996 for procedural guidance.

Arrangements where children arrested

43.—(1) Where a person who is apparently a child is apprehended, with or without warrant, and cannot be brought forthwith before a sheriff, a police officer of the rank of inspector or above or the officer in charge of the police station to which he is brought, shall inquire into the case, and, subject to subsection (3) below, may liberate him—

(a) on a written undertaking being entered into by him or his parent or guardian that he will attend at a court and at a time specified in the undertaking; or

(b) unconditionally.

(2) An undertaking mentioned in subsection (1) above shall be signed by the child or, as the case may be, the parent or guardian and shall be certified by the officer mentioned in that subsection.

(3) A person shall not be liberated under subsection (1) where—

(a) the charge is one of homicide or other grave crime;

(b) it is necessary in his interest to remove him from association with any reputed criminal or prostitute; or

(c) the officer has reason to believe that his liberation would defeat the ends of justice.

(4) Where a person who is apparently a child having been apprehended is not liberated as mentioned in subsection (1) above, the police officer referred to in that subsection shall cause him to be kept in a place of safety other than a police station until he can be brought before a sheriff unless the officer certifies—

(a) that it is impracticable to do so;

(b) that he is of so unruly a character that he cannot safely be so detained; or

(c) that by reason of his state of health or of his mental or bodily condition it is inadvisable so to detain him,

and the certificate shall be produced to the court before which he is brought.

(5) Where a person who is apparently a child has not been liberated as mentioned in subsection (1) above but has been kept under subsection (4) above, and it is decided not to proceed with the charge against him, a constable shall so inform the Principal Reporter.

(6) Any person, who without reasonable excuse fails to appear at the court and at the time specified in the undertaking entered into by him or on his behalf under subsection (1) above, shall be guilty of an offence, and liable on summary conviction of any charge made against him at the time he was liberated under that subsection in addition to any other penalty which it is competent for the court to impose on him, to a fine not exceeding level 3 on the standard scale.

(7) In any proceedings relating to an offence under this section, a writing, purporting to be such an undertaking as is mentioned in subsection (1) above and bearing to be signed and certified, shall be sufficient evidence of the undertaking given by the accused.

AMENDMENTS

Subss.(1) and (6) substituted by the Crime and Punishment (Scotland) Act 1997 (c.48) s.55 with effect from August 1, 1997 in terms of the Crime and Punishment (Scotland) Act 1997 (Commencement and Transitional Provisions) Order 1997 (SI 1997/1712) para.3.

DEFINITIONS

"child": s.307(1) and s.93(2)(b) of the Children (Scotland) Act 1995.
"parent or guardian": s.42(5) and in relation to "guardian" only also refer to s.307(1).
"place of safety": s.307(1) and s.93(1) of the Children (Scotland) Act 1995.
"Principal Reporter": s.93(1) of the Children (Scotland) Act 1995.

GENERAL NOTE

This section repeats the provisions previously contained in ss.295 and 296 of the 1975 Act with account being taken of the introduction of the Children (Scotland) Act 1995 and small, but significant, changes wrought by the Crime and Punishment (Scotland) Act 1997. It is still to be assumed generally that a child arrested for a criminal offence will be brought before a court without delay, or be liberated on his undertaking, or that of his parent or guardian, to appear at court on a specified date. Subs. (1) as now enacted gives greater discretion to the police to withhold an undertaking. Once an undertaking is entered into, failure to appear at the designated time and place becomes an offence but only in the event of conviction of the original charge which gave rise to the undertaking. The terms of the undertaking can be proved in any proceedings by production of a certified copy of the original form and, it is submitted, that the signatory is in a position of special capacity. While the Act does not specify the form the undertaking should take, subs.(7) clearly envisages that it should be in writing.

In more serious cases as defined in subs.(3), the first effort should be to bring the child before a sheriff forthwith. If that is not practicable, then the senior police officer involved must first endeavour to obtain accommodation for the child in a place of safety, namely a local authority residential establishment, a community home, a hospital, surgery or "other suitable place" whose occupier is willing to take in the child.

Note that while the statutory definition of "a place of safety" in the Children (Scotland) Act. s.93(1) includes a police station, this does not hold good for the purposes of s.43(4) of the 1995 Act— police stations are expressly excluded as acceptable accommodation for this purpose. The reason for this apparent anomaly is found later in subs.(4) which stipulates the conditions which must prevail before a child can be held in police custody pending his appearance before the court: broadly, if it is not practical to convey the child to a suitable place of safety or such a place is not available, or the child's character is unruly and militates against his safe detention in an available place of safety, or there are medical grounds which raise concern for his well-being, then continued detention in a police station will be justified. The senior police officer must then certify the reasons for resorting to detention of the child in police custody rather than the preferred option of a place of safety and that certificate must be produced to the court when the child first appears. It will be noted that during such a period of detention, the police are still obliged to keep the child segregated from adult prisoners (see the notes to s.42(9) above).

If the procurator fiscal decides not to proceed with charges against the child, subss.(6) and (7) contain saving provisions to enable the child to be detained pending initial investigation by the principal reporter (see s.56(1) and (6) of the Children (Scotland) Act 1995) and consideration if necessary by a children's hearing within seven days.

Detention of children

44.—(1) Where a child appears before the sheriff in summary proceedings and pleads guilty to, or is found guilty of, an offence to which this section applies, the sheriff may order that he be detained in residential accommodation provided under Part II of the Children (Scotland) Act 1995 by the appropriate local authority for such period not exceeding one year as may be specified in the order in such place (in any part of the United Kingdom) as the local authority may, from time to time, consider appropriate.

(2) This section applies to any offence (other than, if the child is under the age of 16 years, an offence under section 9(1) of the Antisocial Behaviour etc. (Scotland) Act 2004 (asp 8) or that section as applied by section 234AA(11) of this Act) in respect of which it is competent to impose imprisonment on a person of the age of 21 years or more.

(3) Where a child in respect of whom an order is made under this section is detained by the appropriate local authority, that authority shall have the same powers and duties in respect of the child as they would have if he were subject to a supervision requirement.

(4) Where a child in respect of whom an order is made under this section is also subject to a supervision requirement ... the supervision requirement shall be of no effect during any period for which he is required to be detained under the order.

(5) The Secretary of State may, by regulations made by statutory instrument subject to annulment in pursuance of a resolution of either House of Parliament, make such provision as he considers necessary as regards the detention in secure accommodation of children in respect of whom orders have been made under this section.

(6) [...]

(7) [...]

(8) [...]

(9) [...]

(10) Where a local authority consider it appropriate that a child in respect of whom an order has been made under subsection (1) above should be detained in a place in any part of the United Kingdom outside Scotland, the order shall be a like authority as in Scotland to the person in charge of the place to restrict the child's liberty to such an extent as that person may consider appropriate having regard to the terms of the order.

(11) In this section—

"the appropriate local authority" means—

(a) where the child usually resides in Scotland, the local authority for the area in which he usually resides;

(b) in any other case, the local authority for the area in which the offence was committed; and

"secure accommodation" has the meaning assigned to it in Part II of the Children (Scotland) Act 1995.

AMENDMENT

Subss.(6), (7), (8), (9) deleted by the Crime and Punishment (Scotland) Act 1997 (c.48), s.62(1) and Sch.1, para.21(3) with effect from August 1, 1997 in terms of the Crime and Punishment (Scotland) Act 1997 (Commencement and Transitional Provisions) Order 1997 (SI 1997/1712), art.3.

Subss.(4) and (10) as amended by the above Act.

Subs.(2) as amended by the Antisocial Behaviour etc. (Scotland) Act 2004, s.10. Brought into force on October 28, 2004 by the Antisocial Behaviour etc. (Scotland) Act 2004 (Commencement and Savings) Order2004 (SSI 2004/420 (C.31)).

DEFINITIONS

"appropriate local authority": s.44(11).
"child": s.307(1) and s.93(2)(b) of the Children (Scotland) Act 1995.
"offence": s.307(1).
"residential accommodation": s.307(1).
"secure accommodation": s.44(11) and s.93(1) of the Children (Scotland) Act 1995.
"supervision requirement": s.307(1) and s.70(1) of the Children (Scotland) Act 1995.

GENERAL NOTE

This section enables a sheriff sitting summarily to impose a term of detention in residential accommodation of up to one year when an offence, for which imprisonment could competently be imposed upon an adult, is held or admitted to have been committed by a child. The sheriff may then consider immediate use of his powers under s.44 or, in the first instance (and more usually), refer the case under s.49 of the Act to the Principal Reporter for the advice of a children's hearing: when the child is already under a supervision requirement, s.49(3)(b) stipulates that the advice of a children's hearing must be obtained.

Only a minority of cases will be likely to merit a disposal in terms of s.44 without first obtaining the advice of a children's hearing. The use of s.44 powers is perhaps an indication that the paramount consideration in sentencing has been public safety and the preservation of good order rather than the well-being of the child. Most cases involving juveniles found guilty of offences will continue to require the advice of a children's hearing.

Statutory duties of local authority

When the sheriff either with, or less usually without, advice of a children's hearing imposes detention under s.44, it is then the duty of the Scottish local authority within whose area the child lives, to provide such accommodation at a place within the United Kingdom selected by the authority.

However if the child is not ordinarily resident in Scotland then this responsibility falls upon the local authority within whose area the offence was committed. It is not explicitly stated in the Act, but it seems reasonable to assume that, in the event of offences being committed in a number of jurisdictions, responsibility for providing suitable accommodation would rest with the local authority within whose area the sheriff court making the order was situated.

Subsection (3) provides that the powers and responsibilities of a local authority given charge of such a child will be the same as those regulating supervision requirements and reference to s.70(4) of the Children (Scotland) Act shows that this includes such restrictions on the child's liberty as are deemed appropriate.

Where supervision requirements are imposed by a children's hearing, the hearing can direct that the child resides in residential accommodation or (in more extreme cases) in such accommodation but under secure conditions (see s.70(3) and (8) of the Children (Scotland) Act 1995). Subsection (1) of the 1995 Act states that the court can order that the child "be detained" in residential accommodation, while subs.(5) deals with the regulation of secure accommodation. It is unfortunate that the same phraseology has not been employed consistently in both pieces of legislation, but the provisions of subs.(6) suggest that what is envisaged is placement of the child in secure accommodation and not simply local authority residential care.

Subsection (10) permits the Scottish local authority exercising jurisdiction to remit the child into the custody of persons elsewhere in the United Kingdom when this is felt appropriate. The persons then assuming responsibility for the charge of the child have the same duties and powers as would be vested in an individual under s.44 in Scotland.

Early release provisions and effect of further offences

In a manner similar to s.16 of the Prisoners and Criminal Proceedings (Scotland) Act 1993 (c.9) (which deals with the commission of offences by released prisoners during remission), subs.(6) affords a child an opportunity of remission of at least half of the period of detention. This concession can be rescinded if it is established that a further offence has been committed during the remission period and the timescale of the original detention order has not expired (in practice it may be difficult to re-apply the unexpired portion of the detention period since the sentence imposed under s.44 by the sheriff may have been relatively short).

In the event of re-offending being established the court can apply a full range of disposals but subs.(8) makes it competent to return the child to the residential accommodation from which he was earlier released there to serve the unexpired portion of that earlier detention, calculated according to subs.(8). This re-imposition of the order can be instead of, or in addition to, any disposal resulting from the later offence which had been committed during the early release period. Subsection (9) adds that the remaining portion of the original detention order may be served prior to, or concurrent with, the period of detention imposed for the later offence.

Section 44 and existing supervision requirements

Where the child appearing before the court is already the subject of a supervision requirement made by a children's hearing, subs.(4) provides for the suspension of that requirement until the appropriate period of detention has been served by the child.

On release from detention (either at the expiry of the full term of detention imposed by the court, or earlier in accordance with subs.(6)(a)), the pre-existing supervision requirement can be resumed. However, even when detention has been imposed by the court, the local authority still has a statutory duty to review the case of any child subject to a supervision requirement (see s.72(6) of the Children (Scotland) Act 1995) and has a discretionary power under the 1995 Act to conduct such a review for children detained by way of a s.44 order—see subs.(6)(b). Indeed, theoretically, such a s.44 review could constitute the first contact between the hearing and the child offender since, as was noted earlier, the statutory obligation upon the sentencing sheriff to seek the advice of a children's hearing before imposing a period of detention upon the child only applies to children who were already subject to a current supervision requirement.

When reviewing the case of a child detained under a s.44 order, the hearing may, following subs.(6) discharge it altogether or vary its terms once due regard has been paid to both the interests of the child and the protection of the public.

Security for child's good behaviour

45.—(1) Where a child has been charged with an offence the court may order his parent or guardian to give security for his co-operation in securing the child's good behaviour.

(2) Subject to subsection (3) below, an order under this section shall not be made unless the parent or guardian has been given the opportunity of being heard.

(3) Where a parent or guardian has been required to attend and fails to do so, the court may make an order under this section.

(4) Any sum ordered to be paid by a parent or guardian on the forfeiture of any security given under this section may be recovered from him by civil diligence or imprisonment in like manner as if the order had been made on the conviction of the parent or guardian of the offence with which the child was charged.

(5) In this section "parent" means either of the child's parents, if that parent has parental responsibilities or parental rights (within the meaning of sections 1(3) and 2(4) respectively of the Children (Scotland) Act 1995) in relation to him.

DEFINITIONS

"child": s.307(1) and s.93(2)(b) of the Children (Scotland) Act 1995.
"offence": s.307(1).
"parent": s.45(5) and ss.1(3), 2(4) and 3(5) of the Children (Scotland) Act 1995.
"guardian": s.307(1).

GENERAL NOTE

This section permits the court to require caution to be found by the parent or *de facto* guardian of the child as a surety for parental co-operation in assuring the future good conduct of the child. Such a condition can only be imposed after the parent or guardian has been given an opportunity to be heard by the court, but it has been ruled unnecessary for a formal citation to attend there to have been served upon him; notification made by a police officer would probably suffice. See *White v. Jeans* (1911) 6 Adam 489 and *Montgomery v. Grey* (1915) 7 Adam 681. Note that subs. (2) does not stipulate that the parent must have been heard, only that the opportunity to be heard has been given. The court under subs. (3) can order attendance by the parent or guardian and require a finding of security, even in the absence of the person concerned. Failure by the parent or guardian to ensure the orderly conduct of the child can result in forfeiture of the amount of security. This can be recovered by civil diligence or by the imprisonment of the guarantor.

Presumption and determination of age of child

46.—(1) Where a person charged with an offence whose age is not specified in the indictment or complaint in relation to that offence is brought before a court other than for the purpose of giving evidence, and it appears to the court that he is a child, the court shall make due enquiry as to the age of that person, and for that purpose shall take such evidence as may be forthcoming at the hearing of the case, and the age presumed or declared by the court to be the age of that person shall, for the purposes of this Act or the Children and Young Persons (Scotland) Act 1937, be deemed to be the true age of that person.

(2) The court in making any inquiry in pursuance of subsection (1) above shall have regard to the definition of child for the purposes of this Act.

(3) Without prejudice to section 255A of this Act, where in an indictment or complaint for—

(a) an offence under the Children and Young Persons (Scotland) Act 1937;

(b) any of the offences mentioned in paragraphs 3 and 4 of Schedule 1 to this Act; or

(c) an offence under section 1, 10(1) to (3) or 12 of the Criminal Law (Consolidation) (Scotland) Act 1995,

it is alleged that the person by or in respect of whom the offence was committed was a child or was under or had attained any specified age, and he appears to the court to have been at the date of the commission of the alleged offence a child, or to have been under or to have attained the specified age, as the case may be, he shall for the purposes of this Act or the Children and Young Persons (Scotland) Act 1937 or Part I of the Criminal Law (Consolidation) (Scotland) Act 1995 be presumed at that date to have been a child or to have been under or to have attained that age, as the case may be, unless the contrary is proved.

(4) Where, in an indictment or complaint for an offence under the Children and Young Persons (Scotland) Act 1937 or any of the offences mentioned in Schedule 1 to this Act, it is alleged that the person in respect of whom the offence was committed was a child or was a young person, it shall not be a defence to prove that the person alleged to have been a child was a young person or the person alleged to have been a young person was a child in any case where the acts constituting the alleged offence would equally have been an offence if committed in respect of a young person or child respectively.

(5) An order or judgement of the court shall not be invalidated by any subsequent proof that—

(a) the age of a person mentioned in subsection (1) above has not been correctly stated to the court; or

(b) the court was not informed that at the material time the person was subject to a supervision requirement or that his case had been referred to a children's hearing by virtue of regulations made under the Children (Scotland) Act 1995 for the purpose of giving effect to orders made in different parts of the United Kingdom.

(6) Where it appears to the court that a person mentioned in subsection (1) above has attained the age of 17 years, he shall for the purposes of this Act or the Children and Young Persons (Scotland) Act 1937 be deemed not to be a child.

(7) In subsection (3) above, references to a child (other than a child charged with an offence) shall be construed as references to a child under the age of 17 years; but except as aforesaid references in this section to a child shall be construed as references to a child within the meaning of section 307 of this Act.

AMENDMENT

Subss. (1) and (3) inserted by the Crime and Punishment (Scotland) Act 1997 (c. 48) s.62(1) and Sched. 1, para. 21(4) with effect from August 1, 1997 by the Crime and Punishment (Scotland) Act 1997 (Commencement and Transitional Provisions) Order 1997 (S.I. 1997 No. 1712) para. 3.

DEFINITIONS

"child": s.307(1) and s.93(2)(b) of the Children (Scotland) Act 1995. Note that a more restricted definition is employed in relation to subs. (3) only by virtue of subs. (7).

"offence": s.307(1).

GENERAL NOTE

This section repeats the provisions found in the 1975 Act as amended and, in effect, contains saving provisions to prevent proceedings in which children are involved either as witnesses or as accused, being invalidated on account of error as to a child's age. The savings only operate to cure a want of procedure and cannot cure a nullity (note that in addition to the provisions of s.46 which relate specifically to children, the 1995 Act, s.307(7) contains a general saving presumption covering adult persons whose age becomes a material factor during criminal proceedings).

Subss. (1), (5) and (6)

The subsections relate to the age of child offenders appearing before the court and extend to children aged under 16 years, and to any youth up to 18 years of age who at the time of appearing before the court was already the subject of a supervision requirement.

The court should if possible question the child as a means of establishing his age and assess the age by reference to his appearance. Additionally if evidence is led, that too can be scrutinised for indications of the offender's age. The court can then legitimately hold the offender's age to be established and consider the options for disposal of the case if the offence is admitted or proved. Note that if it is concluded on the basis of all the available material that the offender is 17 years old and it is not disclosed that he is subject to local authority supervision, the court can lawfully treat him as a young offender. Subsection (5) enacts that findings or orders pronounced by the court in circumstances where the court has had to deduce the child's age will not be voided if it is subsequently discovered that the court was misled.

Subss. (3) and (7)

These subsections apply when a child is either accused of an offence or is the victim of an offence. The effect of subs. (7) is to distinguish between those who meet the statutory definition of a "child" as promulgated by the 1995 Act and those who fulfil the narrower statutory definition of a "child" found in the Children and Young Persons (Scotland) Act 1937. In relation to the offences specified in Sched. 1 to the 1995 Act: in the first case an offender can be aged 17 years or more and continue to be treated as a "child" within the meaning of the 1995 Act provided he is still the subject of a supervision order. However, as a victim the complainer is to be regarded as a child only until his seventeenth birthday is attained. A rebuttable presumption exists that the complainer is a child in the statutory offences specified in subs. (3) was a child at the time of the incident libelled. Similarly where it is averred in a libel that the accused was a "child" in terms of the 1995 Act's statutory definition at the time of committing an offence, and this allegation appears to be confirmed by his bearing and physical appearance, it will be presumed that the offender's age has been established.

Subs. (4)

This subsection prevents the introduction of purely technical defences in cases involving victims who are either children or young persons.

When charged with contravening either of the statutory provisions specified in relation to a child or a young person, an accused cannot base a defence upon a discrepancy between the age of the victim, as stated in the libel, and the actuality when, in either case, an offence would have been committed.

The amendment introduced to subs. (1) by the Crime and Punishment (Scotland) Act 1997 has the effect of removing the court's duty to enquire into the age of a child when his age has been specified in the complaint or indictment. A further presumption as to proof of age, of broader application to witnesses, has been introduced into the 1995 Act as s.255A.

Restriction on report of proceedings involving children

47.—(1) Subject to subsection (3) below, no newspaper report of any proceedings in a court shall reveal the name, address or school, or include any particulars calculated to lead to the identification, of any person under the age of 16 years concerned in the proceedings, either—

    (a) as being a person against or in respect of whom the proceedings are taken; or

    (b) as being a witness in the proceedings.

(2) Subject to subsection (3) below, no picture which is, or includes, a picture of a person under the age of 16 years concerned in proceedings as mentioned in subsection (1) above shall be published in any newspaper in a context relevant to the proceedings.

(3) The requirements of subsections (1) and (2) above shall be applied in any case mentioned in any of the following paragraphs to the extent specified in that paragraph—

    (a) where a person under the age of 16 years is concerned in the proceedings as a witness only and no one against whom the proceedings are taken is under the age of 16 years, the requirements shall not apply unless the court so directs;

    (b) where, at any stage of the proceedings, the court, if it is satisfied that it is in the public interest so to do, directs that the requirements (including the requirements as applied by a direction under paragraph (a) above) shall be dispensed with to such extent as the court may specify; and

(c) where the Secretary of State, after completion of the proceedings, if satisfied as mentioned in paragraph (b) above, by order dispenses with the requirements to such extent as may be specified in the order.

(4) This section shall, with the necessary modifications, apply in relation to sound and television programmes included in a programme service (within the meaning of the Broadcasting Act 1990) as it applies in relation to newspapers.

(5) A person who publishes matter in contravention of this section shall be guilty of an offence and liable on summary conviction to a fine not exceeding level 4 of the standard scale.

(6) In this section, references to a court shall not include a court in England, Wales or Northern Ireland.

DEFINITION

"witness": s.307(1).

GENERAL NOTE

There is a general prohibition upon identifying anyone involved in criminal proceedings as a victim, a witness or an accused when that person is aged less than 16 years of age. The prohibition is intended to prevent the publication or broadcasting of the person's particulars, home address or educational background as well as any details of the circumstances of the case which would be sufficient to establish this information. It extends to photographs of the child, but not of other persons however closely related to the child. Such prohibitions remain in force until the child reaches 16 years of age. See *Caledonian Newspapers, Petrs*, 1995 S.C.C.R. 576 and the general discussion there of the scope of s.169 of the 1975 Act, whose terms are echoed by s.47 of the 1995 Act.

In interpreting the phrase "proceedings in a court" as used in this section and which arose in reporting of the Jodi Jones murder case, the court applied a literal, and strict, construction which was held not to apply to the reporting of the arrest by means of a petition warrant of a murder suspect then aged under 16 years of age. The court declined to provide any wider guidance as to the meaning of the phrase (*Frame v Aberdeen Journals Ltd*, 2005 S.L.T. 949; 2005 S.C.C.R. 579).

Subsection (3) permits a relaxation of this prohibition where; (i) the accused is older than 16 years and the child appears as a witness only, not as a victim, though even here it must be noted that the court can direct that the provisions of subs.(1) are to apply; (ii) the court decides during the proceedings that it is in the public interest to identify the person concerned and stipulates the extent of material which may be published or broadcast; (iii) the Secretary of State decides after proceedings are concluded that it is in the public interest for such information, as specified, to be disseminated.

Note that the Act of Adjournal (Criminal Procedure Rules), r.6.9 requires the court to specify the persons whose identities are to be protected or, alternatively may be revealed, along with suitable directions in that regard.

For an example of the application of a s.47 order see *Urquhart v Mackenzie*, 2004 G.W.D. 21–454.

Extent

These provisions do not extend to reports of proceedings arising outwith Scotland. The section does apply to any report of such Scottish proceedings published or broadcast in Scotland or elsewhere in Great Britain. The penalties for contravening s.47 are found in subs.(5).

Act of Adjournal

See the Act of Adjournal (Criminal Procedure Rules) 1996, r.6.7 for procedural directions.

Power to refer certain children to reporter

48.—(1) A court by or before which a person is convicted of having committed an offence to which this section applies may refer—

(a) a child in respect of whom an offence mentioned in paragraph (a) or (b) of subsection (2) below has been committed; or

(b) any child who is, or who is likely to become, a member of the same household as the person who has committed an offence mentioned in paragraph (b) or (c) of that subsection or the person in respect of whom the offence so mentioned was committed,

to the Principal Reporter, and certify that the offence shall be a ground established for the purposes of Chapter 3 of Part II of the Children (Scotland) Act 1995.

(2) This section applies to an offence—

(a) under section 21 of the Children and Young Persons (Scotland) Act 1937;

(b) mentioned in Schedule 1 to this Act; or

(c) in respect of a person aged 17 years or over which constitutes the crime of incest.

DEFINITIONS

"offence": s.307(1).
"Principal Reporter": s.93(1) of the Children (Scotland) Act 1995.

GENERAL NOTE

Section 48 entitles the court before which a person is convicted of an offence specified in subs.(2) to take immediate account of the harm done to the child victim, or the risk, or potential risk, of harm to any child who stays or may stay in the same household as the offender. This power also extends to the households of persons convicted of incest.

With a view to preserving the moral and physical well-being of such children, the court is empowered to certify the grounds for a supervision order to be established, without there being any need for a children's hearing to be constituted to consider the matter. The task of the hearing is confined to consideration in terms of ss.69 and 70 of the Children (Scotland) Act 1995, of the measures necessary to safeguard the welfare of the child or children.

Reference or remit to children's hearing

49.—(1) Where a child who is not subject to a supervision requirement pleads guilty to, or is found guilty of, an offence the court—

(a) instead of making an order on that plea or finding, may remit the case to the Principal Reporter to arrange for the disposal of the case by a children's hearing; or

(b) on that plea or finding may request the Principal Reporter to arrange a children's hearing for the purposes of obtaining their advice as to the treatment of the child.

(2) Where a court has acted in pursuance of paragraph (b) of subsection (1) above, the court, after consideration of the advice received from the children's hearing may, as it thinks proper, itself dispose of the case or remit the case as mentioned in paragraph (a) of that subsection.

(3) Where a child who is subject to a supervision requirement pleads guilty to, or is found guilty of, an offence the court dealing with the case if it is—

(a) the High Court, may; and

(b) the sheriff or district court, shall,

request the Principal Reporter to arrange a children's hearing for the purpose of obtaining their advice as to the treatment of the child, and on consideration of that advice may, as it thinks proper, itself dispose of the case or remit the case as mentioned in subsection (1)(a) above except that where section 51A of the Firearms Act 1968 or section 29 of theViolent Crime Reduction Act 2006 applies it shall itself dispose of the case.

(4) Subject to any appeal against any decision to remit made under subsection (1)(a) or (7)(b) below, where a court has remitted a case to the Principal Reporter

under this section, the jurisdiction of the court in respect of the child shall cease, and his case shall stand referred to a children's hearing.

(5) Nothing in this section shall apply to a case in respect of an offence the sentence for which is fixed by law.

(6) Where a person who is—

(a) not subject to a supervision requirement;

(b) over the age of 16; and

(c) not within six months of attaining the age of 18,

is charged summarily with an offence and pleads guilty to, or has been found guilty of, the offence the court may request the Principal Reporter to arrange a children's hearing for the purpose of obtaining their advice as to the treatment of the person.

(7) On consideration of any advice obtained under subsection (6) above, the court may, as it thinks proper—

(a) itself dispose of the case; or

(b) where the hearing have so advised, remit the case to the Principal Reporter for the disposal of the case by a children's hearing.

AMENDMENTS

Subs.(4) inserted by the Crime and Punishment (Scotland) Act 1997, s.23(a) with effect from August 1, 1997 in terms of the Crime and Punishment (Scotland) Act (Commencement and Transitional Provisions) Order 1997 (SI 1997/1712), art.3.

Subs.(3)(b) inserted by the Crime and Disorder Act 1998 (c.37), Sch.8, para.118 (effective September 30, 1998: SI 1998/2327).

Subs.(3) as amended by the Criminal Justice Act 2003 (c.44), s.290(2). Brought into force on January 22, 2004 by the Criminal Justice Act 2003 (Commencement No.2 and Saving Provisions) Order 2004 (SI 2004/81 (C.2)).

Section 49 amended by the Violent Crime Reduction Act 2006 (c.38), s.49 and Sch.1 para.4(2

DEFINITIONS

"child": s.307(1) and s.93(2)(b) of the Children (Scotland) Act 1995.
"children's hearing": s.93(1) of the Children (Scotland) Act 1995.
"High Court": s.307(1).
"offence": s.307(1).
"Principal Reporter": s.93(1) of the Children (Scotland) Act 1995.
"supervision requirement": s.307(1) and ss.70(1) and 93(1) of the Children (Scotland) Act 1995.

GENERAL NOTE

When a child not currently the subject of a supervision requirement admits, or is held to have committed an offence, the court effectively has three options; proceeding to an immediate disposal of the case, or remitting the case to a children's hearing either for their advice or for their consideration and disposal. Subsections (6) and (7) extend these provisions to youths aged up to 17 1/2 years who are convicted on summary complaint. Once the case is remitted to a hearing for disposal, the court's involvement ceases. *S v Miller*, 2001 S.L.T. 531 confirms that since children's hearings are not empowered to impose punishment, their proceedings did not involve the determination of a criminal charge, and as a result are not fully within the ambit of Art. 6 of the European Convention. Nonetheless it is acknowledged that the general right to fairly-conducted proceedings would demand compliance with Art. 6(1). This decision follows *Engel v The Netherlands* (1976) 1 E.H.R.R. 647 which set out the criteria determining whether proceedings are deemed to be criminal proceedings or not, for the purposes of Art. 6.

In cases where the child is the subject of a supervision requirement, and thus can be aged up to 17 1/2 years old, admits or is found guilty of an offence in the sheriff or (following the amendment introduced by the 1998 Act in relation only to children already the subject of supervision) the district court, the court must obtain the advice of a children's hearing. On receipt of the hearing's advice the court can dispose of the case or remit the child to the hearing for their decision and disposal. Note that as subs.(3)(b) reads, this procedure would apply equally to summary or solemn cases but that the provisions of s.44 of the Act (which empower a sheriff sitting summarily to order detention of up to one year's duration in residential accommodation) derogate from this general requirement.

Section 208 of the Act empowers solemn courts to impose periods of detention following conviction on indictment.

When the child is convicted before the High Court it is in the discretion of the court to obtain the advice of a children's hearing except where the conviction is for murder since, in that event, the sentence provided by s.205 is a mandatory one of life imprisonment.

Children and certain proceedings

50.—(1) No child under 14 years of age (other than an infant in arms) shall be permitted to be present in court during any proceedings against any other person charged with an offence unless his presence is required as a witness or otherwise for the purposes of justice or the Court consents to his presence.

(2) Any child present in court when, under subsection (1) above, he is not to be permitted to be so shall be ordered to be removed.

(3) Where, in any proceedings in relation to an offence against, or any conduct contrary to, decency or morality, a person who, in the opinion of the court, is a child is called as a witness, the court may direct that all or any persons, not being—

(a) members or officers of the court;

(b) parties to the case before the court, their counsel or solicitors or persons otherwise directly concerned in the case;

(c) *bona fide* representatives of news gathering or reporting organisations present for the purpose of the preparation of contemporaneous reports of the proceedings; or

(d) such other persons as the court may specially authorise to be present,

shall be excluded from the court during the taking of the evidence of that witness.

(4) The powers conferred on a court by subsection (3) above shall be in addition and without prejudice to any other powers of the court to hear proceedings *in camera*.

(5) Where in any proceedings relating to any of the offences mentioned in Schedule 1 to this Act, the court is satisfied that the attendance before the court of any person under the age of 17 years in respect of whom the offence is alleged to have been committed is not essential to the just hearing of the case, the case may be proceeded with and determined in the absence of that person.

(6) Every court in dealing with a child who is brought before it as an offender shall have regard to the welfare of the child and shall in a proper case take steps for removing him from undesirable surroundings.

AMENDMENT

Subs.(1) as amended by the Access to Justice Act 1999 (c.22), s.73(2) (effective September 27, 1999).

DEFINITIONS

"child": as defined in subs.(1).
"witness": s.307(1).

GENERAL NOTE

The provisions of this section are of a directory character and non-compliance would not render the proceedings null.

It will be noted that ss.271 and 272 of the 1995 Act allow for applications to be made for a child's evidence to be taken by a commissioner, relayed to the court by means of a remote closed-circuit television link, or to be taken in court while the child is screened from sight of the accused.

Remand and committal of children and young persons

51.—(1) Where a court remands or commits for trial or for sentence a person under 21 years of age who is charged with or convicted of an offence and is not released on bail or ordained to appear, then, except as otherwise expressly provided by this section, the following provisions shall have effect—

(a) if he is under 16 years of age but is not a child to whom paragraph (bb) below applies, the court shall, commit him to the local authority which it considers appropriate to be detained—

    (i) where the court so requires, in secure accommodation within the meaning of Part II of the Children (Scotland) Act 1995; and

    (ii) in any other case, in a suitable place of safety chosen by the authority;

(aa) if the person has attained the age of 16 years and is subject to a supervision requirement, the court may commit him to the local authority which it considers appropriate to be detained as mentioned in sub-paragraphs (i) or (ii) of paragraph (a) above or may commit him either to prison or to a young offenders institution;

(b) if he is a person who has attained the age of 16 years and to whom paragraph (aa) above does not apply, then where—

    (i) the court has been notified by the Scottish Ministers that a remand centre is available for the reception from that court of persons of his class or description, it shall commit him to a remand centre; or

    (ii) the court has not been so notified, it may commit him either to prison or to a young offenders institution;

(bb) if he is a child who is under 16 years of age but has attained the age of 14 years and is certified by the court to be unruly or depraved, then where—

    (i) the court has been so notified as is mentioned in paragraph (b)(i) above, it shall commit him to a remand centre; or

    (ii) the court has not been so notified, it may commit him either to prison or to a young offenders institution.

(2) Where any person is committed to a local authority under any provision of this Act, that authority shall be specified in the warrant, and he shall be detained by the authority for the period for which he is committed or until he is liberated in due course of law.

(2A) Subject to subsection (4) below, where any person is committed to a remand centre under any provision of this Act, he shall be detained in a remand centre for the period for which he is committed or until he is liberated in due course of law.

(3) Where any person has been committed to a local authority under any provision of this Act, the court by which he was committed, if the person so committed is not less than 14 years of age and it appears to the court that he is unruly or depraved, may revoke the committal and commit the said person—

(a) if the court has been notified that a remand centre is available for the reception from that court of persons of his class or description, to a remand centre; and

(b) if the court has not been so notified, either to a prison or to a young offenders institution.

(4) Where in the case of a person under 16 years of age who has been committed under this section to prison, to a young offenders institution or to a remand centre, the sheriff is satisfied that his detention in prison or a young offenders institution or remand centre is no longer necessary, he may revoke the committal

and commit the person to the local authority which he considers appropriate to be detained—

    (a) where the court so requires, in secure accommodation within the meaning of Part II of the Children (Scotland) Act 1995; and

    (b) in any other case, in a suitable place of safety chosen by the authority.

(4A) The local authority which may be appropriate in relation to a power to commit a person under paragraphs (a) or (aa) of subsection (1) or subsection (4) above may, without prejudice to the generality of those powers, be—

    (a) the local authority for the area in which the court is situated;

    (b) if the person is usually resident in Scotland, the local authority for the area in which he is usually resident;

    (c) if the person is subject to a supervision requirement, the relevant local authority within the meaning of Part II of the Children (Scotland) Act 1995 in relation to that requirement.

(5) Where by virtue of subsection (1)(aa), (b)(ii), (bb)(ii) or (3)(b) of this section a person is committed either to prison or to a young offenders institution, the warrant issued by the court is warrant also, without further application to the court in that regard, for committal to whichever of the two the court does not specify.

AMENDMENTS

Subss.(1)(a) and (4) substituted by the Crime and Punishment (Scotland) Act 1997 (c.48), s.56 with effect from August 1, 1997 in terms of the Crime and Punishment (Scotland) Act 1997 (Commencement and Transitional Provisions) Order 1997 (SI 1997/1712), art.3.

Subss.(1)(aa) inserted by s.56(2) of the above Act with effect from August 1, 1997 in terms of the above Order.

Sub.(4A) inserted by s.56(4) of the above Act and in terms of the above Order.

Section 51 as amended by Criminal Justice (Scotland) Act 2003 (asp 7), Part 4, s.23. Brought into force on June 27, 2003 by the Criminal Justice (Scotland) Act 2003 (Commencement No.1) Order 2003 (SSI 2003/288 (C.14)).

DEFINITIONS

    "commits for trial": s.307(1).

    "local authority": s.307(1).

    "place of safety": s.307(1) of the 1995 Act and, in relation to children see s.93(1)of the Children (Scotland) Act 1995.

    "prison": s.307(1).

    "remand": s.307(1).

    "remand centre": s.307(1).

    "secure accommodation": s.93(1) of the Children (Scotland) Act 1995.

    "supervision requirement": s.307(1) of the 1995 Act and the Children (Scotland) Act 1995 ss.70(1) and 93(1).

GENERAL NOTE

Section 51 applies equally to summary or solemn proceedings and specifies the forms of remand facilities which are to be utilised when persons under 21 years of age are held in custody awaiting trial or remanded for sentence by the court. The aim, so far as practicable, is not to resort to use of remand facilities either before or after any trial unless the circumstances of the case, or the offender, make this unavoidable. The provisions introduced by the 1997 Act reflect the changes brought about by local government reorganisation and give the courts a degree of flexibility when nominating the local authority to provide suitable remand facilities for children and young offenders. It no longer follows that this function must necessarily be met by the local authority within whose boundaries the court is situated; it is now being left to the court to decide the most appropriate authority in the case of each offender.

In discussing s.43 of the Act it was noted that when it was felt that ordaining or liberating a child to appear at the first diet of the case was considered inappropriate, the options available to the police thereafter would be to remand a child to a place of safety, unless his conduct or circumstances militated against that form of detention. The more stringent restrictions upon the child's liberty, produced by detaining him in police cells pending his appearance before the court from custody could only be justified by the production to the court, on first appearance, of an unruly certificate. A similar philosophy is applied by the courts when it is felt that a child or young person must be remanded in custody for trial or sentence; the broad objective is then to remand the offender to an establishment most suited to the offender's circumstances and so far as possible, to minimise the rigour of the remand regime.

Children Under 16 Years

Prior to the child's appearance from custody before the sheriff, the procurator fiscal and the principal reporter (or their deputes) should already have considered whether such an appearance is necessary or whether the child can instead be referred to the reporter in custody or liberated for the reporter to arrange a later children's hearing. Such a consultation process also applies when the offender is aged between 16 and 17 years and six months old and is the subject of a supervision requirement, but failure on the part of the procurator fiscal to consult with the reporter in these circumstances would not vitiate proceedings: see s.46(5) above.

Section 51 only takes effect when the procurator fiscal, having weighed the interests of the child and the broad public interest, elects to retain the case. If the child has been detained in police cells, the procurator fiscal will receive the unruly certificate from the police and has to produce it to the sheriff when the child appears from custody (following s.142 of the 1995 Act it will be observed that in summary proceedings such an appearance should not occur in an adult court (unless there is an adult co-accused) and must be held in private).

Should the procurator fiscal decide that bail will be opposed because of the nature of the offence or the unruliness of the child, he should have established with the local authority before the case is called, whether suitable remand facilities are available. This information should be put before the court in conjunction with a motion to remand the child in custody. In the absence of suitable accommodation, the court, if it refuses bail, will have no option but to consider whether the child is unruly, and if so, certify the child unruly and remand him to a remand institution or an adult prison albeit subs.(4) does permit later variation of the order. It is submitted that while the nature of the offence may well point to the child being unruly or depraved that is not the test; it is the nature of the child himself which should be assessed by the court. See however *R.M., Petr*, 1996 S.C.C.R. 92 and the editor's commentary thereon in regard to the implications of a lack of suitable secure accommodation.

It ought to be clearly established whether the child is or is not in custody pending trial, since the warrant issued by the court will specify either the centre to which the child is remanded or identify the local authority into whose charge he is placed and (following subs.(1)(a)) the nature of the accommodation to be provided—a place of safety, residential or secure accommodation. The important factor is whether the child is granted bail, and is at liberty, or remanded in custody, since this has an obvious bearing upon the timescale and competency of later proceedings; see ss.65 and 147 of the 1995 Act which re-enact the familiar provisions of ss.101 and 331A of the 1975 Act regarding prevention of delay in proceedings, *i.e* the 110 day and 40 day rules respectively. The warrant issued by the court will not conclusively determine whether a child is in custody or not, that is ultimately an issue of fact in each case, but the warrant will assuredly be a highly persuasive determining factor. The court must be furnished with comprehensive and accurate information about the precise circumstances of the child and the basis upon which he is held. In *X., Petr*, 1996 S.C.C.R. 436 the Crown was criticised for making representations which were based upon inaccurate information provided by the local authority. The court observed that the Crown had a duty to verify the accuracy of such information for itself and should seek an adjournment for that purpose if necessary.

These comments apply with even greater force when the child appearing before the court is already the subject of a residential supervision order: it is then vital that it is determined whether the child is bailed, and returns to the care of the local authority to continue the current supervision order, or is remanded to secure accommodation provided by the local authority as a preferred alternative to a remand or prison place. It is also essential that the local authority seek a review of the case in terms of subs.(4), should the circumstances of the offender change.

The complications which can arise are amply illustrated in *K. v. H.M. Advocate*, 1991 S.C.C.R. 343, where the child was "bailed" to reside at a List D school which in fact contained both secure and residential accommodation. K was bailed to reside in the school's secure unit, instead of being either remanded into the care of the local authority or certified unruly and remanded. The court's well-meant intention was to substitute an earlier warrant which had remanded K to an adult prison with a more suitable regime but, on any view, K was not at liberty and the provisions (then) of s.110 applied, since the bail order had had no practical effect (the solution would have been for the local authority, if it was in agreement, to seek review of the warrant as subs.(4) provides in the 1995 Act).

See also *X., Petr*, 1996 S.C.C.R. 436; following a petition appearance upon a rape charge and refusal of bail, C was held in custody in a remand institution. A review hearing later allowed bail subject to residence in a List D school; although the bail order did not stipulate it, C was kept in secure accommodation by staff solely in execution of the order, and only the issue of instructions by the procurator fiscal for the child's liberation (which were acted upon on the 109th day) stopped the 110 days running. A petition to the *nobile officium* was refused since *de facto* liberty had been obtained before the expiry of the 110 days.

Note that once a child has been certified unruly by the sheriff it is doubtful whether it can be revoked by anyone, even the certifying sheriff, or formally appealed. In *X., Petr, supra*, the child was certified unruly and remanded in a remand institution after absconding from the local authority home to which he had earlier been bailed. A petition to the *nobile officium* for revocation of the certification was lodged, but the High Court doubted that such an order would be competent; in the absence of Crown opposition the court used its inherent equitable powers to grant a bail order specifying residence in a secure unit. The principles which prompted this decision appear in conflict with the *ratio* in *K. v. H.M. Advocate* above.

A similar situation arose in *Y., Petr*, 1995 S.C.C.R. 457, with the court ruling that a petition to the *nobile officium* was not a competent means for review of an unruly certificate.

Nevertheless the court substituted a bail order requiring Y to reside in the secure unit of a List D school.

PART VI

MENTAL DISORDER

Committal of mentally disordered persons

Power of court to commit to hospital an accused suffering from mental disorder

52.—(1) Where it appears to the prosecutor in any court before which a person is charged with an offence that the person may be suffering from mental disorder, it shall be the duty of the prosecutor to bring before the court such evidence as may be available of the mental condition of that person.

(2)–(7) [...]

AMENDMENT

Subss.(2)–(7) repealed by the Mental Health (Care and Treatment) (Scotland) Act 2003 (asp 13), Sch.5, Part I. Brought into force on October 5, 2005 by the Mental Health (Care and Treatment) (Scotland) Act 2003 (Commencement No.4) Order 2005 (SSI 2005/161 (C.6)).

DEFINITIONS

"mental disorder": s.328(1) of the Mental Health (Care and Treatment) (Scotland) Act 2003.
"offence": s.307(1).
"prosecutor": s.307(1).

GENERAL NOTE

This section amends and consolidates the existing provisions of the court to commit to a specified hospital at the pre-trial stage an accused who appears to be suffering from a mental disorder. The section makes express provision for review of that committal. The committal to hospital is an alternative to remanding such an accused in custody pending trial. Thus the committal to hospital is subject to the maximum remand time limits of 40 days in summary proceedings and 110 days in solemn proceedings. Before the court can make the hospital committal order three criteria must be met. First, the court must be satisfied on the written or oral evidence of a registered medical practitioner that the accused appears to be suffering from mental disorder, although at this stage it is not necessary for the nature or degree of mental disorder to be established. Secondly, the court must be satisfied that a hospital is *available* for the accused's admission, and thirdly the court must be satisfied that the hospital is *suitable* for the accused's detention pending trial. Accordingly, the registered medical practitioner should confirm to the court that a suitable hospital is prepared to admit the accused.

It should be noted that it is open to anyone with an interest in the case to raise the possibility of an accused's mental disorder with the court. Such interested parties would include the prosecutor, the police, the defence agent and the judge.

Subs. (1)

The breadth of the definition of the word "prosecutor" should be noted for in solemn proceedings it includes Crown counsel. The flexibility implied by this is such that relevant evidence may be brought at what would otherwise be the trial diet in the High Court of Justiciary. The procedure is not contingent on a conviction because of the phrase "is charged with": see *Herron v McCrimmon*, 1969 S.L.T. (Sh. Ct) 37 for circumstances in which a summary complaint was deserted *pro loco et tempore* to place the accused on petition and yet the phrase was still satisfied.

The provision of a psychiatric report by the Crown in compliance with this section's provisions is to be regarded as the fulfilment of a statutory duty which has been placed on the prosecutor for the protection of the accused, and not as an element of the Crown's investigation in furtherance of its case against the accused. Thus in *Sloan v Crowe*, 1996 S.C.C.R. 200 an objection to the competency of proceedings was repelled, and refused on appeal, the defence having asserted that information provided to the Crown in a psychiatric report on the accused unfairly made reference to the offence itself. In *MacDonald v Munro*, 1996 S.C.C.R. 595 where the psychiatrist had interviewed both the accused and his mother (the complainer) about the circumstances of the offence in compiling his report, it was observed that any prejudicial material would fall to be ignored by the judge and that any attempt by the Crown to found on such material would likely be objectionable.

Whether a person may be suffering from "mental disorder" is a medical question for those qualified to answer the question but that is frequently the most difficult point: in *Allan v H.M. Advocate*, 1983 S.C.C.R. 183 four psychiatrists divided on precisely that aspect and, if the accused was so suffering, what the best method of disposal would be.

A similar division is apparent in *Jessop v Robertson*, 1989 S.C.C.R. 600 (Sh. Ct.) where it was held by a sheriff that: (1) a written report that had been produced by the prosecutor but was not spoken to by a witness at the proof was not admissible; (2) there was an onus on any person alleging unfitness by reason of insanity to satisfy the court of that allegation by corroborated evidence on a balance of probabilities; and (3) in the circumstances of medical division the unfitness had not been proved; and the accused was called upon to plead.

Remit of mentally disordered persons from district court

Remit of certain mentally disordered persons from district court to sheriff court

52A. Where—

(a) a person has been charged in a district court with an offence punishable by imprisonment; and

(b) it appears to the court that the person has a mental disorder,

the district court shall remit the person to the sheriff in the manner provided by section 7(9) and (10) of this Act.

AMENDMENT

Section 52A inserted by the Mental Health (Care and Treatment) (Scotland) Act 2003 (asp 13), s.130. Brought into force on October 5, 2005 by the Mental Health (Care and Treatment) (Scotland) Act 2003 (Commencement No.4) Order 2005 (SSI 2005/161 (C.6)).

DEFINITIONS

"mental disorder": s.328(1) of the Mental Health (Care and Treatment) (Scotland) Act 2003.
"offence": s.307(1).

GENERAL NOTE

Section 52A(a) applies where a person has been "charged" in a district court. It is unnecessary, it seems, to have a finding of guilt or an acquittal to invoke the power of the section. Further, by s.52A(b) the issue of a mental disorder is raised merely by impression on the part of the court.

Assessment orders

Prosecutor's power to apply for assessment order

52B.—(1) Where—

(a) a person has been charged with an offence;

(b) a relevant disposal has not been made in the proceedings in respect of the offence; and

(c) it appears to the prosecutor that the person has a mental disorder,

the prosecutor may apply to the court for an order under section 52D(2) of this Act (in this Act referred to as an "assessment order") in respect of that person.

(2) Where the prosecutor applies for an assessment order under subsection (1) above, the prosecutor shall, as soon as reasonably practicable after making the application, inform the persons mentioned in subsection (3) below of the making of the application.

(3) Those persons are—

(a) the person in respect of whom the application is made;

(b) any solicitor acting for the person; and

(c) in a case where the person is in custody, the Scottish Ministers.

(4) In this section—

"court" means any court, other than a district court, competent to deal with the case; and

"relevant disposal" means—

(a) the liberation in due course of law of the person charged;

(b) the desertion of summary proceedings *pro loco et tempore* or *simpliciter*;

(c) the desertion of solemn proceedings *simpliciter*;

(d) the acquittal of the person charged; or

(e) the conviction of the person charged.

AMENDMENT

Section 52B inserted by the Mental Health (Care and Treatment) (Scotland) Act 2003 (asp 13), s.130. Brought into force on October 5, 2005 by the Mental Health (Care and Treatment) (Scotland) Act 2003 (Commencement No.4) Order 2005 (SSI 2005/161 (C.6)).

DEFINITIONS

"assessment order": s.52B(1)(c).

"court": s.52B(4).

"mental disorder": s.328(1) of the Mental Health (Care and Treatment) (Scotland) Act 2003.

"offence": s.307(1).

"prosecutor": s.307(1).

"relevant disposal": s.52B(4).

GENERAL NOTE

First, the "prosecutor" within the meaning of the 1995 Act is the person prosecuting under solemn procedure or summary procedure in any criminal court and thus applying the terms of the section to all criminal courts: see s.307(1). Secondly, in the conditions specified in s.52B(1) an assessment order may be sought. Reference needs to be made to s.52D(2) and (5) for the nature and effect of such an assessment order.

Scottish Ministers' power to apply for assessment order

52C.—(1) Where—

(a) a person has been charged with an offence;

(b) the person has not been sentenced;

(c) the person is in custody; and

(d) it appears to the Scottish Ministers that the person has a mental disorder,

the Scottish Ministers may apply to the court for an assessment order in respect of that person.

(2) Where the Scottish Ministers apply for an order under subsection (1) above, they shall, as soon as reasonably practicable after making the application, inform the persons mentioned in subsection (3) below of the making of the application.

(3) Those persons are—

(a) the person in respect of whom the application is made;

(b) any solicitor acting for the person; and

(c) in a case where a relevant disposal has not been made in the proceedings in respect of the offence with which the person is charged, the prosecutor.

(4) In this section, "court" and "relevant disposal" have the same meanings as in section 52B of this Act.

AMENDMENT

Section 52C inserted by the Mental Health (Care and Treatment) (Scotland) Act 2003 (asp 13), s.130. Brought into force on October 5, 2005 by the Mental Health (Care and Treatment) (Scotland) Act 2003 (Commencement No.4) Order 2005 (SSI 2005/161 (C.6)).

DEFINITIONS

"assessment order": s.52B(1)(c).
"court": s.52B(4).
"offence": s.307(1).
"relevant disposal": s.52B(4).

GENERAL NOTE

In the conditions specified in s.52C(1), an assessment order may be sought by the Scottish Ministers. Reference needs to be made to s.52D for the nature and effect of such an assessment order.

Assessment order

52D.—(1) This section applies where an application for an assessment order is made under section 52B(1) or 52C(1) of this Act.

(2) If the court is satisfied—

(a) on the written or oral evidence of a medical practitioner, as to the matters mentioned in subsection (3) below; and

(b) that, having regard to the matters mentioned in subsection (4) below, it is appropriate,

it may, subject to subsection (5) below, make an assessment order authorising the measures mentioned in subsection (6) below and specifying any matters to be included in the report under section 52G(1) of this Act.

(3) The matters referred to in subsection (2)(a) above are—

(a) that there are reasonable grounds for believing—

(i) that the person in respect of whom the application is made has a mental disorder;

(ii) that it is necessary to detain the person in hospital to assess whether the conditions mentioned in subsection (7) below are met in respect of the person; and

(iii) that if the assessment order were not made there would be a significant risk to the health, safety or welfare of the person or a significant risk to the safety of any other person;

(b) that the hospital proposed by the medical practitioner is suitable for the purpose of assessing whether the conditions mentioned in subsection (7) below are met in respect of the person;

(c) that, if an assessment order were made, the person could be admitted to such hospital before the expiry of the period of 7 days beginning with the day on which the order is made; and

(d) that it would not be reasonably practicable to carry out the assessment mentioned in paragraph (b) above unless an order were made.

(4) The matters referred to in subsection (2)(b) above are—

(a) all the circumstances (including the nature of the offence with which the person in respect of whom the application is made is charged or, as the case may be, of which the person was convicted); and

(b) any alternative means of dealing with the person.

(5) The court may make an assessment order only if the person in respect of whom the application is made has not been sentenced.

(6) The measures are—

(a) in the case of a person who, when the assessment order is made, has not been admitted to the specified hospital, the removal, before the expiry of the period of 7 days beginning with the day on which the order is made, of the person to the specified hospital by—

    (i) a constable;

    (ii) a person employed in, or contracted to provide services in or to, the specified hospital who is authorised by the managers of that hospital to remove persons to hospital for the purposes of this section; or

    (iii) a specified person;

(b) the detention, for the period of 28 days beginning with the day on which the order is made, of the person in the specified hospital; and

(c) during the period of 28 days beginning with the day on which the order is made, the giving to the person, in accordance with Part 16 of the Mental Health (Care and Treatment) (Scotland) Act 2003 (asp 13), of medical treatment.

(7) The conditions referred to in paragraphs (a)(ii) and (b) of subsection (3) above are—

(a) that the person in respect of whom the application is made has a mental disorder;

(b) that medical treatment which would be likely to—

    (i) prevent the mental disorder worsening; or

    (ii) alleviate any of the symptoms, or effects, of the disorder,

is available for the person; and

(c) that if the person were not provided with such medical treatment there would be a significant risk—

    (i) to the health, safety or welfare of the person; or

    (ii) to the safety of any other person.

(8) The court may make an assessment order in the absence of the person in respect of whom the application is made only if—

(a) the person is represented by counsel or a solicitor;

(b) that counsel or solicitor is given an opportunity of being heard; and

(c) the court is satisfied that it is—

    (i) impracticable; or

    (ii) inappropriate,

for the person to be brought before it.

(9) An assessment order may include such directions as the court thinks fit for the removal of the person subject to the order to, and detention of the person in, a place of safety pending the person's admission to the specified hospital.

(10) The court shall, as soon as reasonably practicable after making an assessment order, give notice of the making of the order to—

(a) the person subject to the order;

(b) any solicitor acting for the person;

(c) in a case where—

    (i) the person has been charged with an offence; and

    (ii) a relevant disposal has not been made in the proceedings in respect of the offence,

the prosecutor;

(d) in a case where the person, immediately before the order was made, was in custody, the Scottish Ministers; and

(e) the Mental Welfare Commission.

(11) In this section—

"court" has the same meaning as in section 52B of this Act;

"medical treatment" has the meaning given by section 329(1) of the Mental Health (Care and Treatment) (Scotland) Act 2003 (asp 13);

"relevant disposal" has the same meaning as in section 52B of this Act; and

"specified" means specified in the assessment order.

AMENDMENT

Section 52D inserted by the Mental Health (Care and Treatment) (Scotland) Act 2003 (asp 13), s.130. Brought into force on October 5, 2005 by the Mental Health (Care and Treatment) (Scotland) Act 2003 (Commencement No.4) Order 2005 (SSI 2005/161 (C.6)).

DEFINITIONS

"assessment order": s.52B(1)(c).
"court": s.52B(4).
"medical treatment": s.329(1) of the Mental Health (Care and Treatment) (Scotland) Act 2003.
"mental disorder": s.328(1) of the Mental Health (Care and Treatment) (Scotland) Act 2003.
"offence": s.307(1).
"prosecutor": s.307(1).
"relevant disposal": s.52B(4).
"specified": s.52D(11).

GENERAL NOTE

This section allows courts to make an assessment order authorising the measures mentioned in s.52D(6). The making of such an order is dependent on the written or oral evidence of a medical practitioner. The relevant measures are (a) the removal of a person to a specified hospital; (b) the detention of that person in a specified hospital for a period of 28 days; and (c) the giving to that person treatment as set out in Part 16 of the Mental Health (Care and Treatment) (Scotland) Act 2003. Prior to making the assessment order there must be reasonable grounds for believing that the person in respect of whom an application is made has mental disorder and that if the assessment order were not made there would be a significant risk to the health, safety or welfare of the person under consideration or a significant risk to the safety of any other person: s.52D(3).

Assessment order made ex proprio motu: application of section 52D

52E.—(1) Where—

(a) a person has been charged with an offence;

(b) the person has not been sentenced; and

(c) it appears to the court that the person has a mental disorder,

the court may, subject to subsections (2) and (3) below, make an assessment order in respect of that person.

(2) The court may make an assessment order under subsection (1) above only if it would make one under subsections (2) to (11) of section 52D of this Act; and those subsections shall apply for the purposes of subsection (1) above as they apply for the purposes of subsection (1) of that section, references in those subsections to the person in respect of whom the application is made being construed as

references to the person in respect of whom it is proposed to make an assessment order.

(3) An assessment order made under subsection (1) above shall, for the purposes of this Act and the Mental Health (Care and Treatment) (Scotland) Act 2003 (asp 13), be treated as if made under section 52D(2) of this Act.

(4) In this section, "court" has the same meaning as in section 52B of this Act.

AMENDMENT

Section 52E inserted by the Mental Health (Care and Treatment) (Scotland) Act 2003 (asp 13), s.130. Brought into force on October 5, 2005 by the Mental Health (Care and Treatment) (Scotland) Act 2003 (Commencement No.4) Order 2005 (SSI 2005/161 (C.6)).

DEFINITIONS

"assessment order": s.52B(1)(c).
"court": s.52B(4).
"mental disorder": s.328(1) of the Mental Health (Care and Treatment) (Scotland) Act 2003.
"offence": s.307(1).
"relevant disposal": s.52B(4).

GENERAL NOTE

This section allows the court *ex proprio motu* to make an assessment order.

Assessment order: supplementary

52F.—(1) If, before the expiry of the period of 7 days beginning with the day on which an assessment order is made—

(a) in the case of a person who, immediately before the order was made, was in custody, it appears to the Scottish Ministers; or

(b) in any other case, it appears to the court,

that, by reason of emergency or other special circumstances, it is not reasonably practicable for the person to be admitted to the hospital specified in the order, the Scottish Ministers, or, as the case may be, the court, may direct that the person be admitted to the hospital specified in the direction.

(2) Where the court makes a direction under subsection (1) above, it shall, as soon as reasonably practicable after making the direction, inform the person having custody of the person subject to the assessment order of the making of the direction.

(3) Where the Scottish Ministers make a direction under subsection (1) above, they shall, as soon as reasonably practicable after making the direction, inform—

(a) the court;

(b) the person having custody of the person subject to the assessment order; and

(c) in a case where—

(i) the person has been charged with an offence; and

(ii) a relevant disposal has not been made in the proceedings in respect of the offence,

the prosecutor,

of the making of the direction.

(4) Where a direction is made under subsection (1) above, the assessment order shall have effect as if the hospital specified in the direction were the hospital specified in the order.

(5) In this section—

"court" means the court which made the assessment order; and

"relevant disposal" has the same meaning as in section 52B of this Act.

AMENDMENT

Section 52F inserted by the Mental Health (Care and Treatment) (Scotland) Act 2003 (asp 13), s.130. Brought into force on October 5, 2005 by the Mental Health (Care and Treatment) (Scotland) Act 2003 (Commencement No.4) Order 2005 (SSI 2005/161 (C.6)).

DEFINITIONS

"assessment order": s.52B(1)(c).
"court": s.52B(4).
"mental disorder": s.328(1) of the Mental Health (Care and Treatment) (Scotland) Act 2003.
"offence": s.307(1).
"relevant disposal": s.52B(4).

Review of assessment order

52G.—(1) The responsible medical officer shall, before the expiry of the period of 28 days beginning with the day on which the assessment order is made, submit a report in writing to the court—

(a) as to whether the conditions mentioned in section 52D(7) of this Act are met in respect of the person subject to the order; and

(b) as to any matters specified by the court under section 52D(2) of this Act.

(2) The responsible medical officer shall, at the same time as such officer submits the report to the court, send a copy of such report—

(a) to the person in respect of whom the report is made;

(b) to any solicitor acting for the person;

(c) in a case where—

(i) the person has been charged with an offence; and

(ii) a relevant disposal has not been made in the proceedings in respect of the offence,

to the prosecutor; and

(d) to the Scottish Ministers.

(3) Subject to subsection (4) below, the court shall, on receiving a report submitted under subsection (1) above, revoke the assessment order and—

(a) subject to subsections (7) and (8) below, make a treatment order; or

(b) commit the person to prison or such other institution to which the person might have been committed had the assessment order not been made or otherwise deal with the person as the court considers appropriate.

(4) If, on receiving a report submitted under subsection (1) above, the court is satisfied that further time is necessary to assess whether the conditions mentioned in section 52D(7) of this Act are met in respect of the person subject to the assessment order, it may, on one occasion only, make an order extending the assessment order for a period not exceeding 7 days beginning with the day on which the order otherwise would cease to authorise the detention of the person in hospital.

(5) The court may, under subsection (4) above, extend an assessment order in the absence of the person subject to the order only if—

(a) the person is represented by counsel or a solicitor;

(b) that counsel or solicitor is given an opportunity of being heard; and

(c) the court is satisfied that it is—

(i) impracticable; or

(ii) inappropriate,

for the person to be brought before it.

(6) Where the court makes an order under subsection (4) above, it shall, as soon as reasonably practicable after making the order, give notice of the making of the order to—

(a) the persons mentioned in paragraphs (a) and (b) of subsection (2) above;
(b) in a case where—
    (i) the person has been charged with an offence; and
    (ii) a relevant disposal has not been made in the proceedings in respect of the offence,
  the prosecutor;
(c) the Scottish Ministers; and
(d) the person's responsible medical officer.

(7) The court shall make a treatment order under subsection (3)(a) above only if it would make one under subsections (2) to (10) of section 52M of this Act; and those subsections shall apply for the purposes of subsection (3)(a) above as they apply for the purposes of that section, references in those subsections to the person in respect of whom the application is made being construed as references to the person in respect of whom it is proposed to make a treatment order.

(8) A treatment order made under subsection (3)(a) above shall, for the purposes of this Act and the Mental Health (Care and Treatment) (Scotland) Act 2003 (asp 13), be treated as if made under section 52M(2) of this Act.

(9) The responsible medical officer shall, where that officer is satisfied that there has been a change of circumstances since the assessment order was made which justifies the variation of the order, submit a report to the court in writing.

(10) Where a report is submitted under subsection (9) above, the court shall—
(a) if satisfied that the person need not be subject to an assessment order, revoke the order and take any action mentioned in subsection (3)(b) above; or
(b) if not so satisfied—
    (i) confirm the order;
    (ii) vary the order; or
    (iii) revoke the order and take any action mentioned in subsection (3)(b) above.

(11) Sections 52D, 52F, 52H and 52J of this Act and subsections (1) to (3) above apply to the variation of an order under subsection (10)(b)(ii) above as they apply to an assessment order.

(12) In this section—
  "court" means the court which made the assessment order;
  "relevant disposal" has the same meaning as in section 52B of this Act; and
  "responsible medical officer" means the person's responsible medical officer appointed under section 230 of the Mental Health (Care and Treatment) (Scotland) Act 2003 (asp 13).

AMENDMENT

Section 52G inserted by the Mental Health (Care and Treatment) (Scotland) Act 2003 (asp 13), s.130. Brought into force on October 5, 2005 by the Mental Health (Care and Treatment) (Scotland) Act 2003 (Commencement No.4) Order 2005 (SSI 2005/161 (C.6)).

DEFINITIONS

"assessment order": s.52B(1)(c).
"court": s.52B(4).
"mental disorder": s.328(1) of the Mental Health (Care and Treatment) (Scotland) Act 2003.
"offence": s.307(1).
"relevant disposal": s.52B(4).
"responsible medical officer": s.230 of the Mental Health (Care and Treatment) (Scotland) Act 2003.
"treatment order": s.52M.

GENERAL NOTE

This section imports restrictions on the duration of the assessment order: the responsible medical officer submits to the court a report in writing within a period of 28 days from the requirement being made: s.52G(1). Thereafter the court "shall" revoke the assessment order: s.52G(3). On revocation the court is required to make a treatment order or commit the person to prison or other institution: s.52G(3)(a) or (b).

Further time for consideration is competent but only under the constraints provided: s.52G(4).

Early termination of assessment order

52H.—(1) This section applies where—

(a) in the case of a person who, when the assessment order is made, has not been removed to the hospital specified in the order, the period of 7 days beginning with the day on which the order is made has not expired;

(b) in the case of a person—

(i) who, when the assessment order is made, has been admitted to the hospital specified in the order; or

(ii) who has been removed under paragraph (a) of subsection (6) of section 52D of this Act to the hospital so specified,

the period of 28 days beginning with the day on which the order is made has not expired; or

(c) in the case of a person in respect of whom the court has made an order under section 52G(4) of this Act extending the assessment order for a period, the period for which the order was extended has not expired.

(2) An assessment order shall cease to have effect on the occurrence of any of the following events—

(a) the making of a treatment order in respect of the person subject to the assessment order;

(b) in a case where—

(i) the person subject to the assessment order has been charged with an offence; and

(ii) a relevant disposal had not been made in the proceedings in respect of that offence when the order was made,

the making of a relevant disposal in such proceedings;

(c) in a case where the person subject to the assessment order has been convicted of an offence but has not been sentenced—

(i) the deferral of sentence by the court under section 202(1) of this Act;

(ii) the making of one of the orders mentioned in subsection (3) below or

(iii) the imposition of any sentence.

(3) The orders are—

(a) an interim compulsion order;

(b) a compulsion order;

(c) a guardianship order;

(d) a hospital direction;

(e) any order under section 57 of this Act; or

(f) a probation order which includes a requirement imposed by virtue of section 230(1) of this Act.

(4) In this section, "relevant disposal" has the same meaning as in section 52B of this Act.

AMENDMENT

Section 52H inserted by the Mental Health (Care and Treatment) (Scotland) Act 2003 (asp 13), s.130. Brought into force on October 5, 2005 by the Mental Health (Care and Treatment) (Scotland) Act 2003 (Commencement No.4) Order 2005 (SSI 2005/161 (C.6)).

DEFINITIONS
"assessment order": s.52B(1)(c).
"court": s.52B(4).
"relevant disposal": s.52B(4).
"treatment order": s.52M.

GENERAL NOTE

This section provides that the making of other orders (specified in the section) has the effect of ending the assessment order.

Power of court on assessment order ceasing to have effect

52J.—(1) Where, otherwise than by virtue of section 52G(3) or (10) or 52H(2) of this Act, an assessment order ceases to have effect the court shall commit the person who was subject to the order to prison or such other institution to which the person might have been committed had the order not been made or otherwise deal with the person as the court considers appropriate.

(2) In this section, "court" has the same meaning as in section 52B of this Act.

AMENDMENT

Section 52J inserted by the Mental Health (Care and Treatment) (Scotland) Act 2003 (asp 13), s.130. Brought into force on October 5, 2005 by the Mental Health (Care and Treatment) (Scotland) Act 2003 (Commencement No.4) Order 2005 (SSI 2005/161 (C.6)).

DEFINITIONS
"assessment order": s.52B(1)(c).
"court": s.52B(4).

Treatment orders

Prosecutor's power to apply for treatment order

52K.—(1) Where—

(a) a person has been charged with an offence;

(b) a relevant disposal has not been made in the proceedings in respect of the offence; and

(c) it appears to the prosecutor that the person has a mental disorder,

the prosecutor may apply to the court for an order under section 52M of this Act (in this Act referred to as a "treatment order") in respect of that person.

(2) Where the prosecutor applies for a treatment order under subsection (1) above, the prosecutor shall, as soon as reasonably practicable after making the application, inform the persons mentioned in subsection (3) below of the making of the application.

(3) Those persons are—

(a) the person in respect of whom the application is made;

(b) any solicitor acting for the person; and

(c) in a case where the person is in custody, the Scottish Ministers.

(4) In this section, "court" and "relevant disposal" have the same meanings as in section 52B of this Act.

AMENDMENT

Section 52K inserted by the Mental Health (Care and Treatment) (Scotland) Act 2003 (asp 13), s.130. Brought into force on October 5, 2005 by the Mental Health (Care and Treatment) (Scotland) Act 2003 (Commencement No.4) Order 2005 (SSI 2005/161 (C.6)).

DEFINITIONS
"assessment order": s.52B(1)(c).

"court": s.52B(4).
"relevant disposal": s.52B(4).
"treatment order": s.52M.

GENERAL NOTE

First, the "prosecutor" within the meaning of the 1995 Act is the person prosecuting under solemn procedure or summary procedure in any criminal court and thus applying the terms of the section to all criminal courts: see s.307(1). The provision on this wide definition allows all prosecutors the power to apply for a treatment order. Secondly, in the conditions specified in s.52K(1) a treatment order may be sought. Reference needs to be made to s.52M for the nature and effect of such a treatment order.

Scottish Ministers' power to apply for treatment order

52L.—(1) Where—

(a) a person has been charged with an offence;

(b) the person has not been sentenced;

(c) the person is in custody; and

(d) it appears to the Scottish Ministers that the person has a mental disorder,

the Scottish Ministers may apply to the court for a treatment order in respect of that person.

(2) Where the Scottish Ministers apply for an order under subsection (1) above, they shall, as soon as reasonably practicable after making the application, inform the persons mentioned in subsection (3) below of the making of the application.

(3) Those persons are—

(a) the person in respect of whom the application is made;

(b) any solicitor acting for the person; and

(c) in a case where a relevant disposal has not been made in the proceedings in respect of the offence with which the person is charged, the prosecutor.

(4) In this section, "court" and "relevant disposal" have the same meanings as in section 52B of this Act.

AMENDMENT

Section 52L inserted by the Mental Health (Care and Treatment) (Scotland) Act 2003 (asp 13), s.130. Brought into force on October 5, 2005 by the Mental Health (Care and Treatment) (Scotland) Act 2003 (Commencement No.4) Order 2005 (SSI 2005/161 (C.6)).

DEFINITIONS

"assessment order": s.52B(1)(c).
"court": s.52B(4).
"mental disorder": s.328(1) of the Mental Health (Care and Treatment) (Scotland) Act 2003.
"offence": s.307(1).
"prosecutor": s.307(1).
"relevant disposal": s.52B(4).
"sentence": s.307(1).
"treatment order": s.52M.

GENERAL NOTE

This section allows the Scottish Ministers under the conditions set out in s.52L(1)(a) to (c) to apply for a treatment order. Intimation to various parties of the making of the application is necessary: s.52L(3).

Treatment order

52M.—(1) This section applies where an application for a treatment order is made under section 52K(1) or 52L(1) of this Act.

(2) If the court is satisfied—

(a) on the written or oral evidence of two medical practitioners, as to the matters mentioned in subsection (3) below; and

(b) that, having regard to the matters mentioned in subsection (4) below, it is appropriate,

it may, subject to subsection (5) below, make a treatment order authorising the measures mentioned in subsection (6) below.

(3) The matters referred to in subsection (2)(a) above are—

(a) that the conditions mentioned in subsection (7) of section 52D of this Act are met in relation to the person in respect of whom the application is made;

(b) that the hospital proposed by the approved medical practitioner and the medical practitioner is suitable for the purpose of giving medical treatment to the person; and

(c) that, if a treatment order were made, such person could be admitted to such hospital before the expiry of the period of 7 days beginning with the day on which the order is made.

(4) The matters referred to in subsection (2)(b) above are—

(a) all the circumstances (including the nature of the offence with which the person in respect of whom the application is made is charged or, as the case may be, of which the person was convicted); and

(b) any alternative means of dealing with the person.

(5) The court may make a treatment order only if the person in respect of whom the application is made has not been sentenced.

(6) The measures are—

(a) in the case of a person who, when the treatment order is made, has not been admitted to the specified hospital, the removal, before the expiry of the period of 7 days beginning with the day on which the order is made, of the person to the specified hospital by—

   (i) a constable;

   (ii) a person employed in, or contracted to provide services in or to, the specified hospital who is authorised by the managers of that hospital to remove persons to hospital for the purposes of this section; or

   (iii) a specified person;

(b) the detention of the person in the specified hospital; and

(c) the giving to the person, in accordance with Part 16 of the Mental Health (Care and Treatment) (Scotland) Act 2003 (asp 13), of medical treatment.

(7) The court may make a treatment order in the absence of the person in respect of whom the application is made only if—

(a) the person is represented by counsel or solicitor;

(b) that counsel or solicitor is given an opportunity of being heard; and

(c) the court is satisfied that it is—

   (i) impracticable; or

   (ii) inappropriate,

   for the person to be brought before it.

(8) A treatment order may include such directions as the court thinks fit for the removal of the person subject to the order to, and detention of the person in, a place of safety pending the person's admission to the specified hospital.

(9) The court shall, as soon as reasonably practicable after making a treatment order, give notice of the making of the order to—

(a) the person subject to the order;

(b) any solicitor acting for the person;

(c) in a case where—

    (i) the person has been charged with an offence; and

    (ii) a relevant disposal has not been made in the proceedings in respect of the offence,

the prosecutor;

(d) in a case where the person, immediately before the order was made—

    (i) was in custody; or

    (ii) was subject to an assessment order and, immediately before that order was made, was in custody,

the Scottish Ministers; and

(e) the Mental Welfare Commission.

(10) In this section—

"court" has the same meaning as in section 52B of this Act;

"medical treatment" has the same meaning as in section 52D of this Act; and

"specified" means specified in the treatment order.

AMENDMENT

Section 52M inserted by the Mental Health (Care and Treatment) (Scotland) Act 2003 (asp 13), s.130. Brought into force on October 5, 2005 by the Mental Health (Care and Treatment) (Scotland) Act 2003 (Commencement No.4) Order 2005 (SSI 2005/161 (C.6)).

DEFINITIONS

"assessment order": s.52B(1)(c).

"court": s.52B(4).

"medical treatment": s.52D.

"mental disorder": s.328(1) of the Mental Health (Care and Treatment) (Scotland) Act 2003.

"offence": s.307(1).

"prosecutor": s.307(1).

"relevant disposal": s.52B(4).

"sentence": s.307(1).

"specified": s.52M(10).

"treatment order": s.52M.

GENERAL NOTE

A treatment order authorises certain measures including (if required) the removal to hospital, the detention of a person there and the giving of specified treatment: s.52M(6). Such a power can only be invoked if a court is satisfied on the written or oral evidence of two medical practitioners as to certain matters: s.52M(2)(a) and (3). The court must also have regard to all the circumstances (including the nature of the offence charged or proved) and any alternative means of dealing with the person: s.52M(2)(b) and (4). It is competent to make a treatment order in the absence of the person in respect of whom the application is made but there are conditions to be met before that may properly be done: s.52M(7). The making of a treatment order requires intimation to various parties: s.52M(9).

Treatment order made ex proprio motu: application of section 52M

52N.—(1) Where—

(a) a person has been charged with an offence;

(b) the person has not been sentenced; and

(c) it appears to the court that the person has a mental disorder,

the court may, subject to subsections (2) and (3) below, make a treatment order in respect of that person.

(2) The court may make a treatment order under subsection (1) above only if it would make one under subsections (2) to (10) of section 52M of this Act; and those subsections shall apply for the purposes of subsection (1) above as they ap-

ply for the purposes of subsection (1) of that section, references in those subsections to the person in respect of whom the application is made being construed as references to the person in respect of whom it is proposed to make a treatment order.

(3) A treatment order made under subsection (1) above shall, for the purposes of this Act and the Mental Health (Care and Treatment) (Scotland) Act 2003 (asp 13), be treated as if made under section 52M(2) of this Act.

(4) In this section, "court" has the same meaning as in section 52B of this Act.

AMENDMENT

Section 52N inserted by the Mental Health (Care and Treatment) (Scotland) Act 2003 (asp 13), s.130. Brought into force on October 5, 2005 by the Mental Health (Care and Treatment) (Scotland) Act 2003 (Commencement No.4) Order 2005 (SSI 2005/161 (C.6)).

DEFINITIONS

"court": s.52B(4).
"mental disorder": s.328(1) of the Mental Health (Care and Treatment) (Scotland) Act 2003.
"offence": s.307(1).
"sentence": s.307(1).
"treatment order": s.52M.

GENERAL NOTE

It is competent for a court itself (without an application from another party) to make a treatment order: s.52N(1).

Treatment order: supplementary

52P.—(1) If, before the expiry of the period of 7 days beginning with the day on which the treatment order is made—

(a) in the case of a person to whom subsection (2) below applies, it appears to the Scottish Ministers; or

(b) in any other case, it appears to the court,

that, by reason of emergency or other special circumstances, it is not reasonably practicable for the person to be admitted to the hospital specified in the order, the Scottish Ministers, or, as the case may be, the court, may direct that the person be admitted to the hospital specified in the direction.

(2) This subsection applies to—

(a) a person who is in custody immediately before the treatment order is made; or

(b) a person—

(i) who was subject to an assessment order immediately before the treatment order is made; and

(ii) who was in custody immediately before that assessment order was made.

(3) Where the court makes a direction under subsection (1) above, it shall, as soon as reasonably practicable after making the direction, inform the person having custody of the person subject to the treatment order of the making of the direction.

(4) Where the Scottish Ministers make a direction under subsection (1) above, they shall, as soon as reasonably practicable after making the direction, inform—

(a) the court;

(b) the person having custody of the person subject to the treatment order; and

(c) in a case where—

(i) the person has been charged with an offence; and

(ii) a relevant disposal has not been made in the proceedings in respect of the offence,

the prosecutor,

of the making of the direction.

(5) Where a direction is made under subsection (1) above, the treatment order shall have effect as if the hospital specified in the direction were the hospital specified in the order.

(6) In this section—

"court" means the court which made the treatment order; and

"relevant disposal" has the same meaning as in section 52B of this Act.

AMENDMENT

Section 52P inserted by the Mental Health (Care and Treatment) (Scotland) Act 2003 (asp 13), s.130. Brought into force on October 5, 2005 by the Mental Health (Care and Treatment) (Scotland) Act 2003 (Commencement No.4) Order 2005 (SSI 2005/161 (C.6)).

DEFINITIONS

"assessment order": s.52B(1)(c).
"court": s.52B(4).
"mental disorder": s.328(1) of the Mental Health (Care and Treatment) (Scotland) Act 2003.
"offence": s.307(1).
"relevant disposal": s.52B(4).
"sentence": s.307(1).
"treatment order": s.52M.

Review of treatment order

52Q.—(1) The responsible medical officer shall, where that officer is satisfied—

(a) that any of the conditions mentioned in section 52D(7) of this Act are no longer met in respect of the person subject to the treatment order; or

(b) that there has otherwise been a change of circumstances since the order was made which makes the continued detention of the person in hospital by virtue of the order no longer appropriate,

submit a report in writing to the court.

(2) Where a report is submitted under subsection (1) above, the court shall—

(a) if satisfied that the person need not be subject to the treatment order—

(i) revoke the order; and

(ii) commit the person to prison or such other institution to which the person might have been committed had the order not been made or otherwise deal with the person as the court considers appropriate; or

(b) if not so satisfied—

(i) confirm the order;

(ii) vary the order; or

(iii) revoke the order and take any action mentioned in paragraph (a)(ii) above.

(3) Sections 52M, 52P, this section and sections 52R and 52S of this Act apply to the variation of a treatment order under subsection (2)(b)(ii) above as they apply to a treatment order.

(4) In this section—

"court" means the court which made the treatment order; and

"responsible medical officer" means the person's responsible medical officer appointed under section 230 of the Mental Health (Care and Treatment) (Scotland) Act 2003 (asp 13).

AMENDMENT
Section 52Q inserted by the Mental Health (Care and Treatment) (Scotland) Act 2003 (asp 13), s.130. Brought into force on October 5, 2005 by the Mental Health (Care and Treatment) (Scotland) Act 2003 (Commencement No.4) Order 2005 (SSI 2005/161 (C.6)).

DEFINITIONS
"assessment order": s.52B(1)(c).
"court": s.52Q(4).
"offence": s.307(1).
"responsible medical officer": s.230 of the Mental Health (Care and Treatment) (Scotland) Act 2003.
"treatment order": s.52M.

Termination of treatment order

52R.—(1) This section applies—

(a) where, in the case of a person who, when the treatment order is made, has not been removed to the hospital specified in the order, the period of 7 days beginning with the day on which the order is made has not expired; or

(b) in the case of a person—

    (i) who, when the treatment order is made, has been admitted to the hospital specified in the order; or

    (ii) who has been removed under paragraph (a) of subsection (6) of section 52M of this Act to the hospital so specified.

(2) A treatment order shall cease to have effect on the occurrence of any of the following events—

(a) in a case where—

    (i) the person subject to the treatment order has been charged with an offence; and

    (ii) a relevant disposal had not been made in the proceedings in respect of such offence when the order was made,

    the making of a relevant disposal in such proceedings;

(b) in a case where the person subject to the treatment order has been convicted of an offence but has not been sentenced—

    (i) the deferral of sentence by the court under section 202(1) of this Act;

    (ii) the making of one of the orders mentioned in subsection (3) below; or

    (iii) the imposition of any sentence.

(3) The orders are—

(a) an interim compulsion order;

(b) a compulsion order;

(c) a guardianship order;

(d) a hospital direction;

(e) any order under section 57 of this Act; or

(f) a probation order which includes a requirement imposed by virtue of section 230(1) of this Act.

(4) In this section, "relevant disposal" has the same meaning as in section 52B of this Act.

AMENDMENT
Section 52R inserted by the Mental Health (Care and Treatment) (Scotland) Act 2003 (asp 13), s.130. Brought into force on October 5, 2005 by the Mental Health (Care and Treatment) (Scotland) Act 2003 (Commencement No.4) Order 2005 (SSI 2005/161 (C.6)).

DEFINITIONS
"assessment order": s.52B(1)(c).

"court": s.52Q(4).
"offence": s.307(1).
"relevant disposal": s.52B(4).
"responsible medical officer": s.230 of the Mental Health (Care and Treatment) (Scotland) Act 2003.
"treatment order": s.52M.

GENERAL NOTE

A treatment order ceases to have effect on the occurrence of certain events: s.52R(2). Where a charge is not proceeded with further or the charge is proved or the person is acquitted of the charge then the treatment order ceases to have effect: s.52R(2)(a) and s.52B(4). Where a person has been convicted but not sentenced then the occurrence of one of three events mean that the treatment order ceases to have effect: s.52R(2)(b). These events are the deferral of a sentence, the making of various orders or the imposition of any sentence: s.52R(2)(b). The various orders that terminate a treatment order are set out in s.52R(3)(a) to (f).

Power of court on treatment order ceasing to have effect

52S.—(1) Where, otherwise than by virtue of section 52Q(2) or 52R(2) of this Act, a treatment order ceases to have effect the court shall commit the person who was subject to the order to prison or such other institution to which the person might have been committed had the order not been made or otherwise deal with the person as the court considers appropriate.

(2) In this section, "court" has the same meaning as in section 52B of this Act.

AMENDMENT

Section 52S inserted by the Mental Health (Care and Treatment) (Scotland) Act 2003 (asp 13), s.130. Brought into force on October 5, 2005 by the Mental Health (Care and Treatment) (Scotland) Act 2003 (Commencement No.4) Order 2005 (SSI 2005/161 (C.6)).

DEFINITIONS

"court": s.52Q(4).
"treatment order": s.52M.

Prevention of delay in trials

Prevention of delay in trials: assessment orders and treatment orders

52T.—(1) Subsections (4) to (9) of section 65 of this Act shall apply in the case of a person charged on indictment who is detained in hospital by virtue of an assessment order or a treatment order as those subsections apply in the case of an accused who is—

(a) committed for an offence until liberated in due course of law; and

(b) detained by virtue of that committal.

(2) Section 147 of this Act shall apply in the case of a person charged with an offence in summary proceedings who is detained in hospital by virtue of an assessment order or a treatment order as it applies in the case of an accused who is detained in respect of that offence.

(3) Any period during which, under—

(a) section 221 (as read with sections 222 and 223) of the Mental Health (Care and Treatment) (Scotland) Act 2003 (asp 13); or

(b) section 224 (as read with sections 225 and 226) of that Act,

a patient's detention is not authorised shall be taken into account for the purposes of the calculation of any of the periods mentioned in subsection (4) below.

(4) Those periods are—

(a) the total periods of 80 days and 110 days referred to respectively in paragraphs (a) and (b) of subsection (4) of section 65 of this Act as applied by subsection (1) above;

(b) those total periods as extended under subsection (5) or (7) respectively or, on appeal, under subsection (8) of that section as so applied;

(c) the total of 40 days referred to in section 147 of this Act (prevention of delay in trials in summary proceedings) as applied by subsection (2) above; and

(d) that period as extended under subsection (2) of that section or, on appeal, under subsection (3) of that section as so applied.

AMENDMENT

Section 52T inserted by the Mental Health (Care and Treatment) (Scotland) Act 2003 (asp 13), s.130. Brought into force on October 5, 2005 by the Mental Health (Care and Treatment) (Scotland) Act 2003 (Commencement No.4) Order 2005 (SSI 2005/161 (C.6)).

DEFINITIONS

"assessment order": s.52B(1)(c).
"court": s.52Q(4).
"indictment": s.307(1).
"offence": s.307(1).
"treatment order": s.52M.

Effect of assessment and treatment orders on pre-existing mental health orders

Effect of assessment order and treatment order on pre-existing mental health order

52U.—(1) This section applies where—

(a) a patient is subject to a relevant order; and

(b) an assessment order or a treatment order is made in respect of the patient.

(2) The relevant order shall, subject to subsection (3) below, cease to authorise the measures specified in it for the period during which the patient is subject to the assessment order or, as the case may be, treatment order.

(3) For the purposes of sections 112 to 120, and Part 20, of the Mental Health (Care and Treatment) (Scotland) Act 2003 (asp 13) (the "2003 Act"), the patient shall be deemed not to be subject to the relevant order during the period mentioned in subsection (2) above.

(4) In this section, a "relevant order" means—

(a) an interim compulsory treatment order made under section 65(2) of the 2003 Act; and

(b) a compulsory treatment order made under section 64(4)(a) of that Act.

AMENDMENT

Section 52U inserted by the Mental Health (Care and Treatment) (Scotland) Act 2003 (asp 13), s.130. Brought into force on October 5, 2005 by the Mental Health (Care and Treatment) (Scotland) Act 2003 (Commencement No.4) Order 2005 (SSI 2005/161 (C.6)).

DEFINITIONS

"assessment order": s.52B(1)(c).
"court": s.52Q(4).
"relevant order": s.52U(4).
"treatment order": s.52M.

Interim compulsion orders

Interim compulsion orders

53.—(1) This section applies where a person (referred to in this section and in sections 53A to 53D of this Act as an "offender")—

(a) is convicted in the High Court or the sheriff court of an offence punishable by imprisonment (other than an offence the sentence for which is fixed by law); or

(b) is remitted to the High Court by the sheriff under any enactment for sentence for such an offence.

(2) If the court is satisfied—

(a) on the written or oral evidence of two medical practitioners—

    (i) that the offender has a mental disorder; and

    (ii) as to the matters mentioned in subsection (3) below; and

(b) that, having regard to the matters mentioned in subsection (4) below, it is appropriate,

it may, subject to subsection (7) below, make an order (in this Act referred to as an "interim compulsion order") authorising the measures mentioned in subsection (8) below and specifying any matters to be included in the report under section 53B(1) of this Act.

(3) The matters referred to in subsection (2)(a)(ii) above are—

(a) that there are reasonable grounds for believing—

    (i) that the conditions mentioned in subsection (5) below are likely to be met in respect of the offender; and

    (ii) that the offender's mental disorder is such that it would be appropriate to make one of the disposals mentioned in subsection (6) below in relation to the offender;

(b) that the hospital to be specified in the order is suitable for the purpose of assessing whether the conditions mentioned in subsection (5) below are met in respect of the offender;

(c) that, were an interim compulsion order made, the offender could be admitted to such hospital before the expiry of the period of 7 days beginning with the day on which the order is made; and

(d) that it would not be reasonably practicable for the assessment mentioned in paragraph (b) above to be made unless an order were made.

(4) The matters referred to in subsection (2)(b) above are—

(a) all the circumstances (including the nature of the offence of which the offender is convicted); and

(b) any alternative means of dealing with the offender.

(5) The conditions referred to in paragraphs (a)(i) and (b) of subsection (3) above are—

(a) that medical treatment which would be likely to—

    (i) prevent the mental disorder worsening; or

    (ii) alleviate any of the symptoms, or effects, of the disorder,

    is available for the offender;

(b) that if the offender were not provided with such medical treatment there would be a significant risk—

    (i) to the health, safety or welfare of the offender; or

    (ii) to the safety of any other person; and

(c) that the making of an interim compulsion order in respect of the offender is necessary.

(6) The disposals are—

(a) both a compulsion order that authorises detention in hospital by virtue of section 57A(8)(a) of this Act and a restriction order; or

(b) a hospital direction.

(7) An interim compulsion order may authorise detention in a state hospital only if, on the written or oral evidence of the two medical practitioners mentioned in subsection (2)(a) above, it appears to the court—

    (a) that the offender requires to be detained in hospital under conditions of special security; and

    (b) that such conditions of special security can be provided only in a state hospital.

(8) The measures are—

    (a) in the case of an offender who, when the interim compulsion order is made, has not been admitted to the specified hospital, the removal, before the expiry of the period of 7 days beginning with the day on which the order is made, of the offender to the specified hospital by—

        (i) a constable;

        (ii) a person employed in, or contracted to provide services in or to, the specified hospital who is authorised by the managers of that hospital to remove persons to hospital for the purposes of this section; or

        (iii) a specified person;

    (b) the detention, for a period not exceeding 12 weeks beginning with the day on which the order is made, of the offender in the specified hospital; and

    (c) during the period of 12 weeks beginning with the day on which the order is made, the giving to the offender, in accordance with Part 16 of the Mental Health (Care and Treatment) (Scotland) Act 2003 (asp 13), of medical treatment.

(9) An interim compulsion order may include such directions as the court thinks fit for the removal of the offender to, and the detention of the offender in, a place of safety pending the offender's admission to the specified hospital.

(10) The court may make an interim compulsion order in the absence of the offender only if—

    (a) the offender is represented by counsel or solicitor;

    (b) that counsel or solicitor is given an opportunity of being heard; and

    (c) the court is satisfied that it is—

        (i) impracticable; or

        (ii) inappropriate,

    for the offender to be brought before it.

(11) The court shall, as soon as reasonably practicable after making an interim compulsion order, give notice of the making of the order to—

    (a) the person subject to the order;

    (b) any solicitor acting for that person;

    (c) the Scottish Ministers; and

    (d) the Mental Welfare Commission.

(12) Where a court makes an interim compulsion order in relation to an offender, the court—

    (a) shall not, at the same time

        (i) make an order under section 200 of this Act;

        (ii) impose a fine;

        (iii) pass sentence of imprisonment;

        (iv) make a compulsion order;

        (v) make a guardianship order;

        (vi) make a probation order; or

        (vii) make a community service order,

in relation of the offender;

(b) may make any other order which it has power to make apart from this section.

(13) In this section—

"medical treatment" has the same meaning as in section 52D of this Act;

"sentence of imprisonment" includes any sentence or order for detention; and

"specified" means specified in the interim compulsion order.

AMENDMENTS

Section 53 substituted by the Mental Health (Care and Treatment) (Scotland) Act 2003 (asp 13), s.131. Brought into force on October 5, 2005 by the Mental Health (Care and Treatment) (Scotland) Act 2003 (Commencement No.4) Order 2005 (SSI 2005/161 (C.6)).

DEFINITIONS

"court": s.53A(4).
"interim compulsion order": s.53(2).
"medical treatment": s.329(1) of the Mental Health (Care and Treatment) (Scotland) Act 2003.
"sentence of imprisonment": s.53(13).
"specified": s.52(13).

GENERAL NOTE

An interim compulsion order may be made competently after conviction if a court is satisfied on the written or oral evidence of two medical practitioners that the offender has a mental disorder: s.53(2). There are other conditions to be met: see s.53(2)(b), (3) and (4).

Interim compulsion order: supplementary

53A.—(1) If, before the expiry of the period of 7 days beginning with the day on which the interim compulsion order is made, it appears to the court, or, as the case may be, the Scottish Ministers, that, by reason of emergency or other special circumstances, it is not reasonably practicable for the offender to be admitted to the hospital specified in the order, the court, or, as the case may be, the Scottish Ministers, may direct that the offender be admitted to the hospital specified in the direction.

(2) Where—

(a) the court makes a direction under subsection (1) above, it shall, as soon as reasonably practicable after making the direction, inform the person having custody of the offender; and

(b) the Scottish Ministers make such a direction, they shall, as soon as reasonably practicable after making the direction, inform—

(i) the court; and

(ii) the person having custody of the offender.

(3) Where a direction is made under subsection (1) above, the interim compulsion order shall have effect as if the hospital specified in the direction were the hospital specified in the order.

(4) In this section, "court" means the court which made the interim compulsion order.

AMENDMENT

Section 53A inserted by the Mental Health (Care and Treatment) (Scotland) Act 2003 (asp 13), s.131. Brought into force on October 5, 2005 by the Mental Health (Care and Treatment) (Scotland) Act 2003 (Commencement No.4) Order 2005 (SSI 2005/161 (C.6)).

Review and extension of interim compulsion order

53B.—(1) The responsible medical officer shall, before the expiry of the period specified by the court under section 53(8)(b) of this Act, submit a report in writing to the court—

(a) as to the matters mentioned in subsection (2) below; and

(b) as to any matters specified by the court under section 53(2) of this Act.

(2) The matters are—

(a) whether the conditions mentioned in section 53(5) of this Act are met in respect of the offender;

(b) the type (or types) of mental disorder that the offender has; and

(c) whether it is necessary to extend the interim compulsion order to allow further time for the assessment mentioned in section 53(3)(b) of this Act.

(3) The responsible medical officer shall, at the same time as such officer submits the report to the court, send a copy of such report to—

(a) the offender; and

(b) any solicitor acting for the offender.

(4) The court may, on receiving the report submitted under subsection (1) above, if satisfied that the extension of the order is necessary, extend the order for such period (not exceeding 12 weeks beginning with the day on which the order would cease to have effect were such an extension not made) as the court may specify.

(5) The court may extend an interim compulsion order under subsection (4) above for a period only if, by doing so, the total period for which the offender will be subject to the order does not exceed 12 months beginning with the day on which the order was first made.

(6) The court may, under subsection (4) above, extend an interim compulsion order in the absence of the offender only if—

(a) the offender is represented by counsel or a solicitor;

(b) that counsel or solicitor is given an opportunity of being heard; and

(c) the court is satisfied that it is—

(i) impracticable; or

(ii) inappropriate,

for the offender to be brought before it.

(7) Subsections (1) to (9) of this section shall apply for the purposes of an interim compulsion order extended under subsection (4) above as they apply for the purposes of an interim compulsion order, references in those subsections to the period specified by the court under section 53(8)(b) of this Act being construed as references to the period specified by the court under subsection (4) above.

(8) Where a report is submitted under subsection (1) above, the court may, before the expiry of the period specified by the court under section 53(8)(b) of this Act—

(a) revoke the interim compulsion order and make one of the disposals mentioned in section 53(6) of this Act; or

(b) revoke the interim compulsion order and deal with the offender in any way (other than by making an interim compulsion order) in which the court could have dealt with the offender if no such order had been made.

(9) In this section—

"court" means the court which made the interim compulsion order; and

"responsible medical officer" means the responsible medical officer appointed in respect of the offender under section 230 of the Mental Health (Care and Treatment) (Scotland) Act 2003 (asp 13).

AMENDMENT

Section 53B inserted by the Mental Health (Care and Treatment) (Scotland) Act 2003 (asp 13), s.131. Brought into force on October 5, 2005 by the Mental Health (Care and Treatment) (Scotland) Act 2003 (Commencement No.4) Order 2005 (SSI 2005/161 (C.6)).

DEFINITIONS

"court": s.53B(9).
"interim compulsion order": s.53(2).
"mental disorder": s.328(1) of the Mental Health (Care and Treatment) (Scotland) Act 2003.
"offence": s.307(1).
"offender": s.53(1).
"relevant disposal": s.52B(4).
"responsible medical officer": s.230 of the Mental Health (Care and Treatment) (Scotland) Act 2003.
"treatment order": s.52M.

Early termination of interim compulsion order

53C.—(1) An interim compulsion order shall cease to have effect if the court—

(a) makes a compulsion order in relation to the offender;

(b) makes a hospital direction in relation to the offender; or

(c) deals with the offender in some other way, including the imposing of a sentence of imprisonment on the offender.

(2) In this section, "court" means the court which made the interim compulsion order.

AMENDMENT

Section 53C inserted by the Mental Health (Care and Treatment) (Scotland) Act 2003 (asp 13), s.131. Brought into force on October 5, 2005 by the Mental Health (Care and Treatment) (Scotland) Act 2003 (Commencement No.4) Order 2005 (SSI 2005/161 (C.6)).

DEFINITIONS

"compulsion order": s.57A.
"court": s.53C(2).
"hospital direction": s.59A(1).
"offender": s.53(1).

Power of court on interim compulsion order ceasing to have effect

53D.—(1) Where, otherwise than by virtue of section 53B(8) or 53C of this Act, an interim compulsion order ceases to have effect the court may deal with the offender who was subject to the order in any way (other than the making of a new interim compulsion order) in which it could have dealt with the offender if no such order had been made.

(2) In this section, "court" means the court which made the interim compulsion order.

AMENDMENT

Section 53D inserted by the Mental Health (Care and Treatment) (Scotland) Act 2003 (asp 13), s.131. Brought into force on October 5, 2005 by the Mental Health (Care and Treatment) (Scotland) Act 2003 (Commencement No.4) Order 2005(SSI 2005/161 (C.6)).

DEFINITIONS

"court": s.53D(2).

"interim compulsion order": s.53(2).
"offender": s.53(1).

Insanity in bar of trial

Insanity in bar of trial

54.—(1) Where the court is satisfied, on the written or oral evidence of two medical practitioners, that a person charged with the commission of an offence is insane so that his trial cannot proceed or, if it has commenced, cannot continue, the court shall, subject to subsection (2) below—

    (a) make a finding to that effect and state the reasons for that finding;

    (b) discharge the trial diet or, in proceedings on indictment where the finding is made at or before the first diet (in the case of proceedings in the sheriff court) or the preliminary hearing (in the case of proceedings in the High Court), that diet or, as the case may be, hearing and order that a diet (in this Act referred to as an "an examination of facts") be held under section 55 of this Act; and

    (c) remand the person in custody or on bail or, where the court is satisfied—

        (i) on the written or oral evidence of two medical practitioners, that the conditions mentioned in subsection (2A) below are met in respect of the person; and

        (ii) that a hospital is available for his admission and suitable for his detention,

make an order (in this section referred to as a "temporary compulsion order") authorising the measures mentioned in subsection (2B) below in respect of the person until the conclusion of the examination of facts.

(2) Subsection (1) above is without prejudice to the power of the court, on an application by the prosecutor, to desert the diet *pro loco et tempore*.

(2A) The conditions referred to in subsection (1)(c)(i) above are—

    (a) that the person has a mental disorder;

    (b) that medical treatment which would be likely to—

        (i) prevent the mental disorder worsening; or

        (ii) alleviate any of the symptoms, or effects, of the disorder,

    is available for the person; and

    (c) that if the person were not provided with such medical treatment there would be a significant risk—

        (a) to the health, safety or welfare of the person; or

        (b) to the safety of any other person.

(2B) The measures referred to in subsection (1)(c)(i) above are—

    (a) in the case of a person who, when the temporary compulsion order is made, has not been admitted to the specified hospital, the removal, before the expiry of the period of 7 days beginning with the day on which the order is made of the person to the specified hospital by—

        (i) a constable;

        (ii) person employed in, or contracted to provide services in or to, the specified hospital who is authorised by the managers of that hospital to remove persons to hospital for the purposes of this section; or

        (iii) a specified person;

    (b) the detention of the person in the specified hospital; and

(c) the giving to the person, in accordance with Part 16 of the Mental Health (Care and Treatment) (Scotland) Act 2003 (asp 13), of medical treatment.

(3) The court may, before making a finding under subsection (1) above as to the insanity of a person, adjourn the case in order that investigation of his mental condition may be carried out.

(4) The court which made a temporary compulsion order may, at any time while the order is in force, review the order on the ground that there has been a change of circumstances since the order was made and, on such review—

(a) where the court considers that such an order is no longer required in relation to a person, it shall revoke the order and may remand him in custody or on bail;

(b) in any other case, the court may—

(i) confirm or vary the order; or

(ii) revoke the order and make such other order, under subsection (1)(c) above or any other provision of this Act, as the court considers appropriate.

(5) Where it appears to a court that it is not practicable or appropriate for the accused to be brought before it for the purpose of determining whether he is insane so that his trial cannot proceed, then, if no objection to such a course is taken by or on behalf of the accused, the court may order that the case be proceeded with in his absence.

(6) Where evidence is brought before the court that the accused was insane at the time of doing the act or making the omission constituting the offence with which he is charged and he is acquitted, the court shall—

(a) in proceedings on indictment, direct the jury to find; or

(b) in summary proceedings, state,

whether the accused was insane at such time as aforesaid, and, if so, to declare whether he was acquitted on account of his insanity at that time.

(7) It shall not be competent for a person charged summarily in the sheriff court to found on a plea of insanity standing in bar of trial unless, before the first witness for the prosecution is sworn, he gives notice to the prosecutor of the plea and of the witnesses by whom he proposes to maintain it; and where such notice is given, the court shall, if the prosecutor so moves, adjourn the case.

(8) In this section,

"medical treatment" has the same meaning as in section 52D of this Act;

"specified" means specified in the temporary compulsion order; and

"the court" means—

(a) as regards a person charged on indictment, the High Court or the sheriff court;

(b) as regards a person charged summarily, the sheriff court.

AMENDMENTS

Subs.(1)(b) as amended by the Criminal Procedure (Amendment) (Scotland) Act 2004 (asp 5), s.25 and Sch.1, para.13. Brought into force on February 1, 2005 by the Criminal Procedure (Amendment) (Scotland) Act 2004 (Commencement, Transitional Provisions and Savings) Order 2004 (SSI 2004/405 (C.28)), art.2.

Subss.(1)(c), (4), (8) as amended, and subss.(2A), (2B) inserted, by the Mental Health (Care and Treatment) (Scotland) Act 2003 (asp 13), Sch.4, para.8(2). Brought into force on October 5, 2005 by the Mental Health (Care and Treatment) (Scotland) Act 2003 (Commencement No.4) Order 2005 (SSI 2005/161 (C.6)).

DEFINITIONS

"bail": s.307(1).

"court": s.54(8).

"examination of facts": s.307(1).

"medical practitioner": s.61(1).

"temporary hospital order": s.54(1)(c).

GENERAL NOTE

It is interesting to note, by way of a preliminary, that s.52 is concerned with "mental disorder", s.53 is concerned with "mental disorder within the meaning of s.1(2) of the Mental Health (Scotland) Act 1984" and s.54 is concerned with "insanity".

The broad question in a plea-in-bar on grounds of insanity is whether the accused has the capacity to instruct his legal representatives as to his defence and to follow proceedings at his trial. The case of *Stewart v H.M. Advocate (No. 1)*, 1997 S.C.C.R. 330, where such a plea was taken at a preliminary diet in relation to a mentally handicapped accused, emphasises that it is for the judge to decide on assessing the medical evidence whether the plea is made out. See also the case of *McLachlan v Brown*, 1997 S.C.C.R. 457, which confirms that s.54(1) applies not only to cases where the accused is unfit to plead due to mental illness, but also to cases where the accused is unfit to plead due to some mental impairment or handicap. It is conceivable that such a plea-in-bar could also extend to extreme physical defects (see *H.M. Advocate v Wilson*, 1942 J.C. 75; 1942 S.L.T. 194 approved in *Stewart (No. 1)* above). Also worthy of note is *Stewart v H.M. Advocate (No. 2)*, 1997 S.C.C.R. 430 where it was held, *inter alia*, that there is nothing in the legislation to exclude the right of an accused to renew a plea of insanity in bar of trial at a preliminary diet following service of a fresh indictment, despite the fact that such a plea was unsuccessful in respect of the original indictment. The decision recognises the fact that an accused's mental condition may fluctuate, and that accordingly insanity for the purposes of s.54 includes not only insanity by reason of some permanent condition but also insanity by reason of a condition which may alter from time to time. These authorities were also cited in *Hughes v H.M. Advocate*, 2001 G.W.D. 15–572 when H unsuccessfully contended that his post-accident amnesia should be treated as a plea in bar of trial on the grounds that he would not be able to instruct his defence about the circumstances. The court noted that H had been found to be sane and fit to plead and fully capable of following proceedings, instructing his defence and testing the Crown case, hence the rejection of H's plea.

Subsection (6) of s.54 deals with the special defence of insanity at the time of the offence, as distinct from insanity in bar of trial. Insanity as a defence rests upon alienation of reason at the time of the wrongful act, such that there can have been no *mens rea* for its commission. Acquittal as a result of a finding of insanity at the time of the offence may arise after trial (s.54(6)) or as a conclusion of an EOF (discussed below and see s.55(4)). In either case the court moves to disposal under s.57 of the Act.

Section 54 requires a court in both solemn and summary proceedings, following a finding that a person is insane so that a trial cannot proceed or continue, to hold an examination of the facts ("EOF") relating to the charges. The section further provides for the court to remand in custody or on bail, or to commit such a person to hospital under a temporary hospital order, until the conclusion of the EOF.

The new procedure very much contrasts with the previous law under which, when a person was found insane in bar of trial, no attempt was made by the court to examine the evidence as to whether the accused did the act with which he is charged. The new procedure requires that there be an examination of the relevant facts. It gives effect to certain recommendations contained in the Second Thomson Report on Criminal Procedure (Cmnd. 6218 (1975)). The only circumstances in which an EOF cannot be held are when the Crown applies for and the court agrees to the diet being deserted *pro loco et tempore*.

The novelty of these proceedings is accentuated by the possibility that the hearing to determine insanity may in some circumstances proceed in the absence of the accused: see s.54(5); but it should be borne in mind that the hearing is to be conducted along the lines of a trial in so far as possible, and accordingly proof of the material fact of identification requires to be considered and addressed.

In relation to solemn proceedings, s.54 should be read together with s.67. The latter section sets out the statutory requirements on the Crown for the witnesses and for intimation in writing of the details of the witnesses and where they can be contacted for the purposes of precognition. For that reason the accused or those advising him should have clear intimation of the availability of the two medical practitioners who may give evidence for the Crown of insanity. If the illness has developed immediately prior to the trial then such medical practitioners may be called with leave of the court: see s.67(5). If the defence seek to raise the issue then they must intimate the details of the two medical practitioners: see s.78(4).

In relation to summary proceedings, the approach to the issue is necessarily different. There appears to be no duty on the Crown to intimate the issue in advance of the trial although one would hope that such an important matter would be intimated in the interests of justice. In any event, an adjournment for inquiry at the first calling in terms of s.145(1) would undoubtedly follow where there had been no intimation. The accused or those advising him are under a clear duty to give notice: see s.54(7).

For the purposes of s.54(1) a written report bearing to be signed by a medical practitioner may, subject to the provisions of s.61 being met, be received in evidence without proof of the signature or qualifications of the practitioner: note that s.61(3) entitles the court, in any case, to call the report's author to give oral evidence. Section 54(1)(b) has been amended to take account of the mandatory preliminary diet proceedings in the High Court. At any point in the proceedings, summary or solemn, trial can be discharged if evidence satisfying the requirements of s.54 is produced; the court has then to fix an examination of facts conform to ss.55 and 56.

Examination of facts

Examination of facts

55.—(1) At an examination of facts ordered under section 54(1)(b) of this Act the court shall, on the basis of the evidence (if any) already given in the trial and such evidence, or further evidence, as may be led by either party, determine whether it is satisfied—

(a) beyond reasonable doubt, as respects any charge on the indictment or, as the case may be, the complaint in respect of which the accused was being or was to be tried, that he did the act or made the omission constituting the offence; and

(b) on the balance of probabilities, that there are no grounds for acquitting him.

(2) Where the court is satisfied as mentioned in subsection (1) above, it shall make a finding to that effect.

(3) Where the court is not so satisfied it shall, subject to subsection (4) below, acquit the person of the charge.

(4) Where, as respects a person acquitted under subsection (3) above, the court is satisfied as to the matter mentioned in subsection (1)(a) above but it appears to the court that the person was insane at the time of doing the act or making the omission constituting the offence, the court shall state whether the acquittal is on the ground of such insanity.

(5) Where it appears to the court that it is not practical or appropriate for the accused to attend an examination of facts the court may, if no objection is taken by or on behalf of the accused, order that the examination of facts shall proceed in his absence.

(6) Subject to the provisions of this section, section 56 of this Act and any Act of Adjournal the rules of evidence and procedure and the powers of the court shall, in respect of an examination of facts, be as nearly as possible those applicable in respect of a trial.

(7) For the purposes of the application to an examination of facts of the rules and powers mentioned in subsection (6) above, an examination of facts—

(a) commences when the indictment or, as the case may be, complaint is called; and

(b) concludes when the court—

(i) acquits the person under subsection (3) above;

(ii) makes an order under subsection (2) of section 57 of this Act; or

(iii) decides, under paragraph (e) of that subsection, not to make an order.

DEFINITIONS

"examination of facts": s.54(1)(b).

"offence": s.307(1).

GENERAL NOTE

Section 54 establishes the competency of an examination of facts ("EOF") and s.55 specifies the procedure and powers of the court, its findings, and a number of detailed ancillary matters. An EOF is to be held along the lines of a trial as far as possible and, again emphasising the novelty, it may proceed in certain circumstances in the absence of the accused.

It seems important to stress that an EOF need not necessarily be a matter wholly separate from a trial in the conventional sense. Section 54(1) refers to "a person charged with the commission of an offence" being insane "so that his trial cannot proceed or, if it has commenced, cannot continue". On that approach it is easy to imagine under solemn procedure a trial commencing in the ordinary way and after the jury has heard some evidence the defence lawyers (or others) intimating that there is concern about the accused's health. Thereafter, a medical examination might produce the necessary evidence leading the court to make the essential finding (s.54(1)(a)) and the trial diet being discharged and an EOF then being held (s.54(1)(b)). Indeed, the citation of the accused and any witnesses to the trial diet is valid citation to the EOF: see s.56(1) and (2). It follows from the discharge of the trial diet and the terms of s.55 that the jury is released.

Thereafter, at the EOF the court must consider both any evidence already given in the trial and the evidence led at the EOF itself, by either party. The court must then determine whether it is satisfied that the accused did the act or made the omission constituting the offence and that there are no grounds for his acquittal. The standard for the first determination is beyond reasonable doubt and for the second it is on a balance of probabilities (s.55(1)(a) and (b)).

If the court is not satisfied that these standards have been made out the accused is acquitted (s.55(3)). However, if the court is satisfied that the accused did the act or made the omission constituting the offence, but on a balance of probabilities it appears to the court that the accused was insane at the time, acquittal on that ground may competently be determined and stated by the court (s.55(4)).

Examination of facts: supplementary provisions

56.—(1) An examination of facts ordered under section 54(1)(b) of this Act may, where the order is made at the trial diet or, in proceedings on indictment, at the first diet (in the case of proceedings in the sheriff court) or the preliminary hearing (in the case of proceedings in the High Court), be held immediately following the making of the order and, where it is so held, the citation of the accused and any witness to the trial diet, first diet or, as the case may be, preliminary hearing shall be a valid citation to the examination of facts.

(2) [*Repealed by the Criminal Procedure (Amendment) (Scotland) Act 2004 (asp 5), s.25 and Sch.1, para.14(b). Brought into force on February 1, 2005 by the Criminal Procedure (Amendment) (Scotland) Act 2004 (Commencement, Transitional Provisions and Savings) Order 2004 (SSI 2004/405 (C.28)), art.2.*]

(3) Where an accused person is not legally represented at an examination of facts the court shall appoint counsel or a solicitor to represent his interests.

(4) The court may, on the motion of the prosecutor and after hearing the accused, order that the examination of facts shall proceed in relation to a particular charge, or particular charges, in the indictment or, as the case may be, complaint in priority to other such charges.

(5) The court may, on the motion of the prosecutor and after hearing the accused, at any time desert the examination of facts *pro loco et tempore* as respects either the whole indictment or, as the case may be, complaint or any charge therein.

(6) Where, and to the extent that, an examination of facts has, under subsection (5) above, been deserted *pro loco et tempore*—

(a) in the case of proceedings on indictment, the Lord Advocate may, at any time, raise and insist in a new indictment; or

(b) in the case of summary proceedings, the prosecutor may at any time raise a fresh libel, notwithstanding any time limit which would otherwise apply in respect of prosecution of the alleged offence.

(7) If, in a case where a court has made a finding under subsection (2) of section 55 of this Act, a person is subsequently charged, whether on indictment or on a complaint, with an offence arising out of the same act or omission as is referred to in subsection (1) of that section, any order made, under section 57(2) of this Act shall, with effect from the commencement of the later proceedings, cease to have effect.

(8) For the purposes of subsection (7) above, the later proceedings are commenced when the indictment or, as the case may be, the complaint is served.

AMENDMENTS

Subs.(1) as amended by the Criminal Procedure (Amendment) (Scotland) Act 2004 (asp 5), s.25 and Sch.1, para.14(a). Brought into force on February 1, 2005 by the Criminal Procedure (Amendment) (Scotland) Act 2004 (Commencement, Transitional Provisions and Savings) Order 2004 (SSI 2004/405 (C.28)), art.2.

DEFINITIONS

"complaint": s.307(1).
"diet": s.307(1).
"examination of facts": s.54(1)(b).
"indictment": s.307(1).
"order": s.307(1).
"prosecutor": s.307(1).

GENERAL NOTE

The section makes supplementary provisions for the conduct of examinations of facts ("EOF") in summary and solemn cases. The existing powers of citation to the trial diet in summary cases, or to the first or preliminary or trial diets in solemn proceedings, hold good for any EOF (s.56(1)). Any time limits which might constrain the Crown following an EOF being deserted *pro loco et tempore* are removed (s.56(6)), and the Crown's rights to serve a new complaint or to re-indict are preserved.

If at the EOF a finding is delivered to the effect that the accused did the act charged as the main offence, thus paving the way for the EOF to move to disposal under s.57, the prosecutor may not wish to prolong the EOF and move to desert the remaining charges under s.56(5). The effect of such desertion *pro loco et tempore* is to terminate the present proceedings, but reserve the Crown's right to reraise proceedings should the accused recover his sanity sufficiently to stand trial. Any disposal order made under s.57 in relation to the previous finding of insanity ceases to have effect from the commencement of the new proceedings, namely when the new indictment or complaint is served (see s.56(7) and (8)). Thus on an accused person sufficiently recovering his sanity, he may be prosecuted in exactly the same terms as those contained in the original indictment or complaint against him, except of course for those charges where he has been acquitted by the court at the EOF. In other words, insanity is no longer a bar to trial. This is in line with case law to the effect that a person found to be insane in bar of trial has not tholed his assize and may be tried upon recovering his sanity or upon it being discovered that he was not insane: see *H.M. Advocate v Bickerstaff*, 1926 J.C. 5 followed in *H.M. Advocate v Graham* (High Court of Justiciary, February 16, 1996, unreported).

Disposal in case of insanity

Disposal of case where accused found to be insane

57.—(1) This section applies where—

(a) a person is, by virtue of section 54(6) or 55(3) of this Act, acquitted on the ground of his insanity at the time of the act or omission; or

(b) following an examination of facts under section 55, a court makes a finding under subsection (2) of that section.

(2) Subject to subsection (3) below, where this section applies the court may, as it thinks fit—

(a) subject to subsection (4) below, make a compulsion order authorising the detention of the person in a hospital;

(b) in addition to making such a compulsion order, subject to subsection (4A) below, make a restriction order in respect of the person;

(bb) subject to subsections (3A) and (4B) below, make an interim compulsion order in respect of the person;

(c) subject to subsections (4C) and (6) below, make a guardianship order in respect of the person;

(d) subject to subsection (5) below, make a supervision and treatment order (within the meaning of paragraph 1(1) of Schedule 4 to this Act) in respect of the person; or

(e) make no order.

(3) Where the court is satisfied, having regard to a report submitted in respect of the person following an interim compulsion order, that, on a balance of probabilities, the risk his being at liberty presents to the safety of the public at large is high, it shall make orders under both paragraphs (a) and (b) of subsection (2) above in respect of that person.

(3A) The court may make an interim compulsion order under paragraph (bb) of subsection (2) above in respect of a person only where it has not previously made such an order in respect of the person under that paragraph.

(4) For the purposes of subsection (2)(a) above—

(a) subsections (2) to (16) of section 57A of this Act shall apply as they apply for the purposes of subsection (1) of that section, subject to the following modifications—

    (i) references to the offender shall be construed as references to the person to whom this section applies; and

    (ii) in subsection (4)(b)(i), the reference to the offence of which the offender was convicted shall be construed as a reference to the offence with which the person to whom this section applies was charged;

(b) section 57B of this Act shall have effect subject to the modification that references to the offender shall be construed as references to the person to whom this section applies;

(c) section 57C of this Act shall have effect subject to the following modifications—

    (i) references to the offender shall be construed as references to the person to whom this section applies; and

    (ii) references to section 57A of this Act shall be construed as references to subsection (2)(a) above; and

(d) section 57D of this Act shall have effect subject to the modification that references to the offender shall be construed as references to the person to whom this section applies.

(4A) For the purposes of subsection (2)(b) above, section 59 of this Act shall have effect.

(4B) For the purposes of subsection (2)(bb) above—

(a) subsections (2) to (13) of section 53 of this Act shall apply as they apply for the purposes of subsection (1) of that section, subject to the following modifications—

    (i) references to the offender shall be construed as references to the person to whom this section applies;

    (ii) in subsection (3)(a)(ii), the reference to one of the disposals mentioned in subsection (6) of that section shall be construed as a reference to the disposal mentioned in subsection (6)(a) of that section;

      (iii) in subsection (4)(a), the reference to the offence of which the offender is convicted shall be construed as a reference to the offence with which the person to whom this section applies is charged; and

      (iv) subsection (6)(b) shall not apply;

  (b) section 53A of this Act shall have effect subject to the modification that references to the offender shall be construed as references to the person to whom this section applies;

  (c) section 53B of this Act shall have effect subject to the following modifications—

      (i) references to the offender shall be construed as references to the person to whom this section applies; and

      (ii) for paragraphs (a) and (b) of subsection (8) there shall be substituted ", revoke the interim compulsion order and

         (a) make an order in respect of the person under paragraph (a), (b), (c) or (d) of subsection (2) of section 57 of this Act; or

         (b) decide, under paragraph (e) of that subsection, to make no order in respect of the person."

  (d) section 53C of this Act shall have effect subject to the following modifications—

      (i) references to the offender shall be construed as references to the person to whom this section applies; and

      (ii) for paragraphs (a) to (c) of subsection (1) there shall be substituted—

         "(a) makes an order in respect of the person under paragraph (a), (b), (c) or (d) of subsection (2) of section 57 of this Act; or

         (b) decides, under paragraph (e) of that subsection, to make no order in respect of the person."

  (e) section 53D of this Act shall have effect subject to the modification that the reference to the offender shall be construed as a reference to the person to whom this section applies.

(4C) For the purposes of subsection (2)(c) above, subsections (1A), (6) to (8) and (11) of section 58 of this Act shall apply, subject to the modifications that the reference to a person convicted and any references to the offender shall be construed as references to the person to whom this section applies.

(5) Schedule 4 to this Act shall have effect as regards supervision and treatment orders.

(6) Section 58A of this Act shall have effect as regards guardianship orders made under subsection (2)(c) of this section.

Amendments

    Section 57 as amended by the Adults with Incapacity (Scotland) Act 2000 (asp 4), s.88 and Sch.5, para.26. Brought into force on April 1, 2002 by the Adults with Incapacity (Scotland) Act 2000 (Commencement No. 1) Order 2001 (SSI 2001/81 (C.2)).

    Subs.(3) substituted by Criminal Justice (Scotland) Act 2003 (asp 7), Part 1, s.2(b). Brought into force on June 27, 2003 by the Criminal Justice (Scotland) Act 2003 (Commencement No.1) Order 2003 (SSI 2003/288 (C.14)).

    Subss.(2), (3) and (4) as amended, and subss.(3A), (4A)–(4C) inserted, by the Mental Health (Care and Treatment) (Scotland) Act 2003 (asp 13), Sch.4, para.8(3). Brought into force on October 5, 2005 by the Mental Health (Care and Treatment) (Scotland) Act 2003 (Commencement No.4) Order 2005 (SSI 2005/161 (C.6)).

Definitions

    "examination of facts": s.54(1)(b).

    "medical practitioner": s.61(1).

"new supervising officer": Sch.4, para.7(1)(b).

"order": s.307(1).

"relevant sheriff court": Sch.4, para.3(2)(b).

"supervised person": Sch.4, para.1(1).

"supervising officer": Sch.4, para.1(1).

"supervision and treatment order": Sch.4, para.1(1).

GENERAL NOTE

This section specifies the disposals available to a court at an examination of facts ("EOF") in both solemn and summary proceedings, and to a court acquitting a person on the grounds of insanity at the time of the commission of the offence charged. It provides for the making of a hospital order, with or without a restriction order, a guardianship order, a new disposal (the Supervision and Treatment Order) in which the recipient resides in the community under the supervision of a social worker and for the purposes of treatment under a medical practitioner, and, finally, the making of no order at all. The power to specify a hospital contained in subs.(2)(a) includes a power to specify a hospital unit, but only where the court also makes an order in terms of subs.(2)(b), subjecting the person to the special restrictions set out in s.62(1) of the Mental Health (Scotland) Act 1984. The power to specify a hospital unit was introduced by s.9 of the Crime and Punishment (Scotland) Act 1997 with effect from January 1, 1998, and thus allows a measure of flexibility in placing patients at distinct, possibly specialist, mental health units.

Section 57 thus provides a court with a wider range of disposals than was available under the previous law when dealing with an accused who is unfit to plead. Only two observations need to be made in regard to these disposals. First, the new disposal of a Supervision and Treatment Order is only new to Scotland as it has been provided for in the Criminal Procedure (Insanity and Unfitness to Plead) Act 1991 (c.25) for England and Wales. The extensive arrangements for the new disposal are set out in Sch.4 to this Act. Secondly, in only one disposal is the discretion of the court restricted.

Subs.(3), effective from June 27, 2003, was substituted by s.2(b) of the Criminal Justice (Scotland) Act 2003. In fact, in practical terms subs.(3) cannot be followed by the court until s.2(a) of the 2003 Act is commenced. Section 2(A) adds the making of an interim hospital order to the list of disposals already available to the court in s.57(2).

Compulsion orders

Compulsion order

57A.—(1) This section applies where a person (in this section and in sections 57C and 57D of this Act, referred to as the "offender")—

(a) is convicted in the High Court or the sheriff court of an offence punishable by imprisonment (other than an offence the sentence for which is fixed by law); or

(b) is remitted to the High Court by the sheriff under any enactment for sentence for such an offence.

(2) If the court is satisfied—

(a) on the written or oral evidence of two medical practitioners, that the conditions mentioned in subsection (3) below are met in respect of the offender; and

(b) that, having regard to the matters mentioned in subsection (4) below, it is appropriate,

it may, subject to subsection (5) below, make an order (in this Act referred to as a "compulsion order") authorising, subject to subsection (7) below, for the period of 6 months beginning with the day on which the order is made such of the measures mentioned in subsection (8) below as may be specified in the order.

(3) The conditions referred to in subsection (2)(a) above are—

(a) that the offender has a mental disorder;

(b) that medical treatment which would be likely to—

    (i) prevent the mental disorder worsening; or

    (ii) alleviate any of the symptoms, or effects, of the disorder,

  is available for the offender;

(c) that if the offender were not provided with such medical treatment there would be a significant risk—

    (i) to the health, safety or welfare of the offender; or

    (ii) to the safety of any other person; and

(d) that the making of a compulsion order in respect of the offender is necessary.

(4) The matters referred to in subsection (2)(b) above are—

(a) the mental health officer's report, prepared in accordance with section 57C of this Act, in respect of the offender;

(b) all the circumstances, including—

    (i) the nature of the offence of which the offender was convicted; and

    (ii) the antecedents of the offender; and

(c) any alternative means of dealing with the offender.

(5) The court may, subject to subsection (6) below, make a compulsion order authorising the detention of the offender in a hospital by virtue of subsection (8)(a) below only if satisfied, on the written or oral evidence of the two medical practitioners mentioned in subsection (2)(a) above, that—

(a) the medical treatment mentioned in subsection (3)(b) above can be provided only if the offender is detained in hospital;

(b) the offender could be admitted to the hospital to be specified in the order before the expiry of the period of 7 days beginning with the day on which the order is made; and

(c) the hospital to be so specified is suitable for the purpose of giving the medical treatment to the offender.

(6) A compulsion order may authorise detention in a state hospital only if, on the written or oral evidence of the two medical practitioners mentioned in subsection (2)(a) above, it appears to the court—

(a) that the offender requires to be detained in hospital under conditions of special security; and

(b) that such conditions of special security can be provided only in a state hospital.

(7) Where the court—

(a) makes a compulsion order in respect of an offender; and

(b) also makes a restriction order in respect of the offender,

the compulsion order shall authorise the measures specified in it without limitation of time.

(8) The measures mentioned in subsection (2) above are—

(a) the detention of the offender in the specified hospital;

(b) the giving to the offender, in accordance with Part 16 of the Mental Health (Care and Treatment) (Scotland) Act 2003 (asp 13), of medical treatment;

(c) the imposition of a requirement on the offender to attend—

    (i) on specified or directed dates; or

    (ii) at specified or directed intervals,

  specified or directed places with a view to receiving medical treatment;

(d) the imposition of a requirement on the offender to attend—

    (i) on specified or directed dates; or

    (ii) at specified or directed intervals,

specified or directed places with a view to receiving community care services, relevant services or any treatment, care or service;

(e) subject to subsection (9) below, the imposition of a requirement on the offender to reside at a specified place;

(f) the imposition of a requirement on the offender to allow—

    (i) the mental health officer;

    (ii) the offender's responsible medical officer; or

    (iii) any person responsible for providing medical treatment, community care services, relevant services or any treatment, care or service to the offender who is authorised for the purposes of this paragraph by the offender's responsible medical officer,

to visit the offender in the place where the offender resides;

(g) the imposition of a requirement on the offender to obtain the approval of the mental health officer to any change of address; and

(h) the imposition of a requirement on the offender to inform the mental health officer of any change of address before the change takes effect.

(9) The court may make a compulsion order imposing, by virtue of subsection (8)(e) above, a requirement on an offender to reside at a specified place which is a place used for the purpose of providing a care home service only if the court is satisfied that the person providing the care home service is willing to receive the offender.

(10) The Scottish Ministers may, by regulations made by statutory instrument, make provision for measures prescribed by the regulations to be treated as included among the measures mentioned in subsection (8) above.

(11) The power conferred by subsection (10) above may be exercised so as to make different provision for different cases or descriptions of case or for different purposes.

(12) No regulations shall be made under subsection (10) above unless a draft of the statutory instrument containing them has been laid before, and approved by a resolution of, the Scottish Parliament.

(13) The court shall be satisfied as to the condition mentioned in subsection (3)(a) above only if the description of the offender's mental disorder by each of the medical practitioners mentioned in subsection (2)(a) above specifies, by reference to the appropriate paragraph (or paragraphs) of the definition of "mental disorder" in section 328(1) of the Mental Health (Care and Treatment) (Scotland) Act 2003 (asp 13), at least one type of mental disorder that the offender has that is also specified by the other.

(14) A compulsion order—

(a) shall specify—

    (i) by reference to the appropriate paragraph (or paragraphs) of the definition of "mental disorder" in section 328(1) of the Mental Health (Care and Treatment) (Scotland) Act 2003 (asp 13), the type (or types) of mental disorder that each of the medical practitioners mentioned in subsection (2)(a) above specifies that the offender has that is also specified by the other; and

    (ii) if the order does not, by virtue of subsection (8)(a) above, authorise the detention of the offender in hospital, the name of the hospital the managers of which are to have responsibility for appointing the offender's responsible medical officer; and

(b) may include—

    (i) in a case where a compulsion order authorises the detention of the offender in a specified hospital by virtue of subsection (8)(a) above; or

(ii) in a case where a compulsion order imposes a requirement on the offender to reside at a specified place by virtue of subsection (8)(e) above,

such directions as the court thinks fit for the removal of the offender to, and the detention of the offender in, a place of safety pending the offender's admission to the specified hospital or, as the case may be, place.

(15) Where the court makes a compulsion order in relation to an offender, the court—

(a) shall not—

(i) make an order under section 200 of this Act;

(ii) make an interim compulsion order;

(iii) make a guardianship order;

(iv) pass a sentence of imprisonment;

(v) impose a fine;

(vi) make a probation order; or

(vii) make a community service order,

in relation to the offender;

(b) may make any other order that the court has power to make apart from this section.

(16) In this section—

"care home service" has the meaning given by section 2(3) of the Regulation of Care (Scotland) Act 2001 (asp 8);

"community care services" has the meaning given by section 5A(4) of the Social Work (Scotland) Act 1968 (c.49);

"medical treatment" has the same meaning as in section 52D of this Act;

"relevant services" has the meaning given by section 19(2) of the Children (Scotland) Act 1995 (c.36);

"responsible medical officer", in relation to an offender, means the responsible medical officer appointed in respect of the offender under section 230 of the Mental Health (Care and Treatment) (Scotland) Act 2003 (asp 13);

"restriction order" means an order under section 59 of this Act;

"sentence of imprisonment" includes any sentence or order for detention; and

"specified" means specified in the compulsion order.

AMENDMENT

Section 57A inserted by the Mental Health (Care and Treatment) (Scotland) Act 2003 (asp 13), s.133. Brought into force on March 21, 2005, only for the purpose of enabling regulations to be made, by the Mental Health (Care and Treatment) (Scotland) Act 2003 (Commencement No.4) Order 2005 (SSI 2005/161 (C.6)). Coming into force for all other purposes on October 5, 2005.

DEFINITIONS

"care home service": s.2(3) of the Regulation of Care (Scotland) Act 2001.
"community care services": s.5A(4) of the Social Work (Scotland) Act 1968.
"compulsion order": s.57A(1).
"court": s.52B(4).
"medical treatment": s.329(1) of the Mental Health (Care and Treatment) (Scotland) Act 2003.
"mental disorder": s.328(1) of the Mental Health (Care and Treatment) (Scotland) Act 2003.
"offence": s.307(1).
"prosecutor": s.307(1).
"relevant services": s.19(2) of the Children (Scotland) Act 1995.
"restriction order": s.59.

"sentence of imprisonment": s.57A(16).
"specified": s.57A(16).

GENERAL NOTE

A compulsion order may be made competently after conviction if a court is satisfied on the written or oral evidence of two medical practitioners that the offender has a mental disorder: s.57A(2). There are other conditions to be met prior to the making of such an order: see s.57A(2)(b), (3) and (5). A compulsion order may authorise detention in a state hospital only if, on the written or oral evidence of two medical practitioners, it appears that the offender requires to be detained in hospital under conditions of special security and that such conditions of special security can be provided only in a state hospital: s.57A(6). Where the court makes a compulsion order in respect of an offender and also makes a restriction order (under s.59) in respect of the offender then the compulsion order shall authorise the measures specified in it "without limitation of time": s.57A(7).

Compulsion order authorising detention in hospital or requiring residence at place: ancillary provision

57B.—(1) Where a compulsion order—

(a) authorises the detention of an offender in a specified hospital; or

(b) imposes a requirement on an offender to reside at a specified place,

this section authorises the removal, before the expiry of the period of 7 days beginning with the day on which the order is made, of the offender to the specified hospital or place, by any of the persons mentioned in subsection (2) below.

(2) Those persons are—

(a) a constable;

(b) a person employed in, or contracted to provide services in or to, the specified hospital who is authorised by the managers of that hospital to remove persons to hospital for the purposes of this section; and

(c) a specified person.

(3) In this section, "specified" means specified in the compulsion order.

AMENDMENT

Section 57B inserted by the Mental Health (Care and Treatment) (Scotland) Act 2003 (asp 13), s.133. Brought into force on March 21, 2005, only for the purpose of enabling regulations to be made, by the Mental Health (Care and Treatment) (Scotland) Act 2003 (Commencement No.4) Order 2005 (SSI 2005/161 (C.6)). Coming into force for all other purposes on October 5, 2005.

DEFINITIONS

"compulsion order": s.57A(1).
"specified": s.57B(3).

Mental health officer's report

57C.—(1) This section applies where the court is considering making a compulsion order in relation to an offender under section 57A of this Act.

(2) If directed to do so by the court, the mental health officer shall—

(a) subject to subsection (3) below, interview the offender; and

(b) prepare a report in relation to the offender in accordance with subsection (4) below.

(3) If it is impracticable for the mental health officer to comply with the requirement in subsection (2)(a) above, the mental health officer need not do so.

(4) The report shall state—

(a) the name and address of the offender;

(b) if known by the mental health officer, the name and address of the offender's primary carer;

(c) in so far as relevant for the purposes of section 57A of this Act, details of the personal circumstances of the offender; and

(d) any other information that the mental health officer considers relevant for the purposes of that section.

(5) In this section—

"carer", and "primary", in relation to a carer, have the meanings given by section 329(1) of the Mental Health (Care and Treatment) (Scotland) Act 2003 (asp 13);

"mental health officer" means a person appointed (or deemed to be appointed) under section 32(1) of that Act; and

"named person" has the meaning given by section 329(1) of that Act.

AMENDMENT

Section 57C inserted by the Mental Health (Care and Treatment) (Scotland) Act 2003 (asp 13), s.133. Brought into force on March 21, 2005, only for the purpose of enabling regulations to be made, by the Mental Health (Care and Treatment) (Scotland) Act 2003 (Commencement No.4) Order 2005 (SSI 2005/161 (C.6)). Coming into force for all other purposes on October 5, 2005.

DEFINITIONS

"carer": s.329(1) of the Mental Health (Care and Treatment) (Scotland) Act 2003.
"compulsion order": s.57A(1).
"mental health officer": s.32(1) of the Mental Health (Care and Treatment) (Scotland) Act 2003.
"named person": s.32(1) of the Mental Health (Care and Treatment) (Scotland) Act 2003.
"offender": s.53(1).
"primary carer": s.329(1) of the Mental Health (Care and Treatment) (Scotland) Act 2003.

Compulsion order: supplementary

57D.—(1) If, before the expiry of the period of 7 days beginning with the day on which a compulsion order authorising detention of the offender in a hospital is made, it appears to the court, or, as the case may be, the Scottish Ministers, that, by reason of emergency or other special circumstances, it is not reasonably practicable for the offender to be admitted to the hospital specified in the order, the court, or, as the case may be, the Scottish Ministers, may direct that the offender be admitted to the hospital specified in the direction.

(2) Where—

(a) the court makes a direction under subsection (1) above, it shall inform the person having custody of the offender; and

(b) the Scottish Ministers make such a direction, they shall inform—

(i) the court; and

(ii) the person having custody of the offender.

(3) Where a direction is made under subsection (1) above, the compulsion order shall have effect as if the hospital specified in the direction were the hospital specified in the order.

(4) In this section, "court" means the court which made the compulsion order.

AMENDMENT

Section 57D inserted by the Mental Health (Care and Treatment) (Scotland) Act 2003 (asp 13), s.133. Brought into force on March 21, 2005, only for the purpose of enabling regulations to be made, by the Mental Health (Care and Treatment) (Scotland) Act 2003 (Commencement No.4) Order 2005 (SSI 2005/161 (C.6)). Coming into force for all other purposes on October 5, 2005.

DEFINITIONS

"compulsion order": s.57A.
"court": s.57D(4).
"offender": s.53(1).

Hospital orders and guardianship

Order for hospital admission or guardianship

58.—(1) [...]

(1A) Where a person is convicted in the High Court or the sheriff court of an offence, other than an offence the sentence for which is fixed by law, punishable by that court with imprisonment, and the court is satisfied—

    (a) on the evidence of two medical practitioners (complying with section 61 of this Act and with any requirements imposed under section 57(3) of the Adults with Incapacity (Scotland) Act 2000 (asp 4)) that the grounds set out in section 58(1)(a) of that Act apply in relation to the offender;

    (b) that no other means provided by or under this Act would be sufficient to enable the offender's interests in his personal welfare to be safeguarded or promoted,

the court may, subject to subsection (2) below, by order place the offender's personal welfare under the guardianship of such local authority or of such other person approved by a local authority as may be specified in the order.

(2) Where the case is remitted by the sheriff to the High Court for sentence under any enactment, the power to make an order under subsection (1A) above shall be exercisable by that court.

(3) Where in the case of a person charged summarily in the sheriff court with an act or omission constituting an offence the court would have power, on convicting him, to make an order under subsection (1A) above, then, if it is satisfied that the person did the act or made the omission charged, the court may, if it thinks fit, make such an order without convicting him.

    (4) [...]

    (5) [...]

(6) An order placing a person under the guardianship of a local authority or of any other person (in this Act referred to as a "guardianship order") shall not be made under this section unless the court is satisfied—

    (a) on the report of a mental health officer (complying with any requirements imposed by section 57(3)of the Adults with Incapacity (Scotland) Act 2000 (asp 4)) giving his opinion as to the general appropriateness of the order sought, based on an interview and assessment of the person carried out not more than 30 days before it makes the order, that it is necessary in the interests of the personal welfare of the person that he should be placed under guardianship;

    (b) that any person nominated to be appointed a guardian is suitable to be so appointed;

    (c) that the authority or person is willing to receive that person into guardianship; and

    (d) that there is no other guardianship order, under this Act or the Adults with Incapacity (Scotland) Act 2000 (asp 4), in force relating to the person.

(7) A guardianship order shall specify (by reference to the appropriate paragraph (or paragraphs) of the definition of "mental disorder" in section 328(1) of the Mental Health (Care and Treatment) (Scotland) Act 2003 (asp 13)) the type (or types) of mental disorder that the offender has; and no such order shall be made unless the descriptions of the offender's mental disorder by each of the medical practitioners, whose evidence is taken into account under subsection (1A)(a) above, specifies at least one type of mental disorder that is also specified by the other.

(8) Where an order is made under this section, the court shall not pass sentence of imprisonment or impose a fine or make a probation order or a community service order in respect of the offence, but may make any other order which the court has power to make apart from this section; and for the purposes of this subsection "sentence of imprisonment" includes any sentence or order for detention.

(9) [...]

(10) [...]

(11) Section 58A of this Act shall have effect as regards guardianship orders made under this section.

AMENDMENTS

Subss.(4) and (9) amended by the Crime and Punishment (Scotland) Act 1997 (c.48), s.62(1) and Sch.1, para.21(6), with effect from January 1, 1998 in terms of the Crime and Punishment (Scotland) Act 1997 (Commencement No.2 and Transitional and Consequential Provisions) Order 1997 (SI 1997/2323), art.4 and Sch.2.

Subs.(7) as amended by the Mental Health (Public Safety and Appeals) (Scotland) Act 1999 (asp 1), s.3(b) (effective September 13, 1999).

Section 58(1), (2), (3), (5)–(7) and (10) as amended by the Adults with Incapacity (Scotland) Act 2000 (asp 4), s.88 and Sch.5, para.26. Brought into force on April 1, 2002 by the Adults with Incapacity (Scotland) Act 2000 (Commencement No.1) Order 2001 (SSI 2001/81 (C.2)).

Subs.(11) inserted by the Adults with Incapacity (Scotland) Act 2000 (asp 4), s.88 and Sch.5, para.26. Brought into force as above.

Subss.(1A) and (7) as amended by the Mental Health (Care and Treatment) (Scotland) Act 2003 (asp 13), Sch.4, para.8(4). Brought into force on October 5, 2005 by the Mental Health (Care and Treatment) (Scotland) Act 2003 (Commencement No.4) Order 2005 (SSI 2005/161 (C.6)).

Subss.(1), (4), (5), (9) and (10) repealed, and subss.(2), (3), (7) and (11) as amended, by the Mental Health (Care and Treatment) (Scotland) Act 2003 (asp 13), Sch.5, Part I. Brought into force on October 5, 2005 as above.

Application of Adults with Incapacity (Scotland) Act 2000

58A.—(1) Subject to the provisions of this section, the provisions of Parts 1, 5, 6 and 7 of the Adults with Incapacity (Scotland) Act 2000 (asp 4) ("the 2000 Act") apply—

(a) to a guardian appointed by an order of the court under section 57(2)(c), 58(1) or 58(1A) of this Act (in this section referred to as a "guardianship order") whether appointed before or after the coming into force of these provisions, as they apply to a guardian with powers relating to the personal welfare of an adult appointed under section 58 of that Act;

(b) to a person authorised under an intervention order under section 60A of this Act as they apply to a person so authorised under section 53 of that Act.

(2) In making a guardianship order the court shall have regard to any regulations made by the Scottish Ministers under section 64(11) of the 2000 Act and—

(a) shall confer powers, which it shall specify in the order, relating only to the personal welfare of the person;

(b) may appoint a joint guardian;

(c) may appoint a substitute guardian;

(d) may make such consequential or ancillary order, provision or direction as it considers appropriate.

(3) Without prejudice to the generality of subsection (2), or to any other powers conferred by this Act, the court may—

(a) make any order granted by it subject to such conditions and restrictions as appear to it to be appropriate;

(b) order that any reports relating to the person who will be the subject of the order be lodged with the court or that the person be assessed or interviewed and that a report of such assessment or interview be lodged;

(c) make such further inquiry or call for such further information as appears to it to be appropriate;

(d) make such interim order as appears to it to be appropriate pending the disposal of the proceedings.

(4) Where the court makes a guardianship order it shall forthwith send a copy of the interlocutor containing the order to the Public Guardian who shall—

(a) enter prescribed particulars of the appointment in the register maintained by him under section 6(2)(b)(iv) of the 2000 Act;

(b) unless he considers that the notification would be likely to pose a serious risk to the person's health notify the person of the appointment of the guardian; and

(c) notify the local authority and the Mental Welfare Commission of the terms of the interlocutor.

(5) A guardianship order shall continue in force for a period of 3 years or such other period (including an indefinite period) as, on cause shown, the court may determine.

(6) Where any proceedings for the appointment of a guardian under section 57(2)(c) or 58(1) of this Act have been commenced and not determined before the date of coming into force of section 84 of, and paragraph 26 of schedule 5 to, the Adults with Incapacity (Scotland) Act 2000 (asp 4) they shall be determined in accordance with this Act as it was immediately in force before that date.

AMENDMENT

Section 58A inserted by the Adults with Incapacity (Scotland) Act 2000 (asp 4), s.84. Brought into force on April 1, 2002 by the Adults with Incapacity (Scotland) Act 2000 (Commencement No. 1) Order 2001 (SSI 2001/81 (C.2)).

Hospital orders: restrictions on discharge

59.—(1) Where a compulsion order authorising the detention of a person in a hospital by virtue of paragraph (a) of section 57A(8) of this Act is made in respect of a person, and it appears to the court—

(a) having regard to the nature of the offence with which he is charged;

(b) the antecedents of the person; and

(c) the risk that as a result of his mental disorder he would commit offences if set at large,

that it is necessary for the protection of the public from serious harm so to do, the court may, subject to the provisions of this section, further order that the person shall be subject to the special restrictions set out in Part 10 of the Mental Health (Care and Treatment) (Scotland) Act 2003 (asp 13), without limit of time.

(2) An order under this section (in this Act referred to as "a restriction order") shall not be made in the case of any person unless the approved medical practitioner, whose evidence is taken into account by the court under section 57A(2)(a) of this Act, has given evidence orally before the court.

(2A) The court may, in the case of a person in respect of whom it did not, before making the compulsion order, make an interim compulsion order, make a restriction order in respect of the person only if satisfied that, in all the circumstances, it was not appropriate to make an interim compulsion order in respect of the person.

(3) [...]

AMENDMENTS

Section 59(2) as amended by the Adults with Incapacity (Scotland) Act 2000 (asp 4), s.88 and Sch.6. Brought into force on April 1, 2002 by the Adults with Incapacity (Scotland) Act 2000 (Commencement No.1) Order 2001 (SSI 2001/81 (C.2)).

Subss.(1) and (2) as amended, and subs.(2A) inserted, by the Mental Health (Care and Treatment) (Scotland) Act 2003 (asp 13), Sch.4, para.8(5). Brought into force on October 5, 2005 by the Mental Health (Care and Treatment) (Scotland) Act 2003 (Commencement No.4) Order 2005 (SSI 2005/161 (C.6)).

Subs.(3) repealed by the Mental Health (Care and Treatment) (Scotland) Act 2003 (asp 13), Sch.5, Part I. Brought into force on October 5, 2005 as above.

DEFINITIONS

"offence": s.307(1).
"restriction order": s.59(2).

GENERAL NOTE

Section 59 makes provision to restrict the discharge of hospital orders made under s.58. As a court may make a further hospital order that amounts to a person being subject to statutory special restrictions without limit of time, the tests to be met are suitably high. Indeed, the aspects of risk and protection in s.59(1) are redolent of the concerns latent in the terms of s.58(5).

In *M v H.M. Advocate*, 1998 G.W.D. 24–1231, an appeal against the making of a restriction order founding upon a change of opinion by one of the examining psychiatrists subsequent to the sheriff's determination, the Appeal Court held that the only relevant material for the purposes of appeal was that which had been laid before the sheriff; M's case might be considered administratively by the Secretary of State.

The making of a restriction order is ultimately a matter for the Court in the circumstances of each particular case—see *Thomson v H.M. Advocate*, 1999 S.C.C.R. 640 where the necessary criteria under s.59(1) was held made out and a restriction order made, despite psychiatric evidence that a restriction order was not necessary.

Reference is made in passing to the Mental Health (Public Safety and Appeals) (Scotland) Act 1999 which received Royal Assent on September 13, 1999 and is effective from September 1, 1999. This Act, *inter alia*, adds public safety to the criteria to be taken into account on an appeal under s.64 of the Mental Health (Scotland) Act 1984 by a person subject to a restriction order. Accordingly, it is provided that the sheriff shall refuse such an appeal if satisfied that the patient is suffering from a mental disorder the effect of which is such that it is necessary, in order to protect the public from serious harm, that the patient continue to be detained in a hospital, "whether for medical treatment or not". The definition of "mental disorder" in s.1(2) of the 1984 Act has been extended to include "personality disorder" (see s.3 of the Mental Health (Public Safety and Appeals) (Scotland) Act 1999, effective from September 1, 1999). This radical provision is subject to a right of appeal to the Court of Session. It is expected that in future greater use will be made of the hospital direction under s.59A of the 1995 Act which allies a period of remedial hospitalisation to a custodial sentence, but of course this hybrid disposal has only been available to the solemn court since January 1, 1998.

Hospital directions

Hospital directions

59A.—(1) This section applies where a person, not being a child, (in this section and in sections 59B and 59C of this Act referred to as the "offender") is convicted on indictment in—

(a) the High Court; or

(b) the sheriff court,

of an offence punishable by imprisonment.

(2) If the court is satisfied—

    (a) on the written or oral evidence of two medical practitioners—

        (i) that the conditions mentioned in subsection (3) below are met in respect of the offender; and

        (ii) as to the matters mentioned in subsection (4) below; and

    (b) that, having regard to the matters mentioned in subsection (5) below, it is appropriate,

the court may, in addition to any sentence of imprisonment which it has the power or the duty to impose, make, subject to subsection (6) below, a direction (in this Act referred to as a "hospital direction") authorising the measures mentioned in subsection (7) below.

(3) The conditions referred to in subsection (2)(a)(i) above are—

    (a) that the offender has a mental disorder;

    (b) that medical treatment which would be likely to—

        (i) prevent the mental disorder worsening; or

        (ii) alleviate any of the symptoms, or effects, of the disorder,

    is available for the offender;

    (c) that if the offender were not provided with such medical treatment there would be a significant risk—

        (i) to the health, safety or welfare of the offender; or

        (ii) to the safety of any other person; and

    (d) that the making of a hospital direction in respect of the offender is necessary.

(4) The matters referred to in subsection (2)(a)(ii) above are—

    (a) that the hospital proposed by the two medical practitioners mentioned in subsection (2)(a) above is suitable for the purpose of giving the medical treatment mentioned in paragraph (b) of subsection (3) above to the offender; and

    (b) that, were a hospital direction made, the offender could be admitted to such hospital before the expiry of the period of 7 days beginning with the day on which the direction is made.

(5) The matters referred to in subsection (2)(b) above are—

    (a) the mental health officer's report, prepared in accordance with section 59B of this Act, in respect of the offender;

    (b) all the circumstances, including—

        (i) the nature of the offence of which the offender was convicted; and

        (ii) the antecedents of the offender; and

    (c) any alternative means of dealing with the offender.

(6) A hospital direction may authorise detention in a state hospital only if, on the written or oral evidence of the two medical practitioners mentioned in subsection (2)(a) above, it appears to the court—

    (a) that the offender requires to be detained in a state hospital under conditions of special security; and

    (b) that such conditions of special security can be provided only in a state hospital.

(7) The measures mentioned in subsection (2) above are—

    (a) in the case of an offender who, when the hospital direction is made, has not been admitted to the specified hospital, the removal, before the expiry of the period of 7 days beginning with the day on which the direction is made, of the offender to the specified hospital by—

    (i) a constable;

   (ii) a person employed in, or contracted to provide services in or to, the specified hospital who is authorised by the managers of that hospital to remove persons to hospital for the purposes of this section; or

  (iii) a specified person;

  (b) the detention of the offender in the specified hospital; and

  (c) the giving to the offender, in accordance with Part 16 of the Mental Health (Care and Treatment) (Scotland) Act 2003 (asp 13), of medical treatment.

(8) The court shall be satisfied as to the condition mentioned in subsection (3)(a) above only if the description of the offender's mental disorder by each of the medical practitioners mentioned in subsection (2)(a) above specifies, by reference to the appropriate paragraph (or paragraphs) of the definition of "mental disorder" in section 328(1) of the Mental Health (Care and Treatment) (Scotland) Act 2003 (asp 13), at least one type of mental disorder that the offender has that is also specified by the other.

(9) A hospital direction—

  (a) shall specify, by reference to the appropriate paragraph (or paragraphs) of the definition of "mental disorder" in section 328(1) of the Mental Health (Care and Treatment) (Scotland) Act 2003 (asp 13), the type (or types) of mental disorder that each of the medical practitioners mentioned in subsection (2)(a) above specifies that is also specified by the other; and

  (b) may include such directions as the court thinks fit for the removal of the offender to, and the detention of the offender in, a place of safety pending the offender's admission to the specified hospital.

(10) In this section—

    "medical treatment" has the same meaning as in section 52D of this Act; and

    "specified" means specified in the hospital direction.

AMENDMENTS

Section 59A substituted by the Mental Health (Care and Treatment) (Scotland) Act 2003 (asp 13), Sch.4, para.8(6). Brought into force on October 5, 2005 by the Mental Health (Care and Treatment) (Scotland) Act 2003 (Commencement No.4) Order 2005 (SSI 2005/161 (C.6)).

DEFINITIONS

    "hospital direction": s.59A(2).

    "indictment": s.307(1).

    "medical treatment": s.329(1) of the Mental Health (Care and Treatment) (Scotland) Act 2003.

    "mental disorder": s.328(1) of the Mental Health (Care and Treatment) (Scotland) Act 2003.

    "sentence": s.307(1).

    "specified": s.59A(10).

GENERAL NOTE

Hospital directions may be made competently after conviction if a court is satisfied on the written or oral evidence of two medical practitioners that the offender has a mental disorder: s.59A(2). There are other conditions to be met: see s.59A(2)(b), (4) and (5). Hospital directions authorise the detention of an offender in a state hospital under conditions of special security where it appears to the court that such conditions of special security can be provided only in a state hospital: s.59A(6). A hospital direction shall specify the type (or types) of mental disorder that each of the medical practitioners specifies and is specified by the other practitioner: s.59A(9).

Hospital direction: mental health officer's report

59B.—(1) This section applies where the court is considering making a hospital direction in relation to an offender under section 59A of this Act.

(2) If directed to do so by the court, the mental health officer shall—

(a) subject to subsection (3) below, interview the offender; and

(b) prepare a report in relation to the offender in accordance with subsection (4) below.

(3) If it is impracticable for the mental health officer to comply with the requirement in subsection (2)(a) above, the mental health officer need not do so.

(4) The report shall state—

(a) the name and address of the offender;

(b) if known by the mental health officer, the name and address of the offender's primary carer;

(c) in so far as relevant for the purposes of section 59A of this Act, details of the personal circumstances of the offender; and

(d) any other information that the mental health officer considers relevant for the purposes of that section.

(5) In this section, "carer", "primary", in relation to a carer, and "mental health officer" have the same meanings as in section 57C of this Act.

AMENDMENT

Section 59B inserted by the Mental Health (Care and Treatment) (Scotland) Act 2003 (asp 13), Sch.4, para.8(6). Brought into force on October 5, 2005 by the Mental Health (Care and Treatment) (Scotland) Act 2003 (Commencement No.4) Order 2005 (SSI 2005/161 (C.6)).

DEFINITIONS

"carer": s.329(1) of Mental Health (Care and Treatment) (Scotland) Act 2003.
"hospital direction": s.59A(2).
"indictment": s.307(1).
"medical treatment": s.329(1) of the Mental Health (Care and Treatment) (Scotland) Act 2003.
"mental disorder": s.328(1) of the Mental Health (Care and Treatment) (Scotland) Act 2003.
"mental health officer": s.32(1) of the Mental Health (Care and Treatment) (Scotland) Act 2003.
"offender": s.53(1).
"primary carer": s.329(1) of the Mental Health (Care and Treatment) (Scotland) Act 2003.
"sentence": s.307(1).

Hospital direction: supplementary

59C.—(1) If, before the expiry of the period of 7 days beginning with the day on which a hospital direction is made, it appears to the court, or, as the case may be, the Scottish Ministers, that, by reason of emergency or other special circumstances, it is not reasonably practicable for the offender to be admitted to the hospital specified in the hospital direction, the court, or, as the case may be, the Scottish Ministers, may direct that the offender be admitted to such other hospital as is specified.

(2) Where—

(a) the court makes a direction under subsection (1) above, it shall inform the person having custody of the offender; and

(b) the Scottish Ministers make such a direction, they shall inform—

(i) the court; and

(ii) the person having custody of the offender.

(3) Where a direction is made under subsection (1) above, the hospital direction shall have effect as if the hospital specified in the hospital direction were the hospital specified by the court, or, as the case may be, the Scottish Ministers, under subsection (1) above.

(4) In this section, "court" means the court which made the hospital direction.

AMENDMENT

Section 59C inserted by the Mental Health (Care and Treatment) (Scotland) Act 2003 (asp 13),

Sch.4, para.8(6). Brought into force on October 5, 2005 by the Mental Health (Care and Treatment) (Scotland) Act 2003 (Commencement No.4) Order 2005 (SSI 2005/161 (C.6)).

DEFINITIONS

"court": s.59C(4).
"hospital direction": s.59A(2).
"offender": s.53(1).

Appeals against hospital orders

60. Where a compulsion order, interim compulsion order (but not an extension thereof), guardianship order, a restriction order or a hospital direction has been made by a court in respect of a person charged or brought before it, he may without prejudice to any other form of appeal under any rule of law (or, where an interim compulsion order has been made, to any right of appeal against any other order or sentence which may be imposed), appeal against that order or, as the case may be, direction in the same manner as against sentence.

AMENDMENTS

Section 60 as amended by the Crime and Punishment (Scotland) Act 1997 (c.48) s.6(2) with effect from January 1, by the Crime and Punishment (Scotland) Act 1997 (Commencement No.2 and Transitional Provisions) Order 1997 (SI 1997/2323) art.4 and Sch.2.

Section 60 as amended by the Mental Health (Care and Treatment) (Scotland) Act 2003 (asp 13), Sch.4, para.8(7). Brought into force on October 5, 2005 by the Mental Health (Care and Treatment) (Scotland) Act 2003 (Commencement No.4) Order 2005 (SSI 2005/161 (C.6)).

DEFINITIONS

"guardianship order": s.58(6).
"hospital direction": s.59A(1).
"restriction order": s.59(2).
"sentence": s.307(1).

GENERAL NOTE

This section conjoins the right of appeal formerly to be found in ss.280 and 443 of the 1975 Act. The right of appeal against these orders is treated as an appeal against sentence so that, for example, an appeal against a finding on fact under s.55(2) by the court cannot be appealed under s.60. Appeals against findings and orders are dealt with by ss.62 and 63. The right of appeal against the making of a hospital direction was inserted into s.60 by virtue of s.6(2) of the Crime and Punishment (Scotland) Act 1997, with effect from January 1, 1998.

Appeal by prosecutor against hospital orders etc.

60A.—(1) This section applies where the court, in respect of a person charged or brought before it, has made—

(a) a compulsion order;

(b) a restriction order;

(c) guardianship order;

(d) a decision under section 57(2)(e) of this Act to make no order; or

(e) a hospital direction.

(2) Where this section applies, the prosecutor may appeal against any such order, decision or direction as is mentioned in subsection (1) above—

(a) if it appears to him that the order, decision or direction was inappropriate; or

(b) on a point of law,

and an appeal under this section shall be treated in the same manner as an appeal against sentence under section 108 of this Act.

AMENDMENTS

Section 60A inserted by the Crime and Punishment (Scotland) Act 1997 (c.48) s.22 with effect from January 1, 1998 by the Crime and Punishment (Scotland) Act 1997 (Commencement No.2 and Transitional and Consequential Provisions) Order 1997 (SI 1997/2323) art.4 and Sch.2.

Subs.(1)(a) and (b) substituted, and subs.(1)(c), (d) and (e) inserted, by the Mental Health (Care and Treatment) (Scotland) Act 2003 (asp 13), Sch.4, para.8(8). Brought into force on October 5, 2005 by the Mental Health (Care and Treatment) (Scotland) Act 2003 (Commencement No.4) Order 2005 (SSI 2005/161 (C.6)).

DEFINITIONS

"court": s.59C(4).
"hospital direction": s.59A(2).
"prosecutor": s.307(1).

GENERAL NOTE

This section was inserted by s.22 of the Crime and Punishment (Scotland) Act 1997, with effect from January 1, 1998. It extends the right of appeal of the prosecutor found in s.63 of this Act, to include a right to appeal against hospital orders, etc. made where an accused is found to be insane.

Intervention orders

60B. The court may instead of making a compulsion order under section 58(1) of this Act or a guardianship order under section 57(2)(c) or 58(1A) of this Act, make an intervention order where it considers that it would be appropriate to do so.

AMENDMENTS

Section 60B inserted by the Adults with Incapacity (Scotland) Act 2000 (asp 4), s.88 and Sch.5, para.26. Brought into force on April 1, 2002 by the Adults with Incapacity (Scotland) Act 2000 (Commencement No.1) Order 2001 (SSI 2001/81 (C.2)).

Section 60B as amended by the Mental Health (Care and Treatment) (Scotland) Act 2003 (asp 13), Sch.4, para.8(9). Brought into force on October 5, 2005 by the Mental Health (Care and Treatment) (Scotland) Act 2003 (Commencement No.4) Order 2005 (SSI 2005/161 (C.6)).

Acquitted persons: detention for medical examination

60C.—(1) Subject to subsection (7) below, this section applies where a person charged with an offence is acquitted.

(2) If the court by or before which the person is acquitted is satisfied—

(a) on the written or oral evidence of two medical practitioners that the conditions mentioned in subsection (3) below are met in respect of the person; and

(b) that it is not practicable to secure the immediate examination of the person by a medical practitioner,

the court may, immediately after the person is acquitted, make an order authorising the measures mentioned in subsection (4) below for the purpose of enabling arrangements to be made for a medical practitioner to carry out a medical examination of the person.

(3) The conditions referred to in subsection (2)(a) above are—

(a) that the person has a mental disorder;

(b) that medical treatment which would be likely to—

    (i) prevent the mental disorder worsening; or

    (ii) alleviate any of the symptoms, or effects, of the disorder, is available for the person; and

(c) that if the person were not provided with such medical treatment there would be a significant risk—

    (i) to the health, safety or welfare of the person; or

    (ii) to the safety of any other person.

(4) The measures referred to in subsection (2) above are—

(a) the removal of the person to a place of safety by—

    (i) a constable; or

    (ii) a person specified by the court; and

(b) the detention, subject to subsection (6) below, of the person in that place of safety for a period of 6 hours beginning with the time at which the order under subsection (2) above is made.

(5) If the person absconds—

(a) while being removed to a place of safety under subsection (4) above; or

(b) from the place of safety,

a constable or the person specified by the court under paragraph (a) of that subsection may, at any time during the period mentioned in paragraph (b) of that subsection, take the person into custody and remove the person to a place of safety.

(6) An order under this section ceases to authorise detention of a person if, following the medical examination of the person, a medical practitioner grants—

(a) an emergency detention certificate under section 36 of the Mental Health (Care and Treatment) (Scotland) Act 2003 (asp 13); or

(b) a short-term detention certificate under section 44 of that Act.

(7) This section does not apply—

(a) in a case where a declaration is made by virtue of section 54(6) of this Act that the person is acquitted on account of the person's insanity at the time of doing the act or making the omission constituting the offence with which the person was charged; or

(b) in a case where the court states under section 55(4) of this Act that the person is so acquitted on the ground of such insanity.

(8) In this section, "medical treatment" has the same meaning as in section 52D of this Act.

AMENDMENT

    Section 60C inserted by the Mental Health (Care and Treatment) (Scotland) Act 2003 (asp 13), s.134. Brought into force on March 21, 2005, only for the purpose of enabling regulations to be made, by the Mental Health (Care and Treatment) (Scotland) Act 2003 (Commencement No.4) Order 2005 (SSI 2005/161 (C.6)). Coming into force for all other purposes on October 5, 2005.

DEFINITIONS

    "mental disorder": s.328(1) of the Mental Health (Care and Treatment) (Scotland) Act 2003.

    "medical treatment": s.329(1) of the Mental Health (Care and Treatment) (Scotland) Act 2003.

    "offender": s.53(1).

GENERAL NOTE

    After a person charged with an offence is acquitted the court may make an order competently to detain that person in a place of safety for a period of six hours if a court is satisfied on the written or oral evidence of two medical practitioners that the offender has a mental disorder: s.60C(2). There are other conditions to be met: see s.60C(2)(b) and (4). This order seems not to have a specific name but it is, rather, a pragmatic power to have the person acquitted seen for consideration for treatment because it is not practicable to secure the immediate examination of that person by a medical practitioner. Section 60D requires the making of such a place of safety order to be intimated to others.

Notification of detention under section 60C

    60D.—(1) This section applies where a person has been removed to a place of safety under section 60C of this Act.

(2) The court shall, before the expiry of the period of 14 days beginning with the day on which the order under section 60C(2) of this Act is made, ensure that the Mental Welfare Commission is given notice of the matters mentioned in subsection (3) below.

(3) Those matters are—

(a) the name and address of the person removed to the place of safety;

(b) the date on and time at which the person was so removed;

(c) the address of the place of safety;

(d) if the person is removed to a police station, the reason why the person was removed there; and

(e) any other matter that the Scottish Ministers may, by regulations made by statutory instrument, prescribe.

(4) The power conferred by subsection (3)(e) above may be exercised so as to make different provision for different cases or descriptions of case or for different purposes.

(5) A statutory instrument containing regulations under subsection (3)(e) above shall be subject to annulment in pursuance of a resolution of the Scottish Parliament.

AMENDMENT

Section 60D inserted by the Mental Health (Care and Treatment) (Scotland) Act 2003 (asp 13), s.134. Brought into force on March 21, 2005, only for the purpose of enabling regulations to be made, by the Mental Health (Care and Treatment) (Scotland) Act 2003 (Commencement No.4) Order 2005 (SSI 2005/161 (C.6)). Coming into force for all other purposes on October 5, 2005.

Medical evidence

Requirements as to medical evidence

61.—(1) Of the medical practitioners whose evidence is taken into account in making a finding under section 54(1)(a) of this Act or under any of the relevant provisions, at least one shall be an approved medical practitioner.

(1A) Of the medical practitioners whose evidence is taken into account under section 52M(2)(a), 53(2)(a), 54(1)(c), 57A(2)(a) or 59A(3)(a) and (b) of this Act, at least one shall be employed at the hospital which is to be specified in the order or, as the case may be, direction.

(2) Written or oral evidence given for the purposes of section 52D(2)(a) or any of the relevant provisions shall include a statement as to whether the person giving the evidence is related to the accused and of any pecuniary interest which that person may have in the admission of the accused to hospital or his reception into guardianship.

(3) For the purposes of making a finding under section 52D(2)(a) or 54(1)(a) of this Act or of any of the relevant provisions a report in writing purporting to be signed by a medical practitioner may, subject to the provisions of this section, be received in evidence without proof of the signature or qualifications of the practitioner; but the court may, in any case, require that the practitioner by whom such a report was signed be called to give oral evidence.

(4) Where any such report as aforesaid is tendered in evidence, otherwise than by or on behalf of the accused, then—

(a) if the accused is represented by counsel or solicitor, a copy of the report shall be given to his counsel or solicitor;

(b) if the accused is not so represented, the substance of the report shall be disclosed to the accused or, where he is a child under 16 years of age, to his parent or guardian if present in court;

(c) in any case, the accused may require that the practitioner by whom the report was signed be called to give oral evidence, and evidence to rebut the evidence contained in the report may be called by or on behalf of the accused,

and where the court is of the opinion that further time is necessary in the interests of the accused for consideration of that report, or the substance of any such report, it shall adjourn the case.

(5) For the purpose of calling evidence to rebut the evidence contained in any such report as aforesaid, arrangements may be made by or on behalf of an accused person detained in a hospital or, as respects a report for the purposes of the said section 54(1), remanded in custody for his examination by any medical practitioner, and any such examination may he made in private.

(6) In this section the "relevant provisions" means sections 52M(2)(a), 53(2)(a), 54(1)(c), 57A(2)(a), 58(1A)(a), 59A(2)(a) and 60C(2)(a).

(7) In this section, "approved medical practitioner" has the meaning given by section 22 of the Mental Health (Care and Treatment) (Scotland) Act 2003 (asp 13).

AMENDMENTS

Subss.(1), (2) and (3) as amended by the Crime and Punishment (Scotland) Act 1997 (c.48), s.10(2) with effect from January 1, 1998 by the Crime and Punishment (Scotland) Act 1997 (Commencement No.2 and Transitional and Consequential Provisions) Order 1997 (SI 1997/2323), art.4, Sch.2.

Subss.(1A) and (6) as inserted by the above Act.

Section 61 as amended by the Adults with Incapacity (Scotland) Act 2000 (asp 4), s.88 and Sch.5, para.26. Brought into force on April 1, 2002 by the Adults with Incapacity (Scotland) Act 2000 (Commencement No.1) Order 2001 (SSI 2001/81 (C.2)). See Ward, *Adult Incapacity* (2003), para.11–87.

Subss.(1), (1A), (2), (3) and (6) as amended, and subs.(7) inserted, by the Mental Health (Care and Treatment) (Scotland) Act 2003 (asp 13), Sch.4, para.8(10). Brought into force on October 5, 2005 by the Mental Health (Care and Treatment) (Scotland) Act 2003 (Commencement No.4) Order 2005 (SSI 2005/161 (C.6)).

DEFINITIONS

"hospital": s.307(1).
"medical practitioner": s.61(1).
"mental disorder": s.58(7).

GENERAL NOTE

Section 61 specifies requirements as to medical evidence in respect of (i) a finding of insanity in bar of trial (s.54(1)(a)), (ii) the making of an interim hospital order (s.53(1)), (iii) the making of a temporary hospital order (s.54(1)(c)), (iv) the making of a hospital or guardianship order (s.58(1)(a)), and (v) the newly introduced hospital direction (s.59A(3)(a) and (b) as inserted by s.6 of the Crime and Punishment (Scotland) Act 1997 as from January 1, 1998).

One of the purposes of this section is to ensure that medical practitioners who give evidence on the mental health of the person in question do so in the capacity of skilled witnesses, or at least one of them must to meet the terms of s.61(1). In addition, by virtue of subs.1(A) at least one of the medical practitioners involved must be employed in the proposed receiving hospital. This requirement is presumably intended to ensure that facilities will be available at that hospital and that at an early stage a practitioner experienced in the treatment of mental illness has had an input to the case.

Appeals under Part VI

Appeal by accused in case involving insanity

62.—(1) A person may appeal to the High Court against—

(a) a finding made under section 54(1) of this Act that he is insane so that his trial cannot proceed or continue, or the refusal of the court to make such a finding;

(b) a finding under section 55(2) of this Act; or

(c) an order made under section 57(2) of this Act.

(2) An appeal under subsection (1) above shall be—

(a) in writing; and

(b) lodged—

    (i) in the case of an appeal under paragraph (a) of that subsection, not later than seven days after the date of the finding or refusal which is the subject of the appeal;

    (ii) in the case of an appeal under paragraph (b), or both paragraphs (b) and (c) of that subsection, not later than 28 days after the conclusion of the examination of facts;

    (iii) in the case of an appeal under paragraph (c) of that subsection against an order made on an acquittal, by virtue of section 54(6) or 55(3) of this Act, on the ground of insanity at the time of the act or omission, not later than 14 days after the date of the acquittal;

    (iv) in the case of an appeal under that paragraph against an order made on a finding under section 55(2), not later than 14 days after the conclusion of the examination of facts,

or within such longer period as the High Court may, on cause shown, allow.

(3) Where the examination of facts was held in connection with proceedings on indictment, subsections (1)(a) and (2)(b)(i) above are without prejudice to section 74(1) of this Act.

(4) Where an appeal is taken under subsection (1) above, the period from the date on which the appeal was lodged until it is withdrawn or disposed of shall not count towards any time limit applying in respect of the case.

(5) An appellant in an appeal under this section shall be entitled to be present at the hearing of the appeal unless the High Court determines that his presence is not practicable or appropriate.

(6) In disposing of an appeal under subsection (1) above the High Court may—

(a) affirm the decision of the court of first instance;

(b) make any other finding, order or other disposal which that court could have made at the time when it made the finding or order which is the subject of the appeal; or

(c) remit the case to that court with such directions in the matter as the High Court thinks fit.

(7) Section 60 of this Act shall not apply in relation to any order as respects which a person has a right of appeal under subsection (1)(c) above.

AMENDMENT

Subs.(6)(b) as amended by the Crime and Punishment (Scotland) Act 1997 (c.48) Sched. 1, para. 21(7) with effect from January 1, 1997 (Commencement No. 2 and Transitional and Consequential Provisions) Order 1997 (S.I. 1997 No. 2323) art. 4, Sched. 2.

DEFINITIONS

"examination of facts": s.54(1)(b).

"High Court": s.307(1).

"order": s.307(1).

GENERAL NOTE

Under the previous law, ss.174(1) and 375(2) of the 1975 Act enabled a court to find a person insane in bar of trial. An accused person had no right of appeal either against such a finding or against the refusal of any plea or motion that such a finding should be made. The only exception was where the finding was made at a preliminary diet in solemn proceedings in which event the accused had a right of appeal by s.76A(1) of the 1975 Act.

The new section provides the accused under solemn or summary procedure with rights of appeal in relation to any findings, or the refusal to make a finding, that the accused is insane in bar of trial and against findings made by, and orders made at, examinations of fact. Although such appeals must be made in comparatively short periods of time, longer periods may be allowed by the High Court of Justiciary on cause shown. The appellate judges have a broad range of powers to affirm or vary decisions and orders appealed against and to remit cases with directions.

Appeal by prosecutor in case involving insanity

63.—(1) The prosecutor may appeal to the High Court on a point of law against—

(a) a finding under subsection (1) of section 54 of this Act that an accused is insane so that his trial cannot proceed or continue;

(b) an acquittal on the ground of insanity at the time of the act or omission by virtue of subsection (6) of that section;

(c) an acquittal under section 55(3) of this Act (whether or not on the ground of insanity at the time of the act or omission); or

(d) ...

(2) An appeal under subsection (1) above shall be—

(a) in writing; and

(b) lodged—

(i) in the case of an appeal under paragraph (a) or (b) of that subsection, not later than seven days after the finding or, as the case may be, the acquittal which is the subject of the appeal;

(ii) in the case of an appeal under paragraph (c) of that subsection, not later than seven days after the conclusion of the examination of facts,

or within such longer period as the High Court may, on cause shown, allow.

(3) Where the examination of facts was held in connection with proceedings on indictment, subsections (1)(a) and (2)(b)(i) above are without prejudice to section 74(1) of this Act.

(4) A respondent in an appeal under this subsection shall be entitled to be present at the hearing of the appeal unless the High Court determines that his presence is not practicable or appropriate.

(5) In disposing of an appeal under subsection (1) above the High Court may—

(a) affirm the decision of the court of first instance;

(b) make any other finding, order or disposal which that court could have made at the time when it made the finding or acquittal which is the subject of the appeal; or

(c) remit the case to that court with such directions in the matter as the High Court thinks fit.

(6) In this section, "the prosecutor" means, in relation to proceedings on indictment, the Lord Advocate.

AMENDMENTS

Subs.(5)(b) as amended by the Crime and Punishment (Scotland) Act 1997 (c.48) Sched. 1. para. 21(8) with effect from January 1, 1998 by the Crime and Punishment (Scotland) Act 1997 (Commencement No. 2 and Transitional and Consequential Provisions) Order 1997 (S.I. 1997 No. 2323) art. 4, Sched. 2.

Subs. (1)(d) as repealed by the above Act.

"examination of facts": s.54(1)(b).
"High Court": s.307(1).
"order": s.307(1).
"prosecutor": s.63(6).

GENERAL NOTE

Under the previous law, ss.174(1) and 375(2) of the 1975 Act enabled a court to find a person insane in bar of trial. The Crown had no right of appeal against such a finding unless it had been made at a preliminary diet in solemn proceedings, in which event the Crown had a right of appeal by s.76A(1) of the 1975 Act.

This section now provides the Crown with a right of appeal similar to those given to the accused under s.62. The Crown may appeal against a finding of insanity in bar of trial, against a trial verdict of acquittal on the ground of insanity, and against any acquittal at an examination of facts. In each of these the appeal may be only on a point of law. Note also s.60A which allows the prosecutor a right of appeal against hospital orders, etc. made where an accused is found to be insane.

PART VII

SOLEMN PROCEEDINGS

The indictment

Prosecution on indictment

64.—(1) All prosecutions for the public interest before the High Court or before the sheriff sitting with a jury shall proceed on indictment in name of Her Majesty's Advocate.

(2) The indictment may be in the forms—

(a) set out in Schedule 2 to this Act; or

(b) prescribed by Act of Adjournal,

or as nearly as may be in such form.

(3) Indictments in proceedings before the High Court shall be signed by the Lord Advocate or one of his deputes.

(4) Indictments in proceedings before the sheriff sitting with a jury shall be signed by the procurator fiscal, and the words "By Authority of Her Majesty's Advocate" shall be prefixed to the signature of the procurator fiscal.

(5) The principal record and service copies of indictments and all notices of citation, lists of witnesses, productions and jurors, and all other official documents required in a prosecution on indictment may be either written or printed or partly written and partly printed.

(6) Schedule 3 to this Act shall have effect as regards indictments under this Act.

DEFINITIONS

"High Court": s.307(1).
"indictment": s.307(1).
"procurator fiscal": s.307(1).

GENERAL NOTE

The provisions dealing with the latitudes as to time, place, capacity and implied terms previously contained in ss.43 to 67 of the 1975 Act, in relation to solemn proceedings, and s.311 relative to summary proceedings, are now incorporated in Sch.3 to the 1995 Act. It remains a moot point what practical benefit is derived from preserving the indictment styles of the 1887 Act as Sch.2 does. The subject of implied charges, or alternative verdicts, was discussed in *McMaster v HM Advocate*, 2001 S.C.C.R. 517 with particular reference to Convention principles.

Section 287 of the 1995 Act makes provision for the maintenance of proceedings in the event of the death of, or demission of office by, the Lord Advocate. Even where the Solicitor General exercised his powers in terms of s.287(2) following the resignation of the Lord Advocate in February 2000, it is of note that conform to subs.(4), sheriff and jury indictments continued to have the words "By Authority of Her Majesty's Advocate" upon them. While the terms of subs.(4) appear mandatory (and reflect the fact that a procurator fiscal's commission was protected under the Sheriff Courts and Legal Officers (Scotland) Act 1927 (c.35)) regard has to be paid to *Christie v HM Advocate*, 2004 J.C. 13 where only the words "By Authority" preceded the fiscal's signature. Having regard to the full narrative of the libel, the Appeal Court held there to be neither a nullity nor material prejudice to the appellants. See the broad discussion in *Hester v MacDonald*, 1961 S.C. 370; 1961 S.L.T. 414. A similarly broad approach was evident in a summary case, *Gates v Donnelly*, 2004 S.L.T. 33 discussed at A4–311 below but the latitude given to the Crown is not unlimited. The decision in *Christie* above has to be read in conjunction with *HM Advocate v Crawford*, 2005 S.L.T. 1056, a case where the indictment served upon the accused was missing the words "By Authority of Her Majesty's Advocate" entirely and was signed by the "Acting Procurator Fiscal". The omission entirely of the first phrase was fatal to proceedings on that indictment; the court did not regard the second phrase [instead of "Procurator Fiscal"] as of any moment and was prepared to regard that error as being excusable in character.

Latitude as to dates in charges is granted to the Crown by Sch.3 to the Act at para.4 but subject to the general tests of fairness—set out in *HM Advocate v Hastings*, 1985 S.L.T. 446—and irreversible prejudice, in *McFadyen v Annan*, 1992 S.L.T. 163. See also the discussion of Convention issues in *Stewart v HM Advocate*, 2005 G.W.D. 27–523.

The extent of the Crown's power to amend the libel to correspond to evidence led or agreed is discussed at A4–299 below.

Section 288 below entitles the Lord Advocate to be advised of, and be heard in relation to, any proposed private prosecution; see *X v Sweeney*, 1983 S.L.T. 48 which proceeded by Bill of Criminal Letters, the Lord Advocate offering no objection, following an earlier formal intimation by the Crown to the accused of no further proceedings.

The complex factors involved in the prosecution of a non-natural person (in this case a public limited company charged with culpable homicide following fatalities in a gas explosion) are discussed at length in *Transco Plc v HM Advocate*, 2004 S.L.T. 41. See the discussion "Corporate Culpable Homicide" by P.W. Ferguson in 2004 S.L.T. 97 noting the particular difficulty in attributing *mens rea* to corporate entities.

Prevention of delay in trials

65.—(1) Subject to subsections (2) and (3) below, an accused shall not be tried on indictment for any offence unless

(a) where an indictment has been served on the accused in respect of the High Court, a preliminary hearing is commenced within the period of 11 months; and

(b) in any case, the trial is commenced within the period of 12 months,

of the first appearance of the accused on petition in respect of the offence.

(1A) If the preliminary hearing (where subsection (1)(a) above applies) or the trial is not so commenced, the accused

(a) shall be discharged forthwith from any indictment as respects the offence; and

(b) shall not at any time be proceeded against on indictment as respects the offence.

(2) Nothing in subsection (1) or (1A) above shall bar the trial of an accused for whose arrest a warrant has been granted for failure to appear at a diet in the case.

(3) On an application made for the purpose,

(a) where an indictment has been served on the accused in respect of the High Court, a single judge of that court may, on cause shown, extend either or

219

both of the periods of 11 and 12 months specified in subsection (1) above; or

(b) in any other case, the sheriff may, on cause shown, extend the period of 12 months specified in that subsection.

(3A) An application under subsection (3) shall not be made at any time when an appeal made with leave under s.74(1) of this Act has not been disposed of by the High Court.

(4) Subject to subsections (5) to (9) below, an accused who is committed for any offence until liberated in due course of law shall not be detained by virtue of that committal for a total period of more than—

(a) 80 days, unless within that period the indictment is served on him, which failing he shall be entitled to be admitted to bail; or

(aa) where an indictment has been served on the accused in respect of the High Court—

(i) 110 days, unless a preliminary hearing in respect of the case is commenced within that period, which failing he shall be entitled to be admitted to bail; or

(ii) 140 days, unless the trial of the case is commenced within that period, which failing he shall be entitled to be admitted to bail;

(b) where an indictment has been served on the accused in respect of the sheriff court, 110 days, unless the trial of the case is commenced within that period, which failing he shall be entitled to be admitted to bail.

(4A) Where an indictment has been served on the accused in respect of the High Court, subsections (1)(a) and (4)(aa)(i) above shall not apply if the preliminary hearing has been dispensed with under section 72B(1) of this Act.

(5) On an application made for the purpose—

(a) in a case where, at the time the application is made, an indictment has not been served on the accused, a single judge of the High Court; or

(b) in any other case, the court specified in the notice served under section 66(6) of this Act,

may, on cause shown, extend any period mentioned in subsection (4) above.

(5A) Before determining an application under subsection (3) or (5) above, the judge or, as the case may be, the court shall give the parties an opportunity to be heard.

(5B) However, where all the parties join in the application, the judge or, as the case may be, the court may determine the application without hearing the parties and, accordingly, may dispense with any hearing previously appointed for the purpose of considering the application.

(6)–(7) [*Repealed by the Criminal Procedure (Amendment) (Scotland) Act 2004 (asp 5), s.6(8). Brought into force on February 1, 2005 by the Criminal Procedure (Amendment) (Scotland) Act 2004 (Commencement, Transitional Provisions and Savings) Order 2004 (SSI 2004/405 (C.28)), art.2.*]

(8) The grant or refusal of any application to extend the periods mentioned in this section may be appealed against by note of appeal presented to the High Court; and that Court may affirm, reverse or amend the determination made on such application.

(8A) Where an accused is, by virtue of subsection (4) above, entitled to be admitted to bail, the accused shall, unless he has been admitted to bail by the Lord Advocate, be brought forthwith before—

(a) in a case where an indictment has not yet been served on the accused, a single judge of the High Court; or

(b) in any other case, the court specified in the notice served under section 66(6) of this Act.

(8B) Where an accused is brought before a judge or court under subsection (8A) above, the judge or, as the case may be, the court shall give the prosecutor an opportunity to make an application under subsection (5) above.

(8C) If the prosecutor does not make such an application or, if such an application is made but is refused, the judge or, as the case may be, the court shall, after giving the prosecutor an opportunity to be heard, admit the accused to bail.

(8D) Where such an application is made but is refused and the prosecutor appeals against the refusal, the accused—

(a) may continue to be detained under the committal warrant for no more than 72 hours from the granting of bail under subsection (8C) above or for such longer period as the High Court may allow; and

(b) on expiry of that period, shall, whether the appeal has been disposed of or not, be released on bail subject to the conditions imposed.

(9) For the purposes of this section,

(a) where the accused is cited in accordance with subsection (4)(b) of section 66 of this Act, the indictment shall be deemed to have been served on the accused;

(b) a preliminary hearing shall be taken to commence when it is called; and

(c) a trial shall be taken to commence when the oath is administered to the jury.

(10) In calculating the periods of 11 and 12 months specified in subsections (1) and (3) above there shall be left out of account any period during which the accused is detained, other than while serving a sentence of imprisonment or detention, in any other part of the United Kingdom or in any of the Channel Islands or the Isle of Man in any prison or other institution or place mentioned in subsection (1) or (1A) of section 29 of the Criminal Justice Act 1961 (transfer of prisoners for certain judicial purposes).

AMENDMENTS

Subs.(3A) inserted by the Crime and Punishment (Scotland) Act 1997, Sch.1, para.21(9) with effect from August 1, 1997 in terms of the Crime and Punishment (Scotland) Act 1997 (Commencement and Transitional Provisions) Order 1997 (SI 1997/1712), art.21(9).

Subs.(1) as amended by the Criminal Procedure and Investigations Act 1996 (c.25), s.73(3).

Subss.(1)(a), (b), (1A), (3)(a), (b), (4)(aa), (4A), (5A), (5B), (8A)–(8D), (9)(a)–(c) inserted, subs.(5) substituted and subss.(1)–(3), (4)(a), (b), (9), (10) as amended by the Criminal Procedure (Amendment) (Scotland) Act 2004 (asp 5), s.6(2)–(7), (9)–(11). Brought into force on February 1, 2005 by the Criminal Procedure (Amendment) (Scotland) Act 2004 (Commencement, Transitional Provisions and Savings) Order 2004 (SSI 2004/405 (C.28)), art.2.

DEFINITIONS

"High Court": s.307(1).
"indictment": s.307(1).
"offence": s.307(1).
"prison": s.307(1).

GENERAL NOTE

While the origins of these provisions can be traced back to the Act Anent Wrongeous Imprisonment of 1701 and provide the mandatory time frames for solemn criminal proceedings in Scotland, they have undergone substantial changes since the Criminal Justice (Scotland) Act 1980. Until the introduction of s.6 of that Act, trial proceedings against anyone accused remanded for solemn trial had to be concluded within 110 days; after 1980 the provision was modified to require trial proceedings to commence within the 110 day period. The 2004 Act further alters the time bars in relation to High Court proceedings and substantial procedural changes.

The comprehensive review into High Court procedures conducted by Lord Bonomy ("Improving Practice: 2002 Review of the Practices and Procedure of the High Court of Justiciary") focused upon the substantial growth in High Court business in recent years and the six-fold rise in motions for adjournment (many in custody cases) since 1995.

The findings of the Bonomy Report led to a Scottish Executive White Paper "Modernising Justice in Scotland: The Reform of the High Court of Justiciary" (2003) and in turn to the Criminal Procedure (Amendment) (Scotland) Act 2004 (asp 5) whose most substantial provisions are to introduce pre-trial preliminary diets in the High Court (drawing heavily upon the first diets long familiar in sheriff solemn cases), a vigorous regime of pre-trial enquiry to ensure that indicted cases are fully prepared for trial, and the reform of the time bar provisions, at least so far as they relate to High Court proceedings. Equally significantly, the outcome for a remanded accused whose case is not commenced within the statutory time scale is that the court may well admit him to bail rather than, as previously, he being forever free of all legal process in relation to the matter.

Following the 2004 Act, there are now several distinct procedural differences between solemn proceedings in the High Court and sheriff courts. These are detailed below.

Subss.(1), (1A) and (2)

Subs.(1) now requires that an accused on bail and indicted for trial in the High Court has to be served with an indictment no later than 10 months after the date of his first petition appearance.

Instead of being indicted to a trial diet in the High Court, the accused is now required to appear at a preliminary diet within 11 months of that first appearance: the purposes of the preliminary diet are set out in s.72 below. (These timescales would not apply to an accused who was indicted without a first petition appearance and, as subs.(2) provides, fly off in any solemn proceedings following a failure to appear at any diet—see *Kelly v HM Advocate*, 2002 S.L.T. 43 and *HM Advocate v Taylor*, 1996 S.L.T. 836).

Section 66(6)(b) stipulates that a period of not less than 29 clear days must separate the preliminary and trial diets.

More familiar rules apply to sheriff solemn proceedings; subs.(1)(b) restates the requirement that such bail proceedings must be commenced by indictment within one year of petition appearance. Reference then has to be made to s.66(6)(a) of the Act which provides for a first diet not less than 15 clear days after service of the indictment and a trial diet not less than 29 clear days after that service. A degree of flexibility exists in fixing the first diet since it must also occur not less than 10 clear days before the trial.

In all solemn proceedings it remains possible to tender an accelerated plea on an agreed libel in terms of s.76 of the Act.

Subs.(1A) of the Act provides a new constraint upon solemn bail proceedings by stipulating that they must be commenced by way of a preliminary diet in the High Court, or a trial diet in the sheriff court, within the 11 and 12 month times respectively, or else the accused is forever free of further proceedings in respect of the offence. As mentioned earlier, subs.(2) qualifies this provision as does subs.(3) which preserves the right of parties to apply to the court for an extension of time.

Subss.(3) and (3A)

The periods set out in subs.(1) commence with the date of the accused's first appearance on petition, whether he is committed for further examination as is usual, or fully committed, and halt in the High Court with the commencement of the preliminary hearing within 11 months and in all solemn proceedings, with the commencement of trial within the year. (Calculation of these dates is *de die in diem* not *de momento in momentum*; see *McCulloch v HM Advocate*, 1995 S.L.T. 918 and the discussion on the general topic at A4–292 below).

Prior to service of an indictment upon an accused on bail, *any* application for an extension falls to be considered by the sheriff having jurisdiction over the petition and he retains that power in relation to sheriff solemn proceedings once they are indicted for trial. (See *HM Advocate v Caulfield*, 1999 S.L.T. 1003). Matters are now more problematic in relation to High Court proceedings; once an accused on bail has been indicted, application has to be made to a High Court judge to extend timebars as necessary. More difficult is the position prior to indictment of a bail case self-evidently destined for the High Court, for example a murder or rape, since subs.(3)(b) only empowers a sheriff to extend the 12 (and not the 11) month period.

Application for a prospective or retrospective extension of these timebars would be competent (*Ashcroft v HM Advocate*, 1996 S.C.C.R. 608) but can only be considered afresh where the facts and circumstances are materially different from those argued originally (*Goldie v HM Advocate*, 2003 S.L.T. 1078). Subs.(3A) ensures that no application can be made while an appeal springing from a preliminary or first diet is ongoing.

Extension of 11-month time-bar in High Court proceedings (subs.(3))

The same broad considerations, and case law, governing extensions of the year time bar upon proceedings apply equally to the statutory 11-month time-bar which has been introduced in High Court proceedings only. Within that 11 month period the court must hold a preliminary hearing diet (see s.72 below). In *HM Advocate v Freeman*, 2006 S.L.T. 35, the Crown in error fixed the preliminary hearing for a Sunday, a *dies non*. Rapidly appreciating the error, a one day extension was sought, and refused, at first instance. The Appeal Court allowed the extension, being critical of the initial lack of clarity of the Crown explanations given to the judge considering the application and doubtful of the defence's stated readiness for trial in a complex case where the libel had been substantially overhauled from the charges in the original petition. No prejudice had been demonstrated by the respondent.

Extension of the one year time bar (subs.(3))

Any such motion will be considered by a single judge and can be granted on cause shown. The judge does not have an absolute discretion when considering a motion to extend the 12-month (or now, by inference, the 11-month) period. Compare *Langan v HM Advocate*, 1997 S.C.C.R. 306, where the Appeal Court could divine no basis for the sheriff's grant of a retrospective extension and reduced the matter to a summary complaint, and *HM Advocate v Brown*, 1984 S.C.C.R. 347 in which it was held that the sheriff acted unreasonably in granting a defence adjournment while refusing an unopposed Crown motion for an extension. *McCulloch v HM Advocate*, 2001 S.L.T. 113 (discussed at A4–153 below) in which an extension of the year was allowed to enable re-indictment of the case, perhaps surprisingly since the Crown had commented upon the failure of a spouse to give evidence, illustrates the competing interests which must be must be weighed in the balance when considering applications for extension.

A degree of fault on the part of the Crown would not be fatal to an application for extension of the year period (*Mallison v HM Advocate*, 1987 S.C.C.R. 320 and *McGill v HM Advocate*, 1997 S.C.C.R. 230), but certainly failure to serve an indictment at a domicile of citation would attract particularly rigorous scrutiny (*HM Advocate v Swift*, 1984 S.C.C.R. 216; 1985 S.L.T. 26) while a libel which constituted a nullity would not generally warrant an extension; *Stenton v HM Advocate*, 1999 S.L.T. 255. Similarly, adjournment of a trial to a non-existent sitting, and efforts to constitute a sitting to overcome the error, led to refusal of a last-minute motion for extension of the year (see *Willoughby v HM Advocate*, 2000 S.C.C.R. 73). *Rennie v HM Advocate*, 1998 S.C.C.R. 191 is probably an extreme example of the excusal of Crown fault, and may have been not unrelated to the fact that the complainer, in what had begun life as an allegation of rape and had been indicted as shameless indecency, was mentally backward; objection to the libel, which the Crown did not defend, was taken just four days prior to trial—the lateness of this challenge being a factor which the Appeal Court felt had wrongly been taken into consideration by the sheriff. Accordingly, the Appeal Court reviewed the decision to extend the time bar, held the fault on the part of the Crown in serving an indictment which they later conceded to be irrelevant was not entirely inexcusable and paid due regard to the seriousness of the allegations. The extension was upheld on appeal but, whether it accurately reflected the anticipated evidence or not, it could be said that the Crown had been too hasty in conceding that the libel was irrelevant. A Crown error in serving an indictment upon the accused to call in Glasgow High Court, but with a Notice of Compearance (see Form 8.2-B at para. B1–97) calling him to appear at Paisley, late into the year was held on appeal not to be a major and fundamental error. The Appeal Court seemed to hint that an appearance by the accused at the Glasgow sitting would have sufficed to cure this defect, but taking account of the lack of prejudice to him and the gravity of the offence, allied to the rapidity of the Crown application for extension, felt able to grant an extension of the 12 month period (*HM Advocate v Fitzpatrick*, 2002 S.C.C.R. 758). Lack of urgency on the part of the Crown can be a factor; see *Palmer v HM Advocate*, 2002 S.C.C.R. 908.

However, failure on the part of the police to execute service of an indictment timeously or to comply with express instructions are not faults of the prosecutor; see *Welsh v HM Advocate*, 1985 S.C.C.R. 404; *HM Advocate v Davies*, 1993 S.C.C.R. 645; *Coutts v HM Advocate*, 1992 S.C.C.R. 87. Even where the Crown instructed service of an indictment on the last available day with unclear instructions and in the knowledge that the accused had no proper domicile of citation, the Appeal Court felt able to uphold the grant of an extension; it was observed that the terms of the indictment were known to him some days before service and that no claim of prejudice had been advanced (*Fin-*

lay v HM Advocate, 1998 S.L.T. 1235). It is clear that failure to intimate a change of domicile which results in service being unsuccessful at the accused's former address will not count against the Crown (*Black v HM Advocate*, 1990 S.C.C.R. 609); similarly the provision of an incomplete or imprecise address as domicile when seeking bail will not benefit an accused when service at that address proves to be defective (*Brown v HM Advocate*, 1998 S.L.T. 971).

In *HM Advocate v Crawford* (High Court of Justiciary, November 22, 2005, unreported) the Court of Appeal overturned an earlier refusal by the sheriff to extend the year time-bar period, this to enable re-indictment of the case. A previous attempt to indict the proceedings had foundered due to defects in the signing of that indictment (see the notes to s.64 above) but it is significant that in considering the later application for extension (necessitated as a result of fault wholly attributable to Crown error) the Appeal Court examined the causes of the error rather than the consequences which resulted from it when measuring the excusability. See too that the court took account of the history of the case which had been adjourned previously on the same charges and generally on defence motion, the gravity of the charges, noted the absence of any prejudice to the accused and the fact that the defects in the libel had not been commented upon by either party until a very late stage in the proceedings, too late indeed for the defect then to be remedied timeously by a fresh indictment.

In *Forrester v HM Advocate*, 1997 S.C.C.R. 9 the year had been extended twice already, on Crown motion, due to the prolonged illness of an essential witness. Before applying for a third extension the prosecutor had intimated to the defence, that if a further extension was opposed the Crown intended to lead the evidence of that witness, through use of the hearsay provisions of s.259 of the 1995 Act. The Crown then sought a last extension arguing that the illness of a vital witness was not its fault. A defence appeal against the grant of that third extension, founding inter alia upon the unwillingness of the Crown to lead evidence by means of s.259 for tactical reasons, was refused by the Appeal Court, which distinguished between the technical sufficiency of evidence available using the provisions in s.259 and the desirability of the jury hearing the testimony of such a vital witness and any cross-examination. Recourse to s.259 was not available to the Crown in *HM Advocate v Lewis* (High Court of Justiciary, May 29, 2002, unreported) where a principal witness, whose evidence was essential to proof of sexual offences using *Moorov*, was persistently unfit psychiatrically to give evidence. It was suggested that this condition was a consequence of those offences against her. Trial was postponed six times with appropriate extensions of the year time bar due to the gravity of the offences. More unusually the sheriff's decision to desert proceedings *pro loco et tempore* and to extend the year time bar were upheld on appeal in a case where both he, and the prosecutor, had gone too far in comforting a child witness who had broken down in the course of her evidence (see *McKie v HM Advocate*, 1997 S.L.T. 1018, discussed more fully at A4–527 below).

An extension of time has been permitted to enable the Crown to indict an offence committed by the accused late during the year after his petition appearance. In *Campbell v Ritchie*, 1999 S.C.C.R. 914 it was of particular significance that *Moorov* could be applied to both groups of offences. An extension of the year time bar was confirmed on appeal where the Crown, having put three persons on petition, had decided for evidential reasons to split trial proceedings only to find that the initial trial diet against the two other accused (who would be necessary witnesses against H) was delayed for reasons outwith the Crown's control. It was held in *Hogg v HM Advocate*, 2002 S.L.T. 639 that the Crown need not be confronted with losing the right to proceed against H when it was obviously necessary and diligent to precognosce the co-accused before indicting H. Similarly, the Crown was not faulted in *Smith v HM Advocate*, 2002 G.W.D. 17–559 in seeking a retrospective extension where a principal witness had changed his evidence against S, and faced prosecution for perjury. The witness reverted to his original account just before his own trial but almost three months elapsed before he was precognosced anew. The court held there to be no prejudice to S and granted the extension.

A breach of Art. 6 was held in *Rimmer v HM Advocate*, 2001 G.W.D. 33–1306 where the presiding judge, before whom pleas were tendered and accepted by the Crown, noted that a restraint order laid before the court ran in his name as a former Lord Advocate. He declined to act further and all subsequent procedure was conducted by a fellow judge who permitted the withdrawal of R's pleas and desertion of the diet. The Crown was compelled to seek a retrospective extension to re-indict, the grant of which was appealed unsuccessfully by R. The Appeal Court intriguingly and rather tenuously held there to be fault on the part of the Crown in placing the indictment before the first judge but granted the extension sought. At no point was it alleged that there had been any partiality or impropriety on the part of the judge.

Pressure of business alone will not justify an extension and even when administrative difficulties are founded upon, the court is under an obligation to make enquiry into their nature (see *Dobbie v HM Advocate*, 1986 S.L.T. 648; *Fleming v HM Advocate*, 1992 S.C.C.R. 575). Note that in *Rudge v HM Advocate*, 1989 S.C.C.R. 105 a Crown motion in such circumstances was granted and one persuasive factor was the lack of real prejudice being demonstrated. In *Beattie v HM Advocate*, 1995 S.C.C.R. 606 where a Crown motion to extend the 110 day period was granted, the Court of Appeal disfavoured the view that the non-availability of the trial judge was itself sufficient cause for extending the statutory time-limits. The court was critical of the lack of enquiry made by the trial judge as to possible alternatives and emphasised that the tests involved in extending the 110 day period are more exacting than those applicable to extending the one year period. An extension was granted to the Crown in *HM Advocate v McNally*, 1999 S.L.T 1377 where insufficient jurors were available to deal with the remaining cases in the sitting but the Appeal Court (at p.1381F) was at pains not to give the Crown *carte blanche* in the event of a repetition. In *Warnes v HM Advocate*, 2001 S.L.T. 34 a Crown motion for extension of the year time-bar was refused following an appeal by the accused. The Crown, which had given precedence to cases which did not time-bar in the sitting over *Warnes* whose case did, had cited pressure of business in a sitting already shortened by Easter holidays. The court was critical of the resources made available by the Scottish Executive and noted that the pressure in the sitting was entirely predictable but had been ignored by the Crown. Efforts to distinguish *Warnes*, by referring to the prior history of adjournments in the case and the pressure of business in its final sitting, failed in *Riaviz v HM Advocate*, 2003 S.L.T. 1110; 2003 S.C.C.R. 444. The complexity of the case allied to Crown efforts both to secure a plea (and broker restitution) in a large fraud case were held to justify extensions of the time bar in *Voudouri v HM Advocate*, 2003 S.C.C.R. 448.

Miscalculation of the time bar period on the Crown's part was rejected by the Appeal Court as a valid ground for extension in *Lyle v HM Advocate*, 1992 S.L.T. 467 and *Bennett v HM Advocate*, 1998 S.C.C.R. 23 (but see *Millar v HM Advocate*, 1994 S.L.T. 461 and *Duke v Lees*, 1997 G.W.D. 15–659 discussed below), as has a realisation too late that essential corroborative evidence had not been secured; see *Stewart v HM Advocate*, 1994 S.L.T. 518 where a successful Crown application for extension was overturned on appeal when it was conceded that such additional evidence could have been obtained within the statutory year. Correction of a misnumbered production on the indictment by the Crown without this being made known to the defence or the court was held in *Brown v HM Advocate*, 1999 S.L.T. 1369 to justify refusal of an extension. Detention in England and consequent absence which necessitated an extension was, on the facts, regarded as attributable to the accused, not the Crown (*Duffy v HM Advocate*, 1991 S.C.C.R. 685). Subsection (10) provides some statutory clarification in this area, by enacting that periods of remand served elsewhere in the United Kingdom shall interrupt the advance of the year time bar, an issue which had surfaced (and caused judicial calls for just such a reform) in *HM Advocate v Rowan*, 1994 S.C.C.R. 801. In *Rowan* the Court of Appeal considered a Crown appeal against a refusal of extension of the year period where R was in custody in England on other matters, and the English authorities lacked any powers to transfer him to Scotland; the appeal was allowed and this anomalous situation resulted in the amendment of the Criminal Justice (Scotland) Act 1995, s.15 at the Report Stage (*Hansard*, H.L. Vol. 561, col.39). However, detention as a serving prisoner in Scotland on other charges is not a factor, which can properly be taken into account by the court, when considering an application for extension (*McGill v HM Advocate*, 1997 S.C.C.R. 230).

While an application for extension may be presented orally to the court, the defence are entitled to be heard (*Sandford v HM Advocate*, 1986 S.C.C.R. 573) and to have warning of the motion to be made, albeit no formal notice is necessary (*Ferguson v HM Advocate*, 1992 S.C.C.R. 480; *Cation v HM Advocate*, 1992 S.C.C.R. 480). These last two cases also serve as warnings to the Crown of the risks associated with excusing witnesses without first securing the agreement of the defence: in both cases appeals against extensions of the year period were successful. By contrast see *Berry v HM Advocate*, 1989 S.L.T. 71 where delays in notifying the Crown that a witness on the indictment could not be excused, or his evidence be agreed, resulted in an extension of time which was upheld on appeal. Equally, where adjournment of the trial was on defence motion and, in an oversight, the Crown failed to seek the necessary time-bar extension to preserve the proceedings, the Appeal Court was unimpressed by defence opposition to extension (*McGinlay v HM Advocate*, 1999 S.C.C.R. 779).

Persistent illness or absence of co-accused may not justify extensions if the Crown have not considered proceeding against the accused who is present on his own (*Mejka v HM Advocate*, 1993 S.L.T. 1321; 1993 S.C.C.R. 978).

Where an accused has appeared on successive petitions, the court has to look to each petition individually in order to determine the effective date of the year time bar (*Ross v HM Advocate*, 1990 S.C.C.R. 182). Thus in *HM Advocate v Muir*, 1998 S.L.T. 1296 where M had been remanded on petition and was later released at the trial diet following the failure to appear of a co-accused, only to fail to appear himself at a later trial resulting in a further period of remand after arrest, it was held on appeal that s.65(4) required that both periods of imprisonment had to be added together in calculating the 80 and 110 day periods; appropriate extensions had to be obtained.

It is possible for the time-bar to be extended retrospectively (*HM Advocate v M*, 1986 S.C.C.R. 624) and as subs.(2) provides the accused's failure to appear at a first or preliminary diet, or a trial diet, immediately stops the operation of the time-bar. Prospective extension of the time-bar is competent even where no indictment has yet been served is competent (*HM Advocate v Caulfield*, 1999 G.W.D. 19–872).

While the provisions of s.65 do not apply directly to private prosecutions by way of a Bill of Criminal Letters, in *G.M.C. v Forsyth*, 1995 S.C.C.R. 553 the court had regard to the spirit of the statutory provisions in refusing a Bill presented 14 months after proceedings were deserted by the Crown.

In computing the time-scale of any extension, the natural interpretation of such a motion is that the extended period runs from the expiry of the original 12 month period, not from the date upon which the motion for extension is made. This applies equally to applications made under subs.(3) and to cases begun on petition and later reduced to summary complaint (see *Millar v HM Advocate*, 1994 S.L.T. 461 and *Duke v Lees*, 1997 G.W.D. 15–659).

The Note of Appeal in relation to an application for extension of the 12 month period should be on Form 8.1-A of the Act of Adjournal (Criminal Procedure Rules).

Subss.(4) to (7)

Unlike the 11 and 12 month time bars in solemn bail cases which run from the date of first appearance on petition, calculation of the 80, 110 (and now 140) day time limits which apply to solemn custody trials run from the date of full committal. Prior to the 2004 Act, Crown applications to extend custody time limits could only be granted if the court was satisfied that there had been no fault on the part of the Crown; and all applications had to be made to the High Court, the sheriff dealing with the petition committal warrant or a subsequent solemn trial having no power to extend these remand time limits.

At the heart of s.65 (and no doubt the reason so much case law has been generated) were the peremptory consequences if a necessary extension of the time limits was not obtained either prospectively or retrospectively—an accused would be forever free from all further proceedings arising from the petition warrant.

Several significant changes have followed the 2004 Act. Most notably in relation to High Court proceedings is the introduction of the 80, 110 and 140 day periods to permit the regime of preliminary diets formulated in the *Bonomy Report*, and the additional time for focused preparation of trial business. Prior to service of an indictment, subs.(5) requires applications for extension of any of the custodial periods in solemn proceedings to be made to a single judge in the High Court; however, once the indictment has been served application for extension now falls to be considered by a judge of the court where the case is to be tried—a reform which avoids the need for adjourned or postponed cases to be referred to the High Court simply to obtain a time bar extension.

Subs.(5) preserves the power of the court to extend all, or any, of these periods as appropriate and subs.(8) implies that the court retains the power to refuse an application for extension, a decision which can be appealed.

Ordinarily, the terms of subs.(4)(aa) appear to require the immediate admission of an accused to bail if the Crown fails to adhere to the prescribed time scales, but closer examination of subs.(8A) shows that while providing a mechanism to admit remanded accused to bail, it also preserves the right of the court to refuse bail on a Crown motion. (Subs.(8A) also restates the right of the Lord Advocate to admit the accused to bail administratively). Subs.(8D) enables the Crown to appeal a decision to grant bail but any such appeal must be heard within 72 hours unless *that* period is itself extended by the High Court. (It may be that the court of first instance will have to deal with this further extension since the committal warrant for the accused will otherwise expire after 72 hours and he will then be admitted to bail as of right).

It is important to appreciate that the previous stringent test applied to any application for extension of the solemn remand period has been relaxed—the test now applied to extensions in all solemn proceedings is on cause shown—whereas the 1995 Act required there be no fault on the part of the Crown. Nonetheless the large volume of case law flowing from interpretation of s.65 has not lost its value.

Failure to serve an indictment timeously is not fatal to the proceedings but might give rise to a civil claim and now, would entitle the accused to bail, subject to the provisions in subs.(8A); see also *Farrell v HM Advocate*, 1 985 S.L.T. 58; *McCluskey v HM Advocate*, 1993 S.L.T. 897; *HM Advocate v McCann*, 1977 S.L.T. (Notes) 19 and *X, Petitioner*, 1995 S.C.C.R. 407.

It remains the case that the statutory remand periods can be interrupted by liberation of the accused or the imposition of a custodial sentence. The period spent in custody has to be referable solely to the committal order giving rise to the indictment charges to count in the calculation (*HM Advocate v Boyle*, 1972 S.L.T. (Notes) 16; *Harley v HM Advocate*, 1970 S.L.T. (Notes) 6).

Where two or more petitions are conjoined on an indictment the dates of each committal have to be weighed separately in any calculation (*Ross v HM Advocate*, 1990 S.C.C.R. 182).

Similarly, where the 110 days are interrupted by a term of imprisonment, they recommence at the prisoner's earliest release date and not by reference to the working practices of the prison authorities which, in the past, released prisoners whose liberation date fell during a weekend on the Friday before

(*Brown v HM Advocate*, 1988 S.C.C.R. 577). The effect of the interaction of subss.(4) to (7) and the revocation of licence provisions contained in s.17 of the Prisoners and Criminal Proceedings (Scotland) Act 1993 was considered in *Follen v HM Advocate*, 2001 S.C.C.R. 255. F had been released on licence following conviction of contravening s.4(3)(b) of the Misuse of Drugs Act 1971. Within a year of this release he was caught in possession of a substantial quantity of cannabis resin and remanded in custody and, within a week of committal until liberation in due course of law, his licence was recalled and revoked. When indicted he raised devolution issues and pled in bar of trial that he had been detained for more than 110 days. It was held that the period was attributable to the s.17 order and detention in relation to the original sentence.

Case authorities

In *HM Advocate v McTavish*, 1974 S.L.T. 246 a Crown motion for extension, to enable the completion of further forensic tests and to allow further treatment of the accused's mental illness, in circumstances where the Crown was admittedly able to proceed to trial upon the matters libelled in the petition was rejected. In *HM Advocate v Bickerstaff*, 1926 J.C. 65 where trial had been unable to proceed due to the accused's supervening insanity, a Full Bench held the delay as being attributable to the accused, not the Crown. Illness of the judge and of co-accused permitted three extensions (upheld on appeal) in *Young v HM Advocate*, 1990 S.C.C.R. 315, the High Court itself admitting the accused to bail on a murder charge. Two extensions of time, once on the motion of a co-accused and once on Crown motion because of illness of a witness, were allowed in *Johnston (R.) v HM Advocate*, 1993 S.C.C.R. 295. Perhaps the most contentious use of these provisions in which no fault was felt to lie with the Crown is found in *Gildea v HM Advocate*, 1983 S.C.C.R. 144 where an extension was granted on account of a case scheduled earlier in the assize having taken longer than could reasonably be foreseen. Fault on the part of the Crown was argued, but rejected by the Appeal Court, in *Cunningham v HM Advocate*, 2002 S.C.C.R. 499. Prison authorities had failed to serve an indictment upon C timeously. The Crown lodged application to extend the time bar but delayed service of a fresh indictment; defence objections centred upon the failure to re-indict without delay. The Appeal Court noted that the practical outcome of granting the application was not materially different from the outcome had a fresh indictment been served timeously—either way such an extension would have been unavoidable. The application had been made before the expiry of the time bar though there had been delay (compare the approach in *Farrell v HM Advocate*, 2001 S.C.C.R. 720 discussed below).

Particular difficulty can arise in cases involving children who are remanded into the custody of the local authority pending trial or who are already subject of supervision requirements. It is essential to establish whether bail has been refused, if the child has been bailed into the care of local authority accommodation be that in secure or open accommodation, and whether the residential regime has been altered as a result of the petition appearance or at the initiative of the local authority exercising separate powers under the Children (Scotland) Act 1995. Refer to the Notes "Children Under 16 Years" at A4–120 and the cases of *X, Petr*, 1996 S.C.C.R. 436 and *M, Petr*, 1996 S.C.C.R. 92.

Subs.(8)

It may seem tautological but an appeal against the grant or refusal of an extension of the periods of 80 or 110 days, or 12 months, can only be competently taken where there has *de facto* been such a grant or refusal. See *McKnight v HM Advocate*, 1996 S.L.T. 834 where an appeal to the *nobile officium* was ruled incompetent, the sheriff having refused to consider an application for extension at an earlier diet (the case being adjourned through lack of time) and there being no decision to appeal statutorily and no judicial acting to justify recourse to the *nobile officium*.

"Retrospective Extensions Generally"

Delay in making such an application may itself tell against the Crown. See, for example, *Farrell v HM Advocate*, 2001 S.C.C.R. 720 where, after failures to appear the Crown did not appreciate following re-arrest of the accused that little of the 110 day period remained.

A failure on the part of others to execute explicit instructions issued by the Crown would not be regarded as a fault attributable to the Crown (*Coutts v HM Advocate*, 1992 S.C.C.R. 87) but see also *HM Advocate v Sands (Andrew)*, 2001 S.C.C.R. 786 where an appeal against refusal of an extension failed, the Crown having relied upon inaccurate information supplied by prison authorities as to the length of a prison sentence but, crucially, were dilatory in acting when alerted to the true position by the defence agent.

It will be recalled that, prior to the 2004 Act, in the former two situations no degree of fault on the part of the prosecutor was acceptable—see *HM Advocate v Bickerstaff*, 1926 S.L.T. 121, *Farrell v HM Advocate*, 1985 S.L.T. 58 and *McDowall v Lees*, 1996 S.C. 214. So far as the year time bar was concerned a degree of fault might be excused—*HM Advocate v Davies (Alexander)*, 1993 S.C.C.R. 645; 1994 S.L.T. 296 and *Finlay (Barry Thomas) v HM Advocate*, 1998 S.L.T. 1235. Now, however, the fact that the Crown has been at fault does not, of itself, determine whether any sort of application to extend a time bar should be refused.

"Loss of principal petition or indictment"

While s.157 of the Act makes statutory provisions to deal with the loss of the principal complaint in summary proceedings, no similar provision exists in solemn procedure. The most obvious solution would be to petition the court for an extension of the time bar under subss.(3) and (5) and note that it may be necessary in cases involving a remand period to extend each of the 80, 110 and 140 day periods. See, however, *HM Advocate v Fox*; *HM Advocate v Wilson* (High Court of Justiciary, December 5, 2001, unreported) in both of which the Crown resorted to a petition to the *nobile officium*. Both cases had been indicted for trial in the same Kilmarnock sitting and had thereafter been adjourned on several occasions until, during a sitting in November 2001, the Clerk could not find the principal indictments and interlocutors. The Crown stance was that no application could be made to the sheriff in accordance with subs.(3) since an indictment had been served on each accused but nor could an application for extension be made to a single High Court judge since there was no principal indictment to lay before the court. The indictments libelled respectively charges of murder and indecent assault and in both cases the Crown was anxious to preserve the trial diet to which witnesses had been cited. Instead, a petition to the *nobile officium* was lodged along with a copy of each indictment certified as true by the advocate depute who had signed the missing principal indictment craving substitution of the copy and an extension of the time bars. The applications were not contested.

In *Bryceland v HM Advocate*, 2002 S.C.C.R. 995 the Crown used the same approach, petitioning the *nobile officium*, when the principal indictment had been destroyed after being returned, in error, to the Crown after service of the indictment. In this instance a certified copy of the original indictment was signed by an advocate depute other than the original signatory and was tendered to the court in substitution for the destroyed copy. It is of passing interest that the single judge held it to be competent to place the *nobile officium* application before a single judge (as had occurred in *BBC, Petitioners (No.3)*, 2002 J.C. 27) rather than before a bench of three judges. In *Bryceland* it was of some moment that the 110 days were running and that the only other course open to the Crown would have been to liberate the accused.

The case is further reported as *Bryceland, Petitioner*, 2003 S.L.T. 54 but that deals with a later application to the *nobile officium* (as distinct from an appeal) lodged by the accused against the decision at first instance. The competency, or otherwise, of the Crown's petition to the single judge disappointingly was not argued.

New Prosecutions and Time Bar Provisions

Quite distinct time bar provisions govern retrials authorised in terms of s.119 of the Act. See A4–264 below. Curiously, given the spirit of the 2004 Act, no explicit provision has been made to incorporate a preliminary or first diet in the retrial proceedings.

Commencement and Transitional Issues

Reference is required to the Criminal Procedure (Amendment) (Scotland) Act 2004 (Commencement, Transitional Provisions and Savings) Order 2004 (SSI 2004/405).

Preliminary hearings in the High Court begin on or after April 1, 2005 but it will be observed that in relation to High Court or sheriff solemn proceedings commenced by, or extended to, a diet occurring before April 1, 2005, procedures will be governed by the 1995 Act as it read before the amendments introduced by the 2004 Act. Thus for a time, the date upon which an indictment was called for a first diet, or trial diet, will dictate the procedural form to be adopted by the court. Plainly, the taking of an apprehension warrant, or desertion *pro loco* of the indictment, will perforce give rise to the need for a fresh libel which will be governed by the procedural regime introduced by the 2004 Act. Particularly too, art.4 allows the High Court a discretion, when adjourning or postponing a High Court trial between February 1 and April 1, 2005, to appoint a floating diet (see s.83A) in the absence now of sittings, rather than a fixed date for trial.

Service and lodging of indictment, etc.

66.—(1) This Act shall be sufficient warrant for—

(a) the citation of the accused and witnesses to—

(i) any diet of the High Court to be held on any day, and at any place, the Court is sitting;

   (ii) any diet of the sheriff court to be held on any day the court is sitting; or

   (iii) any adjournment of a diet specified in sub-paragraph (i) or (ii) above; and

 (b) the citation of jurors for any trial to be held—

   (i) in the High Court; or

   (ii) under solemn procedure in the sheriff court.

(2) The execution of the citation against an accused, witness or juror shall be in such form as may be prescribed by Act of Adjournal, or as nearly as may be in such form.

(3) A witness may be cited by sending the citation to the witness by ordinary or registered post or by the recorded delivery service and a written execution in the form prescribed by Act of Adjournal or as nearly as may be in such form, purporting to be signed by the person who served such citation together with, where appropriate, the relevant post office receipt shall be sufficient evidence of such citation.

(4) The accused may be cited either—

 (a) by being served with a copy of the indictment and of the list of the names and addresses of the witnesses to be adduced by the prosecution and of the list of productions (if any) to be put in evidence by the prosecution; or

 (b) if the accused, at the time of citation, is not in custody, by a constable affixing to the door of the relevant premises a notice in such form as may be prescribed by Act of Adjournal, or as nearly as may be in such form—

   (i) specifying the date on which it was so affixed;

   (ii) informing the accused that he may collect a copy of the indictment and of such lists as are mentioned in paragraph (a) above from a police station specified in the notice; and

   (iii) calling upon him to appear and answer to the indictment at such diet as shall be so specified.

(4ZA) In subsection (4)(b) above, "the relevant premises" means—

 (a) where the accused, at the time of citation, has been admitted to bail, his proper domicile of citation as specified for the purposes of section 25 of this Act; or

 (b) in any other case, any premises which the constable reasonably believes to be the accused's dwelling-house or place of business.

(4A) Where a date is specified by virtue of sub-paragraph (i) of subsection (4)(b) above, that date shall be deemed the date on which the indictment is served; and the copy of the indictment referred to in sub-paragraph (ii) of that subsection shall, for the purposes of subsections (12) and (13) below be deemed the service copy.

(4B) Paragraphs (a) and (b) of subsection (6) below shall apply for the purpose of specifying a diet by virtue of subsection (4)(b)(iii) above as they apply for the purpose of specifying a diet in any notice under subsection (6).

(4C) Where—

 (a) the accused is cited in accordance with subsection (4)(b) above; and

 (b) the charge in the indictment is of committing a sexual offence to which section 288C of this Act applies,

the accused shall, on collecting the indictment, be given a notice containing intimation of the matters specified in subsection (6A)(a) below.

(5) Except in a case to which section 76 of this Act applies, the prosecutor shall on or before the date of service of the indictment lodge the record copy of

the indictment with the clerk of court before which the trial is to take place, together with a copy of the list of witnesses and a copy of the list of productions.

(6) If the accused is cited by being served with a copy of the indictment, then except where such service is under section 76(1) of this Act, a notice shall be served on the accused with the indictment calling upon him to appear and answer to the indictment—

    (a) where the case is to be tried in the sheriff court,

        (i) at a first diet not less than 15 clear days after the service of the indictment and not less than 10 clear days before the trial diet; and

        (ii) at a trial diet not less than 29 clear days after service of the indictment,

    (b) where the indictment is in respect of the High Court, at a diet not less than 29 clear days after the service of the indictment (such a diet being referred to in this Act as a "preliminary hearing").

(6A) Where the charge in the indictment is of committing a sexual offence to which section 288C of this Act applies, the notice served under subsection (6) above shall—

    (a) contain intimation to the accused—

        (zi) where the case is to be tried in the High Court, that his case at or for the purposes of the preliminary hearing may be conducted only by a lawyer;

        (i) that, if he is tried for the offence, his defence (including at any commissioner proceedings) and any proof ordered as is mentioned in section 288C(1) of this Act may be conducted only by a lawyer;

        (ii) that it is, therefore, in his interests, if he has not already done so, to get the professional assistance of a solicitor; and

        (iii) that if he does not engage a solicitor for the purposes of the conduct of his case at or for the purposes of the preliminary hearing or his defence at the tria (or at any related commissioner proceedings), the court will do so;

    (b) [*Repealed by the Criminal Procedure (Amendment) (Scotland) Act 2004 (asp 5), s.1(2). Brought into force on February 1, 2005 by the Criminal Procedure (Amendment) (Scotland) Act 2004 (Commencement, Transitional Provisions and Savings) Order 2004 (SSI 2004/405 (C.28)), art.2.*]

(6AA) A notice affixed under subsection (4)(b) above or served under subsection (6) above shall, where the accused is a body corporate, also contain intimation to the accused—

    (a) where the indictment is in respect of the High Court, that, if it does not appear as mentioned in section 70(4) of this Act or by counsel or a solicitor at the preliminary hearing—

        (i) the hearing may proceed; and

        (ii) a trial diet may be appointed,

    in its absence; and

    (b) in any case (whether the indictment is in respect of the High Court or the sheriff court), that if it does not appear as mentioned in paragraph (a) above at the trial diet, the trial may proceed in its absence.

(6B) A failure to comply with subsection (4C), (6A) or (6AA) above does not affect the validity or lawfulness of any notice affixed under subsection (4)(b) above or served under subsection (6) above or any other element of the proceedings against the accused.

(6C) An accused shall be taken to be served with—

(a) the indictment and lists of witnesses and productions; and

(b) the notice referred to in subsection (6) above,

if they are served on the solicitor specified in subsection (6D) below at that solicitor's place of business.

(6D) The solicitor referred to in subsection (6C) above is any solicitor who—

(a) has notified in writing the procurator fiscal for the district in which the charge against the accused was being investigated that he is engaged by the accused for the purposes of his defence; and

(b) has not informed that procurator fiscal that he has been dismissed by, or has withdrawn from acting for, the accused.

(6E) It is the duty of a solicitor who has, before service of an indictment, notified a procurator fiscal that he is engaged by the accused for the purposes of his defence to inform that procurator fiscal in writing forthwith if he is dismissed by, or withdraws from acting for, the accused.

(7) Subject to subsection (4)(b) above, service of the indictment, lists of witnesses and productions, and any notice or intimation to the accused, and the citation of witnesses, whether for precognition or trial, may be effected by any officer of law.

(8) [*Repealed by the Criminal Procedure (Amendment) (Scotland) Act 2004 (asp 5), s.7(6). Brought into force on February 1, 2005 by the Criminal Procedure (Amendment) (Scotland) Act 2004 (Commencement, Transitional Provisions and Savings) Order 2004 (SSI 2004/405 (C.28)), art.2.*]

(9) The citation of witnesses may be effected by any officer of law duly authorised; and in any proceedings, the evidence on oath of the officer shall, subject to subsection (10) below, be sufficient evidence of the execution of the citation.

(10) [*Repealed by the Criminal Procedure (Amendment) (Scotland) Act 2004 (asp 5), s.25 and Sch.1, para.15(e). Brought into force on February 1, 2005 by the Criminal Procedure (Amendment) (Scotland) Act 2004 (Commencement, Transitional Provisions and Savings) Order 2004 (SSI 2004/405 (C.28)), art.2.*]

(11) No objection to the competency of the officer who served the indictment, or who executed a citation under subsection (4)(b) above, to give evidence in respect of such service or execution shall be upheld on the ground that his name is not included in the list of witnesses served on the accused.

(12) Any deletion or correction made before service on the record or service copy of an indictment shall be sufficiently authenticated by the initials of the person who has signed, or could by law have signed, the indictment.

(13) Any deletion or correction made on a service copy of an indictment, or on any notice of citation, postponement, adjournment or other notice served on an accused shall be sufficiently authenticated by the initials of any procurator fiscal or of the person serving the same.

(14) Any deletion or correction made on any execution of citation or notice or other document so served shall be sufficiently authenticated by the initials of the person serving the same.

(15) In subsection (6A) above, "commissioner proceedings" means proceedings before a commissioner appoointed under section 271I(1) or by virtue of section 272(1)(b) of this Act.

AMENDMENT

Subss.(6A) and (6B) inserted by the Sexual Offences (Procedure and Evidence) (Scotland) Act 2002 (asp 9), Sch.1, para.4. Brought into force by the Sexual Offences (Procedure and Evidence) (Scotland) Act 2002 (Commencement and Transitional Provisions) Order 2002 (SSI 2002/443 (C.24)), art.4 (effective November 1, 2002).

Section 66 as amended by Criminal Justice (Scotland) Act 2003 (asp 7), Part 8, s.61. Brought into force on June 27, 2003 by the Criminal Justice (Scotland) Act 2003 (Commencement No.1) Order 2003 (SSI 2003/288 (C.14)).

Subs.(6A) as amended by Criminal Justice (Scotland) Act 2003 (asp 7), Sch.4, para.3. Brought into force on November 25, 2003 by the Criminal Justice (Scotland) Act 2003 (Commencement No.3 and Revocation) Order 2003 (SSI 2003/475 (C.26)), art.2.

Subs.(1) substituted, subs.(4)(b) as amended and subss.(4ZA), (6C), (6D) and (6E) inserted by the Criminal Procedure (Amendment) (Scotland) Act 2004 (asp 5), s.7. Brought into force on February 1, 2005 by the Criminal Procedure (Amendment) (Scotland) Act 2004 (Commencement, Transitional Provisions and Savings) Order 2004 (SSI 2004/405 (C.28)), art.2.

Subs.(6)(a) as amended, and subs.(6)(b) substituted, by the Criminal Procedure (Amendment) (Scotland) Act 2004 (asp 5), s.1(1). Brought into force on February 1, 2005 as above.

Subs.(6AA) inserted by the Criminal Procedure (Amendment) (Scotland) Act 2004 (asp 5), s.10(5). Brought into force on February 1, 2005 as above.

Subss.(4), (6A)(a)(iii) and (6B) as amended, and subss.(4C), (6A)(a)(zi) inserted, by the Criminal Procedure (Amendment) (Scotland) Act 2004 (asp 5), s.25 and Sch.1, para.15(a)–(d). Brought into force on February 1, 2005 as above.

Section 66(6A) amended and s.66(15) inserted by the Criminal Proceedings etc. (Reform) (Scotland) Act 2007 (asp 6), s.35

DEFINITIONS

"Clerk of Justiciary": s.307(1).
"diet": s.307(1).
"High Court": s.307(1).
"indictment": s.307(1).
"officer of law": s.307(1).
"prosecutor": s.307(1).
"sheriff clerk": s.307(1).
"witness": s.307(1).

GENERAL NOTE

The provisions relating to service of indictments, citations and proof of service were spread over ss.58, 69 to 73, 75 and 78 in the 1975 Act but are now brought together in s.66 of the 1995 Act. Broader, more flexible provisions for service of indictments were introduced by the Criminal Justice (Scotland) Act 2003 (asp 7) and by s.7(2) of the 2004 Act.

Service of the indictment dictates the timetable for all subsequent proceedings; the dual provisions governing solemn proceedings become clearer from subs.(6). In sheriff and jury proceedings trial must occur not less than 29 clear days after service, with a first diet not less than 15 days after service of the indictment and not less than 10 days before a trial. Now in High Court proceedings the only fixed interval is that a preliminary diet must occur not less than 29 clear days after service. Note should, however, be taken of the provisions of s.72B which provide (presumably more rarely) for dispensing with preliminary diets in the High Court and the immediate assignment of a trial diet. Separate provisions govern accelerated plea proceedings under s.76 of the Act

Various technical matters are dealt with by the section: subs.(1) provides an automatic warrant to cite witnesses to any diet (preliminary, first or trial) in the proceedings and for jurors to be cited for any trial; subs.(4) enables service of an indictment to be made upon an accused by affixing a notice at his bail domicile or wheresoever he is believed to reside or work; see subs.(4ZA). This enables an indictment, which may well contain sensitive material, to be collected from a nominated police office rather than having to be left in public view at a domicile. This may be particularly understandable in indictments detailing allegations of a sexual nature. (See the note "*Listed sexual offences*" which follows). The form of notice to be used for this purpose is found as Form 8.2-A in the Act of Adjournal (Criminal Procedure Rules Amendment) (Criminal Procedure (Amendment) (Scotland) Act 2004) 2005 (SSI 2005/44) while the standard intimation to appear is now Form 8.2-B therein. The execution of service now appears as Form 2.6-G.

Substantial new administrative provisions are to be found in subss.(6C) and (6D). The solicitor engaged by the accused is now obliged to notify the procurator fiscal within whose jurisdiction appearance was made on petition that he is so engaged, and to notify if he ceases to act. (More difficulty will inevitably arise where an accused is indicted without first having appeared on petition). The significance of these measures is seen in subs.(6C) which now enables service of an indictment to be effected in the hands of the nominated solicitor at his place of business. This simple measure will remove the absolute need to effect service of the indictment upon the accused but it is suggested that the Crown will ordinarily still seek to do so—in Convention terms the accused must be aware of the allegations he faces; all that appears to be intended is to avoid proceedings falling for a purely technical want of form where no prejudice has been caused to an accused. Attention is directed to *H.M. Advocate v Holbein*, 2005 S.L.T. 242 which addressed the dilemma facing the Crown when the accused's bail domicile has been demolished. It remains the case that service is validly effected nonetheless by depositing the indictment (or notice to collect it) there; the court confined consideration to this narrow issue and did not explore the possible bail contravention committed by the accused's failure to apply to the court for a change of domicile. The new provisions are intended to simplify service of indictments and documents but arguably have still to be shown to fulfil Art.6 Convention requirements.

Subs.(5) repeats a time-honoured duty upon the Crown to lodge a record copy of the indictment with the sheriff clerk or Clerk of Justiciary, but where this could once have been regarded as a directory rather than mandatory provision (see, for example, *H.M. Advocate v Graham*, 1985 S.L.T. 498) lodging now has to be seen as an essential precursor to any solemn diet.

It is competent, though unusual, to run two identical indictments simultaneously against an accused. So in *H.M. Advocate v Dow*, 1992 S.L.T. 577 where a minute of postponement had been lodged by the defence, and granted by the court, and the Crown was given authority under s.77A(2) of the 1975 Act to serve notice of a new trial diet (the equivalent procedure is now contained in s.80(3) of the 1995 Act) but did not do so, service of a fresh indictment in identical terms was held to be neither oppressive nor incompetent. (See also the notes to s.80 *infra*.)

In *Smith v H.M. Advocate*, 1996 S.L.T. 1384 it was discovered, before a preliminary diet, that an error in the minute of notice meant that an incorrect address had been given for the High Court sitting, and a second identical indictment was served. The High Court on appeal held that as the master of the instance it was a matter within the discretion of the Crown which indictment would be called. This suggests that the terms of the indictments themselves (be they identical or not) are not of moment since the Court also indicated that the service of a second indictment implied that the Crown were deserting the first and proceeding on the later indictment.

Provisions relating to service of indictments

New service provisions are found in subs.(4) onwards. Service of an indictment is normally effected upon an accused personally, or by leaving it at his domicile of citation or customary abode, or even *in extremis* by pinning it to a house door. Now it is possible instead to forward a notice to the accused instead of the full indictment (or complaint in summary cases); the notice is dated and informs the accused of the diet (or diets) at which he must appear, and directs him to a specific police office to collect his indictment. As mentioned earlier subs.(6D) allows for an indictment to be taken to be validly served if left at the office of the nominated solicitor.

Either the execution of service of the indictment, or notice, will be sufficient evidence of lawful citation but failure to serve remains fatal to the proceedings on that indictment and cannot be cured by appearance (*McAllister v H.M. Advocate*, 1985 S.L.T. 399; 1985 S.C.C.R. 36, and *Hester v MacDonald*, 1961 S.C. 370). The aim of the extended service provisions is to avoid the need to leave court documents, which by their nature can contain sensitive material, in places where they may fall into the wrong hands or become common currency in the neighbourhood—this protects the Convention rights of the accused and witnesses alike.

A failure to effect service timeously does not cause the committal warrant granted at the time of appearance on petition to fall, but the Crown will still be obliged to obtemper the timebar requirements set out in s.65 of the Act; see *Jamieson v H.M. Advocate*, 1990 S.L.T. 845; 1990 S.C.C.R. 137 and the Notes to s.65 above. Service without giving the requisite 29 clear days notice demanded in subs.(6) would not create a nullity and in the absence of an objection to service, which would be taken at a preliminary diet (or first diet in sheriff solemn proceedings), trial could proceed. That 29-day *induciae* can be waived and can be asserted to have been so in the absence of a preliminary challenge (see *H.M. Advocate v McDonald*, 1984 S.L.T. 426).

Section 66(4A) establishes that the date upon which the notice of an indictment is served upon the accused is to be taken to be the date of service, just as service of the indictment itself would denote.

In *Bryson v H.M. Advocate*, 1961 S.L.T. 289, an accused bailed to a domicile was subsequently remanded in custody for further charges, but the indictment was served at his original domicile not at the prison, a procedure which was upheld. Service of an indictment without giving the requisite 29 clear days notice stipulated in subs.(6) would not create a nullity and in the absence of an objection to service, which should be taken at a preliminary diet (or at the first diet in sheriff and jury cases), trial could proceed: furthermore the *induciae* can be waived and it can be argued that this has occurred in the absence of a preliminary challenge (see *H.M. Advocate v McDonald*, 1984 S.L.T. 426).

Listed sexual offences (s.288C of the Act)

Where the libel contains a sexual offence listed in s.288C of the Act it is provided by s.66(6A) that the accused is to be given an additional notice setting out the special provisions relating to legal representation which apply to such offences, and is to be notified that he has to attend at a mandatory first diet. The form of notice to be used in such cases is now Form 8.2-C in the Act of Adjournal (Criminal Procedure Rules Amendment) (Criminal Procedure (Amendment) (Scotland) Act 2004) 2005 (SSI 2005/44).

Section 66(6B) serves to indicate that the provisions are directory upon the Crown and that a Crown failure to observe them is not fatal to the proceedings themselves (the court having a continuing duty in such cases to ensure that the accused is legally represented throughout the proceedings).

Proof of service

The form of the Notice of Compearance to be served upon the accused with any indictment has been amended by para.2(12) of the Act of Adjournal (Criminal Procedure Rules Amendment No.3) (Sexual Offences (Procedure and Evidence) (Scotland) Act 2002) 2002 (SSI 2002/454). Consequently, the Notice of Compearance accompanying the indictment is signed by the prosecutor when the indictment itself is signed, rather than completed by the police officer serving the documents. See Form 8.2-B at B1–97 below.

An indictment must be served by an officer of law in the presence of a witness in one of the manners specified in rule 2.2 of the 1996 Act of Adjournal, namely (i) by personal service; (ii) by leaving it in the hands of a member of the accused's family, an inmate or employee at the domicile of citation; or (iii) by delivery through, or affixing to the door of the domicile. Similar provisions apply in situations where the accused has no domicile of citation in which event service can be effected at the address which the officer has reasonable cause to believe is occupied by the accused or by personal service.

The execution of service completed by the officer should comply with Form 2.6-A shown in the Appendix to the 1996 Act of Adjournal and be returned to the prosecutor: the execution will in all likelihood require to be produced to the court if the accused fails to appear at any diet before an arrest warrant will be granted. In *Welsh v H.M. Advocate*, 1986 S.L.T. 664 a dispute arose as to whether the police could have served the indictment as claimed, since (it was alleged) the building had been demolished. The claim was refuted by the officers but the court noted that even if the accused's assertion had been correct, there would have been a failure to inform the court of a change of domicile.

It is competent in terms of subss.(8) and (11) for the officers effecting service of the indictment to be heard in evidence without their particulars being added to the indictment, a useful provision in the event of later additional charges for failure to appear at a lawful diet.

Witnesses for precognition or trial can be cited in conformity with subs.(3) but in the event of a failure to appear at trial, it may be difficult to persuade the court to grant an arrest warrant, as subs.(10) allows, unless an execution of personal service conforming to Form 2.6-E of the 1996 Act of Adjournal can be exhibited. However, the same Act of Adjournal has introduced a new Form 8.2-D, a reply form to be returned by witnesses cited in indictment cases acknowledging citation and this should be a factor to be taken into account in the event of non-appearance and, incidentally, may alert the Crown at an early stage to any potential shortcomings in citation (it must be doubted that precognition mentioned in subs.(7) can be regarded as "a diet" for the purposes of subs.(10); it is submitted that a warrant for arrest could not properly be sought following failure to appear for precognition, except precognition on oath. The relevant forms of petition for authority to precognosce on oath, are Forms 29.1-A and 29.1-B in the above Act of Adjournal).

For purposes of computation of time, note that in the case of the time limits specified in subs.(6), s.75 enacts that where the final day falls on a *dies non*, the effective date for calculation is the next working day.

Provisions for planning and disposal of sittings

Guidance in relation to the organisation of business intended to supplement existing statutory provisions for High Court sittings is to be found in Memorandum dated January 9, 2002, issued by the Lord Justice General. These provisions which set out responsibilities before, and during, sittings for defence agents and counsel and the Crown, and for the trial judge at the start of sittings, are intended to improve the flow of business in all High Court sittings and can be found in 2002 S.L.T. (News) 28.

Witnesses

67.—(1) The list of witnesses shall consist of the names of the witnesses together with an address at which they can be contacted for the purposes of precognition.

(2) It shall not be necessary to include in the list of witnesses the names of any witnesses to the declaration of the accused or the names of any witnesses to prove that an extract conviction applies to the accused, but witnesses may be examined in regard to these matters without previous notice.

(3) Any objection in respect of misnomer or misdescription of—

(a) any person named in the indictment; or

(b) any witness in the list of witnesses,

shall be intimated in writing to the court before which the trial is to take place, to the prosecutor and to any other accused, where the case is to be tried in the sheriff court, at or before the first diet and, where the case is to be tried in the High Court, not less than seven clear days before the preliminary hearing; and, except on cause shown, no such objection shall be admitted unless so intimated.

(4) Where such intimation has been given or cause is shown and the court is satisfied that the accused making the objection has not been supplied with sufficient information to enable him to identify the person named in the indictment or to find such witness in sufficient time to precognosce him before the trial, the court may grant such remedy by postponement, adjournment or otherwise as appears to it to be appropriate.

(4A) The prosecutor shall have a duty to cite a witness included in the list only if—

(a) it has been ascertained under—

(i) in the case of proceedings in the High Court, section 72(6)(d); or

(ii) in the case of proceedings in the sheriff court, section 71(1C)(a),

of this Act that the witness is required by the prosecutor or the accused to attend the trial; or

(b) where, in the case of proceedings in the High Court, the preliminary hearing has been dispensed with under subsection (1) of section 72B of this Act, the witness was identified in the application under that subsection as being required by the prosecutor or the accused to attend the trial.

(5) Without prejudice to—

(a) any enactment or rule of law permitting the prosecutor to examine any witness not included in the list of witnesses; or

(b) subsection (6) below,

in any trial it shall be competent with the leave of the court for the prosecutor to examine any witness or to put in evidence any production not included in the lists lodged by him, provided that written notice, containing in the case of a witness his name and address as mentioned in subsection (1) above, has been given to the accused by the relevant time.

(5A) In subsection (5) above, "the relevant time" means—

(a) where the case is to be tried in the High Court—

(i) not less then seven clear days before the preliminary hearing; or

(ii) such later time, before the jury is sworn to try the case, as the court may, on cause shown, allow;

(b) where the case is to be tried in the sheriff court, not less than two clear days before the day on which the jury is sworn to try the case.

(6) It shall be competent for the prosecutor to examine any witness or put in evidence any production included in any list or notice lodged by the accused, and it shall be competent for an accused to examine any witness or put in evidence any production included in any list or notice lodged by the prosecutor or by a co-accused.

AMENDMENT

Subss.(3), (5) as amended, and (4A), (5A) inserted, by the Criminal Procedure (Amendment)

(Scotland) Act 2004 (asp 5), s.25 and Sch.1, para.16. Brought into force on February 1, 2005 by the Criminal Procedure (Amendment) (Scotland) Act 2004 (Commencement, Transitional Provisions and Savings) Order 2004 (SSI 2004/405 (C.28)), art.2.

DEFINITIONS

"diet": s.307(1).
"High Court": s.307(1).
"indictment": s.307(1).
"prosecutor": s.307(1).
"witness": s.307(1).

GENERAL NOTE

Section 67 anticipates that the identity and particulars of most witnesses will be known to the Crown sufficiently early for inclusion in the indictment served upon the accused. Experience suggests otherwise; in custody cases particularly, increasing reliance has been placed upon the use of the provisions in s.67(5) of the Act both for adding witnesses and productions to the indictment.

Objection to any deficiency in the specification of a witness must be intimated in writing to the court and to all parties to the proceedings prior to the first diet in sheriff solemn proceedings and not less than seven days prior to a preliminary hearing in the High Court. Later objection can be made on cause shown (subs.(3)) and distinct time limits apply to both sheriff and jury and High Court proceedings—at or prior to the first diet in the former, seven clear days before the High Court preliminary diet).

Subs.(4A) contains an important reform; whereas previously the inclusion of a witness on an indictment implicitly obliged the Crown to produce that person at the trial diet (even if the witness was hostile, reluctant or had proved uncooperative) or imperil the proceedings, that duty is now a more restricted one; henceforth the obligation is only to cite a witness named on the indictment the need for whose attendance at the trial has been confirmed at the first or preliminary diet. In High Court cases where a preliminary diet has been waived (see s.72B below), the application to dispense with that diet still has to identify the witnesses whose evidence is required at the trial.

Although witnesses are expected to be named in the indictment, later witnesses can be added subject to the provisions in subs.(5A).

Again distinct provisions distinguish High Court and sheriff solemn proceedings: later additions can be made up to seven days prior to the preliminary hearing, or right up until the commencement of the trial with leave of the court in High Court cases, but no later than two clear days before the trial in sheriff and jury cases.

Subs.(6) preserves the right of parties to call as witnesses those listed by either the Crown, the accused or any co-accused.

Subs. (5)

As was noted above, the provisions of s.81 in regard to late intimation of witnesses and productions have been preserved in s.67(5) of the 1995 Act: provided due notice has been given to the accused, such evidence can be added to the indictment with leave of the court. However, while an error in describing a witness in a s.67 notice is probably capable of being remedied by amendment in the course of proceedings, given the grounds of amendment in s.96 of the Act, a misdescription of a production either in the list of productions or, later, in a s.67 notice, cannot be so remedied. In *H.M. Advocate v Swift*, 1983 S.C.C.R. 204 an error in the original list of productions was corrected in a s.81 notice which itself misdescribed the production. The sheriff held the terms of s.81 to be peremptory and held evidence arising from the production, a tape, to be inadmissible. It is observed that it would still be open to parties to have such evidence admitted by way of a Minute of Agreement in the course of the trial if they were so minded.

Subsection (5)(a) entitles the prosecutor to examine certain witnesses without having given intimation to the accused. The most obvious categories of witnesses covered by this concession are co-accused whose pleas have been accepted prior to, or during trial, or even by way of an accelerated plea following service of a common indictment (see *Monaghan v H.M. Advocate*, 1984 S.L.T. 262), witnesses cited by any of the accused, witnesses led in replication in accordance with s.269 of the 1995 Act, police officers proving service of an indictment (s.66(11)), and the officials specified in subs.(2) above.

Failure of witness to attend for, or give evidence on, precognition

67A. [...]

AMENDMENT

Section 67A inserted by the Crime and Punishment (Scotland) Act 1997 (c. 48) s.57(1) with effect from August 1, 1997 in terms of the Crime and Punishment (Scotland) Act 1997 (Commencement and Transitional Provisions) Order 1997 (SI 1997/1712), art.5.

Section 67A repealed by the Criminal Procedure (Amendment) (Scotland) Act 2004 (asp 5), s.25, Sch.1, para.17. Brought into force on October 4, 2004 by the Criminal Procedure (Amendment) (Scotland) Act 2004 (Commencement, Transitional Provisions and Savings) Order 2004 (SSI 2004/405 (C.28)).

Productions

68.—(1) The list of productions shall include the record, made under section 37 of this Act (incorporating any rectification authorised under section 38(1) of this Act), of proceedings at the examination of the accused.

(2) The accused shall be entitled to see the productions according to the existing law and practice in the office of the sheriff clerk of the district in which the court of the trial diet is situated or, where the trial diet is to be in the High Court in Edinburgh, in the Justiciary Office.

(3) Where a person who has examined a production is adduced to give evidence with regard to it and the production has been lodged, where the case is to be tried in the sheriff court, at least eight days before the trial diet or, where the case is to be tried in the High Court, at least 14 days before the preliminary hearing, it shall not be necessary to prove—

(a) that the production was received by him in the condition in which it was taken possession of by the procurator fiscal or the police and returned by him after his examination of it to the procurator fiscal or the police; or

(b) that the production examined by him is that taken possession of by the procurator fiscal or the police,

unless the accused where the case is to be tried in the sheriff court, at least four days before the trial diet or, where the case is to be tried in the High Court, at least seven days before the preliminary hearing, gives in accordance with subsection (4) below written notice that he does not admit that the production was received or returned as aforesaid or, as the case may be, that it is that taken possession of as aforesaid.

(4) The notice mentioned in subsection (3) above shall be given—

(a) where the case is to be tried in the High Court, to the Crown Agent; and

(b) where the case is to be tried in the sheriff court, to the procurator fiscal.

AMENDMENT

Subss.(3), (4)(a), (b) as amended by the Criminal Procedure (Amendment) (Scotland) Act 2004 (asp 5), s.25 and Sch.1, para.18. Brought into force on February 1, 2005 by the Criminal Procedure (Amendment) (Scotland) Act 2004 (Commencement, Transitional Provisions and Savings) Order 2004 (SSI 2004/405 (C.28)), art.2.

DEFINITIONS

"diet": s.307(1).
"High Court": s.307(1).
"procurator fiscal": s.307(1).
"sheriff clerk": s.307(1).

GENERAL NOTE

Subsection (3) contains presumptions that (i) productions examined after their recovery by the police or lodging with the procurator fiscal were produced to the witness in the same condition as when recovered or lodged and (ii) that the articles produced to the witness were those seized by the police or procurator fiscal. The presumption only applies to productions lodged not less than eight days before trial in sheriff solemn proceedings, and 14 days prior to the preliminary hearing in High Court cases.

Any challenge to these presumptions must be made at least four days before a trial in the sheriff court, and no less than seven days prior to the preliminary hearing in the High Court, by notice in accordance with subs.(4).

Note that in *Livingston v HM Advocate*, 1991 S.C.C.R. 350 examination of productions and their comparison against the accused's fingerprint forms, which necessitated a motion for the removal of articles from the court during the course of a trial for that purpose, was upheld on appeal. This was viewed as a matter within the discretion of the trial judge, albeit an exceptional procedure. In that case the Lord Justice-General (at 356C) echoed the view expressed in *William Turner Davies, Petr*, 1973 S.L.T. (Notes) 36 by the Lord Justice-Clerk at p.37, that after service of an indictment;

> "the productions ... are lodged with the sheriff clerk who has a duty to retain them in his custody and make them available at the trial. At that stage, the only body with the authority to allow the productions to be inspected and examined is the court, and the proper procedure is to make application to the court thereanent. It is then for the court to decide whether the application should be granted or refused."

Davies had petitioned the *nobile officium* for authority for a defence expert to examine gloves lodged by the Crown as productions before the trial began, but the same principles apply both prior to, and during, trial. The court has to weigh the potential prejudice to the accused in the preparation and presentation of his case against the public interest in the effective prosecution of crime. See also *MacNeil v HM Advocate*, 1986 S.C.C.R. 288, where productions listed in the indictment had not been lodged it was held that objection should have been taken before the jury was sworn and the appropriate remedy in the event of prejudice was an adjournment. It is notable that in *HM Advocate v Sorrie*, (discussed at Notes to s.65(1)(2) and (3) above), the Court of Appeal held that there had been no want of compliance with s.68(2) on the basis that the productions had been lost or destroyed. The absence of an opportunity to examine the missing banknotes was a matter for comment and appropriate direction (the Crown having already undertaken a fingerprint examination of the bank bags which contained the notes initially and averring no likelihood of prejudice in the whole circumstances). This is surely an extreme interpretation and one wonders what approach could have been taken had a written challenge (subs.(3)(b)) been taken.

The procedures regulating the access of jurors to productions are discussed in the notes to s.99 below.

Lodging of productions and their introduction as evidence is only necessary where they are best evidence bearing distinguishing or peculiar features; otherwise there will be no demonstrable prejudice to the accused and no requirement for the items to be produced to the court. See *Maciver v Mackenzie*, 1942 S.L.T. 144, followed most recently in *Friel v Leonard*, 1997 G.W.D. 12–494. Such prejudice to the accused must be of a substantial degree (see *Anderson v Laverock*, 1976 S.L.T. 62 followed in *Allan v Napier*, 1999 G.W.D. 29–1364); mere speculation of possible prejudice to the defence case is not sufficient (*Duke v HM Advocate*, 2001 G.W.D. 21–795). See also *McQuade v Vannet*, 2000 S.C.C.R. 18 where a plea in bar of trial based upon the unavailability of a CCTV video tape which had been viewed by a police officer, found to contain nothing significant, returned to its owner and reused, was repelled. The video tape had never been considered as a production in the summary trial. The Appeal Court noted that if it transpired in the course of the trial the missing production became significant, and its absence then became gravely prejudicial, it would then be appropriate for the court to desert the diet: see *McFadyen v Annan*, 1992 S.L.T. 163; 1992 S.C.C.R. 186.

HM Advocate v Stuurman, 2003 S.L.T. 1050 establishes that the test to be applied where productions are not produced to the court is whether their absence means that the accused could not receive a fair trial, not simply that there would be a material risk of an unfair trial. See too *Rose v HM Advocate*, 2003 S.L.T. 1050. Requests from the jury to see productions must always be approached with care; again the test to be applied is whether there would be any potential for prejudice to any of the parties; *Barnetson v HM Advocate*, 2003 G.W.D. 30–838.

Notice of previous convictions

69.—(1) No mention shall be made in the indictment of previous convictions; nor shall extracts of previous convictions be included in the list of productions annexed to the indictment.

(2) If the prosecutor intends to place before the court any previous conviction, he shall cause to be served on the accused along with the indictment a notice in the form set out in an Act of Adjournal or as nearly as may be in such form, and

any conviction specified in the notice shall be held to apply to the accused unless he gives, in accordance with subsection (3) below, written intimation objecting to such conviction on the ground that it does not apply to him or is otherwise inadmissible.

(3) Intimation objecting to a conviction under subsection (2) above shall be given—

(a) where the accused is indicted to the High Court, to the Crown Agent not less than seven clear days before the preliminary hearing;

(b) where the accused is indicted to the sheriff court, to the procurator fiscal at least five clear days before the first day of the sitting in which the trial diet is to be held.

(4) Where notice is given by the accused under section 76 of this Act of his intention to plead guilty and the prosecutor intends to place before the court any previous conviction, he shall cause to be served on the accused along with the indictment a notice in the form set out in an Act of Adjournal or as nearly as may be in such form.

(4A) A notice served under subsection (2) or (4) above shall include any details which the prosecutor proposes to provide under section 101(3A) of this Act; and subsection (3) above shall apply in relation to intimation objecting to the provision of such details, on the grounds that they do not apply to the accused or are otherwise inadmissible, as it applies in relation to intimation objecting to a conviction.

(5) Where the accused pleads guilty at any diet, no objection to any conviction of which notice has been served on him under this section, or to the provision of such details as are, by virtue of subsection (4A) above, included in a notice so served, shall be entertained unless he has, at least two clear days before the diet, given intimation to the procurator fiscal of the district to the court of which the accused is cited for the diet.

AMENDMENT

Subss.(3)(a) as amended, and subs.(3)(b) substituted, by the Criminal Procedure (Amendment) (Scotland) Act 2004 (asp 5), s.25 and Sch.1, para.19. Brought into force on February 1, 2005 by the Criminal Procedure (Amendment) (Scotland) Act 2004 (Commencement, Transitional Provisions and Savings) Order 2004 (SSI 2004/405 (C.28)), art.2.

Subs.(4A) inserted, and subs.(5) as amended, by the Criminal Justice (Scotland) Act 2003 (asp 7), Sch.1, para.2(2). Brought into force on June 19, 2006 by the Criminal Justice (Scotland) Act 2003 (Commencement No.9) Order 2006 (SSI 2006/332 (C.30)), art.2(1), subject to art.2(2).

DEFINITIONS

"extract of previous conviction": s.307(1).
"indictment": s.307(1).
"prosecutor": s.307(1).

GENERAL NOTE

The Notice of Previous Convictions which the Crown may place before the court in the event of conviction of the accused should conform to Form 8.3 in the 1996 Act of Adjournal.

Broadly, these provisions echo the terms of s.68 of the 1975 Act but are now specified more clearly. Objection to the accuracy of any previous conviction libelled in an indictment which proceeds to trial now has to be made to the Crown Agent not less than seven days prior to the preliminary hearing in High Court cases, and to the procurator fiscal at least five days before a sheriff and jury trial. In the case of cases which plead, rather than proceeding to trial, any objection to a conviction libelled has to be made to the procurator fiscal not less than two days prior to the diet at which the plea is tendered.

Previous convictions which are under appeal should not be libelled (*McCall v Mitchell* (1911) 6

Adam 303) and no previous conviction omitted from the Notice should be taken into account by the court considering sentence, unless it is disclosed in a social enquiry or other report before the court (*Sharp v Stevenson*, 1948 S.L.T. (Notes) 79).

Although the provisions of subs.(1) appear to be absolute, they must be read in conjunction with s.101(2) of the 1995 Act which permits the leading of evidence of an accused's previous convictions where it is a necessary element of proof of the substantive charge.

The anomalous position of previous convictions libelled against bodies corporate and any named officer in the indictment against that body is discussed in the notes to s.70 below.

Proceedings against bodies corporate

70.—(1) This section applies to proceedings on indictment against a body corporate.

(2) The indictment may be served by delivery of a copy of the indictment together with notice to appear at the registered office or, if there is no registered office or the registered office is not in the United Kingdom, at the principal place of business in the United Kingdom of the body corporate.

(3) Where a letter containing a copy of the indictment has been sent by registered post or by the recorded delivery service to the registered office or principal place of business of the body corporate, an acknowledgement or certificate of the delivery of the letter issued by the postal operator shall be sufficient evidence of the delivery of the letter at the registered office or place of business on the day specified in such acknowledgement or certificate.

(4) A body corporate may, for the purpose of—

(a) stating objections to the competency or relevancy of the indictment or proceedings; or

(b) tendering a plea of guilty or not guilty; or

(c) making a statement in mitigation of sentence,

appear by a representative of the body corporate.

(5) Where at the trial diet the body corporate does not appear as mentioned in subsection (4) above, or by counsel or a solicitor, the court may—

(a) on the motion of the prosecutor; and

(b) if satisfied as to the matters specified in subsection (5A) below,

proceed with the trial and dispose of the case in the absence of the body corporate.

(5A) The matters referred to in subsection (5)(b) above are—

(a) that the body corporate was cited in accordance with section 66 of this Act as read with subsection (2) above; and

(b) that it is in the interests of justice to proceed as mentioned in subsection (5) above.

(6) Where a body corporate is sentenced to a fine, the fine may be recovered in like manner in all respects as if a copy of the sentence certified by the clerk of the court were an extract decree of the Court of Session for the payment of the amount of the fine by the body corporate to the Queen's and Lord Treasurer's Remembrancer.

(7) Nothing in section 77 of this Act shall require a plea tendered by or on behalf of a body corporate to be signed.

(8) In this section, "representative", in relation to a body corporate, means an officer or employee of the body corporate duly appointed by it for the purpose of the proceedings; and a statement in writing purporting to be signed by the managing director of, or by any person having or being one of the persons having the management of the affairs of the body corporate, to the effect that the person named in the statement has been appointed the representative of the body corporate for the purpose of any proceedings to which this section applies shall

be sufficient evidence of such appointment; and "officer" and "any person having or being one of the persons having the management of the affairs of the body corporate", in relation to a limited liability partnership, means a member of the limited liability partnership.

AMENDMENTS

Subs.(3) as amended by the Postal Services Act 2000 (Consequential Modifications No. 1) Order 2001 (SI 2001/1149), art.3 and Sch.1, para.104.

Subs.(8) as amended by the Limited Liability Partnerships (Scotland) Regulations 2001 (SSI 2001/128), reg.5 and Sch.4.

Subs.(5) as amended, and subss.(5)(a), (b), (5A) inserted, by the Criminal Procedure (Amendment) (Scotland) Act 2004 (asp 5), s.10(6). Brought into force on February 1, 2005 by the Criminal Procedure (Amendment) (Scotland) Act 2004 (Commencement, Transitional Provisions and Savings) Order 2004 (SSI 2004/405 (C.28)), art.2.

DEFINITIONS

"diet": s.307(1).
"fine": s.307(1).
"indictment": s.307(1).
"prosecutor": s.307(1).
"representative": s.70(8).

GENERAL NOTE

Provisions in s.70 refer to prosecution on indictment. Section 143 of the Act deals with summary prosecutions of partnerships, trustees in their corporate capacity and companies. A number of statutory provisions, namely the Insurance Companies Act 1982 (c.50), s.92(4), the Companies Act 1985 (c.6), s.734(4), the Financial Services Act 1986 (c.60), s.203(4), the Banking Act 1987 (c.22), s.98(4) and the Companies Act 1989 (c.40), ss.44(4) and 91(4) extended the terms of s.74 of the 1975 Act to unincorporated bodies. In the absence of contrary provisions, s.70 of the 1995 Act is similarly extended. Note that s.28(7) of the Companies Act 1985 (c.6) provides for the preservation and continuity of legal liabilities when a body corporate changes its name or transfers control; a move from registered to unregistered company status does not affect the validity of existing proceedings or preclude the commencement of proceedings (ss.49 and 50 of that Act). Similar provisions govern the move from unlimited to limited status (ss.51 and 52).

Provisions for service are contained in r.8.2 of the Act of Adjournal (Criminal Procedure Rules Amendment) (Criminal Procedure (Amendment) (Scotland) Act 2004) 2005 (SSI 2005/44) and in Form 8.2-H.

Once the court is satisfied that an indictment has been lawfully served upon a limited company or incorporation, it is entitled, on the motion of the prosecutor, to proceed to consider the evidence at a trial diet and dispose of the case at that time even if the body is unrepresented (it seems implicit from the reference to "the trial diet" in subs.(5) that a failure to appear at any earlier diet has to be treated as a plea of not guilty). If the body prosecuted does elect to make an appearance at any diet, this can be made on its behalf by an authorised representative and need not be by a solicitor or counsel.

The prosecutor may opt to prosecute the corporate body alone, proceed against a responsible officer of the company, or both. In the absence of specific statutory provision in regard to the previous convictions of bodies corporate, the general rules expressed in ss.69 and 101(7) would appear to apply. However, if proceedings are taken solely against an officer of the company as its responsible representative, it would surely be inequitable to libel against him previous convictions incurred by the company.

Subsection (6) enacts that fines imposed upon bodies corporate are recoverable by civil diligence.

The growing importance of criminal sanctions in cases of environmental pollution and health and safety offences has made prosecutions on indictment of limited companies more commonplace. See, for example, *HM Advocate v Kettle Produce Ltd*, 1996 G.W.D. 3–159 (unauthorised connection between sewage outflow pipe and the public water supply causing widescale illness in the vicinity; fine £60,000) and *Balmoral Group Ltd v HM Advocate*, 1996 S.L.T. 1230 (death of employee struck by crane chain and death of a second employee in a second, unrelated incident; fines of £35,000 and £10,000 respectively).

In *HM Advocate v Transco Plc* (High Court of Justiciary, August 25, 2005, unreported) after a lengthy trial on health and safety charges following the death in a gas explosion of all four members of a family in Larkhall, the accused company was fined £15 million, the equivalent of 4 per cent of the last declared annual profits of the company.

Pre-trial proceedings

First diet

71.—(A1) At a first diet in proceedings to which subsection (B1) below applies, the court shall, ascertain whether the accused has engaged a solicitor for the purposes of his defence at the trial.

(B1) This subsection applies to proceedings—

(a) in which the accused is charged with a sexual offence to which section 288C of this Act applies,

(b) to which section 288E of this Act applies, or

(c) in which an order under section 288F(2) of this Act has been made before the trial diet.

(1) At a first diet the court shall, so far as is reasonably practicable, ascertain whether the case is likely to proceed to trial on the date assigned as the trial diet and, in particular—

(a) the state of preparation of the prosecutor and of the accused with respect to their cases; and

(b) the extent to which the prosecutor and the accused have complied with the duty under section 257(1) of this Act.

(1A) At a first diet, the court shall also—

(a) ascertain whether subsection (1B) below applies to any person who is to give evidence at or for the purposes of the trial or to the accused, and

(b) if so, consider whether it should make an order under section 271A(7) or 271D(2) of this Act in relation to the person or, as the case may be, the accused.

(1B) This subsection applies—

(a) to a person who is to give evidence at or for the purposes of the trial if that person is, or is likely to be, a vulnerable witness,

(b) to the accused if, were he to give evidence at or for the purposes of the trial, he would be, or would be likely to be, a vulnerable witness.

(1C) At a first diet, the court—

(a) shall ascertain which of the witnesses included in the list of witnesses are required by the prosecutor or the accused to attend the trial; and

(b) shall, where the accused has been admitted to bail, review the conditions imposed on his bail and may—

(i) after giving the parties an opportunity to be heard; and

(ii) if it considers it appropriate to do so,

fix bail on different conditions.

(2) In addition to the matters mentioned in subsection (1), (1A) and (1C) above the court shall, at a first diet, consider any preliminary plea or preliminary issue (within the meanings given to those terms in section 79(2) of this Act) of which a party has, not less than two clear days before the first diet, given notice to the court and to the other parties.

(2XA) At a first diet the court shall also dispose of any child witness notice under section 271A(2) or vulnerable witness application under section 271C(2) appointed to be disposed of at that diet.

(2YA) At a first diet, the court shall also ascertain whether there is any objection to the admissibility of any evidence which any party wishes to raise despite not having given the notice referred to in subsection (2) above, and—

(a) if so, decide whether to grant leave under section 79(1) of this Act for the objection to be raised; and

(b) if leave is granted, dispose of the objection unless it considers it inappropriate to do so at the first diet.

(2ZA) Where the court, having granted leave for the objection to be raised, decides not to dispose of it at the first diet, the court may—

(a) appoint a further diet to be held before the trial diet for the purpose of disposing of the objection; or

(b) appoint the objection to be disposed of at the trial diet.

(2A) At a first diet the court may consider an application for the purposes of subsection (1) of section 275 of this Act.

(3) At a first diet the court may ask the prosecutor and the accused any question in connection with any matter which it is required to ascertain or consider under subsection (1), (1A), (2) or (2YA) above or which is relevant to an application for the purposes of subsection (1), (1C) of the said section 275.

(4) The accused shall attend a first diet of which he has been given notice and the court may, if he fails to do so, grant a warrant to apprehend him.

(5) A first diet may proceed notwithstanding the absence of the accused.

(5A) Where, however—

(a) the proceedings in which the first diet is being held are proceedings to which subsection (B1) above applies;

(b) the court has not ascertained (whether at that diet or earlier) that he has engaged a solicitor for the purposes of his defence at the trial,

a first diet may not proceed in his absence; and, in such a case, the court shall adjourn the diet and ordain the accused then to attend.

(6) The accused shall, at the first diet, be required to state how he pleads to the indictment, and section 77 of this Act shall apply where he tenders a plea of guilty.

(7) Where at a first diet the court concludes that the case is unlikely to proceed to trial on the date assigned for the trial diet, the court—

(a) shall, unless having regard to previous proceedings in the case it considers it inappropriate to do so, postpone the trial diet; and

(b) may fix a further first diet.

(8)–(8A) [*Repealed by the Criminal Procedure (Amendment) (Scotland) Act 2004 (asp 5), s.25, Sch.1, para.20(b). Brought into force on February 1, 2005 by the Criminal Procedure (Amendment) (Scotland) Act 2004 (Commencement, Transitional Provisions and Savings) Order 2004 (SSI 2004/405 (C.28)), art.2.*]

(9) In this section "the court" means the sheriff court.

AMENDMENT

Subss.(A1), (5A) and (8A) inserted by the Sexual Offences (Procedure and Evidence) (Scotland) Act 2002 (asp 9), Sch.1, para.5.

Subs.(2A) inserted by the Sexual Offences (Procedure and Evidence) (Scotland) Act 2002 (asp 9), s.8(2)(a).

Subs.(3) as amended by the Sexual Offences (Procedure and Evidence) (Scotland) Act 2002 (asp 9), s.8(2)(b).

All these changes are brought into force by the Sexual Offences (Procedure and Evidence) (Scotland) Act 2002 (Commencement and Transitional Provisions) Order 2002 (SSI 2002/443 (C.24)), art.4 (effective November 1, 2002).

Subss.(2YA) and (2ZA) inserted, and subs.(3) as amended, by the Criminal Procedure (Amendment) (Scotland) Act 2004 (asp 5), s.14(1). Brought into force on February 1, 2005 by the Criminal Procedure (Amendment) (Scotland) Act 2004 (Commencement, Transitional Provisions and Savings) Order 2004 (SSI 2004/405 (C.28)), art.2.

Subs.(1C) inserted, and subss.(2) and (3) as amended, by the Criminal Procedure (Amendment) (Scotland) Act 2004 (asp 5), s.19. Brought into force on February 1, 2005 as above.

Subs.(2) as amended by the Criminal Procedure (Amendment) (Scotland) Act 2004 (asp 5), s.25, Sch.1, para.20(a). Brought into force on February 1, 2005 as above.

Subss.(1A) and (1B) inserted, and subss.(2) and (3) as amended, by the Vulnerable Witnesses (Scotland) Act 2004 (asp 3), s.2. Brought into force on April 1, 2005 by the Vulnerable Witnesses (Scotland) Act 2004 (Commencement) Order 2005 (SSI 2005/168 (C.7)), art.2 and Sch. Further brought into force on April 1, 2006 by the Vulnerable Witnesses (Scotland) Act 2004 (Commencement No.3, Savings and Transitional Provisions) Order 2006 (SSI 2006/59 (C.8)).

Subs.(B1) inserted, subs.(5A)(a) as substituted and subs.(A1) as amended by the Vulnerable Witnesses (Scotland) Act 2004 (asp 3), s.7(1). Brought into force on April 1, 2005 by the Vulnerable Witnesses (Scotland) Act 2004 (Commencement) Order 2005 (SSI 2005/168 (C.7)), art.2 and Sch. Further brought into force on April 1, 2006 by the Vulnerable Witnesses (Scotland) Act 2004 (Commencement No.3, Savings and Transitional Provisions) Order 2006 (SSI 2006/59 (C.8)).

Subs.(2XA) inserted by the Criminal Procedure (Amendment) (Scotland) Act 2004 (Incidental, Supplemental and Consequential Provisions) Order 2005 (SSI 2005/40), art.4(3). Brought into force on January 31, 2005 in accordance with art.1.

DEFINITIONS

"court": subs.(9).
"diet": s.307(1).
"prosecutor": s.307(1).

GENERAL NOTE

Mandatory first diets in sheriff solemn proceedings were introduced by s.13 of the Criminal Justice (Scotland) Act 1995 (c.20). At that time preliminary hearings were optional (and little-used) in High Court cases but are now mandatory and more rigorous still, and can be waived only exceptionally (see s.72 below). Section 71 deals solely with sheriff and jury proceedings.

Following the advent of the Sexual Offences (Procedure and Evidence) (Scotland) Act 2002 (asp 9), the provisions of ss.275, 275A and 288C were introduced and are now further extended.

Duties of the first diet court

Section 71(A1) obliges the court to ensure that an accused charged with committing a listed sexual offence (as set out in s.288C), or charged with any other of the offences specified in s.288E(3) in which a witness is under 12 years of age, is legally represented for both the preparation and conduct of the proceedings.

More generally the first diet court now has a range of tasks to fulfill in addition to ascertaining whether witnesses are covered by these specific statutory provisions: there is an obligation to consider whether any listed witness may be regarded as vulnerable (refer to s.271 of the Act) or equally whether the accused himself is considered vulnerable and in need of special measures to enable him to follow the proceedings or to give evidence (subs.1B); it must ascertain the preparedness of all parties for trial (subs.1(a)); enquire whether evidence capable of agreement has been identified (subs.1(b)) and identify the witnesses whose parole evidence will be required for any trial or hearing (subs.(1C)(a)); consider whether any variation of existing bail conditions is needed (subs.(1C)(b)) and deal with any preliminary pleas or objections to admissibility of evidence (subss.(2) and (2YA)) and, finally, postpone the trial if it is considered that the trial will be unable to proceed at the assigned trial diet or further continue the first diet to enable any of these matters to be resolved.

If trial is postponed the court has the option of assigning a fresh first diet, a step which sets a new target date for the lodging of notices, witness lists and challenges.

Procedural matters

First diets can proceed in the absence of an accused and, in the event of a failure to appear and on being satisfied of notice of the diet having been served on the accused, the court has a discretion to grant an apprehension warrant (subss.(4) and (5)). A warrant at this stage has the effect of ending the proceedings upon that indictment against the absent accused, as well as halting any statutory timebar affecting his proceedings. In many cases it may prove preferable to maintain the existing indictment (especially where there are other accused involved) by seeking instead a continuation of the first diet.

Attention is directed to the provisions in s.70 governing the citation and trial of bodies corporate; it would for example, be perfectly competent for an officer of the company or other representative to appear instead of a legal representative at the diet. Note too the specific requirements in regard to those charged with listed sexual offences, or who are deemed to be vulnerable, or whose proceedings will involve vulnerable witnesses or witnesses aged less than 12 years; in each of these circumstances the court has to ensure that the accused has been informed of the necessity for legal representation and cannot proceed in his absence until it is satisfied that this has been made known to him.

At the conclusion of the first diet the accused has to be called upon to tender pleas to the charges libelled.

Subs. (7)

While it is clear that the first diet must occur not less than 15 clear days after service of the indictment and more than 10 clear days before any trial (see s.66(6)(a) above), once that strict timescale has been met the diet can be continued up to any date before the trial diet itself (see *O'Connell v H.M. Advocate*, 1996 S.C.C.R. 614). However while the Act stipulates in s.78(4)(a)(i) that, in sheriff solemn cases, the list of defence witnesses and productions must be lodged at or prior to the first diet, it is notable that any special defences or notices of incrimination must be intimated not less than 10 clear days before the trial diet (s.78(1)(ii)) and thereafter can only be accepted on cause shown.

At the first diet it is open to the court to postpone the trial diet (separate procedures are available in s.80 below to adjourn or postpone a trial at the time of calling the indictment for trial); care must be taken to ensure that the diet fixed complies with the statutory time-bars set out in s.65 or that an appropriate extension of time is granted by the court in bail cases, or application made for extension in custody cases (see s.65(3) and (5)). If it is decided that the trial diet is to be postponed three points are noteworthy; first, it will not be necessary to re-indict the case since the original indictment will remain valid; secondly, any additional witnesses or productions will require to be added by way of s.67 notice; thirdly, if the court fixes a further first diet (see s.71(7)(b)) the date of that diet will have to be fixed at the time of postponement, intimated to the accused at that time and, it is submitted, comply with the time constraints imposed under s.66(6)(a) discussed earlier.

Given the potential for error it may be of some comfort to the Crown that following the *ratio* in *H.M. Advocate v Dow* and in *Smith v H.M. Advocate* cited at A4–152 above it would be competent to raise a fresh indictment instead: it will be seen that s.74(3) in allowing the postponement of trial diets after a preliminary diet in High Court cases, enacts that any resultant delay in proceedings shall not count towards any "time limit".

Stewart v H.M. Advocate, 1997 G.W.D. 23–1145 suggests that, where a case is re-indicted for trial, earlier unsuccessful pleas in bar of trial (in *Stewart* a plea in bar of insanity which had been repelled at first instance and on appeal and is reported as *Stewart v H.M. Advocate* (No.1), 1997 S.C.C.R. 330) may competently be restated, the court having the option in terms of s.73(5) and s.80 of the Act to postpone trial to enable further inquiry. It is of course the case that an accused's fitnes for trial can alter between indictments and could thus require to be reconsidered; issues of competency or relevancy, it is submitted, could not be resurrected in the same way.

It will be observed that, adopting the provisions of s.79(1), means that notices specifying any one of the preliminary objections (*i.e.* competency or relevancy of the libel, objections to the validity of any citation, any plea in bar of trial, motions for separation or conjunction of charges or trials, challenges to any special capacity libelled, including the currency of bail orders, and any objection to the admission of the judicial examination transcript or transcript of an accused's declaration) must be notified not less than two days before the first diet or its continuation.

Less familiar grounds for a hearing are now contained in s.79: any party can call for the court at the first diet to review documentary evidence whose contents are felt to be capable of agreement (s.79(2)(b)(v)), or raise a general matter which should be resolved before trial (s.79(2)(b)(vi)). This latter provision could conceivably be deployed to deal with matters which traditionally had to be considered in "a trial within a trial"; there is no authority on the point.

After consideration of any preliminary pleas or other matters raised before the court it is essential that pleas be tendered and recorded to any charges left on the libel.

Notwithstanding this proposition it is of note that in *Roselli v Vannet*, 1997 S.C.C.R. 655, a summary complaint, advocation of proceedings was held to be competent to review events at an intermediate diet.

Act of Adjournal

Chapter 9 of the Act of Adjournal (Criminal Procedure Rules) 1996 regulates procedures in both first diets and preliminary diets. Form 9.1 is the style for any minute of notice; Form 9.9 is the notice of abandonment of matters which were to have been raised at such a diet.

Mandatory first diets (then called pleading diets) were abolished by s.12 of the Criminal Justice

(Scotland) Act 1980 (c.62) when it was perceived that they had been reduced to mere formal appearances. The new first diets are essential elements in retaining public confidence in the courts and it is to be hoped that the Bench exercises its powers in subs.(A1) to (3) vigorously. Note, however, that the court can apply no *compulsitor* upon parties who do not enter into the spirit of s.258(1) and that that provision does not apply to accused who are unrepresented. It is debatable how far the court can venture in its enquiries under s.71 where an accused is not legally represented.

Appeal procedures

Appeals arising from decisions of the court at first diets or preliminary diets are considered by the High Court under s.74 of the Act; in the event of an appeal, part, or all of the postponement period can be discounted by the High Court from any time bar calculation and, by implication, this can be done with retrospective effect. Appeals must be raised within two days upon Form 9.12 given in the Act of Adjournal and, if need be, abandoned by Form 9.17. Note that decisions to adjourn the first, or preliminary, diet or to postpone the trial diet cannot be appealed under s.74 (see subs.(2)(a)) but that such decisions can be challenged by an accused in an appeal against conviction or sentence (s.106) and by the Lord Advocate in an appeal against an unduly lenient sentence (s.108).

Further pre-trial diet: dismissal or withdrawal of solicitor representing accused in case of sexual offence

71A. [...]

AMENDMENT

Section 71A inserted by the Sexual Offences (Procedure and Evidence) (Scotland) Act 2002 (asp 9), Sch.1, para.6. Brought into force by the Sexual Offences (Procedure and Evidence) (Scotland) Act 2002 (Commencement and Transitional Provisions) Order 2002 (SSI 2002/443 (C.24)), art.4 (effective November 1, 2002).

Section 71A repealed by the Criminal Procedure (Amendment) (Scotland) Act 2004 (asp 5), s.25, Sch.1, para.21. Brought into force on December 4, 2004 by the Criminal Procedure (Amendment) (Scotland) Act 2004 (Commencement, Transitional Provisions and Savings) Order 2004 (SSI 2004/405 (C.28)).

Preliminary hearing: procedure up to appointment of trial diet

72.—(1) A preliminary hearing shall be conducted in accordance with this section and section 72A.

(2) The court shall—

(a) where the accused is charged with an offence to which section 288C of this Act applies; or

(b) in any case—

(i) in respect of which section 288E of this Act applies; or

(ii) in which an order has been made under section 288F(2) of this Act,

before taking any further step under this section, ascertain whether the accused has engaged a solicitor for the purposes of the conduct of his case at or for the purposes of the preliminary hearing.

(3) After complying with subsection (2) above, the court shall dispose of any preliminary pleas (within the meaning of section 79(2)(a) of this Act) of which a party has given notice not less than 7 clear days before the preliminary hearing to the court and to the other parties.

(4) After disposing of any preliminary pleas under subsection (3) above, the court shall require the accused to state how he pleads to the indictment.

(5) If the accused tenders a plea of guilty, section 77 of this Act shall apply.

(6) After the accused has stated how he pleads to the indictment, the court shall, unless a plea of guilty is tendered and accepted—

(a) in any case—

    (i) where the accused is charged with an offence to which section 288C of this Act applies;

    (ii) in respect of which section 288E of this Act applies; or

    (iii) in which an order has been made under section 288F(2) of this Act,

ascertain whether the accused has engaged a solicitor for the purposes of his defence at the trial;

(b) unless it considers it inappropriate to do so at the preliminary hearing, dispose of—

    (i) any preliminary issues (within the meaning of section 79(2)(b) of this Act) of which a party has given notice not less than 7 clear days before the preliminary hearing to the court and to the other parties;

    (ii) any child witness notice under section 271A(2) or vulnerable witness application under section 271C(2) appointed to be disposed of at the preliminary hearing;

    (iii) subject to subsection (8) below, any application under section 275(1) or 288F(2) of this Act made before the preliminary hearing; and

    (iv) any other matter which, in the opinion of the court, could be disposed of with advantage before the trial;

(c) ascertain whether there is any objection to the admissibility of any evidence which any party wishes to raise despite not having given the notice referred to in paragraph (b)(i) above, and—

    (i) if so, decide whether to grant leave under section 79(1) of this Act for the objection to be raised; and

    (ii) if leave is granted, dispose of the objection unless it considers it inappropriate to do so at the preliminary hearing;

(d) ascertain which of the witnesses included in the list of witnesses are required by the prosecutor or the accused to attend the trial;

(e) ascertain whether subsection (7) below applies to any person who is to give evidence at or for the purposes of the trial or to the accused and, if so, consider whether it should make an order under section 271A(7) or 271D(2) of this Act in relation to the person or, as the case may be, the accused; and

(f) ascertain, so far as is reasonably practicable—

    (i) the state of preparation of the prosecutor and the accused with respect to their cases; and

    (ii) the extent to which the prosecutor and the accused have complied with the duty under section 257(1) of this Act.

(7) This subsection applies—

(a) to a person who is to give evidence at or for the purposes of the trial if that person is, or is likely to be, a vulnerable witness;

(b) to the accused if, were he to give evidence at or for the purposes of the trial, he would be, or would be likely to be, a vulnerable witness.

(8) Where any application or notice such as is mentioned in subsection (6)(b)(iii) above is required by the provision under which it is made or lodged, or by any other provision of this Act, to be made or lodged by a certain time, the court—

(a) shall not be required under that subsection to dispose of it unless it has been made or lodged by that time; but

(b) shall have power to dispose of it to the extent that the provision under which it was made, or any other provision of this Act, allows it to be disposed of notwithstanding that it was not made or lodged in time.

(9) Where the court decides not to dispose of any preliminary issue, application, notice, objection or other matter referred to in subsection (6)(b) or (c) above at the preliminary hearing, it may—

(a) appoint a further diet, to be held before the trial diet appointed under section 72A of this Act, for the purpose of disposing of the issue, application, notice, objection or matter; or

(b) appoint the issue, application, notice, objection or other matter to be disposed of at the trial diet.

AMENDMENT

Section 72 as substituted by the Criminal Procedure (Amendment) (Scotland) Act 2004 (asp 5), s.1(3). Brought into force, with exceptions, on February 1, 2005 by the Criminal Procedure (Amendment) (Scotland) Act 2004 (Commencement, Transitional Provisions and Savings) Order 2004 (SSI 2004/405 (C.28)), art.2.

DEFINITIONS

"High Court": s.307(1).
"indictment": s.307(1).
"preliminary hearing": s.66(6)(b).
"preliminary issues": s.79(2)(b).
"preliminary pleas": s.79(2)(a).
"prosecutor": s.307(1).
"the court": s.72D(9).
"vulnerable witness": s.307(1).

GENERAL NOTE

Background

The Criminal Justice (Scotland) Act 1995 (c.20) introduced mandatory first diets into sheriff and jury proceedings but made the High Court equivalent (the "preliminary diet") optional. This distinction may have stemmed, at least in part, from the logistical difficulties in ensuring the attendance of accused at the High Court in Edinburgh, but two factors conspired to ensure that the once-rare preliminary diet became commonplace; the advent of the European Convention into domestic law following the Scotland Act 1998 (c.46) and the consequent diets to determine devolution issues, and the provisions enacted in relation to listed sexual offences (see ss.274–275B) which demanded advance determination of the scope of questioning at trial. As can be seen, following upon the recommendations of the Bonomy Committee, ss.72 to 72G now introduce a mandatory (and rigorous) pre-trial regime of judicial scrutiny which is intended to resolve the perceived defects and delays in existing procedures. It is important to recall that with the extended timebars in High Court proceedings introduced by s.67(4)(aa) of the Act, a preliminary diet must be held within 110 days of full committal, and trial within 140 days. Furthermore, earlier notice of any preliminary pleas or objections to admissibility must ordinarily be given in High Court proceedings than apply to sheriff solemn proceedings.

Duties of the preliminary diet court

The duties of the court broadly mirror those described in the notes to s.71 above but it must be appreciated that the scope of enquiry by the court in High Court cases is even more extensive.

First, the court has to consider whether any charge libelled falls within the scope of s.288C of the Act as a listed sexual offence, or failing this, whether any offence falls within the scope of s.288E(3) and involves adducing the evidence of a child aged under 12 years at the time of the trial, or will require the evidence of a vulnerable witness (s.288F). In each of these situations the court has to ensure that the accused is alert to the fact that he cannot either prepare the case personally or represent himself in the *preliminary* diet proceedings, and, if need be, arrange for legal representation: while s.288F(3) of the Act appears to permit departure from the need for legal representation in these cases this is only in relation to the conduct of *trial* proceedings, and then strictly on cause shown.

Next, if the accused does not then plead guilty to the charges, the court has to consider any preliminary pleas of which due notice has been given (s.79(2)(a)) before calling upon the accused to plead to any charges remaining. (Refer to Form 9A.1 in SSI 2005/44 for the style of notice).

With a view specifically to the *trial* proceedings now identified, subs.(6)(a) then revisits witness issues as set out in ss.288C, 288E(3) and 288(F) to ensure that legal representation is available for the conduct of any trial before moving on to consideration of any of the preliminary issues specified in s.79(2)(b) and a more detailed scrutiny of the manner in which evidence will be led by the parties (subs.(6)(b)). This scrutiny will determine the merits of any screen or CCTV applications lodged in relation to child witnesses or vulnerable witnesses, the scope of any application to depart from the general restrictions set down in s.274 of the Act in regard to the questioning of complainers in sexual crimes, and any other matters which could be considered advantageously at that time.

The hearing is also an opportunity for seeking the court's leave to introduce preliminary pleas or preliminary issues (see s.79 below) of which timeous notice has not been given; for the court to resolve with parties which witnesses are required to give parole evidence at the trial (and by implication to identify evidence not in dispute) and to assess what special measures, if any, are necessary for the taking of the evidence of any child or vulnerable witness or, indeed, the accused. It should be noted that s.271(A)(2)(b) expressly requires the party seeking to lead the child's evidence to state explicitly when *no* special measures are deemed necessary.

Subs.(6)(f) re-enacts the duty of the court to ascertain the readiness of parties for trial (s.72E demands that the parties lodge a written record (following Form 9A.4 in SSI 2005/44) of their efforts to discuss issues) and to investigate the degree to which parties have identified evidence capable of agreement (see s.257 below). Subs.(8) underlines the importance of lodging any notices under ss.275 and 288F timeously but leaves the court a residual discretion to consider such waiver applications, or applications for witnesses to be treated as vulnerable, to the court.

As subs.(9) makes patent it is competent for the court either to appoint a later diet to consider any notices or preliminary pleas or issues, or to continue the matter for consideration at the trial diet itself. (It follows that the trial diet is preserved in either event).

Once all these issues have been resolved the court can proceed to assign the trial diet in accordance with s.72A of the Act.

Dispensing with the preliminary diet

Given the exhaustive range of enquiries the court is now obliged to undertake it may be thought difficult to envisage situations in which no preliminary diet would be needed. Nonetheless, s.72B addresses such rare situations, leaving the parties to lodge written application to the court to waive the diet. It should not be imagined that dispensing with the diet can be deployed as a means of escaping scrutiny by the court; the court has to be satisfied that the case is ready for trial, that there are no preliminary pleas or issues to be settled and no vulnerable witnesses or accused in the case, and that the parties have identified the witnesses whose attendance at trial is not deemed necessary, and should be able to refer to the written record which still must be available for examination by the court (s.72E below).

Note that the time limits for lodging notices or intimations of challenges still apply in the absence of a preliminary diet.

Preliminary hearing: appointment of trial diet

72A.—(1) In proceedings to which this section applies, the court shall, at the preliminary hearing—

(a) after complying with that subsection;

(b) having regard to earlier proceedings at the preliminary hearing; and

(c) subject to subsections (3) to (7) below,

appoint a trial diet.

(1A) This section applies to proceedings in the High Court—

(a) in which the accused is charged with a sexual offence to which section 288C of this Act applies,

(b) to which section 288E of this Act applies, or

(c) in which an order under section 288F(2) of this Act has been made before the trial diet.

(2) In appointing a trial diet under subsection (1) above, the court may, if satisfied that it is appropriate to do so, indicate that the diet is to be a floating diet for the purposes of section 83A of this Act.

(3) In any case in which the 12 month period applies (whether or not the 140 day period also applies in the case)—

(a) if the court considers that the case would be likely to be ready to proceed to trial within that period, it shall, subject to subsections (5) to (7) below, appoint a trial diet for a date within that period; or

(b) if the court considers that the case would not be likely to be so ready, it shall give the prosecutor an opportunity to make an application to the court under section 65(3) of this Act for an extension of the 12 month period.

(4) Where paragraph (b) of subsection (3) above applies—

(a) if such an application as is mentioned in that paragraph is made and granted, the court shall, subject to subsections (5) to (7) below, appoint a trial diet for a date within the 12 month period as extended; or

(b) if no such application is made or if one is made but is refused by the court—

    (i) the court may desert the preliminary hearing simpliciter or pro loco et tempore; and

    (ii) where the accused is committed until liberated in due course of law, he shall be liberated forthwith.

(5) Subsection (6) below applies in any case in which—

(a) the 140 day period as well as the 12 month period applies; and

(b) the court is required, by virtue of subsection (3)(a) or (4)(a) above, to appoint a trial diet within the 12 month period.

(6) In such a case—

(a) if the court considers that the case would be likely to be ready to proceed to trial within the 140 day period, it shall appoint a trial diet for a date within that period as well as within the 12 month period; or

(b) if the court considers that the case would not be likely to be so ready, it shall give the prosecutor an opportunity to make an application under section 65(5) of this Act for an extension of the 140 day period.

(7) Where paragraph (b) of subsection (6) above applies—

(a) if such an application as is mentioned in that paragraph is made and granted, the court shall appoint a trial diet for a date within the 140 day period as extended as well as within the 12 month period;

(b) if no such application is made or if one is made but is refused by the court

    (i) the court shall proceed under subsection (3)(a) or, as the case may be, (4)(a) above to appoint a trial diet for a date within the 12 month period; and

    (ii) the accused shall then be entitled to be admitted to bail.

(8) Where an accused is, by virtue of subsection (7)(b)(ii) above, entitled to be admitted to bail, the court shall, before admitting him to bail, give the prosecutor an opportunity to be heard.

(9) On appointing a trial diet under this section in a case where the accused has been admitted to bail (otherwise than by virtue of subsection (7)(b)(ii) above), the court, after giving the parties an opportunity to be heard—

(a) shall review the conditions imposed on his bail; and

(b) having done so, may, if it considers it appropriate to do so, fix bail on different conditions.

(10) In this section—

    "the 12 month period" means the period specified in subsection (1)(b) of section 65 of this Act and, in any case in which that period has been extended under subsection (3) of that section, includes that period as so extended; and "the 140 day period" means the period specified in subsection (4)(aa)(ii) of that section and, in any case in which that period has been extended under subsection (5) of that section, includes that period as so extended.

AMENDMENT

Section 72A inserted by the Sexual Offences (Procedure and Evidence) (Scotland) Act 2002 (asp 9), Sch.1, para.7. Brought into force by the Sexual Offences (Procedure and Evidence) (Scotland) Act 2002 (Commencement and Transitional Provisions) Order 2002 (SSI 2002/443 (C.24)), art.4 (effective November 1, 2002).

Section 72A substituted by the Criminal Procedure (Amendment) (Scotland) Act 2004 (asp 5), s.1(3). Brought into force on February 1, 2005 by the Criminal Procedure (Amendment) (Scotland) Act 2004 (Commencement, Transitional Provisions and Savings) Order 2004 (SSI 2004/405 (C.28)), art.2.

Subs.(1) as amended, and subs.(1A) inserted, by the Vulnerable Witnesses (Scotland) Act 2004 (asp 3), s.7(3). Brought into force on April 1, 2005 by the Vulnerable Witnesses (Scotland) Act 2004 (Commencement) Order 2005 (SSI 2005/168 (C.7)), art.2 and Sch. Further brought into force on April 1, 2006 by the Vulnerable Witnesses (Scotland) Act 2004 (Commencement No.3, Savings and Transitional Provisions) Order 2006 (SSI 2006/59 (C.8)), art.2 and Sch.

DEFINITIONS

"bail": s.307(1).
"diet": s.307(1).
"preliminary hearing": s.66(6)(b).
"the court": s.72D(8).
"the 140 day period": s.72A(10).
"the 12 month period": s.72A(10).

GENERAL NOTE

This section applies only to High Court proceedings (see s.72D(10) below).

Once all preliminary pleas and preliminary issues specified in s.72 have been resolved the accused has to be called upon to tender pleas and, if need be, a trial diet is ordinarily assigned. Subss.(3) to (7) address circumstances where it is considered at the preliminary diet that the case cannot yet proceed to trial and provides mechanisms for extensions of either the 140 day time custody time limit or the year time limit applying to High Court proceedings to be extended. It falls to the prosecutor to make any application necessary to extend the time bar to comply with the terms of s.65(3) or (4) of the Act, failing which the court may opt to desert the indictment *pro loco et tempore* or *simpliciter* (s.72A(4)) and liberate the accused if he is remanded in relation to the charges.

Assuming that the prosecution so moves, the court in granting such a motion (and extending the requisite time bar) has to fix a fresh trial diet falling within the new time frame for proceedings. If the accused was already bailed, subs.(9) enables the court to review and vary the existing bail terms; in situations where the accused's custody trial cannot occur within 140 days the implicit presumption is that the court following subs.(7)(b)(ii) will admit him to bail but must first hear submissions from the prosecutor on the matter (subs.(8)).

It is submitted that any such submissions merely relate to the conditions to attach to the bail order; separate provision is made in subs.6(b) for the prosecutor to seek an extension of the 140 day period itself—so it should not be thought that the Crown now has no *locus* to seek extension of the period of a custodial remand. Indeed, reference to s.65(4) and (5) of the Act makes it clear that an application for extension can be granted on cause shown—the previous stricter test (which permitted *no* fault on the part of the Crown) has now been superseded.

The definitions in subs.(10) of "the twelve month period" and "the 140 day period" clarify that each period is taken to include any extension of that time limit previously permitted by the court.

Finally, it will be noted that in assigning a trial diet at the preliminary hearing the court has two options; either to appoint a fixed trial diet upon which trial is to commence or, in terms of s.83A(2), to identify the case as a floating trial diet to commence within the days stipulated.

Power to dispense with preliminary hearing

72B.—(1) The court may, on an application made to it jointly by the parties, dispense with a preliminary hearing and appoint a trial diet if the court is satisfied on the basis of the application that—

(a) the state of preparation of the prosecutor and the accused with respect to their cases is such that the case is likely to be ready to proceed to trial on the date to be appointed for the trial diet;

(b) there are no preliminary pleas, preliminary issues or other matters which require to be, or could with advantage be, disposed of before the trial; and

(2) An application under subsection (1) above shall identify which (if any) of the witnesses included in the list of witnesses are required by the prosecutor or the accused to attend the trial.

(3) Where a trial diet is to be appointed under subsection (1) above, it shall be appointed in accordance with such procedure as may be prescribed by Act of Adjournal.

(4) Where a trial diet is appointed under subsection (1) above, the accused shall appear at the diet and answer the indictment.

(5) The fact that a preliminary hearing in any case has been dispensed with under subsection (1) above shall not affect the calculation in that case of any time limit for the giving of any notice or the doing of any other thing under this Act, being a time limit fixed by reference to the preliminary hearing.

(6) Accordingly, any such time limit shall have effect in any such case as if it were fixed by reference to the date on which the preliminary hearing would have been held if it had not been dispensed with.

Amendment

Section 72B inserted by the Criminal Procedure (Amendment) (Scotland) Act 2004 (asp 5), s.1(3). Brought into force, with exceptions, on February 1, 2005 by the Criminal Procedure (Amendment) (Scotland) Act 2004 (Commencement, Transitional Provisions and Savings) Order 2004 (SSI 2004/405 (C.28)), art.2.

Definitions

"Clerk of Justiciary": s.307(1).
"diet": s.307(1).
"High Court": s.307(1).
"indictment": s.307(1).
"preliminary hearing": s.66(6)(b).
"preliminary issues": s.79(2)(b).
"preliminary pleas": s.79(2)(a).
"the court": s.72D(8).

General Note

This section enables parties on joint application to dispense with the preliminary diet in High Court proceedings. This should not be thought to be a means of avoiding scrutiny of the case by the court which it is normally obliged to undertake at any preliminary hearing (see s.72 above). Applications to dispense must use Form 9A.2 in the Act of Adjournal (Criminal Procedure Rules Amendment) (Criminal Procedure (Amendment) (Scotland) Act 2004) 2005 (SSI 2005/44) and confirm the absence of any preliminary pleas or preliminary issues, identify witnesses whose evidence is not in dispute, and confirm that neither the accused or any witnesses are considered to be vulnerable witnesses (s.271 of the Act sets out exhaustive definitions).

For the purposes of timebar calculations, subs.(5) makes it clear that the diet originally fixed for the preliminary hearing now dispensed with still obtains for such purposes and remains the operative date also for calculating the dates for lodging notices, defences, challenges and pleas. Note too that since the normal practice at a preliminary hearing is to record the accused's pleas, the absence of that diet when s.72C is applied means that the accused has to be called upon to plead at the commencement of the trial diet. It might be argued that the giving of joint written notice to the court itself implies that the case is intended to proceed to trial.

Procedure where preliminary hearing does not proceed

72C.—(1) The prosecutor shall not raise a fresh libel in any case in which the court has deserted a preliminary hearing *simpliciter* unless the court's decision has been reversed on appeal.

(2) Where a preliminary hearing is deserted *pro loco et tempore*, the court may appoint a further preliminary hearing for a later date and the accused shall appear and answer the indictment at that hearing.

(3) Subsection (4) below applies where, at a preliminary hearing—

(a) the hearing has been deserted *pro loco et tempore* for any reason and no further preliminary hearing has been appointed under subsection (2) above; or

(b) the indictment is for any reason not proceeded with and the hearing has not been adjourned or postponed.

(4) Where this subsection applies, the prosecutor may, at any time within the period of two months after the relevant date, give notice to the accused on another copy of the indictment to appear and answer the indictment—

(a) at a further preliminary hearing in the High Court not less than seven clear days after the date of service of the notice; or

(b) at—

(i) a first diet not less than 15 clear days after the service of the notice and not less than 10 clear days before the trial diet; and

(ii) a trial diet not less than 29 clear days after the service of the notice,

in the sheriff court where the charge is one that can lawfully be tried in that court.

(5) Where notice is given to the accused under subsection (4)(b) above, then for the purposes of section 65(4) of this Act—

(a) the giving of the notice shall be taken to be service of an indictment in respect of the sheriff court; and

(b) the previous service of the indictment in respect of the High Court shall be disregarded.

(6) In subsection (4) above, "the relevant date" means—

(a) where paragraph (a) of subsection (3) above applies, the date on which the diet was deserted as mentioned in that paragraph; or

(b) where paragraph (b) of that subsection applies, the date of the preliminary hearing referred to in that paragraph.

(7) A notice referred to in subsection (4) above shall be in such form as may be prescribed by Act of Adjournal, or as nearly as may be in such form.

<small>AMENDMENT</small>

Section 72C inserted by the Criminal Procedure (Amendment) (Scotland) Act 2004 (asp 5), s.1(3). Brought into force on February 1, 2005 by the Criminal Procedure (Amendment) (Scotland) Act 2004 (Commencement, Transitional Provisions and Savings) Order 2004 (SSI 2004/405 (C.28)), art.2.

<small>DEFINITIONS</small>

"diet": s.307(1).
"High Court": s.307(1).
"indictment": s.307(1).
"preliminary hearing": s.66(6)(b).
"the court": s.72D(8).
"the relevant date": s.72C(4).

<small>GENERAL NOTE</small>

Section 72C applies to proceedings in the High Court (see s.72D(10) below).

The marginal note is perhaps slightly confusing since this section has no application to the most obvious situation where a preliminary hearing does not occur—when the parties jointly dispense with it in proceedings before the High Court in terms of s.72B. Closer scrutiny reveals that s.72C, though primarily relevant (as the reference to a "preliminary hearing" suggests) to the High Court, also applies to sheriff solemn proceedings presumably on the grounds that after preliminary pleas and preliminary issues have been aired the libel remaining might more appropriately proceed in that lower court.

At the preliminary hearing if the case is not ready for trial, the court has several options; an extension of the custody timebars or the year period can be granted to enable the trial then to proceed, the preliminary diet can be continued (and the anticipated trial diet preserved) or the case can be deserted either *pro loco et tempore* or *simpliciter* causing the existing indictment to fall. Of course none of these provisions affects the other option open to the Crown—not to call the indictment at all.

Subs.(4) provides an abbreviated procedure to re-indict to a fresh preliminary diet, echoing the existing procedures found in s.81 which only apply at an abortive *trial* diet. The same cautionary note has to be sounded; any indictment re-served under either s.72C or 81 will not automatically include any s.67 notices previously served upon the accused. Consequently, care has to be taken to ensure that any such notices are timeously served afresh and, in the case of proceedings still remaining in the High Court, that at least seven clear days are allowed before a new preliminary diet to enable compliance with the "relevant time" provisions set out in s.67(5A) of the Act.

Subs.(5) indicates that any timebar calculation required under s.65 of the Act is unaffected by service of an earlier indictment—calculation begins either with the date upon which the proceedings were deserted *pro loco et tempore* or no trial diet has been fixed at the conclusion of the preliminary diet.

Preliminary hearing: further provision

72D.—(1) The court may, on cause shown, allow a preliminary hearing to proceed notwithstanding the absence of the accused.

(2) Where—

(a) the accused is a body corporate;

(b) it fails to appear at a preliminary hearing;

(c) the court allows the hearing to proceed in its absence under subsection (1) above; and

(d) no plea is entered on its behalf at the hearing,

it shall be treated for the purposes of proceedings at the preliminary hearing as having pled not guilty.

(3) Where, at a preliminary hearing, a trial diet is appointed, the accused shall appear at the trial diet and answer the indictment.

(4) At a preliminary hearing, the court—

(a) shall take into account any written record lodged under section 72E of this Act; and

(b) may ask the prosecutor and the accused any question in connection with any matter which it is required to dispose of or ascertain under section 72 of this Act.

(5) The proceedings at a preliminary hearing shall be recorded by means of shorthand notes or by mechanical means.

(6) Subsections (2) to (4) of section 93 of this Act shall apply for the purposes of the recording of proceedings at a preliminary hearing in accordance with subsection (5) above as they apply for the purposes of the recording of proceedings at the trial in accordance with subsection (1) of that section.

(7) The Clerk of Justiciary shall prepare, in such form and manner as may be prescribed by Act of Adjournal, a minute of proceedings at a preliminary hearing, which shall record, in particular, whether any preliminary pleas or issues were disposed of and, if so, how they were disposed of.

(8) In this section, references to a preliminary hearing include an adjourned preliminary hearing.

(9) In this section and sections 72 to 72C, "the court" means the High Court.

AMENDMENT

Section 72D inserted by the Criminal Procedure (Amendment) (Scotland) Act 2004 (asp 5), s.1(3). Brought into force on February 1, 2005 by the Criminal Procedure (Amendment) (Scotland) Act 2004 (Commencement, Transitional Provisions and Savings) Order 2004 (SSI 2004/405 (C.28)), art.2.

DEFINITIONS

"Clerk of Justiciary": s.307(1).
"diet": s.307(1).
"High Court": s.307(1).
"indictment": s.307(1).
"preliminary hearing": s.66(6)(b).
"prosecutor": s.307(1).
"the court": s.72D(8).

GENERAL NOTE

This section, as subs.(9) states, deals with procedural aspects arising from preliminary diets in the High Court. Reference should be made to the General Note to s.72 above. Essentially, the absence of an accused at the preliminary diet does not prevent the court from considering preliminary pleas and preliminary issues provided that a motion to proceed in absence is made to the court and allowed. In the case of a body corporate (s.70 above) in particular, a failure to appear, or be represented, at the preliminary diet would not vitiate further proceedings; instead the court will record a not guilty plea and move to assigning a trial diet or to proceed as accords.

As subs.(4) indicates the court has a duty to investigate the state of readiness of the parties by reference to the written record to be lodged jointly by parties (s.72E and High Court of Justiciary Practice Note No.1 of 2005), and by questioning parties as necessary. The Practice Note envisages that each case hearing will last no more than one hour (para.11), a clear indication that preparation of the written record is intended to concentrate minds on the live issues in the case. The Practice Note (para.30) also addresses the approach to be adopted if parties consider that the diet cannot be concluded within the one hour timespan.

Once preliminary pleas have been resolved, the accused is to be called upon to tender pleas, and in the event of a trial being required, the High Court then has to proceed to deal with the preliminary issues (reference to the general discussions in ss.71 and 72 above may assist—*Duties of the first diet court*; *Duties of the preliminary diet court*).

Written record of state of preparation in certain cases

72E.—(1) This section applies where, in any proceedings in the High Court, a solicitor has notified the Court under section 72F(1) of this Act that he has been engaged by the accused for the purposes of the conduct of his case at the preliminary hearing.

(2) The prosecutor and the accused's legal representative shall, not less than two days before the preliminary hearing—

(a) communicate with each other with a view to jointly preparing a written record of their state of preparation with respect to their cases (referred to in this section as "the written record"); and

(b) lodge the written record with the Clerk of Justiciary.

(3) The High Court may, on cause shown, allow the written record to be lodged after the time referred to in subsection (2) above.

(4) The written record shall—

(a) be in such form, or as nearly as may be in such form;

(b) contain such information; and

(c) be lodged in such manner,

as may be prescribed by Act of Adjournal.

(5) The written record may contain, in addition to the information required by virtue of subsection (4)(b) above, such other information as the prosecutor and the accused's legal representative consider appropriate.

(6) In this section—

"the accused's legal representative" means —

(a) the solicitor referred to in subsection (1) above; or

(b) where the solicitor has instructed counsel for the purposes of the conduct of the accused's case at the preliminary hearing, either the solicitor or that counsel, or both of them; and

"counsel" includes a solicitor who has a right of audience in the High Court of Justiciary under section 25A (rights of audience in various courts including the High Court of Justiciary) of the Solicitors (Scotland) Act 1980 (c.46).

AMENDMENT

Section 72E inserted by the Criminal Procedure (Amendment) (Scotland) Act 2004 (asp 5), s.2. Brought into force on February 1, 2005 by the Criminal Procedure (Amendment) (Scotland) Act 2004 (Commencement, Transitional Provisions and Savings) Order 2004 (SSI 2004/405 (C.28)), art.2.

DEFINITIONS

"a written report": s.72E(2).
"Clerk of Justiciary": s.307(1).
"counsel": s.72E(6).
"High Court": s.307(1).
"preliminary hearing": s.66(6)(b).
"the accused's legal representative": s.72E(6).
"the written record": s.72E(2)(a).

GENERAL NOTE

This section applies to High Court proceedings and should be read in conjunction with the Act of Adjournal (Criminal Procedure Rules Amendment) (Criminal Procedure (Amendment) (Scotland) Act 2004) 2005 (SSI 2005/44), particularly r.9A.4 and Form 9A.4 which sets out the purpose and format of the written record. Note that the form can now be lodged physically or by means of facsimile or e-mail transmission.

Not less than two days before the preliminary diet, it is expected that the parties will have met, discussed preparation of the case and produced a written record conform to Form 9A.4 and lodge this with the Clerk of Justiciary by 2pm two days prior to the hearing. (Later lodging, with leave of the court, is permitted by subs.(3)). High Court of Justiciary Practice Note No.1 of 2005 states that lodging should be with the Clerk of Justiciary in Glasgow for diets scheduled for there; otherwise records are to be lodged with the Clerk of Justiciary in Edinburgh.

The form of the written record is not intended to be exhaustive. If parties consider that other matters could be considered by the court (for example, the transcription of evidence and its availability for ongoing court use rather than purely for appeal purposes, as arose in *Transco Plc v H.M. Advocate*, 2005 S.L.T. 211) this is permissible.

Engagement, dismissal and withdrawal of solicitor representing accused

72F.—(1) In any proceedings on indictment, it is the duty of a solicitor who is engaged by the accused for the purposes of his defence at any part of the proceedings to notify the court and the prosecutor of that fact forthwith in writing.

(2) A solicitor is to be taken to have complied with the duty under subsection (1) to notify the prosecutor of his engagement if, before service of the indictment, he—

(a) notified in writing the procurator fiscal for the district in which the charge against the accused was then being investigated that he was then engaged by the accused for the purposes of his defence; and

(b) had not notified that procurator fiscal in writing that he had been dismissed by the accused or had withdrawn from acting.

(3) Where any such solicitor as is referred to in subsection (1) above—

(a) is dismissed by the accused; or

(b) withdraws,

it is the duty of the solicitor to inform the court and the prosecutor of those facts forthwith in writing.

(4) The prosecutor shall, for the purposes of subsections (1) and (3), be taken to be notified or informed of any fact in accordance with those subsections if—

(a) in proceedings in the High Court, the Crown Agent; or

(b) in proceedings on indictment in the sheriff court, the procurator fiscal for the district in which the trial diet is to be held,

is so notified or, as the case may be, informed of the fact.

(5) On being informed in accordance with subsection (3) above of the dismissal or withdrawal of the accused's solicitor in any case to which subsections (6) and (7) below apply, the court shall order that, before the trial diet, there shall be a further pre-trial diet under this section.

(6) This subsection applies to any case—

(a) where the accused is charged with an offence to which section 288C of this Act applies;

(b) in respect of which section 288E of this Act applies; or

(c) in which an order has been made under section 288F(2) of this Act.

(7) This subsection applies to any case in which–

(a) the solicitor was engaged for the purposes of the defence of the accused—

(i) in the case of proceedings in the High Court, at the time of a preliminary hearing or, if a preliminary hearing was dispensed with under section 72B(1) of this Act, at the time it was so dispensed with;

(ii) in the case of solemn proceedings in the sheriff court, at the time of a first diet;

(iii) at the time of a diet under this section; or

(iv) in the case of a diet which, under subsection (11) below, is dispensed with, at the time when it was so dispensed with; and

(b) the court is informed as mentioned in subsection (3) above after that time but before the trial diet.

(8) At a diet under this section, the court shall ascertain whether or not the accused has engaged another solicitor for the purposes of his defence at the trial.

(9) A diet under this section shall be not less than 10 clear days before the trial diet.

(10) A court may, at a diet under this section, postpone the trial diet for such period as appears to it to be appropriate and may, if it thinks fit, direct that such period (or some part of it) shall not count towards any time limit applying in respect of the case.

(11) The court may dispense with a diet under this section previously ordered, but only if a solicitor engaged by the accused for the purposes of the defence of the accused at the trial has, in writing—

(a) confirmed his engagement for that purpose; and

(b) requested that the diet be dispensed with.

AMENDMENT

Section 72F inserted by the Criminal Procedure (Amendment) (Scotland) Act 2004 (asp 5), s.8. Brought into force on February 1, 2005 by the Criminal Procedure (Amendment) (Scotland) Act 2004 (Commencement, Transitional Provisions and Savings) Order 2004 (SSI 2004/405 (C.28)), art.2.

DEFINITIONS

"diet": s.307(1).
"High Court": s.307(1).
"order": s.307(1).
"preliminary hearing": s.66(6)(b).
"procurator fiscal": s.307(1).

GENERAL NOTE

This section applies to all solemn proceedings and requires the solicitor engaged by the accused to inform both the court and the prosecutor of his identity and contact details. Although subs.(4) stipulates that once a case has been indicted in the High Court intimation should be made to the Crown Agent, prudence would suggest that it would be appropriate to notify the procurator fiscal of first instance of this information. The section also obliges the agent to advise in the event of withdrawal from acting or when dismissed by the accused.

These requirements serve several purposes: identification of the solicitor acting will obviously facilitate communications (particularly important now that High Court proceedings demand the lodging of a written record of discussions between the parties), will immediately alert the court to cases where the accused has not engaged an agent at all (especially vital in cases libelling listed sexual offences under s.288C of the Act where the accused *must* be legally represented) and, as was noted in s.66, service of the indictment may now validly be made in the hands of the defence agent.

Subss.(5) and (9) enable the court to respond to withdrawal or dismissal by fixing a pre-trial hearing for not less than 10 days before the trial diet itself to resolve the issue of legal representation and, as would seem likely, to postpone the trial. Significantly, subs.(10) empowers the court when postponing a trial diet on these grounds to discount any part of the postponement period for calculation of timebars. In keeping with the spirit of this section, it is submitted that the same period could also to be subtracted from any subsequent discount on sentence (see s.196 of the Act), or from any backdate of sentence taking account of the period on remand (s.210 below) but there is no direct authority on the point.

Subs.(11) is a saving provision to permit the cancellation of a diet fixed in terms of subs.(5) once it has been established that an agent has now been engaged for the trial.

Service etc. on accused through a solicitor

72G.—(1) In any proceedings on indictment, anything which is to be served on or given, notified or otherwise intimated to, the accused shall be taken to be so served, given, notified or intimated if it is, in such form and manner as may be prescribed by Act of Adjournal, served on or given, notified or intimated to (as the case may be) the solicitor described in subsection (2) below at that solicitor's place of business.

(2) That solicitor is any solicitor—

(a) who—

    (i) has notified the prosecutor under subsection (1) of section 72F of this Act that he is engaged by the accused for the purposes of his defence; and

    (ii) has not informed the prosecutor under subsection (3) of that section that he has been dismissed by, or has withdrawn from acting for, the accused; or

(b) who—

    (i) has been appointed to act for the purposes of the accused's defence at the trial under section 92 or 288D of this Act; and

    (ii) has not been relieved of the appointment by the court.

Section 72G inserted by the Criminal Procedure (Amendment) (Scotland) Act 2004 (asp 5), s.12. Brought into force on December 4, 2004 by the Criminal Procedure (Amendment) (Scotland) Act 2004 (Commencement, Transitional Provisions and Savings) Order 2004 (SSI 2004/405 (C.28)).

DEFINITIONS

"prosecutor": s.307(1).

GENERAL NOTE

This section applies in any solemn proceedings and entitles parties, once the case has been indicted, to effect lawful service of any notice upon other parties to the proceedings by lodging it in the hands of an accused's solicitor. Reference should be made to s.72F above.

Preliminary diet: procedure
73. [...]

AMENDMENT

Subss.(3) and (4) as amended by the Sexual Offences (Procedure and Evidence) (Scotland) Act 2002 (asp 9), s.8(4). Brought into force by the Sexual Offences (Procedure and Evidence) (Scotland) Act 2002 (Commencement and Transitional Provisions) Order 2002 (SSI 2002/443 (C.24)), art.4 (effective November 1, 2002).

Section 73 repealed by the Criminal Procedure (Amendment) (Scotland) Act 2004 (asp 5), s.1(3). Brought into force on February 1, 2005 by the Criminal Procedure (Amendment) (Scotland) Act 2004 (Commencement, Transitional Provisions and Savings) Order 2004 (SSI 2004/405 (C.28)), art.2.

DEFINITIONS

"indictment": s.307(1).
"prosecutor": s.307(1).

Consideration of matters relating to vulnerable witnesses where no preliminary diet is ordered
73A. [...]

AMENDMENT

Section 73A, as prospectively inserted by Vulnerable Witnesses (Scotland) Act 2004 (asp 3), s.2(3), repealed by the Criminal Procedure (Amendment) (Scotland) Act 2004 (asp 5), s.1(3). Brought into force on February 1, 2005 by the Criminal Procedure (Amendment) (Scotland) Act 2004 (Commencement, Transitional Provisions and Savings) Order 2004 (SSI 2004/405 (C.28)), art.2.

Appeals in connection with preliminary diets

74.—(1) Without prejudice to—

(a) any right of appeal under section 106 or 108 of this Act; and

(b) section 131 of this Act,

and subject to subsection (2) below, a party may with the leave of the court of first instance (granted either on the motion of the party or *ex proprio motu*) in accordance with such procedure as may be prescribed by Act of Adjournal, appeal to the High Court against a decision at a first diet or a preliminary hearing.

(2) An appeal under subsection (1) above—

(a) may not be taken against a decision to adjourn the first diet or, as the case may be, preliminary hearing or to accelerate or postpone the trial diet;

(aa) may not be taken against a decision taken by virtue of—

(i) in the case of a first diet, section 71(1A),

(ii) in the case of a preliminary hearing, section 72(6)(e),

of this Act;

(ab) may not be taken against a decision at a preliminary hearing, in appointing a trial diet, to appoint or not to appoint it as a floating diet for the purposes of section 83A(2) of this Act;

(b) must be taken not later than 2 days after the decision.

(3) Where an appeal is taken under subsection (1) above, the High Court may postpone any trial diet that has been appointed for such period as appears to it to be appropriate and may, if it thinks fit, direct that such period (or some part of it) shall not count towards any time limit applying in respect of the case.

(3A) Where an appeal is taken under subsection (1) above against a decision at a preliminary hearing, the High Court may adjourn, or further adjourn, the preliminary hearing for such period as appears to it to be appropriate and may, if it thinks fit, direct that such period (or some part of it) shall not count towards any time limit applying in respect of the case.

(4) In disposing of an appeal under subsection (1) above the High Court—

(a) may affirm the decision of the court of first instance or may remit the case to it with such directions in the matter as it thinks fit;

(b) where the court of first instance has dismissed the indictment or any part of it, may reverse that decision and direct that the court of first instance fix

  (i) where the indictment is in respect of the High Court, a further preliminary hearing; or

  (ii) where the indictment is in respect of the sheriff court, a trial diet, if it has not already fixed one as regards so much of the indictment as it has not dismissed; and

(c) may on cause shown extend the period mentioned in section 65(1) of this Act.

AMENDMENTS

Subs.(4)(a) words deleted by the Crime and Punishment (Scotland) Act 1997 (c.48), s.62(1) and Sch.1, para.21(10)(a) with effect from August 1, 1997 as provided by the Crime and Punishment (Scotland) Act 1997 (Commencement and Transitional Provisions) Order 1997 (SI 1997/1712), art.3 and Sch.1.

Subs.(4)(c) inserted by Sch.1, para.21(10)(b) of the above-mentioned Act with effect from August 1, 1997 in terms of the above Order.

Subss.(1), (2)(a) and (3) as amended, and subss.(2)(ab), (3A) and (4)(b)(i), (ii) inserted, by the Criminal Procedure (Amendment) (Scotland) Act 2004 (asp 5), s.3. Subs.(2)(a) also as amended by 2004 Act, s.25 and Sch.1, para.22. Brought into force on February 1, 2005 by the Criminal Procedure (Amendment) (Scotland) Act 2004 (Commencement, Transitional Provisions and Savings) Order 2004 (SSI 2004/405 (C.28)), art.2.

Subs.(2)(aa) inserted by the Vulnerable Witnesses (Scotland) Act 2004 (asp 3), s.2(4). Brought into force on April 1, 2005, for certain purposes, by the Vulnerable Witnesses (Scotland) Act 2004 (Commencement) Order 2005 (SSI 2005/168 (C.7)), art.2. Further brought into force by the Vulnerable Witnesses (Scotland) Act 2004 (Commencement No.3, Savings and Transitional Provisions) Order 2006 (SSI 2006/59 (C.8)).

Subs.(2)(aa)(ii) as amended by the Criminal Procedure (Amendment) (Scotland) Act 2004 (asp 5), s.3(b). Brought into force on February 1, 2005 by the Criminal Procedure (Amendment) (Scotland) Act 2004 (Commencement, Transitional Provisions and Savings) Order 2004 (SSI 2004/405 (C.28)), art.2.

DEFINITIONS

"first diet": s.71(1).

"High Court": s.307(1).

"preliminary diet": s.72(1).

GENERAL NOTE

This section applies to all solemn proceedings and permits limited rights of appeal from decisions arising in the preliminary, or first, diet court. Appeals cannot be taken against scheduling decisions (decisions to adjourn the diet, accelerate or postpone the trial) or against the court's determination as to the vulnerability of an accused or a witness, or in High Court cases against a decision to assign either a fixed or floating trial diet.

Appeals in regard to preliminary issues or pleas must be taken within two days of the court's decision either following the motion of a party, granted by the court, or by the court *ex proprio motu*; however, in *H.M. Advocate v Sorrie*, 1997 S.L.T. 250 (discussed at A4–158), the Crown, having failed to appeal a decision upholding S's plea in bar timeously, proceeded by way of bill of advocation, and also secured an extension of the statutory time-bar on proceedings. The relevant forms for s.74 appeals are Forms 9.6 (sheriff solemn appeal), 9.11 (abandonment), 9A.7 (High Court appeal) and 9A.8 (abandonment).

Subs.(3) entitles, but does not oblige, the court to deduct the period (or any part of it) taken for such appeals from calculation of timebars applying to the accused, or to any co-accused.

The powers available to the Appeal Court are set out in subs.(4).

Note that even if leave to appeal is granted at the preliminary or first diet, the accused should nonetheless be called upon to plead.

Computation of certain periods

75. Where the last day of any period mentioned in section 66(6), 67(3) or 74 of this Act falls on a Saturday, Sunday or court holiday, such period shall extend to and include the next day which is not a Saturday, Sunday or court holiday.

AMENDMENT

Section 75 as amended by the Criminal Procedure (Amendment) (Scotland) Act 2004 (asp 5), s.25 and Sch.1, para.23. Brought into force on February 1, 2005 by the Criminal Procedure (Amendment) (Scotland) Act 2004 (Commencement, Transitional Provisions and Savings) Order 2004 (SSI 2004/405 (C.28)), art.2.

GENERAL NOTE

The timescales specified in s.66(6) refer both to the dates within which a first diet must occur in the Sheriff court and the timelapse from service of an indictment until trial; in either event the due date is extended to the next working day. A similar provision covers the time-limit for service of a notice objecting to the description of witnesses in that indictment. The section's reference to s.72 is understandable in that subs.(6) defines "the appropriate period" for notice of the matters to be raised at a preliminary diet. It will be appreciated that s.75's terms do not interfere in any way with the provisions in s.65 against delay.

Adjournment and alteration of diets

Adjournment and alteration of diets

75A.—(1) This section applies where any diet has been fixed in any proceedings on indictment.

(2) The court may, if it considers it appropriate to do so, adjourn the diet.

(3) However—

(a) in the case of a trial diet, the court may adjourn the diet under subsection (2) above only if the indictment is not brought to trial at the diet;

(b) if the court adjourns any diet under that subsection by reason only that, following enquiries for the purpose of ascertaining whether the accused has engaged a solicitor for the purposes of the conduct of his defence at or for the purposes of a preliminary hearing or at a trial, it appears to the court that he has not done so, the adjournment shall be for a period of not more than 48 hours.

261

(4) A trial diet in the High Court may be adjourned under subsection (2) above to a diet to be held at a sitting of the Court in another place.

(5) The court may, on the application of any party to the proceedings made at any time before commencement of any diet—

(a) discharge the diet; and

(b) fix a new diet for a date earlier or later than that for which the discharged diet was fixed.

(6) Before determining an application under subsection (5) above, the court shall give the parties an opportunity to be heard.

(7) However, where all the parties join in an application under that subsection, the court may determine the application without hearing the parties and, accordingly, may dispense with any hearing previously appointed for the purpose of subsection (6) above.

(8) Where there is a hearing for the purpose of subsection (6) above, the accused shall attend it unless the court permits the hearing to proceed notwithstanding the absence of the accused.

(9) In appointing a new trial diet under subsection (5)(b) above, the court—

(a) shall have regard to the state of preparation of the prosecutor and the accused with respect to their cases and, in particular, to the likelihood of the case being ready to proceed to trial on the date to be appointed for the trial diet; and

(b) may, if it appears to the court that there are any preliminary pleas, preliminary issues or other matters which require to be, or could with advantage be, disposed of or ascertained before the trial, appoint a diet to be held before the trial diet for the purpose of disposing of or, as the case may be, ascertaining them.

(10) A date for a new diet may be fixed under subsection (5)(b) above notwithstanding that the holding of the diet on that date would result in any provision of this Act as to the minimum or maximum period within which the diet is to be held or to commence not being complied with.

(11) In subsections (5) to (9) above, "the court" means—

(a) in the case of proceedings in the High Court, a single judge of that Court; and

(b) in the case of proceedings in the sheriff court, that court.

(12) For the purposes of subsection (5) above—

(a) a diet other than a trial diet shall be taken to commence when it is called; and

(b) a trial diet shall be taken to commence when the jury is sworn.

AMENDMENT

Section 75A inserted by the Criminal Procedure (Amendment) (Scotland) Act 2004 (asp 5), s.15. Brought into force on February 1, 2005 by the Criminal Procedure (Amendment) (Scotland) Act 2004 (Commencement, Transitional Provisions and Savings) Order 2004 (SSI 2004/405 (C.28)), art.2(1).

DEFINITIONS

"diet": s.307(1).
"High Court": s.307(1).
"prosecutor": s.307(1).
"the court": s.75A(11).

GENERAL NOTE

This section applies to all solemn proceedings and introduces the flexibility necessary to accommodate the system of fixed and floating trial diets in the High Court by pinpointing, at an early stage, cases which clearly are not ready for trial or cannot be scheduled in the assigned trial date or dates. Not only can public expense and inconvenience to witnesses and jury assize members be reduced by altering diets (including trial diets) but suitably flexible business management, combined with the provisions of the section, could result in more effective use of freed court time.

The section enables diets to be altered by application to the court prior to the trial date. A minute can be initiated by a party (see Form 12.2-A) or jointly (Form 12.2-B) as now inserted in the 1996 Act of Adjournal which is discussed at "*Act of Adjournal*" below.

Subs.(3) limits the time allowed for an unrepresented accused to secure legal representation to 48 hours; thereafter, he is to be represented at the preliminary, or first, diet. Subs.(4) usefully provides for adjournment of High Court trials to sittings elsewhere.

Subss.(5) and (7) make it clear that applications to the court for these purposes can be administrative in nature, and do not necessarily require a formal calling of the case provided it is evident that all preliminaries (pleas and issues) identified by then have been canvassed and resolved between the parties in advance of any hearing. (Situations may, of course, arise—such as the grave illness of an accused—which would preclude a trial or restrict the taking of proper instructions, where parties would necessarily have to reserve their positions, but the underlying ethos is that parties should be proactive in identifying areas of agreement and dispute much earlier than on the date of trial).

Note that a diet can be discharged, and an earlier trial diet fixed, as well as the more familiar later adjourned diet but the court is still directed (subs.(9)) to ascertain the parties' state of readiness for trial at the proposed date and can fix a further preliminary, or first, diet for the purpose and to deal with preliminaries.

While a paper procedure (akin to the summary minute of acceleration) can be used by parties individually or jointly, subs.(5) entitles the court to fix a hearing on the application and allows the option of dispensing with the attendance of the accused. At this hearing the full range of enquiries set out in subs.(9) can be undertaken if it is decided to fix a new diet; that diet can be fixed for either earlier or later than the one discharged by the court.

Act of Adjournal

Refer to the Act of Adjournal (Criminal Procedure Rules Amendment) (Criminal Procedure (Amendment) (Scotland) Act 2004) 2005 (SSI 2005/44) which amends, particularly, Chapter 12 of the 1996 Act of Adjournal (SI 1996/513).

Plea of guilty

Procedure where accused desires to plead guilty

76.—(1) Where an accused intimates in writing to the Crown Agent that he intends to plead guilty and desires to have his case disposed of at once, the accused may be served with an indictment (unless one has already been served) and a notice to appear at a diet of the appropriate court not less than four clear days after the date of the notice; and it shall not be necessary to lodge or give notice of any list of witnesses or productions.

(2) In subsection (1) above, "appropriate court" means—

(a) in a case where at the time of the intimation mentioned in that subsection an indictment had not been served, either the High Court or the sheriff court; and

(b) in any other case, the court specified in the notice served under section 66(6) of this Act on the accused.

(3) If at any such diet the accused pleads not guilty to the charge or pleads guilty only to a part of the charge, and the prosecutor declines to accept such restricted plea, the diet shall be deserted *pro loco et tempore* and thereafter the cause may proceed in accordance with the other provisions of this Part of this Act; except that in a case mentioned in paragraph (b) of subsection (2) above the court may postpone the trial diet or, where the accused has been indicted to the High Court, the preliminary hearing and the period of such postponement shall not count towards any time limit applying in respect of the case.

AMENDMENT

Subs.(3) as amended by the Criminal Procedure (Amendment) (Scotland) Act 2004 (asp 5), s.25 and Sch.1, para.24. Brought into force on February 1, 2005 by the Criminal Procedure (Amendment) (Scotland) Act 2004 (Commencement, Transitional Provisions and Savings) Order 2004 (SSI 2004/405 (C.28)), art.2.

DEFINITIONS

"High Court": s.307(1).
"indictment": s.307(1).
"witnesses": s.307(1).

GENERAL NOTE

Section 76 re-enacts the familiar accelerated plea provisions of s.102 of the 1975 Act. Although the statute requires written intimation of a proposed plea by the accused to the Crown Agent, it is customary for the letter intimating the terms of the plea to be sent to the procurator fiscal at whose instance the petition charges were raised. It is, of course, competent to serve an indictment without any prior petition but in that event it will be difficult to negotiate a satisfactory plea practically.

On receipt of a letter, the procurator fiscal is under a duty to comply with the Procurator Fiscal Service's Book of Regulations and deliver the letter along with a report outlining his views on its merits, or otherwise, to the Crown Agent. While the section stipulates that the letter be sent to the Crown Agent, the Crown as a matter of course indicate the date of its receipt by the procurator fiscal to the court when the plea of guilt is recorded, since this may have a bearing upon any sentence; this is particularly pertinent now given the terms of s.196 of the Act which allows courts discretion to consider as a sentencing parameter, the point in proceedings at which a plea was tendered.

It will be observed that a plea tendered prior to service of any indictment leaves the issue open as to whether the plea should be heard before a sheriff or in the High Court (subs.(2)(a)) and the choice of forum may be a material factor in the plea tendered; by contrast, once an indictment has been served, subs.(2)(b) enacts that a s.76 letter will only have the effect of accelerating the hearing before that court. Rule 10.1-(2) of the 1996 Act of Adjournal provides that cases set down for trial in the High Court, and by necessary inference, charges in which the High Court has exclusive jurisdiction—treason, murder and rape, can be called for disposal in the High Court sitting in Edinburgh instead of at the sitting originally scheduled elsewhere in Scotland. Any charge may be dealt with on a s.76 indictment. It is rare for a murder to be put before the court in this way but it is not unknown: see *HM Advocate v Todd*, 2003 G.W.D. 11–310.

If the plea offered by the accused is acceptable to the Crown, a notice conforming to the style of Form 10.1-A where no indictment has yet been served, or Form 10.1-B, when an indictment has still to be served, will accompany the indictment now served upon the accused. Cases in which a s.76 plea is offered prior to service of an indictment (see subs.(2)(a)) will ordinarily proceed upon an edited indictment which does not include lists of productions and witnesses; this is not an absolute requirement, but obviously economises on Crown resources. Cases which have simply been brought forward after service of the indictment competently proceed on the full indictment previously served on the accused.

The practice of obtaining the accused's written instructions detailing the precise terms of the plea to be tendered is expedient. Refer to A4–178 below for a general discussion of the issue.

Subsection (3) works to the benefit of the Crown; if, at the accelerated diet the accused reneges on his plea, the court can postpone the trial diet or the preliminary diet (in the High Court) and discount the period of the postponement in any calculation of statutory time-bars. This concession only applies to cases proceeding under subs.(2)(b), i.e. where an accelerated plea has been offered after service of the indictment. Note, however, that Rule 10.1-(3) of the 1996 Act of Adjournal only permits such a postponement when all of the accused have tendered s.76 notices and all are present at the accelerated diet and the court grants the postponement in response to a motion made at that time. It is difficult to envisage practical instances in which these circumstances would apply: it may arise where one (or more) accused recants on a "package" deal involving a number of the accused, thus rendering the totality unacceptable to the Crown. Ordinarily the Crown would probably accept pleas from other accused and elect to proceed to trial later against the recalcitrant accused and a subs.(3) motion for postponement could then be made quite properly.

The Induciae

This section proceeds upon an *induciae* between service of the edited form of indictment, and its calling, of four clear days. The *induciae* can be waived by the accused but in *McKnight v HM Advocate*, 1991 S.C.C.R. 751 where the accused pleaded to an indictment served upon him 10 minutes beforehand, the Court of Appeal doubted the wisdom of proceeding in such a summary fashion and indicated that the Crown should be hesitant to accept pleas tendered in such circumstances. It may be said too that with the current re-evaluation by the Appeal Court of the relationship between criminal practitioners and clients (after *Anderson v HM Advocate*, 1996 S.L.T. 155), it could be regarded as imprudent to advise clients to waive the four day *induciae*.

Withdrawal of the Plea

A plea tendered at the accelerated diet can be withdrawn competently at a later diet, but the court would have to be satisfied that the accused had substantially misunderstood his position and had been prejudiced by that misunderstanding. See *Healy v HM Advocate*, 1990 S.C.C.R. 110, where the indictment had been read over to the accused by the sheriff at the first diet and accepted by the accused who sought to withdraw her plea before a different sheriff at the diet of deferred sentence; and *Paul v HM Advocate* (1914) 7 Adam 343 where the accused sought to change his plea following upon a remit to the High Court for sentence. In *Weightman v HM Advocate*, 1997 G.W.D. 3–85 the court looked to the absence of any dissent by the accused, during narration of the facts and mitigation, in rejecting his later claims that he had been bullied or pressured to plead during his trial.

Once a plea of guilt is recorded, it cannot be revisited in light of the outcome of any subsequent trial of a co-accused on those charges (*Reedie v HM Advocate*, 2005 S.C.C.R. 407). Crown consent to amendment of the pleas is irrelevant; by then the Crown has no locus in the matter.

So far as the Crown is concerned, any mitigation tendered which is felt to be inconsistent with a guilty plea, or, it is suggested, any defence explanation of the factual circumstances which is disputed, must be made known to the court of first instance. Otherwise, the Crown will likely be held to have acquiesced and will be barred from raising the matter in any appeal (*Bennett v HM Advocate*, 1996 S.C.C.R. 331 and see also s.118(8) below). In the event of such an unsatisfactory plea the court is obliged to invoke the provisions of subs.(3) (refer to A4–174 above). Guidance on the procedures open to the court where disagreement on the terms of the plea surfaces is given in *McCartney v HM Advocate*, 1997 S.C.C.R. 644.

Sentencing Issues

It has long been tacitly accepted by the courts that the tendering of an acceptable plea utilising this section's provisions can attract a discount on sentence. This reflects a recognition that prosecution resources, court time and witnesses, have all been spared. Nonetheless, there is no automatic entitlement under s.76 to a sentence lower than that which the offence, and offender, would normally merit simply by reason of an early (or accelerated) plea of guilt (see *Tennie v Munro*, 1999 S.C.C.R. 70). Reference to the terms of s.196 below makes it clear that the court has a discretion in *all* cases to have regard to the timing, circumstances and purpose of a guilty plea when imposing sentence (*Du Plooy v HM Advocate*, 2003 S.L.T. 1237) but that the scale of discount normally should not exceed one-third of the sentence otherwise in prospect.

However, it is observed that in *McKenna v HM Advocate*, 2005 G.W.D. 27–527, where the appellant's s.76 plea had attracted a discount on sentence of only 15 per cent, it was held that use of the accelerated plea procedures ordinarily ought to have merited a discount in the region of 30 per cent, the maximum permissible.

Plea of guilty

77.—(1) Where at any diet the accused tenders a plea of guilty to the indictment or any part thereof he shall do so in open court and, subject to section 70(7) of this Act, shall, if he is able to do so, sign a written copy of the plea; and the judge shall countersign such copy.

(2) Where the plea is to part only of the charge and the prosecutor does not accept the plea, such non-acceptance shall be recorded.

(3) Where an accused charged on indictment with any offence tenders a plea of guilty to any other offence of which he could competently be found guilty on the trial of the indictment, and that plea is accepted by the prosecutor, it shall be competent to convict the accused of the offence to which he has so pled guilty and to sentence him accordingly.

"diet": s.307(1).

"indictment": s.307(1).

"prosecutor": s.307(1).

GENERAL NOTE

This section substantially re-enacts the provisions of s.103 of the 1975 Act. Obviously if for some reason the accused is unable to subscribe his plea, the court is under an additional responsibility to ensure that the plea as recorded reflects his intention. Thereafter the judge is required to countersign the plea on the same papers; failure to do so constitutes a nullity (see *HM Advocate v MacDonald* (1896) 3 S.L.T. 317). The prosecutor must ensure that any mitigation offered by the accused whose terms are not accepted by the Crown is objected to at the first diet, failing which the Crown will be taken as having acquiesced in the matter (see A4–174 above).

Prosecutor's refusal of pleas

There is no obligation upon the prosecutor to accept a plea of guilt to the libel (indeed, historically, in capital crimes the Crown always elected to prove its case when a guilty plea was offered).

The rules for such eventualities were stated in *Strathern v Sloan*, 1937 J.C. 76 at 80 but had little practical impact once the 1980 Act abolished mandatory pleading diets. The re-introduction of mandatory first diets, and preliminary diets, in ss.71 and 72 of the 1995 Act may render that judgment more topical. If a guilty plea is tendered at the earlier diet but refused by the Crown, the minute should record that the plea was tendered and rejected; it should not record the plea as one of not guilty. At the trial diet the accused should not be called upon to plead *de novo*, in the interim, unless the prosecutor has decided to accept the plea previously tendered (it will be appreciated that the terms of s.196, which have already been discussed in the notes to s.76 above, may well make it advantageous to tender partial pleas at a first diet even if, at that juncture, they are not acceptable to the Crown). If the trial proceeds, and the plea previously tendered becomes acceptable to the Crown, the accused should then be called upon to state his plea publicly. No reference in the course of a trial should be made by the Crown to the fact that such a plea has been preferred.

Prosecutor's acceptance of pleas

Following upon *Anderson v HM Advocate*, 1996 S.C.C.R. 487 it is submitted to be a prudent practice to secure a client's written instructions before tendering a guilty plea to the court; this view accords with the Faculty of Advocates' Code of Professional Conduct. In *Crossan v HM Advocate*, 1996 S.C.C.R. 279, C appealed his conviction following a guilty plea to a murder charge (his co-accused having pled guilty to assault), and sought to withdraw his plea the following day, a procedure which was not competent to the court. In terms of s.252(d) of the 1975 Act (now s.104 of the 1995 Act) the Court of Appeal remitted the matter to a single judge for a report on the circumstances surrounding the appeal. It will be noted that the evidence to that judge was not given on oath and was heard in chambers outwith the presence of the accused, it being a matter within the sole discretion of the appointed judge to determine procedures necessary for the preparation of his report.

Recording of pleas

In *Fraser v HM Advocate*, 2004 S.L.T. 592 the Appeal Court was critical of the long-established practice of partial pleas of guilt being tendered in the presence of an assize before jurors were selected to hear the trial. Although at that stage no narration would be given to the court as to the nature of the charges admitted by the accused, and the jury would receive jury copies of the indictment which would include only the charges proceeding to trial, nonetheless the potential for prejudice remained: the Court considered that any partial pleas tendered (and by implication, any pleas formally tendered but rejected) should be tendered and recorded outwith the presence of the unempanelled jurors.

Act of Adjournal

Refer to Ch.10 of the 1996 Act of Adjournal.

Sentencing guidance

A most notable use of the authority in s.18(7), *supra*, is the appeal of *Du Plooy v HM Advocate*, 2003 S.L.T. 1237. There guidance was given as to the basis of, and scope for, an allowance in the sentencing of an accused in respect of a guilty plea, and the form that such an allowance might take. Further consideration is given to this matter under ss.196 and 197 of this Act, *infra*.

Notice by accused

Special defences, incrimination and notice of witnesses, etc.

78.—(1) It shall not be competent for an accused to state a special defence or to lead evidence calculated to exculpate the accused by incriminating a co-accused unless—

(a) a plea of special defence or, as the case may be, notice of intention to lead such evidence has been lodged and intimated in writing in accordance with subsection (3) below—

(b) the court, on cause shown, otherwise directs.

(2) Subsection (1) above shall apply to a defence of automatism, coercion or, in a prosecution for an offence to which section 288C of this Act applies, consent as if it were a special defence.

(2A) In subsection (2) above, the reference to a defence of consent is a reference to the defence which is stated by reference to the complainer's consent to the act which is the subject matter of the charge or the accused's belief as to that consent.

(2B) In subsection (2A) above, "complainer" has the same meaning as in section 274 of this Act.

(3) A plea or notice is lodged and intimated in accordance with this subsection—

(a) where the case is to be tried in the High Court, by lodging the plea or notice with the Clerk of Justiciary and by intimating the plea or notice to the Crown Agent and to any co-accused not less than seven clear days before the preliminary hearing;

(b) where the case is to be tried in the sheriff court, by lodging the plea or notice with the sheriff clerk and by intimating it to the procurator fiscal and to any co-accused at or before the first diet.

(4) It shall not be competent for the accused to examine any witnesses or to put in evidence any productions not included in the lists lodged by the prosecutor unless—

(a) written notice of the names and addresses of such witnesses and of such productions has been given—

(i) where the case is to be tried in the sheriff court, to the procurator fiscal of the district of the trial diet at or before the first diet; and

(ii) where the case is to be tried in the High Court, to the Crown Agent at least seven clear days before the preliminary hearing; or

(b) the court, on cause shown, otherwise directs.

(5) A copy of every written notice required by subsection (4) above shall be lodged by the accused with the sheriff clerk of the district in which the trial diet is to be held, or in any case the trial diet of which is to be held in the High Court in Edinburgh with the Clerk of Justiciary, at or before

(a) where the case is to be tried in the High Court, the preliminary hearing;

(b) where the case is to be tried in the sheriff court, the trial diet,

for the use of the court.

AMENDMENT

Subs.(2) as amended by the Sexual Offences (Procedure and Evidence) (Scotland) Act 2002 (asp 9), s.6(1)(a).

Subs.(2A) and (2B) inserted by the Sexual Offences (Procedure and Evidence) (Scotland) Act 2002 (asp 9), s.6(1)(b).

Brought into force by the Sexual Offences (Procedure and Evidence) (Scotland) Act 2002 (Commencement and Transitional Provisions) Order 2002 (SSI 2002/443 (C.24)), art.4 (effective November 1, 2002).

Subss.(1)(a), (3)(a), (b), (4)(a)(ii) and (5) as amended by the Criminal Procedure (Amendment) (Scotland) Act 2004 (asp 5), s.25 and Sch.1, para.25. Brought into force on February 1, 2005 by the Criminal Procedure (Amendment) (Scotland) Act 2004 (Commencement, Transitional Provisions and Savings) Order 2004 (SSI 2004/405 (C.28)), art.2.

DEFINITIONS

"Clerk of Justiciary": s.307(1).
"High Court": s.307(1).
"procurator fiscal": s.307(1).

GENERAL NOTE

Section 78 stipulates the periods of notice to be given by the accused to the prosecutor and any co-accused of any defence, special defence, list of witnesses or productions. Note that different periods of notice apply in sheriff and jury and High Court cases and that these procedures have to be seen in the context of the preliminary diets and first diets introduced by ss.71 and 72 of the 1995 Act. Thus subs.(3)(a) stipulates that such notices in High Court cases must be lodged, and served on all other parties, not less than seven days before the preliminary hearing; subs.(3)(b) governing sheriff solemn cases, requires lodging at, or before, the first diet. Later lodging of special defences, or defences, strictly is not competent but has often been permitted where the Crown consents to late tendering. By contrast, late lodging by the defence of witness lists or productions (which should be lodged to the same timescale) can be permitted on cause shown (subs.(4)(b)).

The insertion of subss.(2) and (3) adds the defence of consent to the special defences, and notices, which must be intimated in advance of trial to the prosecutor and to co-accused. A defence of consent applies to the category of sexual offences set out in s.288C. Note should also be taken of the procedures in respect of sexual offences now introduced by s.275A of the Act. The equivalent summary provision is found in s.149A of the Act. In this context attention is drawn to the clarification provided by subs.(2A); a defence of consent to a sexual offence specified in s.288C of the Act must relate to the subject matter of the charge and to the accused's belief of consent to that act.

Service of Lists and Notices in Sheriff Solemn Cases

Section 71 now stipulates that a first diet has to occur not less than 15 clear days after service of an indictment and not more than 10 days before the trial diet. Section 78(4) enacts that any lists of witnesses or productions (other than those included in the indictment by the prosecutor) must be served upon the Crown, and a copy lodged with the court, no later than at the first diet. Note that there is no obligation to serve these lists upon any co-accused. Failure to lodge the lists timeously renders the examination of either productions or witnesses incompetent unless, in terms of subs.(4)(b), the accused can show cause for this failure. This timescale demands earlier action on the part of the accused than heretofore; s.82(2) of the 1975 Act only stipulated three clear days' notice of witnesses and productions to the prosecutor in any solemn case, calculated by reference to the date on which the jury was sworn.

It will be recalled that at the first diet the sheriff is obliged to enquire as to the state of preparation of the parties for trial (s.71(1)(a)). Accordingly, it may be expected that later lodging of lists will entail a considerable burden in persuading the court that these should still be received. The same can be said for notices of special defences (extended to include defences of coercion and automatism): these have to be served upon the prosecutor and any co-accused at or before the first diet though, again, a discretion is open to the court to permit late lodging on cause shown.

A special defence is a fact which if established must lead to the acquittal of the accused upon the libel (*Adam v McNeill*, 1971 S.L.T. (Notes) 80). The effect of such a defence, if successful, is to divorce the accused from all blame or culpability in the charge libelled and secure his acquittal. Thus in *McQuade v HM Advocate*, 1996 S.C.C.R. 347 where only one of three accused gave evidence, admitted shooting the deceased during a robbery and implicated his co-accused, it was held on appeal that a notice of incrimination had not been necessary since that evidence could not have secured his acquittal. See also *McShane v HM Advocate*, 1989 S.C.C.R. 687 and *Collins v HM Advocate*, 1991 S.C.C.R. 898: unlike other special defences a notice of incrimination does not require to be read to the jury or be referred to in the course of the judge's charge.

A notice of alibi is not required when it is to be asserted that the accused was at the *locus* for an innocent purpose (*Balsillie v HM Advocate*, 1993 S.C.C.R. 760). In relation to special defences of self defence, *O'Connell v HM Advocate*, 1996 S.C.C.R. 614 is authority for the proposition that the particulars of the defence must be properly specified to be received by the court; at an adjourned first diet the special defence had been inspecifically stated causing the sheriff to adjourn the matter further. The defence of coercion or necessity was recognised in *Moss v Howdle*, 1997 S.L.T. 782 following *Thomson v HM Advocate*, 1983 S.L.T. 682; 1983 S.C.C.R. 368. See also the discussion in "Necessity and Coercion in Criminal Law" by P.W. Ferguson, 1997 S.L.T. 127. (The issue of withdrawal of a special defence from a jury where only the thinnest evidence is available is ruled on in *Whyte v HM Advocate*, 1996 G.W.D. 25–1411.)

It is doubtful that a notice of defence, not in proper form, can be treated as complying with the time-limit for notice imposed in subs.(1)(a), but it might serve to indicate a lack of readiness for trial (see s.71(1)(a)) if produced at a first, or preliminary, diet as occurred in *O'Connell*.

Note that in terms of Ch.11 of the 1996 Act of Adjournal notices under s.78(1) and lists of witnesses and productions under s.78(4) can be served on the solicitor acting for a co-accused rather than upon the co-accused personally. Despite their effect upon any trial, pleas of diminished responsibility or provocation, which may focus strongly upon technical or medical evidence and necessitate further investigation by the Crown, need not be intimated before trial. See the critical discussion of recent developments in the law of provocation in "Collapsing the Structure of Criminal Law" by James Chalmers in 2001 S.L.T. 241 following *Drury v HM Advocate*, 2001 S.L.T. 1013 which centred upon the nature of provocation wrought by alleged infidelity.

It remains open to the prosecutor to waive timeous notice, and to the court to consider the broad interests of justice when assessing whether due cause has been shown for notices to be received late, but such an assessment must surely now take account of any potential prejudice to co-accused since they too are entitled to timeous notification. In *Lowson v HM Advocate*, 1943 J.C. 141, where a list of defence witnesses had not been lodged due to a change of trial venue, the trial judge disallowed the evidence on the view (shared by the procurator fiscal who had objected), that there was no discretion to permit examination of unintimated witnesses; the Lord Justice-General (at 145) while noting that the provisions existed to prevent the introduction of evidence which the prosecutor has no means of meeting, stated:

> "But I am clear that rules, being conceived in the interests of the prosecution, may competently, and should, be waived where the interests of justice are better served by waiving them than by insisting on them."

Despite the apparent mandatory nature of many of the 1995 Act's provisions this broad principle should still hold good.

Service of Lists and Notices in the High Court

The advent of preliminary hearings in High Court proceedings has led to the modification of subs.(3)(a); any notices or defences and lists of witnesses and productions need to be lodged, and served upon the prosecutor, at least seven clear days before the preliminary hearing. Notices or defences must also be served on co-accused in the same timescale but there is no obligation to intimate either lists of witnesses or productions to co-accused. Subs.(4)(b) allows these lists to be received late on cause shown, but no such discretion is given to the court to permit late lodging of notices or defences.

Act of Adjournal

Refer to Ch.11 of the 1996 Act of Adjournal and especially note the alteration to r.11.2 effected by the Act of Adjournal (Criminal Procedure Rules Amendment) (Miscellaneous) 1996; this permits service of notices under s.78(4) on the accused's solicitor.

Preliminary pleas and preliminary issues

79.—(1) Except by leave of the court on cause shown, no preliminary plea or preliminary issue shall be made, raised or submitted in any proceedings on indictment by any party unless his intention to do so has been stated in a notice under section 71(2) or, as the case may be, 72(3) or (6)(b)(i) of this Act.

(2) For the purposes of this section and those sections—

(a) the following are preliminary pleas, namely—

(i) a matter relating to the competency or relevancy of the indictment;

(ii) an objection to the validity of the citation against a party, on the ground of any discrepancy between the record copy of the indictment and the copy served on him, or on account of any error or deficiency in such service copy or in the notice of citation; and

    (iii) a plea in bar of trial; and

(b) the following are preliminary issues, namely—

    (i) an application for separation or conjunction of charges or trials;

    (ii) a preliminary objection under section 27(4A)(a), 255 or 255A of this Act, section 9(6) of the Antisocial Behaviour etc. (Scotland) Act 2004 (asp 8) or that section of that Act as applied by section 234AA(11) of this Act;

    (iii) an application under section 278(2) of this Act;

    (iv) an objection by a party to the admissibility of any evidence;

    (v) an assertion by a party that there are documents the truth of the contents of which ought to be admitted, or that there is any other matter which in his view ought to be agreed; and

    (vi) any other point raised by a party, as regards any matter not mentioned in sub-paragraphs (i) to (v) above, which could in his opinion be resolved with advantage before the trial.

(3) No discrepancy, error or deficiency such as is mentioned in subsection (2)(a)(ii) above shall entitle an accused to object to plead to the indictment unless the court is satisfied that the discrepancy, error or deficiency tended substantially to mislead and prejudice the accused.

(4) Where the court, under subsection (1) above, grants leave for a party to make, raise or submit a preliminary plea or preliminary issue (other than an objection to the admissibility of any evidence) without his intention to do so having been stated in a notice as required by that subsection, the court may—

(a) if it considers it appropriate to do so, appoint a diet to be held before the trial diet for the purpose of disposing of the plea or issue; or

(b) appoint the plea or issue to be disposed of at the trial diet.

AMENDMENTS

    Section 79 substituted by the Criminal Procedure (Amendment) (Scotland) Act 2004 (asp 5), s.13(1). Brought into force on February 1, 2005 by the Criminal Procedure (Amendment) (Scotland) Act 2004 (Commencement, Transitional Provisions and Savings) Order 2004 (SSI 2004/405 (C.28)), art.2.

    Subs.(2)(b)(ii) amended by the Antisocial Behaviour etc. (Scotland) Act 2004 (asp 8), s.144 and Sch.4, para.5(2). Brought into force on October 28, 2004 by the Antisocial Behaviour etc. (Scotland) Act 2004 (Commencement and Savings) Order 2004 (SSI 2004/420 (C.31)), art.3.

DEFINITIONS

    "diet": s.307(1).
    "High Court": s.307(1).
    "indictment": s.307(1).
    "preliminary hearing": s.66(6)(b).
    "preliminary issues": s.79(2)(b).
    "preliminary pleas": s.79(2)(a).
    "the court": s.72D(8).

GENERAL NOTE

    This section applies to all solemn proceedings and has been substantially expanded by the 2004 Act, a reflection of the enhanced role of first diets in sheriff solemn cases and the introduction of mandatory preliminary diets in the High Court.

All preliminary pleas (detailed in subs.(2)(a)) and, thereafter, any preliminary issues (as found in subs.(2)(b)) must be intimated in advance of the appropriate diet; not less than two days before a first diet, and at least seven days before any preliminary diet. Subs.(1) does permit later lodging of notices on cause shown but this has to be viewed as an exceptional measure, and will bring the provisions of subs.(4) into play; the court may then fix a further first or preliminary diet or continue the issues for a hearing at the trial diet, before a jury is selected.

Subs.(3) serves notice that any argument of want of citation has to be directed towards showing the prejudice or confusion caused to the accused—minor errors or discrepancies will not be regarded as fatal to the proceedings.

Attention is drawn to the observations of the Appeal Court in *HM Advocate v Crawford*, High Court of Justiciary, November 22, 2005, unreported, a case discussed in the Notes to ss.64 and 65 above. "There have to be very compelling reasons before technicalities in procedure, even of a fundamental nature, can be used to avoid a prosecution. It is a fundamental part of our criminal justice system that if technicalities are available to be taken by the defence, they must have a positive result in a sense of prejudice to the accused".

Objections to admissibility of evidence raised after first diet or preliminary hearing

79A.—(1) This section applies where a party seeks to raise an objection to the admissibility of any evidence after—

(a) in proceedings in the High Court, the preliminary hearing; or

(b) in proceedings on indictment in the sheriff court, the first diet.

(2) The court shall not, under section 79(1) of this Act, grant leave for the objection to be raised if the party seeking to raise it has not given written notice of his intention to do so to the other parties.

(3) However, the court may, where the party seeks to raise the objection after the commencement of the trial, dispense with the requirement under subsection (2) above for written notice to be given.

(4) Where the party seeks to raise the objection after the commencement of the trial, the court shall not, under section 79(1) of this Act, grant leave for the objection to be raised unless it considers that it could not reasonably have been raised before that time.

(5) Where the party seeks to raise the objection before the commencement of the trial and the court, under section 79(1), grants leave for it to be raised, the court shall—

(a) if it considers it appropriate to do so, appoint a diet to be held before the commencement of the trial for the purpose of disposing of the objection; or

(b) dispose of the objection at the trial diet.

(6) In appointing a diet under subsection (5)(a) above, the court may postpone the trial diet for such period as appears to it to be appropriate and may, if it thinks fit, direct that such period (or some part of it) shall not count towards any time limit applying in respect of the case.

(7) The accused shall appear at any diet appointed under subsection (5)(a) above.

(8) For the purposes of this section, the trial shall be taken to commence when the jury is sworn.

AMENDMENT

Section 79A inserted by the Criminal Procedure (Amendment) (Scotland) Act 2004 (asp 5), s.14(2). Brought into force on February 1, 2005 by the Criminal Procedure (Amendment) (Scotland) Act 2004 (Commencement, Transitional Provisions and Savings) Order 2004 (SSI 2004/405 (C.28)), art.2(1).

DEFINITIONS

"diet": s.307(1).
"indictment": s.307(1).
"preliminary issues": s.79(2)(b).
"preliminary pleas": s.79(2)(a).
"prosecutor": s.307(1).

GENERAL NOTE

The Act stipulates in s.79(2)(b)(iv) that an objection to the admissibility of evidence is now a preliminary issue and, as such, ordinarily should be taken by written notice, timeously served on other parties, at a first or preliminary diet. Such an objection can be raised at these diets even without the requisite period of notice but with leave of the court (see ss.71(2)(YA) and 72(6)(c)).

The present section deals with circumstances where objection to admissibility has not been taken by the time of the first, or preliminary, diet. Even in this situation it is envisaged that objection will first be made known by written notice (subs. (2)), but subs.(3) tacitly acknowledges this to be a counsel of perfection in trial situations and permits the court to dispense with written notice.

Objections intimated late

Such objections should be intimated in writing, albeit late, by using Form 9B.1 in the Act of Adjournal (Criminal Procedure Rules Amendment) (Criminal Procedure (Amendment) (Scotland) Act 2004) 2005 (SSI 2005/44).

Subss.(5) and (6) addresses late objections to admissibility intimated before the trial diet: in these circumstances if the court permits late intimation it may fix a fresh first, or preliminary, diet to consider the merits, order the appearance of the accused and postpone the trial diet and discount any part of the intervening period from any time bar calculation; alternatively, defer the issue to be resolved during the trial.

Objections intimated in the course of trial

Subs.(3) preserves the court's long-established power to consider objections to admissibility of evidence in the course of the trial without the prior written notice now demanded in s.79. However, it is important to note that, since it is now expected that such an objection will be taken in advance of the trial, it can only be taken in the course of the trial once the court has been satisfied that it could not reasonably have been raised earlier. Only once this test has been met can the court move on to consider the merits of the objection.

Alteration, etc, of diet

Alteration and postponement of trial diet
80. [...]

AMENDMENT

Section 80 repealed by the Criminal Procedure (Amendment) (Scotland) Act 2004 (asp 4), s.25 and Sch.1, para.26. Brought into force on February 1, 2005 by the Criminal Procedure (Amendment) (Scotland) Act 2004 (Commencement, Transitional Provisions and Savings) Order 2004 (SSI 2004/405 (C.28)), art.2.

Procedure where trial does proceed
81.—(1) The prosecutor shall not raise a fresh libel in a case in which the court has deserted the trial simpliciter unless the court's decision has been reversed on appeal.

(2) Where a trial diet in any proceedings on indictment is deserted pro loco et tempore the court may appoint a further trial diet for a later date and the accused shall appear and answer the indictment at that diet.

(3) In appointing a further trial diet under subsection (2) above, the court—

(a) shall have regard to the state of preparation of the prosecutor and the accused with respect to their cases and, in particular, to the likelihood of the case being ready to proceed to trial on the date to be appointed for the trial diet; and

(b) may, if it appears to the court that there are any preliminary pleas, preliminary issues or other matters which require to be, or could with advantage be, disposed of or ascertained before the trial diet, appoint a diet to be held before the trial diet for the purpose of disposing of or, as the case may be, ascertaining them.

(4) Subsection (5) below applies where, in any proceedings on indictment in which a trial diet has been appointed or the accused has been cited to a trial diet in the sheriff court—

(a) the diet has been deserted pro loco et tempore for any reason and no further trial diet has been appointed under subsection (2) above; or

(b) the indictment falls or is for any other reason not brought to trial and the diet has not been continued, adjourned or postponed.

(5) Where this subsection applies, the prosecutor may, at any time within the period of two months after the relevant date, give notice to the accused on another copy of the indictment to appear and answer the indictment—

(a) where the trial diet referred to in subsection (4) above was in the High Court—

(i) at a further preliminary hearing in that Court not less than seven clear days after service of the notice; or

(ii) where the charge is one that can lawfully be tried in the sheriff court, at a first diet not less than 15 clear days after service of the notice and not less than 10 clear days before the trial diet and at a trial diet not less than 29 clear days after service of the notice; or

(b) where the trial diet referred to in subsection (4) was in the sheriff court—

(i) at a further trial diet in that court not less than seven clear days after service of the notice; or

(ii) at a preliminary hearing in the High Court not less than 21 clear days after service of the notice.

(6) Where notice is given to the accused under paragraph (a)(ii) or (b)(ii) of subsection (5) above, then for the purposes of section 65(4) of this Act—

(a) the giving of the notice shall be taken to be service of an indictment in respect of—

(i) in the case of a notice under paragraph (a)(ii) of subsection (5) above, the sheriff court; or

(ii) in the case of a notice under paragraph (b)(ii) of that subsection, the High Court; and

(b) the previous service of the indictment in respect of—

(i) in the case of a notice under paragraph (a)(ii) of subsection (5), the High Court; or

(ii) in the case of a notice under paragraph (b)(ii) of that subsection, the sheriff court,

shall be disregarded.

(7) A notice under subsection (5) above shall be in such form as may be prescribed by Act of Adjournal, or as nearly as may be in such form.

(8) In subsection (5) above, "the relevant date" means—

(a) where paragraph (a) of subsection (4) applies, the date on which the trial diet was deserted as mentioned in that paragraph; or

(b) where paragraph (b) of that subsection applies, the date of the trial diet referred to in that subsection.

AMENDMENTS

Section 81 substituted by the Criminal Procedure (Amendment) (Scotland) Act 2004 (asp 5), s.9. Brought into force on February 1, 2005 by the Criminal Procedure (Amendment) (Scotland) Act 2004 (Commencement, Transitional Provisions and Savings) Order 2004 (SSI 2004/405 (C.28)), art.2.

Subs.(4) as amended by the Criminal Procedure (Amendment) (Scotland) Act 2004 (Incidental, Supplemental and Consequential Provisions) Order 2005 (SSI 2005/40), art.3.

DEFINITIONS

"diet": s.307(1).
"High Court": s.307(1).
"indictment": s.307(1).
"preliminary hearing": s.66(6)(b).
"preliminary issues": s.79(2)(b).
"preliminary pleas": s.79(2)(a).
"prosecutor": s.307(1).
"the relevant date": s.81A(8).
"witness": s.307(1).

GENERAL NOTE

These provisions apply to all solemn proceedings and set out the options available at the trial diet should trial not proceed.

Subs.(1)

Subs.(1) simply restates the existing law.

Subs.(2)

Subs.(2) introduces a procedural innovation; where traditionally a trial did not proceed in a sitting, it would be adjourned on a Crown motion, with the court having little option but to grant the motion unless it saw fit to desert *simpliciter.*

Now when the Crown opts to desert *pro loco et tempore* it is open to the court to fix a new trial diet there and then with the existing indictment. Whereas service of a fresh indictment would enable any perceived defects in the indictment, and any s.67 material, to be incorporated into the libel, or the *forum* of proceedings to be changed, preservation of the existing indictment using s.81(2) is unlikely to be a particularly flexible procedural instrument; its primary effect would be to avoid the need for service of a new indictment, or it would seem associated s.67 notices, but that is not the benefit it once was now that service can be effected lawfully in the hands of the accused's solicitor (see s.66(6C) above). Note, however, that subs.(3) also enables the court to appoint a fresh preliminary, or first, diet.

Subs.(2) can be used to re-indict for trial (in sheriff solemn cases at least) in the same *sitting* if that becomes necessary. The same indictment, notices and any defences would remain valid and the case could be empanelled using a fresh jury assize. See *H.M. Advocate v Johnstone and Kennedy*, Forfar High Court sitting, March 25, 2002, unreported.

Subss.(3) and (4)

Familiar (but until now little-used) provisions which apply only at the time of the trial diet are repeated, and can be applied when the court either has made no order under subs.(2) or has made no order at all. The Crown is authorised to serve a copy of the indictment on the accused with a reduced *induciae.* A cautionary note is necessary—using these provisions it is submitted that it becomes necessary to re-serve any s.67 notices.

Different timescales affect High Court and sheriff solemn proceedings and reflect the quite different procedural regimes which now figure in each forum subject to the general comment that use of the abbreviated procedures can only occur within two months of the "relevant date" (see subs.(8)). It also becomes possible to switch the case from the higher to the lower court or *vice versa* for trial (see subs.(5)(a)(ii) and (b)(ii)) in either case extending the *induciae*, presumably to effect the transfer of papers. Generally, however, a case can be re-indicted on an *induciae* of as little as seven days—in the High Court to a new preliminary diet—and to a fresh trial diet in the sheriff court; this permits a high degree of flexibility in the allocation of trial business.

Subs.(8)

This sets out the two-month timescale which governs use of the section's provisions. Calculation of that period in High Court cases ought to be straightforward since a trial diet will have been assigned a definite date, but less so in sheriff solemn cases where cases are indicted to a sitting. Some caution will be required in utilising the provisions of subs.(4)(b) in the sheriff court for that reason.

Act of Adjournal

The notice specified in subs.(1) follows the style of Form 8.2-B set out in the 1996 Act of Adjournal. In the case of libels involving "listed sexual offences" under s.288C below, Form 8.2-B is to be used.

Desertion or postponement where accused in custody

82. Where—

(a) a diet is deserted *pro loco et tempore*;

(b) a diet is continued, accelerated, postponed or adjourned; or

(c) an order is issued for the trial to take place at a different place from that first given notice of, or, in the case of proceedings in the High Court, originally appointed by the Court,

the warrant of committal on which the accused is at the time in custody till liberated in due course of law shall continue in force.

AMENDMENT

Subss.(b) and (c) as amended by the Criminal Procedure (Amendment) (Scotland) Act 2004 (asp 5), s.25 and Sch.1, para.27. Brought into force on February 1, 2005 by the Criminal Procedure (Amendment) (Scotland) Act 2004 (Commencement, Transitional Provisions and Savings) Order 2004 (SSI 2004/405 (C.28)), art.2.

GENERAL NOTE

This section keeps the original committal warrant extant in circumstances where the indictment served has not proceeded to trial or a plea.

Circumstances giving rise to the need to keep the original warrant alive occur in cases of postponement under ss.71(7) and 72(4), s.74(3), adjournment of a trial diet by s.80(1) and desertion *pro loco et tempore* in terms of s.81(1)(a); s.82(c) relates both to situations in which the prosecutor alters the forum of trial (s.81(1)), or the court, before trial, in accordance with s.83 below, grants the prosecutor's motion to transfer the trial to another sheriff court in the sheriffdom.

Transfer of sheriff court solemn proceedings

83.—(1) Where an accused person has been cited to attend a diet of the sheriff court the prosecutor may apply to the sheriff for an order for the transfer of the proceedings to a sheriff court in another district in that sheriffdom and for adjournment to a diet of that court.

(1A) Where—

(a) an accused person has been cited to attend a diet of the sheriff court; or

(b) paragraph (a) above does not apply but it is competent so to cite an accused person,

and the prosecutor is informed by the sheriff clerk that, because of exceptional circumstances which could not reasonably have been foreseen, it is not practicable for that court (in subsection (2A)(b)(i) below referred to as the "relevant court") or any other sheriff court in that sheriffdom to proceed with the case, the prosecutor—

(i) may, where paragraph (b) above applies, so cite the accused; and

(ii) shall, where paragraph (a) above applies or the accused is so cited by virtue of paragraph (i) above, as soon as practicable apply to the sheriff principal for an order for the transfer of the proceedings to a sheriff court in another sheriffdom and for adjournment to a diet of that court.

(2) On an application under subsection (1) above the sheriff may—

(a) after giving the accused or his counsel or solicitor an opportunity to be heard; or

(b) on the joint application of the parties,

make such order as is mentioned in that subsection.

(2A) On an application under subsection (1A) above the sheriff principal may make the order sought—

(a) provided that the sheriff principal of the other sheriffdom consents; but

(b) in a case where the trial (or part of the trial) would be transferred, shall do so only—

(i) if the sheriff of the relevant court, after giving the accused or his counsel an opportunity to be heard, consents to the transfer; or

(ii) on the joint application of the parties.

(2B) On the application of the prosecutor, a sheriff principal who has made an order under subsection (2A) above may, if the sheriff principal of the other sheriffdom mentioned in that subsection consents—

(a) revoke; or

(ii) vary so as to restrict the effect of,

that order.

(2C) The sheriff may proceed under subsection (2) above on a joint application of the parties without hearing the parties and, accordingly, he may dispense with any hearing previously appointed for the purposes of considering the application.

(3) [...]

AMENDMENTS

Subs.(1) substituted by the Crime and Punishment (Scotland) Act 1997 (c.48), s.62(1) and Sch.1, para.21(12)(a) with effect from August 1, 1997 in terms of the Crime and Punishment (Scotland) Act 1997 (Commencement and Transitional Provisions) Order 1997 (SI 1997/1712), art.3.

Subss.(2) and (3) inserted by s.62(1) and Sch.1, para.21(12) of the above Act with effect from August 1, 1997 by means of the above Order.

Subss.(1), (2) and (3) as amended, and subss.(1A), (2A) and (2B) inserted, by Criminal Justice (Scotland) Act 2003 (asp 7), Part 8, s.58. Brought into force on June 27, 2003 by the Criminal Justice (Scotland) Act 2003 (Commencement No.1) Order 2003 (SSI 2003/288 (C.14)).

Section 83 as amended by the Criminal Procedure (Amendment) (Scotland) Act 2004 (asp 5), s.25 and Sch.1, para.28. Brought into force on February 1, 2005 by the Criminal Procedure (Amendment) (Scotland) Act 2004 (Commencement, Transitional Provisions and Savings) Order 2004 (SSI 2004/405 (C.28)), art.2.

DEFINITION

"prosecutor": s.307(1).

GENERAL NOTE

This provision was introduced into the 1975 Act by Sch.6, para.41 of the Criminal Justice (Scotland) Act 1995 and is untested. The only changes of note introduced by the 2004 Act are the ability to use these provisions at any point once a case has been indicted; previously, the section only applied to cases due in a trial sitting; and by subs.(2C) to enable the transfer to be effected administratively if parties are agreed. The most obvious use of this section is to permit the transfer of a case to a court equipped to take the evidence of a child via a live television link (see s.271(9) and (10) below), but the section is widely drafted and could, for example, be used to enable the transfer of a sitting to another sheriff court in the sheriffdom if a previous sitting had badly overrun. The amendments introduced by the 1997 Act are of a technical nature, but serve to ensure that the original warrant to cite the accused and witnesses holds good despite any change of venue. Note, however, that s.83 makes no provision for extension of any time bar; reference still has to be had to the general provisions of s.65 above.

The amendments introduced by the Criminal Justice (Scotland) Act 2003 (asp 7) improve mechanisms for the transfer of solemn business to another part of the sheriffdom or, as subs.(1A) now provides, to transfer that business to another sheriffdom in exceptional circumstances. In part this has been a response to the potential for disruption which movement restrictions in areas recently affected by foot and mouth disease had to face. The measures in subs.(1) can be used to deal with pressure of business, or the need for special court facilities available elsewhere in the sheriffdom or perhaps to move proceedings out of the immediate vicinity to preserve public order; by contrast, the provisions in subs.(1A) deal with much less routine situations, are initiated by the sheriff clerk (though it falls to the prosecutor to intimate the application to the accused) and can only be begun with the mutual consent of the affected sheriff principals (subs. (2A)). It falls to the sheriff principal of the original jurisdiction to vary or rescind a transfer order.

(The equivalent summary provisions are set out in ss.137, 137A and 137B of the Act as now amended).

Continuation of trial diet in the High Court

Continuation of trial diet in the High Court

83A.—(1) Where, in any case which is to be tried in the High Court, the trial diet does not commence on the day appointed for the holding of the diet, the indictment shall fall.

(2) However, where, in appointing a day for the holding of the trial diet, the Court has indicated that the diet is to be a floating diet, the diet and, if it is adjourned, the adjourned diet may, without having been commenced, be continued from sitting day to sitting day—

(a) by minute, in such form as may be prescribed by Act of Adjournal, signed by the Clerk of Justiciary; and

(b) up to such maximum number of sitting days after the day originally appointed for the trial diet as may be so prescribed.

(3) If such a trial diet or adjourned diet is not commenced by the end of the last sitting day to which it may be continued by virtue of subsection (2)(b) above, the indictment shall fall.

(4) For the purposes of this section, a trial diet or adjourned trial diet shall be taken to commence when it is called.

(5) In this section, "sitting day" means any day on which the court is sitting, but does not include any Saturday or Sunday or any day which is a court holiday.

AMENDMENT

Section 83A inserted by the Criminal Procedure (Amendment) (Scotland) Act 2004 (asp 5), s.5. Brought into force on February 1, 2005 by the Criminal Procedure (Amendment) (Scotland) Act 2004 (Commencement, Transitional Provisions and Savings) Order 2004 (SSI 2004/405 (C.28)), art.2.

DEFINITIONS

"Clerk of Justiciary": s.307(1).
"diet": s.307(1).
"indictment": s.307(1).
"sitting day": s.83A(5).

GENERAL NOTE

The section applies only to High Court proceedings and contains the mechanisms for the fixed and floating trial diets now in place. Following resolution of preliminary pleas and preliminary issues at the preliminary diet, and the recording of pleas, the court will then have assigned any necessary trial to either a fixed diet or a floating trial diet.

Subss.(1) and (4)

An indictment assigned to a fixed trial diet must call on that day. The intention is that the trial should then commence but subs.(4) requires only that the diet be called, not that either a jury be empanelled or evidence led.

Subss.(2) and (3)

Much like a trial assigned to a traditional sitting, a floating trial diet can call for trial within the window of dates previously determined by the court, without having to call day on day. If the case does not proceed to trial, the Crown will require to consider whether to commence the trial diet, *i.e.* call the case, to seek an adjournment and thus preserve the existing indictment, or simply not call the case at all, bearing in mind the need to comply with the (now) revised timebar provisions in s.65 of the Act.

Jurors for sittings

Juries: returns of jurors and preparation of lists

84.—(1) For the purposes of a trial, the sheriff principal shall return such number of jurors as he thinks fit or, in relation to a trial in the High Court, such other number as the Lord Justice Clerk or any Lord Commissioner of Justiciary may direct.

(2) The Lord Justice General, whom failing the Lord Justice Clerk, may give directions as to the areas from which and the proportions in which jurors are to be summoned for trials to be held in the High Court, and for any such trial the sheriff principal of the sheriffdom in which the trial is to take place shall requisition the required number of jurors from the areas and in the proportions so specified.

(3) Where a sitting of the High Court is to be held at a town in which the High Court does not usually sit, the jury summoned to try any case in such a sitting shall be summoned from the list of potential jurors of the sheriff court district in which the town is situated.

(4) For the purpose of a trial in the sheriff court, the clerk of court shall be furnished with a list of names from lists of potential jurors of the sheriff court district in which the court is held containing the number of persons required.

(5) The sheriff principal, in any return of jurors made by him to a court, shall take the names in regular order, beginning at the top of the list of potential jurors in each of the sheriff court districts, as required; and as often as a juror is returned to him, he shall mark or cause to be marked, in the list of potential jurors of the respective sheriff court districts the date when any such juror was returned to serve; and in any such return he shall commence with the name immediately after the last in the preceding return, without regard to the court to which the return was last made, and taking the subsequent names in the order in which they are entered, as directed by this subsection, and so to the end of the lists respectively.

(6) Where a person whose name has been entered in the lists of potential jurors dies, or ceases to be qualified to serve as a juror, the sheriff principal, in making returns of jurors in accordance with the Jurors (Scotland) Act 1825, shall pass over the name of that person, but the date at which his name has been so passed over, and the reason therefor, shall be entered at the time in the lists of potential jurors.

(7) Only the lists returned in accordance with this section by the sheriffs principal to the clerks of court shall be used for the trials for which they were required.

(8) The persons to serve as jurors at trials in the High Court sitting at a particular place on a particular day shall be listed and their names and addresses shall be inserted in one roll, and the list made up under this section shall be known as the "list of assize".

(9) When more than one case is set down for trial in the High Court sitting at a particular place on a particular day, it shall not be necessary to prepare more than one list of assize, and such list shall be the list of assize for all trials to be held in the High Court sitting in that particular place on that particular day; and the persons included in such list shall be summoned to serve generally for all such trials, and only one general execution of citation shall be returned against them; and a copy of the list of assize, certified by one of the clerks of court, shall have the like effect, for all purposes for which the list may be required, as the principal list of assize authenticated as aforesaid.

(10) No irregularity in—

(a) making up the lists in accordance with the provisions of this Act;

(b) transmitting the lists;

(c) [...]

(d) summoning jurors; or

(e) in returning any execution of citation,

shall constitute an objection to jurors whose names are included in the jury list, subject to the ruling of the court in relation to the effect of an objection as to any criminal act by which jurors may be returned to serve in any case contrary to this Act or the Jurors (Scotland) Act 1825.

AMENDMENT

Subs.(8) and (9) as amended, and subs.10(c) repealed, by the Criminal Procedure (Amendment) (Scotland) Act 2004 (asp 5), s.25 and Sch.1, para.29. Brought into force on February 1, 2005 by the Criminal Procedure (Amendment) (Scotland) Act 2004 (Commencement, Transitional Provisions and Savings) Order 2004 (SSI 2004/405 (C.28)), art.2.

DEFINITIONS

"High Court": s.307(1).
"Lord Commissioner of Justiciary": s.307(1).
"Lord Justice Clerk": s.307(1).
"Lord Justice General": s.1(1).

GENERAL NOTE

This section lays out the administrative procedures to be followed in drawing up and maintaining a list of assize. Particularly note that subs.(9) makes it competent for those who have served on a jury during the sitting to be balloted for later trials in the sitting.

Rule 13.1 of the 1996 Act of Adjournal requires the clerk of court to pay heed to the postponement or adjournment of trials under s.74(5), the postponement of trial following upon the withdrawal of an accelerated plea of guilty (s.76(3)) and the alteration and postponement of a trial during a sitting, when drawing up lists of jurors.

Act of Adjournal

Refer to Chap.13 of the 1996 Act of Adjournal.

Juries: citation and attendance of jurors

85.—(1) It shall not be necessary to serve any list of jurors upon the accused

...

(2) A list of jurors shall—

(a) be prepared and kept in such form and manner; and

(b) contain such minimum number of names,

as may be prescribed by Act of Adjournal.

(2A) The clerk of the court before which the trial is to take place shall, on an application made to him by or on behalf of an accused, supply the accused, free of charge on the day on which the trial diet is called, and before the oath has been administered to the jurors for the trial of the accused, with a copy of a list of jurors prepared under subsection (2) above.

(2B) Where an accused has been supplied under subsection (2A) above with a list of jurors—

(a) neither he nor any person acting on his behalf shall make a copy of that list, or any part thereof; and

(b) he or his representatives shall return the list to the clerk of the court after the oath has been administered to the jurors for his trial.

(2C) A person who fails to comply with subsection (2B) above shall be guilty of an offence and shall be liable on summary conviction to a fine not exceeding level 1 on the standard scale.

(3) It shall not be necessary to summon all the jurors contained in any list of jurors under this Act, but it shall be competent to summon such jurors only, commencing from the top of the list, as may be necessary to ensure a sufficient number for the trial of the cases which remain for trial at the date of the citation of the jurors, and such number shall be fixed by the clerk of the court in which the trial diet is to be called, or in any case in the High Court by the Clerk of Justiciary, and the jurors who are not so summoned shall be placed upon the next list issued, until they have attended to serve.

(4) The sheriff clerk of the sheriffdom in which the High Court is to sit or the sheriff clerk of the sheriff court district in which any juror is to be cited where the citation is for a trial before a sheriff, shall fill up and sign a proper citation addressed to each such juror, and shall cause the same to be transmitted to him by letter, sent to him at his place of residence as stated in the lists of potential jurors by registered post or recorded delivery or to be served on him by an officer of law; and a certificate under the hand of such sheriff clerk of the citation of any jurors or juror in the manner provided in this subsection shall be a legal citation.

(5) The sheriff clerk of the sheriffdom in which the High Court is to sit on any particular day shall issue citations to the whole jurors required for trials to be held in the High Court sitting in the sheriffdom on that day, whether the jurors reside in that or in any other sheriffdom.

(6) Persons cited to attend as jurors may, unless they have been excused in respect thereof under section 1 of the Law Reform (Miscellaneous Provisions) (Scotland) Act 1980, be fined up to level 3 on the standard scale if they fail to attend in compliance with the citation.

(7) A fine imposed under subsection (6) above may, on application, be remitted—

(a) by a Lord Commissioner of Justiciary where imposed in the High Court;

(b) by the sheriff court where imposed in the sheriff court,

and no court fees or expenses shall be exigible in respect of any such application.

(8) A person shall not be exempted by sex or marriage from the liability to serve as a juror.

AMENDMENTS

Subss.(1) and (2) as amended by the Crime and Punishment (Scotland) Act 1997 (c.48), s.58 with effect from August 1, 1997 (Commencement and Transitional Provisions) Order 1997 (SI 1997/1712), art.3.

Subs.(2), (4) and (5) as amended by the Criminal Procedure (Amendment) (Scotland) Act 2004 (asp 5), s.25 and Sch.1, para.30. Brought into force on February 1, 2005 by the Criminal Procedure (Amendment) (Scotland) Act 2004 (Commencement, Transitional Provisions and Savings) Order 2004 (SSI 2004/405 (C.28)), art.2.

DEFINITIONS

"Clerk of Justiciary": s.307(1).
"High Court": s.307(1).
"indictment": s.307(1).
"Lord Commissioner of Justiciary": s.307(1).
"sheriff clerk": s.307(1).

GENERAL NOTE

This section, amended by the 1997 Act, removes the accused's right to receive a copy of the List of Assize once his indictment has been served upon him; from August 1, 1997 the right is limited to sight of the Assize List on the day the case is called for trial.

The modified provision is directed against intimidation of jurors and was introduced into the 1997 Act at a late stage (January 20, 1997) without opposition. "Jury nobbling" has become a recognised phenomenon in other jurisdictions and the potential for abuse which advance access to jurors' particulars could present is obvious. Concern was heightened by the discovery of a current High Court Assize List circulating amongst prisoners.

Both the accused and his agent are only entitled to sight of the Assize List on the day the indictment calls for trial and may neither retain, nor copy, the List which must be returned to the Clerk once the jury is empannelled. It will be noted that subs.(2B) creates a criminal offence for any breach of that provision.

Persons made subject to probation, drug testing and treatment, community service, restriction of liberty and community orders either before or after the coming into force of s.78 of the Criminal Justice (Scotland) Act 2003 (asp 7) on June 27, 2003 are disqualified from jury service. A saving provision in subs.(3) requires the individual cited for service to attend the assize nonetheless.

Jurors: excusal and objections

86.—(1) Where, before a juror is sworn to serve, the parties jointly apply for him to be excused the court shall, notwithstanding that no reason is given in the application, excuse that juror from service.

(2) Nothing in subsection (1) above shall affect the right of the accused or the prosecutor to object to any juror on cause shown.

(3) If any objection is taken to a juror on cause shown and such objection is founded on the want of sufficient qualification as provided by section 1(1) of the Law Reform (Miscellaneous Provisions) (Scotland) Act 1980, such objection shall be proved only by the oath of the juror objected to.

(4) No objection to a juror shall be competent after he has been sworn to serve.

DEFINITION

"prosecutor": s.307(1).

GENERAL NOTE

The right of peremptory challenge to a number of jurors without showing cause was abolished by s.8 of the Criminal Justice (Scotland) Act 1995 and subs.(1) was substituted; where parties concur, jurors can still be excused without cause being shown, a measure largely intended to enable patently unsuitable or unfit jurors to be relieved of possible selection without open challenge. Although the obvious time for such an agreement to be reached is when the assize presents itself for ballot, the section does not rule out an earlier agreement between parties after the list of assize has been inspected. The court has no power to intervene in the matter.

Subsection (2) preserves the traditional right of challenge on cause shown to a juror selected in the ballot. "Cause shown" has to relate to the juror personally and to his inability to try the case impartially or without importing personal knowledge of the circumstances of the alleged offence or of the parties listed in the indictment. So in *H.M. Advocate v Devine* (1962) 78 S.C. Rep. 173, objection on the basis that a juror had already served on a jury in the same assize dealing with a similar incident to that now libelled at the same *locus*, and might thus be against the accused, was repelled.

In *McCadden v H.M. Advocate*, 1985 S.C.C.R. 282 the court disfavoured any suggestion that vetting of a jury was permissible. Objections to jurors must be stated as subs.(4) provides, before the jury is sworn; thereafter they cannot be entertained (also see *McArthur v H.M. Advocate*, 1902 S.L.T. 310).

The Law Reform (Miscellaneous Provisions) (Scotland) Act 1980 (c.55), s.1(1) broadly enacts that persons aged between 18 and 65 years, ordinarily resident in the United Kingdom and registered as an elector are qualified for jury service; those persons exempted, barred or disqualified from jury service are detailed in Sch.I to that Act.

Non-availability of judge

Non-availability of judge

87.—(1) Where the court is unable to proceed owing to the death, illness or absence of the presiding judge, the clerk of court may convene the court (if necessary) and—

    (a) in a case where no evidence has been led, adjourn the diet and any other diet appointed for the same day to—

        (i) a time later the same day, or a date not more than seven days later, when he believes a judge will be available; or

        (ii) a later date not more than two months after the date of the adjournment; or

    (b) in a case where evidence has been led—

        (i) adjourn the diet and any other diet appointed for the same day to a time later the same day, or a date not more than seven days later, when he believes a judge will be available; or

        (ii) with the consent of the parties, desert the diet *pro loco et tempore*.

(2) Where a diet has been adjourned under sub-paragraph (i) of either paragraph (a) or paragraph (b) of subsection (1) above the clerk of court may, where the conditions of that subsection continue to be satisfied, further adjourn the diet under that sub-paragraph; but the total period of such adjournments shall not exceed seven days.

(3) Where a diet has been adjourned under subsection (1)(b)(i) above the court may, at the adjourned diet—

    (a) further adjourn the diet; or

    (b) desert the diet *pro loco et tempore*.

(4) Where a diet is deserted in pursuance of subsection (1)(b)(ii) or (3)(b) above, the Lord Advocate may raise and insist in a new indictment, and—

    (a) where the accused is in custody it shall not be necessary to grant a new warrant for his incarceration, and the warrant or commitment on which he is at the time in custody till liberation in due course of law shall continue in force; and

    (b) where the accused is at liberty on bail, his bail shall continue in force.

AMENDMENT

   Subs.(1) as amended by the Criminal Procedure (Amendment) (Scotland) Act 2004 (asp 5), s.25 and Sch.1, para.31. Brought into force on February 1, 2005 by the Criminal Procedure (Amendment) (Scotland) Act 2004 (Commencement, Transitional Provisions and Savings) Order 2004 (SSI 2004/ 405 (C.28)), art.2.

DEFINITIONS

   "bail": s.307(1).

"indictment": s.307(1).

GENERAL NOTE

This section provides powers to the clerk of court in the event of illness or death of the presiding judge to convene the court and defer the day's business to a later date or dates.

Two different situations are envisaged: first, where no evidence has been led (subs.(1)(a)), the clerk may, in the absence of an available judge, adjourn any such case for a maximum of seven days to enable a judge to attend, or alternatively, *ex proprio motu* adjourn the case for up to two months. Subs.(2) limits the cumulative total of these adjournments to seven days.

On the other hand where evidence has already been led (subs.(1)(b)) the options are to adjourn the case for up to seven days, or with the consent of parties, desert the diet *pro loco et tempore*. In the absence of this consent, resort then has to be had to an adjournment of the trial for up to seven days; in terms of subs.(3) it only becomes competent (in the absence of the parties' concurrence) for the clerk to desert the diet after a first adjournment under subs.(1)(b)(i) has elapsed.

Subs.(4) maintains the right of the Lord Advocate, where a trial has been interrupted through the unavailability of the judge and has been deserted *pro loco et tempore*, to re-indict the case. While the original warrant for committal remains in force, and the Lord Advocate can "insist" upon the proceedings, which surely suggests that there would be no need to extend timebars, prudence would suggest it would be expedient to seek extensions of any timebars for the avoidance of any doubt.

Disposal of preliminary matters at trial diet

87A. Where—

(a) any preliminary plea or issue; or

(b) in a case to be tried in the High Court, any application, notice or other matter referred to in section 72(6)(b)(iii) or (iv) of this Act,

is to be disposed of at the trial diet, it shall be so disposed of before the jury is sworn, unless, where it is a preliminary issue consisting of an objection to the admissibility of any evidence, the court at the trial diet considers it is not capable of being disposed of before then.

AMENDMENT

Section 87A inserted by the Criminal Procedure (Amendment) (Scotland) Act 2004 (asp 5), s.13(2). Brought into force on February 1, 2005 by the Criminal Procedure (Amendment) (Scotland) Act 2004 (Commencement, Transitional Provisions and Savings) Order 2004 (SSI 2004/405 (C.28)), art.2.

DEFINITIONS

"High Court": s.307(1).
"preliminary issues": s.79(2)(b).
"preliminary pleas": s.79(2)(a).

GENERAL NOTE

Preliminary pleas or issues of related matters are now required to be disposed of at preliminary hearings but if they are to be disposed of at the trial diet then this section requires that they are disposed of before the jury is sworn. The section allows for the proviso (in effect a proof before answer) that where a preliminary issue consists of an objection to the admissibility of any evidence then it may be disposed of in the course of the trial diet.

Jury for trial

Plea of not guilty, balloting and swearing of jury, etc.

88.—(1) Where the accused pleads not guilty, the clerk of court shall record that fact and proceed to ballot the jury.

(2) The jurors for the trial shall be chosen in open court by ballot from the list

of persons summoned in such manner as shall be prescribed by Act of Adjournal, and the persons so chosen shall be the jury to try the accused, and their names shall be recorded in the minutes of the proceedings.

(3) It shall not be competent for the accused or the prosecutor to object to a juror on the ground that the juror has not been duly cited to attend.

(4) Notwithstanding subsecction (1) above, the jurors chosen for any particular trial may, when that trial is disposed of, without a new ballot serve on the trials of other accused, provided that—

(a) the accused and the prosecutor consent;

(b) the names of the jurors are contained in the list of jurors; and

(c) the jurors are duly sworn to serve on each successive trial.

(5) When the jury has been balloted, the clerk of court shall inform the jury of the charge against the accused—

(a) by reading the words of the indictment (with the substitution of the third person for the second); or

(b) if the presiding judge, because of the length or complexity of the indictment, so directs, by reading to the jury a summary of the charge approved by the judge,

and copies of the indictment shall be provided for each member of the jury without lists of witnesses or productions.

(6) After reading the charge as mentioned in subsection (5) above and any special defence as mentioned in section 89(1) of this Act, the clerk of court shall administer the oath in common form.

(7) The court may excuse a juror from serving on a trial where the juror has stated the ground for being excused in open court.

(8) Where a trial which is proceeding is adjourned from one day to another, the jury shall not be secluded during the adjournment, unless, on the motion of the prosecutor or the accused or *ex proprio motu* the court sees fit to order that the jury be kept secluded.

DEFINITION

"prosecutor": s.307(1).

GENERAL NOTE

This section deals with the selection of a trial jury from the list of assize prepared beforehand. Ch.14 of the Act of Adjournal 1996 regulates the mechanics of the ballot and Forms 14.3.-A and 14.3.-B respectively stipulate the oath or affirmation to be administered to all jurors. While parties can concur to excuse jurors without showing cause (see the notes to s.86 above), in any other case objection to a juror serving on the jury must be on cause shown: the right to peremptory challenge of jurors has been abolished. It remains the case that a juror who is not exempted or disqualified from service by the provisions of the Law Reform (Miscellaneous Provisions) (Scotland) Act 1980, s.1 must serve on the jury unless he can give reason in terms of subs.(7) why he should be excused. Ordinarily, personal knowledge of the circumstances of the case, or of the accused or witnesses, would be telling factors but ultimately the determining factor has to be whether the court can be assured that the juror can try the accused according to the evidence, without importing outside knowledge or prejudice; if there is any doubt, fairness dictates that the juror should not be called upon to serve. In *Hay v HM Advocate*, 1995 S.C.C.R. 639 an appeal was taken founding on the fact that two of the jurors had knowledge of the accused (a fact made known to the clerk and the sheriff by five of the assize) while a third juror had had dealings with an associate of the accused; no challenge had been given to the selection of the jury. The Appeal Court noted that the sheriff followed the guidance given in *Pullar v HM Advocate*, 1993 S.C.C.R. 514 and emphasised (at 643C) that the issues raised in the appeal should properly have been aired prior to the trial; the appeal against conviction was dismissed.

Before the jury is empanelled, the clerk of court is required to have made the assembled assize aware of the particulars of the accused and of any witness named in the charges on the indictment and to have advised them to inform him of any prior knowledge of these parties which they have (*Pullar v HM Advocate*).

The presiding judge should also make enquiry of the jurors once the indictment has been read to them and before evidence is led, if they know of any reason why they should not serve (*Spink v HM Advocate*, 1989 S.C.C.R. 413 and also *Russell v HM Advocate*, 1992 S.L.T. 25). The ineligibility of a juror for jury service will not of itself nullify a conviction; in the face of the terms of the juror's oath to try the accused solely on the evidence led, an appeal on these grounds would only succeed if it could be demonstrated to an objective standard that there was a lack of impartiality. See *R v HM Advocate*, 2005 G.W.D. 28–521, where a former police officer who had served in another police area, who had served on R's jury was disqualified from jury service, as ineligible, in a later trial in the same sitting.

Following *B v HM Advocate* 2006 S.L.T. 143,it would seem that the presiding sheriff, even before ordering the ballot of jurors, has to be content that there is an adequate number comprising the panel from which a ballot is to be made. The appellant principally objected to the sex mix of the selected jury (7 males and 15 females which, in the event, produced a jury of 3 men and 12 women) and did so when the case was called for trial. This submission was rejected by the sheriff who ordered the jury to be balloted. On appeal the court's approach was that the pool of available jurors for the assize on that day (only 22 from 60, and equal numbers of men and women, the missing 38 having been excused or failing to attend) was far too small; the sheriff ought to have considered an adjournment of the diet until the following day when a much larger pool was due to attend. It takes no prescience to predict primary legislation on the issues identified by the court. Authority was granted to the Crown for a retrial.

Subsection (4) re-enacts the rarely-used provision of s.132 of the 1975 Act: a jury which has just concluded a trial can be selected to sit in the following case in the sitting without the necessity of a ballot. However, this abbreviated procedure can only be used where; (i) the accused and the Crown consent and thus have no challenge on cause shown and; (ii) the jurors themselves pronounce no personal knowledge of the case, the accused or witnesses. Furthermore, it is implicit that the whole of that prior jury must serve in the new case and subs.(4)(c) stipulates that the jury must be put on oath anew. A consent to the use of this shortened procedure can be withdrawn by an objection from the accused which is stated before the jury has been sworn (*Daniel or Donald Stuart, Re* (1829) Bell's Notes 237). Chapter 14 of the Act of Adjournal provides a short form of minute, recording the particulars of the jury by reference to the record of proceedings of the previous trial.

While subs.(5)(b) allows for a summary form of the indictment charges approved by the judge to be read to the jury, it is interesting to note that this is not a matter which has to be addressed expressly at either a first or preliminary diet (the same observation could equally be made in relation to the provision in s.89(2) which allows for a condensed version of any special defence to be read to the jury instead of the notice intimated to the court).

Unempanelled jurors are not released until evidence is begun and the trial is lawfully under way.

Subsection (8) is broadly drafted. The statutory authority for the overnight accommodation of jurors who are deliberating upon their verdict is contained in s.99(4) below. Hence, subs.(8) would appear to be intended for use at earlier points in the trial, while evidence is still being led.

Jury to be informed of special defence

89.—(1) Subject to subsection (2) below, where the accused has lodged a plea of special defence, the clerk of court shall, after informing the jury, in accordance with section 88(5) of this Act, of the charge against the accused, and before administering the oath, read to the jury the plea of special defence.

(2) Where the presiding judge on cause shown so directs, the plea of special defence shall not be read over to the jury in accordance with subsection (1) above; and in any such case the judge shall inform the jury of the lodging of the plea and of the general nature of the special defence.

(3) Copies of a plea of special defences shall be provided for each member of the jury.

DEFINITION

"judge": s.307(1).

GENERAL NOTE

Section 78 of the Act requires that any special defence must be intimated to the court, and all other parties, at or before the first diet in sheriff solemn cases, and not less than seven clear days before the preliminary diet in High Court proceedings. Although it is possible to dispense with the preliminary diet in the High Court (s.72B) except, it is submitted, in cases involving listed sexual offences (see s.288C below), it remains the case in terms of s.72B(5) that the date of that diet still determines when notices have to be lodged and intimated. It will be noted that in addition to the well-understood categories of special defence, s.78(2) adds defences of coercion and automatism (see for the latter *Sorley v HM Advocate*, 1992 S.LT. 867 and *Ross v HM Advocate*, 1991 S.LT. 564) and, in s.288C cases, the defence of consent.

Once the indictment is read to the jury by the clerk of court, the next procedure is to read the terms of any special defence over to the jury. Failure to read over the special defence will not necessarily amount to a miscarriage of justice; see *Moar v HM Advocate*, 1949 J.C. 31. Indeed, it is often asserted that the only purpose of a notice of special defence is to give notice to the Crown of a possible line of defence evidence and, accordingly, the reading over of the terms of a notice which may not ultimately form a part of the defence case is both unnecessary and likely to confuse. Refer to *Mullen v HM Advocate*, 1978 S.L.T. (Notes) 33. Nonetheless, the provisions of s.89 are unequivocal: the terms of the notice must be made known to the jury before the trial begins. Subsection (2) allows the judge following a motion by one or other of the parties to withhold the full terms of the notice from the jury and to substitute a condensed account of the notice's meaning. In this context it has to be assumed that the terms of subs.(3), which instructs the distribution of copies of the notice of special defence, would not be adhered to, since that would appear to defeat the purpose of editing the original notice as lodged.

A plea of insanity must always be made known to the jury since the accused's state of mind at the time of the commission of the crime is a fundamental issue. It is not proper to read over a notice of incrimination of a co-accused; see *Collins v HM Advocate*, 1991 S.C.C.R. 898.

Death or illness of jurors

90.—(1) Where in the course of a trial—

(a) a juror dies; or

(b) the court is satisfied that it is for any reason inappropriate for any juror to continue to serve as a juror,

the court may in its discretion, on an application made by the prosecutor or an accused, direct that the trial shall proceed before the remaining jurors (if they are not less than twelve in number), and where such direction is given the remaining jurors shall be deemed in all respects to be a properly constituted jury for the purpose of the trial and shall have power to return a verdict accordingly whether unanimous or, subject to subsection (2) below, by majority.

(2) The remaining jurors shall not be entitled to return a verdict of guilty by majority unless at least eight of their number are in favour of such verdict and if, in any such case, the remaining jurors inform the court that—

(a) fewer than eight of their number are in favour of a verdict of guilty; and

(b) there is not a majority in favour of any other verdict,

they shall be deemed to have returned a verdict of not guilty.

GENERAL NOTE

This section regulates the composition of the jury which, of course, must comprise of 15 people at the outset of the trial, and stipulates that a majority verdict in any case requires eight of the jury at least to favour a guilty verdict. Once the trial has begun, the size of the jury can be reduced by reason of death, illness or other suitable cause (including misconduct by a juror himself) but in no case can the trial proceed with a jury numbering less than 12 persons. Recent experience in long-running trials might have suggested that the preservation of jurors' numbers is no small feat; see for example the sheriff's note in *MacDonald v HM Advocate*, 1995 S.C.C.R. 663 which lends an insight into the major logistical problems experienced in lengthy trials.

The subsection does not of course require that the trial must proceed with a reduced number of jurors though that is the normal procedure; it would be open to the court to consider motions to desert the trial diet and to exercise such powers as were competent to the court under s.65 of the Act to extend statutory time-bars. However, in *HM Advocate v Khan*, 1997 S.C.C.R. 100 where a juror was certified unfit in the course of a trial, leaving less than 12 jurors to continue, and the sheriff refused a Crown motion to adjourn the trial for a period to permit the juror to return to health, instead deserting the trial *pro loco et tempore*, Crown advocation of that sentence was upheld, the Appeal Court having regard to both the length of proceedings and possible prejudice to the accused in a retrial.

The procedure to be followed when the jury seeks guidance on the calculation of their verdict is described in *Kerr v HM Advocate*, 1992 S.C.C.R. 281; 1992 S.L.T. 1031, where the trial judge was handed a slip of paper from the jury showing a split verdict, eight for acquittal, seven (the arithmetical majority) for guilt and after further direction a conviction resulted; quashed on appeal.

Obstructive witnesses

Apprehension of witnesses in proceedings on indictment

90A.—(1) In any proceedings on indictment, the court may, on the application of any of the parties, issue a warrant for the apprehension of a witness if subsection (2) or (3) below applies in relation to the witness.

(2) This subsection applies if the witness, having been duly cited to any diet in the proceedings, deliberately and obstructively fails to appear at the diet.

(3) This subsection applies if the court is satisfied by evidence on oath that the witness is being deliberately obstructive and is not likely to attend to give evidence at any diet in the proceedings without being compelled to do so.

(4) For the purposes of subsection (2) above, a witness who, having been duly cited to any diet, fails to appear at the diet is to be presumed, in the absence of any evidence to the contrary, to have so failed deliberately and obstructively.

(5) An application under subsection (1) above—

(a) may be made orally or in writing;

(b) if made in writing—

    (i) shall be in such form as may be prescribed by Act of Adjournal, or as nearly as may be in such form; and

    (ii) may be disposed of in court or in chambers after such inquiry or hearing (if any) as the court considers appropriate.

(6) A warrant issued under this section shall be in such form as may be prescribed by Act of Adjournal or as nearly as may be in such form.

(7) A warrant issued under this section in the form mentioned in subsection (6) above shall imply warrant to officers of law—

(a) to search for and apprehend the witness in respect of whom it is issued;

(b) to bring the witness before the court;

(c) in the meantime, to detain the witness in a police station, police cell or other convenient place; and

(d) so far as is necessary for the execution of the warrant, to break open shut and lockfast places.

(8) It shall not be competent, in any proceedings on indictment, for a court to issue a warrant for the apprehension of a witness otherwise than in accordance with this section.

(9) A person apprehended under a warrant issued under this section shall wherever practicable be brought before the court not later than in the course of the first day on which—

(a) in the case of a warrant issued by a single judge of the High Court, that Court;

(b) in any other case, the court,

is sitting after he is taken into custody.

(10) In this section and section 90B, "the court" means, except where the context requires otherwise—

(a) where the witness is to give evidence in proceedings in the High Court, a single judge of that Court; or

(b) where the witness is to give evidence in proceedings on indictment in the sheriff court, any sheriff court with jurisdiction in relation to the proceedings.

AMENDMENT

Section 90A inserted by the Criminal Procedure (Amendment) (Scotland) Act 2004 (asp 5), s.11. Brought into force on February 1, 2005 by the Criminal Procedure (Amendment) (Scotland) Act 2004 (Commencement, Transitional Provisions and Savings) Order 2004 (SSI 2004/405 (C.28)), art.2.

DEFINITIONS

"diet": s.307(1).
"indictment": s.307(1).
"the Court": s.90A(10).
"witness": s.307(1).

GENERAL NOTE

This section applies only to solemn proceedings and is in response to the conclusions of the Bonomy Report, "Modernising Justice in Scotland: The Reform of the High Court of Justiciary" (Scottish Executive, 2003) that witness problems were the cause of the bulk of Crown motions for adjournments of trial.

Thus, a substantial portion of the Criminal Procedure (Amendment) (Scotland) Act 2004 was devoted to policing errant or reluctant witnesses as can be seen from the following sections. It will be noted that the 1995 Act already contains provisions to permit the admission of the evidence of missing witnesses (s.259(2)(c)) and of prior statements by uncooperative witnesses at trial (s.259(2)(e)).

The present section enables any party to apply to the court by means of Form 13A.2-A in the Act of Adjournal (Criminal Procedure Rules Amendment) (Criminal Procedure (Amendment) (Scotland) Act 2004) 2005 (SSI 2005/44), or verbally at a diet, for a witness apprehension warrant. The section applies at any point in the proceedings and the application can be considered, as appropriate, in court or in chambers.

The court has to be satisfied that the witness has misconducted himself as specified in either subss.(2) or (3) and this is without prejudice to any right to reach a subsequent determination of contempt.

In the case of subs.(2) it is noted that a failure to appear at a cited diet will *prima facie* be construed as deliberate or wilful. Subs.(3) depends upon evidence on oath and suggests that conduct both before and after any successful service of a witness citation can be taken into account by the court.

The warrant is granted for execution by officers of law whose powers under warrant are set out in subs.(7); these echo the terms of ordinary search warrants but require the apprehended witness to be produced before a judge of the court which issued the warrant as soon as practicable. Generally, it has to be assumed that warrants will be sought by the Crown but application can competently be made by the defence. Section 90B deals with the options which the court can exercise in relation to the witness.

Orders in respect of witnesses apprehended under section 90A

90B.—(1) Where a witness is brought before the court in pursuance of a warrant issued under section 90A of this Act, the court shall, after giving the parties and the witness an opportunity to be heard, make an order—

(a) detaining the witness until the conclusion of the diet at which the witness is to give evidence;

(b) releasing the witness on bail; or

(c) liberating the witness.

(2) The court may make an order under subsection (1)(a) or (b) above only if it is satisfied that—

(a) the order is necessary with a view to securing that the witness appears at the diet at which the witness is to give evidence; and

(b) it is appropriate in all the circumstances to make the order.

(3) Subsection (1) above is without prejudice to any power of the court to—

(a) make a finding of contempt of court in respect of any failure of a witness to appear at a diet to which he has been duly cited; and

(b) dispose of the case accordingly.

(4) Where—

(a) an order under subsection (1)(a) above has been made in respect of a witness; and

(b) at, but before the conclusion of, the diet at which the witness is to give evidence, the court in which the diet is being held excuses the witness,

that court, on excusing the witness, may recall the order under subsection (1)(a) above and liberate the witness.

(5) On making an order under subsection (1)(b) above in respect of a witness, the court shall impose such conditions as it considers necessary with a view to securing that the witness appears at the diet at which he is to give evidence.

(6) However, the court may not impose as such a condition a requirement that the witness or a cautioner on his behalf deposit a sum of money in court.

(7) Where the court makes an order under subsection (1)(a) above in respect of a witness, the court shall, on the application of the witness—

(a) consider whether the imposition of a remote monitoring requirement would enable it to make an order under subsection (1)(b) above releasing the witness on bail subject to a movement restriction condition; and

(b) if so—

(i) make an order under subsection (1)(b) above releasing the witness on bail subject to such a condition (as well as such other conditions required to be imposed under subsection (5) above); and

(ii) in the order, impose, as a further condition under subsection (5) above, a remote monitoring requirement.

(8) Subsections (7) to (19) of section 24A of this Act apply in relation to remote monitoring requirements imposed under subsection (7)(b)(ii) above and to the imposing of such requirements as they apply to remote monitoring requirements imposed under section 24A(1) or (2) of this Act and the imposing of such requirements, but with the following modifications—

(a) references to a remote monitoring requirement imposed under section 24A(1) or (2) of this Act shall be read as if they included references to a remote monitoring requirement imposed under subsection (7)(b)(ii) above;

(b) references to the accused shall be read as if they were references to the witness in respect of whom the order under subsection (1)(b) above is made.

(9) The powers conferred and duties imposed by sections 24B to 24D of this Act are exercisable in relation to remote monitoring requirements imposed under subsection (7)(b)(ii) above as they are exercisable in relation to remote monitoring requirements imposed under subsection (1) or (2) of section 24A of this Act; and—

(a) references in those sections to remote monitoring requirements shall be read accordingly; and

(b) references to the imposition of any requirement as a further condition of bail shall be read as if they were references to the imposition of the requirement as a further condition under subsection (5) above.

(10) Section 25 of this Act (which makes provision for an order granting bail to specify the conditions imposed on bail and the accused's proper domicile of citation) shall apply in relation to an order under subsection (1)(b) above as it applies to an order granting bail, but with the following modifications—

(a) references to the accused shall be read as if they were references to the witness in respect of whom the order under subsection (1)(b) above is made;

(b) references to the order granting bail shall be read as if they were references to the order under subsection (1)(b) above;

(c) subsection (3) shall be read as if for the words from "relating" to "offence" in the third place where it occurs there were substituted "at which the witness is to give evidence".

(11) In this section—

(a) "a movement restriction condition" means, in relation to a witness released on bail under subsection (1)(b) above, a condition imposed under subsection (5) above restricting the witness's movements, including such a condition requiring the witness to be, or not to be, in any place or description of place for, or during, any period or periods or at any time.

(b) "a remote monitoring requirement" means, in relation to a movement restriction condition, a requirement that compliance with the condition be remotely monitored.

AMENDMENT

Section 90B inserted by the Criminal Procedure (Amendment) (Scotland) Act 2004 (asp 5), s.11. Brought into force (with exceptions) on February 1, 2005 by the Criminal Procedure (Amendment) (Scotland) Act 2004 (Commencement, Transitional Provisions and Savings) Order 2004 (SSI 2004/ 405 (C.28)), art.2.

DEFINITIONS

"a movement restriction condition": s.90A(11)(a).
"a remote monitoring requirement": s.90A(11)(b).
"bail": s.307(1).
"indictment": s.307(1).
"the Court": s.90A(10).
"witness": s.307(1).

GENERAL NOTE

Applying only to solemn proceedings, this section lays out the procedures for the court in dealing with a witness apprehended under a s.90A warrant. Previously, a witness apprehended on warrant was either held in custody to await a point when his evidence could be heard or had to petition the *nobile officium* for bail—a time-consuming, costly and not necessarily swift resolution.

The alternatives open to the court on the appearance from custody of the witness are described in subs.(1) but release on bail or a remand in custody pending the trial proceedings can only be deployed if the court is satisfied that the measure is appropriate to ensure appearance at the diet and no determination can be reached until both the parties and the witness himself have been heard.

Bail conditions much like those which apply to accused persons can be imposed and might, for example, require surrender of passport or signing at given times at a police station, but, following subs.(6), cannot include the finding of money bail or caution by the witness or a guarantor. Review of the conditions is competent; see s.90D of the Act. No less important, s.90E provides mechanisms for appealing decisions of the court, appeals being open to the witness, the Crown and the accused.

Breach of bail under section 90B(1)(b)

90C.—(1) A witness who, having been released on bail by virtue of an order under subsection (1)(b) of section 90B of this Act, fails without reasonable excuse—

(a) to appear at any diet to which he has been cited; or

(b) to comply with any condition imposed under subsection (5) of that section,

shall be guilty of an offence and liable on conviction on indictment to the penalties specified in subsection (2) below.

(2) Those penalties are—

(a) a fine; and

(b) imprisonment for a period not exceeding two years.

(3) Subsection (4) below applies in proceedings against a witness for an offence under paragraph (b) of subsection (1) above where the condition referred to in that paragraph is—

(a) a movement restriction condition (within the meaning of section 90B(11) of this Act) in respect of which a remote monitoring requirement has been imposed under section 90B(7)(b)(ii) of this Act; or

(b) a requirement imposed under section 24D(3)(b) (as extended by section 90B(9)) of this Act.

(4) In proceedings in which this subsection applies, evidence of—

(a) in the case referred to in subsection (3)(a) above, the presence or absence of the witness at a particular place at a particular time; or

(b) in the case referred to in subsection (3)(b) above, any tampering with or damage to a device worn or carried by the witness for the purpose of remotely monitoring his whereabouts,

may, subject to subsections (7) and (8) below, be given by the production of the document or documents referred to in subsection (5) below.

(5) That document or those documents is or are a document or documents bearing to be—

(a) a statement automatically produced by a device specified in regulations made under section 24D(4) (as extended by section 90B(9)) of this Act by which the witness's whereabouts were remotely monitored; and

(b) a certificate signed by a person nominated for the purpose of this paragraph by the Scottish Ministers that the statement relates to—

(i) in the case referred to in subsection (3)(a) above, the whereabouts of the witness at the dates and times shown in the statement; or

(ii) in the case referred to in subsection (3)(b) above, any tampering with or damage to the device.

(6) The statement and certificate mentioned in subsection (5) above shall, when produced in the proceedings, be sufficient evidence of the facts set out in them.

(7) Neither the statement nor the certificate mentioned in subsection (5) above shall be admissible in evidence unless a copy of both has been served on the witness prior to the trial.

(8) Without prejudice to subsection (7) above, where it appears to the court that the witness has had insufficient notice of the statement or certificate, it may adjourn the trial or make an order which it thinks appropriate in the circumstances.

(9) In subsections (7) and (8), "the trial" means the trial in the proceedings against the witness referred to in subsection (3) above.

(10) Section 28 of this Act shall apply in respect of a witness who has been released on bail by virtue of an order under section 90B(1)(b) of this Act as it applies to an accused released on bail, but with the following modifications—

(a) references to an accused shall be read as if they were references to the witness;

(b) in subsection (2), the reference to the court to which the accused's application for bail was first made shall be read as if it were a reference to the court which made the order under section 90B(1)(b) of this Act in respect of the witness; and

(c) in subsection (4)—

(i) references to the order granting bail and original order granting bail shall be read as if they were references to the order under section 90B(1)(b) and the original such order respectively;

(ii) paragraph (a) shall be read as if at the end there were inserted "and make an order under section 90B(1)(a) or (c) of this Act in respect of the witness"; and

(iii) paragraph (c) shall be read as if for the words from "complies" to the end there were substituted "appears at the diet at which the witness is to give evidence".

AMENDMENT

Section 90C inserted by the Criminal Procedure (Amendment) (Scotland) Act 2004 (asp 5), s.11. Brought into force (with exceptions) on February 1, 2005 by the Criminal Procedure (Amendment) (Scotland) Act 2004 (Commencement, Transitional Provisions and Savings) Order 2004 (SSI 2004/ 405 (C.28)), art.2.

DEFINITIONS

"bail": s.307(1).
"diet": s.307(1).
"trial": s.90C(9).
"witness": s.307(1).

GENERAL NOTE

This section creates offences for any breach of bail conditions by a witness and extends to matters of evidential proof where a remote monitoring requirement has been imposed. Powers of arrest without warrant, mirroring those applied to bailed accused by s.28 of the Act, are applied to witnesses by s.90C(10). Significantly, arrest can be used against a witness who, it is anticipated, is *likely* to breach his bail conditions.

Review of orders under section 90B(1)(a) or (b)

90D.—(1) Where a court has made an order under subsection (1)(a) of section 90B of this Act, the court may, on the application of the witness in respect of whom the order was made, on cause shown and after giving the parties and the witness an opportunity to be heard—

(a) recall the order; and

(b) make an order under subsection (1)(b) or (c) of that section in respect of the witness.

(2) Where a court has made an order under subsection (1)(b) of section 90B of this Act, the court may, after giving the parties and the witness an opportunity to be heard—

(a) on the application of the witness in respect of whom the order was made and on cause shown—

(i) review the conditions imposed under subsection (5) of that section at the time the order was made; and

(ii) make a new order under subsection (1)(b) of that section and impose different conditions under subsection (5) of that section;

(b) on the application of the party who made the application under section 90A(1) of this Act in respect of the witness, review the order and the conditions imposed under subsection (5) of that section at the time the order was made, and

(i) recall the order and make an order under subsection (1)(a) of that section in respect of the witness; or

(ii) make a new order under subsection (1)(b) of that section and impose different conditions under subsection (5) of that section.

(3) The court may not review an order by virtue of subsection (2)(b) above unless the party making the application puts before the court material information which was not available to it when it made the order which is the subject of the application.

(4) An application under this section by a witness—

(a) where it relates to the first order made under section 90B(1)(a) or (b) of this Act in respect of the witness, shall not be made before the fifth day after that order is made;

(b) where it relates to any subsequent such order, shall not be made before the fifteenth day after the order is made.

(5) On receipt of an application under subsection (2)(b) above the court shall—

(a) intimate the application to the witness in respect of whom the order which is the subject of the application was made;

(b) fix a diet for hearing the application and cite the witness to attend the diet; and

(c) where it considers that the interests of justice so require, grant warrant to arrest the witness.

(6) Nothing in this section shall affect any right of a person to appeal against an order under section 90B(1).

AMENDMENT

Section 90D inserted by the Criminal Procedure (Amendment) (Scotland) Act 2004 (asp 5), s.11. Brought into force on February 1, 2005 by the Criminal Procedure (Amendment) (Scotland) Act 2004 (Commencement, Transitional Provisions and Savings) Order 2004 (SSI 2004/405 (C.28)), art.2.

DEFINITIONS

"bail": s.307(1).
"diet": s.307(1).
"trial": s.90C(9).
"witness": s.307(1).

GENERAL NOTE

This section applies to witnesses in solemn proceedings and allows for review of the terms of a bail order, the making of a bail order where bail has previously been refused by the court and a material change in circumstances has occurred or fresh information is now available, or the outright removal of a bail order. All parties are entitled to be heard; note too that subs.(1) relates to any such application by the witness himself, while subs.(2)(b) is initiated by the party who originally craved the warrant for the witness' apprehension and has to be read in conjunction with subs.(5). Written application for a warrant in these circumstances should follow the style of Form 13A.2-A in the Act of Adjournal (Criminal Procedure Rules Amendment) (Criminal Procedure (Amendment) (Scotland) Act 2004) 2005 (SSI 2005/44).

By way of clarification, subs.(4) sets out the timescales for applications for review or further review of the court's decision; these apply only to applications by the affected witness.

Appeals in respect of orders under section 90B(1)

90E.—(1) Any of the parties specified in subsection (2) below may appeal to the High Court against—

(a) any order made under subsection (1)(a) or (c) of section 90B of this Act; or

(b) where an order is made under subsection (1)(b) of that section—

(i) the order;

(ii) any of the conditions imposed under subsection (5) of that section on the making of the order; or

(iii) both the order and any such conditions.

(2) The parties referred to in subsection (1) above are—

(a) the witness in respect of whom the order which is the subject of the appeal was made;

(b) the prosecutor; and

(c) the accused.

(3) A party making an appeal under subsection (1) above shall intimate it to the other parties specified in subsection (2) above and, for that purpose, intimation to the Lord Advocate shall be sufficient intimation to the prosecutor.

(4) An appeal under this section shall be disposed of by the High Court or any Lord Commissioner of Justiciary in court or in chambers after such inquiry and hearing of the parties as shall seem just.

(5) Where the witness in respect of whom the order which is the subject of an appeal under this section was made is under 21 years of age, section 51 of this Act shall apply to the High Court or, as the case may be, the Lord Commissioner of Justiciary when disposing of the appeal as it applies to a court when remanding or committing a person of the witness's age for trial or sentence.

AMENDMENT

Section 90E inserted by the Criminal Procedure (Amendment) (Scotland) Act 2004 (asp 5), s.11. Brought into force on February 1, 2005 by the Criminal Procedure (Amendment) (Scotland) Act 2004 (Commencement, Transitional Provisions and Savings) Order 2004 (SSI 2004/405 (C.28)), art.2.

DEFINITIONS

"High Court": s.307(1).
"prosecutor": s.307(1).
"witness": s.307(1).

GENERAL NOTE

Applying to solemn proceedings, this section enables appeals to the High Court by any witness refused witness bail or made subject to bail conditions which he considers to be unduly onerous. As with other bail orders in the Act, the prosecutor has a right of appeal but so too does an accused, or any co-accused. Subs.(5) specifies the form of remand facilities to be used for the detention of witnesses under 21 years of age by drawing upon the provisions of s.51 of the Act which ordinarily apply to accused persons.

Trial

Trial to be continuous

91. Every trial shall proceed from day to day until it is concluded unless the court sees cause to adjourn over a day or days.

GENERAL NOTE

Although it is generally the case that trials will continue from day to day until concluded, this section affords the presiding judge an element of discretion in allowing for variations from that norm when appropriate. See *MacDonald v H.M. Advocate*, 1995 S.C.C.R. 663 for an insight into the conduct of longer trials.

Section 102 below permits the interruption of proceedings to receive the verdict in another case. See also rr.14.8 and 14.9 of the 1996 Act of Adjournal.

Trial in presence of accused

92.—(1) Without prejudice to section 54 of this Act, and subject to subsections (2) and (2A) below, no part of a trial shall take place outwith the presence of the accused.

(2) If during the course of his trial an accused so misconducts himself that in the view of the court a proper trial cannot take place unless he is removed, the court may order—

    (a) that he is removed from the court for so long as his conduct makes it necessary; and

    (b) that the trial proceeds in his absence,

but if he is not legally represented the court shall appoint a solicitor to represent his interests during such absence.

(2A) If—

    (a) after evidence has been led which substantially implicates the accused in respect of the offence charged in the indictment or, where two or more offences are charged in the indictment, any of them, the accused fails to appear at the trial diet; and

    (b) the failure to appear occurred at a point in proceedings where the court is satisfied that it is in the interests of justice to do so,

then the court may, on the motion of the prosecutor and after hearing the parties on the motion, proceed with the trial and dispose of the case in the absence of the accused.

(2B) Where a motion is made under subsection (2A) above, the court shall—

    (a) if satisfied that there is a solicitor with authority to act for the purposes of—

        (i) representing the accused's interests at the hearing on the motion; and

        (ii) if the motion is granted, the accused's defence at the trial

    allow that solicitor to act for those purposes; or

    (b) if there is no such solicitor, at its own hand appoint a solicitor to act for those purposes.

(2C) It is the duty of a solicitor appointed under subsection (2) or (2B)(b) above to act in the best interests of the accused.

(2D) In all other respects, a solicitor so appointed has, and may be made subject to, the same obligations and has, and may be given, the same authority as if engaged by the accused; and any employment of and instructions given to counsel by the solicitor shall proceed and be treated accordingly.

(2E) Where the court is satisfied that—

    (a) a solicitor allowed to act under subsection (2B)(a) above no longer has authority to act; or

    (b) a solicitor appointed under subsection (2) or (2B)(b) above is no longer able to act in the best interests of the accused,

the court may relieve that solicitor and appoint another solicitor for the purposes referred to in subsection (2) or, as the case may be, (2B) above.

(2F) Subsections (2B)(b) and (2E) above shall not apply in the case of proceedings

    (a) in respect of a sexual offence to which section 288C of this Act applies; or

    (b) in respect of which section 288E of this Act applies; or

    (c) in which an order has been made under section 288F(2) of this Act.

(3) From the commencement of the leading of evidence in a trial for rape or the like the judge may, if he thinks fit, cause all persons other than the accused and counsel and solicitors to be removed from the court-room.

(4) In this section—

    (a) references to a solicitor appointed under subsection (2) or (2B)(b) above include references to a solicitor appointed under subsection (2E) above;

(b) "counsel" includes, in relation to the High Court of Justiciary, a solicitor who has a right of audience in that Court under section 25A of the Solicitors (Scotland) Act 1980 (c.46).

AMENDMENT

Subss.(1) and (2) as amended, and subs.(2A)–(2F), (4) inserted, by the Criminal Procedure (Amendment) (Scotland) Act 2004 (asp 5), s.10. Brought into force on February 1, 2005 by the Criminal Procedure (Amendment) (Scotland) Act 2004 (Commencement, Transitional Provisions and Savings) Order 2004 (SSI 2004/405 (C.28)), art.2.

Subs.(2F)(b) as amended, and subs.(2F)(c) inserted, by the Criminal Procedure (Amendment) (Scotland) Act 2004 (Incidental, Supplemental and Consequential Provisions) Order 2005 (SSI 2005/40), art.3.

DEFINITION

"counsel": s.92(4)(b).
"judge": s.307(1).

GENERAL NOTE

The hearing of evidence in all cases should occur in the presence of the accused unless he so misconducts himself as to necessitate his removal from the court. In *Aitken v Wood*, 1921 J.C. 84 magistrates examined alleged injuries on the complainer's arm in private. Breach of this provision, which arose from removal of the accused from court in the course of his evidence due to a legal debate, was held to be fundamental even without any evidence of prejudice in *Drummond v HM Advocate*, 2003 S.L.T. 295; oddly, the Crown was held to be responsible to a significant extent in not reminding the court that such a procedure would be inept and application for a retrial was refused. The conviction was quashed. See also *Livingston v HM Advocate*, 1991 S.C.C.R. 350; 1992 S.L.T. 481, where the removal of productions from the court for expert examination during the trial was held not to breach the general prohibition then contained in s.145 of the 1975 Act. In *McColl v HM Advocate*, 1989 S.C.C.R. 229; 1989 S.L.T. 691 the clerk of court was called to the jury room and was asked for guidance upon the judge's directions which he gave; the conviction was quashed. See also *Kerr v HM Advocate*, 1992 S.C.C.R. 281; 1992 S.L.T. 1031 discussed in the notes to s.90 above.

While the courts are generally public courts, subs.(3) permits the presiding judge in cases involving a charge of rape or other charges of a sexual nature to close the court to the public from the outset of proceedings. Further provisions in regard to the line of questioning permissible in sexual offences are to be found at s.274 below. Specifically in relation to the evidence of children, it will also be recalled that s.50(3) enables the court to be cleared of all but the immediately interested parties during the hearing of that evidence. The general principle need not extend to any proceedings deemed necessary in connection with an appeal: see *Crossan v HM Advocate*, 1996 S.C.C.R. 279 discussed at A4–178 above.

The distinction between matters of an administrative character (which can be dealt with outwith the presence of the accused) and matters intrinsic to the trial itself (where the accused's presence is a prerequisite except in the circumstances set out in s.54 or in s.92(2) above) was discussed in *Thomson v HM Advocate*, 1998 S.L.T. 364. See more recently *Lindsay v HM Advocate*, 2005 S.C.C.R. 515.

Subs.(2A) introduces a contentious measure to deal with an accused who absents himself during the course of his trial on indictment: on the motion of the prosecutor, and after hearing submissions, the court can order that the trial continue in absence. Despite the novelty of the provision, one has to question how readily it can be used to any sustainable effect.

Leaving aside the practicality of such a provision where identification of the accused may still be in issue, subs.(2A) lays out the tests to be applied by the court in considering such a motion—once an accused has been substantially implicated upon a charge (or one of the charges) on the indictment and the court is satisfied that it is in the interests of justice to do so, there is a discretion to proceed with the trial, and if need be to appoint a solicitor to continue with the defence of the case. It is submitted that the court might consider the effects of an aborted trial upon the witnesses who have given, or are still waiting to give, evidence under these circumstances, but would also have to take account of the significance or gravity of the charge in which the accused has been substantially implicated in the context of the entire libel, and the form and content of the defence case up to that point in the proceedings. Bluntly, it is difficult to see how this provision could be applied in solemn proceedings except where the bulk of evidence, including, arguably, defence evidence, had been led before the accused absented himself; further, in the event of a conviction it cannot be assumed that the court would already be in possession of the necessary social enquiry reports to pass sentence competently, a problem which need not arise where an accused had been removed from the court on account of misconduct.

It might be felt better in the circumstances set out in subs.(2A), for the Crown to adopt a robust stance—in seeking withdrawal of bail—where the evidence led has substantially implicated the accused upon grave charges, rather than courting the risk of using a procedure so fraught with jurisprudential difficulty.

Act of Adjournal

See Form 14.7 in the 1996 Act of Adjournal.

Record of trial

93.—(1) The proceedings at the trial of any person who, if convicted, is entitled to appeal under Part VIII of this Act, shall be recorded by means of shorthand notes or by mechanical means.

(2) A shorthand writer shall—

(a) sign the shorthand notes taken by him of such proceedings and certify them as being complete and correct; and

(b) retain the notes.

(3) A person recording such proceedings by mechanical means shall—

(a) certify that the record is true and complete;

(b) specify in the certificate the proceedings or, as the case may be, the part of the proceedings to which the record relates; and

(c) retain the record.

(4) The cost of making a record under subsection (1) above shall be defrayed, in accordance with scales of payment fixed for the time being by Treasury, out of money provided by Parliament.

(5) In subsection (1) above "proceedings at the trial" means the whole proceedings including, without prejudice to that generality—

(a) discussions—

(i) on any objection to the relevancy of the indictment;

(ii) with respect to any challenge of jurors; and

(iii) on all questions arising in the course of the trial;

(b) the decision of the court on any matter referred to in paragraph (a) above;

(c) the evidence led at the trial;

(d) any statement made by or on behalf of the accused whether before or after the verdict;

(e) the judge's charge to the jury;

(f) the speeches of counsel or agent;

(g) the verdict of the jury;

(h) the sentence by the judge.

DEFINITION

"judge": s.307(1).

GENERAL NOTE

A shorthand or recorded record of the entire proceedings in all solemn cases must be maintained and preserved lest a call is made (in terms of s.94) for them to be produced. Additionally Chap.14 of the Act of Adjournal 1996 enacts that the trial judge is obliged to preserve and authenticate his own notes of evidence and produce them (or a certified copy) to the High Court when requested. The same rules stipulate that where reliance is placed on a recording of the proceedings instead of shorthand notes, the clerk of court must record the fact in his minutes of proceedings.

On appeal in *Kyle v H.M. Advocate*, 1987 S.C.C.R. 116, weight was placed by the appellant upon the apparent inconsistency of a part of the judge's charge, the shorthand notes having been certified as accurate. In fact the terms of the notes suggested that the shorthand writer had some doubts about the accuracy of that section of the transcription; the High Court held that while the notes had to be so certified, the court was not bound to accept them as such and that, in any event, no miscarriage of justice had occurred.

However the absence of a shorthand record altogether has been held to have left the Appeal Court in doubt as to additional directions given to the jury, the sheriff having re-convened the court in the absence of the shorthand writer in breach of the provisions of s.274(1) of the 1975 Act. The aggravated element of the conviction which had been the reason for further directions was quashed and a lesser conviction substituted (see *McLaughlan v H.M. Advocate*, 1995 G.W.D. 38–1935).

Comparison of this decision with that in *Carroll v H.M. Advocate*, 1999 S.L.T. 1185; 1999 S.C.C.R. 617 is instructive; on one reading the sheriff had wilfully proceeded with his directions to the jury in the knowledge that no record of the proceedings was being made in *McLaughlan* whereas in *Carroll* none of the parties was aware of a defect in the recording equipment, and this only became an issue when an appeal on entirely unrelated grounds was taken and the defect discovered. The Appeal Court declined to quash the conviction simply on account of the absence of a record of trial, looked to the judge's report and ruled that the appellant would have to point to an irregularity or misdirection to maintain an appeal. The Court declined to regard the absence of a record as fatal to any conviction.

Transcripts of record and documentary productions

94.—(1) The Clerk of Justiciary may direct that a transcript of a record made under section 93(1) of this Act, or any part thereof, be made and delivered to him for the use of any judge.

(2) Subject to subsection (3) below, the Clerk of Justiciary shall, if requested to do so by—

(a) the Secretary of State or, subject to subsection (2B) below, the prosecutor; or

(b) any other person, not being a person convicted at the trial, on payment of such charges as may be fixed for the time being by Treasury,

direct that such a transcript be made and sent to the person who requested it.

(2A) If—

(a) on the written application of a person convicted at the trial and granted leave to appeal; and

(b) on cause shown,

a judge of the High Court so orders, the Clerk of Justiciary shall direct, on payment of such charges as are mentioned in paragraph (b) of subsection (2) above, that such a transcript be made and sent to that person.

(2B) Where, as respects any person convicted at the trial, the Crown Agent has received intimation under section 107(10) of this Act, the prosecutor shall not be entitled to make a request under subsection (2)(a) above; but if, on the written application of the prosecutor and on cause shown, a judge of the High Court so orders, the Clerk of Justiciary shall direct that such a transcript be made and sent to the prosecutor.

(2C) Any application under subsection (2A) above shall—

(a) be made within 14 days after the date on which leave to appeal was granted or within such longer period after that date as a judge of the High Court may, on written application and on cause shown, allow; and

(b) be intimated forthwith by the applicant to the prosecutor.

(2D) The prosecutor may, within 7 days after receiving intimation under subsection (2C)(b) above, make written representations to the court as respects the application under subsection (2A) above (the application being determined without a hearing).

(2E) Any application under subsection (2B) above shall—

(a) be made within 14 days after the receipt of intimation mentioned in that subsection or within such longer period after that receipt as a judge of the High Court may, on written application and on cause shown, allow; and

(b) be intimated forthwith by the prosecutor to the person granted leave to appeal.

(2F) The person granted leave to appeal may, within 7 days after receiving intimation under subsection (2E)(b) above, make written representations to the court as respects the application under subsection (2B) above (the application being determined without a hearing).

(3) The Secretary of State may, after consultation with the Lord Justice General, by order made by statutory instrument provide that in any class of proceedings specified in the order the Clerk of Justiciary shall only make a direction under subsection (2)(b) above if satisfied that the person requesting the transcript is of a class of person so specified and, if purposes for which the transcript may be used are so specified, intends to use it only for such a purpose; and different purposes may be so specified for different classes of proceedings or classes of person.

(4) Where subsection (3) above applies as respects a direction, the person to whom the transcript is sent shall, if purposes for which that transcript may be used are specified by virtue of that subsection, use it only for such a purpose.

(5) A statutory instrument containing an order under subsection (3) above shall be subject to annulment in pursuance of a resolution of either House of Parliament.

(6) A direction under subsection (1) or (2) above may require that the transcript be made by the person who made the record or by such competent person as may be specified in the direction; and that person shall comply with the direction.

(7) A transcript made in compliance with a direction under subsection (1) or (2) above—

(a) shall be in legible form; and

(b) shall be certified by the person making it as being a correct and complete transcript of the whole or, as the case may be, the part of the record purporting to have been made and certified, and in the case of shorthand notes signed, by the person who made the record.

(8) The cost of making a transcript in compliance with a direction under subsection (1) or (2)(a) above shall be defrayed, in accordance with scales of payment fixed for the time being by the Treasury, out of money provided by Parliament.

(9) The Clerk of Justiciary shall, on payment of such charges as may be fixed for the time being by the Treasury, provide a copy of any documentary production lodged in connection with an appeal under this Part of this Act to such of the following persons as may request it—

(a) the prosecutor;

(b) any person convicted in the proceedings;

(c) any other person named in, or immediately affected by, any order made in the proceedings; and

(d) any person authorised to act on behalf of any of the persons mentioned in paragraphs (a) to (c) above.

AMENDMENT

Subs.(2) as amended and subss.(2A)–(2F) inserted by Criminal Justice (Scotland) Act 2003 (asp 7), Part 8, s.65. Brought into force on June 27, 2003 by the Criminal Justice (Scotland) Act 2003 (Commencement No.1) Order 2003 (SSI 2003/288 (C.14)).

DEFINITIONS

"Clerk of Justiciary": s.307(1).

"judge": s.307(1).

"Lord Justice General": s.307(1).

GENERAL NOTE

The effect of certification of a transcript of evidence as correct was raised in *Kyle v H.M. Advocate*, 1987 S.C.C.R. 116. See the discussion in the notes to s.93 above.

In *H.M. Advocate v Nulty*, 2000 S.L.T. 528: 2000 S.C.C.R. 431, a retrial in which the Crown gave notice of its intention to utilise the hearsay provisions found in s.259 of the Act, to lodge the testimony of a principal witness from the abortive trial, she now being unfit to testify, it is of note that use was made of the original tapes of evidence rather than a transcript of evidence. (It could be argued that the tape was now the best evidence.) The admissibility of this evidence was upheld on appeal in *N v H.M. Advocate*, 2003 S.L.T. 761.

Provisions introduced by s.65 of the Criminal Justice (Scotland) Act 2003 (asp 7) would entitle persons other than a convicted accused (or of course the Crown) to apply to the court for a transcript of proceedings, on cause shown. The Crown would be entitled to be heard in response to such an application.

The primary purpose of the transcript of evidence is to provide an official record of the proceedings should an appeal occur: see *Transco Plc v H.M. Advocate*, 2005 S.L.T. 211. The appellant company appealed against the decision of the judge hearing the preliminary diet who refused a motion for simultaneous transcription (LiveNote) of the trial proceedings expected to last at least six months. It was implicit that such a transcription (extended daily) would constitute the official record of the trial proceedings as, indeed, occurred during the Lockerbie trial. *Transco Plc* does not entirely exclude the possibility (all parties and the court agreeing) of such a record being kept of the proceedings but does emphasise the extra-statutory nature of such an arrangement.

See generally the Transcript of Criminal Proceedings (Scotland) Order 1993 (SI 1993/2226 (S.236)) and the Transcripts of Criminal Proceedings (Scotland) Amendment Order 1995 (SI 1995/1751(S.121)).

Verdict by judge alone

95.—(1) Where, at any time after the jury has been sworn to serve in a trial, the prosecutor intimates to the court that he does not intend to proceed in respect of an offence charged in the indictment, the judge shall acquit the accused of that offence and the trial shall proceed only in respect of any other offence charged in the indictment.

(2) Where, at any time after the jury has been sworn to serve in a trial, the accused intimates to the court that he is prepared to tender a plea of guilty as libelled, or such other plea as the Crown is prepared to accept, in respect of any offence charged in the indictment, the judge shall accept the plea tendered and shall convict the accused accordingly.

(3) Where an accused is convicted under subsection (2) above of an offence—

(a) the trial shall proceed only in respect of any other offence charged in the indictment; and

(b) without prejudice to any other power of the court to adjourn the case or to defer sentence, the judge shall not sentence him or make any other order competent following conviction until a verdict has been returned in respect of every other offence mentioned in paragraph (a) above.

DEFINITIONS

"indictment": s.307(1).

"judge": s.307(1).

"offence": s.307(1).

"prosecutor": s.307(1).

GENERAL NOTE

Section 95 deals with situations in the course of a trial in which the jury is not called upon to reach a verdict upon the evidence, either because the Crown has withdrawn a charge (subs.(1)) or acceptable pleas have been tendered (subs.(2)). In the latter case, it is implicit that acceptance of pleas tendered is signified by the prosecutor subscribing his minute of acceptance following the signatures of the accused and the presiding judge. Subsection (2) also deals with the tendering of a partial plea in circumstances where other charges remain outstanding against the accused. In that situation, where the prosecutor is maintaining the other charges on the libel, care must be taken to ensure that the prosecutor's endorsement is restricted solely to the charges in relation to which the plea was tendered.

It will be noted that the onus of assenting to the pleas tendered strictly lies with the trial judge, not with the jury. No sentence can competently be pronounced until a verdict is reached on all the charges on the indictment.

In determining sentence, the court may take account of the point in the proceedings at which a plea or pleas were tendered (see s.196 below).

Particlarly in solemn proceedings the court will not readily consent to the withdrawal of a guilty plea; see *Weightman v H.M. Advocate*, 1997 G.W.D. 3–85 and the discussion at A4–174 and A4–178 above.

Amendment of indictment

96.—(1) No trial shall fail or the ends of justice be allowed to be defeated by reason of any discrepancy or variance between the indictment and the evidence.

(2) It shall be competent at any time prior to the determination of the case, unless the court see just cause to the contrary, to amend the indictment by deletion, alteration or addition, so as to—

(a) cure any error or defect in it;

(b) meet any objection to it; or

(c) cure any discrepancy or variance between the indictment and the evidence.

(3) Nothing in this section shall authorise an amendment which changes the character of the offence charged, and, if it appears to the court that the accused may in any way be prejudiced in his defence on the merits of the case by any amendment made under this section, the court shall grant such remedy to the accused by adjournment or otherwise as appears to the court to be just.

(4) An amendment made under this section shall be sufficiently authenticated by the initials of the clerk of the court.

DEFINITION

"indictment": s.307(1).

GENERAL NOTE

Schedule 3 of the Act states the general rules concerning latitudes in time and place, implied terms and implied alternatives. Section 96 re-enacts the provisions contained in s.123 of the 1975 Act relating to the power of amendment of an indictment in the course of a trial. The Crown may seek leave to amend the terms of the libel at a first, or preliminary, diet to meet any preliminary objection, but s.96 deals with such motions in the course of trial. While wide powers of amendment are available to the Crown this is qualified by the provisos that; (i) they cannot be used to introduce an essential requisite into a criminal charge—a fundamentally defective libel cannot be cured (*Stevenson v McLevy* (1879) 4 Couper 196 and *Thomson, Petr*, 1997 S.L.T. 322 where the libel lacked a *locus delicti*) and (ii) they must not change the character of the charge to such a degree as to prejudice the accused's defence on the merits (see subs.(3)). Any amendment has to be justified to the court, and while amendment of either the libel or the description of a witness can be craved, amendment of the description of a production in the indictment is not competent (see *H.M. Advocate v Swift*, 1983 S.C.C.R. 204 discussed in the notes to s.67(5)). *Thomson, Petr*, cited above also indicates that there can be no question of a tholed assize where the libel itself was a fundamental nullity. The point in proceedings when amendment is moved is a significant factor; see *Phillips v Houston*, 2003 G.W.D. 29–805, a summary case, where objection had been taken promptly to evidence not covered by the libel and amendment was not then sought till the close of the Crown case.

Amendment of an indictment which omitted the accused's name in one of the three charges (the murder charge), when he had been correctly described in the instance, has been allowed (*Keane v H.M. Advocate*, 1986 S.C.C.R. 491); the decision might have been quite different if there had been other accused on the indictment.

In the event that amendment is allowed by the court, the remedy for the accused is ordinarily adjournment. The presiding judge's decision on the issue will only be overturned on appeal if the Appeal Court is satisfied that the public interest or the interest of the accused has been adversely affected (see *Cumming v Frame* (1909) 6 Adam 57).

Customarily, deletions from the libel are made to bring it into line with the extent of corroborated evidence heard by the jury. See however *Clarke v Ruxton*, 1997 G.W.D. 10–408 in relation, at least, to sexual offences discussed at A4–406.1 below.

No case to answer

97.—(1) Immediately after the close of the evidence for the prosecution, the accused may intimate to the court his desire to make a submission that he has no case to answer both—

(a) on an offence charged in the indictment; and

(b) on any other offence of which he could be convicted under the indictment.

(2) If, after hearing both parties, the judge is satisfied that the evidence led by the prosecution is insufficient in law to justify the accused being convicted of the offence charged in respect of which the submission has been made or of such other offence as is mentioned, in relation to that offence, in paragraph (b) of subsection (1) above, he shall acquit him of the offence charged in respect of which the submission has been made and the trial shall proceed only in respect of any other offence charged in the indictment.

(3) If, after hearing both parties, the judge is not satisfied as is mentioned in subsection (2) above, he shall reject the submission and the trial shall proceed, with the accused entitled to give evidence and call witnesses, as if such submission had not been made.

(4) A submission under subsection (1) above shall be heard by the judge in the absence of the jury.

DEFINITIONS

"indictment": s.307(1).
"judge": s.307(1).
"offence": s.307(1).

GENERAL NOTE

The no case to answer submission was introduced into Scots criminal law by the Criminal Justice (Scotland) Act 1980, s.19 and the terms of that section are repeated in s.97 above. A common law submission could always be made at the conclusion of evidence, before the judge's charge but a s.97 submission, unlike the common law type, is concerned only with the sufficiency of evidence, not its quality. The submission is made outwith the presence of the jury and can relate to any, or all, of the charges on the indictment. Note that s.97 refers to "an offence" not "a charge" on the indictment; so where a number of offences are libelled as part of one charge a submission can competently be made upon each offence: the Crown cannot, by creative draftsmanship, withhold the right of an accused to make a s.97 motion (see *Cordiner v H.M. Advocate*, 1991 S.C.C.R. 652).

It will be observed that a submission can be made in regard to the charge libelled or any other offence which is implied by the libel but, in practical terms, the starting point will be the sufficiency, or otherwise, of the charge libelled before proceeding to a consideration of any alternative charge. Any challenge to the competency or admissibility of evidence must be raised at, or prior to, the point in proceedings at which that evidence is being received by the court; it is too late to air such issues at the point of a no case to answer submission when no prior objection has been taken (*McGee v McNaughtan*, 1996 G.W.D. 17–977).

If in terms of subs.(3) the accused's submissions are rejected, he has to decide whether or not to lead evidence, a dilemma heightened by the introduction of the prosecutor's right to comment upon the failure of the accused to lead evidence (see s.32 of the Criminal Justice (Scotland) Act 1995). It remains to be seen what use will be made of this provision and to what effect. What is the position if the judge incorrectly rejects a submission of no case to answer and the accused then leads evidence which confirms the Crown case? The problem was recognised but not addressed in *Little v H.M. Advocate*, 1983 S.C.C.R. 56. The same problems occurred in *Mackie v H.M. Advocate*, 1994 S.C.C.R. 277 and there the judge read the elements of the charge as a unity in what was, by any standard, a complex libel.

It is permissible for the Crown to submit to the jury at the conclusion of evidence that the withdrawal of charges at the submission stage does not necessarily reflect adversely upon prosecution witnesses; it is however one step too far to suggest that the accused might still have committed the offences of which he had been acquitted earlier (see *Dudgeon v H.M. Advocate*, 1988 S.C.C.R. 147). In that case the improper remarks of the prosecutor were held to have been cured by the directions of the trial judge and no miscarriage to have resulted.

Defence to speak last

98. In any trial the accused or, where he is legally represented, his counsel or solicitor shall have the right to speak last.

Seclusion of jury to consider verdict

99.—(1) When the jury retire to consider their verdict, the clerk of court shall enclose the jury in a room by themselves and, except in so far as provided for, or is made necessary, by an instruction under subsection (4) below, neither he nor any other person shall be present with the jury while they are enclosed.

(2) Except in so far as is provided for, or is made necessary, by an instruction under subsection (4) below, while the jury are enclosed and until they intimate that they are ready to return their verdict—

    (a) subject to subsection (3) below, no person shall visit the jury or communicate with them; and

    (b) no juror shall come out of the jury room other than to receive or seek a direction from the judge or to make a request—

        (i) for an instruction under subsection (4)(a), (c) or (d) below; or

        (ii) regarding any matter in the cause.

(3) Nothing in paragraph (a) of subsection (2) above shall prohibit the judge, or any person authorised by him for the purpose, communicating with the jury for the purposes—

    (a) of giving a direction, whether or not sought under paragraph (b) of that subsection; or

    (b) responding to a request made under that paragraph.

(4) The judge may give such instructions as he considers appropriate as regards—

    (a) the provision of meals and refreshments for the jury;

    (b) the making of arrangements for overnight accommodation for the jury and, unless under subsection (7) below the court permits them to separate, for their continued seclusion if such accommodation is provided;

    (c) the communication of a personal or business message, unconnected with any matter in the cause, from a juror to another person (or vice versa); or

    (d) the provision of medical treatment, or other assistance, immediately required by a juror.

(5) If the prosecutor or any other person contravenes the provisions of this section, the accused shall be acquitted of the crime with which he is charged.

(6) During the period in which the jury are retired to consider their verdict, the judge may sit in any other proceedings; and the trial shall not fail by reason only of his so doing.

(7) The court may, if it thinks fit, permit the jury to separate even after they have retired to consider their verdict.

AMENDMENT

Subss.(1), (2) and (4)(b) as amended, and subs.(7) inserted, by Criminal Justice (Scotland) Act 2003 (asp 7), Part 12, s.79. Brought into force on June 27, 2003 by the Criminal Justice (Scotland) Act 2003 (Commencement No.1) Order 2003 (SSI 2003/288 (C.14)).

DEFINITIONS

"judge": s.307(1).
"prosecutor": s.307(1).

GENERAL NOTE

Until the point at which the jury is directed to retire to consider its verdict, all proceedings in a trial must take place in the presence of the accused (see s.92). Once the jury withdraws to the jury room, s.99 stipulates that no contact should be made with its members unless the jury requests directions or has need to seek assistance from the court. The provisions of s.99 are mandatory and conduct constituting a breach (subs.(5)) is fatal to any conviction. The reforms introduced into s.99 by the Criminal Justice (Scotland) Act 2003 (asp 7) substantially relax the provisions which required the seclusion, or supervised corralling, of the jury once it had retired to consider its verdict. Until the passage of the Criminal Justice (Scotland) Act 1980 (c.62) once a jury retired to consider its verdict, no interruptions were permitted until the jury returned. The 1980 Act enabled the jury to break from protracted deliberations and to retire to supervised accommodation until the following day: the latest reforms introduce a judicial discretion to permit jurors to break from deliberations and to "separate", or more prosaically—go home, until directed to return to court to continue consideration of their verdict.

One might be forgiven for sensing the dead hands of misplaced economy and bureaucratic convenience; we may perhaps lament a further dilution of a distinct Scottish legal tradition which underpinned the unique importance, even mystique, of jury service; what cannot be gainsaid is that the new provisions do not explicitly address the sort of problems which no doubt will occur in practice.

First, although it is not evident from the textual changes now introduced into s.99 itself (by dint of some ungainly draftsmanship), the Criminal Justice (Scotland) Act 2003, s.79 stipulates that seclusion of the jury, until a verdict is reached, is no longer mandatory. Thus in each case the matter lies in the discretion of the trial judge.

Secondly, s.88(8) of the 1995 Act contains a power (scarcely used) for the jury to be secluded *throughout* the proceedings; thus a motion for seclusion could be made at any point during the trial where deemed appropriate, but it is submitted that this should certainly be made outwith the presence of either jurors or the potential jurors of an assize—indeed there would be obvious merit in applying to the court by means of a preliminary diet (s.72(d) of the Act) where possible.

Yet the most likely scenario, which can be expected to cast up unprecedented difficulties, is that of the errant juror who fails to return to court after "separation". It is submitted that the priority at this stage is to avoid delay to the jury's deliberations and that the appropriate course, rather than any form of delay or desertion, ought to be for the court to review the position in accordance with s.90 of the Act, and to proceed with a reduced number of jurors so far as this is possible and appropriate.

Points of appeal have arisen from allegations of inappropriate communication between the jury and court officials; the Appeal Court may remit the case for enquiry and report under s.104(d) below (see for example *Squire v HM Advocate*, 1998 G.W.D. 28–1410) but has emphasised that such enquiry should confine itself to establishing the factual background and must not concern itself with the jury's deliberations. In *Simpson v HM Advocate*, 2001 G.W.D. 16–603 an appeal founded on the fact that the sheriff had declined to desert proceedings after a letter discussing the trial evidence and passing comment was found on a stairwell only 10 metres from the jury room. The sheriff in open court asked all jury members if they knew of the letter and in the absence of a positive response allowed trial to continue. The Appeal Court upheld the sheriff's approach, noting that the extent of investigation was one within his discretion and had to be directed to preserving the integrity of the proceedings.

In *Swankie v HM Advocate*, 1999 S.C.C.R. 1, an appeal against conviction rested on the alleged conduct during jury deliberations of a juror in making known a previous conviction of the accused, an incident which was stated to have been disclosed by another juror to an acquaintance of S. (Such a disclosure would have been in breach of s.8 of the Contempt of Court Act 1981). The appeal proceeded by way of an affidavit from the acquaintance. Leaving aside the hearsay nature of the affidavit, the Appeal Court itself examined the quality of the evidence before the jury and the apparent extent of its deliberations, cast doubt on the veracity of the affidavit and declined to initiate a s.104 enquiry.

By contrast in *McLean v HM Advocate*, 2001 S.L.T. 1096, where the sheriff's enquiry confirmed that after the jury had deliberated, but before a verdict was pronounced, a jury member had disclosed knowledge of a previous conviction of the accused, the Appeal Court was not satisfied that an unimpeachable verdict had been achieved. Although the sheriff had directly interrogated the juror as to whether this knowledge had influenced her verdict, and noted that the revealed conviction (of shoplifting) was minor when set against the charges being tried, this could not suffice to remove taint from the proceedings. Authority was granted for a retrial.

The limits for investigation of a jury's deliberations were considered in *Scottish Criminal Cases Review Commission, Petitioners*, 2001 S.L.T. 1198 where the Commission sought to make enquiry of jurors in a murder trial as to events prior to their retiral to consider verdicts. The court confirmed the legitimacy of such enquiries, the Commission being anxious not to fall foul of the contempt of court provisions contained in s.8 of the Contempt of Court Act 1981 (c.49) which bar investigations into any jury's deliberations once it has retired to consider verdicts. It was also made clear that the Commission could not petition the court to carry out investigations on its behalf; the court's own powers of investigation under s.104 of the 1995 Act exist for the limited purpose of dealing with appeals under ss.106 and 108 of that Act.

Subss. (2) and (3)

Unfortunately the cases arising from s.153 (the statutory predecessor to s.99) tend to suggest that in their zeal to provide for the seclusion of the jury, officers of the court have on occasion overlooked the obligations (now) created by s.92 and trespassed into matters which should have been dealt with in open court.

It is the jury's right to examine productions referred to in the evidence but subject to any directions given by the court. The procedure to be followed is laid out in *Hamilton v HM Advocate*, 1980 J.C. 66; the Lord Justice-Clerk (at 69) stated:

"If the jury make a request to see a production, this request should be communicated to the clerk of court who should inform counsel on both sides and then refer the matter to the trial judge for his decision."

A practice has developed, in part to delay the jury's deliberations as little as possible and to avoid the need to reconvene the court repeatedly, of trial judges clarifying with the parties which productions can, and which cannot, be given to the jury on request. This is done in open court immediately after the jury retires and has the merit of focusing this issue even before the event arises and commits parties' views to the record. There is no statutory authority for this procedure but, it is submitted, it complies with the directions in *Hamilton*. Support for this reading can be found in *Bertram v HM Advocate*, 1990 S.C.C.R. 394, where the judge in his charge permitted access to all productions admitted in evidence during the trial. See also *Martin v HM Advocate*, 1989 S.C.C.R. 546 where the sheriff gave directions which were inspecific and were acted upon by the clerk of court without reference to the parties and *Boyle v HM Advocate*, 1990 S.C.C.R. 480 where productions not spoken of in evidence were given to the jurors in error. Once the error was appreciated, the sheriff gave further directions to the jury to ignore the content of these productions; the conviction was upheld in the circumstances.

It is clear that the question of access to productions is one upon which parties should be heard; it is not an administrative matter to be resolved between the clerk of court and the presiding judge. The complex issues which can surface are amply illustrated by *Collins v HM Advocate*, 1991 S.C.C.R. 898 where the trial judge withheld statements by various of the accused on the grounds that they could be misapplied and wrongly used as evidence against other accused. Similar problems arose, but were dealt with quite differently (the judge allowing transcripts of police interviews given by all accused to be made available following a request by the jury, but giving additional directions on the inadmissibility against others of statements made outwith their presence) in *Munro v HM Advocate*, 2000 S.L.T. 950. It is of note that the Appeal Court considered it might well be preferable in such circumstances to lead evidence by means of edited transcripts.

In the past, difficulty has also been caused by the interpretation of the provisions against contact being made with the jury room (subs.(2)). In *Brownlie v HM Advocate* (1966) S.C.C.R. Supp. 14, the clerk of court on the judge's instructions went to the jury room door and asked if the jury had understood the judge's direction. This had followed earlier difficulty and further directions. The appeal, which had founded upon both the recall of the jury for further directions and the judge's actions in causing the clerk to communicate with the jury was refused. The right of the judge to recall the jury for further directions was upheld in *McBeth v HM Advocate* (1976) S.C.C.R. Supp. 123.

In *Cunningham v HM Advocate*, 1984 S.C.C.R. 40 written requests for directions were delivered to the judge in chambers in the presence of both counsel and dealt with by further written directions; these events occurred outwith the presence of the accused and were not recorded in the shorthand notes. While the conviction was quashed, the court held that the Crown was not at fault and gave authority for fresh proceedings, surely the only just solution in the circumstances. An appeal against conviction on grounds of miscarriage was refused where a jury's request for further directions could not be dealt with by the judge for over an hour, since another jury was being empanelled. In the interval the jury reached a verdict and it is of note that the Appeal Court took note of the discriminating nature of that verdict as evidence of a considered, and not a capricious, jury (*Brown v HM Advocate*, 1997 S.C.C.R. 201). *McColl v HM Advocate*, 1989 S.C.C.R. 229 is a rare example of communication of an order so extreme as to constitute a miscarriage, a decision the Court of Appeal reached after granting authority to parties to precognosce the clerk of court. The clerk had given formal directions to the jurors on the instructions of the presiding judge and the court did not reconvene; no record existed of the communings between the clerk and the jurors, all of which had occurred outwith the presence of the accused. It was by no means clear whether the circumstances had been brought to the attention of both counsel but the lack of a record of proceedings was critical and the verdict was overturned.

Difficulties have arisen when the court has been faced with a verdict at odds with the judge's directions: in *Whyte v HM Advocate*, 1999 G.W.D. 16–745 the Crown case rested entirely on application of the *Moorov* doctrine, and the court was advised by the foreman that guidance was needed because the jury was coming to two dissimilar verdicts. Additional directions were given but, on appeal, *Whyte* contended that once such an impasse had been reached in a *Moorov* case he should have been acquitted. The Appeal Court noted that no settled verdict had been reached and, following *Took v HM Advocate*, 1989 S.L.T. 425, indicated that where different verdicts would be mutually inconsistent, further directions would be appropriate. Broadly, where the jury seeks to return a verdict patently at odds with the judge's directions, or returns a verdict which simply is not lawful, it is no part of the court's function to let a verdict based on confusion, error or inconsistency pass unchecked. The judge in such circumstances must consider issuing further directions to assist the jury to reach a clear and sustainable verdict (see *Cameron (J.P.) v HM Advocate*, 1999 S.C.C.R. 476).

In *McGill v HM Advocate*, 2001 S.C.C.R. 28 an unsuccessful appeal founded upon the form of deletions made by the jury to a libel of attempted rape.

A novel problem (but one likely to concern courts in the future) arose in *Matthewson v HM Advocate*, 1989 S.C.C.R. 101 when the jury asked to be shown parts of a video tape produced in evidence. The only operator available was the procurator fiscal depute who, in the presence of counsel for one of the accused and the clerk, showed a juror how to operate the video recorder, the jury having had to return to the court in order to view the tape. In *Gray v HM Advocate*, 1999 S.L.T. 533; 1999 S.C.C.R. 24, an assault and robbery in which video evidence was central to identification of the accused by witnesses who had seen him earlier that day, the trial judge refused a jury request to view the video again. On appeal against conviction the Appeal Court distinguished between the jurors viewing the tape again for the purpose of testing the accuracy and reliability of the witnesses' evidence (which could be permitted in open court) and undertaking an investigation or assessment of the contents of the tape for themselves (which would be unacceptable). *Gray* holds that it is competent to grant such jury requests; however, it has to be doubted that such subtle distinctions will be clear to the jury even after additional directions. The jury also sought assistance from the court in *Moir v HM Advocate*, 1993 S.C.C.R. 1191 to "hear if possible … all or part of the evidence given by [J]". Plainly at that stage in proceedings the witness could not be recalled and, in the absence of a transcript, the judge had declined to read over his own notes of evidence lest this influence the jury's own recall. The Appeal Court (at 1197) followed *Hamilton v HM Advocate*, 1938 S.L.T. 333 at 337 and held that the notes could have been read if the judge so chose, but that the issue was one which fell to the judge's discretion in determining the best way to conduct the case and not subject to review by the Appeal Court. The considerations governing the extent of a jury's access to productions are discussed in *Barnetson v HM Advocate*, 2003 G.W.D. 30–838.

Subs. (4)

At earlier stages in the proceedings, arrangements for accommodating jurors overnight during adjournments of trial can be made (s.88(8)) and it is presumed that the requirements of subs.(4) would then be applied to those situations. Once the jury has been charged there is no doubt that its deliberations should be interrupted only for the purposes of subs.(4). It is implicit that the jury should be unhindered in its deliberations and should in no way be pressured directly or indirectly to hasten to a verdict. See *McKenzie v HM Advocate*, 1986 S.C.C.R. 94 and *Love v HM Advocate*, 1995 S.C.C.R. 501. The distinction between eliciting a report on the jury's progress (necessary for the planning of accommodation) and pressing for a conclusion, can be a fine, but telling, one. Contrast *Robertson v HM Advocate*, 1996 S.C.C.R. 243 and *Sinclair v HM Advocate*, 1996 S.C.C.R. 221. It would seem to be good practice to remind jurors that they should reach a verdict in their own good time and should feel under no pressure to reach a verdict. An alternative, and perhaps less satisfactory, approach was used by the sheriff in *Eraker v HM Advocate*, 1997 G.W.D. 5–183 when the jury was asked if they were happy to consider "at least in the first instance trying to make a decision this evening"; presumably, since this left the jury to resolve whether to try to reach a verdict later that day (as they did) rather than directing them to do so, no element of pressure was evident.

Subsection (7), which was introduced by the 2003 Act, permits the trial judge, where appropriate, to interrupt the jury's deliberations after they have been charged and allow its members to break off and to return home rather than being in continued seclusion (subs.4(b)) and accommodated overnight. The greater element of discretion now found in subs.(7) greatly eases the burden on jurors, and on the court, of having to arrange suitable secluded accommodation at very short notice. The task of securing suitable accommodation (say) in Edinburgh during Festival time is not one for either the faint-hearted or the parsimonious.

It is submitted, though the section is silent on the matter, that it would be prudent when utilising subs.(7)'s powers for the trial judge to make further explicit directions to the jurors not to discuss, or deliberate upon, the evidence until the court has reconvened.

Subs. (6)

This provision was introduced by the Prisoners and Criminal Proceedings (Scotland) Act 1993 (c.9), s.40(1) into the 1975 Act as s.155A. Section 91 enacts that trials shall proceed from day to day until concluded, while the marginal note stipulates "Trial to be continuous". Technical objections as to want of procedure of the sort raised in *Boyle v HM Advocate* above should not occur. The logical corollary of subs.(6) is s.102 below which permits other proceedings to be interrupted for the taking of a verdict, deal with the requests of, or issue further directions to, the jury in a prior trial. Section 158 of the Act allows summary proceedings to be interrupted for the same purposes.

Verdict and conviction

Verdict of jury

100.—(1) The verdict of the jury, whether the jury are unanimous or not, shall be returned orally by the foreman of the jury unless the court directs a written verdict to be returned.

(2) Where the jury are not unanimous in their verdict, the foreman shall announce that fact so that the relative entry may be made in the record.

(3) The verdict of the jury may be given orally through the foreman of the jury after consultation in the jury box without the necessity for the jury to retire.

GENERAL NOTE

The jury's verdict can be returned competently in court immediately on conclusion of the judge's charge; it is not essential that they retire to the jury room (subs.(3)) or deliberate for any length of time (*Crowe v HM Advocate*, 1990 J.C. 112).

The verdict should be delivered orally to the court, a written verdict being competent only when the court has previously directed that the verdict be given to the court in that form. In part this ensures that all proceedings occur within the view and hearing of the accused; see *Kerr v HM Advocate*, 1992 S.L.T. 1031; 1992 S.C.C.R. 281 discussed in the notes to s.90. It has been held in *MacDermid (John Anderson) v HM Advocate*, 1948 J.C. 12 that the judge is not obliged to explain the meaning of the not proven verdict on the grounds that it is well-understood in Scotland. That assessment is questionable but the High Court has repeatedly warned judges against attempting to differentiate between the not proven and not guilty verdicts in jury charges; see most recently *Cussick (Barry) v HM Advocate*, 2001 S.L.T. 1316; 2001 S.C.C.R. 683 and *Sweeney v HM Advocate*, 2002 S.C.C.R. 131.

On rare occasions the nature of evidence can be such as to require the withdrawal of the not proven verdict from the jury; see *Reid v HM Advocate*, 1947 S.L.T. 150. The presiding judge is obliged to explain the meaning of a majority verdict to the jury and it must be made clear that at least eight of the jury are minded to convict: the jury will only be asked whether the verdict is unanimous or by a majority and no further enquiry should be made into the arithmetic involved (*Pullar v HM Advocate*, 1993 J.C. 126). The manner of calculating a majority has to be well understood by jurors particularly because of the availability (usually) of three verdicts and because the size of the jury can be reduced in certain circumstances to consist of as few as 12 jurors (s.90(1)). Refer to *Affleck v HM Advocate*, 1987 S.C.C.R. 150. In *Docherty v HM Advocate*, 1997 J.C. 196 confusion arose in a murder trial where the jury had voted by a majority for a guilty verdict, but were divided as to whether to convict for murder or culpable homicide. The Appeal Court held that those who had voted for an acquittal should not thereafter vote upon which of the alternative verdicts of guilt should be pronounced. Of consent, a conviction of culpable homicide was substituted by the Appeal Court. In the light of *Docherty* it would seem that modification of the standard directions given to juries would be appropriate in cases where alternative charges are libelled.

Once the verdict has been recorded by the clerk of court, read back to them and assented as correct, it cannot be subject to further consideration by the trial court, the verdict being finally pronounced (see *McGarry v HM Advocate*, 1959 J.C. 30). It has been held, however, that failure to read back a verdict to the jury is not itself fatal to the conviction (*Torri v HM Advocate*, 1923 J.C. 52).

How far even an appellate court can venture in exploring the nature of a jury's deliberations is discussed in "Jury Secrecy and Criminal Appeals" by P.W. Ferguson in 2004 S.L.T. 43.

Previous convictions: solemn proceedings

101.—(1) Previous convictions against the accused shall not , subject to subsection (2) below and section 275A(2) of this Act, be laid before the jury, nor shall reference be made to them in presence of the jury before the verdict is returned.

(2) Nothing in subsection (1) above shall prevent the prosecutor—

(a) asking the accused questions tending to show that he has been convicted of an offence other than that with which he is charged, where he is entitled to do so under section 266 of this Act; or

(b) leading evidence of previous convictions where it is competent to do so under section 270 of this Act, and nothing in this section or in section 69 of this Act shall prevent evidence of previous convictions being led in any case where such evidence is competent in support of a substantive charge.

(3) Previous convictions shall not, subject to section 275A(1) of this Act, be laid before the presiding judge until the prosecutor moves—

(a) for sentence; or

(b) for a risk assessment order (or the court at its own instance proposes to make such an order).

and in that event the prosecutor shall lay before the judge a copy of the notice referred to in subsection (2) or (4) of section 69 of this Act

(3A) Where, under paragraph (b) of subsection (3) above, the prosecutor lays previous convictions before the judge, he shall also provide the judge with such details regarding the offences in question as are available to him.

(4) On the conviction of the accused it shall be competent for the court, subject to subsection (5) below, to amend a notice of previous convictions so laid by deletion or alteration for the purpose of curing any error or defect.

(5) [...]

(6) Any conviction which is admitted in evidence by the court shall be entered in the record of the trial.

(7) Where a person is convicted of an offence, the court may have regard to any previous conviction in respect of that person in deciding on the disposal of the case.

(8) Where any such intimation as is mentioned in section 69 of this Act is given by the accused, it shall be competent to prove any previous conviction included in a notice under that section in the manner specified in section 285, or as the case may be 286A, of this Act, and the provisions of the section in question shall apply accordingly.

AMENDMENT

Subs.(5) repealed by the Crime and Punishment (Scotland) Act 1997 (c.48), s.31 with effect from August 1, 1997 (Commencement and Transitional Provisions) Order 1997 (SI 1997/1712), art.3.

Subss.(1) and (3) as amended by the Sexual Offences (Procedure and Evidence) (Scotland) Act 2002 (asp 9), s.10(1). Brought into force by the Sexual Offences (Procedure and Evidence) (Scotland) Act 2002 (Commencement and Transitional Provisions) Order 2002 (SSI 2002/443 (C.24)), art.4 (effective November 1, 2002).

Subs.(8) as amended by the Criminal Justice (Scotland) Act 2003, s.57(2). Brought into force on June 27, 2003 by the Criminal Justice (Scotland) Act 2003 (Commencement No.1) Order 2003 (SSI 2003/288 (C.14)).

Subs.(3) as amended, and subs.(3A) inserted, by the Criminal Justice (Scotland) Act 2003 (asp 7), Sch.1, para.2(3). Brought into force on June 19, 2006 by the Criminal Justice (Scotland) Act 2003 (Commencement No.9) Order 2006 (SSI 2006/332 (C.30)), art.2(1), subject to art.2(2).

DEFINITIONS

"judge": s.307(1).
"previous conviction": s.307(5).
"prosecutor": s.307(1).

GENERAL NOTE

Previous convictions in the course of trial

The previous convictions of the accused should not normally be made known to the court until a conviction is recorded and the prosecutor moves for sentence. There are two accepted exceptions to this general rule: first where proof of the conviction is an essential to proof of the substantive charge (for example, driving while disqualified, or contravening the provisions of the Firearms Act 1968 (c.27), s.21, or prison-breaking—see *Russell v HM Advocate*, 1993 S.L.T. 358; *Varey v HM Advocate*, 1986 S.L.T. 321 and *Harkin v HM Advocate*, 1996 S.L.T. 1004); secondly when the accused has represented himself to be of good character or impugned the character of prosecution witnesses, the complainer or the prosecutor (see ss.266(4) and 270(1)). The prosecutor is also under a duty not to question the accused in a fashion calculated to show that he has been involved in other criminal charges which are not before the court.

The consequences of revealing previous convictions, even when this is done by the prosecutor, are not necessarily fatal; much depends on the circumstances in which the section's provisions were breached, whether the information was wilfully elicited or was imparted unexpectedly, what objection, if any, was offered to the evidence and who sought the evidence in the first place. The approach adopted by the Court of Appeal is to consider whether a miscarriage of justice has occurred (having regard, inter alia, to any steps taken by the trial judge to address the issue, or consciously avoid it, in his charge) and then to consider whether the breach constituted a sufficiently substantial miscarriage to merit the quashing of the conviction or amendment of the verdict. So in *McCuaig v HM Advocate*, 1982 J.C. 59 where a police officer in response to a question from the trial judge read over the full terms of a charge preferred to him, making reference to the accused's previous convictions, it was held that no substantial miscarriage had occurred. Similarly in *Binks v HM Advocate*, 1984 S.C.C.R. 335; 1985 S.L.T. 59 where in reading a statement given by the accused, a Customs officer during his examination-in-chief read the phrase "I don't want to go back to jail again", the court took the view that the mere disclosure of a previous conviction might be of little or no significance in the circumstances of the case. See generally *Kepple v HM Advocate*, 1936 J.C. 76, *HM Advocate v McIlwain*, 1965 S.L.T. 311 and *Penman v Stott*, 2001 S.C.C.R. 911; 2001 G.W.D. 36–1363.

By contrast a very similar reply to caution and charge elicited by the prosecutor in *Graham v HM Advocate*, 1984 S.L.T. 67 was held to be deliberate and fatal to conviction. Compare *McAvoy v HM Advocate*, 1991 S.C.C.R. 123 in which the prosecutor asked a police officer about "known associates" of the accused a question, which though criticised by the Appeal Court, was held not to have breached the provisions. The central issue in studying the conduct of the prosecutor is whether the disclosure came about as a result of calculation or unacceptable want of care on his part, or whether it occurred unexpectedly or as part of a wilful ploy by a witness or co-accused. See *Deeney v HM Advocate*, 1986 S.C.C.R. 393 where a witness mentioned that the accused was on licence at the time of offences, an answer not anticipated from the Crown's question and which was held not to have breached the section's provisions. More recently in *Robertson v HM Advocate*, 1995 S.C.C.R. 497 where a Crown witness repeatedly referred to the accused being provided accommodation by SACRO (Scottish Association for Care and Resettlement of Offenders), using only the acronym and without divulging the objects of the organisation, the disclosure was held to be accidental and to have been dealt with sensitively in the judge's charge to the jury. In *Campbell v HM Advocate*, 1999 S.L.T. 399 (driving while disqualified) the prosecutor's brief questioning of C about his previous conviction notwithstanding that C had stated no preliminary objection to the special capacity, was upheld. The court took the view that the Crown could still elect to prove the terms of the qualifying conviction; see the discussion at A4–495 below.

It will be noted that the section bars any reference to an accused's previous convictions (unless the provisions of subs.(2) apply) but this cannot guard against wilful conduct on the part of co-accused or defence witnesses; in such circumstances this is almost certain to be prejudicial but the court will not rush to hold that a miscarriage has occurred. See *Slane v HM Advocate*, 1984 S.L.T. 293. In the first instance the judge presiding at the trial has to decide whether to mention such inadmissible evidence in order to direct that it be disregarded or whether, in the whole circumstances, it is more discreet, and effective, to say nothing at all and in so doing avoid resurrecting the objectionable evidence (see *Fyfe v HM Advocate*, 1989 S.C.C.R. 429; 1990 S.L.T. 50 and *Gallagher v HM Advocate*, 1992 G.W.D. 6–355).

The deletion of subs.(5) introduced by the 1997 Act means that it is now competent to amend the schedule of previous convictions to correct errors. This concession would have had a considerable impact if the Government had commenced the scheme of automatic sentences set out in Part I of the 1997 Act; in that scheme the precise terms of a prior conviction would have dictated whether a re-offending accused was subject to an automatic sentence on indictment.

Previous convictions and the sentencing process

When moving for sentence the Crown is entitled to place a schedule detailing previous convictions before the court as material relevant to sentence. The question now is what in the way of more detailed information about the nature and circumstances of prior background, including convictions, should be disclosed to the court, and considered by it. Until now the directions laid down in *Connel v Mitchell*, 1909 S.C.(J.) 13 (broadly that the court could not look behind previous convictions) had been applied, albeit previous convictions not libelled by the Crown but revealed in social enquiry reports could be taken into account once the accused had been given the opportunity to challenge them or comment (*Sillars v Copeland*, 1966 J.C. 8). Otherwise the court would seek no more information as to the factual circumstances of previous offences.

In *Riley v HM Advocate*, 1999 J.C. 308; 1999 S.L.T. 1076; 1999 S.C.C.R. 644, the Appeal Court has signalled a broader approach and has approved a practice of the Crown serving extracts of convictions whose factual detail is being founded upon in any narration. Nonetheless it was emphasised that a sentencing court would not wish to become embroiled in disputes over the fine detail of convictions, and would limit scrutiny to the terms of charges, and only then in exceptional cases.

The purpose of schedules of previous convictions and social enquiry reports is to enable the sentencing judge to pass an appropriate disposal having regard to all the known circumstances: thus in *Penman v HM Advocate*, 1999 S.C.C.R. 740 where no previous convictions were put before the court but a report referred to convictions for offences committed subsequent to the sexual misconduct libelled, the Appeal Court approved the use of this information provided that the record was not treated as an aggravating feature. Penman's recent pattern of offending justified the view that he was a danger to the public.

Moving for sentence

Ordinarily following the pronouncement of the jury's verdict, the prosecutor is invited to proceed and will lay any convictions before the court. *Noon v HM Advocate*, 1960 J.C. 52 is authority for the proposition that no particular form of words is required of the prosecutor; his actions in placing any schedule of convictions signals his intention. However in *Arthur, Petitioner*, 2003 S.L.T. 90 a murder trial in which the judge proceeded straight to imposition of the mandatory sentence of life imprisonment on pronouncement of the verdict, without inviting the Crown to address the court, the sentence but, significantly not the conviction, was quashed and the case was remitted to the trial judge to sentence according to law.

Road Traffic Offenders Act 1988 (c.53).

See the notes at A4–359 below.

European Convention on Human Rights

In *Andrew v HM Advocate*, 1999 G.W.D. 32–1517 the Appeal Court rejected the contention that disclosure of an accused's previous conviction in the course of trial necessarily amounted to a breach of Art.6(1) or (2). It is of note that the disclosure arose through no fault of the Crown.

Inclusion of convictions imposed by courts in the European Union

The effect of s.57 of the Criminal Justice (Scotland) Act 2003 (asp 7) is to permit the inclusion of an accused's convictions from these courts in any schedule of convictions served upon an accused in Scottish criminal proceedings. Such convictions can be proved by certification of known fingerprints in much the same manner as was applied to United Kingdom convictions by s.285 of the 1995 Act.

Interruption of trial for other proceedings

102.—(1) When the jury have retired to consider their verdict, and the diet in another criminal cause has been called, then, subject to subsection (3) below, if it appears to the judge presiding at the trial to be appropriate, he may interrupt the proceedings in such other cause—

(a) in order to receive the verdict of the jury in the preceding trial, and thereafter to dispose of the case;

(b) to give a direction to the jury in the preceding trial upon any matter upon which the jury may wish a direction from the judge or to hear any request from the jury regarding any matter in the cause.

(2) Where in any case the diet of which has not been called, the accused intimates to the clerk of court that he is prepared to tender a plea of guilty as libelled or such qualified plea as the Crown is prepared to accept, or where a case is remitted to the High Court for sentence, then, subject to subsection (3) below, any trial then proceeding may be interrupted for the purpose of receiving such plea or dealing with the remitted case and pronouncing sentence or otherwise disposing of any such case.

(3) In no case shall any proceedings in the preceding trial take place in the presence of the jury in the interrupted trial, but in every case that jury shall be directed to retire by the presiding judge.

(4) On the interrupted trial being resumed the diet shall be called *de novo*.

(5) In any case an interruption under this section shall not be deemed an irregularity, nor entitle the accused to take any objection to the proceedings.

DEFINITIONS

"High Court": s.307(1).
"judge": s.307(1).

GENERAL NOTE

This section and, in some circumstances, s.99(6) fall to be read in conjunction. While s.91 of the Act requires that the trial shall proceed from day to day, procedural difficulties can develop when it is necessary to interpose other solemn business. See for example *Boyle v. H.M. Advocate*, 1990 S.C.C.R. 480. These problems became yet more acute when a jury trial had spilled over from a previous sitting; then the disposal of business called to the later (delayed) sitting often demanded dexterity of a high order. Section 102 admits a degree of flexibility into the administration of court business but it will be noted that when a jury trial is interrupted to deal with other business before the court, that jury is to be excluded until the fresh business is concluded.

The section also enables a jury in a later trial to be empanelled while an earlier jury deliberates, a provision which may assist on occasion to utilise court time more effectively.

Rule 14.8. of the 1996 Act of Adjournal enacts that a minute of continuation shall be entered in the minutes of the interrupted trial; Rule 14.9.-(1) permits other matters, which have been deferred for sentence to await the outcome of the jury trial, to be called once a verdict has been reached in that trial without the need to adjourn.

It will be observed that it is still necessary to call the diet anew after any such interruption (subs.(4)).

PART VIII

APPEALS FROM SOLEMN PROCEEDINGS

Appeal sittings

103.—(1) The High Court shall hold both during session and during vacation such sittings as are necessary for the disposal of appeals and other proceedings under this Part of this Act.

(2) Subject to subsection (3) below, for the purpose of hearing and determining any appeal or other proceeding under this Part of this Act three of the Lords Commissioners of Justiciary shall be a quorum of the High Court, and the determination of any question under this Part of this Act by the court shall be according to the votes of the majority of the members of the court sitting, including the presiding judge, and each judge so sitting shall be entitled to pronounce a separate opinion.

(3) For the purpose of hearing and determining any appeal under section 106(1)(b) to (e) of this Act, or any proceeding connected therewith, two of the Lords Commissioners of Justiciary shall be a quorum of the High Court, and each judge shall be entitled to pronounce a separate opinion; but where the two Lords Commissioners of Justiciary are unable to reach agreement on the disposal of the appeal, or where they consider it appropriate, the appeal shall be heard and determined in accordance with subsection (2) above.

(4) Subsections (1) to (3) above shall apply to cases certified to the High Court by a single judge of the said court and to appeals by way of advocation in like manner as they apply to appeals under this Part of this Act.

(5) The powers of the High Court under this Part of this Act—

(a) to extend the time within which intimation of intention to appeal and note of appeal may be given;

(b) to allow the appellant to be present at any proceedings in cases where he is not entitled to be present without leave; and

(c) to admit an appellant to bail,

may be exercised by any judge of the High Court, sitting and acting wherever convenient, in the same manner as they may be exercised by the High Court, and subject to the same provisions.

(6) Where a judge acting under subsection (5) above refuses an application by an appellant to exercise under that subsection any power in his favour, the appellant shall be entitled to have the application determined by the High Court.

(6A) Where a judge acting under subsection (5)(c) above grants an application by an appellant to exercise that power in his favour, the prosecutor shall be entitled to have the application determined by the High Court.

(7) Subject to subsections (5), (6) and (6A) above and without prejudice to it, preliminary and interlocutory proceedings incidental to any appeal or application may be disposed of by a single judge.

(8) In all proceedings before a judge under section (5) above, and in all preliminary and interlocutory proceedings and applications except such as are heard before the full court, the parties may be represented and appear by a solicitor alone.

AMENDMENT

Subss.(3), (4) and (7) as amended by the Crime and Punishment (Scotland) Act 1997 (c.48), s.62(1) and Sch.1, para.21(13) with effect from August 1, 1997 in terms of the Crime and Punishment (Scotland) Act 1997 (Commencement and Transitional Provisions) Order 1997 (SI 1997/1712) art.3.

Subs.(6A) inserted, and subs.(7) as amended, by Criminal Justice (Scotland) Act 2003 (asp 7), Part 8, s.66. Brought into force on June 27, 2003 by the Criminal Justice (Scotland) Act 2003 (Commencement No.1) Order 2003 (SSI 2003/288 (C.14)).

DEFINITIONS

"appellant": s.132.
"bail": s.307(1).
"High Court" s.307(1).
"judge": s.307(1).

"Lords Commissioners of Justiciary": s.307(1).
"sentence": s.132.

The structure of the 1975 Act in regard to solemn appeals was to deal with the right of appeal (ss.228 *et seq.*) and then to consider procedure at the hearing (ss.245 *et seq.*). The 1995 Act considers the sitting of the High Court of Justiciary to deal with appeals and then the law of appeals in general.

One of the most potent changes for practitioners in the appeal court is the quorum of the High Court of Justiciary. By s.245 of the 1975 Act the quorum for "any appeal" was three and the simple logic was that in the event of division there would be a majority. Commendable as this approach is, there was for nearly all appeals no possibility of division because of judicial uniformity in approach, especially to sentencing.

The fundamental split between appeals against conviction and appeals against sentence is now reflected in the necessary quorum. For any appeal under Pt VIII of the 1995 Act the quorum is three judges except that for appeals against sentence alone the quorum is two judges. This includes appeals against a decision not to exercise the power contained in s.205B(3) and a decision to remit to the Principal Reporter in terms of s.49(1)(a).

The effect of this change, especially when taken with the requirement to obtain leave to appeal, is likely to reduce dramatically the extent of appellate business in the High Court of Justiciary and to reduce the time waiting for appeals to appear on the roll.

In cases not covered by the 1995 Act it is for the court to determine the appropriate quorum—*Express Newspapers PLC Petr*, 1999 S.C.C.R. 262.

If one of the judges in a court is subsequently held not to be impartial then proceedings are treated as if he had not been present. If there are insufficient judges remaining to form a quorum then there is no validly constituted court and hence no valid interlocutor in terms of s.124—*Hoekstra v H.M. Advocate (No.2)*, 2000 S.C.C.R. 368.

Subsection (4)—certification is a procedure whereby a judge on circuit can refer a point of law for decision by the High Court: see *H.M. Advocate v Cunningham*, 1963 J.C. 80 and *H.M. Advocate v Burns*, 1967 J.C. 15.

Subsection (5)—The quorum is one judge in relation to the matters of extending the time within which intimation of intention to appeal and note of appeal may be given, of allowing the appellant to be present at any proceedings in cases where leave is necessary and to admit the appellant to bail.

Prior to the incorporation of the ECHR into domestic law submissions regarding delays in the hearing of appeals received short shrift in the Appeal Court—*Ucak v H.M. Advocate*, 1998 J.C. 283. Article 6 and the right to a fair trial within a reasonable time covers appeal proceedings and has already arisen in *H.M. Advocate v McGlinchey*, 2000 S.C.C.R. 593; *Lawrie v H.M. Advocate*, 2000 G.W.D. 28–1081 and *Mills v H.M. Advocate*, 2001 G.W.D. 20–760.

An argument by the Crown in *Clark v Kelly*, 2000 S.C.C.R. 821 that in cases involving minor charges where alleged breaches of Art.6 occurred the opportunity to challenge any conviction by appeal cured the breach was dismissed by the Appeal Court.

Power of High Court in appeals

104.—(1) Without prejudice to any existing power of the High Court, it may for the purposes of an appeal under section 106(1) or 108 of this Act—

(a) order the production of any document or other thing connected with the proceedings;

(b) hear any evidence relevant to any alleged miscarriage of justice or order such evidence to be heard by a judge of the High Court or by such other person as it may appoint for that purpose;

(c) take account of any circumstances relevant to the case which were not before the trial judge;

(d) remit to any fit person to enquire and report in regard to any matter or circumstance affecting the appeal;

(e) appoint a person with expert knowledge to act as assessor to the High Court in any case where it appears to the court that such expert knowledge is required for the proper determination of the case.

(2) The evidence of any witnesses ordered to be examined before the High Court or before any judge of the High Court or other person appointed by the High Court shall be taken in accordance with the existing law and practice as to the taking of evidence in criminal trials in Scotland.

(3) The appellant or applicant and the respondent or counsel on their behalf shall be entitled to be present at and take part in any examination of any witness to which this section relates.

AMENDMENT

Subs.(1)(b) as amended by the Crime and Punishment (Scotland) Act 1997, Sch.1, para.21.

DEFINITIONS

"appellant": s.132.
"High Court": s.307(1).
"judge": s.307(1).

GENERAL NOTE

The central question in appeals against conviction is whether there has been a miscarriage of justice: s.106(3). The essence of s.104 is to allow the High Court of Justiciary, in addition to any existing powers, statutory powers relating to the investigation of an allegation of a miscarriage of justice. The substance of s.104(1) is essentially that of s.252 of the 1975 Act although it is an indication of how allegations have developed that s.104(2) and (3) clarifies doubts, if there were any, about the manner of taking evidence in the presence of the appellant and his lawyer.

Subsection (1)(a): In *Hoekstra v H.M. Advocate (No.1)*, 2000 S.C.C.R. 263 "disclosure minutes" were prepared by the appellants seeking recovery of new material not available at the trial. It was held that "in general terms the court should not order the Crown to disclose new material in the course of an appeal unless the court was satisfied that the material was likely to be of value for the purpose of evaluating the grounds of appeal and determining whether or not there had been a miscarriage of justice, but the court might be prepared to consider ordering the production of new material which was shown to be of potential importance even if it was not material which was, on a strict reading, relevant to an existing ground of appeal, provided that the material sought could provide the basis for a new or amended ground of appeal which the appellant should, at a late stage be allowed to advance". The court declined in that case to order disclosure. A further petition for recovery was presented in respect of the fresh appeal proceedings. It was argued that the general disclosure of documents was appropriate so that the appellants could investigate the whole background of the prosecution and trial. The Appeal Court disagreed holding that the production of material must relate to the grounds of appeal and the statutory requirements of the 1995 Act—*Hoekstra v H.M. Advocate (No.5)*, 2001 S.C.C.R. 121. In *Porter & Smith Petrs*, 2000 G.W.D. 2–46 a petition for commission and diligence was sought and granted in respect of material evidence not heard at the trial, the existence of which did not become known until later confiscation proceedings.

Subsection (1)(b) has been amended by the Crime and Punishment (Scotland) Act 1997, Sch.1, para.21(14). The word "additional" has been removed in light of the new ground of appeal in s.106(3). For cases where evidence was heard by the Appeal Court see *Morland v H.M. Advocate*, 1985 S.C.C.R. 316; *Kinnon v H.M. Advocate*, 1997 S.C.C.R. 552; *O'Neill v H.M. Advocate*, 1996 G.W.D. 29–1728 and *Daly v H.M. Advocate*, 1997 G.W.D. 22–1067; *Jackson v H.M. Advocate*, 1998 S.C.C.R. 539; Subsection (1)(c), see *Rubin v H.M. Advocate*, 1984 S.C.C.R. 96; *Carrington v H.M. Advocate*, 1994 S.C.C.R. 567 and *Tarbett v H.M. Advocate*, 1994 S.C.C.R. 867; Subsection (1)(d), see *McCadden v H.M. Advocate*, 1985 S.C.C.R. 282; *Robertson v H.M. Advocate*, 1996 S.C.C.R. 243; *Crossan v H.M. Advocate*, 1996 S.C.C.R. 279; *Squire v H.M. Advocate*, 1998 G.W.D. 28–1410; *Feely v H.M. Advocate*, 2000 G.W.D. 12–422 and *Kerr v H.M. Advocate*, 1999 S.C.C.R. 763. As Sheriff Gordon points out in his commentary the remit to a single judge required to be specific in its terms so as not to conflict with s.8 of the Contempt of Court Act 1981.

The form an investigation should take is set out in *Squire v H.M. Advocate*, 1998 G.W.D. 28–1410, a case concerning alleged communications between the jury and the clerk of court. In considering the question of an alleged miscarriage of justice, in *Clark v H.M. Advocate*, 2000 S.C.C.R. 767 the tape of part of the judge's charge was played to the Appeal Court.

Appeal against refusal of application

105.—(1) When an application or applications have been dealt with by a judge of the High Court, under section 103(5) of this Act, the Clerk of Justiciary shall—

(a) notify to the applicant the decision in the form prescribed by Act of Adjournal or as nearly as may be in such form; and

(b) where all or any of such applications have been refused, forward to the applicant the prescribed form for completion and return forthwith if he desires to have the application or applications determined by the High Court as fully constituted for the hearing of appeals under this Part of this Act.

(2) Where the applicant does not desire a determination as mentioned in subsection (1)(b) above, or does not return within five days to the Clerk the form duly completed by him, the refusal of his application or applications by the judge shall be final.

(3) Where an applicant who desires a determination by the High Court as mentioned in subsection (1)(b) above—

(a) is not legally represented, he may be present at the hearing and determination by the High Court of the application;

(b) is legally represented, he shall not be entitled to be present without leave of the court.

(4) When an applicant duly completes and returns to the Clerk of Justiciary within the prescribed time the form expressing a desire to be present at the hearing and determination by the court of the applications mentioned in this section, the form shall be deemed to be an application by the applicant for leave to be so present, and the Clerk of Justiciary, on receiving the form, shall take the necessary steps for placing the application before the court.

(4A) An application by a convicted person for a determination by the High Court of a decision of a judge acting under section 103(5)(c) of this Act to refuse to admit him to bail shall be intimated by him immediately and in writing to the Crown Agent.

(5) If the application to be present is refused by the court, the Clerk of Justiciary shall notify the applicant; and if the application is granted, he shall notify the applicant and the Governor of the prison where the applicant is in custody and the Secretary of State.

(6) For the purpose of constituting a Court of Appeal, the judge who has refused any application may sit as a member of the court, and take part in determining the application.

AMENDMENT

Subs.(4A) inserted by Criminal Justice (Scotland) Act 2003 (asp 7), Part 8, s.66. Brought into force on June 27, 2003 by the Criminal Justice (Scotland) Act 2003 (Commencement No.1) Order 2003 (SSI 2003/288 (C.14)).

DEFINITIONS

"clerk of justiciary": s.307(1).
"High Court": s.307(1).
"judge": s.307(1).

GENERAL NOTE

Under s.103(5) the quorum is one judge in relation to the matters of extending the time within which intimation of intention to appeal and note of appeal may be given, of allowing the appellant to be present at any proceedings in cases where leave is necessary and to admit the appellant to bail.

Section 105 prescribes the procedure to appeal against a refusal of an application under s.103(5). Such an appeal (not being an appeal against sentence) requires to be heard by three judges. It is strange to see that for the purposes of constituting a Court of Appeal, the judge who has refused any application may sit as a member of the court, and take part in determining the application: s.105(6).

Appeal against granting of application

105A.—(1) Where the prosecutor desires a determination by the High Court as mentioned in subsection (6A) of section 103 of this Act, he shall apply to the judge immediately after the power in subsection (5)(c) of that section is exercised in favour of the appellant.

(2) Where a judge acting under section 103(5)(c) of this Act has exercised that power in favour of the appellant but the prosecutor has made an application under subsection (1) above—

    (a) the appellant shall not be liberated until the determination by the High Court; and

    (b) that application by the prosecutor shall be heard not more than seven days after the making of the application,

and the Clerk of the Justiciary shall forward to the appellant the prescribed form for completion and return forthwith if he desires to be present at the hearing.

(3) At a hearing and determination as mentioned in subsection (2) above, if the appellant—

    (a) is not legally represented, he may be present;

    (b) is legally represented, he shall not be entitled to be present without leave of the court.

(4) If the appellant completes and returns the form mentioned in subsection (2) above indicating a desire to be present at the hearing, the form shall be deemed to be an application by the appellant for leave to be so present, and the Clerk of Justiciary, on receiving the form, shall take the necessary steps for placing the application before the court.

(5) If the application to be present is refused by the court, the Clerk of Justiciary shall notify the appellant; and if the application is granted, he shall notify the appellant and the Governor of the prison where the applicant is in custody and the Scottish Ministers.

(6) For the purposes of constituting a Court of Appeal, the judge who exercised the power in section 103(5)(c) of this Act in favour of the appellant may sit as a member of the court, and take part in determining the application of the prosecutor.

AMENDMENT

Section 105A inserted by Criminal Justice (Scotland) Act 2003 (asp 7), Part 8, s.66. Brought into force on June 27, 2003 by the Criminal Justice (Scotland) Act 2003 (Commencement No.1) Order 2003 (SSI 2003/288 (C.14)).

Right of appeal

106.—(1) Any person convicted on indictment may, with leave granted in accordance with section 107 of this Act, appeal in accordance with this Part of this Act, to the High Court—

    (a) against such conviction;

    (b) subject to subsection (2) below, against the sentence passed on such conviction;

  (ba) against the making of an order for lifelong restriction;

  (bb) against any decision not to exercise the power conferred by section 205A(3) or 205B(3) of this Act;

    (c) against his absolute discharge or admonition;

    (d) against any probation order, drug treatment and testing order or any community service order;

(da) against any decision to remit made under section 49(1)(a) of this Act;

(db) against any reference proposed under section 10(1) of the Protection of Children (Scotland) Act 2003 (asp 5) in respect of the conviction;

(dc) against such reference and, subject to subsection (2) below, such sentence, disposal or order or any order deferring sentence;

(e) against any order deferring sentence; or

(f) against

    (i) both such conviction and, subject to subsection (2) below, such sentence or disposal or order;

    (ii) both such a conviction and such a reference; or

    (iii) such a conviction, such a reference and, subject to subsection (2) below, such sentence, disposal or order.

(2) There shall be no appeal against any sentence fixed by law.

(3) By an appeal under subsection (1) above a person may bring under review of the High Court any alleged miscarriage of justice, which may include such a miscarriage based on—

(a) subject to subsections (3A) to (3D) below, the existence and significance of evidence which was not heard at the original proceedings; and

(b) the jury's having returned a verdict which no reasonable jury, properly directed, could have returned.

(3A) Evidence such as is mentioned in subsection (3)(a) above may found an appeal only where there is a reasonable explanation of why it was not so heard.

(3B) Where the explanation referred to in subsection (3A) above or, as the case may be, (3C) below is that the evidence was not admissible at the time of the original proceedings, but is admissible at the time of the appeal, the court may admit that evidence if it appears to the court that it would be in the interests of justice to do so.

(3C) Without prejudice to subsection (3A) above, where evidence such as is mentioned in paragraph (a) of subsection (3) above is evidence—

(a) which is—

    (i) from a person; or

    (ii) of a statement (within the meaning of section 259(1) of this Act) by a person,

who gave evidence at the original proceedings; and

(b) which is different from, or additional to, the evidence so given,

it may not found an appeal unless there is a reasonable explanation as to why the evidence now sought to be adduced was not given by that person at those proceedings, which explanation is itself supported by independent evidence.

(3D) For the purposes of subsection (3C) above, "independent evidence" means evidence which—

(a) was not heard at the original proceedings;

(b) is from a source independent of the person referred to in subsection (3C) above; and

(c) is accepted by the court as being credible and reliable.

(4) Any document, production or other thing lodged in connection with the proceedings on the trial of any person who, if convicted, is entitled or may be authorised to appeal under this Part of this Act, shall, in accordance with subsections (5) to (9) below, be kept in the custody of the court in which the conviction took place.

(5) All documents and other productions produced at the trial of a convicted

person shall be kept in the custody of the court of trial in such manner as it may direct until any period allowed under or by virtue of this Part of this Act for lodging intimation of intention to appeal has elapsed.

(6) Where no direction is given as mentioned in subsection (5) above, such custody shall be in the hands of the sheriff clerk of the district of the court of the second diet to whom the clerk of court shall hand them over at the close of the trial, unless otherwise ordered by the High Court on an intimation of intention to appeal being lodged, and if within such period there has been such lodgement under this Part of this Act, they shall be so kept until the appeal, if it is proceeded with, is determined.

(7) Notwithstanding subsections (5) and (6) above, the judge of the court in which the conviction took place may, on cause shown, grant an order authorising any of such documents or productions to be released on such conditions as to custody and return as he may deem it proper to prescribe.

(8) All such documents or other productions so retained in custody or released and returned shall, under supervision of the custodian thereof, be made available for inspection and for the purpose of making copies of documents or productions to a person who has lodged an intimation of intention to appeal or as the case may be, to the convicted person's counsel or agent, and to the Crown Agent and the procurator fiscal or his deputes.

(9) Where no intimation of intention to appeal is lodged within the period mentioned in subsection (6) above, all such documents and productions shall be dealt with as they are dealt with according to the existing law and practice at the conclusion of a trial; and they shall be so dealt with if, there having been such intimation, the appeal is not proceeded with.

AMENDMENTS

Subs.(3) as amended by the Crime and Punishment (Scotland) Act 1997 (c.48), s.17 with effect from August 1, 1997 in terms of the Crime and Punishment (Scotland) Act 1997 (Commencement and Transitional Provisions) Order 1997 (SI 1997/1712), art.3.

Subs.(1)(bb) inserted by the Crime and Punishment (Scotland) Act 1997 (c.48), s.18 with effect from October 20, 1997 in terms of the Crime and Punishment (Scotland) Act 1997 (Commencement No. 2 and Transitional Provisions) Order 1997 (SI 1997/2323), art.3, Sch.1; amended by the Crime and Disorder Act 1998 (c.37), Sch.8, para.119 (effective September 30, 1998: SI 1998/2327).

Subs.(1)(da) inserted by the Crime and Punishment (Scotland) Act 1997 (c.48), s.23 with effect from August 1, 1997 in terms of the Crime and Punishment (Scotland) Act 1997 (Commencement and Transitional Provisions) Order 1997 (SI 1997/1712), art.3.

Subs.(1)(d) as amended by the Crime and Disorder Act 1998 (c.37), s.94 and Sch.6, para.5. Brought into force on September 30, 1998 by the Crime and Disorder Act 1998 (Commencement No.2 and Transitional Provisions) Order 1998 (SI 1998/2327 (C.53)).

Subs.(1)(db)(dc) and (f)(ii)(iii) inserted, and subs.(1)(f) as amended, by the Protection of Children (Scotland) Act 2003 (asp 5), s.16(2). Brought into force on January 10, 2005 by the Protection of Children (Scotland) Act 2003 (Commencement No.1) Order 2004 (SSI 2004/522 (C.38)), art.2.

Subs.(1)(ba) inserted by the Criminal Justice (Scotland) Act 2003, Sch.1, para.2(4). Brought into force on June 19, 2006 by the Criminal Justice (Scotland) Act 2003 (Commencement No.9) Order 2006 (SSI 2006/332 (C.30)), art.2(1), subject to art.2(2).

DEFINITIONS

"community service order": s.238.
"High Court": s.307(1).
"indictment": s.307(1).
"judge": s.307(1).
"probation order": s.228.
"procurator fiscal": s.307(1).
"sentence": s.307(1).
"sheriff court": s.307(1).

The Crime and Punishment Act 1997 radically altered this section and in particular subs.(3) containing the single ground of appeal. The changes followed a report by the Sutherland Committee who were appointed to examine the criteria for consideration of appeals by the Appeal Court and to consider any changes that may be required (Cmnd 3245).

An appeal under s.106 must be "with leave granted in accordance with s.107 of this Act". Reference may be made to that section and the General Note to it for a full understanding of this hurdle to be cleared.

Assuming that leave has been granted, an appeal against conviction alone is possible under s.106(1)(a) and against both conviction and sentence disposal or other order under s.106(1)(f). The hearing of these appeals will be by three judges: s.103(2). Further assuming that leave has been granted, an appeal against sentence and other similar disposals is possible under s.106(1)(b) to (e) inclusive. The hearing of these appeals will be by two judges: s.103(2).

Subs.(1)

From October 20, 1997, a convicted person can also appeal against a decision to impose a minimum sentence for drug trafficking. From August 1, 1997 a convicted person can appeal against any decision by the court to remit to the Principal Reporter in terms of s.49(1)(a) to arrange for disposal by a Children's Hearing.

Subs.(2)

There is no appeal against any sentence fixed by law. The clearest example of this is the sentence of imprisonment for life for murder: s.205(1). A minimum recommendation can be appealed: see s.205(6).

Subs.(3)

The provision implementing the new subs.(3) took effect on August 1, 1997. It applies to all appeals in existence at that date and all appeals raised thereafter. The single ground of appeal remains on the basis of a miscarriage of justice but gone is the one example of the existence and significance of additional evidence. This has been replaced with two examples namely (a) the existence and significance of evidence which was not heard at the original proceedings and (b) a verdict returned by a jury which no reasonable jury properly directed could have returned. The retention of "miscarriage of justice" was recommended by the Sutherland Committee on the basis that the phrase was adaptable to changing circumstances citing the case of *Anderson v HM Advocate*, 1996 S.C.C.R. 114 as an example of this. The miscarriage need no longer occur "in the proceedings". The Sutherland Committee considered that this created room for uncertainty and argument as a miscarriage of justice could arise as a result of an event prior to the trial or evidence emerging post conviction.

The test which the court should apply in determining whether to quash a conviction or to substitute an amended verdict was considered in *Smith v HM Advocate*, 2001 S.L.T. 438. The court held where the Crown accept that a jury's verdict must be set aside but contend that, on the correct factual basis, the court should substitute a different verdict of guilty, the onus of satisfying the court that it should do so must rest on the Crown. When deciding whether to substitute an amended verdict of guilty the Appeal Court should consider what a reasonable jury, properly instructed, would have done. See also *Murray v HM Advocate*, 2001 S.L.T. 435.

The first appeal case to consider the new subss.(3) and (3A) to (3D) was *Campbell and Steele v HM Advocate*, 1998 S.C.C.R. 214.

Subs. 3(a)

The evidence no longer requires to be "additional" as outlined in e.g. *Mitchell v HM Advocate*, 1989 S.C.C.R. 502 and *McCormack v HM Advocate*, 1993 S.C.C.R. 581. Therefore subject to subs.(3A) (see below) recovery of memory could now qualify and so too could change of story by a witness, subject to subs.(3C).

It was held in *Kidd v HM Advocate*, 2000 J.C. 509 that the governing question in any appeal based on fresh evidence is whether the fact that it was not heard at the trial represents a miscarriage of justice. It is not a question of whether the additional evidence is significant but whether it is of such significance as to lead to the conclusion that a verdict returned in ignorance of it must be regarded as a miscarriage of justice. The sole test is miscarriage of justice. The significance of the evidence includes considerations regarding relevance, materiality and importance and quality in the point of credibility and reliability. None of these factors is determinative. It is the overall impression which is created. The court pointed out that the Appeal Court is different in function from the trial court and does not enjoy the advantages of hearing and seeing the original witnesses and that there are inherent limitations in an appeal court determining what the trial court would have made of the additional evidence when considered in the context of the original evidence. It is sufficient that the Appeal Court be satisfied that the evidence is capable of being regarded by a reasonable jury as both credible and reliable but that the importance of its quality must be emphasised and that its cogency is of critical importance.

A discrepancy previously was thought to exist between the criterion set out in *Cameron v HM Advocate*, 1987 S.C.C.R. 608 and *Church v HM Advocate*, 1996 S.C.C.R. 29. In *Kidd, supra* the Appeal Court considered that there was no essential difference between the approach in *Cameron* and *Church*. McCluskey and McBride on "Criminal Appeals" appear to disagree as does Sheriff Gordon in his commentary to *McLay v HM Advocate*, 2000 S.C.C.R. 579. See also *Fraser v HM Advocate*, 2000 S.C.C.R. 755 on the applicable test; *Mills v HM Advocate*, 2001 G.W.D. 20–760 and *Rennie v HM Advocate*, 2001 G.W.D. 21–793.

Subs. 3(b)

Section 2(1) of the Criminal Appeal (Scotland) Act 1926 (c.15) provided inter alia that a verdict of a jury could be set aside on the grounds that it was unreasonable or could not be supported by the evidence, but the proviso to the section required a "substantial miscarriage of justice" before an appeal would be allowed (see *Webb v HM Advocate*, 1927 J.C. 92). The test of unreasonableness was as set out in the current provision namely a verdict which no reasonable jury properly directed could have returned (see *Slater v HM Advocate*, 1928 J.C. 94). In *Macmillan v HM Advocate*, 1927 J.C. 62 and *Webb, supra* the court stated that the Appeal Court was not a court of review and it could not upset a verdict because it disagreed with a jury's view of evidence or credibility of witnesses. There had to be circumstances of a special character before the court would set aside a jury's verdict.

Post 1980 legislation did not contain provision for review of unreasonable verdicts provoking concern about verdicts considered to be unsafe.

The Sutherland Committee recognised that the test to be applied in the current legislation is very similar to the test applied by the Appeal Court under the 1926 legislation. They envisaged that an appeal based on this subsection would succeed only in exceptional cases. They expected however "a broader recognition of the potential for such cases" than with the 1926 Act. Subsection 3(b) was considered by the Appeal Court in *King v HMAdvocate*, 1999 S.C.C.R. 330. It was held that the Appeal Court could quash the verdict of a jury only if satisfied that, on the evidence led at the trial, no reasonable jury could have been satisfied beyond a reasonable doubt that the accused was guilty. (The court observed that this formulation was not dissimilar to that in Webb but gave no indication whether in future cases it would be as strictly interpreted.) At p. 333E to F the Lord Justice-General stated "the test is objective; the court must be able to say that no reasonable jury *could* have returned a guilty verdict on the evidence before them. Since in any case where the provision is invoked the jury will ex hypothesi have returned a guilty verdict, their verdict will have implied they were satisfied beyond a reasonable doubt that the Appellant was guilty. What the appellant must establish therefore is that, on the evidence led at the trial, no reasonable jury could have been satisfied beyond a reasonable doubt that the appellant was guilty." The Appeal Court will not simply substitute their view of the evidence for the jury's view. There will not be a miscarriage of justice simply because the Appeal Court might have entertained a reasonable doubt on the evidence. In determining such cases the Appeal Court will have regard to the fact that the jury had the advantage of seeing and hearing the evidence. In *King* four witnesses led by the Crown contradicted the Crown case in that they claimed to have seen the deceased alive and well some three hours after the murder allegedly occurred. The Appeal Court held that the jury would have been entitled to accept or reject the evidence of the four witnesses and it could not be said that no reasonable jury could have been satisfied beyond a reasonable doubt that the appellant was guilty and appeal refused; see also *McAllan v. H.M. Advocate*, 1999 G.W.D. 18–826 and *Donnelly v. H.M. Advocate*, 2000 S.C.C.R. 861.

A verdict cannot be attacked under this provision on the basis of "fresh evidence" as the attack must be based on evidence actually before the jury: see *Campbell and Steele v. H.M. Advocate, supra.* Otherwise an appellant would be able to circumvent subss. (3A) to (3D).

Subs. (3A)

Additional evidence required to be evidence which was not available and could not have reasonably been made available at the trial. The test was an exacting one and had to be fully satisfied see *Carr v. Lees*, 1993 S.C.C.R. 316 and *Tolmie v. H.M. Advocate*, 1997 G.W.D. 26–1312. The reasonable availability test has now gone and all that is required is that a "reasonable explanation" be provided as to why the evidence was not heard at the original proceedings see subs.(3A).

"Reasonable explanation". The Sutherland Committee recommended no attempt be made to qualify or interpret the term and that it be a matter for the court to decide. They did consider that the comments of Lord Justice-Clerk Thomson in *Gallacher v. H.M. Advocate*, 1951 J.C. 38 regarding an adequate explanation for a failure to produce fresh evidence at a trial were relevant. His Lordship stated:

> "No general rule can possibly be laid down and the explanation in any particular case must be viewed, not in the light of any technicality or rule of practice or procedure but solely in the light of the dominating consideration that we may order new evidence if we think it necessary or expedient in the interests of justice."

The Appeal Court in *Campbell and Steele v. H.M. Advocate, supra,* considered that although the words "necessary or expedient in the interests of justice", which were used by the Lord Justice-Clerk in reference to s.6 of the 1926 Act, were not included in subs.(3A) in determining whether the terms of that subsection were satisfied the court should have regard to the interests of justice according to the circumstances of the particular case. As the Lord Justice-Clerk states "the underlying intention of the new legislation is that the court should take a broad and flexible approach in taking account of the circumstances of the particular case".

A "reasonable explanation" Lord Sutherland defined as an "explanation which, in the circumstances of the particular case is one which the court is persuaded to regard as some justification for the failure to lead the evidence bearing in mind the context that what is being enquired into is an alleged miscarriage of justice which in turn involves the concept of the interests of justice as a whole".

Lord McCluskey considered that "where an appellant is able to tender an explanation which cannot be shown without enquiry to be untrue and which is one that the court can objectively regard as plausible, sufficient and not unreasonable" the Appeal Court would then ask if it was necessary or expedient in the interests of justice to hear the evidence. The L.J.-C. stated that the explanation must be adequate to account for the fact that a witness evidence was not heard.

It is for the appellant to satisfy the test of reasonable explanation in subs.(3A) and reasonable explanation will be interpreted in an objective way. The Court must be persuaded to treat the explanation as genuine rather than as true as the latter would require what Lord McCluskey describes as "preliminary proof as to the truth or otherwise of the explanation" and hence "depart dramatically from the relatively simple approach which the Sutherland Committee recommended, the Government expressly accepted and which Parliament approved and enacted".

The L.J.-C. and Lord Sutherland agreed with the English Court of Appeal in *R. v. Shields and Patrick* [1977] Crim.L.R. 281 that a decision not to call a witness whose evidence was viewed as dangerous would seldom be a reasonable explanation. Their Lordships considered that a tactical decision not to call a witness could not provide a reasonable explanation nor could an appellant being unaware of the existence of a witness or if aware, not aware he was able or willing to give evidence of any significance. The Lord Justice-Clerk did however go on to state that if the appellant could show that at the time of the trial he had no good reason for thinking that the witness existed or as the case might be that he would give the evidence in question then this might amount to a reasonable explanation. It "might depend on the steps which the appellant could reasonably be expected to have taken in the light of what was known at the time". Failure by defence solicitors to precognosce a witness on the Crown list could not, according to Lord Sutherland, amount to a reasonable explanation.

In the English case of *R. v. Beresford* (1971) 56 Cr.App.R. 143 the court confirmed that in order to satisfy the reasonable explanation requirement "the court has in general to be satisfied that the evidence could not with reasonable diligence have been obtained for use at the trial".

In *Hall v. H.M. Advocate*, 1998 S.C.C.R. 525 the Appeal Court accepted that a reasonable explanation existed in respect of a witness who had not been on the Crown list of witnesses, who had given two statements to the police making no mention of the evidence he was now giving and who at the time he was interviewed by the police was anxious to conceal his presence near to the locus. The appellant argued that given the witness' position at the time of the trial the defence could not, in the exercise of reasonable diligence, have been aware of the significance of the witness. The Appeal Court also agreed to hear the evidence of a witness who was on the list of Crown witnesses but who was not called at the trial diet. Her evidence had become significant in the light of the first witness whose evidence was to be heard. Her significance, it was argued, could not have been discovered by the defence at the time. The Appeal Court stressed that even if there is a reasonable explanation provided the evidence will only be heard if it is "significant evidence" in the light of the test set out in *Cameron v. H.M. Advocate*, 1987 S.C.C.R. 608 at 619.

The Appeal Court in *Hall v. H.M. Advocate, supra* observed that adequate specification should be given in the grounds of appeal of what is proposed to be adduced as additional evidence and what is merely a change in the evidence.

In *Hall v. H.M. Advocate (No. 2)*, 1999 S.C.C.R. 130, in quashing the conviction, it was held that the terms of subs.(3A) suggest that the reasonable explanation question should be looked at from the point of view of those who represented the appellant at the time of the trial, which includes the period when the defence was being prepared and that if it was shown that despite reasonable steps having been taken to investigate the case, it did not appear that a person would provide information which would be of assistance, whether by way of challenging the Crown case or advancing the case for the defence, there could be a reasonable explanation of why the witness was not adduced at the trial. In attempting to satisfy the subs.(3A) requirements it is important that the appellant should be able to point to information as to what was known to those who represented the appellant at the time and what steps they took to investigate the defence. Information should also be provided regarding any reason or reasons for thinking no further enquiries were necessary, if appropriate—*Barr v. H.M. Advocate*, 1999 S.C.C.R. 13.

In *Mills v. H.M. Advocate*, 1999 S.C.C.R. 202 it was held that the decision not to call an incriminee as a witness at a trial precluded his evidence and evidence of alleged confessions made by him being led in terms of s.106(3) at the stage of an appeal as the test in subs.(3A) had not been satisfied. The Crown conceded in that case that the fact that a co-accused did not give evidence and could not be compelled to give evidence amounted to a reasonable explanation. The court, however reserved their opinion regarding this concession. They did suggest that in such circumstances a motion for separation of trials would have been appropriate. As Sheriff Gordon notes in his commentary on this case if such a motion was refused it could be argued that the test in subs.(3A) had been satisfied.

In *Karling v. H.M. Advocate*, 1999 S.C.C.R. 359 the Appeal Court observed that a reasonable explanation why evidence was not led from one witness does not necessarily apply to another witness. If a reasonable explanation is advanced regarding part of a witness' evidence it does not necessarily apply to the whole of their evidence. In that case a reasonable explanation for not seeking further expert opinion was held to have been made out where a defence expert provided advice to the appellant's solicitors confirming the Crown evidence as to one possible cause of death. The Court rejected this explanation regarding another possible cause of death which had been raised at the trial. If the existence of a witness is not known this may amount to a reasonable explanation *Fraser v. H.M. Advocate*, 2000 S.C.C.R. 755.

Subs. (3B)

In *Conway v. H.M. Advocate*, 1996 S.C.C.R. 570 the accused was unable to benefit from a change in the hearsay provisions where his trial had been concluded prior to a change in the rules, the court holding that the evidence must have been admissible at the original trial. Under the new provision the law current at the date of the hearing of the appeal would apply.

Subs. (3C)

Mitchell v. H.M. Advocate, 1989 S.C.C.R. 502 and *Brodie v. H.M. Advocate*, 1993 S.C.C.R. 371 established that the Appeal Court will not entertain an appeal on the basis that a witness who has given evidence at the trial wishes to change his story. The Sutherland Committee recommended that this be changed but added the proviso that the reason for the change of testimony be supported by additional credible and reliable evidence. The Government originally rejected this proposal but at the committee stage in the House of Lords introduced the present provision. The section relates not only to oral evidence from a person but also a statement under the exceptions to the hearsay provisions in terms of s.259. The evidence sought to be adduced can be different or additional. A reasonable explanation must be provided as to why the evidence sought to be led was not given by that person at the trial. The section also provides for a check in the form of "independent evidence" which is defined in subs.(3D) to support the reasonable explanation.

The main ground of appeal in *Campbell and Steele v. H.M. Advocate, supra*, was the changing of the evidence of a material witness. The Lord Justice-Clerk and Lord Sutherland considered that in such appeals the words "without prejudice to subs.(3A)" meant that the first hurdle to be overcome was that a reasonable explanation had to be provided by the appellant as to why the evidence was not heard and thereafter a reasonable explanation would be required from the witness as to why the evidence was not given.

Lord McCluskey in his opinion however dissented from the two reasonable explanations requirement. As His Lordship points out there are cases where a witness cannot or will not provide an explanation hence the reference to the hearsay provisions in s.259. Parliament's intention was not to so prejudice an appellant.

Reasonable explanation in this subsection is as defined for subs.(3A).

In *Hall v. H.M. Advocate, supra* the appellant sought to argue that a transcript of a police interview (post conviction) with a witness who gave evidence at the trial was a statement that fell within s.106(3C)(a)(ii), namely evidence different or additional to that given at the trial. As the requirements of s.259(2) had not been satisfied the attempt to rely on subs. (3C)(a)(ii) foundered. The appellant then sought to rely on subs. (3C)(a)(i) namely that it was evidence from a person different or additional to the evidence given at the trial. The reasonable explanation for not giving this evidence at the trial was said to be that the witness was a fantasist or untruthful. Independent evidence was said to come from other false allegations made. The Appeal Court held that the reasonable explanation test was not satisfied. No explanation had been provided by the witness. The Appeal Court considered it unnecessary to express a concluded view on whether the reasonable explanation should come from the witness himself. The Court also held that there was no independent evidence to support the explanation. See also *McLay v. H.M. Advocate*, 2000 S.C.C.R. 579.

Subs. (3D)

The independent evidence must satisfy three requirements. In respect of part (a) it is the evidence which requires not to have been heard, not the witness and therefore if a witness is called to give evidence at a trial diet but not asked about a particular matter then the provision would be satisfied—or as in the case of *Cameron v. H.M. Advocate*, 1994 S.C.C.R. 502 a witness could state that they were not prepared to give evidence to that effect at the trial. The Sutherland Committee considered that the additional supporting evidence could be evidence which was heard at the trial but clearly given the terms of part (a) this could not be the case.

Part (b) provides that the evidence must be independent of the person who is changing his story. This was discussed in some detail at the committee stage in the House of Lords (see *Hansard*, H.L. March 10, 1997 cols 37 to 39). The Lord Advocate explained that independent evidence could derive from a relative or colleague, more importantly however, the independent evidence should relate to the reason why the new evidence was not given at the earlier trial and should not relate to the particulars of the new account. This would cover the situation in *McCormack supra* where an accused was suffering from amnesia (see the comments of L.J. Hope and the Lord Advocate in *Hansard*, H.L. March 10, 1997 col. 39) and the independent evidence could be from a doctor that the accused was suffering from this condition. If however the reasonable explanation is that the witness had been pressurised into withholding evidence it may be difficult to find independent evidence to support this.

In *Campbell and Steele v. H.M. Advocate*, *supra*, the appellants sought to employ, as independent evidence *inter alia* the evidence of police officers of what Love said during interview post conviction of the two accused. The Appeal Court held that this could not be independent evidence as the evidence was of statements from the same source, *i.e.* Love.

Part (c) provides that the evidence must be credible and reliable.

It is for the Appeal Court to decide whether or not the evidence is credible and reliable.

Subss. (4) to (9)

The remaining subsections of s.106 are concerned with the custody of trial documents, productions and related matters. The emphasis in Scotland on real evidence means that there are or can be a substantial quantity of material to be kept safe for the possible consideration of the appellate judges or until such time as it seems reasonable to consider that there is not to be an appeal. In *Strock, Petr*, 1996 S.C.C.R. 432 the court indicated that the proviso in s.270(2) of the 1975 Act now s.106(7) can operate even though an appeal against conviction was pending. If the outstanding appeal relates to the person seeking release of productions conditions might have to be imposed as to custody and return of productions.

Sentence

The foregoing note is directed principally to any alleged miscarriage of justice in relation to conviction but it is competent to bring under review of the High Court of Justiciary any alleged miscarriage of justice, including one which arises in relation to sentence on the basis of evidence not *heard at the original proceedings*: see *Renton and Brown* (5th ed.) para. 11–47, at p.208. At any rate in appeals against sentence the test is no longer (as before 1980) whether the sentence was harsh and oppressive but whether it was excessive: *Addison v. Mackinnon*, 1983 S.C.C.R. 52; *Donaldson v. H.M. Advocate*, 1983 S.C.C.R. 216. A bold statement that a sentence is excessive might reasonably be said to be lacking in specification. There must be an indication of the circumstances to be relied on. One important reason for that is to allow the trial judge or the sheriff to report fully upon them for the appellate judges, see Practice Note "Appeals in Solemn Procedure and Appeals against Sentence in Summary Procedure", March 29, 1985. For an example of an appeal against sentence on the basis of fresh evidence see *Baikie v. H.M. Advocate*, 2000 S.C.C.R. 119. Medical reports obtained post sentence disclosed the appellant was suffering from an undiagnosed mental condition at the time of sentence. A hospital order was substituted.

Appeal against automatic sentences where earlier conviction quashed

106A.—[(1) This subsection applies where—

(a) a person has been sentenced under section 205A(2) of this Act;

(b) he had, at the time at which the offence for which he was so sentenced was committed, only one previous conviction for a qualifying offence or a relevant offence within the meaning of that section; and

(c) after he has been so sentenced, the conviction mentioned in paragraph (b) above has been quashed.]

(2) This subsection applies where—

(a) a person has been sentenced under section 205B(2) of this Act;

(b) he had, at the time at which the offence for which he was so sentenced was committed, only two previous convictions for class A drug trafficking offences within the meaning of that section; and

(c) after he has been so sentenced, one of the convictions mentioned in paragraph (b) above has been quashed.

(3) Where subsection (1) or (2) above applies, the person may appeal under section 106(1)(b) of this Act against the sentence imposed on him under [section 205A(2) or, as the case may be], 205B(2) of this Act.

(4) An appeal under section 106(1)(b) of this Act by virtue of subsection (3) above—

(a) may be made notwithstanding that the person has previously appealed under that section; and

(b) shall be lodged within two weeks of the quashing of the conviction as mentioned in subsection (1)(c) or, as the case may be, (2)(c) above.

(5) Where an appeal is made under section 106(1)(b) by virtue of this section, the following provisions of this Act shall not apply in relation to such an appeal, namely—

(a) section 121; and

(b) section 126.

AMENDMENTS

Section 106A inserted by the Crime and Punishment (Scotland) Act 1997 (c.48) s.19 with effect from October 20, 1997 in terms of the Crime and Punishment (Scotland) Act 1997 (Commencement No.2 and Transitional Provisions) Order 1997 (SI 1997/2323) art.3, Sch.1.

Subs.(1) prospectively inserted by the above.

Subs.(3) inserted by the above and effective except in so far as it refers to s.205(A)(2) of the 1995 Act.

GENERAL NOTE

From the October 20, 1997 where an earlier conviction which qualified an accused of a minimum sentence for drug trafficking is quashed by the Appeal Court, an accused who has received the minimum sentence may appeal. The appeal is in terms of s.106(1)(b) and must be made within two weeks of the conviction being quashed. A previous appeal against sentence does not preclude an appeal under this section.

Subs.(5) provides that suspension of disqualification etc. and the provisions relating to extract convictions shall not apply where there is an appeal under this section.

Leave to appeal

107.—(1) The decision whether to grant leave to appeal for the purposes of section 106(1) of this Act shall be made by a judge of the High Court who shall—

(a) if he considers that the documents mentioned in subsection (2) below disclose arguable grounds of appeal, grant leave to appeal and make such comments in writing as he considers appropriate; and

    (b) in any other case—
        (i) refuse leave to appeal and give reasons in writing for the refusal; and
       (ii) where the appellant is on bail and the sentence imposed on his conviction is one of imprisonment, grant a warrant to apprehend and imprison him.

(2) The documents referred to in subsection (1) above are—

    (a) the note of appeal lodged under section 110(1)(a) of this Act;

    (b) in the case of an appeal against conviction or sentence in a sheriff court, the certified copy or, as the case may be, the record of the proceedings at the trial;

    (c) where the judge who presided at the trial furnishes a report under section 113 of this Act, that report; and

    (d) where, by virtue of section 94(1) of this Act, a transcript of the charge to the jury of the judge who presided at the trial is delivered to the Clerk of Justiciary, that transcript.

(3) A warrant granted under subsection (1)(b)(ii) above shall not take effect until the expiry of the period of 14 days mentioned in subsection (4) below (and if that period is extended under subsection (4A) below before the period being extended expires, until the expiry of the period as so extended) without an application to the High Court for leave to appeal having been lodged by the appellant under that subsection.

(4) Where leave to appeal is refused under subsection (1) above the appellant may, within 14 days of intimation under subsection (10) below, apply to the High Court for leave to appeal.

(4A) The High Court may, on cause shown, extend the period of 14 days mentioned in subsection (4) above, or that period as extended under this subsection, whether or not the period to be extended has expired (and if that period of 14 days has expired, whether or not it expired before section 62 of the Criminal Justice (Scotland) Act 2003 (asp 7) came into force).

(5) In deciding an application under subsection (4) above the High Court shall—

    (a) if, after considering the documents mentioned in subsection (2) above and the reasons for the refusal, the court is of the opinion that there are arguable grounds of appeal, grant leave to appeal and make such comments in writing as the court considers appropriate; and

    (b) in any other case—
        (i) refuse leave to appeal and give reasons in writing for the refusal; and
       (ii) where the appellant is on bail and the sentence imposed on his conviction is one of imprisonment, grant a warrant to apprehend and imprison him.

(6) Consideration whether to grant leave to appeal under subsection (1) or (5) above shall take place in chambers without the parties being present.

(7) Comments in writing made under subsection (1)(a) or (5)(a) above may, without prejudice to the generality of that provision, specify the arguable grounds of appeal (whether or not they are contained in the note of appeal) on the basis of which leave to appeal is granted.

(8) Where the arguable grounds of appeal are specified by virtue of subsection (7) above it shall not, except by leave of the High Court on cause shown, be competent for the appellant to found any aspect of his appeal on any ground of appeal contained in the note of appeal but not so specified.

(9) Any application by the appellant for the leave of the High Court under subsection (8) above—

(a) shall be made not less than seven days before the date fixed for the hearing of the appeal; and

(b) shall, not less that seven days before that date, be intimated by the appellant to the Crown Agent.

(10) The Clerk of Justiciary shall forthwith intimate—

(a) a decision under subsection (1) or (5) above; and

(b) in the case of a refusal of leave to appeal, the reasons for the decision,

to the appellant or his solicitor and to the Crown Agent.

AMENDMENT

Subs.(4) inserted by the Crime and Punishment (Scotland) Act 1997 (c.48) Sch.1, para.21(15) with effect from August 1, 1997 in terms of the Crime and Punishment (Scotland) Act 1997 (Commencement and Transitional Provisions) Order 1997 (SI 1997/1712) art.3.

Subs.(3) as amended, and subs.(4A) inserted, by Criminal Justice (Scotland) Act 2003 (asp 7), Part 8, s.62. Brought into force on June 27, 2003 by the Criminal Justice (Scotland) Act 2003 (Commencement No.1) Order 2003 (SSI 2003/288 (C.14)).

DEFINITIONS

"bail": s.307(1).
"High Court": s.307(1).
"judge": s.307(1).

GENERAL NOTE

It is probably more convenient in seeking to understand the full import of this section to consider the law under the headings of, on the one hand, leave to appeal and, on the other, application for leave to appeal. Separate consideration of the hearing must be made.

Leave to appeal

The procedure of seeking leave to appeal existed prior to this change of the law to the extent that leave to appeal was required for an appeal arising out of a preliminary diet: s.76A(1) of the 1975 Act. However, under the previous law leave to appeal was not required for any appeal after conviction and now that such leave is required there can be said to have been a major change in the law.

Section 106 allows a right of appeal to any person convicted on indictment and such appeal may be against conviction or sentence or both. The right of appeal is conditional on a ground of leave to appeal by a judge of the High Court of Justiciary in terms of s.107. Before the judge can decide the grant he must have documents before him and these are specified as the note of appeal, the certified copy or actual record of proceedings for a sheriff court trial, a judge's report and a transcript of the charge to the jury by the judge, as necessary: subs.(2). Having considered these documents the judge must decide whether they disclose arguable grounds of appeal: subs.(1)(a). The action that follows such a decision depends on which way the decision goes. Before considering the alternatives the turning point requires analysis: what are "arguable grounds of appeal"?

To answer that question one might start with "High Court of Justiciary Practice Note" dated March 29, 1985 (*Renton and Brown* (6th ed.) Appendix E, at p.726). There, judicial criticism is directed predominantly at grounds of appeal which are found in notes of appeal to be "wholly unspecific". The examples given in the Note are, first, an allegation of "misdirection" without any specification whatever. Secondly, "insufficient evidence" without any specification of the particular point, if any, which is to be taken. Examples are also given in relation to appeals against sentence where the ground of appeal is "more often than not equally uninformative" with a bare allegation of a sentence being excessive or severe.

The Practice Note indicated in terms that it was intended to remind practitioners that grounds of appeal must be stated with sufficient specification to identify the particular criticism of the conviction or sentence which the appellant hopes to present at the hearing.

It can readily be seen that appellate judges require detail in the grounds of appeal such as allows some insight as to the appellant's complaint. Detail alone may not take matters far: although the allegation of a miscarriage of justice is the only ground of appeal, there are various particular grounds of appeal, which are commonly advanced as a basis for the conclusion that there has been a miscarriage of justice.

Lord McCluskey in *Criminal Appeals* (1992) at pp.177–189 discusses some of the possible types or categories of appeal: it may be that there is alleged to have been a misdirection by the presiding judge (by omission, with an error of law, or regarding corroboration), that the conduct of the trial judge, the prosecutor or the defence advocate was improper, that the proceedings were incompetent or that there were some other irregularities. There are ample precedents for all these allegations. In short, "arguable grounds of appeal" are such to indicate, in Lord McCluskey's words, *ibid.* at p.177, "clarity, accuracy, brevity and comprehensiveness" and which invite a conclusion that there has been in law a miscarriage of justice.

The judge of the High Court of Justiciary who will consider the documents to decide whether they disclose arguable grounds of appeal does so in chambers without the parties being present: s.107(6). If the judge considers that the documents do disclose arguable grounds of appeal he then grants leave to appeal and he makes such comments in writing as he considers appropriate: s.107(1)(a). If the judge considers that the documents do not disclose arguable grounds of appeal he then refuses leave to appeal and he gives reasons in writing for the refusal: subs.(1)(b)(i).

The appellant, who is at this stage on bail and who had a sentence of imprisonment imposed on conviction, will then be the subject of a warrant to apprehend granted by the judge and on implementation the appellant will be imprisoned: subs.(1)(b)(ii).

The warrant to apprehend and imprison under subs.(1)(b)(ii) shall not take effect until the expiry of the period of 14 days during which period the appellant may, in effect, appeal by making an application to the High Court of Justiciary: subs.(4). If no such application is to be made then the appellant's solicitor has the time available to arrange for the client to surrender to the warrant.

Application for leave to appeal

There can be no doubt that this change in law will end any practice, if there is one, of lodging broad and vague grounds of appeal against conviction or sentence to be supplemented with speculative advocacy before the appellate judges. A clear ground will require to be formulated at a far earlier point in the procedure.

There are no statutory grounds for the reason for, in effect, appealing the decision of the single judge in chambers. The provision merely states that if leave to appeal is refused under subs.(1) then the appellant may within 14 days of intimation apply to the High Court of Justiciary for leave to appeal against the original conviction or sentence or both: subs.(4).

Who decides the application in terms of subs.(4) depends on what is at issue, namely, on appeal against conviction, sentence or conviction and sentence. By s.103(2) "for the purpose of hearing and determining any appeal or other proceeding under this Part of this Act" the quorum is three judges, except that by s.103(3) for appeals against sentence alone the quorum is two judges.

The various judges of the High Court of Justiciary who must consider the documents to decide whether they disclose arguable grounds of appeal do so in chambers without the parties being present: subs.(6).

In deciding the application the judges must consider the documents that had been before the single judge in chambers and also consider the reasons for the earlier refusal but thereafter, if the court is of the opinion that there are arguable grounds of appeal, then the court should grant leave to appeal and make such comments in writing as the court considers appropriate: subs.(5)(a). In any other case, leave to appeal will be refused with reasons in writing and a warrant to apprehend and imprison is to be granted if appropriate: subs.(5)(b).

In *Connolly Petr*, 1997 S.C.C.R. 205 it was held that it was incompetent to invoke the *nobile officium* where an application in terms of s.107(4) was not lodged timeously.

Hearing of appeal

Regard must be paid to the comments in writing made either by the single judge in chambers by subs.(1)(a) or by a greater number of judges in chambers by subs.(5)(a). The importance of the comments in writing lies in the possibility that they "may specify the arguable grounds of appeal (whether or not they are contained in the note of appeal) on the basis of which leave to appeal is granted": subs.(7).

It is very easy to imagine on the wording of subs.(1)(a) a single judge in chambers granting leave to appeal, not on the original grounds in the note of appeal, but on the basis of comments in writing which amend, alter or distil the original grounds in the note of appeal. The new grounds of appeal, having been specified, in effect dictate the ground of appeal to be argued at the hearing: subs.(8).

The appellant who wishes to found any aspect of his appeal on any ground of appeal contained in the note of appeal but not so specified in the comments in writing provided under subs.(1)(a) or subs.(5)(a) may seek leave of the High Court of Justiciary to do so: subs.(8). Application for such leave under subs.(8) must be made not less than seven days before the date fixed for the hearing of the appeal: subs.(9). It is not immediately clear from a reading of the statute as to whom an application under subs.(8) will be directed. As it is not so much an appeal as a request to broaden an approach to an appeal it may simply be returned to those who made the comments in writing under subss.(1)(a) or (5)(a).

In *Milne v H.M. Advocate*, 1998 G.W.D. 17–848, the Appeal Court held that in determining the appeal it was irrelevant that the sifting judge considered the matter arguable.

Lord Advocate's right of appeal against disposal

108.—(1) Where a person has been convicted on indictment, the Lord Advocate may, in accordance with subsection (2) below, appeal against any of the following disposals, namely—

(a) a sentence passed on conviction;

(b) a decision under section 209(1)(b) of this Act not to make a supervised release order;

(c) a decision under section 234A(2) of this Act not to make a non-harassment order;

(ca) a decision under section 92 of the Proceeds of Crime Act 2002 not to make a confiscation order;

(d) a probation order;

(dd) a drug treatment and testing order;

(e) a community service order;

(f) a decision to remit to the Principal Reporter made under section 49(1)(a) of this Act;

(g) an order deferring sentence;

(h) an admonition; or

(i) an absolute discharge.

(2) An appeal under subsection (1) above may be made—

(a) on a point of law;

(b) where it appears to the Lord Advocate, in relation to an appeal under—

(i) paragraph (a), (h) or (i) of that subsection, that the disposal was unduly lenient;

(ii) paragraph (b), (c) or (ca) of that subsection, that the decision not to make the order in question was inappropriate;

(iii) paragraph (d) to (e) of that subsection, that the making of the order concerned was unduly lenient or was on unduly lenient terms;

(iv) under paragraph (f) of that subsection, that the decision to remit was inappropriate;

(v) under paragraph (g) of that subsection, that the deferment of sentence was inappropriate or was on unduly lenient conditions.

(3) For the purposes of subsection (2)(b)(i) above in its application to a confiscation order by virtue of section 92(11) of the Proceeds of Crime Act 2002, the reference to the disposal being unduly lenient is a reference to the amount required to be paid by the order being unduly low.

AMENDMENT

Section 108 substituted by the Crime and Punishment (Scotland) Act 1997 (c.48), s.21 with effect from August 1, 1997 in terms of the Crime and Punishment (Scotland) Act 1997 (Commencement and Transitional Provisions) Order 1997 (SI 1997/1712) art.3.

Subss.(1) and (2) as amended by the Crime and Disorder Act 1998 (c.37), s.94 and Sch.6, para.6. Brought into force on September 30, 1998 by the Crime and Disorder Act 1998 (Commencement No. 2 and Transitional Provisions) Order 1998 (SI 1998/2327 (C.53)).

Subss.(1) and (2) as amended, and subs.(3) inserted, by the Proceeds of Crime Act 2002 (c.29),

Part 3, s.115. Brought into force on March 24, 2003 by the Proceeds of Crime Act 2002 (Commencement No.6, Transitional Provisions and Savings) (Scotland) Order 2003 (SSI 2003/210 (C.44)).

DEFINITIONS

"community service order": s.238.
"indictment": s.307(1).
"probation order": s.228.

GENERAL NOTE

As there was no tariff for sentences in the criminal courts of Scotland the selection of the appropriate sentence was clearly a matter for the individual discretion of the sentencer: *Strawhorn v Mcleod*, 1987 S.C.C.R. 413. The present Act invites the High Court of Justiciary, in appropriate circumstances, to pronounce an opinion on the sentence or other disposal or order which is appropriate in any similar case: ss.118(7) and 189(7). The Crown can appeal on a point of law (*e.g. H.M. Advocate v Foley*, 1999 G.W.D. 17–788) or on the ground that the sentence or other disposal is either unduly lenient or inappropriate as provided in subs.(2).

The Crown right of appeal against an unduly lenient sentence can only proceed in circumstances where "it appears" that a sentence is unduly lenient: s.228A of the 1975 Act as amended, and now s.108 of the present Act. A new reorganised s.108 was introduced by s.21(1) of the Crime and Punishment (Scotland) Act 1997 with effect from August 1, 1997. It introduces a right of appeal by the Lord Advocate against decisions by a court not to make a supervised release order; non harassment order and decision to remit to the principal Reporter. The right to bring an appeal under this section entitles the Crown to take an interest in sentencing which they did not have before—*H.M. Advocate v McKinlay*, 1998 S.C.C.R. 201.

The first appeal taken by the Crown was successful: see *H.M. Advocate v McPhee*, 1994 S.C.C.R. 830. There have been a number of appeals since then and the Appeal Court has indicated that a high standard of care and accuracy is expected of the Crown who do not require leave to appeal: see *H.M. Advocate v Mackay*, 1996 S.C.C.R. 410; *H.M. Advocate v Ross*, 1996 S.C.C.R. 107 and *H.M. Advocate v Wallace*, 1999 S.L.T. 1134. The grounds of appeal must be specific although the Appeal Court have allowed amendments to same: see *H.M. Advocate v Lee*, 1996 S.C.C.R. 205. In *Mackay*, *supra*, the court deplored the Crown's seeking to abandon the appeal at the hearing.

Furthermore the Crown must ensure that if they challenge a sentence as being unduly lenient the basis for the challenge has properly been laid in the trial court: see *H.M. Advocate v Bennett*, 1996 S.C.C.R. 331. If the Crown seek to maintain a sentence was unduly lenient because due consideration had not been given to a particular factor by a trial judge then the Crown have to show that the factor was fully drawn to the trial judge's attention: see *H.M. Advocate v Donaldson*, 1997 S.C.C.R. 738. Relevant factors to be taken into account in the determination of such appeals are the forum in which the Crown choose to proceed—see *H.M. Advocate v Robertson*, 1997 G.W.D. 5–187; the nature of any pleas accepted by the Crown: see *H.M. Advocate v Campbell*, 1997 S.L.T. 354 and if a non custodial option was imposed whether or not it was complied with—*H.M. Advocate v Jamieson*, 1996 S.C.C.R. 836; *H.M. Advocate v Carnall*, 1999 G.W.D. 31–1485; *H.M. Advocate v Paterson*, 2000 S.C.C.R. 309; *H.M. Advocate v Drain*, 2000 S.C.C.R. 256 but *cf. H.M. Advocate v McKinlay*, 1998 S.C.C.R. 201. The Crown are not specifically entitled to ask for a deterrent sentence—*H.M. Advocate v McKinlay*, *supra*.

Before the Appeal Court will interfere with a sentence it must be unduly lenient or inappropriate as provided by the section. Unduly lenient was defined in *H.M. Advocate v Bell*, 1995 S.L.T. 350 and *H.M. Advocate v O'Donnell*, 1995 S.C.C.R. 745 namely "The sentence must be seen to be unduly lenient. That means that it must fall outside the range of sentences which the judge at first instance, applying his mind to all the relevant factors, could reasonably have considered appropriate". It was held in *H.M. Advocate v Carnall*, 1999 G.W.D. 31–1485 even if the Appeal Court considered that an order was unduly lenient the court still has a discretion in terms of s.118(4) as to the course to adopt in determining disposal of the appeal. Due weight will be given by the Appeal Court to the views of the trial judge especially where he has had the advantage of seeing and hearing all the evidence— *H.M. Advocate v Wheldon*, 1998 S.C.C.R. 710. Lord Johnstone in that case described the task facing the Crown in such appeals as "formidable".

In *H.M. Advocate v Lee*, *supra* the court observed that although it was not the practice of the Appeal Court to lay down sentencing guidelines decisions of the Appeal Court in appeals against sentence especially unduly lenient sentence appeals do from time to time provide guidelines as to what is or is not appropriate and that a judge who fails to take account of that guidance cannot be said to have acted within the proper limits of his discretion as a sentencer: see *H.M. Advocate v Lee*, *supra*.

Section 197 of this Act now provides that a court in passing sentence shall have regard to any relevant opinion pronounced in terms of ss.118(7) or 189(7). The question of setting down minimum sentences was rejected in *H.M. Advocate v Mackay, supra*.

Guidelines can be found in *H.M. Advocate v Brough*, 1996 S.C.C.R. 377 (lewd and libidinous practices; teacher; custodial sentence well nigh inevitable); *H.M. Advocate v McPhee*, 1994 S.C.C.R. 830 (supply of Class A drug to teenage girls; custodial sentences must be imposed): *H.M. Advocate v Fallan*, 1996 S.C.C.R. 80 (unprovoked sexual attack on stranger in street at night; custodial sentence should normally be imposed); *H.M. Advocate v Lee*, 1996 S.C.C.R. 205 (being concerned in the supply of a Class A drug; substantial custodial sentence will be inevitable) and *H.M. Advocate v Carnall, supra*; *H.M. Advocate v Jamieson*, 1996 S.C.C.R. 836 (assault to severe injury and danger of life; only in an unusual case should the court refrain from imposing custodial sentence) see also *H.M. Advocate v Smith*, 1998 S.C.C.R. 637; *H.M. Advocate v Spiers*, 1997 S.L.T. 1401 (a custodial sentence was the only appropriate disposal where an assault occurred by stabbing with a broken bottle). The Appeal Court declined to set down a minimum sentence for culpable homicide where death was caused by kicking—*H.M. Advocate v Wheldon, supra*. The Appeal Court has also provided guidelines in appeals under this section as to factors that a judge is entitled to take into account in determining sentence. The fact that an accused pled guilty to a reduced charge is a mitigatory factor which a judge can take into account—*HM Advocate v Brand*, 1998 S.C.C.R. 71. A judge is not obliged to take account of an early plea of guilty but is entitled to give it the weight appropriate in the circumstances—*HM Advocate v Forrest*, 1998 S.C.C.R. 153. In cases involving kicking and punching it is appropriate for a sentencing judge to have regard to the nature of the conduct in determining whether an attack is violent and savage rather than the resulting injuries—*HM Advocate v Allan*, 2000 S.C.C.R. 219. For other Crown appeals see *HM Advocate v Gordon and Foy*, 1996 S.C.C.R. 274; *HM Advocate v McColl*, 1996 S.C.C.R. 523; *HM Advocate v Callaghan*, 1996 S.C.C.R. 709; *HM Advocate v McPherson*, 1996 S.C.C.R. 802; *HM Advocate v Campbell*, 1997 S.L.T. 354; *HM Advocate v McC.*, 1996 S.C.C.R. 842; *HM Advocate v McK.*, 1996 S.C.C.R. 866; *HM Advocate v M.*, 1997 S.L.T. 359; *HM Advocate v Scottish Hydro Electric plc*, 1997 S.L.T. 359 and *HM Advocate v Speirs*, 1997 S.C.C.R. 479; *HM Advocate v Hodgson*, 1998 S.C.C.R. 320; *HM Advocate v Heron*, 1998 S.C.C.R. 449 and *HM Advocate v Carpenter*, 1998 S.C.C.R. 706; *HM Advocate v Duff*, 1999 S.C.C.R. 193; *HM Advocate v Davidson*, 1999 S.C.C.R. 729; *HM Advocate v Millard*, 2000 G.W.D. 25–939 and *HM Advocate v Briody*, 2000 G.W.D. 29–1138.

The Crown has a right under s.121A to seek suspension of a probation order, community service order, supervised attendance order and restriction of liberty order pending determination of the appeal. Failure to exercise this right is a factor which the Appeal Court will take into account in determining appeals against sentence by the Crown—*HM Advocate v Carnall, supra*.

In *Urqhart v Campbell* [2006] HCJAC 76; 2006 S.C.C.R. 656 the court said that, in principle, proceedings in such an appeal where the consequence, if the appeal is allowed, is likely to be the imposition of a more severe sentence, ought not to take place outwith the presence of the respondent and that it would not be satisfactory to hear the appeal in the respondent's absence and, then, if it was successful, continue it to enable the respondent to be present when the new sentence was imposed. Although the context of this was summary proceedings, the court said in terms that the same principle applies in a solemn appeal where the accused is not in custody.

Lord Advocate's appeal against decision not to impose automatic sentence in certain cases

108A. Where the court has exercised the power conferred by section 205A(3) or 205B(3) of this Act, the Lord Advocate may appeal against that decision.

AMENDMENT

Section 108A inserted by the Crime and Punishment (Scotland) Act 1997 (c.48), s.18(2) with effect from October 20, 1997 in terms of the Crime and Punishment (Scotland) Act 1997 (Commencement No.2 and Transitional Provisions) Order 1997 (SI 1997/2323), art.3 and Sch.1; as amended by the Crime and Disorder Act 1998 (c.37), Sch.8 para.120 (effective September 30, 1998: SI 1998/2327).

Section 108A as amended by the Crime and Disorder Act 1998, Sch.8 para.120.

GENERAL NOTE

Some account of the origins of this involved section has to be attempted; it involves a provision on the statute book not brought into force, a provision now live and a third which has been repealed without ever coming into force.

Section 108A was introduced into the 1995 Act by the Crime and Punishment (Scotland) Act 1997 (c.48), s.18(2) to afford the Lord Advocate a specific right of appeal against the court's decision not to impose: (i) an automatic life sentence on conviction of a qualifying offence (s.205A of the 1995 Act as prospectively inserted by the 1997 Act s.1); (ii) an automatic minimum sentence on a third solemn conviction for drug trafficking (s.205B of the 1995 Act as now in force); or (iii) a supervised release order on conviction of a qualifying offence (s.209 of the 1995 Act as prospectively substituted by s.4 of the 1997 Act).

To date only the second provision, s.205B has been brought into force but it remains open for the regime of automatic life sentences to be activated should this be desired. The 1998 amendment to s.108A takes account of the fact that s.4 of the 1997 Act has been repealed; see Sch.10 of the 1998 Act.

Intimation of intention to appeal

109.—(1) Subject to section 111(2) of this Act and to section 99 of the Proceeds of Crime Act 2002 (postponement), where a person desires to appeal under section 106(1)(a) or (f) of this Act, he shall within two weeks of the final determination of the proceedings, lodge with the Clerk of Justiciary written intimation of intention to appeal which shall identify the proceedings and be in as nearly as may be the form prescribed by Act of Adjournal.

(2) A copy of intimation given under subsection (1) above shall be sent to the Crown Agent.

(3) On intimation under subsection (1) above being lodged by a person in custody, the Clerk of Justiciary shall give notice of the intimation to the Secretary of State.

(4) Subject to subsection (5) below, for the purposes of subsection (1) above and section 106(5) to (7) of this Act, proceedings shall be deemed finally determined on the day on which sentence is passed in open court.

(5) Where in relation to an appeal under section 106(1)(a) of this Act sentence is deferred under section 202 of this Act, the proceedings shall be deemed finally determined on the day on which sentence is first so deferred in open court.

(6) Without prejudice to section 10 of the said Act of 1995, the reference in subsection (4) above to "the day on which sentence is passed in open court" shall, in relation to any case in which, under subsection (1) of that section, a decision has been postponed for a period, be construed as a reference to the day on which that decision is made, whether or not a confiscation order is then made or any other sentence is then passed.

AMENDMENT

Subs.(1) as amended by the Proceeds of Crime Act 2002 (c.29), Sch.11 para.29(2). Brought into force on March 24, 2003 by the Proceeds of Crime Act 2002 (Commencement No.6, Transitional Provisions and Savings) (Scotland) Order 2003 (SSI 2003/210 (C.44)).

DEFINITIONS

"Clerk of Justiciary": s.307(1).
"sentence": s.307(1).

GENERAL NOTE

It is crucial to recall that the right of appeal under s.106(1) relates to all convictions on indictment. It is as important to know that all appeals following conviction on indictment are initiated in the justiciary office and not in the sheriff court. The intimation of an intention to appeal required under this section is important for it gives an office in Edinburgh notice of an appeal from a trial that may have occurred in any one of the sheriff courts of Scotland or one of the towns where the High Court has been on circuit. Those who may be required to produce notes or reports can thus be put on notice. Where there are several accused on one indictment the trial of all of them must be brought to a finality before any one of them can exercise the right of appeal: see *Evans, Petr*, 1991 S.C.C.R. 160.

Once an intimation of intention to appeal against conviction is lodged a transcript of the charge to the jury will be ordered to enable the grounds of appeal to be prepared. The unavailabilty of the transcript will not necessarily result in the appeal being allowed. Prejudice must be shown—*Carroll v HM Advocate*, 1999 J.C. 302.

Note of appeal

110.—(1) Subject to section 111(2) of this Act—

(a) within eight weeks of lodging intimation of intention to appeal or, in the case of an appeal under section 106(1)(b) to (e) of this Act or, in the case of an appeal under section 106(1)(db) or (dc) of this Act, the date on which the proposal to make a reference is made, within two weeks of the appropriate date (being, as the case may be, the date on which sentence was passed, the order disposing of the case was made, sentence was deferred or the previous conviction was quashed as mentioned in section 106A(1)(c) or (2)(c) of this Act) (or, as the case may be, of the making of the order disposing of the case or deferring sentence) in open court, the convicted person may lodge a written note of appeal with the Clerk of Justiciary who shall send a copy to the judge who presided at the trial and to the Crown Agent; or, as the case may be,

(b) within four weeks of the passing of the sentence in open court, the Lord Advocate may lodge such a note with the Clerk of Justiciary, who shall send a copy to the said judge and to the convicted person or that person's solicitor.

(2) The period of eight weeks mentioned in paragraph (a) of subsection (1) above may be extended, before it expires, by the Clerk of Justiciary.

(3) A note of appeal shall—

(a) identify the proceedings;

(b) contain a full statement of all the grounds of appeal; and

(c) be in as nearly as may be the form prescribed by Act of Adjournal.

(4) Except by leave of the High Court on cause shown, it shall not be competent for an appellant to found any aspect of his appeal on a ground not contained in the note of appeal.

(5) Subsection (4) above shall not apply as respects any ground of appeal specified as an arguable ground of appeal by virtue of subsection (7) of section 107 of this Act.

(6) On a note of appeal under section 106(1)(b) to (e) of this Act being lodged by an appellant in custody the Clerk of Justiciary shall give notice of that fact to the Secretary of State.

AMENDMENT

Subs.(1)(a) as amended by the Crime and Punishment (Scotland) Act 1997 (c.48), s.19(2) with effect from October 20, 1997 in terms of the Crime and Punishment (Scotland) Act 1997 (Commencement No.2 and Transitional Provisions) Order 1997 (SI 1997/2323), art.3 and Sch.1.

Subss.(1)(a) and (2) as amended by the Act of Adjournal (Criminal Appeals) 2002 (SSI 2002/387), art.2 with effect from August 26, 2002 in accordance with art.1(2).

Subs.(1) as amended by the Criminal Procedure (Amendment) (Scotland) Act 2004 (asp 5), s.24(2). Brought into force on October 4, 2004 by the Criminal Procedure (Amendment) (Scotland) Act 2004 (Commencement, Transitional Provisions and Savings) Order 2004 (SSI 2004/405 (C.28)).

DEFINITIONS

"Clerk of Justiciary": s.307(1).
"judge": s.307(1).

Three periods of time are envisaged by this section. First, for all solemn appeals against conviction or conviction and sentence written intimation of intention to appeal should be lodged within two weeks of the final determination with the Clerk of Justiciary by s.109(1). Thereafter a convicted person has six weeks to lodge a written note of appeal. Alternatively, and secondly, if the appeal is only against sentence then the period is two weeks from the date sentence was passed, or order disposing of the case was made, or sentence deferred etc.: subs.(1)(a). It is clear that if conviction is accepted fewer papers are required and less preparatory work is necessary. Thirdly, if the Crown wishes to appeal (against, for example, what appears to be an unduly lenient sentence) a note of appeal must be lodged within four weeks: subs.(1)(b).

Those lodging notes of appeal must have regard to two important points. The note of appeal must contain a full statement of all the grounds of appeal: subs.(3)(b). There are a number of reported cases that emphasise the importance of specification; see, for example, *Mitchell v HM Advocate*, 1991 S.C.C.R. 216. *Smith v HM Advocate*, 1983 S.C.C.R. 30: *Lindsay v HM Advocate*, 1993 S.C.C.R. 868, and *McGregor v HM Advocate*, 1996 G.W.D. 9–471. If the grounds of appeal are deficient the presiding judge may be unable to fully comment on the appeal—*MacLeay v HM Advocate*, 2000 G.W.D. 8–278. In *HM Advocate v Bagan*, 1996 G.W.D. 29–1734 the court observed that there was a professional responsibility to ensure that grounds of appeal were formulated which had a sound basis in fact. The importance is accentuated by the new requirement to disclose arguable grounds of appeal in the note of appeal for the consideration of a single judge in chambers to obtain leave to appeal: s.107(1)(a) and (2)(a).

Further, it is not competent, except by leave of the High Court of Justiciary on cause shown, for an appellant to found any aspect of his appeal on a ground not contained in the note of appeal: subs.(4). The narrow approach is also emphasised earlier in the Act: s.107(8). If a ground of appeal is abandoned it cannot be resurrected at a later stage—*McGinty v HM Advocate*, 2000 J.C. 277.

Subsection (1) has been amended by s.19(2) of the Crime and Punishment (Scotland) Act 1997 with effect from October 20, 1997 to take account of the provisions in s.106A that an accused can appeal against sentence where he no longer qualifies for an automatic sentence. He has two weeks from the sentence being quashed to appeal.

Provisions supplementary to sections 109 and 110

111.—(1) Where the last day of any period mentioned in sections 109(1) and 110(1) of this Act falls on a day on which the office of the Clerk of Justiciary is closed, such period shall extend to and include the next day on which such office is open.

(2) Any period mentioned in section 109(1) or 110(1)(a) of this Act may be extended at any time by the High Court in respect of any convicted person; and an application for such extension may be made under this subsection and shall be in as nearly as may be the form prescribed by Act of Adjournal.

(3) Subsection (2) above does not allow the High Court to extend any such period which relates to an appeal under section 106(1)(db), (dc) or (f)(ii) or (iii) of this Act

Subs.(3) inserted by the Criminal Procedure (Amendment) (Scotland) Act 2004 (asp 5), s.24(3). Brought into force on October 4, 2004 by the Criminal Procedure (Amendment) (Scotland) Act 2004 (Commencement, Transitional Provisions and Savings) Order 2004 (SSI 2004/405 (C.28)).

"Clerk of Justiciary": s.307(1).
"High Court": s.307(1).

For examples of extensions considered, see *Spence v HM Advocate*, 1945 J.C. 65 and *Birrell v HM Advocate*, 1993 S.C.C.R. 812. See *Grant v HM Advocate*, 1996 G.W.D. 19–1077—an appeal against refusal to extend the time.

Admission of appellant to bail

112.—(1) Subject to subsections (2), (2A) and (9) below, the High Court may, if it thinks fit, on the application of a convicted person, admit him to bail pending the determination of—

    (a) his appeal; or

    (b) any relevant appeal by the Lord Advocate under section 108 or 108A of this Act.

(2) The High Court shall not admit a convicted person to bail under subsection (1) above unless—

    (a) the application for bail—

        (i) states reasons why it should be granted; and

        (ii) where he is the appellant and has not lodged a note of appeal in accordance with section 110(1)(a) of this Act, sets out the proposed grounds of appeal; and

    (b) the prosecutor has had an opportunity to be heard on the application.

(2A) Where—

    (a) the convicted person is the appellant and has not lodged a note of appeal in accordance with section 110(1)(a) of this Act; or

    (b) the Lord Advocate is the appellant,

the High Court shall not admit the convicted person to bail under subsection (1) above unless it considers there to be exceptional circumstances justifying admitting him to bail.

(3) A person who is admitted to bail under subsection (1) above shall, unless the High Court otherwise directs, appear personally in court on the day or days fixed for the hearing of the appeal.

(4) Where an appellant fails to appear personally in court as mentioned in subsection (3) above, the court may—

    (a) if he is the appellant—

        (i) decline to consider the appeal; and

        (ii) dismiss it summarily; or

    (b) whether or not he is the appellant—

        (i) consider and determine the appeal; or

        (ii) without prejudice to section 27 of this Act, make such other order as the court thinks fit.

(5) For the purposes of subsections (1), (3) and (4) above, "appellant" includes not only a person who has lodged a note of appeal but also one who has lodged an intimation of intention to appeal.

(6) Subject to subsections (7) and (9) below, the High Court may, if it thinks fit, on the application of a convicted person, admit him to bail pending the determination of any appeal under paragraph 13(a) of Schedule 6 to the Scotland Act 1998 and the disposal of the proceedings by the High Court thereafter.

(7) The High Court shall not admit a convicted person to bail under subsection (6) above unless

    (a) the application for bail states reasons why it should be granted and the High Court considers there to be exceptional circumstances justifying admitting the convicted person to bail, and

    (b) where the appeal relates to conviction on indictment, the prosecutor has had an opportunity to be heard on the application.

(8) A person who is admitted to bail under subsection (6) above shall, unless the High Court otherwise directs, appear personally in the High Court at any subsequent hearing in the High Court in relation to the proceedings; and if he fails to do so the court may, without prejudice to section 27 of this Act, make such order as it thinks fit.

(9) An application for the purposes of subsection (1) or (6) above by a person convicted on indictment shall be—

(a) intimated by him immediately and in writing to the Crown Agent; and

(b) heard not less than seven days after the date of that intimation.

AMENDMENTS

Subs.(1)(b) as amended by the Crime and Punishment (Scotland) Act 1997 (c.48), s.18(3) with effect from October 20, 1997 in terms of the Crime and Punishment (Scotland) Act 1997 (Commencement No. 2 and Transitional Provisions) Order 1997 (SI 1997/2323) art.3, Sch.1.

Subss.(6), (7) and (8) inserted by the Scotland Act 1998 (Consequential Modifications) (No.1) Order 1999 (SI 1999/1042) art.3, Sch., para.13 (effective May 6, 1999).

Subss.(1), (2), (6) and (7) as amended, and subss.(2A) and (9) inserted, by Criminal Justice (Scotland) Act 2003 (asp 7), Part 8, s.66. Brought into force on June 27, 2003 by the Criminal Justice (Scotland) Act 2003 (Commencement No.1) Order 2003 (SSI 2003/288 (C.14)).

DEFINITIONS

"appellant": s.112(5).
"bail": s.307(1).
"High Court": s.307(1).

GENERAL NOTE

This section follows earlier authorities that allowed the High Court of Justiciary, if it thought fit, to admit an appellant to bail pending determination of the appeal. It is, however, for the appellant to show cause why he should be admitted to bail: *Young v H.M. Advocate*, 1946 J.C.5. The Appeal Court in *Ogilvie Petr*, 1998 S.C.C.R. 187, held that there was no rule that bail could only be granted under this section in exceptional circumstances, thereby clarifying any doubts arising from *Young*, *supra*. The mere fact, however, that a person has been given leave to appeal is not in itself sufficient to show cause why bail should be granted. It is just another factor to be taken into account, *e.g.* the prospects of success of the appeal.

With effect from October 20, 1997 s.112(1)(b) has been extended to allow a convicted person to be admitted to bail pending appeal by the Lord Advocate against a decision to appeal against the failure to impose a minimum sentence in terms of s.205B.

Judge's report

113.—(1) As soon as is reasonably practicable after receiving the copy note of appeal sent to him under section 110(1) of this Act, the judge who presided at the trial shall furnish the Clerk of Justiciary with a written report giving the judge's opinion on the case generally and on the grounds contained in the note of appeal.

(2) The Clerk of Justiciary shall send a copy of the judge's report—

(a) to the convicted person or his solicitor;

(b) to the Crown Agent; and

(c) in a case referred under Part XA of this Act, to the Commission.

(3) Where the judge's report is not furnished as mentioned in subsection (1) above, the High Court may call for the report to be furnished within such period as it may specify or, if it thinks fit, hear and determine the appeal without the report.

(4) Subject to subsection (2) above, the report of the judge shall be available only to the High Court, the parties and, on such conditions as may be prescribed by Act of Adjournal, such other persons or classes of persons as may be so prescribed.

AMENDMENT

Subs.(2)(c) as amended by the Crime and Punishment (Scotland) Act 1997, Sch.1, para.21(16) (effective April 1, 1999: SI 1999/652).

DEFINITIONS
"Clerk of Justiciary": s.307(1).
"High Court": s.307(1).
"judge": s.307(1).

GENERAL NOTE

In *McLaren v H.M. Advocate*, 1994 S.C.C.R. 855 the Appeal Court observed that where more than one accused has appealed against conviction or sentence the trial judge should prepare separate reports and it is desirable these be self-contained and set out points the judge considers appropriate in response to the grounds of appeal.

Where the ground of appeal is based on the wrongful rejection of a no case to answer submission the form of the judge's report should be as set out in *Horne v H.M. Advocate*, 1991 S.C.C.R. 248 and *Vetters v H.M. Advocate*, 1994 S.C.C.R. 305. It was observed in *McPhelim v H.M. Advocate*, 1996 S.C.C.R. 647 that judges should comment on all grounds of appeal and not just those raising questions of fact. Delay by a trial judge in producing a report for the Appeal Court was only one factor to be considered in assessing the issue of reasonable time in terms of Art.6—*H.M. Advocate v McGlinchey*, 2000 S.C.C.R. 593.

The duties of a trial judge, in furnishing a report in terms of this section were emphasised in *McCutcheon v H.M. Advocate*, 2001 G.W.D. 18–694. In *Ogilvie v Heywood*, 2001 G.W.D. 18–695 the Appeal Court disapproved of comments by a trial judge regarding the bringing of the appeal. In *Megrahi v H.M. Advocate*, 2001 G.W.D. 26–1014 it was held that the requirement upon the judge to produce a report was mandatory.

Applications made orally or in writing

114. Subject to any provision of this Part of this Act or to rules made under section 305 of this Act to the contrary, any application to the High Court may be made by the appellant or respondent as the case may be or by counsel on his behalf, orally or in writing.

AMENDMENT

Section 114 as amended by the Act of Adjournal (Criminal Appeals) 2003 (SSI 2003/387), art.2. Brought into force on September 1, 2003 in accordance with art.1.

DEFINITIONS

"appellant": s.132.
"High Court": s.307(1).

Presentation of appeal in writing

115.—(1) Subject to rules made under section 305 of this Act, if an appellant desires to present his case and his argument in writing instead of orally he shall, at least four days before the diet fixed for the hearing of the appeal—

(a) intimate this desire to the Clerk of Justiciary;

(b) lodge with the Clerk of Justiciary three copies of his case and argument; and

(c) send a copy of the intimation, case and argument to the Crown Agent.

(2) Any case or argument presented as mentioned in subsection (1) above shall be considered by the High Court.

(3) Unless the High Court otherwise directs, the respondent shall not make a written reply to a case and argument presented as mentioned in subsection (1) above, but shall reply orally at the diet fixed for the hearing of the appeal.

(4) Unless the High Court otherwise allows, an appellant who has presented his case and argument in writing shall not be entitled to submit in addition an oral argument to the court in support of the appeal.

AMENDMENT

Section 115 as amended by the Act of Adjournal (Criminal Appeals) 2003 (SSI 2003/387), art.2. Brought into force on September 1, 2003 in accordance with art.1.

DEFINITIONS

"appellant": s.132.
"Clerk of Justiciary": s.307(1).
"High Court": s.307(1).

GENERAL NOTE

It is interesting to note the willingness of the Appeal Court in certain cases to entertain written submissions both from appellants and the Lord Advocate: see *Anderson v H.M. Advocate*, 1996 S.C.C.R. 114. In *Campbell v H.M. Advocate*, 1998 S.C.C.R. 214, the court ordered the Crown to lodge a written history of the case.

Abandonment of appeal

116.—(1) An appellant may abandon his appeal by lodging with the Clerk of Justiciary a notice of abandonment in as nearly as may be the form prescribed by Act of Adjournal; and on such notice being lodged the appeal shall be deemed to have been dismissed by the court.

(2) A person who has appealed under section 116(1)(dc) or (f) of this Act may abandon the appeal in so far as it is against conviction, reference or sentence, decision, disposal or order and may proceed with it against—

(a) both reference and sentence, decision, disposal or order; or

(b) reference alone; or, as the case may be

(c) sentence, decision, disposal or order alone.

AMENDMENT

Subs.(2) as amended by the Crime and Punishment (Scotland) Act 1997 (c.48), s.18(4) with effect from October 20, 1997 in terms of the Crime and Punishment (Scotland) Act 1997 (Commencement No. 2 and Transitional Provisions) Order 1997 (SI 1997/2323), art.3 and Sch.1.

Subs.(2) substituted by the Protection of Children (Scotland) Act 2003 (asp 5), s.16(3). Brought into force on January 10, 2005 by the Protection of Children (Scotland) Act 2003 (Commencement No.1) Order 2004 (SSI 2004/522 (C.38)), art.2.

DEFINITIONS

"appellant": s.132.
"Clerk of Justiciary": s.307(1).
"sentence": s.132.

GENERAL NOTE

In *Ferguson, Petr*, 1980 S.L.T. 21 the petitioner made a motion to abandon the appeal at the calling of the case before the Appeal Court. The court refused the motion and increased the sentence. At the hearing of a subsequent petition to the nobile officium the court indicated that formal abandonment under the then s.244 of the Criminal Procedure (Scotland) Act 1975 could be made at any time prior to the calling of the case by the Appeal Court, but if not done any oral motion to abandon is subject to the discretion of the court. See also *West v H.M. Advocate*, 1955 S.L.T. 425.

Where a Notice of Abandonment has been lodged the competent mode of reinstating the appeal is by petition to the nobile officium: see *Young, Petr*, 1994 S.L.T. 269 and *McIntosh, Petr*, 1995 S.C.C.R. 327.

The Crown seeking to abandon an appeal against an unduly lenient sentence at the hearing was deplored in the case of *H.M. Advocate v Mackay*: see s.108, *supra*.

An appellant who has appealed against conviction and the imposition of a minimum sentence may abandon the appeal against conviction and proceed only with the appeal against sentence—s.18(4) of the Crime and Punishment (Scotland) Act 1997.

Presence of appellant or applicant at hearing

117.—(1) Where an appellant or applicant is in custody the Clerk of Justiciary shall notify—

(a) the appellant or applicant;

(b) the Governor of the prison in which the appellant or applicant then is; and

(c) the Secretary of State,

of the probable day on which the appeal or application will be heard.

(2) The Secretary of State shall take steps to transfer the appellant or applicant to a prison convenient for his appearance before the High Court at such reasonable time before the hearing as shall enable him to consult his legal adviser, if any.

(3) A convicted appellant, notwithstanding that he is in custody, shall be entitled to be present if he desires it, at the hearing of his appeal.

(4) When an appellant or applicant is to be present at any diet—

(a) before the High Court or any judge of that court; or

(b) for the taking of additional evidence before a person appointed for that purpose under section 104(1)(b) of this Act, or

(c) for an examination or investigation by a special commissioner in terms of section 104(1)(d) of this Act,

the Clerk of Justiciary shall give timeous notice to the Secretary of State, in the form prescribed by Act of Adjournal or as nearly as may be in such form.

(5) A notice under subsection (4) above shall be sufficient warrant to the Secretary of State for transmitting the appellant or applicant in custody from prison to the place where the diet mentioned in that subsection or any subsequent diet is to be held and for reconveying him to prison at the conclusion of such diet.

(6) The appellant or applicant shall appear at any diet mentioned in subsection (4) above in ordinary civilian clothes.

(7) Where the Lord Advocate is the appellant, subsections (1) to (6) above shall apply in respect of the convicted person, if in custody, as they apply to an appellant or applicant in custody.

(8) The Secretary of State shall, on notice under subsection (4) above from the Clerk of Justiciary, ensure that sufficient male and female prison officers attend each sitting of the court, having regard to the list of appeals for the sitting.

(9) When the High Court fixes the date for the hearing of an appeal or of an application under section 111(2) of this Act, the Clerk of Justiciary shall give notice to the Crown Agent and to the solicitor of the convicted person, or to the convicted person himself if he has no known solicitor.

DEFINITIONS

"appellant": s.132.
"Clerk of Justiciary": s.307(1).
"diet": s.307(1).
"governor": s.307(1).
"High Court": s.307(1).
"judge": s.307(1).

GENERAL NOTE

An appellant who is in custody need not be present at his appeal hearing: see *Manuel v H.M. Advocate*, 1958 J.C. 41 where the accused accepted counsel's advice that it was not in his best interest to be there. However if an appellant does wish to be present subs.(3) entitles him to be there.

Disposal of appeals

118.—(1) The High Court may, subject to subsection (4) below, dispose of an appeal against conviction by—

(a) affirming the verdict of the trial court;

(b) setting aside the verdict of the trial court and either quashing the conviction or, subject to subsection (2) below, substituting therefor an amended verdict of guilty; or

(c) setting aside the verdict of the trial court and quashing the conviction and granting authority to bring a new prosecution in accordance with section 119 of this Act.

(2) An amended verdict of guilty substituted under subsection (1) above must be one which could have been returned on the indictment before the trial court.

(3) In setting aside, under subsection (1) above, a verdict the High Court may quash any sentence imposed on the appellant (or, as the case may be, any disposal or order made) as respects the indictment, and—

(a) in a case where it substitutes an amended verdict of guilty, whether or not the sentence (or disposal or order) related to the verdict set aside; or

(b) in any other case, where the sentence (or disposal or order) did not so relate,

may pass another (but not more severe) sentence or make another (but not more severe) disposal or order in substitution for the sentence, disposal or order so quashed.

(4) The High Court may, subject to subsection (5) below, dispose of an appeal against sentence by—

(a) affirming such sentence; or

(b) if the Court thinks that, having regard to all the circumstances, including any evidence such as is mentioned in section 106(3) of this Act, a different sentence should have been passed, quashing the sentence and passing another sentence whether more or less severe in substitution therefor,

and, in this subsection, "appeal against sentence" shall, without prejudice to the generality of the expression, be construed as including an appeal under section 106(1)(bb) to (e), and any appeal under section 108, of this Act; and other references to sentence shall be construed accordingly.

(4AA) The High Court may dispose of an appeal against a reference proposed under subsection (1) of section 10 of the Protection of Children (Scotland) Act 2003 (asp 5)—

(a) by dismissing the appeal and affirming such reference; or

(b) if it thinks—

(i) in a case to which subsection (3) of that section applies, that the court which is proposing to make the reference should not have been satisfied as to the condition mentioned in that subsection;

(ii) in a case to which subsection (4) of that section applies, that the court which is proposing to make the reference should have been satisfied as to the condition mentioned in that subsection,

by directing the court not to make the reference.

(4A) On an appeal under section 108A of this Act, the High Court may dispose of the appeal—

(a) by affirming the decision and any sentence or order passed;

(b) where it is of the opinion mentioned in section 205A(3) or, as the case may be, 205B(3) of this Act but it considers that a different sentence or order should have been passed, by affirming the decision but quashing any sentence or order passed and passing another sentence or order whether more or less severe in substitution therefor; or

  (c) in any other case, by setting aside the decision appealed against and any sentence or order passed by the trial court and where the decision appealed against was taken under—

     (i) subsection (3) of section 205A of this Act, by passing the sentence mentioned in subsection (2) of that section;

    (ii) subsection (3) of section 205B of this Act, by passing a sentence of imprisonment of at least the length mentioned in subsection (2) of that section; or

   (iii) [...]

(5) In relation to any appeal under section 106(1) of this Act, the High Court shall, where it appears to it that the appellant committed the act charged against him but that he was insane when he did so, dispose of the appeal by—

  (a) setting aside the verdict of the trial court and substituting therefor a verdict of acquittal on the ground of insanity; and

  (b) quashing any sentence imposed on the appellant (or disposal or order made) as respects the indictment and—

    (i) making, in respect of the appellant, any order mentioned in section 57(2)(a) to (d) of this Act; or

    (ii) making no order.

(6) Subsections (3) to (6) of section 57 of this Act shall apply to an order made under subsection (5)(b)(i) above as they apply to an order made under subsection (2) of that section.

(7) In disposing of an appeal under section 106(1)(b) to (f) or 108 of this Act the High Court may, without prejudice to any other power in that regard, pronounce an opinion on

  (a) the sentence or other disposal or order which is appropriate in any similar case;

  (b) whether a reference is appropriate in any similar case.

(8) No conviction, sentence, judgment, order of court or other proceeding whatsoever in or for the purposes of solemn proceedings under this Act—

  (a) shall be quashed for want of form; or

  (b) where the accused had legal assistance in his defence, shall be suspended or set aside in respect of any objections to—

    (i) the relevancy of the indictment, or the want of specification therein; or

    (ii) the competency or admission or rejection of evidence at the trial in the inferior court,

    unless such objections were timeously stated.

(9) The High Court may give its reasons for the disposal of any appeal in writing without giving those reasons orally.

AMENDMENTS

Subs.(4)(b) as amended by the Crime and Punishment (Scotland) Act 1997 (c.48), Sch.1, para.21(17) with effect from August 1, 1997 in terms of the Crime and Punishment (Scotland) Act 1997 (Commencement and Transitional Provisions) Order 1997 (SI 1997/1712), art.3. As amended by the Crime and Punishment (Scotland) Act 1997 (c.48), s.18(5) with effect from October 20, 1997 in terms of the Crime and Punishment (Scotland) Act 1997 (Commencement No. 2 and Transitional Provisions) Order 1997 (SI 1997/2323), art.3, Sch.1.

Subs.(4A) inserted by the Crime and Punishment (Scotland) Act 1997 (c.48), s.18(5) with effect from October 20, 1997 in terms of the Crime and Punishment (Scotland) Act 1997 (Commencement No. 2 and Transitional Provisions) Order 1997 (SI 1997/2323), art.3, Sch.1.

Subs.(9) inserted by the Crime and Punishment (Scotland) Act 1997 (c.48), Sch.1, para.21(17) with effect from August 1, 1997 in terms of the Crime and Punishment (Scotland) Act 1997 (Commencement and Transitional Provisions) Order 1997 (SI 1997/1712), art.3.

Subs.(4A)(c)(iii) repealed by the 1998 Act, Sch.8, para.121.

Subss.(4AA) and (7)(b) inserted, and subs.(7) as amended, by the Protection of Children (Scotland) Act 2003 (asp 5), s.16(4). Brought into force on January 10, 2005 by the Protection of Children (Scotland) Act 2003 (Commencement No.1) Order 2004 (SSI 2004/522 (C.38)), art.2.

Subs.(6) as amended by the Mental Health (Care and Treatment) (Scotland) Act 2003 (asp 13), Sch.4, para.8(11). Brought into force on October 5, 2005 by the Mental Health (Care and Treatment) (Scotland) Act 2003 (Commencement No.4) Order 2005 (SSI 2005/161 (C.6)).

DEFINITIONS

"appeal against sentence": s.118(4).

"High Court": s.307(1).

"sentence": s.307(1).

GENERAL NOTE

Appeal against conviction

Subsection (1) is concerned with appeals against conviction following solemn proceedings. The High Court of Justiciary may dispose of an appeal by affirming the verdict of the trial court: subs.(1)(a). Alternatively, the High Court of Justiciary may dispose of an appeal by setting aside the verdict of the trial court: subs.(1)(b) and (c). What follows after setting aside the verdict depends on what has gone wrong and how that is to be corrected. The Appeal Court is not obliged to give effect to a concession by the Crown at the appeal. It is for the court to determine if there has been a miscarriage of justice—*Duffy v H.M. Advocate*, 1999 G.W.D. 37–1791. In *Santini v H.M. Advocate*, 2000 S.C.C.R. 726 the Appeal Court declined to accept a Crown concession to restrict the libel to 2 days on the basis that there was no justification in law for this.

The High Court of Justiciary may set aside the verdict and quash the conviction and that may be done where the irregularity was substantial: *e.g. Gardiner v H.M. Advocate*, 1978 S.L.T. 118. Alternatively, the High Court of Justiciary may set aside the verdict and substitute therefor an amended verdict of guilty: *e.g. Salmond v H.M. Advocate*, 1991 S.C.C.R. 43 in which it was clear that the jury held some criminal behaviour proved but returned an incorrect verdict owing to a misunderstanding of the law. See *White v H.M. Advocate*, 1989 S.C.C.R. 553 and *Ainsworth v. H.M. Advocate*, 1996 S.C.C.R. 631.

The Appeal Court has a discretionary power to quash a conviction where a miscarriage of justice has occurred. Prior to the Criminal Justice (Scotland) Act 1980 the court was under a duty to do so providing that the miscarriage was a substantial one. The duty and proviso were removed by the 1980 Act. In *McCuaig* the amendments introduced by the 1980 Act were interpreted as giving a wider power to the Appeal Court than the previous legislation. See Sir Gerald Gordon's full commentary thereon at pp.128–129 and *McAvoy & anr v H.M. Advocate*, 1982 S.C.C.R. 263. The test which the court should apply in determining whether to quash a conviction or to substitute an amended verdict was considered in *Smith v H.M. Advocate*, 2001 S.C.C.R. 143.

The High Court of Justiciary may set aside the verdict of the trial court and quash the conviction and grant, on statutory grounds, authority to bring a new prosecution: *e.g. Mackenzie v H.M. Advocate*, 1982 S.C.C.R. 499 through many cases to *McDade v H.M. Advocate*, 1994 S.C.C.R. 627. See *Sinclair v H.M. Advocate*, 1996 S.C.C.R. 221; *O'Neill v H.M. Advocate*, 1996 G.W.D. 4–183; *Hutton v H.M. Advocate*, 1996 G.W.D. 31–1907; *Hobbins v H.M. Advocate*, 1996 S.C.C.R. 637, *McPhelim v H.M. Advocate*, 1996 S.C.C.R. 647; *Hoy v H.M. Advocate*, 1997 S.L.T. 26; *Hemphill v H.M. Advocate*, 2001 S.C.C.R. 361 and *McLean v H.M. Advocate*, 2001 G.W.D. 7–24.

The setting aside of the verdict of the trial court and the quashing of the conviction in the context of a misdirection to the jury does not necessarily lead to the grant of authority to bring a new prosecution. In *Farooq v H.M. Advocate*, 1993 S.L.T. 1271 the ages of child witnesses and the generally unsatisfactory nature of the evidence resulted in such authority being refused. In *Jones v H.M. Advocate*, 1991 S.C.C.R. 290 the appellants were convicted of murder. They then gave evidence for the Crown at the trial of another on the same charge having been called as socii. The appellants' convictions were set aside on appeal. Authority to bring prosecution was refused as the setting aside of the conviction operated retroactively and as the appellants had given evidence for the Crown as socii they were immune from prosecution. See also *Kerr v H.M. Advocate*, 1992 S.C.C.R. 281. In

Hoy v H.M. Advocate, 1998 S.C.C.R. 8, authority for a second retrial was refused on the basis that there had been insufficient evidence before the jury to convict of murder. Repeated indictments do not necessarily preclude authority being granted for a new prosecution—*Callan v H.M. Advocate*, 1999 S.C.C.R. 57 (murder charge and no fault on the part of the Crown) but see *Cameron v H.M. Advocate*, 1999 S.C.C.R. 11 (appellant previously undergone two trials and long delay in proceedings—authority refused). See also *Muirhead v H.M. Advocate*, 1999 G.W.D. 4–176 and *Cathcart v H.M. Advocate*, 1999 G.W.D. 5–241. In *Glancy v H.M. Advocate*, 2001 S.C.C.R. 385 authority for a fresh prosecution was refused due to the age of the offence and the fact the accused had been in custody for four months, the equivalent of a nine month sentence. The power in subs.(1) to set aside the verdict of the court necessarily requires a comparable power to deal with the question of sentence. Subsection (3) allows variation of sentence but whenever a sentence is varied a substituted sentence may only be the same or less than the original sentence. An appeal against conviction alone does not allow a variation of sentence for the imposition of a more severe sentence: *cf.* the earlier position, *e.g.* in *O'Neil v H.M. Advocate*, 1976 S.L.T. (Notes) 7.

Appeals against sentence

Subsection (4) is concerned with appeals against sentence following solemn proceedings. The High Court of Justiciary may dispose of an appeal by affirming the sentence complained of: subs.(4)(a). Alternatively, the High Court of Justiciary may dispose of an appeal by quashing the sentence complained of and passing another sentence "whether more or less severe" in substitution. In doing the latter, the High Court of Justiciary may have regard to additional evidence such as that mentioned in s.106(3) of this Act.

An example of a more severe sentence being substituted is to be found in *Donnelly v H.M. Advocate*, 1988 S.C.C.R. 386 where 18 months' detention was quashed and two years' detention substituted for a youth who had a CS gas canister at a football match. In contrast, a less serious sentence was substituted in *McIntyre v H.M. Advocate*, 1994 G.W.D. 28–1687 where 20 years' imprisonment was quashed and was substituted with 14 years' imprisonment for culpable homicide for throwing or pouring acid on another. See also *Donnell v H.M. Advocate*, 1997 G.W.D. 17–762 where the Appeal Court declined to exercise its power under subs.(4). The new subs.(4A) was added by s.18(5) of the Crime and Punishment Act 1997 with effect from October 20, 1997. This provides that on appeal by the prosecutor in terms of s.108A the court can (1) affirm the original decision; or (2) whilst agreeing that the minimum sentence should not be imposed for the reasons set out in s.205B(3) alter the sentence or (3) impose the appropriate sentence prescribed by the Act.

Sentencing guidance

A most notable use of the authority in s.18(7), *supra*, is the appeal of *Du Plooy v H.M. Advocate*, 2003 S.L.T. 1237. There guidance was given as to the basis of, and scope for, an allowance in the sentencing of an accused in respect of a guilty plea, and the form that such an allowance might take. Further consideration is given to this matter under ss.196 and 197 of this Act, *infra*.

Supplementary provisions

In relation to any appeal under s.106(1) of this Act, the High Court of Justiciary is required to set aside the verdict of the trial court and quash the sentence and make an order where it appears that the appellant committed the act charged against him but that he was insane when he did so: subss. (5) and (6).

When disposing of appeals against sentence generally, the High Court of Justiciary may pronounce an opinion on the sentence or other disposal or order which is appropriate in any similar case: subs.(7). In *O'Neill v H.M. Advocate*, 1998 S.C.C.R. 644 the Appeal Court set out guidelines for dealing with confidential material in mitigation. In *H.M. Advocate v Carnall*, 1999 G.W.D. 31–1485 the Appeal Court observed that although reference in the course of an appeal hearing to disposals in previous, similar appeals against sentence may indicate to some extent the appropriate level of sentence for an offence they could not provide guidance to the whole range of sentences appropriate. See also *H.M. Advocate v Wheldon*, 1999 J.C. 5.

Two other matters may have important consequences for appeals. First, no conviction, sentence, judgment, order of court or other proceedings whatsoever in or for the purposes of solemn proceedings shall be quashed for want of form: subs.(8)(A).

Secondly, and similarly, no conviction, sentence, judgment, order of court or other proceeding whatsoever in or for the purposes of solemn proceedings, where the accused had legal assistance in his defence, shall be suspended or set aside in respect of any objection to, either, the relevancy of the indictment, or the want of specification, or, the competency or admission or rejection of evidence at trial in the lower court, unless such objections were timeously stated: subs.(8)(b)(i) and (ii).

The concept of timeous objection was to be found in s.454 of the 1975 Act in relation to summary trials and it was said to be "special to summary trials": Renton and Brown (5th ed.) para.14–61 at p.300. For a recent case of how the section worked, see *McPherson v McNaughton*, 1992 S.L.T. 600. See notes at s.192.

Subsection (9) was introduced by para.21(17) of Sch.1 to the Crime and Punishment Act with effect from August 1, 1997. This provides that the High Court may give written reasons without giving these reasons orally. This does away with the necessity of having advisings.

The deletion of s.118(4A)(c)(iii) occurs as a consequence of the repeal of s.4 of the 1997 Act wrought by the 1998 Act, Sch.10.

Provision where High Court authorises new prosecution

119.—(1) Subject to subsection (2) below, where authority is granted under section 118(1)(c) of this Act, a new prosecution may be brought charging the accused with the same or any similar offence arising out of the same facts; and the proceedings out of which the appeal arose shall not be a bar to such new prosecution.

(2) In a new prosecution under this section the accused shall not be charged with an offence more serious than that of which he was convicted in the earlier proceedings.

(3) No sentence may be passed on conviction under the new prosecution which could not have been passed on conviction under the earlier proceedings.

(4) A new prosecution may be brought under this section, notwithstanding that any time limit, other than the time limit mentioned in subsection (5) below, for the commencement of such proceedings has elapsed.

(5) Proceedings in a prosecution under this section shall be commenced within two months of the date on which authority to bring the prosecution was granted.

(6) In proceedings in a new prosecution under this section it shall, subject to subsection (7) below, be competent for either party to lead any evidence which it was competent for him to lead in the earlier proceedings.

(7) The indictment in a new prosecution under this section shall identify any matters as respects which the prosecutor intends to lead evidence by virtue of subsection (6) above which would not have been competent but for that subsection.

(8) For the purposes of subsection (5) above, proceedings shall be deemed to be commenced—

    (a) in a case where a warrant to apprehend the accused is granted—

        (i) on the date on which the warrant is executed; or

        (ii) if it is executed without unreasonable delay, on the date on which it is granted;

    (b) in any other case, on the date on which the accused is cited.

(9) Where the two months mentioned in subsection (5) above elapse and no new prosecution has been brought under this section, the order under section 118(1)(c) of this Act setting aside the verdict shall have the effect, for all purposes, of an acquittal.

(10) On granting authority under section 118(1)(c) of this Act to bring a new prosecution, the High Court shall, after giving the parties an opportunity of being heard, order the detention of the accused person in custody or admit him to bail.

(11) Subsections (4)(b) and (7) to (9) of section 65 of this Act (prevention of delay in trials) shall apply to an accused person who is detained under subsection (10) above as they apply to an accused person detained by virtue of being committed until liberated in due course of law.

AMENDMENT

Subs.(8)(a), (b) as amended by the Criminal Procedure (Amendment) (Scotland) Act 2004 (asp 5), s.25 and Sch.1, para.32. Brought into force on February 1, 2005 by the Criminal Procedure (Amendment) (Scotland) Act 2004 (Commencement, Transitional Provisions and Savings) Order 2004 (SSI 2004/405 (C.28)), art.2.

DEFINITIONS

"High Court": s.307(1).
"offence": s.307(1).
"prosecutor": s.307(1).
"sentence": s.307(1).

GENERAL NOTE

Section 119 sets out the procedures for retrial following the quashing of a conviction on appeal but the critical issue is the form of libel which the Crown may use when re-indicting. A number of different situations may arise from the original trial: as well as being convicted of the offence since successfully appealed, the accused may have plead to other charges, have been acquitted, or the Crown may have withdrawn some parts of the libel either due to a perceived insufficiency, or because these had been included for evidential purposes only or to focus issues for the jury.

Subs. (1)

There have been a considerable number of new prosecutions on statutory authority in its earlier form: see, *e.g. Mackenzie v H.M. Advocate*, 1982 S.C.C.R. 499, *King v H.M. Advocate*, 1985 S.C.C.R. 322, *McGhee v H.M. Advocate*, 1991 S.C.C.R. 510, and *Allison v H.M. Advocate*, 1994 S.C.C.R. 464. The grant of such authority does not mean that the Crown is bound to initiate new proceedings: see *e.g. Sinclair v H.M. Advocate*, 1990 S.C.C.R. 412.

Subs. (2)

In a new prosecution under s.119 the accused is not to be *charged* with an offence more serious than that of which he was convicted in the earlier proceedings. The clearest example of this restriction is the case of Daniel Boyle. He had been charged with murder and after trial in the High Court of Justiciary at Glasgow he was convicted of culpable homicide in November 1991. He was sentenced to 10 years' detention. He appealed against conviction and that verdict was set aside in July 1992: *Boyle v H.M. Advocate*, 1993 S.L.T. 577. The High Court of Justiciary, in setting aside that verdict, granted authority to the Crown to bring a new prosecution in accordance with s.254(1)(c) of the 1975 Act.

A new indictment with a charge of murder was served on Boyle on July 30, 1992 for trial on August 31, 1992 but the trial diet was overtaken by an appeal by the Crown against a decision at a preliminary diet: see s.76A of the 1975 Act. The Crown appeal arose in this way: at the preliminary diet the accused argued that the jury, having returned a verdict of culpable homicide, had barred the Crown from indicting Boyle for the more serious crime of murder. The Crown argued otherwise.

At the preliminary diet the judge held that the action of the Crown was competent in law but unfair in the circumstances and dismissed the indictment. The Crown appeal from the preliminary diet was allowed, it being for the Crown not the court to decide any charges brought, and the indictment for murder was remitted to the trial court to proceed: *H.M. Advocate v Boyle*, 1992 S.C.C.R. 939.

Thereafter, Boyle petitioned the *nobile officium* of the High Court of Justiciary to complain that that court had exceeded its own authority in the original appeal in setting aside certain charges on the indictment which Boyle had been convicted of but had not appealed. The petition was refused: *Boyle, Petr*, 1993 S.L.T. 1085.

For the sake of completeness it should be added that at the adjourned trial diet in November 1992 the trial was again adjourned to January 1993 because of difficulties that the Crown had with citing witnesses. Boyle had been in custody since August 1991 and he again petitioned the *nobile officium* of the High Court of Justiciary, this time for bail. That was granted (unusually for those on a murder charge) in terms of s.35 of the 1975 Act: *Boyle, Petr*, 1993 S.C.C.R. 251. Daniel Boyle was acquitted at his second murder trial.

Subs. (3)

This provision ensures that at a second trial in the event of conviction a sentence cannot competently be passed if it could not have been passed on conviction under the earlier proceedings.

Subs. (4)

This provision permits a new prosecution notwithstanding any existing time-limits except for that in subs.(5). It is submitted that calculation of the two month time bar specified falls to be calculated *de die in diem*, the normal rule; see *Lees v Lovell*, 1992 S.L.T. 967 discussed at A4–291 below. It will be noted that the summary provision for fresh proceedings following illness of a judge is drafted in almost identical terms.

Subs. (5)

Proceedings in a prosecution under s.119 must be commenced within two months of the date on which authority to bring the prosecution was granted. Authority for a new prosecution was granted in *Maillie v H.M. Advocate*, 1993 S.C.C.R. 535. Delay in implementing a subsequent petition warrant results in that petition being dismissed: *Friel v Mailley*, 1993 S.C.C.R. 928.

Where an accused has been remanded in custody pending a retrial this provision has the effect of requiring the Crown to re-indict within 60 days of the date upon which the court grants authority for a retrial, rather than the customary 80 day period, following full committal on petition, as set out in s.65 above. It is submitted that, while there would be no time bar upon proceedings in a retrial where the accused is on bail, once an indictment has been served the position in custody cases is quite different; the authority for retrial would become the operative date for calculation of a 110 day period. Thus in *H.M. Advocate v Donnelly*, (High Court of Justiciary, December 2000, unreported) the Crown obtained a retrospective extension of the 110 days when D's trial was adjourned on defence motion beyond the period without an extension having been granted at the time. The Appeal Court's warrant for a retrial was by that time the only authority the Crown had for keeping D in custody or serving an indictment, the original petition warrant having long since expired.

Subss. (6) to (7)

The requirements of s.119(7) apply to cases where evidence could be led only in terms of s.119(6). If the evidence is admissible in terms of *e.g.Nelson v H.M. Advocate*, 1994 S.C.C.R. 192 and *Cairns v H.M. Advocate*, 1967 J.C. 37 then subs.(7) does not apply—*Diamond v H.M. Advocate*, 1999 S.C.C.R. 411.

Subss. (8) to (11)

In *McPhelim v H.M. Advocate*, 1997 S.C.C.R. 87 the Crown raised an indictment within the statutory two months but the indictment was thereafter deserted *pro loco et tempore*. A fresh indictment was raised outwith the two month period. This was held to be competent as proceedings had been commenced timeously.

The competency by subs.(10) of bail for the accused reflects the position that Boyle found himself in and that resulted in his petition to the *nobile officium*: see *Boyle, Petr*, 1993, above.

Appeals: supplementary provisions

120.—(1) Where—

(a) intimation of the diet appointed for the hearing of the appeal has been made to the appellant;

(b) no appearance is made by or on behalf of an appellant at the diet; and

(c) no case or argument in writing has been timeously lodged,

the High Court shall dispose of the appeal as if it had been abandoned.

(2) The power of the High Court to pass any sentence under this Part of this Act may be exercised notwithstanding that the appellant (or, where the Lord Advocate is the appellant, the convicted person) is for any reason not present.

(3) When the High Court has heard and dealt with any application under this Part of this Act, the Clerk of Justiciary shall (unless it appears to him unnecessary so to do) give to the applicant if he is in custody and has not been present at the hearing of such application notice of the decision of the court in relation to the said application.

(4) On the final determination of any appeal under this Part of this Act or of any matter under section 103(5) of this Act, the Clerk of Justiciary shall give notice of such determination—

(a) to the appellant or applicant if he is in custody and has not been present at such final determination;

(b) to the clerk of the court in which the conviction took place; and

(c) to the Secretary of State.

DEFINITIONS
"appellant": s.132.
"diet": s.307(1).
"High Court": s.307(1).

GENERAL NOTE
These supplementary provisions in practice are important because a not inconsiderable number of appeals are refused for want of insistence. The appellant cannot, however, fail to meet any obligation placed on him and expect to have the court overlook it. In *Manson, Petr*, 1991 S.L.T. 96 the petitioner sought to have heard an appeal against sentence which had been dismissed for want of insistence. Manson claimed not to have been notified of the date of appeal but he had failed to notify the court of a change of address as required by s.2(2) of the 1980 Act and the petition was refused.

In *Boyle, Petr*, 1992 S.C.C.R. 949 the Appeal Court held that intimation under the then s.261 of the Criminal Procedure (Scotland) Act 1975 was not an interlocutor and is open to correction by the court, the opinion of the court being the best evidence of what was decided by the court.

Suspension of disqualification, forfeiture, etc.

121.—(1) Any disqualification, forfeiture or disability which attaches to a person by reason of a conviction shall not attach—

(a) for the period of four weeks from the date of the verdict against him; or

(b) where an intimation of intention to appeal or, in the case of an appeal under section 106(1)(b) to (e), 108 or 108A of this Act, a note of appeal is lodged, until the appeal, if it is proceeded with, is determined.

(2) The destruction or forfeiture or any order for the destruction or forfeiture of any property, matter or thing which is the subject of or connected with any prosecution following upon a conviction shall be suspended—

(a) for the period of four weeks after the date of the verdict in the trial; or

(b) where an intimation of intention to appeal or, in the case of an appeal under section 106(1)(b) to (e), 108 or 108A of this Act, a note of appeal is lodged, until the appeal, if it is proceeded with, is determined.

(3) This section does not apply in the case of any disqualification, destruction or forfeiture or order for destruction or forfeiture under or by virtue of any enactment which makes express provision for the suspension of the disqualification, destruction or forfeiture or order for destruction or forfeiture pending the determination of an appeal against conviction or sentence.

(4) Where, upon conviction, a fine has been imposed on a person or a compensation order has been made against him under section 249 of this Act, then, for a period of four weeks from the date of the verdict against such person or, in the event of an intimation of intention to appeal (or in the case of an appeal under section 106(1)(b) to (e), 108 or 108A of this Act a note of appeal) being lodged under this Part of this Act, until such appeal, if it is proceeded with, is determined—

(a) the fine or compensation order shall not be enforced against that person and he shall not be liable to make any payment in respect of the fine or compensation order; and

(b) any money paid by that person under the compensation order shall not be paid by the clerk of court to the person entitled to it under subsection (9) of the said section 249.

(5) In this section—

(a) "appeal" includes an appeal under paragraph 13(a) of Schedule 6 to the Scotland Act 1998; and

(b) in relation to such an appeal, references to an appeal being determined are to be read as references to the disposal of the proceedings by the High Court following determination of the appeal.

AMENDMENT

Subss.(1)(b), (2)(b) and (4) as amended by the Crime and Punishment (Scotland) Act 1997 (c.48), s.18(6) with effect from October 20, 1997 in terms of the Crime and Punishment (Scotland) Act 1997 (Commencement No. 2 and Transitional Provisions) Order 1997 (SI 1997/2323), art.3, Sch.1.

Subs.(5) inserted by the Scotland Act 1998 (Consequential Modifications) (No.1) Order 1999 (SI 1999/1042), art.3, Sch.1, para.13(3) (effective May 6, 1999).

DEFINITION

"fine": s.307(1).

Suspension of certain sentences pending determination of appeal

121A.—(1) Where an intimation of intention to appeal or, in the case of an appeal under section 106(1)(b) to (e) (other than an appeal under section 106(1)(db) or (dc)), 108 or 108A of this Act, a note of appeal is lodged, the court may on the application of the appellant direct that the whole, or any remaining part, of a relevant sentence shall be suspended until the appeal, if it is proceeded with, is determined.

(2) Where the court has directed the suspension of the whole or any remaining part of a person's relevant sentence, the person shall, unless the High Court otherwise directs, appear personally in court on the day or days fixed for the hearing of the appeal.

(3) Where a person fails to appear personally in court as mentioned in subsection (2) above, the court may—

(a) if he is the appellant—

(i) decline to consider the appeal; and

(ii) dismiss it summarily; or

(b) whether or not he is the appellant—

(i) consider and determine the appeal; or

(ii) make such other order as the court thinks fit.

(4) In this section "relevant sentence" means any one or more of the following—

(a) a probation order;

(b) a supervised attendance order made under section 236(6) of this Act;

(c) a community service order;

(d) a restriction of liberty order.

(5) Subsections (1), (2) and (4) above apply to an appeal under paragraph 13(a) of Schedule 6 to the Scotland Act 1998 and, in relation to such an appeal—

(a) references to an appeal being determined are to be read as references to the disposal of the proceedings by the High Court following determination of the appeal; and

(b) the reference in subsection (2) to the hearing of the appeal is to be read as a reference to any subsequent hearing in the High Court in relation to the proceedings.

(6) Where a person fails to appear personally in court as mentioned in subsection (2) as read with subsection (5) above, the court may make such order as it thinks fit.

AMENDMENTS

Section 121A inserted by the Crime and Punishment (Scotland) Act 1997 (c.48), s.24 with effect from August 1, 1997 in terms of the Crime and Punishment (Scotland) Act 1997 (Commencement and Transitional Provisions) Order 1997 (SI 1997/1712), art.3.

Subs.(4)(d) inserted by the Crime and Punishment (Scotland) Act 1997 (c.48), s.24 (effective July 1, 1998: SI 1998/2323).

Subss.(5) and (6) inserted by the Scotland Act 1998 (Consequential Modifications) (No.1) Order 1999 (SI 1999/1042), art.3, Sch.1, para.13(4) (effective May 6, 1999).

Subs.(1) as amended by the Protection of Children (Scotland) Act 2003 (asp 5), s.16(5). Brought into force on January 10, 2005 by the Protection of Children (Scotland) Act 2003 (Commencement No.1) Order 2004 (SSI 2004/522 (C.38)), art.2.

GENERAL NOTE

With effect from August 1, 1997 sentences detailed in subs.(4) are to be suspended pending the determination of an appeal. This should prevent the situation as arose in *H.M. Advocate v Jamieson*, 1996 S.C.C.R. 836 where an accused had completed the majority of a community service order and paid most of a compensation order prior to the hearing of an appeal. The Crown appeal against sentence was refused. In *H.M. Advocate v McKinlay*, 1998 S.C.C.R. 201, however, the Appeal Court upheld a Crown appeal against sentence despite completion of community service. Partial completion of probation and community service will be taken into account in any subsequent unduly lenient sentence appeal *H.M. Advocate v Paterson*, 2000 S.C.C.R. 309 and *H.M. Advocate v Drain*, 2000 S.C.C.R. 256. The fact that the Crown failed to exercise its right under s.121A is a relevant factor in determining unduly lenient sentence appeals—*H.M. Advocate v Carnall*, 1999 G.W.D. 31–1485.

Fines and caution

122.—(1) Where a person has on conviction been sentenced to payment of a fine and in default of payment to imprisonment, the person lawfully authorised to receive the fine shall, on receiving it, retain it until the determination of any appeal in relation to the conviction or sentence.

(2) If a person sentenced to payment of a fine remains in custody in default of payment of the fine he shall be deemed, for the purposes of this Part of this Act, to be a person sentenced to imprisonment.

(3) An appellant who has been sentenced to the payment of a fine, and has paid it in accordance with the sentence, shall, in the event of his appeal being successful, be entitled, subject to any order of the High Court, to the return of the sum paid or any part of it.

(4) A convicted person who has been sentenced to the payment of a fine and has duly paid it shall, if an appeal against sentence by the Lord Advocate or any appeal by the Lord Advocate or the Advocate General for Scotland under paragraph 13(a) of Schedule 6 to the Scotland Act 1998 results in the sentence being quashed and no fine, or a lesser fine than that paid, being imposed, be entitled, subject to any order of the High Court, to the return of the sum paid or as the case may be to the return of the amount by which that sum exceeds the amount of the lesser fine.

(5) In subsections (1) and (3) above, "appeal" includes an appeal under paragraph 13(a) of Schedule 6 to the Scotland Act 1998.

AMENDMENTS

Subs. (4) as amended by the Scotland Act 1998 (Consequential Modifications) (No.1) Order 1999 (S.I. 1999 No.1042) art.3, Sched.1, para.13(5)(a) (effective May 6, 1999).

Subs. (5) inserted by the Scotland Act 1998 (Consequential Modifications) (No.1) Order 1999 (S.I. 1999 No.1042) art.3, Sched.1, para.13(5)(b) (effective May 6, 1999).

DEFINITIONS

"appellant": s.132.
"fine": s.307(1).
"High Court": s.307(1).

Lord Advocate's reference

123.—(1) Where a person tried on indictment is acquitted or convicted of a charge, the Lord Advocate may refer a point of law which has arisen in relation to that charge to the High Court for their opinion; and the Clerk of Justiciary shall send to the person and to any solicitor who acted for the person at the trial, a copy of the reference and intimation of the date fixed by the Court for a hearing.

(2) The person may, not later than seven days before the date so fixed, intimate in writing to the Clerk of Justiciary and to the Lord Advocate either—

(a) that he elects to appear personally at the hearing; or

(b) that he elects to be represented thereat by counsel,

but, except by leave of the Court on cause shown, and without prejudice to his right to attend, he shall not appear or be represented at the hearing other than by and in conformity with an election under this subsection.

(3) Where there is no intimation under subsection (2)(b) above, the High Court shall appoint counsel to act at the hearing as *amicus curiae*.

(4) The costs of representation elected under subsection (2)(b) above or of an appointment under subsection (3) above shall, after being taxed by the Auditor of the Court of Session, be paid by the Lord Advocate.

(5) The opinion on the point referred under subsection (1) above shall not affect the acquittal or, as the case may be, conviction in the trial.

DEFINITIONS

"Clerk of Justiciary": s.307(1).
"High Court": s.307(1).
"indictment": s.307(1).

GENERAL NOTE

There is no appeal against acquittal in solemn proceedings: see the terms of s.106(1) of this Act. It is incompetent in such proceedings to advocate either a verdict of acquittal by a jury, or an acquittal by a judge on a submission of no case to answer. However, should there then be a doubt about the law to be applied then the Lord Advocate may invoke the reference procedure provided by s.123. The expression "a point of law which has arisen in relation to that charge" in subsection (1) relates "not merely to points of law which are in some general way inherent in the charge itself but also to points of law which have actually arisen in the proceedings which led to acquittal or conviction ... including points of law which arise from any defence which is advanced against the charge", *Lord Advocate's Reference (No. 1 of 2000)*, 2001 S.C.C.R. 296 at 333. It was open to the court to hear arguments on what were contended by the defence to be the real issues in the case.

A few such references have been taken on a diverse range of points of law: see *Lord Advocate's Reference No. 1 of 1983*, 1984 S.C.C.R. 62 (taped interviews); *Lord Advocate's Reference No. 1 of 1985*, 1987 S.L.T. 187 (perjury); *Lord Advocate's Reference No. 1 of 1992*, 1992 S.L.T. 1010 (building societies); *Lord Advocate's Reference No. 2 of 1992*, 1992 S.C.C.R. 960 (joke as motive); *Lord Advocate's Reference No. 1 of 1994*, 1995 S.L.T. 248 (supply of a controlled drug), *Lord Advocate's Reference No. 1 of 1996*, 1996 S.C.C.R. 516 (bankers' books) and *Lord Advocate's Reference (No.1 of 2000)*, 2001 S.C.C.R.296 (malicious mischief, necessity and international law).

The costs of representation elected under s.123(2)(b) are, after being taxed by the Auditor of the Court of Session, paid by the Lord Advocate: s.123(4).

Finality of proceedings and Secretary of State's reference

124.—(1) Nothing in this Part or Part XA of this Act shall affect the prerogative of mercy.

(2) Subject to Part XA of this Act and paragraph 13(a) of Schedule 6 to the Scotland Act 1998, every interlocutor and sentence pronounced by the High Court under this Part of this Act shall be final and conclusive and not subject to review by any court whatsoever and, except for the purposes of an appeal under paragraph 13(a) of that Schedule, it shall be incompetent to stay or suspend any execution or diligence issuing from the High Court under this Part of this Act.

(3)–(5) [...]

AMENDMENTS

Subss. (1) and (2) as amended by the Crime and Punishment (Scotland) Act 1997, Sched. 1, para. 21(18).

Subs. (2) as amended by the Scotland Act 1998 (Consequential Modifications) (No.1) Order 1999 (S.I. 1999 No.1042) art.3, Sched.1, para.13(6) (effective May 6, 1999).

Subss. (3)–(5) repealed by the Crime and Punishment (Scotland) Act 1997, Sched. 1, para.21(18) and Sched. 3 (effective April 1, 1999: S.I. 1999 No. 652).

DEFINITIONS

"High Court": s.307(1).
"sentence": s.132.

GENERAL NOTE

Subs. (1)

The prerogative of mercy remains unaffected by the provisions in Pt VIII of the 1995 Act. Precisely what this subsection means, in the context of subs.(3), is a matter of some interest. Some assistance may be found in *H.M. Advocate v. Waddell*, 1976 S.L.T. (Notes) 61 and C. Gane "The Effect of a Pardon in Scots Law", 1980 J.R. 18.

Subs. (2)

This limitation applies to interlocutors and sentences pronounced by the High Court in appeals from solemn proceedings—*Express Newspapers PLC Petrs*, 1999 S.C.C.R. 262. Subsection (2) has been amended to permit appeals to the Judicial Committee of the Privy Council in terms of the Scotland Act 1998.

The *nobile officium* cannot be invoked to review the merits of decisions of the court exercising its appellate jurisdiction but it can be used to alter or correct an order pronounced by the Appeal Court where the court has exceeded its powers. See *Perrie Petr*, 1991 S.C.C.R. 475; *Beattie Petr*, 1997 S.C.C.R. 949; *Windsor Petr*, 1994 S.C.C.R. 59 and *Granger, Petr*, 2001 S.C.C.R. 337. In that case not even a decision by the ECtHR that failure to provide legal aid for an appeal constituted a breach of G's human rights permitted the appellant to use the nobile officium to review the merits of the Appeal Court's refusal of an appeal against conviction. In *Express Newspapers PLC Petrs, supra*, a petition to the *nobile officium* was used to appeal fines imposed for contempt of court.

A valid interlocutor cannot be pronounced if a quorum of the Appeal Court is not constituted— *Hoekstra v. H.M. Advocate (No.2)*, 2000 S.C.C.R. 368. The resulting setting aside of the courts interlocutor was thereafter held not to amount to an attempt by the Appeal Court to amend s.124(2) (finality of interlocutors) and did not give rise to a devolution issue. The Privy Council confirmed "except in regard to devolution issues as defined by para. 1 the position remains that every interlocutor of the High Court of Justiciary is final and conclusive and not subject to review by any court whatsoever", *Hoekstra v. H.M. Advocate (No. 4)*, 2000 S.C.C.R. 1121.

Reckoning of time spent pending appeal

125.—(1) Subject to subsection (2) below, where a convicted person is admitted to bail under section 112 of this Act, the period beginning with the date of his admission to bail and ending on the date of his readmission to prison in consequence of the determination or abandonment of—

(a) his appeal; or, as the case may be,

(b) any relevant appeal by the Lord Advocate under section 108 or 108A of this Act, shall not be reckoned as part of any term of imprisonment under his sentence.

(2) The time, including any period consequent on the recall of bail during which an appellant is in custody pending the determination of his appeal or, as the case may be, of any relevant appeal by the Lord Advocate under section 108 or 108A of this Act shall, subject to any direction which the High Court may give to the contrary, be reckoned as part of any term of imprisonment under his sentence.

(3) Subject to any direction which the High Court may give to the contrary, imprisonment of an appellant or, where the appellant is the Lord Advocate, of a convicted person—

(a) who is in custody in consequence of the conviction or sentence appealed against, shall be deemed to run as from the date on which the sentence was passed;

(b) who is in custody other than in consequence of such conviction or sentence, shall be deemed to run or to be resumed as from the date on which his appeal was determined or abandoned;

(c) who is not in custody, shall be deemed to run or to be resumed as from the date on which he is received into prison under the sentence.

(4) In this section references to a prison and imprisonment shall include respectively references to a young offenders institution or place of safety or, as respects a child sentenced to be detained under section 208 of this Act, the place directed by the Secretary of State and to detention in such institution, centre or place of safety, or, as respects such a child, place directed by the Secretary of State and any reference to a sentence shall be construed as a reference to a sentence passed by the court imposing sentence or by the High Court on appeal as the case may require.

AMENDMENT

Subss. (1)(b) and (2) as amended by the Crime and Punishment (Scotland) Act 1997 (c. 48), s.18(7) with effect from October 20, 1997 in terms of the Crime and Punishment (Scotland) Act 1997 (Commencement and Transitional Provisions) Order 1997 (S.I. 1997 No. 2323) art. 3, Sched. 1.

DEFINITIONS

"bail": s.307(1).
"prison": s.307(1).
"sentence": s.132.
"young offender's institution": s.307(1).

GENERAL NOTE

Subsections 1 and 2 have been amended with effect from October 20, 1997 to provide that where an appellant is released on bail pending an appeal under s.108A by the Lord Advocate this shall not be reckoned towards the calculation of the period of imprisonment.

Subsection (2)—see *Scott v. H.M. Advocate*, 1946 J.C. 68 where an accused made a frivolous application for extension of time. The court refused to direct that the time he was treated as an appellant should count as part of his sentence.

Extract convictions

126. No extract conviction shall be issued—

(a) during the period of four weeks after the day on which the conviction took place, except in so far as it is required as a warrant for the detention of the person convicted under any sentence which has been pronounced against him; nor

(b) where an intimation of intention to appeal or, in the case of an appeal under section 106(1)(b) to (e), 108 or 108A of this Act, a note of appeal is lodged, until the appeal, if it is proceeded with, is determined.

AMENDMENT

Subs. (b) as amended by the Crime and Punishment (Scotland) Act 1997 (c. 48), s.18(8) with effect from October 20, 1997 in terms of the Crime and Punishment (Scotland) Act 1997 (Commencement and Transitional Provisions) Order 1997 (S.I.1997 No.2323), art.3, Sched. 1.

DEFINITIONS

"extract conviction": s.307(1).
"sentence": s.132.

GENERAL NOTE

This has been amended with effect from October 20, 1997 to include appeals under s.108A.

Forms in relation to appeals

127.—(1) The Clerk of Justiciary shall furnish the necessary forms and, instructions in relation to intimations of intention to appeal, notes of appeal or notices of application under this Part of this Act to—

(a) any person who demands them; and

(b) to officers of courts, governors of prisons, and such other officers or persons as he thinks fit.

(2) The governor of a prison shall cause the forms and instructions mentioned in subsection (1) above to be placed at the disposal of prisoners desiring to appeal or to make any application under this Part of this Act.

(3) The governor of a prison shall, if requested to do so by a prisoner, forwarded on the prisoner's behalf to the Clerk of Justiciary any intimation, note or notice mentioned in subsection (1) above given by the prisoner.

DEFINITIONS

"Clerk of Justiciary": s.307(1).
"governor": s.307(1).
"prison": s.307(1).

Fees and expenses

128. Except as otherwise provided in this Part of this Act, no court fees, or other fees or expenses shall be exigible from or awarded against an appellant or applicant in respect of an appeal or application under this Part of this Act.

Non-compliance with certain provisions may be waived

129.—(1) Non-compliance with—

(a) the provisions of this Act set out in subsection (3) below; or

(b) any rule of practice for the time being in force under this Part of this Act relating to appeals,

shall not prevent the further prosecution of an appeal if the High Court or a judge thereof considers it just and proper that the non-compliance is waived or, in the manner directed by the High Court or judge, remedied by amendment or otherwise.

(2) Where the High Court or a judge thereof directs that the non-compliance is to be remedied, and the remedy is carried out, the appeal shall proceed.

(3) The provisions of this Act referred to in subsection (1) above are:—
    section 94
    section 103(1), (4), (6) and (7)
    section 104(2) and (3)
    section 105
    section 106(4)
    section 111
    section 114
    section 115
    section 116
    section 117
    section 120(1), (3) and (4)
    section 121
    section 122
    section 126
    section 128.

(4) This section does not apply to any rule of practice relating to appeals under section 60 of this Act.

DEFINITIONS

"High Court": s.307(1).
"judge": s.307(1).

GENERAL NOTE

This general saving power permits an appeal against conviction or sentence to proceed notwithstanding non-compliance with the rules specified in s.129(3) if it appears just and proper to proceed or if a consequential problem can be remedied.

Bill of suspension not competent

130. It shall not be competent to appeal to the High Court by bill of suspension against any conviction, sentence, judgement or order pronounced in any proceedings on indictment in the sheriff court.

DEFINITIONS

"indictment": s.307(1).
"sentence": s.132.

GENERAL NOTE

The origins of this section lie in the Criminal Appeal (Scotland) Act 1926 which, by s.13, abolished appeal by suspension, but appeal by advocation from the sheriff in solemn procedure remained competent. A bill of suspension for an appeal by a witness found in contempt in the course of solemn proceedings in the sheriff court was held competent in *Butterworth v Herron*, 1975 S.L.T. (Notes) 56. This was later over-ruled when five judges held in *George Outram & Co. v Lees*, 1992 S.L.T. 32 that the correct mode of appeal was a petition to the *nobile officium*. In *Mellors v Normand (No.2)*, 1996 J.C. 148 the Appeal Court held it was appropriate to use a bill of suspension to suspend a committal warrant.

Prosecution appeal by bill of advocation

131.—(1) Without prejudice to section 74 of this Act, the prosecutor's right to bring a decision under review of the High Court by way of bill of advocation in accordance with existing law and practice shall extend to the review of a decision of any court of solemn jurisdiction.

(2) Where a decision to which a bill of advocation relates is reversed on the review of the decision the prosecutor may, whether or not there has already been a trial diet at which evidence has been led, proceed against the accused by serving him with an indictment containing, subject to subsection (3) below, the charge or charges which were affected by the decision.

(3) The wording of the charge or charges referred to in subsection (2) above shall be as it was immediately before the decision appealed against.

DEFINITIONS

"High Court": s.307(1).
"prosecutor": s.307(1).

GENERAL NOTE

In *HM Advocate v Sinclair*, 1987 S.L.T. 161 a shrieval decision to desert an indictment *pro loco et tempore* was successfully challenged by the Crown. The competency of the use of advocation by the Crown to review a sheriff's decision during the currency, rather than at the conclusion, of proceedings, and before final judgment was upheld in *HM Advocate v Khan*, 1997 S.C.C.R. 100 and in *HM Advocate v Shepherd*, 1997 S.C.C.R. 246 (see A4–207 and A4–55 above). In *HM Advocate v Sorrie*, 1996 S.C.C.R. 778 the Appeal Court indicated that if the Crown seek to use a bill of advocation rather than an appeal in terms of s.74 of the Act the accused should be alerted to the fact. In *HM Advocate v Khan*, 1997 S.C.C.R. 100 the Crown successfully brought a Bill of Advocation against a sheriff's refusal to adjourn a diet and to grant a defence motion to discharge a juror while in *HM Advocate v Fleming*, 2005 S.C.C.R. 324, a decision by the trial judge in High Court proceedings, unusually, to desert *simpliciter* rather than *pro loco et tempore* was advocated.

Interpretation of Part VIII

132. In this Part of this Act, unless the context otherwise requires—

"appellant" includes a person who has been convicted and desires to appeal under this Part of the Act;

"sentence" includes any order of the High Court made on conviction with reference to the person convicted or his wife or children, and any recommendation of the High Court as to the making of a deportation order in the case of a person convicted and the power of the High Court to pass a sentence includes a power to make any such order of the court or recommendation, and a recommendation so made by the High Court shall have the same effect for the purposes of Articles 20 and 21 of the Aliens Order 1953 as the certificate and recommendation of the convicting court.

PART IX

SUMMARY PROCEEDINGS

General

Application of Part IX of Act

133.—(1) This Part of this Act applies to summary proceedings in respect of any offence which might prior to the passing of this Act, or which may under the provisions of this or any Act, whether passed before or after the passing of this Act, be tried summarily.

(2) Without prejudice to subsection (1) above, this Part of this Act also applies

to procedure in all courts of summary jurisdiction in so far as they have jurisdiction in respect of—

(a) any offence or the recovery of a penalty under any enactment or rule of law which does not exclude summary procedure as well as, in accordance with section 211(3) and (4) of this Act, to the enforcement of a fine imposed in solemn proceedings; and

(b) any order *ad factum praestandum*, or other order of court or warrant competent to a court of summary jurisdiction.

(3) Where any statute provides for summary proceedings to be taken under any public general or local enactment, such proceedings shall be taken under this Part of this Act.

(4) Nothing in this Part of this Act shall—

(a) extend to any complaint or other proceeding under or by virtue of any statutory provision for the recovery of any rate, tax, or impost whatsoever; or

(b) affect any right to raise any civil proceedings.

(5) Except where any enactment otherwise expressly provides, all prosecutions under this Part of this Act shall be brought at the instance of the procurator fiscal.

DEFINITIONS

"court of summary jurisdiction":s5(1) and (2) and s.307(1).
"offence":s.307(1).
"statute":s.307(1).
"summarily":s.5(1) and (2) and s.7(5) and (6).

GENERAL NOTE

Part IX of the Act regulates the procedure in all summary cases including proceedings raised under local enactments as well as statutory provisions which apply generally. Revenue offences involving the Inland Revenue and H.M. Customs and Excise only adopt the procedures in Pt IX of the Act insofar as expressly stipulated within their relevant statutes.

It will be seen that subs. (2)(a) provides that summary provisions also apply to the enforcement of monetary fines imposed following solemn convictions and to the enforcement of fines imposed by other courts in Scotland, England and Wales unless such a jurisdiction is specifically excluded.

Incidental applications

134.—(1) This section applies to any application to a court for any warrant or order of court—

(a) as incidental to proceedings by complaint; or

(b) where a court has power to grant any warrant or order of court, although no subsequent proceedings by complaint may follow thereon.

(2) An application to which this section applies may be made by petition at the instance of the prosecutor in the form prescribed by Act of Adjournal.

(3) Where it is necessary for the execution of a warrant or order granted under this section, warrant to break open shut and lockfast places shall be implied.

DEFINITION

"complaint":s.307(1).

GENERAL NOTE

This section determines that the form specified in the 1996 Act of Adjournal (Form 16.4.-A) shall be used for applications to the court by the prosecutor or the accused when summary proceedings have begun (subs. (1)(a)) or when the prosecutor, in carrying out his investigative role, seeks a search warrant, or other warrant, from a sheriff or magistrate even before any person has been charged with an offence (subs. (1)(b)); this latter provision will doubtless remain the most common use of this section. Examples of the range of warrants sought, can be found in *Carmichael, Complainer*, 1993 S.L.T. 305 (to precognosce a complainer on oath); *Frame v. Houston*, 1992 S.L.T. 205 (warrant for hair samples of accused sought after indictment served); *Normand, Complainer*, 1992 S.L.T. 478 (warrant at common law to inspect bankers' books before proceedings have begun). Applications made under s.31 of the Criminal Law (Consolidation) (Scotland) Act 1995 by the prosecutor for an "inspection order" or a "production order" are made by such an incidental application; see para. A1–62 above.

Summary warrants to apprehend which are used to commence proceedings and empower the arrest of a known accused are granted under s.139(1)(c) below.

In addition to the statutory power of apprehension and search enacted in s.135 below, a multiplicity of statutes contain their own express powers of search, detention and arrest, notably the Misuse of Drugs Act 1971, the Road Traffic Act 1988 and the Firearms Act 1968: these express provisions override the general powers contained in s.134.

In *Douglas v. Procurator Fiscal, Kirkcaldy* (High Court, November 1991) the procurator fiscal resorted to incidental application procedure to have citations as defence witnesses for himself and the Law Officers rescinded on the grounds that they had no evidence to offer pertinent to the case; the accused, on appeal, stated that citations had been served because he had a separate grievance against the procurator fiscal. His appeal by advocation was refused.

Note that where one of the parties has declined to make a joint application to the court to alter a diet as enabled by s.137 below, s.137(4) permits the use of an incidental application to put the matter before the court for consideration.

Reduction of incidental applications is by way of a bill of suspension. See, for example, *McIntyre v. Munro*, 1999 G.W.D. 9–419 where an inept apprehension warrant was quashed.

Warrants of apprehension and search

135.—(1) A warrant of apprehension or search may be in the form prescribed by Act of Adjournal or as nearly as may be in such form, and any warrant of apprehension or search shall, where it is necessary for its execution, imply warrant to officers of law to break open shut and lockfast places.

(2) A warrant of apprehension of an accused in the form mentioned in subsection (1) above shall imply warrant to officers of law to search for and to apprehend the accused, and to bring him before the court issuing the warrant, or before any other court competent to deal with the case, to answer to the charge on which such warrant is granted, and, in the meantime, until he can be so brought, to detain him in a police station, police cell, or other convenient place.

(3) A person apprehended under a warrant or by virtue of power under any enactment or rule of law shall wherever practicable be brought before a court competent to deal with the case not later than in the course of the first day after he is taken into custody.

(4) The reference in subsection (3) above to the first day after he is taken into custody shall not include a Saturday, a Sunday or a court holiday prescribed for that court under section 8 of this Act; but nothing in this subsection shall prevent a person being brought before the court on a Saturday, a Sunday or such a court holiday where the court is, in pursuance of the said section 8, sitting on such day for the disposal of criminal business.

(5) A warrant of apprehension or other warrant shall not be required for the purpose of bringing before the court an accused who has been apprehended without a written warrant or who attends without apprehension in answer to any charge made against him.

DEFINITION

"officers of law": s.307(1).

As subs.(5) makes clear, the provisions of this section are intended to initiate proceedings against an accused whose identity is known to the prosecutor but who, for one reason or another, has not been apprehended and brought before the court to answer the charge against him. Rule 16.5.-(1) of the 1996 Act of Adjournal stipulates that such warrants are to follow the styles shown as Forms 16.5-A and B (Warrants to apprehend following a failure to appear at a diet are granted under s.150 of the Act).

While the power granted by warrant under subs.(2) is to arrest the accused, it is competent for the prosecutor instead to exercise a discretion to invite the accused to appear at a specified court or police station on a given date and thus avoid the pains of arrest; see *Spowart v Burr* (1895) 1 Adam 539. It was held in *Young v Smith*, 1981 S.L.T. (Notes) 101; 1981 S.C.C.R. 85 that where an accused attended voluntarily in response to such an invitation the warrant had not been executed. Similarly failure to respond to such an invitation with the result that a warrant is executed, cannot work to the benefit of the accused (*Young v McLeod*, 1993 S.C.C.R. 479 where pleas of undue delay were repelled).

The wording of subss.(3) and (4) paraphrases the terms of s.321(3) of the 1975 Act and, following *Robertson v MacDonald*, 1993 S.L.T. 1337; 1992 S.C.C.R. 916 would appear to be directory rather than mandatory in its effect. In *Robertson*, the accused had been arrested upon a petition warrant, granted at Wick Sheriff Court, in Glasgow. He was conveyed to Wick and made his appearance on summary complaint four days later when he took objection to the competency of proceedings. Albeit a breach of the subsection had occurred, the court upheld Crown submissions that itself did not vitiate proceedings.

So far as search warrants are concerned it is well-understood that it is incompetent to look behind the grant of a warrant (*Allan v Tant*, 1986 S.C.C.R. 175; *H.M. Advocate v Rae*, 1992 S.C.C.R. 1) and there is a general presumption of regularity where the warrant appears *ex facie* valid (*MacNeill, Complainer*, 1984 S.L.T. 157 and *H.M. Advocate v Beggs (No.4)*, 2002 S.L.T. 163). Refer also to the Notes to ss.296 and 297 below.

Time limit for certain offences — *COMPETENCY* *Offences created by statute triable summarily*

136.—(1) Proceedings under this Part of this Act in respect of any offence to which this section applies shall be commenced—

(a) within six months after the contravention occurred;

(b) in the case of a continuous contravention, within six months after the last date of such contravention,

and it shall be competent in a prosecution of a contravention mentioned in paragraph (b) above to include the entire period during which the contravention occurred.

(2) This section applies to any offence triable only summarily and consisting of the contravention of any enactment, unless the enactment fixes a different time limit.

(3) For the purposes of this section proceedings shall be deemed to be commenced on the date on which a warrant to apprehend or to cite the accused is granted, if the warrant is executed without undue delay.

DEFINITION

"offence": s.307(1).

GENERAL NOTE

The peremptory nature of these provisions in the 1975 Act inevitably produced a substantial volume of case law. Section 136 appears to re-enact the terms of s.331 of the 1975 Act which applied a six-month time bar to the raising of summary prosecutions of statutory offences; however subs.(2) now restricts the operation of the provisions to cases which are triable summarily only, and to statutory enactments which contain their own express time bar provisions. See for example *Gilday v Ritchie*, 1999 G.W.D. 32–1528, a prosecution under the Misuse of Drugs Act 1971 on summary complaint, where it was held that the statute's specific time bar was not set aside by the terms of s.136 above.

Note that this time-bar provision, which now applies to a more limited number of statutory offences than were affected by s.331 of the 1975 Act, does not apply to the libelling of common law offences. While pleas to the competency of proceedings on the grounds of time-bar should now be less commonplace, it may be noted that a delay on the part of the Crown in initiating proceedings could well justify a plea of *mora*. (For *mora* see generally *Tudhope v McCarthy*, 1985 J.C. 48; 1985 S.L.T. 395; *McFarlane v Jessop*, 1988 S.L.T. 596; 1988 S.C.C.R. 186; *Connachan v Douglas*, 1990 S.L.T. 563; 1990 S.C.C.R. 101).

The issue of *mora* was not argued explicitly in *Higson v Morrison*, 2001 G.W.D. 16–600 where M had taken objection, on Convention grounds, to proceedings against him under the Road Traffic Act 1988. These had been initiated by means of certification by the Lord Advocate specifying the date upon which sufficient information came to his knowledge to justify proceedings. M's challenge to proceedings failed under s.136 since the offence was not triable only summarily but the sheriff expressed some unease about the conclusive nature of such certification—the court having no power to look behind it—and opined that proceedings initiated so long after the event might be capable of reduction on the basis that they offended against Convention rights. The court did not review the public interest considerations which arguably underpin the kinds of offence which can be certified by the Lord Advocate; these tend to be offences, for example driving without insurance, or driving while disqualified, where discovery of the offence might take some time.

Proceedings will normally be commenced by the postal service of a citation and service copy complaint upon the accused, but can also be started by an initiating warrant or by obtaining an assigned diet within the six-month period for a diet outwith that period; the question of whether the prosecutor has complied with the statutory timebar provisions has to be approached differently in each of these situations. Service by post of a complaint timeously to call at a diet within the six-month date offers no difficulty; the proceedings commence on the date of posting of the complaint. The same rule applies to the service of a complaint to call at a diet after the expiry of six-months; in that event the proceedings are still competent, provided that the complaint is sent and received within the six-month date and calls at the cited diet (see *Keily v Tudhope*, 1986 S.C.C.R. 351; 1987 S.L.T. 99; *Orr v Lowdon*, 1987 S.C.C.R. 515 and *Slater v Howdle*, 2002 G.W.D. 31–1063); it is desirable that the prosecutor is able to produce an execution of service of the complaint in that latter situation.

Different considerations apply when the prosecutor elects to proceed instead by way of either an initiating warrant or by a warrant to cite the accused to an assigned diet. The grant of either form of warrant signals the commencement of the proceedings and to preserve those proceedings the warrant must in either case be executed without undue delay. It must be emphasised however that while an initiating warrant may well be a valid basis for proceedings months later (if the prosecutor can show that there was no undue delay on his part, a matter discussed later), in the case of a warrant to cite the complaint will either stand or fall on the date of the assigned diet (*Tudhope v. Buckner*, 1985 S.C.C.R. 352).

If service has not been effected upon the accused prior to the diet then the complaint necessarily falls. The only option available to the prosecutor should he learn of difficulty in effecting service of a warrant to cite, is to withdraw the warrant and reraise by means of an initiating warrant if this can be done before the expiry of the timebar.

Once an initiating warrant or a warrant to cite has been obtained, any undue delay in its execution must not be attributable to the actions (or inactions) of the prosecutor. Generally, reported cases have focused upon what constitutes "undue delay" and it has to be stressed that even where a warrant to cite an accused to a diet outwith the six-month period is granted timeously, the prosecutor must still effect service of the complaint swiftly. The onus of proof of "no undue delay" rests with the Crown and if facts are in dispute, the court should hear evidence of the steps taken to execute the warrant (*McCartney v. Tudhope*, 1985 S.C.C.R. 373; 1986 S.L.T. 159). An incorrect address in the instance of the complaint and frustrated efforts to serve at the correct address by post and personally were held not to constitute "undue delay"; see *McKay v. Normand*, 1995 G.W.D. 39–1995.

Statutory Exceptions

It is well understood that where a statute provides specific time limits for procedures or proceedings, then those time limits apply and are not affected by the generality of s.136; see for example *Gilday v. Ritchie*, 2000 S.C.C.R. 53, a Misuse of Drugs Act 1971 prosecution which was time-barred.

Computation of Time

The six-month period is calculated *de die in diem* and not *de momento in momentum* (see *Tudhope v. Lawson*, 1983 S.C.C.R. 435; *Lees v. Lovell*, 1992 S.L.T. 967; 1992 S.C.C.R. 557 following *Keenan v. Carmichael*, 1991 S.C.C.R. 680), *i.e.* excluding the date of offence.

In the exceptional circumstances produced by the death, illness or absence of the judge, which has interrupted a part-heard trial, s.151(2) permits a new prosecution of a statutory complaint raised within two months of its desertion, notwithstanding the usual timebar on statutory proceedings.

Undue Delay

Warrants are sought for arrest or for the assignment of a diet for a date usually outwith the normal prescriptive period. Undue delay where established is fatal to proceedings on that complaint and the result of such a finding is to preclude any further proceedings on a statutory (but not a common law) charge. The delay has to be attributable to the prosecutor alone and will be assessed according to the facts of each case. The presiding judge has a broad discretion in deciding the issue. Execution of the warrant extends to any action taken by the prosecutor to effect citation whether by post or other means (*Lockhart v. Bradley*, 1977 S.L.T. 5); "undue delay" was defined in *Smith v. Peter Walker and Son (Edinburgh)*, 1978 J.C. 44.

Examples of undue delay are found in *Carmichael v. Sardar and Sons*, 1983 S.C.C.R. 433 (unexplained period of six days), *Harvey v. Lockhart*, 1991 S.C.C.R. 83; 1992 S.L.T. 68 (14 days but the sheriff had erred in reaching a decision without hearing explanations for the delay), *Robertson v. Carmichael*, 1993 S.C.C.R. 841 (four days unexplained and not investigated).

Undue delay was not established in *Stagecoach v. MacPhail*, 1986 S.C.C.R. 184 (seven days between warrant to cite and service), *Anderson v. Lowe*, 1991 S.C.C.R. 712 (warrant mislaid in Sheriff Clerk's office for three days), *Buchan v. McNaughtan*, 1990 S.C.C.R. 688; 1991 S.L.T. 410 (delay attributed to conduct of accused), *Young v. MacPhail*, 1991 S.C.C.R. 630; 1992 S.L.T. 98 (a warrant granted for accused then serving a prison sentence in England not being executed until his date of release), or in *Melville v. Normand*, 1996 G.W.D. 10–542 (a combination of public holidays, the warrant being sent to the wrong police office and execution being delayed by the police until the conclusion of the accused's High Court trial on other charges, this last practice being viewed as a sound one), *Alexander v. Normand*, 1997 S.L.T. 370 (a delay of 13 days before issuing the warrant to the police where the time-bar was still two months away followed by three abortive attempts to execute the warrant), *McGlennan v. Singh*, 1993 S.C.C.R. 341 (16 days lapsed from grant of warrant till its execution, but the sheriff had moved too summarily in finding against the Crown).

The period to be taken into account in assessing delay is from the date of granting of the warrant until its execution, not the time from the expiry of the prescriptive period until the execution of the warrant (see *MacNeill v. Cowie*, 1984 S.C.C.R. 449; *McNellie v. Walkingshaw*, 1990 S.C.C.R. 428; 1991 S.L.T. 892) but it must be emphasised that the issue of delay will only arise where service is effected outwith the six-month time-bar period. Hence in *Chow v. Lees*, 1997 S.C.C.R. 253, where the prosecutor was granted an apprehension warrant shortly before expiry of the time-bar and elected to invite the accused to appear voluntarily on a date after that expiry, the Appeal Court directed the sheriff (who had repelled a plea to the competency) to consider the issue of undue delay; it had taken Crown over a week to instruct an invitation to be sent to the accused and a further week to intimate to him a date for his appearance.

Reduction of Proceedings to Summary Complaint

The anticipated impact of the decision in *Gardner v. Lees* 1996 S.C.C.R. 168, which required that any petition proceedings later reduced to a summary complaint had to be concluded within a year of the original appearance on petition, has been blunted by the express provisions of the Criminal Procedure and Investigations Act 1996 (c. 25), s.73(3). This statutory provision, which amended s.65(1) of the 1995 Act, has the effect of removing any time-bar on such summary proceedings while restating the time-bar applicable to solemn proceedings (carried over from s.101 of the 1975 Act, *i.e.* one year from petition appearance to the date of commencement of indictment proceedings).

While *Gardner v. Lees* may assist in understanding the constitutional origins of the statutory time-bar, the jurisprudential justification for applying those principles equally to non-custodial summary proceedings was, to say the least, doubtful; the leap of logic which required summary trial proceedings to be concluded within a year (rather than commenced as s.101 demanded of solemn proceedings) was more questionable still. Effectively the statutory amendment to s.65 brings the law back to that stated in *MacDougall v. Russell*, 1985 S.C.C.R. 441 and *Whitelaw v. Dickinson*, 1993 S.C.C.R. 164. See A4.149 in relation to the computation of the time of such proceedings and *Duke v. Lees*, 1997 G.W.D. 15–659.

Alteration of diets

137.—(1) Where a diet has been fixed in a summary prosecution, it shall be competent for the court, on a joint application in writing by the parties or their solicitors, to discharge the diet and fix an earlier diet in lieu.

Adjournment

(2) Where the prosecutor and the accused make joint application to the court (orally or in writing) for postponement of a diet which has been fixed, the court shall discharge the diet and fix a later diet in lieu unless the court considers that it should not do so because there has been unnecessary delay on the part of one of more of the parties.

(3) Where all the parties join in an application under subsection (2) above, the court may proceed under that subsection without hearing the parties.

(4) Where the prosecutor has intimated to the accused that he desires to postpone or accelerate a diet which has been fixed, and the accused refuses, or any of the accused refuse, to make a joint application to the court for that purpose, the prosecutor may make an incidental application for that purpose under section 134 of this Act; and after giving the parties an opportunity to be heard, the court may discharge the diet and fix a later diet or, as the case may be, an earlier diet in lieu.

(5) Where an accused had intimated to the prosecutor and to all the other accused that he desires such postponement or acceleration and the prosecutor refuses, or any of the other accused refuse, to make a joint application to the court for that purpose, the accused who has so intimated may apply to the court for that purpose; and, after giving the parties an opportunity to be heard, the court may discharge the diet and fix a later diet or, as the case may be, an earlier diet in lieu.

DEFINITIONS

"diet": s.307(1).
"prosecutor": s.307(1).

GENERAL NOTE

This section provides procedures for applications to the court for alteration of summary diets on joint motion, and for such applications to be made by a party in the absence of agreement of all parties. Subsection (1) permits acceleration of a diet by means of a joint written application; subs.(2) relates to joint applications to postpone a summary diet and gives expression to the right of the court to refuse such an application which, unlike a motion for acceleration, can be made either orally or in writing. Where all parties concur in making a written application timeously, the court can dispose of it administratively. Note however that the court's power to refuse an application for postponement on grounds of unnecessary delay by one of the parties suggests that a hearing would be required before the motion could be decided by the court.

Subsections (4) and (5) respectively provide for the prosecutor and the accused to make application individually to the court for variation of the diet in situations where other parties will not concur. The prosecutor should make application by way of an incidental application (see s.134 above) while the accused, although it is not stipulated in subs.(5), can petition using Form 16.7 provided in the 1996 Act of Adjournal.

In *White v Ruxton*, 1996 S.C.C.R. 427 it was held in the absence of a court minute recording a new diet of trial fixed by Joint Minute of Acceleration that the minute itself, whose terms were not in dispute, was sufficient for the purpose. Objections to the competency of the proceedings were rejected.

Transfer of sheriff court summary proceedings within sheriffdom

137A.—(1) Where an accused person has been cited to attend a diet of the sheriff court the prosecutor may apply to the sheriff for an order for the transfer of the proceedings to a sheriff court in any other district in that sheriffdom and for adjournment to a diet of that court.

(2) On an application under subsection (1) above the sheriff may make such order as is mentioned in that subsection.

AMENDMENT

Section 137A inserted by Criminal Justice (Scotland) Act 2003 (asp 7), Part 8, s.58. Brought into

force on June 27, 2003 by the Criminal Justice (Scotland) Act 2003 (Commencement No.1) Order 2003 (SSI 2003/288 (C.14)).

GENERAL NOTE

This new provision entitles the prosecutor, at any point in the proceedings, to apply to the sheriff for authority to cite accused persons, and transfer the proceedings to elsewhere in the sheriffdom. Section 137B enables the sheriff clerk to inform the prosecutor of exceptional factors which would justify the transfer of existing business, and cited diets, to another sheriffdom. (Some assistance may be found in the General Notes to s.83 above). The transfer arrangements between sheriffdoms are contingent upon there being agreement between the sheriff principals involved *before* any application by the prosecutor is granted. In summary proceedings it is conceivable that joint minute procedures could be utilised to transfer ongoing proceedings under both these sections.

Transfer of sheriff court summary proceedings outwith sheriffdom

137B.—(1) Where—

(a) an accused person has been cited to attend a diet of the sheriff court; or

(b) paragraph (a) does not apply but it is competent so to cite an accused person,

and the prosecutor is informed by the sheriff clerk that, because of exceptional circumstances which could not reasonably have been foreseen, it is not practicable for that court or any other sheriff court in that sheriffdom to proceed with the case, the prosecutor—

(i) may, where paragraph (b) above applies, so cite the accused; and

(ii) shall, where paragraph (a) above applies or the accused is so cited by virtue of paragraph (i) above, as soon as practicable apply to the sheriff principal for an order for the transfer of the proceedings to a sheriff court in another sheriffdom and for adjournment to a diet of that court.

(2) On an application under subsection (1) above the sheriff principal may make the order sought, provided that the sheriff principal of the other sheriffdom consents.

(3) On the application of the prosecutor, a sheriff principal who has made an order under subsection (2) above may, if the sheriff principal of the other sheriffdom mentioned in that subsection consents—

(a) revoke; or

(b) vary so as to restrict the effect of,

that order.

AMENDMENT

Section 137B inserted by Criminal Justice (Scotland) Act 2003 (asp 7), Part 8, s.58. Brought into force on June 27, 2003 by the Criminal Justice (Scotland) Act 2003 (Commencement No.1) Order 2003 (SSI 2003/288 (C.14)).

Complaints - Form g Summary Complaint

Complaints

138.—(1) All proceedings under this Part of this Act for the trial of offences or recovery of penalties shall be instituted by complaint signed by the prosecutor or by a solicitor on behalf of a prosecutor other than the procurator fiscal.

(2) The complaint shall be in the form—

(a) set out in Schedule 5 to this Act; or

(b) prescribed by Act of Adjournal,

or as nearly as may be in such form.

(3) A solicitor may appear for and conduct any prosecution on behalf of a prosecutor other than the procurator fiscal.

(4) Schedule 3 to this Act shall have effect as regards complaints under this Act.

DEFINITIONS

"complaint": s.307(1).
"judge": s.307(1).
"procurator fiscal": s.307(1).
"prosecutor": s.307(1).

GENERAL NOTE

The complaint will ordinarily proceed at the instance of the procurator fiscal having jurisdiction over a locus where it is alleged an offence was committed. Section 138 also permits other authorised prosecutors (for example the local education authority) to initiate proceedings by a complaint and to prosecute such cases. *P.926*

Form of Complaint The form of complaint should correspond to Form 16.1.-A in the 1996 Act of Adjournal, a style identical to the format used under the 1975 Act. The citation form now shown in Form 16.1.-B is similarly familiar. Examples of statutory charges are given in Sch.5 to the Act which in turn adopts the somewhat esoteric charges listed as indictment styles in Sch.2; Sch.5 may lack some of the colour of the earlier schedule but at least has the merit of being of some practical (if limited) use. More importantly, the provisions of Sch.3 in relation to implied terms and alternative verdicts, which were previously contained in s.312 of the 1975 Act are applied to all summary complaints. See for example *MacQueen v Hingston*, 1997 S.C.C.R. 561, a Skye Bridge case in which, on appeal, it was held that the Crown was not obliged to lead proof of the currency of an Order where no preliminary plea to relevancy had been taken. The subject of implied charges, and alternative verdicts, was fully discussed in *McMaster v HM Advocate*, 2001 S.C.C.R. 517. No *nomen juris* need be stipulated in a complaint (see *Lippe v Wilson*, 1997 G.W.D. 17–766 and A4–146 above).

The scope of the Crown's extensive powers of amendment were illustrated in *Robertson v Klos* [2005] HCJAC 136, dated December 1, 2005, a case notable not least for the video recorded speed of the vehicle driven on public roads—156 miles per hour—while its driver used a mobile phone. The sheriff had held during trial that no Notice of Intended Prosecution had been served timeously on the accused, as registered owner of the vehicle, the Crown being unable to rebut the claim. The Appeal Court held that the sheriff had erred in refusing a Crown motion to amend the charge to one at common law of culpable and reckless conduct on the facts proved, in place of the original charge of dangerous driving. (*Wimpey Homes Holdings Ltd v Lees*, 1993 S.L.T. 564; 1991 S.C.C.R. 447 discussed at A4–313 and A4–495, distinguished).

Amendment Note that the court has no power *ex proprio motu* to amend the libel and has to be moved to do so by the Crown, and consider defence submissions, before an amendment is permissible; see *Anderson v Griffiths*, 2005 S.L.T. 86; 2005 S.C.C.R. 41 discussed at A1–102.3 above.

Essential Elements of a Complaint

Signing The principal complaint has to be signed by the prosecutor but only the citation form to the accused need be signed (1996 Act of Adjournal, Rule 16.2.-(1)). Rule 16.2.-(2) suggests that signature of any part of the papers sent to an accused as a service copy complaint would be sufficient to render proceedings competent. Failure by the prosecutor to sign the principal complaint creates a nullity (*Lowe v Bee*, 1989 S.C.C.R. 476): loss of the principal complaint has till now been held to be fatal to proceedings and could not be remedied by seeking to substitute a certified copy (*McSeveney v Annan*, 1990 S.C.C.R. 573; *Wilson v Carmichael*, 1992 S.L.T. 54; 1991 S.C.C.R. 587; *Scott v MacKay*, 1983 S.C.C.R. 210). However, s.157 of the Act now permits the substitution of a certified copy of the complaint in the event of such loss.

A discrepancy between the libel in the principal complaint and the service copy is no more than a technical defect unless it can be shown that the variation has caused substantial prejudice (*Fletcher v Webster*, 1991 S.L.T. 256; 1991 S.C.C.R. 379 following *Dunsmore v Threshie* (1896) 2 Adam 202).

Rule 16.1. above directs that the copy complaint should include a reply form and a means form, which again are familiar in appearance; failure to include these two forms will not vitiate proceedings on that complaint (Rule 16.3.).

It will be noted that this section does not require a complaint to include notices of penalty; such notices were previously essential to any sentence upon conviction of a statutory offence on summary complaint. The complaint should include any previous convictions to be founded upon by the prosecutor in the event of a conviction of the accused; previous convictions are discussed in notes to s.166 below.

Although it is statutorily enacted that any proceedings must be initiated by the procurator fiscal or an authorised prosecutor, the cases of *Thomson v Scott; Walker v Emslie* (1899) 3 Adam 102 and *Hill v Finlayson* (1883) 5 Couper 284 support the view that the court itself has an inherent power to appoint a prosecutor *pro hac vice* to conduct those proceedings in the event of the death, illness or unavoidable absence of the prosecutor.

Complaints: orders and warrants

139.—(1) On any complaint under this Part of this Act being laid before a judge of the court in which the complaint is brought, he shall have power on the motion of the prosecutor—

    (a) to pronounce an order assigning a diet for the disposal of the case to which the accused may be cited as mentioned in section 141 of this Act;

    (b) to grant warrant to apprehend the accused where this appears to the judge expedient;

    (c) to grant warrant to search the person, dwelling-house and repositories of the accused and any place where he may be found for any documents, articles, or property likely to afford evidence of his guilt of, or guilty participation in, any offence charged in the complaint, and to take possession of such documents, articles or property;

    (d) to grant any other order or warrant of court or warrant which may be competent in the circumstances.

    (2) The power of a judge under subsection (1) above—

    (a) to pronounce an order assigning a diet for the disposal of the case may be exercised on his behalf by the clerk of court;

    (b) to grant a warrant to apprehend the accused shall be exercisable notwithstanding that there is power whether at common law or under any Act to apprehend him without a warrant.

DEFINITIONS

    "complaint": s.307(1).
    "judge": s.307(1).
    "prosecutor": s.307(1).

GENERAL NOTE

As subs.(2)(a) provides, cited diets are normally assigned administratively by the clerk of court, the judge initially needing only to be involved in considering the grant of an expediency or initiating warrant (subs.(1)(b)) or search warrants (subs.(1)(c)). It is the responsibility of the prosecutor to indicate to the clerk whether a specific date for the complaint to be called is needed; the complaint itself will show whether an assigned diet is craved and it then falls to the prosecutor to ensure that service is effected timeously (see notes to s.136 above).

When the prosecutor decides to begin proceedings by means of an initiating warrant the practice is for the complaint to be considered by the judge in chambers without hearing the prosecutor; it is unusual, but perfectly competent for the judge to require the prosecutor to specify the grounds which lie behind the application for a warrant. Commonly an initiating warrant will be necessary in order to obtain the accused's fingerprints or other samples in an admissible fashion or to place him before an identification parade.

As its name suggests, an expediency warrant is granted at the discretion of the court where a complaint is already current before the court and serves to keep the proceedings on it alive, provided that there are then reasonable grounds for believing that the complaint has been validly served: such a warrant cannot be used to validate a defect in the service of a complaint or as a means of overcoming a statutory timebar which would otherwise nullify the proceedings. In *Heywood v McLennan*, 1994 S.C.C.R. 1 where a complaint had been continued without plea, and later was established not to have been served, the depute moved to desert the case *pro loco et tempore* and sought an initiating warrant on that complaint. In such circumstances the proper course should have been to raise a fresh complaint craving an initiating warrant, the first complaint having fallen. See also *Lees v Malcolm*, 1992 S.C.C.R. 589.

The extent of the procurator fiscal's common law power to apply for a search warrant as part of his investigative role, before proceedings are initiated, was discussed in *MacNeill, Complainer*, 1983 S.C.C.R. 450.

Citation

Citation

140.—(1) This Act shall be a sufficient warrant for

(a) [...]

(b) the citation of the accused and witnesses in a summary prosecution to any ordinary sitting of the court or to any special diet fixed by the court or any adjournment thereof.

(2) Without prejudice to section 141(2A) of this Act, such citation shall be in the form prescribed by Act of Adjournal or as nearly as may be in such form and shall, in the case of the accused, proceed on an induciae of at least 48 hours unless in the special circumstances of the case the court fixes a shorter induciae.

(2A) Where the charge in the complaint in respect of which an accused is cited is of committing a sexual offence to which section 288C of this Act applies, the citation shall include or be accompanied by notice to the accused—

(a) that, if he is tried for the offence, his defence (including at any commissioner proceedings) and any proof ordered as is mentioned in section 288C(1) of this Act may be conducted only by a lawyer;

(b) that it is, therefore, in his interests, if he has not already done so, to get the professional assistance of a solicitor; and

(c) that, if he does not engage a solicitor for the purposes of his defence at the trial (or at any related commissioner proceedings), the court will do so.

(2B) A failure to comply with subsection (2A) above does not affect the validity or lawfulness of any such citation or any other element of the proceedings against the accused.

(2C) In subsection (2A) above, "commissioner proceedings" means proceedings before a commissioner appointed under section 271I(1) or by virtue of section 272(1)(b) of this Act,

(3) [...]

AMENDMENTS

Subss.(1) and (1)(a) inserted by the Crime and Punishment (Scotland) Act 1997 (c.48), s.57(2) with effect from August 1, 1997 in terms of the Crime and Punishment (Scotland) Act 1997 (Commencement and Transitional Provisions) Order 1997 (SI 1997/1712), art.3.

Subs.(3) deleted by s.57(2)(b) of the Act above in terms of the above Order.

Subss.(2A) and (2B) inserted by the Sexual Offences (Procedure and Evidence) (Scotland) Act 2002 (asp 9), Sch.1, para.8. Brought into force by the Sexual Offences (Procedure and Evidence) (Scotland) Act 2002 (Commencement and Transitional Provisions) Order 2002 (SSI 2002/443 (C.24)), art.4 (effective November 1, 2002).

Subs.(2) as amended by Criminal Justice (Scotland) Act 2003 (asp 7), Part 8, s.61. Brought into force on June 27, 2003 by the Criminal Justice (Scotland) Act 2003 (Commencement No.1) Order 2003 (SSI 2003/288 (C.14)).

Subs.(2A) as amended by Criminal Justice (Scotland) Act 2003 (asp 7), Sch.4, para.3. Brought into force on November 25, 2003 by the Criminal Justice (Scotland) Act 2003 (Commencement No.3 and Revocation) Order 2003 (SSI 2003/475 (C.26)), art.2.

Subs.(1)(a) repealed by the Criminal Procedure (Amendment) (Scotland) Act 2004 (asp 5), s.25, Sch.1, para.33. Brought into force on October 4, 2004 by the Criminal Procedure (Amendment) (Scotland) Act 2004 (Commencement, Transitional Provisions and Savings) Order 2004 (SSI 2004/405 (C.28)).

Section 140 amended and s.140(2C) inserted by the Criminal Proceedings etc. (Reform) (Scotland) Act 2007 (asp 6), s.35

Definitions

"diet": s.307(1).
"judge": s.307(1).
"prosecutor": s.307(1).

General Note

Chapter 16 of the 1996 Act of Adjournal provides that the citation of an accused shall be by Form 16.1-B while witnesses should be cited by post using Form 16.6-A and, personally, by Form 16.6-C. Omission of the date of the diet from the accused's citation creates a nullity (*Beattie v MacKinnon*, 1977 J.C. 64).

As with solemn witness citations, the Act of Adjournal envisages that any witness cited postally to attend, will acknowledge receipt of the citation by returning a pre-paid envelope with a further form (Form 16.6-B) within 14 days of citation. The objective of this reform, particularly now that intermediate diets are to be mandatory in summary cases (see s.148 below), is to enable parties to be in a position to advise the court confidently about their readiness for trial; however well-intended this provision may be, serious doubts must remain as to its practical worth. No citation of a witness or an accused is valid until the principal complaint has been signed (*Stewart v Lang* (1894) 1 Adam 493).

Subsection (2) prescribes an *induciae* in the case of service of a citation upon an accused of at least 48 hours. This period, in the case of postal citation, is reckoned from 24 hours after the time of posting (see s.141(6) below). The *induciae* can of course be waived by the accused or, exceptionally, be reduced by the court itself on cause shown, but must not be so shortened as to prejudice the accused in the conduct of his defence. No such time scale is applied to the citation of witnesses but Rule 16.6 in the Act of Adjournal plainly envisages a greater period of notice being given to witnesses.

As well as providing for the citation of accused and witnesses in summary prosecutions, subs.(1) as now amended provides a mechanism for the prosecutor to obtain a warrant to cite witnesses for precognition even before any proceedings are active before the court. See also s.67A of Act dealing with the failure of a witness to attend for precognition by the prosecutor. Both petition and summary warrants as a matter of course give power to the prosecutor to cite for precognition but subs.(1) enables the Crown to make preliminary investigations even before proceedings are initiated; it is usual to petition the court by way of an incidental application in circumstances where it is believed that witnesses will not attend for precognition voluntarily. This procedure is rarely used.

Manner of citation

141.—(1) The citation of the accused and witnesses in a summary prosecution to any ordinary sitting of the court or to any special diet fixed by the court or to any adjourned sitting or diet shall be effected by delivering the citation to him personally or leaving it for him at his dwelling-house or place of business with a resident or, as the case may be, employee at that place or, where he has no known dwelling-house or place of business, at any other place in which he may be resident at the time.

(2) Notwithstanding subsection (1) above, citation may also be effected—

(a) where the accused or witness is the master of, or a seaman or person employed in a vessel, if the citation is left with a person on board the vessel and connected with it;

(b) where the accused is a partnership, association or body corporate—

(i) if the citation is left at its ordinary place of business with a partner, director, secretary or other official; or

(ii) if it is cited in the same manner as if the proceedings were in a civil court; or

(c) where the accused is a body of trustees, if the citation is left with any one of them who is resident in Scotland or with their known solicitor in Scotland; and

in sub-paragraph (b)(i) of this subsection references to the director or secretary or other official, in relation to a limited liability partnership, are to any member of the limited liability partnership.

(2A) Notwithstanding subsection (1) above and section 140(2) of this Act, citation of the accused may also be effected by an officer of law affixing to the door of the accused's dwelling-house or place of business a notice in such form as may be prescribed by Act of Adjournal, or as nearly as may be in such form—

(a) specifying the date on which it was so affixed;

(b) informing the accused that he may collect a copy of the complaint from a police station specified in the notice; and

(c) calling upon him to appear and answer the complaint at such diet as shall be so specified.

(2B) Where the citation of the accused is effected by notice under subsection (2A) above, the induciae shall be reckoned from the date specified by virtue of paragraph (a) of that subsection.

(3) Subject to subsection (4) below and without prejudice to the effect of any other manner of citation, the citation of the accused or a witness to a sitting or diet or adjourned sitting or diet as mentioned in subsection (1) above shall be effective if it is—

(a) in the case of the accused signed by the prosecutor and sent by post in a registered envelope or through the recorded delivery service; and

(b) in the case of a witness, sent by or on behalf of the prosecutor by ordinary post,

to the dwelling-house or place of business of the accused or witness or, if he has no known dwelling-house or place of business, to any other place in which he may be resident at the time.

(4) Where the accused fails to appear at a diet or sitting or adjourned diet or sitting to which he has been cited in the manner provided by this section, subsections (3) and (5) to (7) of section 150 of this Act shall not apply unless it is proved to the court that he received the citation or that its contents came to his knowledge.

(5) The production in court of any letter or other communication purporting to be written by or on behalf of an accused who has been cited as mentioned in subsection (2A) or (3) above in such terms as to infer that the contents of such citation came to his knowledge, shall be admissible as evidence of that fact for the purposes of subsection (4) above.

(5A) The citation of a witness to a sitting or diet or adjourned sitting or diet as mentioned in subsection (1) above shall be effective if it is sent by the accused's solicitor by ordinary post to the dwelling house or place of business of the witness or if he has no known dwelling house or place of business, to any other place in which he may be resident at the time.

(6) When the citation of any person is effected by post in terms of this section or any other provision of this Act to which this section is applied, the induciae shall be reckoned from 24 hours after the time of posting.

(7) It shall be sufficient evidence that—

(a) a citation has been sent by post in terms of this section or any other provision of this Act mentioned in subsection (6) above, if there is produced in court a written execution, signed by the person who signed the citation in the form prescribed by Act of Adjournal, or as nearly as may be in such form, together with the post office receipt for the relative registered or recorded delivery letter; or

(b) citation has been effected by notice under subsection (2A) above, if there is produced in court a written execution, in such form as may be prescribed by Act of Adjournal, or as nearly as may be in such form, signed by the officer of law who affixed the notice.

AMENDMENTS

Subs.(3) as amended by the Crime and Punishment (Scotland) Act 1997 (c.48), s.62(1) and Sch.1, para.21(19)(a) with effect from August 1, 1997 in terms of the Crime and Punishment (Scotland) Act 1997 (Commencement and Transitional Provisions) Order 1997 (SI 1997/1712), art.3.

Subss.(3)(a), (b) as amended, and (5A) inserted, by the 1997 Act s.62 and Sch.1, para.21(19) with effect from August 1, 1997 in terms of the above Order.

Subs.(2) as amended by the Limited Liability Partnerships (Scotland) Regulations 2001 (SSI 2001/128), reg.5 and Sch.4.

Subs.(2A) and (2B) inserted, and subss.(3), (5) and (7) as amended, by Criminal Justice (Scotland) Act 2003 (asp 7), Part 8, s.61. Brought into force on June 27, 2003 by the Criminal Justice (Scotland) Act 2003 (Commencement No.1) Order 2003 (SSI 2003/288 (C.14)).

DEFINITIONS

"diet": s.307(1).
"prosecutor": s.307(1).

GENERAL NOTE

This section deals with the methods of citation of both accused and any witnesses to court in criminal proceedings. Minor changes introduced by the 1997 Act have brought a measure of clarity, and economy, to this procedure; subs.(3) relates to citations to be served by the Crown, while subs.(5A) makes distinct provisions for citation of defence witnesses and makes postal service an acceptable form of citation. The section does not preclude personal service by either police or sheriff officers, but indicates that postal service should normally be sufficient. Section 61 of the Criminal Justice (Scotland) Act 2003 (asp 7) now also entitles the prosecution to intimate proceedings to an accused by means of a notice calling upon him to call at a specified police office to collect his complaint. A dated notice is intended to have the same effect, for the commencement of proceedings, as service of the complaint itself. See too the general discussion at s.66 above but note that in summary proceedings a defect in service can be cured by the appearance of the accused.

The date of postal citation is the date of posting, not receipt, of a citation (*Lockhart v Bradley*, 1977 S.L.T. 5) and no warrant for citation exists until the principal citation has been signed (see the discussion "Essential Elements of a Complaint" at A4–298 and *Stewart v Lang* (1894) 1 A. 493). *Failure*

Section 150 entitles the court to grant a warrant to arrest an accused following failure to appear at a diet to which he has been cited or notified to appear. The prosecutor must satisfy the court that service has been validly effected in accordance with this section and may found upon the recorded delivery execution of service of the complaint or any letter sent by, or on behalf of the accused which indicates the accused's awareness of the diet (see *Aitchison v Wringe*, 1985 S.L.T. 449; 1985 S.C.C.R. 134; *Orr v Lowdon*, 1987 S.C.C.R. 515 while in *Normand v Harkins*, 1996 S.C.C.R. 355 service was upheld where the complaint was left in the hands of a person bearing to be a flatmate of the accused and accepted service, the process server having acted in good faith. Compare *Normand v Buchanan*, 1996 S.C.C.R. 363 where service was not effected at the accused's address, the complaint being left elsewhere in the hands of relatives (also accused) to pass to the accused, which they duly did; in that case the prosecutor failed to prove valid service of a complaint and penalty notices). In certain statutory enactments it may be competent to proceed to trial in the absence of the accused (s.150(5)) but again this is contingent upon the court being satisfied that the accused knew of the diet.

In the case of limited companies, partnerships or other bodies, citation can be effected at the home of a responsible officer of that entity at his home address as well as at the place of business (*Kirkcudbright Scallop Gear Ltd v Walkingshaw*, 1994 S.C.C.R. 372).

Kelly v Rae, 1917 J.C. 12 is still authority for the view that neither the accused apprehended *in flagrante delicto* nor his agentneed receive a copy complaint at least when the accused has been brought before the first available custody court; the case is mentioned tentatively since no previous convictions could be put before the court, and. it has to be said, that any conviction would be liable to be quashed if it was shown that the defence had suffered substantial prejudice as a result of this omission.

Children

Summary proceedings against children

142.—(1) Where summary proceedings are brought in respect of an offence alleged to have been committed by a child, the sheriff shall sit either in a different building or room from that in which he usually sits or on different days from those on which other courts in the building are engaged in criminal proceedings: and no person shall be present at any sitting for the purposes of such proceedings except—

(a) members and officers of the court;

(b) parties to the case before the court, their solicitors and counsel, and witnesses and other persons directly concerned in that case;

(c) *bona fide* representatives of news gathering or reporting organisations present for the purpose of the preparation of contemporaneous reports of the proceedings;

(d) such other persons as the court may specially authorise to be present.

(2) A sheriff sitting summarily for the purpose of hearing a charge against, or an application relating to, a person who is believed to be a child may, if he thinks fit to do so, proceed with the hearing and determination of the charge or application, notwithstanding that it is discovered that the person in question is not a child.

(3) When a sheriff sitting summarily has remanded a child for information to be obtained with respect to him, any sheriff sitting summarily in the same place—

(a) may in his absence extend the period for which he is remanded provided that he appears before a sheriff or a justice at least once every 21 days;

(b) when the required information has been obtained, may deal with him finally,

and where the sheriff by whom he was originally remanded has recorded a finding that he is guilty of an offence charged against him it shall not be necessary for any court which subsequently deals with him under this subsection to hear evidence as to the commission of that offence, except in so far as it may consider that such evidence will assist the court in determining the manner in which he should be dealt with.

(4) Any direction in any enactment that a charge shall be brought before a juvenile court shall be construed as a direction that he shall be brought before the sheriff sitting as a court of summary jurisdiction, and no such direction shall be construed as restricting the powers of any justice or justices to entertain an application for bail or for a remand, and to hear such evidence as may be necessary for that purpose.

(5) This section does not apply to summary proceedings before the sheriff in respect of an offence where a child has been charged jointly with a person who is not a child.

Definitions

"justice": s.307(1).
"offence": s.307(1).
"sheriff": s.5(1).

GENERAL NOTE

Section 42 stipulates that where criminal offences alleged to have been committed by children are prosecuted by the criminal courts, rather than being referred to the Principal Reporter, such offences must be prosecuted in the sheriff court or a higher court (see generally the discussion in the notes to s.42 above). This stipulation does not extend to cases in which a co-accused is over 16 years old; in that event the proceedings can be taken in any court if it is felt that referring the child to the children's panel is inappropriate and proceedings must be taken against both parties.

The district court will not have jurisdiction over complaints against juvenile offenders but subs.(4) provides that this is without prejudice to any right of a justice (as defined in s.307(1) this includes sheriffs, stipendiary magistrates and justices of the peace) to determine applications for bail or remand.

The object of subs.(1) is to ensure that the juvenile criminal proceedings brought against children are conducted in court facilities distinct from those used in the course of summary proceedings against young persons and adults. This is intended to prevent the child coming into contact with older offenders and means that a separate juvenile court should convene to hear any custody, diet or trial business whose accused are solely children. The provision is directory in character and non-observance of it is not fatal to a finding of guilt (*Heywood v B*, 1994 S.C.C.R. 554).

Chapter 6 of the 1996 Act of Adjournal also provides that efforts be made to prevent the mixing of children attending any juvenile court hearing.

In addition to requiring separate courts for juvenile hearings, s.142 enacts that those proceedings will not be held in open court; access is restricted to the parties specified by subs.(1)(a) to (c) and is otherwise at the discretion of the court.

Subsection (2) preserves the validity of any finding made by a court which has proceeded on the mistaken belief that the accused, or one of the accused, is a child.

Subsection (3) provides for an administrative continuation of a juvenile's case by another sheriff in the absence of the sheriff who made the original remand for information and, in situations where the latter sheriff is unavailable at the time of receipt of that information, his colleague may dispose of the case. A period of remand of a juvenile can exceed 21 days provided that the child is brought before a justice at least once every 21 days.

Companies

Prosecution of companies, etc.

143.—(1) Without prejudice to any other or wider powers conferred by statute, this section shall apply in relation to the prosecution by summary procedure of a partnership, association, body corporate or body of trustees.

(2) Proceedings may be taken against the partnership, association body corporate or body of trustees in their corporate capacity, and in that event any penalty imposed shall be recovered by civil diligence in accordance with section 221 of this Act.

(3) Proceedings may be taken against an individual representative of a partnership, association or body corporate as follows:—

(a) in the case of a partnership or firm, any one of the partners, or the manager or the person in charge or locally in charge of its affairs;

(b) in the case of an association or body corporate, the managing director or the secretary or other person in charge, or locally in charge, of its affairs,

may be dealt with as if he was the person offending, and the offence shall be deemed to be the offence of the partnership, association or body corporate; and in paragraph 3(b) of this subsection references to the managing director or the secretary, in relation to a limited liability partnership, are to any member of the limited liability partnership.

AMENDMENT

Subs.(3) as amended by the Limited Liability Partnerships (Scotland) Regulations 2001 (SSI 2001/128), reg.5 and Sch.4.

DEFINITION

"offence": s.307(1).

GENERAL NOTE

The leading discussion of the extent of culpability of a limited company, as distinct from its officers, managers or employees, is found in *Transco Plc v HM Advocate*, 2004 S.L.T. 41.

See generally the notes to s.70 above.

An unincorporated company may be charged in the name of the company or the partners' names or both (*City and Suburban Dairies v Mackenna*, 1918 J.C. 105). The same approach can be followed against partnerships.

Proceedings against a registered club can be taken against its office bearers (*Burnette v Mackenna*, 1917 J.C. 20).

It is competent to proceed against directors of a limited company or against a manager or employee locally responsible for its affairs (*Bean v Sinclair*, 1930 J.C. 31) but previous convictions libelled against the company cannot be used against that individual (*Campbell v MacPherson* (1910) 6 Adam 394). A manager can competently represent the company at any diet (*McAlpine v Ronaldson* (1901) 3 Adam 405). Only convictions libelled against the accused company can be founded upon by the Crown, but where such convictions exist and have not been libelled against the company, it is not open to the defence to make claims at odds with the terms of those convictions; *Massily Packaging (U.K.) Ltd v MacDonald*, 1997 G.W.D. 3–87.

Amendment of the complaint where the company is incorrectly named is problematical; see *Hoyers (U.K.) v Houston*, 1991 S.L.T. 934; 1991 S.C.C.R. 919 where the description of the accused was amended at the trial diet, by which time a new complaint would have been timebarred. In *Ralston v Carmichael*, 1995 G.W.D. 38–1933 a complaint against "Henry Ralston Ltd" was amended to "Henry Ralston" when it was discovered that the limited company did not exist; an appearance and correspondence had already passed before the amendment was sought and it could not be contended that prejudice was caused by the amendment. The issues are whether the error in the name or designation is trivial and if an appearance is made in answer to the complaint (*Poli v Thomson* (1910) 5 Adam 261); in that event amendment is competent.

For service of citations against bodies corporate, see s.141 above.

First diet

Procedure at first diet

144.—(1) Where the accused is present at the first calling of the case in a summary prosecution and—

(a) the complaint has been served on him, or

(b) the complaint or the substance thereof has been read to him, or

(c) he has legal assistance in his defence,

he shall, unless the court adjourns the case under the section 145 of this Act and subject to subsection (4) below, be asked to plead to the charge.

(2) Where the accused is not present at a calling of the case in a summary prosecution and either—

(a) the prosecutor produces to the court written intimation that the accused pleads not guilty or pleads guilty and the court is satisfied that the intimation has been made or authorised by the accused; or

(b) counsel or a solicitor, or a person not being counsel or a solicitor who satisfies the court that he is authorised by the accused, appears on behalf of the accused and tenders a plea of not guilty or a plea of guilty,

subsection (3) below shall apply.

(3) Where this subsection applies—

(a) in the case of a plea of not guilty, this Part of this Act except section 146(2) shall apply in like manner as if the accused had appeared and tendered the plea; and

(b) in the case of a plea of guilty, the court may, if the prosecutor accepts the plea, proceed to hear and dispose of the case in the absence of the accused in like manner as if he had appeared and pled guilty, or may, if it thinks fit, continue the case to another diet and require the attendance of the accused with a view to pronouncing sentence in his presence.

(3A) Where an accused charged with a sexual offence to which section 288C of this Act applies is present, whether or not with a solicitor, at a calling of the case in a summary prosecution, he shall be told—

(a) that if he is tried for the offence, his defence and any proof ordered as is mentioned in section 288C(1) of this Act at his trial may be conducted only by a lawyer;

(b) that it is, therefore, in his interests, if he has not already done so, to get the professional assistance of a solicitor; and

(c) that if he does not engage a solicitor for the purposes of his defence at the trial, the court will do so.

(3B) A failure to comply with subsection (3A) above does not affect the validity or lawfulness of anything done at the calling of the case or any other element of the proceedings against the accused.

(4) Any objection to the competency or relevancy of a summary complaint or the proceedings thereon, or any denial that the accused is the person charged by the police with the offence shall be stated before the accused pleads to the charge or any plea is tendered on his behalf.

(5) No objection or denial such as is mentioned in subsection (4) above shall be allowed to be stated or issued at any future diet in the case except with the leave of the court, which may be granted only on cause shown.

(6) Where in pursuance of subsection (3)(b) above the court proceeds to hear and dispose of a case in the absence of the accused, it shall not pronounce a sentence of imprisonment or of detention in a young offenders institution, remand centre or other establishment.

(7) In this section a reference to a plea of guilty shall include a reference to a plea of guilty to only part of the charge, but where a plea of guilty to only part of a charge is not accepted by the prosecutor it shall be deemed to be a plea of not guilty.

(8) It shall not be competent for any person appearing to answer a complaint, or for counsel or a solicitor appearing for the accused in his absence, to plead want of due citation or informality therein or in the execution thereof.

(9) In this section, a reference to the first calling of a case includes a reference to any adjourned diet fixed by virtue of section 145 or 145A of this Act.

AMENDMENT

Subss.(3A) and (3B) inserted by the Sexual Offences (Procedure and Evidence) (Scotland) Act 2002 (asp 9), Sch.1, para.9. Brought into force by the Sexual Offences (Procedure and Evidence) (Scotland) Act 2002 (Commencement and Transitional Provisions) Order 2002 (SSI 2002/443 (C.24)), art.4 (effective November 1, 2002).

Subs.(9) as amended by Criminal Justice (Scotland) Act 2003 (asp 7), Part 8, s.63. Brought into force on June 27, 2003 by the Criminal Justice (Scotland) Act 2003 (Commencement No.1) Order 2003 (SSI 2003/288 (C.14)).

Subs.(3A) as amended by Criminal Justice (Scotland) Act 2003 (asp 7), Sch.4, para.3. Brought into force on November 25, 2003 by the Criminal Justice (Scotland) Act 2003 (Commencement No.3 and Revocation) Order 2003 (SSI 2003/475 (C.26)), art.2.

DEFINITIONS

"complaint": s.307(1).
"diet": s.307(1).
"imprisonment": s.308.
"prosecutor": s.307(1).
"sentence": s.307(1).
"young offenders institution": s.307(1).

Appearance at a first diet cures any deficiency in citation (subs.(8)); the accused can make an appearance in person, by way of attendance at court by a solicitor or other authorised representative or by letter. Want of form, which is curable by appearance, should not be confused with a nullity; an unsigned complaint (*Lowe v Bee*, 1989 S.C.C.R. 476; *McLeod v Millar*, 2004 S.C.C.R. 419), a complaint which failed to specify a date or locus or in which the court had no jurisdiction (*McMillan v Grant*, 1924 J.C. 13; *Duffy v Ingram*, 1987 S.C.C.R. 286) or a missing principal complaint (*McSeveney v Annan*, 1990 S.C.C.R. 573) are all fundamental procedural defects which cannot be remedied. Note in the last instance, the terms of s.157 which appear to permit the use of a certified copy complaint to preserve proceedings. See too *Gates v Donnelly*, 2004 S.L.T. 13 where the accused appeared at the pleading diet to voice objection to an unsigned citation; held appearance had cured any want of citation.

While the law does not go so far as to hold that any want or defect in citation is cured by the appearance of the accused or his law agent, when it is asserted that a complaint has not been proceeded with or served timeously (see s.136 above) there is some onus upon him to establish the facts giving rise to the preliminary plea (*Shaw v Dyer*, 2002 S.L.T. 826).

Before any plea is tendered any plea in bar, plea to the competency or relevancy (including any allegation of undue delay in executing any warrant to apprehend or cite), notice that the accused disputes having been cautioned and charged with the offences libelled should be stated (subs.(4)), as should any objection to the libelling of a special capacity (s.255).

Failure to sign the citation of an accused, unlike a failure to sign the principal complaint, does not create a nullity. In *Gates v Donnelly*, 2004 S.L.T. 13 the Appeal Court approved the reasoning of the sheriff in holding that the purpose of the complaint is to inform the accused of the allegations he faces, and that such a defect—an unsigned citation, would be of little moment unless particular prejudice could be shown to have been suffered by the accused.

Mental Disorder

Section 52 expressly, and s.145 impliedly, require both the prosecutor and the court to ensure that the accused is not suffering any mental disorder and the diet should be adjourned without plea for the purpose of investigation (in the former section the prosecutor should place medical evidence before the court; in the latter the court itself may adjourn without plea, to enable the prosecutor to obtain a medical report). Until the issue is resolved, any continuation is to be treated as a first diet (subs.(9)). See generally the notes at A4–122 above, *Sloan v Crowe*, 1996 S.C.C.R. 200 and *MacDonald v Munro*, 1996 S.C.C.R. 595 for discussion of the Crown's obligations under this section.

Pleas to Competency and Relevancy and Special Capacity

Subsection (5) stipulates that any such pleas must normally be stated at the first diet, though subs.(9) has the effect of permitting a continuation without plea under s.145, to permit proper formulation of any such objections. After the first diet, any objection can only be heard on cause shown; in *H.M. Advocate v Bell* (1892) 3 White 313, the court at a second diet was held to be entitled to consider such objections not previously stated where otherwise a gross injustice would result. See also *McLeay v Hingston*, 1994 S.L.T. 720; 1994 S.C.C.R. 116 where objection to a complaint devoid of a locus was stated only part way through a trial, the Appeal Court noting that the case could have been adjourned pending resolution of an appeal, the sheriff having repelled objections and granted leave to appeal. The introduction of mandatory intermediate diets in all summary cases (see s.148 below) may serve to limit the late introduction of any such motion.

The Appeal Court has indicated that it is primarily a matter for the discretion of the trial judge whether or not to entertain late pleas to competency, relevancy or capacity (which of course necessarily involve the withdrawal of any pleas previously tendered in regard to the charges) and that that discretion will only be reviewed in light of fundamental objections (*Henderson v Ingram*, 1982 S.C.C.R. 135). See also *Scott v Annan*, 1981 S.C.C.R. 172; 1982 S.L.T. 90; *Wimpey Homes Holdings v Lees*, 1993 S.L.T. 564.

The principal ground for consideration of a plea to relevancy of a complaint is whether the libel is sufficiently specific to give the defence fair notice of the offences (*Clydesdale Group v Normand*, 1994 S.L.T. 1302).

If a preliminary plea is wholly sustained, then the complaint falls. In the event that the complaint is upheld in whole or part, ordinarily the accused should then be called upon to plead to the charges (a continuation without plea, for example to obtain further instructions, would be competent in terms of s.145). It is important to note that even if the defence move for, or are granted, leave to appeal against the decision relating to the preliminary plea (by way of s.174 below), a plea of guilty or not guilty should be tendered and recorded and a trial diet assigned as necessary (see *Lafferty v Jessop*, 1989

S.L.T. 846; 1989 S.C.C.R. 451 and *Jessop v First National Securities*, 1988 S.C.C.R. 1). Note that in the latter case having decided the issue of relevancy, the sheriff, no doubt conscious that his decision was likely to be appealed, canvassed the views of parties and decided to issue a written note of his judgment. Procedurally the proper course would have been to give no decision and continue the case to a later diet for the judgment or, alternatively, give his decision and defer any written comment for his Report, should an appeal be taken against the judgment and the call upon the accused to plead.

Although the court may continue a case for the personal appearance of the accused for sentence (subs.(3)(b)), it does not follow that sentence is contingent upon such an appearance (see *Taylor v Lees*, 1993 S.C.C.R. 947). The only stricture upon sentence in absence is stated in subs.(6); a sentence of imprisonment or detention can only be imposed when an accused is personally present.

The prosecutor is never obliged to accept a plea of guilty either to the whole or part of a complaint: (*Kirkwood v Coalburn District Cooperative Society*, 1930 J.C. 38). However where a plea of guilt is tendered, it has been held that appeal by way of bill of suspension will rarely be appropriate; see *Aitken v Reith*, 1996 G.W.D. 2–79 where following a letter plea of guilty and a personal appearance for sentence, the accused subsequently claimed to have been unaware that he had been charged with dangerous, rather than careless, driving and had been too timid to withdraw his plea at the deferred diet.

The court would require to be satisfied that the accused had substantially misunderstood his position and been prejudiced, or had been unreasonably pressured by his solicitor into pleading and had been prejudiced as a result (see *McGuire v Normand*, 1997 G.W.D. 3–86; *Simpson v McKay*, 1997 G.W.D. 14–588 where the Crown's narration went unchallenged; *Kerr v Friel*, 1997 S.C.C.R. 317 a "plea of convenience" case; and *Bieniwoski v Ruxton*, 1997 G.W.D. 23–1143 a plea to dangerous driving by speeding, allegedly tendered in ignorance of the penalties, the conviction was not suspended, the Appeal Court noting the service of a penalty notice on the accused).

Crombie v Clark, 2001 S.L.T. 635 is something of a curiosity, being referred to the Appeal Court by the Scottish Criminal Cases Review Commission (see s.194C below) as a possible miscarriage of justice without any further investigation of the factual background. C's objection had been to the *quantum* in his guilty plea to evasion of betting and gaming duties, rather than to a plea tendered in error; indeed he had failed to consult further with a solicitor despite an adjournment being granted by the sheriff for that express purpose. For its part the court examined the whole history of the case and was not content that the conviction or sentence would have been materially different if C's contentions had been aired at the time.

Where the accused is present in court, the terms of his plea should be confirmed directly from him, even if he is represented; failure to follow the procedure set out in the Act of Adjournal (Criminal Procedure Rules) 1996, r.18.1(1) creates a nullity (*McGowan v Ritchie*, 1997 S.C.C.R. 332 where authority for fresh proceedings on the original charges libelled was granted).

In *Ettinger v McFadyen*, 2000 G.W.D. 22–851 the Appeal Court held it to be a breach of natural justice for the sheriff, having found an unexplained period of delay on the part of the Crown in initiating proceedings, to permit an adjournment for the Crown to produce further evidence after parties had concluded submissions. See also *McAnea v H.M. Advocate*, 2001 S.L.T. 12; 2000 S.C.C.R. 779 where the trial judge, having ruled upon defence objections to a line of evidence, was held to have wrongly permitted further Crown submissions on the point thereafter.

Adjournment for inquiry at first calling   *— Where Accused Present*

145.—(1) Where the accused is present at the first calling of a case in a summary prosecution the court may, in order to allow time for inquiry into the case or for any other cause which it considers reasonable, adjourn the case under this section, for such period as it considers appropriate, without calling on the accused to plead to any charge against him but remanding him in custody or on bail or ordaining him to appear at the diet thus fixed; and, subject to subsections (2) and (3) below, the court may from time to time so adjourn the case.

(2) Where the accused is remanded in custody, the total period for which he is so remanded under this section shall not exceed 21 days and no one period of adjournment shall, except on special cause shown, exceed 7 days.

(3) Where the accused is remanded on bail or ordained to appear, no one period of adjournment shall exceed 28 days.

AMENDMENT

Subs.(1) as amended by Criminal Justice (Scotland) Act 2003 (asp 7), Part 8, s.63. Brought into

force on June 27, 2003 by the Criminal Justice (Scotland) Act 2003 (Commencement No.1) Order 2003 (SSI 2003/288 (C.14)).

DEFINITIONS

"bail": s.307(1).
"diet": s.307(1).
"remand": s.307(1).

GENERAL NOTE

The court's power to continue a case without plea on the motion of a party or *ex proprio motu* is preserved. However where an accused is remanded in custody in relation to the complaint before the court, no continuation should exceed seven days save on cause shown, and the total period of continuations cannot exceed 21 days (subs.(2)). It will be remembered that the period involved in any such continuation has to be included in the calculation of time spent in custody awaiting summary trial since the bringing of the complaint (see s.147 below).

The maximum period of adjournment allowed at any one time in cases where the accused is bailed or ordained to appear is 28 days (subs.(3)). A continuation without plea for debate would appear not to be subject to the time limit imposed by subs.(3) following the *ratio* in *Pearson v Crowe*, 1994 S.L.T. 378, but is obviously affected by the strictures imposed in custody cases by subs.(2).

Adjournment at first calling to allow accused to appear etc.

145A.—(1) Without prejudice to section 150(1) to (7) of this Act, where the accused is not present at the first calling of the case in a summary prosecution, the court may (whether or not the prosecutor is able to provide evidence that the accused has been duly cited) adjourn the case under this section for such period as it considers appropriate; and subject to subsections (2) and (3) below, the court may from time to time so adjourn the case.

(2) An adjournment under this section shall be—

(a) for the purposes of allowing—

(i) the accused to appear in answer to the complaint; or

(ii) time for inquiry into the case; or

(b) for any other cause the court considers reasonable.

(3) No one period of adjournment under this section shall exceed 28 days.

AMENDMENT

Section 145A inserted by Criminal Justice (Scotland) Act 2003 (asp 7), Part 8, s.63. Brought into force on June 27, 2003 by the Criminal Justice (Scotland) Act 2003 (Commencement No.1) Order 2003 (SSI 2003/288 (C.14)).

DEFINITIONS

"prosecutor": s.307(1) of the 1995 Act.

GENERAL NOTE

Section 145A of the 1995 Act permits the court to adjourn a case at the first calling where the accused is not present and irrespective of whether the procurator fiscal is able to provide evidence that the accused has been cited to court. This is subject to the restrictions in subss.(2) and (3).

Subs.(2) specifies that the court may permit the adjournment where the purpose is to allow the accused the opportunity of answering the complaint or for further time for enquiry into the case or for any other reasonable cause. Subs.(3) restricts any single adjournment granted under this subsection to a period of 28 days irrespective of whether the accused is in custody.

The practical effect of s.145A is to permit the court to continue the case in the absence of the accused or where the prosecutor is unable to provide evidence to the court that the accused has been cited to appear at the diet. In addition s.145A permits adjournments of up to 28 days in order to allow the accused to answer the complaint, for further inquiry or for any other reasonable cause.

Plea of not guilty

146.—(1) This section applies where the accused in a summary prosecution—

(a) pleads not guilty to the charge; or

(b) pleads guilty to only part of the charge and the prosecutor does not accept the partial plea.

(2) The court may proceed to trial at once unless either party moves for an adjournment and the court considers it expedient to grant it.

(3) The court may adjourn the case for trial to as early a diet as is consistent with the just interest of both parties, and the prosecutor shall, if requested by the accused, furnish him with a copy of the complaint if he does not already have one.

(3A) Where, under subsection (3) above, the prosecutor furnishes an accused charged with a sexual offence to which section 288C of this Act applies with a copy of the complaint, it shall be accompanied by a notice to the accused—

(a) that, if he is tried for the offence, his defence and any proof ordered as is mentioned in section 288C(1) of this Act at his trial may be conducted only by a lawyer;

(b) that it is, therefore, in his interests, if he has not already done so, to get the professional assistance of a solicitor; and

(c) that, if he does not engage a solicitor for the purposes of his defence at the trial, the court will do so.

(3B) A failure to comply with subsection (3A) above does not affect the validity or lawfulness of any such copy complaint or any other element of the proceedings against the accused.

(4) Where the accused is brought before the court from custody the court shall inform the accused of his right to an adjournment of the case for not less than 48 hours and if he requests such adjournment before the prosecutor has commenced his proof, subject to subsection (5) below, the adjournment shall be granted.

(5) Where the court considers that it is necessary to secure the examination of witnesses who otherwise would not be available, the case may proceed to trial at once or on a shorter adjournment than 48 hours.

(6) Where the accused is in custody, he may be committed to prison or to legalised police cells or to any other place to which he may lawfully be committed pending trial—

(a) if he is neither granted bail nor ordained to appear; or

(b) if he is granted bail on a condition imposed under section 24(6) of this Act that a sum of money is deposited in court, until the accused or a cautioner on his behalf has so deposited that sum.

(7) The court may from time to time at any stage of the case on the motion of either party or *ex proprio motu* grant such adjournment as may be necessary for the proper conduct of the case, and where from any cause a diet has to be continued from day to day it shall not be necessary to intimate the continuation to the accused.

(8) It shall not be necessary for the prosecutor to establish a charge or part of a charge to which the accused pleads guilty.

(9) The court may, in any case where it considers it expedient, permit any witness for the defence to be examined prior to evidence for the prosecution having been led or concluded, but in any such case the accused shall be entitled to lead additional evidence after the case for the prosecution is closed.

AMENDMENT

Subss.(3A) and (3B) inserted by the Sexual Offences (Procedure and Evidence) (Scotland) Act

2002 (asp 9), Sch.1, para.10. Brought into force by the Sexual Offences (Procedure and Evidence) (Scotland) Act 2002 (Commencement and Transitional Provisions) Order 2002 (SSI 2002/443 (C.24)), art.4 (effective November 1, 2002).

Subs.(3A) as amended by Criminal Justice (Scotland) Act 2003 (asp 7), Sch.4, para.3. Brought into force on November 25, 2003 by the Criminal Justice (Scotland) Act 2003 (Commencement No.3 and Revocation) Order 2003 (SSI 2003/475 (C.26)), art.2.

DEFINITIONS

"bail": s.307(1).
"diet": s.307(1).
"legalised police cells": s.307(1).
"prison": s.307(1).
"prosecutor": s.307(1).

GENERAL NOTE

Provided that any preliminary pleas have been repelled, the accused should then be called upon to plead to the charges still current on the complaint. The prosecutor may, but is not obliged to, accept any partial pleas tendered. Subject to the exceptional provisions of subs.(5), in custody cases the accused is entitled to an *induciae* of 48 hours before his trial occurs, an *induciae* which he may waive, but his right to which the court must make known to him; failure to do so will almost certainly vitiate any conviction (see *Ferguson v Brown*, 1942 J.C. 113). The refusal of an adjournment which is needed, in order to enable the accused to lead evidence in support of his alibi defence once trial has begun, may constitute oppression: *McKellar v Dickson* (1898) 2 Adam 504.

In accordance with subs.(2), the court can proceed to trial immediately unless any of the parties moves for an adjournment. In practice, such a peremptory diet of trial is rare though subs.(5) allows for such a trial then or within 48 hours, where this is essential to secure witnesses' evidence even in custody cases. It is perfectly competent to adjourn the trial once such evidence has been heard or at any point in any summary trial (subs.(7)).

Subsection (6) permits a remand in custody in cases where bail is either not granted or not sought, or more unusually, where a sum of money bail is required to be deposited with the court as an additional bail condition in terms of s.24(6).

Subsection (7) allows for adjournments. An adjournment occurs when a case calls at a settled diet, being a date fixed earlier, and then is put back: see *Mitchell v Reith*, 2004 S.C.C.R. 433 at 435 (para.6). This is contrasted with a postponement that occurs when the date of the diet is altered in advance of the date set originally: *ibid*.

Guidance on the courses which the court may follow where there is disagreement between the parties in the factual narration is given in *McCartney v H.M. Advocate*, 1997 S.C.C.R. 644.

Subsection (9) echoes the little-used terms of s.337(h) of the 1975 Act and permits the calling of defence evidence prior to, or during, Crown evidence. It is suggested that this provision envisages the leading of defence evidence, a preferable alternative to the Crown, as an expedient means of assisting the defence—calling defence witnesses during the Crown case formally, then leaving the defence to lead the witness' evidence in cross-examination.

Pre-trial procedure

Prevention of delay in trials

147.—(1) Subject to subsections (2) and (3) below, a person charged with an offence in summary proceedings shall not be detained in that respect for a total of more than 40 days after the bringing of the complaint in court unless his trial is commenced within that period, failing which he shall be liberated forthwith and thereafter he shall be for ever free from all question or process for that offence.

(2) The sheriff may, on application made to him for the purpose, extend the period mentioned in subsection (1) above and order the accused to be detained awaiting trial for such period as he thinks fit where he is satisfied that delay in the commencement of the trial is due to—

(a) the illness of the accused or of a judge;
(b) the absence or illness of any necessary witness; or

(c) any other sufficient cause which is not attributable to any fault on the part of the prosecutor.

(3) The grant or refusal of any application to extend the period mentioned in subsection (1) above may be appealed against by note of appeal presented to the High Court; and that Court may affirm, reverse or amend the determination made on such application.

(4) For the purposes of this section, a trial shall be taken to commence when the first witness is sworn.

DEFINITIONS

"complaint": s.307(1).
"High Court": s.307(1).
"judge": s.307(1).
"offence": s.307(1).
"prosecutor": s.307(1).
"sheriff": s.5(1).
"witness": s.307(1).

GENERAL NOTE

This section preserves the provisions introduced into the 1975 Act by s.14(2) of the Criminal Justice (Scotland) Act 1980 to limit the period of remand affecting persons awaiting summary trial. A person remanded in custody in terms of s.146(6) may only be held in custody pending trial for 40 days in relation to that complaint.

Note that the period only begins from "the bringing of the complaint" so a period on remand following an appearance on petition would not, it is submitted, be included in calculation of the 40 days, notwithstanding the recent decision in *Gardner v. Lees*, 1996 S.C.C.R. 186 (itself since superseded by the terms of s.65(1) as now amended) which dealt with a non-custodial reduction of petition proceedings to summary proceedings.

Similarly, the period spent in custody must be attributable wholly to matters awaiting trial; a person serving a sentence, or a person remanded for trial but who then becomes a serving prisoner thus effectively interrupting the remand period, cannot benefit from the protection of the provisions against delay in trial. However in *Lockhart v. Robb*, 1988 S.C.C.R. 381 it was held by the sheriff that a remand for pre-sentencing reports on another complaint did not interrupt the running of 40 days in a custody complaint.

Two extensions were permitted where the accused's plea in bar on grounds of insanity had to be investigated by the Crown, and through no fault on the Crown's part one of the reports was not available to the court; the accused was remanded awaiting trial for 70 days (*Sweeney v. Douglas*, 1997 G.W.D. 28–1408).

In calculating the 40 day period, the whole of the day on which the remand order is made is discounted, while the whole of the final day is included: see *Hazlett v. McGlennan*, 1992 S.C.C.R. 799; 1993 S.L.T. 74 and the discussion "Computation of Time" in notes to s.136 above. As subs.(4) enacts, the period expires when the trial begins. In *Grugen v. Jessop*, 1988 S.C.C.R. 182 the accused took a Bill of Advocation founding upon the actions of the prosecutor who commenced his trial on the fortieth day, in the knowledge that the trial would have to be adjourned only part-heard due to the known unavailability of Crown witnesses. The Appeal Court refused the Bill and declined to hold these procedures to be an abuse of process.

The court on application can extend the 40 day period on the grounds specified in subs. (2); considerations similar to those applying to s.65(4) in solemn procedure are relevant. Appeal to the High Court against such extension proceeds on Form 17.1 while Rule 17.1.-(2) of the 1996 Act of Adjournal stipulates service of copies of the Form upon the prosecutor and the clerk of court. Appeals against extensions of the 40 day period are marked using Form 17.1 in the Act of Adjournal.

Subsection (4) was interpreted in *Mitchell v. Vannet*, 1999 G.W.D. 20–928.

See A4–329 below.

Intermediate diet

148.—(1) The court may, when adjourning a case for trial in terms of section 146(3) of this Act, and may also, at any time thereafter, whether before, on or after any date assigned as a trial diet, fix a diet (to be known as an intermediate diet) for the purpose of ascertaining, so far as is reasonably practicable, whether the case is likely to proceed to trial on any date assigned as a trial diet and, in particular—

(a) the state of preparation of the prosecutor and of the accused with respect to their cases;

(b) whether the accused intends to adhere to the plea of not guilty; and

(c) the extent to which the prosecutor and the accused have complied with the duty under section 257(1) of this Act. secure agreement - evidence not in dispute

(1A) At an intermediate diet in summary proceedings in the sheriff court, the court shall also:

(a) ascertain whether subsection (1B) below applies to any person who is to give evidence at or for the purposes of the trial or to the accused, and

(b) if so, consider whether it should make an order undersection 271A(7) or 271D(2) of this Act in relation to person or, as the case may be, the accused.

(1B) This subsection applies:

(a) to a person who is to give evidence at or for the purposes of the trial if that person is, or is likely to be, a vulnerable witness,

(b) to the accused if, were he to give evidence at or for the purposes of the trial, he would be, or would be likely to be, a vulnerable witness.

postpone trial diet (2) Where at an intermediate diet the court concludes that the case is unlikely to proceed to trial on the date assigned for the trial diet, the court—

(a) shall, unless having regard to previous proceedings in the case it considers it inappropriate to do so, postpone the trial diet; and

(b) may fix a further intermediate diet.

(3) Subject to subsection (2) above, the court may, if it considers it appropriate to do so, adjourn an intermediate diet.

(3A) At an intermediate diet, the court may consider an application for the purposes of subsection (1) of section 275 of this Act; and, notwithstanding subsection (1) above, the court may fix a diet under that subsection for the purpose only of considering such an application.

(3B) Subsection (3A) above shall not operate so as to relieve any court prescribed by order under subsection (7) below of its duty, which arises by virtue of the operation of that subsection, to fix an intermediate diet for the purpose mentioned in subsection (1) above.

(4) At an intermediate diet, the court may ask the prosecutor and the accused any question for the purposes mentioned in subsection (1) or (3A) above [or for the purpose of ascertaining or considering any matter mentioned in subsection (1A) above].

(5) The accused shall attend an intermediate diet of which he has received intimation or to which he has been cited unless—

(a) he is legally represented; and

(b) the court considers that there are exceptional circumstances justifying him not attending.

Guilty Plea (6) A plea of guilty may be tendered at the intermediate diet.

(7) The foregoing provisions of this section shall have effect as respects any court prescribed by the Secretary of State by order, in relation to proceedings commenced after such date as may be so prescribed, with the following modifications—

(a) in subsection (1), for the word "may" where it first appears there shall be substituted "shall, subject to subsection (1A) below,"; and

(b) after subsection (1) there shall be inserted the following subsections—

"(1A) If, on a joint application by the prosecutor and the accused made at any time before the commencement of the intermediate diet, the court considers it inappropriate to have such a diet, the duty under subsection (1) above shall not apply and the court shall discharge any such diet already fixed.

(1B) The court may consider an application under subsection (1A) above without hearing the parties.".

(8) An order under subsection (7) above shall be made by statutory instrument, which shall be subject to annulment in pursuance of a resolution of either House of Parliament.

AMENDMENT

Subss.(1) and (7)(a) as amended by the Criminal Procedure (Intermediate Diets) (Scotland) Act 1998 (c. 10) s.1 (effective April 8, 1998).

Subss.(3A) and (3B) inserted by the Sexual Offences (Procedure and Evidence) (Scotland) Act 2002 (asp 9), s.8(5)(a). Brought into force by the Sexual Offences (Procedure and Evidence) (Scotland) Act 2002 (Commencement and Transitional Provisions) Order 2002 (SSI 2002/443 (C.24)), art.4 (effective November 1, 2002).

Subs.(4) as amended by the Sexual Offences (Procedure and Evidence) (Scotland) Act 2002 (asp 9), s.8(5)(b). Brought into force as above.

s.148(4) as ammended, and (1A) and (1B) inserted by the Vulnerable Witnesses (Scotland) Act 2004 (asp3), s.2(5). Brought into force on April 1, 2007 (only in respect of child witness and referred to in s.27(1)(a) of the 1995 Act) by the Vulnerable Witnesses (Scotland) Act 2004 (Commencement No.4, Savings and Transitional Provisions) Order 2007(SSI 2007/101 (C.13)) , art.2.

DEFINITIONS

"diet": s.307(1).
"prosecutor": s.307(1).

GENERAL NOTE

The Criminal Procedure (Intermediate Diets) (Scotland) Act 1998 (c.10) received Royal Assent on April 9, 1998 and was a legislative response to the High Court's decisions in *Mackay v Ruxton*, 1998 S.C.C.R. 790 and *Kerr v Carnegie*, 1998 S.C.C.R. 168, both of which explored the consequences of failure to fix an intermediate diet, and *Vannet v Milligan*, 1998 S.C.C.R. 305, dealing with a purported alteration of a trial diet at an incompetent intermediate diet. (The practice had developed in summary courts of assigning an intermediate diet prior to the trial diet as s.148(1) dictates and further such diets, ostensibly under s.148(1), where the trial did not proceed and had to be adjourned to a later trial diet.)

It is some measure of the uncertainty which these decisions engendered and the far-reaching implications for a large volume of summary trial business that the new Act was treated by Parliament as emergency legislation and, most unusually, came into force with retrospective effect. The new provisions require summary courts to fix an intermediate diet when a trial diet is first assigned and give those courts a discretion to fix further intermediate diets, as necessary, during the currency of any criminal complaint which is proceeding to trial. Generally however there is likely to be little practical benefit in assigning a further intermediate diet once a trial diet has been adjourned unless there has been a tangible change in circumstances; joint minute procedures arguably provide a more flexible tool for the purpose, at least where parties agree the need for the court to consider afresh (see s.137 above).

Intermediate diets were introduced in 1980 in a drive to avoid the waste of court resources, the expense and the needless inconvenience to the public caused by the large numbers of cases which, for one reason or another, did not proceed at trial diets.

Section 14 of the Criminal Justice (Scotland) Act 1995 (c.20) extended the scope of intermediate diets and envisaged a more pro-active role on the part of the Bench in ascertaining the state of preparation of parties for the impending trial. It will be remembered that s.196 of the Criminal Procedure (Scotland) Act 1995 allowed the courts to take account of the point in proceedings at which the accused tendered a guilty plea: a formal diet calling prior to the trial, but after the parties had concluded their preparation, could materially assist both in speeding the flow of court business and disposing of pleas.

Subsections (2) and (3) enable the courts to ascertain whether a trial will proceed or not and, if not, to postpone the trial diet (with or without a further intermediate diet being fixed) or adjourn the intermediate diet while preserving the trial diet.

The Appeal Court has held that the purpose of intermediate (or first) diets is an administrative one rather than being a fundamental, and necessary, process any procedural lapse in which would vitiate proceedings (*Hogg v H.M. Advocate*, 1999 S.L.T. 371 applying *Kerr v Carnegie*, 1998 S.C.C.R. 168). In *Kerr*, a custody trial, no intermediate diet was fixed, an omission which the Appeal Court declined to view as an irremediable defect. Indeed the Court went on to point to the fact that it was s.148(7) of the Act which required mandatory, rather than discretionary, intermediate diets and that that only took effect at the behest of the Secretary of State by order—clearly the exercise of an administrative function. It may also be significant in this context that s.146(2) of the Act entitles a summary court to proceed immediately to trial as soon as a plea of not guilty is tendered, a long-standing provision wholly at odds with *Kerr* contentions, but one which underlines the incidental rather than fundamental nature of intermediate diets. See too *Reith v Bates*, 1998 S.C.C.R. 426; 1999 S.L.T. 380, a case in which at a second intermediate diet the court was minuted as having adjourned the imminent trial diet; the Appeal Court looked to the intention of the prosecutor and the sheriff to postpone the trial and thus repelled the accused's objection to the competency of the proceedings which was founded on inaccurate minutes.

The essentially administrative character of intermediate diets is underlined by *Brown v Vannet*, 1999 G.W.D. 19–873 in which an unsuccessful appeal founded upon the availability of an interpreter at the intermediate diet for a deaf-mute accused. Compare the position at trial; see *Mikhailitchenko v Normand*, 1993 S.L.T. 1138. The role of an interpreter at intermediate, and trial, diets is discussed in *Erkurt v Higson*, 2004 S.L.T. 21.

The amendments introduced by the Sexual Offences (Procedure and Evidence) (Scotland) Act 2002 (asp 9) now add mechanisms for the hearing of applications, under s.275 of the 1995 Act, to lift the general restrictions on questioning of victims of sexual crimes. Such applications must be lodged at least 14 clear days before trial (unless special cause can be shown) and may well be considered separately from other matters raised at a preliminary diet. The reasons for this are discussed in the General Note to ss.275 and 275A. It is appropriate to direct attention to s.148A whose purpose is to ensure that any accused charged with a listed sexual offence or offence containing a substantial sexual element (s.288C) is legally represented.

A summary court is obliged to ensure that such an accused is not defending himself since this could result in him subjecting his victim both to precognition and cross-examination. It will be seen that any appointed solicitor in such cases has duties to the court to intimate in writing if he is dismissed by the accused or withdraws from acting. (The section does not bar an agent from withdrawing from acting). Hearings in relation to these issues can be dispensed with if the court receives intimation that the accused has benefit of legal representation but otherwise it will be necessary for the accused to attend personally at the diet (or at a continued diet fixed for the purpose) to confirm that he is legally represented.

Interim diet: sexual offence to which section 288C of this Act applies

148A.—(1) Where, in a case which is adjourned for trial, the charge is of committing a sexual offence to which section 288C of this Act applies, the court shall order that, before the trial diet, there shall be a diet under this section and ordain the accused then to attend.

(2) At a diet under this section, the court shall ascertain whether or not the accused has engaged a solicitor for the purposes of his defence at the trial.

(3) Where, following inquiries for the purposes of subsection (2) above, it appears to the court that the accused has not engaged a solicitor for the purposes of his defence at his trial, it may adjourn the diet under this section for a period of not more than 48 hours and ordain the accused then to attend.

(4) A diet under this section may be conjoined with an intermediate diet.

(5) A court may, at a diet under this section, postpone the trial diet.

(6) The court may dispense with a diet under this section previously ordered, but only if a solicitor engaged by the accused for the purposes of the defence of the accused at the trial has, in writing—

(a) confirmed his engagement for that purpose; and

(b) requested that the diet be dispensed with.

(7) Where—

(a) a solicitor has requested, under subsection (6) above, that a diet under this section be dispensed with; and

(b) before that diet has been held or dispensed with, the solicitor—

(i) is dismissed by the accused; or

(ii) withdraws,

the solicitor shall forthwith inform the court in writing of those facts.

(8) It is the duty of a solicitor who—

(a) was engaged for the purposes of the defence of the accused at the trial—

(i) at the time of a diet under this section; or

(ii) in the case of a diet which, under subsection (6) above, is dispensed with, at the time when it was so dispensed with; and

(b) after that time but before the trial diet—

(i) is dismissed by the accused; or

(ii) withdraws,

forthwith to inform the court in writing of those facts.

(9) On being so informed, the court shall order a further diet under this section.

AMENDMENT

Section 148A inserted by the Sexual Offences (Procedure and Evidence) (Scotland) Act 2002 (asp 9), Sch.1, para.11. Brought into force by the Sexual Offences (Procedure and Evidence) (Scotland) Act 2002 (Commencement and Transitional Provisions) Order 2002 (SSI 2002/443 (C.24)), art.4 (effective November 1, 2002).

GENERAL NOTE

Refer to discussion at A4–321 above.

Pre-trial procedure in sheriff court where no intermediate diet is fixed

148B—(1) Where, in any summary proceedings in the sheriff court, no intermediate diet is fixed, the court shall, at the trial diet before the first witness is sworn—

(a) ascertain whether subsection (2) below applies to any person who is to give evidence at or for the purposes of the trial or to the accused and, if so, consider whether it should make an order under section 271A(7) or 271D(2) of this Act in relation to the person or, as the case may be, the accused, and

(b) if—

(i) section 288E of this Act applies to the proceedings, or

(ii) an order under section 288F(2) has been made in the proceedings,

ascertain whether or not the accused has engaged a solicitor for the purposes of his defence at the trial.

(2) This subsection applies—

(a) to a person who is to give evidence at or for the purposes of the trial if that person is, or is likely to be, a vulnerable witness,

(b) to the accused if, were he to give evidence at or for the purposes of the trial, he would be, or be likely to be, a vulnerable witness.

(3) Where, following inquiries for the purposes of subsection (1)(b) above, it appears to the court that the accused has not engaged a solicitor for the purposes of his defence at the trial, the court may adjourn the trial diet for a period of not more than 48 hours and ordain the accused then to attend.

(4) At the trial diet, the court may ask the prosecutor and the accused any

question in connection with any matter which it is required to ascertain or consider under subsection (1) above.

AMENDMENT

Section 148Binserted by the Vulnerable Witnesses (Scotland) Act 2004 (asp 3), s.9.Brought into force on April 1, 2007 (only in respect of child witness and referred to in s.27(1)(a) of the 1995 Act) by the Vulnerable Witnesses (Scotland) Act 2004 (Commencement No.4, Savings and Transitional Provisions) Order 2007(SSI 2007/101 (C.13)) , art.2

DEFINITIONS

"diet": s.307(1).
"prosecutor": s.307(1).
"vulnerable witness": s.271.

GENERAL NOTE

This section covers the procedural possible event of a trial in a summary case that has not been preceded by an intermediate diet. Section 148B applies to a vulnerable witness or to an accused who (if giving evidence) would be a vulnerable witness: see s.148B(2). In these circumstances the court must, at the trial diet before the first witness is sworn, see if s.148B(2) does apply and whether there may be a prohibition on an accused personally cross-examining a complainer and ascertain whether or not the accused has engaged a solicitor for the purposes of his defence at the trial. If it appears that there is no solicitor so engaged then the court may adjourn the trial diet for a period of not more than 48 hours: s.148B(3).

Alibi — *Summary Procedure*

149. It shall not be competent for the accused in a summary prosecution to found on a plea of alibi unless he gives, at any time before the first witness is sworn, notice to the prosecutor of the plea with particulars as to time and place and of the witnesses by whom it is proposed to prove it; and, on such notice being given, the prosecutor shall be entitled, if he so desires, to an adjournment of the case.

DEFINITIONS

"prosecutor": s.307(1).
"witness": s.307(1).

GENERAL NOTE

Sch.6, para.121 of the Criminal Justice (Scotland) Act 1995 introduced only one small clarifying amendment to s.339 of the 1975 Act, which carried over into s.149 of the current Act. An alibi has now to be intimated before the first witness is sworn, whereas in the 1975 Act intimation had to be made "prior to the examination of the first witness". Special note has to be taken of the markedly different provision applying to a defence of consent in a summary trial. This arises in sexual offences. See s.149A below.

Notice of defence plea of consent — *Sexual Offences*

149A.—(1) It shall not be competent for the accused in a summary prosecution for an offence to which section 288C of this Act applies to found on a defence of consent unless, not less than 10 clear days before the trial diet, he gives notice to the prosecutor of the defence and of the witnesses by whom he proposes to maintain it.

(2) The court may, however, on cause shown, allow the accused to maintain such a defence after giving such notice although given after the time limit specified in subsection (1) above.

(3) In subsection (1) above, the reference to a defence of consent is a reference to the defence which is stated by reference to the complainer's consent to the act which is the subject matter of the charge or the accused's belief as to that consent.

(4) In subsection (3) above, "complainer" has the same meaning as in section 274 of this Act.

AMENDMENT

Section 149A inserted by the Sexual Offences (Procedure and Evidence) (Scotland) Act 2002 (asp 9), s.6(2). Brought into force by the Sexual Offences (Procedure and Evidence) (Scotland) Act 2002 (Commencement and Transitional Provisions) Order 2002 (SSI 2002/443 (C.24)), art.4 (effective November 1, 2002).

GENERAL NOTE

Advance notice is necessary not less than 10 clear days before trial if it is intended to rely upon a defence of consent to any of the category of sexual offences specified in s.288C of the Act. Additional procedures in relation to advance notice of attacks on character are set out in s.275A. The equivalent provision governing solemn procedure is found in s.78 of the Act.

Failure of accused to appear

Failure of accused to appear

150.—(1) This section applies where the accused in a summary prosecution fails to appear at any diet of which he has received intimation, or to which he has been cited other than a diet which, by virtue of section 148(5) of this Act, he is not required to attend.

(2) The court may adjourn the proceedings to another diet, and order the accused to attend at such diet, and appoint intimation of the diet to be made to him.

(3) The court may grant warrant to apprehend the accused.

(3A) The grant, under subsection (3) above, at an intermediate diet, or a diet under section 148A of this Act, of a warrant to apprehend the accused has the effect of discharging the trial diet as respects that accused.

(3B) Subsection (3A) above is subject to any order to different effect made by the court when granting the warrant.

(4) Intimation under subsection (2) above shall be sufficiently given by an officer of law, or by letter signed by the clerk of court or prosecutor and sent to the accused at his last known address by registered post or by the recorded delivery service, and the production in court of the written execution of such officer or of an acknowledgement or certificate of the delivery of the letter issued by the postal operator shall be sufficient evidence of such intimation having been duly given.

(5) Where the accused is charged with a statutory offence for which a sentence of imprisonment cannot be imposed in the first instance, or where the statute founded on or conferring jurisdiction authorises procedure in the absence of the accused, the court, on the motion of the prosecutor and upon being satisfied that the accused has been duly cited, or has received due intimation of the diet where such intimation has been ordered, may subject to subsections (6) and (7) below, proceed to hear and dispose of the case in the absence of the accused.

(6) Unless the statute founded on authorises conviction in default of appearance, proof of the complaint must be led to the satisfaction of the court.

(7) In a case to which subsection (5) above applies, the court may, if it considers it expedient, allow counsel or a solicitor who satisfies the court that he has authority from the accused so to do, to appear and plead for and defend him.

see s. 150 (8)

P. TO.

Make him subject to an additional complaint of failing to appear ↓

(8) An accused who without reasonable excuse fails to attend any diet of which he has been given due notice, shall be guilty of an offence and liable on summary conviction—

(a) to a fine not exceeding level 3 on the standard scale; and

(b) to a period of imprisonment not exceeding—

    (i) in the district court, 60 days; or

    (ii) in the sheriff court, 3 months.

(9) The penalties provided for in subsection (8) above may be imposed in addition to any other penalty which it is competent for the court to impose, notwithstanding that the total of penalties imposed may exceed the maximum penalty which it is competent to impose in respect of the original offence.

(10) An accused may be dealt with for an offence under subsection (8) above either at his diet of trial for the original offence or at a separate trial.

AMENDMENTS

Subs.(4) as amended by the Postal Services Act 2000 (Consequential Modifications No.1) Order 2001 (SI 2001/1149), art.3 and Sch.1, para.104.

Subss.(3A) and (3B) inserted by the Criminal Procedure (Amendment) (Scotland) Act 2002 (asp 4), s.1 (effective March 9, 2002).

Subs.(3A) as amended by the Sexual Offences (Procedure and Evidence) (Scotland) Act 2002 (asp 9), Sch.1, para.12. Brought into force by the Sexual Offences (Procedure and Evidence) (Scotland) Act 2002 (Commencement and Transitional Provisions) Order 2002 (SSI 2002/443 (C.24)), art.4 (effective November 1, 2002).

DEFINITIONS

"complaint": s.307(1).

"diet": s.307(1).

"imprisonment": s.307(6).

"offence": s.307(1).

"officer of law": s.307(1).

"prosecutor": s.307(1).

GENERAL NOTE

Section 141, which specifies the methods of citation of accused, and this section which deals with the consequences of a failure by an accused to appear at a summary diet need to be considered together. Intimation of any diet can be made by notice sent by registered or recorded post, by personal service of such a notice by an officer of law, or by the fixing of the diet in the accused's presence. While s.141 relates to the way in which proceedings are launched, s.150 has general application once a complaint has been placed before the court until the proceedings are concluded.

The failure by an accused to attend a diet of which he has been given notice lawfully, entitles the prosecutor to seek an apprehension warrant in terms of s.150 and to libel a further complaint founding upon failure to appear. The penalties disclosed in subs. (8) are in addition to any penalty the court may impose on the original complaint and, cumulatively, the penalties exacted on the original and second complaint can competently exceed the statutory ceilings fixed in summary proceedings; these are defined in s.5(2) and (3) for the sheriff court, and in s.7(6) and (7) in relation to the district court.

On proof of citation or notice of a diet being produced to the court, the prosecutor may seek a warrant to apprehend the accused. The court may grant a warrant or continue the diet to a later diet and order intimation of the diet on the accused as provided by subs.(2). This underlines the importance of the Crown being able to exhibit evidence of service of the complaint or of intimation of the diet when required by the court. See *Beattie v. Mackinnon*, 1977 J.C. 64 where no date of citation had been placed on the accused's citation and service copy complaint, a fact unknown to the court when a warrant to apprehend was granted following an apparent failure to appear.

The court is not obliged to issue a warrant following failure to appear by the accused (subs.(2) permits adjournment of proceedings) but must pronounce some order and cannot simply refrain from action; see *Skeen v. Sullivan*, 1980 S.L.T. (Notes) 11. Equally the prosecutor can only proceed under this section to take a warrant, when he is satisfied that service of the complaint has been effected and, hence, that it is validly before the court for further procedure; see *Lees v. Malcolm*, 1992 S.L.T. 1137; 1992 S.C.C.R. 589 where a fresh complaint was raised to maintain proceedings, and *Heywood v. McLennan*, 1994 S.C.C.R. 1 where efforts were made to "convert" an unserved complaint into an initiating warrant, despite the complaint having fallen.

Subsections (5), (6) and (7) provide for trial proceedings in the absence of the accused only once the court is satisfied that the accused has either been cited or received an intimation of the diet deemed necessary by the court.

Subs. (3A) and (3B)

In *Reynolds v. Dyer*, 2002 S.L.T. 331 it was held that the discharge of a trial diet, which was a peremptory diet, should not be left to implication and that the granting of a warrant at an intermediate diet did not *per se* discharge a trial diet. The statutory changes in the Criminal Procedure (Amendment) (Scotland) Act 2002 reversed that decision and thereby reinstated the usual practice in the summary courts.

Non-availability of judge

Death, illness or absence of judge

151.—(1) Where the court is unable to proceed owing to the death, illness or absence of the presiding judge, it shall be lawful for the clerk of court—

(a) where the diet has not been called, to convene the court and adjourn the diet;

(b) where the diet has been called but no evidence has been led, to adjourn the diet; and

(c) where the diet has been called and evidence has been led—

    (i) with the agreement of the parties, to desert the diet *pro loco et tempore*; or

    (ii) to adjourn the diet.

(2) Where, under subsection (1)(c)(i) above, a diet has been deserted *pro loco et tempore*, any new prosecution charging the accused with the same or any similar offence arising out of the same facts shall be brought within two months of the date on which the diet was deserted notwithstanding that any other time limit for the commencement of such prosecution has elapsed.

(3) For the purposes of subsection (2) above, a new prosecution shall be deemed to commence on the date on which a warrant to apprehend or to cite the accused is granted, if such warrant is executed without undue delay.

DEFINITIONS

    "judge": s.307(1).
    "offence": s.307(1).

GENERAL NOTE

The purpose of this section is to provide for the adjournment, or desertion *pro loco et tempore*, of summary proceedings where the court cannot proceed due to the death, illness or absence of the "presiding judge", a phrase equally applicable to sheriff or district court proceedings. Similar provisions, taking due account of differences in procedure, apply to solemn proceedings by s.87 above.

In summary proceedings the court has a common law authority to fix a new diet when a judge is taken ill during a trial and therefore the possibility of postponement of a trial, for that same reason, was acknowledged in s.331A(2)(a) of the 1975 Act. However until the passage of s.30 of the Criminal Justice (Scotland) Act 1995, no statutory provision existed in summary cases to regulate proceedings in the event of the death of a judge. In *Clarke v. Fraser*, 2002 S.L.T. 745, the Appeal Court refused to uphold a purported adjournment of a District Court proof where the court could not convene due to severe weather and the clerk and the judge having spoken over the phone, the clerk opted to adjourn in the absence of the judge at a place other than the court itself. The Appeal Court noted that since the court could not convene the remedy would have been for the Crown to petition the *nobile officium* as a means of preserving the complaint.

Desertion of the diet necessarily means that the instance in the complaint falls. To preserve the public interest, particularly in cases which would otherwise be time-barred in accordance with s.136 above, subs.(2) permits the re-raising of any proceedings deserted in terms of s.151. In that event proceedings can be initiated anew, but must be effected upon the accused without undue delay (for "undue delay" see generally the notes to s.136 above).

A separate provision dealing with the illness or death of a judge in the course of preparation of an appeal by stated case is found at s.176(4).

Trial diet

Desertion of diet

152.—(1) It shall be competent at the diet of trial, at any time before the first witness is sworn, for the court, on the application of the prosecutor, to desert the diet *pro loco et tempore*.

(2) If, at a diet of trial, the court refuses an application by the prosecutor to adjourn the trial or to desert the diet *pro loco et tempore*, and the prosecutor is unable or unwilling to proceed with the trial, the court shall desert the diet *simpliciter*.

(3) Where the court has deserted a diet *simpliciter* under subsection (2) above (and the court's decision in that regard has not been reversed on appeal), it shall not be competent for the prosecutor to raise a fresh libel.

DEFINITIONS

"diet": s.307(1).
"prosecutor": s.307(1).
"trial": s.307(1).
"witness": s.307(1).

GENERAL NOTE

The terms of s.338A of the 1975 Act are preserved. Section 147(4) of this Act enacts that a trial begins when the first witness is sworn; until that time it is open to the prosecutor to move the court to desert the diet *pro loco et tempore*, or to move to adjourn the trial. Once either of these motions has been made however, the court can refuse the motion and, instead, desert the trial *simpliciter*, a step which brings proceedings to an end. In some instances the Crown might better achieve its purpose simply by not calling the case for trial at all, since, although the instance in the current complaint would fall, the right to proceed might still be retained. It remains the case, as subs.(3) states, that the unreasonable refusal by the judge of a Crown motion to adjourn or desert *pro loco et tempore* can still be appealed.

In *Tudhope v Gough*, 1982 S.C.C.R. 157 it was held competent for the Crown to move to desert *pro loco* even after the refusal of a motion to adjourn and see *Fay v Vannet*, 1998 S.L.T. 1099, where desertion of a complaint of police assault by the prosecutor following the sheriff's refusal of adjournment was competently followed by a fresh complaint of common law assault, a step which was held not to be oppressive. In *Fay v Vannet*, 1998 S.L.T. 1099 it was affirmed that desertion *simpliciter* could only be exercised by the court in terms of s.152(2) after refusal of both of the prosecutor's motions to adjourn and to desert *pro loco et tempore*. A more novel, but inappropriate, use of desertion *simpliciter* is found in *MacLeod v Williamson*, 1993 S.L.T. 144 where the sheriff did so *ex proprio motu* having overheard witnesses during an adjournment and having drawn the nature of the eavesdropping to the attention of the prosecutor.

The Appeal Court indicated that if the sheriff had come to the view that he could no longer preside over the trial, he should have discharged the trial diet and fixed a new diet to go before another sheriff; desertion *simpliciter* was invalid. In a similar vein, see *Carmichael v Monaghan*, 1986 S.C.C.R. 598.

In *McMahon v Hamilton*, 1992 S.C.C.R. 351, the prosecutor deserted one of two charges on a complaint *simpliciter*, a plea of not guilty being recorded for the second charge. Issue was thereafter taken with the competency of proceeding on the latter charge. The plea to competency was repelled but the Appeal Court, rather than express any view on the competency of deserting a charge (as distinct from a complaint) *simpliciter* elected to treat both charges as live and to treat the minuting of the pleas as *pro non scripto*: it remains unresolved whether such a motion is competent or not, though the simplest solution is surely to accept a plea of not guilty to the charge in normal circumstances. In *Mitchell v H.M. Advocate*, 2004 S.L.T. 151 the Crown's decision to desert not one, but two, prior complaints to enable substitution of a complaint containing still more serious charges was upheld; only if the accused can demonstrate oppression, *i.e.* that he cannot now receive a fair trial due to the gravity of the prejudice resulting from the proceedings, could a motion to desert *pro loco et tempore* be refused.

See *Normand v West*, 1992 S.C.C.R. 76 as an example of an unreasonable refusal by the court to permit an adjournment in the absence of essential witnesses. Desertion *simpliciter* by the court and the premature ending of a prosecution is a step which, in *Tudhope v Laurie*, 1979 S.L.T. (Notes) 13 at 14, "must be exercised only after the most careful consideration on weighty grounds and with due and accurate regard to the interests which will be affected or prejudiced by that exercise".

See also *Normand v Milne*, 1996 G.W.D. 19–1078, where the Crown succeeded on appeal by advocation against the sheriff's refusal to permit a desertion *pro loco*. The Appeal Court may have signalled a more rigorous (and less tolerant) approach to repeated Crown motions to adjourn caused by failure to trace or cite witnesses; see *Donaldson v Kelly* 2004 S.C.C.R. 153.

Ruxton v Borland, 2000 S.L.T. 612; 2000 S.C.C.R. 484 re-introduces a measure of familiarity, and clarity, to summary proceedings after the uncertainties produced by the Appeal Court in *Mitchell v Vannet*, 1999 S.L.T 934, which bore to follow *Handley v Pirie*, 1977 S.L.T. 30, both of which *Ruxton v Borland*, a five judge decision, has overruled. Following this decision and its three judge precursor (found at 2000 G.W.D. 9–326) it can be said that after the tendering of a plea of not guilty on a summary complaint, it is only necessary thereafter to ascertain whether the plea previously tendered is adhered to, and that unless there is evident prejudice to the accused, there is no necessity for the same judge to deal with the case at all times once it has been put down for trial.

Trial in presence of accused

153.—(1) Without prejudice to section 150 of this Act, and subject to subsection (2) below, no part of a trial shall take place outwith the presence of the accused.

(2) If during the course of his trial an accused so misconducts himself that in the view of the court a proper trial cannot take place unless he is removed, the court may order—

(a) that he is removed from the court for so long as his conduct makes it necessary; and

(b) that the trial proceeds in his absence,

but if he is not legally represented the court shall appoint counsel or a solicitor to represent his interests during such absence.

DEFINITION

"trial": s.307(1).

GENERAL NOTE

Subject to the statutory enactments which permit trial in the absence of the accused (see s.150(5)), it is generally the case that any trial can only competently proceed in the accused's presence (see *Aitken v Wood*, 1921 J.C. 84) for justice to be seen to be done. Section 153 introduces a further exception to the generality in circumstances where the accused so misconducts himself as to preclude proper conduct of the case. In that event the accused can be removed from the court and trial continue with the accused represented by his solicitor or counsel, or if he has not been legally represented, by an agent appointed by the court to act on his behalf, during the period of absence. This provision does not, of course, resolve what action the court may take at the conclusion of the trial to deal with any contempt.

The general principle that justice must not only be done, but be seen to be done, underpins this provision. Unreasonable fetters upon an accused's ability to cross-examine, as in *McGeechan v Higson*, 2000 G.W.D. 39–1445 where the magistrate had restricted the accused, who was defending himself, to cross-examining witnesses only on their answers to Crown questions, offend against that principle. Similarly in *McKee v Brown*, 2001 S.C.C.R. 6, where the trial judge accidentally saw the schedule of convictions which had been left with the complaint after withdrawal of an earlier guilty plea, and expressed misgivings but still felt bound by the decision in *Tudhope v O'Neill*, 1984 S.L.T. 424; 1984 S.C.C.R. 276 (discussed at A4–359 below), conviction was quashed. The obligation to ensure the fairness of proceedings persists even after a verdict has been reached on the evidence. In *Doherty v McGlennan*, 1997 S.L.T. 444 a conviction was quashed where the sheriff, having convicted the accused, then deferred sentence and invited the complainer (a local Member of Parliament) to meet in chambers. *Harper v Heywood*, 1998 G.W.D. 3–110, is perhaps an extreme example of unjudicial conduct which resulted in the quashing of the conviction and authority being granted for a new prosecution. However expressions of sympathy towards a victim during sentence of an accused, which caused an accused to aver that his conviction had resulted from the sheriff's sympathy, were held not to be improper, the court having moved from weighing the evidence to sentence (*Bagan v Normand*, 1997 G.W.D. 14–596). Compare *Ogilvie v Heywood*, 2001 G.W.D. 18–695 where the judge expressed regret to a witness at the conclusion of her evidence that she had had to travel from England by saying "In fact, I am sorry that this happened at all". The Appeal Court accepted that an impartial observer would have felt that the sheriff had already reached a concluded view on the evidence. In *Lowe v Brown*, 1997 S.C.C.R. 341, the Appeal Court observed that judges should question witnesses with restraint and avoid any indication of disbelieving a witness' account during examination. In *Clark v H.M. Advocate*, 2000 S.L.T. 1107; 2000 S.C.C.R. 767 the Appeal Court listened to the tape of the sheriff's charge to the jury and quashed the accused's conviction on the ground that the tone used in posing a series of rhetorical questions was such as to intrude into the jury's role as masters of fact. Injudicious comment by the sheriff in the course of trial, hastening defence cross-examination, and giving a clear impression that his mind was made up resulted in the quashing of conviction in *Murray v Watt*, 2002 G.W.D. 2–64.

Section 153(1)'s principles need not apply however in relation to enquiries conducted in connection with appeals where further evidence is heard; see *Crossan v H.M. Advocate*, 1996 S.C.C.R. 279 and the discussion at A4–179 above. It is noted that the accused's counsel and solicitor were present in chambers during the appointed judge's examination of evidence.

The equivalent provision in solemn proceedings is found at s.92(2) above.

Proof of official documents
154. [...]

AMENDMENT

Repealed by the Crime and Punishment (Scotland) Act 1997 (c.48), s.28.

GENERAL NOTE

This section was deleted by s.28(1) of the Crime and Punishment (Scotland) Act 1997 and its provisions are now to be found in s.279A of the Act which extends the provisions in relation to official documents to all criminal proceedings. Section 154, which only applied to summary proceedings, ceased to have effect from August 1, 1997 in terms of SI 1997/1712.

Punishment of witness for contempt
155.—(1) If a witness in a summary prosecution—

(a) wilfully fails to attend after being duly cited; or

(b) unlawfully refuses to be sworn; or

(c) after the oath has been administered to him refuses to answer any question which the court may allow; or

(d) prevaricates in his evidence,

he shall be deemed guilty of contempt of court and be liable to be summarily punished forthwith for such contempt by a fine not exceeding level 3 on the standard scale or by imprisonment for any period not exceeding 21 days.

(2) Where punishment is summarily imposed as mentioned in subsection (1) above, the clerk of court shall enter in the record of the proceedings the acts constituting the contempt or the statements forming the prevarication.

(3) Subsections (1) and (2) above are without prejudice to the right of the prosecutor to proceed by way of formal complaint for any such contempt where a summary punishment, as mentioned in the said subsection (1), is not imposed.

(4) Any witness who, having been duly cited in accordance with section 140 of this Act—

(a) fails without reasonable excuse, after receiving at least 48 hours' notice, to attend for precognition by a prosecutor at the time and place mentioned in the citation served on him; or

(b) refuses when so cited to give information within his knowledge regarding any matter relative to the commission of the offence in relation to which such precognition is taken,

shall be liable to the like punishment as is provided in subsection (1) above.

DEFINITIONS   *or punished by separate Complaint or failing to*

"prosecutor": s.307(1). *appear*

"witness": s.307(1).

GENERAL NOTE

A finding of contempt will only be justified where there has been wilful or deliberate conduct or an affront or challenge to the court's authority (*Johnston v Normand*, 1997 G.W.D. 3–81, *McTavish v Hamilton*, 1997 G.W.D. 11–451 and, generally, *McMillan v Carmichael*, 1993 S.C.C.R. 943; 1994 S.L.T. 510). A measure of magnanimity was shown to the accused in *Williams v Clark*, 2001 G.W.D. 20–758, W having been held in contempt for having a mobile phone ringing while in the dock despite clear warning notices in the court building. One might be moved to sympathy for the judge but the Appeal Court felt that he might well have concluded disrespect on W's part also from earlier conduct in the court and upon which submissions had not then been sought. A solicitor can be held in contempt, in the course of proceedings applying the same test, should he refuse to comply with the clear ruling of the court (*Blair-Wilson, Petr*, 1997 S.L.T. 621).

The court must indicate that consideration is being given to making a finding of contempt and afford the party an opportunity to explain the circumstances and submit why such a finding should not be made (*Johnston v Normand* above, *Harkness v Westwater*, 1997 G.W.D. 15–650 and *Dickson v Reith*, 1997 G.W.D. 23–1139). The broad lesson from all these cases is that the court has to proceed with cool deliberation, specify the nature of the misconduct, give the offending party ample opportunity to explain himself and, possibly, purge any contempt, rather than leaping too swiftly to an untenable conclusion which will not be supported.

In minuting the act which constituted the contempt, care must be taken to specify in detail the nature of the misconduct; see *Strang v Annan*, 1991 S.L.T. 676; *Sze v Wilson*, 1992 S.L.T. 569; 1992 S.C.C.R. 54. In *Riaviz v Howdle*, 1996 S.L.T. 747 the Appeal Court proceeded to deal with a bill of suspension (following a finding of prevarication) despite the absence of minutes recording the witness' misconduct; the court founded upon the contents of the sheriff's report and applied a purposive, rather than literal, reading of this section. Since s.155(1) refers to punishment "forthwith", there is no necessity to obtain social enquiry reports and the punishment imposed is not a "sentence" (see *Forrest v Wilson*, 1994 S.L.T. 490; 1993 S.C.C.R. 631 and the statutory definition of "sentence" at s.307(1)). Although subs.(4) refers back to the provisions of subs.(1), it would appear that the same comments would apply. As subs.(1) states the maximum penalty following a finding of contempt or prevarication is a sentence of 21 days' imprisonment; see *Logan v McGlennan*, 1999 G.W.D. 22–1041.

The factors justifying precognition on oath are set out in *Carmichael, Complainer*, 1992 S.C.C.R. 553, where a Bill of Advocation followed refusal of an application to precognosce on oath. Precognition on oath applications by the defence proceed by way of s.291 below.

European Convention on Human Rights

In *Mair (Bryan), Petitioner*, 2002 S.L.T. (Sh.Ct) 2 it was submitted that this section's provisions contravened Art.6 of the European Convention since the presiding judge was simultaneously accuser, prosecutor and judge, roles incompatible with Convention rights. The court acknowledged the apparent contradictions inherent in s.155 but recognised that the competing public interest in preserving the authority of the court had to prevail. In any event even had it been decided that the section was incompatible with Art.6 this could have been justified in terms of s.6(2)(b) of the Human Rights Act 1998 (c.42). See too *Little (Cheryl)*, 2002 S.L.T. 12. In summary it is submitted that provided the well-established procedures set out in case law are adhered to, then the requirements of Art.6 will be satisfied.

Memorandum by the Lord Justice-General on Contempt of Court

Attention is drawn to the memorandum, dated April 1, 2005 which provides general directions on the subject. The full text is found at para.C1–26 in Division C, Practice Notes, and also in *Renton and Brown's Criminal Procedure* at Appendix C.

Apprehension of witness

156.—(1) Where a witness in a summary prosecution, having been duly cited, fails to appear at the diet fixed for his attendance and no just excuse is offered by him or on his behalf, the court may, if it is satisfied that he received the citation or that its contents came to his knowledge, issue a warrant for his apprehension.

(2) Where the court is satisfied by evidence on oath that a witness in a summary prosecution is not likely to attend to give evidence without being compelled so to do, it may issue a warrant for his apprehension.

(3) A warrant of apprehension of a witness in a summary prosecution in the form mentioned in section 135(1) of this Act shall imply warrant to officers of law to search for and apprehend the witness, and to detain him in a police station, police cell, or other convenient place, until—

(a) the date fixed for the hearing of the case; or

(b) the date when security to the amount fixed under subsection (4) below is found,

whichever is the earlier.

(4) A witness apprehended under a warrant under subsection (1) or (2) above shall, wherever practicable, be brought immediately by the officer of law who executed that warrant before a justice, who shall fix such sum as he considers appropriate as security for the appearance of the witness at all diets.

AMENDMENT

Subs.(1)–(3) as amended by the Criminal Procedure (Amendment) (Scotland) Act 2004 (asp 5), s.25 and Sch.1, para.34. Brought into force on February 1, 2005 by the Criminal Procedure (Amendment) (Scotland) Act 2004 (Commencement, Transitional Provisions and Savings) Order 2004 (SSI 2004/405 (C.28)), art.2.

DEFINITIONS

"diet": s.307(1).
"justice": s.307(1).
"officers of law": s.307(1).
"witness": s.307(1).

GENERAL NOTE

This section now applies solely to summary proceedings. The much more extensive powers available to solemn courts to deal with errant witnesses are contained in ss.90A to 90E above. Note that there is no pre-emptive power of apprehension in s.156—the section's provisions are only triggered by a failure to appear at the intimated diet—so any earlier inkling of non-attendance would have to proceed by means of an incidental application for a warrant to apprehend. In contrast to the solemn provisions mentioned above, a witness apprehended after a failure to appear should be placed before a justice on the next lawful day but can be kept in custody until the next diet of the case or until money bail is found.

The 1996 Act of Adjournal Form 18.3 sets out the style of a warrant to apprehend a witness.

Record of proceedings

157.—(1) Proceedings in a summary prosecution shall be conducted summarily *viva voce* and, except where otherwise provided and subject to subsection (2) below, no record need be kept of the proceedings other than the complaint, or a copy of the complaint certified as a true copy by the procurator fiscal, the plea, a note of any documentary evidence produced, and the conviction and sentence or other finding of the court.

(2) Any objection taken to the competency or relevancy of the complaint or proceedings, or to the competency or (subject to subsection (3) below) admissibility of evidence, shall, if either party desires it, be entered in the record of the proceedings.

(3) An application for the purposes of subsection (1) of section 275 of this Act, together with the court's decision on it, the reasons stated therefor and any conditions imposed and directions issued under subsection (7) of that section shall be entered in the record of the proceedings.

AMENDMENT

Subs.(2) as amended by the Sexual Offences (Procedure and Evidence) (Scotland) Act 2002 (asp 9), s.8(6)(a).

Subs.(3) inserted by the Sexual Offences (Procedure and Evidence) (Scotland) Act 2002 (asp 9), s.8(6)(b). Brought into force by the Sexual Offences (Procedure and Evidence) (Scotland) Act 2002 (Commencement and Transitional Provisions) Order 2002 (SSI 2002/443 (C.24)), art.4 (effective November 1, 2002).

DEFINITIONS

"complaint": s.307(1).
"procurator fiscal": s.307(1).

GENERAL NOTE

s.157(1)

"except where otherwise provided, no record need be kept of [summary] proceedings other than" In *Barr v Ingram*, 1977 S.L.T. 173 an appeal was taken after summary trial on the ground that the proceedings prior to conviction were irregular and vitiated by fundamental nullity. The accused had attended for trial at the time and date appointed by the court. After the calling of the case, it was adjourned three times in the course of the day and these adjournments were not minuted.

The accused argued on appeal that such adjournments must be minuted otherwise the proceedings fell. It was held that adjournments within the date of citation (as opposed to adjournments to a later date) did not require to be minuted. The appeal was refused.

In *Higson v Clark*, 2003 S.L.T. 253; 2004 S.C.C.R. 161 the respondent was charged on summary complaint and pleaded not guilty. A trial diet and an intermediate diet were fixed, but the minutes made no reference to the intermediate diet, and the case did not appear on the court roll for the date of the intermediate diet. The case did not call on the date of the intermediate diet.

When the case called at the trial diet the sheriff amended the minutes to include the fixing of the intermediate diet, and then dismissed the complaint as incompetent in the light of the failure of the Crown to call the case at the intermediate diet. The Crown appealed to the High Court, and submitted that the purported amendment came too late. Parties accepted that an intermediate diet was a peremptory diet.

It was held, applying *Barr v Ingram, supra*, that on the hypothesis that an intermediate diet was peremptory there was no reason not to apply to it the same stringency as applied to adjourned diets, including the formal requirement that it be constituted in writing, and that there had been no effectual fixing of the intermediate diet and the sheriff had erred in upholding the plea to the competency. The appeal was allowed and the case remitted to the sheriff to proceeds as accords.

"or a copy of the complaint certified as a true copy by the Procurator Fiscal" These words were inserted into s.359 of the 1995 Act by the Criminal Justice (Scotland) Act 2003, Sch.6, para.128. The current s.157 is derived from s.359. The loss of the principal or court copy of a summary complaint would have previously vitiated proceedings may now be cured. Although no similar statutory provision exists for the loss of an indictment there have been authorities on the problem: see the note "Loss of indictment" at A4–150 above.

Interruption of summary proceedings for verdict in earlier trial

158. Where the sheriff is sitting in summary proceedings during the period in which the jury in a criminal trial in which he has presided are retired to consider their verdict, it shall be lawful, if he considers it appropriate to do so, to interrupt those proceedings—

(a) in order to receive the verdict of the jury and dispose of the cause to which it relates;

(b) to give a direction to the jury on any matter on which they may wish one from him, or to hear a request from them regarding any matter,

and the interruption shall not affect the validity of the proceedings nor cause the instance to fall in respect of any person accused in the proceedings.

DEFINITION

"sheriff": s.307(1).

GENERAL NOTE

This section was introduced by the Prisoners and Criminal Proceedings (Scotland) Act 1993 (c.9) s.40. It provides for more efficient use of court time by enabling the sheriff to deal with summary business while a jury charged by him earlier is considering its verdict. Chapter 18 of the 1996 Act of Adjournal makes provision for the interruption of summary proceedings on conviction of the accused, to enable the court to consider conviction or sentence in other cases proceeding before the court (see r.18.5).

Section 102 of this Act enacts equivalent provisions relative to the interruption of sheriff and jury trials.

Competency + Relevancy

Amendment of complaint

159.—(1) It shall be competent at any time prior to the determination of the case, unless the court see just cause to the contrary, to amend the complaint or any notice of previous conviction relative thereto by deletion, alteration or addition, so as to—

(a) cure any error or defect in it;

(b) meet any objection to it; or

(c) cure any discrepancy or variance between the complaint or notice and the evidence.

(2) Nothing in this section shall authorise an amendment which changes the character of the offence charged, and, if it appears to the court that the accused may in any way be prejudiced in his defence on the merits of the case by any amendment made under this section, the court shall grant such remedy to the accused by adjournment or otherwise as appears to the court to be just.

(3) An amendment made under this section shall be sufficiently authenticated by the initials of the clerk of the court.

DEFINITIONS

"complaint": s.138 and Sched. 5.
"offence": s.307(1).
"previous conviction": s.307(5).

GENERAL NOTE

The Act permits wide powers of amendment to a summary complaint but subject to the proviso that the amendment proposed must not alter the character of the offence charged, and cannot be used *Fundamental Nullity* to validate a complaint which is radically defective in its essentials (*Stevenson v McLevy* (1879) 4 Couper 196; *Lowe v Bee*, 1989 S.C.C.R. 476). Note that no one can be competently convicted upon a complaint which is a fundamental nullity and, accordingly, there has been no tholed assize (*Thomson, Petr*, 1997 S.L.T. 322).

The court cannot amend the complaint *ex proprio motu* in the absence of such a motion from the prosecutor (*Grant v Lockhart*, Crown Office Circular A3/91). The refusal or grant of a proposed amendment rests in the discretion of the trial judge and will not readily be interfered with by the Appeal Court (*Cumming v Frame* (1909) 6 Adam 57). Such a motion can be made at any point in the case prior to the determination of proceedings (see *Cochrane v The West Calder Cooperative Society*, 1978 S.L.T. (Notes) 22 and *Matheson v Ross* (1885) 5 Couper 582, where the date libelled was found to be incorrect after the close of the Crown case, the accused not being prejudiced and declining an adjournment). The point in the proceedings at which amendment is moved can itself be significant; in *MacArthur v MacNeill*, 1986 S.C.C.R. 552; 1987 S.L.T. 299 the Crown sought to amend a road traffic complaint, substituting failure to supply a blood specimen in a libel which originally averred failure to provide breath specimens at the close of evidence, a manoeuvre which the Appeal Court held to have changed the character of the offence (compare with *Fenwick v Valentine*, 1994 S.L.T. 485; 1993 S.C.C.R. 892).

See also *Phillips v Houston*, 2003 S.C.C.R. 653 where a Crown motion to amend the libel to add previously unspecified sexual misconduct at the close of the Crown evidence was rejected on appeal. The Appeal Court observed that amendment might properly have been allowed if it had been moved when the evidence first came out and objection to it had been taken.

Amendment of the Preamble and Instance

Adding a heading to the complaint to read "Under the Summary Jurisdiction (Scotland) Acts 1864 and 1881, and the Criminal Procedure (Scotland) Act 1887" by amendment, was allowed in *Finlayson v Bunbury* (1898) 2 Adam 478; correction of the heading on a complaint which referred to a District Court jurisdiction when the accused had been cited to, and the case called in, the relevant sheriff court was upheld on appeal (*Doonin Plant v Lees*, 1994 S.L.T. 313; 1993 S.C.C.R. 511).

Altering the name of the accused even after the statutory time bar has expired was allowed in *Hoyers (U.K.) v Houston*, 1991 S.L.T. 934; 1991 S.C.C.R. 919 and see also *Ralston v Carmichael*, 1995 G.W.D. 38–1933 discussed in Notes to s.143 above. More curiously in *Montgomery Transport v Walkingshaw*, 1992 S.C.C.R. 17 the complainers brought a Bill of Suspension following a guilty plea to a complaint which, it was later discovered, had libelled the wrong section of the statute albeit the narrative accurately set out the offence: they argued the complaint to be a nullity, but the High Court treated it as merely irrelevant and capable of amendment noting that the complainers had not taken objection before the sheriff.

However in *Lockhart v British School of Motoring*, 1982 S.C.C.R. 118, amendment to the libel was refused on the grounds that, if allowed, it would deprive co-accused of a statutory defence. Amendment to change the identity of the accused was refused in *Valentine v Thistle Leisure*, 1983 S.C.C.R. 515; by contrast, amendment of a nature which altered the capacity of the accused was allowed on appeal in *Tudhope v Chung*, 1985 S.C.C.R. 139.

Amendment of Offence Dates

See *Matheson v Ross* cited above. In *Duffy v Ingram* (also cited above), where the offence date was omitted in the first charge and adopted in the second charge and detailed as "said 30 November 1985" in the last charge on the complaint, an objection to relevancy was repelled by the sheriff who allowed amendments to cure the defects in the libel. In *McFadyen v Kerr*, 2002 G.W.D. 9-281, following dismissal of a complaint as a nullity which did not contain the year in an offence date, a Crown Bill of Advocation succeeded. In fact the complaint contained a bail aggravation dated October 5, 2000 and the trial occurred on November 20 of that year; on that basis *Duffy v Ingram* was binding, and the bill was passed and case remitted to the sheriff to proceed.

Amendment of Locus

It is generally competent to amend the locus stated in a summary charge so as to bring the libel into accord with the evidence, and amendment should be permitted unless it alters the nature of the charge. Amendment is permissible even if it involves including a locus outwith the court's jurisdiction (see *Craig v Keane*, 1982 S.L.T. 198; 1981 S.C.C.R. 166 and, more generally, *Belcher v MacKinnon*, 1987 S.L.T. 298).

In *Herron v Gemmell*, 1975 S.L.T. (Notes) 93 the sheriff refused an amendment to add "Glasgow" to the specification "on the road on the Glasgow Inner Ring Road, at a part thereof near Charing Cross underpass" a decision which was overturned on appeal.

A more radical amendment in *Brown v McLeod*, 1986 S.C.C.R. 615 had the effect of extending the locus to include driving between two towns. In response, the sheriff offered the defence the opportunity of an adjournment to lead additional evidence in light of the amendment but this was declined. His decision was upheld on appeal. Similarly in *Tudhope v Fulton*, 1986 S.C.C.R. 567 amendment of the *locus delicti*, where the offence was failure to provide breath specimens at an incorrectly specified police office, was allowed on appeal; this follows reasoning similar to that employed in *Belcher v MacKinnon* cited above.

Where the *locus* is inspecific, as above, the acid test is whether the details specified in the libel are sufficient to enable the court to ascertain whether it has jurisdiction or not; see *Yarrow Shipbuilders Ltd v Normand*, 1995 S.L.T. 1215; 1995 S.C.C.R. 224 and *Caven v Cumming*, 1998 S.L.T. 768.

Amendment and Statutory Offences

Amendment may be used to alter an incorrectly specified contravention of statute or regulations, but must not change the nature of the offence libelled. In *MacKenzie v Brougham*, 1985 S.L.T. 276; 1984 S.C.C.R. 434, the charge narrated the statute and regulations contravened but omitted reference to the precise regulation which created a criminal offence and was poorly specified; it was held that the complaint was not a nullity and could be cured by amendment. Amendment of a complaint to reflect the terms of the current statutory legislation is competent even where this renders an accused liable, on conviction, to an increased penalty (*Wadbister Offshore Ltd v Adam*, 1998 S.L.T. 33 following *Cook v Jessop* cited below). The broad test to be applied is whether the charge as specified affords the defence fair notice of what the Crown was seeking to prove; see *Blair v Keane*, 1981 S.L.T. (Notes) 4; *Clydesdale Group v Normand*, 1994 S.L.T. 1302; 1993 S.C.C.R. 958; *Gullett v Hamilton*, 1997 G.W.D. 14–592.

In *Sterling-Winthrop Group v Allan*, 1987 S.C.C.R. 25, a prosecution under the Health and Safety at Work etc. Act 1974 (c.37), objections to the relevancy of charges were repelled by the sheriff. Before the Appeal Court the Crown sought, and were permitted, to amend the charges to meet the objections previously stated. Even where a repealed statute has been libelled, amendment of the charge to make reference to the correct statutory provision is permissible, despite the greater penalties which can be imposed. See *Cook v Jessop*, 1990 S.C.C.R. 211, where a charge of harbouring an escaper from an approved school was made, contrary to the Children and Young Persons (Scotland) Act 1937, a statute which had been repealed and replaced by the Social Work (Scotland) Act 1968: it will be noted however that the libel gave clear warning of the character of the offence and there could be little cause to argue prejudice or lack of specification of the *species facti* (see also *High-Clad Roofing v Carmichael*, "The Scotsman" Law Reports, February 24, 1989, where the wrong regulation under the Factories Act 1961 (c.34) had been libelled).

Schedule 3 of the Act contains the provisions relating to latitudes in time and place and alternative verdicts which previously appeared in s.312 of the 1975 Act. Particularly, the terms of paras 11 to 14 are of significance in relation to the libelling of statutory offences.

The Nomen Juris

It is well accepted that the charge in an indictment need not specify the *nomen juris* of the alleged crime, it being sufficient that the facts described in the libel are relevant and set forth a crime known to the law of Scotland (*Cameron v H.M. Advocate*, 1971 S.L.T. 333 (piracy)). By the same token, since it is the *species facti* which indicate the nature of the crime complained of, and not the *nomen juris* attached (*Lippe v Wilson*, 1997 G.W.D. 17–766), it follows that amendment of the *nomen juris* is competent (see *Dyce v Aitchison*, 1985 S.C.C.R. 184 (contempt of court libelled)).

No case to answer

160.—(1) Immediately after the close of the evidence for the prosecution, the accused may intimate to the court his desire to make a submission that he has no case to answer both—

  (a) on an offence charged in the complaint; and

  (b) on any other offence of which he could be convicted under the complaint were the offence charged the only offence so charged.

(2) If, after hearing both parties, the judge is satisfied that the evidence led by the prosecution is insufficient in law to justify the accused being convicted of the offence charged in respect of which the submission has been made or of such other offence as is mentioned, in relation to that offence, in paragraph (b) of subsection (1) above, he shall acquit him of the offence charged in respect of which the submission has been made and the trial shall proceed only in respect of any other offence charged in the complaint.

(3) If, after hearing both parties, the judge is not satisfied as is mentioned in subsection (2) above, he shall reject the submission and the trial shall proceed, with the accused entitled to give evidence and call witnesses, as if such submission had not been made.

DEFINITIONS
"complaint": s.307(1).
"judge": s.307(1).
"offence": s.307(1).

GENERAL NOTE

The sufficiency in law of evidence presented by the prosecution falls to be considered at the close of the Crown case. The criteria for acceptance or rejection of a no case to answer submission were set out in *Williamson v Wither*, 1981 S.C.C.R. 214, but the court must also assess the admissibility at that stage of evidence led in support of the prosecution case (see *Jessop v Kerr*, 1989 S.C.C.R. 417) and make known the result of this assessment. See also *Gonshaw v Bamber*, 2004 S.L.T. 1270 where the Appeal Court held that the sheriff had erred in rejecting a submission of no case to answer and the accused simply should not have been placed in a dilemma as to whether or not to lead evidence in his defence. In the absence of a sufficiency of evidence at that point in the proceedings a miscarriage of justice had occurred.

The court must give both parties the opportunity to make submissions before reaching a decision on sufficiency, and cannot consider the issue in the absence of a motion from the accused (*Stewart v Lowe*, 1991 S.C.C.R. 317—a case in which the sheriff had rejected a submission without having heard from the prosecutor, and convicted the accused without first hearing from the defence agent; see also *Taylor v Douglas*, 1984 S.L.T. 69). Where a number of submissions are advanced, the court is obliged to determine upon them all, rather than dismissing the case upon a consideration of only one. Consideration of all submissions avoids needless duplication of appeal procedures in the event of the Crown successfully appealing the court's original decision on sufficiency (*Lockhart v Milne*, 1992 S.C.C.R. 864). In *Duffin v Normand*, 1993 S.C.C.R. 864, the court having rejected a submission under the section, and there being no defence evidence, proceeded to convict without hearing further from the parties: the court is obliged to hear submissions at the close of evidence upon the quality of evidence, an issue which cannot be considered at the time of a s.160 submission. The conviction was quashed.

The form of questions to be posed in stated cases challenging decisions on submissions of no case to answer are discussed in the commentary to *Cassidy v Normand*, 1994 S.C.C.R. 325, while guidance on the form of the stated case itself is given in *Keane v Bathgate*, 1983 S.L.T. 651, since at that stage in the case the court cannot state findings-in-fact.

It will be noted that in *Tudhope v Stewart*, 1986 S.L.T. 659; 1986 S.C.C.R. 384 it was held that use of a no case to answer submission, founding upon the inadmissibility of evidence which had earlier been led without objection, was inappropriate (see also *Skeen v Murphy*, 1978 S.L.T. (Notes) 2 and *McGee v McNaughton*, 1996 G.W.D. 17–977, discussed at A4–227 and A4–227.1 above; as a general rule objections to the admissibility of evidence should be taken at the time when that evidence is tendered).

In *Walls v Heywood*, 2000 S.L.T. 841; 2000 S.C.C.R. 21 where the lay magistrate returned a guilty verdict at the s.160 stage, and had to be corrected by the assessor, it was held on appeal, following *Lorimar v Normand*, 1997 S.L.T.1277; 1997 S.C.C.R. 582 that the necessity for an intervention by the assessor might lead an impartial observer to conclude that the judge had reached a verdict prematurely.

Defence to speak last

161. In any trial the accused or, where he is legally represented, his counsel or solicitor shall have the right to speak last.

GENERAL NOTE

"There is no doubt that the panel is entitled to the last word in criminal trials": *Watson v Stuart* (1878) 4 Couper 67. See also *Duffin v Normand* discussed in the notes to s.160 above. Similarly, following conviction the defence must be offered the opportunity to plead in mitigation, before sentence is considered (*Meikle v Lees*, 1997 G.W.D. 3–88).

In *Watson v Griffiths*, 2004 G.W.D 34–694 it was held that even if there had been a breach of s.161 any such breach did not automatically lead to the proceedings being regarded as null. It was seriously doubted in the circumstances of this case whether there had been a breach and it was held that there had been no oppression

Verdict and conviction

Judges equally divided

162. In a summary prosecution in a court consisting of more than one judge, if the judges are equally divided in opinion as to the guilt of the accused, the accused shall be found not guilty of the charge or part thereof on which such division of opinion exists.

DEFINITION

"judge": s.307(1).

GENERAL NOTE

Where two judges sit and reach different verdicts, no conviction can follow (*Dorward v Mackay* (1870) 1 Couper 392).

Conviction: miscellaneous provisions

163.—(1) Where imprisonment is authorised by the sentence of a court of summary jurisdiction, an extract of the finding and sentence in the form prescribed by Act of Adjournal shall be a sufficient warrant for the apprehension and commitment of the accused, and no such extract shall be void or liable to be set aside on account of any error or defect in point of form.

(2) In any proceedings in a court of summary jurisdiction consisting of more than one judge, the signature of one judge shall be sufficient in all warrants or other proceedings prior or subsequent to conviction, and it shall not be necessary that the judge so signing shall be one of the judges trying or dealing with the case otherwise.

DEFINITIONS

"court of summary jurisdiction": s.307(1).
"imprisonment": s.307(1).
"judge": s.307(1).

Conviction of part of charge

164. A conviction of a part or parts only of the charge or charges libelled in a complaint shall imply dismissal of the rest of the complaint.

DEFINITIONS

"complaint": s.307(1).

"Conviction" and "sentence" not to be used for children

165. The words "conviction" and "sentence" shall not be used in relation to children dealt with summarily and any reference in any enactment, whether passed before or after the commencement of this Act, to a person convicted, a conviction or a sentence shall in the case of a child be construed as including a reference to a person found guilty of an offence, a finding of guilt or an order made upon such a finding as the case may be.

DEFINITIONS

"child": s.307(1) and the Children (Scotland) Act 1995, s.93(2)(b).
"enactment": s.307(1).
"finding of guilt": s.307(8).
"sentence": s.307(1).

Previous convictions: summary proceedings

166.—(1) This section shall apply where the accused in a summary prosecution has been previously convicted of any offence and the prosecutor has decided to lay a previous conviction before the court.

(2) A notice in the form prescribed by Act of Adjournal or as nearly as may be in such form specifying the previous conviction shall be served on the accused with the complaint where he is cited to a diet, and where he is in custody the complaint and such a notice shall be served on him before he is asked to plead.

(3) The previous conviction shall not, subject to section 275A(1) of this Act, be laid before the judge until he is satisfied that the charge is proved.

(4) If a plea of guilty is tendered or if, after a plea of not guilty, the accused is convicted the prosecutor shall lay the notice referred to in subsection (2) above before the judge, and—

(a) in a case where the plea of guilty is tendered in writing the accused shall be deemed to admit any previous conviction set forth in the notice, unless he expressly denies it in the writing by which the plea is tendered;

(b) in any other case the judge or the clerk of court shall ask the accused whether he admits the previous conviction,

and if such admission is made or deemed to be made it shall be entered in the record of the proceedings; and it shall not be necessary for the prosecutor to produce extracts of any previous convictions so admitted.

(5) Where the accused does not admit any previous conviction, the prosecutor unless he withdraws the conviction shall adduce evidence in proof thereof either then or at any other diet.

(6) A copy of any notice served on the accused under this section shall be entered in the record of the proceedings.

(7) Where a person is convicted of an offence, the court may have regard to any previous conviction in respect of that person in deciding on the disposal of the case.

(8) Nothing in this section shall prevent the prosecutor—

(a) asking the accused questions tending to show that the accused has been convicted of an offence other than that with which he is charged, where he is entitled to do so under section 266 of this Act; or

(b) leading evidence of previous convictions where it is competent to do so—

(i) as evidence in support of a substantive charge; or

(ii) under section 270 of this Act.

AMENDMENT

Subs.(3) as amended by the Sexual Offences (Procedure and Evidence) (Scotland) (Act) 2002 (asp 9), s.10(2). Brought into force by the Sexual Offences (Procedure and Evidence) (Scotland) Act 2002 (Commencement and Transitional Provisions) Order 2002 (SSI 2002/443 (C.24)), art.4 (effective November 1, 2002).

DEFINITIONS

"complaint": s.307(1).
"diet": s.307(1).
"judge": s.307(1).
"offence": s.307(1).
"previous conviction": s.307(1).
"prosecutor": s.307(1).

GENERAL NOTE

The general principles of placing previous convictions before the court are discussed in the notes to s.101 above. Unless adducing a previous conviction is necessary to prove the substantive charge, or the accused has either attacked the character of Crown witnesses or misrepresented his own character, no reference can be made to the accused's criminal record until he has been convicted.

Any previous convictions to be founded upon by the Crown for the purposes of sentence must accompany the citation and service copy complaint (see Rule 16.1.–(4) and Form 16.1–E in the 1996

Act of Adjournal) and have to be laid before the court by the prosecutor; see *Clark v Connell*, 1952 J.C. 119; 1952 S.L.T. 421; convictions which have not been libelled cannot be considered by the court (*Adair v Hill*, 1943 J.C. 9 and *Massily Packaging (U.K.) Ltd. v MacDonald*, 1997 G.W.D. 3–87 discussed at A4–309 above) except where they are referred to in a social enquiry report prepared for the purpose of sentence (*Sharp v Stevenson*, 1948 S.L.T. (Notes) 79; *Sillars v Copeland*, 1966 C.L.R. 686); in such circumstances the accused should be afforded the opportunity of admitting or denying such additional convictions. The growth of European Union legislation raises previously unconsidered issues. In *Redman v Sehmel*, 1997 G.W.D. 9–370, the accused plead guilty to contravening Articles of the Sea Fishing (Enforcement of Community Control Measures) Order 1994, by failing to record his vessel's true catch and admitted a prior conviction for the same offence only weeks earlier imposed by an Irish court. While not a conviction imposed by a UK court, it is submitted that the earlier conviction was competently libelled in the circumstances; attention is drawn to the terms of s.57(5) of the Criminal Justice (Scotland) Act 2003 (asp 7) which has extended the definition of "previous conviction" to include previous convictions imposed upon an accused by courts in member states of the European Union. European convictions can competently be libelled in a schedule of previous convictions, and can be proved by certification of fingerprints as set out in s.286A of the Act in any criminal proceedings with effect from June 27, 2003.

It will be noted that subs.(4)(a) continues the presumption that any convictions not expressly disputed by the accused when tendering a letter plea are held to be admitted. Difficulty can arise where the plea contained in a letter is rejected by the prosecutor; care then has to be taken to ensure that any schedule of convictions is not retained with the complaint at any subsequent diet, though this has been held not to amount to laying of convictions before the court by the prosecutor (see *O'Neill v Tudhope*, 1984 S.L.T. 424; 1984 S.C.C.R. 276). See also *McKee v Brown*, 2000 G.W.D. 34–1302 where, after a change of plea, the accused's schedule of convictions remained with the complaint and was seen and troubled the trial judge, the conviction was quashed. It would have been preferable for the proceedings to be deserted but parties may have felt compelled to proceed with the trial because the case (which centred on Road Traffic Act offences) would otherwise be timebarred.

The use of extract convictions as evidence in support of a substantive charge, for example the Road Traffic Act 1988 (c.52), s.103 (driving while disqualified) has generated a considerable volume of case law. The cardinal rule is that so far as practicable, the extract used must disclose only the minimum necessary to prove the currency of a disqualification and nothing more (see *Mitchell v Dean*, 1979 S.L.T. (Notes) 12; *Boustead v McLeod*, 1979 S.L.T. (Notes) 48) but note also *Moffat v Robertson*, 1983 S.C.C.R. 392 in which a defence appeal against conviction, founding upon the use of an extract conviction which libelled both driving without a licence and without insurance, was held *not* to be prejudicial.

The general principles applicable to the disclosure either wilfully or inadvertently by the prosecutor are discussed in the notes to s.101; see also *Kerr v Jessop*, 1991 S.C.C.R. 27, an instance of questioning too far and thus breaching the provision and *Carmichael v Monaghan*, 1987 S.L.T. 338; 1986 S.C.C.R. 598, where the sheriff's decision that there had been a breach by the unanticipated revelation that the accused had been apprehended in relation to a means warrant, was overruled. *Kerr v Jessop* was followed in *MacLean v Buchanan*, 1997 S.L.T. 91, the sheriff holding that the adducing of a reply in breach of this provision (but which had been led without objection) was the result of inexperience or lack of preparation, a careless incident which had not been pressed further.

Section 32 of the Road Traffic Offenders Act 1988 (c.53) permits a court, when considering discretionary or obligatory disqualification from driving, to refer to a DVLA printout where the accused does not produce his driving licence. *Hamilton v Ruxton*, 2001 S.L.T. 351; 2001 S.C.C.R. 1 clarifies that such a printout can be founded upon whether the accused fails to produce his licence, has already been disqualified or has never held a licence at all. Similarly in *Clampett v Stott*, 2001 S.C.C.R. 860; 2001 G.W.D. 33–1307 no breach of the section occurred where the Crown had lodged copy papers in support of an allegation that the accused had been subject of a (disputed) bail order which disclosed previous convictions. The Appeal Court ruled that the convictions had not been produced in pursuance of s.166 and, in any event, the convictions had been unknown to the sheriff until the accused directed attention to them in support of a motion for acquittal. The Crown's actions were considered to be careless, not deliberate.

Refer to s.285 in relation to proof of previous convictions by means of a certificate completed on behalf of the Chief Constable and s.286, which provides means by which the service of extract convictions upon the accused can be treated as sufficient evidence.

Forms of finding and sentence

167.—(1) Every sentence imposed by a court of summary jurisdiction shall unless otherwise provided be pronounced in open court in the presence of the accused, but need not be written out or signed in his presence.

(2) The finding and sentence and any order of a court of summary jurisdiction, as regards both offences at common law and offences under any enactment, shall be entered in the record of the proceedings in the form, as nearly as may be, prescribed by Act of Adjournal.

(3) The record of the proceedings shall be sufficient warrant for all execution on a finding, sentence or order and for the clerk of court to issue extracts containing such executive clauses as may be necessary for implement thereof.

(4) When imprisonment forms part of any sentence or other judgement, warrant for the apprehension and interim detention of the accused pending his being committed to prison shall, where necessary, be implied.

(5) Where a fine imposed by a court of summary jurisdiction is paid at the bar it shall not be necessary for the court to refer to the period of imprisonment applicable to the non-payment thereof.

(6) Where several charges at common law or under any enactment are embraced in one complaint, a cumulo penalty may be imposed in respect of all or any of such charges of which the accused is convicted.

(7) Subject to section 204A of this Act, a court of summary jurisdiction may frame—

(a) a sentence following on conviction; or

(b) an order for committal in default of payment of any sum of money or for contempt of court,

so as to take effect on the expiry of any previous sentence for a term or order which, at the date of the later conviction or order, the accused is undergoing.

(7A) Where the court imposes a sentence as mentioned in paragraph (a) of subsection (7) above for an offence committed after the coming into force of this subsection, the court may—

(a) if the person is serving or is liable to serve the punishment part of a previous sentence, frame the sentence to take effect on the day after that part of that sentence is or would be due to expire; or

(b) if the person is serving or is liable to serve the punishment parts of two or more previous sentences, frame the sentence to take effect on the day after the later or (as the case may be) latest expiring of those parts is or would be due to expire.

(7B) Where it falls to the court to sentence a person who is subject to a previous sentence in respect of which a punishment part requires to be (but has not been) specified, the court shall not sentence the person until such time as the part is either specified or no longer requires to be specified.

(7C) In subsections (7A) and (7B) above, any reference to a punishment part of a sentence shall be construed by reference to—

(a) the punishment part of the sentence as is specified in an order mentioned in section 2(2) of the 1993 Act; or

(b) any part of the sentence which has effect, by virtue of section 10 of the 1993 Act or the schedule to the Convention Rights (Compliance) (Scotland) Act 2001 (asp 7), as if it were the punishment part so specified,

and "the 1993 Act" means the Prisoners and Criminal Proceedings (Scotland) Act 1993 (c.9).

(8) It shall be competent at any time before imprisonment has followed on a sentence for the court to alter or modify it; but no higher sentence than that originally pronounced shall be competent, and—

(a) the signature of the judge or clerk of court to any sentence shall be sufficient also to authenticate the findings on which such sentence proceeds; and

(b) the power conferred by this subsection to alter or modify a sentence may be exercised without requiring the attendance of the accused.

AMENDMENT

Subs.(7) inserted by the Crime and Disorder Act 1998 (c.37), Sch.8, para.122 (effective September 30, 1998: SI 1998/2327).

Subs.(7) as amended, and subss.(7A)–(7C) inserted, by Criminal Justice (Scotland) Act 2003 (asp 7), Part 4, s.26. Brought into force on December 1, 2003 by the Criminal Justice (Scotland) Act 2003 (Commencement No.3 and Revocation) Order 2003 (SSI 2003/475 (C.26)), art.2.

DEFINITIONS

"complaint": s.307(1).
"court of summary jurisdiction": s.307(1).
"enactment": s.307(1).
"fine": s.307(1).
"imprisonment": s.307(6).
"judge": s.307(1).
"offences": s.307(1).
"prison": s.307(1).
"sentence": s.307(1).

GENERAL NOTE

While sentence is normally pronounced in the accused's presence this does not apply to the circumstances covered by s.150(5) or, arguably, where the accused misconducts himself in the course of his trial (s.153(2)) provided he is legally represented. Section 144(6) of the Act provides that sentences of imprisonment or detention cannot be imposed in the absence of the accused. Confusion over findings or correction of findings, following the justice's evident confusion over the role played by each of the accused, resulted in the quashing of convictions in *Taylor v Craigen*, 2002 G.W.D. 38–1251.

Subsection (6) enacts that *cumulo* sentences can be imposed in relation to all the charges libelled on a complaint; conversely if the Crown elects to place on separate complaints, matters which could properly have been incorporated in one complaint, then consecutive sentences should not be imposed; *Kesson v Heatly*, 1964 J.C. 40. See also *Noble v Guild*, 1987 S.C.C.R. 518 where a delay in imposing a sentence of imprisonment rendered it incompetent to apply imprisonment consecutive to a term which by then was already being served. However, where an accused was sentenced on indictment to 18-months' detention and had outstanding fines, the Appeal Court upheld the imposition of the alternative periods of detention in lieu of the fines, these being effective consecutive to each other, and to the 18-months' sentence (*Cartledge v McLeod*, 1988 S.L.T. 389; 1988 S.C.C.R. 129). The fact that an earlier sentence is the subject of appeal, and thus is not being "undergone", does not debar a court sentencing in respect of other matters from imposing a consecutive sentence to begin at such time as the matter under appeal is resolved (*Thorne v Stott*, 1999 G.W.D. 28–1332).

The appropriateness and effect upon eligibility for licence of consecutive terms of detention were discussed in *Clayton, Petr*, 1992 S.L.T. 404.

Section 218(2) sets out the table of fines and alternative periods of imprisonment applicable to proceedings under the Act. The minimum period of imprisonment which can be imposed summarily is five days (see s.205).

Caution

168.—(1) This section applies with regard to the finding, forfeiture, and recovery of caution in any proceedings under this Part of this Act.

(2) Caution may be found by consignation of the amount with the clerk of court, or by bond of caution signed by the cautioner.

(3) Where caution becomes liable to forfeiture, forfeiture may be granted by the court on the motion of the prosecutor, and, where necessary, warrant granted for the recovery of the caution.

(4) Where a cautioner fails to pay the amount due under his bond within six days after he has received a charge to that effect, the court may—

(a) order him to be imprisoned for the maximum period applicable in pursuance of section 219 of this Act to that amount or until payment is made; or

(b) if it considers it expedient, on the application of the cautioner grant time for payment; or

(c) instead of ordering imprisonment, order recovery by civil diligence in accordance with section 221 of this Act.

DEFINITIONS

"imprisonment": s.306(7).
"prosecutor": s.307(1).

Detention in precincts of court

169.—(1) Where a court of summary jurisdiction has power to impose imprisonment or detention on an offender it may, in lieu of so doing and subject to subsection (2) below, order that the offender be detained within the precincts of the court or at any police station, till such hour, not later than eight in the evening on the day on which he is convicted, as the court may direct.

(2) Before making an order under this section a court shall take into consideration the distance between the proposed place of detention and the offender's residence (if known to, or ascertainable by, the court), and shall not make any such order under this section as would deprive the offender of a reasonable opportunity of returning to his residence on the day on which the order is made.

DEFINITIONS

"court of summary jurisdiction": s.307(1).
"impose imprisonment or detention": s.307(1).
"imprisonment": s.307(6).

GENERAL NOTE

This is a rarely-used sentencing provision and would appear to escape the restrictions placed upon the imposition of sentences of imprisonment or detention contained in s.203(1) and (2) below. The style of the order of detention is contained in Form 18.6 of the 1996 Act of Adjournal.

Miscellaneous

Damages in respect of summary proceedings

170.—(1) No judge, clerk of court or prosecutor in the public interest shall be found liable by any court in damages for or in respect of any proceedings taken, act done, or judgment, decree or sentence pronounced in any summary proceedings under this Act, unless—

(a) the person suing has suffered imprisonment in consequence thereof; and

(b) such proceedings, act, judgment, decree or sentence has been quashed; and

(c) the person suing specifically avers and proves that such proceeding, act, judgment, decree or sentence was taken, done or pronounced maliciously and without probable cause.

(2) No such liability as aforesaid shall be incurred or found where such judge,

clerk of court or prosecutor establishes that the person suing was guilty of the offence in respect whereof he had been convicted, or on account of which he had been apprehended or had otherwise suffered, and that he had undergone no greater punishment than was assigned by law to such offence.

(3) No action to enforce such liability as aforesaid shall lie unless it is commenced within two months after the proceeding, act, judgment decree or sentence founded on, or in the case where the Act under which the action is brought fixes a shorter period, within that shorter period.

(4) In this section "judge" shall not include "sheriff", and the provisions of this section shall be without prejudice to the privileges and immunities possessed by sheriffs.

DEFINITIONS

"imprisonment": s.307(6).
"judge": ss.170(6) and 307(1).
"prosecutor": s.307(1).
"sentence": s.307(1).

GENERAL NOTE

In the conduct of proceedings on indictment the Lord Advocate, and subordinates appointed by him to prepare and conduct such proceedings, enjoy absolute privilege and thus immunity from actions for damages (see *Hester v MacDonald*, 1961 S.C. 370; 1961 S.L.T. 414). This immunity extends to procurators fiscal in solemn proceedings but is restricted in summary proceedings by the operation of s.170: the right to seek damages from the criminal authorities in relation to any summary proceedings is available to an accused person who can satisfy all the requirements of subs.(1); see *Graham v Strathern*, 1924 S.C. 699. Any proceedings must be commenced within two months of the conduct complained of or any shorter period specifically stated. Subsection (2) provides immunity from civil liability for court officials only while they are proceeding under the Act (*Graham v Strathern* at 724; *Ferguson v MacDonald* (1885) 12 Rettie 1083). The practical effect of subs.(4) is to afford a sheriff sitting in summary proceedings a greater degree of immunity at common law, than was conferred on other judges in summary proceedings. See the extensive discussion of the issue in *Russell v Dickson*, 1997 G.W.D. 22–1058.

See *Bell v McGlennan*, 1992 S.L.T. 237, where proceedings were held to have been competently raised against the prosecutor as vicariously liable over the retention of property as evidence in a case which did not proceed, due to the intervention of the statutory time bar.

Maliciously and without probable cause

The most difficult legal obstacle for a pursuer seeking damages in respect of summary proceedings is the requirement to aver and prove that the action complained of had been taken or done *maliciously and without probable cause*: see s.170(1)(c) *supra*. The difficulty lies in the requirement that the standard of averment and proof is high, requiring the basis of any claim of malice to be described with particular clarity in the pleadings: *McKie v Strathclyde Joint Police Board*, 2004 G.W.D. 2–38

Recovery of penalties

171.—(1) All penalties, for the recovery of which no special provision has been made by any enactment may be recovered by the public prosecutor in any court having jurisdiction.

(2) Where a court has power to take cognisance of an offence the penalty attached to which is not defined, the punishment therefore shall be regulated by that applicable to common law offences in that court.

DEFINITIONS

"offence": s.307(1).
"prosecutor": s.307(1).

Unless it is expressly stipulated to the contrary by statute, the public prosecutor holds a general title to prosecute for the recovery of penalties (subs.(1)). In the absence of any express provision, the competent punishment in summary proceedings shall be dictated by reference to the penalties applicable to common law offences (see s.21).

Forms of procedure

172.—(1) The forms of procedure for the purposes of summary proceedings under this Act and appeals therefrom shall be in such forms as are prescribed by Act of Adjournal or as nearly as may be in such forms.

(2) All warrants (other than warrants of apprehension or search), orders of court, and sentences may be signed either by the judge or by the clerk of court, and execution upon any warrant, order of court, or sentence may proceed either upon such warrant, order of court, or sentence itself or upon an extract thereof issued and signed by the clerk of court.

(3) Where, preliminary to any procedure, a statement on oath is required, the statement may be given before any judge, whether the subsequent procedure is in his court or another court.

DEFINITIONS

"judge": s.307(1).
"sentence": s.307(1).

GENERAL NOTE

The 1996 Act of Adjournal substantially revises the format of many forms to be utilised in criminal proceedings.

Although subs.(2) provides that all warrants (except those for apprehension or search) may be subscribed by the judge or the clerk of court, and that extracts thereof shall be equally valid, this presupposes that the order or warrant must first have been granted by a judge (see *Skeen v Ives Cladding*, 1976 S.L.T. (Notes) 31). Failure to complete proper minutes of proceedings and thus maintain a proper record of the proceedings is a fundamental defect (*Heywood v Stewart* C.O. Circ. A54/91).

PART X

APPEALS FROM SUMMARY PROCEEDINGS

General

Quorum of High Court in relation to appeals

173.—(1) For the purpose of hearing and determining any appeal under this Part of this Act, or any proceeding connected therewith, three of the Lords Commissioners of Justiciary shall be a quorum of the High Court, and the determination of any question under this Part of this Act by the court shall be according to the votes of the majority of the members of the court sitting, including the presiding judge, and each judge so sitting shall be entitled to pronounce a separate opinion.

(2) For the purpose of hearing and determining appeals under section 175(2)(b) or (c) or (cb) of this Act, or any proceeding connected therewith, two of the Lords Commissioners of Justiciary shall be a quorum of the High Court, and each judge shall be entitled to pronounce a separate opinion; but where the two Lords Commissioners of Justiciary are unable to reach agreement on the disposal of the appeal, or where they consider it appropriate, the appeal shall be heard and determined in accordance with subsection (1) above.

AMENDMENT

AMENDMENT

Subs.(2) as amended by the Protection of Children (Scotland) Act 2003 (asp 5), s.16(6). Brought into force on January 10, 2005 by the Protection of Children (Scotland) Act 2003 (Commencement No.1) Order 2004 (SSI 2004/522 (C.38)), art.2.

DEFINITIONS

"High Court": s.307(1).
"judge": s.307(1).
"Lords Commissioners of Justiciary": s.307(1).

GENERAL NOTE

Part X of this Act is concerned with appeals from summary proceedings. For the purpose of hearing and determining any appeal under this Part of this Act the quorum of judges is three: s.173(1). However, for the purpose of hearing and determining appeals against sentence or against absolute discharge or admonition or any probation order or any community service order or any order deferring sentence the quorum of judges is two: s.173(2). If the two judges cannot agree or consider it appropriate for another reason, *e.g.* consideration of a point of law by a larger court they can remit to three judges, *e.g. Bain v. Wilson*, 1998 S.C.C.R. 454. This provision, particularly the latter, is likely to reduce the considerable burden that has been placed on appellate judges because of the enormous increase in appeals, and especially appeals against summary sentences.

Appeals relating to preliminary pleas — *Competency, Relevancy etc*

174.—(1) Without prejudice to any right of appeal under section 175(1) to (6) or 191 of this Act, a party may, with the leave of the court (granted either on the motion of the party or *ex proprio motu*) and in accordance with such procedure as may be prescribed by Act of Adjournal, appeal to the High Court against a decision of the court of first instance (other than a decision not to grant leave under this subsection) which relates to such objection or denial as is mentioned in section 144(4) of this Act; but such appeal must be taken not later than two days after such decision.

(2) Where an appeal is taken under subsection (1) above, the High Court may postpone the trial diet (if one has been fixed) for such period as appears to it to be appropriate and may, if it thinks fit, direct that such period (or some part of it) shall not count towards any time limit applying in respect of the case.

(3) If leave to appeal under subsection (1) above is granted by the court it shall not proceed to trial at once under subsection (2) of section 146 of this Act; and subsection (3) of that section shall be construed as requiring sufficient time to be allowed for the appeal to be taken.

(4) In disposing of an appeal under subsection (1) above the High Court may affirm the decision of the court of first instance or may remit the case to it with such directions in the matter as it thinks fit; and where the court of first instance had dismissed the complaint, or any part of it, may reverse that decision and direct that the court of first instance fix a trial diet (if it has not already fixed one as regards so much of the complaint as it has not dismissed.)

DEFINITIONS

"diet": s.307(1).
"High Court": s.307(1).

GENERAL NOTE

Section 184(4) of this Act follows on the provision in s.334(2A) of the 1975 Act. These subsections require any objection to the competency, relevancy of a summary complaint or the proceedings thereon, or any denial that the accused is the person charged by the police with the offence shall be stated before the accused pleads to the charge or any plea is tendered on his behalf.

Section 174(1) allows "a party" with leave of the court to appeal to the High Court of Justiciary against a decision of the court of first instance which relates to such objection or denial as is mentioned in s.144(4). This appeal must be taken within two days after that decision. Refusal of leave to appeal is not applicable.

Practitioners should remember that there are two hurdles in relation to appeals relating to preliminary pleas. First, appeal must be made with the leave of the court although such leave may be either on the motion of the party or *ex proprio motu*. Secondly, a note of appeal is required to be lodged with the sheriff clerk. For the procedure under the 1975 Act, see Act of Adjournal (Consolidation) 1988, rr.34 and 35. Form 17 of Sch.1 sets out the angle for the note of appeal.

For examples of the substantive and procedural complexities that can arise in this regard see *Johnston v MacGillivray*, 1993 S.L.T. 120 and *McLeay v Hingston*, 1994 S.L.T. 720. The Crown is a party and has a right of appeal: see *Walkingshaw v Robison & Davidson Ltd*, 1989 S.C.C.R. 359. In *HMA Advocate v Sorrie*, 1996 G.W.D. 30–1795 the Appeal Court indicated that if the Crown seek to use a Bill of Advocation rather than an appeal under the section the accused should be alerted to the fact. An accused person need not appeal a preliminary matter immediately but can appeal post-conviction by Stated Case or Bill of Suspension: see *Harvey v Lockhart*, 1991 J.C. 9.

Subsections (2), (3) and (4) make consequential provision for postponing the trial diet, allowing time for the appeal and setting out the powers of the High Court of Justiciary in relation to affirming the decision at first instance or remitting the case with directions. The Appeal Court in *MacNeill v Sutherland*, 1998 S.C.C.R. 474 observed that a sheriff should reach conclusions on all submissions made to him as part of a preliminary plea.

Subsection (2) allows for postponements. Postponements and adjournments are different. An adjournment occurs when a case calls at a settled diet, being a date fixed earlier, and then is put back: see *Mitchell v Reith*, 2004 S.C.C.R. 433 at 435 (para.6). This is contrasted with a postponement that occurs when the date of the diet is altered in advance of the date set originally: *ibid*.

Right of appeal

175.—(1) This section is without prejudice to any right of appeal under section 191 of this Act.

(2) Any person convicted, or found to have committed an offence, in summary proceedings may, with leave granted in accordance with section 180 or, as the case may be, 187 of this Act, appeal under this section to the High Court—

    (a) against such conviction, or finding;

    (b) against the sentence passed on such conviction;

    (c) against his absolute discharge or admonition or any probation order, drug treatment and testing order or any community service order or any order deferring sentence;

    (ca) against any decision to remit made under section 49(1)(a) or (7)(b) of this Act;

    (cb) against any reference proposed under section 10(1) of the Protection of Children (Scotland) Act 2003 (asp 5) in respect of the conviction or, as the case may be, against such reference and such sentence, disposal or order; or

    (d) against

        (i) both such conviction and such sentence or disposal or order;

        (ii) both such a conviction and such a reference; or

        (iii) such a conviction, such a reference and such sentence, disposal or order.

(3) The prosecutor in summary proceedings may appeal under this section to the High Court on a point of law—

    (a) against an acquittal in such proceedings; or

    (b) against a sentence passed on conviction in such proceedings.

(4) The prosecutor in summary proceedings, in any class of case specified by order made by the Secretary of State, may, in accordance with subsection (4A) below, appeal to the High Court against any of the following disposals, namely—

Prosecutor's right of appeal against sentence

(a) a sentence passed on conviction;

(b) a decision under section 209(1)(b) of this Act not to make a supervised release order;

(c) a decision under section 234A(2) of this Act not to make a non-harassment order;

(ca) a decision under section 92 of the Proceeds of Crime Act 2002 not to make a confiscation order;

(d) a probation order;

(dd) a drug treatment and testing order;

(e) a community service order;

(f) a decision to remit to the Principal Reporter made under section 49(1)(a) or (7)(b) of this Act;

(g) an order deferring sentence;

(h) an admonition; or

(i) an absolute discharge.

(4A) An appeal under subsection (4) above may be made—

(a) on a point of law;

(b) where it appears to the Lord Advocate, in relation to an appeal under—

(i) paragraph (a), (h) or (i) of that subsection, that the disposal was unduly lenient;

(ii) paragraph (b), (c) or (ca) of that subsection, that the decision not to make the order in question was inappropriate:

(iii) paragraph (d) to (e) of that subsection, that the making of the order concerned was unduly lenient or was on unduly lenient terms;

(iv) under paragraph (f) of that subsection, that the decision to remit was inappropriate;

(v) under paragraph (g) of that subsection, that the deferment of sentence was inappropriate or was on unduly lenient conditions.

(4B) For the purposes of subsection (4A)(b)(i) above in its application to a confiscation order by virtue of section 92(11) of the Proceeds of Crime Act 2002, the reference to the disposal being unduly lenient is a reference to the amount required to be paid by the order being unduly low.

(5) By an appeal under subsection (2) above, an appellant may bring under review of the High Court any alleged miscarriage of justice which may include such a miscarriage based, subject to subsections (5A) to (5D) below, on the existence and significance of evidence which was not heard at the original proceedings.

(5A) Evidence which was not heard at the original proceedings may found an appeal only where there is a reasonable explanation of why it was not so heard.

(5B) Where the explanation referred to in subsection (5A) above or, as the case may be, (5C) below is that the evidence was not admissible at the time of the original proceedings, but is admissible at the time of the appeal, the court may admit that evidence if it appears to the court that it would be in the interests of justice to do so.

(5C) Without prejudice to subsection (5A) above, where evidence such as is mentioned subsection (5) above is evidence—

(a) which is—

(i) from a person; or

(ii) of a statement (within the meaning of section 259(1) of this Act) by a person, who gave evidence at the original proceedings; and

(b) which is different from, or additional to, the evidence so given,

it may not found an appeal unless there is a reasonable explanation as to why the evidence now sought to be adduced was not given by that person at those proceedings, which explanation is itself supported by independent evidence.

(5D) For the purposes of subsection (5C) above, "independent evidence" means evidence which—

(a) was not heard at the original proceedings;

(b) is from a source independent of the person referred to in subsection (5C) above; and

(c) is accepted by the court as being credible and reliable.

(5E) By an appeal against acquittal under subsection (3) above a prosecutor may bring under review of the High Court any alleged miscarriage of justice.

(6) The power of the Secretary of State to make an order under subsection (4) above shall be exercisable by statutory instrument; and any order so made shall be subject to annulment in pursuance of a resolution of either House of Parliament.

(7) Where a person desires to appeal under subsection (2)(a) or (d) or (3) above, he shall pursue such appeal in accordance with sections 176 to 179, 181 to 185, 188, 190 and 192(1) and (2) of this Act.

(8) A person who has appealed under subsection (2)(cb) or (d) above may abandon the appeal in so far as it is against conviction, reference or sentence and may proceed with it against—

(a) both reference and sentence; or

(b) reference alone; or, as the case may be

(c) sentence alone,

subject to such procedure as may be prescribed by Act of Adjournal.

(9) Where a convicted person or as the case may be a person found to have committed an offence desires to appeal under subsection (2)(b) or (c) or (cb) above, or the prosecutor desires so to appeal by virtue of subsection (4) above, he shall pursue such appeal in accordance with sections 186, 189(1) to (6), 190 and 192(1) and (2) of this Act; but nothing in this section shall prejudice any right to proceed by bill of suspension, or as the case may be advocation, against an alleged fundamental irregularity relating to the imposition of sentence.

(10) Where any statute provides for an appeal from summary proceedings to be taken under any public general or local enactment, such appeal shall be taken under this Part of this Act.

AMENDMENTS

Subs.(2)(a) inserted by the Crime and Punishment (Scotland) Act 1997 (c.48), s.23 with effect from August 1, 1997 in terms of the Crime and Punishment (Scotland) Act 1997 (Commencement and Transitional Provisions) Order 1997 (SI 1997/1712), art.3.

Subs.(4) inserted by the Crime and Punishment (Scotland) Act 1997 (c.48), s.21 with effect from August 1, 1997 in terms of the Crime and Punishment (Scotland) Act 1997 (Commencement and Transitional Provisions) Order 1997 (SI 1997/1712), art.3.

Subs.(5) inserted by the Crime and Punishment (Scotland) Act 1997 (c.48), s.17(2) with effect from August 1, 1997 in terms of the Crime and Punishment (Scotland) Act 1997 (Commencement and Transitional Provisions) Order 1997 (SI 1997/1712) art.3.

Subs.(5C) as amended by the Crime and Disorder Act 1998 (c.37), Sch.8, para.123 (effective September 30, 1998: SI 1998/2327).

Subss.(2)(c), (4) and (4A) as amended by the Crime and Disorder Act 1998 (c.37), s.94 and Sch.6, para.7. Brought into force on September 30, 1998 by the Crime and Disorder Act 1998 (Commencement No. 2 and Transitional Provisions) Order 1998 (SI 1998/2327 (C.53)).

Subss.(4) and (4A) as amended, and subs.(4B) inserted, by the Proceeds of Crime Act 2002 (c.29),

Part 3, s.115. Brought into force on March 24, 2003 by the Proceeds of Crime Act 2002 (Commencement No.6, Transitional Provisions and Savings) (Scotland) Order 2003 (SSI 2003/210 (C.44)).

Subs.(2)(cb), (d)(ii)(iii) inserted, and subss.(2)(c), (d), (8), (9) as amended, by the Protection of Children (Scotland) Act 2003 (asp 5), s.16(7). Brought into force on January 10, 2005 by the Protection of Children (Scotland) Act 2003 (Commencement No.1) Order 2004 (SSI 2004/522 (C.38)), art.2.

DEFINITIONS

"community service order": s.238.
"offence": s.307(1).
"probation order": s.228.
"prosecutor": s.307(1).
"sentence": s.307(1).

GENERAL NOTE

Subs.(1)

The right of appeal from summary proceedings to the High Court of Justiciary may be exercised without prejudice to an appeal by suspension or advocation on the ground of miscarriage of justice: see s.191.

Subs.(2)

Section 175 relies heavily on the terms of s.442 of the 1975 Act but with several crucial differences. The most important in law and in practice is undoubtedly the qualification that an appeal under s.175 must be "with leave granted in accordance with s.180 or, as the case may be, s.187 of this Act". Reference should be made to these two sections and the General Notes to them.

Assuming that leave has been granted, an appeal against conviction alone is possible under s.175(1)(a) and against sentence under s.175(1)(b) and against orders by way of sentence under s.175(1)(c) or against both conviction and sentence or orders under s.175(1)(d).

Appeals in terms of s.175(1)(a) and s.175(1)(d) will be heard by three judges: s.173(1). Appeals in terms of s.175(1)(b) and s.175(1)(c) will be heard by two judges: s.173(2). Paragraph (ca)—with effect from August 1, 1997 a right of appeal is introduced against a decision to remit under s.49(1)(a) or (7)(b) of the Act. A supervised attendance order is not a sentence passed on conviction and cannot be appealed under this section—*McGregor Petr*, 1999 S.C.C.R. 225.

Subs.(3)

This provision allows for a Crown appeal against acquittal on a point of law or against a sentence passed on conviction, again on a point of law. The second head appears to be designed to catch incompetent sentences.

Subss.(4) and (4A)

These subsections equate with the Lord Advocate's appeal against sentence under s.108 of this Act, but there is a crucial distinction. A sentence passed after conviction on indictment or summary complaint must appear to the Lord Advocate to be unduly lenient or inappropriate depending on the nature of the sentence imposed. A sentence passed after conviction on summary complaint must also be "in any class of case specified by order made by the Secretary of State". Classes of cases where the prosecutor can appeal against sentence or other disposal were specified by the Secretary of State in the Prosecutors Right of Appeal in Summary Proceedings (Scotland) Order 1996 (SI 1996/2548) namely—where a sentence is passed or a probation order, community service order or order made deferring sentence or admonition or absolute discharge is made.

Subsection 4 was reorganised by s.21 of the Crime and Punishment (Scotland) Act 1997 with effect from August 1, 1997 introducing the new s.4A. A right of appeal by the Lord Advocate against a decision by a court not to make a supervised release order; non-harassment order and decision to remit to the Principal Reporter has been introduced. In *MacGlennan v McKinnon*, 1998 S.C.C.R. 285, the Crown unsuccessfully appealed the failure by the sheriff to make a non-harassment order. In *Urqhart v Campbell* [2006] HCJAC 76; 2006 S.C.C.R. 656 the court said that, in principle, proceedings in such an appeal where the consequence, if the appeal is allowed, is likely to be the imposition of a more severe sentence, ought not to take place outwith the presence of the respondent and that it would not be satisfactory to hear the appeal in the respondent's absence and, then, if it was successful, continue it to enable the respondent to be present when the new sentence was imposed.

Subs. (5)

As with s.106(3) the Crime and Punishment (Scotland) Act 1997 has radically altered this subsection. With effect from August 1997 the single ground of appeal in summary proceedings remains on the basis of a miscarriage of justice. The one example previously given of additional evidence has been amended to the existence and significance of evidence which was not heard at the original proceedings. The test to be applied is one of reasonable explanation and as with solemn appeals change of testimony by a witness can now form the basis for such an appeal: See subsections (5A) to (5E). For further comment on this see s.106. In *Ward v Crowe*, 1999 S.C.C.R. 219 it was held that an averment in an initial writ in a subsequent civil action did not constitute "evidence" in terms of s.175(5). The error in subs.(5C) referred to by the court in their opinion was rectified by Sch.8 of the Crime and Disorder Act 1998.

Subs.(5c)

The deletion introduced by the 1998 Act serves only to remedy an error in draftsmanship.

Appeal by *Stated case*

Stated case: manner and time of appeal

176.—(1) An appeal under section 175(2)(a) or (d) or (3) of this Act shall be by application for a stated case, which application shall—

(a) be made within one week of the final determination of the proceedings;

(b) contain a full statement of all the matters which the appellant desires to bring under review and, where the appeal is also against sentence or disposal or order, the ground of appeal against that sentence or disposal or order; and

(c) be signed by the appellant or his solicitor and lodged with the clerk of court,

and a copy of the application shall, within the period mentioned in paragraph (a) above, be sent by the appellant to the respondent or the respondent's solicitor.

(2) The clerk of court shall enter in the record of the proceedings the date when an application under subsection (1) above was lodged.

(3) The appellant may, at any time within the period of three weeks mentioned in subsection (1) of section 179 of this Act, or within any further period afforded him by virtue of section 181 (1) of this Act, amend any matter stated in his application or add a new matter; and he shall intimate any such amendment, or addition, to the respondent or the respondent's solicitor.

(4) Where such an application has been made by the person convicted, and the judge by whom he was convicted dies before signing the case or is precluded by illness or other cause from doing so, it shall be competent for the convicted person to present a bill of suspension to the High Court and to bring under the review of that court any matter which might have been brought under review by stated case.

(5) The record of the procedure in the inferior court in an appeal mentioned in subsection (1) above shall be as nearly as may be in the form prescribed by Act of Adjournal.

GENERAL NOTE

Subs. (1)

An application for stated case is not competent until the cause has been finally determined and sentence pronounced: see *Lee v. Lasswade Local Authority* (1893) 5 Couper 329 and *Torrance v. Miller* (1892) 3 White 254.

A case is finally determined when particulars of conviction and sentence are entered in the record of proceedings: see *Tudhope v. Colbert*, 1978 S.L.T. (Notes) 57 and *Tudhope v. Campbell*, 1979 J.C. 24. Where sentence is deferred in terms of s.202 then the final determination for summary proceedings is the date on which sentence is first deferred.

An application for a stated case is an application for a document that sets forth "the particulars of any matters competent for review which the appellant desires to bring under the review of the High Court, and of the facts, if any, proved in the case, and any point of law decided, and the grounds of the decision": subs.(2).

The nature and content of a stated case is emphasised because of the requirement in subs.(1)(b) that the application for a stated case contain "a full statement of all the matters which the appellant desires to bring under review". If the application does not have a comprehensive and accurate description of the point at issue the stated case will in the fullness of time reflect that.

Superficial applications can be held not to have met the requirements of the section: hence "insufficient evidence for conviction" did not lead to a stated case being issued: *Galloway v. Hillary*, 1983 S.C.C.R. 119. An allegation of insufficient evidence must proceed to highlight the part of the evidence said to be insufficient: *Durant v. Lockhart*, 1986 S.L.T. 312 and *Anderson v. McClory*, 1991 S.C.C.R. 571. See also *McDougall, Petr*, 1986 S.C.C.R., 128: *McTaggart, Petr*, 1987 S.C.C.R. 638; *McQuarry v. Carmichael*, 1989 S.C.C.R. 371, and *Anderson v. McClory* 1991 S.C.C.R. 571.

It may be that notwithstanding the brevity of an application a sheriff can state a case although not obliged to do so. The High Court of Justiciary would then proceed to hear an appeal: *Dickson v. Valentine*, 1988 S.C.C.R. 325. See also *McTaggart, Petr*, 1987 S.C.C.R. 638, *Crowe, Petr*, 1994 S.C.C.R. 784 and *Leonard, Petr*, 1995 S.C.C.R. 39. *H.M. Advocate Petr*, 1996 G.W.D. 20–1155 and *Reid Petr*, 1996 G.W.D. 33–1965.

A further concern arising from applications for stated cases that do not contain full statements relates to the hearing of the appeal. An application for a stated case, and in turn the stated case itself, that does not properly focus the real issue can unduly hamper those presenting the appeal: *Cameron v. Normand*, 1997 G.W.D. 9–367. In *Walton v. Crowe*, 1993 S.C.C.R. 885 an attempt by the appellant to raise an issue which had not been mentioned in the application was refused. That restriction can also apply to the Crown: *Normand v. Walker*, 1994 S.C.C.R. 875.

The main practical problem is the failure to meet the requirements of subs.(1)(b) about a full statement. Making an application within one week of the final determination is less of a general problem: see subs.(1)(a) which must be read with s.194(3) for the meaning of "final determination".

Subs. (3)

The draft stated case that follows from a proper application may on authority be amended or added to and if that is done there must be intimation to the other side.

Subs. (4)

An appeal cannot proceed on the basis of a draft stated case. Either there is a signed stated case to found the appeal or there is not. If there is no stated case in the terms set out in this subsection then the correct mode is a bill of suspension: see *Brady v. Barbour*, 1994 S.C.C.R. 890 and *Clark v. Ruxton*, 1997 G.W.D. 10–408.

Procedure where appellant in custody

177.—(1) If an appellant making an application under section 176 of this Act is in custody, the court of first instance may—

(a) grant bail;

(b) grant a sist of execution;

(c) make any other interim order.

(2) An application for bail shall be disposed of by the court within 24 hours after such application has been made.

(3) If bail is refused or the appellant is dissatisfied with the conditions imposed, he may, within 24 hours after the judgment of the court, appeal against it by a note of appeal written on the complaint and signed by himself or his solicitor, and the complaint and proceedings shall thereupon be transmitted to the Clerk of Justiciary, and the High Court or any judge thereof, either in court or in

chambers, shall, after hearing parties, have power to review the decision of the inferior court and to grant bail on such conditions as the Court or judge may think fit, or to refuse bail.

(4) No clerks' fees, court fees or other fees or expenses shall be exigible from or awarded against an appellant in custody in respect of an appeal to the High Court against the conditions imposed or on account of refusal of bail by a court of summary jurisdiction.

(5) If an appellant who has been granted bail does not thereafter proceed with his appeal, the inferior court shall have power to grant warrant to apprehend and imprison him for such period of his sentence as at the date of his bail remained unexpired and, subject to subsection (6) below, such period shall run from the date of his imprisonment under the warrant or, on the application of the appellant, such earlier date as the court thinks fit, not being a date later than the date of expiry of any term or terms of imprisonment imposed subsequently to the conviction appealed against.

(6) Where an appellant who has been granted bail does not thereafter proceed with his appeal, the court from which the appeal was taken shall have power, where at the time of the abandonment of the appeal the person is in custody or serving a term or terms of imprisonment imposed subsequently to the conviction appealed against, to order that the sentence or, as the case may be, the unexpired portion of that sentence relating to that conviction should run from such date as the court may think fit, not being a date later than the date on which any term or terms of imprisonment subsequently imposed expired.

(7) The court shall not make an order under subsection (6) above to the effect that the sentence or, as the case may be, unexpired portion of the sentence shall run other than concurrently with the subsequently imposed term of imprisonment without first notifying the appellant of its intention to do so and considering any representations made by him or on his behalf.

(8) Subsections (6) and (7) of section 112 of this Act (bail pending determination of appeals under paragraph 13(a) of Schedule 6 to the Scotland Act 1998) shall apply to appeals arising in summary proceedings as they do to appeals arising in solemn proceedings.

AMENDMENT

Subs. (8) inserted by the Scotland Act 1998 (Consequential Modifications) (No.1) Order 1999 (S.I. 1999 No.1042) art.3, Sched.1, para.13(7) (effective May 6, 1999).

DEFINITIONS

"bail": s.307(1).
"Clerk of Justiciary": s.307(1).
"High Court": s.307(1).
"order": s.307(1).

GENERAL NOTE

This section sets out the immediate procedure if the appellant makes an application for a stated case and is in custody. If bail is sought an application would be disposed of within 24 hours of such an application or, if refused, a note of appeal may be lodged to review the decision to refuse: subss. (2) and (3).

Appeals are frequently not pursued despite the initial enthusiasm. Where the appellant is at liberty when he abandons his appeal the warrant to imprison him in accordance with his sentence shall run from the date of his imprisonment under the warrant or, on application, such earlier date as the court thinks fit, not being a date later than the date of expiry of any term of imprisonment imposed subsequently to the conviction appealed against: subs. (5).

This may be contrasted with the circumstances where the appellant is in custody when he abandons his appeal, then the unexpired portion of that sentence should run from such date as the court thinks fit, not being a date later than the date on which any term of imprisonment subsequently imposed expired: subs. (6).

Subsection (7) gives statutory effect to *Proudfoot v. Wither*, 1990 S.L.T. 742 and requires sentences under subs. (6) to be served concurrently but if the court is minded to do otherwise then the appellant must be notified and the court must consider any representations he wishes to make.

Stated case: preparation of draft

178.—(1) Within three weeks of the final determination of proceedings in respect of which an application for a stated case is made under section 176 of this Act—

(a) where the appeal is taken from the district court and the trial was presided over by a justice of the peace or justices of the peace, the Clerk of Court; or

(b) in any other case the judge who presided at the trial,

shall prepare a draft stated case, and the clerk of the court concerned shall forthwith issue the draft to the appellant or his solicitor and a duplicate thereof to the respondent or his solicitor.

(2) A stated case shall be, as nearly as may be, in the form prescribed by Act of Adjournal, and shall set forth the particulars of any matters competent for review which the appellant desires to bring under the review of the High Court, and of the facts, if any, proved in the case, and any point of law decided, and the grounds of the decision.

DEFINITION

"judge": s.307(1).

GENERAL NOTE

In the district court the draft stated case is prepared by the clerk of court: see *Mackinnon v. McGarry*, 1987 S.C.C.R. 522. If the justice fails to comply with the statutory provisions the conviction will be quashed: see *Mitchell v. Smith*, Crown Office circular A2/81. In *Clarke v. Ruxton*, 1997 G.W.D. 10–408 the accused had to proceed by way of a bill of suspension following the death of the sheriff before a stated case could be prepared.

Subs. (2)

The form of the draft stated case has been considered a number of times and the following guidelines have been given: (1) it is not necessary to narrate the charges; (2) the facts proved should be fully set out: see *Gordon v. Hansen* (1914) 7 Adam 441; *Waddell v. Kinnaird*, 1922 J.C. 40; *Gordon v. Allan*, 1987 S.L.T. 400; *Duncan v. MacLeod*, 1997 G.W.D. 13–550; (3) it should set out objections taken to admissibility or rejection of evidence and the reasons for upholding or repelling same should be explained: see *Falconer v. Brown* (1893) 1 Adam 96; (4) any findings in fact made should be based on the whole evidence: see *Jordan v. Allan*, 1989 S.C.C.R. 202 and *Bowman v. Jessop*, 1989 S.C.C.R. 597; (5) where a no case to answer submission is made then the form of the stated case should be as set out in *Wingate v. MacGlennan*, 1991 S.C.C.R. 133. See also *MacDonald v. Normand*, 1994 S.C.C.R. 121; *Cassidy v. Normand*, 1994 S.C.C.R. 325, and *Thomson v. Barber*, 1994 S.C.C.R. 485; (6) the reasons for the final decision should be set out: see *Lyon v. Don Brothers, Buist & Co*, 1944 J.C. 1 including the reasons the evidence was believed or disbelieved. See *Petrovich v. Jessop*, 1990 S.C.C.R. 1; *Roberton v. McGlennan*, 1994 S.C.C.R. 394, and *Leask v. Vannet*, 1996 G.W.D. 36–1960; (7) questions should be stated for the opinion of the court: see *Needes v. MacLeod*, November 7 1984, unreported. Notwithstanding that questions are not properly framed the court may proceed: see *Robertson v. Aitchison*, 1981 S.C.C.R. 149; *Marshall v. Smith*, 1983 S.C.C.R. 156, and *Waddell v. MacPhail*, 1986 S.C.C.R. 593. In *Jackson v. Vannet*, 1997 G.W.D. 23–1146 the stated case was sent back for restatement where the justice did not summarise the entire evidence of a number of essential witnesses.

Stated case: adjustment and signature

179.—(1) Subject to section 181(1) of this Act, within three weeks of the issue of the draft stated case under section 178 of this Act, each party shall cause to be transmitted to the court and to the other parties or their solicitors a note of any adjustments he proposes be made to the draft case or shall intimate that he has no such proposal.

(2) The adjustments mentioned in subsection (1) above shall relate to evidence heard or purported to have been heard at the trial and not to such evidence as is mentioned in section 175(5) of this Act.

(3) Subject to section 181(1) of this Act, if the period mentioned in subsection (1) above has expired and the appellant has not lodged adjustments and has failed to intimate that he has no adjustments to propose, he shall be deemed to have abandoned his appeal; and subsection (5) of section 177 of this Act shall apply accordingly.

(4) If adjustments are proposed under subsection (1) above or if the judge desires to make any alterations to the draft case there shall, within one week of the expiry of the period mentioned in that subsection or as the case may be of any further period afforded under section 181(1) of this Act, be a hearing (unless the appellant has, or has been deemed to have, abandoned his appeal) for the purpose of considering such adjustments or alterations.

(5) Where a party neither attends nor secures that he is represented at a hearing under subsection (4) above, the hearing shall nevertheless proceed.

(6) Where at a hearing under subsection (4) above—

(a) any adjustment proposed under subsection (1) above by a party (and not withdrawn) is rejected by the judge; or

(b) any alteration proposed by the judge is not accepted by all the parties,

that fact shall be recorded in the minute of the proceedings of the hearing.

(7) Within two weeks of the date of the hearing under subsection (4) above or, where there is no hearing, within two weeks of the expiry of the period mentioned in subsection (1) above, the judge shall (unless the appellant has been deemed to have abandoned the appeal) state and sign the case and shall append to the case—

(a) any adjustment, proposed under subsection (1) above, which is rejected by him, a note of any evidence rejected by him which is alleged to support that adjustment and the reasons for his rejection of that adjustment and evidence; and

(b) a note of the evidence upon which he bases any finding of fact challenged, on the basis that it is unsupported by the evidence, by a party at the hearing under subsection (4) above.

(8) As soon as the case is signed under subsection (7) above the clerk of court—

(a) shall send the case to the appellant or his solicitor and a duplicate thereof to the respondent or his solicitor; and

(b) shall transmit the complaint, productions and any other proceedings in the cause to the Clerk of Justiciary.

(9) Subject to section 181(1) of this Act, within one week of receiving the case the appellant or his solicitor, as the case may be, shall cause it to be lodged with the Clerk of Justiciary.

(10) Subject to section 181(1) of this Act, if the appellant or his solicitor fails to comply with subsection (9) above the appellant shall be deemed to have abandoned the appeal; and subsection (5) of section 177 of this Act shall apply accordingly.

AMENDMENT

Subs. (2) as amended by the Crime and Punishment (Scotland) Act 1997 (c. 48) Schedule. 1, para.

21(20) with effect from August 1, 1997 in terms of the Crime and Punishment (Scotland) Act 1997 (Commencement and Transitional Provisions) Order 1997 (S.I. 1997 No. 1712) art.3.

<small>DEFINITIONS</small>

"Clerk of Justiciary": s.307(1).
"judge": s.307(1).

<small>GENERAL NOTE</small>

Section 179 consolidates s.448 of the 1975 Act which had been much amended. There are only two practical points which need to be emphasised. First, many appeals are deemed to be abandoned because adjustments are not lodged or because the appellant does not intimate that he has no adjustments to propose. This requirement still exists in subs. (3). Similarly, within one week of receiving the stated case itself it should be lodged with the Clerk of Justiciary: subs. (9). Failure to comply with that requirement also results in an appeal being deemed to be abandoned: subs. (10).

Secondly, adjustments must relate to the evidence heard or purported to have been heard at trial not to any fresh evidence: subs. (2). Adjustments can be proposed to: (1) findings in fact: see *Wilson v. Carmichael*, 1982 S.C.C.R. 528; (2) the trial judge's note: see *Ballantyne v. McKinnon*, 1983 S.C.C.R. 97, and *MacDonald v. Scott*, 1993 S.C.C.R. 78; and (3) questions of law: see *O'Hara v. Tudhope*, 1984 S.C.C.R. 283. However, if any adjustments are rejected by the judge then reasons for that rejection must be given: subs. (7)(a). The court can take account of material rejected by the sheriff: see *Wilson v. Carmichael, supra*, and s.182 below.

Where reasons are not given the case may be remitted for the purpose of having reasons given. That was done in *Owens v. Crowe*, 1994 S.C.C.R. 310 and on reporting the sheriff gave sound reasons.

Leave to appeal against conviction etc.

180.—(1) The decision whether to grant leave to appeal for the purposes of section 175(2)(a) or (d) of this Act shall be made by a judge of the High Court who shall—

(a) if he considers that the documents mentioned in subsection (2) below disclose arguable grounds of appeal, grant leave to appeal and make such comments in writing as he considers appropriate; and

(b) in any other case—

(i) refuse leave to appeal and give reasons in writing for the refusal; and

(ii) where the appellant is on bail and the sentence imposed on his conviction is one of imprisonment, grant a warrant to apprehend and imprison him.

(2) The documents referred to in subsection (1) above are—

(a) the stated case lodged under subsection (9) of section 179 of this Act; and

(b) the documents transmitted to the Clerk of Justiciary under subsection (8)(b) of that section.

(3) A warrant granted under subsection (1)(b)(ii) above shall not take effect until the expiry of the period of 14 days mentioned in subsection (4) below without an application to the High Court for leave to appeal having been lodged by the appellant under that subsection.

(4) Where leave to appeal is refused under subsection (1) above the appellant may, within 14 days of intimation under subsection (10) below, apply to the High Court for leave to appeal.

(5) In deciding an application under subsection (4) above the High Court shall—

(a) if, after considering the documents mentioned in subsection (2) above and the reasons for the refusal, the court is of the opinion that there are arguable grounds of appeal, grant leave to appeal and make such comments in writing as the court considers appropriate; and

(b) in any other case—

    (i) refuse leave to appeal and give reasons in writing for the refusal; and

    (ii) where the appellant is on bail and the sentence imposed on his conviction is one of imprisonment, grant a warrant to apprehend and imprison him.

(6) The question whether to grant leave to appeal under subsection (1) or (5) above shall be considered and determined in chambers without the parties being present.

(7) Comments in writing made under subsection (1)(a) or (5)(a) above may, without prejudice to the generality of that provision, specify the arguable grounds of appeal (whether or not they are contained in the stated case) on the basis of which leave to appeal is granted.

(8) Where the arguable grounds of appeal are specified by virtue of subsection (7) above it shall not, except by leave of the High Court on cause shown, be competent for the appellant to found any aspect of his appeal on any ground of appeal contained in the stated case but not so specified.

(9) Any application by the appellant for the leave of the High Court under subsection (8) above—

(a) shall be made not less than seven days before the date fixed for the hearing of the appeal; and

(b) shall, not less that seven days before that date, be intimated by the appellant to the Crown Agent.

(10) The Clerk of Justiciary shall forthwith intimate—

(a) a decision under subsection (1) or (5) above; and

(b) in the case of a refusal of leave to appeal, the reasons for the decision,

to the appellant or his solicitor and to the Crown Agent.

DEFINITIONS

    "bail": s.307(1).
    "High Court": s.307(1).
    "judge": s.307(1).

GENERAL NOTE

    This section mirrors so far as possible the provisions for solemn appeals which are to be found in s.107. Reference therefore might conveniently be made to the general note to that section.

Leave to appeal

    The requirement to obtain a grant of appeal is likely to reduce substantially the number of summary appeals against conviction and, separately, appeals against conviction and sentence actually heard in court. For many years a considerable volume of these sorts of cases have got to a hearing more in hope than expectation of a setting aside of the conviction.

    Section 175(2)(a) and (d) has provided for a right of appeal against conviction and, separately, appeal against conviction and sentence. The right of appeal is conditional on a grant of leave to appeal by a judge of the High Court of Justiciary in terms of s.180. Before the judge can decide the grant he must have documents before him and these are specified as the stated case, the complaint, the productions and any other proceedings: subs.(2). Having considered these documents the judge must decide whether they disclose arguable grounds of appeal: subs.(1)(a). The action that follows such a decision depends on which way the decision goes.

    In the General Note to s.107 some thought was given to what is meant by "arguable grounds of appeal". On the principle that the greater (solemn procedure) includes the lesser (summary procedure) the considerations in relation to s.107 also apply to s.180. There are two procedural differences that may affect the meaning of "arguable grounds of appeal". First, in solemn procedure the presence of a jury means that there are aspects, *e.g.* the judge's charge to the jury, that do not apply to summary appeals: Renton and Brown (5th ed.) para. 11–38 at pp.199–200 sets out the law on the point.

Secondly, the pivotal role of the stated case in summary appeals is emphasised repeatedly in the case law, and the scrutiny applied to its terms gives rise to different issues: *e.g.* the nature of irregularity will be different: Renton and Brown (5th ed.) para. 16–28 at p. 337.

To return to the appeal, the judge of the High Court of Justiciary who must consider the documents to decide whether they disclose arguable grounds of appeal does so in chambers without the parties being present: subs.(6). If the judge considers that the documents do disclose arguable grounds of appeal he then grants leave to appeal and he makes such comments in writing as he considers appropriate: subs.(1)(a). If the judge considers that the documents do not disclose arguable grounds of appeal he then refuses leave to appeal and he gives reasons in writing for the refusal: subs.(1)(b)(i), *e.g. MacNeill v Skelly*, 1997 G.W.D. 6–230. The appellant, who is at this stage on bail and the sentence imposed on his conviction was one of imprisonment, will then be the subject of a warrant to apprehend granted by the judge and on implementation the appellant will be imprisoned: subs.(1)(b)(ii).

The warrant to apprehend and imprison under subs.(1)(b)(ii) shall not take effect until the expiry of the period of 14 days during which period the appellant may, in effect, appeal by making an application to the High Court of Justiciary: subs.(4). If no such application is to be made then the appellant's solicitor has the time available to arrange for the client to surrender to the warrant.

Application for leave to appeal

The refusal of leave to appeal by a single judge in chambers may therefore be followed by an application to the High Court of Justiciary for leave to appeal; subs. (4). This is in effect an appeal in itself. Who decides the application depends on what is at issue, namely an appeal against conviction, sentence or both.

By s.173(1) "for the purpose of hearing and determining any appeal under this Part of this Act or any proceeding connected therewith" the quorum is three judges, except that by s.173(2) for appeals against sentence alone the quorum is two judges. Accordingly, an application in terms of subs.(4) will generally be decided by three judges unless the appeal concerns sentence alone, in which event the quorum is two.

The various judges of the High Court of Justiciary who must consider the documents to decide whether they disclose arguable grounds of appeal do so in chambers without the parties being present: subs.(6). In deciding the application the judges must consider the documents that had been before the single judge in chambers and also consider the reasons for the earlier refusal but, thereafter, if the court is of the opinion that there are arguable grounds of appeal then the court should grant leave to appeal and make such comments in writing as the court considers appropriate: subs.(5)(a).

In any other case, leave to appeal will be refused with reasons in writing, and a warrant to apprehend and imprison is to be granted if appropriate: subs.(5)(b).

Hearing of appeal

Regard must be paid to the comments in writing made either by the single judge in chambers by subs.(1)(a) or by a greater number of judges in chambers by subs.(5)(a). The importance of the comments in writing lies in the possibility that they "may specify the arguable grounds of appeal (whether or not they are contained in the note of appeal) on the basis of which leave to appeal is granted": subs.(7).

It is very easy to imagine on the wording of subs.(1)(a) a single judge in chambers granting leave to appeal, not on the original ground in the note of appeal, but on the basis of comments in writing which amend, alter or distil the original grounds in the note of appeal. The new grounds of appeal, having been specified, in effect dictate the ground of appeal to be argued at the hearing: subs.(8).

The appellant who wishes to found any aspect of his appeal on any ground of appeal contained in the stated case but not so specified in the comments in writing provided under subs.(1)(a) or subs.(5)(a) may seek leave to do so: subs.(8). Application for such leave under subs.(8) must be made not less than seven days before the date fixed for the hearing of the appeal: subs.(9). It is not immediately clear from a reading of the statute as to whom an application under subs.(8) will be directed. As it is not so much an appeal as a request to broaden an approach to an appeal, it may simply be returned to those who made the comments in writing under subs.(1)(a) or subs.(5)(a).

Stated case: directions by High Court

181.—(1) Without prejudice to any other power of relief which the High Court may have, where it appears to that court on application made in accordance with subsection (2) below, that the applicant has failed to comply with any of the requirements of—

(a) subsection (1) of section 176 of this Act; or

(b) subsection (1) or (9) of section 179 of this Act,

the High Court may direct that such further period of time as it may think proper be afforded to the applicant to comply with any requirement of the aforesaid provisions.

(2) Any application for a direction under subsection (1) above shall be made in writing to the Clerk of Justiciary and shall state the ground for the application, and, in the case of an application for the purposes of paragraph (a) of subsection (1) above, notification of the application shall be made by the appellant or his solicitor to the clerk of the court from which the appeal is to be taken, and the clerk shall thereupon transmit the complaint, documentary productions and any other proceedings in the cause to the Clerk of Justiciary.

(3) The High Court shall dispose of any application under subsection (1) above in like manner as an application to review the decision of an inferior court on a grant of bail, but shall have power—

(a) to dispense with a hearing; and

(b) to make such enquiry in relation to the application as the court may think fit,

and when the High Court has disposed of the application the Clerk of Justiciary shall inform the clerk of the inferior court of the result.

(4) Subsection (1) above does not allow the High Court to make a direction in relation to an appeal under section 175(2)(cb) or (d)(ii) or (iii) of this Act.

AMENDMENT

Subs.(4) inserted by the Criminal Procedure (Amendment) (Scotland) Act 2004 (asp 5), s.24(4). Brought into force on October 4, 2004 by the Criminal Procedure (Amendment) (Scotland) Act 2004 (Commencement, Transitional Provisions and Savings) Order 2004 (SSI 2004/405 (C.28)).

DEFINITIONS

"Clerk of Justiciary": s.307(1).
"High Court": s.307(1).

GENERAL NOTE

The complex arrangements for applying for a stated case and thereafter attending to adjustments and hearings will all be done within a short time frame: see s.176(1) and s.179(1) to (9). A pragmatic power is granted to the High Court of Justiciary to afford an appropriate further time to comply with these arrangements: s.181(1). An application for a grant is made in writing: s.181(2). A hearing is not necessary and the High Court may make enquiry: subs.(5).

Stated case: hearing of appeal

182.—(1) A stated case under this Part of this Act shall be heard by the High Court on such date as it may fix.

(2) For the avoidance of doubt, where an appellant, in his application under section 176(1) of this Act (or in a duly made amendment or addition to that application), refers to an alleged miscarriage of justice, but in stating a case under section 179(7) of this Act the inferior court is unable to take the allegation into account, the High Court may nevertheless have regard to the allegation at a hearing under subsection (1) above.

(3) Except by leave of the High Court on cause shown, it shall not be competent for an appellant to found any aspect of his appeal on a matter not contained in his application under section 176(1) of this Act (or in a duly made amendment or addition to that application).

417

(4) Subsection (3) above shall not apply as respects any ground of appeal specified as an arguable ground of appeal by virtue of subsection (7) of section 180 of this Act.

(5) Without prejudice to any existing power of the High Court, that court may in hearing a stated case—

(a) order the production of any document or other thing connected with the proceedings;

(b) hear any evidence relevant to any alleged miscarriage of justice or order such evidence to be heard by a judge at the High Court or by such other person as it may appoint for that purpose;

(c) take account of any circumstances relevant to the case which were not before the trial judge;

(d) remit to any fit person to enquire and report in regard to any matter or circumstance affecting the appeal;

(e) appoint a person with expert knowledge to act as assessor to the High Court in any case where it appears to the court that such expert knowledge is required for the proper determination of the case;

(f) take account of any matter proposed in any adjustment rejected by the trial judge and of the reasons for such rejection;

(g) take account of any evidence contained in a note of evidence such as is mentioned in section 179(7) of this Act.

(6) The High Court may at the hearing remit the stated case back to the inferior court to be amended and returned.

AMENDMENT

Subs.(5)(b) as amended by the Crime and Punishment (Scotland) Act 1997 (c.48), Sch.1, para.21(21) with effect from August 1, 1997 in terms of the Crime and Punishment (Scotland) Act 1997 (Commencement and Transitional Provisions) Order 1997 (SI 1997/1712), art.3.

DEFINITIONS

"judge": s.307(1).
"single court": s.307(1).

GENERAL NOTE

The court in *Egan v Normand*, 1997 S.C.C.R. 211 observed that it was unacceptable for an appellant at the hearing of an appeal to seek a postponement to allow enquiries to be made into a possible ground of appeal based on *Anderson v H.M. Advocate*. It remains the position (notwithstanding earlier strictures) that if in an application for a stated case a miscarriage of justice is alleged but for some reason has not been dealt with in the stated case itself, the High Court of Justiciary at a hearing of the appeal may still have regard to the earlier allegation: subs.(2). An appellant cannot himself found on a matter not contained in the application for a stated case without the leave of the court: subs.(3). See *West v McNaughton*, 1990 S.C.C.R. 439; *Stein v Lowe*, 1991 S.C.C.R. 692; *Fulton v Lees*, 1992 S.C.C.R. 923; *Normand v Walker*, 1994 S.C.C.R. 875, and *Campbell v McClory*, 1996 G.W.D. 28–1659. However, if the appellant wishes to extend his position beyond any ground of appeal specified as an arguable ground of appeal then he may not do so: subs.(4).

Prior to disposing of the appeal the High Court of Justiciary has a wide range of powers to assist in attaining justice: subs.(5). Re para.(b) see *MacLeod v Lowe*, 1993 S.L.T. 475 and *Marshall v MacDougall*, 1987 S.L.T. 123. Re para.(c) see *Hogg v Heattle*, 1961 S.L.T. 38. Re para.(d) *Marshall v MacDougall, supra*, but see also *Faroux v Brown*, 1996 S.C.C.R. 891. Paragraph (f) see *Wilson v Carmichael*, 1982 S.C.C.R. 528; *Paterson v Lees*, 1992 S.C.C.R. 300; *Ballantyne v McKinnon*, 1983 S.C.C.R. 97 and *MacDonald v Scott*, 1993 S.C.C.R. 78. Subsection 6—see *Jackson v Vannet*, 1997 G.W.D. 23–1146.

Stated case: disposal of appeal — *In disposing of the Appeal*

183.—(1) The High Court may, subject to subsection (3) below and to section 190(1) of this Act, dispose of a stated case by—

(a) remitting the ca~~u~~se to the inferior court with its opinion and any direction thereon; *[as to how to proceed* `lower` `on`

(b) affirming the verdict of the inferior court;

(c) setting aside the verdict of the inferior court and either quashing the conviction or, subject to subsection (2) below, substituting therefor an amended verdict of guilty; or *provided that verdict was within powers of*

(d) setting aside the verdict of the inferior court and granting authority to bring a new prosecution in accordance with section 185 of this Act. `lower` `court` `to` `return`

(2) An amended verdict of guilty substituted under subsection (1)(c) above must be one which could have been returned on the complaint before the inferior court.

(3) The High Court shall, in an appeal—

(a) against both conviction and sentence, subject to section 190(1) of this Act, dispose of the appeal against sentence; or

(b) by the prosecutor, against sentence, dispose of the appeal,

by exercise of the power mentioned in section 189(1) of this Act.

(4) In setting aside, under subsection (1) above, a verdict the High Court may quash any sentence imposed on the appellant as respects the complaint, and—

(a) in a case where it substitutes an amended verdict of guilty, whether or not the sentence related to the verdict set aside; or

(b) in any other case, where the sentence did not so relate,

may pass another (but not more severe) sentence in substitution for the sentence so quashed.

(5) For the purposes of subsections (3) and (4) above, "sentence" shall be construed as including disposal or order.

(6) Where an appeal against acquittal is sustained, the High Court may—

(a) convict and, subject to subsection (7) below, sentence the respondent;

(b) remit the case to the inferior court with instructions to convict and sentence the respondent, who shall be bound to attend any diet fixed by the court for such purpose; or

(c) remit the case to the inferior court with their opinion thereon.

(7) Where the High Court sentences the respondent under subsection (6)(a) above it shall not in any case impose a sentence beyond the maximum sentence which could have been passed by the inferior court.

(8) Any reference in subsection (6) above to convicting and sentencing shall be construed as including a reference to—

(a) convicting and making some other disposal; or

(b) convicting and deferring sentence.

(9) The High Court shall have power in an appeal under this Part of this Act to award such expenses both in the High Court and in the inferior court as it may think fit.

(10) Where, following an appeal, other than an appeal under section 175(2)(b) or (3) of this Act, the appellant remains liable to imprisonment or detention under the sentence of the inferior court, or is so liable under a sentence passed in the appeal proceedings the High Court shall have the power where at the time of disposal of the appeal the appellant—

(a) was at liberty on bail, to grant warrant to apprehend and imprison or detain the appellant for a term, to run from the date of such apprehension, not longer than that part of the term or terms of imprisonment or detention specified in the sentence brought under review which remained unexpired at the date of liberation;

(b) is serving a term or terms of imprisonment or detention imposed in relation to a conviction subsequent to the conviction appealed against, to exercise the like powers in regard to him as may be exercised, in relation to an appeal which has been abandoned, by a court of summary jurisdiction in pursuance of section 177(6) of this Act.

DEFINITIONS

"High Court": s.307(1).
"sentence": s.183(5).

GENERAL NOTE

The general approach to disposing of appeals by way of stated case in s.183 is very similar to the general approach to disposing of solemn appeals in s.118. Reference may be made to the General Note to that section.

It should be emphasised that the different nature of the procedure means that the cause under this section may be remitted to the lower court with any necessary direction: subs.(1)(a). This includes an instruction to convict where an appeal against acquittal has been successful: subs.(6)(b). For examples under sub.(1): Para.(c) see *Robertson v Scott*, 1993 S.C.C.R. 450 and *McCusker v Whitelaw*, 1993 S.C.C.R. 198; Para.(d) see *Miller v Lees*, 1991 S.C.C.R. 799; *Stewart v Normand*, 1991 S.C.C.R. 940; *McSorley v Normand*, 1991 S.C.C.R. 949, and *Brims v MacDonald*, 1993 S.C.C.R. 1061. But see also *Kelly v Docherty*, 1991 S.C.C.R. 312 and *O'Brien v Ruxton*, 1999 S.C.C.R. 216. For a case under subs.(4)(b) see *Robertson v Scott*, 1993 S.C.C.R. 450. Subsection (6) see *Aitchison v Rizza*, 1985 S.C.C.R. 299 and *Heywood v Ross* 1993 S.C.C.R. 101.

Abandonment of appeal

184.—(1) An appellant in an appeal such as is mentioned in section 176(1) of this Act may at any time prior to lodging the case with the Clerk of Justiciary abandon his appeal by minute signed by himself or his solicitor, written on the complaint or lodged with the clerk of the inferior court, and intimated to the respondent or the respondent's solicitor, but such abandonment shall be without prejudice to any other competent mode of appeal, review, advocation or suspension.

(2) Subject to section 191 of this Act, on the case being lodged with the Clerk of Justiciary, the appellant shall be held to have abandoned any other mode of appeal which might otherwise have been open to him.

DEFINITION

"Clerk of Justiciary": s.307(1).

New prosecution

Authorisation of new prosecution

185.—(1) Subject to subsection (2) below, where authority is granted under section 183(1)(d) of this Act, a new prosecution may be brought charging the accused with the same or any similar offence arising out of the same facts; and the proceedings out of which the stated case arose shall not be a bar to such prosecution.

(2) In a new prosecution under this section the accused shall not be charged with an offence more serious than that of which he was convicted in the earlier proceedings.

(3) No sentence may be passed on conviction under the new prosecution which could not have been passed on conviction under the earlier proceedings.

(4) A new prosecution may be brought under this section, notwithstanding that any time limit (other than the time limit mentioned in subsection (5) below) for the commencement of such proceedings has elapsed.

(5) Proceedings in a prosecution under this section shall be commenced within two months of the date on which authority to bring the prosecution was granted.

(6) In proceedings in a new prosecution under this section it shall, subject to subsection (7) below, be competent for either party to lead any evidence which it was competent for him to lead in the earlier proceedings.

(7) The complaint in a new prosecution under this section shall identify any matters as respects which the prosecutor intends to lead evidence by virtue of subsection (6) above which would not have been competent but for that subsection.

(8) For the purposes of subsection (5) above, proceedings shall be deemed to be commenced—

(a) in a case where such warrant is executed without unreasonable delay, on the date on which a warrant to apprehend or to cite the accused is granted; and

(b) in any other case, on the date on which the warrant is executed.

(9) Where the two months mentioned in subsection (5) above elapse and no new prosecution has been brought under this section, the order under section 183(1)(d) of this Act setting aside the verdict shall have the effect, for all purposes, of an acquittal.

(10) On granting authority under section 183(1)(d) of this Act to bring a new prosecution, the High Court may, after giving the parties an opportunity of being heard, order the detention of the accused person in custody; but an accused person may not be detained by virtue of this subsection for a period of more than 40 days.

GENERAL NOTE

See notes to s.183, para.(d) above, for examples. In *Heywood, Petr*, 1998 S.C.C.R. 335, the Crown brought a petition to the nobile officium to amend the record of the interlocutor pronounced by the court which did not reflect the fact that the Crown had been granted leave to raise a fresh prosecution in respect of all charges. In granting the petition the court held that as the order granting authority had been pronounced in open court the Crown needed no further authority to bring a fresh prosecution.

Appeals against sentence

Appeals against sentence only

186.—(1) An appeal under section 175(2)(b) or (c) or (cb), or by virtue of section 175(4), of this Act shall be by note of appeal, which shall state the ground of appeal.

(2) The note of appeal shall, where the appeal is—

(a) under section 175(2)(b) or (c) or (cb) be lodged, within one week of—
   (i) the passing of the sentence;
   (ii) the making of the order disposing of the case or deferring sentence; or
   (iii) in the case of an appeal under section 175(2)(cb), the date on which it is proposed that a reference be made,
   with the clerk of the court from which the appeal is to be taken; or

(b) by virtue of section 175(4) be so lodged within four weeks of such passing or making.

(3) The clerk of court on receipt of the note of appeal shall—

(a) send a copy of the note to the respondent or his solicitor; and

(b) obtain a report from the judge who sentenced the convicted person or, as the case may be, who disposed of the case or deferred sentence.

(4) Subject to subsection (5) below, the clerk of court shall within two weeks of the passing of the sentence or within two weeks of the disposal or order against which the appeal is taken—

(a) send to the Clerk of Justiciary the note of appeal, together with the report mentioned in subsection (3)(b) above, a certified copy of the complaint, the minute of proceedings and any other relevant documents; and

(b) send copies of that report to the appellant and respondent or their solicitors.

(5) Where a judge—

(a) is temporarily absent from duty for any cause;

(b) is a part-time sheriff; or

(c) is a justice of the peace,

the sheriff principal of the sheriffdom in which the judgment was pronounced may extend the period of two weeks specified in subsection (4) above for such period as he considers reasonable.

(6) Subject to subsection (4) above, the report mentioned in subsection (3)(b) above shall be available only to the High Court, the parties and, on such conditions as may be prescribed by Act of Adjournal, such other persons or classes of persons as may be so prescribed.

(7) Where the judge's report is not furnished within the period mentioned in subsection (4) above or such period as extended under subsection (5) above, the High Court may extend such period, or, if it thinks fit, hear and determine the appeal without the report.

(8) Section 181 of this Act shall apply where an appellant fails to comply with the requirement of subsection (2)(a) above as they apply where an applicant fails to comply with any of the requirements of section 176(1) of this Act.

(9) An appellant under section 175(2)(b) or (c) or (cb), or by virtue of section 175(4), of this Act may at any time prior to the hearing of the appeal abandon his appeal by minute, signed by himself or his solicitor, lodged—

(a) in a case where the note of appeal has not yet been sent under subsection (4)(a) above to the Clerk of Justiciary, with the clerk of court;

(b) in any other case, with the Clerk of Justiciary,

and intimated to the respondent.

(10) Sections 176(5), 177 and 182(5)(a) to (e) of this Act shall apply to appeals under section 175(2)(b) or (c) or (cb), or by virtue of section 175(4), of this Act as they apply to appeals under section 175(2)(a) or (d) of this Act, except that, for the purposes of such application to any appeal by virtue of section 175(4), references in subsections (1) to (4) of section 177 to the appellant shall be construed as references to the convicted person and subsections (6) and (7) of that section shall be disregarded.

AMENDMENT

Subs.(5) as amended by the Bail, Judicial Appointments etc. (Scotland) Act 2000 (asp 9), s.12 and Sch., para.7(4).

Subs.(2) as amended by the Criminal Procedure (Amendment) (Scotland) Act 2004 (asp 5), s.24(5). Brought into force on October 4, 2004 by the Criminal Procedure (Amendment) (Scotland) Act 2004 (Commencement, Transitional Provisions and Savings) Order 2004 (SSI 2004/405 (C.28)).

Subss.(1), (2), (9), (10) as amended by the Protection of Children (Scotland) Act 2003 (asp 5), s.16(8). Brought into force on January 10, 2005 by the Protection of Children (Scotland) Act 2003 (Commencement No.1) Order 2004 (SSI 2004/522 (C.38)), art.2.

DEFINITIONS

"High Court": s.307(1).
"judge": s.307(1).
"sentence": s.307(1).

GENERAL NOTE

A brief glance at the vast number of criminal cases reported in Green's Weekly Digest will reveal that in all probability the single biggest category of cases is appeals against summary sentences. Whether this remains the position is open to doubt with the new procedure.

A note of appeal stating the ground of appeal commences the action: subs.(1). Merely to complain of an excessive sentence will not suffice and the High Court of Justiciary is very likely to support sheriffs who complain of minimal specification: *Campbell v MacDougall*, 1991 S.C.C.R. 218. The sheriff's report is required to set out the circumstances of the offence and of the appellants. See *Henry v Docherty*, 1989 S.C.C.R. 426. In *Mullins v Walkingshaw*, 1996 G.W.D. 27–159 it was observed that each of the three justices did not have to prepare a report. Confusion as to the facts of a case in a Sheriff's report was a factor taken into account by the Appeal Court in allowing an appeal against sentence—*Scott v Fraser*, 1998 G.W.D. 11–533.

Leave to appeal against sentence

187.—(1) The decision whether to grant leave to appeal for the purposes of section 175(2)(b) or (c) or (cb) of this Act shall be made by a judge of the High Court who shall—

(a) if he considers that the note of appeal and other documents sent to the Clerk of Justiciary under section 186(4)(a) of this Act disclose arguable grounds of appeal, grant leave to appeal and make such comments in writing as he considers appropriate; and

(b) in any other case—
    (i) refuse leave to appeal and give reasons in writing for the refusal; and
    (ii) where the appellant is on bail and the sentence imposed on his conviction is one of imprisonment, grant a warrant to apprehend and imprison him.

(2) A warrant granted under subsection (1)(b)(ii) above shall not take effect until the expiry of the period of 14 days mentioned in subsection (3) below without an application to the High Court for leave to appeal having been lodged by the appellant under that subsection.

(3) Where leave to appeal is refused under subsection (1) above the appellant may, within 14 days of intimation under subsection (9) below, apply to the High Court for leave to appeal.

(4) In deciding an application under subsection (3) above the High Court shall—

(a) if, after considering the note of appeal and other documents mentioned in subsection (1) above and the reasons for the refusal, it is of the opinion that there are arguable grounds of appeal, grant leave to appeal and make such comments in writing as he considers appropriate; and

(b) in any other case—
    (i) refuse leave to appeal and give reasons in writing for the refusal; and
    (ii) where the appellant is on bail and the sentence imposed on his conviction is one of imprisonment, grant a warrant to apprehend and imprison him.

(5) The question whether to grant leave to appeal under subsection (1) or (4) above shall be considered and determined in chambers without the parties being present.

(6) Comments in writing made under subsection (1)(a) or (4)(a) above may, without prejudice to the generality of that provision, specify the arguable grounds of appeal (whether or not they are contained in the note of appeal) on the basis of which leave to appeal is granted.

(7) Where the arguable grounds of appeal are specified by virtue of subsection (6) above it shall not, except by leave of the High Court on cause shown, be competent for the appellant to found any aspect of his appeal on any ground of appeal contained in the note of appeal but not so specified.

(8) Any application by the appellant for the leave of the High Court under subsection (7) above—

(a) shall be made not less than seven days before the date fixed for the hearing of the appeal; and

(b) shall, not less that seven days before that date, be intimated by the appellant to the Crown Agent.

(9) The Clerk of Justiciary shall forthwith intimate—

(a) a decision under subsection (1) or (4) above; and

(b) in the case of a refusal of leave to appeal, the reasons for the decision,

to the appellant or his solicitor and to the Crown Agent.

AMENDMENT

Subs.(1) as amended by the Protection of Children (Scotland) Act 2003 (asp 5), s.16(9). Brought into force on January 10, 2005 by the Protection of Children (Scotland) Act 2003 (Commencement No.1) Order 2004 (SSI 2004/522 (C.38)), art.2.

DEFINITIONS

"bail": s.307(1).
"High Court": s.307(1).
"judge": s.307(1).
"sentence": s.307(1).

GENERAL NOTE

The procedure to be followed in regard to appeals against summary sentences necessarily requires leave to appeal. The note of appeal containing the ground of appeal is placed before a single judge in chambers along with, principally, the trial judge's report: subs.(1)(a). There is consideration and determination without the parties being present: subs. (5). As there is no longer the opportunity to explain or expand upon the grounds of appeal by advocacy the written note of appeal assumes far greater significance: such a note no longer merely initiates an appeal, it is now the substance of the leave to appeal. When leave to appeal is refused further application can be made: subs.(3) which follows identical procedure under, *e.g.* s.180(3).

Disposal of appeals

Setting aside conviction or sentence: prosecutor's consent or application

188.—(1) Without prejudice to section 175(3) or (4) of this Act, where—

(a) an appeal has been taken under section 175(2) of this Act or by suspension or otherwise and the prosecutor is not prepared to maintain the judgment appealed against he may, by a relevant minute, consent to the conviction or sentence or, as the case may be, conviction and sentence ("sentence" being construed in this section as including disposal or order) being set aside either in whole or in part; or

(b) no such appeal has been taken but the prosecutor is, at any time, not prepared to maintain the judgment on which a conviction is founded or the sentence imposed following such conviction he may, by a relevant minute, apply for the conviction or sentence or, as the case may be, conviction and sentence to be set aside.

(2) For the purposes of subsection (1) above, a "relevant minute" is a minute, signed by the prosecutor—

  (a) setting forth the grounds on which he is of the opinion that the judgment cannot be maintained; and

  (b) written on the complaint or lodged with the clerk of court.

(3) A copy of any minute under subsection (1) above shall be sent by the prosecutor to the convicted person or his solicitor and the clerk of court shall—

  (a) thereupon ascertain and note on the record, whether that person or solicitor desires to be heard by the High Court before the appeal, or as the case may be application, is disposed of; and

  (b) thereafter transmit the complaint and relative proceedings to the Clerk of Justiciary.

(4) The Clerk of Justiciary, on receipt of a complaint and relative proceedings transmitted under subsection (3) above, shall lay them before any judge of the High Court either in court or in chambers who, after hearing parties if they desire to be heard, may—

  (a) set aside the conviction or the sentence, or both, either in whole or in part and—

    (i) award such expenses to the convicted person, both in the High Court and in the inferior court, as the judge may think fit;

    (ii) where the conviction is set aside in part, pass another (but not more severe) sentence in substitution for the sentence imposed in respect of that conviction; and

    (iii) where the sentence is set aside, pass another (but not more severe) sentence; or

  (b) refuse to set aside the conviction or sentence or, as the case may be, conviction and sentence, in which case the complaint and proceedings shall be returned to the clerk of the inferior court.

(5) Where an appeal has been taken and the complaint and proceedings in respect of that appeal returned under subsection (4)(b) above, the appellant shall be entitled to proceed with the appeal as if it had been marked on the date of their being received by the clerk of the inferior court on such return.

(6) Where an appeal has been taken and a copy minute in respect of that appeal sent under subsection (3) above, the preparation of the draft stated case shall be delayed pending the decision of the High Court.

(7) The period from an application being made under subsection (1)(b) above until its disposal under subsection (4) above (including the day of application and the day of disposal) shall, in relation to the conviction to which the application relates, be disregarded in any computation of time specified in any provision of this Part of this Act.

DEFINITIONS

  "complaint": s.307(1).
  "High Court": s.307(1).
  "prosecutor": s.307(1).
  "relevant minute": s.188(2).
  "sentence": s.188(1)(a).

A set of procedural or other circumstances may have arisen resulting in a clear and unequivocal miscarriage of justice having occurred so that the Crown would not wish to maintain a judgment. This section provides for a conviction being set aside with the prosecutor's consent or on the prosecutor's application depending on the circumstances.

Subsection (2)(a)—in *MacRae v Hingston*, 1992 S.C.C.R. 911 the Appeal Court made it clear that where the procedure under this section is to be used any minute should be accompanied by sufficient material to satisfy the single judge that grounds of law exist to set aside the conviction.

Subs.(4)(b)—see *O'Brien v Adair*, 1947 J.C. 180 where the court refused to set aside a conviction.

Disposal of appeal against sentence

189.—(1) An appeal against sentence by note of appeal shall be heard by the High Court on such date as it may fix, and the High Court may, subject to section 190(1) of this Act, dispose of such appeal by—

(a) affirming the sentence; or

(b) if the Court thinks that, having regard to all the circumstances, including any evidence such as is mentioned in section 175(5) of this Act, a different sentence should have been passed, quashing the sentence and, subject to subsection (2) below, passing another sentence, whether more or less severe, in substitution therefor.

(2) In passing another sentence under subsection (1)(b) above, the Court shall not in any case increase the sentence beyond the maximum sentence which could have been passed by the inferior court.

(2A) The High Court may dispose of an appeal against a reference proposed under subsection (1) of section 10 of the Protection of Children (Scotland) Act 2003 (asp 5) by—

(a) dismissing the appeal and affirming such reference; or

(b) if it thinks—

(i) in a case to which subsection (3) of that section applies, that the court which is proposing to make the reference should not have been satisfied as to the condition mentioned in that subsection;

(ii) in a case to which subsection (4) of that section applies, that the court which is proposing to make the reference should have been satisfied as to the condition mentioned in that subsection,

by directing the court not to make the reference.

(3) The High Court shall have power in an appeal by note of appeal to award such expenses both in the High Court and in the inferior court as it may think fit.

(4) Where, following an appeal under section 175(2)(b) or (c), or by virtue of section 175(4), of this Act, the convicted person remains liable to imprisonment or detention under the sentence of the inferior court or is so liable under a sentence passed in the appeal proceedings, the High Court shall have power where at the time of disposal of the appeal the convicted person—

(a) was at liberty on bail, to grant warrant to apprehend and imprison or detain the appellant for a term, to run from the date of such apprehension, not longer than that part of the term or terms of imprisonment or detention specified in the sentence brought under review which remained unexpired at the date of liberation; or

(b) is serving a term or terms of imprisonment or detention imposed in relation to a conviction subsequent to the conviction in respect of which the sentence appealed against was imposed, to exercise the like powers in regard to him as may be exercised, in relation to an appeal which has been abandoned, by a court of summary jurisdiction in pursuance of section 177(6) of this Act.

(5) In subsection (1) above, "appeal against sentence" shall, without prejudice to the generality of the expression, be construed as including an appeal under section 175(2)(c), and any appeal by virtue of section 175(4), of this Act; and without prejudice to subsection (6) below, other references to sentence in that subsection and in subsection (4) above shall be construed accordingly.

(6) In disposing of any appeal in a case where the accused has not been convicted, the High Court may proceed to convict him; and where it does, the reference in subsection (4) above to the conviction in respect of which the sentence appealed against was imposed shall be construed as a reference to the disposal or order appealed against.

(7) In disposing of an appeal under section 175(2)(b) to (d), (3)(b) or (4) of this Act the High Court may, without prejudice to any other power in that regard, pronounce an opinion on

(a) the sentence or other disposal or order which is appropriate in any similar case;

(b) whether a reference is appropriate in any similar case.

AMENDMENT

Subs.(1)(b) as amended by the Crime and Punishment (Scotland) Act 1997 (c. 48), Sch.1 para.21(22) with effect from August 1, 1997 in terms of the Crime and Punishment (Scotland) Act 1997 (Commencement and Transitional Provisions) Order 1997 (SI 1997/1712), art.3.

Subss.(2A), (7)(b) inserted, and (7) as amended, by the Protection of Children (Scotland) Act 2003 (asp 5), s.16(10). Brought into force on January 10, 2005 by the Protection of Children (Scotland) Act 2003 (Commencement No.1) Order 2004 (SSI 2004/522 (C.38)), art.2.

DEFINITIONS

"appeal against sentence": s.189(5).
"High Court": s.307(1).
"sentence": s.307(1).

GENERAL NOTE

Subs. (1)

The sole test for appeals is whether there has been a miscarriage of justice and the question in relation to sentence is whether the sentence complained of is excessive: *Addison v Mackinnon*, 1983 S.C.C.R. 52: *Donaldson v H.M. Advocate*, 1983 S.C.C.R. 216. The High Court of Justiciary may affirm the sentence or quash it and impose another of greater or lesser severity. The latter option is not often used to increase a summary sentence although it has been done: *Briggs v Guild*, 1987 S.C.C.R. 141. The Court of Appeal is not authorised to alter a sentence on a charge which has not been appealed: see *Allan, Petr*, 1993 S.C.C.R. 686. In *Kelly v Vannet*, 2000 S.L.T. 75 in an appeal against sentence it was held that the appellant had pled to a non offence and an absolute discharge was substituted.

Disposal of appeal where appellant insane

190.—(1) In relation to any appeal under section 175(2) of this Act, the High Court shall, where it appears to it that the appellant committed the act charged against him but that he was insane when he did so, dispose of the appeal by—

(a) setting aside the verdict of the inferior court and substituting therefor a verdict of acquittal on the ground of insanity; and

(b) quashing any sentence imposed on the appellant as respects the complaint and—

(i) making, in respect of the appellant, any order mentioned in section 57(2)(a) to (d) of this Act; or

(ii) making no order.

(2) Subsections (3) to (6) of section 57 of this Act shall apply to an order made under subsection (1)(b)(i) above as it applies to an order made under subsection (2) of that section.

AMENDMENT

Subs.(2) as amended by the Mental Health (Care and Treatment) (Scotland) Act 2003 (asp 13), Sch.4, para.8(12). Brought into force on October 5, 2005 by the Mental Health (Care and Treatment) (Scotland) Act 2003 (Commencement No.4) Order 2005 (SSI 2005/161 (C.6)).

Miscellaneous

Appeal by suspension or advocation on ground of miscarriage of justice

191.—(1) Notwithstanding section 184(2) of this Act, a party to a summary prosecution may, where an appeal under section 175 of this Act would be incompetent or would in the circumstances be inappropriate, appeal to the High Court, by bill of suspension against a conviction or, as the case may be, by advocation against an acquittal on the ground of an alleged miscarriage of justice in the proceedings.

(2) Where the alleged miscarriage of justice is referred to in an application under section 176(1) of this Act, for a stated case as regards the proceedings (or in a duly made amendment or addition to that application), an appeal under subsection (1) above shall not proceed without the leave of the High Court until the appeal to which the application relates has been finally disposed of or abandoned.

(3) Sections 182(5)(a) to (e), 183(1)(d) and (4) and 185 of this Act shall apply to appeals under this section as they apply to appeals such as are mentioned in section 176(1) of this Act.

(4) This section is without prejudice to any rule of law relating to bills of suspension or advocation in so far as such rule of law is not inconsistent with this section.

GENERAL NOTE

For examples see *Pettigrew v Ingram*, 1982 S.L.T. 435; *MacKinnon v Craig*, 1983 S.L.T. 475 and *Durant v Lockhart*, 1985 S.C.C.R. 72. In *Clarke v Ruxton* 1997 G.W.D. 10–408 the accused proceeded by bill of suspension following the death of the sheriff before a stated case could be prepared. This last case is of broader evidential interest, since C's partial admissions of sexual misconduct with a child were held to corroborate evidence of the full libel given by the child.

Appeals: miscellaneous provisions

192.—(1) Where an appellant has been granted bail, whether his appeal is under this Part of this Act or otherwise, he shall appear personally in court at the diet appointed for the hearing of the appeal.

(2) Where an appellant who has been granted bail does not appear at such a diet, the High Court shall either—

(a) dispose of the appeal as if it had been abandoned (in which case subsection (5) of section 177 of this Act shall apply accordingly); or

(b) on cause shown permit the appeal to be heard in his absence.

(3) No conviction, sentence, judgement, order of court or other proceeding whatsoever in or for the purposes of summary proceedings under this Act—

(a) shall be quashed for want of form; or

(b) where the accused had legal assistance in his defence, shall be suspended or set aside in respect of any objections to—

    (i) the relevancy of the complaint, or to the want of specification therein; or

    (ii) the competency or admission or rejection of evidence at the trial in the inferior court,

unless such objections were timeously stated.

(4) The provisions regulating appeals shall, subject to the provisions of this Part of this Act, be without prejudice to any other mode of appeal competent.

(5) Any officer of law may serve any bill of suspension or other writ relating to an appeal.

DEFINITIONS

"bail": s.307(1).
"High Court": s.307(1).
"officer of law": s.307(1).
"sentence": s.307(1).

GENERAL NOTE

Subsection (3)(a)—see *Paterson v. MacLennan* (1914) 7 Adam 128 where the accused was found guilty but not as libelled. The appeal was refused. See also *Ogilvie v. Mitchell* (1903) 4 Adam 273; *Miller v. Brown*, 1941 J.C. 2, and *Gilmour v. Gray*, 1951 J.C. 70.

Subsection (2)—in *Gemmell v. MacDougall*, 1993 S.C.C.R. 238 the appeal by stated case was continued on a number of occasions because the appellant was medically unfit to attend. On the motion of the Crown and in the presence of counsel for the appellant the appeal was heard in the absence of the appellant, the view being taken that as the appeal was on a question of law the appellant would not be prejudiced by his absence.

In *Pratt v. Normand*, 1995 S.C.C.R. 881 the appellant failed to appear at the hearing of his appeal. The case was continued to give him an opportunity to appear. At the continued hearing he appeared and gave an explanation with which the Appeal Court were not satisfied. They refused the appeal for want of insistence: see also *Flynn v. Vannet*, 1997 G.W.D. 31–1555.

First, highly pedantic points cannot be taken on procedural or other matters as no conviction, sentence, judgment, order of court or other proceedings in or for the purposes of summary proceedings can be quashed for want of form: subs. (3)(a).

Secondly, the failure to object timeously to the relevancy of the complaint or to the want of specification or to the competency or admission or rejection of evidence prevents later suspension of a conviction or sentence if the accused had legal assistance: subs. (3)(b). See *e.g. Jardine v. Howdle*, 1997 S.C.C.R. 294 where an appeal against conviction, founding on the sheriff's placing a 13-year-old child on oath without ascertaining the age of a child witness or satisfying himself that the child understood the nature of the oath, was refused, no objection having been taken at the time.

If however the objection amounts to a fundamental nullity then this can be challenged at any time: see *Czajkowski v. Lewis*, 1956 J.C. 8; *Coventry v. Douglas*, 1944 J.C. 13; *Rendle v. Muir*, 1952 J.C. 115; *Aitkenhead v. Cuthbert*, 1961 J.C. 12, and *Shaw v. Smith*, Crown Office circular A43/78.

Suspension of disqualification, forfeiture etc.

193.—(1) Where upon conviction of any person—

(a) any disqualification, forfeiture or disability attaches to him by reason of such conviction; or

(b) any property, matters or things which are the subject of the prosecution or connected therewith are to be or may be ordered to be destroyed or forfeited,

if the court before which he was convicted thinks fit, the disqualification, forfeiture or disability or, as the case may be, destruction or forfeiture or order for destruction or forfeiture shall be suspended pending the determination of any appeal against conviction or sentence (or disposal or order).

(2) Subsection (1) above does not apply in respect of any disqualification, forfeiture or, as the case may be, destruction or forfeiture or order for destruction or forfeiture under or by virtue of any enactment which contains express provision for the suspension of such disqualification, forfeiture or, as the case may be, destruction or forfeiture or order for destruction or forfeiture pending the determination of any appeal against conviction or sentence (or disposal or order).

(3) Where, upon conviction, a fine has been imposed upon a person or a compensation order has been made against him under section 249 of this Act—

- (a) the fine or compensation order shall not be enforced against him and he shall not be liable to make any payment in respect of the fine or compensation order; and
- (b) any money paid under the compensation order shall not be paid by the clerk of court to the entitled person under subsection (9) of that section,

pending the determination of any appeal against conviction or sentence (or disposal or order).

Suspension of certain sentences pending determination of appeal

193A.—(1) Where a convicted person or the prosecutor appeals to the High Court under section 175 of this Act (other than by way of an appeal under section 175(2)(cb) of this Act against a reference only), the court may on the application of the appellant direct that the whole, or any remaining part, of a relevant sentence shall be suspended until the appeal, if it is proceeded with, is determined.

(2) Where the court has directed the suspension of the whole or any remaining part of a person's relevant sentence, the person shall, unless the High Court otherwise directs, appear personally in court on the day or days fixed for the hearing of the appeal.

(3) Where a person fails to appear personally in court as mentioned in subsection (2) above, the court may—

- (a) if he is the appellant—
  - (i) decline to consider the appeal; and
  - (ii) dismiss it summarily; or
- (b) whether or not he is the appellant—
  - (i) consider and determine the appeal; or
  - (ii) make such other order as the court thinks fit.

(4) In this section "relevant sentence" means any one or more of the following—

- (a) a probation order;
- (b) a supervised attendance order made under section 236(6) of this Act;
- (c) a community service order;
- (d) a restriction of liberty order;
- (e) a community reparation order.

AMENDMENTS

Section 193A inserted by the Crime and Punishment (Scotland) Act 1997 (c.48), s.24(2) with effect from August 1, 1997 in terms of the Crime and Punishment (Scotland) Act 1997 (Commencement and Transitional Provisions) Order 1997 (SI 1997/1712), art.3.

Subs.(4)(d) inserted by the Crime and Punishment (Scotland) Act 1997 (c.48), s.24(2) (effective July 1, 1998: SI 1998/2323).

Subs.(4)(e) inserted by the Antisocial Behaviour etc. (Scotland) Act 2004 (asp 8), s.144(1), Sch.4, para.5(3). Brought into force on October 28, 2004 by the Antisocial Behaviour etc. (Scotland) Act 2004 (Commencement and Savings) Order 2004 (SSI 2004/420 (C.31)).

Subs.(1) as amended by the Protection of Children (Scotland) Act 2003 (asp 5), s.16(11). Brought into force on January 10, 2005 by the Protection of Children (Scotland) Act 2003 (Commencement No.1) Order 2004 (SSI 2004/522 (C.38)), art.2.

GENERAL NOTE

With effect from August 1, 1997 certain sentences as detailed in subs. 4 can be suspended pending the determination of an appeal. Prevents a situation as arose in *H.M. Advocate v Jamieson*, 1996 S.C.C.R. 836.

Computation of time

194.—(1) If any period of time specified in any provision of this Part of this Act relating to appeals expires on a Saturday, Sunday or court holiday prescribed for the relevant court, the period shall be extended to expire on the next day which is not a Saturday, Sunday or such court holiday.

(2) Where a judge against whose judgment an appeal is taken—

(a) is temporarily absent from duty for any cause;

(b) is a part-time sheriff; or

(c) is a justice of the peace,

the sheriff principal of the sheriffdom in which the court at which the judgment was pronounced is situated may extend any period specified in sections 178(1) and 179(4) and (7) of this Act for such period as he considers reasonable.

(3) For the purposes of sections 176(1)(a) and 178(1) of this Act, summary proceedings shall be deemed to be finally determined on the day on which sentence is passed in open court; except that, where in relation to an appeal—

(a) under section 175(2)(a) or (3)(a); or

(b) in so far as it is against conviction, under section 175(2)(d),

of this Act sentence is deferred under section 202 of this Act, they shall be deemed finally determined on the day on which sentence is first so deferred in open court.

AMENDMENT

Subs.(2) as amended by Bail, Judicial Appointments etc. (Scotland) Act 2000 (asp 9), s.12 and Sch., para.7(5).

PART XA

SCOTTISH CRIMINAL CASES REVIEW COMMISSION

The Scottish Criminal Cases Review Commission

Scottish Criminal Cases Review Commission

194A.—(1) There shall be established a body corporate to be known as the Scottish Criminal Cases Review Commission (in this Act referred to as "the Commission").

(2) The Commission shall not be regarded as the servant or agent of the Crown or as enjoying any status, immunity or privilege of the Crown; and the Commission's property shall not be regarded as property of, or held on behalf of, the Crown.

(3) The Commission shall consist of not fewer than three members.

(4) The members of the Commission shall be appointed by Her Majesty on the recommendation of the Secretary of State.

(5) At least one third of the members of the Commission shall be persons who are legally qualified; and for this purpose a person is legally qualified if he is an advocate or solicitor of at least ten years' standing.

(6) At least two thirds of the members of the Commission shall be persons who appear to the Secretary of State to have knowledge or experience of any aspect of the criminal justice system; and for the purposes of this subsection the criminal justice system includes, in particular, the investigation of offences and the treatment of offenders.

(7) Schedule 9A to this Act, which makes further provision as to the Commission, shall have effect.

AMENDMENT

Section 194A inserted by s.25 of the Crime and Punishment (Scotland) Act 1997 with effect from January 1, 1998 as provided by the Crime and Punishment (Scotland) Act 1997 (Commencement No.4) Order 1997 (SI 1997/3004 (C.110) (S.190)).

GENERAL NOTE

This part of the Act provides for a Scottish Criminal Cases Review Commission. The Sutherland Commission recommended the setting up of a new body to consider alleged miscarriages of justice and to refer deserving cases to the Court of Appeal. The Secretary of State would be removed from this process. The Committee was of the view that the Secretary of State's role was incompatible with the constitutional separation of powers between the executive and the courts. An independent body would be seen to be impartial. The Committee recognised that the Secretary of State was however accountable to Parliament whilst the Commission would be subject to judicial review.

The Sutherland Committee reported there was a strong body of opinion that there was no need for change, and defects in the system would be remedied by the amended ground of appeal. The Government latched onto this and made no provision for the Commission in the Bill. Despite the best efforts of Lord McCluskey at the committee stage in the House of Lords, the Government resisted amendments to remedy the omission (see *Hansard*, HL, March 10, 1997, cols 56 to 62). The legislative timetable however resulted in a Government concession (see *Hansard*, HL, March 10, 1997, cols 945 to 952). The provisions on the whole follow the Sutherland Committee's recommendations.

Further provisions for the workings of the Commission can be found in Sch.9A.

s.194A

Provision is made for at least three members of the Commission and the Sutherland Committee envisaged that these will be part-time appointments. At least one-third of the members requires to be legally qualified and at least two-thirds need knowledge or experience of the investigation of offences and treatment of offenders. There are currently seven commissioners.

References to High Court

Cases dealt with on indictment

194B.—(1) The Commission on the consideration of any conviction of a person or of the sentence (other than sentence of death) passed on a person who has been convicted on indictment or complaint may, if they think fit, at any time, and whether or not an appeal against such conviction or sentence has previously been heard and determined by the High Court, refer the whole case to the High Court and the case shall be heard and determined, subject to any directions the High Court may make, as if it were an appeal under Part VIII or, as the case may be, Part X of this Act.

(2) The power of the Commission under this section to refer to the High Court the case of a person convicted shall be exercisable whether or not that person has petitioned for the exercise of Her Majesty's prerogative of mercy.

(3) This section shall apply in relation to a finding under section 55(2) and an order under section 57(2) of this Act as it applies, respectively, in relation to a conviction and a sentence.

(4) For the purposes of this section "person" includes a person who is deceased.

AMENDMENTS

Section 194B inserted by s.25 of the Crime and Punishment (Scotland) Act 1997 with effect from April 1, 1999 as provided by the Crime and Punishment (Scotland) Act 1997 (Commencement No. 5 and Transitional Provisions and Savings) Order 1999 (SI 1999/652).

Subs.(1) as amended by SI 1999/1181, para.3 (effective April 1, 1999).

GENERAL NOTE

s.194B

Subs.(1) A reference can be made at any time (in *Preece v HM Advocate* [1981] Crim.L.R. 783, the reference by the Secretary of State was made seven years after conviction) **post conviction**, whether or not the case has been previously heard by the Appeal Court. The appeal is then treated as an ordinary appeal. The Commission may, as could the Secretary of State, refer the whole case or part thereof to the Appeal Court (see e.g. *Slater v HM Advocate*, 1928 J.C. 94; *Gallacher v HM Advocate*, 1951 J.C. 38 and *Beattie v HM Advocate*, 1995 J.C. 33). The first reference by the SCCRC was *Bonca-Tomaszewski v HM Advocate*, 2000 J.C. 586. It was held that the Appeal Court in considering the reference would proceed on the basis of current understanding of common law and present day standards although that could result in the court criticising their predecessors by reference to different criteria than applied then.

Once a reference is made the provisions relating to either solemn or summary appeals apply as applicable. In e.g. *Bonca Tomaszewski v HM Advocate* following the Commission's reference the applicant proceeded by lodging grounds of appeal. In *Crombie v Clark*, 2001 S.L.T. 635 the applicant lodged a Bill of Suspension following the reference.

Subs.(2) The prerogative of mercy is still exercisable by the Secretary of State but the Commission may refer a case even if a petition for the Royal Prerogative has previously been made.

Subs.(3) A reference can be made in respect of a finding that an accused committed an act where he is insane in bar of trial and also in respect of disposals where an accused is insane at the time of the offence.

Subs.(4) A reference can be made in respect of a deceased.

Grounds for reference

194C. The grounds upon which the Commission may refer a case to the High Court are that they believe—

(a) that a miscarriage of justice may have occurred; and

(b) that it is in the interests of justice that a reference should be made.

AMENDMENT

Section 194C inserted by s.25 of the Crime and Punishment (Scotland) Act 1997 with effect from April 1, 1999 as provided by the Crime and Punishment (Scotland) Act 1997 (Commencement No. 5 and Transitional Provisions and Savings) Order 1999 (SI 1999/652).

GENERAL NOTE

s.194C

The administrative criteria by which the Secretary of State assessed cases involving a miscarriage of justice was considered by the Sutherland Committee. The criteria were whether there was relevant material to suggest a miscarriage of justice and further, would the Appeal Court as a matter of law entertain the case on a reference.

The Committee considered that the criteria for references by the commission should reflect the "broad and flexible miscarriage of justice" ground of appeal. It appears that part (a) incorporates the previous criteria used by the Secretary of State, there being no point in referring an alleged miscarriage of justice which the appeal court as a matter of law would not entertain.

The Committee also recommended that the normal appeal procedures should have been exhausted but this has not been incorporated in the current provisions.

In *Crombie v Clark*, 2001 S.L.T. 635 the Appeal Court held that the question of whether or not it was in the interests of justice for a reference to be made was a matter for the Commission and not the Appeal court. As Sir Gerald Gordon comments at pages 240–241 the Commission only requires "to believe there may have been" a miscarriage of justice. The Appeal Court require to be satisfied that there has. The reasons for the Commission's belief or material on which it is based are not considered by the Court. The Appeal Court in *Crombie* expressed surprise that the merits of the applicant's defence were not considered when the Commission determined whether they believed there had been a miscarriage of justice.

Further provision as to references

194D.—(1) A reference of a conviction, sentence or finding may be made under section 194B of this Act whether or not an application has been made by or on behalf of the person to whom it relates.

(2) In considering whether to make a reference the Commission shall have regard to—

(a) any application or representations made to the Commission by or on behalf of the person to whom it relates;

(b) any other representations made to the Commission in relation to it; and

(c) any other matters which appear to the Commission to be relevant.

(3) In considering whether to make a reference the Commission may at any time refer to the High Court for the Court's opinion any point on which they desire the Court's assistance; and on a reference under this subsection the High Court shall consider the point referred and furnish the Commission with their opinion on the point.

(4) Where the Commission make a reference to the High Court under section 194B of this Act they shall—

(a) give to the Court a statement of their reasons for making the reference; and

(b) send a copy of the statement to every person who appears to them to be likely to be a party to any proceedings on the appeal arising from the reference.

(5) In every case in which—

(a) an application has been made to the Commission by or on behalf of any person for the reference by them of any conviction, sentence or finding; but

(b) the Commission decide not to make a reference of the conviction, sentence or finding,

they shall give a statement of the reasons for their decision to the person who made the application.

AMENDMENT

Section 194D inserted by s.25 of the Crime and Punishment (Scotland) Act 1997 with effect from April 1, 1999 as provided by the Crime and Punishment (Scotland) Act 1997 (Commencement No. 5 and Transitional Provisions and Savings) Order 1999 (SI 1999/652).

s.194D

Subs.(1)   This allows an application to be made to the Commission on someone's behalf, e.g. someone who is mentally ill or deceased. Although the Sutherland Committee recommended that this should be allowed only if there was a good reason, this requirement has not been incorporated.

Subs.(2)   In *R. v Secretary of State for Home Department, ex p. Hickey (No.2)* [1995] 1 All E.R. 490, it was held that prior to the Secretary of State's decision regarding a referral, a petitioner should be given the opportunity to make representations upon whatever material had been revealed by the Secretary of State's enquiries and that sufficient disclosure should be given to enable the petitioner to present his case.

It may well be that the Commission will have to disclose relevant material to enable the applicant to make full representations.

Subs.(3)   This is not limited to a point of law. Hopefully this may be used to clarify points such as mentioned above.

Subs.(4)   A statement of reasons for making the reference must be sent to every person the Commission considers likely to be a party to any proceedings. In most cases this will just be the Crown and the accused but there is also the possibility of a co-accused. The principal statement of reasons is given to the court.

In *Bonca-Tomaszewski v HM Advocate*, 2000 J.C. 586 after the reference was lodged by the SC-CRC the appellant lodged fresh grounds of appeal. Following a procedural hearing the court suggested that the grounds of appeal be amended to include the original grounds of appeal and ordered written submissions. In *Crombie v Clark*, 2001 S.L.T. 635 once the reference was made by the Commission, the complainer lodged a Bill of Suspension. The Appeal Court held that the court must proceed on the material in the Bill and not in the letter of referral.

Subs.(5)   If a decision is taken not to make a reference, a statement of reasons must be given to the applicant. The decision will no doubt be subject to judicial review.

Extension of Commission's remit to summary cases

194E.—(1) The Secretary of State may by order provide for this Part of this Act to apply in relation to convictions, sentences and findings made in summary proceedings as they apply in relation to convictions, sentences and findings made in solemn proceedings, and may for that purpose make in such an order such amendments to the provisions of this Part as appear to him to be necessary or expedient.

(2) An order under this section shall be made by statutory instrument, and shall not have effect unless a draft of it has been laid before and approved by a resolution of each House of Parliament.

Section 194E inserted by s.25 of the Crime and Punishment (Scotland) Act 1997 with effect from January 1, 1998 as provided by the Crime and Punishment (Scotland) Act 1997 (Commencement No. 4) Order 1997 (SI 1997/3004 (C.110) (S.190)).

s.194E

The Sutherland Committee considered that the Commission should also be able to consider summary cases but that to ensure that priority was given to solemn cases and to ensure that the Commission was not overwhelmed, then the Secretary of State could extend the Commission's remit at a later stage to summary cases. The Committee envisaged that the Commission would rarely have to consider summary cases as the existing appeal procedures for summary cases were well established. The Commission remit was extended to summary cases by means of the Scottish Criminal Cases Review Commission (Application to Summary Proceedings) Order 1999 (SI 1999/1181).

In *Crombie v Clark*, 2001 S.L.T. 635 proceedings commenced by a reference by the Commission in a summary case. C subsequently appealed by Bill of Suspension.

Further powers

194F. The Commission may take any steps which they consider appropriate for assisting them in the exercise of any of their functions and may, in particular—

(a) themselves undertake inquiries and obtain statements, opinions or reports; or

(b) request the Lord Advocate or any other person to undertake such inquiries or obtain such statements, opinions and reports.

AMENDMENT

Section 194F inserted by s.25 of the Crime and Punishment (Scotland) Act 1997 with effect from April 1, 1999 as provided by the Crime and Punishment (Scotland) Act 1997 (Commencement No. 5 and Transitional Provisions and Savings) Order 1999 (SI 1999/652).

GENERAL NOTE

s.194F

The Commission has power to undertake enquiries, obtain statements, opinions or reports or request the Lord Advocate or others to do so. As the emphasis is on independence and justice being seen to be done the Commission undertakes the majority of enquiries themselves employing a number of case workers. Previously, investigations were dealt with through Crown Office, the Procurator Fiscal or the police—including the precognition of witnesses, obtaining forensic reports, etc. One of the major criticisms of the old procedure was that those bodies responsible for prosecuting a person thereafter were involved in investigating any alleged miscarriage of justice.

Supplementary provision

194G.—(1) The Secretary of State may by order make such incidental, consequential, transitional or supplementary provisions as may appear to him to be necessary or expedient for the purpose of bringing this Part of this Act into operation, and, without prejudice to the generality of the foregoing, of dealing with any cases being considered by him under section 124 of this Act at the time when this Part comes into force, and an order under this section may make different provision in relation to different cases or classes of case.

(2) An order under this section shall be made by statutory instrument subject to annulment in pursuance of a resolution of either House of Parliament.

AMENDMENT

Section 194G inserted by s.25 of the Crime and Punishment (Scotland) Act 1997 with effect from January 1, 1998 as provided by the Crime and Punishment (Scotland) Act 1997 (Commencement No. 4) Order 1997 (SI 1997/3004 (C.110) (S.190)).

Powers of investigation of Commission

Power to request precognition on oath

194H.—(1) Where it appears to the Commission that a person may have information which they require for the purposes of carrying out their functions, and the person refuses to make any statement to them, they may apply to the sheriff under this section.

(2) On an application made by the Commission under this section, the sheriff may, if he is satisfied that it is reasonable in the circumstances, grant warrant to cite the person concerned to appear before the sheriff in chambers at such time or place as shall be specified in the citation, for precognition on oath by a member of the Commission or a person appointed by them to act in that regard.

(3) Any person who, having been duly cited to attend for precognition under subsection (2) above and having been given at least 48 hours notice, fails without reasonable excuse to attend shall be guilty of an offence and liable on summary conviction to a fine not exceeding level 3 on the standard scale or to imprisonment for a period not exceeding 21 days; and the court may issue a warrant for the apprehension of the person concerned ordering him to be brought before a sheriff for precognition on oath.

(4) Any person who, having been duly cited to attend for precognition under subsection (2) above, attends but—

(a) refuses to give information within his knowledge or to produce evidence in his possession; or

(b) prevaricates in his evidence,

shall be guilty of an offence and shall be liable to be summarily subjected to a fine not exceeding level 3 on the standard scale or to imprisonment for a period not exceeding 21 days.

AMENDMENT

Section 194H inserted by s.25 of the Crime and Punishment (Scotland) Act 1997 with effect from April 1, 1999 as provided by the Crime and Punishment (Scotland) Act 1997 (Commencement No. 5 and Transitional Provisions and Savings) Order 1999 (SI 1999/652).

GENERAL NOTE

New s.194H

This allows for precognition on oath. Other parties would not be entitled to be present (see Hume Vol. ii. 82).

Power to obtain documents etc.

194I.—(1) Where the Commission believe that a person or a public body has possession or control of a document or other material which may assist them in the exercise of any of their functions, they may apply to the High Court for an order requiring that person or body—

(a) to produce the document or other material to the Commission or to give the Commission access to it; and

(b) to allow the Commission to take away the document or other material or to make and take away a copy of it in such form as they think appropriate,

and such an order may direct that the document or other material must not be destroyed, damaged or altered before the direction is withdrawn by the Court.

(2) The duty to comply with an order under this section is not affected by any obligation of secrecy or other limitation on disclosure (including any such obligation or limitation imposed by or by virtue of any enactment) which would otherwise prevent the production of the document or other material to the Commission or the giving of access to it to the Commission.

(3) The documents and other material covered by this section include, in par-

ticular, any document or other material obtained or created during any investigation or proceedings relating to—

(a) the case in relation to which the Commission's function is being or may be exercised; or

(b) any other case which may be in any way connected with that case (whether or not any function of the Commission could be exercised in relation to that other case).

(4) In this section—

"Minister" means a Minister of the Crown as defined by section 8 of the Ministers of the Crown Act 1975;

"police force" means any police force maintained for a local government area under section 1(1) of the Police (Scotland) Act 1967 and references to a chief constable are references to the chief constable of such a force within the meaning of that Act; and

"public body" means

(a) any police force;

(b) any government department, local authority or other body constituted for the purposes of the public service, local government or the administration of justice; or

(c) any other body whose members are appointed by Her Majesty, any Minister, the Scottish Minister or any government department or whose revenues consist wholly or mainly of money provided by Parliament.

AMENDMENTS

Section 194I inserted by s.25 of the Crime and Punishment (Scotland) Act 1997 with effect from April 1, 1999 as provided by the Crime and Punishment (Scotland) Act 1997 (Commencement No.5 and Transitional Provisions and Savings) Order 1999 (SI 1999/652).

Subs.(4)(c) as amended by the Scotland Act 1998 (Consequential Modifications) (No.2) Order 1999 (SI 1999/1820), art.4 and Sch.2, para.122(2) (effective July 1, 1999).

GENERAL NOTE

The Commission's broad rights to recover and examine documents were upheld in *Scottish Criminal Cases Review Commission v HM Advocate*, 2001 S.L.T. 905; 2000 S.C.C.R. 842, where the Crown had opposed access to its papers. The Appeal Court held that SCCRC were not precluded from recovering e.g. departmental documents, the nature and circumstance of the creation of the document not being sufficient objection to recovery. While the court accepted that there might be certain classes of documents which would warrant denial of access to the Commission, the Crown still had to justify refusal of a request for materials by the Commission. On the other hand it would be difficult for the Commission to make out a case for access to documents whose contents were entirely unknown to it. The court held that averments setting out the history of the case satisfied the requirements of s.194I. It was recognised that it was only when the SCCRC saw the documents they would be able to ascertain if they were material.

Disclosure of information

Offence of disclosure

194J.—(1) A person who is or has been a member or employee of the Commission shall not disclose any information obtained by the Commission in the exercise of any of their functions unless the disclosure of the information is excepted from this section by section 194K of this Act.

(2) A member of the Commission shall not authorise the disclosure by an employee of the Commission of any information obtained by the Commission in the exercise of any of their functions unless the authorisation of the disclosure of the information is excepted from this section by section 194K of this Act.

(3) A person who contravenes this section is guilty of an offence and liable on summary conviction to a fine of an amount not exceeding level 5 on the standard scale.

AMENDMENT

Section 194J inserted by s.25 of the Crime and Punishment (Scotland) Act 1997 with effect from April 1, 1999 as provided by the Crime and Punishment (Scotland) Act 1997 (Commencement No. 5 and Transitional Provisions and Savings) Order 1999 (SI 1999/652).

Exceptions from obligations of non-disclosure

194K.—(1) The disclosure of information, or the authorisation of the disclosure of information, is excepted from section 194J of this Act by this section if the information is disclosed, or is authorised to be disclosed—

(a) for the purposes of any criminal, disciplinary or civil proceedings;

(b) in order to assist in dealing with an application made to the Secretary of State for compensation for a miscarriage of justice;

(c) by a person who is a member or an employee of the Commission to another person who is a member or an employee of the Commission;

(d) in any statement or report required by this Act;

(e) in or in connection with the exercise of any function under this Act; or

(f) in any circumstances in which the disclosure of information is permitted by an order made by the Secretary of State.

(2) The disclosure of information is also excepted from section 194J of this Act by this section if the information is disclosed by an employee of the Commission who is authorised to disclose the information by a member of the Commission.

(3) The disclosure of information, or the authorisation of the disclosure of information, is also excepted from section 194J of this Act by this section if the information is disclosed, or is authorised to be disclosed, for the purposes of—

(a) the investigation of an offence; or

(b) deciding whether to prosecute a person for an offence,

unless the disclosure is or would be prevented by an obligation or other limitation on disclosure (including any such obligation or limitation imposed by, under or by virtue of any enactment) arising otherwise than under that section.

(4) Where the disclosure of information is excepted from section 194J of this Act by subsection (1) or (2) above, the disclosure of the information is not prevented by any obligation of secrecy or other limitation on disclosure (including any such obligation or limitation imposed by, under or by virtue of any enactment) arising otherwise than under that section.

(5) The power to make an order under subsection (1)(f) above is exercisable by statutory instrument which shall be subject to annulment in pursuance of a resolution of either House of Parliament.

AMENDMENT

Section 194K inserted by s.25 of the Crime and Punishment (Scotland) Act 1997 with effect from April 1, 1999 as provided by the Crime and Punishment (Scotland) Act 1997 (Commencement No. 5 and Transitional Provisions and Savings) Order 1999 (SI 1999/652).

Consent of disclosure

194L.—(1) Where a person or body is required by an order under section 194I of this Act to produce or allow access to a document or other material to the Commission and notifies them that any information contained in the document or other material to which the order relates is not to be disclosed by the Commission without his or its prior consent, the Commission shall not disclose the information without such consent.

(2) Such consent may not be withheld unless—

(a) (apart from section 194I of this Act) the person would have been prevented by any obligation of secrecy or other limitation on disclosure from disclosing the information without such consent; and

(b) it is reasonable for the person to withhold his consent to disclosure of the information by the Commission.

(3) An obligation of secrecy or other limitation on disclosure which applies to a person only where disclosure is not authorised by another person shall not be taken for the purposes of subsection (2)(a) above to prevent the disclosure by the person of information to the Commission unless—

(a) reasonable steps have been taken to obtain the authorisation of the other person; or

(b) such authorisation could not reasonably be expected to be obtained.".

AMENDMENT

Section 194L inserted by s.25 of the Crime and Punishment (Scotland) Act 1997 with effect from April 1, 1999 as provided by the Crime and Punishment (Scotland) Act 1997 (Commencement No. 5 and Transitional Provisions and Savings) Order 1999 (SI 1999/652).

PART XI

SENTENCING

General

Remit to High Court for sentence

195.—(1) Where at any diet in proceedings on indictment in the sheriff court, sentence falls to be imposed but the sheriff holds that any competent sentence which he can impose is inadequate or it appears to him that the criteria mentioned in section 210E of this Act (that is to say, the risk criteria) may be met so that, in either case, the question of sentence is appropriate for the High Court, he shall—

(a) endorse upon the record copy of the indictment a certificate of the plea or the verdict, as the case may be;

(b) by interlocutor written on the record copy remit the convicted person to the High Court for sentence; and

(c) append to the interlocutor a note of his reasons for the remit,

and a remit under this section shall be sufficient warrant to bring the accused before the High Court for sentence and shall remain in force until the person is sentenced.

(2) Where under any enactment an offence is punishable on conviction on indictment by imprisonment for a term exceeding five years but the enactment either expressly or impliedly restricts the power of the sheriff to impose a sentence of imprisonment for a term exceeding five years, it shall be competent for the sheriff to remit the accused to the High Court for sentence under subsection (1) above; and it shall be competent for the High Court to pass any sentence which it could have passed if the person had been convicted before it.

(3) When the Clerk of Justiciary receives the record copy of the indictment he shall send a copy of the note of reasons to the convicted person or his solicitor and to the Crown Agent.

(4) Subject to subsection (3) above, the note of reasons shall be available only to the High Court and the parties.

AMENDMENT

Subs.(2) as amended by the Crime and Punishment (Scotland) Act 1997 (c.48), s.13(3). Brought into force on May 1, 2004 by the Crime and Punishment (Scotland) Act 1997 (Commencement No. 6 and Savings) Order 2004 (SSI 2004/176 (C.12)).

Subs.(1) as amended by the Criminal Justice (Scotland) Act 2003 (asp 7), Sch.1, para.2(5). Brought into force on June 19, 2006 by the Criminal Justice (Scotland) Act 2003 (Commencement No.9) Order 2006 (SSI 2006/332 (C.30)), art.2(1), subject to art.2(2).

DEFINITIONS

"Clerk of Justiciary": s.307(1).
"diet": s.307(1).
"enactment": s.307(1).
"High Court": s.307(1).
"indictment": s.307(1).
"sentence": s.307(1).

GENERAL NOTE

Subs. (1)

This subsection reproduces the terms of s.104(1) of the 1975 Act in requiring a remit where "the sheriff holds that any competent sentence which he can impose is inadequate so that the question of sentence is appropriate for the High Court". This contrasts with the original position in s.31 of the Criminal Procedure (Scotland) Act 1887 (c.35) which required a remit if the sheriff held that if the case was "of so grave a nature" that the question of punishment should be disposed of by the High Court of Justiciary. Care must be taken that the plea and remit are properly authenticated: *HM Advocate v Galloway*, (1894) 1 Adam 375 and *HM Advocate v McDonald*, (1896) 3 S.L.T. 317. The sheriff who remits the accused merely means the sheriff who has the duty to sentence: *Borland v HM Advocate*, 1976 S.L.T. (Notes) 12.

Subs. (2)

This subsection reproduces the terms of s.104(1A) of the 1975 Act as amended. The maximum competent sentence must be considered by the sheriff before remit, and where there are two or more indictments, each indictment must be considered separately. Where the maximum sentence which could be imposed on an indictment was within the competence of the sheriff then he must deal with that indictment: *HM Advocate v Anderson*, 1946 J.C. 81. Each of several indictments must be considered separately: *HM Advocate v Stern*, 1974 S.L.T. 2.

Sentence following guilty plea

196.—(1) In determining what sentence to pass on, or what other disposal or order to make in relation to, an offender who has pled guilty to an offence, a court shall take into account—

(a) the stage in the proceedings for the offence at which the offender indicated his intention to plead guilty, and

(b) the circumstances in which that indication was given.

(1A) In passing sentence on an offender referred to in subsection (1) above, the court shall—

(a) state whether, having taken account of the matters mentioned in paragraphs (a) and (b) of that subsection, the sentence imposed in respect of the offence is different from that which the court would otherwise have imposed; and

(b) if it is not, state reasons why it is not.

(2) Where the court is passing sentence on an offender under section 205B(2) of this Act and that offender has pled guilty to the offence for which he is being so sentenced, the court may, after taking into account the matters mentioned in paragraphs (a) and (b) of subsection (1) above, pass a sentence of less than seven years imprisonment or, as the case may be, detention but any such sentence shall not be of a term of imprisonment or period of detention of less than five years, two hundred and nineteen days.

AMENDMENT

Subs.(2) inserted by the Crime and Punishment (Scotland) Act 1997 (c.48), s.2(2) with effect from October 20, 1997 in terms of the Crime and Punishment (Scotland) Act 1997 (Commencement No. 2 and Transitional Provisions) Order 1997 (SI 1997/2323), art.3 and Sch.1.

Subs.(1) as amended, and (1A) inserted, by the Criminal Procedure (Amendment) (Scotland) Act 2004 (asp 5), s.20. Brought into force on October 4, 2004 by the Criminal Procedure (Amendment) (Scotland) Act 2004 (Commencement, Transitional Provisions and Savings) Order 2004 (SSI 2004/405 (C.28)).

DEFINITION

"sentence": s.307(1).

GENERAL NOTE

For the modern policy on sentencing following a guilty plea the beginning of wisdom is now *Du Plooy v HM Advocate*, 2003 S.L.T. 1237. There guidance was given as to the basis of, and scope for, an allowance in the sentencing of an accused in respect of a guilty plea, and the form that such an allowance might take.

It was held that it is desirable that, where a plea of guilty and related matters call for an allowance, the sentencer should use a distinct discount in the process of arriving at the appropriate sentence, and should state in court the extent to which he or she has discounted the sentence (opinion at para 25). An elegant, and brief, discussion of the competing factors to be considered when this section's provisions arise during proceedings is found in *HM Advocate v Booth*, 2005 S.L.T. 337 (opinion at paras 21 and 22).

Moreover, since the significance of the timing and circumstances of the tendering of the plea of guilty will vary, it would not be appropriate for there to be a fixed or 'normal' discount. What should be the discount in the individual case is plainly a matter for the discretion of the sentencer. For the same reason the court did not consider it appropriate to indicate a maximum or a minimum discount. However, the court considered that the discount should normally not exceed a third of the sentence that would otherwise have been imposed (opinion at para 26).

More subtle distinctions will doubtless emerge from future sentencing appeals but some general comments should hold good; henceforth, it will be important for prosecution and defence alike to preserve careful notes of the terms, and precise timing, of pleas offered and to be in a position to address the court on the matter; tactical pleas, for example to lesser alternatives, or partial pleas from an individual accused, may well not merit a *Du Plooy*-type discount on sentence once evidence has been led; it would seem necessary for the court to stipulate the extent of any discount applied in the sentence; and the whole issue will be much more complex in cases involving several accused, especially when the Crown refuses otherwise acceptable pleas from an accused for its own tactical purposes. Finally, a discount on sentence need not be confined to the calculation of a custodial sentence—it might validly reduce say, a probation period or hours of community service, but it is a matter of conjecture whether it could justify the substitution of a lesser form of sentence.

One aspect which has not been clarified is the interplay between *Du Plooy* considerations and the imposition of extended sentences as set out in s.210A of the Act. Since the paramount consideration in such circumstances is the long-term need to protect the public as part of the sentencing process, it is submitted that in such cases there would be limited scope for discounting sentence.

Subs.(a)

The court may take into account the stage in the proceedings for the offence at which the offender indicated his intention to plead guilty. There are various stages from arrest to a letter of intention to plead guilty to an instruction to a solicitor at which the intention may be stated: see *Backdating Sen-*

tences and Imprisonment (1995) 40 J.L.S. 383 and especially at p.384 for a discussion of these stages and various authorities.

Subs.(b)

The court may take into account the circumstances in which the indication was given. Context is important because a guilty plea may save children from giving evidence: *Khaliq v HM Advocate*, 1984 J.C. 23. Similar considerations must apply to other vulnerable witnesses but there can be little thought for an accused who puts such witnesses to the test and then pleads guilty at the end of the Crown case without having diminished the Crown case in any way.

In *Johnston v Wilson*, 1996 G.W.D. 17–986 the Appeal Court further backdated a sentence from the date upon which the accused had pled guilty to the date of his incarceration on remand, J having faced 40 charges originally and pleas having been accepted to only 13 of those charges.

Subs.(1A)

This subsection requires a court to state openly any discount that is being allowed for in passing a sentence following a guilty plea: see *Du Plooy v HM Advocate*, 2003 S.L.T. 1237.

Subs.(2)

It was only after the Committee stage of the Crime and Punishment Bill that the Government moved the amendments, now found in subs.(2), to enable the High Court to mitigate the automatic minimum sentences introduced as s.205B of the 1995 Act in cases where a timeous guilty plea has been tendered. The mandatory sentence of seven years may in such circumstances be reduced to a period of not less than 5 years 219 days, a 20 per cent discount. Clarification of the interplay between subs.(2) above and s.205B(3) which relates to the extent of judicial discretion in sentencing after trial is found in s.199(3)(c) below. Section 199 serves to limit the range of sentencing options available at the judge's discretion in the circumstances set out in s.205B; accordingly, it is submitted that the sentencing options specified in s.199(2) of the Act do not apply to a third conviction before the High Court for a class A drug trafficking offence—an offender has to be incarcerated for a term of imprisonment, or detention, of at least 5 years 219 days in any such case.

Sentencing guidelines

197. Without prejudice to any rule of law, a court in passing sentence shall have regard to any relevant opinion pronounced under section 118(7) or section 189(7) of this Act.

GENERAL NOTE

Sections 254 and 455 of the 1975 Act (and now ss.118 and 189 of this Act) provided powers for the disposal of appeals by the High Court of Justiciary. These powers were concerned only with the individual appeal then before the court. On one view, for the court to give an exposition of sentencing policy in generality for similar cases would be ultra vires. However, by ss.118(7) and 189(7) of this Act the High Court of Justiciary may pronounce an opinion in relation to similar cases. By s.197, in sentencing a court must have regard to any such opinion.

Form of sentence

198.—(1) In any case the sentence to be pronounced shall be announced by the judge in open court and shall be entered in the record in the form prescribed by Act of Adjournal.

(2) In recording a sentence of imprisonment, it shall be sufficient to minute the term of imprisonment to which the court sentenced the accused, without specifying the prison in which the sentence is to be carried out; and an entry of sentence, signed by the clerk of court, shall be full warrant and authority for any subsequent execution of the sentence and for the clerk to issue extracts for the purposes of execution or otherwise.

(3) In extracting a sentence of imprisonment, the extract may be in the form set out in an Act of Adjournal or as nearly as may be in such form.

DEFINITION

"sentence": s.307(1).

GENERAL NOTE

O'Neill v H.M. Advocate, 1999 S.L.T. 364 establishes that all information which an accused seeks to place before a sentencing court as mitigation must be produced in open court. (In *O'Neill's* case information showing his previous co-operation with the police was produced to the trial judge who declined to consider the papers on the basis that the contents could not be discussed publicly.)

In *Steele v H.M. Advocate*, 2002 S.L.T. 868 the court was reconvened after sentence had been imposed upon the accused when it was realised that no disqualification from driving had been pronounced. On appeal the accused's contention was that no such disqualification could be imposed upon him by the judge; it was argued that the judge was by that stage *functus officio* and enjoyed no *locus* to sentence. The Appeal Court was satisfied that a valid sentence had been passed in open court.

Power to mitigate penalties

199.—(1) Subject to subsection (3) below, where a person is convicted of the contravention of an enactment and the penalty which may be imposed involves—

(a) imprisonment;

(b) the imposition of a fine;

(c) the finding of caution for good behaviour or otherwise whether or not imposed in addition to imprisonment or a fine,

subsection (2) below shall apply.

(2) Where this subsection applies, the court, in addition to any other power conferred by statute, shall have power—

(a) to reduce the period of imprisonment;

(b) to substitute for imprisonment a fine (either with or without the finding of caution for good behaviour);

(c) to substitute for imprisonment or a fine the finding of caution;

(d) to reduce the amount of the fine;

(e) to dispense with the finding of caution.

(3) Subsection (2) above shall not apply—

(a) in relation to an enactment which carries into effect a treaty, convention, or agreement with a foreign state which stipulates for a fine of a minimum amount;

(b) to proceedings taken under any Act relating to any of Her Majesty's regular or auxiliary forces; or

(c) to any proceedings in which the court on conviction is under a duty to impose a sentence under section 205A(2) or 205B(2) of this Act.

(4) Where, in summary proceedings, a fine is imposed in substitution for imprisonment, the fine—

(a) in the case of an offence which is triable either summarily or on indictment, shall not exceed the prescribed sum; and

(b) in the case of an offence triable only summarily, shall not exceed level 4 on the standard scale.

(5) Where the finding of caution is imposed under this section—

(a) in respect of an offence which is triable only summarily, the amount shall not exceed level 4 on the standard scale and the period shall not exceed that which the court may impose under this Act; and

(b) in any other case, the amount shall not exceed the prescribed sum and the period shall not exceed 12 months.

AMENDMENT

Subs.(3)(c) inserted by the Crime and Punishment (Scotland) Act 1997, Sch.1, para.21 with effect from October 20, 1997 as provided by the Crime and Punishment (Scotland) Act 1997 (Commencement No. 2) and Transitional and Consequential Provisions) Order 1997 (SI 1997/2323).

DEFINITIONS

"fine": s.307(1).
"indictment": s.307(1).
"level 4": s.225(2) [*i.e.* £2,500].
"prescribed sum": s.225(8).
"standard scale": s.225(1).

GENERAL NOTE

This section applies to all proceedings, subject to the express restrictions set out in subs.(3), and empowers the court to modify or amend sentences previously imposed. As the section description makes clear, the provisions can only be used to mitigate (reduce) sentence. Subs.(3) specifies the circumstances in which no exercise of this general post-sentencing discretion is permissible.

Pre-sentencing procedure

Remand for inquiry into physical or mental condition

200.—(1) Without prejudice to any powers exercisable by a court under section 201 of this Act, where—

(a) the court finds that an accused has committed an offence punishable with imprisonment; and

(b) it appears to the court that before the method of dealing with him is determined an inquiry ought to be made into his physical or mental condition,

subsection (2) below shall apply.

(2) Where this subsection applies the court shall—

(a) for the purpose of inquiry solely into his physical condition, remand him in custody or on bail;

(b) for the purpose of inquiry into his mental condition (whether or not in addition to his physical condition), remand him in custody or on bail or, where the court is satisfied—

(i) on the written or oral evidence of a medical practitioner, that the person appears to be suffering from a mental disorder; and

(ii) that the accused could be admitted to a hospital that is suitable for his detention,

make an order committing him to that hospital,

for such period or periods, no single period exceeding three weeks, as the court thinks necessary to enable a medical examination and report to be made.

(3) Where the court is of the opinion that a person ought to continue to be committed to hospital for the purpose of inquiry into his mental condition following the expiry of the period specified in an order for committal to hospital under paragraph (b) of subsection (2) above, the court may—

(a) if the condition in sub-paragraph (i) of that paragraph continues to be satisfied and he could be admitted to a hospital that is suitable for his continued detention, renew the order for such further period not exceeding three weeks as the court thinks necessary to enable a medical examination and report to be made; and

(b) in any other case, remand the person in custody or on bail in accordance with subsection (2) above.

(4) An order under subsection (3)(a) above may, unless objection is made by or on behalf of the person to whom it relates, be made in his absence.

(5) Where, before the expiry of the period specified in an order for committal

to hospital under subsection (2)(b) above, the court considers, on an application made to it, that committal to hospital is no longer required in relation to the person, the court shall revoke the order and may make such other order, under subsection (2)(a) above or any other provision of this Part of this Act, as the court considers appropriate.

(6) Where an accused is remanded on bail under this section, it shall be a condition of the order granting bail that he shall—

(a) undergo a medical examination by a duly qualified registered medical practitioner or, where the inquiry is into his mental condition, and the order granting bail so specifies, two such practitioners; and

(b) for the purpose of such examination, attend at an institution or place, or on any such practitioner specified in the order granting bail and, where the inquiry is into his mental condition, comply with any directions which may be given to him for the said purpose by any person so specified or by a person of any class so specified,

and, if arrangements have been made for his reception, it may be a condition of the order granting bail that the person shall, for the purpose of the examination, reside in an institution or place specified as aforesaid, not being an institution or place to which he could have been remanded in custody, until the expiry of such period as may be so specified or until he is discharged therefrom, whichever first occurs.

(7) On exercising the powers conferred by this section to remand in custody or on bail the court shall—

(a) where the person is remanded in custody, send to the institution or place in which he is detained; and

(b) where the person is released on bail, send to the institution or place at which or the person by whom he is to be examined,

a statement of the reasons for which it appears to the court that an inquiry ought to be made into his physical or mental condition, and of any information before the court about his physical or mental condition.

(8) On making an order of committal to hospital under subsection (2)(b) above the court shall send to the hospital specified in the order a statement of the reasons for which the court is of the opinion that an inquiry ought to be made into the mental condition of the person to whom it relates, and of any information before the court about his mental condition.

(9) A person remanded under this section may, before the expiry of the period of 24 hours beginning with his remand, appeal against the refusal of bail or against the conditions imposed and a person committed to hospital under this section may, at any time during the period when the order for his committal, or, as the case may be, renewal of such order, is in force, appeal against the order of committal by note of appeal presented to the High Court, and the High Court, either in court or in chambers, may after hearing parties—

(a) review the order and grant bail on such conditions as it thinks fit; or

(b) confirm the order; or

(c) in the case of an appeal against an order of committal to hospital, revoke the order and remand the person in custody.

(10) The court may, on cause shown, vary an order for committal to hospital under subsection (2)(b) above by substituting another hospital for the hospital specified in the order.

(11) Subsection (2)(b) above shall apply to the variation of an order under subsection (10) above as it applies to the making of an order for committal to hospital.

AMENDMENTS

Subss.(2)(b) and (3)(a) as amended by the Mental Health (Care and Treatment) (Scotland) Act 2003 (asp 13), Sch.4, para.8(13). Brought into force on October 5, 2005 by the Mental Health (Care and Treatment) (Scotland) Act 2003 (Commencement No.4) Order 2005(SSI 2005/161 (C.6)).

Subs.(9) as amended by the Mental Health (Care and Treatment) (Scotland) Act 2003 (asp 13), s.132 and Sch.5. Brought into force on October 5, 2005 as above.

DEFINITIONS

"bail": s.307(1).
"hospital": s.307(1).
"registered medical practitioner": s.2 of the Medical Act 1983 (c. 54).

Power of court to adjourn case before sentence   ← Social Enquiry Report

201.—(1) Where an accused has been convicted or the court has found that he committed the offence and before he has been sentenced or otherwise dealt with, subject to subsection (3) below, the court may adjourn the case for the purpose of enabling inquiries to be made or of determining the most suitable method of dealing with his case.

(2) Where the court adjourns a case solely for the purpose mentioned in subsection (1) above, it shall remand the accused in custody or on bail or ordain him to appear at the adjourned diet.

(3) Subject to section 21(9) of the Criminal Justice (Scotland) Act 2003 (asp 7), a court shall not adjourn the hearing of a case as mentioned in subsection (1) above for any single period exceeding four weeks or, on cause shown, eight weeks.

(4) An accused who is remanded under this section may appeal against the refusal of bail or against the conditions imposed within 24 hours of his remand, by note of appeal presented to the High Court, and the High Court, either in court or in chambers, may, after hearing parties—

(a) review the order appealed against and either grant bail on such conditions as it thinks fit or ordain the accused to appear at the adjourned diet; or

(b) confirm the order.

AMENDMENT

Subs.(3) as amended by Criminal Justice (Scotland) Act 2003 (asp 7), Part 8, s.67. Brought into force on June 27, 2003 by the Criminal Justice (Scotland) Act 2003 (Commencement No.1) Order 2003 (SSI 2003/288 (C.14)).

Subs.(3) as amended by the Criminal Justice (Scotland) Act 2003 (asp 7), Part 3, s.21(10). Brought into force on June 10, 2004 by the Criminal Justice (Scotland) Act 2003 (Commencement No.4) Order 2004 (SSI 2004/240 (C.16)).

DEFINITIONS

"bail": s.307(1).
"diet": s.307(1).
"remand": s.307(1).

GENERAL NOTE

The antecedent provisions conjoined for this section have produced a considerable number of authorities, those provisions being ss.179 and 380 of the 1975 Act as amended. The principal point to note is that it is of paramount importance for courts at first instance to have in mind the clear statutory distinction between adjourning a case before sentence and deferring sentence. In *H.M. Advocate v Clegg*, 1991 S.L.T. 192 it was held that to obtain various reports for sentencing the correct approach is to adjourn the case and not to defer sentence, a distinction that was emphasised in *McRobbie v H.M. Advocate*, 1990 S.C.C.R 767. Refer also to *Airlie v Heywood*, 1996 S.C.C.R. 562 where sentence had been deferred for good behaviour, social inquiry reports and to ascertain the effect of conviction upon the accused's taxi licence; it was held that the adjournment had been at common law and was not a statutory one limited to eight weeks.

At the very least when adjourning a case for sentence in excess of four weeks, it must be recorded in the minutes that the adjournment was on cause shown otherwise the Appeal Court can have no inkling of its purpose (*Dingwall v Vannet*, 1997 S.C.C.R. 515). Although there is no requirement that the reason for such a length of adjournment be stated either in court or in the minutes themselves, it would seem sensible (if only as a means of answering any points taken on appeal) that such steps be taken. See too *Napier v Dyer*, 2001 S.L.T. 1298 in which following a guilty plea and deferment of sentence, the accused was permitted to tender a late plea to the competency of proceedings founding upon the role of a temporary sheriff at an earlier point in the case (see *Starrs v Ruxton*, 2000 S.L.T. 42; 1999 S.C.C.R. 1052). Rather than the court permitting withdrawal of earlier pleas, the diet was adjourned; the accused later asserted that further proceedings were now incompetent in his bill of advocation. The Appeal Court agreed that procedure had gone awry but held that no particular form of wording was necessary in minuting such an adjournment where the court's intention was clear.

The necessity of abiding by the statutory time-limits was shown in *Wilson v Donald*, 1993 S.L.T. 31 because, while the continuation was recorded as a deferred sentence, the obtaining of a DVLA printout during a period greater than three weeks was an adjournment to which the time-limits applied. This point was applied in *Holburn v Lees*, 1993 S.C.C.R. 426 and *Burns v Wilson*, 1993 S.C.C.R. 418 although it was held that convictions were unaffected by these appeals on procedural points although the sentences were suspended: see also *McCulloch v Scott*, 1993 S.L.T. 901.

A further distinction became apparent in *Douglas v Jamieson*, 1993 S.L.T. 816 and *Douglas v Peddie*, 1993 S.C.C.R. 717 where it was held that with a combination of guilty and not guilty pleas leading to an adjourned trial diet the court was exercising its power at common law to adjourn at any stage when it seemed appropriate to do so. See also *Mcleod v Hutton* (Sh.Ct), 1993 S.C.C.R. 747.

The statutory distinction was also held not to apply in *Johnstone v Lees*, 1994 S.L.T. 551 where an adjournment of eight weeks to await the outcome of other cases was deemed competent at common law. A continuation for a proof of a previous conviction is a matter at common law: *Burns v Lees*, 1994 S.C.C.R. 780. "Cause shown" (subs.(3)(9b)) was held to extend to an extension of the four week period of deferment at Christmas where a social worker had requested additional time to obtain additional material for the accused's report (*Porteous v Hamilton*, 1996 G.W.D. 21–1199).

In the authorities cited, objection to the competency of the various proceedings was taken timeously and to delay without explanation a complaint about competency may amount to acquiescence especially with a long passage of time and a payment of fines as ordered: *Storie v Friel*, 1993 S.C.C.R. 955.

Finally, in *Long v HM Advocate*, 1984 S.C.C.R. 161 it was held that review of the court's decision on bail (s.30 of the 1975 Act and this Act) had no application to bail in relation to the power of the court to adjourn a case before sentence.

Deferred sentence

202.—(1) It shall be competent for a court to defer sentence after conviction for a period and on such conditions as the court may determine.

(2) If it appears to the court which deferred sentence on an accused under subsection (1) above that he has been convicted during the period of deferment, by a court in any part of Great Britain of an offence committed during that period and has been dealt with for that offence, the court which deferred sentence may—

(a) issue a warrant for the arrest of the accused; or

(b) instead of issuing such a warrant in the first instance, issue a citation requiring him to appear before it at such time as may be specified in the citation,

and on his appearance or on his being brought before the court it may deal with him in any manner in which it would be competent for it to deal with him on the expiry of the period of deferment.

(3) Where a court which has deferred sentence on an accused under subsection (1) above convicts him of another offence during the period of deferment, it may deal with him for the original offence in any manner in which it would be competent for it to deal with him on the expiry of the period of deferment, as well as for the offence committed during the said period.

DEFINITION

"sentence": s.307(1).

GENERAL NOTE

It is of paramount importance for courts at first instance to have in mind the clear statutory distinction between adjourning a case before sentence and deferring sentence. Regard might be had to the cases in the General Note to s.201 of this Act for the authorities arising from this distinction. The note by A.D. Smith on *Deferred Sentences in Scotland*, 1968 S.L.T. (Notes) 153 is still of interest.

In *Valentine v Parker*, 1992 S.C.C.R. 695 an appeal was taken during a deferred sentence but in the absence of the court papers the sheriff held the calling of the case on the appropriate date for consideration was incompetent. A Crown Bill of Advocation was passed and it was held by the High Court of Justiciary that the deferred sentence had been superceded by the appeal proceedings and the case was remitted to the sheriff for sentence.

In *Maitland v McNaughtan*, 1996 G.W.D. 22–1261 sentence had been deferred for good behaviour. The Appeal Court held that the sheriff erred in holding M to be in breach, when a conviction, for an offence which predated the deferment, and a pending trial, for an offence alleged to have occurred during the period of deferment, were disclosed: the correct approach would have been to defer to await the outcome of the trial.

In *Hart v Hingston*, 2001 G.W.D. 16–620 where following upon a deferment of sentence for good behaviour, and H having failed to maintain payments of other fines, this was held not to be sufficient to entitle the sheriff to conclude that there had been a breach of good behaviour.

In *Fletcher v Walkingshaw*, 1997 G.W.D. 8–327 where sentences of imprisonment were imposed upon the accused, after an initial deferment for restitution had not been complied with, the Appeal Court took account of a non-analogous record and the social enquiry report obtained before deferral, which had concluded that a custodial sentence was inappropriate; a probation order allied to community service (as proposed in the report) was substituted.

When deferring sentence it is probably unwise for the judge either to predict or promise a particular disposal. Any such statement would not be binding on the judge himself or any other judge called upon to dispose of the case (*Laing v Heywood*, 1998 S.L.T. 458). When deferring sentence for good behaviour the conditions imposed should not be unduly restrictive—the aim is to confirm that the accused is capable of behaving "in ordinary life in an acceptable way"; see *Islam v Heywood*, 1999 S.C.C.R. 68.

Reports

203.—(1) Where a person specified in section 27(1)(b)(i) to (vi) of the Social Work (Scotland) Act 1968 commits an offence, the court shall not dispose of the case without obtaining from the local authority in whose area the person resides a report as to—

(a) the circumstances of the offence; and

(b) the character of the offender, including his behaviour while under the supervision, or as the case may be subject to the order, so specified in relation to him.

(2) In subsection (1) above, "the court" does not include a district court.

(3) Where, in any case, a report by an officer of a local authority is made to the court with a view to assisting the court in determining the most suitable method of dealing with any person in respect of an offence, a copy of the report shall be given by the clerk of the court to the offender or his solicitor.

DEFINITIONS

"local authority": s.307(1).
"offence": s.307(1).

GENERAL NOTE

This section requires the court to obtain a report targeted on new offences by an offender who is subject to statutory supervision. So in *Hendry v HM Advocate*, 1999 G.W.D. 21–1004, a sentence of imprisonment was suspended on appeal where the sheriff had failed to obtain a local authority report on H who was on probation at the time of the offence. The obligation to obtain such a report exists even where the accused lives outwith Scotland, as in *Williams v Kennedy*, 2002 G.W.D. 15-496, where the accused who resided in Wales and was there subject of a probation order had been convicted of a further offence in Scotland. The provisions of the section only apply when the person committing the offences libelled is already subject to the provisions of s.27(1)(b) of the Social Work (Scotland) Act 1968 (see *Townsley v McGlennan*, 1998 S.L.T. 104). The circumstances of the new offences are an aspect distinct from the offender's behaviour on supervision.

Imprisonment, etc.

Restrictions on passing sentence of imprisonment or detention

204.—(1) A court shall not pass a sentence of imprisonment or of detention in respect of any offence, nor impose imprisonment, or detention, under section 214(2) of this Act in respect of failure to pay a fine, on an accused who is not legally represented in that court and has not been previously sentenced to imprisonment or detention by a court in any part of the United Kingdom, unless the accused either—

(a) applied for legal aid and the application was refused on the ground that he was not financially eligible; or

(b) having been informed of his right to apply for legal aid, and having had the opportunity, failed to do so.

(2) A court shall not pass a sentence of imprisonment on a person of or over twenty-one years of age who has not been previously sentenced to imprisonment or detention by a court in any part of the United Kingdom unless the court considers that no other method of dealing with him is appropriate ...

(2A) For the purpose of determining under subsection (2) above whether any other method of dealing with such a person is appropriate, the court, unless it has made a risk assessment order in respect of the person, shall take into account—

(a) such information as it has been able to obtain from an officer of a local authority or otherwise about his circumstances;

(b) any information before it concerning his character and mental and physical condition;

(c) its power to make a hospital direction in addition to imposing a sentence of imprisonment.

(3) Where a court of summary jurisdiction passes a sentence of imprisonment on any such person as is mentioned in subsection (2) above, the court shall state the reason for its opinion that no other method of dealing with him is appropriate, and shall have that reason entered in the record of the proceedings.

(4) The court shall, for the purpose of determining whether a person has been previously sentenced to imprisonment or detention by a court in any part of the United Kingdom—

(a) disregard a previous sentence of imprisonment which, having been suspended, has not taken effect under section 23 of the Powers of Criminal Courts Act 1973 or under section 19 of the Treatment of Offenders Act (Northern Ireland) 1968;

(b) construe detention as meaning—

(i) in relation to Scotland, detention in a young offenders institution or detention centre;

(ii) in relation to England and Wales a sentence of youth custody, borstal training or detention in a young offender institution or detention centre; and

(iii) in relation to Northern Ireland, detention in a young offenders centre.

(5) This section does not affect the power of a court to pass sentence on any person for an offence the sentence for which is fixed by law.

(6) In this section—

"legal aid" means legal aid for the purposes of any part of the proceedings before the court;

"legally represented" means represented by counsel or a solicitor at some stage after the accused is found guilty and before he is dealt with as referred to in subsection (1) above.

AMENDMENTS

Subs.(2): words deleted by s.6(3) of the Crime and Punishment (Scotland) Act 1997 with effect from January 1, 1998 as provided by the Crime and Punishment (Scotland) Act 1997 (Commencement No. 2 and Transitional and Consequential Provisions) Order 1997 (SI 1997/2323), art. 4 and Sch.2.

Subs.(2A) inserted by s.6(3) of the above Act and commenced on January 1, 1998 in terms of the above Order.

Subs.(2A) as amended by the Criminal Justice (Scotland) Act 2003 (asp 7), Sch.1, para.2(6). Brought into force on June 19, 2006 by the Criminal Justice (Scotland) Act 2003 (Commencement No.9) Order 2006 (SSI 2006/332 (C.30)), art.2(1), subject to art.2(2).

DEFINITIONS

"court of summary jurisdiction": s.307(1).
"fine": s.307(1).
"impose imprisonment": s.307(1).
"legal aid": s.204(6).
"legally represented": s.204(6).
"offence": s.307(1).
"sentence": s.307(1).

GENERAL NOTE

This section conjoins the provisions in ss.41 and 42 of the 1980 Act. Imprisonment as a sentence or as a penalty for fine default can only be imposed once the accused has been legally represented in the proceedings (subs.(1)). In addition the court can now impose a hospital direction (discussed at ss.59 and 60 above) as part of such sentence or penalty. In all cases there is a general obligation to have regard to any information about the accused's character, physical and mental condition.

Two authorities are worth considering here. First, the duty (in subs.(2)) to obtain information from a local authority "or otherwise" is not fulfilled by obtaining information from the prosecution or the defence: *Auld v Herron*, 1969 J.C. 4. It should be noted that the duty is qualified by the phrase "such information as it can" although that is not defined. Secondly, the imprisonment or detention relates only to the UK and that necessarily excludes the Republic of Ireland: *Mawhinney v HM Advocate*, 1950 S.L.T. 135. It is difficult to see why imprisonment or detention elsewhere is excluded in this way but it may be information bearing on the accused's character. While it is not necessary for the sentencing judge to enumerate the other disposals considered before arriving at a custodial sentence, for the purposes of compliance with the requirements of subs.(2), and particularly in preparing a report for any appeal, a judge should indicate that the sentencing options have been fully considered (*Keogh v Watt*, 2000 S.C.C.R. 443).

Should the report contain material which is disputed, care has to be taken to assess whether this can be dealt with by means of a proof in mitigation or whether the material really contains fresh allegations of criminality which must be considered separately; see *Ross v HM Advocate*, 2002 S.L.T. 925.

Restriction on consecutive sentences for released prisoners

204A. A court sentencing a person to imprisonment or other detention shall not order or direct that the term of imprisonment or detention shall commence on the expiration of any other such sentence from which he has been released at any time under the existing or new provisions within the meaning of Schedule 6 to the Prisoners and Criminal Proceedings (Scotland) Act 1993.

AMENDMENT

Section 204A inserted by the Crime and Disorder Act 1998 (c.37) s.112 (effective September 30, 1998: SI 1998/2327).

DEFINITIONS

"imprisonment": s.307(1) of the 1995 Act.
"detention": s.307(1) of the 1995 Act.
"sentence": s.307(1) of the 1995 Act.

GENERAL NOTE

In keeping with the provisions in s.111(1) of the 1998 Act, which added s.1A to the Prisoners and Criminal Proceedings (Scotland) Act 1993 (c.9), this section stipulates that prisoners released on licence who are sentenced, in relation to other offences, to another term of imprisonment should not receive a sentence running consecutive to the expiry of that imprisonment term. Only by imposing an immediate and concurrent sentence of further imprisonment (which may of course result in incarceration beyond the end of the earlier sentence) can the release provisions set down in the 1993 Act, as amended, function effectively.

This provision came into force on September 30, 1998 in terms of SI 1998/ 2327.

See for example, *H.M. Advocate v Graham*, 1999 G.W.D. 26–1235 and *Thomson, Petr*, 2000 G.W.D. 8–289.

In *McIntosh v H.M. Advocate*, 2003 G.W.D. 31–868 the Appeal Court approved the practice of the Crown drawing the attention of the court imposing sentence to a pre-existing sentence, the balance of which had been re-imposed upon the accused.

Consecutive sentences: life prisoners etc.

204B.—(1) This section applies in respect of sentencing for offences committed after the coming into force of this section.

(2) Where, in solemn proceedings, the court sentences a person to imprisonment or other detention, the court may—

  (a) if the person is serving or is liable to serve the punishment part of a previous sentence, frame the sentence to take effect on the day after that part of that sentence is or would be due to expire; or

  (b) if the person is serving or is liable to serve the punishment parts of two or more previous sentences, frame the sentence to take effect on the day after the later or (as the case may be) latest expiring of those parts is or would be due to expire.

(3) Where, in such proceedings, it falls to the court to sentence a person who is subject to a previous sentence in respect of which a punishment part requires to be (but has not been) specified, the court shall not sentence the person until such time as the part is either specified or no longer requires to be specified.

(4) Where the court sentences a person to a sentence of imprisonment or other detention for life, for an indeterminate period or without limit of time, the court may, if the person is serving or is liable to serve for any offence—

  (a) a previous sentence of imprisonment or other detention the term of which is not treated as part of a single term under section 27(5) of the 1993 Act; or

  (b) two or more previous sentences of imprisonment or other detention the terms of which are treated as a single term under that section of that Act,

frame the sentence to take effect on the day after the person would (but for the sentence so framed and disregarding any subsequent sentence) be entitled to be released under the provisions referred to in section 204A of this Act as respects the sentence or sentences.

AMENDMENT

Section 204B inserted by Criminal Justice (Scotland) Act 2003 (asp 7), Part 4, s.26. Brought into force on December 1, 2003 by the Criminal Justice (Scotland) Act 2003 (Commencement No.3 and Revocation) Order 2003 (SSI 2003/475 (C.26)), art.2.

DEFINITIONS

"detention": s.307(1) of the 1995 Act.
"imprisonment": s.307(1) of the 1995 Act.
"sentence": s.307(1) of the 1995 Act.

GENERAL NOTE

This new section provides a court, when sentencing a person for an offence committed after the section comes into force and where that person is already serving a sentence of imprisonment, to order that: (a) a life sentence may commence, in the existing life prisoner, on the expiry of the punishment part of the existing life sentence or, if the prisoner is already serving a determinate sentence, at the point at which the Scottish Ministers would otherwise be required to release the prisoner; and (b) a determinate sentence may commence, in the case of an existing life prisoner, on the expiry of the punishment of the existing life sentence. This provision applies only to solemn proceedings as summary proceedings are dealt with in terms of s.167 of the 1995 Act as amended.

Punishment for murder

205.—(1) Subject to subsections (2) and (3) and section 205D below, a person convicted of murder shall be sentenced to imprisonment for life.

(2) Where a person convicted of murder is under the age of 18 years he shall not be sentenced to imprisonment for life but to be detained without limit of time and shall be liable to be detained in such place, and under such conditions, as the Secretary of State may direct.

(3) Where a person convicted of murder has attained the age of 18 years but is under the age of 21 years he shall not be sentenced to imprisonment for life but to be detained in a young offenders institution and shall be liable to be detained for life.

(4)–(6) ...

AMENDMENT

Section 205 as amended by the Convention Rights (Compliance) (Scotland) Act 2001 (asp 7), s.2. Brought into force on October 8, 2001 by the Convention Rights (Compliance) (Scotland) Act 2001 (Commencement) Order 2001 (SSI 2001/274 (C.12)).

DEFINITIONS

"judge": s.307(1).
"sentence": s.307(1).

GENERAL NOTE

The recommendation permitted by subs.(4) appears to be fairly common now. A good example is *Birrell v H.M. Advocate*, 1993 S.C.C.R. 812 where previous convictions were held not to be a factor of significance in this case. The important factors had been the method used to commit the crime, the degree of planning and premeditation and the ruthlessness exhibited in the acts which had been perpetrated. A recommendation of a minimum of 15 years was held to be correctly decided. This approach was followed in *Greenfield v H.M. Advocate*, 1996 S.L.T. 1214 it being noted that the trial judge had given weight to the fact that the accused had lain in wait for his victim, a factor not libelled in the murder charge and expressly deliberated upon by the jury but consistent with the evidence. A similar period was imposed on appeal in *Casey v H.M. Advocate*, 1994 S.L.T. 54 where it was observed by the Appeal Court that it would not expect a recommendation to be made for a period of less than 12 years.

By contrast in *McKay v H.M. Advocate*, 2001 S.C.C.R. 341, a concerted attack on a total stranger with a pogo stick inflicting grievous injuries, a minimum 14 year recommendation was quashed where the trial judge could not identify factors which indicated that M posed a risk to the public.

In *Brown v H.M. Advocate*, 2002 G.W.D. 2–68, where two accused were convicted of murder and a minimum recommendation was made for them both, the Appeal Court quashed the recommendation in M's case, contrasting his role in the offence with that of his co-accused for whom a recommendation was justified.

Minimum sentence for third conviction of certain offences relating to drug trafficking

205B.—(1) This section applies where—
- (a) a person is convicted on indictment in the High Court of a class A drug trafficking offence committed after the commencement of section 2 of the Crime and Punishment (Scotland) Act 1997;
- (b) at the time when that offence was committed, he had attained the age of at least 18 years and had been convicted in any part of the United Kingdom of two other class A drug trafficking offences, irrespective of—
  - (i) whether either of those offences was committed before or after the commencement of section 2 of the Crime and Punishment (Scotland) Act 1997;
  - (ii) the court in which any such conviction was obtained; and
  - (iii) his age at the time of the commission of either of those offences; and
- (c) one of the offences mentioned in paragraph (b) above was committed after he had been convicted of the other.

(2) Subject to subsection (3) below, where this section applies the court shall sentence the person—
- (a) where he has attained the age of 21 years, to a term of imprisonment of at least seven years; and
- (b) where he has attained the age of 18 years but is under the age of 21 years, to detention in a young offenders institution for a period of at least seven years.

(3) The court shall not impose the sentence otherwise required by subsection (2) above where it is of the opinion that there are specific circumstances which—
- (a) relate to any of the offences or to the offender; and
- (b) would make that sentence unjust.

(4) For the purposes of section 106(2) of this Act a sentence passed under subsection (2) above in respect of a conviction for a class A drug trafficking offence shall not be regarded as a sentence fixed by law for that offence.

(5) In this section "class A drug trafficking offence" means a drug trafficking offence committed in respect of a class A drug; and for this purpose—

"class A drug" has the same meaning as in the Misuse of Drugs Act 1971;

"drug trafficking offence" means an offence specified in paragraph 2 or (so far as it relates to that paragraph) paragraph 10 of Schedule 4 to the Proceeds of Crime Act 2002.

AMENDMENT

Section 205B inserted by the Crime and Punishment (Scotland) Act 1997 (c.48), s.2 with effect from January 20, 1998 as provided by the Crime and Punishment (Scotland) Act 1997 (Commencement No.2 and Transitional and Consequential Provisions) Order 1997 (SI 1997/2323) art.3, Sch.1.

Subs.(5) as amended by the Proceeds of Crime Act 2002 (c.29), Sch.11, para.29(3). Brought into force on March 24, 2003 by the Proceeds of Crime Act 2002 (Commencement No.6, Transitional Provisions and Savings) (Scotland) Order 2003 (SSI 2003/210 (C.44)).

DEFINITIONS

"indictment": s.307(1) of the 1995 Act.

"High Court": s.307(1) of the Act.

"class A drug": s.2(1) and Sch.2, Part I of the Misuse of Drugs Act 1971 (c.38).

"drug trafficking offence": s.49(5)of the Proceeds of Crime (Scotland) Act 1995 (c.43); s.1(3) of the Drug Trafficking Act 1994 (c.37); Proceeds of Crime (Northern Ireland) Order 1996.

"offence": s.307(1) of the 1995 Act.

"United Kingdom": Schedule 1 of the Interpretation Act 1978 (c. 30).

"conviction": s.3 of the 1997 Act.

"young offenders institutution": s.307(1) of the 1995 Act.

"sentence": s.307(1) of the 1995 Act.

GENERAL NOTE

This section was introduced into the 1995 Act by s.2 of the Crime and Punishment (Scotland) Act with effect from October 20, 1997 as provided by the Crime and Punishment (Scotland) Act 1997 (Commencement No. 2 and Transitional and Consequential Provisions) 1997 (SI 1997/2323).

Section 205B provides that, where a person convicted of a drug trafficking offence before the High Court in relation to a class A drug, has two distinct prior convictions for trafficking in class A drugs (a number of incidents conjoined in one conviction would not suffice), he shall be sentenced to a minimum period of imprisonment or detention of seven years. Reference to the legislation mentioned in subs.(5) shows that "drug trafficking offence" has a much wider meaning than merely dealing in, or being concerned in, the supply of controlled drugs. It is important to note that the two prior convictions can have been imposed by any United Kingdom court at any time—these provisions can operate retrospectively. Subsection (1)(b) stipulates that such a minimum sentence can only be imposed upon an offender who had reached 18 years of age at the time of committing the third offence.

Reservations have to be expressed, however, as to whether information currently available in previous convictions will highlight that the prior convictions related specificaly to class A drugs. This problem may lead the Crown to lodge certified copies of the complaints or indictments, and related Minutes of Procedure, and perhaps a s.285 certificate (now a Secretary of State's rather than a Chief Constable's certificate, following s.59 of the 1997 Act) to lay out the provenance of previous convictions.

It will be appreciated that the broad intention of s.205B is to limit the sentencing discretion available to judges when dealing with recidivist drug trafficking offenders but the wording of s.205B(3) is not free of difficulty, particularly when read along with s.196(2) of the 1995 Act. While the Government adhered to the familiar notion that a sentencing court would have to look to the circumstances of the current offence before it, and to any previous convictions, the Lord Advocate did concede that "the procedure for laying details of the circumstances of the first qualifying offence before the court will have to be addressed" (*Hansard*, March 4, 1997, col. 1821). It is submitted that it would be quite proper for the court to have regard to the sentences imposed in relation to the earlier convictions, and that in something of a departure from current sentencing practices, subs.(3) suggests that some investigation of the factual background to those convictions could be undertaken by the court. This is a marked departure from the principles set out in *Connell v Mitchell* (1908) 5 A. 641 and *Baker v Mc-Fadyean*, 1952 S.L.T. (Notes) 69 which disapproved of "looking behind convictions". See, however, the discussion at A4–228 above.

Interestingly, it was only after the Committee stage of the Crime and Punishment (Scotland) Bill that the Government moved an amendment to s.196 of the 1995 Act to permit the sentencing court to pass a lower sentence where a guilty plea had been tendered. (This it will be noted pre-dated *Du Plooy v H.M. Advocate*, 2003 S.L.T 1237; 2003 S.C.C.R. 640 which formulated general rules on the discounting of sentences following a guilty plea as permitted by s.196 of the Act). The prescriptive tone of s.205B, with its limited admission of judicial sentencing discretion, and the broader, permissive approach in s.196 do not sit together comfortably. Section 196(2) of the Act makes express provision for a statutory reduction in sentence to one of 5 years, 219 days, a figure which, not by chance, reflects a 20 per cent discount against the mandatory minimum which a third Class A drug dealing offence would ordinarily attract. The issue is whether the sentencing court can exercise its discretionary powers (in s.205B(3)) irrespective of whether an accused pleads guilty or is convicted after trial and, in the former case, also permit a broad s.196 discount for the guilty plea.

In *H.M. Advocate v McGale* (High Court of Justiciary, April 7, 2005, unreported) the court held that it could exercise that discretion and apply a s.196 discount on that sentence and take account of time spent on remand awaiting trial (s.210). It has to be doubted that this was the form of sentencing regime envisaged when s.205B was introduced by Parliament (the court was not referred to *Hansard* and, almost uniquely, s.199 of the Act, which generally permits the court to mitigate a sentence previously passed, is expressly disapplied to s.205B(2) by s.199(3)). Arguably, a preferable approach would be to disregard s.196 entirely in imposing sentence and proceed simply by exercising the discretion vested in the court by s.205B(3). In doing so, the factors giving rise to the reduction to the otherwise mandatory sentence would have to be stated and could properly include the timing of the plea if that was appropriate.

Section 205B(4) preserves the right of appeal against sentence since s.205B provides for an automatic, not a mandatory sentence; by definition the latter form of sentence cannot be appealed.

Meaning of "conviction"

Reference to s.205C below reveals that the automatic sentence for a third relevant drug trafficking offence will apply even if one, or both, of the earlier convictions was disposed of by way of admonition or a probation order. Such a disposal would, in the event of conviction after trial for a third drug trafficking offence, still fall to be considered under subs.(3) above as a ground for refraining from imposing the seven year minimum sentence.

Meaning of "conviction" for purposes of sections 205A and 205B

205C.—(1) For the purposes of paragraph (b) of subsection (1) of each sections 205A and 205B of this Act "conviction" includes—

    (a) a finding of guilt in respect of which the offender was admonished under section 181 of the Criminal Procedure (Scotland) Act 1975 (admonition); and

    (b) a conviction for which an order is made placing the offender on probation,

and related expressions shall be construed accordingly.

AMENDMENT

Section 205C inserted by the Crime and Punishment (Scotland) Act 1997 (c.48), s.3 (in part) with effect from October 20, 1997 as provided by the Crime and Punishment (Scotland) Act 1997 (Commencement No. 2 and Transitional and Consequential Provisions) Order 1997 (SI 1997/2323), art.3, Sch.1.

DEFINITIONS

"admonished": s.246 of the Criminal Procedure (Scotland) Act 1995.

"probation": s.247 of said Act.

"offence": s.307(1) of said Act.

"Class A drug": s.2(1) and Sch.2, Part I of the Misuse of Drugs Act 1971.

"drug trafficking offence": s.49(5) of the Proceeds of Crime (Scotland) Act 1995, s.1(3) of the Drug Trafficking Act 1994 and s.1(3) of the Proceeds of Crime (Northern Ireland) Order 1996.

GENERAL NOTE

This section defines the meaning of "conviction", a concept central to the operation of Part I of the 1997 Act. It will be recalled that the 1997 Act introduced two "automatic" sentences, requiring the High Court to impose life sentences in a range of serious offences and minimum sentences for class A drug trafficking offences. The incoming Government has not commenced the regime of automatic life sentences specified in s.1 of the 1997 Act, and has commenced only part of s.205B (the full text of the section appears as s.3 of the 1997 Act) with effect from October 20, 1997.

The ethos of the 1997 Act, which sought to impose more severe penalties upon offenders by removing large elements of sentencing discretion from judges, is still to be found in s.205B: it will be noted that the imposition of a probation order, an order which as s.247(1) of the 1995 Act provides, is not deemed to be a conviction, is nonetheless a disposal for the purposes of s.205B, counting as a conviction. (As originally drafted even absolute and conditional discharges were included also as "convictions" but this was withdrawn late in the life of the Bill).

Although the mechanism is in place to permit drug trafficking convictions imposed by military courts martial to count as prior convictions for the purposes of s.205B (see subs.(2) of s.205B as it appears in the 1997 Act) no steps have been taken to activate that provision as yet.

Only one sentence of imprisonment for life to be imposed in any proceedings

205D. Where a person is convicted on the same indictment of more than one offence for which the court must impose or would, apart from this section, have imposed a sentence of imprisonment for life, only one such sentence shall be imposed in respect of those offences.

AMENDMENT

Section 205D inserted by the Convention Rights (Compliance) (Scotland) Act 2001 (asp 7), s.2.

Brought into force on October 8, 2001 by the Convention Rights (Compliance) (Scotland) Act 2001 (Commencement) Order 2001 (SSI 2001/274 (C.12)).

Minimum periods of imprisonment

206.—(1) No person shall be sentenced to imprisonment by a court of summary jurisdiction for a period of less than five days.

(2) Where a court of summary jurisdiction has power to impose imprisonment on an offender, it may, if any suitable place provided and certified as mentioned in subsection (4) below is available for the purpose, sentence the offender to be detained therein, for such period not exceeding four days as the court thinks fit, and an extract of the finding and sentence shall be delivered with the offender to the person in charge of the place where the offender is to be detained and shall be a sufficient authority for his detention in that place in accordance with the sentence.

(3) The expenses of the maintenance of offenders detained under this section shall be defrayed in like manner as the expenses of the maintenance of prisoners under the Prisons (Scotland) Act 1989.

(4) The Secretary of State may, on the application of any police authority, certify any police cells or other similar places provided by the authority to be suitable places for the detention of persons sentenced to detention under this section, and may by statutory instrument make regulations for the inspection of places so provided, the treatment of persons detained therein and generally for carrying this section into effect.

(5) No place certified under this section shall be used for the detention of females unless provision is made for their supervision by female officers.

(6) In this section the expression "police authority" has the same meaning as in the Police (Scotland) Act 1967.

DEFINITIONS

"court of summary jurisdiction": s.307(1).
"imprisonment": s.307(1).
"police authority": s.206(6).

Act of Adjournal

The style of the extract for detention in police custody is set out in Form 20.2 in the 1996 Act of Adjournal.

Detention of young offenders

207.—(1) It shall not be competent to impose imprisonment on a person under 21 years of age.

(2) Subject to section 205(2) and (3), 205A(2)(b) and 205B(2)(b) of this Act and to subsections (3) and (4) below, a court may impose detention (whether by way of sentence or otherwise) on a person, who is not less than 16 but under 21 years of age, where but for subsection (1) above the court would have power to impose a period of imprisonment; and a period of detention imposed under this section on any person shall not exceed the maximum period of imprisonment which might otherwise have been imposed.

(3) The court shall not under subsection (2) above impose detention on an offender unless it is of the opinion that no other method of dealing with him is ap-

propriate; and the court shall state its reasons for that opinion, and, except in the case of the High Court, those reasons shall be entered in the record of proceedings.

(3A) Subsections (2) and (3) above are subject to-

(a) Section 51A(2) of the Firearms Act 1968 (minimum sentences for certain firearms offences); and

(b) Section 29(8) of the Violent Crime Reduction Act 2006 (minimum sentence of detention for certain offences relating to dangerous weapons).

(4) To enable the court to form an opinion under subsection (3) above, it shall obtain from an officer of a local authority or otherwise such information as it can about the offender's circumstances; and it shall also take into account any information before it concerning the offender's character and physical and mental condition.

(4A) In forming an opinion under subsection (3) above the court shall take into account its power to make a hospital direction in addition to imposing a period of detention.

(4B) Subsections (4) and (4A) above apply to the forming of an opinion under the enactments mentioned in subsection Criminal Procedure (Scotland) Act above as they apply to the forming of an opinion under subsection (3) above.]

(5) A sentence of detention imposed under this section shall be a sentence of detention in a young offenders institution.

AMENDMENTS

Subs.(2) as amended by the Crime and Punishment (Scotland) Act 1997 (c.48), Sch.1, para.21(25) with effect from October 20, 1997 in terms of the Crime and Punishment (Scotland) Act 1997 (Commencement No.2 and Transitional and Consequential Provisions) Order 1997 (SI 1997/2323), art.3 and Sch.1.

Subs.(4A) inserted by the Crime and Punishment (Scotland) Act 1997, s.6(4) with effect from January 1, 1998 in terms of the Crime and Punishment (Scotland) Act 1997 (Commencement No.2 and Transitional and Consequential Provisions) Order 1997 (SI 1997/2323), art.4 and Sch.2.

Sections 207(3A) and (4B) inserted by the Violent Crime Reduction Act (c.38), s.49 and Sch.1 para.4(3):

DEFINITIONS

"imprisonment": s.307(1).
"hospital direction": s.9A of the 1997 Act.
"local authority": s.307(1).
"young offender's institution": s.307(1).

GENERAL NOTE

The correct approach for the court in deciding the issue of detention for a young offender is to ask, in terms of subs.(3), what methods of dealing with the accused are appropriate. If the court is of the opinion that no method other than detention is appropriate then detention should be imposed: see *Milligan v Jessop*, 1988 S.C.C.R. 137; *Dunsmore v Allan*, 1991 S.C.C.R. 946 and *Divers v Friel*, 1994 S.L.T. 247 in which the approaches were flawed. Having formed the opinion that no other method of dealing with the accused is appropriate, the court is required to state its reasons for that opinion and those reasons shall be entered in the record of proceedings. For the effect of failure to obtemper an earlier version of this subsection, see *Binnie v Farrell*, 1972 S.L.T. 212. The common reasons so stated are "character, gravity or nature of the offence" and "previous record of the accused", variations of which were used in *Dunsmore v Allan*, above. Some support for these are to be found in s.214(4) of this Act.

It is not sufficient for the purposes of subs.(3) for the sentencing judge to recall the terms of earlier reports upon the accused. The Appeal Court did approve the use of an up-to-date report prepared in regard to other proceedings provided that a copy of that report is placed before the court; see *Bain v McNaughtan*, 1999 S.L.T. 410. Some care has to be taken when considering previously undisclosed material in such a report; thus in *Ross v HM Advocate*, 2002 S.L.T. 925 where the report discussed allegations about the accused's conduct while on remand awaiting sentence, the sheriff wrongly proceeded to hold a proof upon matters which were plainly fresh criminal allegations. This procedure was held to be flawed by the Appeal Court which emphasised that at that stage there could only be a proof in mitigation upon factors relevant to sentence.

The court may now incorporate a hospital direction into any sentence of detention imposed upon a young offender. See generally s.59A above.

Detention of children convicted on indictment

208.—(1) Subject to section 205 of this Act and subsection (3) below, where a child is convicted on indictment and the court is of the opinion that no other method of dealing with him is appropriate, it may sentence him to be detained for a period which it shall specify in the sentence; and the child shall during that period be liable to be detained in such place and on such conditions as the Secretary of State may direct.

(2) Subsection (1) above is subject to-

(a) Section 51A(2) of the Firearms Act 1968 (Minimum sentences for certain firearms offences);

and

(b) Section 29(9) of the Violent Crime Reduction Act 2006 (Minimum sentence of detention for certain offences relating to dangerous weapons).

(3) If the child is under the age of 16 years, the power conferred by subsection (1) above shall not be exercisable in respect of a conviction for an offence under section 9(1) of the Antisocial Behaviour etc. (Scotland) Act 2004 (asp 8) or that section as applied by section 234AA(11) of this Act.

AMENDMENTS

Section 208 as amended by the Criminal Justice Act 2003 (c.44), s.290(3). Brought into force on January 22, 2004 by the Criminal Justice Act 2003 (Commencement No.2 and Savings Provisions) Order 2004 (SI 2004/81 (C.2)), art.3.

Section 208 as amended by the Antisocial Behaviour etc. (Scotland) Act 2004 (asp 8), s.10(3) and (4). Brought into force on October 28, 2004 by the Antisocial Behaviour etc. (Scotland) Act 2004 (Commencement and Savings) Order 2004 (SSI 2004/420 (C.31)).

Section.208(2) substituted by the Violent Crime Reduction Act 2006 (c.38), s.49 and Sch.1 para.4(4).

DEFINITIONS

"child": s.307(1).
"indictment": s.307(1).
"sentence": s.307(1).

GENERAL NOTE

The correct approach for the court in deciding the issue of detention for a child convicted on indictment is the same as that for young offenders, namely to ask what methods of dealing with the child are appropriate. If the court is of the opinion that no method other than detention is appropriate then the child shall be detained for a specified period. See for example *Sneddon v HM Advocate*, 1998 G.W.D. 22–1131.

In *R.J.K. v HM Advocate*, 1993 S.L.T. 237 it was held that (in relation to s.206 of the 1975 Act from which this section is derived) the sentence of detention "without limit of time" is a specified sentence and the absence of those words from the section did not impose any restriction on a court to pass such a sentence. Such a sentence, however, is in effect a life sentence: *R.F. v HM Advocate*, 1994 S.C.C.R. 71.

Supervised release orders

209.—(1) Where a person is convicted on indictment of an offence other than a sexual offence within the meaning of section 210A of this Act and is sentenced to imprisonment for a term of less than four years, the court on passing sentence may, if it considers that it is necessary to do so to protect the public from serious harm from the offender on his release, make such order as is mentioned in subsection (3) below.

(2) A court shall, before making an order under subsection (1) above, consider a report by a relevant officer of a local authority about the offender and his circumstances and, if the court thinks it necessary, hear that officer.

(3) The order referred to in subsection (1) above (to be known as a "supervised release order") is that the person, during a relevant period—

    (a) be under the supervision either of a relevant officer of a local authority or of an officer of a local probation board appointed for or assigned to a petty sessions area (such local authority or the justices for such area to be designated under section 14(4) or 15(1) of the Prisoners and Criminal Proceedings (Scotland) Act 1993);

    (b) comply with;

        (i) such requirements as may be imposed by the court in the order; and

        (ii) such requirements as that officer may reasonably specify,

    for the purpose of securing the good conduct of the person or preventing, or lessening the possibility of, his committing a further offence (whether or not an offence of the kind for which he was sentenced); and

    (c) comply with the standard requirements imposed by virtue of subsection (4)(a)(i) below.

(4) A supervised release order—

    (a) shall—

        (i) without prejudice to subsection (3)(b) above, contain such requirements (in this section referred to as the "standard requirements"); and

        (ii) be as nearly as possible in such form,

    as may be prescribed by Act of Adjournal;

    (b) for the purposes of any appeal or review constitutes part of the sentence of the person in respect of whom the order is made; and

    (c) shall have no effect during any period in which the person is subject to a licence under Part I of the said Act of 1993.

(5) Before making a supervised release order as respects a person the court shall explain to him, in as straightforward a way as is practicable, the effect of the order and the possible consequences for him of any breach of it.

(6) The clerk of the court by which a supervised release order is made in respect of a person shall—

    (a) forthwith send a copy of the order to the person and to the Secretary of State; and

    (b) within seven days after the date on which the order is made, send to the Secretary of State such documents and information relating to the case and to the person as are likely to be of assistance to a supervising officer.

(7) In this section—

    "relevant officer" has the same meaning as in Part I of the Prisoners and Criminal Proceedings (Scotland) Act 1993;

    "relevant period" means such period as may be specified in the supervised release order, being a period—

        (a) not exceeding twelve months after the date of the person's release; and

        (b) no part of which is later than the date by which the entire term of imprisonment specified in his sentence has elapsed; and "supervising officer" means, where an authority has or justices have been designated as is mentioned in subsection (3)(a) above for the purposes of the order, any relevant officer or, as the case may be, officer of a local probation board who is for the time being supervising for those purposes the person released.

(7A) Where a person—

(a) is serving a sentence of imprisonment and on his release from that sentence will be subject to a supervised release order; and

(b) is sentenced to a further term of imprisonment, whether that term is to run consecutively or concurrently with the sentence mentioned in paragraph (a) above,

the relevant period for any supervised release order made in relation to him shall begin on the date when he is released from those terms of imprisonment; and where there is more than one such order he shall on his release be subject to whichever of them is for the longer or, as the case may be, the longest period.

(8) This section applies to a person sentenced under section 207 of this Act as it applies to a person sentenced to a period of imprisonment.

AMENDMENTS

Subs.(1) as amended by the Crime and Disorder Act 1998 (c.37), s.86(2) (effective September 30, 1998: SI 1998/2327).

Subs.(7A) inserted by the Crime and Punishment (Scotland) Act 1997, Sch.1, para.21(26) (effective April 1, 1999: SI 1999/652).

Subs.(3)(a) as amended by the Criminal Justice and Court Services Act 2000 (c. 43), s.74 and Sch.7, para.4. Brought into force by the Criminal Justice and Court Services Act 2000 (Commencement No.4) Order 2001 (SI 2001/919 (C.33)), art.2(f)(ii) (effective April 1, 2001).

Subs.(7) as amended by the Criminal Justice and Court Services Act 2000 (c.43), s.74 and Sch.7, para.121. Brought into force as above.

DEFINITIONS

"local authority": s.307(1).
"relevant officer": s.209(7).
"relevant period": s.209(7).
"supervised release order": s.209(3).
"supervising officer": s.209(7).

GENERAL NOTE

These minor amendments to s.209 of the 1995 Act serve two purposes: firstly, supervised release orders are not available to solemn courts when sentencing offenders for any sexual offence now specified in s.210A(8) of the 1995 Act (see the General Notes to s.210); in *Craig v H.M. Advocate*, 2000 G.W.D. 34–1313 the Appeal Court accepted Crown submissions that, having been convicted of sexual offences, the accused should have been made subject of an extended sentence order in terms of s.210A of the Act, not a supervised release order (see also *O'Hare v H.M. Advocate*, 2002 S.L.T. 925 (Note)). Note however that the court declined to impose an extended sentence on appeal on the grounds that the social enquiry report prepared originally had not addressed the risk to the public posed by the accused; secondly, it is s.209 that empowers solemn courts to make such orders in relation to offenders sentenced to imprisonment for a period of less than four years. Separate provisions, introducing extended sentences for sexual offenders, and for violent offenders sentenced to more than four years imprisonment, are to be found in s.210A. These provisions came into force on September 30, 1998 in terms of the Crime and Disorder Act 1998 (Commencement No.2 and Transitional Provisions) Order 1998 (SI 1998/2327); the provisions do not apply to sex offences committed before September 30, 1998—supervised release orders could still be imposed in such circumstances.

Act of Adjournal

The style of supervised release order is set out in Form 20.3 in the 1996 Act of Adjournal as amended by the Act of Adjournal (Criminal Procedure Rules Amendment) (Miscellaneous) 2000 (SSI 2000/65) which came into force on April 7, 2000; whose text is found in 2000 S.L.T. 121.

Consideration of time spent in custody

210.—(1) A court, in passing a sentence of imprisonment or detention on a person for an offence, shall—

(a) in determining the period of imprisonment or detention, have regard to any period of time spent in custody by the person on remand awaiting trial or sentence, or spent in custody awaiting extradition to the United Kingdom, or spent in hospital awaiting trial or sentence by virtue of an assessment order, a treatment order or an interim compulsion order or by virtue of an order made under section 200 of this Act;

(b) specify the date of commencement of the sentence; and

(c) if the person—

  (i) has spent a period of time in custody on remand awaiting trial or sentence; or

  (ii) is an extradited prisoner for the purposes of this section, or

  (iii) has spent a period of time in hospital awaiting trial or sentence by virtue of an assessment order, a treatment order or an interim compulsion order or by virtue of an order under section 200 of this Act,

and the date specified under paragraph (b) above is not earlier than the date on which sentence was passed, state its reasons for not specifying an earlier date so however that a period of time spent both in custody on remand and, by virtue of section 47(1) of the Crime (International Co-operation) Act 2003, abroad is not for any reason to be discounted in a determination under paragraph (a) above or specification under paragraph (b) above.

(2) A prisoner is an extradited prisoner for the purposes of this section if—

(a) he was tried for the offence in respect of which his sentence of imprisonment was imposed—

  (i) after having been extradited to the United Kingdom; and

  (ii) without having first been restored to the state from which he was extradited or having had an opportunity of leaving the United Kingdom; and

(b) he was for any period in custody while awaiting such extradition.

(3) In this section "extradited to the United Kingdom" means returned to the United Kingdom—

(a) in pursuance of extradition arrangements (as defined in section 3 of the Extradition Act 1989);

(b) under any law which corresponds to that Act and is a law of a designated Commonwealth country (as defined in section 5(1) of that Act);

(c) under that Act as extended to a colony or under any corresponding law of a colony;

(d) in pursuance of arrangements with a foreign state in respect of which an Order in Council under section 2 of the Extradition Act 1870 is in force; or

(e) in pursuance of a warrant of arrest endorsed in the Republic of Ireland under the law of that country corresponding to the Backing of Warrants (Republic of Ireland) Act 1965.

AMENDMENTS

Subss.(1)(a) and (1)(c)(iii) inserted by the Crime and Punishment (Scotland) Act 1997 (c.48), s.12 and commenced on August 1, 1997 by the Crime and Punishment (Scotland) Act 1997 (Commencement and Transitional Provisions) Order 1997 (SI 1997/1712), art.3.

Subs.(1)(c) as amended by the Crime (International Co-operation) Act 2003 (c.32), Sch.5, para.65.

Brought into force on April 26, 2004 by the Crime (International Co-operation) Act 2003 (Commencement No.1) Order 2004 (SI 2004/786 (C.32)).

Subs.(1)(a) and (c) as amended by the Mental Health (Care and Treatment) (Scotland) Act 2003 (asp 13), Sch.4, para.8(13) and Sch.5. Brought into force on October 5, 2005 by the Mental Health (Care and Treatment) (Scotland) Act 2003 (Commencement No.4) Order 2005 (SSI 2005/161 (C.6)).

DEFINITION

"sentence": s.307(1).

GENERAL NOTE

The obligation placed on a court by this section is to "have regard to any period of time spent in custody by the person awaiting trial or sentence, or spent in custody awaiting extradition to the United Kingdom". The 1997 Act extended this obligation to any prisoner spending time on remand in hospital prior to plea or trial to ascertain his mental state (s.52 of the 1995 Act), prior to sentence when an interim hospital order had been made (s.53 of that Act as amended) or when remanded to hospital during a deferment of sentence (s.200 of the 1995 Act). This obligation normally exists even when the conviction is one of murder which, of course, carries a mandatory life sentence; while subs.(1)(a) has no application in such a case the remaining provisions do, and can affect the date upon which a prisoner might first be eligible for parole (*Elliott v H.M. Advocate,* 1997 G.W.D. 1–15).

In effect, it is submitted, the court should have such a period in mind when selecting a sentence: it does not follow that such a period should be deducted automatically or that the sentence passed should be backdated to a commencement date that in effect deducts the period in mind. In practice, however, many sentences are backdated to a suitable commencement date: for a survey of the very considerable number of authorities on this point see *Backdating Sentences of Imprisonment* (1995) 40 J.L.S. 383.

While the extent and seriousness of the accused's previous convictions and the gravity of the offences before the court are factors which would justify not backdating a term of imprisonment (see for example *Robertson v H.M. Advocate*, 1996 G.W.D. 14–836; *Wilson v Lees*, 1996 G.W.D. 8–441, and *Grant v H.M. Advocate*, 1996 G.W.D. 25–1421), due attention has to be paid to the extent of the charges where the accused has been convicted when set against those libelled originally: see *Johnston v Wilson*, 1996 G.W.D. 17–986; *Craig v H.M. Advocate*, 1997 G.W.D. 8–306 and *Blacklock v H.M. Advocate*, 1998 G.W.D. 7–328 and *Pugh v Hingston*, 1999 G.W.D. 13–605.

Time spent on remand resulting from an accused's own failure to appear for trial is unlikely to merit backdating (*Galbraith v Vannet*, 1998 G.W.D. 5–215 following *Wojciechowski v McLeod*, 1992 S.C.C.R. 563) but backdating only to the date of intimation of an acceptable plea, rather than to the date of being taken into custody, will only be upheld if reasons for so doing are stated (*Taylor v H.M. Advocate*, 1998 G.W.D. 28–1415). However contrast *McAuley v McLeod*, 1998 G.W.D. 37–1918 where a breach of bail and an appalling record of shoplifting offences was held to justify a refusal to backdate sentence.

Even following a conviction for murder, the mandatory sentence of life imprisonment should be backdated unless there are sound reasons stated to the contrary (*Elliott v H.M. Advocate (No.2)*, 1997 S.L.T. 1229).

Ordinarily the reasons for refraining from backdating have to be noted when sentence is imposed (subs.(1)(c)) as in *Young v H.M. Advocate*, 1996 G.W.D. 15–667 and *McGhee v H.M. Advocate*, 1997 G.W.D. 17–772, cases in which regard was had to offending while on bail or very soon after the commission of other offences; failure to state them generally results in sentence being backdated on appeal (*Egan v McGlennan*, 1996 G.W.D. 17–985 and *Dailly v H.M. Advocate*, 1996 S.C.C.R. 580). In the latter case matters were further complicated by the need to take account of s.16 of the Prisoners and Criminal Proceedings (Scotland) 1993 which makes no provision for backdating; such sentences either must be served before any additional sentence imposed by the court or concurrently with such additional sentence. See also *McLaughlin v H.M. Advocate*, 1996 G.W.D. 23–1315 in which the sheriff refrained from backdating on the basis that, had he done so, he would have remitted the accused to the High Court for sentence. The Court of Appeal paid the same regard to the accused's record, albeit that had not been expressly referred to in the sentencing minutes.

In *Hutcheson v H.M. Advocate*, 2001 S.C.C.R. 43, which might seem to follow upon *Douglas v H.M. Advocate*, 1997 S.C.C.R. 671 (where the sentencing judge had refrained from backdating as an alternative to remitting to the High Court for sentence), the sentencing High Court judge adopted an idiosyncratic approach, and one which the Appeal Court seemed reluctant to commend; H's sentence for assault to severe injury and danger of life committed while on bail, was not backdated on the basis that such a brutal attack truly merited a more severe punishment, the time spent in custody being used to offset the sentence which would otherwise have been imposed. It would surely have been more satisfactory to have imposed an appropriate sentence first, then consider whether or not to backdate.

Sexual or violent offenders

Extended sentences for sex and violent offenders

210A.—(1) Where a person is convicted on indictment of a sexual or violent offence, the court may, if it—

(a) intends, in relation to—

    (i) a sexual offence, to pass a determinate sentence of imprisonment; or

    (ii) a violent offence, to pass such a sentence for a term of four years or more; and

(b) considers that the period (if any) for which the offender would, apart from this section, be subject to a licence would not be adequate for the purpose of protecting the public from serious harm from the offender,

pass an extended sentence on the offender.

(2) An extended sentence is a sentence of imprisonment which is the aggregate of—

(a) the term of imprisonment ("the custodial term") which the court would have passed on the offender otherwise than by virtue of this section; and

(b) a further period ("the extension period") for which the offender is to be subject to a licence and which is, subject to the provisions of this section, of such length as the court considers necessary for the purpose mentioned in subsection (1)(b) above.

(3) The extension period shall not exceed, in the case of—

(a) a sexual offence, ten years; and

(b) a violent offence, ten years.

(4) A court shall, before passing an extended sentence, consider a report by a relevant officer of a local authority about the offender and his circumstances and, if the court thinks it necessary, hear that officer.

(5) The term of an extended sentence passed for a statutory offence shall not exceed the maximum term of imprisonment provided for in the statute in respect of that offence.

(6) Subject to subsection (5) above, a sheriff may pass an extended sentence which is the aggregate of a custodial term not exceeding the maximum term of imprisonment which he may impose and an extension period not exceeding five years.

(7) The Secretary of State may by order—

(a) amend paragraph (b) of subsection (3) above by substituting a different period, not exceeding ten years, for the period for the time being specified in that paragraph; and

(b) make such transitional provision as appears to him to be necessary or expedient in connection with the amendment.

(8) The power to make an order under subsection (7) above shall be exercisable by statutory instrument; but no such order shall be made unless a draft of the order has been laid before, and approved by a resolution of, each House of Parliament.

(9) An extended sentence shall not be imposed where the sexual or violent offence was committed before the commencement of section 86 of the Crime and Disorder Act 1998.

(10) For the purposes of this section—

"licence" and "relevant officer" have the same meaning as in Part Iof the Prisoners and Criminal Proceedings (Scotland) Act 1993;

"sexual offence" means—

    (i) rape;

    (ii) clandestine injury to women;

    (iii) abduction of a woman or girl with intent to rape or ravish;

    (iv) assault with intent to rape or ravish;

    (v) indecent assault;

    (vi) lewd, indecent or libidinous behaviour or practices;

    (vii) shameless indecency;

    (viii) sodomy;

    (ix) an offence under section 170 of the Customs and Excise Management Act 1979 in relation to goods prohibited to be imported under section 42 of the Customs Consolidation Act 1876, but only where the prohibited goods include indecent photographs of persons;

    (x) an offence under section 52 of the Civic Government (Scotland) Act 1982 (taking and distribution of indecent images of children);

    (xi) an offence under section 52A of that Act (possession of indecent images of children);

    (xii) an offence under section 1 of the Criminal Law (Consolidation) (Scotland) Act 1995 (incest);

    (xiii) an offence under section 2 of that Act (intercourse with a stepchild);

    (xiv) an offence under section 3 of that Act (intercourse with child under 16 by person in position of trust);

    (xv) an offence under section 5 of that Act (unlawful intercourse with girl under 16);

    (xvi) an offence under section 6 of that Act (indecent behaviour towards girl between 12 and 16);

    (xvii) an offence under section 8 of that Act (abduction of girl under 18 for purposes of unlawful intercourse);

    (xviii) an offence under section 10 of that Act (person having parental responsibilities causing or encouraging sexual activity in relation to a girl under 16);

    (xix) an offence under subsection (5) of section 13 of that Act (homosexual offences);

    (xx) an offence under section 3 of the Sexual Offences (Amendment) Act 2000 (abuse of position of trust);

    (xxi) an offence under section 311(1) of the Mental Health (Care and Treatment) (Scotland) Act 2003 (asp 13) (non-consensual sexual acts).

"imprisonment" includes—

    (i) detention under section 207 of this Act; and

    (ii) detention under section 208 of this Act; and

"violent offence" means any offence (other than an offence which is a sexual offence within the meaning of this section) inferring personal violence.

(11) Any reference in subsection (10) above to a sexual offence includes—

(a) a reference to any attempt, conspiracy or incitement to commit that offence; and

(b) except in the case of an offence in paragraphs (i) to (viii) of the definition of "sexual offence" in that subsection, a reference to aiding and abetting, counselling or procuring the commission of that offence.

AMENDMENTS

Section 210A inserted by the Crime and Disorder Act 1998 (c.37), s.86 (effective September 30, 1998: SI 1998/2327).

Subs.(10)(xx) inserted by the Sexual Offences (Amendment) Act 2000 (c.44), s.6(2).

Subs.(3)(b) as amended by Extended Sentences for Violent Offenders (Scotland) Order 2003 (SSI 2003/48), art.2 (effective January 28, 2003).

Subs.(6) as amended by the Criminal Procedure (Amendment) (Scotland) Act 2004 (asp 5), s.21. Brought into force on October 4, 2004 by the Criminal Procedure (Amendment) (Scotland) Act 2004 (Commencement, Transitional Provisions and Savings) Order 2004 (SSI 2004/405 (C.28)).

Subs.(10) as amended by the Mental Health (Care and Treatment) (Scotland) Act 2003 (asp 13), s.312. Brought into force on October 5, 2005 by the Mental Health (Care and Treatment) (Scotland) Act 2003 (Commencement No.4) Order 2005(SSI 2005/161 (C.6)).

DEFINITIONS

"indictment": s.307(1) of the 1995 Act.

"sexual offence": s.210A(8) of the 1995 Act as inserted by s.86(1) of the 1998 Act.

"violent offence": as last above.

"imprisonment": s.307(1) of the 1995 Act and s.210A(8) of that Act as inserted by s.86(1) of the 1998 Act.

GENERAL NOTE

These provisions came into force on September 30, 1998 in terms of the Crime and Disorder Act 1998 (Commencement No.2 and Transitional Provisions) Order 1998 (SI 1998/2327).

This section inserted into the 1995 Act as s.210A has to be read in conjunction with s.26A of the Prisoners and Criminal Proceedings (Scotland) Act 1993 (c.9) which, confusingly, inserts "extended sentence" provisions into that latter Act.

Solemn courts imposing imprisonment for serious sexual offences or violent crimes attracting a term of imprisonment of four years or more now have a discretion to place the offender on licence, and thus subject to recall, when it is considered that the offender may pose a serious threat to public safety after his release.

(Section 87 of the 1998 Act is inserted into Pt I of the Prisoners and Criminal Proceedings (Scotland) Act 1993 and ss.12 and 17 of the 1993 Act set out the meaning of "licence"; however, Schs 1 and 3 of the Crime and Punishment (Scotland) Act 1997 (c.48) contain prospective changes to these sections.)

Henceforth, courts opting to place an offender on licence for a qualifying offence will impose an extended sentence comprising the period of imprisonment or detention (dubbed "the custodial term") and a period of licence ("the extension term"). Subsection (10) by defining "imprisonment" under reference to ss.207 and 208 of the 1995 Act stipulates that these discretionary sentencing powers can be applied to children and young offenders as well as to adult offenders. The provisions can only apply to determinate sentences—those serving indeterminate sentences, i.e. life imprisonment, are dealt with separately. While subs.(4) requires the court to obtain and consider both a social enquiry report and an offender risk assessment before imposing an extended sentence (*Robertson v HM Advocate*, 2004 S.L.T. 888), no such stricture applies to offenders sentenced to life imprisonment for violent, as opposed to sexual, offences—see *Hamilton v HM Advocate*, 2005 S.C.C.R. 316.

It has to be emphasised that extended sentences are discretionary and, necessarily, only operate in circumstances where a term of imprisonment has been imposed on indictment and it is felt that the offender will constitute a threat to public safety on release and, then, subject to several qualifications. While it is proper to impose an extended sentence, when it is felt that the period of licence after early release is insufficient to protect the public from serious harm, consideration has still to be given to the extension period necessary for that purpose (*Fleming v HM Advocate*, 2002 G.W.D. 2–69). A common law "sexual offence" as defined by s.210A(10) can involve a period of licence of up to 10 years, while the extended sentence for a statutory "sexual offence" is to be not more than the maximum period of imprisonment statutorily provided for that offence, or the 10 year ceiling already mentioned, whichever is lower. It will be recalled that some statutory sexual offences, notably contraventions of ss.1 to 3 of the Criminal Law (Consolidation) (Scotland) Act 1995 (c.39) can attract life imprisonment. It is submitted that s.210A(3) and (4) have to be read in conjunction.

The new provisions in s.210A in regard to violent offences only apply to sentences of over four years'imprisonment, the point at which prisoners are regarded as long-term prisoners (see s.27 of the 1993 Act) and in such cases the "extension period" cannot exceed five years. If the violent offence has been a statutory crime then, again, the extension period will be the lower of either the maximum period of imprisonment available under statute, or five years, due to the interaction of s.210A(3) and (4). It is worth noting that subs.(7) empowers the Secretary of State to increase "the extension period" in relation to violent offences (but not sexual offences) from the five years set out in subs.(3)(b) up to 10 years, by order.

For those convicted of a violent offence and sentenced to less than four years' imprisonment the option open to the court is to impose a supervised release order; see s.209 above.

See the discussion of *Craig v HM Advocate*, 2000 G.W.D. 34–1313 and *O'Hare v HM Advocate*, 2002 S.L.T. 925 (Note) at A4–435.2 above.

Extended sentences for certain other offenders

210AA. Where a person is convicted on indictment of abduction but the offence is other than is mentioned in paragraph (iii) of the definition of "sexual offence" in subsection (10) of section 210A of this Act, that section shall apply in relation to the person as it applies in relation to a person so convicted of a violent offence.

AMENDMENT

Section 210AA inserted by Criminal Justice (Scotland) Act 2003 (asp 7), Part 3, s.20. Brought into force on June 27, 2003 by the Criminal Justice (Scotland) Act 2003 (Commencement No.1) Order 2003 (SSI 2003/288 (C.14)).

Risk assessment

Risk assessment order

210B.—(1) This subsection applies where it falls to the High Court to impose sentence on a person convicted of an offence other than murder and that offence—

(a) is (any or all)—

   (i) a sexual offence (as defined in section 210A(10) of this Act);

   (ii) a violent offence (as so defined);

   (iii) an offence which endangers life; or

(b) is an offence the nature of which, or circumstances of the commission of which, are such that it appears to the court that the person has a propensity to commit any such offence as is mentioned in sub-paragraphs (i) to (iii) of paragraph (a) above.

(2) Where subsection (1) above applies, the court, at its own instance or (provided that the prosecutor has given the person notice of his intention in that regard) on the motion of the prosecutor, if it considers that the risk criteria may be met, shall make an order under this subsection (a "risk assessment order") unless—

(a) the court makes an interim hospital order by virtue of section 210D(1) of this Act in respect of the person; or

(b) the person is subject to an order for lifelong restriction previously imposed.

(3) A risk assessment order is an order—

(a) for the convicted person to be taken to a place specified in the order, so that there may be prepared there—

   (i) by a person accredited for the purposes of this section by the Risk Management Authority; and

   (ii) in such manner as may be so accredited,

a risk assessment report (that is to say, a report as to what risk his being at liberty presents to the safety of the public at large); and

(b) providing for him to be remanded in custody there for so long as is necessary for those purposes and thereafter there or elsewhere until such diet as is fixed for sentence.

(4) On making a risk assessment order, the court shall adjourn the case for a period not exceeding ninety days.

(5) The court may on one occasion, on cause shown, extend the period mentioned in subsection (4) above by not more than ninety days; and it may exceptionally, where by reason of circumstances outwith the control of the person to whom it falls to prepare the risk assessment report (the "assessor"), or as the case may be of any person instructed under section 210C(5) of this Act to prepare such a report, the report in question has not been completed, grant such further extension as appears to it to be appropriate.

(6) There shall be no appeal against a risk assessment order or against any refusal to make such an order.

AMENDMENT

Section 210B inserted by the Criminal Justice (Scotland) Act 2003 (asp 7), s.1(1). Brought into force on June 19, 2006 by the Criminal Justice (Scotland) Act 2003 (Commencement No.9) Order 2006 (SSI 2006/332 (C.30)), art.2(1), subject to art.2(2).

Risk assessment report

210C.—(1) The assessor may, in preparing the risk assessment report, take into account not only any previous conviction of the convicted person but also any allegation that the person has engaged in criminal behaviour (whether or not that behaviour resulted in prosecution and acquittal).

(2) Where the assessor, in preparing the risk assessment report, takes into account any allegation that the person has engaged in criminal behaviour, the report is to—

(a) list each such allegation;

(b) set out any additional evidence which supports the allegation; and

(c) explain the extent to which the allegation and evidence has influenced the opinion included in the report under subsection (3) below.

(3) The assessor shall include in the risk assessment report his opinion as to whether the risk mentioned in section 210B(3)(a) of this Act is, having regard to such standards and guidelines as are issued by the Risk Management Authority in that regard, high, medium or low.

(4) The assessor shall submit the risk assessment report to the High Court by sending it, together with such documents as are available to the assessor and are referred to in the report, to the Principal Clerk of Justiciary, who shall then send a copy of the report and of those documents to the prosecutor and to the convicted person.

(5) The convicted person may, during the period of his detention at the place specified in the risk assessment order, himself instruct the preparation (by a person other than the assessor) of a risk assessment report; and if such a report is so prepared then the person who prepares it shall submit it to the court by sending it, together with such documents as are available to him (after any requirement under subsection (4) above is met) and are referred to in the report, to the Principal Clerk of Justiciary, who shall then send a copy of it and of those documents to the prosecutor.

(6) When the court receives the risk assessment report submitted by the assessor a diet shall be fixed for the convicted person to be brought before it for sentence.

(7) If, within such period after receiving a copy of that report as may be prescribed by Act of Adjournal, the convicted person intimates, in such form, or as nearly as may be in such form, as may be so prescribed—

(a) that he objects to the content or findings of that report; and

(b) what the grounds of his objection are,

the prosecutor and he shall be entitled to produce and examine witnesses with regard to—

    (i) that content or those findings; and

    (ii) the content or findings of any risk assessment report instructed by the person and duly submitted under subsection (5) above.

AMENDMENT

Section 210C inserted by the Criminal Justice (Scotland) Act 2003 (asp 7), s.1(1). Brought into force on June 19, 2006 by the Criminal Justice (Scotland) Act 2003 (Commencement No.9) Order 2006 (SSI 2006/332 (C.30)), art.2(1), subject to art.2(2).

Interim hospital order and assessment of risk

210D.—(1) Where subsection (1) of section 210B of this Act applies, the High Court, if—

    (a) it may make an interim hospital order in respect of the person under section 53 of this Act; and

    (b) it considers that the risk criteria may be met,

shall make such an order unless the person is subject to an order for lifelong restriction previously imposed.

(2) Where an interim hospital order is made by virtue of subsection (1) above, a report as to the risk the convicted person's being at liberty presents to the safety of the public at large shall be prepared by a person accredited for the purposes of this section by the Risk Management Authority and in such manner as may be so accredited.

(3) Section 210C(1) to (4) and (7) (except paragraph (ii)) of this Act shall apply in respect of any such report as it does in respect of a risk assessment report.

AMENDMENT

Section 210D inserted by the Criminal Justice (Scotland) Act 2003 (asp 7), s.1(1). Brought into force on June 19, 2006 by the Criminal Justice (Scotland) Act 2003 (Commencement No.9) Order 2006 (SSI 2006/332 (C.30)), art.2(1), subject to art.2(2).

The risk criteria

210E. For the purposes of sections 195(1), 210B(2), 210D(1) and 210F(1) and (3) of this Act, the risk criteria are that the nature of, or the circumstances of the commission of, the offence of which the convicted person has been found guilty either in themselves or as part of a pattern of behaviour are such as to demonstrate that there is a likelihood that he, if at liberty, will seriously endanger the lives, or physical or psychological well-being, of members of the public at large.

AMENDMENT

Section 210E inserted by the Criminal Justice (Scotland) Act 2003 (asp 7), s.1(1). Brought into force on June 19, 2006 by the Criminal Justice (Scotland) Act 2003 (Commencement No.9) Order 2006 (SSI 2006/332 (C.30)), art.2(1), subject to art.2(2).

Application of certain sections of this Act to proceedings under section 210C(7)

210EA.—(1) Sections 271 to 271M, 274 to 275C and 288C to 288F of this Act (in this section referred to as the "applied sections") apply in relation to proceedings under section 210C(7) of this Act as they apply in relation to proceedings in or for the purposes of a trial, references in the applied sections to the "trial" and to the "trial diet" being construed accordingly.

(2) But for the purposes of this section the references—

    (a) in sections 271(1)(a) and 271B(1)(b) to the date of commencement of the proceedings in which the trial is being held or is to be held; and

(b) in section 288E(2)(b) to the date of commencement of the proceedings,
are to be construed as references to the date of commencement of the proceedings in which the person was convicted of the offence in respect of which sentence falls to be imposed (such proceedings being in this section referred to as the "original proceedings").

(3) And for the purposes of this section any reference in the applied sections to—

(a) an "accused" (or to a person charged with an offence) is to be construed as a reference to the convicted person except that the reference in section 271(2)(e)(iii) to an accused is to be disregarded;

(b) an "alleged" offence is to be construed as a reference to any or all of the following—

    (i) the offence in respect of which sentence falls to be imposed;

    (ii) any other offence of which the convicted person has been convicted;

    (iii) any alleged criminal behaviour of the convicted person; and

(c) a "complainer" is to be construed as a reference to any or all of the following—

    (i) the person who was the complainer in the original proceedings;

    (ii) in the case of any such offence as is mentioned in paragraph (b)(ii) above, the person who was the complainer in the proceedings relating to that offence;

    (iii) in the case of alleged criminal behaviour if it was alleged behaviour directed against a person, the person in question.

(4) Where—

(a) any person who is giving or is to give evidence at an examination under section 210C(7) of this Act gave evidence at the trial in the original proceedings; and

(b) a special measure or combination of special measures was used by virtue of section 271A, 271C or 271D of this Act for the purpose of taking the person's evidence at that trial,

that special measure or, as the case may be, combination of special measures is to be treated as having been authorised, by virtue of the same section, to be used for the purpose of taking the person's evidence at or for the purposes of the examination.

(5) Subsection (4) above does not affect the operation, by virtue of subsection (1) above, of section 271D of this Act.

AMENDMENT

Section 210EA inserted by the Management of Offenders etc. (Scotland) Act 2005 (asp 14), s.19. Brought into force on June 20, 2006 by the Management of Offenders etc. (Scotland) Act 2005 (Commencement No.2) Order 2006 (SSI 2006/331 (C.29)), art.3 (1), subject to art.3(2).

Order for lifelong restriction etc.

Order for lifelong restriction or compulsion order

210F.—(1) The High Court, at its own instance or on the motion of the prosecutor, if it is satisfied, having regard to—

(a) any risk assessment report submitted under section 210C(4) or (5) of this Act;

(b) any report submitted by virtue of section 210D of this Act;

(c) any evidence given under section 210C(7) of this Act; and

(d) any other information before it,

that, on a balance of probabilities, the risk criteria are met, in a case where it may make a compulsion order in respect of the convicted person under section 57A of this Act, either make such an order or make an order for lifelong restriction in respect of that person and in any other case make an order for lifelong restriction in respect of that person.

(2) An order for lifelong restriction constitutes a sentence of imprisonment, or as the case may be detention, for an indeterminate period.

(3) The prosecutor may, on the grounds that on a balance of probabilities the risk criteria are met, appeal against any refusal of the court to make an order for lifelong restriction.

AMENDMENT

Section 210F inserted by the Criminal Justice (Scotland) Act 2003 (asp 7), s.1(1). Brought into force on June 19, 2006 by the Criminal Justice (Scotland) Act 2003 (Commencement No.9) Order 2006 (SSI 2006/332 (C.30)), art.2(1), subject to art.2(2).

Subs.(1) as amended by the Management of Offenders etc. (Scotland) Act 2005 (asp 14), s.14(2) and (3). Brought into force on June 20, 2006 by the Management of Offenders etc. (Scotland) Act 2005 (Commencement No.2) Order 2006 (SSI 2006/331 (C.29)), art.3(1), subject to art.3(2).

Disposal of case where certain orders not made

210G.—(1) Where, in respect of a convicted person—

(a) a risk assessment order is not made under section 210B(2) of this Act, or (as the case may be) an interim hospital order is not made by virtue of section 210D(1) of this Act, because the court does not consider that the risk criteria may be met; or

(b) the court considers that the risk criteria may be met but a risk assessment order, or (as the case may be) an interim hospital order, is not so made because the person is subject to an order for lifelong restriction previously imposed,

the court shall dispose of the case as it considers appropriate.

(2) Where, in respect of a convicted person, an order for lifelong restriction is not made under section 210F of this Act because the court is not satisfied (in accordance with subsection (1) of that section) that the risk criteria are met, the court, in disposing of the case, shall not impose on the person a sentence of imprisonment for life, detention for life or detention without limit of time.

AMENDMENT

Section 210G inserted by the Criminal Justice (Scotland) Act 2003 (asp 7), s.1(1). Brought into force on June 19, 2006 by the Criminal Justice (Scotland) Act 2003 (Commencement No.9) Order 2006 (SSI 2006/332 (C.30)), art.2(1), subject to art.2(2).

Report of judge

Report of judge

210H.—(1) This subsection applies where a person falls to be sentenced—

(a) in the High Court for an offence (other than murder) mentioned in section 210B(1) of this Act; or

(b) in the sheriff court for such an offence prosecuted on indictment.

(2) Where subsection (1) above applies, the court shall, as soon as reasonably practicable, prepare a report in writing, in such form as may be prescribed by Act of Adjournal—

(a) as to the circumstances of the case; and

(b) containing such other information as it considers appropriate, but no such report shall be prepared if a report is required to be prepared under section 21(4) of the Criminal Justice (Scotland) Act 2003 (asp 7).

AMENDMENT

Section 210H inserted by the Criminal Justice (Scotland) Act 2003 (asp 7), s.1(1). Brought into force on June 19, 2006 by the Criminal Justice (Scotland) Act 2003 (Commencement No.9) Order 2006 (SSI 2006/332 (C.30)), art.2(1), subject to art.2(2).

Fines

Fines

211.—(1) Where an accused who is convicted on indictment of any offence (whether triable only on indictment or triable either on indictment or summarily other than by virtue of section 292(6) of this Act) would apart from this subsection be liable to a fine of or not exceeding a specified amount, he shall by virtue of this subsection be liable to a fine of any amount.

(2) Where any Act confers a power by subordinate instrument to make a person liable on conviction on indictment of any offence mentioned in subsection (1) above to a fine or a maximum fine of a specified amount, or which shall not exceed a specified amount, the fine which may be imposed in the exercise of that power shall by virtue of this subsection be a fine of an unlimited amount.

(3) Any sentence or decree for any fine or expenses pronounced by a sheriff court or district court may be enforced against the person or effects of any party against whom the sentence or decree was awarded—

(a) in the district where the sentence or decree was pronounced; or

(b) in any other such district.

(4) A fine imposed by the High Court shall be remitted for enforcement to, and shall be enforceable as if it had been imposed by—

(a) where the person upon whom the fine was imposed resides in Scotland, the sheriff for the district where that person resides; and

(b) where that person resides outwith Scotland, the sheriff before whom he was brought for examination in relation to the offence for which the fine was imposed.

(5) Any fine imposed in the High Court on the accused, and on a juror for non-attendance, and any forfeiture for non-appearance of a party, witness or juror in the High Court shall be payable to and recoverable by the Treasury, except where the High Court orders that the whole or any part of the fine shall be otherwise disposed of.

(6) All fines and expenses imposed in summary proceedings under this Act shall be paid to the clerk of court to be accounted for by him to the person entitled to such fines and expenses, and it shall not be necessary to specify in any sentence the person entitled to payment of such fines or expenses unless it is necessary to provide for the division of the penalty.

(7) A court in determining the amount of any fine to be imposed on an offender shall take into consideration, amongst other things, the means of the offender so far as known to the court.

DEFINITIONS

"fine": s.307(1).
"High Court": s.307(1).
"indictment": s.307(1).

"sentence": s.307(1).
"witness": s.307(1).

GENERAL NOTE

This section presumes as a generality the proposition that fines following conviction on indictment are unlimited subject to statutory maxima for certain offences. It is of some interest that the only item which is specified as being required to be taken into consideration in imposing a fine is "the means of the offender so far as known to the court": subs. (7).

Fines in summary proceedings

212.—(1) Where a court of summary jurisdiction imposes a fine on an offender, the court may order him to be searched, and any money found on him on apprehension or when so searched or when taken to prison or to a young offenders institution in default of payment of the fine, may, unless the court otherwise directs and subject to subsection (2) below, be applied towards payment of the fine, and the surplus if any shall be returned to him.

(2) Money shall not be applied as mentioned in subsection (1) above if the court is satisfied that it does not belong to the person on whom it was found or that the loss of the money will be more injurious to his family than his imprisonment or detention.

(3) When a court of summary jurisdiction, which has adjudged that a sum of money shall be paid by an offender, considers that any money found on the offender on apprehension, or after he has been searched by order of the court, should not be applied towards payment of such sum, the court, shall make a direction in writing to that effect which shall be written on the extract of the sentence which imposes the fine before it is issued by the clerk of the court.

(4) An accused may make an application to such a court either orally or in writing, through the governor of the prison in whose custody he may be at that time, that any sum of money which has been found on his person should not be applied in payment of the fine adjudged to be paid by him.

(5) A person who alleges that any money found on the person of an offender is not the property of the offender, but belongs to that person, may apply to such court either orally or in writing for a direction that the money should not be applied in payment of the fine adjudged to be paid, and the court after enquiry may so direct.

(6) A court of summary jurisdiction, which has adjudged that a sum of money shall be paid by an offender, may order the attendance in court of the offender, if he is in prison, for the purpose of ascertaining the ownership of money which has been found on his person.

(7) A notice in the form prescribed by Act of Adjournal, or as nearly as may be in such form, addressed to the governor of the prison in whose custody an offender may be at the time, signed by the judge of a court of summary jurisdiction shall be a sufficient warrant to the governor of such prison for conveying the offender to the court.

DEFINITIONS

"court of summary jurisdiction": s.307(1).
"fine": s.307(1).

Act of Adjournal

The procedure set out in subs. (1) uses Form 20.4–A in the 1996 Act of Adjournal. The notice described in subs.(7) follows the style of Form 20.4–B in that Act of Adjournal.

Remission of fines

213.—(1) A fine may at any time be remitted in whole or in part by—

   (a) in a case where a transfer of fine order under section 222 of this Act is effective and the court by which payment is enforceable is, in terms of the order, a court of summary jurisdiction in Scotland, that court; or

   (b) in any other case, the court which imposed the fine or, where that court was the High Court, by which payment was first enforceable.

(2) Where the court remits the whole or part of a fine after imprisonment has been imposed under section 214(2) or (4) of this Act, it shall also remit the whole period of imprisonment or, as the case may be, reduce the period by an amount which bears the same proportion to the whole period as the amount remitted bears to the whole fine.

(3) The power conferred by subsection (1) above shall be exercisable without requiring the attendance of the accused.

Definitions

   "court of summary jurisdiction": s.307(1).
   "fine": s.307(1).
   "High Court": s.307(1).

General Note

   In *Tudhope v. Furphy*, 1982 S.C.C.R. 575 a sheriff held *inter alia* that he has power to reduce or extinguish a compensation order in circumstances where it had subsequently been discovered that the payee had died before the order was made.

Fines: time for payment and payment by instalments

214.—(1) Where a court has imposed a fine on an offender or ordered him to find caution the court shall, subject to subsection (2) below, allow him at least seven days to pay the fine or the first instalment thereof or, as the case may be, to find caution; and any reference in this section and section 216 of this Act to a failure to pay a fine or other like expression shall include a reference to a failure to find caution.

(2) If on the occasion of the imposition of a fine—

   (a) the offender appears to the court to possess sufficient means to enable him to pay the fine forthwith; or

   (b) on being asked by the court whether he wishes to have time for payment, he does not ask for time; or

   (c) he fails to satisfy the court that he has a fixed abode; or

   (d) the court is satisfied for any other special reason that no time should be allowed for payment,

the court may refuse him time to pay the fine and, if the offender fails to pay, may exercise its power to impose imprisonment and, if it does so, shall state the special reason for its decision.

(3) In all cases where time is not allowed by a court for payment of a fine, the reasons of the court for not so allowing time shall be stated in the extract of the finding and sentence as well as in the finding and sentence itself.

(4) Where time is allowed for payment of a fine or payment by instalments is ordered, the court shall not, on the occasion of the imposition of a fine, impose imprisonment in the event of a future default in paying the fine or an instalment thereof unless the offender is before it and the court determines that, having regard to the gravity of the offence or to the character of the offender, or to other

special reason, it is expedient that he should be imprisoned without further in-quiry in default of payment; and where a court so determines, it shall state the special reason for its decision.

(5) Where a court has imposed imprisonment in accordance with subsection (4) above, then, if at any time the offender asks the court to commit him to prison, the court may do so notwithstanding subsection (1) of this section.

(6) Nothing in the foregoing provisions of this section shall affect any power of the court to order a fine to be recovered by civil diligence.

(7) Where time has been allowed for payment of a fine imposed by the court, it may, on an application by or on behalf of the offender, and after giving the prosecutor an opportunity of being heard, allow further time for payment.

(8) Without prejudice to subsection (2) above, where a court has imposed a fine on an offender, the court may, of its own accord or on the application of the offender, order payment of that fine by instalments of such amounts and at such time as it may think fit.

(9) Where the court has ordered payment of a fine by instalments it may—

(a) allow further time for payment of any instalment thereof;

(b) order payment thereof by instalments of lesser amounts, or at longer intervals, than those originally fixed,

and the powers conferred by this subsection shall be exercisable without requir-ing the attendance of the accused.

Definitions

"caution": s.227.
"fine": s.307(1).

General Note

Subs. (1)

Although the references are to both fines and cautions in practice it is rare for cautions to be imposed. It is incompetent to offer the accused the alternative of making a donation to charity in lieu of a monetary fine (*Wilson v. Transorganics*, 1996 G.W.D. 10–560). The guidelines applicable to the length of time over which a fine may be paid do not apply when compensation orders are imposed (*Ely v. Donnelly*, 1996 S.C.C.R. 537).

Subs. (2)(a) and (d)

In *Barbour v. Robertson* and *Ram v. Robertson*, 1943 J.C. 46 it was observed that in applying these provisions the nature of the offence can never be a relevant consideration when determining whether time should be allowed for payment where a substantial monetary penalty is imposed; the only relevant matters are the means of the offender and similar considerations. Where the nature of the offence is such as to warrant a sentence of imprisonment, the proper course to adopt is to impose such a sentence either without the option of a fine or with a fine in addition, and not to impose merely a pecuniary penalty of such an amount that when no time is allowed for payment the imposition of the fine is equivalent to a sentence of imprisonment without the option of a fine. Accordingly, where a fine is felt to be appropriate it should be imposed even if the accused, rather than seeking no time to pay, states his intention not to pay (*Sheridan v. MacDonald*, 1996 G.W.D. 9–481).

On the other hand the imposition of an unrealistic fine, and period to pay it, in conjunction with a period of imprisonment or detention will not be supported; in *McCorkindale v. McGlennan*, 2001 G.W.D. 1–31 a sentence of 60 days imprisonment (which was not appealed) and a fine of £1,200 pay-able within two months of release was set aside by the Appeal Court. (Presumably the accused had not sought no time to pay).

Subs. (2)(b)

A court of summary jurisdiction, when imposing a fine, has a discretion to allow or refuse time to pay and may allow time for payment where that has not been requested by the accused: *Fraser v. Herron*, 1968 S.L.T. 149.

Subs. (2)(d)

For an example of special reasons being recorded in the minutes see *Sullivan v. Mcleod*, 1980 S.L.T. (Notes) 99.

Subs. (4)

The relevant cases may be considered under the different parts of the subsection.

"*Unless the offender is before it*". The decision in *Campbell v. Jessop*, 1988 S.L.T. 160 made it clear that the accused had to be present when a sentence of imprisonment was imposed. Not least of the reasons is that the absence of the accused meant that there was no opportunity for representations to be made by or for the accused.

"*Having regard to the offence*". In *Finnie v. Mcleod*, 1983 S.C.C.R. 387 "barefaced shoplifting" justified an immediate alternative of imprisonment in default of payment of the fine by instalments but in *Dunlop v. Allan*, 1984 S.C.C.R. 329 careless driving did not allow such action nor did drunk driving in *Buchanan v. Hamilton*, 1988 S.C.C.R. 379.

"*The character of the offender*". *Paterson v. McGlennan*, 1991 S.L.T. 832 illustrates the error of proceeding under this head with only one minor road traffic previous conviction.

"*Other special reason*". Merely to have time still to serve in prison and to be unable to pay fines are not to be regarded as "special reasons"; *Robertson v. Jessop*, 1989 S.L.T. 843.

Act of Adjournal

Form 20.5 in the 1996 Act of Adjournal is used for the purposes of subs. (7) above and for s.215(3) below. See r. 20.5.

Application for further time to pay fine

215.—(1) An application by an offender for further time in which to pay a fine imposed on him by a court, or of instalments thereof, shall be made, subject to subsection (2) below, to that court.

(2) Where a transfer of fine order has been made under section 222 of this Act, section 90 of the Magistrates' Courts Act 1980 or Article 95 of the Magistrates' Courts (Northern Ireland) Order 1981, an application under subsection (1) above shall be made to the court specified in the transfer order, or to the court specified in the last transfer order where there is more than one transfer.

(3) A court to which an application is made under this section shall allow further time for payment of the fine or of instalments thereof, unless it is satisfied that the failure of the offender to make payment has been wilful or that the offender has no reasonable prospect of being able to pay if further time is allowed.

(4) An application made under this section may be made orally or in writing.

DEFINITION

"fine": s.307(1).

Act of Adjournal

Orders under subs. (3) follow the style set out in Form 20.5 to the 1996 Act of Adjournal. See r. 20.5.

Fines: restriction on imprisonment for default

216.—(1) Where a court has imposed a fine or ordered the finding of caution without imposing imprisonment in default of payment, subject to subsection (2) below, it shall not impose imprisonment on an offender for failing to make payment of the fine or, as the case may be, to find caution, unless on an occasion subsequent to that sentence the court has enquired into in his presence the reason why the fine has not been paid or, as the case may be, caution has not been found.

(2) Subsection (1) above shall not apply where the offender is in prison.

(3) A court may, for the purpose of enabling enquiry to be made under this section—

(a) issue a citation requiring the offender to appear before the court at a time and place appointed in the citation; or

(b) issue a warrant of apprehension.

(4) On the failure of the offender to appear before the court in response to a citation under this section, the court may issue a warrant of apprehension.

(5) The citation of an offender to appear before a court in terms of subsection (3)(a) above shall be effected in like manner, *mutatis mutandis*, as the citation of an accused to a sitting or diet of the court under section 141 of this Act, and—

(a) the citation shall be signed by the clerk of the court before which the offender is required to appear, instead of by the prosecutor; and

(b) the forms relating to the citation of an accused shall not apply to such citation.

(6) The following matters shall be, or as nearly as may be, in such form as is prescribed by Act of Adjournal—

(a) the citation of an offender under this section;

(b) if the citation of the offender is effected by an officer of law, the written execution, if any, of that officer of law;

(c) a warrant of apprehension issued by a court under subsection (4) above; and

(d) the minute of procedure in relation to an enquiry into the means of an offender under this section.

(7) Where a child would, if he were an adult, be liable to be imprisoned in default of payment of any fine the court may, if it considers that none of the other methods by which the case may legally be dealt with is suitable, order that the child be detained for such period, not exceeding one month, as may be specified in the order in a place chosen by the local authority in whose area the court is situated.

DEFINITIONS

"caution": s.227.
"fine": s.307(1).
"officer of law": s.307(1).
"prosecutor": s.307(1).

GENERAL NOTE

The power to imprison under this authority may be constrained by statute: see *Fraser v. Herron*, 1968 S.L.T. 149. The imposition of consecutive custodial sentences in default of payment has been doubted: *Stevenson v. McGlennan*, 1990 S.L.T. 842 and *Robertson v. Jessop*, 1989 S.L.T. 843. Imprisonment under this authority must be immediate imprisonment: *Craig v. Smith*, 1990 S.C.C.R. 328.

Act of Adjournal

Refer to r. 20.6 and to Forms 20.6–A to 20.6–C.

Fines: supervision pending payment

217.—(1) Where an offender has been allowed time for payment of a fine, the court may, either on the occasion of the imposition of the fine or on a subsequent occasion, order that he be placed under the supervision of such person, in this section referred to as the "supervising officer", as the court may from time to time appoint for the purpose of assisting and advising the offender in regard to payment of the fine.

(2) An order made in pursuance of subsection (1) above shall remain in force so long as the offender to whom it relates remains liable to pay the fine or any part of it unless the order ceases to have effect or is discharged under subsection (3) below.

(3) An order under this section shall cease to have effect on the making of a transfer of fine order under section 222 of this Act in respect of the fine or may be discharged by the court that made it without prejudice, in either case, to the making of a new order.

(4) Where an offender under 21 years of age has been allowed time for payment of a fine, the court shall not order the form of detention appropriate to him in default of payment of the fine unless—

(a) he has been placed under supervision in respect of the fine; or

(b) the court is satisfied that it is impracticable to place him under supervision.

(5) Where a court, on being satisfied as mentioned in subsection (4)(b) above, orders the detention of a person under 21 years of age without an order under this section having been made, the court shall state the grounds on which it is so satisfied.

(6) Where an order under this section is in force in respect of an offender, the court shall not impose imprisonment in default of the payment of the fine unless before doing so it has—

(a) taken such steps as may be reasonably practicable to obtain from the supervising officer a report, which may be oral, on the offender's conduct and means, and has considered any such report; and

(b) in a case where an enquiry is required by section 216 of this Act, considered such enquiry.

(7) When a court appoints a different supervising officer under subsection (1) above, a notice shall be sent by the clerk of the court to the offender in such form, as nearly as may be, as is prescribed by Act of Adjournal.

(8) The supervising officer shall communicate with the offender with a view to assisting and advising him in regard to payment of the fine, and unless the fine or any instalment thereof is paid to the clerk of the court within the time allowed by the court for payment, the supervising officer shall report to the court without delay after the expiry of such time, as to the conduct and means of the offender.

DEFINITION

"fine": s.307(1).

Act of Adjournal

The notice specified in subs. (7), in accordance with r. 20.7 in the 1996 Act of Adjournal, is in the style set out in Form 20.7.

Fines: supplementary provisions as to payment

218.—(1) Where under the provisions of section 214 or 217 of this Act a court is required to state a special reason for its decision or the grounds on which it is satisfied that it is undesirable or impracticable to place an offender under supervision, the reason or, as the case may be, the grounds shall be entered in the record of the proceedings along with the finding and sentence.

(2) Any reference in the said sections 214 and 217 to imprisonment shall be construed, in the case of an offender on whom by reason of his age imprisonment may not lawfully be imposed, as a reference to the lawful form of detention in default of payment of a fine appropriate to that person, and any reference to prison shall be construed accordingly.

(3) Where a warrant has been issued for the apprehension of an offender for non-payment of a fine, the offender may, notwithstanding section 211(6) of this Act, pay such fine in full to a constable; and the warrant shall not then be enforced and the constable shall remit the fine to the clerk of court.

DEFINITIONS

"fine": s.307(1).
"impose imprisonment": s.307(1).

Fines: periods of imprisonment for non-payment

219.—(1) Subject to sections 214 to 218 of this Act and subsection (1A) below—

(a) a court may, when imposing a fine, impose a period of imprisonment in default of payment; or

(b) where no order has been made under paragraph (a) above and a person fails to pay a fine, or any part or instalment of a fine, by the time ordered by the court (or, where section 214(2) of this Act applies, immediately) the court may, subject to section 235(1) of this Act, impose a period of imprisonment for such failure either with immediate effect or to take effect in the event of the person failing to pay the fine or any part or instalment of it by such further time as the court may order,

whether or not the fine is imposed under an enactment which makes provision for its enforcement or recovery.

(1A) Subsection (1) shall not apply to a fine imposed for an offence under section 107 of the Antisocial Behaviour etc. (Scotland) Act 2004 (asp 8).

(2) Subject to the following subsections of this section, the maximum period of imprisonment which may be imposed under subsection (1) above or for failure to find caution, shall be as follows—

Amount of Fine or Caution	Maximum Period of Imprisonment
Not exceeding £200	7 days
Exceeding £200 but not exceeding £500	14 days
Exceeding £500 but not exceeding £1,000	28 days
Exceeding £1,000 but not exceeding £2,500	45 days
Exceeding £2,500 but not exceeding £5,000	3 months
Exceeding £5,000 but not exceeding £10,000	6 months
Exceeding £10,000 but not exceeding £20,000	12 months
Exceeding £20,000 but not exceeding £50,000	18 months
Exceeding £50,000 but not exceeding £100,000	2 years

Amount of Fine or Caution	Maximum Period of Imprisonment
Exceeding £100,000 but not exceeding £250,000	3 years
Exceeding £250,000 but not exceeding £1 Million	5 years
Exceeding £1 Million	10 years

(3) Where an offender is fined on the same day before the same court for offences charged in the same indictment or complaint or in separate indictments or complaints, the amount of the fine shall, for the purposes of this section, be taken to be the total of the fines imposed.

(4) Where a court has imposed a period of imprisonment in default of payment of a fine, and—

(a) an instalment of the fine is not paid at the time ordered; or

(b) part only of the fine has been paid within the time allowed for payment,

the offender shall be liable to imprisonment for a period which bears to the period so imposed the same proportion, as nearly as may be, as the amount outstanding at the time when warrant is issued for imprisonment of the offender in default bears to the original fine.

(5) Where no period of imprisonment in default of payment of a fine has been imposed and—

(a) an instalment of the fine is not paid at the time ordered; or

(b) part only of the fine has been paid within the time allowed for payment,

the offender shall be liable to imprisonment for a maximum period which bears, as nearly as may be, the same proportion to the maximum period of imprisonment which could have been imposed by virtue of the Table in subsection (2) above in default of payment of the original fine as the amount outstanding at the time when he appears before the court bears to the original fine.

(6) If in any sentence or extract sentence the period of imprisonment inserted in default of payment of a fine or on failure to find caution is in excess of that competent under this Part of this Act, such period of imprisonment shall be reduced to the maximum period under this Part of this Act applicable to such default or failure, and the judge who pronounced the sentence shall have power to order the sentence or extract to be corrected accordingly.

(7) The provisions of this section shall be without prejudice to the operation of section 220 of this Act.

(8) Where in any case—

(a) the sheriff considers that the imposition of imprisonment for the number of years for the time being specified in section 3(3) of this Act would be inadequate; and

(b) the maximum period of imprisonment which may be imposed under subsection (1) above (or under that subsection as read with either or both of sections 252(2) of this Act and section 118(2) of the Proceeds of Crime Act 2002) exceeds that number of years,

he shall remit the case to the High Court for sentence.

AMENDMENT

Subs.(8)(b) as amended by the Proceeds of Crime Act 2002 (c.29), Sch.11, para.29(4). Brought into force by the Proceeds of Crime Act 2002 (Commencement No.6, Transitional Provisions and Savings) (Scotland) Order 2003 (SSI 2003/210 (C.44)).

Subs.(1) as amended, and (1A) inserted, by the Antisocial Behaviour etc. (Scotland) Act 2004 (asp

8), s.144(1) and Sch.4, para.5(4). Brought into force on April 4, 2005 by the Antisocial Behaviour etc. (Scotland) Act 2004 (Commencement and Savings) Order 2004 (SSI 2004/420 (C.31)).

DEFINITIONS

"caution": s.227.
"fine": s.307(1).
"impose imprisonment": s.307(1).
"order": s.307(1).

GENERAL NOTE

The imposition of an immediate alternative of imprisonment (subs.(1)) was criticised by the Appeal Court in *Stephen v McKay*, 1997 G.W.D. 21–1024, since although the accused had a bad record, there was no indication of a history of failure to pay fines. For an example of the failure to pay because of means, see *Webster v Necheporeko*, 2004 G.W.D. 30–615.

Subsection (8) provides a power of remit from the sheriff court to the High Court of Justiciary in addition to that under s.195(1). The general directions on the imposition of concurrent and consecutive sentences arising from several complaints or indictments are found in *Nicholson v Lees*, 1996 S.C.C.R. 551.

Fines: part payment by prisoners

220.—(1) Where a person committed to prison or otherwise detained for failure to pay a fine imposed by a court pays to the governor of the prison, under conditions prescribed by rules made under the Prisons (Scotland) Act 1989, any sum in part satisfaction of the fine, the term of imprisonment imposed under section 219 of this Act in respect of the fine shall be reduced (or as the case may be further reduced) by a number of days bearing as nearly as possible the same proportion to such term as the sum so paid bears to the amount of the fine outstanding at the commencement of the imprisonment.

(2) The day on which any sum is paid as mentioned in subsection (1) above shall not be regarded as a day served by the prisoner as part of the said term of imprisonment.

(3) All sums paid under this section shall be handed over on receipt by the governor of the prison to the clerk of the court in which the conviction was obtained, and thereafter paid and applied *pro tanto* in the same manner and for the same purposes as sums adjudged to be paid by the conviction and sentence of the court, and paid and recovered in terms thereof, are lawfully paid and applied.

(4) In this section references to a prison and to the governor thereof shall include respectively references to any other place in which a person may be lawfully detained in default of payment of a fine, and to an officer in charge thereof.

AMENDMENT

Subs.(1) as amended by Criminal Justice (Scotland) Act 2003 (asp 7), Sch.4, para.3. Brought into force on June 27, 2003 by the Criminal Justice (Scotland) Act 2003 (Commencement No.1) Order 2003 (SSI 2003/288 (C.14)).

DEFINITIONS

"fine": s.307(1).
"governor": s.307(1).
"prison": s.307(1).

Fines: recovery by civil diligence

221.—(1) Where any fine falls to be recovered by civil diligence in pursuance of this Act or in any case in which a court may think it expedient to order a fine to be recovered by civil diligence, there shall be added to the finding of the court imposing the fine a warrant for civil diligence in a form prescribed by Act of Adjournal which shall have the effect of authorising—

    (a) the charging of the person who has been fined to pay the fine within the period specified in the charge and, in the event of failure to make such payment within that period, the execution of an earnings arrestment and the attachment of articles belonging to him and, if necessary for the purpose of executing the attachment, the opening of shut and lockfast places;

    (b) an arrestment other than an arrestment of earnings in the hands of his employer,

and such diligence, whatever the amount of the fine imposed, may be executed in the same manner as if the proceedings were on an extract decree of the sheriff in a summary cause.

(2) Subject to subsection (3) below, proceedings by civil diligence under this section may be taken at any time after the imposition of the fine to which they relate.

(3) No such proceedings shall be authorised after the offender has been imprisoned in consequence of his having defaulted in payment of the fine.

(4) Where proceedings by civil diligence for the recovery of a fine or caution are taken, imprisonment for non-payment of the fine or for failure to find such caution shall remain competent and such proceedings may be authorised after the court has imposed imprisonment for, or in the event of, the non-payment or the failure but before imprisonment has followed such imposition.

AMENDMENT

    Subs.(1)(a) as amended by the Debt Arrangement and Attachment (Scotland) Act 2002 (asp 17), Sch.3, para.25. Brought into force on December 30, 2002 by Royal Assent.

DEFINITION

    "fine": s.307(1).

GENERAL NOTE

    Prior to the 1995 Act the primary use of civil diligence as a criminal sanction was against bodies corporate. Note however that s.303(2)(a)(i) below now provides that in the event of default in payment of a fiscal fine, recovery of sums outstanding is enforced by civil diligence rather than by means courts.

Act of Adjournal

    Form 20.8 in the 1996 Act of Adjournal appears to be the style approved for the purposes of subs.(1) above.

Transfer of fine orders

222.—(1) Where a court has imposed a fine on a person convicted of an offence and it appears to the court that he is residing—

    (a) within the jurisdiction of another court in Scotland; or

    (b) in any petty sessions area in England and Wales; or

    (c) in any petty sessions district in Northern Ireland,

the court may order that payment of the fine shall be enforceable by that other court or in that petty sessions area or petty sessions district as the case may be.

(2) An order under this section (in this section referred to as a "transfer of fine order") shall specify the court by which or the petty sessions area or petty ses-

sions district in which payment is to be enforceable and, where the court to be specified in a transfer of fine order is a court of summary jurisdiction, it shall, in any case where the order is made by the sheriff court, be a sheriff court.

(3) Subject to subsections (4) and (5) below, where a transfer of fine order is made with respect to any fine under this section, any functions under any enactment relating to that sum which, if no such order had been made, would have been exercisable by the court which made the order or by the clerk of that court shall cease to be so exercisable.

(4) Where—

(a) the court specified in a transfer of fine order is satisfied, after inquiry, that the offender is not residing within the jurisdiction of that court; and

(b) the clerk of that court, within 14 days of receiving the notice required by section 223(1) of this Act, sends to the clerk of the court which made the order notice to that effect,

the order shall cease to have effect.

(5) Where a transfer of fine order ceases to have effect by virtue of subsection (4) above, the functions referred to in subsection (3) above shall again be exercisable by the court which made the order or, as the case may be, by the clerk of that court.

(6) Where a transfer of fine order under this section, section 90 of the Magistrates' Courts Act 1980 or Article 95 of the Magistrates' Courts (Northern Ireland) Order 1981 specifies a court of summary jurisdiction in Scotland, that court and the clerk of that court shall have all the like functions under this Part of this Act in respect of the fine or the sum in respect of which that order was made (including the power to make any further order under this section) as if the fine or the sum were a fine imposed by that court and as if any order made under this section, the said Act of 1980 or the said Order of 1981 in respect of the fine or the sum before the making of the transfer of fine order had been made by that court.

(7) The functions of the court to which subsection (6) above relates shall be deemed to include the court's power to apply to the Secretary of State under any regulations made by him under section 24(1)(a) of the Criminal Justice Act 1991 (power to deduct fines etc. from income support).

(8) Where a transfer of fine order under section 90 of the Magistrates' Courts Act 1980, Article 95 of the Magistrates' Courts (Northern Ireland) Order 1981, or this section provides for the enforcement by a sheriff court in Scotland of a fine imposed by the Crown Court, the term of imprisonment which may be imposed under this Part of this Act shall be the term fixed in pursuance of section 31 of the Powers of Criminal Courts Act 1973 by the Crown Court or a term which bears the same proportion to the term so fixed as the amount of the fine remaining due bears to the amount of the fine imposed by that court, notwithstanding that the term exceeds the period applicable to the case under section 219 of this Act.

DEFINITIONS

"fine": s.307(1).
"order": s.222(2).
"transfer of fine order": s.307(1).

Act of Adjournal

See r. 20.9 and Forms 20.9–A to 20.9–C in the 1996 Act of Adjournal.

Transfer of fines: procedure for clerk of court

223.—(1) Where a court makes a transfer of fine order under section 222 of this Act, the clerk of the court shall send to the clerk of the court specified in the order—

    (a) a notice in the form prescribed by Act of Adjournal, or as nearly as may be in such form;

    (b) a statement of the offence of which the offender was convicted; and

    (c) a statement of the steps, if any, taken to recover the fine,

and shall give him such further information, if any, as, in his opinion, is likely to assist the court specified in the order in recovering the fine.

(2) In the case of a further transfer of fine order, the clerk of the court which made the order shall send to the clerk of the court by which the fine was imposed a copy of the notice sent to the clerk of the court specified in the order.

(3) The clerk of the court specified in a transfer of fine order shall, as soon as may be after he has received the notice mentioned in subsection (1)(a) above, send an intimation to the offender in the form prescribed by Act of Adjournal or as nearly as may be in such form.

(4) The clerk of court specified in a transfer of fine order shall remit or otherwise account for any payment received in respect of the fine to the clerk of the court by which the fine was imposed, and if the sentence has been enforced otherwise than by payment of the fine, he shall inform the clerk of court how the sentence was enforced.

DEFINITIONS

    "fine": s.307(1).
    "order": s.307(1).
    "transfer of fine order": s.222(2).

Act of Adjournal

    See r. 20.9 and Forms 20.9–A for subs. (1) and Form 20.9–B for subs. (2).

Discharge from imprisonment to be specified

224. All warrants of imprisonment in default of payment of a fine, or on failure to find caution, shall specify a period at the expiry of which the person sentenced shall be discharged, notwithstanding the fine has not been paid, or caution found.

DEFINITIONS

    "caution": s.307(1).
    "fine": s.307(1).

Penalties: standard scale, prescribed sum and uprating

225.—(1) There shall be a standard scale of fines for offences triable only summarily, which shall be known as "the standard scale".

(2) The standard scale is shown below—

Level on the scale	Amount of Fine
1	£ 200
2	£ 500

Level on the scale	Amount of Fine
3	£1,000
4	£2,500
5	£5,000

(3) Any reference in any enactment, whenever passed or made, to a specified level on the standard scale shall be construed as referring to the amount which corresponds to that level on the standard scale referred to in subsection (2) above.

(4) If it appears to the Secretary of State that there has been a change in the value of money since the relevant date, he may by order substitute for the sum or sums for the time being specified in the provisions mentioned in subsection (5) below such other sum or sums as appear to him justified by the change.

(5) The provisions referred to in subsection (4) above are—

(a) subsection (2) above;

(b) subsection (8) below;

(c) section 219(2) of this Act;

(d) column 5 or 6 of Schedule 4 to the Misuse of Drugs Act 1971 so far as the column in question relates to the offences under provisions of that Act specified in column 1 of that Schedule in respect of which the maximum fines were increased by Part II of Schedule 8 to the Criminal Justice and Public Order Act 1994.

(6) In subsection (4) above "the relevant date" means—

(a) in relation to the first order made under that subsection, the date the last order was made under section 289D(1) of the Criminal Procedure (Scotland) Act 1975; and

(b) in relation to each subsequent order, the date of the previous order.

(7) An order under subsection (4) above—

(a) shall be made by statutory instrument subject to annulment in pursuance of a resolution of either House of Parliament and may be revoked by a subsequent order thereunder; and

(b) without prejudice to Schedule 14 to the Criminal Law Act 1977, shall not affect the punishment for an offence committed before that order comes into force.

(8) In this Act "the prescribed sum" means £5,000 or such sum as is for the time being substituted in this definition by an order in force under subsection (4) above.

DEFINITIONS

"fine": s.307(1).
"prescribed sum": s.225(8).
"relevant date": s.225(4).
"standard scale": s.225(1).

Penalties: exceptionally high maximum fines

226.—(1) The Secretary of State may by order amend an enactment specifying a sum to which this subsection applies so as to substitute for that sum such other sum as appears to him—

(a) to be justified by a change in the value of money appearing to him to have taken place since the last occasion on which the sum in question was fixed; or

(b) to be appropriate to take account of an order altering the standard scale which has been made or is proposed to be made.

(2) Subsection (1) above applies to any sum which—

(a) is higher than level 5 on the standard scale; and

(b) is specified as the fine or the maximum fine which may be imposed on conviction of an offence which is triable only summarily.

(3) The Secretary of State may by order amend an enactment specifying a sum to which this subsection applies so as to substitute for that sum such other sum as appears to him—

(a) to be justified by a change in the value of money appearing to him to have taken place since the last occasion on which the sum in question was fixed; or

(b) to be appropriate to take account of an order made or proposed to be made altering the statutory maximum.

(4) Subsection (3) above applies to any sum which—

(a) is higher than the statutory maximum; and

(b) is specified as the maximum fine which may be imposed on summary conviction of an offence triable either on indictment or summarily.

(5) An order under this section—

(a) shall be made by statutory instrument subject to annulment in pursuance of a resolution of either House of Parliament; and

(b) shall not affect the punishment for an offence committed before that order comes into force.

(6) In this section "enactment" includes an enactment contained in an Act or subordinate instrument passed or made after the commencement of this Act.

DEFINITIONS

"enactment": s.226(6) and s.307(1).
"fine": s.307(1).
"standard scale": s.225(1).

Caution

Caution

227. Where a person is convicted on indictment of an offence (other than an offence the sentence for which is fixed by law) the court may, instead of or in addition to imposing a fine or a period of imprisonment, ordain the accused to find caution for good behaviour for a period not exceeding 12 months and to such amount as the court considers appropriate.

DEFINITIONS

"fine": s.307(1).
"impose imprisonment": s.307(1).
"indictment": s.307(1).
"offence": s.307(1).

Probation orders

228.—(1) Subject to subsection (2) below and without prejudice to sections 234J and 245D of this Act, where an accused is convicted of an offence (other than an offence the sentence for which is fixed by law) the court if it is of the opinion that it is expedient to do so—

(a) having regard to the circumstances, including the nature of the offence and the character of the offender; and

(b) having obtained a report as to the circumstances and character of the offender,

may, instead of sentencing him, make an order requiring the offender to be under supervision for a period to be specified in the order of not less than six months nor more than three years; and such an order is, in this Act, referred to as a "probation order".

(2) A court shall not make a probation order under subsection (1) above unless it is satisfied that suitable arrangements for the supervision of the offender can be made—

(a) in a case other than that mentioned in paragraph (b) below, by the local authority in whose area he resides or is to reside; or

(b) in a case where, by virtue of section 234(1) of this Act, subsections (3) and (4) below would not apply, by the local probation board for the area which contains the petty sessions area which would be named in the order.

(3) A probation order shall be as nearly as may be in the form prescribed by Act of Adjournal, and shall—

(a) name the local authority area in which the offender resides or is to reside; and

(b) subject to subsection (4) below, make provision for the offender to be under the supervision of an officer of the local authority of that area.

(4) Where the offender resides or is to reside in a local authority area in which the court which makes the order has no jurisdiction, the court shall name the appropriate court (being such a court as could have been named in any amendment of the order in accordance with Schedule 6 to this Act) in the area of residence or intended residence, and the appropriate court shall require the local authority for that area to arrange for the offender to be under the supervision of an officer of that authority.

(5) Before making a probation order, the court shall explain to the offender in ordinary language—

(a) the effect of the order, including any additional requirements proposed to be inserted under section 229 or 230 of this Act; and

(b) that if he fails to comply with the order or commits another offence during the probation period he will be liable to be sentenced for the original offence or may be dealt with under the powers provided for in section 42(4) of the Criminal Justice (Scotland) Act 2003 (asp 7) (powers of drugs court),

and the court shall not make the order unless the offender expresses his willingness to comply with the requirements thereof.

(6) The clerk of the court by which a probation order is made or of the appropriate court, as the case may be, shall—

(a) cause copies of the probation order to be given to the officer of the local authority who is to supervise the probationer and to the person in charge of any institution or place in which the probationer is required to reside under the probation order; and

(b) cause a copy thereof to be given to the probationer or sent to him by registered post or by the recorded delivery service; and an acknowledgement or certificate of delivery of a letter containing such copy order issued by the postal operator shall be sufficient evidence of the delivery of the letter on the day specified in such acknowledgement or certificate.

AMENDMENTS

Subs.(1) as amended by the Crime and Punishment (Scotland) Act 1997 (c.48), s.62 and Sch.1, para.21(27). Brought into force on July 1, 1998 by SI 1997/2323.

Subs.(1) as amended by the Crime and Disorder Act 1998 (c.37), s.94 and Sch.6, para.1. Brought into force on September 30, 1998 by the Crime and Disorder Act 1998 (Commencement No.2 and Transitional Provisions) Order 1998 (SI 1998/2327 (C.53)).

Subs.(2)(b) as amended by the Criminal Justice and Court Services Act 2000 (c.43), s.74 and Sch.7, para.122. Brought into force by the Criminal Justice and Court Services Act 2000 (Commencement No.4) Order 2001 (SI 2001/919 (C.33)), art.2(f)(ii) (effective April 1, 2001).

Subs.(6)(b) as amended by the Postal Services Act 2000 (Consequential Modifications No.1) Order 2001 (SI 2001/1149), art.3 and Sch.1, para.104.

Subs.(5)(b) as amended by Criminal Justice (Scotland) Act 2003 (asp 7), Part 5, s.42. Brought into force on June 27, 2003 by the Criminal Justice (Scotland) Act 2003 (Commencement No.1) Order 2003 (SSI 2003/288 (C.14)).

DEFINITIONS

"local authority": s.307(1).
"offence": s.307(1).
"probation order": s.228(1).

GENERAL NOTE

In *Downie v Irvine*, 1964 J.C. 52 it was held that a probation order and a sentence of imprisonment were wholly inconsistent and could not stand together. However, in *Walker v McGlennan*, 1997 G.W.D. 8–310, such a sentence was approved by the Appeal Court (albeit the term of imprisonment was reduced from six to three months) where the accused had been drunk and threatening when attending a social work office, in relation to the preparation of a report for earlier offences; the object was to provide a drying out period and early probation support.

In *McLaughlin v McQuaid* 2005 S.L.T. 972 it was held, as a generality, that in absence of express statutory authority a court is *functus* once it has finally disposed of a case by passing sentence and as a consequence a court has no power to sit again in the same case. In the particular circumstances of the case and given the statutory basis of probation orders, the fixing of a further hearing was held to be incompetent.

Act of Adjournal

Refer to r.20.10 of the 1996 Act of Adjournal. The form for a probation order is laid out in Form 20.10–A in the 1996 Act of Adjournal.

Probation orders: additional requirements

229.—(1) Subject to section 230 of this Act, a probation order may require the offender to comply during the whole or any part of the probation period with such requirements as the court, having regard to the circumstances of the case, considers—

(a) conducive to securing the good conduct of the offender or for preventing a repetition by him of the offence or the commission of other offences; or

(b) where the probation order is to include such a requirement as is mentioned in subsection (4) or (6) below, conducive to securing or, as the case may be, preventing the matters mentioned in paragraph (a) above.

(2) Without prejudice to the generality of subsection (1) above, a probation order may, subject to subsection (3) below, include requirements relating to the residence of the offender.

(3) In relation to a probation order including a requirement such as is mentioned in subsection (2) above—

   (a) before making the order, the court shall consider the home surroundings of the offender; and

   (b) if the order requires the offender to reside in any institution or place, the name of the institution or place and the period for which he is so required to reside shall be specified in the order, and that period shall not extend beyond 12 months from the date of the requirement or beyond the date when the order expires.

(4) Without prejudice to the generality of subsection (1) above, where an offender has been convicted of an offence punishable by imprisonment and a court which is considering making a probation order—

   (a) is satisfied that the offender is of or over 16 years of age and that the conditions specified in paragraphs (a) and (c) of section 238(2) of this Act for the making of a community service order have been met;

   (b) has been notified by the Secretary of State that arrangements exist for persons who reside in the locality where the offender resides, or will be residing when the probation order comes into force, to perform unpaid work as a requirement of a probation order; and

   (c) is satisfied that provision can be made under the arrangements mentioned in paragraph (b) above for the offender to perform unpaid work under the probation order,

it may include in the probation order, in addition to any other requirement, a requirement that the offender shall perform unpaid work for such number of hours (being in total not less than 40 nor more than 240) as may be specified in the probation order.

(5) Sections 238 (except subsections (1), (2)(b) and (d) and (4)(b)), 239(1) to (3), and 240 of this Act shall apply, subject to any necessary modifications, to a probation order including a requirement such as is mentioned in subsection (4) above as they apply to a community service order, and in the application of subsection (5) of the said section 238 for the words "subsection (1) above" there shall be substituted the words "subsection (4) of section 229 of this Act".

(6) Without prejudice to the generality of subsection (1) above, where a court is considering making a probation order it may include in the probation order, in addition to any other requirement, a requirement that the offender shall pay compensation either in a lump sum or by instalments for any personal injury, loss or damage caused (whether directly or indirectly) by the acts which constituted the offence; and the following provisions of this Act shall apply to such a requirement as if any reference in them to a compensation order included a reference to a requirement to pay compensation under this subsection—

   section 249(3) to (5), (8) to (10);

   section 250(2);

   section 251(1) and (2)(b);

   section 253.

(7) Where the court imposes a requirement to pay compensation under subsection (6) above—

   (a) it shall be a condition of a probation order containing such a requirement that payment of the compensation shall be completed not more than 18 months after the making of the order or not later than two months before the end of the period of probation, whichever first occurs;

(b) the court, on the application of the offender or the officer of the local authority responsible for supervising the offender, may vary the terms of the requirement, including the amount of any instalments, in consequence of any change which may have occurred in the circumstances of the offender; and

(c) in any proceedings for breach of a probation order where the breach consists only in the failure to comply with a requirement to pay compensation, a document purporting to be a certificate signed by the clerk of the court for the time being having jurisdiction in relation to the order that the compensation or, where payment by instalments has been allowed, any instalment has not been paid shall be sufficient evidence of such breach.

DEFINITIONS

"compensation": s.229(6).
"offence": s.307(1).
"probation order": s.228(1).

GENERAL NOTE

In *HM Advocate v Jamieson*, 1997 S.L.T. 955, a conviction of assault to severe injury and danger of life, the Crown appealed as unduly lenient, a probation order for 12 months allied to 240 hours community service and a compensation order of £3,000 payable within 12 months. The Appeal Court upheld the Crown contention that s.229(7)(a) required that the compensation order should have been ordered to be paid in full within 10 months, i.e. two months before the expiry of the probation order. While agreeing that the sentence imposed was indeed unduly lenient, the Court paid heed to the substantial number of hours of community service the accused had completed and the fact that £2,200 had not only been paid by him, but mistakenly had been paid to the victim by the Sheriff Clerk; the appeal was refused. An additional probation condition which barred the accused from visiting her boyfriend in prison, following a conviction for attempting to supply him with controlled drugs there, was upheld on appeal as being appropriate and humane in her circumstances (*Reid v Napier*, 2002 S.L.T. 1229).

In imposing other requirements it is not competent to include periodic reviews of progress as a means of ensuring the continued compliance of the accused. Once an order has been fixed the court is *functus* unless, or until, the order is breached. In *McLaughlin v McQuaid*, 2005 S.L.T. 972 such a purported condition was quashed by bill of suspension.

Note that the minimum and maximum numbers of hours of community service which can be linked to a probation order, set out in subs.(4), were unaffected by the Community Service by Offenders (Hours of Work) (Scotland) Order 1996 (SI 1996/1938) whose general effect was to raise the hours which had to be imposed in community service orders.

While a probation order can be allied to other disposals, for example a community service order, it is apparent that the other elements of the sentence have to be capable of being completed within the timescale set by the probation order; see *Lynn v Howdle*, 2002 S.L.T. 970. In *Lynn* it was held that a community service order could not competently be linked to a probation order of less than 12 months duration.

Probation progress review

229A.—(1) A court may, in making a probation order, provide for the order to be reviewed at a hearing held for the purpose by the court.

(2) The officer responsible for the probationer's supervision is, before the hearing, to make a report in writing to the court on the probationer's progress under the order.

(3) The probationer must, and that officer may, attend the hearing.

(4) The hearing may be held whether or not the prosecutor elects to attend.

(5) Where the probationer fails to attend the hearing the court may issue a warrant for his arrest.

(6) At the hearing the court, after considering the report made under subsection (2) above, may amend the probation order.

(7) But before amending the order the court is to explain to the probationer, in ordinary language, the effect of making the amendment; and may proceed to make it only if the probationer expresses his willingness to comply with the requirements of the order as amended.

(8) Sub-paragraph (2) of paragraph 3 of Schedule 6 to this Act applies to amending under subsection (6) above as that sub-paragraph applies to amending under sub-paragraph (1) of that paragraph.

(9) At the hearing the court may provide for the order to be reviewed again at a subsequent hearing held for the purpose by the court; and subsections (2) to (8) above and this subsection apply in relation to a review under this subsection as they apply in relation to a review under subsection (1) above.

Amendment

Section 229A as inserted by the Management of Offenders etc. (Scotland) Act 2005 (asp 14), s.12(2). Brought into force on February 8, 2006 by the Management of Offenders etc. (Scotland) Act 2005 (Commencement No.1) Order 2006 (SSI 2006/48 (C.6)), art.3(1) and Sch.

Probation orders: requirement of treatment for mental condition

230.—(1) Subject to subsection (3) below, where the court is satisfied, on the evidence of an approved medical practitioner, that the mental condition of an offender is such as requires and may be susceptible to treatment but is not such as to warrant his detention in pursuance of a compulsory treatment order under section 64 of the Mental Health (Care and Treatment) (Scotland) Act 2003 (asp 13) or a compulsion order, the court may, if it makes a probation order, include a requirement that the offender shall submit, for such period as may be specified in the order, to treatment by or under the direction of a registered medical practitioner or chartered psychologist with a view to the improvement of the offender's mental condition.

(2) The treatment required by virtue of subsection (1) above shall be such one of the following kinds of treatment as may be specified in the order, that is to say—

(a) treatment as a resident patient in a hospital within the meaning of the said Act of 2003, not being a State hospital within the meaning of the Act;

(b) treatment as a non-resident patient at such institution or place as may be specified in the order; or

(c) treatment by or under the direction of such registered medical practitioner or chartered psychologist as may be specified in the order,

but otherwise the nature of the treatment shall not be specified in the order.

(3) A court may make a probation order including a requirement under subsection (1) above only if it is satisfied—

(a) on the written or oral evidence of the registered medical practitioner or chartered psychologist by whom or under whose direction the treatment intended to be specified in the order is to be provided, that the treatment is appropriate; and

(b) that arrangements have been made for that treatment, including, where the offender is to be treated as a resident patient, arrangements for his reception in the hospital intended to be specified in the order.

(4) Where the registered medical practitioner or chartered psychologist by whom or under whose direction a probationer is receiving any of the kinds of treatment to which he is required to submit in pursuance of a probation order is of the opinion—

(a) that the probationer requires, or that it would be more appropriate for him to receive, a different kind of treatment (whether in whole or in part) from that which he has been receiving, being treatment of a kind which subject to subsection (5) below could have been specified in the probation order; or

(b) that the treatment (whether in whole or in part) can be more appropriately given in or at a different institution or place from that where he has been receiving treatment in pursuance of the probation order,

he may, subject to subsection (6) below, make arrangements for the probationer to be treated accordingly.

(5) Arrangements made under subsection (4) above may provide for the probationer to receive his treatment (in whole or in part) as a resident patient in an institution or place notwithstanding that it is not one which could have been specified for that purpose in the probation order.

(6) Arrangements shall not be made under subsection (4) above unless—

(a) the probationer and any officer responsible for his supervision agree;

(b) the treatment will be given by or under the direction of a registered medical practitioner or chartered psychologist who has agreed to accept the probationer as his patient; and

(c) where such treatment entails the probationer's being a resident patient, he will be received as such.

(7) Where any such arrangements as are mentioned in subsection (4) above are made for the treatment of a probationer—

(a) any officer responsible for the probationer's supervision shall notify the appropriate court of the arrangements; and

(b) the treatment provided for by the arrangements shall be deemed to be treatment to which he is required to submit in pursuance of the probation order.

(8) Subsections (3) to (5) of section 61 of this Act shall apply for the purposes of this section as if for the reference in subsection (3) to section 58(1)(a) of this Act there were substituted a reference to subsection (1) above.

(9) Except as provided by this section, a court shall not make a probation order requiring a probationer to submit to treatment for his mental condition.

AMENDMENTS

Section 230(1) as amended by the Adults with Incapacity (Scotland) Act 2000 (asp 4), s.88 and Sch.6. Brought into force on April 1, 2002 by Adults with Incapacity (Scotland) Act 2000 (Commencement No.1) Order 2001 (SSI 2001/81 (C.2)).

Subss.(1) and (2) as amended, and subs.(3) substituted, by the Mental Health (Care and Treatment) (Scotland) Act 2003 (asp 13), s.135, Sch.4, para.8(15) and Sch.5. Brought into force on October 5, 2005 by the Mental Health (Care and Treatment) (Scotland) Act 2003 (Commencement No.4) Order 2005 (SSI 2005/161 (C.6)).

DEFINITIONS

"chartered psychologist": s.307(1).
"hospital": s.307(1).
"probation order": s.228(1).
"registered medical practitioner": s.2 of the Medicine Act 1968.
"State hospital": s.307(1).

Requirement for remote monitoring in probation order

230A.—(1) Without prejudice to section 245D of this Act, a probation order may include a requirement that during such period as may be specified in the requirement, being a period not exceeding twelve months, the probationer comply with such restrictions as to his movements as the court thinks fit; and paragraphs (a) and (b) of subsection (2) of section 245A of this Act (with the qualification of paragraph (a) which that subsection contains) shall apply in relation to any such requirement as they apply in relation to a restriction of liberty order.

(2) The clerk of the court shall cause a copy of a probation order which includes such a requirement to be sent to the person who is to be responsible for monitoring the probationer's compliance with the requirement.

(3) If, within the period last specified by virtue of subsection (1) above or section 231(1) of this Act, it appears to the person so responsible that the probationer has failed to comply with the requirement the person shall so inform the supervising officer appointed by virtue of section 228(3) of this Act, who shall report the matter to the court.

(4) Section 245H shall apply in relation to proceedings under section 232 of this Act as respects a probation order which includes such a requirement as it applies in relation to proceedings under section 245F of this Act.

(5) Sections 245A(6) and (8) to (11), 245B and 245C of this Act shall apply in relation to the imposition of, or as the case may be compliance with, requirements included by virtue of subsection (1) above in a probation order as those sections apply in relation to the making of, or as the case may be compliance with, a restriction of liberty order.

(6) In relation to a probation order which includes such a requirement—

(a) the persons who may make an application under paragraph 3(1) of Schedule 6 to this Act shall include the person responsible for monitoring the probationer's compliance with the requirement, but only in so far as the application relates to the requirement; and

(b) a copy of any application under that paragraph by—

(i) the probationer or the supervising officer shall be sent by the applicant to the person so responsible; or

(ii) the person so responsible shall be sent by the applicant to the probationer and the supervising officer.

(7) Where under section 232(2)(c) of, or Schedule 6 to, this Act the court varies such a requirement, the clerk of court shall cause a copy of the amended probation order to be sent—

(a) to the person so responsible; and

(b) where the variation comprises a change in who is designated for the purposes of such monitoring, to the person who, immediately before the order was varied, was so responsible.

AMENDMENT

Section 230A inserted by Criminal Justice (Scotland) Act 2003 (asp 7), Part 6, s.46. Brought into force on June 27, 2003 by the Criminal Justice (Scotland) Act 2003 (Commencement No.1) Order 2003 (SSI 2003/288 (C.14)).

GENERAL NOTE

This section makes provision for so-called "tagging" of offenders as part of a probation order. It should be borne in mind that s.228(5) of the Criminal Procedure (Scotland) Act 1995 provides that the court must not make a probation order unless the offender expresses his willingness to comply with its requirements. A requirement for remote monitoring is subject to that provision like all other requirements. Remote monitoring, which arguably involves significant inroads on the right to respect for the private life, cannot therefore be imposed against the will of the person affected.

Probation orders: amendment and discharge

231.—(1) Schedule 6 to this Act shall have effect in relation to the discharge and amendment of probation orders.

(2) Where, under section 232 of this Act, a probationer is sentenced for the offence for which he was placed on probation, the probation order shall cease to have effect.

DEFINITION

"probation order": s.228(1).

GENERAL NOTE

In *McLaughlin v McQuaid*, 2005 S.L.T. 972 it was held, as a generality, that in the absence of express statutory authority a court is *functus* once it has finally disposed of a case by passing sentence and as a consequence a court has no power to sit again in the same case. In the particular circumstances of the case and given the statutory basis of probation orders, the fixing of a further hearing was held to be incompetent.

Probation orders: failure to comply with requirement

232.—(1) If, on information from—

(a) the officer supervising the probationer;

(b) the chief social work officer of the local authority whose officer is supervising the probationer; or

(c) an officer appointed by the chief social work officer to act on his behalf for the purposes of this subsection,

it appears to the court which made the probation order or to the appropriate court that the probationer has failed to comply with any requirement of the order, that court may issue a warrant for the arrest of the probationer, or may, if it thinks fit, instead of issuing such a warrant in the first instance, issue a citation requiring the probationer to appear before the court at such time as may be specified in the citation.

(2) If it is proved to the satisfaction of the court before which a probationer appears or is brought in pursuance of subsection (1) above or of section 229A of this Act that he has failed to comply with a requirement of the probation order, the court may—

(a) except in the case of a failure to comply with a requirement to pay compensation and without prejudice to the continuance in force of the probation order, impose a fine not exceeding level 3 on the standard scale; or

(b) sentence the offender for the offence for which the order was made; or

(c) vary any of the requirements of the probation order, so however that any extension of the probation period shall terminate not later than three years from the date of the probation order and any extension to the period of a requirement imposed by virtue of section 230A of this Act shall not increase that period above the maximum mentioned in subsection (1) of that section; or

(d) without prejudice to the continuance in force of the probation order, in a case where the conditions required by sections 238 to 244 of this Act are satisfied, make a community service order, and those sections shall apply to such an order as if the failure to comply with the requirement of the probation order were the offence in respect of which the order had been made.

(2A) Subsections (6) and (11) of section 245A of this Act apply to the variation, under paragraph (c) of subsection (2) above, of a requirement such as is mentioned in that paragraph as they apply to the making of a restriction of liberty order.

(3) For the purposes of subsection (2) above, evidence of one witness shall be sufficient evidence.

(3A) Where the court intends to sentence an offender under subsection (2)(b) above, and the offender is by virtue of section 245D of this Act subject to,

(a) a restriction of liberty order; or

(b) a restriction of liberty order and a drug treatment and testing order,

it shall, before sentencing the offender under that paragraph, revoke the restriction of liberty order or, as the case may be, the restriction of liberty order and the drug treatment and testing order.

(3B) Where the court intends to sentence an offender under subsection (2)(b) above and the offender is by virtue of section 234J of this Act subject to a drug treatment and testing order, it shall, before sentencing the offender under that paragraph, revoke the drug treatment and testing order.

(4) A fine imposed under this section in respect of a failure to comply with the requirements of a probation order shall be deemed for the purposes of any enactment to be a sum adjudged to be paid by or in respect of a conviction or a penalty imposed on a person summarily convicted.

(5) A probationer who is required by a probation order to submit to treatment for his mental condition shall not be deemed for the purpose of this section to have failed to comply with that requirement on the ground only that he has refused to undergo any surgical, electrical or other treatment if, in the opinion of the court, his refusal was reasonable having regard to all the circumstances.

(6) Without prejudice to section 233 of this Act, a probationer who is convicted of an offence committed during the probation period shall not on that account be liable to be dealt with under this section for failing to comply with any requirement of the probation order.

(7) The unified citation provisions apply in relation to a citation under this section as they apply in relation to a citation under section 216(3)(a) of this Act.

(8) This section is subject to section 42(9) of the Criminal Justice (Scotland) Act 2003 (asp 7) (powers of drugs court).

AMENDMENTS

Subs.(3A) inserted by the Crime and Punishment (Scotland) Act 1997 (c.48), s.62 and Sch.1, para.21(28). Brought into force on July 1, 1998 by the Crime and Punishment (Scotland) Act 1997 (Commencement No.2 and Transitional and Consequential Provisions) Order 1997 (SI 1997/2323 (C.89)).

Subs.(3A) as amended, and subs.(3B) inserted, by the Crime and Disorder Act 1998 (c.37), s.94 and Sch.6, para.2. Brought into force on September 30, 1998 by the Crime and Disorder Act 1998 (Commencement No.2 and Transitional Provisions) Order 1998 (SI 1998/2327 (C.53)).

Subs.(2) as amended, and subs.(2A) inserted, by the Criminal Justice (Scotland) Act 2003 (asp 7), Part 6, s.46. Brought into force on June 27, 2003 by the Criminal Justice (Scotland) Act 2003 (Commencement No.1) Order 2003 (SSI 2003/288 (C.14)).

Subs.(7) substituted by the Criminal Justice (Scotland) Act 2003 (asp 7), Part 8, s.60. Brought into force on October 27, 2003 by the Criminal Justice (Scotland) Act 2003 (Commencement No.3 and Revocation) Order 2003 (SSI 2003/475 (C.26)), art.2.

Subs.(8) inserted by the Criminal Justice (Scotland) Act 2003 (asp 7), Part 5, s.42. Brought into force on June 27, 2003 by the Criminal Justice (Scotland) Act 2003 (Commencement No.1) Order 2003 (SSI 2003/288 (C.14)).

Subs.(2) as amended by the Management of Offenders etc. (Scotland) Act 2005 (asp 14), s.12(3). Brought into force on February 8, 2006 by the Management of Offenders etc. (Scotland) Act 2005 (Commencement No.1) Order 2006 (SSI 2006/48 (C.6)), art.3(1) and Sch.

"community service order": s.307(1).
"court of summary jurisdiction": s.307(1).
"fine": s.307(1).
"local authority": s.307(1).
"probation order": s.228(1).
"probationer": s.307(1).
"sentence": s.307(1).
"standard scale": s.225(1).

GENERAL NOTE

In *McLaughlin v McQuaid*, 2005 S.L.T. 972 it was held, as a generality, that in the absence of express statutory authority a court is *functus* once it has finally disposed of a case by passing sentence and as a consequence a court has no power to sit again in the same case. In the particular circumstances of the case and given the statutory basis of probation orders, the fixing of a further hearing was held to be incompetent.

Act of Adjournal

Refer to r.20.10 in the 1996 Act of Adjournal.

The form used for citing an offender for failure to comply with a probation order, or for further offending, is Form 20.10–B in the 1996 Act of Adjournal.

Note that r.20.17 permits the use of certified copies of probation orders in any relevant proceedings before a court other than the court which imposed the order.

Probation orders: commission of further offence

233.—(1) If it appears to—

(a) the court which made a probation order; or, as the case may be,

(b) the appropriate court,

in this section referred to as "the court", that the probationer to whom the order relates has been convicted by a court in any part of Great Britain of an offence committed during the probation period and has been dealt with for that offence, the court may issue a warrant for the arrest of the probationer, or may, if it thinks fit, instead of issuing such a warrant in the first instance issuing a citation requiring the probationer to appear before the court at such time as may be specified in the citation, and on his appearance or on his being brought before the court, the court may, if it thinks fit, deal with him under section 232(2)(b) of this Act.

(1A) The unified citation provisions apply in relation to a citation under this section as they apply in relation to a citation under section 216(3)(a) of this Act.

(2) Where a probationer is convicted by the court of an offence committed during the probation period, the court may, if it thinks fit, deal with him under section 232(2)(b) of this Act for the offence for which the order was made as well as for the offence committed during the period of probation.

(3) Where—

(a) a court has, under section 229(4) of this Act, included in a probation order a requirement that an offender shall perform unpaid work; and

(b) the offender is convicted of an offence committed in the circumstances mentioned in subsection (4) below,

the court which sentences him for the offence shall, in determining the appropriate sentence for that offence, have regard to the fact that the offence was committed in those circumstances.

(4) The circumstances referred to in subsection (3) above are that the offence was committed—

(a) during the period that the offender was subject to a requirement to perform unpaid work or within the period of three months following the expiry of that period; and

(b) in any place where the unpaid work was being or had previously been performed.

(5) The court shall not, under subsection (3) above, have regard to the fact that the offence was committed in the circumstances mentioned in subsection (4) above unless that fact is libelled in the indictment or, as the case may be, specified in the complaint.

(6) The fact that the offence mentioned in subsection (3)(b) above was committed in the circumstances mentioned in subsection (4) above shall, unless challenged—

(a) in the case of proceedings on indictment, by giving notice of a preliminary objection under paragraph (b) of section 72(1) of this Act or under that paragraph as applied by section 71(2) of this Act; or

(b) in summary proceedings, by preliminary objection before his plea is recorded,

be held as admitted.

AMENDMENT

Subs.(1A) by Criminal Justice (Scotland) Act 2003 (asp 7), Part 8, s.60. Brought into force on October 27, 2003 by the Criminal Justice (Scotland) Act 2003 (Commencement No.3 and Revocation) Order 2003 (SSI 2003/475 (C.26)), art.2.

Subs.(6) inserted by the the Crime and Punishment (Scotland) Act 1997 (c.48), s.26(1) and given effect from August 1, 1997 by the Crime and Punishment (Scotland) Act 1997 (Commencement and Transitional Provisions) Order 1997 (SI 1997/1712).

DEFINITIONS

"complaint": s.307(1).
"indictment": s.307(1).
"probation order": s.228(1).
"probationer": s.307(1).

GENERAL NOTE

Subsection (2) above empowers a court before which the probationer appears for offending during the period of probation to sentence both the offences in respect of which the order had been made, and the fresh offences. Subsection (3), which originated in s.40 of the Criminal Justice (Scotland) Act 1995 creates a specific aggravating offence where a probationer on placement, during its currency or within three months of its expiry, commits an offence at that place. (A similar provision in relation to community service order placements is found in s.241(2), below); it is vital to note that the aggravation only arises if it is expressly libelled in the body of the complaint or indictment, failing which the court can have no regard to the aggravating factor. Two points spring to mind; first, it is submitted that like a disqualification from driving, the fact of being a probationer in terms of subs.(3) would fall to be regarded as a special capacity; secondly, that the commission of a relevant offence under subs.(3) would have to be libelled on a separate complaint or indictment from other charges much as is done with charges of disqualified driving. Neither point is yet settled but it is not difficult to envisage situations, for example where the Crown was relying upon the *Moorov* doctrine, in which the prosecutor might have to make a conscious decision to sacrifice the aggravating nature of the offence simply to achieve a conviction; it is doubtful that that was what the legislature had in mind.

The introduction of subs.(6) goes a little way towards easing the burden of proof by, in effect, treating the commission of an offence at a designated workplace within three months as a special capacity which, unless challenged need not be proved by the Crown. However the fact remains that the special capacity will have to be libelled in the body of the charge.

Act of Adjournal

See the note at A4–465 above.

Probation orders: persons residing in England and Wales

234.—(1) Where the court which made a probation order to which this subsection applies is satisfied that the offender has attained the age of 16 years and resides or will reside in England and Wales, subsections (3) and (4) of section 228 of this Act shall not apply to the order, but—

    (a) the order shall contain a requirement that he be under the supervision of an officer of a local probation board appointed for or assigned to the local justice area in which the offender resides or will reside; and

    (b) that area shall be named in the order.

(2) Subsection (1) above applies to any probation order made under section 228 unless the order includes requirements which are more onerous than those which a court in England and Wales could impose on an offender under section 177 of the Criminal Justice Act 2003.

(3) Where a probation order has been made under the said section 228 and the court in Scotland which made the order or the appropriate court is satisfied—

    (a) that the probationer has attained the age of 16 years;

    (b) that he proposes to reside, or is residing, in England and Wales; and

    (c) that suitable arrangements for his supervision can be made by the local probation board for the area which contains the local justice area in which he resides or will reside,

the power of that court to amend the order under Schedule 6 to this Act shall include power to insert the provisions required by subsection (1) above, and the court may so amend the order without summoning the probationer and without his consent.

(4) A probation order made or amended by virtue of this section may, notwithstanding section 230(9) of this Act, include a requirement that the probationer shall submit to treatment for his mental condition, and—

    (a) subsections (1), (3) and (8) of the said section 230 and section 207(2) of the Criminal Justice Act 2003 (all of which regulate the making of probation orders or, as the case may be, community orders under Part 12 of that Act which include any such requirement) shall apply to the making of an order which includes any such requirement by virtue of this subsection as they apply to the making of an order which includes any such requirement by virtue of the said section 230 and section 207 of the Criminal Justice Act 2003 respectively; and

    (b) sections 207(4) and 208(1) and (2) of the Criminal Justice Act 2003 (functions of supervising officer and registered medical practitioner where such a requirement has been imposed) shall apply in relation to a probationer who is undergoing treatment in England and Wales in pursuance of a requirement imposed by virtue of this subsection as they apply in relation to a probationer undergoing such treatment in pursuance of a requirement imposed by virtue of that section.

(4A) A probation order made or amended under this section must specify as the corresponding requirements for the purposes of this section requirements which could be included in a community order made under section 177 of the Criminal Justice Act 2003.

(5) Sections 231(1) and 232(1) of this Act shall not apply to any order made or amended under this section; but subject to subsection (6) below, Schedule 8 to the Criminal Justice Act 2003 shall apply as if it were a community order made by a magistrates' court under section 177 of that Act and imposing the requirements specified under subsection (4A) above.

(6) In its application to a probation order made or amended under this section, Schedule 8 to the Criminal Justice Act 2003 has effect subject to the following modifications—

(a) any reference to the responsible officer has effect as a reference to the person appointed or assigned under subsection (1)(a) above,

(b) in paragraph 9—

    (i) paragraphs (b) and (c) of sub-paragraph (1) are omitted,

    (ii) in sub-paragraph (6), the first reference to the Crown Court has effect as a reference to a court in Scotland, and

    (iii) any other reference in sub-paragraphs (6) or (7) to the Crown Court has effect as a reference to the court in Scotland, and

(c) Parts 3 and 5 are omitted.

(7) If it appears on information to a justice acting in the local justice area named in a probation order made or amended under this section that the person to whom the order relates has been convicted by a court in any part of Great Britain of an offence committed during the period specified in the order he may issue—

(a) a summons requiring that person to appear, at the place and time specified in the summons, before the court in Scotland which made the probation order; or

(b) if the information is in writing and on oath, a warrant for his arrest, directing that person to be brought before the last-mentioned court.

(8) If a warrant for the arrest of a probationer issued under section 233 of this Act by a court is executed in England and Wales and the probationer cannot forthwith be brought before that court, the warrant shall have effect as if it directed him to be brought before a magistrates' court; and the magistrates' court shall commit him to custody or release him on bail (with or without sureties) until he can be brought or appear before the court in Scotland.

(9) The court by which a probation order is made or amended in accordance with the provisions of this section shall send three copies of the order to the designated officer for the local justice area named in the order, together with such documents and information relating to the case as it considers likely to be of assistance to the court acting in that local justice area.

(10) Where a probation order which is amended under subsection (3) above is an order to which the provisions of this Act apply by virtue of paragraph 8 of Schedule 9 (which relates to community orders under that Act relating to persons residing in Scotland) then, notwithstanding anything in that Schedule or this section, the order shall, as from the date of the amendment, have effect in all respects as if it were a community order made under Part 12 in the case of a person residing in England and Wales.

(11) [...]

AMENDMENTS

Subs.(9) as amended by the Access to Justice 1999 (c.22), s.90 and Sch.13, para.175 (effective April 1, 2001).

Subs.(2) as amended by the Powers of Criminal Courts (Sentencing) Act 2000 (c.6), s.165 and Sch.9, para.176(2)(a) and (b).

Subs.(4) as amended by the Powers of Criminal Courts (Sentencing) Act 2000 (c.6), s.165 and Sch.9, para.176(3)(a) and (b).

Subs.(5) as amended by the Powers of Criminal Courts (Sentencing) Act 2000 (c.6), s.165 and Sch.9, para.176(4)(a), (b) and (c).

Subs.(6) as amended by the Powers of Criminal Courts (Sentencing) Act 2000 (c.6), s.165 and Sch.9, para.176(5)(a), (b) and (c).

Subs.(10) as amended by the Powers of Criminal Courts (Sentencing) Act 2000 (c.6), s.165 and Sch.9, para.176(6)(a) and (b).

Subs.(11) as substituted by the Powers of Criminal Courts (Sentencing) Act 2000 (c.6), s.165 and Sch.9, para.176(7).

Subss.(2), (3)(c), (4)(a), (5) and (10) as amended by the Criminal Justice and Court Services Act 2000 (c.43), s.74 and Sch.7, para.123. Brought into force by the Criminal Justice and Court Services Act 2000 (Commencement No. 4) Order 2001 (SI 2001/919 (C.33)), art.2(f)(ii) (effective April 1, 2001).

Subs.(1)(a) as amended by the Criminal Justice and Court Services Act 2000 (c.43), s.74 and Sch.7, para.4. Brought into force on April 1, 2001 by the Criminal Justice and Court Services Act 2000 (Commencement No.4) Order 2001 (SI 2001/919 (C.33)).

Subss.(2), (6) as substituted, subss.(4), (5), (10) as amended and subs.(4A) inserted by the Criminal Justice Act 2003 (c.44), s.304 and Sch.32, para.70. Brought into force on April 4, 2005 by the Criminal Justice Act 2003 (Commencement No.8 and Transitional and Saving Provisions) Order 2005 (SI 2005/950 (C.42)), art.2 and Sch.1.

Subss.(1) and (3) partially repealed, and subs.(11) repealed, by the Criminal Justice Act 2003 (c.44), ss.304, 332, Sch.32, para.70 and Sch.37, Part VII. Brought into force on April 4, 2005 by the Criminal Justice Act 2003 (Commencement No.8 and Transitional and Saving Provisions) Order 2005 (SI 2005/950 (C.42)), art.2 and Sch.1.

Subss.(1)(a), (3)(c), (7)–(9) as amended by the Courts Act 2003 (Consequential Provisions) Order 2005 (SI 2005/886), art.2 and Sch.1, para.52. In force April 1, 2005.

DEFINITIONS

"probation order": s.307(1).
"probationer": s.307(1).

Non-harassment orders

234A.—(1) Where a person is convicted of an offence involving harassment of a person ("the victim"), the prosecutor may apply to the court to make a non-harassment order against the offender requiring him to refrain from such conduct in relation to the victim as may be specified in the order for such period (which includes an indeterminate period) as may be so specified, in addition to any other disposal which may be made in relation to the offence.

(2) On an application under subsection (1) above the court may, if it is satisfied on a balance of probabilities that it is appropriate to do so in order to protect the victim from further harassment, make a non-harassment order.

(3) A non-harassment order made by a criminal court shall be taken to be a sentence for the purposes of any appeal and, for the purposes of this subsection "order" includes any variation or revocation of such an order made under subsection (6) below.

(4) Any person who is in breach of a non-harassment order shall be guilty of an offence and liable—

(a) on conviction on indictment, to imprisonment for a term not exceeding 5 years or to a fine, or to both such imprisonment and such fine; and

(b) on summary conviction, to imprisonment for a period not exceeding 6 months or to a fine not exceeding the statutory maximum, or to both such imprisonment and such fine.

(4A) A constable may arrest without warrant any person he reasonably believes is committing or has committed an offence under subsection (4) above.

(4B) Subsection (4A) above is without prejudice to any power of arrest conferred by law apart from that subsection.

(5) […]

(6) The person against whom a non-harassment order is made, or the prosecutor at whose instance the order is made, may apply to the court which made the order for its revocation or variation and, in relation to any such application the

court concerned may, if it is satisfied on a balance of probabilities that it is appropriate to do so, revoke the order or vary it in such manner as it thinks fit, but not so as to increase the period for which the order is to run.

(7) For the purposes of this section "harassment" shall be construed in accordance with section 8 of the Protection from Harassment Act 1997.

AMENDMENTS

Section 234A inserted by the Protection from Harassment Act 1997 (c.40), s.11.

Subs.(5) repealed by the Crime and Punishment (Scotland) Act 1997 (c.48), s.62(1) and Sch.1, para.21(30) with effect from August 1, 1997 in terms of the Crime and Punishment (Scotland) Act 1997 (Commencement and Transitional Provisions) Order (SI 1997/1712) art.3.

Subs.(4) as amended, and subss.(4A) and (4B) inserted, by Criminal Justice (Scotland) Act 2003 (asp 7), Part 6, s.49. Brought into force on June 27, 2003 by the Criminal Justice (Scotland) Act 2003 (Commencement No.1) Order 2003 (SSI 2003/288 (C.14)).

DEFINITIONS

"offence": s.307(1)

"harassment": s.8 of the Protection from Harassment Act 1997 (c. 40)

"prosecutor": s.307(1)

"sentence": s.307(1)

"indictment": s.307(1)

"imprisonment": s.307(1)

"fine": s.307(1)

GENERAL NOTE

The Protection from Harassment Act 1997 was directed at the prevention of stalking, anti-social behaviour by neighbours and racial harassment: *Tuppen v Microsoft Corporation Ltd*, The Times Law Reports, November 15, 2000. This decision was based on a study of the relevant speeches in Hansard of the Government Ministers at the time the Bill was going through the Westminster Parliament.

This section, inserted by s.11 of the Protection from Harassment Act 1997, empowers both civil and criminal courts in Scotland to make a "non-harassment order" against an offending party. In the criminal courts, an order may only be granted on the motion of the prosecutor with the object of preventing any future misconduct, but can be made in addition to, or as, the disposal imposed in the proceedings. It is clear that an order can only be imposed when the conviction indicates misconduct on at least two occasions—the "course of conduct" specified in s.8(3) of the Protection from Harassment Act 1997; see *McGlennan v McKinnon*, 1998 S.L.T. 494. It is notable that the Appeal Court rejected Crown attempts to found upon extract complaints and previous convictions as evidencing a course of conduct and that the Lord Justice General highlighted the need for carefully considered drafting of charges where a non-harassment order was likely to be sought. Given these limitations, in some instances it may well be more fruitful for a complainer to raise civil proceedings under the Protection from Harassment Act 1997.

A number of features are notable: firstly, the court has to be satisfied of the need for an order only on the balance of probabilities as a means of protecting an identified victim (subs.(2)); secondly, it is open to the prosecutor to appeal to the High Court against a court's refusal to impose an order, or it is submitted, to appeal the terms of the order itself—this based on a broad reading of "application" as defined in subs.(1); thirdly, either the prosecutor at whose initiative the order was imposed or the offender subject of the order (but not the victim specified in it) may apply to the court for variation or revocation of the order. It is not competent to extend the duration of an order by application, appeal in terms of subs.(5) being the only method by which this can be done.

A broad construction of subs.(1), and practice, would suggest that the Appeal Court can impose a non-harassment order as an element of sentence, even where the issue had not been raised in the court of first instance, provided that an appropriate motion is made by the prosecutor to the Appeal Court.

Breach of a non-harassment order, as subs.(4) provides, is a crime triable summarily or on indictment.

Robertson v Vannet, 1999 S.L.T. 1081 underlines that an order can be imposed on criminal conviction even where the victim already holds an interdict or interim interdict against the accused. (By contrast, in the civil context s.8(5) of the Protection from Harrassment Act 1997 (c.40) precludes the currency, simultaneously, of both a non-harrassment order and an interdict (or interim interdict) arising from the same *species facti*). Interestingly, in *Robertson* too the Appeal Court construed reference to "the victim" as extending to the complainer's father who had not been expressly identified in the breach of the peace charges libelled, but had been alarmed by the accused's actions; it appears that the procurator fiscal when moving for the order had highlighted the effects on both the complainer and her father.

Although it has not been inserted into the 1995 Act, reference should also be made to s.12 of the Protection from Harassment Act and to the sweeping powers of certification vested in the Secretary of State. The section entitles the Secretary of State to certify conclusively that conduct which might otherwise constitute harassment of a person, on specific occasions by a specified person, related to national security, the economic well-being of the UK or the prevention or detection of serious crime. It would appear that the intention is to exempt legitimate surveillance operations from claims under the Act of harassment. Some assistance in reaching an understanding of the nature of the statutory offences may be derived from English decisions, although the statutory provision may differ between the jurisdictions. In *R. v Henley* [2000] Crim.L.R. 582 it was held that causing the victim to be in fear is not enough to meet the terms of s.4 of the 1997 Act, and nor even is causing the victim to be "seriously frightened". Again with reference to s.4, it was held in *R. v DPP* [2001] Crim.L.R. 396 that whether or not the conduct of a person had given cause to another to fear that violence would be used against him or her was a question of fact to be established in each case. Words or conduct ostensibly directed to something or someone other than the person it was alleged was caused to be put in fear of violence did not, because so directed, fall outside conduct which could support a conviction. This case has other *obiter* remarks of assistance.

The Protection from Harassment Act 1997 received Royal Assent on March 19, 1997 and was commenced for Scottish proceedings by the Protection from Harassment Act 1997 (Commencement) (No.1) Order 1997 (SI 1997/1418) on June 16, 1997. The Act of Adjournal (Criminal Procedure Rules Amendment No.2) (Non-harassment order) 1997 (SI 1997/1526) inserts rr.20.10A and 20.10B into the 1996 Act of Adjournal. Forms 20.10A and 20.10B set out the forms of orders and applications for revocation. Civil proceedings are regulated by the Act of Sederunt (Rules of the Court of Session Amendment No.6) (Actions of harassment) 1997 (SI 1997/1527).

In *Donaldson v Gallacher*, 1999 G.W.D. 31–1460 a condition not to "approach" the complainer was held to include circumstances that amounted to following. There are several examples of non-harassment orders being made, *e.g. Robertson v Vannet*, 1998 G.W.D. 36–1865 (5 years), *Lees v Rys*, 1998 G.W.D. 28–1431 (10 years), *McFadyen v Clarke*, 1999 G.W.D. 19–890 (6 years), *Dickson v Main*, 2001 G.W.D. 4–155 (2 years) and *Stott v Marshall*, 2002 G.W.D. 40–1344 (indeterminate period) and *H.M. Advocate v Lawrence*, 2003 G.W.D. 35–987 (10 years).

Antisocial behaviour orders

234AA.—(1) Where subsection (2) below applies, the court may, instead of or in addition to imposing any sentence which it could impose, make an antisocial behaviour order in respect of a person (the "offender").

(2) This subsection applies where—

(a) the offender is convicted of an offence;

(b) at the time when he committed the offence, the offender was at least 12 years of age;

(c) in committing the offence, he engaged in antisocial behaviour; and

(d) the court is satisfied, on a balance of probabilities, that the making of an antisocial behaviour order is necessary for the purpose of protecting other persons from further antisocial behaviour by the offender.

(3) For the purposes of subsection (2)(c) above, a person engages in antisocial behaviour if he—

(a) acts in a manner that causes or is likely to cause alarm or distress; or

(b) pursues a course of conduct that causes or is likely to cause alarm or distress,

to at least one person who is not of the same household as him.

(4) Subject to subsection (5) below, an antisocial behaviour order is an order which prohibits, indefinitely or for such period as may be specified in the order, the offender from doing anything described in the order.

(5) The prohibitions that may be imposed by an antisocial behaviour order are

those necessary for the purpose of protecting other persons from further antisocial behaviour by the offender.

(6) Before making an antisocial behaviour order, the court shall explain to the offender in ordinary language—

(a) the effect of the order and the prohibitions proposed to be included in it;

(b) the consequences of failing to comply with the order;

(c) the powers the court has under subsection (8) below; and

(d) the entitlement of the offender to appeal against the making of the order.

(7) Failure to comply with subsection (6) shall not affect the validity of the order.

(8) On the application of the offender in respect of whom an antisocial behaviour order is made under this section, the court which made the order may, if satisfied on a balance of probabilities that it is appropriate to do so—

(a) revoke the order; or

(b) subject to subsection (9) below, vary it in such manner as it thinks fit.

(9) Where an antisocial behaviour order specifies a period, the court may not, under subsection (8)(b) above, vary the order by extending the period.

(10) An antisocial behaviour order made under this section, and any revocation or variation of such an order under subsection (8) above, shall be taken to be a sentence for the purposes of an appeal.

(11) Sections 9 and 11 of the Antisocial Behaviour etc. (Scotland) Act 2004 (asp 8) (which provide that breach of an antisocial behaviour order made under that Act is an offence for which a person is liable to be arrested without warrant) shall apply in relation to antisocial behaviour orders made under this section as those sections apply in relation to antisocial behaviour orders made under section 4 of that Act.

(12) In this section, "conduct" includes speech; and a course of conduct must involve conduct on at least two occasions.

AMENDMENT

Section 234AA inserted by the Antisocial Behaviour etc. (Scotland) Act 2004 (asp 8), s.118. Brought into force on October 28, 2004 by the Antisocial Behaviour etc. (Scotland) Act 2004 (Commencement and Savings) Order 2004 (SSI 2004/420 (C.31)).

DEFINITIONS

"antisocial behaviour": s.234AA(3) of the 1995 Act and s.143(1) of the 2004 Act.
"conduct": s.234AA(12) of the 1995 Act and see also s.143(2) of the 2004 Act.
"offender": s.234AA(1) of the 1995 Act.

GENERAL NOTE

Antisocial behaviour orders

Amongst the various options now available to the court at the sentencing stage is that of an antisocial behaviour order: s.234AA(1). That provision provides that the court "may, instead of or in addition to imposing any sentence which it could impose" make such an order. There are conditions to satisfy but as the offender must be at least 10 years of age when the offence was committed and the test is one of a balance of probabilities that is necessary to prevent further such behaviour then the court is left with a wide discretion: s.234AA(2).

"Conduct"

The phrase "antisocial behaviour" includes a course of conduct that causes or is likely to cause alarm or distress: s.234AA(3)(b). "Conduct" includes speech and a course of conduct must involve conduct on at least two occasion: s.234AA(12).

Antisocial behaviour orders: notification

234AB.—(1) Upon making an antisocial behaviour order under section 234AA of this Act, the court shall—

(a) serve a copy of the order on the offender; and

(b) give a copy of the order to the local authority it considers most appropriate.

(2) Upon revoking an antisocial behaviour order under subsection (8)(a) of that section, the court shall notify the local authority to whom a copy of the order was given under subsection (1)(b) above.

(3) Upon varying an antisocial behaviour order under subsection (8)(b) of that section, the court shall—

(a) serve a copy of the order as varied on the offender; and

(b) give a copy of the order as varied to the local authority to whom a copy of the order was given under subsection (1)(b) above.

(4) For the purposes of this section, a copy is served on an offender if—

(a) given to him; or

(b) sent to him by registered post or the recorded delivery service.

(5) A certificate of posting of a letter sent under subsection (4)(b) issued by the postal operator shall be sufficient evidence of the sending of the letter on the day specified in such certificate.

(6) In this section, "offender" means the person in respect of whom the antisocial behaviour order was made.

AMENDMENT

Section 234AB inserted by the Antisocial Behaviour etc. (Scotland) Act 2004 (asp 8), s.118. Brought into force on October 28, 2004 by the Antisocial Behaviour etc. (Scotland) Act 2004 (Commencement and Savings) Order 2004 (SSI 2004/420 (C.31)).

DEFINITIONS

"conduct": s.234AA(12) of the 1995 Act and see also s.143(2) of the 2004 Act.
"local authority": s.143(1) of the 2004 Act.
"offender": s.234AB(6) of the 1995 Act.

GENERAL NOTE

This section provides for the procedure to be adopted when making an antisocial behaviour order.

Drug treatment and testing order

234B.—(1) This section applies where a person of 16 years of age or more is convicted of an offence, other than one for which the sentence is fixed by law, committed on or after the date on which section 89 of the Crime and Disorder Act 1998 comes into force.

(2) Subject to the provisions of this section, the court by or before which the offender is convicted may, if it is of the opinion that it is expedient to do so instead of sentencing him, make an order (a "drug treatment and testing order") which shall—

(a) have effect for a period specified in the order of not less than six months nor more than three years ("the treatment and testing period"); and

(b) include the requirements and provisions mentioned in section 234C of this Act.

(3) A court shall not make a drug treatment and testing order unless it—

(a) has been notified by the Secretary of State that arrangements for implementing such orders are available in the area of the local authority proposed to be specified in the order under section 234C(6) of this Act and the notice has not been withdrawn;

(b) has obtained a report by, and if necessary heard evidence from, an officer of the local authority in whose area the offender is resident about the offender and his circumstances; and

(c) is satisfied that—

    (i) the offender is dependent on, or has a propensity to misuse, drugs;

    (ii) his dependency or propensity is such as requires and is susceptible to treatment; and

    (iii) he is a suitable person to be subject to such an order.

(4) For the purpose of determining for the purposes of subsection (3)(c) above whether the offender has any drug in his body, the court may by order require him to provide samples of such description as it may specify.

(5) A drug treatment and testing order or an order under subsection (4) above shall not be made unless the offender expresses his willingness to comply with its requirements.

(6) The Secretary of State may by order—

(a) amend paragraph (a) of subsection (2) above by substituting a different period for the minimum or the maximum period for the time being specified in that paragraph; and

(b) make such transitional provisions as appear to him necessary or expedient in connection with any such amendment.

(7) The power to make an order under subsection (6) above shall be exercisable by statutory instrument; but no such order shall be made unless a draft of the order has been laid before and approved by resolution of each House of Parliament.

(8) A drug treatment and testing order shall be as nearly as may be in the form prescribed by Act of Adjournal.

AMENDMENT

Section 234B inserted by the Crime and Disorder Act 1998 (c.37), s.89 (effective September 30, 1998: SI 1998/2327).

DEFINITIONS

"offence": s.307(1) of the 1995 Act.

"sentence": s.307(1) of the 1995 Act.

"drug treatment and testing order": ss.234B(2) and 234C(1) of the 1995 Act as inserted by ss.89 and 90 of the 1998 Act.

GENERAL NOTE

The provisions contained in ss.89 to 95 of the 1998 Act introduced a new form of court disposal for Scottish courts, the drug treatment and testing order (referred to henceforth as a DTTO), and echo the measures applied to England and Wales by ss.58 to 60 of that Act. The Scottish measures are all inserted in the 1995 Procedure Act as ss.234B to 234J and came into force on September 30, 1998 in terms of the Crime and Disorder Act 1998 (Commencement No.2 and Transitional Provisions) Order 1998 (SI 1998/2327.)

It will be observed that the provisions owe much to existing procedures used in relation to probation orders, a clear signal that the object of a DTTO is rehabilitation, rather than punishment, of the offender. A DTTO is an alternative to a criminal sentence, cannot be imposed following conviction of murder, and can be for a specified period of between six months and three years duration (subs.(2)) subject to several criteria being met. A DTTO can be imposed on its own or combined concurrently with either a probation order (see s.234J(1)) or a restriction of liberty order, or combined with both such orders (implied by s.234H(3)). The court must first receive a report indicating that the offender, who has to be aged 16 years or older, abuses drugs and that his condition is amenable to treatment (subs.(3)) aimed at reducing or ending his susceptibility to misuse drugs (s.234C(1)).

Secondly, the offender must express willingness to comply with the order which will be supervised by an officer nominated by the local authority and, particularly, must consent to attend an establishment for appropriate medical treatment (as an in-patient or out-patient or both), make himself available to the supervising officer as necessary and provide appropriate samples to enable his compliance with the order, and his progress, to be monitored (s.234C(2) and (3)).

The court can only impose a DTTO once the Secretary of State has given notice that suitable arrangements have been put in place in the locale (s.234B(3)) and once satisfied that appropriate medical care facilities are available there to provide the treatment proposed (s.234B(3)). In addition to the background report which must be furnished to it, the court is empowered to require the offender to provide samples for the purpose of confirming the presence of drugs in his body (s.234B(4)). This power is intended only for use at the investigative stage; once a DTTO has been imposed, samples for monitoring compliance are got using s.234C(2) and (3) of the Act.

Subsection (6) entitles the Secretary of State to alter the length of DTTOs, which can be imposed, by Statutory Instrument and gives a broad discretion to enact transitional arrangements.

Two points are worthy of note: it is not necessary that the offence giving rise to the DTTO was itself drug-related (though that will often be so)—what matters are the offender's circum stances; secondly, subs.(3)(b) stipulates that the duty of providing a report to the court rests with the local authority within whose area the offender resides—it does not follow that any element of the DTTO has to be provided in that area. However for practical purposes, like probation, a DTTO depends upon the offender having a regular abode, a qualification which may exclude rootless offenders with drug problems unless suitable in-patient or residential facilities are available.

Section 234G provides penalties for failure to comply with the requirements of a DTTO and entitles the court to issue either a citation or an apprehension warrant to bring an offender before it.

Reference should also be made to Sch.6 to the 1998 Act which imports a number of amendments to enable DTTOs to be combined with both probation and restriction of liberty orders. Part II of the same Schedule contains provisions to deal with appeals arising from a sentence which includes a DTTO.

Requirements and provisions of drug treatment and testing orders

234C.—(1) A drug treatment and testing order shall include a requirement ("the treatment requirement") that the offender shall submit, during the whole of the treatment and testing period, to treatment by or under the direction of a specified person having the necessary qualifications or experience ("the treatment provider") with a view to the reduction or elimination of the offender's dependency on or propensity to misuse drugs.

(2) The required treatment for any particular period shall be

(a) treatment as a resident in such institution or place as may be specified in the order; or

(b) treatment as a non-resident in or at such institution or place, and at such intervals, as may be so specified;

but the nature of the treatment shall not be specified in the order except as mentioned in paragraph (a) or (b) above.

(3) A court shall not make a drug treatment and testing order unless it is satisfied that arrangements have been made for the treatment intended to be specified in the order (including arrangements for the reception of the offender where he is required to submit to treatment as a resident).

(4) A drug treatment and testing order shall include a requirement ("the testing requirement") that, for the purpose of ascertaining whether he has any drug in his body during the treatment and testing period, the offender shall provide during that period, at such times and in such circumstances as may (subject to the provisions of the order) be determined by the treatment provider, samples of such description as may be so determined.

(5) The testing requirement shall specify for each month the minimum number of occasions on which samples are to be provided.

(6) A drug treatment and testing order shall specify the local authority in whose area the offender will reside when the order is in force and require that authority to appoint or assign an officer (a "supervising officer") for the purposes of subsections (7) and (8) below.

(7) A drug treatment and testing order shall—

(a) provide that, for the treatment and testing period, the offender shall be under the supervision of a supervising officer;

(b) require the offender to keep in touch with the supervising officer in accordance with such instructions as he may from time to time be given by that officer, and to notify him of any change of address; and

(c) provide that the results of the tests carried out on the samples provided by the offender in pursuance of the testing requirement shall be communicated to the supervising officer.

(8) Supervision by the supervising officer shall be carried out to such extent only as may be necessary for the purpose of enabling him—

(a) to report on the offender's progress to the appropriate court;

(b) to report to that court any failure by the offender to comply with the requirements of the order; and

(c) to determine whether the circumstances are such that he should apply to that court for the variation or revocation of the order.

AMENDMENT

Section 234C inserted by the Crime and Disorder Act 1998 (c.37), s.90 (effective September 30, 1998: SI 1998/2327).

DEFINITIONS

"drug treatment and testing order": ss.234B(2) and 234C(1) of the 1995 Act as inserted by ss.89 and 90 of the 1998 Act.

"offender": s.5 of the Crime and Punishment (Scotland) Act 1997 (c.48).

"local authority": s.234K of the 1995 Act as inserted by s.95(1) of the 1998 Act.

GENERAL NOTE

This section indicates that the purpose of a drug treatment and testing order (hereafter referred to as a "DTTO") is to provide the offender with a programme to curb, or end, his propensity to misuse drugs. It came into force on September 30, 1998; see generally the Note to s.234B above.

Section 234C(2) enacts that appropriate treatment may be delivered by in-patient or out-patient treatment as directed, or varied, by the treatment provider specified in the order. The treatment provider is responsible for monitoring the medical aspects, including the regime of periodic sampling for drug testing purposes—a compulsory element in all DTTOs (subs.(4)), while a nominated member of the social work department is given the general duty to oversee the offender's conduct and to provide compulsory reports on the progress of the offender to the court (s.234F(1)).

In addition to the general requirements set out in s.234B(3) above, the court has to satisfy itself that satisfactory arrangements for the form of treatment identified as necessary in the report to combat the offender's misuse of drugs are in place (s.234C(3)); to stipulate the minimum number of testing samples to be provided monthly by the offender; to set the timescale (at least initially) for reviews of the order and require the supervising officer to provide a written progress report for consideration at each review (s.234F(1)). Each report must incorporate the results of drug tests and an assessment of the offender's progress by the treatment provider.

It may be appreciated that DTTOs will draw heavily upon medical and social work resources and demand similar commitment from the offenders involved. Failure to comply with the terms of a DTTO are to be reported to the court by the supervising officer who is also empowered to seek variation or revocation of the order (s.234C(8)). The offender himself can also apply to the court for variation or revocation of the order—see s.234E as inserted by s.92 of the 1998 Act.

Requirement for remote monitoring in drug treatment and testing order

234CA—(1) A drug treatment and testing order may include a requirement that during such period as may be specified in the requirement, being a period not exceeding twelve months, the offender comply with such restrictions as to his movements as the court thinks fit; and paragraphs (a) and (b) of subsection (2) of section 245A of this Act (with the qualification of paragraph (a) which that subsection contains) shall apply in relation to any such requirement as they apply in relation to a restriction of liberty order.

(2) The clerk of the court shall cause a copy of a drug treatment and testing order which includes such a requirement to be sent to the person who is to be responsible for monitoring the offender's compliance with the requirement.

(3) If, within the period last specified by virtue of subsection (1) above or (6)(d) below, it appears to the person so responsible that the offender has failed to comply with the requirement the person shall so inform the supervising officer appointed by virtue of section 234C(6) of this Act, who shall report the matter to the court.

(4) Section 245H shall apply in relation to proceedings under section 234G of this Act as respects a drug treatment and testing order which includes such a requirement as it applies in relation to proceedings under section 245F of this Act.

(5) Sections 245A(6) and (8) to (11), 245B and 245C of this Act shall apply in relation to the imposition of, or as the case may be compliance with, requirements included by virtue of subsection (1) above in a drug treatment and testing order as those sections apply in relation to the making of, or as the case may be compliance with, a restriction of liberty order.

(6) In relation to a drug testing order which includes such a requirement, section 234E of this Act shall apply with the following modifications—

(a) the persons who may make an application under subsection (1) of that section shall include the person responsible for monitoring the offender's compliance with the requirement, but only in so far as the application relates to the requirement;

(b) the reference in subsection (2) of that section to the supervising officer shall be construed as a reference to either that officer or the person so responsible;

(c) where an application is made under subsection (1) of that section and relates to the requirement, the persons to be heard under subsection (3) of that section shall include the person so responsible;

(d) the ways of varying the order which are mentioned in subsection (3)(a) of that section shall include increasing or decreasing the period specified by virtue of subsection (1) above (or last specified by virtue of this paragraph) but not so as to increase that period above the maximum mentioned in subsection (1) above; and

(e) the reference in subsection (5) of that section—

(i) to the supervising officer shall be construed as a reference to either that officer or the person so responsible; and

(ii) to sections 234B(5) and 234D(1) shall be construed as including a reference to section 245A(6) and (11).

(7) Where under section 234E or 234G(2)(b) of this Act the court varies such a requirement, the clerk of court shall cause a copy of the amended drug treatment and testing order to be sent—

(a) to the person responsible for monitoring the offender's compliance with the requirement; and

(b) where the variation comprises a change in who is designated for the purposes of such monitoring, to the person who, immediately before the order was varied, was so responsible.

AMENDMENT

Section 234CA inserted by Criminal Justice (Scotland) Act 2003 (asp 7), Part 6, s.47. Brought into force on June 27, 2003 by the Criminal Justice (Scotland) Act 2003 (Commencement No.1) Order 2003 (SSI 2003/288 (C.14)).

GENERAL NOTE

Drug treatment and testing orders may be made in terms of s.234B of the Criminal Procedure (Scotland) Act 1995 and require the offender to submit to treatment designed to reduce or eliminate drug dependency. The present section makes it possible to add a requirement for remote monitoring, much as in relation to probation orders.

Procedural matters relating to drug treatment and testing orders

234D.—(1) Before making a drug treatment and testing order, a court shall explain to the offender in ordinary language—

(a) the effect of the order and of the requirements proposed to be included in it;

(b) the consequences which may follow under section 234G of this Act or 42(4) of the Criminal Justice (Scotland) Act 2003 (asp 7) (powers of drugs court) if he fails to comply with any of those requirements;

(c) that the court has power under section 234E of this Act to vary or revoke the order on the application of either the offender or the supervising officer; and

(d) that the order will be periodically reviewed at intervals provided for in the order.

(2) Upon making a drug treatment and testing order the court shall—

(a) give, or send by registered post or the recorded delivery service, a copy of the order to the offender;

(b) send a copy of the order to the treatment provider;

(c) send a copy of the order to the chief social work officer of the local authority specified in the order in accordance with section 234C(6) of this Act; and

(d) where it is not the appropriate court, send a copy of the order (together with such documents and information relating to the case as are considered useful) to the clerk of the appropriate court.

(3) Where a copy of a drug treatment and testing order has under subsection (2)(a) been sent by registered post or by the recorded delivery service, an acknowledgement or certificate of delivery of a letter containing a copy order issued by the postal operator shall be sufficient evidence of the delivery of the letter on the day specified in such acknowledgement or certificate.

AMENDMENTS

Section 234D inserted by the Crime and Disorder Act 1998 (c.37), s.91 (effective September 30, 1998: SI 1998/2327).

Subs.(3) as amended by the Postal Services Act 2000 (Consequential Modifications No. 1) Order 2001 (SI 2001/1149), art.3 and Sch.1, para.104.

Subs.(1)(b) as amended by Criminal Justice (Scotland) Act 2003 (asp 7), Part 5, s.42. Brought into force on June 27, 2003 by the Criminal Justice (Scotland) Act 2003 (Commencement No.1) Order 2003 (SSI 2003/288 (C.14)).

DEFINITIONS

"drug treatment and testing order": ss.234B(2) and 234C(1) as inserted by ss.89 and 90 of the 1998 Act.

"offender": s.5 of the Crime and Punishment (Scotland) Act 1997 (c.48).

"supervising officer": s.234C(6) of the 1995 Act as inserted by s.90 of the 1998 Act.

GENERAL NOTE

In addition to the provisions of s.234B(2) and s.234C which specify the nature of a drug treatment and testing order and the court's powers, this section sets out the obligation of the court to explain (as it would when imposing a probation order) the effects of the order and his obligations. Subs.(2) permits personal or postal intimation of the order upon the offender, and stipulates that notification has also to be given to the treatment provider (see s.234C(1)), to the local authority and, where necessary, to the sheriff clerk or clerk of court of the court within whose jurisdiction the offender will reside while subject to the drug treatment and testing order—a situation which will arise where the order has to be transferred from the court which dealt with the original offences.

This section came into force on September 30, 1998 in terms of SI 1998/2327; see the Notes to s.234B above.

Amendment of drug treatment and testing order

234E.—(1) Where a drug treatment and testing order is in force either the offender or the supervising officer may apply to the appropriate court for variation or revocation of the order.

(2) Where an application is made under subsection (1) above by the supervising officer, the court shall issue a citation requiring the offender to appear before the court.

(2A) The unified citation provisions apply in relation to a citation under this section as they apply in relation to a citation under section 216(3)(a) of this Act.

(3) On an application made under subsection (1) above and after hearing both the offender and the supervising officer, the court may by order, if it appears to it in the interests of justice to do so—

    (a) vary the order by—

        (i) amending or deleting any of its requirements or provisions;

        (ii) inserting further requirements or provisions; or

        (iii) subject to subsection (4) below, increasing or decreasing the treatment and testing period; or

    (b) revoke the order.

(4) The power conferred by subsection (3)(a)(iii) above shall not be exercised so as to increase the treatment and testing period above the maximum for the time being specified in section 234B(2)(a) of this Act, or to decrease it below the minimum so specified.

(5) Where the court, on the application of the supervising officer, proposes to vary (otherwise than by deleting a requirement or provision) a drug treatment and testing order, sections 234B(5) and 234D(1) of this Act shall apply to the variation of such an order as they apply to the making of such an order.

(6) If an offender fails to appear before the court after having been cited in accordance with subsection (2) above, the court may issue a warrant for his arrest.

(7) This section is subject to section 234CA(6) of this Act.

AMENDMENT

Section 234E inserted by the Crime and Disorder Act 1998 (c.37), s.92 (effective September 30, 1998: SI 1998/2327).

Subs.(7) inserted by Criminal Justice (Scotland) Act 2003 (asp 7), Part 6, s.47. Brought into force on June 27, 2003 by the Criminal Justice (Scotland) Act 2003 (Commencement No.1) Order 2003 (SSI 2003/288 (C.14)).

Subs.(2A) inserted by Criminal Justice (Scotland) Act 2003 (asp 7), Part 8, s.60. Brought into force on October 27, 2003 by the Criminal Justice (Scotland) Act 2003 (Commencement No.3 and Revocation) Order 2003 (SSI 2003/475 (C.26)), art.2.

DEFINITIONS

"drug treatment and testing order": ss.234B(2) and 234C(1) of the 1995 Act as inserted by ss.89 and 90 of the 1998 Act.

"offender": s.5 of the Crime and Punishment (Scotland) Act 1997 (c.48).

"supervising officer": s.234C(6) of the 1995 Act as inserted by s.90 of the 1998 Act.

"citation": s.141 of the 1995 Act.

"appropriate court": s.234K of the 1995 Act as inserted by s.95 of the 1998 Act.

GENERAL NOTE

On the application of either the offender, or his supervising officer, the court can be requested to vary the terms of a drug treatment and testing order (hereafter referred to as a "DTTO") or to revoke the order entirely. Note that while the court may continue, vary or revoke the order (or indeed specify additional requirements) after hearing parties, it must adhere to the terms of s.234B(2), *i.e.* it cannot alter the period of a DTTO which must be of not less than six months and not more than three years' duration.

On receipt of an application from the supervising officer for amendment or revocation of the DTTO, the court, if it considers there to be merit in the application, shall cite the offender to attend a hearing (subs.(4)). Note however that it is not mandatory to cite the offender to appear if the court intends only to delete a requirement or vary a provision of the order.

These procedures are in addition to, and distinct from, the mandatory programme of periodic reviews of all DTTOs set out in s.234F below; and came into force on September 30, 1998 in terms of SI 1998/2327; see generally the Notes to s.234B above.

Periodic review of drug treatment and testing order

234F.—(1) A drug treatment and testing order shall—

(a) provide for the order to be reviewed periodically at intervals of not less than one month;

(b) provide for each review of the order to be made, subject to subsection (5) below, at a hearing held for the purpose by the appropriate court (a "review hearing");

(c) require the offender to attend each review hearing;

(d) provide for the supervising officer to make to the court, before each review, a report in writing on the offender's progress under the order; and

(e) provide for each such report to include the test results communicated to the supervising officer under section 234C(7)(c) of this Act and the views of the treatment provider as to the treatment and testing of the offender.

(1A) A review hearing may be held whether or not the prosecutor elects to appear.

(2) At a review hearing the court, after considering the supervising officer's report, may amend any requirement or provision of the order.

(3) The court—

(a) shall not amend the treatment or testing requirement unless the offender expresses his willingness to comply with the requirement as amended;

(b) shall not amend any provision of the order so as reduce the treatment and testing period below the minimum specified in section 234B(2)(a) of this Act or to increase it above the maximum so specified; and

(c) except with the consent of the offender, shall not amend any requirement or provision of the order while an appeal against the order is pending.

(4) If the offender fails to express his willingness to comply with the treatment or testing requirement as proposed to be amended by the court, the court may revoke the order.

(5) If at a review hearing the court, after considering the supervising officer's report, is of the opinion that the offender's progress under the order is sastisfactory, the court may so amend the order as to provide for each subsequent review to be made without a hearing.

(6) A review without a hearing shall take place in chambers without the parties being present.

(7) If at a review without a hearing the court, after considering the supervising officer's report, is of the opinion that the offender's progress is no longer satisfactory, the court may issue a warrant for the arrest of the offender or may, if it thinks fit, instead of issuing a warrant in the first instance, issue a citation requiring the offender to appear before that court as such time as may be specified in the citation.

(8) Where an offender fails to attend—

(a) a review hearing in accordance with a requirement contained in a drug treatment and testing order; or

(b) a court at the time specified in a citation under subsection (7) above, the court may issue a warrant for his arrest.

(9) Where an offender attends the court at a time specified by a citation issued under subsection (7) above—

(a) the court may exercise the powers conferred by this section as if the court were conducting a review hearing; and

(b) so amend the order as to provide for each subsequent review to be made at a review hearing.

AMENDMENT

Section 234F inserted by the Crime and Disorder Act 1998 (c.37), s.92 (effective September 30, 1998: SI 1998/2327).

Subs.(1A) inserted by Criminal Justice (Scotland) Act 2003 (asp 7), Part 8, s.64. Brought into force on June 27, 2003 by the Criminal Justice (Scotland) Act 2003 (Commencement No.1) Order 2003 (SSI 2003/288 (C.14)).

DEFINITIONS

"drug treatment and testing order": ss.234B(2) and 234C(1) of the 1998 Act as inserted by ss.89 and 90 of the 1998 Act.

"review hearing": s.234F(1)(b) of the 1998 Act.

"offender": s.5 of the Crime and Punishment (Scotland) Act 1997 (c.48).

"the appropriate court": s.234K of the 1995 Act as inserted by s.95(1) of the 1998 Act.

GENERAL NOTE

This section sets out the mandatory procedures for review of an offender's performance of a drug treatment and testing order at a hearing. Each such order must specify the timescale for hearings, a process which operates separately from the right of either the offender, or the supervising officer, to apply to the court for variation or revocation of an order (see s.234E as inserted by s.92(1) of the 1998 Act).

Prior to the due review date the supervising officer is required to furnish a written report on the offender's progress to the court. Subsection (3) stipulates that the results of all "testing requirements" made by the "treatment officer" and any observations should be incorporated in each review report. Although the offender is required to attend all review hearings until that requirement is waived by the court in terms of subs.(5), nothing expressly stipulates that he be provided with a copy of the supervising officer's report.

The court is empowered to review, and amend, the terms of the existing order's treatment or testing requirements only with the offender's consent (subs.(3)(a)). Failing consent at this stage, the DTTO must proceed unaltered or be revoked but it should be noted that different considerations apply once the offender is held to have been in breach of his order; see s.234G(2) below.

As has been mentioned the offender's attendance at review hearings is mandatory until such time as the court itself resolves that his progress is sufficiently satisfactory to vary the DTTO, and dispense with such attendance. Future reviews would then be held in chambers and based solely on consideration of the supervising officer's report.

In the event of an adverse report being placed before the court in chambers, subs.(7) entitles the court either to cite the offender to appear at a specified time or, alternatively, to issue an arrest warrant. Failure to appear at a review as specified in the DTTO (subs.(1)(c)) or in answer to a citation issued by the court following receipt of an unsatisfactory report (subs.(7)) will entitle the court to issue an arrest warrant. A failure to appear on being given due notice can be treated as a breach of the order and attract the penalties set out in s.234G(2) of the 1995 Act (inserted by s.93 of the 1998 Act). Once a DTTO has been established to have been breached the court may elect to continue the order but strictly, in those circumstances, no longer needs the consent of the offender, albeit it would seem fairly fruitless to persist with treatment in the absence of consent.

These provisions came into force on September 30, 1998; see SI 1998/2327.

Breach of drug treatment testing order

234G.—(1) If at any time when a drug treatment and testing order is in force it appears to the appropriate court that the offender has failed to comply with any requirement of the order, the court may issue a citation requiring the offender to appear before the court at such time as may be specified in the citation or, if it appears to the court to be appropriate, it may issue a warrant for the arrest of the offender.

(1A) The unified citation provisions apply in relation to a citation under this section as they apply in relation to a citation under section 216(3)(a) of this Act.

(2) If it is proved to the satisfaction of the appropriate court that the offender has failed without reasonable excuse to comply with any requirement of the order, the court may by order—

(a) without prejudice to the continuation in force of the order, impose a fine not exceeding level 3 on the standard scale;

(b) vary the order so however that any extension of the period of a requirement imposed by virtue of section 234CA of this Act shall not increase that period above the maximum mentioned in subsection (1) of that section; or

(c) revoke the order.

(2A) Subsections (6) and (11) of section 245A of this Act apply to the variation, under paragraph (b) of subsection (2) above, of a requirement imposed as is mentioned in that paragraph as they apply to the making of a restriction of liberty order.

(3) For the purposes of subsection (2) above, the evidence of one witness shall be sufficient evidence.

(4) A fine imposed under this section in respect of a failure to comply with the requirements of a drug treatment and testing order shall be deemed for the purposes of any enactment to be a sum adjudged to be paid by or in respect of a conviction or a penalty imposed on a person summarily convicted.

AMENDMENT

Section 234G inserted by the Crime and Disorder Act 1998 (c.37), s.93 (effective September 30, 1998: SI 1998/ 2327).

Subs.(2)(b) as amended, and subs.(2A) inserted, by Criminal Justice (Scotland) Act 2003 (asp 7), Part 6, s.47. Brought into force on June 27, 2003 by the Criminal Justice (Scotland) Act 2003 (Commencement No.1) Order 2003 (SSI 2003/288 (C.14)).

Subs.(1A) inserted by Criminal Justice (Scotland) Act 2003 (asp 7), Part 8, s.60. Brought into force on October 27, 2003 by the Criminal Justice (Scotland) Act 2003 (Commencement No.3 and Revocation) Order 2003 (SSI 2003/475 (C.26)), art.2.

DEFINITIONS

"drug treatment and testing order": ss.234B(2) and 234C(1) of the 1995 Act as inserted by ss.89 and 90 of the 1998 Act.

"the appropriate court": s.234K of the 1998 Act as inserted by s.95(1) of the 1998 Act.

"offender": s.5 of the Crime and Punishment (Scotland) Act 1997 (c.48).

"citation": s.141 of the 1995 Act.

"fine": s.307(1) of the 1995 Act.

"standard scale": s.225(1) of the 1995 Act.

"witness": s.307(1) of the 1995 Act.

GENERAL NOTE

Failure to comply with the requirements of a drug treatment and testing order (hereafter referred to as a "DTTO") which, it is submitted, can include a failure to appear at a review hearing as well as refusal to provide test samples or to co-operate with either the supervising or treatment officers, is an offence which can be proved on the evidence of one witness, *i.e.* without the necessity of corroborated evidence. Conviction attracts a monetary penalty up to Level 3 on the standard scale, and also entitles the court, as subs.(3) provides, to vary or revoke the order. In the latter case reference then has to be made to s.234H below which entitles the court to impose any other disposal competent at the time of the making of the DTTO.

Once the court has received information pointing to a breach of a DTTO it can either cite the offender to appear at a designated time or issue an arrest warrant. Plainly, when the offender subsequently appears before the court, he will be called upon to admit or deny breaching the order (a procedure already familiar in relation to alleged breaches of probation or community service orders) and, in the case of a denial, a proof will require to be fixed. The procedures for dealing with a reported breach were considered in *Tweedie v Higson*, 2002 S.L.T. 443 a case in which the purported order did not specify the particulars of those to be responsible for providing treatment.

Subsection (4) provides that any fine imposed after a breach has been established shall fall subject to the fine provisions of the 1995 Act (see ss.211 to 223), and the offence itself may be libelled as a conviction.

It is submitted, with hesitation, that once a DTTO has been breached and the court decides to vary the terms of the order (rather than revoking it), and proceeds "by order" as subs.(2) allows, it is no longer necessary to secure the offender's willingness to comply with the revised terms of the order. Nonetheless, having regard to the resource implications of DTTOs, it would seem sensible to obtain an undertaking from the offender as to his future conduct, failing which to consider the range of alternative sentencing disposals.

These provisions came into force on September 30, 1998; see SI 1998/2327.

Disposal on revocation of drugs treatment and testing order

234H.—(1) Where the court revokes a drugs treatment and testing order under section 234E(3)(b), 234F(4) or 234G(2)(c) of this Act, it may dispose of the offender in any way which would have been competent at the time when the order was made.

(2) In disposing of an offender under subsection (1) above, the court shall have regard to the time for which the order has been in operation.

(3) Where the court revokes a drug treatment and testing order as mentioned in subsection (1) above and the offender is subject to—

(a) a probation order, by virtue of section 234J of this Act; or

(b) a restriction of liberty order, by virtue of section 245D of this Act; or

(c) a restriction of liberty order and a probation order, by virtue of the said section 245D,

the court shall, before disposing of the offender under subsection (1) above—

(i) where he is subject to a probation order, discharge that order;

(ii) where he is subject to a restriction of liberty order, revoke that order; and

(iii) where he is subject to both such orders, discharge the probation order and revoke the restriction of liberty order.

(4) This section is subject to section 42(8) of the Criminal Justice (Scotland) Act 2003 (asp 7) (powers of drugs court).

AMENDMENT

Section 234H inserted by the Crime and Disorder Act 1998 (c.37), s.93 (effective September 30, 1998: SI 1998/2327).

Subs.(4) inserted by Criminal Justice (Scotland) Act 2003 (asp 7), Part 5, s.42(11). Brought into force on June 27, 2003 by the Criminal Justice (Scotland) Act 2003 (Commencement No.1) Order 2003 (SSI 2003/288 (C.14)).

Concurrent drug treatment and testing and probation orders

234J.—(1) Notwithstanding sections 228(1) and 234B(2) of this Act, where the court considers it expedient that the offender should be subject to a drug treatment and testing order and to a probation order, it may make both such orders in respect of the offender.

(2) In deciding whether it is expedient for it to exercise the power conferred

by subsection (1) above, the court shall have regard to the circumstances, including the nature of the offence and the character of the offender and to the report submitted to it under section 234B(3)(b) of this Act.

(3) Where the court makes both a drug treatment and testing order and a probation order by virtue of subsection (1) above, the clerk of the court shall send a copy of each of the orders to the following—

(a) the treatment provider within the meaning of section 234C(1);

(b) the officer of the local authority who is appointed or assigned to be the supervising officer under section 234C(6) of this Act; and

(c) if he would not otherwise receive a copy of the order, the officer of the local authority who is to supervise the probationer.

(4) Where the offender by an act or omission fails to comply with a requirement of an order made by virtue of subsection (1) above—

(a) if the failure relates to a requirement contained in a probation order and is dealt with under section 232(2)(c) of this Act, the court may, in addition, exercise the power conferred by section 234G(2)(b) of this Act in relation to the drug treatment and testing order; and

(b) if the failure relates to a requirement contained in a drug treatment and testing order and is dealt with under section 234G(2)(b) of this Act, the court may, in addition, exercise the power conferred by section 232(2)(c) of this Act in relation to the probation order.

(5) Where an offender by an act or omission fails to comply with both a requirement contained in a drug treatment and testing order and in a probation order to which he is subject by virtue of subsection (1) above, he may, without prejudice to subsection (4) above, be dealt with as respects that act or omission either under section 232(2) of this Act or under section 234G(2) of this Act but he shall not be liable to be otherwise dealt with in respect of that act or omission.

(6) Schedule 6 to this Act (Part I of which makes further provision in relation to the combination of drug treatment and testing orders with other orders and Part II of which makes provision in relation to appeals) shall have effect.

AMENDMENT

Section 234J inserted by the Crime and Disorder Act 1998 (c.37), s.94 (effective September 30, 1998: SI 1998/2327).

Drug treatment and testing orders: interpretation

234K. In sections 234B to 234J of this Act—

"the appropriate court" means—

(a) where the drug treatment and testing order has been made by the High Court, that court;

(b) in any other case, the court having jurisdiction in the area of the local authority for the time being specified in the order under section 234C(6) of this Act, being a sheriff or district court according to whether the order had been made by a sheriff or district court, but in a case where an order has been made by a district court and there is no district court in that area, the sheriff court; and

"local authority" means a council constituted under section 2 of the Local Government etc. (Scotland) Act 1994 and any reference to the area of such an authority is a reference to the local government area within the meaning of that Act for which it is so constituted.

AMENDMENT

Section 234K inserted in terms of the Crime and Disorder Act 1998 (c.37), s.95(1) (effective September 30, 1998: SI 1998/2327).

GENERAL NOTE

It is evident that drug treatment and testing orders can be imposed by any Scottish criminal court, and that for the purposes of delivering the appropriate measures of treatment and supervision, it is competent for the offender to be supervised by a local authority other than that within whose area he offended. It should not be assumed that the local authority within whose area the offender resides (and which must furnish a background report—see s.234B(3) of the 1995 Act as inserted by s.89 of the 1998 Act) will necessarily be the authority named in the DTTO; much will depend upon the availability of suitable treatment facilities, residential or otherwise.

Supervised attendance

Supervised attendance orders

235.—(1) A court may make a supervised attendance order in the circumstances specified in subsection (3) below and shall, subject to paragraph 1 of Schedule 7 to this Act, make such an order where subsection (4) or (4A) below applies.

(2) A supervised attendance order is an order made by a court in respect of an offender requiring him—

(a) to attend a place of supervision for such period, being a period of not less than 10 hours and not more than—

   (i) where the amount of the fine, part or instalment which the offender has failed to pay does not exceed level 1 on the standard scale, 50 hours; and

   (ii) in any other case, 100 hours, as is specified in the order; and

(b) during that period, to carry out such instructions as may be given to him by the supervising officer.

(2A) In making a supervised attendance order where subsection (4A) below applies, a court shall take into consideration the best interests of any person under the age of 16 in respect of whom the offender has parental responsibilities within the meaning of Part I of the Children (Scotland) Act 1995 (c.36).

(3) The circumstances referred to in subsection (1) above are where—

(a) the offender is of or over 16 years of age; and

(b) having been convicted of an offence, he has had imposed on him a fine which (or any part or instalment of which) he has failed to pay and the court, but for this section, would also have imposed on him a period of imprisonment under subsection (1) of section 219 of this Act; and

(c) the court considers a supervised attendance order more appropriate than the serving of or, as the case may be, imposition of such a period of imprisonment.

(4) This subsection applies where—

(a) the court is a court prescribed for the purposes of this subsection by order made by the Secretary of State;

(b) the offender is of or over 16 years of age and is not serving a sentence of imprisonment;

(c) having been convicted of an offence, he has had imposed on him a fine which (or any part or instalment of which) he has failed to pay and the court, but for this section, would have imposed on him a period of imprisonment under section 219(1)(b) of this Act; and

(d) the fine, or as the case may be, the part or instalment, is of an amount not exceeding level 2 on the standard scale.

(4A) This subsection applies where, having been convicted of an offence under section 107 of the Antisocial Behaviour etc. (Scotland) Act 2004 (asp 8), the offender has had imposed on him a fine which (or any part or instalment of which) he has failed to pay.

(5) An order under subsection (4)(a) above shall be made by statutory instrument, which shall be subject to annulment in pursuance of a resolution of either House of Parliament.

(6) The coming into force of a supervised attendance order shall have the effect of discharging the fine referred to in subsection (3)(b), (4)(c) or (4A) above or, as the case may be, section 236(3)(a) or 237(1) of this Act.

(7) Schedule 7 to this Act has effect for the purpose of making further and qualifying provision as to supervised attendance orders.

(8) In this section—

"imprisonment" includes detention;

"place of supervision" means such place as may be determined for the purposes of a supervised attendance order by the supervising officer; and

"supervising officer", in relation to a supervised attendance order, means a person appointed or assigned under Schedule 7 to this Act by the local authority whose area includes the locality in which the offender resides or will be residing when the order comes into force.

AMENDMENT

Subss.(3)(a) and (4)(b) as amended by Criminal Justice (Scotland) Act 2003 (asp 7), Part 6, s.50. Brought into force on June 27, 2003 by the Criminal Justice (Scotland) Act 2003 (Commencement No.1) Order 2003 (SSI 2003/288 (C.14)).

Subss.(1) and (6) as amended, and subss.(2A) and (4A) inserted by the Antisocial Behaviour etc. (Scotland) Act 2004 (asp 8), s.144(1) and Sch.4, para.5. Brought into force on April 4, 2005 by the Antisocial Behaviour etc. (Scotland) Act 2004 (Commencement and Savings) Order 2004 (SSI 2004/420 (C.31)).

DEFINITIONS

"appropriate court": Sch.7, para.8.
"imprisonment": s.235(8).
"place of supervision": s.235(8).
"standard scale": s.225(1).
"supervised attendance order": s.235(2).
"supervising officer": s.235(8).

GENERAL NOTE

Section 62 of, and Sch.6 to, the 1990 Act introduced supervised attendance orders ("SAOs") as an alternative to imprisonment for fine default. Under the provisions of the 1990 Act a court, with the consent of the offender, may impose an SAO where it would otherwise have imposed a term of imprisonment for fine default and where it has been notified by the Secretary of State that the appropriate arrangements exist in the area where the offender resides.

This provision extends the existing arrangements to provide that SAOs may be used as an alternative to, or replacement for, imprisonment for fine default. Under this section a court prescribed by the Secretary of State would be required to make an SAO for failure to pay a fine of less than the equivalent of level two on the standard scale (at present, £500: see s.225(2)) instead of imposing a period of imprisonment. The consent of the offender would no longer be required.

Prescribed courts

A supervised attendance prder requires an offender to attend a place of supervision for a specified period and, during that period, to carry out such supervised instructions as may be given to the offender by the supervising officer. All sheriff courts, district courts and justice of the peace courts in Scotland are prescribed (with effect from September 1, 2007) as the courts that must make a supervised attendance order in the circumstances set out in s.235(4) of the 1995 Act: The Supervised Attendance Order (Prescribed Courts) (Scotland) Order 2007 (SSI/120): Art 3.

Act of Adjournal

The form of a supervised attendance order is shown in Form 20.11–A in the 1996 Act of Adjournal. A separate form (Form 20.11–B) is used in the case of orders imposed upon 16 and 17 year olds. Rule 20.17 permits the use of certified copies of such orders in relevant proceedings before a court other than the one which imposed the order.

Supervised attendance orders in place of fines for 16 and 17 year olds

236.—(1) This section applies where a person of or over 16 years of age is convicted of an offence by a court of summary jurisdiction and the court considers that, but for this section, the appropriate sentence is a fine.

(2) Where this section applies, the court shall determine the amount of the fine and shall consider whether the person is likely to pay a fine of that amount within 28 days.

(3) If the court considers that the person is likely to pay the fine as mentioned in subsection (2) above, it shall—

(a) impose the fine; and

(b) subject to paragraph 1 of Schedule 7 to this Act, make a supervised attendance order in default of payment of the fine within 28 days.

(4) A supervised attendance order made under subsection (3)(b) above—

(a) shall come into force on such date, not earlier than 28 days after the making of the order, as may be specified in the order, unless the person pays the fine within that period;

(b) shall, for the purposes of the said Schedule 7, be deemed to be made on the date when it comes into force.

(5) Where, before the coming into force of a supervised attendance order made under subsection (3)(b) above, the person pays part of the fine, the period specified in the order shall be reduced by the proportion which the part of the fine paid bears to the whole fine, the resulting figure being rounded up or down to the nearest 10 hours; but this subsection shall not operate to reduce the period to less than 10 hours.

(6) If the court considers that the person is not likely to pay the fine as mentioned in subsection (2) above, it shall—

(a) if it considers that the person is likely to pay the fine within a reasonable period of more than 28 days, impose the fine;

(b) in any other case, subject to paragraph 1 of Schedule 7 to this Act, make a supervised attendance order in respect of that person.

(7) Sections 211(3), 213, 214(1) to (7), 215, 216(1) to (6), 217 to 219, 222 and 223 of this Act shall not apply in respect of a person to whom this section applies.

(8) For the purposes of any appeal or review, a supervised attendance order made under this section is a sentence.

(9) In this section "supervised attendance order" means an order made in accordance with section 235(2), (7) and (8) of this Act.

AMENDMENT

Subss.(1) and (6) as amended by Criminal Justice (Scotland) Act 2003 (asp 7), Part 6, s.50. Brought into force on June 27, 2003 by the Criminal Justice (Scotland) Act 2003 (Commencement No.1) Order 2003 (SSI 2003/288 (C.14)).

DEFINITIONS

"court of summary jurisdiction": s.307(1).
"fine": s.307(1).
"sentence": s.307(1).
"supervised attendance order": s.235(2).

GENERAL NOTE

This section extends the use of SAOs as respects 16 and 17 year olds as a replacement for a sentence of a fine. Refer to the General Note at A4–469, above.

Supervised attendance orders where court allows further time to pay fine

237.—(1) Where a court, on an application to it under section 215(1) of this Act, allows a person further time for payment of a fine or instalments thereof it may, in addition, subject to paragraph 1 of Schedule 7 to this Act, impose a supervised attendance order in default of payment of the fine or any instalment of it on the due date.

(2) A supervised attendance order made under subsection (1) above shall—

(a) if the person fails to pay the fine or any instalment of it on the due date, come into force on the day after the due date; and

(b) for the purposes of the said Schedule 7, be deemed to be made on the date when it comes into force.

(3) Where, before the coming into force of a supervised attendance order under subsection (1) above, the person pays part of the fine, the period specified in the order shall be reduced by the proportion which the part of the fine paid bears to the whole fine, the resulting figure being rounded up or down to the nearest 10 hours; but this subsection shall not operate to reduce the period to less than 10 hours.

(4) In this section "supervised attendance order" means an order made in accordance with section 235(2), (7) and (8) of this Act.

DEFINITIONS

"fine": s.307(1).
"offence": s.307(1).
"sentence": s.307(1).
"supervised attendance order": s.235(2).

Community service by offenders

Community service orders

238.—(1) Subject to the provisions of this Act, where a person of or over 16 years of age is convicted of an offence punishable by imprisonment, other than an offence the sentence for which is fixed by law, the court may, instead of imposing on him a sentence of, or including, imprisonment or any other form of detention, make an order (in this Act referred to as "a community service order") requiring him to perform unpaid work for such number of hours (being in total not less than 80 nor more than 300 on conviction on indictment, and not less than 80 nor more than 240 in any other case) as may be specified in the order.

(2) A court shall not make a community service order in respect of any offender unless—

(a) the offender consents;

(b) the court has been notified by the Secretary of State that arrangements exist for persons who reside in the locality in which the offender resides, or will be residing when the order comes into force, to perform work under such an order;

(c) the court is satisfied, after considering a report by an officer of a local authority about the offender and his circumstances, and, if the court thinks it necessary, hearing that officer, that the offender is a suitable person to perform work under such an order; and

(d) the court is satisfied that provision can be made under the arrangements mentioned in paragraph (b) above for the offender to perform work under such an order.

(3) A copy of the report mentioned in subsection (2)(c) above shall be supplied to the offender or his solicitor.

(4) Before making a community service order the court shall explain to the offender in ordinary language—

(a) the purpose and effect of the order and in particular the obligations on the offender as specified in subsections (1) to (3) of section 239 of this Act;

(b) the consequences which may follow under subsections (4) to (6) of that section if he fails to comply with any of those requirements; and

(c) that the court has under section 240 of this Act the power to review the order on the application either of the offender or of an officer of the local authority in whose area the offender for the time being resides.

(5) The Secretary of State may by order direct that subsection (1) above shall be amended by substituting, for the maximum or minimum number of hours specified in that subsection as originally enacted or as subsequently amended under this subsection, such number of hours as may be specified in the order; and an order under this subsection may specify a different maximum or minimum number of hours for different classes of case.

(6) An order under subsection (5) above shall be made by statutory instrument, but no such order shall be made unless a draft of it has been laid before, and approved by a resolution of, each House of Parliament; and any such order may be varied or revoked by a subsequent order under that subsection.

(7) Nothing in subsection (1) above shall be construed as preventing a court which makes a community service in respect of any offence from—

(a) imposing any disqualification on the offender;

(b) making an order for forfeiture in respect of the offence;

(c) ordering the offender to find caution for good behaviour.

(8) A community service order shall—

(a) specify the locality in which the offender resides or will be residing when the order comes into force;

(b) require the local authority in whose area the locality specified under paragraph (a) above is situated to appoint or assign an officer (referred to in this section and sections 239 to 245 of this Act as "the local authority officer") who will discharge the functions assigned to him by those sections; and

(c) state the number of hours of work which the offender is required to perform.

(9) Where, whether on the same occasion or on separate occasions, an offender is made subject to more than one community service order, or to both a community service order and a probation order which includes a requirement that that offender shall perform any unpaid work, the court may direct that the hours of work specified in any of those orders shall be concurrent with or additional to those specified in any other of those orders, but so that at no time shall the offender have an outstanding number of hours of work to perform in excess of the maximum provided for in subsection (1) above.

(10) Upon making a community service order the court shall—

(a) give, or send by registered post or the recorded delivery service, a copy of the order to the offender;

(b) send a copy of the order to the chief social work officer of the local authority in whose area the offender resides or will be residing where the order comes into force; and

(c) where it is not the appropriate court, send a copy of the order (together with such documents and information relating to the case as are considered useful) to the clerk of the appropriate court.

(11) Where a copy of a community service order has, under subsection (10)(a) above, been sent by registered post or by the recorded delivery service, an acknowledgement or certificate of delivery of a letter containing the copy order issued by the postal operator shall be sufficient evidence of the delivery of the letter on the day specified in such acknowledgement or certificate.

AMENDMENTS

Subs.(1) substituted by the Community Service by Offenders (Hours of Work) (Scotland) Order 1996 (SI 1996/1938), art.3.

Subs.(11) as amended by the Postal Services Act 2000 (Consequential Modifications No. 1) Order 2001 (SI 2001/1149), art.3 and Sch.1, para. 104.

DEFINITIONS

"caution": s.227.
"local authority": s.307(1).
"local authority officer": s.238(8)(b).
"offence": s.307(1).
"sentence": s.307(1).

GENERAL NOTE

With effect from July 18, 1996, the Community Service by Offenders (Hours of Work) (Scotland) Order raised the minimum number of hours which could be imposed in a community service order from 40 to 80 in summary and solemn cases, and raised the maximum number of hours on indictment only from 240 to 300 hours. (The maximum length of an order imposed summarily remains at 240 hours.)

It is mandatory, following subs.(2) that a community service order cannot be imposed either alone, or in conjunction with another order, unless the court has first obtained a CSO report (see *Boyle v McGlennan*, 1999 G.W.D. 28–1337).

Note that a community service order can be allied to a probation order (see s.229 above) but in such a case the minimum and maximum hours are 40 and 240 hours; these were not affected by SI 1996/1938 discussed above. It is not competent to combine a community service order with a restriction of liberty order.

It is not an absolute requirement that the accused be given a copy of the order. In *McCusker v Speirs*, 2003 S.L.T. 1263 there was held to be no prejudice to the accused who had had the nature of the disposal and his obligations fully explained, though he had not been provided with his intimation copy of the order.

Act of Adjournal

See Form 20.12–A for the style of community service orders. The citation for breach of such an order is set out in Form 20.12–B in the 1996 Act of Adjournal. Refer to r.20.17 for use of certified copy documents in breach proceedings before any court other than the one which imposed the original order.

Community service orders: requirements

239.—(1) An offender in respect of whom a community service order is in force shall—

(a) report to the local authority officer and notify him without delay of any change of address or in the times, if any, at which he usually works; and

(b) perform for the number of hours specified in the order such work at such times as the local authority officer may instruct.

(2) Subject to section 240(1) of this Act, the work required to be performed under a community service order shall be performed during the period of 12 months beginning with the date of the order; but, unless revoked, the order shall remain in force until the offender has worked under it for the number of hours specified in it.

(3) The instructions given by the local authority officer under this section shall, so far as practicable, be such as to avoid any conflict with the offender's religious beliefs and any interference with the times, if any, at which he normally works (or carries out voluntary work) or attends a school or other educational establishment.

(4) If at any time while a community service order is in force in respect of any offender it appears to the appropriate court, on information from the local authority officer, that that offender has failed to comply with any of the requirements of subsections (1) to (3) above (including any failure satisfactorily to perform the work which he has been instructed to do), that court may issue a warrant for the arrest of that offender, or may, if it thinks fit, instead of issuing a warrant in the first instance issue a citation requiring that offender to appear before that court at such time as may be specified in the citation.

(4A) The unified citation provisions apply in relation to a citation under this section as they apply in relation to a citation under section 216(3)(a) of this Act.

(5) If it is proved to the satisfaction of the court before which an offender appears or is brought in pursuance of subsection (4) above that he has failed without reasonable excuse to comply with any of the requirements of the said subsections (1) to (3), that court may—

(a) without prejudice to the continuance in force of the order, impose on him a fine not exceeding level 3 on the standard scale;

(b) revoke the order and deal with that offender in any manner in which he could have been dealt with for the original offence by the court which made the order if the order had not been made; or

(c) subject to section 238(1) of this Act, vary the number of hours specified in the order.

(6) The evidence of one witness shall, for the purposes of subsection (5) above, be sufficient evidence.

AMENDMENT

Subs.(4A) inserted by Criminal Justice (Scotland) Act 2003 (asp 7), Part 8, s.60. Brought into force on October 27, 2003 by the Criminal Justice (Scotland) Act 2003 (Commencement No.3 and Revocation) Order 2003 (SSI 2003/475 (C.26)), art.2.

Subs.(3) as amended by the Antisocial Behaviour etc. (Scotland) Act 2004 (asp 8), s.144(1) and Sch.4, para.5(6). Brought into force on October 28, 2004 by the Antisocial Behaviour etc. (Scotland) Act 2004 (Commencement and Savings) Order 2004 (SSI 2004/420 (C.31)).

"community service order": s.238(1).
"local authority officer": s.238(8)(b).
"standard scale": s.225(2).

GENERAL NOTE

Failure to comply with a community service order invokes the procedures set out in subs.(5). In *Gilbert v Buchanan*, 1998 S.L.T. 303, the sheriff revoked G's order and proceeded to sentence him to three months imprisonment in respect of the original offence and imposed a consecutive sentence of two months imprisonment for breach of the order. The latter sentence was held to be incompetent.

Community service orders: amendment and revocation etc.

240.—(1) Where a community service order is in force in respect of any offender and, on the application of that offender or of the local authority officer, it appears to the appropriate court that it would be in the interests of justice to do so having regard to circumstances which have arisen since the order was made, that court may—

(a) extend, in relation to the order, the period of 12 months specified in section 239(2) of this Act;

(b) subject to section 238(1) of this Act, vary the number of hours specified in the order;

(c) revoke the order; or

(d) revoke the order and deal with the offender for the original offence in any manner in which he could have been dealt with for that offence by the court which made the order if the order had not been made.

(2) If the appropriate court is satisfied that the offender proposes to change, or has changed, his residence from the locality for the time being specified under section 238(8)(a) of this Act to another locality and—

(a) that court has been notified by the Secretary of State that arrangements exist for persons who reside in that other locality to perform work under community service orders; and

(b) it appears to that court that provision can be made under those arrangements for him to perform work under the order,

that court may, and on the application of the local authority officer shall, amend the order by substituting that other locality for the locality for the time being specified in the order; and sections 238 to 245 of this Act shall apply to the order as amended.

(3) Where the court proposes to exercise its powers under subsection (1)(a), (b) or (d) above otherwise than on the application of the offender, it shall issue a citation requiring him to appear before the court and, if he fails to appear, may issue a warrant for his arrest.

(4) The unified citation provisions apply in relation to a citation under this section as they apply in relation to a citation under section 216(3)(a) of this Act.

AMENDMENT

Subs.(4) inserted by Criminal Justice (Scotland) Act 2003 (asp 7), Part 8, s.60. Brought into force on October 27, 2003 by the Criminal Justice (Scotland) Act 2003 (Commencement No.3 and Revocation) Order 2003 (SSI 2003/475 (C.26)), art.2.

DEFINITIONS

"community service order": s.238(1).
"local authority officer": s.228(8)(b).

Community service order: commission of offence while order in force

241.—(1) Where—

(a) a court has made a community service order in respect of an offender; and

(b) the offender is convicted of an offence committed in the circumstances mentioned in subsection (2) below,

the court which sentences him for that offence shall, in determining the appropriate sentence for that offence, have regard to the fact that the offence was committed in those circumstances.

(2) The circumstances referred to in subsection (1) above are that the offence was committed—

(a) during the period when the community service order was in force or within the period of three months following the expiry of that order; and

(b) in any place where unpaid work under the order was being or had previously been performed.

(3) The court shall not, under subsection (1) above, have regard to the fact that the offence was committed in the circumstances mentioned in subsection (2) above unless that fact is libelled in the indictment or, as the case may be, specified in the complaint.

(4) The fact that the offence mentioned in subsection (1)(b) above was committed in the circumstances mentioned in subsection (2) above shall, unless challenged—

(a) in the case of proceedings on indictment, by giving notice of a preliminary objection under paragraph (b) of section 72(1) of this Act or under that paragraph as applied by section 71(2) of this Act; or

(b) in summary proceedings, by preliminary objection before his plea is recorded,

be held as admitted.

AMENDMENT

Subs.(4) inserted by the Crime and Punishment (Scotland) Act 1997 (c.48), s.26(2) with effect from August 1, 1997 in terms of the Crime and Punishment (Scotland) Act 1997 (Commencement and Transitional Provisions) Order 1997 (SI 1997/1712), art.3.

DEFINITIONS

"community service order": s.238(1).
"complaint": s.307(1).
"indictment": s.307(1).
"offence": s.307(1).

GENERAL NOTE

It seems a clear inference from the terms of this section that if an offence should be committed by an individual then performing unpaid work under a community service order at a relevant place, then that is an aggravation for the purposes of sentence. The court can only have regard to these facts if they have been libelled by the Crown: see subs. (3). However, reference to a community service order in the libel of a charge in itself implies previous convictions and may thus contravene ss.101(1) and 166(3) of this Act.

The introduction of subs. (4), in effect creating a special capacity in these circumstances eases the evidential burden on the Crown but it seems unfortunate that the application of these provisions could not have been made known to the accused outwith the libel itself.

It would seem that for a court to have regard to the accused's behaviour in relation to this statutory aggravation the Crown will require to be particularly circumspect in drafting the charge or place the single charge on a separate indictment or complaint if there are several charges. See also the discussion at A4–466, above.

Community service orders: persons residing in England and Wales

242.—(1) Where a court is considering the making of a community service order and it is satisfied that the offender has attained the age of 16 years and resides, or will be residing when the order comes into force, in England or Wales, then—

(a) section 238 of this Act shall have effect as if subsection (2) were amended as follows—

  (i) paragraph (b) shall be omitted;

  (ii) in paragraph (c) for the words "such an order" there shall be substituted the words "an unpaid work requirement imposed by a community order (within the meaning of Part 12 of the Criminal Justice Act 2003)"; and

  (iii) for paragraph (d) there shall be substituted the following paragraph—

  "(d) it appears to that court that provision can be made for the offender to perform work under the order made under subsection (1) above under the arrangements which exist in the petty sessions area in which he resides or will be residing for persons to perform work under unpaid work requirements imposed by community orders made under section 177 of the Criminal Justice Act 2003;"
     ; and

(b) the order shall specify that the unpaid work required to be performed by the order shall be performed under the arrangements mentioned in section 238(2)(d) of this Act as substituted by paragraph (a) above.

(2) Where a community service order has been made and—

(a) the appropriate court is satisfied that the offender has attained the age of 16 years and proposes to reside or is residing in England or Wales; and

(b) it appears to that court that provision can be made for the offender to perform work under the order made under the arrangements which exist in the petty sessions area in which he proposes to reside or is residing for persons to perform work under unpaid work requirements imposed by community orders made under section 177 of the Criminal Justice Act 2003,

it may amend the order by specifying that the unpaid work required to be performed by the order shall be performed under the arrangements mentioned in paragraph (b) of this subsection.

(3) A community service order made under section 238(1) as amended by or in accordance with this section shall—

(a) specify the petty sessions area in England or Wales in which the offender resides or will be residing when the order or the amendment comes into force; and

(b) require the local probation board for that area to appoint or assign an officer of the board who will discharge in respect of the order the functions conferred on responsible officers by Part 12 of the Criminal Justice Act 2003 in respect of unpaid work requirements imposed by community orders (within the meaning of that Part).

AMENDMENTS

Subss.(1)(a), (2)(b) and (3)(b) as amended by the Powers of Criminal Courts (Sentencing) Act 2000 (c.6), s.165 and Sch.9, para.177.

Subs.(1)(a), (2)(b) and (3)(b) as amended by the Criminal Justice and Court Services Act 2000 (c.43), s.74 and Sch.7, para.124. Brought into force by the Criminal Justice and Court Services Act 2000 (Commencement No. 4) Order 2001 (SI 2001/919 (C.33)), art.2(f)(ii) (effective April 1, 2001).

Subss.(1)(a)(ii), (iii), (2)(b), (3)(b) as amended by the Criminal Justice Act 2003 (c.44), s.304 and

Sch.32, para.71. Brought into force on April 4, 2005 by the Criminal Justice Act 2003 (Commencement No.8 and Transitional and Saving Provisions) Order 2005 (SI 2005/950 (C.42)), art.2 and Sch.1.

DEFINITION
"community service order": s.238(1).

Community service orders: persons residing in Northern Ireland

243.—(1) Where a court is considering the making of a community service order and it is satisfied that the offender resides, or will be residing when the order comes into force, in Northern Ireland, then—

(a) section 238 of this Act shall have effect as if subsection (2) were amended as follows—

    (i) paragraph (b) shall be omitted;

    (ii) for paragraph (d) there shall be substituted the following paragraph—

    "(d) it appears to the court that provision can be made by the Probation Board for Northern Ireland for him to perform work under such an order;";

(b) the order shall specify that the unpaid work required to be performed by the order shall be performed under the provision made by the Probation Board for Northern Ireland and referred to in section 238(2)(d) of this Act as substituted by paragraph (a) above.

(2) Where a community service order has been made and—

(a) the appropriate court is satisfied that the offender proposes to reside or is residing in Northern Ireland; and

(b) it appears to that court that provision can be made by the Probation Board for Northern Ireland for him to perform work under the order,

it may amend the order by specifying that the unpaid work required to be performed by the order shall be performed under the provision made by the Probation Board for Northern Ireland and referred to in paragraph (b) of this subsection.

(3) A community service order made under section 238(1) of this Act as amended by or in accordance with this section shall—

(a) specify the petty sessions district in Northern Ireland in which the offender resides or will be residing when the order or the amendment comes into force; and

(b) require the Probation Board for Northern Ireland to select an officer who will discharge in respect of the order the functions in respect of community service orders conferred on the relevant officer by the Treatment of Offenders (Northern Ireland) Order 1976.

DEFINITION
"community service order": s.238(1).

Community service orders: general provisions relating to persons living in England and Wales or Northern Ireland

244.—(1) Where a community service order is made or amended in the circumstances specified in section 242 or 243 of this Act, the court which makes or amends the order shall send three copies of it as made or amended to the home court, together with such documents and information relating to the case as it considers likely to be of assistance to that court.

(2) In this section—

"home court" means—

(a) if the offender resides in England or Wales, or will be residing in England or Wales at the relevant time, the magistrates' court acting for the petty sessions area in which he resides or proposes to reside; and

(b) if he resides in Northern Ireland, or will be residing in Northern Ireland, at the relevant time, the court of summary jurisdiction acting for the petty sessions district in which he resides or proposes to reside; and

"the relevant time" means the time when the order or the amendment to it comes into force.

(3) Subject to the following provisions of this section—

(a) a community service order made or amended in the circumstances specified in section 242 shall be treated as if it were a community order (within the meaning of Part 12 of the Criminal Justice Act 2003) made in England and Wales and the legislation relating to such community orders which has effect in England and Wales shall apply accordingly; and

(b) a community service order made or amended in the circumstances specified in section 243 shall be treated as if it were a community service order made in Northern Ireland and the legislation relating to community service orders which has effect in Northern Ireland shall apply accordingly.

(4) Before making or amending a community service order in those circumstances the court shall explain to the offender in ordinary language—

(a) the requirements of the legislation relating to community service orders or, as the case may be, community orders (within the meaning of Part 12 of the Criminal Justice Act 2003) which has effect in the part of the United Kingdom in which he resides or will be residing at the relevant time;

(b) the powers of the home court under that legislation, as modified by this section; and

(c) its own powers under this section,

and an explanation given in accordance with this section shall be sufficient without the addition of an explanation under section 238(4) of this Act.

(5) The home court may exercise in relation to the community service order any power which it could exercise in relation to a community service order or, as the case may be, a community order (within the meaning of Part 12 of the Criminal Justice Act 2003) made by a court in the part of the United Kingdom in which the home court exercises jurisdiction, by virtue of the legislation relating to such orders which has effect in that part of the United Kingdom, except—

(a) a power to vary the order by substituting for the number of hours' work specified in it any greater number than the court which made the order could have specified;

(b) a power to revoke the order; and

(c) a power to revoke the order and deal with the offender for the offence in respect of which it was made in any manner in which he could have been dealt with for that offence by the court which made the order if the order had not been made.

(6) If at any time while legislation relating to community service orders or, as the case may be, community orders (within the meaning of Part 12 of the Crimi-

nal Justice Act 2003) which has effect in one part of the United Kingdom applies by virtue of subsection (3) above to a community service order made in another part—

(a) it appears to the home court—

    (i) if that court is in England or Wales, on information to a justice of the peace acting for the petty sessions area for the time being specified in the order; or

    (ii) if it is in Northern Ireland, upon a complaint being made to a justice of the peace acting for the petty sessions district for the time being specified in the order,

that the offender has failed to comply with any of the requirements of the legislation applicable to the order; or

(b) it appears to the home court on the application of—

    (i) the offender; or

    (ii) if that court is in England and Wales, the responsible officers by Part 12 of the Criminal Justice Act 2003; or

    (iii) if that court is in Northern Ireland, the relevant officer under the Treatment of Offenders (Northern Ireland) Order 1976,

that it would be in the interests of justice to exercise a power mentioned in subsection (5)(b) or (c) above,

the home court may require the offender to appear before the court by which the order was made.

(7) Where an offender is required by virtue of subsection (6) above to appear before the court which made a community service order, that court—

(a) may issue a warrant for his arrest; and

(b) may exercise any power which it could exercise in respect of the community service order if the offender resided in the part of the United Kingdom where the court has jurisdiction,

and any enactment relating to the exercise of such powers shall have effect accordingly.

AMENDMENTS

    Subs.(6)(b) as amended by the Powers of Criminal Courts (Sentencing) Act 2000 (c.6), s.165 and Sch.9, para.178.

    Subss.(4), (5) and (6) as amended by the Criminal Justice and Court Services Act 2000 (c.43), s.74 and Sch.7, para.125. Brought into force by the Criminal Justice and Court Services Act 2000 (Commencement No. 4) Order 2001 (SI 2001/919 (C.33)), art2(f)(ii) (effective April 1, 2001).

    Subs.(3) substituted by the Criminal Justice and Court Services Act 2000 (c.43), s.74 and Sch.7, para.125. Brought into force as above.

    Section 244 is prospectively amended by the Justice (Northern Ireland) Act 2002 (c.26), Sch.4, para.37.

    Subss.(3)(a), (4)(a), (5), (6), (b)(ii) as amended by the Criminal Justice Act 2003 (c.44), s.304 and Sch.32, para.72. Brought into force on April 4, 2005 by the Criminal Justice Act 2003 (Commencement No.8 and Transitional and Saving Provisions) Order 2005 (SI 2005/950 (C.42)), art.2 and Sch.1.

DEFINITIONS

    "community service order": s.238(1).
    "home court": s.244(2).
    "relevant time": s.244(2).

Community service orders: rules, annual report and interpretation

245.—(1) The Secretary of State may make rules for regulating the performance of work under community service orders or probation orders which include a requirement that the offender shall perform unpaid work.

(2) Without prejudice to the generality of subsection (1) above, rules under this section may—

(a) limit the number of hours' work to be done by a person under such an order on any one day;

(b) make provision as to the reckoning of time worked under such orders;

(c) make provision for the payment of travelling and other expenses in connection with the performance of work under such orders;

(d) provide for records to be kept of the work done by any person under such an order.

(3) Rules under this section shall be made by statutory instrument subject to annulment in pursuance of a resolution of either House of Parliament.

(4) The Secretary of State shall lay before Parliament each year, or incorporate in annual reports he already makes, a report of the working of community service orders.

(5) In sections 238 to 243 of this Act, "the appropriate court" means—

(a) where the relevant community service order has been made by the High Court, the High Court;

(b) in any other case, the court having jurisdiction in the locality for the time being specified in the order under section 238(8)(a) of this Act, being a sheriff or district court according to whether the order has been made by a sheriff or a district court, but in a case where the order has been made by a district court and there is no district court in that locality, the sheriff court.

DEFINITIONS

"appropriate court": s.245(5).
"community service orders": s.238(1).
"probation orders": s.308(1).

Restriction of Liberty Orders

Restriction of liberty orders

245A.—(1) Without prejudice to section 245D of this Act, where a person is convicted of an offence punishable by imprisonment (other than an offence the sentence for which is fixed by law) the court may, instead of imposing on him a sentence of, or including, imprisonment or any other form of detention, make an order under this section (in this Act referred to as a "restriction of liberty order") in respect of him.

(2) A restriction of liberty order may restrict the offender's movements to such extent as the court thinks fit and, without prejudice to the generality of the foregoing, may include provision—

(a) requiring the offender to be in such place as may be specified for such period or periods in each day or week as may be specified;

(b) requiring the offender not to be in such place or places, or such class or classes of place or places, at such time or during such periods, as may be specified,

but the court may not, under paragraph (a) above, require the offender to be in any place or places for a period of periods totalling more than 12 hours in any one day.

(3) A restriction of liberty order may be made for any period up to 12 months.

(4) Before making a restriction of liberty order, the court shall explain to the offender in ordinary language—

(a) the effect of the order, including any requirements which are to be included in the order under section 245C of this Act;

(b) the consequences which may follow any failure by the offender to comply with the requirements of any order; and

(c) that the court has power under section 245E of this Act to review the order on the application either of the offender or of any person responsible for monitoring the order,

and the court shall not make the order unless the offender agrees to comply with its requirements.

(5) The clerk of the court by which a restriction of liberty order is made shall—

(a) cause a copy of the order to be sent—

    (i) to any person who is to be responsible for monitoring the offender's compliance with the order; and

    (ii) if the offender resides (or is to reside) in a place outwith the jurisdiction of the court making the order, to the clerk of a court within whose jurisdiction that place is; and

(b) cause a copy of the order to be given to the offender or sent to him by registered post or by the recorded delivery service; and an acknowledgment or certificate of delivery of a letter containing such copy order issued by the Post Office shall be sufficient evidence of the delivery of the letter on the day specified in such acknowledgment or certificate.

(6) Before making a restriction of liberty order which will require the offender to remain in a specified place or places the court shall—

(a) obtain and consider a report by an officer of a local authority about—

    (i) the place or places proposed to be specified; and

    (ii) be affected by the enforced presence there of the offender; and

(b) if it considers it necessary, hear the officer who prepared the report.

(7) A restriction of liberty order shall be taken to be a sentence for the purposes of this Act and of any appeal.

(8) The Secretary of State may by regulations prescribe—

(a) which courts, or class or classes of courts, may make restriction of liberty orders;

(b) what method or methods of monitoring compliance with such orders may be specified in any such order by any such court; and

(c) the class or classes of offenders in respect of which restriction of liberty orders may be made,

and different provision may be made in relation to the matters mentioned in paragraphs (b) and (c) above in relation to different courts or classes of court.

(9) Without prejudice to the generality of subsection (8) above, in relation to district courts, regulations under that subsection may make provision as respects such courts by reference to whether the court is constituted by a stipendiary magistrate or by one or more justices.

(10) Regulations under subsection (8) above may make such transitional and consequential provisions, including provision in relation to the continuing effect of any restriction of liberty order in force when new regulations are made, as the Secretary of State considers appropriate.

(11) A court shall not make a restriction of liberty order which requires an offender to be in or, as the case may be, not to be in, a particular place or places unless it is satisfied that his compliance with that requirement can be monitored by the means of monitoring which it intends to specify in the order.

(11A) A court shall not make a restriction of liberty order in respect of an offender who is under 16 years of age unless, having obtained a report on the offender from the local authority in whose area he resides, it is satisfied as to the services which the authority will provide for his support and rehabilitation during the period when he is subject to the order.

(12) The Secretary of State may by regulations substitute for the period of—

(a) hours for the time being mentioned in subsection (2) above; or

(b) months for the time being mentioned in subsection (3) above,

such period of hours or, as the case may be, months as may be prescribed in the regulations.

(13) Regulations under this section shall be made by statutory instrument.

(14) A statutory instrument containing regulations made under subsection (8) above shall be subject to annulment in pursuance of a resolution of either House of Parliament.

(15) No regulations shall be made under subsection (12) above unless a draft of the regulations has been laid before, and approved by a resolution of, each House of Parliament.

AMENDMENTS

Section 245A inserted by the Crime and Punishment (Scotland) Act 1997 (c.48), s.5 (in part) with (effective July 1, 1998: SI 1997/2323).

Subss.(8)–(15) inserted by the Crime and Punishment (Scotland) Act 1997 (c.48), s.5 (in part) with effect from October 20, 1997 in terms of the Crime and Punishment (Scotland) Act 1997 (Commencement No.2 and Transitional and Consequential Provisions) Order 1997 (SI 1997/2323 (S.155)), art.3 and Sch.1.

Subs.(1) as amended by Criminal Justice (Scotland) Act 2003 (asp 7), Part 6, s.50. Brought into force on June 27, 2003 by the Criminal Justice (Scotland) Act 2003 (Commencement No.1) Order 2003 (SSI 2003/288 (C.14)).

Subs.(5) as amended by Criminal Justice (Scotland) Act 2003 (asp 7), Part 6, s.43. Brought into force on June 27, 2003 by the Criminal Justice (Scotland) Act 2003 (Commencement No.1) Order 2003 (SSI 2003/288 (C.14)).

Subs.(6) as amended by the Criminal Procedure(Amendment) (Scotland) Act 2004 (asp 5), s.25 and Sch.1, para.35. Brought into force on October 4, 2004 by the Criminal Procedure (Amendment) (Scotland) Act 2004 (Commencement, Transitional Provisions and Savings) Order 2004 (SSI 2004/405 (C.28)).

Subs.(11A) inserted by the Antisocial Behaviour etc. (Scotland) Act 2004 (asp 8), s.121(3). Brought into force on April 4, 2005 by the Antisocial Behaviour etc. (Scotland) Act 2004 (Commencement and Savings) Order 2004 (SSI 2004/420 (C.31)).

Subs.(1) as amended by the Antisocial Behaviour etc. (Scotland) Act 2004 (asp 8), s.121(2), s.144(2) and Sch.5. Brought into force on April 4, 2005 as above.

DEFINITIONS

"restriction of liberty order": s.5 of the 1997 Act.

"offender": s.5 of the 1997 Act.

"stipendiary magistrate": s.5 of the District Courts (Scotland) Act 1975 and s.7(5) of the 1995 Act.

"justice": ss.6 and 307(1) of the 1995 Act.

"probation order": s.228 of the 1995 Act.

"fine": s.307(1) of the 1995 Act.

"standard scale": s.225(1) of the 1995 Act.

GENERAL NOTE

This section was brought into the 1995 Act by the Crime and Punishment (Scotland) Act 1997 (c.48), s.5 and introduced the concept of curfew into Scottish criminal procedure and, more controversially, aimed to monitor compliance by means of electronic tagging. The provisions apply to adults and young offenders but not to child offenders.

Orders can stand alone or operate in conjunction with community service or probation orders or the newer drug testing and treatment orders found in s.234B of the Act but (as with these other alternatives to custodial sentences) can only be imposed with the consent of the accused. The duration of the order can be for up to 12 months and for up to 12 hours in a day, can restrict the accused's movements so as to prohibit his attendance, or require his attendance, at specified premises. Thus a restriction of liberty order (henceforth "RLO") can be used to bar an individual from licensed premises or football grounds, or to require attendance elsewhere. Monitoring of compliance is by way of electronic tagging and the broad aim has been to use the disposal as an alternative to custody in fairly minor cases with attendant cost savings; it is estimated that the costs of such schemes run at about half the level of custodial alternatives. Monitoring services have been provided by private contractors both in England and in three Scottish pilot schemes in Hamilton, Peterhead and Aberdeen. Recently the Government announced an extension of the RLO scheme to other Scottish courts; see 2001 S.L.T. (News) 209. The section does not permit one condition, at least, in combination with any RLO; it is not competent to link a community service order with any RLO, the two being distinct forms of penalty (*Macauley v Houston*, 2005 S.L.T. 834).

Note that RLOs cannot be imposed in murder cases where the sentence is fixed by law and, as with other non-custodial alternatives, must be assented to by the accused once its workings have been explained to him in plain language. Unusually, subs.(6) also requires the court to take soundings from, and consider the impact upon, persons likely to be affected by the nomination of a place where the RLO is to be served. It seems probable that this would involve consultation with social work services.

Delegated legislation

The means of enforcing the restriction of liberty orders is brought into effect by the Restriction of Liberty Order (Scotland) Regulations 2006 (SSI 2006/8) which by reg.2 came into force on April 16, 2006.

Monitoring of restriction of liberty orders

245B.—(1) Where the Secretary of State, in regulations made under section 245A(8) of this Act, empowers a court or a class of court to make restriction of liberty orders he shall notify the court or each of the courts concerned of the person or class or description of persons who may be designated by that court for the purpose of monitoring an offender's compliance with any such order.

(2) A court which makes a restriction of liberty order in respect of an offender shall include provision in the order for making a person notified by the Secretary of State under subsection (1) above, or a class or description of persons so notified, responsible for the monitoring of the offender's compliance with it.

(3) Where the Secretary of State changes the person or class or description of persons notified by him under subsection (1) above, any court which has made a restriction of liberty order shall, if necessary, vary the order accordingly and shall notify the variation to the offender.

AMENDMENT

Section 245B inserted by the Crime and Punishment (Scotland) Act 1997 (c.48), s.5 (effective July 1, 1998: SI 1997/2323).

GENERAL NOTE

s.245B

In addition to his general regulatory duties set out in s.245A(10), the Secretary of State is required to intimate to any court empowered to make restriction of liberty orders the particulars of the individual person or category of persons who shall monitor offenders' compliance with orders. This provision would permit the nomination of a named individual or a generic description, say, employees of an authorised monitoring organisation.

In the event of a change of monitor it is the court's responsibility to notify the offender of this alteration. Observe that s.254B is not explicit as to how such notification is to be effected but, it is suggested, that guidance may be had from s.254A(6) above. It is submitted that although subs.(3) refers to "variation" of the order this is a quite distinct procedure from variation of an order as set out in s.245E: in the former case the court simply intimates a change of monitor to an offender without any court hearing.

Remote monitoring

245C.—(1) The Secretary of State may make such arrangements, including contractual arrangements, as he considers appropriate with such persons, whether legal or natural, as he thinks fit for the remote monitoring of the compliance of offenders with restriction of liberty orders, and different arrangements may be made in relation to different areas or different forms of remote monitoring.

(2) A court making a restriction of liberty order which is to be monitored remotely may include in the order a requirement that the offender—

(a) shall, either continuously or for such periods as may be specified, wear or carry a device for the purpose of enabling the remote monitoring of his compliance with the order to be carried out, and

(b) shall not tamper with or intentionally damage the device or knowingly allow it to be tampered with or intentionally damaged.

(3) The Secretary of State shall by regulations specify devices which may be used for the purpose of remotely monitoring the compliance of an offender with the requirements of a restriction of liberty order.

(4) Regulations under this section shall be made by statutory instrument subject to annulment in pursuance of a resolution of either House of Parliament.

AMENDMENT

Section 245C inserted by the Crime and Punishment (Scotland) Act 1997 (c.48), s.5 (effective July 1, 1998: SI 1997/2323).

Subs.(2) as amended by the Criminal Procedure (Amendment) (Scotland) Act 2004 (asp 5), s.25 and Sch.1, para.36. Brought into force on October 4, 2004 by the Criminal Procedure (Amendment) (Scotland) Act 2004 (Commencement, Transitional Provisions and Savings) Order 2004 (SSI 2004/405 (C.28)).

GENERAL NOTE

s.245C

This section empowers the Secretary of State to select contractors to carry out electronic tagging of offenders and remote monitoring, and to designate the types of electronic devices which may be placed on the person of offenders.

Delegated legislation

The means of enforcing the restriction of liberty orders is brought into effect by the Restriction of Liberty Order (Scotland) Regulations 2006 (SSI 2006/8) which by reg.2 came into force on April 16, 2006.

Combination of restriction of liberty order with other orders

245D.—(1) Subsection (3) applies where the court—

(a) intends to make a restriction of liberty order under section 245A(1) of this Act; and

(b) considers it expedient that the offender should also be subject to

(i) in the case of an offender who is under 16 years of age, a probation order made under section 228(1) of this Act

(ii) in the case of an offender who is 16 years of age or more, a probation order made under section 228(1) of this Act, a drug treatment and testing order made under section 234B(2) of this Act or both such orders.

(2) In deciding whether it is expedient to make a probation order or drug treatment and testing order by virtue of paragraph (b) of subsection (1) above, the court shall—

(a) have regard to the circumstances, including the nature of the offence and the character of the offender; and

(b) obtain a report as to the circumstances and character of the offender.

(3) Where this subsection applies, the court, notwithstanding sections 228(1), 234(2) and 245A(1) of this Act, may make a restriction of liberty order and

(a) in the case of an offender who is under 16 years of age, a probation order;

(b) in the case of an offender who is 16 years of age or more, either or both of a probation order and a drug treatment and testing order.

(4) Where the court makes a restriction of liberty order and a probation order by virtue of subsection (3) above, the clerk of court shall send a copy of each order to—

(a) any person responsible for monitoring the offender's compliance with the restriction of liberty order; and

(b) the officer of the local authority who is to supervise the probationer.

(5) Where the court makes a restriction of liberty order and a drug treatment and testing order by virtue of subsection (3) above, the clerk of court shall send a copy of each order to—

(a) any person responsible for monitoring the offender's compliance with the restriction of liberty order;

(b) the treatment provider, within the meaning of section 234C(1) of this Act; and

(c) the officer of the local authority who is appointed or assigned to be the supervising officer under section 234C(6) of this Act.

(6) Where the court makes a restriction of liberty order, a probation order and a drug treatment and testing order the clerk of the court shall send copies of each of the orders to the persons mentioned—

(a) in subsection (4) above;

(b) in paragraph (b) of subsection (5) above; and

(c) in paragraph (c) of that subsection, if that person would not otherwise receive such copies.

(7) Where the offender by an act or omission fails to comply with a requirement of an order made by virtue of subsection (3) above—

(a) if the failure relates to a requirement contained in a probation order and is dealt with under section 232(2)(c) of this Act, the court may, in addition, exercise the powers conferred by section 234G(2)(b) of this Act in relation to a drug treatment and testing order to which the offender is subject by virtue of subsection (3) above and by section 245F(2) of this Act in relation to the restriction of liberty order;

(b) if the failure relates to a requirement contained in a drug treatment and testing order and is dealt with under section 234G(2)(b) of this Act, the court may, in addition, exercise the powers conferred by section 232(2)(c) of this Act in relation to a probation order to which the offender is subject by virtue of subsection (3) above and by section 245F(2)(b) of this Act in relation to the restriction of liberty order; and

(c) if the failure relates to a requirement contained in a restriction of liberty order and is dealt with under section 245F(2)(b) of this Act, the court may, in addition, exercise the powers conferred by section 232(2)(c) of this Act in relation to a probation order and by section 234G(2)(b) of this Act in relation to a drug treatment and testing order to which, in either case, the offender is subject by virtue of subsection (3) above.

(8) In any case to which this subsection applies, the offender may, without prejudice to subsection (7) above, be dealt with as respects that case under section 232(2) or, as the case may be, section 234G or section 245F(2) of this Act but he shall not be liable to be otherwise dealt with as respects that case.

(9) Subsection (8) applies in a case where—

(a) the offender by an act or omission fails to comply with both a requirement contained in a restriction of liberty order and in a probation order to which he is subject by virtue of subsection (3) above;

(b) the offender by an act or omission fails to comply with both a requirement contained in a restriction of liberty order and in a drug treatment and testing order to which he is subject by virtue of subsection (3) above;

(c) the offender by an act or omission fails to comply with a requirement contained in each of a restriction of liberty order, a probation order and a drug treatment and testing order to which he is subject by virtue of subsection (3) above.

AMENDMENT

Section 245D inserted by the Crime and Punishment (Scotland) Act 1997 (c.48), s.5 (effective July 1, 1998: SI 1997/2323).

Section 245D as substituted by the Crime and Disorder Act 1998 (c.37), s.94 and Sch.6, para.3. Brought into force on September 30, 1998 by the Crime and Disorder Act 1998 (Commencement No.2 and Transitional Provisions) Order 1998 (SI 1998/2327 (C.53)).

Subs.(1)(b) as amended, and subss.(1)(b)(i), (3)(a), (b) inserted, by the Antisocial Behaviour etc. (Scotland) Act 2004 (asp 8), s.144(1), Sch.4, para.5(7). Brought into force on April 4, 2005 by the Antisocial Behaviour etc. (Scotland) Act 2004 (Commencement and Savings) Order 2004 (SSI 2004/420 (C.31)).

GENERAL NOTE

s.245D

The well-established principle that a probation order is an alternative to sentence is adhered to in s.228(1) of the 1995 Act but, practically, is considerably eroded in the current Act. For the purposes of an automatic sentence under ss.1 and 2 of the Act, probation, following conviction of a qualifying offence, is viewed no differently from any other sentencing disposal. A restriction of liberty order can be imposed in conjunction with other non-custodial disposals, including probation, and is held to be a sentence (s.245A(10)). It has already been noted that the procedures which a court must follow before imposing a restriction of liberty order (s.245A(4)) draw heavily upon the existing practices in relation to probation orders, albeit additional conditions have to be met before a tagging order can be initiated.

Where a court opts to impose a probation order along with a restriction of liberty order it imposes two separate orders and thus, must specify both the person to be responsible for operating remote monitoring of the offender and the local authority responsible for supervising probation. It will be recalled that a restriction of liberty order can only subsist for a year (s.245A(3)) whereas a probation order can exceptionally last up to three years from the date of the order.

These dual orders inevitably create difficulty when one or other order, or both, needs to be breached or varied. Subsection (3) enacts that where a "linked" probation order is held not to have been complied with, the court may also vary the RLO but, it is postulated that it will then be necessary to ensure that the RLO complies with the time limits laid out in s.245A(3). Similarly where a "linked" RLO is varied following non-compliance, the court is also empowered to call up and vary the terms of the concurrent probation order. The provisions of subs.(3) do not apply to breaches of unassociated probation and restriction of liberty orders which contain the same requirements; these are dealt with once only in accordance with subs.(4), thus avoiding double jeopardy.

Variation of restriction of liberty order

245E.—(1) Where a restriction of liberty order is in force either the offender or any person responsible for monitoring his compliance with the order may—

(a) except in a case to which paragraph (b) below applies, apply to the court which made the order, or

(b) where a copy of the order was, under section 245A(5)(a)(ii) of this Act or subsection (7)(a) below, sent to the clerk of a different court, apply to that different court (or, if there has been more than one such sending, the different court to which such a copy has most recently been so sent), for a review of it.

(2) On an application made under subsection (1) above, and after hearing both the offender and any person responsible for monitoring his compliance with the order, the court may by order, if it appears to it to be in the interests of justice to do so—

    (a) vary the order by—

        (i) amending or deleting any of its requirements;

        (ii) inserting further requirements; or

        (iii) subject to subsection (3) of section 245A of this Act, increasing the period for which the order has to run; or

    (b) revoke the order.

(3) Where the court, on the application of a person other than the offender, proposes to—

    (a) exercise the power conferred by paragraph (a) of subsection (2) above to vary (otherwise than by deleting a requirement) a restriction of liberty order, it shall issue a citation requiring the offender to appear before the court and section 245A(4) shall apply to the variation of such an order as it applies to the making of an order; and

    (b) exercise the power conferred by subsection (2)(b) above to revoke such an order and deal with the offender under section 245G of this Act, it shall issue a citation requiring him to appear before the court.

(3A) The unified citation provisions apply in relation to a citation under this section as they apply in relation to a citation under section 216(3)(a) of this Act.

(4) If an offender fails to appear before the court after having been cited in accordance with subsection (3) above, the court may issue a warrant for his arrest.

(4A) Before varying a restriction of liberty order so as to require the offender to remain in a specified place or places or so as to specify a different place or different places in which the offender is to remain, the court shall—

    (a) obtain and consider a report by an officer of a local authority about—

        (i) the place or places proposed to be specified, and

        (ii) the attitude of persons likely to be affected by any enforced presence there of the offender; and

    (b) if it considers it necessary, hear the officer who prepared the report.

(5) Where a reason for an application by the offender under subsection (1) above is that he proposes to reside in a place outwith the jurisdiction of the court to which that application is made, and the court is satisfied that suitable arrangements can be made, in the district where that place is, for monitoring his compliance with the order it may—

    (a) vary the order to permit or make practicable such arrangements; and

    (b) where the change in residence necessitates or makes desirable a change in who is designated for the purpose of such monitoring, vary the order accordingly.

(6) Before varying a restriction of liberty order for the reason mentioned in subsection (5) above, the court shall—

    (a) if the order will require the offender to remain in a specified place or in specified places—

        (i) obtain and consider a report by an officer of a local authority about the place or places proposed to be specified and be affected by any enforced presence there of the offender; and

        (ii) if it considers it necessary, hear the officer who prepared the report; and

(b) satisfy itself that his compliance with that requirement can be monitored by the means of monitoring specified, or which it intends to specify, in the order.

(7) Where a restriction of liberty order is varied as is mentioned in subsection (5) above, the clerk of the court shall send a copy of the order as so varied to—

(a) the clerk of a court within whose jurisdiction the place of proposed residence is;

(b) the person who, immediately before the order was varied, was responsible for monitoring the person's compliance with it; and

(c) the person who, in consequence of the variation, is to have that responsibility.

(8) If, in relation to an application made for such reason as is mentioned in subsection (5) above, the court is not satisfied as is mentioned in that subsection, it may—

(a) refuse the application; or

(b) revoke the order.

AMENDMENT

Section 245E inserted by the Crime and Punishment (Scotland) Act 1997 (c.48), s.5 (effective July 1, 1998: SI 1997/2323).

Subs.(1) as amended, and subss.(5)–(8) inserted, by Criminal Justice (Scotland) Act 2003 (asp 7), Part 6, s.43. Brought into force on June 27, 2003 by the Criminal Justice (Scotland) Act 2003 (Commencement No.1) Order 2003 (SSI 2003/288 (C.14)).

Subs.(3A) inserted by Criminal Justice (Scotland) Act 2003 (asp 7), Part 8, s.60. Brought into force on October 27, 2003 by the Criminal Justice (Scotland) Act 2003 (Commencement No.3 and Revocation) Order 2003 (SSI 2003/475 (C.26)), art.2.

Subs.(4A) inserted, and subs.(6) as amended, by the Criminal Procedure (Amendment) (Scotland) Act 2004 (asp 5), s.25 and Sch.1, para.37. Brought into force on October 4, 2004 by the Criminal Procedure (Amendment) (Scotland) Act 2004 (Commencement, Transitional Provisions and Savings) Order 2004 (SSI 2004/405 (C.28)).

Subs.(1)(b) as amended by the Antisocial Behaviour etc. (Scotland) Act 2004 (asp 8), s.144(1), Sch.4, para.5(8). Brought into force on April 4, 2005 by the Antisocial Behaviour etc. (Scotland) Act 2004 (Commencement and Savings) Order 2004 (SSI 2004/420 (C.31)).

GENERAL NOTE

s.245E

During the currency of a restriction of liberty order it is open to both the offender and his monitoring supervisor to apply to the court for its review. As was noted at s.245B(3) it is not necessary to make an application for review when all that is sought is variation of the particulars of the monitoring supervisor. (The court has its own intrinsic power to deal with alleged failures to comply with the terms of an RLO in s.245F below).

Where application is made by the supervisor for a purpose other than revocation of the order or deletion of a requirement, subs.(3)(a) makes it clear that it is necessary to specify what variation is proposed. Thereafter the court, if it considers that alteration of the order could be in the interests of justice, shall cite the offender to appear before it; on varying the order the court is obliged to comply with s.245A(5) and explain the effects plainly to the offender.

If the supervisor seeks revocation of the RLO, the court if satisfied that this in the interests of justice, shall issue a citation ordering the offender to appear. Failure to appear after being duly cited will entitle the court to issue an apprehension warrant (s.245E(4)).

At the review hearing the court requires to hear both parties and is only obliged to vary the order if it is felt to be in the interests of justice. In that event the RLO can be revoked or altered by adding to, amending or deleting requirements but subject to the requirements set out in s.245A(3) that it must be completed in a 12 month period—six months in the case of a child offender.

On revocation of the RLO the court can pronounce any other disposal competent at the time the order was made but is obliged to take account of the length of time for which the RLO operated. Where dual tagging and probation orders had been imposed on the offender, the court when revoking the RLO has also to discharge the probation order (s.245G below).

Breach of restriction of liberty order

245F.—(1) If at any time when a restriction of liberty order is in force it appears—

(a) except in a case to which paragraph (b) below applies, to the court which made the order, or

(b) where a copy of the order was, under section 245A(5)(a)(ii) or 245E(7)(a) of this Act, sent to the clerk of a different court, to that different court (or, if there has been more than one such sending, the different court to which such a copy has most recently been so sent),

that the offender has failed to comply with any of the requirements of the order the court in question may issue a citation requiring the offender to appear before the it at such time as may be specified in the citation or, if it appears to that court to be appropriate, it may issue a warrant for the arrest of the offender.

(1A) The unified citation provisions apply in relation to a citation under this section as they apply in relation to a citation under section 216(3)(a) of this Act.

(2) If it is proved to the satisfaction of that court that the offender has failed without reasonable excuse to comply with any of the requirements of the order it may by order—

(a) without prejudice to the continuance in force of the order, impose a fine not exceeding level 3 on the standard scale;

(b) vary the restriction of liberty order; or

(c) revoke that order.

A fine imposed under this section in respect of a failure to comply with the requirements of a restriction of liberty order shall be deemed for the purposes of any enactment to be a sum adjudged to be paid by or in respect of a conviction or a penalty imposed on a person summarily convicted.

(4) Where a court varies a restriction of liberty order under subsection (2) above it may do so in any of the ways mentioned in paragraph (a) of section 245E(2) of this Act.

AMENDMENT

Section 245F inserted by the Crime and Punishment (Scotland) Act 1997 (c.48), s.5 (effective July 1, 1998: SI 1997/2323).

Subss.(1), (2) and (4) as amended by Criminal Justice (Scotland) Act 2003 (asp 7), Part 6, s.43. Brought into force on June 27, 2003 by the Criminal Justice (Scotland) Act 2003 (Commencement No.1) Order 2003 (SSI 2003/288 (C.14)).

Subs.(1A) inserted by Criminal Justice (Scotland) Act 2003 (asp 7), Part 8, s.60. Brought into force on October 27, 2003 by the Criminal Justice (Scotland) Act 2003 (Commencement No.3 and Revocation) Order 2003 (SSI 2003/475 (C.26)), art.2.

GENERAL NOTE

s.245F

The court's own powers to initiate breach proceedings are contained in this section. It will be noted that s.245E deals with the rights of both the offender and the monitoring supervisor to seek review of the terms of an order. Where the court has reason to believe that the offender has failed to comply with the terms of the order, it may cite him or issue an arrest warrant.

Once it is proved or admitted that a breach of a requirement has occurred, the court may impose a fine up to level 3, before resolving whether to continue or revoke the order or vary it in any of the ways specified in s.245E(2)(a) to (c). Any fine is governed by the provisions of Pt XI of the 1995 Act.

Disposal on revocation of restriction of liberty order

245G.—(1) Where the court revokes a restriction of liberty order under section 245E(2)(b) or 245F(2) of this Act, it may dispose of the offender in any way which would have been competent at the time when the order was made, but in so doing the court shall have regard to the time for which the order has been in operation.

(2) Where the court revokes a restriction of liberty order as mentioned in subsection (1) above, and the offender is, by virtue of section 245D(3) of this Act, subject to a probation order or a drug treatment and testing order or to both such orders, it shall, before disposing of the offender under subsection (1) above—

(a) where he is subject to a probation order, discharge that order;
(b) where he is subject to a drug treatment and testing order, revoke that order; and
(c) where he is subject to both such orders, discharge the probation order and revoke the drug treatment and testing order.

(3) Where the court orders a probation order discharged or a drug treatment and testing order revoked the clerk of the court shall forthwith give copies of that order to the persons mentioned in subsection (4) or, as the case may be, (5) of section 245D of this Act.

(4) Where the court orders a probation order discharged and a drug treatment and testing order revoked, the clerk of court shall forthwith give copies of that order to the persons mentioned in section 245D(6) of this Act.

AMENDMENT

Section 245G inserted by the Crime and Punishment (Scotland) Act 1997 (c.48), s.5 (effective July 1, 1998: SI 1997/2323).

Section 245G as amended by the Crime and Disorder Act 1998 (c.37), s.94 and Sch.6, para.3. Brought into force on September 30, 1998 by the Crime and Disorder Act 1998 (Commencement No.2 and Transitional Provisions) Order1998 (SI 1998/2327 (C.53)).

Subs.(2) as amended by the Antisocial Behaviour etc. (Scotland) Act 2004 (asp 8), s.144(1), Sch.4, para.5(9). Brought into force on April 4, 2005 by the Antisocial Behaviour etc. (Scotland) Act 2004 (Commencement and Savings) Order 2004 (SSI 2004/420 (C.31)).

GENERAL NOTE

s.245G

On revocation of an RLO the court can dispose of the offender's case in any way competent at the time of the imposition of the order. In cases where an RLO has been initiated in association with a probation order, the court when revoking the RLO must also discharge the probation order.

Note that when revoking an order, the court is obliged to pay heed to the time during which the order operated; it is a matter of interpretation whether this is intended to take account of the arithmetical duration of the order or its effective duration, the period during which the offender complied satisfactorily with the order.

Documentary evidence in proceedings under section 245F

245H.—(1) Evidence of the presence or absence of the offender at a particular place at a particular time may, subject to the provisions of this section, be given by the production of a document or documents bearing to be—

(a) a statement automatically produced by a device specified in regulations made under section 245C of this Act, by which the offender's whereabouts were remotely monitored; and
(b) a certificate signed by a person nominated for the purpose of this paragraph by the Secretary of State that the statement relates to the whereabouts of the offender at the dates and times shown in the statement.

(2) The statement and certificate mentioned in subsection (1) above shall, when produced at a hearing, be sufficient evidence of the facts set out in them.

(3) Neither the statement nor the certificate mentioned in subsection (1) above

shall be admissible in evidence unless a copy of both has been served on the offender prior to the hearing and, without prejudice to the foregoing, where it appears to the court that the offender has had insufficient notice of the statement or certificate, it may adjourn a hearing or make any order which it thinks appropriate in the circumstances.

AMENDMENT

Section 245H inserted by the Crime and Punishment (Scotland) Act 1997 (c.48), s.5 (effective July 1, 1998: SI 1997/2323).

Subs.(1)(b) as amended by the Antisocial Behaviour etc. (Scotland) Act 2004 (asp 8), s.144(1), Sch.4, para.5(10). Brought into force on April 4, 2005 by the Antisocial Behaviour etc. (Scotland) Act 2004 (Commencement and Savings) Order2004 (SSI 2004/420 (C.31)).

GENERAL NOTE

s.245H

This section provides for a certificated statement showing the presence or absence of the offender at a specified place on a specific occasion to be used as evidence in proceedings.

The statement, automatically generated by an approved monitoring device and certified by an authorised official, will be sufficient evidence if it has been served along with the certificate upon the offender prior to the court hearing. The court may adjourn the hearing to allow sufficient time for the offender to consider the material laid before him.

Procedure on variation or revocation of restriction of liberty order

245I. Where a court exercises any power conferred by sections 232(3A), 245E(2) or 245F(2)(b) or (c) of this Act, the clerk of the court shall forthwith give copies of the order varying or revoking the restriction of liberty order to any person responsible for monitoring the offender's compliance with that order and that person shall give a copy of the order to the offender.".

AMENDMENT

Section 245I inserted by the Crime and Punishment (Scotland) Act 1997 (c.48), s.5 (effective July 1, 1998: SI 1997/2323).

GENERAL NOTE

s.245I

At any time when the court varies or revokes an RLO or an RLO linked to a probation order, it is obliged to issue a copy of its interlocutor to the monitoring supervisor who, in turn, is responsible for ensuring that notification is served upon the offender.

Breach of certain orders: adjourning hearing and remanding in custody etc.

245J.—(1) Where a probationer or offender appears before the court in respect of his apparent failure to comply with a requirement of, as the case may be, a probation order, drug treatment and testing order, supervised attendance order, community service order or restriction of liberty order the court may, for the purpose of enabling inquiries to be made or of determining the most suitable method of dealing with him, adjourn the hearing.

(2) Where, under subsection (1) above, the court adjourns a hearing it shall remand the probationer or offender in custody or on bail or ordain him to appear at the adjourned hearing.

(3) A court shall not so adjourn a hearing for any single period exceeding four weeks or, on cause shown, eight weeks.

(4) A probationer or offender remanded under this section may appeal against the refusal of bail, or against the conditions imposed, within 24 hours of his remand.

(5) Any such appeal shall be by note of appeal presented to the High Court, who, either in court or in chambers, may after hearing the prosecutor and the appellant—

(a) review the order appealed against and either grant bail on such conditions as it thinks fit or ordain the appellant to appear at the adjourned hearing; or

(b) confirm the order.

AMENDMENT

Section 245J inserted by Criminal Justice (Scotland) Act 2003 (asp 7), Part 6, s.48. Brought into force on June 27, 2003 by the Criminal Justice (Scotland) Act 2003 (Commencement No.1) Order 2003 (SSI 2003/288 (C.14)).

GENERAL NOTE

Proceedings for breach of various sentencing orders has always been rather *ad hoc*. The present section makes it possible for courts to do what they have tended to do anyway—that is, to adjourn the hearing for up to four weeks (eight on cause shown) for inquiries to be made (a euphemism for a proof) or to determine the most suitable way to deal with the offender. The offender may be remanded in custody, "remanded" on bail (the creeping anglicisation of the language of the statute is to be regretted—elsewhere in the Act, a person is "admitted to" bail) or ordained to appear. A bail appeal is available (but not, it seems, a bail review).

Community reparation orders

Community reparation orders

245K.—(1) Where subsection (2) below applies, the court may, instead of imposing any sentence which, but for this subsection, it could impose, make a community reparation order in respect of a person ("the offender").

(2) This subsection applies where—

(a) the offender is convicted in summary proceedings of an offence;

(b) at the time when he committed the offence, he was at least 12 years old;

(c) he committed the offence by engaging to any extent in antisocial behaviour; and

(d) in relation to the local authority that would be specified in the order, the Scottish Ministers have notified the court that the authority has made arrangements that would enable an order to be complied with.

(3) For the purposes of subsection (2)(c) above, a person engages in antisocial behaviour if he—

(a) acts in a manner that causes or is likely to cause alarm or distress; or

(b) pursues a course of conduct that causes or is likely to cause alarm or distress,

to at least one person who is not of the same household as him.

(4) A community reparation order is an order—

(a) requiring the specified local authority to appoint a supervising officer for the purposes of—

(i) determining which prescribed activities the offender should undertake for the specified number of hours (being at least 10 and not exceeding 100) during the period of 12 months beginning with the day on which the order is made;

(ii) determining at what times and in which localities he should undertake those activities; and

(iii) giving the offender directions during that period to undertake activities in accordance with determinations under sub-paragraphs (i) and (ii) above; and

(b) requiring the offender, during that period, to comply with those directions.

(5) In subsection (4) above—

"prescribed activities" means activities designed—

    (a) to enable reparation to be made (whether to a particular person or to a group of persons and whether such a person, or any person in the group, has been affected by the antisocial behaviour or otherwise) by persons who have engaged in antisocial behaviour; or

    (b) to reduce the likelihood of persons engaging in such behaviour, which are of such description as the Scottish Ministers may by regulations prescribe; and

"specified" means specified in the order.

(6) The Scottish Ministers may by regulations make provision about determinations made, and directions given, by virtue of paragraph (a) of subsection (4) above.

(7) In giving directions by virtue of subsection (4)(a)(iii) above, a supervising officer shall, as far as practicable, avoid—

(a) any conflict with the offender's religious beliefs;

(b) any interference with the times at which the offender normally works (or carries out voluntary work) or attends an educational establishment.

(8) Before making a community reparation order in respect of an offender, the court shall explain to him in ordinary language—

(a) the purpose and effect of the order;

(b) the consequences of failure to comply with the order; and

(c) the powers the court has under section 245P of this Act.

(9) For the purposes of any appeal or review, a community reparation order is a sentence.

(10) Regulations under subsections (5) and (6) above shall be made by statutory instrument; and any such instrument shall be subject to annulment in pursuance of a resolution of the Scottish Parliament.

AMENDMENT

Section 245K inserted by the Antisocial Behaviour etc. (Scotland) Act 2004 (asp 8), s.120. Brought into force on October 28, 2004 by the Antisocial Behaviour etc. (Scotland) Act 2004 (Commencement and Savings) Order 2004 (SSI 2004/420 (C.31)).

DEFINITIONS

"antisocial behaviour": s.245K(3) of the 1995 Act.
"community reparation order": s.245K(4) of the 1995 Act.
"local authority": s.143(1) of the 2004 Act.
"prescribed activities": s.245K(5) of the 1995 Act.
"specified": s.245K(5) of the 1995 Act.
"the offender": s.245K(1) of the 1995 Act.

GENERAL NOTE

Community reparation order

This is a new sentencing option available in summary proceedings where the offender is at least 12 years of age and has committed the offence by engaging "to any extent" in antisocial behaviour: s.245K(2). The community reparation order requires the specified local authority to appoint a supervising order to determine which prescribed activities the offender should undertake for a certain number of hours (being at least 10 and not exceeding 100) in a period of 12 months: s.245K(4). While prescribed activities are those designed to enable reparation to be made no further statutory definition is given to such activities in the Act although the Scottish Ministers may prescribe what that is to be: s.245K(5).

Community reparation order: notification

245L. Where the court makes a community reparation order it shall intimate the making of the order to—

(a) the offender;

(b) the chief social work officer of the local authority specified in the order; and

(c) where it is not the appropriate court, the clerk of the appropriate court.

AMENDMENT

Section 245L inserted by the Antisocial Behaviour etc. (Scotland) Act 2004 (asp 8), s.120. Brought into force on October 28, 2004 by the Antisocial Behaviour etc. (Scotland) Act 2004 (Commencement and Savings) Order 2004 (SSI 2004/420 (C.31)).

DEFINITIONS

"appropriate court": s.245Q of the 1995 Act.
"community reparation order": s.245K(4) of the 1995 Act.
"local authority": s.143(1) of the 2004 Act.
"the offender": s.245K(1) of the 1995 Act.

Failure to comply with community reparation order: extension of 12 month period

245M. Subject to sections 245N(4) and 245P(2)(c) and (d) of this Act, if—

(a) a community reparation order is made in respect of an offender; and

(b) the offender fails to comply with a direction given by the supervising officer appointed by virtue of the order,

then the order shall, notwithstanding section 245K(4)(a)(i), remain in force until the offender has complied with the direction.

AMENDMENT

Section 245M inserted by the Antisocial Behaviour etc. (Scotland) Act 2004 (asp 8), s.120. Brought into force on October 28, 2004 by the Antisocial Behaviour etc. (Scotland) Act 2004 (Commencement and Savings) Order 2004 (SSI 2004/420 (C.31)).

DEFINITIONS

"community reparation order": s.245K(4) of the 1995 Act.
"the offender": s 245K(1) of the 1995 Act.

Failure to comply with community reparation order: powers of court

245N.—(1) Subsection (2) below applies where—

(a) a community reparation order is made in respect of an offender; and

(b) on information from the offender's supervising officer, it appears to the appropriate court that the offender has failed to comply with the order or any direction given under it.

(2) The court may issue—

(a) a warrant for the arrest of the offender; or

(b) a citation requiring the offender to appear before the court at such time as may be specified in the citation.

(3) The unified citation provisions shall apply in relation to a citation under this section as they apply in relation to a citation under section 216(3)(a) of this Act.

(4) If it is proved to the satisfaction of the court before which the offender is brought or appears in pursuance of subsection (2) above that the offender has failed without reasonable excuse to comply with the order or any direction given under it, the court may revoke the order and deal with the offender in any manner in which he could have been dealt with for the original offence if the order had not been made.

(5) The evidence of one witness shall, for the purposes of subsection (4) above, be sufficient evidence.

AMENDMENT

Section 245N inserted by the Antisocial Behaviour etc. (Scotland) Act 2004 (asp 8), s.120. Brought into force on October 28, 2004 by the Antisocial Behaviour etc. (Scotland) Act 2004 (Commencement and Savings) Order 2004 (SSI 2004/420 (C.31)).

DEFINITIONS

"appropriate court": s.245Q of the 1995 Act.
"community reparation order": s.245K(4) of the 1995 Act.
"the offender": s.245K(1) of the 1995 Act.

GENERAL NOTE

The failure of an offender to comply with the requirements of a community reparation order allows the court a variety of options to then deal with that offender: s.245N.

Extension, variation and revocation of order

245P.—(1) Subsection (2) below applies where a community reparation order is made in respect of an offender.

(2) On the application of the offender or the offender's supervising officer, the appropriate court may, if it appears to it that it would be in the interests of justice to do so having regard to circumstances which have arisen since the order was made—

(a) extend, in relation to the order, the period of 12 months specified in section 245K(4)(a)(i) of this Act;
(b) vary the numbers of hours specified in the order;
(c) revoke the order; or
(d) revoke the order and deal with the offender in any manner in which he could have been dealt with for the original offence if the order had not been made.

(3) If the court proposes to exercise its powers under subsection (2)(a), (b) or (d) above otherwise than on the application of the offender, it shall issue a citation requiring the offender to appear before the court at such time as may be specified in the citation and, if he fails to appear, may issue a warrant for his arrest.

(4) The unified citation provisions shall apply in relation to a citation under this section as they apply in relation to a citation under section 216(3)(a) of this Act.

AMENDMENT

Section 245P inserted by the Antisocial Behaviour etc. (Scotland) Act 2004 (asp 8), s.120. Brought into force on October 28, 2004 by the Antisocial Behaviour etc. (Scotland) Act 2004 (Commencement and Savings) Order 2004 (SSI 2004/420 (C.31)).

DEFINITIONS

"appropriate court": s.245Q of the 1995 Act.
"community reparation order": s.245K(4) of the 1995 Act.
"the offender": s.245K(1) of the 1995 Act.

GENERAL NOTE

The failure of an offender to comply with the requirements of a community reparation order allows the court (in the interests of justice in new circumstances) to vary that community reparation order in a number of different ways in order to deal with that offender: s.245P.

Sections 245L, 245N and 245P: meaning of "appropriate court"

245Q. In sections 245L, 245N and 245P of this Act, "appropriate court", in relation to a community reparation order, means the court having jurisdiction in the area of the local authority specified in the order, being a sheriff or district court according to whether the order is made by a sheriff or district court (except that, in the case where an order is made by a district court and there is no district court in that area, it means the sheriff).

AMENDMENT

Section 245Q inserted by the Antisocial Behaviour etc. (Scotland) Act 2004 (asp 8), s.120. Brought into force on October 28, 2004 by the Antisocial Behaviour etc. (Scotland) Act 2004 (Commencement and Savings) Order 2004 (SSI 2004/420 (C.31)).

DEFINITIONS

"appropriate court": s.245Q of the 1995 Act.
"community reparation order": s.245K(4) of the 1995 Act.
"local authority": s.143(1) of the 2004 Act; and "area" in relation to a local authority: s.143(2) of the 2004 Act.
"the offender": s.245K(1) of the 1995 Act.

Admonition and absolute discharge

Admonition and absolute discharge

246.—(1) A court may, if it appears to meet the justice of the case, dismiss with an admonition any person convicted by the court of any offence.

(2) Where a person is convicted on indictment of an offence (other than an offence the sentence for which is fixed by law), if it appears to the court, having regard to the circumstances including the nature of the offence and the character of the offender, that it is inexpedient to inflict punishment and that a probation order is not appropriate it may instead of sentencing him make an order discharging him absolutely.

(3) Where a person is charged before a court of summary jurisdiction with an offence (other than an offence the sentence for which is fixed by law) and the court is satisfied that he committed the offence, the court, if it is of the opinion, having regard to the circumstances including the nature of the offence and the character of the offender, that it is inexpedient to inflict punishment and that a

probation order is not appropriate may without proceeding to conviction make an order discharging him absolutely.

"court of summary jurisdiction": s.307(1).
"indictment": s.307(1).
"offence": s.307(1).
"probation order": s.307(1).

General Note

The legal effect of an absolute discharge is stipulated in s.247, below. In *McLay v Ruxton*, 1996 G.W.D. 23–1311 the Appeal Court granted an absolute discharge after allowing a motion to appeal against conviction to be made at the bar.

Effect of probation and absolute discharge

247.—(1) Subject to the following provisions of this section, a conviction of an offence for which an order is made placing the offender on probation or discharging him absolutely shall be deemed not to be a conviction for any purpose other than the purposes of the proceedings in which the order is made and of laying it before a court as a previous conviction in subsequent proceedings for another offence.

(2) Without prejudice to subsection (1) above, the conviction of an offender who is placed on probation or discharged absolutely as aforesaid shall in any event be disregarded for the purposes of any enactment which imposes any disqualification or disability upon convicted persons, or authorises or requires the imposition of any such disqualification or disability.

(3) Subsections (1) and (2) above shall not affect any right to appeal.

(4) Where a person charged with an offence has at any time previously been discharged absolutely in respect of the commission by him of an offence it shall be competent, in the proceedings for that offence, to lay before the court the order of absolute discharge in like manner as if the order were a conviction.

(5) Where an offender is discharged absolutely by a court of summary jurisdiction, he shall have the like right of appeal against the finding that he committed the offence as if that finding were a conviction.

(6) Where an offender, being not less than 16 years of age at the time of his conviction of an offence for which he is placed on probation as mentioned in subsection (1) above, is subsequently sentenced under this Act for that offence, the provisions of that subsection shall cease to apply to the conviction.

Definitions

"court of summary jurisdiction": s.307(1).
"offence": s.307(1).
"probation": s.307(1).

Disqualification

Disqualification where vehicle used to commit offence

248.—(1) Where a person is convicted of an offence (other than one triable only summarily) and the court which passes sentence is satisfied that a motor vehicle was used for the purposes of committing or facilitating the commission of that offence, the court may order him to be disqualified for such a period as the court thinks fit from holding or obtaining a licence to drive a motor vehicle granted under Part III of the Road Traffic Act 1988.

(2) A court which makes an order under subsection (1) above disqualifying a person from holding or obtaining a licence under Part III of the Road Traffic Act 1988 shall require him to produce—

(a) any such licence;

(b) any Community licence (within the meaning of that Part); and

(c) any counterpart of a licence mentioned in paragraph (a) or (b) above, held by him.

(3) Any reference in this section to facilitating the commission of an offence shall include a reference to the taking of any steps after it has been committed for the purpose of disposing of any property to which it relates or of avoiding apprehension or detection.

(4) In relation to licences, other than Community licences which came into force before 1st June 1990, the reference in subsection (2) above to the counterpart of a licence shall be disregarded.

AMENDMENT

Subs.(2) substituted, and subs.(4) as amended, by the Driving Licences (Community Driving Licences) Regulations 1996 (SI 1996/1974) (effective January 1, 1997).

DEFINITIONS

"offence": s.307(1).
"order": s.307(1).

General power to disqualify offenders

248A.—(1) Subject to subsection (2) below, the court by or before which a person is convicted of an offence may, in addition to or instead of dealing with him in any other way, order him to be disqualified from holding or obtaining a licence to drive a motor vehicle granted under Part III of the Road Traffic Act 1988 for such period as it thinks fit.

(2) Where the person is convicted of an offence for which the sentence is fixed by law, subsection (1) above shall have effect as if the words "or instead of" were omitted.

(3) Subsections (2) and (4) of section 248 of this Act shall apply for the purposes of this section as they apply for the purposes of that section.

AMENDMENT

Section 248A inserted by the Crime and Punishment (Scotland) Act 1997 (c.48), s.15 with effect from January 1, 1998 in terms of the Crime and Punishment (Scotland) Act 1977 (Commencement No. 2 and Transitional and Consequential Provisions) Order 1997 (SI 1997/2323), art.3 and Sch.1.

DEFINITIONS

"offence": s.307(1) of the 1995 Act.
"disqualified": s.98(1) of the Road Traffic Offenders Act 1988.
"motor vehicle": s.185(1) of the Road Traffic Act 1988.

GENERAL NOTE

This section, introduced at a late stage in the life of the Crime and Punishment (Scotland) Bill, gives courts or categories of courts selected by the Secretary of State, a general power of disqualification from driving as an element of sentence on conviction of any offence. This power is quite distinct from the specific provisions found in s.248 and may be used even where the offence leading to conviction was neither a road traffic contravention nor a crime involving the use of a motor vehicle in its commission. The section took effect on January 1, 1998 but only for offences committed after that date.

Section 248B of the Act, which took effect on the same date, provides for disqualification as a sentencing alternative to imprisonment in cases of fine default. It has to be said that these two provisions passed into law with little or no Parliamentary discussion.

A s.248A disqualification can be imposed as an element of any sentence including a sentence fixed by law (subs.(2)), and applies to an offender irrespective of whether or not he possesses a driving licence; subs.(3) serves to make it clear that any driving licence held by an accused will require to be produced to the court and it may now be necessary for agents to advise clients to ensure that driving licences are available at any court diet, and for agents to be ready to address the court on this aspect of sentence.

It is important to observe that this general power of disqualification may be imposed even where the original offence did not involve the use of a motor vehicle in the commission of the offence.

It remains to be seen how far, if at all, the sentencing principles, already established in relation to disqualification for Road Traffic offences, can properly apply to s.248A or s.248B disqualifications: notably where a conviction or sentence is under appeal, what mechanism, if any, exists for suspension of disqualification? It does not appear that the general provisions of ss.39 to 41 of the Road Traffic Offenders Act 1988 (c.53) can be read into ss.248A and 248B. A fuller discussion is found in the annotations to s.15 of the Crime and Punishment (Scotland) Act 1997 below.

Power to disqualify fine defaulters

248B.—(1) This section applies where the court has power to impose a period of imprisonment in default of payment of a fine, or any part or instalment of a fine.

(2) Where this section applies, the court may, instead of imposing such a period of imprisonment as is mentioned in subsection (1) above, order that where the offender is in default he shall be disqualfied from holding a licence to drive a motor vehicle granted under Part III of the Road Traffic Act 1988 for such period not exceeding twelve months as the court thinks fit.

(3) Where an order has been made under subsection (2) above in default of payment of any fine, or any part or instalment of a fine—

    (a) on payment of the fine to any person authorised to receive it, the order shall cease to have effect; and

    (b) on payment of any part of that fine to any such person, the period of disqualification to which the order relates shall be reduced (or, as the case may be, further reduced) by a number of days bearing as nearly as possible the same proportion to such period as the sum so paid bears to the amount of the fine outstanding at the commencement of that period.

(4) Subsections (2) and (4) of section 248 of this Act shall apply for the purposes of this section as they apply for the purposes of that Section.

(5) Section 19 of the Road Traffic Offenders Act 1988 (proof of disqualification in Scottish proceedings) shall apply to an order under subsection (2) above as it applies to a conviction or extract conviction.

(6) The Secretary of State may by order made by statutory instrument vary the period specified in subsection (2) above; but not such order shall be made unless a draft of the order has been laid before, and approved by a resolution of, each House of Parliament.

AMENDMENT

Section 248B inserted by the Crime and Punishment (Scotland) Act 1997 (c.48), s.15 with effect from January 1, 1998 in terms of the Crime and Punishment (Scotland) Act 1997 (Commencement No. 2 and Transitional and Consequential Provisions) Order 1997 (SI 1997/2323), art.3 and Sch.1.

DEFINITIONS

"imprisonment": s.307(1) of the 1995 Act.

"fine": s.307(1).
"extract conviction": s.307(1) above.

Application of sections 248A and 248B

248C.—(1) The Secretary of State may by order prescribe which courts, or class or classes of courts, may make orders under section 248A or 248B of this Act and, without prejudice to that generality, in relation to district courts an order under this subsection may make provision as respects such courts by reference to whether the court is constituted by a stipendiary magistrate or by one or more justices.

(2) An order made under subsection (1) above shall be made by statutory instrument and any such instrument shall be subject to annulment in pursuance of a resolution of either House of Parliament.

(3) Where an order has been made under subsection (1) above, section 248(1) of this Act shall not apply as respects any court, or class or classes of court prescribed by the order.

AMENDMENT

Section 248C inserted by the Crime and Punishment (Scotland) Act 1997 (c.48), s.15 with effect from October 20, 1997 in terms of the Crime and Punishment (Scotland) Act 1997 (Commencement No. 2 and Transitional and Consequential Provisions) Order 1997 (SI 1997/2323), art.3 and Sch.1.

GENERAL NOTE

Section 248C was brought into force on October 20, 1997 and empowers the Secretary of State to make orders to prescribe the particular courts, or categories of courts, which will ultimately have power to impose driving disqualification as a penalty on conviction of any offence (s.248A) or as an alternative to imprisonment following fine default (s.248B). The main provisions came into effect on January 1, 1998.

The purpose of this section, introduced at a late stage to the Bill, is to make disqualification from driving available as a punishment for a broad range of offences, including fine default. The majority of s.15 is inserted into the 1995 Procedure Act as ss.248A, 248B and 248C and to s.252, with only a small addition (subs.(3)) to the Proceeds of Crime (Scotland) Act 1995. Despite, or perhaps because of, the brevity of the draftsmanship, the mechanics of this new legislation are by no means clear and much depends upon the extent to which the provisions of the Road Traffic Offenders Act 1988 are held to apply to it.

Some concern was expressed during debate of this provision that the court should not impose a s.248 disqualification until suitability reports had first been considered; while social enquiry reports would usually have been sought before the court could consider imprisonment, such reports are not generally obtained in respect of fine defaulters who can now be disqualified under s.248B, as an alternative to imprisonment, for fine default. The Lord Advocate indicated that the new disqualification provisions would be tested by a number of pilot schemes in both urban and rural areas before consideration is given to their more widespread introduction. (*Hansard*, H.L., March 19, 1997, col. 942).

Compensation

Compensation order against convicted person

249.—(1) Subject to subsections (2) and (4) below, where a person is convicted of an offence the court, instead of or in addition to dealing with him in any other way, may make an order (in this Part of this Act referred to as "a compensation order") requiring him to pay compensation for any personal injury, loss or damage caused, whether directly or indirectly, by the acts which constituted the offence.

(2) It shall not be competent for a court to make a compensation order—

(a) where, under section 246(2) of this Act, it makes an order discharging him absolutely;

(b) where, under section 228 of this Act, it makes a probation order; or

(c) at the same time as, under section 202 of this Act, it defers sentence.

(3) Where, in the case of an offence involving dishonest appropriation, or the unlawful taking and using of property or a contravention of section 178(1) of the Road Traffic Act 1988 (taking motor vehicle without authority etc.) the property is recovered, but has been damaged while out of the owner's possession, that damage, however and by whomsoever it was in fact caused, shall be treated for the purposes of subsection (1) above as having been caused by the acts which constituted the offence.

(4) No compensation order shall be made in respect of—

(a) loss suffered in consequence of the death of any person; or

(b) injury, loss or damage due to an accident arising out of the presence of a motor vehicle on a road, except such damage as is treated, by virtue of subsection (3) above, as having been caused by the convicted person's acts.

(5) In determining whether to make a compensation order against any person, and in determining the amount to be paid by any person under such order, the court shall take into consideration his means so far as known to the court.

(6) For the purposes of subsection (5) above, in assessing the means of a person who is serving, or is to serve, a period of imprisonment or detention, no account shall be taken of earnings contingent upon his obtaining employment after release.

(7) In solemn proceedings there shall be no limit on the amount which may be awarded under a compensation order.

(8) In summary proceedings—

(a) a sheriff, or a stipendiary magistrate appointed under section 5 of the District Courts (Scotland) Act 1975, shall have power to make a compensation order awarding in respect of each offence an amount not exceeding the prescribed sum;

(b) a judge of a district court (other than such stipendiary magistrate) shall have power to make a compensation order awarding in respect of each offence an amount not exceeding level 4 on the standard scale.

(9) Payment of any amount under a compensation order shall be made to the clerk of the court who shall account for the amount to the person entitled thereto.

(10) Only the court shall have power to enforce a compensation order.

DEFINITIONS

"compensation order": s.249(1).
"offence": s.307(1).
"probation order": s.307(1).
"prescribed sum": s.225(8)
"standard scale": s.225(1).

GENERAL NOTE

Compensation orders have probably not been sought for as many offences as they might have but that may merely reflect the impecunious state of most convicted people in Scotland. Nevertheless the law to date has been clarified by several decisions: in *Stewart v H.M. Advocate*, 1982 S.C.C.R. 203 it was held on appeal that an order made in respect of "inconvenience suffered" was not open to criticism.

In *Carmichael v Siddique*, 1985 S.C.C.R. 145 a sheriff rejected an argument that a compensation order was competent and appropriate only where the legal position was clear and bereft of complexities and the damage was capable of precise valuation and was not great. Such an argument has not, apparently, been put forward again. In *Collins v Lowe*, 1990 S.C.C.R. 605 it was held on appeal that it was competent to make a compensation order in addition to custodial sentences, an approach followed in *Moses v MacDonald*, 1996 G.W.D. 1–62 where compensation was fixed to cover a vehicle insurance excess and other costs in addition to a maximum custodial sentence. In *Robertson v Lees*, 1992 S.C.C.R. 545 the Appeal Court observed that the fact that the accused was a first offender was not a relevant factor when setting the amount of compensation: equally it has been held to be irrelevant that the complainer was insured (see *Ely v Donnelly*, 1996 S.C.C.R. 537 which also holds that the guidelines relating to the period of time allowable for repayment of fines, have no bearing upon repayment of compensation orders). See also *Galbraith v Gilchrist*, 2001 G.W.D. 31–1231 where a £250 fine and £500 compensation order was imposed payable at the rate of £5 weekly; the fine was reduced to £150 with an order for £350 solely having regard to the excessive time needed for repayment.

In *Sullivan v McLeod*, 1998 S.L.T. 552, the construction of "at the same time" in subs.(2)(c) was raised: S had been convicted on a summary complaint containing two charges and a deferred sentence was imposed on one charge, a compensation order on the other. While observing that such a disposal would only rarely be appropriate, the Appeal Court held that all that subs.(2)(c) sought to prevent was the imposition of both a deferment of sentence and a compensation order for the same offence. Where a number of offences appeared on the same complaint, separate disposals could be considered in relation to each charge but *no cumulo* sentence could incorporate both a deferred sentence and a compensation order.

Compensation cannot be awarded simply for causing a complainer fear and alarm (see *Smillie v Wilson*, 1990 S.L.T. 582, *Simpson v Carmichael*, 1996 G.W.D. 32–1916 and *Armit v Ruxton*, 1998 G.W.D. 26–1305) nor for racial harassment (see *Brown v Laing*, 2004 S.L.T. 646; 2004 S.C.C.R. 132), there must be loss, damage or injury. It is not necessary however for the libel to include an allegation of injury before a compensation order can be imposed; it was sufficient that the facts narrated (if not challenged in any plea), or the facts held as proved after trial, included mention of injury. See *Campbell v Stott*, 2001 S.L.T. 112; 2001 S.C.C.R. 10. By the same token compensation cannot be awarded to a group or individual unconnected with the events prompting a compensation award; in *H.M. Advocate v Nelson*, 1996 S.L.T. 1073 the Crown successfully appealed against a compensation award to Victim Support, where that organisation had no involvement in the incidents libelled, the award being quashed as incompetent. Imposition of a compensation order by the court may present practical difficulties should the Crown elect to appeal a sentence as unduly lenient; see *H.M. Advocate v Jamieson*, 1997 S.L.T. 955, discussed at para.A4–462.1 above.

In *Heafey v Craigen*, 2001 G.W.D. 16–615 a compensation order of £200 had been imposed. An appeal against sentence was allowed on the basis that the appellant had not been given the opportunity to dispute the valuation or been informed that the compensation might be ordered. It was observed, while not wishing to lay down a general rule, that it appeared that at least in many cases where there was a plea of guilty by letter or the accused was not present, it might be right to continue the matter if compensation was contemplated given potential disputes about the valuation of damages and circumstances where it might be proper to ask whether a complainer should receive compensation. See also *Shaw v Donnelly*, 2002 S.C.C.R. 805 where a compensation order was imposed without sufficient enquiry into the accuracy of a repair estimate, or any opportunity to challenge same. Similar issues of assessing compensation for damage to a car arose in *Grant v Griffiths*, 2004 S.C.C.R. 136, where the court also paid heed to the extent to which the complainer had provoked the criminal conduct.

Questions of causation must be examined closely, especially from the accused's point of view, for in *Nazir v Normand*, 1994 S.C.C.R. 265 the appellant caused and permitted another to drive an uninsured car and the appellant's appeal against a consequential compensation order was refused.

Finally, Parliament has not given the court power to make a compensation order where the impact of an offender's behaviour falls short of the infliction of personal injury: *Brown v Laing*, 2004 S.L.T. 647.

Compensation orders: supplementary provisions

250.—(1) Where a court considers that in respect of an offence it would be appropriate to impose a fine and to make a compensation order but the convicted person has insufficient means to pay both an appropriate fine and an appropriate amount in compensation the court should prefer a compensation order.

(2) Where a convicted person has both been fined and had a compensation order made against him in respect of the same offence or different offences in the same proceedings, a payment by the convicted person shall first be applied in satisfaction of the compensation order.

(3) For the purposes of any appeal or review, a compensation order is a sentence.

(4) Where a compensation order has been made against a person, a payment made to the court in respect of the order shall be retained until the determination of any appeal in relation to the order.

DEFINITIONS

"compensation order": s.249(1).
"offence": s.307(1).

GENERAL NOTE

There are, having regard to subs.(3), several reported cases in which a compensation order has been appealed. For example, in *Brown v Normand*, 1988 S.C.C.R. 229 a sentence of a fine and a compensation order was appealed on the ground that the sentence was excessive and it was allowed. Appeals were similarly allowed in *Smillie v Wilson*, 1990 S.C.C.R. 133, *Hughes v Brown*, 1990 G.W.D. 13–670, *Crawford v McGlennan*, 1990 G.W.D 21–1170, *McMahon v Hamilton*, 1990 G.W.D. 37–2124, *Wilson v Brown*, 1992 G.W.D. 6–288, *Currie v Webster*, 1992 G.W.D. 13–722 and *Clark v O'Brien*, 1995 G.W.D. 20–1130. Such appeals were refused in *McPhail v Hamilton*, 1991 G.W.D. 24–1375 and *Barclay v Douglas*, 1994 G.W.D. 1–37.

Review of compensation order

251.—(1) Without prejudice to the power contained in section 213 of this Act, (as applied by section 252 of this Act), at any time before a compensation order has been complied with or fully complied with, the court, on the application of the person against whom the compensation order was made, may discharge the compensation order or reduce the amount that remains to be paid if it appears to the court that—

(a) the injury, loss or damage in respect of which the compensation order was made has been held in civil proceedings to be less than it was taken to be for the purposes of the compensation order; or

(b) that property the loss of which is reflected in the compensation order has been recovered.

(2) In subsection (1) above "the court" means—

(a) in a case where, as respects the compensation order, a transfer of fine order under section 222 of this Act (as applied by the said section 252) is effective and the court by which the compensation order is enforceable is in terms of the transfer of fine order a court of summary jurisdiction in Scotland, that court; or

(b) in any other case, the court which made the compensation order or, where that court was the High Court, by which the order was first enforceable.

DEFINITIONS

"compensation order": s.249(1).
"court": s.251(2).

Enforcement of compensation orders: application of provisions relating to fines

252.—(1) The provisions of this Act specified in subsection (2) below shall, subject to any necessary modifications and to the qualifications mentioned in that subsection, apply in relation to compensation orders as they apply in relation to fines; and section 91 of the Magistrates' Courts Act 1980 and article 96 of the Magistrates' Courts (Northern Ireland) Order 1981 shall be construed accordingly.

(2) The provisions mentioned in subsection (1) above are—

section 211(3), (4) and (7) to (9) (enforcement of fines);

section 212 (fines in summary proceedings);

section 213 (power to remit fines), with the omission of the words "or (4)" in subsection (2) of that section;

section 214 (time for payment) with the omission of—

(a) the words from "unless" to "its decision" in subsection (4); and

(b) subsection (5);

section 215 (further time for payment);

section 216 (reasons for default);

section 217 (supervision pending payment of fine);

section 218 (supplementary provisions), except that subsection (1) of that section shall not apply in relation to compensation orders made in solemn proceedings;

subject to subsection (3) below, section 219(1)(b), (2), (3), (5), (6) and (8) (maximum period of imprisonment for non-payment of fine);

section 220 (payment of fine in part by prisoner);

section 221 (recovery by civil diligence);

section 222 (transfer of fine orders);

section 223 (action of clerk of court on transfer of fine order);

section 224 (discharge from imprisonment to be specified); and

section 248B (driving disqualification for fine defaulters) so far as it relates to the power conferred by section 219(1)(b).

(3) In the application of the provisions of section 219 of this Act mentioned in subsection (2) above for the purposes of subsection (1) above—

(a) a court may impose imprisonment in respect of a fine and decline to impose imprisonment in respect of a compensation order but not vice versa; and

(b) where a court imposes imprisonment both in respect of a fine and of a compensation order the amounts in respect of which imprisonment is imposed shall, for the purposes of subsection (2) of the said section 219, be aggregated.

AMENDMENTS

Subs. (2) amended by the Crime and Punishment (Scotland) Act 1997 (c. 48) s.15(2) with effect from January 1, 1998 in terms of the Crime and Punishment (Scotland) Act 1997 (Commencement No. 2 and Transitional and Consequential Provisions) Order 1997 (S.I. 1997 No. 2323) art. 4 and Sched. 2.

Subs. (2) inserted by the above provisions.

DEFINITION

"fines": s.307(1).

Effect of compensation order on subsequent award of damages in civil proceedings

253.—(1) This section shall have effect where a compensation order or a service compensation order or award has been made in favour of any person in respect of any injury, loss or damage and a claim by him in civil proceedings for damages in respect thereof subsequently falls to be determined.

(2) The damages in the civil proceedings shall be assessed without regard to the order or award; but where the whole or part of the amount awarded by the order or award has been paid, the damages awarded in the civil proceedings shall be restricted to the amount (if any) by which, as so assessed, they exceed the amount paid under the order or award.

(3) Where the whole or part of the amount awarded by the order or award remains unpaid and damages are awarded in a judgment in the civil proceedings, then, unless the person against whom the order or award was made has ceased to be liable to pay the amount unpaid (whether in consequence of an appeal, or of his imprisonment for default or otherwise), the court shall direct that the judgment—

(a) if it is for an amount not exceeding the amount unpaid under the order or award, shall not be enforced; or

(b) if it is for an amount exceeding the amount unpaid under the order or award, shall not be enforced except to the extent that it exceeds the amount unpaid,

without the leave of the court.

(4) In this section a "service compensation order or award" means—

(a) an order requiring the payment of compensation under paragraph 11 of—

(i) Schedule 5A to the Army Act 1955;

(ii) Schedule 5A to the Air Force Act 1955; or

(iii) Schedule 4A to the Naval Discipline Act 1957; or

(b) an award of stoppages payable by way of compensation under any of those Acts.

DEFINITIONS

"compensation orders": s.249(1).
"order": s.307(1).
"service compensation order": s.253(4).

GENERAL NOTE

Following *Goodhall v. Carmichael*, 1984 S.C.C.R. 247 it is clear that credible though uncorroborated evidence is sufficient to settle the value of the loss to be compensated, a practice that is now consistent with the civil law of evidence. The appeal by Goodhall was dismissed without Opinions being delivered. However, in an article following that appeal it was said that Lord Wheatley had commented during the appeal that "the whole point of compensation orders was to save victims the need to go to the civil courts": C.J. Docherty and G. Maher, "Corroboration and Compensation Orders", 1984 S.L.T. (News) 125 at p.126.

Forfeiture

Search warrant for forfeited articles

254. Where a court has made an order for the forfeiture of an article, the court or any justice may, if satisfied on information on oath—

(a) that there is reasonable cause to believe that the article is to be found in any place or premises; and

(b) that admission to the place or premises has been refused or that a refusal of such admission is apprehended,

issue a warrant of search which may be executed according to law.

PART XII

EVIDENCE

Special capacity

Special capacity

255. Where an offence is alleged to be committed in any special capacity, as by the holder of a licence, master of a vessel, occupier of a house, or the like, the fact that the accused possesses the qualification necessary to the commission of the offence shall, unless challenged—

(a) in the case of proceedings on indictment, by giving notice of a preliminary objection in accordance with section 71(2) or 72(6)(b)(i) of this Act; or

(b) in summary proceedings, by preliminary objection before his plea is recorded,

be held as admitted.

AMENDMENT

Subs.(a) as amended by the Criminal Procedure (Amendment) (Scotland) Act 2004 (asp 5), s.25 and Sch.1, para.38. Brought into force on February 1, 2005 by the Criminal Procedure (Amendment) (Scotland) Act 2004 (Commencement, Transitional Provisions and Savings) Order 2004 (SSI 2004/ 405 (C.28)), art.2.

DEFINITIONS

"indictment": s.307(1).
"offence": s.307(1).

GENERAL NOTE

This section relates both to solemn and summary procedure. A special capacity is a capacity which is special to the accused and is necessary to the commission of the offence.

In order to take advantage of this evidential concession, a prosecutor has to give notice in the libel of the capacity upon which he intends to found. Failure to do so will compel the prosecution to lead sufficient evidence to establish that the accused did possess the capacity essential to the commission of the offence. Furthermore, if the Crown libels a special capacity and then proceeds to conduct its case by leading evidence of the fact, it risks being held to have waived the benefit of the presumption (*Wimpey Homes Holdings v Lees*, 1993 S.L.T. 564; 1991 S.C.C.R. 447; *Smith v Ross*, 1937 J.C. 65). Note that production of an extract conviction in support of a charge of driving while disqualified does not constitute a waiver of the presumption by the Crown (*Paton v Lees*, 1992 S.C.C.R. 212).

A special capacity is not implied in any charge so while no express formula of words is required, it must be patent that the accused was acting in that capacity at the time of the offence (*Ross v Simpson*, 1994 S.C.C.R. 847).

Any denial of a special capacity must be stated at the first calling of a summary complaint (s.144(4)) and will only be permitted at future diets on cause shown (s.144(5)): in solemn proceedings s.72(1)(b)(iii) applies rather untidily to both sheriff and jury and High Court proceedings. (It will be remembered that first diets are mandatory in the case of sheriff and jury trials; while preliminary diets were once optional in High Court cases—such a diet is essential to intimate a challenge under s.72(1)(b)(iii).)

Examples of special capacity are: being subject to bail conditions in terms of the Bail etc. (Scotland) Act 1980 and, now, in terms of s.27(4) of the 1996 Act as amended, being subject of bail conditions imposed after July 4, 1996; being a common prostitute (*Allan v McGraw*, 1986 S.C.C.R. 257); being a known thief as defined in s.58 of the Civic Government (Scotland) Act 1982 (c.45) (*Newlands v MacPhail*, 1991 S.C.C.R. 88); being a disqualified driver (*Paton v Lees*, cited above); ownership of a vessel (*Thomas W. Ward Ltd v Waugh*, 1934 J.C. 13); and in certain circumstances, being the parent of a child (*Ross v Simpson*, 1994 S.C.C.R. 847). It is submitted that ss.233 and 241 above which relate to offences committed at placements by those subject to probation or community service orders equally create categories of special capacity as well as being aggravated offences. See *McClory v MacKinnon*, 1996 S.C.C.R. 367 in relation to the construction of "occupier".

Proof of age

255A. Where the age of any person is specified in an indictment or complaint, it shall, unless challenged—

(a) in the case of proceedings on indictment by giving notice of a preliminary objection in accordance with section 71(2) or 72(6)(b)(i) of this Act; or

(b) in summary proceedings—

    (i) by preliminary objection before the plea of the accused is recorded; or

    (ii) by objection at such later time as the court may in special circumstances allow,

be held as admitted.

AMENDMENT

Section 255A inserted by the Crime and Punishment (Scotland) Act 1997 (c.48) s.27 with effect from August 1, 1997 by the Crime and Punishment (Scotland) Act 1997 (Commencement and Transitional Provisions) Order 1997 (SI 1997/1712), art.3.

Subs.(a) as amended by the Criminal Procedure (Amendment) (Scotland) Act 2004 (asp 5), s.25 and Sch.1, para.39. Brought into force on February 1, 2005 by the Criminal Procedure (Amendment) (Scotland) Act 2004 (Commencement, Transitional Provisions and Savings) Order 2004 (SSI 2004/405 (C.28)), art.2.

DEFINITIONS

"complaint": s.307(1) of the 1995 Act.
"indictment": s.307(1) of the 1995 Act.

GENERAL NOTE

This provision was introduced into the 1997 Act at a relatively late stage and would apply to witness particulars in cases where the age of a witness is a necessary element of the offence, notably the broad range of sexual offences now contained in Part I of the Criminal Law (Consolidation) (Scotland) Act 1995, and in the Licensing (Scotland) Act 1976. This provision is sufficiently broadly drafted to apply to circumstances where the libel indicates the age of the victim as an aggravating factor, for example in assaults or housebreakings, as well as where the age of the accused is a necessary element of the offence, as in the Firearms Act 1968 s.22 (acquisition and possession of firearms by minors).

It may be that specification of a witness's age in the list of witnesses on an indictment could create a rebuttable presumption. Any objection to specification of the age of a victim, witness or accused must be specified at a preliminary (or first) diet in solemn proceedings, or, in summary proceedings, by preliminary objection prior to tendering any plea (s.144(4) of the 1995 Act).

Agreed evidence

Agreements and admissions as to evidence

256.—(1) In any trial it shall not be necessary for the accused or for the prosecutor—

(a) to prove any fact which is admitted by the other; or

(b) to prove any document, the terms and application of which are not in dispute between them,

and, without prejudice to paragraph 1 of Schedule 8 to this Act, copies of any documents may, by agreement of the parties, be accepted as equivalent to the originals.

(2) For the purposes of subsection (1) above, any admission or agreement shall be made by lodging with the clerk of court a minute in that behalf signed—

(a) in the case of an admission, by the party making the admission or, if that party is the accused and he is legally represented, by his counsel or solicitor; and

(b) in the case of an agreement, by the prosecutor and the accused or, if he is legally represented, his counsel or solicitor.

(3) Where a minute has been signed and lodged as aforesaid, any facts and documents admitted or agreed thereby shall be deemed to have been duly proved.

DEFINITIONS

Facts once agreed in the minute are established.

"prosecutor": s.307(1).
"trial": s.307(1).

GENERAL NOTE

This section applies to both solemn and summary procedure and provides for the lodging of Minutes of Agreement or Minutes of Admissions describing facts accepted as established in the proceedings. Documentary evidence or copies thereof can be admitted in this way; where such evidence is not formally agreed, or is not agreed with sufficient celerity, then recourse can be had to the provisions of s.258 which permits service of a statement of what is felt to be uncontroversial evidence upon other parties or, alternatively, the use of the procedures for setting up documentary evidence contained in Sch.8 (this preserves the terms of Sch.3 of the Prisoners and Criminal Proceedings (Scotland) Act 1993 (c.9)).

It will be recalled that there is no timescale stipulated for agreement of evidence by Minutes of Agreement or Admission and, indeed, these can be prepared and lodged at any point in proceedings before evidence is closed; by contrast s.258 demands a response from the other party in seven days to any statement of facts served validly and is only available prior for use more than 14 days before trial.

Duty to seek agreement of evidence

257.—(1) Subject to subsection (2) below, the prosecutor and the accused (or each of the accused if more than one) shall each identify any facts which are facts—

(a) which he would, apart from this section, be seeking to prove;

(b) which he considers unlikely to be disputed by the other party (or by any of the other parties); and

(c) in proof of which he does not wish to lead oral evidence,

and shall, without prejudice to section 258 of this Act, take all reasonable steps to secure the agreement of the other party (or each of the other parties) to them; and the other party (or each of the other parties) shall take all reasonable steps to reach such agreement.

(2) Subsection (1) above shall not apply in relation to proceedings as respects which the accused (or any of the accused if more than one) is not legally represented.

(3) The duty under subsection (1) above applies—

(a) in relation to proceedings on indictment, from the date of service of the indictment until the swearing of the jury or, where intimation is given under section 76 of this Act, the date of that intimation; and

(b) in relation to summary proceedings, from the date on which the accused pleads not guilty until the swearing of the first witness or, where the accused tenders a plea of guilty at any time before the first witness is sworn, the date when he does so.

(4) Without prejudice to subsection (3) above, in the case of proceedings in the High Court, the parties to the proceedings shall, in complying with the duty under subsection (1) above, seek to ensure that the facts to be identified, and the

steps to be taken in relation to those facts, by that subsection are identified and taken before the preliminary hearing.

AMENDMENT

Subs.(4) inserted by the Criminal Procedure (Amendment) (Scotland) Act 2004 (asp 5), s.25 and Sch.1, para.40. Brought into force on February 1, 2005 by the Criminal Procedure (Amendment) (Scotland) Act 2004 (Commencement, Transitional Provisions and Savings) Order 2004 (SSI 2004/ 405 (C.28)), art.2.

DEFINITIONS

"indictment": s.307(1).
"prosecutor": s.307(1).

GENERAL NOTE

This section applies to both solemn and summary proceedings. The purpose of this, and the following section, is to identify evidence which is capable of being received without the need for its introduction by parole evidence and the need for witnesses to attend court. Prior to the introduction of these provisions there was no onus upon any party to identify, or agree, formal or uncontroversial evidence and while a duty is now placed on parties to consider such material, there is no sanction for failure to do so. The prosecutor and, only where he is legally represented the accused, are each required to identify factual evidence felt to be capable of agreement and to take all reasonable steps to agree these matters before trial.

Section 256 provides a mechanism for agreement of evidence, or for the admission of facts by one party; s.258 enacts a procedure for service of statements of fact upon other parties. Subsection (3) provides two different timescales during which the duties imposed on parties persist: in solemn proceedings this is the period from service of the indictment until the commencement of trial (see s.64(9)) or, in the case of accelerated pleas, until the accused gives notice in writing of a plea which is accepted by the Crown (see s.76(1)); in summary proceedings, the period from the date of the plea being recorded (s.146(1)) until trial begins (s.147(4)) or a plea of guilty is intimated.

Uncontroversial evidence

258.—(1) This section applies where, in any criminal proceedings, a party (in this section referred to as "the first party") considers that facts which that party would otherwise be seeking to prove are unlikely to be disputed by the other parties to the proceedings.

(2) Where this section applies, the first party may prepare and sign a statement—

(a) specifying the facts concerned; or

(b) referring to such facts as set out in a document annexed to the statement,

and shall, not less than 14 days before the relevant diet, serve a copy of the statement and any such document on every other party.

(2A) In subsection (2) above, "the relevant diet" means—

(a) in the case of proceedings in the High Court, the preliminary hearing;

(b) in any other case, the trial diet.

(3) Unless any other party serves on the first party, not more than seven days after the date of service of the copy on him under subsection (2) above or by such later time as the court may in special circumstances allow, a notice that he challenges any fact specified or referred to in the statement, the facts so specified or referred to shall be deemed to have been conclusively proved.

(4) Where a notice is served under subsection (3) above, the facts specified or referred to in the statement shall be deemed to have been conclusively proved only in so far as unchallenged in the notice.

(4A) Where a notice is served under subsection (3) above in any solemn proceedings, the court may, on the application of any party to the proceedings made not less than 48 hours before the relevant diet, direct that any challenge in the notice to any fact is to be disregarded for the purposes of subsection (4) above if the court considers the challenge to be unjustified.

(4B) In subsection (4A) above, "the relevant diet" means—

(a) in proceedings in the High Court, the preliminary hearing; and

(b) in proceedings in the sheriff court, the first diet.

(4C) In proceedings in the High Court, the Court may, on cause shown, allow an application under subsection (4A) above to be made after the time limit specified in that subsection.

(5) Subsections (3) and (4) above shall not preclude a party from leading evidence of circumstances relevant to, or other evidence in explanation of, any fact specified or referred to in the statement.

(6) Notwithstanding subsections (3) and (4) above, the court—

(a) may, on the application of any party, where it is satisfied that there are special circumstances; and

(b) shall, on the joint application of all the parties,

direct that the presumptions in those subsections shall not apply in relation to such fact specified or referred to in the statement as is specified in the direction.

(7) An application under subsection (6) above may be made at any time after the commencement of the trial and before the commencement of the prosecutor's address to the court on the evidence.

(8) Where the court makes a direction under subsection (6) above it shall, unless all the parties otherwise agree, adjourn the trial and may, without prejudice to section 268 of this Act, permit any party to lead evidence as to any such fact as is specified in the direction, notwithstanding that a witness or production concerned is not included in any list lodged by the parties and that the notice required by sections 67(5) and 78(4) of this Act has not been given.

(9) A copy of a statement or a notice required, under this section, to be served on any party shall be served in such manner as may be prescribed by Act of Adjournal; and a written execution purporting to be signed by the person who served such copy or notice together with, where appropriate, the relevant post office receipt shall be sufficient evidence of such service.

AMENDMENT

Subss.(4A)–(4C) inserted, by the Criminal Procedure (Amendment) (Scotland) Act 2004 (asp 5), s.16. Subs.(2) as amended and subs.(2A) inserted by s.25 and Sch.1, para.41 of the 2004 Act. Brought into force on February 1, 2005 by the Criminal Procedure (Amendment) (Scotland) Act 2004 (Commencement, Transitional Provisions and Savings) Order 2004 (SSI 2004/405 (C.28)), art.2.

DEFINITIONS

"diet": s.307(1).
"prosecutor": s.307(1).
"the relevant diet": s.258(2A) and (4B).

GENERAL NOTE

This section applies to solemn and summary proceedings. It introduces a new procedure for evidence, which a party regards as "unlikely to be disputed", to be held as admitted after a statement of facts has been served in conformity to subs.(2) and not challenged by its recipient as provided by subs.(3). At best this provision can be seen as a further means of securing agreement of evidence but, on a cautionary note, great vigilance will have to be exercised by parties to ensure that any evidence which would be disputed does not slip through without challenge. Subsection (3) does permit a notice of challenge to be tendered late but its acceptance by the court is far from automatic.

This procedure was introduced in the Criminal Justice (Scotland) Act 1995 (c.20) and followed a recommendation by the Scottish Law Commission Report No. 137 *"Evidence: Report on Documentary Evidence and Proof of Undisputed Facts in Criminal Proceedings"* of such a procedure for use by the prosecution; it will be observed that s.258 is available for use by both prosecution and defence.

It will be noted that there seems to be no limit on the number of s.258 notices which can be served more than 14 days prior to trial, and that subs.(5) still enables the leading of evidence in clarification or explanation of the statement of facts. Subsection (6) operates as a saving provision to enable the court, or the parties, during the trial to override the terms of a statement of facts which is not in accordance with the evidence, and where the court exercises these powers, to adjourn the trial to permit parties to lead evidence struck at by that operation (see subs.(7)). Note that such evidence can be received in solemn proceedings even when it has not been specified on Crown or defence lists of witnesses or productions.

Rules 21.1 and 21.2 in the 1996 Act of Adjournal specify that Forms 21.1–A and 21.2 are to be used to introduce a statement of fact or challenge same. Form 21.1–B provides a docquet for documents referred to in a statement of facts. The Act is silent as to how statements of fact, modified or unmodified by challenge, are to be introduced into the record of proceedings; they may be treated in the same way as a Minute of Agreement, being read to a jury by the clerk of court, or received by the judge in summary cases but this is not settled. It is apparent that parties serving statements of fact will need to preserve, and be able to produce to the court a copy notice and completed execution of service.

Hearsay

Exceptions to the rule that hearsay evidence is inadmissible

259.—(1) Subject to the following provisions of this section, evidence of a statement made by a person otherwise than while giving oral evidence in court in criminal proceedings shall be admissible in those proceedings as evidence of any matter contained in the statement where the judge is satisfied—

(a) that the person who made the statement will not give evidence in the proceedings of such matter for any of the reasons mentioned in subsection (2) below;

(b) that evidence of the matter would be admissible in the proceedings if that person gave direct oral evidence of it;

(c) that the person who made the statement would have been, at the time the statement was made, a competent witness in such proceedings; and

(d) that there is evidence which would entitle a jury properly directed, or in summary proceedings would entitle the judge, to find that the statement was made and that either—

    (i) it is contained in a document; or

    (ii) a person who gave oral evidence in the proceedings as to the statement has direct personal knowledge of the making of the statement.

(2) The reasons referred to in paragraph (a) of subsection (1) above are that the person who made the statement—

(a) is dead or is, by reason of his bodily or mental condition, unfit or unable to give evidence in any competent manner;

(b) is named and otherwise sufficiently identified, but is outwith the United Kingdom and it is not reasonably practicable to secure his attendance at the trial or to obtain his evidence in any other competent manner;

(c) is named and otherwise sufficiently identified, but cannot be found and all reasonable steps which, in the circumstances, could have been taken to find him have been so taken;

(d) having been authorised to do so by virtue of a ruling of the court in the proceedings that he is entitled to refuse to give evidence in connection with the subject matter of the statement on the grounds that such evidence might incriminate him, refuses to give such evidence; or

(e) is called as a witness and either—
    (i) refuses to take the oath or affirmation; or
    (ii) having been sworn as a witness and directed by the judge to give evidence in connection with the subject matter of the statement refuses to do so,

and in the application of this paragraph to a child, the reference to a witness refusing to take the oath or affirmation or, as the case may be, to having been sworn shall be construed as a reference to a child who has refused to accept an admonition to tell the truth or, having been so admonished, refuses to give evidence as mentioned above.

(3) Evidence of a statement shall not be admissible by virtue of subsection (1) above where the judge is satisfied that the occurrence of any of the circumstances mentioned in paragraphs (a) to (e) of subsection (2) above, by virtue of which the statement would otherwise be admissible, is caused by—

(a) the person in support of whose case the evidence would be given; or

(b) any other person acting on his behalf,

for the purpose of securing that the person who made the statement does not give evidence for the purposes of the proceedings either at all or in connection with the subject matter of the statement.

(4) Where in any proceedings evidence of a statement made by any person is admitted by reference to any of the reasons mentioned in paragraphs (a) to (c) and (e)(i) of subsection (2) above—

(a) any evidence which, if that person had given evidence in connection with the subject matter of the statement, would have been admissible as relevant to his credibility as a witness shall be admissible for that purpose in those proceedings;

(b) evidence may be given of any matter which, if that person had given evidence in connection with the subject matter of the statement, could have been put to him in cross-examination as relevant to his credibility as a witness but of which evidence could not have been adduced by the cross-examining party; and

(c) evidence tending to prove that that person, whether before or after making the statement, made in whatever manner some other statement which is inconsistent with it shall be admissible for the purpose of showing that he has contradicted himself.

(5) Subject to subsection (6) below, where a party intends to apply to have evidence of a statement admitted by virtue of subsection (1) above he shall, by the relevant time, give notice in writing of—

(a) that fact;

(b) the witnesses and productions to be adduced in connection with such evidence; and

(c) such other matters as may be prescribed by Act of Adjournal,

to every other party to the proceedings and, for the purposes of this subsection, such evidence may be led notwithstanding that a witness or production concerned is not included in any list lodged by the parties and that the notice required by sections 67(5) and 78(4) of this Act has not been given.

(5A) In subsection (5) above, "the relevant time" means—

(a) in the case of proceedings in the High Court—
    (i) not less than 7 days before the preliminary hearing; or
    (ii) such later time, before the trial diet, as the judge may on cause shown allow;

(b) in any other case, before the trial diet.

(6) A party shall not be required to give notice as mentioned in subsection (5) above where—

(a) the grounds for seeking to have evidence of a statement admitted are as mentioned in paragraph (d) or (e) of subsection (2) above; or

(b) he satisfies the judge that there was good reason for not giving such notice.

(7) If no other party to the proceedings objects to the admission of evidence of a statement by virtue of subsection (1) above, the evidence shall be admitted without the judge requiring to be satisfied as mentioned in that subsection.

(8) For the purposes of the determination of any matter upon which the judge is required to be satisfied under subsection (1) above—

(a) except to the extent that any other party to the proceedings challenges them and insists in such challenge, it shall be presumed that the circumstances are as stated by the party seeking to introduce evidence of the statement; and

(b) where such a challenge is insisted in, the judge shall determine the matter on the balance of probabilities, and he may draw any reasonable inference—

(i) from the circumstances in which the statement was made or otherwise came into being; or

(ii) from any other circumstances, including, where the statement is contained in a document, the form and contents of the document.

(9) Where evidence of a statement has been admitted by virtue of subsection (1) above on the application of one party to the proceedings, without prejudice to anything in any enactment or rule of law, the judge may permit any party to lead additional evidence of such description as the judge may specify, notwithstanding that a witness or production concerned is not included in any list lodged by the parties and that the notice required by sections 67(5) and 78(4) of this Act has not been given.

(10) Any reference in subsections (5), (6) and (9) above to evidence shall include a reference to evidence led in connection with any determination required to be made for the purposes of subsection (1) above.

AMENDMENT

Subs.(5) as amended, and subs.(5A) inserted, by the Criminal Procedure (Amendment) (Scotland) Act 2004 (asp 5), s.25 and Sch.1, para.42. Brought into force on February 1, 2005 by the Criminal Procedure (Amendment) (Scotland) Act 2004 (Commencement, Transitional Provisions and Savings) Order 2004 (SSI 2004/405 (C.28)), art.2.

DEFINITIONS

"child": s.307(1).
"criminal proceedings": s.262(3).
"document": s.262(3).
"judge": s.307(1).
"statement": s.262(1).
"witness": s.307(1).

GENERAL NOTE

This section statutorily extends the grounds for the admission of hearsay evidence in criminal proceedings and, in subs.(5) onwards, sets out the procedures necessary in most circumstances for such evidence to be received. It is important to note that while a "statement" is very widely defined in s.262(1), anything by nature of a precognition, save for a precognition on oath, is excluded from the ambit of s.259. The distinction between a statement and a precognition was revisited in *H.M. Advocate v Beggs (No.3)*, 2002 S.L.T. 153; 2001 S.C.C.R. 891 in which a police statement taken in the course of enquiries was held not to be a precognition; the statement had been taken from the witness on the initiative of the police (not on the instructions of the fiscal) and the witness had been given the opportunity to read it over and correct it. It is stressed that the section's provisions operate in addition to, and do not replace, the categories of hearsay evidence which can be accepted by the courts at common law (see s.262(4), below); for that reason some mention is necessary of the pre-existing categories of hearsay evidence which were recognised as exceptions to the general bar on hearsay evidence.

Following *H.M. Advocate v Bain*, 2002 S.L.T. 340 it would appear that although a judge is bound to permit the admission of hearsay evidence if it complies with the requirements of subs.(7) that does not debar the judge from considering whether the statement, or statements, can be fairly put before the jury. In *Bain* the Crown had given due notice of the leading of evidence from a deceased witness at the outset of the trial and no objection had been taken by the defence. Nonetheless, the Crown accepted that elements of at least one of the statements were contradicted by other evidence the Crown founded upon; on that basis the trial judge had to consider how the Crown interpreted this evidence for the jury and, indeed, assess afresh whether it could fairly be considered as sufficiently reliable for the jury to found upon. See too *McKenna v H.M. Advocate*, 2003 S.L.T. 769, the appeal arising from *H.M. Advocate v McKenna*, 2000 S.L.T. 508; 2000 S.C.C.R. 159 discussed below.

The trial judge has a continuing duty, as any trial in which hearsay evidence has been led continues, to assess whether the admission of that evidence should be permitted in the light of the evidence as it unfolds. If it becomes clear that the evidence is unfair to the party (or parties) against whom it is admitted, the trial judge may have to direct, at the very least, that the jury disregard the evidence.

In the case of evidence led by the Crown it might also be necessary to uphold a submission of no case to answer, or to desert the trial *ex proprio motu*, or direct the jury to acquit; see *N v H.M. Advocate*, 2003 S.L.T. 761. This function can only properly be exercised by the trial judge in the light of the evidence. Once it is established that the qualifications set out in subss.(1) and (2) have been met, the court has no power to refuse to allow the evidence to be led, but can withdraw it from consideration as evidence (once led) if its admission would result in unfairness.

(The self-evident fact that other parties cannot cross-examine this chapter of evidence does not, of itself, constitute unfairness since Scottish courts will still require corroboration of essential facts before any conviction is possible).

Categories of hearsay admissible at common law

First, it is well-established that statements made by a deceased witness, while hearsay in character, are admissible; see *H.M. Advocate v Irving*, 1978 J.C. 28, but it is unsettled whether this exception extends either as far as writings of a deceased, particularly if authorship is in dispute (the *Lauderdale Peerage* case (1885) 10 App. Cas. 692), or to a dying deposition. More tentatively, a statement made by a witness deemed permanently insane since its making could perhaps be adduced as evidence provided that it could be established that he had been lucid at the time when it was made (*H.M. Advocate v Monson* (1893) 1 Adam 114). It is thought that a statement by a prisoner of war might be received as evidence.

It is well-established that statements forming part of the *res gestae* are admissible as are incriminating or mixed statements made by an accused, and that hearsay evidence can be admitted where it would be impossible to lead primary evidence, this on the basis that such hearsay now qualifies as best evidence. The making of prior inconsistent statements can be used as a means of discrediting a witness, but previous consistent statements cannot be used to bolster credibility; in neither case, however, is the prior statement admissible as evidence of its contents. In addition to statutory exceptions such as the Bankers' Book Evidence Act 1879 and the provisions now contained in Sch.8 to the 1996 Act concerning categories of business documents, case law has also allowed evidence at second hand—of identification or description of an accused (*Muldoon v Herron*, 1970 J.C. 30), of a vehicle (*Frew v Jessop*, 1990 J.C. 15), and more recently, of a statement whose detail had been forgotten by a witness but assented to in evidence (*Jamieson v H.M. Advocate (No.2)*, 1994 S.C.C.R. 610).

While it might seem that the list of expected categories of hearsay evidence which can be adduced as evidence is endless, the fact remains that Scottish courts have exercised extreme caution before admitting such evidence largely on the grounds that it cannot be subjected to cross-examination and must be inherently less reliable than parole evidence. Yet the bar on admissible hearsay may cause unnecessary expense, probably smacks of pettifoggery and contrivance to lay witnesses whose flow of testimony is artificially constrained, and certainly can militate against the broader interests of justice: see especially the cases of *Perrie v H.M. Advocate*, 1991 S.C.C.R. 255 and *McLay v H.M. Advocate*, 1994 S.C.C.R. 397 in both of which it had been held inadmissible to lead evidence made to third parties by an incriminee.

The Scottish Law Commission's Report, *"Hearsay Evidence in Criminal Proceedings"* (No. 149) and, to an extent, the experience of English courts in applying Pt 2 of the Criminal Justice Act 1988 (c.33) (which drew heavily upon the Roskill Report, *"Report of the Departmental Inquiry on Fraud Trials"*, Lord Chancellor's Department 1986), as well as the *Perrie* and *McLay* cases, have all influenced the shape of Pt 12 of the 1995 Act. Section 259 broadens the categories of hearsay evidence which can be introduced into proceedings but provides a right to other parties to challenge such evidence—in which event the court will require to adjudicate prior to the commencement of a trial, and to lead counter-evidence in rebuttal.

Subs. (1)

Subsection (1) sets out several tests which any hearsay material has to meet before it can be founded upon, namely, the unavailability of the maker of the statement (for one of the reasons specified in subs.(2) below); the admissibility of the evidence had it been given in parole form (a ground which demands both that the evidence adduced is competent and does not contain hearsay, and that the maker of the statement would have qualified as a witness); and finally that the making of the statement can itself be proved by direct evidence. The witness' statement need not be in written form provided that other witnesses can speak to its contents but nor can it be by nature a precognition (a distinction itself often more apparent than real nowadays).

In *H.M. Advocate v Beggs (No.3)*, 2002 S.L.T. 153 the Crown moved to lead evidence, of the accused's general interest in picking up young men, in the form of a statement from a witness since deceased. Following a trial within a trial (on which now see *Crooks v Russell*, 2002 S.L.T. 221; 2002 S.C.C.R. 216), the Crown's contention that the statement was not a precognition since it had been taken by a police officer in the course of enquiries into the movements of the accused after an apprehension warrant had been granted (and then was incorporated into extradition proceedings against the accused), was accepted. The defence had founded upon *Kerr v H.M. Advocate*, 1958 J.C. 14 both as setting out the general test of a precognition and as authority for the view that it was for the Crown to satisfy the court that the account being tendered was not by way of being a precognition. In the interest of clarity it may be noted that the issue of lifting the veil of confidentiality on the precognition process was discussed in *Kerr v H.M. Advocate*, 2002 S.L.T. 582; 2002 S.C.C.R. 275.

Subs. (2)

Following on from subs.(1)(a) the permissible grounds for the unavailability of a witness are defined. It is submitted that these statutory provisions are in addition to, and without prejudice to, the common law rules described above. In *H.M. Advocate v Clancy* (High Court, Glasgow, February 9, 1997, unreported) the Crown sought to lead evidence in a murder trial of a statement from the victim without use of the statutory notice set out in subs.(5). Defence objections were upheld, but the indictment fell due to the illness of the judge, though it had been indicated that there was some sympathy for the Crown in the instant case for proceeding under common law and, in any event, there had been no prejudice to the accused. While this unreported case should spur parties to rely upon the statutory notice procedures, it will be noted that subs.(6)(b) does permit hearsay evidence to be adduced without prior notice where just cause can be shown: the deliberate disappearance, or the sudden death, of a witness in the course of a trial would surely justify such a motion. It is unclear whether dying depositions are to be considered competent for the purposes of s.259. In *H.M. Advocate v Johnston*, 2004 S.L.T. 1055, a murder trial, where the Crown sought to lead the police statement of the now-deceased boyfriend of the victim which had become significant in conjunction with DNA evidence, the trial judge repelled objections that there was an inherent unfairness in Art.6 Convention terms in using the statement in evidence. Paragraph (b) enables the statement of a witness abroad to be received in evidence, but only if it can be shown, if required, that is is not reasonable to use other competent evidential devices, such as live television links, letters of request or commission.

Paragraph (c), in a fashion similar to the last paragraph, enables statements of identifiable witnesses who have disappeared to be admitted as evidence but only if it can be shown, if required, that all reasonable steps have been taken to trace the witness beforehand. Paragraph (d) deals with admissions of incriminees; it will now be possible to tender evidence of statements allegedly made by an incriminee who has been brought before the court but refuses to testify on grounds of self-incrimination.

Subtle differences exist between the last provision and the next, contained in para. (e)(i), which deals with a witness who simply misconducts himself and refuses to testify, or prevaricates. Paragraph (e) can apply to the evidence of a child "who has refused an admonition to tell the truth or, having been so admonished, refuses to give evidence"; this phrase would obviously apply to a recalcitrant child witness but would not apply to situations in which the child proved to be unable to give evidence or was tongue-tied. From *MacDonald v H.M. Advocate*, 1999 S.L.T. 533; 1999 S.C.C.R. 146 it is clear that before subs.(2)(e)(ii) can operate in the case of a child, the judge must have directed the witness to answer and have been met with a refusal. It also seems that recourse to the s.259 provision would only be appropriate after some effort had been made to ascertain whether the child might adopt a prior admissible statement (see s.260 below). A further category of child witness has to be recognised—the child who does not understand the nature of the admonition; in such a case it is doubtful that an earlier statement could be taken in evidence at all, since the child was not a "competent witness" when the statement was made (subs.(1)(c)).

Several caveats have to be entered: first, subs.(3) precludes the application of s.259's provisions where the judge is satisfied the party tendering the evidence, or his followers, have colluded in bringing about the unavailability or recalcitrance of the witness identified. This provision would readily apply to assisting in, or engineering the disappearance of a witness (arguably an attempt to pervert the course of justice in many circumstances) but more complex issues might arise for example in child abuse cases where emotional pressures may be brought to bear on the child.

Secondly, subs.(5) stipulates that for hearsay evidence to be admitted in most circumstances notice of the intention to do so must be served on all other parties before the trial. (The form of notice is found in Form 21.3 in the 1996 Act of Adjournal.) The notice has to be in the proper form and relate to the correct statement: in *McPhee (William McAllister) v H.M. Advocate*, 2002 S.L.T. 90; 2001 S.C.C.R. 674 the Crown had attached the wrong statement to the s.259 notice served upon the accused but was permitted to lead the evidence in question on the basis that the accused had suffered no prejudice. The Appeal Court quashed the conviction upon that charge on the grounds that no "good reason" had been shown for the omission as subs.(6)(b) demanded and prejudice (or its lack) was not a relevant factor. Broadly, notice has to be served where it is anticipable that a witness will be unavailable; subs.(6) exempts situations described in para.(2)(d) and (e) namely, failures to testify by incriminees or by witnesses who misconduct themselves, from the normal requirement of advance notice. Thirdly, a failure to challenge appropriate notice under subs.(5) means that the statement's contents can be lead in evidence without further ado (subs.(7)). Nonetheless, it is submitted that some circumspection is necessary here: it cannot be right that the terms of subs.(7) would preclude a common law challenge during the proceedings if it is demonstrable that the evidence being adduced would ordinarily be incompetent or otherwise inadmissible.

Only in the event of a challenge does the presiding judge have to decide the issue before the trial commences (subs.(8)) and it will be noted that it is presumed that the terms of the Form 21.3 are correct, a presumption which is capable of rebuttal, and that the issue is determined on the balance of probabilities. The main benefit of subs.(8) is that a "trial within a trial" to resolve the admissibility of the statement can be avoided, thus saving time and inconvenience to all involved since the issue will be aired, possibly by leading evidence, before trial. Subsection (4) permits parties to lead evidence to support the credibility of the absent witness, challenge his credibility, or demonstrate prior inconsistent statements. (The only exceptions to this generality occur in the circumstances outlined in subs.(2)(d) and (e)(i) where, by definition, no evidence has been heard from the witness.) Reference to "any proceedings" suggests that such evidence could well be adduced before the judge determining the admissibility of a challenged notice.

Although it may be self-evident, the above hearsay provisions do not extend to statements made by an accused in his favour (see s.261(1) below). Less obviously, given the terms of s.261(2) of the Act, a statement by a co-accused B can be adduced as evidence by an accused A where B declines to give evidence: the statement can be used as evidence by A but not by B. Section 261(4) provides that this can only occur where A has given notice in terms of s.259(5) and, it is submitted, where it can be shown that no pressure was exerted by A to prevent B testifying, and the Crown itself has not lead B's statement. To say the least the interplay of ss.259 and 261 is likely to create situations of byzantine complexity, particularly in cases involving several accused; will all accused founding upon B's statement require to serve a s.259 notice as prudence might suggest?

Finally, it will be noted that both s.259(5) and (9) permit the leading of witnesses or productions, not formally intimated, either for the purpose of setting up a hearsay statement or, with leave of the court, as additional evidence.

European Convention on Human Rights

The introduction of the Convention into Scots criminal law has undoubtedly led to a re-appraisal of many well-accepted practices. For that reason the discussion which follows is necessarily of some length, albeit the basic issue—the need to achieve a proper balance between a fair trial for the accused and the need to detect and suppress serious crime (*Irving v H.M. Advocate*, 1998 J.C. 28)—remains unchanged.

H.M. Advocate v McKenna, 2000 S.L.T. 508; 2000 S.C.C.R. 159 was an early challenge under the Convention to the Crown's stated intention to lead hearsay evidence and was notable also because objection was permitted to be taken prior to trial in its exceptional circumstances. Ordinarily it is expected that the leading of s.259 evidence will be considered by the court at the outset of the trial proceedings after service of the appropriate notices. Following upon *H.M. Advocate v Bain*, 2001 G.W.D. 21–693 it is submitted that it is essential (particularly where no objection has been taken in terms of subs.(7)) to determine from the outset whether the court has, or has not, accepted that the hearsay evidence identified can be led. In *Bain* the Crown laid an application under subs.(2)(a) before the court without objection from the defence before the jury was sworn only to be met with an objection at the point in evidence when the statement was about to be lead. The trial judge doubted, despite the lack of objection at the outset, that he had granted the application and, in any event, the grant of an application as admissible in the proceedings would not itself settle issues of evidential admissibility. Rejecting defence submissions that Convention rights were being breached because the deceased's accounts were at odds with each other and that this evidence could not be cross-examined (much as had occurred in *McKenna*), Lord Reed noted that the question of fairness could be revisited as the evidence emerged.

In *McKenna* the Crown advanced seven broad principles to be applied to the leading of hearsay evidence in a manner compatible with Convention rights. Particularly, it was significant that leading such evidence was not *per se* in conflict with such rights provided that the accused had the opportunity to challenge the statement and, more important, following *Kostovski v The Netherlands* (1989) 12 E.H.R.R. 434 and *Asch v Austria* (1992) 15 E.H.R.R.597 that this is not either the sole or main evidence. In his judgment Lord Caplan noted that the European Court has not laid down prescriptive rules (a difficult, if not impossible, task given the variety of criminal law systems) but proceeds by an overall assessment of the whole proceedings, not individual elements.

The defence minutes were repelled in *McKenna*; the accused raised objection by preliminary diet to the Crown leading evidence of a statement from the third person present at the scene of a murder, and since identified as a suspect but who had since died, on grounds that not only could this evidence not be subject to cross-examination but that there was evidence that the witness would likely have given a partial and self-serving account. Particular emphasis was placed upon alleged oppression on the part of the Crown (in contravention of the European Convention) in seeking to lead evidence of this sort; the Crown responded by outlining seven general principles (which the Court approved) in relation to the leading of hearsay evidence from a deceased person foremost of which was the fact that this was neither the sole or principal evidence against the accused. On appeal, the Appeal Court indicated that only on rare occasions could the issue of the potential for prejudice to the achievement of a fair trial be determined in advance of the trial itself (compare the approach in *Brown v Stott*, 2000 S.C.C.R. 314 where the fundamental issue, as a matter of law, of a suspect's right not to be called upon to incriminate himself, notwithstanding the terms of the Road Traffic Act 1988 (c.52), s.172, was so resolved).

In *Patterson v H.M. Advocate*, 2000 S.L.T. 302 the Appeal Court ruled as competent evidence for the purposes of the section, the statement of a deceased witness who had intimated to the defence that she was an alcoholic and had given her police statement while under the influence of drink. It was held that the reliability of the witness was not a determining factor in assessing the competency of her statement. Note that the Court also held that it was not necessary for the Crown to meet an inspecific challenge to the witness' mental capacity by proving her sanity; the general evidential presumption (that witnesses are deemed to have the ordinary physical and mental faculties) applied.

In *H.M. Advocate v Nulty*, 2000 S.L.T. 528 the Crown sought to lead evidence of a complainer in a rape trial by reference to her taped evidence from an earlier trial diet which had, unfortunately, been deserted for procedural reasons. Since giving her evidence and being cross-examined at the first trial, the complainer had become mentally unwell and was unfit to give evidence, causing the Crown to use the best evidence available, her prior testimony. Two points are of note; first, the court apparently had no difficulty in reconciling this approach with the terms of subs.(1) which excludes from the ambit of s.259 oral evidence given in the course of criminal proceedings, no doubt on the basis that the evidence to be received had not been given in the instant proceedings; second, the trial judge was unwilling to hold that unfairness necessarily arose because the accused could not cross-examine the complainer. Following *Doorson v Netherlands* (1996) 22 E.H.R.R. 330 fairness had to be assessed overall and had to take account of the balance between the defence's interests and those of the victims.

It will only rarely be proper for the judge at a preliminary diet to determine conclusively whether hearsay evidence should be allowed in terms of s.259. Such a decision can only be reached where the court can, at that stage, pre-emptively determine that the admission of that evidence would inevitably result in the entire proceedings being rendered unfair; *H.M. Advocate v M*, 2003 S.L.T. 1151.

Convention arguments were aired in *Campbell v H.M. Advocate*, 2004 S.L.T. 135; 2003 S.C.C.R. 779 with little success, but this appeal succeeded on grounds of the inadequate directions given to the jury as to how to approach hearsay evidence which was of an essential corroborative character.

Admissibility of prior statements of witnesses

260.—(1) Subject to the following provisions of this section, where a witness gives evidence in criminal proceedings, any prior statement made by the witness shall be admissible as evidence of any matter stated in it of which direct oral evidence by him would be admissible if given in the course of those proceedings.

(2) A prior statement shall not be admissible under this section unless—

(a) the statement is contained in a document;

(b) the witness, in the course of giving evidence, indicates that the statement was made by him and that he adopts it as his evidence; and

(c) at the time the statement was made, the person who made it would have been a competent witness in the proceedings.

(3) For the purposes of this section, any reference to a prior statement is a reference to a prior statement which, but for the provisions of this section, would not be admissible as evidence of any matter stated in it.

(4) Subsections (2) and (3) above do not apply to a prior statement—

(a) contained in a precognition on oath; or

(b) made in other proceedings, whether criminal or civil and whether taking place in the United Kingdom or elsewhere,

and, for the purposes of this section, any such statement shall not be admissible unless it is sufficiently authenticated.

(5) A prior statement made by a witness shall not, in any proceedings on indictment, be inadmissible by reason only that it is not included in any list of productions lodged by the parties.

AMENDMENT

Subs.(5) inserted by the Criminal Procedure (Amendment) (Scotland) Act 2004 (asp 5), s.23. Brought into force on October 4, 2004 by the Criminal Procedure (Amendment) (Scotland) Act 2004 (Commencement, Transitional Provisions and Savings) Order 2004 (SSI 2004/405 (C.28)).

DEFINITIONS

"criminal proceedings": s.262(3).
"statement": s.262(1).
"witness": s.307(1).

GENERAL NOTE

This section applies to solemn and summary proceedings and permits the introduction of prior statements, as specified by subs.(2), by a witness in criminal proceedings as evidence of any matter therein of which direct oral evidence from him would have been admissible in the course of those proceedings. In essence the section permits the adoption of earlier statements, suitably authenticated, and is perceptibly influenced by the decision of the High Court in *Jamieson v H.M. Advocate (No. 2)*, 1995 S.L.T. 666.

Note that the witness has both to acknowledge being the originator of the statement and adopt it as his evidence (subs.(2)(b)), circumstances which did not prevail in either *Muldoon v Herron*, 1970 J.C. 30; 1970 S.L.T. 228 (a judgment which the court founded upon in *Jamieson*) or in *Smith v H.M. Advocate*, 1986 S.C.C.R. 135. In both those cases police witnesses' accounts of the witness' evidence replaced the testimony of the witnesses themselves. If a witness can adopt a prior statement as this section provides, *McNee v Ruxton*, 1997 G.W.D. 13–545 is authority perhaps for the proposition that witness B can adopt the statement of another witness, witness A, as his own. The corollary however surely must be that either witness can have a prior inconsistent statement made by either witness put to him.

The distinction between this section, which in effect enables witnesses to rely upon accurate statements made earlier (but whose details are now forgotten) such that these can form part of the evidence, and section 263 which enables a prior statement to be put as a means, at least initially, only of challenging the credibility or reliability of a witness, can quickly become blurred; see *Ogilvie v H.M. Advocate*, 1999 S.L.T. 1068. In this case the Crown plainly utilised the (rarely used) power in s.263(2) of the Act to interpose another witness during the witness' evidence, albeit prematurely. See also *Pupkis v Thomson*, 2002 G.W.D. 17-554; if the witness does not adopt his statement, its contents cannot be available as evidence even if confirmed by the officer who noted its terms.

The effect of subs. (4) is to remove the need for a witness to adopt the terms of his precognition on oath (which of course had to be signed as an acknowledgment of its accuracy by the witness at the conclusion of the precognition proceedings) or for him to confirm the accuracy of testimony given in earlier judicial proceedings.

Reference to r.21.4 and Form 21.4 in the 1996 Act of Adjournal indicates that only statements of the type specified in subs. (4) require to be certified with such an authentication docquet; authentication need not be docquetted by the originator of the statement, the certificate of a party present at the making of the statement would suffice. Note that any prior statement by a witness would be admissible if given as a precognition on oath or in the course of any court proceedings once properly authenticated.

The above certification procedures are not required for any other sort of statement; in such cases it would be sufficient for the witness to assent to the truth of an earlier account which is produced to the court in document form. See s.262(2) and (3) for definitions. It will be noted that nothing in either ss.260 or 262 would permit the use of a precognition.

The different evidential significance of a s.260 and s.263 statement is discussed at A4–511 below.

Statements by accused

261.—(1) Subject to the following provisions of this section, nothing in sections 259 and 260 of this Act shall apply to a statement made by the accused.

(2) Evidence of a statement made by an accused shall be admissible by virtue of the said section 259 at the instance of another accused in the same proceedings as evidence in relation to that other accused.

(3) For the purposes of subsection (2) above, the first mentioned accused shall be deemed—

(a) where he does not give evidence in the proceedings, to be a witness refusing to give evidence in connection with the subject matter of the statement as mentioned in paragraph (e) of subsection (2) of the said section 259; and

(b) to have been, at the time the statement was made, a competent witness in the proceedings.

(4) Evidence of a statement shall not be admissible as mentioned in subsection (2) above unless the accused at whose instance it is sought to be admitted has given notice of his intention to do so as mentioned in subsection (5) of the said section 259; but subsection (6) of that section shall not apply in the case of notice required to be given by virtue of this subsection.

DEFINITIONS

"made": s.262(3).
"statement": s.262(1).
"witness": s.307(1).

GENERAL NOTE

This section applies to solemn and summary proceedings. Its effect is to exclude a statement made by the accused from the provisions of ss.259 and 260. However, statements made by an accused, which are hearsay, may become admissible against that accused when introduced by another accused in the same proceedings. Use of this procedure will normally require a Notice in terms of s.259(5) prior to trial (see notes to s.259 above).

Construction of sections 259 to 261

262.—(1) For the purposes of sections 259 to 261 of this Act, a "statement" includes—

(a) any representation, however made or expressed, of fact or opinion; and

(b) any part of a statement, but does not include a statement in a precognition other than a precognition on oath.

(2) For the purposes of the said sections 259 to 261 a statement is contained in a document where the person who makes it—

(a) makes the statement in the document personally;

(b) makes a statement which is, with or without his knowledge, embodied in a document by whatever means or by any person who has direct personal knowledge of the making of the statement; or

(c) approves a document as embodying the statement.

(3) In the said sections 259 to 261—

"criminal proceedings" include any hearing by the sheriff of an application made under Chapter 3 of Part II of the Children (Scotland) Act 1995 for a finding as to whether grounds for the referral of a child's case to a children's hearing are established, in so far as the application relates to the commission of an offence by the child, or for a review of such a finding;

"document" includes, in addition to a document in writing—

(a) any map, plan, graph or drawing;

(b) any photograph;

(c) any disc, tape, sound track or other device in which sounds or other data (not being visual images) are recorded so as to be capable (with or without the aid of some other equipment) of being reproduced therefrom; and

(d) any film, negative, tape, disc or other device in which one or more visual images are recorded so as to be capable (as aforesaid) of being reproduced therefrom;

"film" includes a microfilm;

"made" includes allegedly made.

(4) Nothing in the said sections 259 to 261 shall prejudice the admissibility of a statement made by a person other than in the course of giving oral evidence in court which is admissible otherwise than by virtue of those sections.

DEFINITIONS

"child": s.307(1).
"indictment": s.307(1).
"sheriff": ss.4(4) and 5(1).

GENERAL NOTE

The section makes provision for the construction of ss.259 to 261 of the Act. Subsection (4) enacts that the section's provisions do not prejudice any other rule allowing the admissibility of statements in the course of giving oral evidence in court; see for example s.263(4) which deals with prior inconsistent statements in solemn and summary proceedings. See *Rollo v. H.M. Advocate*, 1997 S.L.T. 958, a prosecution under the Misuse of Drugs Act 1971 (c. 23) in which, for the purposes of search under that Act, an electronic personal organiser was held to be "a document". See *H.M. Advocate v. Beggs (No.3)*, 2002 S.L.T. 153; 2001 S.C.C.R. 891 discussed at para. A4–503 above.

Witnesses

Examination of witnesses

263.—(1) In any trial, it shall be competent for the party against whom a witness is produced and sworn *in causa* to examine such witness both in cross and *in causa*.

(2) The judge may, on the motion of either party, on cause shown order that the examination of a witness for that party ("the first witness") shall be interrupted to permit the examination of another witness for that party.

(3) Where the judge makes an order under subsection (2) above he shall, after the examination of the other witness, permit the recall of the first witness.

(4) In a trial, a witness may be examined as to whether he has on any specified occasion made a statement on any matter pertinent to the issue at the trial different from the evidence given by him in the trial; and evidence may be led in the trial to prove that the witness made the different statement on the occasion specified.

(5) In any trial, on the motion of either party, the presiding judge may permit a witness who has been examined to be recalled.

DEFINITIONS

(4) Where prior statement differs from evidence given at trial

"judge": s.307(1).
"trial": s.307(1).
"witness": s.307(1).

GENERAL NOTE

This section applies to solemn and summary proceedings. Subsections (2) and (3) which permit the interruption of a witness' testimony to allow evidence to be taken from another of the party's witnesses was introduced by the Criminal Justice (Scotland) Act 1980 (c.62), Sch.6, para.54. By implication such a motion could only be made during the examination or re-examination of the first witness, not during cross-examination.

Subsection (4) repeats the familiar terms of ss.147 and 349 of the 1975 Act in relation to prior inconsistent statements by witnesses. This rule does not apply to precognitions which cannot, of course, be put to witnesses unless they are precognitions on oath (see *Kerr v H.M. Advocate*, 1958 J.C. 14; *K.J.C. v H.M. Advocate*, 1994 S.C.C.R. 560). See also *Coll, Petr*, 1977 S.L.T. 58, a petition to the nobile officium by a witness to order destruction of his precognition on oath before giving evidence at the trial proceedings.

The second part of subs.(4) does not become operative until the witness has been specifically asked whether he made the statement (*McTaggart v H.M. Advocate*, 1934 J.C. 33) and that it was made on a specified occasion (*Paterson v H.M. Advocate*, 1998 S.L.T. 117). Subsection (4) has to be read in conjunction with s.269(1) and (2); with leave of the court it is competent to lead additional evidence (to prove the making of the prior statement) by way of productions and witnesses' evidence even if no notice has been given of them in the trial indictment. Following *Leckie v. H.M. Advocate*, 2002 S.L.T. 595 it is not necessary that the entire terms of the prior statement be lead in evidence; what matters is that the gist of the earlier account be put in unequivocal terms for the witness to admit or dispute. In *Leckie* the Crown had objected to defence efforts to put anything other than a full statement, line by line. It is competent to examine a witness upon the terms of another witness' statement where the former witness has previously adopted that statement, or its terms, as his own; see *McNee v Ruxton* 1998 S.L.T. 140. In *H.M. Advocate v Hislop*, 1994 S.L.T. 333 a Crown witness, who claimed to be unable to recall events, stated that she had told the police what had happened. The prosecutor put her account to her by means of her earlier tape-recorded interview and a transcript of it, both of which were listed as productions. Objections to this use of the section's provisions were repelled. See also the notes to s.260 at A4–505 above. The distinction between the admission of a prior statement by means of s.263 and s.260 is vital: a s.263 statement used in the course of proceedings does not itself constitute evidence against the accused but serves only as a test of the credibility and reliability of the maker of the statement once its provenance has been proved; by contrast a s.260 statement (or indeed a *Jamieson* statement) will be primary evidence but only once it has been adopted by the witness as his evidence (see *Ogilvie*, 1999 G.W.D. 14–632).

In *Hemming v H.M. Advocate*, 1998 S.L.T. 213, H was charged with attempted murder and petitioned the High Court for a commission and diligence to recover witness statements. The object was to attack the credibility of Crown witnesses by demonstrating variations in their accounts as the police investigation proceeded. In the instant case the Court held there to be compelling grounds for overriding the public interest objections raised by the Crown. Compare the approach taken by a court of five judges in *McLeod, Petr*, 1998 S.L.T. 234 (at 244J–L) in which the parameters to be met by an accused seeking a diligence to recover documents are formulated.

Refer also to the discussion of *Ogilvie v H.M. Advocate*, 1999 S.L.T. 1068 in the Notes to s.260 above.

It is well understood that a *socius criminis* once called to give evidence for the Crown, enjoys immunity from prosecution in relation to the matter. The defence are entitled to criticise the witness' testimony on the grounds of that immunity and, if they do so, it is generally proper for the trial judge to direct attention to this immunity; see generally *Docherty v H.M. Advocate*, 1987 S.L.T. 784. In *Mason v H.M. Advocate*, 2000 S.L.T. 1004 no such criticism of a witness' evidence had been voiced by the defence and it was held that there was no automatic duty incumbent upon the trial judge to give such directions; indeed it might be risky to do so without an appreciation of the considerations giving rise to the defence approach.

In *H.M. Advocate v Megrahi (No.2)*, 2000 S.L.T. 1399 a transcript of evidence given by a witness before a magistrate in a foreign jurisdiction (in this instance, Malta) was admitted as evidence, the Scottish Court in the Netherlands rejecting defence objections that the statement being put to the witness was akin to a precognition.

In *Trotter v H.M. Advocate*, 2000 G.W.D. 32–1246 the accused, who had been charged with possessing controlled drugs with intent to supply during a visit to prison, had called his father, a serving prisoner, as a witness. The witness gave evidence in court in handcuffs; while the Appeal Court rejected claims that T had been deprived of a fair trial, since the jury could not fail to be aware of his father's status, an opinion was delivered that handcuffs should only be used where security was a real concern and then only after the issues had been considered between the Crown and the judge.

In *Jeffrey v H.M. Advocate*, 2002 S.L.T. 1407; 2002 S.C.C.R 822, which centred upon the adequacy of defence representation (following *Anderson v H.M. Advocate*, 1996 J.C. 29; 1999 S.L.T. 155; 1999 S.C.C.R. 114), a secondary point of appeal was the decision of the sheriff not to exercise his discretion to recall the complainer, a seven year old child, to enable an (apparently) inconsistent earlier statement to be put to her. The statement, of which the defence had a copy at the time, had not been put to the child in cross-examination. The Appeal Court upheld the sheriff's approach to the issue.

Spouse of accused a competent witness

264.—(1) The spouse of an accused may be called as a witness—

(a) by the accused;

(b) by a co-accused or by the prosecutor without the consent of the accused.

(2) Nothing in this section shall—

(a) make the spouse of an accused a compellable witness for a co-accused or for the prosecutor in a case where such spouse would not be so compellable at common law;

(b) compel a spouse to disclose any communication made between the spouses during the marriage.

(3) The failure of the spouse of an accused to give evidence shall not be commented on by the defence or the prosecutor.

(4) The spouse of a person charged with bigamy may be called as a witness either for the prosecution or the defence and without the consent of the person charged.

DEFINITIONS

"prosecutor": s.307(1).
"witness": s.307(1).

GENERAL NOTE

The term "spouse" can only be applied to persons married to each other, not to those who simply co-habit (*Casey v H.M. Advocate*, 1993 S.L.T. 33). In *R. v Pearce* (Court of Appeal, Criminal Division, December 11, 2001) it was argued in the light of changing social mores, and the impact of the European Convention, that this concession (found in s.80(1) of the Police and Criminal Evidence Act 1984 (c.60) in English law) should extend to long-term partners, and that the free use of a partner's testimony by the Crown in a murder trial offended against the right to privacy enshrined in Art.8. In rejecting these submissions the Court of Appeal also asserted that the public interest in the prevention of serious crime would have justified the use of the exception in Art.8(2). A spouse is a compellable witness for the accused to whom she is married, and is competent but not compellable when called by any other party in proceedings (*Hunter v H.M. Advocate*, 1984 S.L.T. 434); once she elects to give evidence, she must answer all relevant questions and cannot refrain from answering on the grounds that they might incriminate her spouse (see *Hunter* above and *Bates v H.M. Advocate*, 1989 S.L.T. 701; 1989 S.C.C.R. 338).

This rule also applies to an estranged spouse who, unless she is the complainer, must be advised that she is not a compellable witness (see *Hay v McClory*, 1993 S.C.C.R. 1040; 1994 S.L.T. 520).

In *McCulloch v H.M. Advocate*, 2000 S.C.C.R. 1115 an extension of the 12 month time-bar was allowed to enable the Crown to re-indict after the trial diet had been deserted, *pro loco et tempore*, by the sheriff following his ruling that the Crown had, in ignorance, commented upon the failure of the spouse to give evidence. It is of note that the sheriff had balanced the public interest in the prosecution of a serious offence against the rights of the accused and had been persuaded by the lack of any prejudice to the accused were the extension to be granted.

Witnesses not excluded for conviction, interest, relationship, etc.

265.—(1) Every person adduced as a witness who is not otherwise by law disqualified from giving evidence, shall be admissible as a witness, and no objection to the admissibility of a witness shall be competent on the ground of—

(a) conviction of or punishment for an offence;

(b) interest;

(c) agency or partial counsel;

(d) the absence of due citation to attend; or

(e) his having been precognosced subsequently to the date of citation.

(2) Where any person who is or has been an agent of the accused is adduced and examined as a witness for the accused, it shall not be competent for the accused to object, on the ground of confidentiality, to any question proposed to be put to such witness on matter pertinent to the issue of the guilt of the accused.

(3) No objection to the admissibility of a witness shall be competent on the ground that he or she is the father, mother, son, daughter, brother or sister, by consanguinity or affinity, or uncle, aunt, nephew or niece, by consanguinity of any party adducing the witness in any trial.

(4) It shall not be competent for any witness to decline to be examined and give evidence on the ground of any relationship mentioned in subsection (3) above.

DEFINITIONS

"conviction": s.307(5).
"witness": s.307(1).

GENERAL NOTE

This section permits parties' evidence to be heard irrespective of their character or interest or relationship. See generally *Dow v McKnight*, 1949 J.C. 38. Subsection (2) provides that the accused's solicitor, or former solicitor, can be adduced as a witness by the accused; the agent cannot be objected to on the grounds that he has been present in court (*Campbell v Cochrane*, 1928 J.C. 25).

Accused as witness

266.—(1) Subject to subsections (2) to (8) below, the accused shall be a competent witness for the defence at every stage of the case, whether the accused is on trial alone or along with a co-accused.

(2) The accused shall not be called as a witness in pursuance of this section except upon his own application or in accordance with subsection (9) or (10) below.

(3) An accused who gives evidence on his own behalf in pursuance of this section may be asked any question in cross-examination notwithstanding that it would tend to incriminate him as to the offence charged.

(4) An accused who gives evidence on his own behalf in pursuance of this section shall not be asked, and if asked shall not be required to answer, any question tending to show that he has committed, or been convicted of, or been charged with, any offence other than that with which he is then charged, or is of bad character, unless—

(a) the proof that he has committed or been convicted of such other offence is admissible evidence to show that he is guilty of the offence with which he is then charged; or

(b) the accused or his counsel or solicitor has asked questions of the witnesses for the prosecution with a view to establishing the accused's good character or impugning the character of the complainer, or the accused has given evidence of his own good character, or the nature or conduct of the defence is such as to involve imputations on the character of the prosecutor or of the witnesses for the prosecution or of the complainer; or

(c) the accused has given evidence against any other person charged in the same proceedings.

(5) In a case to which paragraph (b) of subsection (4) above applies, the prosecutor shall be entitled to ask the accused a question of a kind specified in that subsection only if the court, on the application of the prosecutor, permits him to do so.

(5A) Nothing in subsections (4) and (5) above shall prevent the accused from being asked, or from being required to answer, any question tending to show that he has been convicted of an offence other than that with which he is charged if his conviction for that other offence has been disclosed to the jury, or is to be taken into consideration by the judge, under section 275A(2) of this Act.

(6) An application under subsection (5) above in proceedings on indictment shall be made in the course of the trial but in the absence of the jury.

(7) In subsection (4) above, references to the complainer include references to a victim who is deceased.

(8) Every person called as a witness in pursuance of this section shall, unless otherwise ordered by the court, give his evidence from the witness box or other place from which the other witnesses give their evidence.

(9) The accused may—

(a) with the consent of a co-accused, call that other accused as a witness on the accused's behalf; or

(b) ask a co-accused any question in cross-examination if that co-accused gives evidence,

but he may not do both in relation to the same co-accused.

(10) The prosecutor or the accused may call as a witness a co-accused who has pleaded guilty to or been acquitted of all charges against him which remain before the court (whether or not, in a case where the co-accused has pleaded guilty to any charge, he has been sentenced) or in respect of whom the diet has been deserted; and the party calling such co-accused as a witness shall not require to give notice thereof, but the court may grant any other party such adjournment or postponement of the trial as may seem just.

(11) Where, in any trial, the accused is to be called as a witness he shall be so called as the first witness for the defence unless the court, on cause shown, otherwise directs.

AMENDMENT

Subs.(5A) inserted by the Sexual Offences (Procedure and Evidence) (Scotland) Act 2002 (asp 9), s.10(3). Brought into force by the Sexual Offences (Procedure and Evidence) (Scotland) Act 2002

(Commencement and Transitional Provisions) Order 2002 (SSI 2002/443 (C.24)), art.4 (effective November 1, 2002).

DEFINITIONS

"diet": s.307(1).
"offence": s.307(1).
"prosecutor": s.307(1).
"trial": s.307(1).
"witness": s.307(1).

GENERAL NOTE

The accused cannot be compelled to give evidence on his own behalf in his own trial, but his failure to do so can be the subject of comment, with restraint, by the trial judge in solemn proceedings when charging the jury (see *Scott (A.T.) v H.M. Advocate*, 1946 J.C. 90; *Brown v Macpherson*, 1918 J.C. 3; *McIntosh v H.M. Advocate*, 1997 S.L.T. 1320): s.32 of the Criminal Justice (Scotland) Act 1995 removed the long-standing general prohibition against comment by the prosecutor upon such a failure to give evidence, which was found in the 1975 Act, s.141(1)(b) (*Dempsey v H.M. Advocate*, 1995 S.C.C.R. 431 is a rare example of convictions being set aside on account of such improper comment by a prosecutor).

There was previous authority that in some cases, the proved facts may raise a presumption that the accused committed the crime libelled, and failure by the accused to put forward an explanation sufficient to raise a reasonable doubt in the minds of the jury could occasion comment legitimately (see *H.M. Advocate v Hardy*, 1938 J.C. 144; *McIlhargey v Herron*, 1972 J.C.).

Barnes v H.M. Advocate, 2000 G.W.D. 35–1330 demonstrates the sort of complex issues which can arise when an accused is exposed to cross-examination by others' counsel. It is one thing for a prior record to be revealed inadvertently in the course of questioning but in *Barnes*, the Appeal Court held that his counsel had expressly questioned a co-accused about *Barnes'* involvement in the assault libelled (a fact clearly evident from earlier evidence) solely as a means of drawing out the co-accused's criminal history. Such a tactic flew in the face of the section's purpose, and during the trial, *Barnes'* counsel had been refused the right to cross-examine on record; (*Murdoch v H.M. Advocate*, 1978 S.L.T. 10 distinguished). *Hanlin v McFadyen*, 2000 S.C.C.R. 428 confirms that no witness citation is necessary when it is intended to call a co-accused upon whom the court has already deferred sentence. In *Hanlin* the sheriff had declined an accused's motion to adjourn trial founded upon the failure of the co-accused to appear for sentence, no witness citation having been served.

With regard to the reform which became s.32 of the Criminal Justice (Scotland) Act 1995, during the Committee Stage of the Bill (*Hansard*, H.L. Vol. 560, col. 416), the Lord Advocate observed: "Where the law itself only allows comment with restraint, and only for inferences to be drawn in narrow circumstances, it would be a foolish prosecutor indeed who went further than that."

Subss. (2) and (3)

No other party can compel an accused person to give evidence in any trial unless he has already been convicted or acquitted of all charges libelled. The accused may give evidence on his own behalf but ordinarily should do so before leading any other evidence (s.263(2) permits application to be made only for the interruption of evidence to enable the examination of another witness). Once he elects to give evidence the accused can be cross-examined on any issue subject only to the limitations imposed upon the prosecutor by subs.(4); these restrictions do not apply to co-accused who are entitled to cross-examine an accused as to his criminal record if the accused, directly or impliedly, gives evidence against them (*McCourtney v H.M. Advocate*, 1978 S.L.T. 10; *Burton v H.M. Advocate*, 1979 S.L.T. (Notes) 59). Much of the case law originates from the problems created by cross-incrimination of accused (see *Sandlan v H.M. Advocate*, 1983 S.L.T. 519 which involved prejudicial evidence against first accused elicited in cross-examination of Crown witnesses by second accused without adequate opportunity for first accused to examine anew; in *H.M. Advocate v Ferrie*, 1983 S.C.C.R. 1 the use, by the Crown, as a witness of an accused who tendered partial pleas during trial was upheld; *Dodds v H.M. Advocate*, 1987 S.C.C.R. 678; 1988 S.L.T. 194; an accused who had had his partial pleas accepted, then gave evidence in relation to the outstanding charge and was cross-examined by the co-accused in relation to all charges libelled, unsuccessfully appealed.

If in the conduct of his defence, either in cross-examination of prosecution witnesses or in his own evidence, the accused attacks the character of the complainer, impugns the conduct of the prosecutor or represents himself falsely to be of good character, the accused is liable to lose the customary protection of subs.(4). As subs.(5) makes clear, that protection can only properly be withdrawn by the court after the prosecutor has made that motion outwith the presence of any jury. The court must consider the motion (see *Leggate v H.M. Advocate*, 1988 S.L.T. 665; 1988 S.C.C.R. 391).

The prosecutor has to exercise care to avoid breaching the statutory provisions, particularly in the heat of cross-examination: in *Cordiner v H.M. Advocate*, 1993 S.L.T. 2; 1991 S.C.C.R. 652 the prosecutor challenged the accused that he had sought to instigate another witness to pervert the course of justice by false testimony, a crime not charged. No objection had been taken at the time and the Court of Appeal held that while the section had been breached technically, the appellant had waived compliance. The difficulties involved for prosecutor and defence alike in the face of fingerprint evidence are apparent in *Robertson v H.M. Advocate*, 2003 S.L.T. 127. The Appeal Court, following *Jones v D.P.P.* [1962] A.C. 635; [1962] 1 All E.R. 569, considered that the words "tending to show" in subs.(4) meant "to suggest to the jury".

Note that subs.(7) has the effect of extending the protection given to the character of the complainer by subs.(4)(b) to deceased victims; it is not necessary that the deceased died as a result of being the victim of the crime charged. A curious variation upon subs.(4)(c) is found in *Marshall v H.M. Advocate*, 1996 G.W.D. 27–1577 where the jury was provided a copy of a co-accused's 22 page police interview transcript which made reference to M having previously being released from jail. M's appeal against conviction was refused, it being noted that the relevant passage had not been referred to in evidence and the sheriff had consciously decided not to draw attention to it or issue directions. See also *Sinclair v MacDonald*, 1996 J.C. 145; 1996 S.C.C.R. 466 where defence cross-examination had gone too far and amounted to attacks on character.

Witnesses in court during trial

267.—(1) The court may, on an application by any party to the proceedings, permit a witness to be in court during the proceedings or any part of the proceedings before he has given evidence if it appears to the court that the presence of the witness would not be contrary to the interests of justice.

(2) Without prejudice to subsection (1) above, where a witness has, without the permission of the court and without the consent of the parties to the proceedings, been present in court during the proceedings, the court may, in its discretion, admit the witness, where it appears to the court that the presence of the witness was not the result of culpable negligence or criminal intent, and that the witness has not been unduly instructed or influenced by what took place during his presence, or that injustice will not be done by his examination.

DEFINITION

"witness": s.307(1).

GENERAL NOTE

It is a matter for the court whether the evidence of a witness present in court during the trial should be taken into account. The court should consider whether there has been any criminative intent or wilful neglect on the part of the witness, the likely effect upon his testimony of his earlier presence in court and the likelihood of injustice being done by the exclusion of that evidence in the case.

See *MacDonald v Mackenzie*, 1947 J.C. 169; it is the task of the party tendering the witness' evidence to satisfy the court that the evidence should be admitted notwithstanding the improper presence in court. The evidence of a solicitor engaged in the case cannot be objected to on the ground of his earlier presence in court (*Campbell v Cochrane*, 1928 J.C. 25).

Citation of witnesses for precognition

267A.—(1) This Act shall be sufficient warrant for the citation of witnesses for precognition by the prosecutor, whether or not any person has been charged with the offence in relation to which the precognition is taken.

(2) Such citation shall be in the form prescribed by Act of Adjournal or as nearly as may be in such form.

(3) A witness who, having been duly cited—

(a) fails without reasonable excuse, after receiving at least 48 hours notice, to attend for precognition by a prosecutor at the time and place mentioned in the citation served on him; or

(b) refuses when so cited to give information within his knowledge regarding any matter relative to the commission of the offence in relation to which the precognition is taken,

shall be guilty of an offence and shall be liable on summary conviction to a fine not exceeding level 3 on the standard scale or to a term of imprisonment not exceeding 21 days.

AMENDMENT

Section 267A inserted by the Criminal Procedure (Amendment) (Scotland) Act 2004 (asp 5), s.22. Brought into force on October 4, 2004 by the Criminal Procedure (Amendment) (Scotland) Act 2004 (Commencement, Transitional Provisions and Savings) Order 2004 (SSI 2004/405 (C.28)).

DEFINITIONS

"fine": s.307(1).
"level 3": s.225(2).
"offence": s.307(1).
"prosecutor": s.307(1).
"standard scale": s.225(1).

GENERAL NOTE

New s.267A re-enacts in an updated form what was s.67A of the 1995 Act. In particular, s.267A provides that the 1995 Act is itself sufficient warrant to cite a witness for precognition and that citation shall be in the form prescribed by Act of Adjournal or as nearly as possible in such form. It is an offence for a witness fail to attend or to give information within his knowledge: s.267A(3).

Additional evidence, etc.

Additional evidence

268.—(1) Subject to subsection (2) below, the judge may, on a motion of the prosecutor or the accused made—

(a) in proceedings on indictment, at any time before the commencement of the speeches to the jury;

(b) in summary proceedings, at any time before the prosecutor proceeds to address the judge on the evidence,

permit him to lead additional evidence.

(2) Permission shall only be granted under subsection (1) above where the judge—

(a) considers that the additional evidence is *prima facie* material; and

(b) accepts that at the commencement of the trial either—

(i) the additional evidence was not available and could not reasonably have been made available; or

(ii) the materiality of such additional evidence could not reasonably have been foreseen by the party.

(3) The judge may permit the additional evidence to be led notwithstanding that—

(a) in proceedings on indictment, a witness or production concerned is not included in any list lodged by the parties and that the notice required by sections 67(5) and 78(4) of this Act has not been given; or

(b) in any case, a witness must be recalled.

(4) The judge may, when granting a motion in terms of this section, adjourn or postpone the trial before permitting the additional evidence to be led.

(5) In this section "the commencement of the trial" means—

   (a) in proceedings on indictment, the time when the jury is sworn; and

   (b) in summary proceedings, the time when the first witness for the prosecution is sworn.

DEFINITIONS

   "commencement of proceedings": s.268(5).
   "indictment": s.307(1).
   "judge": s.307(1).
   "prosecutor": s.307(1).

GENERAL NOTE

   Additional evidence can be led in both solemn or summary proceedings provided that the criteria in subs.(2) are satisfied. In solemn proceedings such evidence can be received notwithstanding that the relevant productions or witnesses have not been specified in the indictment (subs.(3)(a)); in either solemn or summary trials the additional evidence can be taken from witnesses whose evidence has already been heard. In making a motion for additional evidence to be heard, the party has to demonstrate some knowledge of the likely content of that evidence and its potential materiality, as well as persuade the court that the conditions set out in subs.(2) can be satisfied. Even then the judge retains an overall discretion not to admit the additional evidence (*Kerr v. H.M. Advocate*, 2002 G.W.D. 5-157).

   In *Cushion v. H.M. Advocate*, 1994 S.L.T. 410; 1993 S.C.C.R. 356 a review of the trial judge's refusal to admit additional evidence was appealed under the explanation that the court had not been given a full background, and that the judge's decision might have been more favourable to the application; the Appeal Court declined to review the application under s.149(1) of the 1975 Act.

Evidence in replication

269.—(1) The judge may, on a motion of the prosecutor made at the relevant time, permit the prosecutor to lead additional evidence for the purpose of—

   (a) contradicting evidence given by any defence witness which could not reasonably have been anticipated by the prosecutor; or

   (b) providing such proof as is mentioned in section 263(4) of this Act.

(2) The judge may permit the additional evidence to be led notwithstanding that—

   (a) in proceedings on indictment, a witness or production concerned is not included in any list lodged by the parties and that the notice required by sections 67(5) and 78(4) of this Act has not been given; or

   (b) in any case, a witness must be recalled.

(3) The judge may when granting a motion in terms of this section, adjourn or postpone the trial before permitting the additional evidence to be led.

(4) In subsection (1) above, "the relevant time" means—

   (a) in proceedings on indictment, after the close of the defence evidence and before the commencement of the speeches to the jury; and

   (b) in summary proceedings, after the close of the defence evidence and before the prosecutor proceeds to address the judge on the evidence.

DEFINITIONS

   "indictment": s.307(1).
   "judge": s.307(1).
   "prosecutor": s.307(1).
   "relevant time, the": s.269(4).

Evidence in replication may be led with leave of the court to contradict defence evidence which could not be anticipated by the prosecutor, or for the purpose of proving a prior statement of a witness whose evidence is now at variance (s.263(4)).

In assessing whether the prosecutor could have expected the testimony led by the defence, the court may well enquire about the preparations for trial; in both *MacGillivray v. Johnston (No. 2)*, 1994 S.L.T. 1012 and *Neizer v. Johnston*, 1993 S.C.C.R. 772 a decisive factor in refusing such a motion in each case was the Crown's awareness of the existence of witnesses who had been precognosced but had not been led in evidence.

Note that replication can only be used to counter defence evidence and cannot be used by the Crown to contradict earlier prosecution evidence (see *Campbell v. Allan*, 1988 S.C.C.R. 47).

Evidence of criminal record and character of accused

270.—(1) This section applies where—

(a) evidence is led by the defence, or the defence asks questions of a witness for the prosecution, with a view to establishing the accused's good character or impugning the character of the prosecutor, of any witness for the prosecution or of the complainer; or

(b) the nature or conduct of the defence is such as to tend to establish the accused's good character or to involve imputations on the character of the prosecutor, of any witness for the prosecution or of the complainer.

(2) Where this section applies the court may, without prejudice to section 268 of this Act, on the application of the prosecutor, permit the prosecutor to lead evidence that the accused has committed, or has been convicted of, or has been charged with, offences other than that for which he is being tried, or is of bad character, notwithstanding that, in proceedings on indictment, a witness or production concerned is not included in any list lodged by the prosecutor and that the notice required by sections 67(5) and 78(4) of this Act has not been given.

(3) In proceedings on indictment, an application under subsection (2) above shall be made in the course of the trial but in the absence of the jury.

(4) In subsection (1) above, references to the complainer include references to a victim who is deceased.

DEFINITIONS

"prosecutor": s.307(1).
"witness": s.307(1).

GENERAL NOTE

The purpose of this section is to provide a balanced picture where the defence, as a matter of tactics, elects to present the accused as being of good character or brings out the faults of witnesses or a deceased person. A cursory examination might suggest that subs. (2) is very similar to the more familiar terms of s.266(4)(b) and (c). Section 266 only enables the prosecutor or other accused to question the accused as to his history and character where such defence tactics have been pursued by the accused and the prosecutor, at least, may only do so with leave of the court (s.266(5)). It is important to note that s.266(4) is limited in scope: it is only activated when the accused gives evidence on his own behalf.

By contrast, subs. (2) is much more radical and enables the prosecution to lead evidence (without prior notice but with leave of the court) in rebuttal to demonstrate the history and character of the accused, if the defence has led evidence of his good character, or attacked the character of Crown witnesses or the prosecutor. The introduction of this provision in the Criminal Justice (Scotland) Act 1995, s.24 was not without controversy, given its nature, but it is clear that the conduct of the defence case in the future may require a good deal more circumspection than was necessary hitherto, even where the accused does not give evidence. It may also be said that subs. (1)(b) by its reference to "the nature or conduct of the defence" lacks both the familiarity and clarity of subs. (1)(a).

While the accused may found upon the previous convictions of Crown witnesses, it is clear that only in exceptional circumstances will the court permit scrutiny of, or questioning about, the factual circumstances giving rise to a previous conviction (see *Brady v. H.M. Advocate*, 1986 S.C.C.R. 191): only when the previous conviction relates directly to the circumstances of the current trial can questioning be extended.

Special measures for child witnesses and other vulnerable witnesses

Vulnerable witnesses: main definitions

271.—(1) For the purposes of this Act, a person who is giving or is to give evidence at, or for the purposes of, a trial is a vulnerable witness if—

(a) the person is under the age of 16 on the date of commencement of the proceedings in which the trial is being or to be held (such a vulnerable witness being referred to in this Act as a "child witness"), or

(b) where the person is not a child witness, there is a significant risk that the quality of the evidence to be given by the person will be diminished by reason of—

(i) mental disorder (within the meaning of section 328 of the Mental Health (Care and Treatment) (Scotland) Act 2003 (asp 13)), or

(ii) fear or distress in connection with giving evidence at the trial.

(2) In determining whether a person is a vulnerable witness by virtue of subsection (1)(b) above, the court shall take into account—

(a) the nature and circumstances of the alleged offence to which the proceedings relate,

(b) the nature of the evidence which the person is likely to give,

(c) the relationship (if any) between the person and the accused, *child*

(d) the person's age and maturity,

(e) any behaviour towards the person on the part of—

(i) the accused,

(ii) members of the family or associates of the accused,

(iii) any other person who is likely to be an accused or a witness in the proceedings, and

(f) such other matters, including—

(i) the social and cultural background and ethnic origins of the person,

(ii) the person's sexual orientation,

(iii) the domestic and employment circumstances of the person,

(iv) any religious beliefs or political opinions of the person, and

(v) any physical disability or other physical impairment which the person has,

as appear to the court to be relevant.

(3) For the purposes of subsection (1)(a) above and section 271B(1)(b) below, proceedings shall be taken to have commenced when the indictment or, as the case may be, complaint is served on the accused.

(4) In subsection (1)(b) above, the reference to the quality of evidence is to its quality in terms of completeness, coherence and accuracy.

(5) In this section and sections 271A to 271M of this Act—

"court" means the High Court or the sheriff court,

"trial" means a trial under solemn procedure in any court or under summary procedure in the sheriff court.

(6) In sections 271A to 271M of this Act, "special measure" means any of the special measures set out in, or prescribed under, section 271H below.

AMENDMENT

Section 271 substituted by the Vulnerable Witnesses (Scotland) Act 2004 (asp 3), s.1(1). Brought into force (except for the reference to s.271I in subss.(5) and(6)), for specified purposes, on April 1, 2005 by the Vulnerable Witnesses (Scotland) Act 2004 (Commencement) Order 2005 (SSI 2005/168 (C.7)), art.2 and Sch.

Further brought into force for specified purposes on November 30, 2005 by the Vulnerable Witnesses (Scotland) Act 2004 (Commencement No.2, Saving and Transitional Provisions) Order 2005 (SSI 2005/590), art.2 and Sch.1.

Further brought into force for specified purposes on April 1, 2006 by the Vulnerable Witnesses (Scotland) Act 2004 (Commencement No.3, Savings and Transitional Provisions) Order 2006 (SSI 2006/59 (C.8)).

Further brought into force for specified purposes on April 1, 2007 by the Vulnerable Witnesses (Scotland) Act 2004 (Commencement No.4, Savings and Transitional Provisions) Order 2007 (SSI 2007/101 (C.13)), art.2.

DEFINITIONS

    "court": s.271(5).
    "proceedings": s.271(3).
    "quality of evidence": s.271(4).
    "special measures": s.271H.
    "trial": s.271(5).
    "vulnerable witness": s.271(1).

GENERAL NOTE

It is recognised that some witnesses need extra help to enable them to give their evidence to a court. There was no automatic entitlement to assistance prior to this legislation on vulnerable witnesses. Specific application was required for special measures for individual witnesses.

One of the aims of the new provisions is to widen the categories of witnesses eligible to use special measures. There are now two categories of witness: first, those witnesses entitled automatically to use special measures; and, secondly, those witnesses entitled on a discretionary basis to use special measures.

Automatic entitlement to use special measures when giving evidence is extended to children, being persons under the age of 16 years at the commencement of the proceedings: s.271(1)(a).

Discretionary entitlement to use special measures when giving evidence may be extended to any person who has a mental disorder that affects their ability to give evidence: s.271(1)(b)(i). Alternatively, such measures may be extended to any person experiencing fear or distress in connection with giving evidence at the trial: s.271(1)(b)(ii).

It has to be emphasised that before the discretionary entitlement is excused by the court there requires to be a significant risk that the quality of the evidence to be given will be diminished by reason of that mental disorder or fear or distress: s.271(1).

In determining whether a person is a vulnerable witness with discretionary entitlement there is a wide range of various circumstances that the court may weigh in the balance: see s.271(2)(a) to (f) for the full range. These wider circumstances mean that assistance may now be extended to, amongst others, victims of sexual offences, domestic abuse or witnesses who have been intimidated.

Child witnesses

271A.—(1) Where a child witness is to give evidence at or for the purposes of a trial, the child witness is entitled, subject to—

    (a) subsections (2) to (13) below, and

    (b) section 271D of this Act,

to the benefit of one or more of the special measures for the purpose of giving evidence.

(2) A party citing or intending to cite a child witness shall, by the required time, lodge with the court a notice (referred to in this Act as a "child witness notice")—

    (a) specifying the special measure or measures which the party considers to be the most appropriate for the purpose of taking the child witness's evidence, or

(b) if the party considers that the child witness should give evidence without the benefit of any special measure, stating that fact.

(3) A child witness notice shall contain or be accompanied by—

(a) a summary of any views expressed for the purposes of section 271E(2)(b) of this Act, and

(b) such other information as may be prescribed by Act of Adjournal.

(4) The court may, on cause shown, allow a child witness notice to be lodged after the required time.

(5) The court shall, not later than 7 days after a child witness notice has been lodged, consider the notice in the absence of the parties and, subject to section 271B(3) of this Act—

(a) in the case of a notice under subsection (2)(a) above—

    (i) if a standard special measure is specified in the notice, make an order authorising the use of that measure for the purpose of taking the child witness's evidence, and

    (ii) if any other special measure is specified in the notice and the court is satisfied on the basis of the notice that it is appropriate to do so, make an order authorising the use of the special measure (in addition to any authorised by virtue of an order under sub-paragraph (i) above) for the purpose of taking the child witness's evidence,

(b) in the case of a notice under subsection (2)(b) above, if—

    (i) the summary of views accompanying the notice under subsection (3)(a) above indicates that the child witness has expressed a wish to give evidence without the benefit of any special measure, and

    (ii) the court is satisfied on the basis of the notice that it is appropriate to do so,

make an order authorising the giving of evidence by the child witness without the benefit of any special measure, or

(c) if—

    (i) paragraph (a)(ii) or (b) above would apply but for the fact that the court is not satisfied as mentioned in that paragraph, or

    (ii) in the case of a notice under subsection (2)(b), the summary of views accompanying the notice under subsection (3)(a) above indicates that the child witness has not expressed a wish to give evidence without the benefit of any special measure,

make an order under subsection (5A) below.

(5A) That order is an order—

(a) in the case of proceedings in the High Court where the preliminary hearing is yet to be held, appointing the child witness notice to be disposed of at that hearing;

(b) in the case of proceedings on indictment in the sheriff court where the first diet is yet to be held, appointing the child witness notice to be disposed of at that diet; or

(c) in any other case, appointing a diet to be held before the trial diet and requiring the parties to attend the diet.

(6) Subsection (7) below applies where—

(a) it appears to the court that a party intends to call a child witness to give evidence at or for the purposes of the trial,

(b) the party has not lodged a child witness notice in respect of the child witness by the time specified in subsection (2) above, and

(c) the court has not allowed a child witness notice in respect of the child witness to be lodged after that time under subsection (4) above.

(7) Where this subsection applies, the court shall—

(a) order the party to lodge a child witness notice in respect of the child witness by such time as the court may specify, or

(b) where the court does not so order—

    (i) in the case of proceedings on indictment where this subsection applies at or before the preliminary hearing or, as the case may be, the first diet, at that hearing or diet make an order under subsection (9) below; or

    (ii) in any other case, make an order appointing a diet to be held before the trial diet and requiring the parties to attend the diet.

(8) On making an order under subsection (5A)(c) or (7)(b)(ii) above, the court may postpone the trial diet.

(8A) Subsection (9) below applies to—

(a) a preliminary hearing or first diet, so far as the court is—

    (i) by virtue of an order under subsection (5A)(a) or (b) above, disposing of a child witness notice at the hearing or diet; or

    (ii) by virtue of subsection (7)(b)(i) above, to make an order under subsection (9) above at the hearing or diet; and

(b) a diet appointed under subsection (5A)(c) or (7)(b)(ii) above.

(9) At a hearing or diet to which this subsection applies, the court, after giving the parties an opportunity to be heard—

(a) in a case where any of the standard special measures has been authorised by an order under subsection (5)(a)(i) above, may make an order authorising the use of such further special measure or measures as it considers appropriate for the purpose of taking the child witness's evidence, and

(b) in any other case, shall make an order—

    (i) authorising the use of such special measure or measures as the court considers to be the most appropriate for the purpose of taking the child witness's evidence, or

    (ii) that the child witness is to give evidence without the benefit of any special measure.

(10) The court may make an order under subsection (9)(b)(ii) above only if satisfied—

(a) where the child witness has expressed a wish to give evidence without the benefit of any special measure, that it is appropriate for the child witness so to give evidence, or

(b) in any other case, that—

    (i) the use of any special measure for the purpose of taking the evidence of the child witness would give rise to a significant risk of prejudice to the fairness of the trial or otherwise to the interests of justice, and

    (ii) that risk significantly outweighs any risk of prejudice to the interests of the child witness if the order is made.

(11) A hearing or diet to which subsection (9) above applies may—

(a) on the application of the party citing or intending to cite the child witness in respect of whom the diet is to be held, or

(b) of the court's own motion,

be held in chambers.

(12) A diet appointed under subsection (5A)(c) or (7)(b)(ii) above in any case may be conjoined with any other diet to be held before the trial diet in the case.

(13) A party lodging a child witness notice shall, at the same time, intimate the notice to the other parties to the proceedings.

(13A) In subsections (2) and (4) above, "the required time" means—

(a) in the case of proceedings in the High Court, no later than 14 clear days before the preliminary hearing;

(b) in the case of proceedings on indictment in the sheriff court, no later than 7 clear days before the first diet;

(c) in any other case, no later than 14 clear days before the trial diet.

(14) In this section, references to a standard special measure are to any of the following special measures—

(a) the use of a live television link in accordance with section 271J of this Act where the place from which the child witness is to give evidence by means of the link is another part of the court building in which the court-room is located,

(b) the use of a screen in accordance with section 271K of this Act, and

(c) the use of a supporter in accordance with section 271L of this Act in conjunction with either of the special measures referred to in paragraphs (a) and (b) above.

AMENDMENT

Sections 271A inserted by the Vulnerable Witnesses (Scotland) Act 2004 (asp 3), s.1(1). Brought into force, for specified purposes, on April 1, 2005 by the Vulnerable Witnesses (Scotland) Act 2004 (Commencement) Order 2005 (SSI 2005/168 (C.7)), art.2 and Sch.

Subss.(2), (4), (5), (8), (9), (11), (12) as amended, subs.(7)(b) substituted and subss.(5A), (8A), (13A) inserted by the Criminal Procedure (Amendment) (Scotland) Act 2004 (asp 5), s.25, Sch.1, para.43. Brought into force on April 1, 2005 by the Criminal Procedure (Amendment) (Scotland) Act 2004 (Commencement, Transitional Provisions and Savings) Order 2004 (SSI 2004/405 (C.28)), art.2 and Sch.2.

Further brought into force for specified purposes on April 1, 2007 by the Vulnerable Witnesses (Scotland) Act 2004 (Commencement No.4, Savings and Transitional Provisions) Order 2007 (SSI 2007/101 (C.13)), art.2

DEFINITIONS

"child witness notice": s.271A(2).
"court": s.271(5).
"proceedings": s.271(3).
"special measures": s.271H.
"trial": s.271(5).

GENERAL NOTE

This section sets out the various powers in regard to the method by which a child witness may competently give evidence.

Subs.(1)

This entitles all child witnesses to give their evidence with the help of at least one of the special measures.

Subss.(2) and (13)

This requires the party calling the child witness to submit a notice to the court and at the same time intimate it to all other parties at least 14 clear days before the trial. That notice must set out the special measures that the party calling the witness considers to be the most appropriate.

Subs.(3)

Where a child has expressed a view then details of that view must be included in the notice.

Subs.(4)

The time limit specified in s.271A(2) may on cause shown be disregarded.

Subss.(5) and (6)

This provides that a court must consider a child witness notice within seven days of that notice being lodged. If the court is satisfied that there are necessary special measures or that the child has expressed a wish not to have special measures then the appropriate authority for either option may be given: s.271A(5)(a) and (6). If the court is not satisfied that there are necessary special measures or that the child has not expressed a wish to give evidence without special measures then a diet may be set down under s.271A(10) and parties may be ordained to attend: s.271A(5)(b) and (6).

Subss.(7) and (8)

If a child witness order is not lodged in time a court has power to order that such a notice is lodged or to arrange for a diet to be held before the trial.

Subs.(9)

The making of an order to hold a diet to consider a child witness order may also be accompanied by an order to postpone the trial diet.

Subs.(10)

The court must give parties the opportunity to be heard on the question of a child witness order. Thereafter, special measures may be authorised or the evidence of a child may be authorised to be given without special measures. The conditions for making such an order are set out in s.271A(11).

Subs.(11)

The effect of this provision is that an order can only be made in one of the two sets of circumstances. First, if a child wishes to give evidence without the benefit of special measures then that may be authorised if it is appropriate to do so: s.271A(11)(a). Secondly, in any other case, a child may be required to give evidence without the benefit of special measures where there is the risk of prejudicing the fairness of the trial significantly outweighs any risk of prejudice to the child: s.271A(11)(b).

Subs.(12)

It is competent to have child witness notice hearings concurrent with other hearings prior to the trial.

Further special provision for child witnesses under the age of 12

271B.—(1) This section applies where a child witness—

(a) is to give evidence at, or for the purposes of, a trial in respect of any offence specified in subsection (2) below, and

(b) is under the age of 12 on the date of commencement of the proceedings in which the trial is being or to be held.

(2) The offences referred to in subsection (1)(a) above are—

(a) murder,

(b) culpable homicide,

(c) any offence to which section 288C of this Act applies,

(d) any offence which involves an assault on, or injury or a threat of injury to, any person (including any offence involving neglect or ill-treatment of, or other cruelty to, a child),

(e) abduction, and

(f) plagium.

(3) Where this section applies, the court shall not make an order under section 271A or 271D of this Act which has the effect of requiring the child witness to be present in the court-room or any part of the court building in which the court-room is located for the purpose of giving evidence unless satisfied—

(a) where the child witness has expressed a wish to be so present for the purposes of giving evidence, that it is appropriate for the child witness to be so present for that purpose, or

(b) in any other case, that—

    (i) the taking of the evidence of the child witness without the child witness being so present would give rise to a significant risk of prejudice to the fairness of the trial or otherwise to the interests of justice, and

    (ii) that risk significantly outweighs any risk of prejudice to the interests of the child witness if the order is made.

AMENDMENT

Section 271B inserted by the Vulnerable Witnesses (Scotland) Act 2004 (asp 3), s.1(1). Brought into force, for specified purposes, on April 1, 2005 by the Vulnerable Witnesses (Scotland) Act 2004 (Commencement) Order 2005 (SSI 2005/168 (C.7)), art.2 and Sch.

Further brought into force for specified purposes on April 1, 2007 by the Vulnerable Witnesses (Scotland) Act 2004 (Commencement No.4, Savings and Transitional Provisions) Order 2007 (SSI 2007/101 (C.13)), art.2

DEFINITION

"trial": s.271(5).

GENERAL NOTE

Section 271B applies to the most serious and violent of cases or those that are of the most sensitive nature. The general principle is that a court may not make an order that has the effect of requiring a child witness to be present in the courtroom or any part of the court building in which the courtroom is located in order to give evidence. The two exceptions for such a requirement are, first, where a child ought to be present where the risk of prejudicing the fairness of the trial significantly outweighs any risk of prejudice to the child. Secondly, the child may be present where the child witness has asked to be there and the court considers it appropriate. For the approach to be taken with s.271B when an accused is a vulnerable person see s.271F(2)(b).

Vulnerable witnesses other than child witnesses

271C.—(1) This section applies where a party citing or intending to cite a person (other than a child witness) to give evidence at, or for the purposes of, a trial (such a person being referred to in this section as "the witness") considers—

(a) that the witness is likely to be a vulnerable witness, and

(b) that a special measure or combination of special measures ought to be used for the purpose of taking the witness's evidence.

(2) Where this section applies, the party citing or intending to cite the witness shall, by the required time, make an application (referred to as a "vulnerable witness application") to the court for an order authorising the use of one or more of the special measures for the purpose of taking the witness's evidence.

(3) A vulnerable witness application shall—

(a) specify the special measure or measures which the party making the application considers to be the most appropriate for the purpose of taking the evidence of the witness to whom the application relates, and

(b) contain or be accompanied by—

    (i) a summary of any views expressed for the purposes of section 271E(2)(b) of this Act, and

    (ii) such other information as may be prescribed by Act of Adjournal.

(4) The court may, on cause shown, allow a vulnerable witness application to be made after the required time.

(5) The court shall, not later than 7 days after a vulnerable witness application is made to it, consider the application in the absence of the parties and—

(a) make an order authorising the use of the special measure or measures specified in the application if satisfied on the basis of the application that—

    (i) the witness in respect of whom the application is made is a vulnerable witness,

    (ii) the special measures or measures specified in the application are the most appropriate for the purpose of taking the witness's evidence, and

    (iii) it is appropriate to do so after having complied with the duty in subsection (8) below, or

(b) if not satisfied as mentioned in paragraph (a) above, make an order under subsection (5A) below.

(5A) That order is an order—

(a) in the case of proceedings in the High Court where the preliminary hearing is yet to be held, appointing the vulnerable witness application to be disposed of at that hearing,

(b) in the case of proceedings on indictment in the sheriff court where the first diet is yet to be held, appointing the vulnerable witness application to be disposed of at that diet, or

(c) in any other case, appointing a diet to be held before the trial diet and requiring the parties to attend the diet.

(6) On making an order under subsection (5A)(c) above, the court may postpone the trial diet.

(6A) Subsection (7) below applies to—

(a) a preliminary hearing or first diet so far as the court is, by virtue of an order under subsection (5A)(a) or (b) above disposing of a vulnerable witness application at the hearing or diet, and

(b) a diet appointed under subsection (5A)(c) above.

(7) At a hearing or diet to which this subsection applies, the court may—

(a) after giving the parties an opportunity to be heard, and

(b) if satisfied that the witness in respect of whom the application is made is a vulnerable witness,

make an order authorising the use of such special measure or measures as the court considers to be the most appropriate for the purpose of taking the witness's evidence.

(8) In deciding whether to make an order under subsection (5)(a) or (7) above, the court shall—

(a) have regard to—

    (i) the possible effect on the witness if required to give evidence without the benefit of any special measure, and

    (ii) whether it is likely that the witness would be better able to give evidence with the benefit of a special measure, and

(b) take into account the matters specified in subsection (2)(a) to (f) of section 271 of this Act.

(9) A hearing or diet to which subsection (7) above applies may—

(a) on the application of the party citing or intending to cite the witness in respect of whom the diet is to be held, or

(b) of the court's own motion,

be held in chambers.

(10) A diet appointed under subsection (5A)(c) above in any case may be conjoined with any other diet to be held before the trial diet in the case.

(11) A party making a vulnerable witness application shall, at the same time, intimate the application to the other parties to the proceedings.

(12) In subsections (2) and (4) above, "the required time" means—

(a) in the case of proceedings in the High Court, no later than 14 clear days before the preliminary hearing,

(b) in the case of proceedings on indictment in the sheriff court, no later than 7 clear days before the first diet,

(c) in any other case, no later than 14 clear days before the trial diet.

AMENDMENT

Section 271C inserted by the Vulnerable Witnesses (Scotland) Act 2004 (asp 3), s.1(1). Brought into force on April 1, 2006 by the Vulnerable Witnesses (Scotland) Act 2004 (Commencement No.3, Savings and Transitional Provisions) Order 2006 (SSI 2006/59 (C.8)).

Subss.(2), (4), (5)(b), (6), (7), (9), (10) as amended, and subss.(5A), (6A), (12) inserted, by the Criminal Procedure (Amendment) (Scotland) Act 2004, s.25, Sch.1, para.44. Brought into force on April 1, 2006 by the Criminal Procedure (Amendment) (Scotland) Act 2004 (Commencement, Transitional Provisions and Savings) Order 2004(SSI 2004/405 (C.28)), art.2(2) and Sch.2.

DEFINITIONS

"special measures": s.271H.
"vulnerable witness": s.271(1).
"vulnerable witness application": s.271C(2).

GENERAL NOTE

This section sets out the various powers in regard to the method by which a vulnerable witness may competently give evidence.

Subs.(1)

This entitles a witness likely to be a vulnerable witness to give evidence with a special measure or a combination of special measures.

Subs.(2)

Where it is proposed to take evidence from a vulnerable witness by means of a special measure then not less than 14 clear days before the trial diet a vulnerable witness application should be made to obtain the necessary authority of the court.

Subs.(3)

A vulnerable witness application is required to specify the special measure sought and should be accompanied by relevant papers.

Subs.(4)

Notwithstanding the time limit set for a vulnerable witness application a court may allow such an application to be heard on other days.

Subs.(5)

Not later than seven days after a vulnerable witness application is made the court must consider the application in the absence of parties. If the court is satisfied with the application then an order is to be made authorising the use of special measures. If the court is not satisfied in regard to any of the specified aspects then the parties should be ordained to attend at a diet.

Subs.(6)

The court at a diet must give parties an opportunity to be heard and then, if satisfied that the relevant witness is a vulnerable witness, make an order authorising the use of a special measure.

Subs.(7)

The court in deciding whether to make an order must have regard to the possible effect on a witness if required to give evidence without the benefit of any special measure and whether it is likely that the witness would be better able to give evidence with the benefit of a special measure. Various circumstances are to be taken into consideration: see s.271(2)(a) to (f) inclusive.

Subs.(8)

It is competent to hear a vulnerable witness application concurrent with other hearings prior to the trial.

A party making a vulnerable witness application must intimate that to the other parties to the proceedings.

Review of arrangements for vulnerable witnesses

271D.—(1) In any case in which a person who is giving or is to give evidence at or for the purposes of the trial (referred to in this section as the "witness") is or appears to the court to be a vulnerable witness, the court may at any stage in the proceedings (whether before or after the commencement of the trial or before or after the witness has begun to give evidence)—

(a) on the application of the party citing or intending to cite the witness, or

(b) of its own motion,

review the current arrangements for taking the witness's evidence and, after giving the parties an opportunity to be heard, make an order under subsection (2) below.

(2) The order which may be made under this subsection is—

(a) where the current arrangements for taking the witness's evidence include the use of a special measure or combination of special measures authorised by an order under section 271A or 271C of this Act or under this subsection (referred to as the "earlier order"), an order varying or revoking the earlier order, or

(b) where the current arrangements for taking the witness's evidence do not include any special measure, an order authorising the use of such special measure or measures as the court considers most appropriate for the purpose of taking the witness's evidence.

(3) An order under subsection (2)(a) above varying an earlier order may—

(a) add to or substitute for any special measure authorised by the earlier order such other special measure as the court considers most appropriate for the purpose of taking the witness's evidence, or

(b) where the earlier order authorises the use of a combination of special measures for that purpose, delete any of the special measures so authorised.

(4) The court may make an order under subsection (2)(a) above revoking an earlier order only if satisfied—

(a) where the witness has expressed a wish to give or, as the case may be, continue to give evidence without the benefit of any special measure, that it is appropriate for the witness so to give evidence, or

(b) in any other case, that—

(i) the use, or continued use, of the special measure or measures authorised by the earlier order for the purpose of taking the witness's evidence would give rise to a significant risk of prejudice to the fairness of the trial or otherwise to the interests of justice, and

(ii) that risk significantly outweighs any risk of prejudice to the interests of the witness if the order is made.

(5) Subsection (8) of section 271C of this Act applies to the making of an order under subsection (2)(b) of this section as it applies to the making of an order under subsection (5)(a) or (7) of that section but as if the references to the witness were to the witness within the meaning of this section.

(6) In this section, "current arrangements" means the arrangements in place at the time the review under this section is begun.

AMENDMENT

Section 271D inserted by the Vulnerable Witnesses (Scotland) Act 2004 (asp 3), s.1(1). Brought into force (except for subs.(5) and the reference to s.271C in subs.(2)(a)), for specified purposes, on April 1, 2005 by the Vulnerable Witnesses (Scotland) Act 2004 (Commencement) Order 2005 (SSI 2005/168 (C.7)), art.2 and Sch.

Further brought into force for specified purposes on April 1, 2006 by the Vulnerable Witnesses (Scotland) Act 2004 (Commencement No.3, Savings and Transitional Provisions) Order 2006 (SSI 2006/59 (C.8)).

Further brought into force (except for subs.(5) and the reference to s.271C in subs.(2)(a)) for specified purposes on April 1, 2007 by the Vulnerable Witnesses (Scotland) Act 2004 (Commencement No.4, Savings and Transitional Provisions) Order 2007 (SSI 2007/101 (C.13)), art.2.

DEFINITIONS

"court": s.271(5).
"current arrangements": s.271D(6).
"earlier order": s.271D(2)(a).
"special measures": s.271H.
"vulnerable witness": s.271(1).
"witness": s.271D(2).

GENERAL NOTE

This section enables the court at any time, up to and including when a vulnerable witness is giving evidence in a trial, to review the arrangements for the taking of their evidence. The court may make an order regarding the arrangements at the request of the party who is calling the witness or of its own accord: s.271D(1). The court may make an order for a special measure to be used by a vulnerable witness in circumstances where an order has not previously been made: s.271D(2)(b). Such an order may add a special measure, or substitute a special measure in the previous order for another special measure that is considered more appropriate: s.271D(3)(a). Where a previous order contains a combination of special measures, the number of measures to be used can be used: s.271D(3)(b).

An order that special measures may no longer be used can only be made in two instances: first, where the court is satisfied that it is appropriate to revoke the use of special measures as the witness does not wish to use them: s.271D(4)(a). Secondly, where the court is satisfied that there is a risk of prejudice to the fairness of the trial that significantly outweighs the risk of prejudice to the witness: s.271D(4)(b). In making an order the court must take into account the circumstances in s.271(2)(a) to (f) inclusive.

Vulnerable witnesses: supplementary provision

271E.—(1) Subsection (2) below applies where—

(a) a party is considering for the purposes of a child witness notice or a vulnerable witness application which of the special measures is or are the most appropriate for the purpose of taking the evidence of the person to whom the notice or application relates, or

(b) the court is making an order under section 271A(5)(a)(ii) or (b) or (9), 271C or 271D of this Act.

(2) The party or, as the case may be, the court shall—

(a) have regard to the best interests of the witness, and

(b) take account of any views expressed by—

(i) the witness (having regard, where the witness is a child witness, to the witness's age and maturity), and

(ii) where the witness is a child witness, the witness's parent (except where the parent is the accused).

(3) For the purposes of subsection (2)(b) above, where the witness is a child witness—

(a) the witness shall be presumed to be of sufficient age and maturity to form a view if aged 12 or older, and

(b) in the event that any views expressed by the witness are inconsistent with any views expressed by the witness's parent, the views of the witness shall be given greater weight.

(4) In this section—

"parent", in relation to a child witness, means any person having parental responsibilities within the meaning of section 1(3) of the Children (Scotland) Act 1995 (c.36) in relation to the child witness,

"the witness" means—

(a) in the case referred to in subsection (1)(a) above, the person to whom the notice or application relates,

(b) in the case referred to in subsection (1)(b) above, the person to whom the order would relate.

AMENDMENT

Section 271E inserted by the Vulnerable Witnesses (Scotland) Act 2004 (asp 3), s.1(1). Brought into force (except for the reference to s.271C in subs.(1)(b)), for specified purposes, on April 1, 2005 by the Vulnerable Witnesses (Scotland) Act 2004 (Commencement) Order 2005 (SSI 2005/168 (C.7)), art.2 and Sch.

Further brought into force for specified purposes on April 1, 2006 by the Vulnerable Witnesses (Scotland) Act 2004 (Commencement No.3, Savings and Transitional Provisions) Order 2006 (SSI 2006/59 (C.8)).

Further brought into force (except for the reference to s.271C in subs.(1)(b))for specified purposes on April 1, 2007 by the Vulnerable Witnesses (Scotland) Act 2004 (Commencement No.4, Savings and Transitional Provisions) Order 2007 (SSI 2007/101 (C.13)), art.2.

DEFINITIONS

"child witness notice": s.271A(2).
"court": s.271(5).
"parent": s.271E(4).
"special measures": s.271H.
"the witness": s.271E(4).
"vulnerable witness": s.271(1).
"vulnerable witness application": s.271C(2).

GENERAL NOTE

Section 271E(1) to (3) require the party calling the witness and the court in determining a special measures order to consider the best interests and views of the witness when deciding the special measures most appropriate for the purpose of taking the evidence. With regard to child witnesses the views of the parents of the child are also to be considered unless that person is the accused.

The section ensures that children over 12 years are presumed to be able to give a view, and in the case of children under 12 years, the age and maturity of the child are to be considered in determining whether they can express a view on the special measures to be used. In the event that the views of the child and the parent differ then the views of the child are to be given greater weight.

The accused

271F.—(1) For the purposes of the application of subsection (1) of section 271 of this Act to the accused (where the accused is giving or is to give evidence at or for the purposes of the trial), subsection (2) of that section shall have effect as if—

(a) for paragraph (c) there were substituted—

"(c) whether the accused is to be legally represented at the trial and, if not, the accused's entitlement to be so legally represented,", and

(b) for paragraph (e) there were substituted—

"(e) any behaviour towards the accused on the part of—

(i) any co-accused or any person who is likely to be a co-accused in the proceedings,

(ii) any witness or any person who is likely to be a witness in the proceedings, or

(iii) members of the family or associates of any of the persons mentioned in sub-paragraphs (i) and (ii) above.".

(2) Where, if the accused were to give evidence at or for the purposes of the trial, he would be a child witness—

  (a) section 271A of this Act shall apply in relation to the accused subject to the following modifications—

    (i) references to a child witness (except in the phrase "child witness notice") shall be read as if they were references to the accused,

    (ii) references to the party citing or intending to cite a child witness shall be read as if they were references to the accused, and

    (iii) subsection (6) shall have effect as if for paragraph (a) there were substituted—

      "(a) it appears to the court that the accused, if he were to give evidence at or for the purposes of the trial, would be a child witness,", and

  (b) section 271B of this Act shall apply in relation to the accused as if—

    (i) for subsection (1) there were substituted—

    "(1) This section applies where the accused—

      (a) if he were to give evidence at or for the purposes of the trial would be a child witness, and

      (b) is under the age of 12 on the date of commencement of the proceedings.", and

    (ii) in subsection (3), references to the child witness were references to the accused.

(3) Subsection (4) below applies where the accused—

  (a) considers that, if he were to give evidence at or for the purposes of the trial, he would be a vulnerable witness other than a child witness, and

  (b) has not decided to give evidence without the benefit of any special measures.

(4) Where this subsection applies, subsections (2) to (11) of section 271C of this Act shall apply in relation to the accused subject to the following modifications—

  (a) references to the witness shall be read as if they were references to the accused,

  (b) references to the party citing or intending the cite the witness shall be read as if they were references to the accused, and

  (c) in subsection (8)(b), the reference to subsection (2)(a) to (f) of section 271 of this Act shall be read as if it were a reference to that subsection as modified by subsection (1) above.

(5) Section 271D of this Act shall apply in any case where it appears to the court that the accused, if he were to give evidence at or for the purposes of the trial, would be a vulnerable witness as it applies in the case referred to in subsection (1) of that section but subject to the following modifications—

  (a) references to the witness shall be read as if they were references to the accused,

  (b) references to the party citing or intending to cite the witness shall be read as if they were references to the accused.

(6) Where the witness within the meaning of section 271E of this Act is the accused, that section shall have effect in relation to the witness as if—

  (a) in subsection (1), paragraph (a) were omitted, and

  (b) in subsection (2), the words "The party or, as the case may be," were omitted.

(7) Section 271M of this Act shall have effect, where the vulnerable witness is

the accused, as if the reference in subsection (2) to the party citing the vulnerable witness were a reference to the accused.

(8) The following provisions of this Act shall not apply in relation to a vulnerable witness who is the accused—

(a) section 271H(1)(c),

(b) section 271I(3).

AMENDMENT

Section 271F inserted by the Vulnerable Witnesses (Scotland) Act 2004 (asp 3), s.1(1). Brought into force (except for subss.(3), (4), (8)(b)), for specified purposes, on April 1, 2005 by the Vulnerable Witnesses (Scotland) Act 2004 (Commencement) Order 2005 (SSI 2005/168 (C.7)), art.2 and Sch.

Subs.(8)(b) brought into force for specified purposes on November 30, 2005 by the Vulnerable Witnesses (Scotland) Act 2004 (Commencement No.2, Saving and Transitional Provisions) Order 2005 (SSI 2005/590), art.2 and Sch.1.

Further brought into force for specified purposes on April 1, 2006 by the Vulnerable Witnesses (Scotland) Act 2004 (Commencement No.3, Savings and Transitional Provisions) Order 2006 (SSI 2006/59 (C.8)).

Further brought into force for specified purposes on April 1, 2007 by the Vulnerable Witnesses (Scotland) Act 2004 (Commencement No.4, Savings and Transitional Provisions) Order 2007 (SSI 2007/101 (C.13)), art.2.

DEFINITIONS

"child witness notice": s.271A(2).

"court": s.271(5).

"vulnerable witness": s.271(1).

GENERAL NOTE

This section sets out the provisions for allowing an accused, if considered to be vulnerable, to give his or her evidence with the use of a special measure. The provisions of ss.271 to 271M will apply to the accused as a vulnerable witness but with certain modifications. Section 271 is modified for the accused by amending the factors to be taken into account under s.271(2) in determining vulnerability, including the fact that the accused is entitled to or will have legal representation. The accused is also not entitled to use screens as a special measure for the giving of his or her evidence.

Saving provision

271G. Nothing in sections 271A to 271F of this Act affects any power or duty which a court has otherwise than by virtue of those sections to make or authorise any special arrangements for taking the evidence of any person.

AMENDMENT

Section 271G inserted by the Vulnerable Witnesses (Scotland) Act 2004 (asp 3), s.1(1). Brought into force (except in respect of s.271C), for specified purposes, on April 1, 2005 by the Vulnerable Witnesses (Scotland) Act 2004 (Commencement) Order 2005 (SSI 2005/168 (C.7)), art.2 and Sch.

Further brought into force for specified purposes on April 1, 2006 by the Vulnerable Witnesses (Scotland) Act 2004 (Commencement No.3, Savings and Transitional Provisions) Order 2006 (SSI 2006/59 (C.8)).

Further brought into force for specified purposes on April 1, 2007 by the Vulnerable Witnesses (Scotland) Act 2004 (Commencement No.4, Savings and Transitional Provisions) Order 2007 (SSI 2007/101 (C.13)), art.2.

DEFINITIONS

"court": s.271(5).

GENERAL NOTE

This section ensures that the existing common law powers to make or authorise special arrangements for vulnerable witnesses' evidence are not removed by the new ss.271A to 271F. In *Hampson v HM Advocate*, 2003 S.L.T. 94 the court established common law power to regulate proceedings and permitted the complainer, who did not fall within the statutory provisions set out in s.271, to give evidence from behind screens but visible to the accused. The test in an application made prior to the commencement of a trial was whether if the application was granted the proposed arrangement would affect the right of the accused to such an extent that the trial would inevitably be unfair: *HM Advocate v Smith*, 2000 S.C.C.R. 910.

The special measures

271H.—(1) The special measures which may be authorised to be used under section 271A, 271C or 271D of this Act for the purpose of taking the evidence of a vulnerable witness are—

(a) taking of evidence by a commissioner in accordance with section 271I of this Act,

(b) use of a live television link in accordance with section 271J of this Act,

(c) use of a screen in accordance with section 271K of this Act,

(d) use of a supporter in accordance with section 271L of this Act,

(e) giving evidence in chief in the form of a prior statement in accordance with section 271M of this Act, and

(f) such other measures as the Scottish Ministers may, by order made by statutory instrument, prescribe.

(2) An order under subsection (1)(f) above shall not be made unless a draft of the statutory instrument containing the order has been laid before and approved by a resolution of the Scottish Parliament.

(3) Provision may be made by Act of Adjournal regulating, so far as not regulated by sections 271I to 271M of this Act, the use in any proceedings of any special measure authorised to be used by virtue of section 271A, 271C or 271D of this Act.

AMENDMENT

Section 271H inserted by the Vulnerable Witnesses (Scotland) Act 2004 (asp 3), s.1(1). Brought into force (except for subs.(1)(a) and the references in subss.(1) and (3) to s.271C), for specified purposes, on April 1, 2005 by the Vulnerable Witnesses (Scotland) Act 2004 (Commencement) Order 2005 (SSI 2005/168 (C.7)), art.2 and Sch.

Subs.(1)(a) brought into force for specified purposes on November 30, 2005 by the Vulnerable Witnesses (Scotland) Act 2004 (Commencement No.2, Saving and Transitional Provisions) Order 2005 (SSI 2005/590), art.2 and Sch.1.

Further brought into force for specified purposes on April 1, 2006 by the Vulnerable Witnesses (Scotland) Act 2004 (Commencement No.3, Savings and Transitional Provisions) Order 2006 (SSI 2006/59 (C.8)).

Further brought into force for specified purposes on April 1, 2007 by the Vulnerable Witnesses (Scotland) Act 2004 (Commencement No.4, Savings and Transitional Provisions) Order 2007 (SSI 2007/101 (C.13)), art.2.

DEFINITIONS

"court": s.271(5).
"vulnerable witness": s.271(1).

GENERAL NOTE

The special measures that may be made available to vulnerable witnesses in order that they may give their evidence are listed in this section. The various competent measures in s.271H(1)(a) to (e) inclusive probably represent the best available measures but there may yet be others. Section 271H(1)(f) allows the Scottish Ministers a power to make provision for other special measures by way of statutory instrument.

Taking of evidence by a commissioner

271I.—(1) Where the special measure to be used is taking of evidence by a commissioner, the court shall appoint a commissioner to take the evidence of the vulnerable witness in respect of whom the special measure is to be used.

(1A) Proceedings before a commissioner appointed under subsection (1) above shall, if the court so directed when authorising such proceedings, take place by means of a live television link between the place where the commissioner is taking, and the place from which the witness is giving, evidence.

(2) Proceedings before a commissioner appointed under subsection (1) above shall be recorded by video recorder.

(3) An accused—

(a) shall not, except by leave of the court on special cause shown, be present-

    (i) in the room where such proceedings are taking place; or

    (ii) if such proceedings are taking placeby means of a live television link, in the same room as the witness

(b) is entitled by such means as seem suitable to the court to watch and hear the proceedings.

(4) The recording of the proceedings made in pursuance of subsection (2) above shall be received in evidence without being sworn to by witnesses.

(5) Sections

(a) 274;

(b) 275;

(c) 275B except subsection (2)(b);

(d) 275C;

(e) 288C;

(f) 288E; and

(g) 288F,

of this Act apply in relation to proceedings before a commissioner appointed under subsection (1)(b) above as they apply in relation to a trial.

(6) In the application of those sections in relation to such proceedings-

(a) the commissioner acting in the proceedings is to perform the functions of the court as provided for in thoses sections;

(b) references-

    (i) in thoses sections, except sections 275(3)(c) and (7)(c), to a trial or a trial diet;

    (ii) in those sections, except sections 275(3)(e) and 288F(2), (3) and (4), to the court, shall be read accordingly;

(c) the reference in section 275B(1) to 14 days shall be read as reference to 7 days.

(7) In a case where it falls to the court to appoint a commissioner under subsection (1) above, the commissioner shall be a person described in subsection (8) below.

(8) The persons are-

(a) where the proceedings before the commissioner are for the purposes of a trial in the High Court, a judge of the Hight Court; or

(b) in any other case, a sheriff.

AMENDMENT

    Section 271I inserted by the Vulnerable Witnesses (Scotland) Act 2004 (asp 3), s.1(1). Brought into force, for specified purposes, on November 30, 2005 by the Vulnerable Witnesses (Scotland) Act 2004 (Commencement No.2, Saving and Transitional Provisions) Order 2005 (SSI 2005/590), art.2 and Sch.1.

    Further brought into force for specified purposes on April 1, 2007 by the Vulnerable Witnesses (Scotland) Act 2004 (Commencement No.4, Savings and Transitional Provisions) Order 2007 (SSI 2007/101 (C.13)), art.2.

    Section 271I amended and s.271I(1A) and s.271(5)–(8) inserted by the Criminal Proceedings etc. (Reform) (Scotland) Act 2007 (asp 6), s.35.

DEFINITIONS
    "court": s.271(5).
    "special measures": s.271H.
    "vulnerable witness": s.271(1).

GENERAL NOTE

    This section allows evidence on commission to be used as a special measure for vulnerable witnesses. The court may appoint a commissioner to take the evidence of a vulnerable witness in advance of the trial. An accused may be present with the agreement of the commissioner but at least must be able to watch and listen by some means while the evidence of that witness is taken. Proceedings heard before a commissioner must be recorded by video. That recording of proceedings must be received in evidence at a trial without necessarily being sworn to by a witness.

Live television link

271J.—(1) Where the special measure to be used is a live television link, the court shall make such arrangements as seem to it appropriate for the vulnerable witness in respect of whom the special measure is to be used to give evidence from a place outside the court-room where the trial is to take place by means of a live television link between that place and the court-room.

    (2) The place from which the vulnerable witness gives evidence by means of the link—

    (a) may be another part of the court building in which the court-room is located or any other suitable place outwith that building, and

    (b) shall be treated, for the purposes of the proceedings at the trial, as part of the court-room whilst the witness is giving evidence.

    (3) Any proceedings conducted by means of a live television link by virtue of this section shall be treated as taking place in the presence of the accused.

    (4) Where—

    (a) the live television link is to be used in proceedings in a sheriff court, but

    (b) that court lacks accommodation or equipment necessary for the purpose of receiving such a link,

the sheriff may by order transfer the proceedings to any other sheriff court in the same sheriffdom which has such accommodation or equipment available.

    (5) An order may be made under subsection (4) above—

    (a) at any stage in the proceedings (whether before or after the commencement of the trial), or

    (b) in relation to any part of the proceedings.

AMENDMENT

    Section 271J inserted by the Vulnerable Witnesses (Scotland) Act 2004 (asp 3), s.1(1). Brought into force, for specified purposes, on April 1, 2005 by the Vulnerable Witnesses (Scotland) Act 2004 (Commencement) Order 2005 (SSI 2005/168 (C.7)), art.2 and Sch.

    Further brought into force for specified purposes on April 1, 2006 by the Vulnerable Witnesses (Scotland) Act 2004 (Commencement No.3, Savings and Transitional Provisions) Order 2006 (SSI 2006/59 (C.8)).

    Further brought into force for specified purposes on April 1, 2007 by the Vulnerable Witnesses (Scotland) Act 2004 (Commencement No.4, Savings and Transitional Provisions) Order 2007 (SSI 2007/101 (C.13)), art.2.

DEFINITIONS
    "court": s.271(5).
    "special measures": s.271H.
    "trial": s.271(5).
    "vulnerable witness": s.271(1).

GENERAL NOTE

    The giving of evidence by means of a live television link is known already: see *HM Advocate v*

Cinci, 2002 G.W.D. 27–934. This new provision refers to the use of a live television link as a special measure for vulnerable witnesses. Section 271J(1) imposes a duty on the court to make suitable arrangements for the evidence of a vulnerable witness to be given from outside the courtroom by a live television link. Section 271J(2) allows for this to happen from either another part of the courtroom building or any suitable place that can be identified away from the court building.

Section 271J(3) provides that when a live link is used in these proceedings it will be treated as taking place in the presence of the accused. Section 271J(4) makes it competent for the sheriff to transfer a case or part of a case in which it is intended that a live television link be used from a sheriff court that does not have either the suitable accommodation needed or the necessary equipment to another sheriff court within the same sheriffdom that does.

Screens

271K.—(1) Where the special measure to be used is a screen, the screen shall be used to conceal the accused from the sight of the vulnerable witness in respect of whom the special measure is to be used.

(2) However, the court shall make arrangements to ensure that the accused is able to watch and hear the vulnerable witness giving evidence.

(3) Subsections (4) and (5) of section 271J of this Act apply for the purpose of the use of a screen under this section as they apply for the purpose of the use of a live television link under that section but as if—

(a) references to the live television link were references to the screen, and

(b) the reference to receiving such a link were a reference to the use of a screen.

AMENDMENT

Section 271K inserted by the Vulnerable Witnesses (Scotland) Act 2004 (asp 3), s.1(1). Brought into force, for specified purposes, on April 1, 2005 by the Vulnerable Witnesses (Scotland) Act 2004 (Commencement) Order 2005 (SSI 2005/168 (C.7)), art.2 and Sch.

Further brought into force for specified purposes on April 1, 2006 by the Vulnerable Witnesses (Scotland) Act 2004 (Commencement No.3, Savings and Transitional Provisions) Order 2006 (SSI 2006/59 (C.8)).

Further brought into force for specified purposes on April 1, 2007 by the Vulnerable Witnesses (Scotland) Act 2004 (Commencement No.4, Savings and Transitional Provisions) Order 2007 (SSI 2007/101 (C.13)), art.2.

DEFINITIONS

"court": s.271(5).
"vulnerable witness": s.271(1).

GENERAL NOTE

This section provides for the use of screens where a vulnerable witness is giving evidence in a criminal trial. The purpose of the screen is to conceal the accused from the sight of the vulnerable person while the latter is giving evidence. There is a duty on the court to ensure that the accused is able to see and hear the witness giving evidence.

Supporters

271L.—(1) Where the special measure to be used is a supporter, another person ("the supporter") nominated by or on behalf of the vulnerable witness in respect of whom the special measure is to be used may be present alongside the witness to support the witness while the witness is giving evidence.

(2) Where the person nominated as the supporter is to give evidence at the trial, that person may not act as the supporter at any time before giving evidence.

(3) The supporter shall not prompt or otherwise seek to influence the witness in the course of giving evidence.

AMENDMENT

Section 271L inserted by the Vulnerable Witnesses (Scotland) Act 2004 (asp 3), s.1(1). Brought into force, for specified purposes, on April 1, 2005 by the Vulnerable Witnesses (Scotland) Act 2004 (Commencement) Order 2005 (SSI 2005/168 (C.7)), art.2 and Sch.

Further brought into force for specified purposes on April 1, 2006 by the Vulnerable Witnesses (Scotland) Act 2004 (Commencement No.3, Savings and Transitional Provisions) Order 2006 (SSI 2006/59 (C.8)).

Further brought into force for specified purposes on April 1, 2007 by the Vulnerable Witnesses (Scotland) Act 2004 (Commencement No.4, Savings and Transitional Provisions) Order 2007 (SSI 2007/101 (C.13)), art.2.

DEFINITIONS

"supporter": s.271L.
"vulnerable witness": s.271(1).

GENERAL NOTE

This section allows for a person to be nominated by a vulnerable witness to accompany the witness into the courtroom or the room where the witness is to give evidence by live television link. The nominated person is known as the supporter. The person nominated as a supporter may not act as such at any time prior to giving evidence. The supporter cannot be allowed to prompt the vulnerable witness when the latter is giving evidence.

Giving evidence in chief in the form of a prior statement

271M.—(1) This section applies where the special measure to be used in respect of a vulnerable witness is giving evidence in chief in the form of a prior statement.

(2) A statement made by the vulnerable witness which is lodged in evidence for the purposes of this section by or on behalf of the party citing the vulnerable witness shall, subject to subsection (3) below, be admissible as the witness's evidence in chief, or as part of the witness's evidence in chief, without the witness being required to adopt or otherwise speak to the statement in giving evidence in court.

(3) Section 260 of this Act shall apply to a statement lodged for the purposes of this section as it applies to a prior statement referred to in that section but as if—

(a) references to a prior statement were references to the statement lodged for the purposes of this section,

(b) in subsection (1), the words "where a witness gives evidence in criminal proceedings" were omitted, and

(c) in subsection (2), paragraph (b) were omitted.

(4) This section does not affect the admissibility of any statement made by any person which is admissible otherwise than by virtue of this section.

(5) In this section, "statement" has the meaning given in section 262(1) of this Act.

AMENDMENT

Section 271M inserted by the Vulnerable Witnesses (Scotland) Act 2004 (asp 3), s.1(1). Brought into force, for specified purposes, on April 1, 2005 by the Vulnerable Witnesses (Scotland) Act 2004 (Commencement) Order 2005 (SSI 2005/168 (C.7)), art.2 and Sch.

Further brought into force for specified purposes on April 1, 2006 by the Vulnerable Witnesses (Scotland) Act 2004 (Commencement No.3, Savings and Transitional Provisions) Order 2006(SSI 2006/59 (C.8)).

Further brought into force for specified purposes on April 1, 2007 by the Vulnerable Witnesses (Scotland) Act 2004 (Commencement No.4, Savings and Transitional Provisions) Order 2007 (SSI 2007/101 (C.13)), art.2.

DEFINITIONS

"special measures": s.271H.
"statement": ss.271M(5) and 262(1).

"vulnerable witness": s.271(1).

GENERAL NOTE

Section 271M(1) and (2) allow for a previous statement made by a vulnerable witness and which has been reliably recorded on video or in some other way to be used as their main evidence without the need for the witness having to adopt the statement: cf. *Jamieson v HM Advocate*, 1994 S.L.T. 537 and also s.260(2)(b) of the 1995 Act.

Evidence on commission and from abroad

Evidence by letter of request or on commission

272.—(1) In any criminal proceedings in the High Court or the sheriff court the prosecutor or the defence may, at an appropriate time, apply to a judge of the court in which the trial is to take place (or, if that is not yet known, to a judge of the High Court) for—

  (a) the issue of a letter of request to a court, or tribunal, exercising jurisdiction in a country or territory outside the United Kingdom, Channel Islands and Isle of Man for the examination of a witness resident in that country or territory; or

  (b) the appointment of a commissioner to examine, at any place in the United Kingdom, Channel Islands, or Isle of Man, a witness who—

   (i) by reason of being ill or infirm is unable to attend the trial diet; or

   (ii) is not ordinarily resident in, and is, at the time of the trial diet, unlikely to be present in, the United Kingdom, Channel Islands or the Isle of Man.

(2) A hearing, as regards any application under subsection (1) above by a party, shall be conducted in chambers but may be dispensed with if the application is not opposed.

(3) An application under subsection (1) above may be granted only if the judge is satisfied that—

  (a) the evidence which it is averred the witness is able to give is necessary for the proper adjudication of the trial; and

  (b) there would be no unfairness to the other party were such evidence to be received in the form of the record of an examination conducted by virtue of that subsection.

(4) Any such record as is mentioned in paragraph (b) of subsection (3) above shall, without being sworn to by witnesses, be received in evidence in so far as it either accords with the averment mentioned in paragraph (a) of that subsection or can be so received without unfairness to either party.

(5) Where any such record as is mentioned in paragraph (b) of subsection (3) above, or any part of such record, is not a document in writing, that record or part shall not be received in evidence under subsection (4) above unless it is accompanied by a transcript of its contents.

(6) The procedure as regards the foregoing provisions of this section shall be prescribed by Act of Adjournal; and without prejudice to the generality of the power to make it, such an Act of Adjournal may provide for the appointment of a person before whom evidence may be taken for the purposes of this section.

(7) In subsection (1) above, "appropriate time" means as regards—

  (a) solemn proceedings, any time before the oath is administered to the jury;

(b) summary proceedings, any time before the first witness is sworn,

or (but only in relation to an application under paragraph (b) of that subsection) any time during the course of the trial if the circumstances on which the application is based had not arisen, or would not have merited such application, within the period mentioned in paragraph (a) or, as the case may be, (b) of this subsection.

(8) In subsection (3) and (4) above, "record" includes, in addition to a document in writing—

(a) any disc, tape, soundtrack or other device in which sounds or other data (not being visual images) are recorded so as to be capable (with or without the aid of some other equipment) of being reproduced therefrom; and

(b) any film (including microfilm), negative, tape, disc or other device in which one or more visual images are recorded so as to be capable (as aforesaid) of being reproduced therefrom.

(9) This section is without prejudice to any existing power at common law to adjourn a trial diet to the place where a witness is.

(10) Sections

(a) 274;

(b) 275;

(c) 275B except subsection (2)(b);

(d) 275C;

(e) 288C;

of this Act apply in relation to proceedings in which a commissioner examines a witness under subsection (1)(b) above as they apply in relation to a trial.

(11) In the application of those sections in relation to such proceedings-

(a) the commissioner acting in the proceedings is to perform the functions of the court as provided for in thoses sections;

(b) references-

(i) in thoses sections, except sections 275(3)(c) and (7)(c), to a trial or a trial diet;

(ii) in those sections, except sections 275(3)(e), to the court, shall be read accordingly;

(c) the reference in section 275B(1) to 14 days shall be read as reference to 7 days.

(12) In a case where it falls to the court to appoint a commissioner under subsection (1)(b) above, the commissioner shall be a person described in subsection (13) below.

(13) The persons are-

(a) where the proceedings before the commissioner are for the purposes of a trial in the High Court, a judge of the Hight Court; or

(b) in any other case, a sheriff.

AMMENDMENTS

Section 272 amended and s.272(10)–(13) inserted by the Criminal Proceedings etc. (Reform) (Scotland) Act 2007 (asp 6), s.35

DEFINITIONS

"appropriate time": s.272(7).

"High Court": s.307(1).

"judge": s.307(1).

"prosecutor": s.307(1).

"record": s.272(8).
"trial": s.307(1).
"witness": s.307(1).

GENERAL NOTE

This section applies to solemn and summary proceedings and can apply in circumstances in which the court might otherwise have to convene elsewhere in order to hear a witness' testimony. Chapters 23 and 24 of the 1996 Act of Adjournal regulates the form in which applications for Letters of Request of the taking of evidence on Commission are to be made. The procedures only operate in the Sheriff and High Courts.

Subsection (7) stipulates that such applications can normally only be made before trial proceedings have begun (although see the exceptional provisions available for applications which of necessity need to be made in the course of the trial). As subs.(1) states, any application should be made to a judge within whose jurisdiction the trial is due to take place, or, if no trial diet has been assigned, to a High Court judge. This requirement will be of limited applicability to summary cases since it would only rarely be necessary to seek Letters or a Commission once a trial had been fixed. The application in terms of Rule 23.1.–(4) has to be intimated to other parties and any hearing will occur in chambers if the application is opposed.

The classes of witness in relation to whom applications can be made are set out in subs.(1) but the judge has to be satisfied that the factors stipulated in subs.(3) are met before the application is allowed. Furthermore the granting of the application does not of itself mean that the testimony obtained has to be admitted as evidence: the court on receipt of the record (which must be accompanied by a written transcript) still has to consider whether its contents can be fairly admitted in accordance with the rules of evidence.

In considering the grant of an application, the court has to consider the test set out in subs.(3). It is essential that due weight is given to the potential unfairness to those in the trial who are deprived of the opportunity of oral cross-examination should Letters or a Commission be permitted (see *Muirhead v HM Advocate*, 1983 S.C.C.R. 133). In *Land, Petr*, 1991 S.L.T. 931; 1991 S.C.C.R. 138 while an application by the Crown to take the evidence on commission of a 91-year old witness was granted, and it was conceded that the sheriff's discretion was not subject to review, it was held that the issue of fairness to the accused still fell to be considered at the trial and, if necessary, on appeal.

See also *HM Advocate v Lesacher*, 1982 S.C.C.R. 418 where the trial had to be delayed to allow for the presentation of Letters of Request to West Germany through diplomatic channels.

Refer to Ch.23 of the 1996 Act of Adjournal for provisions as to expenses, transmission of Letters and custody of documents. Note in particular that Rule 23.6. specifies that such evidence cannot be led or referred to in trial proceedings until a motion to that effect has been made and granted.

It will be observed that requests for live television links for evidence to be taken contemporaneously from abroad during proceedings (s.273 below) are initiated by way of the Letter of Request procedures described above.

Television link evidence from abroad

273.—(1) In any solemn proceedings in the High Court or the sheriff court a person other than the accused may give evidence through a live television link if—

(a) the witness is outside the United Kingdom;

(b) an application under subsection (2) below for the issue of a letter of request has been granted; and

(c) the court is satisfied as to the arrangements for the giving of evidence in that manner by that witness.

(2) The prosecutor or the defence in any proceedings referred to in subsection (1) above may apply to a judge of the court in which the trial is to take place (or, if that court is not yet known, to a judge of the High Court) for the issue of a letter of request to—

(a) a court or tribunal exercising jurisdiction in a country or territory outside the United Kingdom where a witness is ordinarily resident; or

(b) any authority which the judge is satisfied is recognised by the government of that country or territory as the appropriate authority for receiving requests for assistance in facilitating the giving of evidence through a live television link,

requesting assistance in facilitating the giving of evidence by that witness through a live television link.

(3) An application under subsection (2) above shall be granted only if the judge is satisfied that—

    (a) the evidence which it is averred the witness is able to give is necessary for the proper adjudication of the trial; and

    (b) the granting of the application—

        (i) is in the interests of justice; and

        (ii) in the case of an application by the prosecutor, is not unfair to the accused.

DEFINITIONS

    "High Court": s.307(1).
    "judge": s.307(1).
    "prosecutor": s.307(1).
    "sheriff": s.307(1).
    "trial": s.307(1).
    "witness": s.307(1).

GENERAL NOTE

    In solemn proceedings only, application by way of the Letter of Request procedure outlined in s.272 above can be made for a live television link to take the evidence of witnesses who are outwith the United Kingdom. The factors determining whether such an application should be allowed by the court are laid out in subs.(2). For an example of the application of this section see *HM Advocate v Cinci*, 2002 G.W.D. 27–934.

Evidence relating to sexual offences

Restrictions on evidence relating to sexual offences

    274.—(1) In the trial of a person charged with an offence to which section 288C of this Act applies, the court shall not admit, or allow questioning designed to elicit evidence which shows or tends to show that the complainer—

    (a) is not of good character (whether in relation to sexual matters or otherwise);

    (b) has, at any time, engaged in sexual behaviour not forming part of the subject matter of the charge;

    (c) has, at any time (other than shortly before, at the same time as or shortly after the acts which form part of the subject matter of the charge), engaged in such behaviour, not being sexual behaviour, as might found the inference that the complainer—

        (i) is likely to have consented to those acts; or

        (ii) is not a credible or reliable witness; or

    (d) has, at any time, been subject to any such condition or predisposition as might found the inference referred to in sub-paragraph (c) above.

    (2) In subsection (1) above, "complainer" means the person against whom the offence referred to in that subsection is alleged to have been committed; and the reference to engaging in sexual behaviour includes a reference to undergoing or being made subject to any experience of a sexual nature.

AMENDMENT

    Section 274 substituted by the Sexual Offences (Procedure and Evidence) (Scotland) Act 2002 (asp 9), s.7. Brought into force by the Sexual Offences (Procedure and Evidence) (Scotland) Act 2002 (Commencement and Transitional Provisions) Order 2002 (SSI 2002/443 (C.24)), art.4 (effective November 1, 2002).

GENERAL NOTE

This section applies equally to summary and solemn proceedings and introduces entirely new procedures to limit the scope of questioning relating to a complainer's character, sexual behaviour or history. Offences covered by these provisions are set out in s.288C(2) of the Act and, it should be noted, in subs.(4) of that section which adds offences held to contain a substantial sexual element in the offence. Significantly too the general definition here applies equally to the Crown and the defence and extends to the complainer's history as a victim of sexual conduct just as much as a willing participant in sexual conduct.

In order to lift the prohibition, a party has to make application in writing in accordance with s.275, setting out the grounds which are argued to justify an exception being made to the general bar on such questioning, unless special cause can be shown, not less than 14 clear days before trial. So far as an accused is concerned, as s.275A makes clear, the corollary is that the Crown will be obliged to place any relevant previous conviction, served on the accused, before the court on conclusion of its consideration of the application. The intention is that any such conviction, unless its accuracy is challenged, will be admitted in evidence during the trial proceedings. Procedures are established for proof of previous convictions or for showing that a conviction has a substantial sexual element. Issues may become more complex in cases involving co-accused.

Act of Adjournal

The Act of Adjournal (Criminal Procedure Rules Amendment No.3) (Sexual Offences (Procedure and Evidence) (Scotland) Act 2002) 2002 (SSI 2002/454) adds procedural rules and new forms of intimation covering solemn and summary cases involving sexual offences.

Exceptions to restrictions under section 274

275.—(1) The court may, on application made to it, admit such evidence or allow such questioning as is referred to in subsection (1) of section 274 of this Act if satisfied that—

(a) the evidence or questioning will relate only to a specific occurrence or occurrences of sexual or other behaviour or to specific facts demonstrating—

    (i) the complainer's character; or

    (ii) any condition or predisposition to which the complainer is or has been subject;

(b) that occurrence or those occurrences of behaviour or facts are relevant to establishing whether the accused is guilty of the offence with which he is charged; and

(c) the probative value of the evidence sought to be admitted or elicited is significant and is likely to outweigh any risk of prejudice to the proper administration of justice arising from its being admitted or elicited.

(2) In subsection (1) above—

(a) the reference to an occurrence or occurrences of sexual behaviour includes a reference to undergoing or being made subject to any experience of a sexual nature;

(b) "the proper administration of justice" includes—

    (i) appropriate protection of a complainer's dignity and privacy; and

    (ii) ensuring that the facts and circumstances of which a jury is made aware are, in cases of offences to which section 288C of this Act applies, relevant to an issue which is to be put before the jury and commensurate to the importance of that issue to the jury's verdict,

and, in that subsection and in sub-paragraph (i) of paragraph (b) above, "complainer" has the same meaning as in section 274 of this Act.

 (3) An application for the purposes of subsection (1) above shall be in writing and shall set out—

(a) the evidence sought to be admitted or elicited;

(b) the nature of any questioning proposed;

(c) the issues at the trial to which that evidence is considered to be relevant;

(d) the reasons why that evidence is considered relevant to those issues;

(e) the inferences which the applicant proposes to submit to the court that it should draw from that evidence; and

(f) such other information as is of a kind specified for the purposes of this paragraph in Act of Adjournal.

(4) The party making such an application shall, when making it, send a copy of it—

(a) when that party is the prosecutor, to the accused; and

(b) when that party is the accused, to the prosecutor and any co-accused.

(5) The court may reach a decision under subsection (1) above without considering any evidence; but, where it takes evidence for the purposes of reaching that decision, it shall do so as if determining the admissibility of evidence.

(6) The court shall state its reasons for its decision under subsection (1) above, and may make that decision subject to conditions which may include compliance with directions issued by it.

(7) Where a court admits evidence or allows questioning under subsection (1) above, its decision to do so shall include a statement—

(a) of what items of evidence it is admitting or lines of questioning it is allowing;

(b) of the reasons for its conclusion that the evidence to be admitted or to be elicited by the questioning is admissible;

(c) of the issues at the trial to which it considers that that evidence is relevant.

(8) A condition under subsection (6) above may consist of a limitation on the extent to which evidence—

(a) to be admitted; or

(b) to be elicited by questioning to be allowed,

may be argued to support a particular inference specified in the condition.

(9) Where evidence is admitted or questioning allowed under this section, the court at any time may—

(a) as it thinks fit; and

(b) notwithstanding the terms of its decision under subsection (1) above or any condition under subsection (6) above,

limit the extent of evidence to be admitted or questioning to be allowed.

AMENDMENT

Section 275 substituted by the Sexual Offences (Procedure and Evidence) (Scotland) Act 2002 (asp 9), s.8(1). Brought into force by the Sexual Offences (Procedure and Evidence) (Scotland) Act 2002 (Commencement and Transitional Provisions) Order 2002 (SSI 2002/443 (C.24)), art.4 (effective November 1, 2002).

DEFINITION

"trial": s.307(1).

GENERAL NOTE

Refer to the discussion at A4–533. Where a party seeks to lead evidence about the complainer's sexual history or behaviour in face of the general prohibition laid down in s.274 of the Act, notice must be given in writing, ordinarily, not less than 14 clear days before trial. The section applies equally to the Crown and the defence and the object of the section is to ensure that the thrust of questioning is relevant to the issues of fact before the court rather than merely calculated to belittle or humiliate the complainer by raising tangential issues. Several factors are noteworthy: the purpose of

Applies to both crown + defence

the 14 day *induciae* specified in s.275B below is to ensure that the application is raised as far as possible, before the trial rather than at the point when evidence, especially that of the complainer, is being lead so applications should be considered at first or preliminary diets in solemn proceedings (see ss.71 and 72 of the Act as now amended) or at intermediate diets in summary trials; secondly, the court has to consider a broad test—the proper administration of justice—and, to do so, must weigh the comparative benefit to the accused in having such evidence against the impact it might have upon the privacy and dignity of the complainer; third, in considering the application the court may hear evidence and, fourth, while imposing any conditions or limits upon questioning the court nonetheless has to maintain a watching brief (subs.(9)) to limit the evidence admitted under s.275 in the course of the trial. From all of this it follows that in dealing with s.275 applications the court may well seek evidence from parties who were not originally listed as witnesses at all, for example medical practitioners, psychologists or social workers, the aim being to minimise the procedural interruptions which might otherwise occur during the trial itself.

In response to a successful application the Crown is directed to lay before the court any relevant previous convictions. See the fuller discussion on this aspect in the General Note to s.275A below.

Case law

While much depends upon the facts in individual cases, some propositions can now be tentatively advanced: the earlier permissive approach adopted by the courts, where applications were rarely challenged or argued, is now much less evident. A general discussion of the development of these procedures is found in *MM v HM Advocate*, 2004 S.C.C.R. 658 which also held the provisions to be ECHR compliant.

Broadly, any application has to found upon specific and directly relevant allegations, from identifiable sources, which are demonstrated to be necessary to challenge the reliability or credibility of the complainer's testimony (*Cumming v HM Advocate*, 2003 S.C.C.R. 261). Thus, evidence of an earlier predispositon of the complainer to lie or fabricate demonstrably fantastical stories can be brought out (*Mackay v HM Advocate*, 2005 J.C. 24). If the defence elects to produce expert evidence of "false memory syndrome" as a means of challenging the veracity of the complainer, the Crown is entitled to lead evidence in rebuttal. (The diagnosis is one which is still controversial in psychiatric opinion.) A thorough analysis of the range of case law in this field was provided in Lord MacPhail's judgment in *HM Advocate v A*, 2005 S.L.T. 975.

Expert evidence as to the psychiatric condition of the witness, in so far as it would impinge on truthfulness, or explain the response to questioning, or accurate recall was discussed in *Green v HM Advocate*, 1983 S.C.C.R. 42 and in *McBrearty v HM Advocate*, 2004 S.L.T. 917; 2004 S.C.C.R. 337. Where it can be shown to be material to an accused's defence, questions about earlier consensual intercourse between the parties may be permitted (*Tant v HM Advocate*, 2003 S.C.C.R. 506), as may earlier false allegations of rape but only where it is intended to do more than proceed by bald assertions—colourable evidence has to be identified in support of an application (*Thomson v HM Advocate*, 2001 S.C.C.R. 162).

In any application it has to be emphasised that there has to be a soundly-argued basis for the line of evidence being sought and that speculative "fishing", or evidence solely directed towards demeaning or distressing the complainer will not be permitted. Since s.275, applications have to be lodged for consideration at the first diet, or preliminary hearing, the applicant may well have to be ready at that stage in the proceedings to lead evidence in support of the application. Refusal of an application at that point does not necessarily prevent the trial court reconsidering issues as evidence emerges, and the relevance of the questioning proposed earlier in the s.275 application emerges: the court's broader duty to ensure the fairness of the proceedings as the trial develops, remains.

Disclosure of accused's previous convictions where court allows questioning or evidence under section 275

275A.—(1) Where, under section 275 of this Act, a court (or, in proceedings before a commissioner appointed under section 271I(1) or by virtue of section 272(1)(b) of this Act, a commissioner) on the application of the accused allows such questioning or admits such evidence as is referred to in section 274(1) of this Act, the prosecutor shall forthwith place before the presiding judge any previous relevant conviction of the accused.

(2) Any conviction placed before the judge under subsection (1) above shall, unless the accused objects, be—

(a) in proceedings on indictment, laid before the jury;

(b) in summary proceedings, taken into consideration by the judge.

(3) An extract of such a conviction may not be laid before the jury or taken into consideration by the judge unless such an extract was appended to the notice, served on the accused under section 69(2) or, as the case may be, 166(2) of this Act, which specified that conviction.

(4) An objection under subsection (2) above may be made only on one or more of the following grounds—

(a) where the conviction bears to be a relevant conviction by virtue only of paragraph (b) of subsection (10) below, that there was not a substantial sexual element present in the commission of the offence for which the accused has been convicted;

(b) that the disclosure or, as the case may be, the taking into consideration of the conviction would be contrary to the interests of justice;

(c) in proceedings on indictment, that the conviction does not apply to the accused or is otherwise inadmissible;

(d) in summary proceedings, that the accused does not admit the conviction.

(5) Where—

(a) an objection is made on one or more of the grounds mentioned in paragraphs (b) to (d) of subsection (4) above; and

(b) an extract of the conviction in respect of which the objection is made was not appended to the notice, served on the accused under section 69(2) or, as the case may be, 166(2) above, which specified that conviction,

the prosecutor may, notwithstanding subsection (3) above, place such an extract conviction before the judge.

(6) In summary proceedings, the judge may, notwithstanding subsection (2)(b) above, take into consideration any extract placed before him under subsection (5) above for the purposes only of considering the objection in respect of which the extract is disclosed.

(7) In entertaining an objection on the ground mentioned in paragraph (b) of subsection (4) above, the court shall, unless the contrary is shown, presume that the disclosure, or, as the case may be, the taking into consideration, of a conviction is in the interests of justice.

(8) An objection on the ground mentioned in paragraph (c) of subsection (4) above shall not be entertained unless the accused has, under subsection (2) of section 69 of this Act, given intimation of the objection in accordance with subsection (3) of that section.

(9) In entertaining an objection on the ground mentioned in paragraph (d) of subsection (4) above, the court shall require the prosecutor to withdraw the conviction or adduce evidence in proof thereof.

(10) For the purposes of this section a "relevant conviction" is, subject to subsection (11) below—

(a) a conviction for an offence to which section 288C of this Act applies by virtue of subsection (2) thereof; or

(b) where a substantial sexual element was present in the commission of any other offence in respect of which the accused has previously been convicted, a conviction for that offence,

which is specified in a notice served on the accused under section 69(2) or, as the case may be, 166(2) of this Act.

(11) A conviction for an offence other than an offence to which section 288C of this Act applies by virtue of subsection (2) thereof is not a relevant conviction for the purposes of this section unless an extract of that conviction containing information which indicates that a sexual element was present in the commission

of the offence was appended to the notice, served on the accused under section 69(2) or, as the case may be, 166(2) of this Act, which specified that conviction.

AMENDMENT

Section 275A inserted by the Sexual Offences (Procedure and Evidence) (Scotland) Act 2002 (asp 9), s.10(4). Brought into force by the Sexual Offences (Procedure and Evidence) (Scotland) Act 2002 (Commencement and Transitional Provisions) Order 2002 (SSI 2002/443 (C.24)), art.4 (effective November 1, 2002).

Section 275(A) amended by the Criminal Proceedings etc. (Reform) (Scotland) Act 2007 (asp 6), s.35

GENERAL NOTE

Refer to the General Notes to ss.274 and 275 above. It is noted that the corollary of success for an accused with a s.275 application is that the Crown is obliged to place any relevant convictions and supporting extract convictions if the sexual context is not self-evident. All such convictions must first have been served upon the accused by the customary notice, and will then be placed before the trial court in the course of evidence unless the accused at the s.275 hearing can successfully challenge their validity or show that he had not been served with them. The only other ground for ignoring a relevant conviction would be that its disclosure in trial proceedings would be contrary to the interests of justice (subs.(4)(b)). In *HM Advocate v S*, 2005 G.W.D. 26–504 it was held that this section's provisions did not offend against Art.6 of ECHR. An accused whose application under s.275 has been granted by the court can still argue that disclosure of his relevant previous convictions should not follow automatically. Essentially the argument is that disclosure would be disproportionately harmful to his fair trial when set against the (limited) purpose of his application (*HM Advocate v S*, 2005 G.W.D. 26–504). See, generally, *Leggate v HM Advocate*, 1988 S.L.T. 665; 1988 S.C.C.R. 391.

Section 275A is densely drafted and looks likely to attract more than its fair share of procedural appeals and case decisions as well as proofs of previous convictions. This assessment does not even begin to take account of the labyrinthine complexities which will develop in cases involving more than a single accused. For these reasons attention is directed to the discussion of *Riley v HM Advocate*, 1999 J.C. 308; 1999 S.L.T. 1076; 1999 S.C.C.R. 644 at A4–228 above, in relation to the uses of relevant extract convictions, and to the provisions for proof of previous convictions found at ss.285 and 286 below.

One important qualification to this discussion must be noted in solemn proceedings—the accused can only dispute a conviction for the purpose of s.275A if he has already challenged the accuracy of the notice of previous convictions served upon him with his indictment. See s.69(3) of the Act. Failure to comply with this provision would not, it is submitted, nullify any subsequent conviction.

Provisions supplementary to sections 275 and 275A

275B.—(1) An application for the purposes of subsection (1) of section 275 of this Act shall not, unless on special cause shown, be considered by the court unless made

(a) in the case of proceedings in the High Court, not less than 7 clear days before the preliminary hearing; or

(b) in any other case, not less than 14 clear days before the trial diet.

(2) Where—

(a) such an application is considered; or

(b) any objection under subsection (2) of section 275A of this Act is entertained,

during the course of the trial, the court shall consider that application or, as the case may be, entertain that objection in the absence of the jury, the complainer, any person cited as a witness and the public.

AMENDMENT

Section 275B inserted by the Sexual Offences (Procedure and Evidence) (Scotland) Act 2002 (asp 9), s.10(4). Brought into force by the Sexual Offences (Procedure and Evidence) (Scotland) Act 2002 (Commencement and Transitional Provisions) Order 2002 (SSI 2002/443 (C.24)), art.4 (effective November 1, 2002).

Subs.(1)(a) and (b) inserted by the Criminal Procedure (Amendment) (Scotland) Act 2004 (asp 5), s.25 and Sch.1, para.45. Brought into force on February 1, 2005 by the Criminal Procedure (Amendment) (Scotland) Act 2004 (Commencement, Transitional Provisions and Savings) Order 2004 (SSI 2004/405 (C.28)), art.2.

GENERAL NOTE

Ordinarily any application to the court to waive the restrictions upon evidence relating to the sexual history or background of the complainer must be intimated at least 14 clear days before trial. This timing enables such applications to be considered at first or preliminary diets in solemn proceedings, or at the intermediate diet in summary proceedings. Although later notice may be permitted, this will only be on special cause shown, an indication that this has to be seen as available only in exceptional circumstances. Subs.(2) stipulates that if notice is first given at the trial diet then any consideration of an application, or any resultant s.275A hearing in relation to relevant convictions, must be considered by the court *in camera*.

Expert evidence as to subsequent behaviour of complainer

Expert evidence as to subsequent behaviour of complainer in certain cases

275C.—(1) This section applies in the case of proceedings in respect of any offence to which section 288C of this Act applies.

(2) Expert psychological or psychiatric evidence relating to any subsequent behaviour or statement of the complainer is admissible for the purpose of rebutting any inference adverse to the complainer's credibility or reliability as a witness which might otherwise be drawn from the behaviour or statement.

(3) In subsection (2) above—

"complainer" means the person against whom the offence to which the proceedings relate is alleged to have been committed,

"subsequent behaviour or statement" means any behaviour or statement subsequent to, and not forming part of the acts constituting, the offence to which the proceedings relate and which is not otherwise relevant to any fact in issue at the trial.

(4) This section does not affect the admissibility of any evidence which is admissible otherwise than by virtue of this section.

AMENDMENT

Section 275C inserted by the Vulnerable Witnesses (Scotland) Act 2004 (asp 3), s.5. Brought into force, for all purposes, on April 1, 2005 by the Vulnerable Witnesses (Scotland) Act 2004 (Commencement) Order 2005 (SSI 2005/168 (C.7)), art.2 and Sch.

DEFINITIONS

"complainer": s.275C(3).
"statement": ss.271M(5) and 262(1).
"subsequent behaviour or statement": s.275C(3).

GENERAL NOTE

Section 288C of the 1995 Act introduced a prohibition on the personal conduct by the accused of the defence case in certain specified sexual offences. This new s.275C allows for certain expert witness evidence to be admitted in cases involving relevant sexual offences. That evidence may only be admitted for the purpose of explaining the behaviour of the complainer in order to rebut any inference adverse to the credibility and reliability of the complainer that might otherwise be drawn from that behaviour. The new provision does not restrict the use of expert evidence that is admissible by existing law.

Biological material

Evidence of biological material

276.—(1) Evidence as to the characteristics and composition of any biological material deriving from human beings or animals shall, in any criminal proceedings, be admissible notwithstanding that neither the material nor a sample of it is lodged as a production.

(2) A party wishing to lead such evidence as is referred to in subsection (1) above shall, where neither the material nor a sample of it is lodged as a production, make the material or a sample of it available for inspection by the other party unless the material constitutes a hazard to health or has been destroyed in the process of analysis.

GENERAL NOTE

This section dispenses with the need to produce in court certain biological materials in relation to which evidence is to be led in proceedings. Ordinarily in solemn proceedings the accused is entitled to inspect any productions (see s.68(2)); no such provision is found in summary proceedings given their character. Section 276 arises from considerations of public health and constitutes an exception to the authority that allows an accused to see productions.

Transcripts and records

Transcript of police interview sufficient evidence

277.—(1) Subject to subsection (2) below, for the purposes of any criminal proceedings, a document certified by the person who made it as an accurate transcript made for the prosecutor of the contents of a tape (identified by means of a label) purporting to be a recording of an interview between—

(a) a police officer and an accused person; or

(b) a person commissioned, appointed or authorised under section 6(3) of the Customs and Excise Management Act 1979 and an accused person,

shall be received in evidence and be sufficient evidence of the making of the transcript and of its accuracy.

(2) Subsection (1) above shall not apply to a transcript—

(a) unless a copy of it has been served on the accused not less than 14 days before
   (i) in the case of proceedings in the High Court, the preliminary hearing;
   (ii) in any other case, his trial; or

(b) if the accused, not less than
   (i) in the case of proceedings in the High Court, seven days before the preliminary hearing;
   (ii) in any other case, six days before his trial;
   or (in either case) by such later time before his trial as the court may in special circumstances allow, has served notice on the prosecutor that the accused challenges the making of the transcript or its accuracy.

(3) A copy of the transcript or a notice under subsection (2) above shall be served in such manner as may be prescribed by Act of Adjournal; and a written execution purporting to be signed by the person who served the transcript or notice, together with, where appropriate, the relevant post office receipt shall be sufficient evidence of such service.

(4) Where subsection (1) above does not apply to a transcript, if the person who made the transcript is called as a witness his evidence shall be sufficient evidence of the making of the transcript and of its accuracy.

AMENDMENT

Subss.(2)(a)(i), (ii) and (b)(i), (ii) inserted, and subs.(2)(b) as amended, by the Criminal Procedure (Amendment) (Scotland) Act 2004 (asp 5), s.25 and Sch.1, para.46. Brought into force on February 1, 2005 by the Criminal Procedure (Amendment) (Scotland) Act 2004 (Commencement, Transitional Provisions and Savings) Order 2004 (SSI 2004/405 (C.28)), art.2.

DEFINITION
"prosecutor": s.307(1).

GENERAL NOTE

This section permits the admission as evidence of a transcript of any interview conducted by the police or Customs officers with the accused on tape. The transcript, prepared by a person appointed by the procurator fiscal, has to be certified by that person and a copy of it has to be served (subs. (3)) on the accused not less than 14 days before trial (subs. (2)(a)). Any challenge to the accuracy of the transcript has to be intimated to the prosecutor not less than six days before trial normally, or later on cause shown. It appears that a challenge to the accuracy of the transcript can be met conclusively by calling the person who prepared it but this would not preclude the alternative of playing the tape, provided its contents did not breach ss.101(1) and 166(3) and disclose previous convictions or contain other inadmissible material. These factors explain why the prosecution will often prepare and lodge an edited transcript deleting any such untoward references: in that event the jury, or the judge in summary proceedings, should only be referred to the edited transcript in the course of evidence.

Note that, unlike the transcript of any judicial examination, which must be lodged in solemn proceedings (see the notes to ss.36 and 37), this section does not oblige the prosecutor to lodge a transcript of taped interview.

Record of proceedings at examination as evidence

278.—(1) Subject to subsection (2) below, the record made, under section 37 of this Act (incorporating any rectification authorised under section 38(1) of this Act), of proceedings at the examination of an accused shall be received in evidence without being sworn to by witnesses, and it shall not be necessary in proceedings on indictment to insert the names of any witnesses to the record in any list of witnesses, either for the prosecution or for the defence.

(2) On the application of either an accused or the prosecutor—

(a) in proceedings on indictment, subject to sections 37(5) and 79(1) of this Act, the court may determine that the record or part of the record shall not be read to the jury; and

(b) in summary proceedings, subject to the said section 37(5) and to subsection (4) below, the court may refuse to admit the record or some part of the record as evidence.

(3) At the hearing of an application under subsection (2) above, it shall be competent for the prosecutor or the defence to adduce as witnesses the persons who were present during the proceedings mentioned in subsection (1) above and for either party to examine those witnesses upon any matters regarding the said proceedings.

(4) In summary proceedings, except on cause shown, an application under subsection (2)(b) above shall not be heard unless notice of at least 10 clear days has been given to the court and to the other parties.

(5) In subsection (2) above, the "record" comprises—

(a) as regards any trial of an indictment, each record included, under section 68(1) of this Act, in the list of productions; and

(b) as regards a summary trial, each record which it is sought to have received under subsection (1) above.

AMENDMENT

Subs.(2)(a) as amended by the Criminal Procedure (Amendment) (Scotland) Act 2004 (asp 5), s.25 and Sch.1, para.47. Brought into force on February 1, 2005 by the Criminal Procedure (Amendment) (Scotland) Act 2004 (Commencement, Transitional Provisions and Savings) Order 2004 (SSI 2004/405 (C.28)), art.2.

DEFINITIONS

"indictment": s.307(1).

"prosecutor": s.307(1).
"record": s.278(5).
"witness": s.307(1).

GENERAL NOTE

Section 278 specifies the principles to be applied to the use of transcripts of judicial examination at trial. Section 38(1) allows for rectification of the transcript after which procedure the accuracy of the transcript is settled conclusively (see s.38(4)): s.279 is concerned with the admissibility, or otherwise, of material in the transcript. On the motion of any party, the court has to determine which parts of the transcript may be read to the jury or court in the subsequent trial. See also Chap. 25 of the 1996 Act of Adjournal in relation to the use of transcripts in evidence.

Any motion to restrict the material in a judicial examination has to be made in compliance with subs.(2), at a first or preliminary diet in solemn procedure (see s.72(1)(b)), or not less than 10 clear days before a summary trial (it is not essential that the issue be raised at the intermediate diet (see s.148) but this would obviously be a sensible time for it to be considered). Since it cannot be certain in a summary case whether the Crown intends to found upon the transcript of judicial examination until trial proceeds, there is obviously an element of anticipation involved in making such a motion.

Note that in *Hendry v H.M. Advocate*, 1985 S.C.C.R. 275, a Five Bench decision, it was held to be illegitimate to use a self-serving statement made in a judicial examination as a substitute for parole evidence on oath. See *Robertson v H.M. Advocate*, 1996 S.C.C.R. 243 discussed at A4.88. The case of *McEwan v H.M. Advocate*, 1990 S.C.C.R. 401 gives directions as to how the contents of a judicial examination should be presented to a jury.

In considering whether a transcript of judicial examination should be admitted as evidence, a relevant factor is likely to be the similarity or otherwise between the petition charges, which formed the basis of the examination, and the charges ultimately libelled. Similar considerations will apply to any alleged admissions put to the accused at examination and their fairness and admissibility in the light of evidence. The prosecutor is now required to lodge a certified copy of the petition (and by implication any transcript of alleged admissions put to the accused at the judicial examination) as well as any transcript of judicial examination as a production.

Documentary evidence

Evidence from documents

279. Schedule 8 to this Act, which makes provision regarding the admissibility in criminal proceedings of copy documents and of evidence contained in business documents, shall have effect.

GENERAL NOTE

Schedule 8 to the Act restates the terms of Sched. 3 to the Prisoners and Criminal Proceedings (Scotland) Act 1993 which provides for the certification of documentary evidence, particularly business documents, and validates the use of certified copies of documents (as defined in Sched. (8)), which may in some instances contain hearsay material, as best evidence in criminal proceedings. It will be noted that the provisions of this section would not preclude use of the Bankers' Books Evidence Act 1879 (c. 11) in suitable circumstances; there are two means of proving entries in bankers' books though it has to be said that generally the Sched. 8 provisions are more widely drafted (see *Lord Advocate's Reference No. 1 of 1996*, 1996 G.W.D. 21–1189).

Act of Adjournal

Forms 26.1–A to 26.1–C are provided in the 1996 Act of Adjournal for authentication of documents, and setting up business documents, and providing a means for certification of evidence which is not to be found in business documents. This last class of certificate can be tendered in proceedings without the need for the person certifying to attend court as a witness.

Evidence from certain official documents

279A.—(1) Any letter, minute or other official document issuing from the office of or in custody of any of the departments of state or government in the United Kingdom or any part of the Scottish Administration which—

(a) is required to be produced in evidence in any prosecution; and

(b) according to the rules and regulations applicable to such departments may competently be so produced,

shall when so produced be *prima facie* evidence of the matters contained in it without being produced or sworn to by any witness.

(2) A copy of any such document as is mentioned in subsection (1) above bearing to be certified by any person having authority to certify it shall be treated as equivalent to the original of that document and no proof of the signature of the person certifying the copy or of his authority to certify it shall be necessary.

(3) Any order made by any of the departments of state or government or the Scottish Parliament or any local authority or public body made under powers conferred by any statute or a print or a copy of such order, shall when produced in a prosecution be received as evidence of the due making, confirmation, and existence of the order without being sworn to by any witness and without any further or other proof.

(4) Subsection (3) above is without prejudice to any right competent to the accused to challenge any order such as is mentioned in that subsection as being *ultra vires* of the authority making it or any other competent ground.

(5) Where an order such as is mentioned in subsection (3) above is referred to in the indictment or, as the case may be, the complaint, it shall not be necessary to enter it in the record of the proceedings as a documentary production.

(6) The provisions of this section are in addition to, and not in derogation of, any powers of proving documents conferred by statute or existing at common law.

AMENDMENTS

Section 279A inserted by the Crime and Punishment (Scotland) Act 1997 (c.48), s.28(2); commenced with effect from August 1, 1997 in terms of the Crime and Punishment (Scotland) Act 1997 (Commencement and Transitional Provisions) Order 1997 (SI 1997/1712), art.3.

Subss.(1) and (3) as amended by the Scotland Act 1998 (Consequential Modifications) (No. 2) Order 1999 (SI 1999/1820), art.4 and Sch.2, para.122(4) (effective July 1, 1999).

DEFINITIONS

"document": s.279 and Sch.8, para.8 to the 1995 Act.
"order": s.307(1) of the 1995 Act.
"United Kingdom": s.5 of and Sch.1 to the Interpretation Act 1978 (c.30).

GENERAL NOTE

This section supercedes s.154 of the 1995 Act and makes provisions for the admissibility of official documents as evidence in any criminal proceedings. Apart from minor rewording, and associated renumbering of subsections, the new provision is all but identical to the old but, importantly, extends to solemn proceedings.

Either the original document or a certified copy of it can be used in proceedings without the need for it to be listed as a production or set up by parole evidence: the only proviso is that there must be valid certification of the document or a copy of it. These specific evidential concessions go beyond the provisions found in Schedule 8 to the 1995 Act; particularly note that there is no requirement to lodge the relevant Order, Local Government Order or Statutory Instrument as a production in proceedings. Reference should also be made to the statutory presumptions found in Sch.3, para.12 of the 1995 Act.

The procedure to be followed when a challenge is made to the validity of an Order was discussed in *Johnston v McGillivray*, 1993 S.L.T. 120 and in *Neizer v Johnston*, 1993 S.C.C.R. 772.

Routine evidence

Routine evidence

280.—(1) For the purposes of any proceedings for an offence under any of the enactments specified in column 1 of Schedule 9 to this Act, a certificate purporting to be signed by a person or persons specified in column 2 thereof, and certifying the matter specified in column 3 thereof shall, subject to subsection (6) below, be sufficient evidence of that matter and of the qualification or authority of that person or those persons.

(2) The Secretary of State may by order—

(a) amend or repeal the entry in Schedule 9 to this Act in respect of any enactment; or

(b) insert in that Schedule an entry in respect of a further enactment.

(3) An order under subsection (2) above may make such transitional, incidental or supplementary provision as the Secretary of State considers necessary or expedient in connection with the coming into force of the order.

(4) For the purposes of any criminal proceedings, a report purporting to be signed by two authorised forensic scientists shall, subject to subsection (5) below, be sufficient evidence of any fact or conclusion as to fact contained in the report and of the authority of the signatories.

(5) A forensic scientist is authorised for the purposes of subsection (4) above if—

(a) he is authorised for those purposes by the Secretary of State; or

(b) he—

(i) is a constable or is employed by a police authority under section 9 of the Police (Scotland) Act 1967;

(ii) possesses such qualifications and experience as the Secretary of State may for the purposes of that subsection by order prescribe; and

(iii) is authorised for those purposes by the chief constable of the police force maintained for the police area of that authority.

(6) Subsections (1) and (4) above shall not apply to a certificate or, as the case may be, report tendered on behalf of the prosecutor or the accused—

(a) unless a copy has been served on the other party not less than fourteen days before

(i) in the case of proceedings in the High Court, the preliminary hearing;

(ii) in any other case, the trial; or

(b) where the other party, not more than seven days after the date of service of the copy on him under paragraph (a) above or by such later time as the court may in special circumstances allow, has served notice on the first party that he challenges the matter, qualification or authority mentioned in subsection (1) above or as the case may be the fact, conclusion or authority mentioned in subsection (4) above.

(7) A copy of a certificate or, as the case may be, report required by subsection (6) above, to be served on the accused or the prosecutor or of a notice required by that subsection or by subsection (1) or (2) of section 281 of this Act to be served on the prosecutor shall be served in such manner as may be prescribed by Act of Adjournal; and a written execution purporting to be signed by the person who served such certificate or notice, together with, where appropriate, the relevant post office receipt shall be sufficient evidence of service of such a copy.

(8) Where, following service of a notice under subsection (6)(b) above, evidence is given in relation to a report referred to in subsection (4) above by both of the forensic scientists purporting to have signed the report, the evidence of those forensic scientists shall be sufficient evidence of any fact (or conclusion as to fact) contained in the report.

(9) At any trial of an offence it shall be presumed that the person who appears

in answer to the complaint is the person charged by the police with the offence unless the contrary is alleged.

(10) An order made under subsection (2) or (5)(b)(ii) above shall be made by statutory instrument.

(11) No order shall be made under subsection (2) above unless a draft of the order has been laid before, and approved by a resolution of, each House of Parliament.

(12) A statutory instrument containing an order under subsection (5)(b)(ii) above shall be subject to annulment pursuant to a resolution of either House of Parliament.

AMENDMENT

Subs.(6)(b) amended by the Crime and Punishment (Scotland) Act 1997 (c.48), s.62(1) and Sch.1, para.21(32) with effect from August 1, 1997 in terms of the Crime and Punishment (Scotland) Act (Commencement and Transitional Provisions) Order 1997 (SI 1997/1712), art.3.

Subs.6(a) as amended by the Criminal Procedure (Amendment) (Scotland) Act 2004 (asp 5), s.25 and Sch.1, para.48. Brought into force on February 1, 2005 by the Criminal Procedure (Amendment) (Scotland) Act 2004 (Commencement, Transitional Provisions and Savings) Order 2004 (SSI 2004/405 (C.28)), art.2.

DEFINITIONS

"complaint": s.307(1).
"constable": s.307(1) and s.51(1) of the Police (Scotland) Act 1967 (c. 77).
"offence": s.307(1).
"prosecutor": s.307(1).
"trial": s.307(1).

GENERAL NOTE

Unlike s.26(2) of the Criminal Justice (Scotland) Act 1980 which applied only to summary proceedings, the effect of subs.(4) is to apply these provisions relating to routine evidence prepared by authorised forensic scientists to both summary and solemn proceedings. The provisions of s.281 are equally available to prosecution and defence alike provided the authors of the report are authorised scientists.

It will be noted that subs.(5) broadens the definition of "forensic scientist" to include police constables or police employees appointed by their Chief Constable. The provisions in regard to service of forensic reports are repeated in subs.(6) and the form of certificate, as provided by Chap.27 of the 1996 Act of Adjournal, may broadly follow the style of Form 27.2.

Challenges to the contents of a report must be by notice served on the other party not more than seven days after service of the report (note that by contrast, s.26(3) of the 1980 Act allowed challenge up to six days before the trial). Failing such challenge, the contents of the report shall be received as sufficient evidence. Much of the case law generated by s.26 of the 1980 Act related to attacking certificated evidence, which had not been formally challenged, on the basis that the facts contained in the reports did not themselves satisfy the statutory requirements. See *Normand v Wotherspoon*, 1994 S.L.T. 487; 1993 S.C.C.R. 912; *Straker v Orr*, 1994 S.C.C.R. 251; *McCrindle v Walkingshaw*, 1994 S.C.C.R. 299; *O'Brien v McCreadie*, 1994 S.C.C.R. 516. For more recent discussion of the presumptions as to service of such reports see *Lawrence v Vannet*, 1998 G.W.D. 40–2041. Objection to the contents of a forensic report served under s.280 (on the basis that the authors had not stated that they had analysed the drugs identified) without having intimated a challenge under subs.(6)(b) was repelled on appeal in *Meek v H.M. Advocate*, 2000 G.W.D. 9–323.

The section makes various other provisions intended to reduce the unnecessary attendance of witnesses at court. The Secretary of State may add to the list of matters which may be introduced into evidence by certificate, by way of subordinate legislation. This will enable suitable matters to be added to the list as they are identified without the need to wait for a suitable opportunity to incorporate them in primary legislation (subss.(2) and (3)).

This section puts it beyond doubt that the facts and conclusions as to facts spoken to either in the report or in subsequent oral evidence based on the report, are sufficient for the purpose of proving those facts. Such evidence can still be attacked on the grounds of credibility or unreliability.

Subsection (9) repeats the terms of s.26(5) and enacts a presumption that the party answering the complaint is the person charged by the police. Unless a challenge is intimated on behalf of the accused before a plea has been tendered, the presumption will hold good and it then becomes unnecessary to identify the accused in the course of the trial, always provided that it has been established that the person responsible for the offence had been charged. See *Rollo v Wilson*, 1988 S.C.C.R. 312 where the sheriff recalled a police witness to confirm evidence of identification; on appeal it was held that the s.26(5) presumption had in any event rendered the recall unnecessary: in *Hamilton v Ross*, 1992 S.L.T. 384; 1991 S.C.C.R. 165 the Appeal Court raised the issue of the presumption in response to a Crown appeal against a no case to answer motion; the issue had not been aired before that time but the Crown was still entitled to benefit from the provision.

Routine evidence: autopsy and forensic science reports

281.—(1) Where in a trial an autopsy report is lodged as a production by the prosecutor it shall be presumed that the body of the person identified in that report is the body of the deceased identified in the indictment or complaint, unless the accused not less than

  (i) in the case of proceedings in the High Court, seven days before the preliminary hearing;

  (ii) in any other case, six days before the trial;

or (in either case) by such later time before the trial as the court may in special circumstances allow, gives notice that the contrary is alleged.

(2) At the time of lodging an autopsy or forensic science report as a production the prosecutor may intimate to the accused that it is intended that only one of the pathologists or forensic scientists purporting to have signed the report shall be called to give evidence in respect thereof; and, where such intimation is given, the evidence of one of those pathologists or forensic scientists shall be sufficient evidence of any fact or conclusion as to fact contained in the report and of the qualifications of the signatories, unless the accused, not less than

  (i) in the case of proceedings in the High Court, seven days before the preliminary hearing;

  (ii) in any other case, six days before the trial;

or (in either case) by such later time before the trial as the court may in special circumstances allow, serves notice on the prosecutor that he requires the attendance at the trial of the other pathologist or forensic scientist also.

(3) Where, following service of a notice by the accused under subsection (2) above, evidence is given in relation to an autopsy or forensic science report by both of the pathologists or forensic scientists purporting to have signed the report, the evidence of those pathologists or forensic scientists shall be sufficient evidence of any fact (or conclusion as to fact) contained in the report.

Amendment

Subss.(1), (2) as amended, and subss.(1)(i), (ii), (2)(i), (ii) inserted, by the Criminal Procedure (Amendment) (Scotland) Act 2004 (asp 5), s.25 and Sch.1, para.49. Brought into force on February 1, 2005 by the Criminal Procedure (Amendment) (Scotland) Act 2004 (Commencement, Transitional Provisions and Savings) Order 2004 (SSI 2004/405 (C.28)), art.2.

Definitions

  "indictment": s.307(1).
  "complaint": s.307(1).
  "prosecutor": s.307(1).
  "trial": s.307(1).

General Note

It is presumed, unless a challenge is notified to the prosecutor not less than six days before any trial (or later on cause shown), that the person referred to in any autopsy report founded upon in the proceedings is the same person as specified in the libel. Subsection (2) entitles the prosecutor to serve notice that he will call only one of the joint authors of a forensic of autopsy report, a concession designed to minimise inconvenience to such witnesses if their evidence is not in dispute. Again, a challenge to such a notice has to be intimated not less than six days before trial (or later on cause shown). Rule 27.1 in the 1996 Act of Adjournal requires that such notice will be in writing.

The practice has developed in solemn cases of incorporating the subs.(2) notice to the accused in the List of Productions incorporated in the indictment.

The evidential impact of the presumption in subs.(2) was discussed in *Bermingham v H.M. Advocate*, 2004 S.L.T. 692; 2004 S.C.C.R. 354 which recognises that it is competent for forensic scientists to incorporate elements of hearsay evidence in their reports in relation to work or findings generated by supervised assistants.

Routine evidence: reports of identification prior to trial

281A.—(1) Where in a trial the prosecutor lodges as a production a report naming—

(a) a person identified in an identification parade or other identification procedure by a witness, and

(b) that witness,

it shall be presumed, subject to subsection (2) below, that the person named in the report as having been identified by the witness is the person of the same name who appears in answer to the indictment or complaint.

(2) That presumption shall not apply—

(a) unless the prosecutor has, by the required time, served on the accused a copy of the report and a notice that he intends to rely on the presumption, or

(b) if the accused—

(i) not more than 7 days after the date of service of the copy of the report, or

(ii) by such later time as the court may in special circumstances allow,

has served notice on the prosecutor that he intends to challenge the facts stated in the report.

(3) In subsection (2)(a) above, "the required time" means—

(a) in the case of proceedings in the High Court—

(i) not less than 14 clear days before the preliminary hearing; or

(ii) such later time, being not less than 14 clear days before the trial, as the court may, in special circumstances, allow;

(b) in any other case, not less than 14 clear days before the trial.

AMENDMENT

Section 281A inserted by the Vulnerable Witnesses (Scotland) Act 2004 (asp 3), s.4. Brought into force, for all purposes, on April 1, 2005 by the Vulnerable Witnesses (Scotland) Act 2004 (Commencement) Order 2005 (SSI 2005/168 (C.7)), art.2 and Sch.

Subs.(2)(a) as amended and subs.(3) inserted by the Criminal Procedure (Amendment) (Scotland) Act 2004 (asp 5), s.25 and Sch.1, para.50. Brought into force on April 1, 2005 by the Criminal Procedure (Amendment) (Scotland) Act 2004 (Commencement, Transitional Provisions and Savings) Order 2004 (SSI 2004/405 (C.28)), art.2 and Sch.2.

Subs.(3) as amended by the Criminal Procedure (Amendment) (Scotland) Act 2004 (Incidental, Supplemental and Consequential Provisions) Order 2005 (SSI 2005/40), art.3.

DEFINITIONS

"prosecutor": s.307(1).
"trial": s.307(1).
"witness": s.271E(4).

GENERAL NOTE

First, s.281A(1) provides that if the witness has previously identified the accused in an identification procedure before the start of the trial then that witness need not make a dock identification at the trial. A report is lodged naming the person that the witness has identified in the procedure as the accused. That report becomes a production in the case.

Secondly, the presumption of correct identification does not apply unless the prosecutor has served a copy of the report on the accused with a notice that it is intended to rely upon that statutory presumption. The prosecutor has not less than 14 clear days before the trial to serve the documents. The accused may not more than seven days after the service of the copy report serve a notice on the prosecutor that it is intended to challenge the facts stated in the report. Special circumstances may allow a later service of such a notice by an accused.

Sufficient evidence

Evidence as to controlled drugs and medicinal products

282.—(1) For the purposes of any criminal proceedings, evidence given by an authorised forensic scientist, either orally or in a report purporting to be signed by him, that a substance which satisfies either of the conditions specified in subsection (2) below is—

(a) a particular controlled drug or medicinal product; or

(b) a particular product which is listed in the British Pharmacopoeia as containing a particular controlled drug or medicinal product,

shall, subject to subsection (3) below, be sufficient evidence of that fact notwithstanding that no analysis of the substance has been carried out.

(2) Those conditions are—

(a) that the substance is in a sealed container bearing a label identifying the contents of the container; or

(b) that the substance has a characteristic appearance having regard to its size, shape, colour and manufacturer's mark.

(3) A party proposing to rely on subsection (1) above ("the first party") shall, not less than 14 days before the relevant diet, serve on the other party ("the second party")—

(a) a notice to that effect; and

(b) where the evidence is contained in a report, a copy of the report,

and if the second party serves on the first party, not more than seven days after the date of service of the notice on him, a notice that he does not accept the evidence as to the identity of the substance, subsection (1) above shall not apply in relation to that evidence.

(3A) In subsection (3) above, "the relevant diet" means—

(a) in the case of proceedings in the High Court, the preliminary hearing;

(b) in any other case, the trial diet.

(4) A notice or copy report served in accordance with subsection (3) above shall be served in such manner as may be prescribed by Act of Adjournal; and a written execution purporting to be signed by the person who served the notice or copy together with, where appropriate, the relevant post office receipt shall be sufficient evidence of such service.

(5) In this section—

"controlled drug" has the same meaning as in the Misuse of Drugs Act 1971; and

"medicinal product" has the same meaning as in the Medicines Act 1968.

AMENDMENT

Subs.(3) as amended, and subs.(3A) inserted, by the Criminal Procedure (Amendment) (Scotland)

Act 2004 (asp 5), s.25 and Sch.1, para.51. Brought into force on February 1, 2005 by the Criminal Procedure (Amendment) (Scotland) Act 2004 (Commencement, Transitional Provisions and Savings) Order 2004 (SSI 2004/405 (C.28)), art.2.

DEFINITIONS

"controlled drug": s.282(5) and s.2(1)(a) of the Misuse of Drugs Act 1971 (c. 38).
"medicinal product": s.282(5) and s.130(1) of the Medicines Act 1968 (c. 67).
"trial": s.307(1).

GENERAL NOTE

This section, introduced by the Criminal Justice (Scotland) Act 1995, s.25, enables evidence to be given, in certain circumstances, by an authorised forensic scientist in any criminal proceedings to the effect that a substance is listed in British Pharmacopoiea as being, or containing, a controlled drug or medicinal product. Instead of demanding the conduct of a chemical examination to establish identification, s.282 allows forensic identification to be achieved by reference either to the label on a sealed container or, as is more common, to the size, colour, shape and markings on the substance; this latter method is commonplace in medical practice and in the pharmaceutical industry and there seems little virtue in requiring a higher standard than that in criminal proceedings particularly when subs.(3)(b) preserves the rights of the other party to give formal notice of challenge to that evidence.

Any such forensic report can be served in accordance with subs.(3) not less than 14 days prior to trial may broadly follow the style of Form 27, and must be challenged within seven days of the date of service, not receipt. Such a report must be served on all other parties in the proceedings.

Evidence as to time and place of video surveillance recordings

283.—(1) For the purposes of any criminal proceedings, a certificate purporting to be signed by a person responsible for the operation of a video surveillance system and certifying—

(a) the location of the camera;

(b) the nature and extent of the person's responsibility for the system; and

(c) that visual images recorded on a particular video tape are images, recorded by the system, of events which occurred at a place specified in the certificate at a time and date so specified,

shall, subject to subsection (2) below, be sufficient evidence of the matters contained in the certificate.

(2) A party proposing to rely on subsection (1) above ("the first party") shall, not less than 14 days before the relevant diet, serve on the other party ("the second party") a copy of the certificate and, if the second party serves on the first party, not more than seven days after the date of service of the copy certificate on him, a notice that he does not accept the evidence contained in the certificate, subsection (1) above shall not apply in relation to that evidence.

(2A) In subsection (2) above, "the relevant diet" means—

(a) in the case of proceedings in the High Court, the preliminary hearing;

(b) in any other case, the trial diet.

(3) A copy certificate or notice served in accordance with subsection (2) above shall be served in such manner as may be prescribed by Act of Adjournal; and a written execution purporting to be signed by the person who served the copy or notice together with, where appropriate, the relevant post office receipt shall be sufficient evidence of such service.

(4) In this section, "video surveillance system" means apparatus consisting of a camera mounted in a fixed position and associated equipment for transmitting and recording visual images of events occurring in any place.

AMENDMENT

Subs.(2) amended, and subs.(2A) inserted, by the Criminal Procedure (Amendment) (Scotland)

Act 2004 (asp 5), s.25 and Sch.1, para.52. Brought into force on February 1, 2005 by the Criminal Procedure (Amendment) (Scotland) Act 2004 (Commencement, Transitional Provisions and Savings) Order 2004 (SSI 2004/405 (C.28)), art.2.

DEFINITION

"video surveillance systems": s.283(4).

GENERAL NOTE

This section provides for evidence as to certain matters to be given by certificate by a person who is responsible for the operation of a video surveillance system, and was adopted from s.26 of the Criminal Justice (Scotland) Act 1995. The evidential matters which may be dealt with in the certificate are specified in subs.(1), and any such certificate shall be sufficient evidence of the matters stated. The form of certificate is stipulated in Chap.27 of the 1996 Act of Adjournal (see Form 27.2). As elsewhere in Pt XII of the Act, any certificate must be served not less than 14 days prior to trial and any challenge to the sufficiency of the evidence certified must be intimated within seven days of service.

The prime purpose of this provision is to provide a convenient means of leading the evidence of operators of city centre surveillance systems without requiring the unnecessary attendance at court of personnel. If the accused wishes to challenge this video evidence, the operator can be called upon to attend court.

Evidence in relation to fingerprints

284.—(1) For the purposes of any criminal proceedings, a certificate purporting to be signed by a person authorised in that behalf by a chief constable and certifying that relevant physical data (within the meaning of section 18(7A) of this Act) was taken from or provided by thereon were taken from a person designated in the certificate at a time, date and place specified therein shall, subject to subsection (2) below, be sufficient evidence of the facts contained in the certificate.

(2) A party proposing to rely on subsection (1) above ("the first party") shall, not less than 14 days before the relevant diet, serve on any other party to the proceedings a copy of the certificate, and, if that other party serves on the first party, not more than seven days after the date of service of the copy on him, a notice that he does not accept the evidence contained in the certificate, subsection (1) above shall not apply in relation to that evidence.

(2A) Where the first party does not serve a copy of the certificate on any other party as mentioned in subsection (2) above, he shall not be entitled to rely on subsection (1) above as respects that party.

(2B) In subsection (2) above, "the relevant diet" means—

(a) in the case of proceedings in the High Court, the preliminary hearing;

(b) in any other case, the trial diet.

(3) A copy certificate or notice served in accordance with subsection (2) above shall be served in such manner as may be prescribed by Act of Adjournal; and a written execution purporting to be signed by the person who served the copy or notice together with, where appropriate, the relevant post office receipt shall be sufficient evidence of such service.

AMENDMENTS

Subs.(1) substituted by the Crime and Punishment (Scotland) Act 1997, s.47(4)(a) with effect from August 1, 1997 in terms of the Crime and Punishment (Scotland) Act 1997 (Commencement and Transitional Provisions) order 1997 (SI 1997/1712), art.3.

Subss.(2) and (2A) substituted by s.47(4)(b) of the 1997 Act and effected by the Order specified above.

Subs.(2) as amended by Criminal Justice (Scotland) Act 2003 (asp 7), Part 8, s.54. Brought into

force on June 27, 2003 by the Criminal Justice (Scotland) Act 2003 (Commencement No.1) Order 2003 (SSI 2003/288 (C.14)).

Subs.(2) as amended, and subs.(2B) inserted, by the Criminal Procedure (Amendment) (Scotland) Act 2004 (asp 5), s.25 and Sch.1, para.53. Brought into force on February 1, 2005 by the Criminal Procedure (Amendment) (Scotland) Act 2004 (Commencement, Transitional Provisions and Savings) Order 2004 (SSI 2004/405 (C.28)), art.2.

DEFINITIONS

"constable": s.307(1) and s.51(1) of the Police (Scotland) Act 1967.
"relevant physical data": s.18(7A) of the 1995 Act.

GENERAL NOTE

The reforms to s.284 introduced by the Crime and Punishment (Scotland) Act 1997, s.47(4) further abbreviates the procedures for presentation of fingerprint evidence in the Scottish criminal courts. Formerly certificates signed by two police constables on any fingerprint report, giving details of the obtaining of the prints from the person named in the certificate, provided a sufficiency of evidence unless challenged timeously: from August 1, 1997 certification of the taking of relevant physical data can be made by one authorised person, a role which can obviously be undertaken by nominated civilian staff. Ultimately the aim seems to be for a member of staff at the database end, rather than the officers present with the person being fingerprinted, to certify the form produced by the Livescan equipment.

Subsections (2) and (2A) require the party relying upon this provision to serve a copy of the signed certificate on the affected party to the proceedings and, once served, the evidence in the copy shall be sufficient, cannot be challenged and will be conclusive as to its contents. With effect from June 27, 2003, subs.(2) reinstates the right of an accused to challenge the sufficiency of the certificate evidence served upon him; the Crime and Punishment (Scotland) Act 1997, s.47(4) had created a conclusive presumption which it was felt (on an admittedly narrow construction) might not be Convention-compliant.

Any party relying upon these provisions (almost invariably the Crown) will have to be able to produce executions of service of documentation to the court.

Proof of previous convictions

Previous convictions: proof, general

285.—(1) A previous conviction may be proved against any person in any criminal proceedings by the production of such evidence of the conviction as is mentioned in this subsection and subsections (2) to (6) below and by showing that his fingerprints and those of the person convicted are the fingerprints of the same person.

(2) A certificate purporting to be signed by or the Secretary of State or by a person authorised by him to sign such a certificate or the Commissioner of Police of the Metropolis, containing particulars relating to a conviction extracted from the criminal records kept in pursuance of a service provided and maintained by the Secretary of State under or by virtue of Section 36 of the Police (Scotland) Act 1967 or by or on behalf of the Commissioner of Police of the Metropolis, and certifying that the copies of the fingerprints contained in the certificate are copies of the fingerprints appearing from the said records to have been taken in pursuance of rules for the time being in force under sections 12 and 39 of the Prisons (Scotland) Act 1989, or regulations for the time being in force under section 16 of the Prison Act 1952, from the person convicted on the occasion of the conviction or on the occasion of his last conviction, shall be sufficient evidence of the conviction or, as the case may be, of his last conviction and of all preceding convictions and that the copies of the fingerprints produced on the certificate are copies of the fingerprints of the person convicted.

(3) Where a person has been apprehended and detained in the custody of the

police in connection with any criminal proceedings, a certificate purporting to be signed by the chief constable concerned or a person authorised on his behalf, certifying that the fingerprints produced thereon were taken from him while he was so detained, shall be sufficient evidence in those proceedings that the fingerprints produced on the certificate are the fingerprints of that person.

(4) A certificate purporting to be signed by or on behalf of the governor of a prison or of a remand centre in which any person has been detained in connection with any criminal proceedings, certifying that the fingerprints produced thereon were taken from him while he was so detained, shall be sufficient evidence in those proceedings that the fingerprints produced on the certificate are the fingerprints of that person.

(5) A certificate purporting to be signed by the Secretary of State or by a person authorised by him to sign such a certificate, and certifying that the fingerprints, copies of which are certified as mentioned in subsection (2) above by the Secretary of State or by a person authorised by him to sign such a certificate or by or on behalf of or the Commissioner of Police of the Metropolis to be copies of the fingerprints of a person previously convicted and the fingerprints certified by or on behalf of a chief constable or a governor as mentioned in subsection (3) or (4) above, or otherwise shown, to be the fingerprints of the person against whom the previous conviction is sought to be proved, are the fingerprints of the same person, shall be sufficient evidence of the matter so certified.

(6) An extract conviction of any crime committed in any part of the United Kingdom bearing to have been issued by an officer whose duties include the issue of extract convictions shall be received in evidence without being sworn to by witnesses.

(7) It shall be competent to prove a previous conviction or any fact relevant to the admissibility of the conviction by witnesses, although the name of any such witness is not included in the list served on the accused; and the accused shall be entitled to examine witnesses with regard to such conviction or fact.

(8) An official of any prison in which the accused has been detained on such conviction shall be a competent and sufficient witness to prove its application to the accused, although he may not have been present in court at the trial to which such conviction relates.

(9) The method of proving a previous conviction authorised by this section shall be in addition to any other method of proving the conviction.

(10) In this section "fingerprint" includes any record of the skin of a person's finger created by a device approved by the Secretary of State under section 18(7B) of this Act.

AMENDMENTS

Subs.(2) substituted by the Crime and Punishment (Scotland) Act 1997 (c.48), s.59(2) with effect from August 1, 1997 as enacted by the Crime and Punishment (Scotland) Act 1997 (Commencement and Transitional Provisions) Order 1997 (SI 1997/1712), art.3.

Subs.(5) substituted by the 1997 Act s.59(3) and enacted from August 1, 1997 by the above Order.

Subs.(10) inserted by the 1997 Act s.47(5) and enacted from August 1, 1997 by the above Order.

DEFINITION

"conviction": s.307(5).

GENERAL NOTE

This section carries over the provisions relating to proof of previous convictions by use of proved fingerprints. This procedure can be deployed to prove previous convictions which have been disputed by the accused or, in limited circumstances, as evidence in support of a substantive charge (see also s.286 below). Use is made of the fingerprint forms completed at the time of the accused's admission to a prison (subs.(4)) or when routinely detained in police custody in relation to the charges libelled (subs.(3)).

It is not necessary to list as witnesses those prison officials or court officers whose only role is to speak to the fact of a previous conviction or extract conviction.

Certification was previously the responsibility of the Chief Constable of Strathclyde Police but, following amendments to the Police (Scotland) Act 1967 (c.77) made by s.46 of the 1997 Act, responsibility for this core service now lies with the Scottish Secretary.

The development of "livescan" electronic fingerprinting is reflected in subs.(10). See the discussion at A4–49 above. The Electronic Fingerprinting etc. Device Approval (Scotland) Order 1997 (SI 1997/1939) approved the use of the Digital Biometrics Corporation (D.B.I.) Tenprinter 1133S with effect from August 8, 1997.

Previous convictions: proof in support of substantive charge

286.—(1) Without prejudice to section 285(6) to (9) or, as the case may be, section 166 of this Act, where proof of a previous conviction is competent in support of a substantive charge, any such conviction or an extract of it shall, if—

    (a) it purports to relate to the accused and to be signed by the clerk of court having custody of the record containing the conviction; and

    (b) a copy of it has been served on the accused not less than 14 days before the relevant diet,

be sufficient evidence of the application of the conviction to the accused unless, within seven days of the date of service of the copy on him, he serves notice on the prosecutor that he denies that it applies to him.

(1A) In subsection (1)(b) above, "the relevant diet" means—

    (a) in the case of proceedings in the High Court, the preliminary hearing;

    (b) in any other case, the trial diet.

(2) A copy of a conviction or extract conviction served under subsection (1) above shall be served on the accused in such manner as may be prescribed by Act of Adjournal, and a written execution purporting to be signed by the person who served the copy together with, where appropriate, the relevant post office receipt shall be sufficient evidence of service of the copy.

(3) The reference in subsection (1)(a) above to "the clerk of court having custody of the record containing the conviction" includes, in relation to a previous conviction by a court in another member State of the European Union, a reference to any officer of that court or of that State having such custody.

AMENDMENT

    Subs.(3) inserted by Criminal Justice (Scotland) Act 2003 (asp 7), Part 8, s.57. Brought into force on June 27, 2003 by the Criminal Justice (Scotland) Act 2003 (Commencement No.1) Order 2003 (SSI 2003/288 (C.14)).

    Subs.(1)(b) as amended, and subs.(1A) inserted, by the Criminal Procedure (Amendment) (Scotland) Act 2004 (asp 5), s.25 and Sch.1, para.54. Brought into force on February 1, 2005 by the Criminal Procedure (Amendment) (Scotland) Act 2004 (Commencement, Transitional Provisions and Savings) Order 2004 (SSI 2004/405 (C.28)), art.2.

DEFINITIONS

    "previous conviction": s.307(5).
    "trial": s.307(1).

GENERAL NOTE

    Where it is necessary to lead evidence of a conviction in support of a substantive charge, this section provides for the use in evidence, of a relevant certified extract conviction. A copy of the extract conviction has to be served on the accused not less than 14 days before trial and any challenge to it must be intimated within seven days of service. Use of a s.286 certificate may well serve to pre-empt any such challenge. In solemn proceedings the completed execution of service should be lodged as a production.

See generally the discussion on the admissibility of evidence of previous convictions in the notes to ss.101 and 166 above and, in regard to European Union convictions, the notes to ss.285 and 286A of the Act.

Proof of previous conviction by court in other member State

286A.—(1) A previous conviction by a court in another member State of the European Union may be proved against any person in any criminal proceedings by the production of evidence of the conviction and by showing that his fingerprints and those of the person convicted are the fingerprints of the same person.

(2) A certificate—

(a) bearing—

    (i) to have been sealed with the official seal of a Minister of the State in question; and

    (ii) to contain particulars relating to a conviction extracted from the criminal records of that State; and

(b) including copies of fingerprints and certifying that those copies—

    (i) are of fingerprints appearing from those records to have been taken from the person convicted on the occasion of the conviction, or on the occasion of his last conviction; and

    (ii) would be admissible in evidence in criminal proceedings in that State as a record of the skin of that person's fingers,

shall be sufficient evidence of the conviction or, as the case may be, of the person's last conviction and of all preceding convictions and that the copies of the fingerprints included in the certificate are copies of the fingerprints of the person convicted.

(3) A conviction bearing to have been—

(a) extracted from the criminal records of the State in question; and

(b) issued by an officer of that State whose duties include the issuing of such extracts,

shall be received in evidence without being sworn to by witnesses.

(4) Subsection (9) of section 285 of this Act applies in relation to this section as it does in relation to that section.

AMENDMENT

Section 286A inserted by Criminal Justice (Scotland) Act 2003 (asp 7), Part 8, s.57. Brought into force on June 27, 2003 by the Criminal Justice (Scotland) Act 2003 (Commencement No.1) Order 2003 (SSI 2003/288 (C.14)).

GENERAL NOTE

This section provides for proof by fingerprint certificate of a previous conviction imposed upon an accused by a member state of the European Union, when included in a schedule of convictions. The provision follows the terms of s.285 of the Act which apply to proof of United Kingdom convictions.

PART XIII

MISCELLANEOUS

Lord Advocate

Demission of office by Lord Advocate

287.—(1) All indictments which have been raised by a Lord Advocate shall remain effective notwithstanding his subsequently having died or demitted office and may be taken up and proceeded with by his successor.

(2) During any period when the office of Lord Advocate is vacant it shall be lawful to indict accused persons in name of the Solicitor General then in office.

(3) The advocates depute shall not demit office when a Lord Advocate dies or demits office but shall continue in office until their successors receive commissions.

(4) The advocates depute and procurators fiscal shall have power, notwithstanding any vacancy in the office of Lord Advocate, to take up and proceed with any indictment which—

(a) by virtue of subsection (1) above, remains effective; or

(b) by virtue of subsection (2) above, is in the name of the Solicitor General.

(5) For the purposes of this Act, where, but for this subsection, demission of office by one Law Officer would result in the offices of both being vacant, he or, where both demit office on the same day, the person demitting the office of Lord Advocate shall be deemed to continue in office until the warrant of appointment of the person succeeding to the office of Lord Advocate is granted.

(6) The Lord Advocate shall enter upon the duties of his office immediately upon the grant of his warrant of appointment.

AMENDMENT

Subs.(6) as amended by the Scotland Act 1998 (Consequential Modifications) (No.1) Order 1999 (S.I. 1999 No. 1042) art.4 and Sched.2, para.11 and Sched. 2, Pt III.

DEFINITIONS

"indictment": s.307(1).
"procurator fiscal": s.307(1).

GENERAL NOTE

The Lord Advocate has the universal and exclusive title to prosecute on indictment. This section is concerned with the consequences of the decession of office by Lord Advocate. This section puts into statutory form a variety of authorities that have evolved or been passed over the years: see Macdonald *Criminal Law of Scotland* (5th ed.) (W. Green, Edinburgh) at p.212. In short, the section provides for the continuity of Crown business notwithstanding a change of Lord Advocate.

Two points are worth noting. First, during any period when the office of Lord Advocate is vacant it shall be lawful to indict accused persons in the name of the Solicitor General then in office: subs.(2). It is clear that such indictments may be taken up by the new Lord Advocate on his appointment: *H.M. Solicitor General v Lavelle* (1913) 7 Adam 255. Secondly, the Lord Advocate shall enter upon the duties of his office immediately upon the grant of his warrant: subs.(6). Before this provision the Lord Advocate could not act until the Royal Warrant appointing him reached Crown Office, he was not entitled to act merely on notice of his appointment appearing in the Edinburgh Gazette: *Halliday v Wilson* (1891) 3 White 38.

Only in the most exceptional, and unequivocal, of circumstances can an indication as to the form, and forum, of proceedings by the Procurator Fiscal to a defence agent fetter the Lord Advocate's discretion. See *Murphy v HM Advocate*, 2002 S.L.T. 1416; 2002 S.C.C.R. 969 in which a letter was sent by the Fiscal to the defence agent providing an assessment of the evidence and an indication that petition proceedings would be reduced to summary complaint; this pronouncement had been communicated to the accused without the knowledge or authority of Crown counsel. (The separate issue of whether, given the background, it would be oppressive for the Crown to maintain the proceedings in any form was not explored in this appeal). Refer also to *Cook v HM Advocate*, 2003 G.W.D. 3–66.

Intimation of proceedings in High Court to Lord Advocate

288.—(1) In any proceeding in the High Court (other than a proceeding to which the Lord Advocate or a procurator fiscal is a party) it shall be competent for the court to order intimation of such proceeding to the Lord Advocate.

(2) On intimation being made to the Lord Advocate under subsection (1) above, the Lord Advocate shall be entitled to appear and be heard in such proceeding.

DEFINITIONS

"High Court": s.307(1).
"procurator fiscal": s.307(1).

GENERAL NOTE

This section is probably concerned with Bill of Criminal letters which have not been presented to the Lord Advocate for concurrence or with petitions to the *nobile officium* of the High Court of Justiciary. The ordinary practice would be to intimate to the Lord Advocate but individuals proceeding without legal representation, for example, might not know of that practice.

Devolution issues

Rights of appeal for Advocate General: devolution issues

288A.—(1) This section applies where—

(a) a person is acquitted or convicted of a charge (whether on indictment or in summary proceedings), and

(b) the Advocate General for Scotland was a party to the proceedings in pursuance of paragraph 6 of Schedule 6 to the Scotland Act 1998 (devolution issues).

(2) The Advocate General for Scotland may refer any devolution issue which has arisen in the proceedings to the High Court for their opinion; and the Clerk of Justiciary shall send to the person acquitted or convicted and to any solicitor who acted for that person at the trial, a copy of the reference and intimation of the date fixed by the Court for a hearing.

(3) The person may, not later than seven days before the date so fixed, intimate in writing to the Clerk of Justiciary and to the Advocate General for Scotland either—

(a) that he elects to appear personally at the hearing, or

(b) that he elects to be represented by counsel at the hearing,

but, except by leave of the Court on cause shown, and without prejudice to his right to attend, he shall not appear or be represented at the hearing other than by and in conformity with an election under this subsection.

(4) Where there is no intimation under subsection (3)(b), the High Court shall appoint counsel to act at the hearing as amicus curiae.

(5) The costs of representation elected under subsection (3)(b) or of an appointment under subsection (4) shall, after being taxed by the Auditor of the Court of Session, be paid by the Advocate General for Scotland out of money provided by Parliament.

(6) The opinion on the point referred under subsection (2) shall not affect the acquittal or (as the case may be) conviction in the trial.

AMENDMENT

Section 288A inserted by the Scotland Act 1998 (c.46) Sch.8, para.32 and brought into force by the Scotland Act 1998 (Commencement) Order 1998, art.2, Sch.3 (SI 1998/3178: effective May 6, 1999).

GENERAL NOTE

The Advocate General for Scotland is to be the new law officer with the responsibility for Scottish legal matters in regard to the United Kingdom. Where questions arise as to the competency of legislation, or the actings of some members of the Scottish Executive or related questions, the Advocate General may institute proceedings for the determination of such a devolution issue. It follows then that there requires to be a mode of appeal and that is provided for by s.288A and s.288B of the 1995 Act.

Appeals to Judicial Committee of the Privy Council

288B.—(1) This section applies where the Judicial Committee of the Privy Council determines an appeal under paragraph 13(a) of Schedule 6 to the Scotland Act 1998 against a determination of a devolution issue by the High Court in the ordinary course of proceedings.

(2) The determination of the appeal shall not affect any earlier acquittal or earlier quashing of any conviction in the proceedings.

(3) Subject to subsection (2) above, the High Court shall have the same powers in relation to the proceedings when remitted to it by the Judicial Committee as it would have if it were considering the proceedings otherwise than as a trial court.

AMENDMENT

Section 288B inserted by the Scotland Act 1998 (c.46) Sch.8, para.32 and brought into force by the Scotland Act 1998 (Commencement) Order 1998, art.2, Sch.3 (SI 1998/3178: effective May 6, 1999).

Trials for sexual offences

Prohibition of personal conduct of defence in cases of certain sexual offences

288C.—(1) An accused charged with a sexual offence to which this section applies is prohibited from conducting

(a) his case in person at or for the purposes of a preliminary hearing; and

(b) his defence in person at the trial and in any victim statement proof relating to any such offence.

(2) This section applies to the following sexual offences—

(a) rape;

(b) sodomy;

(c) clandestine injury to women;

(d) abduction of a woman or girl with intent to rape;

(e) assault with intent to rape;

(f) indecent assault;

(g) indecent behaviour (including any lewd, indecent or libidinous practice or behaviour);

(h) an offence under section 311 (non-consensual sexual acts) or 313 (persons providing care services: sexual offences) of the Mental Health (Care and Treatment) (Scotland) Act 2003;

(i) an offence under any of the following provisions of the Criminal Law (Consolidation) (Scotland) Act 1995 (c.39)—

(i) sections 1 to 3 (incest and related offences);

(ii) section 5 (unlawful sexual intercourse with girl under 13 or 16);

(iii) section 6 (indecent behaviour toward girl between 12 and 16);

(iv) section 7(2) and (3) (procuring by threats etc.);

(v) section 8 (abduction and unlawful detention);

(vi) section 10 (seduction, prostitution, etc. of girl under 16);

(vii) section 13(5)(b) or (c) (homosexual offences);

(j) attempting to commit any of the offences set out in paragraphs (a) to (i) above.

(3) This section applies also to an offence in respect of which a court having jurisdiction to try that offence has made an order under subsection (4) below.

(4) Where, in the case of any offence, other than one set out in subsection (2) above, that court is satisfied that there appears to be such a substantial sexual element in the alleged commission of the offence that it ought to be treated, for the purposes of this section, in the same way as an offence set out in that subsection, the court shall, either on the application of the prosecutor or *ex proprio motu*, make an order under this subsection.

(5) The making of such an order does not affect the validity of anything which—

(a) was done in relation to the alleged offence to which the order relates; and

(b) was done before the order was made.

(6) The Scottish Ministers may by order made by statutory instrument vary the sexual offences to which this section applies by virtue of subsection (2) above by modifying that subsection.

(7) No such statutory instrument shall be made, however, unless a draft of it has been laid before and approved by resolution of the Scottish Parliament.

(8) In subsection (1)(b) above, "victim statement proof" means any proof ordered in relation to—

(a) a victim statement made by virtue of subsection (2) (or by virtue of that subsection and subsection (6)) of section 14 of the Criminal Justice (Scotland) Act 2003 (asp 7); or

(b) a statement made by virtue of subsection (3) of that section in relation to such a victim statement.

AMENDMENTS

Section 288C inserted by the Sexual Offences (Procedure and Evidence) (Scotland) Act 2002 (asp 9), s.1. Brought into force by the Sexual Offences (Procedure and Evidence) (Scotland) Act 2002 (Commencement and Transitional Provisions) Order 2002 (SSI 2002/443 (C.24)), art.4 (effective November 1, 2002).

Subs.(1) as amended by the Criminal Justice (Scotland) Act 2003 (asp 7), Part 2, s.15(2). Brought into force on November 25, 2003 by the Criminal Justice (Scotland) Act 2003 (Commencement No.3 and Revocation) Order 2003 (SSI 2003/475 (C.26)), art.2.

Subs.(1)(a), (b) inserted by the Criminal Procedure (Amendment) (Scotland) Act 2004 (asp 5), s.4(1). Subs.(1)(b) as amended and subs.(8) inserted by s.25 and Sch.1, para.55 of the 2004 Act. Brought into force on February 1, 2005 by the Criminal Procedure (Amendment) (Scotland) Act 2004 (Commencement, Transitional Provisions and Savings) Order 2004 (SSI 2004/405 (C.28)), art.2.

Subs.(2)(h) as amended by the Mental Health (Care and Treatment) (Scotland) Act 2003 (Modification of Enactments) Order 2005 (SSI 2005/465), art.2 and Sch.1, para.27(5) (effective September 27, 2005).

Following strongly adverse press comment upon the case of *HM Advocate v Anderson* (Perth High Court, June 8, 2000, unreported), the Scottish Parliament rapidly responded with the Sexual Offences (Procedure and Evidence) (Scotland) Act 2002 (asp 9). Anderson had defended himself and cross-examined the complainers at considerable length. Coming as this did after several highly-publicised trials of a similar nature south of the border, it was felt that reliance upon judicial discretion to marshall cross-examination was not enough. This section sets out procedures to prevent accused representing themselves in trials for a sexual offence or in cases which appear to involve a substantial sexualised element (some species of breach of the peace, for example). It will be noted that these provisions apply to proceedings in any Scottish criminal court and that restrictions are also introduced to debar such an accused from conducting precognition on oath of the complainer (see s.291(4) below).

The onus is generally upon the Crown to identify the proceedings as fulfilling the demands of s.288C at the time of indicting or serving a complaint by serving notice upon the accused. The only exception to this general rule is found in subs.(4) where the court, *ex proprio motu* or on application of the prosecutor, can initiate an order. Only if the accused asserts that he is not so represented will a s.288C hearing be necessary but in that situation, the court must follow the directions in s.288D and ensure that legal representation, and legal aid, are in place (see the Legal Aid (Scotland) Act 1986, s.22 as now amended).

Due to the differences between summary and solemn procedures, and between procedures in sheriff and jury and High Court trials, different mechanisms exist to meet the demands of s.288C. In summary proceedings the citation is accompanied by a notice from the prosecutor indicating that the accused cannot conduct his own defence, or the accused is advised personally or through his law agent during a personal appearance. Individuals tendering a letter pleading not guilty would have to attend an intermediate diet in due course. Adjournment for the purpose of enquiry as to legal representation is competent for up to 48 hours.

It is submitted that a s.288C hearing has no other purpose and cannot be used as an means to introduce other preliminary issues.

Appointment of solicitor by court in such cases

288D.—(1) This section applies in the case of proceedings in respect of a sexual offence to which section 288C above applies.

(2) Where the court ascertains that—

(a) the accused has not engaged a solicitor for the purposes of

    (i) the conduct of his case at or for the purposes of a preliminary hearing; or

    (ii) his defence at the trial or as the case may be at any victim statement proof as is mentioned in section 288C(1)(b) of this Act; or

    (iii) the conduct of his case at any commissioner proceedings; or

(b) having engaged a solicitor for those purposes, the accused has dismissed him; or

(c) the accused's solicitor has withdrawn,

then, where the court is not satisfied that the accused intends to engage a solicitor or, as the case may be, another solicitor for those purposes, it shall, at its own hand, appoint a solicitor for those purposes.

(3) A solicitor so appointed is not susceptible to dismissal by the accused or obliged to comply with any instruction by the accused to dismiss counsel.

(4) Subject to subsection (3) above, it is the duty of a solicitor so appointed—

(a) to ascertain and act upon the instructions of the accused; and

(b) where the accused gives no instructions or inadequate or perverse instructions, to act in the best interests of the accused.

(5) In all other respects, a solicitor so appointed has, and may be made subject to, the same obligations and has, and may be given, the same authority as if engaged by the accused; and any employment of and instructions given to counsel by the solicitor shall proceed and be treated accordingly.

(6) Where the court is satisfied that a solicitor so appointed is no longer able to act upon the instructions, or in the best interests, of the accused, the court may relieve that solicitor of his appointment and appoint another solicitor for the purposes of the accused's defence at the trial (or at any related commissioner proceedings).

(6A) Where, in realation to commissioner proceedings, the commissioner is satisfied that a solicitor so appointed is no longer able to act upon the instructions, or in the best interests, of the accused, the commissioner is (for the purpose of the application of subsection (6) above) to refer the case to the court.

(7) The references in subsections (3) to (6A) above to "a solicitor so appointed" include references to a solicitor appointed under subsection (6) above.

(8) In this section "counsel" includes a solicitor who has right of audience in the High Court of Justiciary under section 25A (rights of audience in various courts including the High Court of Justiciary) of the Solicitors (Scotland) Act 1980 (c.46).

(9) In this section, "commissioner proceedings" means proceedings before a commissioner appointed under section 271I(1) or by virtue of section 272(1)(b) of this Act.

Amendments

Section 288D inserted by the Sexual Offences (Procedure and Evidence) (Scotland) Act 2002 (asp 9), s.2(1). Brought into force by the Sexual Offences (Procedure and Evidence) (Scotland) Act 2002 (Commencement and Transitional Provisions) Order 2002 (SSI 2002/443 (C.24)), art.4 (effective November 1, 2002).

Subs.(2)(a) as amended by the Criminal Justice (Scotland) Act 2003 (asp 7), Part 2, s.15. Brought into force on November 25, 2003 by the Criminal Justice (Scotland) Act 2003 (Commencement No.3 and Revocation) Order 2003 (SSI 2003/475 (C.26)), art.2.

Subs.288D(2)(a)(i), (ii) inserted by the Criminal Procedure (Amendment) (Scotland) Act 2004 (asp 5), s.4(2). Subs.(2)(a)(ii) as amended by s.25 and Sch.1, para.56 of the 2004 Act. Brought into force on February 1, 2005 by the Criminal Procedure (Amendment) (Scotland) Act 2004 (Commencement, Transitional Provisions and Savings) Order 2004 (SSI 2004/405 (C.28)), art.2.

Section 288D amended and s.288D(2)(iii) and s.288D(6A) and s.288(9) inserted by the Criminal Proceedings etc. (Reform) (Scotland) Act 2007 (asp 6), s.35

General Note

The purpose of this provision is discussed at A4–561.5.1 above.

Trials involving vulnerable witnesses

Prohibition of personal conduct of defence in certain cases involving child witnesses under the age of 12

288E.—(1) In proceedings to which this section applies, the accused is prohibited from conducting

(a) his case in person at or for the purposes of a preliminary hearing; and

(b) his defence in person at the trial and in any victim statement proof relating to any offence to which the trial relates.

(2) This section applies to any proceedings (other than proceedings in the district court)—

(a) in respect of any offence specified in subsection (3) below, and

(b) in which a child witness who is under the age of 12 on the date of commencement of the proceedings is to give evidence at or for the purposes of the trial.

(3) The offences referred to in subsection (2)(a) above are—

(a) murder,

(b) culpable homicide,

(c) any offence which—

(i) involves an assault on, or injury or threat of injury to, any person (including any offence involving neglect or ill-treatment of, or other cruelty to, a child), but

(ii) is not an offence to which section 288C of this Act applies,

(d) abduction, and

(e) plagium.

(4) Section 288D of this Act applies in the case of proceedings to which this section applies as it applies in the case of proceedings in respect of a sexual offence to which section 288C of this Act applies.

(5) In proceedings to which this section applies, the prosecutor shall, at the same time as intimating to the accused under section 271A(13) of this Act a child witness notice in respect of a child witness referred to in subsection (2)(b) above, serve on the accused a notice under subsection (6).

(6) A notice under this subsection shall contain intimation to the accused—

(za) where he is indicted to the High Court in respect of the offence, that his case at or for the purposes of the preliminary hearing may be conducted only by a lawyer,

(a) that if he is tried for the offence, his defence may be conducted only by a lawyer,

(b) that it is therefore in his interests, if he has not already done so, to get the professional assistance of a solicitor, and

(c) that if he does not engage a solicitor for the purposes of the conduct of his case at or for the purposes of the preliminary hearing (if he is indicted to the High Court in respect of the offence) or his defence at the trial, the court will do so.

(7) A failure to comply with subsection (5) or (6) above does not affect the validity or lawfulness of any child witness notice or any other element of the proceedings against the accused.

(8) In subsection (1) above, "victim statement proof" means any proof ordered in relation to—

(a) a victim statement made by virtue of subsection (2) (or by virtue of that subsection and subsection (6)) of section 14 of the Criminal Justice (Scotland) Act 2003 (asp 7), or

(b) a statement made by virtue of subsection (3) of that section in relation to such a victim statement.

(9) For the purposes of subsection (2)(b) above, proceedings shall be taken to have commenced when the indictment or, as the case may be, the complaint is served on the accused.

AMENDMENTS

Section 288E inserted by the Vulnerable Witnesses (Scotland) Act 2004 (asp 3), s.6. Brought into force, for specified purposes, on April 1, 2005 by the Vulnerable Witnesses (Scotland) Act 2004 (Commencement) Order 2005 (SSI 2005/168 (C.7)), art.2 and Sch. Further brought into force for specified purposes on April 1, 2006 by the Vulnerable Witnesses (Scotland) Act 2004 (Commencement No.3, Savings and Transitional Provisions) Order 2006 (SSI 2006/59 (C.8)), art.2 and Sch.

Subss.(1) and (6)(c) as amended and subss.(1)(a), (b) and (6)(za) inserted by the Criminal Procedure (Amendment) (Scotland) Act 2004 (asp 5), s.4(3). Brought into force on April 1, 2005 by the Criminal Procedure (Amendment) (Scotland) Act 2004 (Commencement, Transitional Provisions and Savings) Order 2004 (SSI 2004/405 (C.28)), art.2 and Sch.2.

Further brought into force for specified purposes on April 1, 2007 by the Vulnerable Witnesses (Scotland) Act 2004 (Commencement No.4, Savings and Transitional Provisions) Order 2007 (SSI 2007/101 (C.13)), art.2.

DEFINITIONS

"court": s.271(5).
"prosecutor": s.307(1).
"trial": s.307(1).
"vulnerable witness": s.271(7).

GENERAL NOTE

Section 288C of the 1995 Act introduced a prohibition on the personal conduct of the defence case by an accused in the trial of certain specified sexual offences. The new s.288E applies to murder, culpable homicide and other offences that involve generally speaking assaults (excluding matters covered by s.288C). The new s.288E, if such a matter is charged, covers a child witness who is under 12 years on the date of the commencement of proceedings and who is to give evidence. The test is whether the use of this procedure is in the best interests of the child witness. The prosecutor must serve a child witness notice on an accused by s.271A(3) and at the same time serve a notice by s.288E(6). The latter notice advises an accused that for the offence charged the defence may only be conducted by a lawyer.

Power to prohibit personal conduct of defence in other cases involving vulnerable witnesses

288F.—(1) This section applies in the case of proceedings in respect of any offence, other than proceedings—

(a) in the district court,

(b) in respect of a sexual offence to which section 288C of this Act applies, or

(c) to which section 288E of this Act applies,

where a vulnerable witness is to give evidence at, or for the purposes of, the trial.

(2) If satisfied that it is in the interests of the vulnerable witness to do so, the court may—

(a) on the application of the prosecutor, or

(b) of its own motion,

make an order prohibiting the accused from conducting his defence in person at the trial and in any victim statement proof relating to any offence to which the trial relates.

(3) However, the court shall not make an order under subsection (2) above if it considers that—

(a) the order would give rise to a significant risk of prejudice to the fairness of the trial or otherwise to the interests of justice, and

(b) that risk significantly outweighs any risk of prejudice to the interests of the vulnerable witness if the order is not made.

(4) The court may make an order under subsection (2) above after, as well as before, proceedings at the trial have commenced.

(4A) Where, in any proceedings in the High Court, an order is made under subsection (2) above before or at the preliminary hearing, the accused is also prohibited from conducting or, as the case may be, continuing to conduct, his case in person at or for the purposes of the preliminary hearing.

(5) Section 288D of this Act applies in the case of proceedings in respect of which an order is made under this section as it applies in the case of proceedings in respect of a sexual offence to which section 288C of this Act applies.

(6) In subsection (2) above, "victim statement proof" means any proof ordered in relation to—

(a) a victim statement made by virtue of subsection (2) (or by virtue of that subsection and subsection (6)) of section 14 of the Criminal Justice (Scotland) Act 2003 (asp 7), or

(b) a statement made by virtue of subsection (3) of that section in relation to such a victim statement.

AMENDMENTS

Section 288F inserted by the Vulnerable Witnesses (Scotland) Act 2004 (asp 3), s.6. Brought into force, for specified purposes, on April 1, 2005 by the Vulnerable Witnesses (Scotland) Act 2004 (Commencement) Order 2005 (SSI 2005/168 (C.7)), art.2 and Sch. Further brought into force for specified purposes on April 1, 2006 by the Vulnerable Witnesses (Scotland) Act 2004 (Commencement No.3, Savings and Transitional Provisions) Order 2006 (SSI 2006/59 (C.8)), art.2 and Sch.

Subs.(4A) inserted by the Criminal Procedure (Amendment) (Scotland) Act 2004 (asp 5), s.4(4). Brought into force on April 1, 2005 by the Criminal Procedure (Amendment) (Scotland) Act 2004 (Commencement, Transitional Provisions and Savings) Order 2004 (SSI 2004/405 (C.28)), art.2 and Sch.2.

Further brought into force for specified purposes on April 1, 2007 by the Vulnerable Witnesses (Scotland) Act 2004 (Commencement No.4, Savings and Transitional Provisions) Order 2007 (SSI 2007/101 (C.13)), art.2.

DEFINITIONS

"court": s.271(5).
"prosecutor": s.307(1).
"trial": s.307(1).
"vulnerable statement proof": s.288E(5A).
"vulnerable witness": s.271(7).

GENERAL NOTE

Section 288C of the 1995 Act introduced a prohibition on the personal conduct of the defence case by an accused in the trial of certain specified sexual offences. The new s.288F extends that type of prohibition to cases (other than ones with sexual offences and those specified in s.288F(3)) if a vulnerable witness is giving evidence in the trial. The test is whether the use of this procedure is in the best interests of the vulnerable witness. There seems to be a balance that requires to be found in this as no such order of prohibition can be made if there is a significant risk of prejudice to the fairness of the trial and that risk outweighs any prejudice to the interests of the vulnerable witness. If an order is made the court also appoints a solicitor for the accused.

Application of vulnerable witnesses provisions to proceedings in the district court

Application of vulnerable witnesses provisions to proceedings in the district court

[288G.—(1) The Scottish Ministers may by order made by statutory instrument provide for any of sections—

(a) 271 to 271M,

(b) 288E, and

(c) 288F,

of this Act to apply, subject to such modifications (if any) as may be specified in the order, to proceedings in the district court.

(2) An order under subsection (1) may—

(a) make such incidental, supplemental, consequential, transitional, transitory or saving provision as the Scottish Ministers think necessary or expedient,

(b) make different provision for different district courts or descriptions of district court or different proceedings or types of proceedings,

(c) modify any enactment.

(3) An order under this section shall not be made unless a draft of the statutory instrument containing the order has been laid before, and approved by resolution of, the Scottish Parliament.]

AMENDMENT

Section 288G prospectively inserted by the Vulnerable Witnesses (Scotland) Act 2004 (asp 3), s.10.

"vulnerable witness": s.271(7).

GENERAL NOTE

There is no reason in principle as to why cases tried in the district courts should not proceed where there are or may be vulnerable witnesses. This is all the more so given the existence of stipendiary magistrates in the district court with the summary powers of a sheriff: see s.7(5) of the 1995 Act. This new s.288G allows the Scottish Ministers a power to apply the vulnerable witness provisions to the district court.

Treason trials

Procedure and evidence in trials for treason

289. The procedure and rules of evidence in proceedings for treason and misprision of treason shall be the same as in proceedings according to the law of Scotland for murder.

GENERAL NOTE

It has been the rule in England since the Treason Act 1800 (see now the Criminal Law Act 1967, s.12(7)) that trials for treason and misprision should be governed by the rules applicable to trials for murder. This section restates the position in Scotland which was clarified in s.39 of the 1980 Act. The substantive law of trespass remains English, but the Treason Acts of 1800 and 1945 were repealed by s.83(3) of and Sch.8 to the 1980 Act, along with what remained of the Treason Act 1708.

Certain rights of accused

Accused's right to request identification parade

290.—(1) Subject to subsection (2) below, the sheriff may, on an application by an accused at any time after the accused has been charged with an offence, order that, in relation to the alleged offence, the prosecutor shall hold an identification parade in which the accused shall be one of those constituting the parade.

(2) The sheriff shall make an order in accordance with subsection (1) above only after giving the prosecutor an opportunity to be heard and only if—

(a) an identification parade, such as is mentioned in subsection (1) above, has not been held at the instance of the prosecutor;

(b) after a request by the accused, the prosecutor has refused to hold, or has unreasonably delayed holding, such an identification parade; and

(c) the sheriff considers the application under subsection (1) above to be reasonable.

DEFINITIONS
"offence": s.307(1).
"prosecutor": s.307(1).
"sheriff": s.4(1) and (4).

GENERAL NOTE

This section re-enacts the provisions of s.10 of the Criminal Justice (Scotland) Act 1980. It is open to the accused to make an application for an identification parade to be held by the prosecutor; (i) where no such parade has been conducted; (ii) where the prosecutor has refused a request by the accused for such a parade, or else been dilatory in organising the parade;and (iii) where the application appears reasonable to the sheriff. An application under s.290 can only be made after charges have been preferred against the accused and once the sheriff has heard the prosecutor on the merits of the charge.

The style of application is found in the 1996 Act of Adjournal, Chap.28; note that the style applies to circumstances where either an indictment has been served or summary proceedings have begun.

In *Wilson v Tudhope*, 1985 S.C.C.R. 339 two Crown attempts to hold an identification parade failed because witnesses were unwilling to attend. The defence craved, and were granted, an identification parade, the sheriff opining that it would be competent to cite witnesses to attend such a parade.

See *Beattie v Hingston*, 1999 S.L.T. 362, where the Appeal Court suspended the sheriff's refusal of B's petition for a parade, the s.290 hearing having had to be fixed too early (in view of the imminent trial diet) for intimation to be given to B. Consequently B. was not present and, more importantly, the local agent who had been instructed to lodge the application had only slight knowledge of the factual background to the case. Note that the Appeal Court reserved opinion upon defence submissions that the s.290 hearing should have been held in open court; it is submitted that given that identification of an accused is plainly to be an issue at trial, there would be little to be gained (and much to be risked) by arguing the merits of an application in open court.

On a general note attention is directed to *Holland v H.M. Advocate* (Privy Council DRA No.1 of 2004) which discusses the use of dock identification and how far it can be said to intrude upon an accused's art.6 Convention rights to a fair trial.

Precognition on oath of defence witnesses

291.—(1) The sheriff may, on the application of an accused, grant warrant to cite any person (other than a co-accused), who is alleged to be a witness in relation to any offence of which the accused has been charged, to appear before the sheriff in chambers at such time or place as shall be specified in the citation, for precognition on oath by the accused or his solicitor in relation to that offence, if the court is satisfied that it is reasonable to require such precognition on oath in the circumstances.

(2) Any person who, having been duly cited to attend for precognition under subsection (1) above and having been given at least 48 hours notice, fails without reasonable excuse to attend shall be guilty of an offence and shall be liable on summary conviction to a fine not exceeding level 3 on the standard scale or to imprisonment for a period not exceeding 21 days; and the court may issue a warrant for the apprehension of the person concerned, ordering him to be brought before a sheriff for precognition on oath.

(3) Any person who, having been duly cited to attend for precognition under subsection (1) above, attends but—

(a) refuses to give information within his knowledge or to produce evidence in his possession; or

(b) prevaricates in his evidence,

shall be guilty of an offence and shall be liable to be summarily subjected forthwith to a fine not exceeding level 3 on the standard scale or to imprisonment for a period not exceeding 21 days.

(4) This section does not, however, extend to the citation of the complainer for precognition by the accused in person.

(5) In subsection (4) above, "complainer" has the same meaning as in section 274 of this Act.

(6) A warrant is not to be granted under this section for the citation for precognition by the accused in person of any child under the age of 12 on the relevant date where the offence in relation to which the child is alleged to be a witness is one specified in section 288E(3) of this Act.

(7) In subsection (6) above, "the relevant date" means—

(a) where an indictment or complaint in respect of the offence has been served on the accused at the time of the application, the date on which the indictment or complaint was so served, or

(b) where an indictment or complaint in respect of the offence has not been so served, the date on which the application under subsection (1) above is made.

AMENDMENT

Subss.(4) and (5) inserted by the Sexual Offences (Procedure and Evidence) (Scotland) Act 2002 (asp 9), s.4. Brought into force by the Sexual Offences (Procedure and Evidence) (Scotland) Act 2002 (Commencement and Transitional Provisions) Order 2002 (SSI 2002/443 (C.24)), art.4 (effective November 1, 2002).

Subss.(6) and (7) inserted by the Vulnerable Witnesses (Scotland) Act 2004 (asp 3), s.8. Brought into force on April 1, 2005 by the Vulnerable Witnesses (Scotland) Act 2004 (Commencement) Order 2005 (SSI 2005/168 (C.7)), art.2 and Sch.

Further brought into force for specified purposes on April 1, 2007 by the Vulnerable Witnesses (Scotland) Act 2004 (Commencement No.4, Savings and Transitional Provisions) Order 2007 (SSI 2007/101 (C.13)), art.2.

DEFINITIONS

"enactment": s.307(1).
"imprisonment": ss.307(6) and 309.
"indictment": s.307(1).
"offence": s.307(1).

GENERAL NOTE

A warrant to cite a witness for precognition on oath may be craved by the defence once charges have been preferred and cause can be shown to justify the use of this *compulsitor*; the power should be exercised with caution (*Low v MacNeill*, 1981 S.C.C.R. 243).

In *Drummond, Petr*, 1998 S.L.T. 757 where an unrepresented accused petitioned the *nobile officium* for authority to interview police witnesses on tape, the High Court observed, in refusing the application, that the appropriate course would have been to make an application under s.291.

It is not competent to make an application of this sort prior to full committal on petition, since, in the period between committal for further examination and full committal the Crown are still completing enquiries; see *Cirignaco, Petr*, 1985 S.C.C.R. 157 where precognition on oath of the complainer was sought with a view to secure early release on bail. Refusal on the part of potential witnesses to assist defence investigations, even after joint approaches by both the defence and the Crown, resulted in the grant of warrant to cite for precognition (*Brady v Lockhart*, 1985 S.C.C.R. 349). It is likely that an application for precognition on oath without first having sought the assistance of the Crown will be treated as premature.

A warrant for precognition on oath can only be sought prior to the trial (and conviction or acquittal) of the accused (see *Gilmour, Petr*, 1994 S.C.C.R. 872). In *Campbell v H.M. Advocate*, 1997 S.L.T. 577 the Appeal Court, with some hesitation, refused Crown advocation of a warrant to precognose a police officer who was not a witness in a murder trial, in relation to earlier dealings with a Crown witness; the broad intention was to undermine the credibility of the Crown witness. It is of note that the original warrant was entirely unqualified, and that the warrant for precognition was upheld by the Appeal Court largely on the basis of the case being a murder trial and of undertakings given by counsel to the court.

Failure to attend for precognition after lawful citation, prevarication, or failure to furnish information is an offence liable to peremptory punishment (subs.(3)); in such circumstances the court is not obliged to obtain social enquiry or other reports before sentencing such misconduct.

Pleas of legal privilege will not necessarily be conclusive where application is made to precognosce an accused's solicitor on oath; see *Kelly v Vannet*, 1999 G.W.D. 4–175. Crown applications proceed as incidental applications in terms of s.134 of the 1995 Act.

Refer to Chap.29 of the 1996 Act of Adjournal for directions on procedures and styles.

The intention of the Sexual Offences (Procedure and Evidence) (Scotland) Act 2002 (asp 9) was to prevent either cross-examination or precognition of victims of sexual offences by the alleged perpetrator. (See the General Note to s.288C above). The addition of subs.(4) extends these prohibitions to precognition on oath of a victim by the accused. Note too that s.24(5) of the Act introduces a specific bail condition in these circumstances precluding such precognition.

Mode of trial

Mode of trial of certain offences

292.—(1) Subject to subsection (6) below, the offences mentioned (and broadly described) in Schedule 10 to this Act shall be triable only summarily.

(2) An offence created by statute shall be triable only summarily if—

(a) the enactment creating the offence or any other enactment expressly so provides (in whatever words); or

(b) subject to subsections (4) and (5)(a) below, the offence was created by an Act passed on or before 29 July 1977 (the date of passing of the Criminal Law Act 1977) and the penalty or maximum penalty in force immediately before that date, on any conviction of that offence, did not include any of the following—

  (i) a fine exceeding £400;

  (ii) subject to subsection (3) below, imprisonment for a period exceeding 3 months;

  (iii) a fine exceeding £50 in respect of a specified quantity or number of things, or in respect of a specified period during which a continuing offence is committed.

(3) In the application of paragraph (b)(ii) of subsection (2) above, no regard shall be paid to the fact that section 5(3) of this Act permits the imposition of imprisonment for a period exceeding 3 months in certain circumstances.

(4) An offence created by statute which is triable only on indictment shall continue only to be so triable.

(5) An offence created by statute shall be triable either on indictment or summarily if—

(a) the enactment creating the offence or any other enactment expressly so provides (in whatever words); or

(b) it is an offence to which neither subsection (2) nor subsection (4) above applies.

(6) An offence which may under any enactment (including an enactment in this Act or passed after this Act) be tried only summarily, being an offence which, if it had been triable on indictment, could competently have been libelled as an additional or alternative charge in the indictment, may (the provisions of this or any other enactment notwithstanding) be so libelled, and tried accordingly.

(7) Where an offence is libelled and tried on indictment by virtue of subsection (6) above, the penalty which may be imposed for that offence in that case shall not exceed that which is competent on summary conviction.

DEFINITIONS

  "enactment": s.307(1).
  "fine": s.307(1).
  "imprisonment": s.307(6).
  "indictment": s.307(1).
  "offence": s.307(1).

GENERAL NOTE

Offences triable summarily only are listed in Sch.10 and in subs.(2) and can extend to offences defined in s.5(3) notwithstanding the fact that these create liability to a sentence of six months' imprisonment on a second or subsequent conviction in the sheriff court. It will be recalled that s.136(2) enacts that the six-month time limit for the commencement of statutory offences applies only to offences triable summarily only.

Offences which by statute may only be prosecuted summarily can be libelled along with other charges on an indictment but, in that event, any sentence which may be imposed on conviction of that offence shall be restricted to that which could have been passed summarily (subs.(6)).

Art and part and attempt

Statutory offences: art and part and aiding and abetting

293.—(1) A person may be convicted of, and punished for, a contravention of any enactment, notwithstanding that he was guilty of such contravention as art and part only.

(2) Without prejudice to subsection (1) above or to any express provision in any enactment having the like effect to this subsection, any person who aids, abets, counsels, procures or incites any other person to commit an offence against the provisions of any enactment shall be guilty of an offence and shall be liable on conviction, unless the enactment otherwise requires, to the same punishment as might be imposed on conviction of the first-mentioned offence.

DEFINITIONS

"enactment": s.307(1).
"offence": s.307(1).

GENERAL NOTE

Art and part guilt can apply equally to common law and statutory offences. See *Vaughan v HM Advocate*, 1979 S.L.T. 49 where the accused though not himself within the forbidden degrees, was convicted under the Incest Act 1567 as an actor.

Attempt at crime

294.—(1) Attempt to commit any indictable crime is itself an indictable crime.

(2) Attempt to commit any offence punishable on complaint shall itself be an offence punishable on complaint.

Legal custody

Legal custody

295. Without prejudice to section 13 of the Prisons (Scotland) Act 1989 (c.45) (legal custody of prisoners), any person required or authorised by or under this Act or any other enactment to be taken to any place, or to be detained or kept in custody is, while being so taken or detained or kept, in legal custody.

AMENDMENT

Section 295 as amended by Criminal Justice (Scotland) Act 2003 (asp 7), Part 4, s.24. Brought into force on June 27, 2003 by the Criminal Justice (Scotland) Act 2003 (Commencement No.1) Order 2003 (SSI 2003/288 (C.14)).

DEFINITION

"enactment": s.307(1).

GENERAL NOTE

The definition of legal custody applies to the status of persons either detained or arrested under the Act or other statutory powers. The anomalous position of a person suspected of committing an offence and required to remain where found by police officers (see s.13(1) and (2) above) has already been discussed; such an individual is not then in legal custody.

Warrants

Warrants for search and apprehension to be signed by judge

296. Any warrant for search or apprehension granted under this Act shall be signed by the judge granting it, and execution upon any such warrant may proceed either upon the warrant itself or upon an extract of the warrant issued and signed by the clerk of court.

DEFINITION

"judge": s.307(1).

GENERAL NOTE

This section applies to the grant of warrants of apprehension or search by a justice of the peace, sheriff or High Court judge. Ordinarily such warrants are craved from judges in the lower courts. See s.135 of the Act and the notes thereto.

The status of the judge granting a warrant was unsuccessfully challenged in *McFarlane v Gilchrist*, 2002 S.L.T. 521. Objection had been taken in the light of *Starrs v Ruxton*, 2000 S.L.T. 42; 1999 S.C.C.R. 1052 which had centred upon the impartiality of temporary judges in the context of trial proceedings. A common law warrant, dated only "November 2000", was upheld as valid. The Crown appealed against the sheriff's decision to uphold preliminary objections to the validity of search. The Appeal Court took account of the fact that, unlike statutory warrants, no time limits applied to the execution of a common law warrant; the warrant under question was *ex facie* valid.

A distinction has to be drawn between statutory warrants, the execution of which must comply with the statutory time limit stated in the relevant legislation, and common law warrants which carry no time limit; in *HMAdvocate v Foulis*, 2002 S.L.T. 761 objection was taken to evidence recovered under an undated common law warrant. The Appeal Court ruled this warrant to be *ex facie* valid, there being no prescription applying to common law warrants. (Since by their very nature search warrants are intended to be executed swiftly, Convention issues of delay would be unlikely to be germane).

In *Lord Advocate's Reference (No.1 of 2002)*, 2002 S.L.T. 1017, following *Hepburn v Brown*, 1998 J.C. 63; 1997 S.C.C.R. 698, it was held on appeal that the sheriff erred in disallowing evidence obtained following an examination of computer equipment and images by a police civilian specialist who had not been specified in the body of the search warrant. (Prudence would suggest that the warrant ought to be sufficiently broadly drafted to avoid such objections, since the court stressed that the regularity or otherwise of a warrant depended upon the circumstances in each case). Different considerations had applied in relation to a warrant obtained under statute by Customs and Excise officers since the Customs and Excise Management Act 1979 (c.2) required that the *number* of officers involved in the search had to be stipulated in the body of the warrant; see *Singh (Manjit) v H.M. Advocate*, 2001 S.L.T. 812; 2001 S.C.C.R. 348.

In *Graham v Higson*, 2002 S.L.T. 1382 the accused proceeded by means of a Bill of Suspension after having precognosced the justice who had granted a statutory search warrant. The Appeal Court ordered a report from the justice who could not recall the information given to him in support of the warrant. G argued unsuccessfully that the justice had not exercised his judicial duty of scrutiny properly and that the warrant should be quashed. Paradoxically, given the oft-expressed unwillingness of the Court to look behind the circumstances leading to grant of warrants, no comment was made about the propriety of precognition here.

A Bill of Suspension, rather than a preliminary plea, was raised in *Knaup v Hutchison*, 2002 S.C.C.R. 879 following service of an indictment alleging contravention of the Misuse of Drugs Act 1971, s.4(3)(b), and precognition of the Crown witnesses. Precognition disclosed that the officer craving the warrant did so on the basis that the accused was concerned in the supplying of controlled drugs and was suspected to be due to take delivery of drugs imminently; the defence contention was that the sheriff could not recall the circumstances giving rise to grant of the warrant and, in any event, that grant was premature, the accused not then being in possession of such drugs. The court proceeded on the customary basis that the warrant was *ex facie* valid and the sheriff's lack of recall was of no moment almost two years on, but accepted that a warrant could not be granted prospectively.

Ex facie valid warrants were attacked, unsuccessfully, by Bill of Suspension in *Crawford v Dyer*, 2003 G.W.D. 1–18, where C, whose rented premises had been searched previously, contended that this information ought to have been disclosed to the sheriff when the warrant was sought and that C should have been given notice of the warrant and the opportunity then to be heard.

Attention is directed to the terms of s.9A of the Act which now enable justices (a definition which applies equally to justices of the peace and to sheriffs) to sign warrants which they could competently grant, but while outwith their territorial jurisdiction. This provision came into force from June 27, 2003; warrants granted before that date would still be subject to the caveats set out in *Shields v Donnelly*, 2000 S.L.T. 147; 1999 S.C.C.R. 890.

Execution of warrants and service of complaints, etc.

297.—(1) Any warrant granted by a justice may, without being backed or endorsed by any other justice, be executed throughout Scotland in the same way as it may be executed within the jurisdiction of the justice who granted it.

(2) Any complaint, warrant, or other proceeding for the purposes of any summary proceedings under this Act may without endorsation be served or executed at any place within Scotland by any officer of law, and such service or execution may be proved either by the oath in court of the officer or by production of his written execution.

(3) A warrant issued in the Isle of Man for the arrest of a person charged with an offence may, after it has been endorsed by a justice in Scotland, be executed there by the person bringing that warrant, by any person to whom the warrant was originally directed or by any officer of law of the sheriff court district where the warrant has been endorsed in like manner as any such warrant issued in Scotland.

(4) In subsection (3) above, "endorsed" means endorsed in the like manner as a process to which section 4 of the Summary Jurisdiction (Process) Act 1881 applies.

(5) The Indictable Offences Act Amendment Act 1868 shall apply in relation to the execution in Scotland of warrants issued in the Channel Islands.

DEFINITIONS

"justice": s.307(1).
"offence": s.307(1).
"officer of law": s.307(1).

GENERAL NOTE

This section reflects the reform introduced by s.9 of the Criminal Justice (Scotland) Act 1995 and applies to all warrants granted in Scotland. It removes the need for a warrant, granted by a justice for execution outwith his jurisdiction, to be "backed" by another justice. A degree of caution is necessary since this reform does not extend to warrants granted in Scotland for execution in England and Wales.

Historically, a warrant granted for execution within the jurisdiction of a justice could always be executed without further ado, but matters were less straightforward when the warrant was granted for execution elsewhere in Scotland, and thoroughly byzantine when the warrant had to be executed in England and Wales: these are discussed in turn below.

Warrants craved for execution outwith the jurisdiction of the court, but in Scotland, included a crave requesting the concurrence of judges in that other place in the granting of the warrant. This necessitated application to be made to two courts before the warrant could be executed, an anachronistic, time-consuming, and invariably unnecessary, procedure. Following *Shields v Donnelly*, 2000 S.L.T. 147; 2000 S.C.C.R. 890 it was established that a warrant had to be granted within the territorial jurisdiction of the court; but see now s.9A at para. A4–18.2.

Warrants craved in Scotland for execution in England and Wales require to be "backed" and "endorsed" in accordance with the Summary Jurisdiction (Process) Act 1881 (c.24): in those circumstances the warrant obtained from the Scottish court has to be docquetted in compliance with the Act and then presented to the relevant magistrates' court having jurisdiction. However in England and Wales warrant procedures are generally regulated by Pt II of the Police and Criminal Evidence Act 1984 (c.60) and, thus, the court competent to grant warrants under PACE is determined by whether it is "special procedure" material (which requires a Crown Court warrant), or not.

PACE failed to take account of cross-border warrants, or the need to preserve the position of warrants granted, and backed, by Scottish courts, when it repealed the 1881 Act's provisions for England and Wales and introduced the Pt II provisions. These shortcomings have now been remedied for warrants granted by English and Welsh courts in relation to materials lying within Scotland by s.86 of the Criminal Justice and Police Act 2001; for practical purposes a Circuit judge is placed on the same footing as a magistrate and the wording of the 1881 docquet is used.

The position in relation to the cross-border execution of Scottish warrants in England and Wales is set out in *R. v Manchester Stipendiary Magistrate, ex p. Granada Television Ltd* [2000] 2 W.L.R. 1, H.L.(E) by the judgement of Lord Hope of Craighead. This case involved the use of a Scottish common law search warrant, endorsed in accordance with the 1881 Act by the Manchester Stipendiary Magistrate, to search a broadcaster's premises for evidential materials arising from a television programme. The competency of the warrant was upheld on final appeal. Note that following upon the reforms wrought by the Criminal Justice and Police Act 2001, the decision in *H.M. Advocate (for Duncan Hodge)*, 2000 S.C.C.R. 439 has been superseded. In that decision, which centred upon efforts to execute an English Circuit Court warrant in Scotland, the Appeal Court reserved opinion upon whether a petition to the *nobile officium* could have been used to meet the shortcomings. It is submitted that matters might still be dealt with satisfactorily in many instances by means of a common law warrant obtained by the Procurator Fiscal for the public interest.

Note should also be taken of the terms of s.81 of the Criminal Justice (Scotland) Act 2003 (asp 7) which enables "backed" search warrants issued in Northern Irish courts, authorising the search of premises in Scotland, to be endorsed by the relevant Scottish court. One could be forgiven for pondering why this straightforward provision could not simply have been incorporated into s.297 rather than standing alone in the 2003 Act.

Trial judge's report

Trial judge's report

298.—(1) Without prejudice to sections 113 and 186(3)(b) of this Act, the High Court may, in relation to—

(a) an appeal under section 106(1), 108, 108A or 175(2) to (4) of this Act;

(b) an appeal by way of bill of suspension or advocation; or

(c) a petition to the nobile officium,

at any time before the appeal is finally determined or, as the case may be, petition finally disposed of, order the judge who presided at the trial, passed sentence or otherwise disposed of the case to provide to the Clerk of Justiciary a report in writing giving the judge's opinion on the case generally or in relation to any particular matter specified in the order.

(2) The Clerk of Justiciary shall send a copy of a report provided under subsection (1) above to the convicted person or his solicitor, the Crown Agent and, in relation to cases referred under Part XA of this Act, the Commission.

(3) Subject to subsection (2) above, the report of the judge shall be available only to the High Court, the parties and, on such conditions as may be prescribed by Act of Adjournal, such other persons or classes of persons as may be so prescribed.

AMENDMENTS

Subs.(1)(a) inserted by the Crime and Punishment (Scotland) Act 1997 (c.48), Sch.1, para. 21(33)(a) with effect from October 20, 1997 in terms of the Crime and Punishment (Scotland) Act 1997 (Commencement No. 2 and Transitional and Consequential Provisions) Order 1997 (SI 1997/ 2323), art.3 and Sch.1.

Subs.(2) as amended by the Crime and Punishment (Scotland) Act 1997 (c.48), Sch.1, para.21(33)(b) (effective April 1, 1999: SI 1999/652).

DEFINITIONS

"Clerk of Justiciary": s.307(1).
"judge": s.307(1).

GENERAL NOTE

This new provision reinforces the statutory duty on judges at first instance to provide a report in the event of an appeal: the section allows the High Court of Justiciary to order further reports of a general or specific nature. This may be necessary because, for example, the note of appeal may not contain, as is required by s.110(3)(b), a full statement of all the grounds of appeal. Alternatively, difficulty or uncertainty in relation to a material point may have arisen at the hearing of the appeal and the trial judge's opinion may be thought necessary in the circumstances. In *Brady v Barbour*, 1994 S.C.C.R. 890 the sheriff, for whatever reason, did not produce a draft stated case and thus placed the High Court of Justiciary in some difficulty. This provision allows further orders to be made for reports. The role of s.298 was commented on in *Megrahi v H.M. Advocate*, 2001 G.W.D. 26–1014.

Correction of entries

Correction of entries

299.—(1) Subject to the provisions of this section, it shall be competent to correct any entry in—

(a) the record of proceedings in a prosecution; or

(b) the extract of a sentence passed or an order of court made in such proceedings,

in so far as that entry constitutes an error of recording or is incomplete.

(2) An entry mentioned in subsection (1) above may be corrected—

(a) by the clerk of the court, at any time before either the sentence or order of the court is executed or, on appeal, the proceedings are transmitted to the Clerk of Justiciary;

(b) by the clerk of the court, under the authority of the court which passed the sentence or made the order, at any time after the execution of the sentence or order of the court but before such transmission as is mentioned in paragraph (a) above; or

(c) by the clerk of the court under the authority of the High Court in the case of a remit under subsection (4)(b) below.

(3) A correction in accordance with paragraph (b) or (c) of subsection (2) above shall be intimated to the prosecutor and to the former accused or his solicitor.

(4) Where during the course of an appeal, the High Court becomes aware of an erroneous or incomplete entry, such as is mentioned in subsection (1) above, the court—

(a) may consider and determine the appeal as if such entry were corrected; and

(b) either before or after the determination of the appeal, may remit the proceedings to the court of first instance for correction in accordance with subsection (2)(c) above.

(5) Any correction under subsections (1) and (2) above by the clerk of the court shall be authenticated by his signature and, if such correction is authorised by a court, shall record the name of the judge or judges authorising such correction and the date of such authorisation.

DEFINITIONS

"clerk of Court": s.114 of the Criminal Justice (Scotland) Act 1995.

"Clerk of Justiciary": s.307(1).

"High Court": s.307(1).

"judge": s.307(1).

"order": s.307(1).

"sentence": s.307(1).

GENERAL NOTE

See *Heywood, Petr*, 1998 G.W.D. 13–639. An unauthenticated correction has no effect (see *Fitzgerald v Vannet*, 2000 S.C.C.R. 422) where corrections made in error, but not initialled, were disregarded. The Appeal Court utilised its power under s.299(4)(a) to remit the complaint back to the court of first instance having directed correction of defective minutes.

Amendment of records of conviction and sentence in summary proceedings

300.—(1) Without prejudice to section 299 of this Act, where, on an application in accordance with subsection (2) below, the High Court is satisfied that a record of conviction or sentence in summary proceedings inaccurately records the identity of any person, it may authorise the clerk of the court which convicted or, as the case may be, sentenced the person to correct the record.

(2) An application under subsection (1) above shall be made after the determination of the summary prosecution and may be made by any party to the summary proceedings or any other person having an interest in the correction of the alleged inaccuracy.

(3) The High Court shall order intimation of an application under subsection (1) above to such persons as it considers appropriate and shall not determine the application without affording to the parties to the summary proceedings and to any other person having an interest in the correction of the alleged inaccuracy an opportunity to be heard.

(4) The power of the High Court under this section may be exercised by a single judge of the High Court in the same manner as it may be exercised by the High Court, and subject to the same provisions.

DEFINITIONS

"clerk of Court": s.114(1) of the Criminal Justice (Scotland) Act 1995.
"Clerk of Justiciary": s.308(1).

Rights of audience

Rights of audience

301.—(1) Without prejudice to section 103(8) of this Act, any solicitor who has, by virtue of section 25A (rights of audience) of the Solicitors (Scotland) Act 1980, a right of audience in relation to the High Court of Justiciary shall have the same right of audience in that court as is enjoyed by an advocate.

(2) Any person who has complied with the terms of a scheme approved under section 26 of the Law Reform (Miscellaneous Provisions) (Scotland) Act 1990 (consideration of applications made under section 25) shall have such rights of audience before the High Court of Justiciary as may be specified in an Act of Adjournal made under subsection (7)(b) of that section.

Fixed penalties

Fixed penalty: conditional offer by procurator fiscal

302.—(1) Where a procurator fiscal receives a report that a relevant offence has been committed he may send to the alleged offender a notice under this section (referred to in this section as a conditional offer); and where he issues a conditional offer the procurator fiscal shall notify the clerk of court specified in it of the issue of the conditional offer and of its terms.

(2) A conditional offer—

(a) shall give such particulars of the circumstances alleged to constitute the offence to which it relates as are necessary for giving reasonable information about the alleged offence;

(b) shall state—

(i) the amount of the appropriate fixed penalty for that offence;

 (ii) the amount of the instalments by which the penalty may be paid; and

 (iii) the intervals at which such instalments should be paid;

(c) shall indicate that if, within 28 days of the date on which the conditional offer was issued, or such longer period as may be specified in the conditional offer, the alleged offender accepts the offer by making payment of the fixed penalty or of the first instalment thereof to the clerk of court specified in the conditional offer at the address therein mentioned, any liability to conviction of the offence shall be discharged;

(d) shall state that proceedings against the alleged offender shall not be commenced in respect of that offence until the end of a period of 28 days from the date on which the conditional offer was issued, or such longer period as may be specified in the conditional offer; and

(e) shall state that acceptance of the offer in the manner described in paragraph (c) above by the alleged offender shall not be a conviction nor be recorded as such.

(3) A conditional offer may be made in respect of more than one relevant offence and shall, in such a case, state the amount of the appropriate fixed penalty for all the offences in respect of which it is made.

(4) Where payment of the appropriate fixed penalty or of the first instalment has not been made to the clerk of court, he shall, upon the expiry of the period of 28 days referred to in subsection (2)(c) above or such longer period as may be specified in the conditional offer, notify the procurator fiscal who issued the conditional offer that no payment has been made.

(5) Proceedings shall not be brought against any person for the offence to which a conditional offer relates until the procurator fiscal receives notification from the clerk of court in accordance with subsection (4) above.

(6) Where an alleged offender makes payment of the appropriate fixed penalty or of the first instalment to the clerk of court specified in the conditional offer no proceedings shall be brought against the alleged offender for the offence.

(7) The Secretary of State shall, by order, prescribe a scale of fixed penalties for the purpose of this section, the amount of the maximum penalty on the scale being a sum not exceeding level 1 on the standard scale.

(8) An order under subsection (7) above—

(a) may contain provision as to the payment of fixed penalties by instalments; and

(b) shall be made by statutory instrument, which shall be subject to annulment in pursuance of a resolution of either House of Parliament.

(9) In this section—

(a) "a relevant offence" means any offence in respect of which an alleged offender could competently be tried before a district court, but shall not include a fixed penalty offence within the meaning of section 51 of the Road Traffic Offenders Act 1988 nor any other offence in respect of which a conditional offer within the meaning of sections 75 to 77 of that Act may be sent; and

(b) "the appropriate fixed penalty" means such fixed penalty on the scale prescribed under subsection (7) above as the procurator fiscal thinks fit having regard to the circumstances of the case.

AMENDMENTS

 s.302(9) as amended by the Wireless Telegraphy Act 2006(c.36), s.123 and Sch.7 para.16 (effective February 8, 2007)

"appropriate fixed penalty": s.302(9).
"offence": s.307(1).
"procurator fiscal": s.307(1).
"relevant offence": s.302(9).
"standard scale": s.225(1).

GENERAL NOTE

This section extends the range of fixed penalties which the procurator fiscal can offer to persons reported to him for offences other than Road Traffic offences. The "fiscal fine" was introduced by the Criminal Justice (Scotland) Act 1987 and then permitted procurator fiscals to use the offer of a £25 fixed fine to alleged offenders as an alternative to prosecution. Payment or part-payment of such a fine brought an end to the procurator fiscal's involvement and was not recorded as a criminal conviction. In 1987 the £25 fine, fixed by statutory instrument, equalled half the Level 1 fine on the standard scale; Level 1 is now a sum of £200. Section 302 permits the Secretary of State by statutory instrument, to set a range of fixed penalty bands from which the procurator fiscal can choose, according to the circumstances of the case as reported, when offering the option of a fiscal fine. Subsection (7) enacts that the bands must not exceed Level 1 on the standard scale.

One of the difficulties identified in the operation of the earlier fiscal fine system was that where several offences were reported against an accused as a result of an incident, the fiscal, if he chose to offer the option of such a fine, had to select one charge only from those reported. In the event of non-payment only the single charge selected previously could later be libelled against the accused; subs. (3) statutorily permits the offer of more than one fiscal fine against an accused following an incident and, hence, in the event of refusal of the offer it will be open to the prosecutor to libel several charges, not just one as before.

The administration and collection of fines remains the responsibility of the clerk of court. Whereas the old fiscal fine system required payment of the entire £25 fine within 28 days, and to an extent limited the range of offenders who could be offered that option, subs. (1)(c) enacts that payment of the full amount or a pre-determined instalment is to be made within 28 days, or a specified longer period. Once either sort of payment is received, the prosecutor is barred from prosecuting those offences. It is then the task of the clerk of court to enforce collection of any unpaid balance (see s.303 below).

It will be appreciated that the thrust of s.302 is to extend the use of fiscal fines as an alternative to prosecution. If successful, the broadened fixed penalty conditional offer scheme may reduce the pressure of criminal business in the lower courts. Failure to pay a fixed penalty timeously can be expected to result in a prosecution for the offence highlighted in the notice. The court convicting of that offence should reach its own view upon the appropriate sentence and need not take account of the fine level stipulated in the unpaid fixed penalty; see *Fyfe v. Walker*, 1998 G.W.D. 16–828.

Fixed penalty: enforcement

303.—(1) Subject to subsection (2) below, where an alleged offender accepts a conditional offer by paying the first instalment of the appropriate fixed penalty, any amount of the penalty which is outstanding at any time shall be treated as if the penalty were a fine imposed by the court, the clerk of which is specified in the conditional offer.

(2) In the enforcement of a penalty which is to be treated as a fine in pursuance of subsection (1) above—

(a) any reference, howsoever expressed, in any enactment whether passed or made before or after the coming into force of this section to—

  (i) the imposition of imprisonment or detention in default of payment of a fine shall be construed as a reference to enforcement by means of civil diligence;

  (ii) the finding or order of the court imposing the fine shall be construed as a reference to a certificate given in pursuance of subsection (3) below;

  (iii) the offender shall be construed as a reference to the alleged offender;

  (iv) the conviction of the offender shall be construed as a reference to the acceptance of the conditional offer by the alleged offender;

(b) the following sections of this Act shall not apply—

section 211(7);

section 213(2);

section 214(1) to (6);

section 216(7);

section 219, except subsection (1)(b);

section 220;

section 221(2) to (4);

section 222(8); and

section 224.

(3) For the purposes of any proceedings in connection with, or steps taken for, the enforcement of any amount of a fixed penalty which is outstanding, a document purporting to be a certificate signed by the clerk of court for the time being responsible for the collection or enforcement of the penalty as to any matter relating to the penalty shall be conclusive of the matter so certified.

(4) The Secretary of State may, by order made by statutory instrument subject to annulment in pursuance of a resolution of either House of Parliament, make such provision as he considers necessary for the enforcement in England and Wales or Northern Ireland of any penalty, treated in pursuance of subsection (1) above as a fine, which is transferred as a fine to a court in England and Wales or, as the case may be, Northern Ireland.

DEFINITIONS

"appropriate fixed penalty: s.302(9)(b).

"enactment": s.307(1).

"fine": s.307(1).

"impose detention": s.307(1).

"impose imprisonment": s.307(1).

GENERAL NOTE

The collection of fiscal fines remains the responsibility of the clerk of court. In the event of only partial payment of the instalments due to meet such a fine, subs. (2) allows recovery of the balance due by way of civil diligence. Subsection (3) provides that for the purpose of such enforcement the clerk of court is empowered to certify conclusively the sums due.

Subsection (2) has the effect of removing criminal sanctions for the enforcement of unpaid fiscal fines.

Transfer of rights of appeal of deceased person

303A.—(1) Where a person convicted of an offence has died, any person may, subject to the provisions of this section, apply to the High Court for an order authorising him to institute or continue any appeal which could have been or has been instituted by the deceased.

(2) An application for an order under this section may be lodged with the Clerk of Justiciary within three months of the deceased's death or at such later time as the Court may, on cause shown, allow.

(3) Where the Commission makes a reference to the High Court under section 194B of this Act in respect of a person who is deceased, any application under this section must be made within one month of the reference.

(4) Where an application is made for an order under this section and the applicant—

(a) is an executor of the deceased; or

(b) otherwise appears to the Court to have a legitimate interest, the Court shall make an order authorising the applicant to institute or continue any appeal which could have been instituted or continued by the deceased; and, subject to the provisions of this section, any such order may include such ancillary or supplementary provision as the Court thinks fit.

(5) The person in whose favour an order under this section is made shall from the date of the order be afforded the same rights to carry on the appeal as the deceased enjoyed at the time of his death and, in particular, where any time limit had begun to run against the deceased the person in whose favour an order has been made shall have the benefit of only that portion of the time limit which remained unexpired at the time of the death.

(6) In this section "appeal" includes any sort of application, whether at common law or under statute, for the review of any conviction, penalty or other order made in respect of the deceased in any criminal proceedings whatsoever.

AMENDMENT

Section 303A inserted by the Crime and Punishment (Scotland) Act 1997 (c.48), s.20 with effect from August 1, 1997 in terms of the Crime and Punishment (Scotland) Act 1997 (Commencement and Transitional Provisions) Order 1997 (S.I. 1997 No. 1712) art.3.

GENERAL NOTE

This introduces provision whereby an executor or a person with a legitimate interest can institute or continue an appeal (of any kind) where an accused person dies. Such a person has three months from the date of death to apply to the High Court. An application can be allowed at a later time on cause shown. It appears that it does not apply where a person is applying to the SCCRC, as an appeal would not be instituted until a reference was made by the Commission.

Where the Criminal Review Commission makes a reference in respect of a deceased person then within one month of the reference an application under this section must be made.

Subsection (5) only allows the applicant the remainder of any time limit running against the deceased. This would appear harsh but given that the person is afforded the same rights as a deceased, they too would be entitled to apply for extensions of time under the relevant statutory provisions, *e.g.* s.11 of the Criminal Procedure (Scotland) Act 1995 (c. 46).

The procedure under s.303A was followed in *Cowan v. H.M. Advocate*, 2001 G.W.D. 18–692 and the conviction quashed.

PART XIV

GENERAL

Criminal Courts Rules Council

304.—(1) There shall be established a body, to be known as the Criminal Courts Rules Council (in this section referred to as "the Council") which shall have the functions conferred on it by subsection (9) below.

(2) The Council shall consist of—

(a) the Lord Justice General, the Lord Justice Clerk and the Clerk of Justiciary;

(b) a further Lord Commissioner of Justiciary appointed by the Lord Justice General;

(c) the following persons appointed by the Lord Justice General after such consultation as he considers appropriate—

  (i) two sheriffs;

  (ii) two members of the Faculty of Advocates;

  (iii) two solicitors;

  (iv) one sheriff clerk; and

    (v) one person appearing to him to have a knowledge of the procedures and practices of the district court;

  (d) two persons appointed by the Lord Justice General after consultation with the Lord Advocate, at least one of whom must be a procurator fiscal;

  (e) two persons appointed by the Lord Justice General after consultation with the Secretary of State, at least one of whom must be a person appearing to the Lord Justice General to have—

    (i) a knowledge of the procedures and practices of the courts exercising criminal jurisdiction in Scotland; and

    (ii) an awareness of the interests of victims of crime and of witnesses in criminal proceedings; and

  (f) any persons appointed under subsection (3) below.

(3) The Lord Justice General may appoint not more than two further persons, and the Secretary of State may appoint one person, to membership of the Council.

(4) The chairman of the Council shall be the Lord Justice General or such other member of the Council, being a Lord Commissioner of Justiciary, as the Lord Justice General may nominate.

(5) The members of the Council appointed under paragraphs (b) to (f) of subsection (2) above shall, so long as they retain the respective qualifications mentioned in those paragraphs, hold office for three years and be eligible for reappointment.

(6) Any vacancy in the membership of the Council by reason of the death or demission of office, prior to the expiry of the period for which he was appointed, of a member appointed under any of paragraphs (b) to (f) of subsection (2) above shall be filled by the appointment by the Lord Justice General or, as the case may be, the Secretary of State, after such consultation as is required by the paragraph in question, of another person having the qualifications required by that paragraph, and a person so appointed shall hold office only until the expiry of that period.

(7) The Council shall meet—

  (a) at intervals of not more than 12 months; and

  (b) at any time when summoned by the chairman or by three members of the Council,

but shall, subject to the foregoing, have power to regulate the summoning of its meetings and the procedure at such meetings.

(8) At any meeting of the Council six members shall be a quorum.

(9) The functions of the Council shall be—

  (a) to keep under general review the procedures and practices of the courts exercising criminal jurisdiction in Scotland (including any matters incidental or relating to those procedures or practices); and

  (b) to consider and comment on any draft Act of Adjournal submitted to it by the High Court, which shall, in making the Act of Adjournal, take account to such extent as it considers appropriate of any comments made by the Council under this paragraph.

(10) In the discharge of its functions under subsection (9) above the Council may invite representations on any aspect of the procedures and practices of the courts exercising criminal jurisdiction in Scotland (including any matters incidental or relating to those procedures or practices) and shall consider any such representations received by it, whether or not submitted in response to such an invitation.

DEFINITIONS

    "Lord Commissioner of Justiciary": s.307(1).
    "procurator fiscal": s.307(1).

GENERAL NOTE

This innovation established a Rules Council for criminal court proceedings with functions broadly comparable to the existing Scottish Rules Council for civil court proceedings. The new body will assist the High Court of Justiciary in the discharge of its existing court procedural rule-making functions.

Acts of Adjournal

305.—(1) The High Court may by Act of Adjournal—

(a) regulate the practice and procedure in relation to criminal procedure;

(b) make such rules and regulations as may be necessary or expedient to carry out the purposes and accomplish the objects of any enactment (including an enactment in this Act) in so far as it relates to criminal procedure;

(c) subject to subsection (5) below, to fix and regulate the fees payable in connection with summary criminal proceedings; and

(d) to make provision for the application of sums paid under section 220 of this Act and for any matter incidental thereto.

(2) The High Court may by Act of Adjournal modify, amend or repeal any enactment (including an enactment in this Act) in so far as that enactment relates to matters with respect to which an Act of Adjournal may be made under subsection (1) above.

(3) No rule, regulation or provision which affects the governor or any other officer of a prison shall be made by Act of Adjournal except with the consent of the Secretary of State.

(4) The Clerk of Justiciary may, with the sanction of the Lord Justice General and the Lord Justice Clerk, vary the forms set out in an Act of Adjournal made under subsection (1) above or any other Act whether passed before or after this Act from time to time as may be found necessary for giving effect to the provisions of this Act relating to solemn procedure.

(5) Nothing in paragraph (c) of subsection (1) above shall empower the High Court to make any regulation which the Secretary of State is empowered to make by the Courts of Law Fees (Scotland) Act 1895.

DEFINITIONS

"governor": s.307(1).
"High Court": s.307(1).
"officer of a prison": s.307(1).

GENERAL NOTE

The High Court of Justiciary is best placed to know how to regulate its own procedure and it does so by Act of Adjournal on statutory authority. The previous powers of ss.282 and 457 of the 1975 Act have been combined in this single provision which relates to "criminal procedure". Variations in the wording of these sections have been removed. Differences as between other statutory powers to make Acts of Adjournal have been removed with this single provision: see, e.g. s.32A of the 1980 Act which allowed provisions the court thought "necessary and expedient", a wider power than that of necessity under the 1975 Act. A lengthy examination of the nature of the powers vested in the High Court to regulate its proceedings was undertaken in *Dickson v HM Advocate*, 2001 S.L.T. 674; 2001 S.C.C.R. 397, a five judge decision which followed upon a three judge hearing convened in the course of trial. The issues had not been raised earlier by devolution minute. D submitted that the court could not independently and impartially deliberate upon whether the Act of Adjournal (Devolution Rules) 1999 (SI 1999/1346) were Convention compliant, arguing that the matter had to be resolved by the Privy Council, and in any event, D had been prejudiced on the merits by the lack of a full judgment during the trial. The thrust of s.305 was summarised by Lord Hope of Craighead in *Montgomery v HM Advocate*, 2001 S.L.T. 37; 2000 S.C.C.R. 1044.

Information for financial and other purposes

306.—(1) The Secretary of State shall in each year publish such information as he considers expedient for the purpose of—

(a) enabling persons engaged in the administration of criminal justice to become aware of the financial implications of their decisions; or

(b) facilitating the performance by such persons of their duty to avoid discriminating against any persons on the ground of race or sex or any other improper ground.

(2) Publication under subsection (1) above shall be effected in such manner as the Secretary of State considers appropriate for the purpose of bringing the information to the attention of the persons concerned.

Interpretation

307.—(1) In this Act, unless the context otherwise requires—

"appropriate court" means a court named as such in pursuance of section 228(4) of this Act or of Schedule 6 to this Act in a probation order or in an amendment of any such order made on a change of residence of a probationer;

"assessment order" has the meaning given by section 52D of this Act;

"bail" means release of an accused or an appellant on conditions, or conditions imposed on bail, as the context requires;

"chartered psychologist" means a person for the time being listed in the British Psychological Society's Register of Chartered Psychologists;

"child", except in section 46(3) of and Schedule 1 to this Act, has the meaning assigned to that expression for the purposes of Chapters 2 and 3 of Part II of the Children (Scotland) Act 1995;

[1]["child witness" shall be construed in accordance with section 271(1)(a) of this Act;]

"children's hearing" has the meaning assigned to it in Part II of the Children (Scotland) Act 1995;

"Clerk of Justiciary" shall include assistant clerk of justiciary and shall extend and apply to any person duly authorised to execute the duties of Clerk of Justiciary or assistant clerk of justiciary;

"commit for trial" means commit until liberation in due course of law;

"community service order" means an order made under section 238 of this Act;

"complaint" includes a copy of the complaint laid before the court;

"compulsion order" has the meaning given by section 57A of this Act;

"constable" has the same meaning as in the Police (Scotland) Act 1967;

"court of summary jurisdiction" means a court of summary criminal jurisdiction;

"court of summary criminal jurisdiction" includes the sheriff court and district court;

"crime" means any crime or offence at common law or under any Act of Parliament whether passed before or after this Act, and includes an attempt to commit any crime or offence;

"devolution issue" has the same meaning as in Schedule 6 to the Scotland Act 1998;

"diet" includes any continuation of a diet;

"drug treatment and testing order" has the meaning assigned to it in section 234B(2) of this Act;

"enactment" includes an enactment contained in a local Act and any order, regulation or other instrument having effect by virtue of an Act;

"examination of facts" means an examination of facts held under section 55 of this Act;

"existing" means existing immediately before the commencement of this Act;

"extract conviction" and "extract of previous conviction" include certified copy conviction, certificate of conviction, and any other document lawfully issued from any court of justice of the United Kingdom as evidence of a conviction and also include a conviction extracted and issued as mentioned in section 286A(3)(a) and (b) of this Act;

"fine" includes—

(a) any pecuniary penalty, (but not a pecuniary forfeiture or pecuniary compensation); and

(b) an instalment of a fine;

"governor" means, in relation to a contracted out prison within the meaning of section 106(4) of the Criminal Justice and Public Order Act 1994, the director of the prison;

"guardian", in relation to a child, includes any person who, in the opinion of the court having cognizance of any case in relation to the child or in which the child is concerned, has for the time being the charge of or control over the child;

"guardianship order" has the meaning assigned to it by section 58 of this Act;

"High Court" and "Court of Justiciary" shall mean "High Court of Justiciary" and shall include any court held by the Lords Commissioners of Justiciary, or any of them;

"hospital" means—

(a) any hospital vested in the Secretary of State under the National Health Service (Scotland) Act 1978;

(aa) any hospital managed by a National Health Service Trust established under section 12A of that Act;

(b) any private hospital as defined in section 12(2) of the Mental Health (Scotland) Act 1984; and

(c) any State hospital;

"hospital direction" has the meaning assigned to it by section 59A(1) of this Act.

"impose detention" or "impose imprisonment" means pass a sentence of detention or imprisonment, as the case may be, or make an order for committal in default of payment of any sum of money or for contempt of court;

"indictment" includes any indictment whether in the sheriff court or the High Court framed in the form set out an Act of Adjournal or as nearly as may be in such form;

"interim compulsion order" has the meaning given by section 53 of this Act;

"judge", in relation to solemn procedure, means a judge of a court of solemn criminal jurisdiction and, in relation to summary procedure, means any sheriff or any judge of a district court;

"justice" includes the sheriff and any stipendiary magistrate or justice of the peace;

"justice of the peace" means any of Her Majesty's justices of the peace for any commission area in Scotland within such commission area;

"legalised police cells" has the like meaning as in the Prisons (Scotland) Act 1989;

"local authority" has the meaning assigned to it by section 1(2) of the Social Work (Scotland) Act 1968;

"local probation board" means a local probation board established under section 4 of the Criminal Justice and Court Services Act 2000;

"Lord Commissioner of Justiciary" includes Lord Justice General and Lord Justice Clerk;

"mental disorder" has the meaning given by section 328(1) of the Mental Health (Care and Treatment) (Scotland) Act 2003 (asp 13);

"Mental Welfare Commission" means the Mental Welfare Commission for Scotland;

"offence" means any act, attempt or omission punishable by law;

"officer of law" includes, in relation to the service and execution of any warrant, citation, petition, indictment, complaint, list of witnesses, order, notice, or other proceeding or document—

(a) any macer, messenger-at-arms, sheriff officer or other person having authority to execute a warrant of the court;

(b) any constable;

(ba) any person commissioned by the Commissioners of Customs and Excise;

(c) any person who is employed or appointed under section 9 of the Police (Scotland) Act 1967 for the assistance of the constables of a police force and who either is authorised by the chief constable of that police force in relation to service and execution as mentioned above or is a police custody and security officer;

(d) where the person upon whom service or execution is effected is in prison at the time of service on him, any prison officer; and

(e) any person or class of persons authorised in that regard for the time being by the Lord Advocate or by the Secretary of State;

"order" means any order, byelaw, rule or regulation having statutory authority;

"order for lifelong restriction" means an order under section 210F(1) of this Act;

"patient" means a person suffering or appearing to be suffering from mental disorder;

"place of safety", in relation to a person not being a child, means any police station, prison or remand centre, or any hospital the board of management of which are willing temporarily to receive him, and in relation to a child means a place of safety within the meaning of Part II of the Children (Scotland) Act 1995;

"postal operator" has the meaning assigned to it by section 125(1) of the Postal Services Act 2000;

"preliminary hearing" shall be construed in accordance with section 66(6)(b) of this Act and, where in any case a further preliminary hearing is held or to be held under this Act, includes the diet consisting of that further preliminary hearing;

"preliminary issue" shall be construed in accordance with section 79(2)(b) of this Act;

"preliminary plea" shall be construed in accordance with section 79(2)(a) of this Act;

"the prescribed sum" has the meaning given by section 225(8) of this Act;

"prison" does not include a naval, military or air force prison;

"prison officer" and "officer of a prison" means, in relation to a contracted out prison within the meaning of section 106(4) of the Criminal Justice and Public Order Act 1994, a prisoner custody officer within the meaning of section 114(1) of that Act;

"probationer" means a person who is under supervision by virtue of a probation order or who was under such supervision at the time of the commission of any relevant offence or failure to comply with such order;

"probation order" has the meaning assigned to it by section 228 of this Act;

"probation period" means the period for which a probationer is placed under supervision by a probation order;

"procurator fiscal" means the procurator fiscal for a sheriff court district, and includes assistant procurator fiscal and procurator fiscal depute and any person duly authorised to execute the duties of the procurator fiscal;

"prosecutor" —

   (a) for the purposes of proceedings other than summary proceedings, includes Crown Counsel, procurator fiscal, any other person prosecuting in the public interest and any private prosecutor; and

   (b) for the purposes of summary proceedings, includes procurator fiscal, and any other person prosecuting in the public interest and complainer and any person duly authorised to represent or act for any public prosecutor;

"remand" means an order adjourning the proceedings or continuing the case and giving direction as to detention in custody or liberation during the period of adjournment or continuation and references to remanding a person or remanding in custody or on bail shall be construed accordingly;

"remand centre" has the like meaning as in the Prisons (Scotland) Act 1989;

"restriction order" has the meaning assigned to it by section 59 of this Act;

"risk assessment order" means an order under section 210B(2) of this Act;

"risk assessment report" has the meaning given by section 210B(3)(a) of this Act;

"sentence", whether of detention or of imprisonment, means a sentence passed in respect of a crime or offence and does not include an order for committal in default of payment of any sum of money or for contempt of court;

"sheriff clerk" includes sheriff clerk depute, and extends and applies to any person duly authorised to execute the duties of sheriff clerk;

"sheriff court district" extends to the limits within which the sheriff has jurisdiction in criminal matters whether by statute or at common law;

"State hospital" has the meaning assigned to it in Part VIII of the Mental Health (Scotland) Act 1984;

"statute" means any Act of Parliament, public general, local, or private, and any Provisional Order confirmed by Act of Parliament;

"supervision requirement" has the meaning assigned to it in Part II of the Children (Scotland) Act 1995;

"training school order" has the same meaning as in the Social Work (Scotland) Act 1968;

"treatment order" has the meaning given by section 52M of this Act;

[1]["vulnerable witness" shall be construed in accordance with section 271(1) of this Act;]

"witness" includes haver;

"the unified citation provisions" means section 216(5) and (6)(a) and (b) of this Act;

"young offenders institution" has the like meaning as in the Prisons (Scotland) Act 1989.

(2) References in this Act to a court do not include references to a court-martial; and nothing in this Act shall be construed as affecting the punishment which may be awarded by a court-martial under the Naval Discipline Act 1957, the Army Act 1955 or the Air Force Act 1955 for a civil offence within the meaning of those Acts.

(3) For the purposes of this Act, except section 228(6), where a probation order has been made on appeal, the order shall be deemed to have been made by the court from which the appeal was brought.

(4) Any reference in this Act to a previous sentence of imprisonment shall be construed as including a reference to a previous sentence of penal servitude; any such reference to a previous sentence of Borstal training shall be construed as including a reference to a previous sentence of detention in a Borstal institution.

(5) Any reference in this Act to a previous conviction or sentence shall be construed as a reference to a previous conviction by a court in any part of the United Kingdom and to a previous sentence passed by any such court except—

(a) where the context otherwise requires; and

(b) in sections 69(2) and 166, where such a reference includes a reference to a previous conviction, by a court in another member State of the European Union, of an act punishable under the law in force in that State (an act so punishable being taken to constitute an offence under that law however described in that law).

(6) References in this Act to an offence punishable with imprisonment shall be construed, in relation to any offender, without regard to any prohibition or restriction imposed by or under any enactment, including this Act, upon the imprisonment of offenders of his age.

(7) Without prejudice to section 46 of this Act, where the age of any person at any time is material for the purposes of any provision of this Act regulating the powers of a court, his age at the material time shall be deemed to be or to have been that which appears to the court, after considering any available evidence, to be or to have been his age at that time.

(8) References in this Act to findings of guilty and findings that an offence has been committed shall be construed as including references to pleas of guilty and admissions that an offence has been committed.

AMENDMENTS

Subs.(1) as amended by the Crime and Punishment (Scotland) Act 1997 (c.48), s.62(1) and Sch.1, para.21(34)(b) with effect from August 1, 1997 in terms of the Crime and Punishment (Scotland) Act 1997 (Commencement and Transitional Provisions) Order 1997 (SI 1997/1712) art.3.

Subs.(1) as amended by the Crime and Punishment (Scotland) Act 1997 (c.48), s.6(5) with effect from January 1, 1998 in terms of the Crime and Punishment (Scotland) Act 1997 (Commencement No.2 and Transitional and Consequential Provisions) Order 1997 (SI 1997/2323), Sch.2.

Section 307 as amended by the Crime and Disorder Act 1998 (c.37), Sch.8, para.124 (effective September 30, 1998: SI 1998/2327).

Subs.(1) as amended by the Crime and Disorder Act 1998 (c.37), s.95.

Subs.(1) as amended by the Scotland Act 1998 (c.46), s.125(1) and Sch.8, para.31(3).

Subs.(1) as amended by the Criminal Justice and Court Services Act 2000 (c.43), s.74 and Sch.7, para.126. Brought into force by the Criminal Justice and Court Services Act 2000 (Commencement No.4) Order 2001 (SI 2001/919 (C.33)), art.2(f)(ii) (effective April 1, 2001).

Subs.(1) as amended by the Postal Services Act 2000 (Consequential Modifications No.1) Order 2001 (SI 2001/1149), art.3 and Sch.1, para.104.

Section 307 as amended by the Regulation of Care (Scotland) Act 2001 (asp 8), s.79 and Sch.3, para.20. Brought into force on October 1, 2001 by the Regulation of Care (Scotland) Act 2001 (Commencement No.1) Order 2001 (SSI 2001/304 (C.13)).

Subss.(1) and (5) as amended by Criminal Justice (Scotland) Act 2003 (asp 7), Part 8, s.57(5). Brought into force on June 27, 2003 by the Criminal Justice (Scotland) Act 2003 (Commencement No.1) Order 2003 (SSI 2003/288 (C.14)).

Subs.(1) as amended by Criminal Justice (Scotland) Act 2003 (asp 7), Part 12, s.76(11). Brought into force on June 27, 2003 by the Criminal Justice (Scotland) Act 2003 (Commencement No.1) Order 2003 (SSI 2003/288 (C.14)).

Subs.(1) as amended by Criminal Justice (Scotland) Act 2003 (asp 7), Part 8, s.60(2). Brought into force on October 27, 2003 by the Criminal Justice (Scotland) Act 2003 (Commencement No.3 and Revocation) Order 2003 (SSI 2003/475 (C.26)), art.2.

Subs.(1) as amended by the Criminal Justice (Scotland) Act 2003 (asp 7), Sch.1, para.2(7). Brought into force on June 19, 2006 by the Criminal Justice (Scotland) Act 2003 (Commencement No.9) Order 2006 (SSI 2006/332 (C.30)), art.2(1), subject to art.2(2).

Subs.(1) as amended by the Criminal Procedure (Amendment) (Scotland) Act 2004 (asp 5), s.25 and Sch.1, para.57. Brought into force on February 1, 2005 by the Criminal Procedure (Amendment) (Scotland) Act 2004 (Commencement, Transitional Provisions and Savings) Order 2004 (SSI 2004/405 (C.28)), art.2.

Subs.(1) as amended by the Mental Health (Care and Treatment) (Scotland) Act 2003 (asp 13), Sch.4, para.8(16) and Sch.5. Brought into force on October 5, 2005 by the Mental Health (Care and Treatment) (Scotland) Act 2003 (Commencement No.4) Order 2005(SSI 2005/161 (C.6)).

[1]Subs.(1) as prospectively amended by the Vulnerable Witnesses (Scotland) Act 2004 (asp 3), s.1(2).

Construction of enactments referring to detention etc.

308. In any enactment—

(a) any reference to a sentence of imprisonment as including a reference to a sentence of any other form of detention shall be construed as including a reference to a sentence of detention under section 207 of this Act; and

(b) any reference to imprisonment as including any other form of detention shall be construed as including a reference to detention under that section.

Short title, commencement and extent

309.—(1) This Act may be cited as the Criminal Procedure Act 1995.

(2) This Act shall come into force on 1 April 1996.

(3) Subject to subsections (4) and (5) below, this Act extends to Scotland only.

(4) The following provisions of this Act and this section extend to England and Wales—

section 44;

section 47;

section 209(3) and (7);

section 234(4) to (11);

section 244;

section 252 for the purposes of the construction mentioned in subsection (1) of that subsection;

section 303(4).

(5) The following provisions of this Act and this section extend to Northern Ireland—

section 44;

section 47;

section 244;

section 252 for the purposes of the construction mentioned in subsection (1) of that subsection;

section 303(4).

(6) Section 297(3) and (4) of this Act and this section also extend to the Isle of Man.

SCHEDULES

SCHEDULE 1

OFFENCES AGAINST CHILDREN UNDER THE AGE OF 17 YEARS TO WHICH SPECIAL PROVISIONS APPLY

1. Any offence under Part I of the Criminal Law (Consolidation) (Scotland) Act 1995.

2. Any offence under section 12, 15, 22 or 33 of the Children and Young Persons (Scotland) Act 1937.

2A. Any offence under the Prohibition of Female Genital Mutilation (Scotland) Act 2005 where the person mutilated or, as the case may be, proposed to be mutilated, is a child under the age of 17 years.

2B. Any offence under section 52 or 52A of the Civic Government (Scotland) Act 1982 in relation to an indecent photograph of a child under the age of 17 years.

2C. Any offence under section 1, 9, 10, 11 or 12 of the Protection of Children and Prevention of Sexual Offences (Scotland) Act 2005 in respect of a child under the age of 17 years.

3. Any other offence involving bodily injury to a child under the age of 17 years.

4. Any offence involving the use of lewd, indecent or libidinous practice or behaviour towards a child under the age of 17 years.

AMENDMENT

Para.2A inserted by the Prohibition of Female Genital Mutilation (Scotland) Act 2005 (asp 8), s.7(1). Brought into force on September 1, 2005 in accordance with s.8.

Paras 2B and 2C inserted by the Protection of Children and Prevention of Sexual Offences (Scotland) Act 2005 (asp 9), Sch., para.2. Brought into force on October 7, 2005 by the Protection of Children and Prevention of Sexual Offences (Scotland) Act 2005 (Commencement and Savings) Order 2005 (SSI 2005/480 (C.24)).

Sections 34 & 64(2)   SCHEDULE 2

Complete RELEVANCY

EXAMPLES OF INDICTMENTS

"A.B. (*name and address, that given in the declaration being sufficient*), you are indicted at the instance of A. F. R. (*name of Lord Advocate*), Her Majesty's Advocate, and the charge against you is that on 20th 199, in a shop in George Street, Edinburgh, occupied by John Cruikshank, draper, you did steal a shawl and a boa."

"...You did rob Charles Doyle, a cattle dealer, of Biggar, Lanarkshire, of a watch and chain and £36 of money..."

"...You did break into the house occupied by Andrew Howe, banker's clerk, and did there steal twelve spoons, a ladle, and a candlestick..."

"...You did force open (*or* attempt to force open) a lockfast cupboard and did thus attempt to steal therefrom..."

"...You did place your hand in one of the packets of Thomas Kerr, commercial traveller, 115 Main Street, Perth, and did thus attempt to steal..."

"...You did assault Lewis Mann, station-master of Earlston, and compress his throat and attempt to take from him a watch and chain..."

"...You did, while in the employment of James Pentland, accountant in Frederick Street, Edinburgh, embezzle £4,075 of money..."

"...You did, while acting as commercial traveller to Brown and Company, merchants in Leith, at the times and places specified in the inventory hereto subjoined, receive from the persons therein set forth the respective sums of money therein specified for the said Brown and Company, and did embezzle the same (*or* did embezzle £470 of money, being part thereof)…"

"…You did pretend to Norah Omond, residing there, that you were a collector of subscriptions for a charitable society, and did thus induce her to deliver to you £15 of money as a subscription thereto, which you appropriated to your own use…"

"…You did reset a watch and chain, pocket book and £15.55 of money, the same having been dishonestly appropriated by theft or robbery…"

"…You did utter as genuine a bill, on which the name of John Jones bore to be signed as acceptor, such signature being forged by (*here describe in general terms how the bill was uttered, and add where the bill is produced*), and said bill of exchange is No. of the productions lodged herewith…"

"…You did utter as genuine a letter bearing to be a certificate of character of you, as a domestic servant, by Mary Watson, of 15 Bon Accord Street, Aberdeen, what was written above the signature of Mary Watson having been written there by some other person without her authority by handing it to Ellen Chisholm of Panmore Street, Forfar, to whom you were applying for a situation (*here add when the letter is produced*), and said letter is No. of the productions lodged herewith…"

"…You did utter a cheque signed by Henry Smith for £8 sterling, which had been altered without his authority by adding the letter Y to eight and the figure 0 to figure 8, so as to make it read as a cheque for XC11,480 sterling, by presenting such altered cheque for payment to Allen Brown, Cashier of the Bank of Scotland at Callander (*here add when the cheque is produced*), and said cheque is No. of the productions lodged herewith…"

"…You did, when examined under section 45 of the Bankruptcy (Scotland) Act 1985 before Hubert Hamilton Esquire, sheriff of the Lothians and Borders, depone (*here state the general nature of the false statement*), in order to defraud your creditors…"

"…You did, sequestration having been awarded on your estate on the 20th March 1991, conceal property consisting of (*here state generally the property concealed*), falling under your sequestration, in order to defraud your creditor, by burying it in the garden of your house in Troon Street, Kilmarnock (*or* by removing it to the house of James Kidd, your son, No. 17 Greek Street, Port-Glasgow)…"

"…You did set fire to a warehouse occupied by Peter Cranston in Holly Lane, Greenock, and the fire took effect on said warehouse, and this you did wilfully (*or* culpably and recklessly)…"

"…You did set fire to the shop in Brown Street, Blairgowrie, occupied by you, with intent to defraud the Liverpool, London, and Globe Insurance Company, and the fire took effect on said shop…"

"…You did assault Theresa Unwin, your wife, and did beat her and did murder her…"

"…You did stab Thomas Underwood, baker, of Shiels Place, Oban, and did murder him…"

"…You did administer poison to Vincent Wontner, your son, and did murder him…"

"…You did strangle Mary Shaw, mill-worker, daughter of John Shaw, residing at Juniper Green, in the county of Midlothian, and did murder her…"

"…You were delivered of a child now dead or amissing, and you did conceal your pregnancy and did not call for or use assistance at the birth, contrary to the Concealment of Birth (Scotland) Act 1809…"

"…You did assault Hector Morrison, carter, of 20 Buccleuch Street, Dalkeith, and did beat him with your fists and with a stick, and did break his arm…"

"…You did ravish Harriet Cowan, mill-worker, of 27 Tweed Row, Peebles…"

"…You did attempt to ravish Jane Peters, servant, at Glen House, near Dunbar…"

"…You did, when acting as railway signalman, cancel a danger signal and allow a train to enter on a part of the line protected by the signals under your charge, and did cause a collision, and did kill William Peters, commercial traveller, of Brook Street, Carlisle, a passenger in said train…"

"…You formed part of a riotous mob, which, acting of common purpose, obstructed A. B., C. D., and E. F., constables of the Northern constabulary on duty, and assaulted them, and forcibly took two persons whom they had arrested from their custody…"

"…You did, being the lawful husband of Helen Hargreaves, of 20 Teviot Row, Edinburgh, and she being still alive, bigamously marry Dorothy Rose, a widow, of 7 Blacks Row, Brechin, and did cohabit with her as her husband…"

"…You being sworn as a witness in a civil cause, then proceeding in the sheriff court, deponed (*here set forth the statements said to be false*) the truth as you knew being that (*here state the true facts*)…"

"…You did suborn James Carruthers, scavenger, 12 Hercles Street, Edinburgh, to depone as a witness in the sheriff court of Edinburgh, that (*here set forth the statements said to be false*), and he did (*time and place*) depone to that effect, the truth as you knew being (*here state the true facts*)…"

"…You did deforce John Macdonald, a sheriff officer of Renfrewshire, and prevent him serving a summons issued by the sheriff of Renfrewshire upon Peter M'Innes, market gardener in Renfrew…"

Sections 64(6) and 138(4)   SCHEDULE 3

INDICTMENTS AND COMPLAINTS

1. An accused may be named and designed—
   (a) according to the existing practice; or
   (b) by the name given by him and designed as of the place given by him as his residence when he is examined or further examined; or
   (c) by the name under which he is committed until liberated in due course of law.

2. It shall not be necessary to specify by any *nomen juris* the offence which is charged, but it shall be sufficient that the indictment or complaint sets forth facts relevant and sufficient to constitute an indictable offence or, as the case may be, an offence punishable on complaint.

3. It shall not be necessary to allege that any act or commission or omission charged was done or omitted to be done "wilfully" or "maliciously", or "wickedly and feloniously", or "falsely and fraudulently" or "knowingly", or "culpably and recklessly", or "negligently", or in "breach of duty", or to use such words as "knowing the same to be forged", or "having good reason to know", or "well knowing the same to have been stolen", or to use any similar words or expressions qualifying any act charged, but such qualifying allegation shall be implied in every case.

4.—(1) The latitude formerly used in stating time shall be implied in all statements of time where an exact time is not of the essence of the charge.

(2) The latitude formerly used in stating any place by adding to the word "at", or to the word "in", the words "or near", or the words "or in the near neighbourhood thereof" or similar words, shall be implied in all statements of place where the actual place is not of the essence of the charge.

(3) Subject to sub-paragraph (4) below, where the circumstances of the offence charged make it necessary to take an exceptional latitude in regard to time or place it shall not be necessary to set forth the circumstances in the indictment, or to set forth that the particular time or the particular place is to the prosecutor unknown.

(4) Where exceptional latitude is taken as mentioned in sub-paragraph (3) above, the court shall, if satisfied that such exceptional latitude was not reasonable in the circumstances of the case, give such remedy to the accused by adjournment of the trial or otherwise as shall seem just.

(5) Notwithstanding sub-paragraph (4) above, nothing in any rule of law shall prohibit the amendment of an indictment or, as the case may be, a complaint to include a time outwith the exceptional latitude if it appears to the court that the amendment would not prejudice the accused.

(6) The latitude formerly used in describing quantities by the words "or thereby", or the words "or part thereof", or the words "or some other quantity to the prosecutor unknown" or similar words, shall be implied in all statements of quantities.

(7) The latitude formerly used in stating details connected with the perpetration of any act regarding persons, things or modes by inserting general alternative statements followed by the words "to the prosecutor unknown" or similar words, shall be implied in every case.

(8) In this paragraph references to latitude formerly used are references to such use before the commencement of—
   (a) in the case of proceedings on indictment, the Criminal Procedure (Scotland) Act 1887; and
   (b) in the case of summary proceedings, the Summary Jurisdiction (Scotland) Act 1908.

5. The word "money" shall include cheques, banknotes, postal orders, money orders and foreign currency.

6. Any document referred to shall be referred to by a general description and, where it is to be produced in proceedings on indictment, by the number given to it in the list of productions for the prosecution.

7. In an indictment which charges a crime importing personal injury inflicted by the accused, resulting in death or serious injury to the person, the accused may be lawfully convicted of the aggravation that the assault or other injurious act was committed with intent to commit such crime.

8.—(1) In an indictment or a complaint charging the resetting of property dishonestly appropriated—
   (a) having been taken by theft or robbery; or
   (b) by breach of trust, embezzlement or falsehood, fraud and wilful imposition,
it shall be sufficient to specify that the accused received the property, it having been dishonestly appropriated by theft or robbery, or by breach of trust and embezzlement, or by falsehood, fraud and wilful imposition, as the case may be.

(2) Under an indictment or a complaint for robbery, theft, breach of trust and embezzlement or falsehood, fraud and wilful imposition, an accused may be convicted of reset.

(3) Under an indictment or a complaint for robbery, breach of trust and embezzlement, or falsehood, fraud and wilful imposition, an accused may be convicted of theft.

(4) Under an indictment or a complaint for theft, an accused may be convicted of breach of trust and embezzlement, or of falsehood, fraud and wilful imposition, or may be convicted of theft, although the circumstances proved may in law amount to robbery.

(5) The power conferred by sub-paragraphs (2) to (4) above to convict a person of an offence other than that with which he is charged shall be exercisable by the sheriff court before which he is tried notwithstanding that the other offence was committed outside the jurisdiction of that sheriff court.

9.—(1) Where two or more crimes or acts of crime are charged cumulatively, it shall be lawful to convict of any one or more of them.

(2) Any part of the charge in an indictment or complaint which itself constitutes an indictable offence or, as the case may be an offence punishable on complaint, shall be separable and it shall be lawful to convict the accused of that offence.

(3) Where any crime is charged as having been committed with a particular intent or with particular circumstances of aggravation, it shall be lawful to convict of the crime without such intent or aggravation.

10.—(1) Under an indictment or, as the case may be, a complaint which charges a completed offence, the accused may be lawfully convicted of an attempt to commit the offence.

(2) Under an indictment or complaint charging an attempt, the accused may be convicted of such attempt although the evidence is sufficient to prove the completion of the offence said to have been attempted.

(3) Under an indictment or complaint which charges an offence involving personal injury inflicted by the accused, resulting in death or serious injury to the person, the accused may be lawfully convicted of the assault or other injurious act, and may also be lawfully convicted of the aggravation that the assault or other injurious act was committed with intent to commit such offence.

11. In an indictment or complaint charging a contravention of an enactment the description of the offence in the words of the enactment contravened, or in similar words, shall be sufficient.

12. In a complaint charging a contravention of an enactment—

    (a) the statement that an act was done contrary to an enactment shall imply a statement—

        (i) that the enactment applied to the circumstances existing at the time and place of the offence;

        (ii) that the accused was a person bound to observe the enactment;

        (iii) that any necessary preliminary procedure had been duly gone through; and

        (iv) that all the circumstances necessary to a contravention existed,

        and, in the case of the contravention of a subordinate instrument, such statement shall imply a statement that the instrument was duly made, confirmed, published and generally made effectual according to the law applicable, and was in force at the time and place in question; and

    (b) where the offence is created by more than one section of one or more statutes or subordinate instruments, it shall be necessary to specify only the leading section or one of the leading sections.

13. In the case of an offence punishable under any enactment, it shall be sufficient to allege that the offence was committed contrary to the enactment and to refer to the enactment founded on without setting out the words of the enactment at length.

14. Where—

    (a) any act alleged in an indictment or complaint as contrary to any enactment is also criminal at common law; or

    (b) where the facts proved under the indictment or complaint do not amount to a contravention of the enactment, but do amount to an offence at common law,

it shall be lawful to convict of the common law offence.

15. Where the evidence in a trial is sufficient to prove the identity of any person, corporation or company, or of any place, or of anything, it shall not be a valid objection to the sufficiency of the evidence that any particulars specified in the indictment or complaint relating to such identity have not been proved.

16. Where, in relation to an offence created by or under an enactment any exception, exemption, proviso, excuse, or qualification, is expressed to have effect whether by the same or any other enactment, the exception, exemption, proviso, excuse or qualification need not be specified or negatived in the indictment or complaint, and the prosecution is not required to prove it, but the accused may do so.

17. It shall be competent to include in one indictment or complaint both common law and statutory charges.

18. In any proceedings under the Merchant Shipping Acts it shall not be necessary to produce the official register of the ship referred to in the proceedings in order to prove the nationality of the ship,

but the nationality of the ship as stated in the indictment or, as the case may be, complaint shall, in the absence of evidence to the contrary, be presumed.

19. In offences inferring dishonest appropriation of property brought before a court whose power to deal with such offences is limited to cases in which the value of such property does not exceed level 4 on the standard scale it shall be assumed, and it shall not be necessary to state in the charge, that the value of the property does not exceed that sum.

Section 57(5)   SCHEDULE 4

SUPERVISION AND TREATMENT ORDERS

PART I

PRELIMINARY

1.—(1) In this Schedule "supervision and treatment order" means an order requiring the person in respect of whom it is made ("the supervised person")—

    (a) to be under the supervision of a social worker who is an officer of the local authority for the area where the supervised person resides or is to reside (in this Schedule referred to as "the supervising officer") for such period, not being more than three years, as is specified in the order;

    (b) to comply during that period with instructions given to him by the supervising officer regarding his supervision; and

    (c) to submit during that period to treatment by or under the direction of a medical practitioner with a view to the improvement of his mental condition.

(2) The Secretary of State may by order amend sub-paragraph (1) above by substituting, for the period for the time being specified in that sub-paragraph, such period as may be specified in the order.

(3) An order under sub-paragraph (2) above may make any amendment to paragraph 8(2) below which the Secretary of State considers necessary in consequence of the order.

(4) The power of the Secretary of State to make orders under sub-paragraph (2) above shall be exercisable by statutory instrument subject to annulment in pursuance of a resolution of either House of Parliament.

PART II

MAKING AND EFFECT OF ORDERS

Circumstances in which orders may be made

2.—(1) The court shall not make a supervision and treatment order unless it is satisfied—

    (a) that, having regard to all the circumstances of the case, the making of such an order is the most suitable means of dealing with the person; and

    (b) on the written or oral evidence of two or more approved medical practitioners, that the mental condition of the person—

        (i) is such as requires and may be susceptible to treatment; but

        (ii) is not such as to warrant the making of an order under paragraph (a) of subsection (2) of section 57 of this Act (whether with or without an order under paragraph (b) of that subsection) or an order under paragraph (c) of that subsection.

(2) The court shall not make a supervision and treatment order unless it is also satisfied—

    (a) that the supervising officer intended to be specified in the order is willing to undertake the supervision; and

    (b) that arrangements have been made for the treatment intended to be specified in the order.

(3) Subsections (3) to (5) of section 61 of this Act shall have effect with respect to proof of a person's mental condition for the purposes of sub-paragraph (1) above as they have effect with respect to proof of an offender's mental condition for the purposes of section 58(1)(a) of this Act.

(4) In this Schedule "approved medical practitioner" has the meaning given by section 22(4) of the Mental Health (Care and Treatment) (Scotland) Act 2003 (asp 13).

AMENDMENT

Para.2(1)(b) as amended by the Adults with Incapacity (Scotland) Act 2000 (asp 4), Sch.6. Brought into force on April 1, 2002 by the Adults with Incapacity (Scotland) Act 2000 (Commencement No.1) Order 2001 (SSI 2001/81 (C.2)).

Para.2(1)(b) as amended, and para.2(4) inserted, by the Mental Health (Care and Treatment) (Scotland) Act 2003 (Modification of Enactments) Order 2005 (SSI 2005/465), art.2and Sch.1, para.27(6) (effective September 27, 2005).

Making of orders and general requirements

3.—(1) A supervision and treatment order shall specify the local authority area in which the supervised person resides or will reside.

(2) Before making such an order, the court shall explain to the supervised person in ordinary language—

(a) the effect of the order (including any requirements proposed to be included in the order in accordance with paragraph 5 below); and

(b) that the sheriff court for the area in which the supervised person resides or will reside (in this Schedule referred to as "the relevant sheriff court") has power under paragraphs 6 to 8 below to review the order on the application either of the supervised person or of the supervising officer.

(3) After making such an order, the court shall forthwith give a copy of the order to—

(a) the supervised person;

(b) the supervising officer; and

(bb) the medical practitioner by whom or under whose supervision the supervised person is to be treated under the order;

(c) the person in charge of any institution in which the supervised person is required by the order to reside.

(4) After making such an order, the court shall also send to the relevant sheriff court—

(a) a copy of the order; and

(b) such documents and information relating to the case as it considers likely to be of assistance to that court in the exercise of its functions in relation to the order.

(5) Where such an order is made, the supervised person shall comply with such instructions as he may from time to time be given by the supervising officer regarding his supervision and shall keep in touch with that officer and notify him of any change of address.

Obligatory requirements as to medical treatment

4.—(1) A supervision and treatment order shall include a requirement that the supervised person shall submit, during the period specified in the order, to treatment by or under the direction of a medical practitioner with a view to the improvement of his mental condition.

(2) The treatment required by the order shall be such one of the following kinds of treatment as may be specified in the order, that is to say—

(a) treatment as a non-resident patient at such institution or place as may be specified in the order; and

(b) treatment by or under the direction of such medical practitioner as may be so specified;

but the nature of the treatment shall not be specified in the order except as mentioned in paragraph (a) or (b) above.

(3) Where the medical practitioner by whom or under whose direction the supervised person is being treated for his mental condition in pursuance of a supervision and treatment order is of the opinion that part of the treatment can be better or more conveniently given at an institution or place which—

(a) is not specified in the order; and

(b) is one at which the treatment of the supervised person will be given by or under the direction of a medical practitioner,

he may, with the consent of the supervised person, make arrangements for him to be treated accordingly.

(4) Where any such arrangements as are mentioned in sub-paragraph (3) above are made for the treatment of a supervised person—

(a) the medical practitioner by whom the arrangements are made shall give notice in writing to the supervising officer, specifying the institution or place at which the treatment is to be carried out; and

(b) the treatment provided for by the arrangements shall be deemed to be treatment to which he is required to submit in pursuance of the supervision and treatment order.

Optional requirements as to residence

5.—(1) Subject to sub-paragraphs (2) to (4) below, a supervision and treatment order may include requirements as to the residence of the supervised person.

(2) Such an order may not require the supervised person to reside as a resident patient in a hospital.

(3) Before making such an order containing any such requirement, the court shall consider the home surroundings of the supervised person.

(4) Where such an order requires the supervised person to reside in any institution, the period for which he is so required to reside shall be specified in the order.

PART III

REVOCATION AND AMENDMENT OF ORDERS

Revocation of order in interests of health or welfare

6. Where a supervision and treatment order is in force in respect of any person and, on the application of the supervised person or the supervising officer, it appears to the relevant sheriff court that, having regard to circumstances which have arisen since the order was made, it would be in the interests of the health or welfare of the supervised person that the order should be revoked, the court may revoke the order.

Amendment of order by reason of change of residence

7.—(1) This paragraph applies where, at any time while a supervision and treatment order is in force in respect of any person, the relevant sheriff court is satisfied that—

  (a) the supervised person proposes to change, or has changed, his residence from the area specified in the order to the area of another local authority;

  (b) a social worker who is an officer of the other local authority ("the new supervising officer") is willing to undertake the supervision; and

  (c) the requirements of the order as respects treatment will continue to be complied with.

(2) Subject to sub-paragraph (3) below the court may, and on the application of the supervising officer shall, amend the supervision and treatment order by substituting the other area for the area specified in the order and the new supervising officer for the supervising officer specified in the order.

(3) Where a supervision and treatment order contains requirements which, in the opinion of the court, can be complied with only if the supervised person continues to reside in the area specified in the order, the court shall not amend the order under this paragraph unless it also, in accordance with paragraph 8 below, either—

  (a) cancels those requirements; or

  (b) substitutes for those requirements other requirements which can be complied with if the supervised person ceases to reside in that area.

Amendment of requirements of order

8.—(1) Without prejudice to paragraph 7 above, but subject to sub-paragraph (2) below, the relevant sheriff court may, on the application of the supervised person or the supervising officer, by order amend a supervision and treatment order—

  (a) by cancelling any of the requirements of the order; or

  (b) by inserting in the order (either in addition to or in substitution for any such requirement) any requirement which the court could include if it were the court by which the order was made and were then making it.

(2) The power of the court under sub-paragraph (1) above shall not include power to amend an order by extending the period specified in it beyond the end of three years from the date of the original order.

Amendment of requirements in pursuance of medical report

9.—(1) Where the medical practitioner by whom or under whose direction the supervised person is being treated for his mental condition in pursuance of any requirement of a supervision and treatment order—

  (a) is of the opinion mentioned in sub-paragraph (2) below; or

  (b) is for any reason unwilling to continue to treat or direct the treatment of the supervised person,

he shall make a report in writing to that effect to the supervising officer and that officer shall apply under paragraph 8 above to the relevant sheriff court for the variation or cancellation of the requirement.

(2) The opinion referred to in sub-paragraph (1) above is—

  (a) that the treatment of the supervised person should be continued beyond the period specified in the supervision and treatment order;

(b) that the supervised person needs different treatment, being treatment of a kind to which he could be required to submit in pursuance of such an order;

(c) that the supervised person is not susceptible to treatment; or

(d) that the supervised person does not require further treatment.

Supplemental

10.—(1) On the making under paragraph 6 above of an order revoking a supervision and treatment order, the sheriff clerk shall forthwith give a copy of the revoking order to the supervising officer and to the medical practitioner by whom or under whose supervision the supervised person was treated under the supervision and treatment order.

(2) On receipt of a copy of the revoking order the supervising officer shall give a copy to the supervised person and to the person in charge of any institution in which the supervised person was required by the order to reside.

11.—(1) On the making under paragraph 7 or 8 above of an order amending a supervision and treatment order, the sheriff clerk shall forthwith—

(a) if the order amends the supervision and treatment order otherwise than by substituting a new area or a new place for the one specified in that order, give a copy of the amending order to the supervising officer and to the medical practitioner by whom or under whose supervision the supervised person has been treated under the supervision and treatment order;

(b) if the order amends the supervision and treatment order in the manner excepted by paragraph (a) above, send to the new relevant sheriff court—

(i) a copy of the amending order; and

(ii) such documents and information relating to the case as he considers likely to be of assistance to that court in exercising its functions in relation to the order;

and in a case falling within paragraph (b) above, the sheriff clerk shall give a copy of the amending order to the supervising officer.

(2) On receipt of a copy of an amending order the supervising officer shall give a copy to the supervised person and to the person in charge of any institution in which the supervised person is or was required by the order to reside.

12. On the making, revocation or amendment of a supervision and treatment order the supervising officer shall give a copy of the order or, as the case may be, of the order revoking or amending it, to the Mental Welfare Commission for Scotland.

AMENDMENTS

Para.3(3)(bb) inserted by the Crime and Punishment (Scotland) Act 1997 (c. 48), Sched. 1, para. 21(35) with effect from January 1, 1998 as provided by the Crime and Punishment (Scotland) Act 1997 (Commencement No. 2 and Transitional and Consequential Provisions) Order 1997 (S.I. 1997 No. 2323) art. 4, Sched. 2.

Paras 10(1) and 11(1)(a) as amended by the above provisions with effect from January 1, 1998.

Section 138(2)	SCHEDULE 5	

FORMS OF COMPLAINT AND CHARGES

The following Forms are additional to those contained in Schedule 2 to this Act, *all of which, in so far as applicable to charges which may be tried summarily, are deemed to be incorporated in this* Schedule:—

You did assault A.L. and strike him with your fists.

You did conduct yourself in a disorderly manner and commit a breach of the peace.

You did threaten violence to the lieges and commit a breach of the peace.

You did fight and commit a breach of the peace.

You did publicly expose your person in a shameless and indecent manner in presence of the lieges.

You did obtain from A.N. board and lodging to the value of £16 without paying and intending not to pay therefor.

You did maliciously knock down 20 metres of the coping of a wall forming the fence between two fields on the said farm.

You did maliciously place a block of wood on the railway line and attempt to obstruct a train.

You did drive a horse and cart recklessly to the danger of the lieges.

You did break into a poultry house and steal three fowls.

You did steal a coat which you obtained from R.O. on the false representation that you had been sent for it by her husband.

having received from D.G. £6 to hand to E.R., you did on (date) at (place) steal the said sum.

having received from G.R. a watch in loan, you did on at, sell it to E.G., and steal it.

having found a watch, you did, without trying to discover its owner, sell it on at, to O.R., and steal it.

You did acquire from K.O., a private in the Third Battalion a military jacket and waist belt, contrary to section 195 of the Army Act 1955.

You, being a person whose estate has been sequestrated, did obtain credit from W.A. to the extent of £260 without informing him that your estate had been sequestrated and that you had not received your discharge, contrary to section 67(9) of the Bankruptcy (Scotland) Act 1985.

You, being the occupier of the said house, did use the same for the purpose of betting with persons resorting thereto, contrary to section 1 of the Betting, Gaming and Lotteries Act 1963.

You did frequent and loiter in the said street for the purpose of betting and receiving bets, contrary to section 8 of the Betting, Gaming and Lotteries Act 1963.

You did assault L.S., a constable of the Police, while engaged in the execution of his duty, and with a stick strike him on the face to the great effusion of blood contrary to section 41 of the Police (Scotland) Act 1967.

You did wilfully neglect your children K.I., aged seven years; J.I., aged five years; and H.I., aged three years, by failing to provide them with adequate food and clothing, and by keeping them in a filthy and verminous condition, contrary to section 12 of the Children and Young Persons (Scotland) Act 1937.

You are the owner of a dog which is dangerous and not kept under proper control, and which on in did chase a flock of sheep, contrary to section 2 of the Dogs Act 1871, section 2, as amended by section 1 of the Dogs Act 1906, whereby you are liable to be ordered to keep the said dog under proper control or to destroy it.

You, being a parent of D.U., a child of school age, aged, who has attended school, and the said child having failed, between and, without reasonable excuse, to attend regularly at the said school, you are thereby guilty of an offence against section 35 of the Education (Scotland) Act 1980.

You did sell and deliver to N.C. to his prejudice an article of food namely; gallons of sweet milk which was not of the nature, substance and quality of the article demanded by him and was not genuine sweet milk in respect that it was deficient in milk fat to the extent of per cent, or thereby in that it contained only per cent, of milk fat, conform to certificate of analysis granted on (date) by A.N. analytical chemist (address), public analyst for (a copy of which certificate of analysis is annexed hereto) of a sample of the said milk taken (specify time and place) by L.O., duly appointed sampling officer for, acting under the direction of the local authority for the said burgh, while the said milk was in course of delivery to the said N.C. contrary to the Food Act 1984, and the Sale of Milk Regulations 1901.

You did take part in gaming in the street contrary to sections 5 and 8 of the Gaming Act 1968.

You did by night enter on the said land with nets for the purpose of taking game, contrary to section 1 of the Night Poaching Act 1828; or

You did by night unlawfully take six rabbits, contrary to, etc.

You did in the daytime trespass on the said land in search of pursuit of game (*or* rabbits), contrary to section 1 of the Game (Scotland) Act 1832.

You were found in the possession of five hares, a net and six net pins, which hares you had obtained by unlawfully going on land in search or pursuit of game, and which net and nets pins you had used for unlawfully killing or taking game, or you had been accessory thereto, contrary to section 2 of the Poaching Prevention Act 1862.

You did present or cause to be presented to W.E., Assessors for a return in which you falsely stated that the yearly rent of your House. No. Street, was £20, instead of £30, contrary to section 7 of the Lands Valuation (Scotland) Act 1854.

You did sell a half gill of whisky to J.M., who was then a drunken person, contrary to your certificate and section 76 of the Licensing (Scotland) Act 1976.

You were found drunk and incapable of taking care of yourself, and not under the care or protection of some suitable person, contrary to section 74(2) of the Licensing (Scotland) Act 1976.

You did drive a motor car recklessly contrary to section 2 of the Road Traffic Act 1988.

You did act as a pedlar without having obtained a certificate, contrary to section 4 of the Pedlars' Act 1871.

...

You did travel in a railway carriage without having previously paid your fare, and with intent to avoid payment thereof, contrary to section 5(3)(a) of the Regulation of Railways Act 1889.

Having on within the house No. Street, given birth to a female child, you did fail, within twenty-one days thereafter, to attend personally and give information to C.W., registrar of births, deaths, and marriages for (Registration District), of the particulars required to be registered concerning the birth, contrary to sections 14 and 53 of the Registration of Births, Deaths, and Marriages (Scotland) Act 1965.

You did take two salmon during the annual close time by means of cobles and sweep nets, contrary to section 15 of the Salmon Fisheries (Scotland) Act 1868.

You had in your possession for use for trade a counter balance which was false, and two weights, which were unjust, contrary to the Weights and Measures Act 1985, section 17.

AMENDMENT

Sch.5 as amended by the Postal Services Act 2000 (Consequential Modifications No. 1) Order 2001 (SI 2001/1149), art. 3 and Sch.2.

Sch.5 as amended by the Manufacture and Storage of Explosives Regulations 2005 (SI 2005/1082), reg.28(1), Sch.5, para.21. Brought into force on April 26, 2005 in accordance with reg.1.

Sch.5 as amended by the Animal Health and Welfare (Scotland) Act 2006 (Consequential Provisions) Order 2006 (SSI 2006/536), art.2(3) andSch.3 (effective November 3, 2006).

Section 231(1)   SCHEDULE 6

DISCHARGE OF AND AMENDMENT TO PROBATION ORDERS

Discharge

1. A probation order may on the application of the officer supervising the probationer or of the probationer be discharged—

    (a) by the appropriate court; or

    (b) if no appropriate court has been named in the original or in any amending order, by the court which made the order.

Amendment

2.—(1) If the court by which a probation order was made, or the appropriate court, is satisfied that the probationer proposes to change or has changed his residence from the area of a local authority named in the order to the area of another local authority, the court may, and if application is made in that behalf by the officer supervising the probationer shall, by order, amend the probation order by—

    (a) substituting for the area named therein that other area; and

    (b) naming the appropriate court to which all the powers of the court by which the order was made shall be transferred and shall require the local authority for that other area to arrange for the probationer to be under the supervision of an officer of that authority.

(2) Subject to sub-paragraphs (3) and (4) below, the court to be named as the appropriate court in any amendment of a probation order in pursuance of sub-paragraph (1) above shall be a court exercising jurisdiction in the place where the probationer resides or is to reside and shall be a sheriff court or district court according to whether the probation order was made by a sheriff court or district court.

(3) If the probation order was made by a district court and there is no district court exercising jurisdiction in the place mentioned in sub-paragraph (2) above, the court to be named shall be the sheriff court.

(4) If the probation order contains requirements which in the opinion of the court cannot be complied with unless the probationer continues to reside in the local authority area named in the order, the court shall not amend the order as mentioned in sub-paragraph (2) above unless, in accordance with the following provisions of this Schedule, it cancels those requirements or substitutes therefor other requirements which can be so complied with.

(5) Where a probation order is amended under this paragraph, the clerk of the court amending it shall send to the clerk of the appropriate court four copies of the order together with such documents and information relating to the case as the court amending the order considers likely to be of assistance to the appropriate court, and the clerk of that court shall send one copy of the probation order to the local authority of the substituted local authority area and two copies to the officer supervising the probationer, one of which the supervising officer shall give to the probationer.

(6) The foregoing provisions of this paragraph shall, in a case where the probation order was made by the High Court, have effect subject to the following modifications—

    (a) the court shall not name an appropriate court, but may substitute for the local authority named in the order, the local authority for the area in which the probationer is to reside;

    (b) the Clerk of Justiciary shall send to the chief social work officer of that area in which the probationer is to reside three copies of the amending order together with such documents and information relating to the case as is likely to be of assistance to the chief social work officer, and the chief social work officer shall send two copies of the amending order to the officer supervising the probationer, one of which the supervising officer shall give to the probationer.

3.—(1) Without prejudice to paragraph 2 above, the court by which a probation order was made or the appropriate court may, upon application made by the officer supervising the probationer or by the probationer, subject to sub-paragraph (2) below, by order amend a probation order by cancelling any of the requirements thereof or by inserting therein (either in addition to or in substitution for any such requirement) any requirement which could be included in the order if it were then being made by that court in accordance with sections 228 to 230A of this Act.

(2) The court shall not amend a probation order under sub-paragraph (1) above—

    (a) by reducing the probation period, or by extending that period beyond the end of three years from the date of the original order;

    (b) so that the probationer is thereby required to reside in any institution or place, or to submit to treatment for his mental condition, for any period or periods exceeding 12 months in all;

    (c) by inserting in it a requirement that the probationer shall submit to treatment for his mental condition unless the amending order is made within three months after the date of the original order.

(3) This paragraph is subject to section 230A(6)(a) of this Act.

4. Where the medical practitioner or chartered psychologist by whom or under whose direction a probationer is being treated for his mental condition in pursuance of any requirement of the probation order is of the opinion—

    (a) that the treatment of the probationer should be continued beyond the period specified for that purpose in the order; or

    (b) that the probationer needs a different kind of treatment (whether in whole or in part) from that which he has been receiving in pursuance of the probation order, being treatment of a kind which could have been specified in the probation order but to which the probationer or his supervising officer has not agreed under section 230(6) of this Act; or

    (c) that the probationer is not susceptible to treatment; or

    (d) that the probationer does not require further treatment,

or where the practitioner or psychologist is for any reason unwilling to continue to treat or direct the treatment of the probationer, he shall make a report in writing to that effect to the officer supervising the probationer and the supervising officer shall apply to the court which made the order or to the appropriate court for the variation or cancellation of the requirement.

AMENDMENT

Para.3 as amended by Criminal Justice (Scotland) Act 2003 (asp 7), Part 6, s.46. Brought into force on June 27, 2003 by the Criminal Justice (Scotland) Act 2003 (Commencement No.1) Order 2003 (SSI 2003/288 (C.14)).

General

5.—(1) Where the court which made the order or the appropriate court proposes to amend a probation order under this Schedule, otherwise than on the application of the probationer, it shall cite him to appear before the court; and the court shall not amend the probation order unless the probationer expresses his willingness to comply with the requirements of the order as amended.

(2) Sub-paragraph (1) above shall not apply to an order cancelling a requirement of the probation order or reducing the period of any requirement, or substituting a new area of a local authority for the area named in the probation order.

(3) The unified citation provisions apply in relation to a citation under sub-paragraph (1) above as they apply in relation to a citation under section 216(3)(a) of this Act

6. On the making of an order discharging or amending a probation order, the clerk of the court shall forthwith give copies of the discharging or amending order to the officer supervising the probationer; and the supervising officer shall give a copy to the probationer and to the person in charge of any institution in which the probationer is or was required by the order to reside.

AMENDMENT

Para.5(3) inserted by Criminal Justice (Scotland) Act 2003 (asp 7), Part 8, s.60. Brought into force on October 27, 2003 by the Criminal Justice (Scotland) Act 2003 (Commencement No.3 and Revocation) Order 2003 (SSI 2003/475 (C.26)), art.2.

SCHEDULE 7

SUPERVISED ATTENDANCE ORDERS: FURTHER PROVISIONS

1.—(1) A court shall not make a supervised attendance order in respect of any offender unless—

   (a) the court has been notified by the Secretary of State that arrangements exist for persons of a class which includes the offender who reside in the locality in which the offender resides, or will be residing when the order comes into force, to carry out the requirements of such an order.

   (b) the court is satisfied that provision can be made under the arrangements mentioned in sub-sub-paragraph (a) above for the offender to carry out such requirements.

(2) Before making a supervised attendance order, the court shall explain to the offender in ordinary language—

   (a) the purpose and effect of the order and in particular the obligations on the offender as specified in paragraph 3 below;

   (b) the consequences which may follow under paragraph 4 below if he fails to comply with any of those requirements; and

   (c) that the court has, under paragraph 5 below, the power to review the order on the application either of the offender or of an officer of the local authority in whose area the offender for the time being resides.

(3) The Secretary of State may by order direct that subsection (2) of section 235 of this Act shall be amended by substituting, for any number of hours specified in that subsection such other number of hours as may be specified in the order; and an order under this subsection may in making such amendment specify different such numbers of hours for different classes of case.

(4) An order under sub-paragraph (3) above shall be made by statutory instrument, but no such order shall be made unless a draft of it has been laid before, and approved by a resolution of, each House of Parliament.

2.—(1) A supervised attendance order shall—

   (a) specify the locality in which the offender resides or will be residing when the order comes into force; and

   (b) require the local authority in whose area the locality specified under sub-sub-paragraph (a) above is situated to appoint or assign a supervising officer.

(2) Where, whether on the same occasion or on separate occasions, an offender is made subject to more than one supervised attendance order, the court may direct that the requirements specified in any of those orders shall be concurrent with or additional to those specified in any other of those orders, but so that at no time shall the offender have an outstanding number of hours during which he must carry out the requirements of these orders in excess of the largest number specified in section 235 of this Act.

(3) Upon making a supervised attendance order the court shall—

   (a) give, or send by registered post or by the recorded delivery service, a copy of the order to the offender;

   (b) send a copy of the order to the chief social work officer of the local authority in whose area the offender resides or will be residing when the order comes into force; and

   (c) where it is not the appropriate court, send a copy of the order (together with such documents and information relating to the case as are considered useful) to the clerk of the appropriate court.

(4) Where a copy of a supervised attendance order has, under sub-paragraph (3)(a) above, been sent by registered post or by the recorded delivery service, an acknowledgement or certificate of delivery of a letter containing the copy order issued by the Post Office shall be sufficient evidence of the delivery of the letter on the day specified in such acknowledgement or certificate.

3.—(1) An offender in respect of whom a supervised attendance order is in force shall report to the supervising officer and notify him without delay of any change of address or in the times, if any, at which he usually works.

(2) Subject to paragraph 5(1) below, instructions given under a supervised attendance order shall be carried out during the period of twelve months beginning with the date of the order; but, unless revoked, the order shall remain in force until the offender has carried out the instructions given under it for the number of hours specified in it.

(3) The instructions given by the supervising officer under the order shall, so far as practicable, be such as to avoid any conflict with the offender's religious beliefs and any interference with the times, if any, at which he normally works or attends a school or other educational establishment.

4.—(1) If at any time while a supervised attendance order is in force in respect of any offender it appears to the appropriate court, on information from the supervising officer, that that offender has failed to comply with any of the requirements of paragraph 3 above or of the order (including any failure satisfactorily to carry out any instructions which he has been given by the supervising officer under the order), the court may issue a warrant for the arrest of that offender, or may, if it thinks fit, instead of issuing a warrant in the first instance issue a citation requiring the offender to appear before that court at such time as may be specified in the citation.

(2) If it is proved to the satisfaction of the court before which an offender is brought or appears in pursuance of sub-paragraph (1) above that he has failed without reasonable excuse to comply with any of the requirements of paragraph 3 above or of the order (including any failure satisfactorily to carry out any instructions which he has been given by the supervising officer under the order) the court may—

    (a) revoke the order and impose such period of imprisonment not exceeding—

        (i) in the case of a sheriff court, 30 days; and

        (ii) in the case of a district court, 20 days,

          as the court considers appropriate; or

    (b) subject to section 235 of this Act and paragraph 2(2) above, vary the number of hours specified in the order.

(3) The evidence of one witness shall, for the purposes of sub-paragraph (2) above, be sufficient evidence.

5.—(1) Where a supervised attendance order is in force in respect of any offender and, on the application of that offender or of the supervising officer, it appears to the appropriate court that it would be in the interests of justice to do so having regard to circumstances which have arisen since the order was made, that court may—

    (a) extend, in relation to the order, the period of twelve months specified in paragraph 3 above;

    (b) subject to section 235 of this Act and paragraph 2(2) above, vary the numbers of hours specified in the order;

    (c) revoke the order; or

    (d) revoke the order and impose such period of imprisonment not exceeding—

        (i) in the case of a sheriff court, 30 days; and

        (ii) in the case of a district court, 20 days,

          as the court considers appropriate.

(2) If the appropriate court is satisfied that the offender proposes to change, or has changed, his residence from the locality for the time being specified under paragraph 2(1)(a) above to another locality and—

    (a) that court has been notified by the Secretary of State that arrangements exist for persons who reside in that other locality to carry out instructions under supervised attendance orders; and

    (b) it appears to that court that provision can be made under those arrangements for him to carry out instructions under the order,

that court may, and on application of the supervising officer shall, amend the order by substituting that other locality for the locality for the time being specified in the order; and section 235 of this Act and this Schedule shall apply to the order as amended.

(3) Where the court proposes to exercise its powers under sub-paragraph (1)(a), (b) or (d) above otherwise than on the application of the offender, it shall issue a citation requiring him to appear before the court and, if he fails to appear, may issue a warrant for his arrest.

5A. The unified citation provisions apply in relation to a citation under paragraph 4(1) or 5(3) of this Schedule as they apply in relation to a citation under section 216(3)(a) of this Act.

6.—(1) The Secretary of State may make rules for regulating the carrying out of the requirements of supervised attendance orders.

(2) Without prejudice to the generality of sub-paragraph (1) above, rules under this paragraph may—

    (a) limit the number of hours during which the requirements of an order are to be met on any one day;

    (b) make provision as to the reckoning of time for the purposes of the carrying out of these requirements;

    (c) make provision for the payment of travelling and other expenses in connection with the carrying out of these requirements;

    (d) provide for records to be kept of what has been done by any person carrying out these requirements.

(3) Rules under this paragraph shall be made by statutory instrument subject to annulment in pursuance of a resolution of either House of Parliament.

7. The Secretary of State shall lay before Parliament each year, or incorporate in annual reports he already makes, a report of the operation of section 235 of this Act and this Schedule.

8. In this Schedule—

"the appropriate court" in relation to a supervised attendance order, means the court having jurisdiction in the locality for the time being specified in the order under paragraph 2(1)(a) above, being a sheriff or district court according to whether the order has been made by a sheriff or district court, but in the case where an order has been made by a district court and there is no district court in that locality, the sheriff court;

"supervising officer" has the same meaning as in section 235 of this Act.

Amendment

Paras 4 and 5 as amended by Criminal Justice (Scotland) Act 2003 (asp 7), Part 6, s.50. Brought into force on June 27, 2003 by the Criminal Justice (Scotland) Act 2003 (Commencement No.1) Order2003 (SSI 2003/288 (C.14)).

Para.5A inserted by Criminal Justice (Scotland) Act 2003 (asp 7), Part 8, s.60. Brought into force on October 27, 2003 by the Criminal Justice (Scotland) Act 2003 (Commencement No.3 and Revocation) Order 2003 (SSI 2003/475 (C.26)), art.2.

Section 279   SCHEDULE 8

DOCUMENTARY EVIDENCE IN CRIMINAL PROCEEDINGS

Production of copy documents

1.—(1) For the purposes of any criminal proceedings a copy of, or of a material part of, a document, purporting to be authenticated in such manner and by such person as may be prescribed, shall unless the court otherwise directs, be—

(a) deemed a true copy; and

(b) treated for evidential purposes as if it were the document, or the material part, itself,
whether or not the document is still in existence.

(2) For the purposes of this paragraph it is immaterial how many removes there are between a copy and the original.

(3) In this paragraph "copy" includes a transcript or reproduction.

Statements in business documents

2.—(1) Except where it is a statement such as is mentioned in paragraph 3(b) and (c) below, a statement in a document shall be admissible in criminal proceedings as evidence of any fact or opinion of which direct oral evidence would be admissible, if the following conditions are satisfied—

(a) the document was created or received in the course of, or for the purposes of, a business or undertaking or in pursuance of the functions of the holder of a paid or unpaid office;

(b) the document is, or at any time was, kept by a business or undertaking or by or on behalf of the holder of such an office; and

(c) the statement was made on the basis of information supplied by a person (whether or not the maker of the statement) who had, or may reasonably be supposed to have had, personal knowledge of the matters dealt with in it.

(2) Sub-paragraph (1) above applies whether the information contained in the statement was supplied directly or indirectly unless, in the case of information supplied indirectly, it appears to the court that any person through whom it was so supplied did not both receive and supply it in the course of a business or undertaking or as or on behalf of the holder of a paid or unpaid office.

(3) Where in any proceedings a statement is admitted as evidence by virtue of this paragraph—

(a) any evidence which, if—

(i) the maker of the statement; or

(ii) where the statement was made on the basis of information supplied by another person, such supplier,

had been called as a witness, would have been admissible as relevant to the witness's credibility shall be so admissible in those proceedings;

(b) evidence may be given of any matter which, if the maker or as the case may be the supplier had been called as a witness, could have been put to him in cross-examination as relevant to his credibility but of which evidence could not have been adduced by the cross-examining party; and

(c) evidence tending to prove that the maker or as the case may be the supplier, whether before or after making the statement or supplying the information on the basis of which the statement was made, made (in whatever manner) some other representation which is inconsistent with the statement shall be admissible for the purpose of showing that he has contradicted himself.

(4) In sub-paragraph (3)(c) above, "representation" does not include a representation in a precognition.

3. A statement in a document shall be admissible in criminal proceedings as evidence of the fact that the statement was made if—

    (a) the document satisfies the conditions mentioned in sub-paragraph (1)(a) and (b) of paragraph 2 above;

    (b) the statement is made, whether directly or indirectly, by a person who in those proceedings is an accused; and

    (c) the statement, being exculpatory only, exculpates the accused.

Documents kept by businesses etc.

4. Unless the court otherwise directs, a document may in any criminal proceedings be taken to be a document kept by a business or undertaking or by or on behalf of the holder of a paid or unpaid office if it is certified as such by a docquet in the prescribed form and purporting to be authenticated, in such manner as may be prescribed—

    (a) by a person authorised to authenticate such a docquet on behalf of the business or undertaking by which; or

    (b) by, or by a person authorised to authenticate such a docquet on behalf of, the office-holder by whom,

the document was kept.

Statements not contained in business documents

5.—(1) In any criminal proceedings, the evidence of an authorised person that—

    (a) a document which satisfies the conditions mentioned in paragraph 2(1)(a) and (b) above does not contain a relevant statement as to a particular matter; or

    (b) no document, within a category of documents satisfying those conditions, contains such a statement,

shall be admissible evidence whether or not the whole or any part of that document or of the documents within that category and satisfying those conditions has been produced in the proceedings.

(2) For the purposes of sub-paragraph (1) above, a relevant statement is a statement which is of the kind mentioned in paragraph 2(1)(c) above and which, in the ordinary course of events—

    (a) the document; or

    (b) a document within the category and satisfying the conditions mentioned in that sub-paragraph,

might reasonably have been expected to contain.

(3) The evidence referred to in sub-paragraph (1) above may, unless the court otherwise directs, be given by means of a certificate by the authorised person in the prescribed form and purporting to be authenticated in such manner as may be prescribed.

(4) In this paragraph, "authorised person" means a person authorised to give evidence—

    (a) on behalf of the business or undertaking by which; or

    (b) as or on behalf of the office-holder by or on behalf of whom,

the document is or was kept.

Additional evidence where evidence from business documents challenged

6.—(1) This sub-paragraph applies where—

    (a) evidence has been admitted by virtue of paragraph 2(3) above: or

    (b) the court has made a direction under paragraph 1(1), 4 or 5(3) above.

(2) Where sub-paragraph (1) above applies the judge may. without prejudice to sections 268 and 269 of this Act—

    (a) in solemn proceedings, on a motion of the prosecutor or defence at any time before the commencement of the speeches to the jury:

    (b) in summary proceedings, on such a motion at any time before the prosecutor proceeds to address the judge on the evidence,

permit him to lead additional evidence of such description as the judge may specify.

(3) Subsections (3) and (4) of section 268 of this Act shall apply in relation to sub-paragraph (2) above as they apply in relation to subsection (1) of that section.

General

7.—(1) Nothing in this Schedule—

(a) shall prejudice the admissibility of a statement made by a person other than in the course of giving oral evidence in court which is admissible otherwise than by virtue of this Schedule;

(b) shall affect the operation of the Bankers' Books Evidence Act 1879;

(c) shall apply to—

    (i) proceedings commenced; or

    (ii) where the proceedings consist of an application to the sheriff by virtue of section 42(2)(c) of the Social Work (Scotland) Act 1968, an application made.

before this Schedule comes into force.

For the purposes of sub-paragraph (1)(c)(i) above, solemn proceedings are commenced when the indictment is served.

8. In this Schedule—

"business" includes trade, profession or other occupation:

"criminal proceedings" includes any hearing by the sheriff under section 62 of the Children (Scotland) Act 1995 of an application for a finding as to whether grounds for the referral of a child's case to a children's hearing are established, in so far as the application relates to the commission of an offence by the child:

"document" includes, in addition to a document in writing—

    (a) any map, plan, graph or drawing;

    (b) any photograph;

    (c) any disc, tape, sound track or other device in which sounds or other data (not being visual images) are recorded so as to be capable, with or without the aid of some other equipment, of being reproduced therefrom; and

    (d) any film, negative, tape, disc or other device in which one or more visual images are recorded so as to be capable (as aforesaid) of being produced therefrom;

"film" includes a microfilm;

"made" includes allegedly made;

"prescribed" means prescribed by Act of Adjournal:

"statement" includes any representation (however made or expressed) of fact or opinion, including an instruction, order or request, but, except in paragraph 7(1)(a) above, does not include a statement which falls within one or more of the following descriptions—

    (a) a statement in a precognition;

    (b) a statement made for the purposes of or in connection with—

        (i) pending or contemplated criminal proceedings; or

        (ii) a criminal investigation; or

    (c) a statement made by an accused person in so far as it incriminates a co-accused; and

"undertaking" includes any public or statutory undertaking, any local authority and any government department.

SCHEDULE 9

CERTIFICATES AS TO PROOF OF CERTAIN ROUTINE MATTERS

Enactment	Persons who may purport to sign certificates	Matters which may be certified
The Parks Regulations Acts 1872 to 1974.	An officer authorised to do so by the Secretary of State.	That, on a date specified in the certificate— (a) copies of regulations made under those Acts, prohibiting such activity as may be so specified, were displayed at a location so specified; (b) in so far as those regulations prohibited persons from carrying out a specified activity in the park without written permission, such permission had not been given to a person so specified.
The Firearms Act 1968 (c. 27).	[1]As respects the matters specified in paragraph (a) of column 3, a constable or a person employed by a police authority, if the constable or person is authorised to do so by the chief constable of the police force maintained for the authority's area; and as respects the matters specified in paragraph (b) of column 3, an officer authorised to do so by the Secretary of State or a member of staff of the Scottish Administration who is authorised to do so by the Scottish Ministers.	In relation to a person identified in the certificate, that on a date specified therein— (a) he held, or as the case may be did not hold, a firearm certificate or shotgun certificate (within the meaning of that Act); (b) [1]he possessed, or as the case may be did not possess, an authority (which as regards as possessed authority, shall be described in the certificate) given under section 5 of that Act by the Secretary of State or, by virtue of provision made under section 63 of the Scotland Act 1998, the Scottish Ministers.
The Misuse of Drugs Act 1971 (c. 38) Sections 4, 5, 6, 8, 9, 12, 13, 19 and 20 (various offences concerning controlled drugs).	Two analysts who have analysed the substance and each of whom is either a person possessing the qualifications (qualifying persons for appointments as public analysts) prescribed by regulations made under section 76 of the Food Act 1984 (c. 30), or section 30 of	

670

Enactment	Persons who may purport to sign certificates	Matters which may be certified
	the Food Safety Act 1990 (c. 16), or a person authorised by the Secretary of State to make analyses for the purposes of the provisions of the Misuse of Drugs Act 1971 mentioned in column 1.	The type, classification, purity, weight and description of any particular substance identified in the certificate by reference to a label or otherwise, which is alleged to be a controlled drug within the meaning of section 2 of the Act referred to in column 1.
The Immigration Act 1971 (c. 77) Section 24(1)(a) in so far as it relates to entry in breach of a deportation order, section 24(1)(b) and section 26(1)(f) in so far as it relates to a requirement of regulations (various offences concerning persons entering, or remaining in, the United Kingdom).	An officer authorised to do so by the Secretary of State.	In relation to a person identified in the certificate— (a) the date, place or means of his arrival in, or any removal of him from, the United Kingdom; (b) any limitation on, or condition attached to, any leave for him to enter or remain in the United Kingdom; (c) the date and method of service of any notice of, or of variations of conditions attached to, such leave.
The Licensing (Scotland) Act 1976 (c. 66).	A person authorised to do so by the Secretary of State.	In relation to a person identified in the certificate, that on a date specified therein he held, or as the case may be did not hold, a licence granted under that Act.
Customs and Excise Management Act 1979 The following provisions in so far as they have effect in relation to the prohibitions contained in sections 20 and 21 of the Forgery and Counterfeiting Act 1981 namely— Sections 50(2) and (3) Section 68; and Section 170 (various offences committed in connection with contraventions of prohibitions on the import and export of counterfeits or currency notes or protected coins). The Forgery and Counterfeiting Act 1981	Two officials authorised to do so by the Secretary of State, being officials of the authority or body which may lawfully issue the currency notes or protected coins referred to in column 3 hereof.	That the coin or note identified in the certificate by reference to a label or otherwise is a counterfeit of a currency note or protected coin; where "currency note" has the meaning assigned to it by section 27(1)(a) of the Forgery and Counterfeiting Act 1981, and "protected coin" means any coin which is customarily used as money in the United Kingdom, any of the Channel Islands, the Isle of Man or the Republic of Ireland.

Enactment	Persons who may purport to sign certificates	Matters which may be certified
Sections 14 to 16 (certain offences relating to counterfeiting).	Two officials authorised to do so by the Secretary of State, being officials of the authority or body which may lawfully issue the currency notes or protected coins referred to in column 3 hereof.	That the coin or note identified in the certificate by reference to a label or otherwise is a counterfeit of a currency note or protected coin; where "currency note" has the meaning assigned to it by section 27(1)(a) of the Forgery and Counterfeiting Act 1981, and "protected coin" means any coin which is customarily used as money in the United Kingdom, any of the Channel Islands, the Isle of Man or the Republic of Ireland.
The Wildlife and Countryside Act 1981 (c. 69) Sections 1, 5, 6(1) to (3), 7, 8, 9(1), (2), (4) and (5), 11(1) and (2), 13(1) and (2) and 14 (certain offences relating to protection of wild animals or wild plants).	An officer of the appropriate authority (within the meaning of section 16(9) of that Act) authorised to do so by the authority.	In relation to a person specified in the certificate that, on a date so specified, he held, or as the case may be did not hold, a licence under section 16 of that Act and, where he held such a licence— (a) the purpose for which the licence was granted; and (b) the terms and conditions of the licence.
The Civic Government (Scotland) Act 1982 (c. 45).	A person authorised to do so by the Secretary of State.	In relation to a person identified in the certificate, that on a date specified therein he held, or as the case may be, did not hold, a licence under a provision so specified of that Act.
The Road Traffic Regulation Act 1984 (c. 27).	Two police officers who have tested the apparatus.	The accuracy of any particular— (a) speedometer fitted to a police vehicle; (b) odometer fitted to a police vehicle; (c) radar meter; or (d) apparatus for measuring speed, time or distance, identified in the certificate by reference to its number or otherwise.
The Video Recordings Act 1984 (c. 39)		

Enactment	Persons who may purport to sign certificates	Matters which may be certified
Sections 9 to 14 (offences relating to the supply and possession of video recordings in contravention of that Act).	²A person authorised to do so by the Secretary of State, being a person who has examined the record maintained in pursuance of arrangements made by the designated authority and in the case of a certificate in terms of— (a) sub-paragraph (a) in column 3, the video work mentioned in that sub-paragraph; (b) sub-paragraph (b) in that column, both video works mentioned in that sub-paragraph.	²That the record shows any of the following— (a) in respect of a video work (or part of a video work) contained in a video recording identified by the certificate, that by a date specified no classification certificate has been issued; (b) in respect of a video work which is the subject of a certificate under sub-paragraph (a) above, that the video work differs in a specified way from another video work contained in a video recording identified in the certificate under this sub-paragraph and that, on a date specified, a classification certificate was issued in respect of that other video work; (c) that, by a date specified, no classification certificate had been issued in respect of a video work having a particular title; (d) that, on a date specified, a classification certificate was issued in respect of a video work having a particular title and that a document which is identified in the certificate under this sub-paragraph is a copy of the classification certificate so issued; expressions used in column 2, or in this column, of this entry being construed in accordance with that Act; and in each of sub-paragraphs (a) to (d) above "specified" means specified in the certificate under that sub-paragraph.
The Road Traffic Act 1988 (c. 52) Section 165(3) (offence of failure to give name and address and to produce vehicle documents when required by constable).	A constable.	In relation to a person specified in the certificate, that he failed, by such date as may be so specified, to produce such documents as may be so specified at a police station so specified.

673

Enactment	Persons who may purport to sign certificates	Matters which may be certified
The Control of Pollution (Amendment) Act 1989 (c. 14)		
Section 1 (offence of transporting controlled waste without registering).	An officer of a regulation authority within the meaning of that Act authorised to do so by the authority.	In relation to a person specified in the certificate, that on a date so specified he was not a registered carrier of controlled waste within the meaning of that Act.
The Environmental Protection Act 1990 (c. 43)		
Section 33(1)(a) and (b) (prohibition on harmful depositing, treatment or disposal of waste).	An officer of a waste regulation authority within the meaning of that Act authorised to do so by the authority.	In relation to a person specified in the certificate that, on a date so specified, he held, or as the case may be he did not hold, a waste management licence.
Section 34(1)(c) (duty of care as respects transfer of waste).	An officer of a waste regulation authority within the meaning of that Act authorised to do so by the authority.	In relation to a person specified in the certificate, that on a date so specified he was not an authorised person within the meaning of section 34(3)(b) or (d) of that Act.
[3]The Social Security Administration Act 1992 (c. 5)		
Section 112(1) (false statements etc. to obtain payments).	Any officer authorised to do so by the Secretary of State.	In relation to a person identified in the certificate— (a) the assessment, award, or nature of any benefit applied for by him; (b) the transmission or handing over of any payment to him.
The Criminal Justice and Public Order Act 1994 (c. 33)		
Paragraph 5 of Schedule 6 (offence of making false statements to obtain certification as prisoner custody officer).	An officer authorised to do so by the Secretary of State.	That— (a) on a date specified in the certificate, an application for a certificate under section 114 of that Act was received from a person so specified; (b) the application contained a statement so specified; (c) a person so specified made, on a date so specified, a statement in writing in terms so specified.
This Act		

Enactment	Persons who may purport to sign certificates	Matters which may be certified
[6]Sections 24(3) to (8), 25, 27 to 29 and 90C(1)	The Clerk of Justiciary or the clerk of court.	In relation to a person specified in the certificate, that— (a) an order granting bail under that Act was made on a date so specified by a court so specified; (b) the order or a condition of it so specified was in force on a date so specified; (c) notice of the time and place appointed for a diet so specified was given to him in a manner so specified; (d) as respects a diet so specified, he failed to appear.
Section 150(8) (offence of failure of accused to appear at diet after due notice).	The clerk of court.	That, on a date specified in the certificate, he gave a person so specified, in a manner so specified, notice of the time and place appointed for a diet so specified.
[4]The Communications Act 2003		
Section 363(1) and (2) (offence of unauthorised installation or use of a television receiver)	A person authorised to do so by the British Broadcasting Corporation	In relation to premises at an address specified in the certificate, whether on a date so specified any television licence (for the purposes of that section) was, in records maintained on behalf of the Corporation in relation to such licences, recorded as being in force; and, if so, particulars so specified of such record of that licence.
[7]The Building (Scotland) Act 2003 (asp 8).		
Section 8(1) and (2) (prohibition of work for construction or demolition of, or provision of services, fittings or equipment for, building, or conversion of building, without warrant)	An officer of a local authority authorised to do so by the authority.	In relation to a building specified in the certificate, that on a date so specified, the local authority had not— (a) granted a warrant under section 9 for the work or, as the case may be, conversion, or (b) received a copy of such a warrant granted by a verifier other than the authority

Enactment	Persons who may purport to sign certificates	Matters which may be certified
Section 21(5) (offence of occupying building when no completion certificate has been accepted)	An officer of a local authority authorised to do so by the authority	That, on a date specified in the certificate, the local authority had not— (a) accepted under section 18(1) a completion certificate in respect of construction or conversion in relation to a building so specified, (b) received a copy of such a certificate accepted under section 18(1) by a verifier other than the authority, or (c) received a copy of a permission for temporary occupation or use of the building so specified granted under section 21(3)
Section 43(1) (offence of occupying building, following evacuation, without notice from local authority)	An officer of a local authority authorised to do so by the authority	That, on a date specified in the certificate, the local authority had not given a person notice under section 42(7)
[5]The Antisocial Behaviour etc. (Scotland) Act 2004 (asp 8), section 45(1).	An officer of a local authority within the meaning of that Act authorised to do so by the authority.	That a level of noise specified in the certificate was measured at a time and in a place specified in the certificate using an approved device within the meaning of that Act.
[8]The Water Environment (Controlled Activities) (Scotland) Regulations 2005 Regulation 40.	Two persons authorised to do so by the Scottish Environment Protection Agency.	That they have analysed a sample identified in the certificate (by label or otherwise) and that the sample is of a nature and composition specified in the certificate.

NOTES

[1]As amended by the Scotland Act 1998 (Consequential Modifications) (No. 2) Order 1999 (SI 1999/1820), art.4 and Sch.2, para.122(5) (effective July 1, 1999).

[2]Substituted by the Crime and Punishment (Scotland) Act 1997 (c.48), s.30 with effect from August 1, 1997 in terms of the Crime and Punishment (Scotland) Act 1997 (Commencement and Transitional Provisions) Order 1997 (SI 1997/1712), para.3.

[3]Amended by the Criminal Procedure and Investigations Act 1996 (c.25), s.73(4).

[4]Inserted by the Communications Act 2003 (c.21), Sch.17, para.133. Brought into force on April 1, 2004 by the Office of Communications Act 2002 (Commencement No.3) and Communications Act 2003 (Commencement No.2) Order 2003 (SI 2003/3142 (C.125)). Entry relating to the Wireless Telegraphy Act 1949 repealed by the Communications Act 2003 (c.21), Sch.19. Brought into force as previous.

[5]Inserted by the Antisocial Behaviour etc. (Scotland) Act 2004 (asp 8), s.144(1) and Sch.4, para.5(12). Brought into force on November 5, 2004 by the Antisocial Behaviour etc. (Scotland) Act 2004 (Commencement and Savings) Order 2004 (SSI 2004/420 (C.31)).

[6]Amended by the Criminal Procedure (Amendment) (Scotland) Act 2004 (asp 5), s.25 and Sch.1, para.58. Brought into force on February 1, 2005 by the Criminal Procedure (Amendment) (Scotland) Act 2004 (Commencement, Transitional Provisions and Savings) Order 2004 (SSI 2004/405 (C.28)), art.2.

[7]Inserted by the Building (Scotland) Act 2003 (asp 8), Sch.6, para.22. Entry relating to the Building (Scotland) Act 1959 (c.24) repealed. Brought into force on May 1, 2005 by the Building (Scotland) Act 2003 (Commencement No.1, Transitional Provisions and Savings) Order 2004 (SSI 2004/404 (C.27)).

[8]Inserted by the Water Environment (Consequential Savings and Provisions) (Scotland) order 2006 (SSI 2006/181), art.2, Sch.1, para.9 (effective April 1, 2006). Entry relating to the Control of Pollution Act 1974 (c.40) repealed by the same provision.

"SCHEDULE 9A

THE COMMISSION: FURTHER PROVISIONS

Membership

1. Her Majesty shall, on the recommendation of the Secretary of State, appoint one of the members of the Commission to be the chairman of the Commission.

2.—(1) Subject to the following provisions of this paragraph, a person shall hold and vacate office as a member of the Commission, or as chairman of the Commission, in accordance with the terms of his appointment.

(2) An appointment as a member of the Commission may be full-time or part-time.

(3) The appointment of a person as a member of the Commission, or as chairman of the Commission, shall be for a fixed period of not longer than five years.

(4) Subject to sub-paragraph (5) below, a person whose term of appointment as a member of the Commission, or as chairman of the Commission, expires shall be eligible for re-appointment.

(5) No person may hold office as a member of the Commission for a continuous period which is longer than ten years.

(6) A person may at any time resign his office as a member of the Commission, or as chairman of the Commission, by notice in writing addressed to Her Majesty.

(7) Her Majesty may at any time remove a person from office as a member of the Commission if satisfied—

(a) that he has without reasonable excuse failed to discharge his functions as a member for a continuous period of three months beginning not earlier than six months before that time;

(b) that he has been convicted of a criminal offence;

(c) that a bankruptcy order has been made against him, or his estate has been sequestrated, or he has made a composition or arrangement with, or granted a trust deed for, his creditors; or

(d) that he is unable or unfit to discharge his functions as a member.

(8) If the chairman of the Commission ceases to be a member of the Commission he shall also cease to be chairman.

Members and employees

3.—(1) The Commission shall—

(a) pay to members of the Commission such remuneration;

(b) pay to or in respect of members of the Commission any such allowances, fees, expenses and gratuities; and

(c) pay towards the provisions of pensions to or in respect of members of the Commission any such sums,

as the Commission are required to pay by or in accordance with directions given by the Secretary of State.

(2) Where a member of the Commission was, immediately before becoming a member, a participant in a scheme under section 1 of the Superannuation Act 1972, the Minister for the Civil Service may determine that his term of office as a member shall be treated for the purposes of the scheme as if it were service in the employment or office by reference to which he was a participant in the scheme; and his rights under the scheme shall not be affected by sub-paragraph (1)(c) above.

(3) Where—

(a) a person ceases to hold office as a member of the Commission otherwise than on the expiry of his term of appointment; and

(b) it appears to the Secretary of State that there are special circumstances which make it right for him to receive compensation,

the Secretary of State may direct the Commission to make to him a payment of such amount as the Secretary of State may determine.

4.—(1) The Commission may appoint a chief executive and such other employees as the Commission think fit, subject to the consent of the Secretary of State as to their number and terms and conditions of service.

(2) The Commission shall—

(a) pay to employees of the Commission such remuneration; and

(b) pay to or in respect of employees of the Commission any such allowances, fees, expenses and gratuities,

as the Commission may, with the consent of the Secretary of State, determine.

(3) Employment by the Commission shall be included among the kinds of employment to which a scheme under section 1 of the Superannuation Act 1972 may apply.

5. The Commission shall pay to the Minister for the Civil Service, at such times as he may direct, such sums as he may determine in respect of any increase attributable to paragraph 3(2) or 4(3) above in the sums payable out of money provided by Parliament under the Superannuation Act 1972.

Procedure

6.—(1) The arrangements for the procedure of the Commission including the quorum for meetings) shall be such as the Commission may determine.

(2) The arrangements may provide for the discharge, under the general direction of the Commission, of any function of the Commission—

(a) in the case of the function specified in sub-paragraph (3) below, by a committee consisting of not fewer than three members of the Commission; and

(b) in any other case, by any committee of, or by one or more of the members or employees of, the Commission.

(3) The function referred to in sub-paragraph (2)(a) above is making a reference to the High Court under section 194B of this Act.

(4) The validity of any proceedings of the Commission (or of any committee of the Commission) shall not be affected by—

(a) any vacancy among the members of the Commission or in the office of chairman of the Commission; or

(b) any defect in the appointment of any person as a member of the Commission or as chairman of the Commission.

(5) Where—

(a) a document or other material has been produced to the Commission under section 194I of this Act, or they have been given access to a document or other material under that section, and the Commission have taken away the document or other material (or a copy of it); and

(b) the person who produced the document or other material to the Commission, or gave them access to it, has notified the Commission that he considers that its disclosure to others may be contrary to the interests of national security,

the Commission shall, after consulting that person, deal with the document or material (or copy) in a manner appropriate for safeguarding the interests of national security.

Evidence

7. A document purporting to be—

(a) duly executed under the seal of the Commission; or

(b) signed on behalf of the Commission,

shall be received in evidence and, unless the contrary is proved, taken to be so executed or signed.

Annual reports and accounts

8.—(1) As soon as possible after the end of each financial year of the Commission, the Commission shall send to the Secretary of State a report on the discharge of their functions during that year.

(2) Such a report may include an account of the working of the provisions of Part XA of this Act and recommendations relating to any of those provisions.

(3) The Secretary of State shall lay before each House of Parliament, and cause to be published, a copy of every report sent to him under sub-paragraph (1).

9.—(1) The Commission shall—

(a) keep proper accounts and proper records in relation to the accounts; and

(b) prepare a statement of accounts in respect of each financial year of the Commission.

(2) The statement of accounts shall contain such information and shall be in such form as the Secretary of State may direct.

(3) The Commission shall send the statement of accounts to the Secretary of State within such period after the end of the financial year to which the statement relates as the Secretary of State may direct.

(3A) The Scottish Ministers shall send the statement of accounts to the Auditor General for Scotland for auditing.

(4) [...]

10. For the purposes of this Schedule the Commission's financial year shall be the period of twelve months ending with 31st March; but the first financial year of the Commission shall be the period beginning with the date of establishment of the Commission and ending with the first 31st March which falls at least six months after that date.

Expenses

11. The Secretary of State shall defray the expenses of the Commission up to such amount as may be approved by him.".

AMENDMENTS

Schedule 9A inserted by s.25 of the Crime and Punishment (Scotland) Act 1997 with effect from April 1, 1999 as provided by the Crime and Punishment (Scotland) Act 1997 (Commencement No. 5 and Transitional Provisions and Savings) Order 1999 (S.I. 1999 No. 652).

Para.9(2) as amended by the Scotland Act 1998 (Consequential Modifications) (No. 2) Order 1999 (S.I. 1999 No. 1820) art. 4 and Sched. 2, para.122(3) (effective July 1, 1999).

Para.9(3) as amended by the Public Finance and Accountability (Scotland) Act 2000 (asp 1), s.26 and Sched. 4, para. 14(a).

Para.9(3A) as inserted by the Public Finance and Accountability (Scotland) Act 2000 (asp 1), s.26 and Sched. 4, para. 14(b).

Para.9(4) repealed by the Public Finance and Accountability (Scotland) Act 2000 (asp 1), s.26 and Sched. 4, para. 14(c).

Section 292(1)   SCHEDULE 10

CERTAIN OFFENCES TRIABLE ONLY SUMMARILY

Night Poaching Act 1828 (c. 69)

1. Offences under section 1 of the Night Poaching Act 1828 (taking or destroying game or rabbits by night or entering land for that purpose).

Public Meeting Act 1908 (c. 66)

2. Offences under section 1(1) of the Public Meeting Act 1908 (endeavour to break up a public meeting).

Post Office Act 1953 (c. 36)

3. [*Repealed by the Postal Services Act 2000 (Consequential Modifications No. 1) Order 2001 (S.I. 2001 No. 1149), art. 3 and Sched. 2.*]

Betting, Gaming and Lotteries Act 1963 (c. 2)

4. Offences under the following provisions of the Betting, Gaming and Lotteries Act 1963—
   (a) section 7 (restriction of betting on dog racecourses);
   (b) section 10(5) (advertising licensed betting offices);
   (c) section 11(6) (person holding bookmaker's or betting agency permit employing a person disqualified from holding such a permit);
   (d) section 18(2) (making unauthorised charges to bookmakers on licensed track);
   (e) section 19 (occupiers of licensed tracks not to have any interest in bookmaker thereon);
   (f) section 21 (betting with young persons); and
   (g) section 22 (betting circulars not to be sent to young persons).

Theatres Act 1968 (c. 54)

5. Offences under section 6 of the Theatres Act 1968 (provocation of breach of the peace by means of public performance of play).

Criminal Law (Consolidation) (Scotland) Act 1995 (c. 39)

6. Offences under section 12(1) of the Criminal Law (Consolidation) (Scotland) Act 1995 (allowing child under 16 to be in brothel).

ACT OF ADJOURNAL (CRIMINAL PROCEDURE RULES) 1996

(S.I. 1996 No. 513 (S.47))

Made   *29th February 1996*
Coming into force   *1st April 1996*

The Lord Justice General, Lord Justice-Clerk and Lords Commissioners of Justiciary under and by virtue of the powers conferred on them by section 305 of the Criminal Procedure (Scotland) Act 1995, the provisions specified in Schedule 1 to this Act of Adjournal and of all other powers enabling them in that behalf, do hereby enact and declare:

Citation and commencement

1.—(1) This Act of Adjournal may be cited as the Act of Adjournal (Criminal Procedure Rules) 1996 and shall come into force on 1st April 1996.

(2) This Act of Adjournal shall be inserted in the Books of Adjournal.

Criminal Procedure Rules

2. Schedule 2 to this Act of Adjournal shall have effect for the purpose of providing new rules of procedure in the High Court of Justiciary, in the sheriff court in exercise of its criminal jurisdiction, and in the district court.

Revocations

3. The Acts of Adjournal mentioned in Schedule 3 to this Act of Adjournal are revoked to the extent specified in the third column of that Schedule.

INTRODUCTION AND GENERAL NOTE

[1]On the foundation of the High Court of Justiciary in 1672 the High Court was given the power "to regulate the inferior officers thereof, and order every other thing concerning the said Court" (see s.6 of the Act 1672 c.40 (now repealed)). The High Court under this power has passed various Acts of Adjournal relating to the forms of procedure in that Court, the organisation of circuits of the Court and sundry other matters. However, by the Act of Adjournal (Consolidation) 1988 (SI 1988/110) of January 21, 1988, all previous Acts of Adjournal were revoked and since that date subsequent alterations in criminal procedure have been effected by amendment of the consolidating Act of Adjournal which provided a detailed code of rules of criminal procedure (hereinafter referred to as "the 1988 Rules").

With the enactment of the Criminal Procedure (Scotland) Act 1995 which repealed the Criminal Procedure (Scotland) Act 1975, itself a consolidation statute, a new Act of Adjournal became necessary. The Act of Adjournal (Criminal Procedure Rules) 1996 provides a new set of rules which are contained in Sch.2 to the Act of Adjournal and are to be known as the Criminal Procedure Rules 1996 (see r.1.1). These rules, as the 1988 Rules did, make provision for criminal procedure both in solemn and summary proceedings. The same policy is adopted with the Criminal Procedure Rules 1996 as was followed with the 1988 Rules and accordingly when the need for change in the rules becomes evident, an Act of Adjournal is passed to amend the consolidating Act of Adjournal of 1996. This process was commenced within just six months of the coming into force of the Criminal Procedure Rules 1996 and has continued on a regular basis. However, as a result of the Criminal Procedure (Amendment) (Scotland) Act 2004 (asp 5) which has effected significant changes to the procedure to be followed in High Court cases, a substantial amendment of the Criminal Procedure Rules 1996 became recently necessary. This was effected by the Act of Adjournal (Criminal Procedure Rules Amendment) (Criminal Procedure (Amendment) (Scotland) Act 2004) 2005 (SSI 2005/44) which came into force on February 1, 2005. Allied with this statutory instrument is the Act of Adjournal (Criminal Procedure Rules Amendment No.3) (Vulnerable Witnesses (Scotland) Act 2004) 2005 (SSI 2005/188) which came into force on April 1, 2005. The principal purpose of the latter Act of Adjournal is to substitute a new Ch.22 for the previous chapter which dealt with the evidence of children. The new chapter is much more extensive because it requires to reflect the considerable extension in

---

[1] Annotations by Peter W. Ferguson, Q.C.

the scope of protection afforded to the now enlarged category of "vulnerable witnesses" for whom provision is made in the Vulnerable Witnesses (Scotland) Act 2004 (asp 3).

One provision in the 1995 Act which requires special notice is s.305(2) which provides that the High Court may by Act of Adjournal "modify, amend or repeal any enactment (including an enactment in this Act) in so far as that enactment relates to matters in respect to which an Act of Adjournal may be made under subs.(1) above." For all material purposes the matters with respect to which this Act of Adjournal has been made are given in s.305(1) and are (a) the regulation of the practice and procedure in relation to criminal procedure and (b) the making of such rules and regulations "as may be necessary or expedient to carry out the purposes and accomplish the objects of any enactment (including an enactment in this Act) in so far as it relates to criminal procedure". An example of the exercise of this power to amend primary legislation is to be found in the Act of Adjournal (Extension of Time Limit for Service of Transcript of Examination) 1998 (SI 1998/2635) which came into force on December 1, 1998 and amended s.37(9) of the 1995 Act to allow for the disposal of applications for extension by the High Court or a single judge either in chambers or in public. A very recent example is the Act of Adjournal (Criminal Appeals) 2003 (SSI 2003/387), para.2 which amends ss.114 and 115(1) of the 1995 Act so as to allow for appeals against sentence in both solemn and summary cases (including the Lord Advocate's appeals against unduly lenient disposals) to be presented in writing only.

Section 305(2) is in its terms a "Henry VIII clause" because it gives to the High Court by way of statutory instrument the power to change the law as Parliament has expressed it in statute. This gives rise to difficulty. Virtually the same provision was contained in the 1975 Act (see ss.282(2) and 457(d)) and it has been stated that having regard to the limits placed upon the High Court's powers by these provisions, an Act of Adjournal may be ultra vires (see (Lord) McCluskey, *Criminal Appeals*, para.1.06). To the extent that an Act of Adjournal sought to make provision for matters which did not relate to criminal procedure, that is no doubt true although Lord McCluskey did also note that Lord Justice-Clerk Ross received with little enthusiasm a submission that the 1988 Rules were ultra vires (see *Wither v Cowie*, 1991 S.L.T. 401 at 405K). However, standing the power of the High Court by Act of Adjournal to amend, modify or repeal the 1995 Act, is it permissible to have regard to the terms of the Act of Adjournal when construing the 1995 Act? Usually a statutory instrument is of no assistance since it exists only as a creature of its parent statute. But by virtue of s.305(2) it is arguable that this progeny can refashion its parent. Indeed, the more precise question may be whether, when there is conflict between the Act of Adjournal and the 1995 Act, the 1995 Act is to be treated as impliedly repealed on the principle *leges posteriores priores abrogant*.

This issue has been considered (although perhaps not fully considered) in some recent decisions. In *McLeay v Hingston*, 1994 S.L.T. 720 at 723J-K Lord Justice-General Hope said: "the purpose of the rules in the Act of Adjournal is to give effect to the provisions of the [1975] statute, not control their meaning or to provide an aid to their interpretation. The meaning and effect of s.334(2A) is to be found by examining the words used by Parliament, not by construing the terms of the Act of Adjournal." In *Walkingshaw v Robison and Davidson Ltd*, 1989 S.C.C.R. 359 Lord Justice-Clerk Ross said at 362B: "Certainly it is not correct to hold that the Act of Adjournal has in some way limited the scope of the subsection of the Act of Parliament." However, one can set against these dicta what Lord Justice-Clerk Ross said in *Lafferty v Jessop*, 1989 S.L.T. 846 at 848K that the terms of r.128 in the 1988 Rules "make it perfectly clear that leave to appeal against a decision under s.334 (2A) cannot be sought or granted until after the accused has stated how he pleads to the charge or charges set out in the complaint." (See also *Stevenson v McGlennan*, 1990 S.L.T. 842.)

Human Rights Act 1998, press reporting and contempt of court

Section 4(2) of the Contempt of Court Act 1981 provides the court with a power to order that publication of any report of any proceedings, or part of such proceedings, should be postponed for such period as the court thinks necessary for the purpose of avoiding a substantial risk of prejudice to the administration of justice. As a result of the "cardinal importance" which the courts now attach to freedom of the press and (because of the incorporation of Art. 10 of the European Convention) the need for any restriction on that freedom to be proportionate and no more than is necessary to promote the legitimate object of the restriction (*McCartan Turkington Breen (A Firm) v Times Newspapers Ltd* [2000] 3 W.L.R. 1670 at 1679H–1680, *per* Lord Bingham of Cornhill) s.12 of the Human Rights Act 1998 was enacted. Section 12(2) requires that before relief which might affect the right to freedom of expression is granted the court should be satisfied that if any affected person is not present or represented, all practicable steps to notify him have been taken or that there are compelling reasons why he should not be notified. Section 12 does not, however, apply to remedies or orders pronounced in criminal proceedings (s.12(5)).

Notwithstanding that deliberate omission and no doubt in view of the cardinal importance of a free press, which was implicitly recognised prior to the Human Rights Act 1998 by the Appeal Court in *Scottish Daily Record and Sunday Mail Ltd, Petrs*, 1999 S.L.T. 624 at 628C (when the right of the press to be heard in any decision to pronounce an order under s.4(2) or the terms in which it should be couched (whether before or after it was pronounced) was emphasised on an analogy with proceedings for interim interdict pronounced on an *ex parte* basis: see 628F-G), the Appeal Court recently took an unusual step. In *Galbraith v HM Advocate*, 2000 S.C.C.R. 935 in the course of an appeal against a murder conviction in which the appellant gave notice of an intention to seek an order under s.4(2) prohibiting reporting of the appeal proceedings until determination of the appeal or of any retrial, the Appeal Court informed the agents for various media interests of the motion. At the resumed hearing the media were represented. The Appeal Court again recognised that "[p]rima facie ... the media have a substantial interest in the making or refusal of such orders and in their scope" (at 941A) but reserved its opinion on whether any order should be made for an initially limited period so as to allow the media to make representations on the order and its terms at a later hearing. The court also observed that the Scottish Courts website was the place for journalists and others to look when concerned to know whether an order had been made (941D-E). In *BBC, Petitioners*, 2002 S.L.T. 2 (para.4), the trial judge (Lord Osborne) made an order under s.4(2) but provided that, while it was to be immediately effective, it should only become "final" at 5 pm on the second working day after it was pronounced, in order to give the media and other interested parties the opportunity to move for recall or variation of the order. A similar practice was adopted by Lord Hodge when he made an order under s.11 of the Contempt of Court Act 1981 in *HM Advocate v M*, 2007 S.L.T. 462; 2007 S.C.C.R. 124 (sub nom HM Advocate v Mola).The present practice is for copies of s.4(2) orders to be immediately sent by e-mail to various newspapers and broadcasting organisations and their agents: see para. 4.

This area of practice seems, with respect, to be an appropriate matter for which provision should be made in the Criminal Procedure Rules. The Rules could set out a procedure to be followed for motions for s.4(2) orders to be raised and for them to be intimated to the media by various means, the manner of, and time for, representations to be made, the holding of a hearing on the motion, the notification to all interested persons of the terms of the order and the duration of the order.

Preamble   SCHEDULE 1

POWERS UNDER AND BY VIRTUE OF WHICH THIS ACT OF ADJOURNAL IS MADE

Column 1	Column 2	Column 3
Relevant enactment conferring power	*Relevant amending enactment*	*Relevant provision in* Schedule 2
Section 1 of the Public Records (Scotland) Act 1937 (c. 43)		Rule 3.6
Section 2A(3) of the Backing of Warrants (Republic of Ireland) Act 1965 (c. 45)	Inserted by paragraph 5 of Schedule 1 to the Criminal Justice Act 1988 (c. 33) and continued by section 37(5) of the Extradition Act 1989 (c. 33)	Rule 30.3(2) and (6)
Section 8 of the Backing of Warrants (Republic of Ireland) Act 1965 (c. 45)	Amended by paragraph 5 of Schedule 4 to the Criminal Procedure (Consequential Provisions) (Scotland) Act 1995 (c. 40)	Chapter 30
Section 38 of the Legal Aid (Scotland) Act 1986 (c. 47)		Chapter 33
Section 90(4) of the Debtors (Scotland) Act 1987 (c. 18)		Rule 20.8(2)
Section 10(3) of the Extradition Act 1989 (c. 33)		Rule 34.2(2) to (8)
Section 14(3) of, and paragraph 9(3) of Schedule 1 to, the Extradition Act 1989 (c. 33)		Rule 34.5
Section 8(5) of the Computer Misuse Act 1990 (c. 18)		Rule 35.1
Section 10 of the Criminal Justice (International Co-operation) Act 1990 (c. 5)		Chapter 36

Column 1	Column 2	Column 3
Relevant enactment conferring power	*Relevant amending enactment*	*Relevant provision in* Schedule 2
Section 19(2) of the Prisoners and Criminal Proceedings (Scotland) Act 1993 (c. 9)		Rule 15.2(6)
Section 18(7) of the Proceeds of Crime (Scotland) Act 1995 (c. 43)		Rule 37.2

Paragraph 2   SCHEDULE 2

CRIMINAL PROCEDURE RULES 1996

ARRANGEMENT OF RULES
Part I—Preliminary and administration

CHAPTER 1

CITATION, INTERPRETATION ETC.

RULE

CHAPTER 19A

ADJOURNMENT BEFORE SENTENCE UNDER SECTION 201 OR DEFERRED SENTENCE UNDER SECTION 202 OF THE ACT OF 1995

CHAPTER 19B

CASES REFERRED BY THE SCOTTISH CRIMINAL CASES REVIEW COMMISSION UNDER SECTION 194B OF THE ACT OF 1995

CHAPTER 19C

RISK ASSESSMENT

CHAPTER 20

SENTENCING

CHAPTER 21

UNCONTROVERSIAL EVIDENCE, HEARSAY AND PRIOR STATEMENTS

CHAPTER 22

EVIDENCE OF VULNERABLE WITNESSES

CHAPTER 23

LETTERS OF REQUEST

CHAPTER 23A

TELEVISION LINK EVIDENCE FROM ABROAD

Part I

Preliminary and administration

Chapter 1

Citation, Interpretation Etc.

Citation of these Rules

1.1. These Rules may be cited as the Criminal Procedure Rules 1996.

Interpretation

1.2.—(1) In these Rules, unless the context otherwise requires—

"the Act of 1995" means the Criminal Procedure (Scotland) Act 1995;

"counsel" means a practising member of the Faculty of Advocates or a so-licitor having a right of audience before the High Court by virtue of section 25A of the Solicitors (Scotland) Act 1980;

(2) Unless the context otherwise requires, a reference to a specified Chapter, Part, rule or form is a reference to the Chapter, Part, rule, or form in the appendix to these Rules, so specified in these Rules; and a reference to a specified paragraph, sub-paragraph or head is a reference to that paragraph of the rule or form, that sub-paragraph of the paragraph or that head of the sub-paragraph, in which the reference occurs.

Forms

1.3. Where there is a reference to the use of a form in these Rules, that form in the appendix to these Rules, or a form substantially to the same effect, shall be used with such variation as circumstances may require.

Direction relating to Advocate General

1.4. The Lord Justice General may, by direction, specify such arrangements as he considers necessary for, or in connection with, the appearance in court of the Advocate General for Scotland.

Amendments

Chapter 1 as amended by the Act of Adjournal (Criminal Procedure Rules Amendment No. 3) 1999 (SI 1999/1387) para.2(2)(a) (effective May 19, 1999).

Rule 1.4 inserted by the Act of Adjournal (Criminal Procedure Rules Amendment No. 3) 1999 (SI 1999/1387) para.2(2)(b) (effective May 19, 1999).

General Note

Rule 1.3 gives a degree of latitude to individual courts to adapt the forms set out in the Appendix to the Rules (as r.2(3) of the 1988 Rules did). Moreover, special power is given by s.305(4) of the 1995 Act to the Clerk of Justiciary, with the sanction of the Lord Justice-General and the Lord Justice-Clerk to vary the forms which are set out in the Appendix to the Rules. This power is, however, confined to variations necessary for giving effect to the provisions of the 1995 Act relating to solemn procedure only. It should also be noted that where the form has not been followed, care should be taken, when effecting variations, to ensure that the substance of the rule is followed: see *Stevenson v McGlennan*, 1990 S.L.T. 842.

Chapter 2

Service of Documents

Service on Crown

2.1. Any document that requires to be sent to or served on the Lord Advocate or the prosecutor under any enactment or rule of law shall be sent to or served on, as the case may be—

(a) if it relates to a case set down for trial in the High Court, the Crown Agent;

(b) if it relates to a case set down for trial in the sheriff court or district court, the appropriate procurator fiscal.

Citation in solemn proceedings

2.2.—(1) Subject to rule 2.4 (service on witnesses), this rule applies to the citation of, and service on, an accused under section 66(4)(a) of the Act of 1995 (service and lodging of indictment, etc.).

(2) Service shall be effected by an officer of law—

(a) delivering the document to the accused personally;

(b) leaving the document in the hands of a member of the family of the accused or other occupier or employee at the proper domicile of citation of the accused;

(c) affixing the document to the door of, or depositing it in, the proper domicile of citation of the accused; or

(d) where the officer of law serving the document has reasonable grounds for believing that the accused, for whom no proper domicile of citation has been specified, is residing at a particular place but is unavailable—

(i) leaving the document in the hands of a member of the family of the accused or other occupier or employee at that place; or

(ii) affixing the document to the door of, or depositing it in, that place.

(3) In this rule, "proper domicile of citation" means the address at which the accused may be cited to appear at any diet relating to the offence with which he is charged or an offence charged in the same proceedings as that offence or to which any other intimation or document may be sent.

Citation in solemn proceedings by service on solicitor

2.2A. Where the documents mentioned in section 66(6C) of the Act of 1995 (citation by service on solicitor) are to be served on a solicitor under that section, they shall be—

(a) delivered to the solicitor personally at the solicitor's place of business;

(b) left for the solicitor with an employee or partner of the solicitor at the solicitor's place of business; or

(c) posted to the solicitor's place of business by the first class recorded delivery service,

with a notice in Form 2.2A.

Amendment

Rule 2.2A inserted by the Act of Adjournal (Criminal Procedure Rules Amendment) (Criminal Procedure (Amendment) (Scotland) Act) 2005 (SSI 2005/44), r.2(5) (subject to r.2(2)–(4)) (effective February 1, 2005).

General provisions for service

2.3.—(1) Subject to the following paragraphs of this rule and to rul 2.3A, the citation of, or the service of any document on, a person under or by virtue of the Act of 1995, these Rules or any other enactment shall, unless otherwise provided in the relevant enactment, be effected in the same manner, with the necessary modifications, as the citation of an accused in summary proceedings under section 141 of that Act (manner of citation) or under rule 2.2 of these Rules (citation in solemn proceedings).

(2) [...]

(3) The citation in Form 29.3 of a person to attend a diet fixed for taking his precognition on oath under section 291 of the Act of 1995 (precognition on oath of defence witnesses) shall be made by personal service on him by an officer of law acting on the instructions of the accused or his solicitor.

AMENDMENT

Rule 2.3(1) as amended by the Act of Adjournal (Criminal Procedure Rules Amendment No.4) (Criminal Procedure (Amendment) (Scotland) Act 2004) 2004 (SSI 2004/434), r.2 (effective October 4, 2004).

Service etc. on accused through a solicitor

2.3A. Where in proceedings on indictment anything is to be served on, given, notified or intimated to a solicitor under section 72G of the Act of 1995 it shall be—

(a) delivered to the solicitor personally;

(b) left for the solicitor with an employee or partner of the solicitor at the solicitor's place of business; or

(c) posted to the solicitor's place of business by the first class recorded delivery service, with a notice in Form 2.3A.

AMENDMENT

Rule 2.3A inserted by the Act of Adjournal (Criminal Procedure Rules Amendment No.4) (Criminal Procedure (Amendment) (Scotland) Act 2004) 2004 (SSI 2004/434), r.2 (effective October 4, 2004).

Service on witnesses

2.4.—(1) Service of a citation by the prosecution or defence on a witness in any proceedings may, in the first instance, be by post.

(2) Where citation of a witness has been attempted by post but has not been effected, or the witness has not returned Form 8.2-D or Form 16.6-B, as the case may be, within the period prescribed in rule 8.2(3) or 16.6(1), as the case may be, citation of that witness shall be effected by an officer of law delivering the document to the witness personally.

Service by post

2.5.—(1) Subject to any provision in the Act of 1995 or of these Rules, service by post shall be by registered post, ordinary first class post or the first class recorded delivery service.

(2) Where the citation of, or service on, any person is effected by post under these Rules, the date of citation shall be deemed to be the day after the date of posting.

AMENDMENT

Rule 2.5(1) as amended by the Act of Adjournal (Criminal Procedure Rules Amendment No.4) (Criminal Procedure (Amendment) (Scotland) Act 2004) 2004 (SSI 2004/434), r.2 (effective October 4, 2004).

Forms of execution of service

2.6.—(1) The execution of service of a citation and notice to appear of a person accused on indictment referred to in rule 8.2(1) (citation of accused and witnesses) shall be in Form 2.6-A.

(1A) The execution of a citation of a person accused on indictment referred to in rule 8.2(1A) (citation of accused by affixing a notice) shall be in Form 2.6-AA.

(2) The execution of service of a complaint on an accused shall be in Form 2.6-B.

(2A) The execution of a citation of an accused referred to in rule 16.1(2A) (citation of accused by affixing a notice) shall be in Form 2.6-BA.

(3) The execution of personal service of a citation of a witness cited to appear at a trial on indictment shall be in Form 2.6-C.

(4) The execution of personal service of a citation of a witness cited to appear at a trial on summary complaint shall be in Form 2.6-D.

(5) The execution of a citation referred to in—

(a) rule 20.3(2) or (3) (supervised release orders: form of citation of offender) shall be in Form 2.6-EA;

(b) rule 20.10(2) or (3) (probation orders: forms of citation of probationer) shall be in Form 2.6-EB;

(c) rule 20.11(3) or (4) (supervised attendance orders: forms of citation of offender) shall be in Form 2.6-EC;

(d) rule 20.12(2) (community service orders: forms of citation of offender) shall be in Form 2.6-ED;

(e) rule 20.12A(3) or (4) (restriction of liberty orders: forms of citation of offender) shall be in Form 2.6-EE;

(f) rule 20.12B(2) or (3) (drug treatment and testing orders: forms of citation of offender) shall be in Form 2.6-EF; and

(g) rule 20.12C(2) or (3) (community reparation orders: forms of citation of offender) shall be in Form 2.6-EG.

(6) The execution of a citation or service under rule 2.3(1) (general provisions for service) shall, with the necessary modifications, be in Form 2.6-F.

(7) The execution of service of documents under rule 2.2A (citation in solemn proceedings by service on solicitor) or rule 2.3A (service etc. on accused through a solicitor) shall be in Form 2.6-G.

AMENDMENT

Rule 2.6(7) inserted by the Act of Adjournal (Criminal Procedure Rules Amendment) (Criminal Procedure (Amendment) (Scotland) Act) 2005 (SSI 2005/44), r.2(6) (subject to r.2(2)–(4)) (effective February 1, 2005).

Rule 2.6(5) as amended by the Act of Adjournal (Criminal Procedure Rules Amendment No.2) (Miscellaneous) 2005 (SSI 2005/160), r.2 (effective March 31, 2005).

Proof of service furth of Scotland

2.7. Where any citation of an accused is served in England, Wales or Northern Ireland by an officer effecting such service in accordance with section 39(3) of the Criminal Law Act 1977 (citation of person charged with crime or offence to appear before a court in Scotland), the evidence of—

(a) that officer on oath, or

(b) written execution of service by him,

shall be sufficient evidence of that service.

AMENDMENTS

Rules 2.2, 2.3 and 2.6 as amended by the Act of Adjournal (Criminal Procedure Rules Amendment No.2) (Miscellaneous) 2003 (SSI 2003/468), r.2. Brought into force on October 27, 2003 in accordance with art.1.

GENERAL NOTE

Chapter 2 deals with the appropriate modes of service of any document which, under the 1995 Act or the 1996 Rules, requires to be served on accused, witnesses, jurors or other persons to whom notice must be given. Separate rules are provided for service on the Crown as represented by the Lord Advocate in solemn proceedings or the procurator fiscal in sheriff and jury trials and summary proceedings; for service on accused persons charged on indictment; and for service on accused persons in summary proceedings and for all witnesses (who should, in the first instance, be served by post).

This chapter is concerned with how service is to be effected on accused persons, whether natural or legal, and not with whether certain persons are amenable to criminal prosecution. In summary procedure, s.143 of the 1995 Act makes provision for prosecution of legal persons including legal non-persons. Partnerships (including limited liability partnerships: see s.1(2) of the Limited Liability Partnerships Act 2000), unincorporated associations, companies and bodies of trustees may be prosecuted by way of summary procedure. When this is to be done, these entities are to be cited in "their corporate capacity" (1995 Act, s.143(2); see *Aitkenhead v Fraser* [2006] HCJAC 51; 2006 S.L.T. 711; 2006 S.C.C.R. 411) although proceedings may also be taken against specified individuals of the partnership, association or company (but not trustees) and in such a case the offence shall be deemed to be the offence of the partnership, association or company (s.143(3)).

So far as solemn proceedings are concerned, s.70 of the 1995 Act makes special provision for service of indictments on "bodies corporate" and specifies special rules which are adapted to accommodate the non-natural character of the corporate accused (such as appearance, representation and tendering of pleas). The forebear of s.70 has been held to apply to firms (see *Mackay Bros v Gibb*, 1969 J.C. 26; *Douglas v Phoenix Motors*, 1970 S.L.T. (Sh. Ct.) 57). The High Court has also expressed the tentative opinion that the rules prescribed by s.143 for bodies of trustees would be likely "to apply equally to cases on indictment against trustees" (*Aitkenhead v Fraser*, 2006 S.L.T. 711 (para.6); see Ferguson, "Trusts and criminal liability", 2006 S.L.T. (News) 175).

The Crown

Rule 2.1 repeats the terms of r.166 of the 1988 Rules with the omission, however, of reference to the Act of Adjournal as being itself a rule of law but it is thought that no significance can be attached to that omission. Accordingly, when an application is made, for example, under r.4.1(1) to alter the accused's address specified in his bail order, service of the application should be made in accordance with r.2.1. Failure by a sheriff clerk to give notice to the procurator fiscal under r.4.1(5) of the accused's new bail address would justify an extension of the 12 month period under s.65(3) if the Crown encountered difficulties in effecting service of the indictment (see *Black v HM Advocate*, 1990 S.C.C.R. 609). Unlike r.166 of the 1988 Rules, r.2.1(b) expressly refers to the district court now.

It is specifically provided that the provisions in r.2.1 have no application to service on the "relevant authority" (i.e. the Lord Advocate, where appropriate, and the Advocate General for Scotland) of minutes which seek to raise devolution issues in terms of Part I of Schedule 6 to the Scotland Act 1998 (c.46): see r.40.1(3). In such cases the relevant provisions are set out in rr.40.2, 40.3 and 40.4 (which includes proceedings for contempt of court: Practice Note of May 6, 1999 (see C1.14, *infra*)).

Service of indictment, Notice of previous convictions, etc.

Section 66(2) provides that the execution of the citation against an accused in solemn proceedings shall be in such form as may be prescribed by Act of Adjournal, or as nearly as may be in such form. The indictment should be served by an officer of law who must be a macer, messenger-at-arms, sheriff officer or other officer having authority to execute a warrant of court; any constable and any other person employed by the appropriate chief constable under s.9 of the Police (Scotland) Act 1967 for the assistance of constables and who has been authorised by the chief constable to effect service and execution of documents; any person or class of persons authorised to effect service and execution by the Lord Advocate or Secretary of State; and any prison officer when the accused is in prison (see s.307(1) of the 1995 Act). Three principal modes of service are provided: (1) personal service on the accused wherever he is found within the jurisdiction; (2) service at his bail address on a family member who must be an occupier of that address, or an occupier such as a tenant of that address, or an employee. It is submitted that reference to employee is reference to the accused's employee or an employee of a member of the accused's family or of an occupier of that address and is not restricted to the accused's domestic servants; (3) leaving the document attached to the door or behind the door at the accused's bail address. This list (which is identical to r.167 of the 1988 Rules) is exhaustive of the manner of citation and (3) is apt when no family member, occupier or appropriate employee is present. A fourth manner of citation is also specified (in r.2.2(2)(3)) but applies only where there is no bail address and the accused is not on remand in respect of the charges in the indictment.

Once an accused has been granted bail on condition inter alia that he reside at a specified address, that address is the accused's "proper domicile of citation" and can only be altered with the leave of the sheriff under s.25(2) of the 1995 Act (see Chapter 4). The Appeal Court has explained that the "whole point" of the bail address being specified by the court in the bail order granted under ss.24 and 25 of the 1995 Act is that it then becomes the address at which the accused may be cited to appear (see *Brown v HM Advocate*, 1998 S.L.T. 971). The Crown is therefore under no obligation to look behind the address and thus, if the accused has given the incorrect address on being admitted to bail, he cannot later found on that fact to complain of defective citation when resisting the Crown's application for an extension of the 12-month period. Service will be validly effected on the accused at that address whether or not it is the accused's correct address (see *Reilly v HM Advocate*, 1995 S.C.C.R. 45). Moreover,r.2.2(b) has been held to give an option to the Crown as to how service might be effected and service of an indictment at the accused's bail address was held to be valid even though by the time of service the accused had been arrested and detained in prison on unrelated charges (see *Jamieson v HM Advocate*, 1990 S.L.T. 845).

However, where the proper domicile of citation has ceased to exist because it has been demolished, unless the accused has been permitted to alter his domicile of citation under s.25(2) of the 1995 Act, the correct course for the Crown to take is to affix the indictment and citation to "the nearest place as could reasonably be regarded as the equivalent" of that address (see *Welsh v HM Advocate*, 1986 S.C.C.R. 233). The Crown is not entitled to rely on r.2.2(2)(d)(ii) and put the service copy through the letterbox of the residence to which the police have subsequently come to understand the accused has removed. That is because that particular rule is intended to cover cases where the sheriff court has not specified a domicile of citation (e.g. where the accused has never appeared on petition). Since the bail address has not been altered, it remains—even though no longer physically in existence—the proper domicile of citation (see *HM Advocate v Holbein* (unreported), December 15, 2004 (para.7)).

Service generally

In practice an accused in summary proceedings, as well as witnesses in both solemn and summary proceedings, will be cited in accordance with the rules relating to citation in summary proceedings under s.141 of the 1995 Act. Effective citation is achieved by (1) delivering the citation to the accused or witness personally wherever he is found within the jurisdiction; or (2) leaving it for that person at his dwelling-house or place of business with a resident or employee at that place; or (3) where that person has no known dwelling-house or place of business, at any other place in which he may be resident at the time (see e.g. *HM Advocate v Finlay*, 1998 S.C.C.R. 103). In *Garrow v HM Advocate*, 1999 S.L.T. 1202 the Appeal Court held that s.66(3) of the 1995 Act did not operate to interfere with the right of the Crown to proceed by the traditional means of personal citation of witnesses in solemn cases. Rule 2.2 provided a variety of methods for service of a citation of a witness and all such methods were usually available subject to the qualification in r.2.4 that citation might, in the first instance, be by post. It is a matter for the Crown but once postal service has failed they are obliged next to attempt personal citation. When an accused person following upon his conviction on indictment is placed on probation and either fails to comply with the requirement of his probation order (see s.232 of the 1995 Act) or commits a further offence during the probation period (see s.233 of the 1995 Act), citation to attend a diet in respect of breach of his probation order should also be as aforesaid. However, when a witness has been cited to a diet under a warrant from the sheriff in order for his precognition to be taken on oath, personal service is required no doubt because an execution of personal service is the best evidence that a witness knew of the diet and his obligation to attend and such knowledge is essential to proof of guilt on a charge of failing to attend under s.291(2) of the 1995 Act.

Postal service

Postal service is a most cost-effective means of service and r.2.5 provides the types of postal service which are valid and makes express the rule that the date of receipt of a citation through the post is not the date of citation (see *Lockhart v Bradley*, 1977 S.L.T. 5). Where postal service has been selected in respect of a witness but has been ineffective, r.2.4(2) requires that personal service be thereafter attempted. Repeated attempts at postal service are irrelevant. Thus where, for example, the defence maintain at a trial diet that an essential witness is absent and has not been successfully served with a citation by post, the court will be entitled to refuse an adjournment if the defence has failed to attempt personal service and has simply attempted postal service again.

CHAPTER 3

COURT RECORDS

Books of Adjournal

3.1.—(1) The Edinburgh Book of Adjournal and the Book of Adjournal for cases heard outwith Edinburgh shall respectively contain—

   (a) in the case of a trial in the High Court—
       (i) the record copy of the indictment;
      (ii) the minute of proceedings prepared by the Clerk of Justiciary;
     (iii) the relative printed list of assize;
   (b) in the case of a petition to the High Court—
       (i) the record copy of the petition;
      (ii) the minute of proceedings prepared by the Clerk of Justiciary;

(2) The Edinburgh Book of Adjournal shall contain the Acts of Adjournal.

(3) The minute of proceedings referred to in paragraph (1) shall be signed by the Clerk of Justiciary; and, on being so signed, shall have effect and shall be treated for all purposes, including extracts, as a true and sufficient record of the proceedings to which it relates.

Form of minuting in solemn proceedings

3.2. Subject to the provisions of any other enactment, the forms of minuting in solemn proceedings before the sheriff shall be in accordance with the forms used in the High Court.

Interlocutors in High Court to be signed by clerk of court

3.3. In the High Court, an interlocutor shall be distinctly minuted or entered in the record, and that entry shall be signed by the clerk of court.

Record copies of indictments etc. to be inserted in record books

3.4.—(1) The record copies of indictments brought before the High Court, and the record copies of all printed proceedings in that court, shall be inserted in the books of adjournal, either at their proper place in the body of such books, or at the end of the volume in which the relative procedure is recorded (in which case they shall be distinctly referred to as so appended); and the books of adjournal so made up and completed shall be and be taken to be and be used as the books of adjournal of that court.

(2) Where an indictment in solemn proceedings in a sheriff court is either wholly or partly printed, a copy of it, either wholly or partly printed, shall be inserted in the record book of court, either in its proper place in the body of that book or at the end of the volume in which the relative procedure is recorded (in which case it shall be distinctly referred to as so appended).

Form of recording warrants for remission of sentences

3.5. The Clerk of Justiciary shall cause all warrants under the royal sign manual for remission of sentences received by him to be bound in volumes and indexed, and a note of each warrant referring to a High Court sentence shall be entered in the margin of the minute book opposite the case to which it relates.

Registers kept by High Court

3.5A. Any register kept by the High Court, whether or not under or by virtue of these Rules, may be kept either—
   (a) in documentary form; or
   (b) in electronic form (that is to say in a form accessible only by electronic means).

Custody and transmission of records

3.6.—(1) Subject to the following provisions of this rule, the records of the High Court shall, after the Keeper of the Records of Scotland and the Clerk of Justiciary have consulted as to what records or parts of them may first be destroyed as not being considered to have a value for legal purposes or for historical or other research, be transmitted to the Keeper of the Records of Scotland under arrangements to be agreed between him and the Clerk of Justiciary.

(2) The Clerk of Justiciary and the Keeper of the Records of Scotland shall arrange for such transmissions at intervals of not less than five years nor more than 10 years from the date of the immediately preceding transmission and after similar consultation, for such periods as may be deemed by them to be appropriate.

(3) The Lord Justice General or Lord Justice-Clerk may make a direction from time to time in relation to the retention, disposal, transmission or destruction by the Clerk of Justiciary of any document or category of document in the records of the High Court.

AMENDMENT

Rule 3.5A inserted by the Act of Adjournal (Criminal Procedure Rules Amendment No. 3) 1999 (SI 1999/1387), para.2(3) (effective May 19, 1999).

Rule 3.1 as amended by Act of Adjournal (Criminal Procedure Rules Amendment No.2) (Miscellaneous) 2003 (SSI 2003/468), r.2. Brought into force on October 27, 2003 in accordance with art.1.

GENERAL NOTE

Chapter 3 provides mainly for the administration of the court records of the High Court but also assimilates the sheriff court to the High Court in respect of the forms of minuting to be employed in proceedings on indictment.

Rule 3.1

The rule retains the historic distinction between sittings of the High Court at Edinburgh and circuits of the High Court outside the capital. The books of record in the High Court were described (see *Green's Encyclopaedia of the Laws of Scotland*, Vol. 8, *s.v.* "Justiciary, High Court of", para.1496) as consisting of the Minute Book written in court by the clerk of court and the Books of Adjournal. A full and correct copy of the minute book at Edinburgh was written out and bound with relative principal indictments and petitions in an appendix. This volume was known as the "Books of Adjournal" (*Encyclopaedia, supra*, para.1501). This rule now seems of only historic significance because of the computerisation of High Court records. When an accused now pleads guilty he has to sign a sheet of paper attesting to that fact because there is no physical Minute Book for him to sign.

Rule 3.1(1)(b)

Provides for petitions which can either be heard by a single judge of the High Court as in a petition under r.15.11(1)(b) (application to suspend *ad interim* a disqualification imposed by the High Court pending determination of an appeal against sentence) or be heard by a quorum of judges of the High Court as in a petition to the *nobile officium*. Historically the record of proceedings of the High Court in its appellate jurisdiction was kept under the title "Justiciary Appeal Book" and a separate minute book was kept for solemn criminal appeals (which were heard under the Criminal Justice (Scotland) Act 1926) (*Encyclopaedia, supra*, para.1504). No provision is made in r.3.1 for court records relating to appeals (*e.g.* stated cases, bills of suspension or advocation, notes of appeal against decisions on competency or relevancy or in respect of conviction on indictment) which are all heard by the High Court sitting in its appellate capacity. Rule 15.1(1) does however provide that the Clerk of Justiciary shall keep a register of all cases in which he receives intimation of intention to appeal in solemn proceedings or in which notes of appeal are lodged under s.108 by the Crown against unduly lenient sentences or under s.106 by the accused who has been granted leave by the High Court to appeal against his conviction and/or sentence in solemn proceedings under s.107.

Rule 3.1(2)

Confirms the historic practice of inserting all Acts of Adjournal in the Books of Adjournal kept for sittings of the High Court at Edinburgh.

Rule 3.1(3)

"[H]ave effect and shall be treated for all purposes ... as a true ... record": it is unclear whether this rule entails, for example, that the summary of proceedings, if it incorrectly recorded a sentence, would take precedence over a judge's report to the High Court setting out the sentence which he actually imposed. Section 299(4)(b) empowers the High Court on appeal, when it becomes aware of an erroneous entry in the record of the proceedings, to remit the proceedings to the court of first instance for correction. It is however suggested that r.3.1(3) is not intended to alter the import of s.299(4)(b) and that the summary of proceedings is true only when the High Court considers that it is accurate.

Rule 3.2

Minuting is the recording of the significant details of the proceedings such as the place, date, judge's name, the Crown and Defence Counsel's name, whether a plea has been taken to the competency or relevancy of the indictment or proceedings, the jury members, the verdict, the sentence, etc. Form 3.1-A is the form of summary of the proceedings prescribed for High Court trials by r.3.1(1)(a)(ii) and should accordingly be employed in sheriff and jury trials also.

Rule 3.3

The term "interlocutor" is not defined in s.307(1) of the 1995 Act notwithstanding the fact that s.124(2) of the 1995 Act reproduces ss.262 and 281 of the 1975 Act and declares that "every interlocutor and sentence pronounced by the High Court ... shall be final and conclusive". The High Court has observed that "it is not the practice of the High Court in appeals under solemn procedure to issue interlocutors signed by the presiding judge" (*Perrie, Petitioner*, 1992 S.L.T. 655 at 657J; 1991 S.C.C.R. 475 at 480L; and *Boyle, Petitioner*, 1993 S.L.T. 1085 at 1088I–J) although in petitions to the *nobile officium* interlocutors are pronounced, presumably on the view that such petitions are proceedings *sui generis* and neither solemn nor summary in character (see *Express Newspapers plc, Petitioners*, 1999 S.L.T. 644 (Five Judges)). The reference to "interlocutor" has been described as unfortunate (see *Windsor, Petitioner*, 1994 S.L.T. 604 at 612H; 1994 S.C.C.R. 59 at 69C, *per* Lord Sutherland) but it was accepted in both *Perrie* and *Windsor* that "interlocutor" in s.262 (1995 Act, s.124(2)) covers any judgment or order pronounced by the High Court (*cf. Church v H.M. Advocate*, 1996 S.C.C.R. 29 at 31A-B) but does not include a notice of determination under s.120(4) of the 1995 Act of an appeal given by the Clerk of Justiciary. Where there is conflict between the notice of determination and the opinion of the court, the opinion is the best evidence of what was decided by the court (see, *Boyle, Petitioner*, *supra*). A minimum recommendation in a mandatory life sentence case is not an "interlocutor" (see *Draper, Petitioner*, 1996 S.C.C.R. 324). In *Heywood, Petitioner*, 1998 G.W.D. 13–639, it was held that the interlocutor pronounced in open court in a summary appeal was the court's order and that the document subsequently issued by the Clerk of Justiciary was merely the record of the interlocutor. Accordingly it is unnecessary to seek rectification of the record when the order pronounced in open court accurately expresses the court's decision in the appeal although for the avoidance of doubt, such rectification can be granted.

Prior to the radical reforms of criminal procedure effected by the Criminal Procedure (Scotland) Act 1887, it was the practice of the High Court sitting as a trial court to issue interlocutors (*e.g.* sustaining the relevancy of the indictment or repelling the defences, before remitting the libel to "the knowledge of the assize") but now orders pronounced by the High Court as a trial court are not generally termed "interlocutors". Practice does, however, vary on occasion. For example, at present where the trial court appoints a hearing on an accused's minute for postponement of the forthcoming trial diet in terms of s.80 of the 1995 Act, the order assigning the diet is recorded as an interlocutor.

It is unclear what the effect of a total failure to comply with r.3.3 would be in appeal proceedings. So far as minuting of adjournments at first instance from day to day (outwith a sitting of the court) is concerned, the rule is that this must be done in order to preserve the instance (Renton and Brown, *Criminal Procedure* (6th ed.), paras 18–17 and 21–13), either before the expiry of midnight on the day of the adjournment or, perhaps, before the case next calls in court (see *Pettigrew v Ingram*, 1982 S.L.T. 435; *Heywood v Stewart*, 1992 S.L.T. 1106). This rule of the common law requires that the adjournment be to a fixed time and place. If the minute is not signed it is held to be no minute at all (*McLean v Falconer* (1895) 22 R. (J.) 39; 1 Adam 564) and the instance falls at midnight on the day of the purported adjournment. This rule applies only to trial proceedings because diets in appeal proceedings are not peremptory (see Notes to r.15.9) but if the minute in, for example, a Crown bill of advocation, is not signed, is the effect the same? It is suggested that it is not; the rule, though couched in mandatory terms, is directory only and does not entail that the Crown appeal fails.

Rule 3.4(1)

This rule confirms the practice of the High Court as to the inclusion of record copies of indictments in the Books of Adjournal (see, note on r.3.1, above).

Rule 3.4(2)

This rule applies the High Court practice in respect of indictments to the record books of the sheriff court.

Rule 3.5

Where a convicted person has successfully petitioned for the exercise of Her Majesty's Mercy his sentence is remitted (though his conviction stands: *H.M. Advocate v Waddell*, 1976 S.L.T. (Notes) 61). The more common name now for such remission of sentence is a royal pardon which is only granted where there is no other remedy for rectifying a miscarriage of justice (see *Stair Memorial Encyclopaedia of the Laws of Scotland*, "Criminal Procedure", paras 1.54 and 8.73). The fact that a sentence has been remitted is to be recorded in the appropriate minute book. The rule apparently envisages that only High Court sentences will be remitted as no reference is made to sheriff court sentences.

Rule 3.6

Not all records or proceedings in the High Court are of legal or historical interest and only those which can be considered to be in one or other of these two categories will be preserved by the Keeper of the Records of Scotland.

PART II

GENERAL

CHAPTER 4

BAIL

Application to alter address in bail order

4.1.—(1) An application under section 25(2) of the Act of 1995 (alteration of address specified in the order granting bail) shall—

(a) include the following information—

    (i) identification of the proceedings in which the order was made;

    (ii) details of the new address; and

    (iii) reasons for the proposed change of address; and

(b) be served on—

    (i) the clerk of the court which made the order; and

    (ii) the prosecutor.

(2) The prosecutor shall, within seven days of receipt of the copy of the application, notify the clerk of court in writing whether or not he intends to oppose the application.

(3) Where the prosecutor notifies the clerk of court that he does not intend to oppose the application, the court shall proceed to dispose of the application and may do so in the absence of the applicant.

(4) Where the prosecutor notifies the clerk of court that he intends to oppose the application, the clerk of court shall arrange a hearing before the court in chambers at which the applicant and the prosecutor may appear or be represented.

(5) The clerk of court shall give notice in writing of the decision of the court on an application referred to in paragraph (1) to—

(a) the applicant;

(b) the prosecutor; and

(c) any co-accused.

(6) Where—

(a) the application is made by a witness who has been granted bail under section 90B(1)(b) of the Act of 1995; and

(b) the warrant to apprehend the witness under section 90A(1) of the Act of 1995 was issued on the application of a party other than the prosecutor, paragraphs (1) to (5) shall also apply to that party as they apply to the prosecutor.

AMENDMENT

Rule 4.1(6) inserted by the Act of Adjournal (Criminal Procedure Rules Amendment) (Criminal Procedure (Amendment) (Scotland) Act) 2005 (SSI 2005/44), r.2(7) (subject to r.2(2)–(4)) (effective February 1, 2005).

GENERAL NOTE

Apart from previous convictions, the most important factor in the refusal of bail in most cases is the suitability of the accused's bail address which becomes his "domicile of citation" under s.25(1)(b) of the 1995 Act. For accused persons the bail address is the place at which service of most documents is effected. That has been described as "the whole point" of the bail address being specified in the bail order granted to the accused (see *Brown v H.M. Advocate*, 1998 S.L.T. 971 at 973, *per* Lord Justice General Rodger). Accordingly, alteration of the bail address can only be effected with leave of the sheriff. All applications for alteration in the bail address must be served on both the clerk of the court which made the order and the procurator fiscal of the appropriate sheriff court district. The procurator fiscal is entitled to oppose the application and, if he does so, the sheriff will hear the application in chambers. It is imperative that an alteration in the bail address should be intimated to the Crown and any co-accused since they require to be advised of the new bail address at which documents should be served. Failure to give the Crown notice of the alteration of the bail address can have serious consequences under s.65(3) of the 1995 Act for the accused (see, *e.g. Black v H.M. Advocate*, 1990 S.C.C.R. 609).

CHAPTER 5

JUDICIAL EXAMINATION

Procedure in examination

5.1. Subject to the following provisions of this Chapter, the procedure to be followed in relation to examination of the accused under sections 35 to 39 of the Act of 1995 (which relate to judicial examination) on any charge shall be in accordance with existing law and practice.

Record of examination

5.2.—(1) The record of all proceedings under the sections of the Act of 1995 mentioned in rule 5.1 (procedure in examination) shall be kept by the sheriff clerk in Form 5.2, and shall be kept by him with the petition containing the charge or charges in respect of which the accused is brought before the sheriff for examination.

(2) The sheriff clerk shall transmit to the prosecutor a certified copy of the petition under section 34 of the Act of 1995 (petition for warrant) and the record of proceedings—

(a) in relation to proceedings at which the accused is liberated in due course of law, on the conclusion of those proceedings; and

(b) in relation to any further examination, on the conclusion of that examination.

Verbatim record

5.3.—(1) Where the prosecutor provides a shorthand writer for the purposes of section 37(1) of the Act of 1995 (verbatim record of proceedings), the shorthand writer shall be—

(a) a person recognised by a court as a shorthand writer for the purposes of section 93 of the Act of 1995 (record of trial) or rule 29.18 of Schedule 1 to the Sheriff Courts (Scotland) Act 1907 (recording of evidence); or

(b) a person, other than a person mentioned in sub-paragraph (a) of this paragraph, who is skilled in the writing of shorthand (whether or not in the service of the prosecutor).

(2) In proceedings where a verbatim record is made by a person mentioned in paragraph (1)(b), a tape-recorded record of the proceedings shall also be made by the sheriff clerk in accordance with rule 5.4(1) and (2) (use of tape recorders).

(3) The name and address of the shorthand writer or the person recording the questions, answers and declarations by mechanical means shall be recorded in the record of proceedings.

(4) The shorthand writer shall record the whole proceedings relating to—

(a) the emitting by the accused of a declaration under section 35(4) of the Act of 1995; and

(b) any questions the accused is asked and any answers given including his declining to answer, under section 35(5) (accused brought before sheriff for further examination), or section 36 (judicial examination: questioning by prosecutor), of the Act of 1995.

(5) The shorthand writer shall not include in the transcript he makes of the proceedings any questions disallowed by the sheriff and any answers to such questions.

(6) The shorthand writer shall, in addition to the transcript of proceedings he makes under paragraph (4), also make such further transcript of the record made by him as either the judge at a first diet or, as the case may be, preliminary diet, or the High Court of Justiciary on an appeal, may direct for the purposes of considering an application under section 278(2) of the Act of 1995 (application that record of judicial examination not be read or be held inadmissible).

(7) The shorthand writer shall, as soon as possible after the conclusion of the proceedings, deliver to the prosecutor the transcript signed and certified by him in accordance with section 37(4)(b) of the Act of 1995.

Use of tape recorders

5.4.—(1) Any tape-recorded record of the proceedings made under rule 5.3(2), shall be made on two separate tapes simultaneously which shall be marked (and in this rule referred to as) "tape A" and "tape B" respectively.

(2) The sheriff clerk shall record on both tapes any proceedings mentioned in rule 5.3(5) (questions disallowed by sheriff), and for the purposes of maintaining a continuous record of the proceedings on both tapes, the proceedings may be interrupted at the instance of the sheriff clerk for such reasonable period as he may require.

(3) The sheriff clerk shall note in the record of proceedings the time of commencement and the time of termination of the tape-recording.

(4) On the conclusion of the proceedings in question, the sheriff clerk shall—

(a) cause tape A to be sealed in an envelope or other similar container on which the following information shall be endorsed—

(i) the name of the accused;

(ii) the date of examination;

(iii) the name of the presiding sheriff;

(iv) the name of the shorthand writer;

(v) the time of commencement and of termination of the tape; and

(vi) the time and date of sealing of the tape; and

(b) deliver tape B to the prosecutor.

(5) The sheriff clerk shall retain tape A until he is informed in writing by the prosecutor that the proceedings against the accused in respect of the charge or charges in relation to which he was examined have come to an end.

(6) The sheriff clerk shall not permit the seal on the container of tape A to be broken while he retains it except on being authorised to do so by a judge.

(7) On being so authorised the sheriff clerk shall only permit such access to tape A for such period as may be required for the purposes of the authorisation and, on the expiry of that period, shall again comply with the requirements of paragraphs (4)(a) and (5).

(8) The sheriff clerk shall, on being informed in writing by the prosecutor that the proceedings mentioned in paragraph (5) have come to an end, return tape A to the prosecutor.

(9) For the purposes of paragraph (8), the circumstances in which the proceedings have come to an end include—

(a) a decision by the prosecutor to take no further action against the accused in respect of the charge in question;

(b) following conviction and sentence of the accused in respect of the charge in question, the expiry of any statutory period of appeal without an appeal being taken; and

(c) the final disposal of any appeal which has been taken.

Questions by prosecutor

5.5—(1) The sheriff before whom the accused is brought for examination shall, if the prosecutor proposes to ask the accused questions regarding the alleged making by the accused of an extrajudicial confession to which section 36(3) of the Act of 1995 (confession in the hearing of constable) applies, be provided by the prosecutor before the commencement of the examination with a copy of the written record of the confession allegedly made.

(2) If the sheriff has not been provided with the written record required under paragraph (1), the prosecutor shall not ask the accused any such questions.

(3) The accused shall not be put on oath in the course of any proceedings on examination.

(4) The judge presiding at the trial of an accused who has declined to answer any question under section 36(1) of the Act of 1995 (prosecutor's questions as to matters in the charge or as to confession or declaration) may, in determining whether his having so declined may be commented upon by virtue of section 36(8) of the Act of 1995 (comments at trial), have regard to the terms of the charge to which the question related.

(5) The petition containing the terms of the charge to which the question referred to in paragraph (4) related, or a copy of the petition certified by the sheriff clerk as such, shall be sufficient evidence of the terms of that charge for the purposes of that paragraph; but the petition or a certified copy of the petition need not be included in any list of productions made available at the trial.

(6) The prosecutor shall, if the presiding judge proposes to have regard to the terms of that charge for the purposes of paragraph (4), provide the presiding judge with the petition or certified copy of the petition referred to in paragraph (5).

Rectification of errors in transcript

5.6.—(1) A notice served under section 38(1)(a) of the Act of 1995 (notice of error or incompleteness in transcript) shall be in Form 5.6-A.

(2) The prosecutor shall, on serving or receiving such a notice, immediately lodge with the sheriff clerk the transcript certified in accordance with section 37(4)(b) of the Act of 1995.

(3) An application to the sheriff under section 38(1)(b) of the Act of 1995 (rectification of error or incompleteness) shall be in Form 5.6-B.

(4) The application referred to in paragraph (3) shall be lodged with the sheriff clerk with—

(a) a copy of the notice served under section 38(1)(a) of the Act of 1995; and

(b) an execution of service of that notice.

(5) Where the person on whom notice is served under section 38(1)(a) of the Act of 1995 agrees with the opinion to which that notice relates—

(a) he may intimate his agreement in Form 5.6-C to the person serving notice; and

(b) he shall, at the same time as intimating his agreement, send a copy of that form to the sheriff clerk.

(6) On the lodging of an application under paragraph (3), the sheriff shall, unless he dispenses with a hearing, by an order endorsed on the application—

(a) fix a date for a hearing; and

(b) order intimation of the date of the hearing to be made by the sheriff clerk to the prosecutor and to the accused person to whose examination the transcript relates.

(7) Where the sheriff authorises rectification of the transcript, he shall by an order endorsed on the application and signed by him specify the rectification authorised.

(8) The sheriff clerk shall give effect to any authorised rectification by amending the signed and certified transcript in accordance with the terms of the order of the sheriff and by initialling any amendment.

(9) On making any such amendment, the sheriff clerk shall—

(a) attach to the rectified transcript a copy of the order of the sheriff certified by the sheriff clerk;

(b) return the rectified transcript to the prosecutor;

(c) retain the application for rectification and the order of the sheriff made in respect of the application; and

(d) attach the documents mentioned in sub-paragraph (c) of this paragraph to the record of proceedings mentioned in rule 5.2 (record of examination).

Alteration of time limits by sheriff

5.7. Any direction made by the sheriff under section 37(7)(a) of the Act of 1995 (modifications as to time limits) shall be entered in the record of proceedings mentioned in rule 5.2 (record of examination) and authenticated by the sheriff subscribing his signature.

Postponement of trial diet by sheriff

5.8.—(1) The sheriff shall not make an order under section 37(7)(b) of the Act of 1995 (postponement of trial diet) in respect of a case set down for trial in the High Court.

(2) Any order by a sheriff under section 37(7)(b) of the Act of 1995 in a case not set down for trial in the High Court shall be—

(a) endorsed on the record copy of the indictment;

(b) authenticated by the signature of the sheriff; and

(c) intimated—

    (i) by the prosecutor to any co-accused by serving on him an intimation of postponement in Form 5.8; and

    (ii) by the sheriff clerk to the governor of any institution in which any co-accused is detained.

Postponement of trial diet by High Court

5.9.—(1) If the sheriff considers that it may be appropriate to make an order under section 37(7)(b) of the Act of 1995 (postponement of trial diet) in respect of a case set down for trial in the High Court, he shall report the circumstances (including the making of any direction under section 37(7)(a) (modifications as to time limits)) to the Clerk of Justiciary.

(2) The Clerk of Justiciary, on receiving the report of the sheriff, shall—

(a) fix a diet (to which the trial diet shall be treated as being postponed) for the determination by a single judge of the High Court of the diet to which the trial shall be postponed; and

(b) intimate that diet to the prosecutor, the accused and the governor of any institution in which any accused is detained.

(3) The single judge of the High Court, in determining the diet to which the trial shall be postponed, shall have regard to the terms of the report of the sheriff.

Alteration of time limits by High Court

5.10.—(1) An application to the High Court for a direction to extend a time limit referred to in section 37(9) of the Act of 1995 shall be made by petition.

(2) A petition under paragraph (1) shall be intimated to the other party and lodged with a certificate of intimation with the sheriff clerk.

(3) The sheriff clerk shall, on the lodging of a petition, transmit it to the Clerk of Justiciary with a certified copy of the relative petition and record of proceedings.

(4) A petition under paragraph (1) may be disposed of by a single judge of the High Court.

(5) The Clerk of Justiciary shall, as soon as possible after he receives the petition—

(a) fix a diet for the hearing; and

(b) intimate the diet to the prosecutor and the accused.

(6) The Clerk of Justiciary shall, on the disposal of the petition by the High Court, transmit a certified copy of the order of the High Court to the sheriff clerk.

(7) The sheriff clerk shall, on receiving the certified copy of the order, attach it to the record of proceedings.

GENERAL NOTE

Sections 35 to 39 of the 1995 Act provide at the Crown's discretion for the accused to be judicially examined before the sheriff at his first or subsequent appearance on petition in respect of the charge or charges contained in the petition and in respect of any extra-judicial confession (whether incriminatory in whole or in part) made to or in the hearing of a constable as defined in the Police (Scotland) Act 1967. The accused is also entitled, if he chooses, to emit a declaration made in his own words at such appearance (see *Robertson v H.M. Advocate*, 1994 S.C.C.R. 152 for an example of a declaration being emitted by an accused). Section 36(9) provides that the procedure in relation to judicial examination by the Crown shall be prescribed by Act of Adjournal.

Rule 5.1

Existing law and practice has been established principally since 1980 when judicial examination was reintroduced by the Criminal Justice (Scotland) Act 1980 but the 1995 Act has widened the prosecutor's right to question the accused so that he may now ask the accused whether he admits any or a part of the charge(s). The prosecutor is not entitled to cross-examine the accused or to reiterate questions which the accused has declined to answer. The sheriff's duty is to ensure fairness to the accused and he must advise the accused that he is not obliged to answer any questions but that his failure to do so may be commented on at his trial by the court, the Crown or any co-accused if he has advanced a defence at his trial which he could appropriately have stated but had not stated at judicial examination. It is suggested here that if the sheriff fails to administer this caution to the accused, the answers which the accused gives to questions at judicial examination will be inadmissible in evidence at his trial on the same principle as governs the admissibility of extra-judicial confessions. The accused should also be told by the sheriff that he is entitled to consult his solicitor before answering any questions (although the solicitor is not entitled to intervene either by way of objection to the prosecutor's questions or to volunteer advice to the accused) and that if his answers disclose an ostensible defence, the Crown is under a duty (under s.36(10)) to investigate the defence so far as is reasonably practicable (see s.36(6)). The duty under s.36(10) is administrative in character and requires the Crown to divulge the results of their investigations but only if requested to do so before trial: see *McDermott v. H.M. Advocate*, 2000 S.L.T. 366. It seems unlikely however that a failure to give such advice under s.36(6) will automatically render inadmissible evidence of what was said at judicial examination. An omission of this nature is in an entirely different position from a failure to administer the caution.

Rule 5.2

A certified copy of the petition is crucial to judicial examination as it is the basis on which the prosecutor may question the accused. In the event of comment at the trial being made about the accused's silence or statements at judicial examination, the trial court will require to examine the petition in order to determine the legitimacy of such comment in the light of the charges which the accused originally faced at judicial examination. The certified copy petition need not however be lodged by the Crown and included with the list of productions annexed to the indictment (see r.5.5(5)).

Rule 5.3

Rule 5.3(1) and (2). There is no obligation to record the judicial examination by means of both a shorthand writer and a tape recorder but when a shorthand writer is employed, the sheriff clerk should also operate a tape recorder.

Rule 5.3(4). A declaration by the accused should also be recorded in full: see *Robertson v H.M. Advocate*, 1995 S.C.C.R. 153.

Rule 5.3(7). It is the Crown's duty to serve the transcript of the judicial examination on the accused and a failure to do so precludes use of the transcript as evidence at the trial.

Rule 5.4

When a tape recorder is employed, two tapes should be simultaneously recorded so that Tape A which is retained by the sheriff clerk until the criminal process is concluded, can be used to verify the accuracy of Tape B which is delivered to the Crown.

Rule 5.5

Rule 5.5(1) and (2). If the sheriff does not receive a copy of the extra-judicial confession, no questioning of the accused about it can be permitted at the judicial examination.

Rule 5.5(3). As the accused is not put on oath any untruths told at judicial examination by an accused will not warrant prosecution for perjury although they could warrant a charge of attempting to pervert the course of justice or of perverting the course of justice.

Rule 5.5(4). Section 36(8) of the 1995 Act permits a prosecutor, judge and any co-accused to comment on the accused's having declined to answer a question put to him at judicial examination, only where and in so far as the accused or any of his witnesses in evidence have averred something which could have been stated appropriately in answer to a question which the accused declined to answer at judicial examination. It is here suggested that the judge should be invited by the Crown or counsel for the co-accused, outwith the presence of the jury, to permit comment to be made before adverse comment is in fact made. The 1995 Act does not expressly give to the trial judge a controlling discretion but the rule clearly envisages that the trial judge's permission should be applied for. The procedure followed should accordingly be the same procedure as is followed when the Crown seeks leave of the court to cross-examine an accused on his criminal record. The trial judge's discretion when it is exercised to allow adverse comment to be made on the accused's silence, will be capable of challenge on appeal as a ground for alleging a miscarriage of justice because it has been held that comment should be made only with restraint and without undue emphasis: see *McEwan v H.M. Advocate*, 1992 S.L.T. 317; 1990 S.C.C.R. 401.

Rule 5.6

Section 38 of the 1995 Act permits the sheriff to order rectification of the transcript of the judicial examination if it contains an error or is incomplete. The Crown or the accused must within 10 days of service of the transcript, serve notice on the other party that the Crown or accused considers that there is an error or that the transcript is incomplete. Within 14 days of service of that notice the party seeking rectification must apply to the sheriff for an order rectifying the transcript and the sheriff must within seven days of that application to him hear parties in chambers although, if there is agreement between the Crown and the accused that the transcript is defective the sheriff may dispense with the hearing. There is no appeal against the sheriff's decision which is declared by s.38(4) to be final but presumably that declaration only applies at the pre-trial stage to avoid delay which could be occasioned by appeal and does not prevent the accused from raising the matter in the Appeal Court in the event that he is convicted. It would be odd indeed if the sheriff's decision could not be challenged on the basis that it had caused a miscarriage of justice.

Rules 5.7 and 5.8

Where the time available before trial does not permit the Crown to comply with the requirement in s.36(6) to serve the transcript of the judicial examination on the accused and his solicitor (where appropriate) within 14 days of the judicial examination, or does not allow compliance with the time-limits under s.38(1) (see r.5.6), the sheriff can direct that those time-limits should be modified. In an extreme case the sheriff can also postpone the trial diet under s.37(7)(b) but r.5.8 prohibits such an order when the case is set down for trial in the High Court. The sheriff in such a case must (under r.5.9) report the case to the Clerk of Justiciary so that the High Court can determine whether or not to postpone the trial diet. The sheriff is directed by s.77(8) of the 1995 Act that postponement of the trial diet is incompetent *unless* he considers that modification of the time-limit would not be practicable. Presumably the same consideration applies when the High Court has to determine whether or not the trial diet should be postponed although s.37(8) refers only to sheriffs.

Rule 5.10

Section 37(9) permits the High Court to extend the time-limits referred to in the preceding note. A single judge of the High Court will hear the application which must be made by way of petition. Although no form of petition is provided for by the Rules, it is suggested here that the petition should set forth (i) the name(s) of the accused; (ii) the date of the judicial examination; (iii) the dates of service of the transcript (where appropriate) or service of the notice under s.38(1); (iv) the error or incompleteness which is complained of in the transcript of the judicial examination (where appropriate); (v) the date of the trial diet; and (vi) the circumstances necessitating alteration of the relevant time-limit.

Chapter 6

Proceedings involving Children

Interpretation of this Chapter

6.1. In this Chapter—

"the Act of 1937" means the Children and Young Persons (Scotland) Act 1937;

"court" means the sheriff sitting as a court of summary jurisdiction.

Application of summary procedure

6.2. The procedure in summary proceedings shall apply, in relation to proceedings against a child as it applies to proceedings against an adult, subject to the provisions of the Act of 1937, the Act of 1995 and this Chapter.

Assistance for unrepresented child

6.3.—(1) Where a child is unrepresented in any proceedings, the parent or guardian of the child may assist him in conducting his defence.

(2) Where the parent or guardian of the child cannot be found, or cannot in the opinion of the court reasonably be required to attend, the court may allow a relative or other responsible person to assist the child in conducting his defence.

Procedure in summary proceedings

6.4. In a case where a child is brought before a court on a complaint, the sheriff—

(a) shall explain to the child the substance of the charge in simple language suitable to his age and understanding, and shall then ask the child whether he admits the charge;

(b) if satisfied, after trial or otherwise, that the child has committed an offence, shall so inform the child and—
   (i) the child and his parent, guardian, relative or other responsible person assisting the child, or the person representing the child, shall be given an opportunity to make a statement, and
   (ii) shall obtain such information as to the general conduct, home sur-roundings, school record, health and character of the child as may en-able the sheriff to deal with the case in the best interests of the child and may remand the child for such enquiry as may be necessary; and
(c) if the sheriff considers it necessary in the interests of the child while considering disposal after conviction, may require the parent, guardian, relative or other responsible person assisting the child, or the person representing the child, or the child, as the case may be, to withdraw from the court.

Failure to comply with probation order

6.5.—(1) Any citation requiring the appearance of a child before the court in respect of a failure to comply with a probation order shall be accompanied by a notice—

(a) giving the reasons for the issue of such citation, and
(b) stating in what respects it is alleged that any one or more of the require-ments of the probation order has or have not been complied with by him;

and, in any case where the child has been apprehended without prior citation, such a notice shall be handed to him in court.

(2) On the child appearing in court, the sheriff shall explain to the child in simple language suitable to his age and understanding the effect of the notice, and shall then ask him whether he admits having failed to comply with the require-ments of the probation order as alleged.

(3) Where the child does not admit the alleged failure to comply with the requirements of the probation order, the proceedings shall thereafter be conducted and the matter shall be determined by the court in the same manner as if the same were a matter which had arisen for determination on the original complaint.

Separation of children at sittings

6.6.—(1) The court shall take steps, so far as possible, to prevent children at-tending sittings of the court from mixing with one another.

(2) If this cannot be achieved by holding separate sittings or fixing different hours for the different cases and types of cases coming before it, the court may order additional waiting rooms to be brought into use or may provide for an at-tendant in the waiting room.

Restrictions on reports of proceedings involving children

6.7.—(1) Any direction made by a court under subsection (3)(a) (person under 16 is a witness only) of section 47 (restriction on report of proceedings involving children) of the Act of 1995 shall specify the person in respect of whom the direction is made.

(2) Any direction made by a court under subsection (3)(b) of section 47 of the Act of 1995 (restrictions dispensed with) shall specify the person in respect of whom the direction is made and the extent to which the provisions of the section are dispensed with in relation to that person.

(3) Any such direction shall be pronounced in open court and its terms shall be recorded in the record of proceedings; and the direction as so recorded shall be authenticated by the signature of the clerk of court.

GENERAL NOTE

Sections 41 to 51 of the 1995 Act contain special provisions for cases involving children who are under 16 years of age. Chapter 6 provides rules which relate only to the sheriff court exercising its summary jurisdiction (r. 6.1). Children cannot competently be prosecuted in the district court (see s.42(1)). Section 42(4) provides that for the purpose of enforcing the attendance of a parent or guardian of a child who is being prosecuted, and for enabling the parent or guardian to take part in the conduct of the child's defence and enabling orders to be made against the parent or guardian (see s.45(1)—order that parent or guardian give security for his co-operation in securing his child's good behaviour), rules may be made by Act of Adjournal for applying, with the necessary adaptations and modifications, such of the provisions of the 1995 Act relating to summary procedure as appear appropriate for the purpose. Rule 6.2 provides that the procedures for children are to be the same as the procedures for adults except in so far as the 1995 Act, the Children and Young Persons (Scotland) Act 1937 and Chapter 6 provide different or additional rules.

Rule 6.3

Section 42(2) of the 1995 Act provides that where a child under 16 years is charged, his parent (who is the person having parental responsibilities or parental rights under s.1(3) and s.2(4)respectively of the Children (Scotland) Act 1995) or his guardian having actual possession and control of the child (see s.42(5)) may be required to attend at the court during all stages of the proceedings and, if such parent or guardian can be found and resides within a reasonable distance of the court, he *shall* require to attend. When a child is arrested a warning must be given to the parent or guardian by the police that he should attend at court (see s.42(3)). It is suggested here that the purpose of these provisions is two-fold: (i) to inform the parent or guardian of what is happening to his child, and (ii) to allow him the opportunity to assist his child both in the conduct of his defence in court and in the child being of good behaviour. Rule 6.3(1) obliges the sheriff to allow the parent or guardian to assist in his child's defence but only where his child has no legal representation. Rule 6.3(2) goes further than the 1995 Act because another relative or responsible person can be permitted to assist in the defence even though no requirement to attend court can be made in respect of that relative or responsible person.

Rule 6.4

This rule imposes duties on the sheriff irrespective of whether the child is legally represented or not. It is open to question, however, whether failure to explain the charge, or to afford the parent an opportunity to make a statement, would respectively vitiate conviction or sentence. See *Heywood v. B*, 1993 S.C.C.R. 554. The local authority responsible for the particular sheriff court district will by the stage of conviction have received notification from the chief constable of the area in which the offence was committed, of the day and time when and the nature of the charge on which the child is brought before the court (see s.42(7)). That local authority is placed under a duty (by s.42(8)) to make investigations and to submit a report to the court. The report should deal with the child's home surroundings, school record (which the appropriate education authority is under a duty to supply), health and character.

Rule 6.5

The duties to serve the notice on the child either with the citation or personally and to explain to the child the effect of the notice, are no doubt important but it is open to question whether failure to discharge these duties would necessarily vitiate the proceedings. These duties also apply whether or not the child has legal representation or is accompanied by his parent, guardian, other relative or responsible person.

Rule 6.6

Section 42(9) requires *inter alia* that while a child accused is waiting at court he should be prevented from associating with an adult (not being a relative) who is charged with any offence other than an offence with which the child is jointly charged. This rule applies to all children whether they are witnesses, accused or complainers. When an attendant is required, at least for a child accused, the attendant must be female if the child is female.

Rule 6.7

No newspaper report of any court proceedings should reveal the name, address or school, or include any particulars which are calculated to lead to the identification of the child who is concerned in the proceedings either as an accused or as a witness (see s.47(1)). Furthermore, no picture which is or includes a picture of such a child should be published in a context relevant to the proceedings (see s.47(2)). These restrictions apply *mutatis mutandis* to radio and television broadcasts (see s.47(4)). However, where the child is concerned in the proceedings only as a witness, these restrictions do not apply unless the court so directs (see s.47(3)). The court can also dispense with these restrictions when at any stage in the proceedings it is satisfied that it is in the public interest to lift reporting restrictions. In both the imposing of the restrictions in respect of a child who is a witness only, and the lifting of the restrictions in respect of any child concerned in the proceedings, the order is specific to named individuals.

Article 10(1) of the European Convention on Human Rights guarantees the right to freedom of expression but subject to certain limited qualifications (set out in Art. 10(2)) which must be prescribed by law and necessary in a democratic society. Two such justifications are "the protection of health or morals ... [or] the reputation or rights of others". The effect of European jurisprudence is that when there is a violation of the right, the burden is cast on the violator to show that the restriction is legitimate and proportionate to one of the objects set out in Art. 10(2) such as the protection of the reputation of others. It is for consideration whether the restrictions on press reporting of summary cases involving children as accused are compatible with Art. 10 since they apply a blanket ban on reporting subject to a discretionary power in the court to disapply them on being asked to do so. The press have an interest in asking for the reporting restrictions to be disapplied. No doubt the press could not be prevented from appearing in the course of the proceedings (or even after the conclusion of them?) to ask for the restrictions to be lifted and it may be that they could also invoke the *nobile officium* in order to appeal against a refusal by the court to lift reporting restrictions. See Introduction and General Note at B1–02.

CHAPTER 7

MENTAL DISORDER

Application for assessment orders

7.1.—(1) A written application under—

(a) section 52B(1) of the Act of 1995 (assessment order: prosecutor); or

(b) section 52C(1) of the Act of 1995 (assessment order: Scottish Ministers),

shall be in Form 7.1.

(2) Where an application is made under paragraph (1)—

(a) the court shall appoint a diet for hearing the application; and

(b) the clerk of court shall intimate the diet to the applicant, the person in respect of whom the application is made or the solicitor for that person, the governor of any institution in which the person in respect of whom the application is made is detained and, where the application is by the Scottish Ministers, the prosecutor.

Assessment orders ex proprio motu

7.2. Where the court considers making an assessment order under section 52E of the Act of 1995 (assessment order: *ex proprio motu*) and considers it appropriate to do so—

(a) the court shall appoint a diet for parties to be heard; and

(b) the clerk of court shall intimate the diet to the prosecutor, the person in respect of whom the order may be made or the solicitor for that person, and the governor of any institution in which the person in respect of whom the application is made is detained.

Applications for treatment orders

7.3.—(1) A written application under—

(a) section 52K(1) of the Act of 1995 (treatment order: prosecutor); or

(b) section 52L(1) of the Act of 1995 (treatment order: Scottish Ministers),

shall be in Form 7.3.

(2) Where an application is made under paragraph (1)—

(a) the court shall appoint a diet for hearing the application; and

(b) the clerk of court shall intimate the diet to the applicant, the person in respect of whom the application is made or the solicitor for that person, the governor of any institution in which the person in respect of whom the application is made is detained, and where the application is by the Scottish Ministers, the prosecutor.

Treatment orders ex proprio motu

7.4. Where the court considers making a treatment order under section 52N of the Act of 1995 (treatment order: *ex proprio motu*) and considers it appropriate to do so—

(a) the court shall appoint a diet for parties to be heard; and

(b) the clerk of court shall intimate the diet to the prosecutor, the person in respect of whom the order may be made or the solicitor for that person, and the governor of any institution in which the person in respect of whom the application is made is detained.

Variation of assessment orders or review of treatment orders

7.5. Where the court receives a report under section 52G(9) (report for variation of assessment order) or section 52Q(1) (report for review of treatment order) of the Act of 1995—

(a) the court shall, by interlocutor in Form 7.5, appoint a hearing for parties to be heard and where appropriate, grant warrant to authorised officers of the hospital or officers of law, to bring the offender from the hospital to the court for that diet; and

(b) the clerk of court shall intimate the diet to the prosecutor, the person in respect of whom the order has been made or the solicitor for that person.

Interim compulsion order

7.6.—(1) Subject to paragraph (2), where the court receives a report under section 53B(1) of the Act of 1995 (interim compulsion order)—

(a) the court shall—

(i) by interlocutor in Form 7.6, appoint a hearing for parties to be heard and where appropriate, grant warrant to authorised officers of the hospital or officers of law, to bring the offender from the hospital to the court for that diet;

(ii) discharge the diet already fixed; and

(b) the clerk of court shall intimate the diet to the prosecutor, the person in respect of whom the order has been made or the solicitor for that person.

(2) Where the report referred to in paragraph (1) is received within 14 days before the diet already fixed, paragraph (1) shall not apply.

Assessment, treatment and interim compulsion orders: specified hospital

7.7. Where the court makes a direction under section 52F(1)(b) (assessment order: specified hospital), section 52P(1)(b) (treatment order: specified hospital) or section 53A(1) (interim compulsion order: specified hospital) of the Act of 1995 the court shall send a copy of the direction to the person in respect of whom the order has been made, the solicitor for that person, the prosecutor and the Scottish Ministers.

Compulsion orders and hospital directions: specified hospital

7.8. Where the court makes a direction under 57D(1) (compulsion order: specified hospital) or specifies another hospital in a direction under section 59C(1) (hospital direction: specified hospital) of the Act of 1995 the court shall send a copy of the direction or specification, as the case may be, to the person in respect of whom the order has been made and the solicitor for that person.

Appeals

7.9—(1) An appeal under:

(a) section 62 of the Act of 1995 (appeal by accused in case involving insanity); or

(b) section 63 of the Act of 1995 (appeal by prosecutor in case involving insanity),

shall be made by lodging a note of appeal in Form 7.9.

(2) At the same time as lodging a note of appeal under paragraph (1), the applicant shall send a copy to the other parties.

(3) As soon as possible after the lodging of a note of appeal under paragraph (1), the Clerk of Justiciary shall request a report from the judge who made the finding, order or acquittal which is the subject of the appeal.

GENERAL NOTE

This chapter was substituted for the previous and much briefer Ch.7 by para.2 of the Act of Adjournal (Criminal Procedure Rules Amendment No.4) (Mental Health (Care and Treatment) (Scotland) Act 2003) 2005 (SSI 2005/457) with effect from October 5, 2005. The 2003 Act introduced a new procedure to be followed when persons charged with an offence suffer from a mental disorder. These procedures are to be found in ss.52B–52U of the 1995 Act and introduce two new forms of order. Both orders can only be made in respect of a person charged with an offence but not yet sentenced for it (see ss.52D(5) and 52M(5)).

Assessment orders

An assessment order under s.52D can be made by any court other than the district court (which must remit to the sheriff court any person charged with an offence when it appears to the court that that person has a mental disorder: s.52A) when the court is satisfied on the evidence (written or oral) of one medical practitioner (who need not be a psychiatric specialist) that there are reasonable grounds for believing (1) that the person charged has a mental disorder; (2) that it is necessary to detain him in hospital to assess him to determine whether he has a mental disorder which is amenable to treatment and would, were he not to receive treatment, pose a significant risk either to his health, safety and welfare or to another person's safety (s.52D(7)); (3) that if the assessment order were not made there would be a significant risk to his health, safety and welfare or such a risk to the safety of another person; (4) that the proposed hospital is suitable for such assessment; (5) that if the order were made, the person could be admitted to the specific hospital before the expiry of seven days beginning with the day on which the order is made; and (6) that it would not be reasonably practicable to carry out the assessment unless the order were made.

An assessment order can be sought by both the prosecutor (s.52B) and the Scottish Ministers (s.52C), although in the latter case the person must be in custody, and it can also be made by the court *ex proprio motu* (s.52E). The order confines the person for a period of 28 days (which can be extended on one occasion only for a further period not exceeding seven days: s.52G(4)) during which time a psychiatric specialist (the "responsible medical officer" appointed under s.230 of the Mental Health (Care and Treatment) (Scotland) Act 2003 to treat the person) will assess the person and prepare a report which is to be submitted to the court making the order *before* the expiry of the 28-day period (s.52G(1)). No provision is made for the effect of a failure to submit the report timeously but in light of the House of Lords' decisions in *R. v Soneji* [2005] 3 W.L.R. 303 and *R. v Knights* [2005] 3 W.L.R. 330 (as to the proper construction of apparently mandatory statutory provisions in penal legislation) it seems likely that the assessment order would not be thereby invalidated and that accordingly the court would be entitled to consider the terms of the report and proceed as allowed by s.52G(3).

Treatment orders

The court can make a treatment order under s.52M. That order is envisaged as one of the outcomes of an assessment order followed by a report to the court on the condition of the person charged with but not yet sentenced for an offence (see s.52G(3)(a)). As with assessment orders, both the prosecutor (s.52K) and the Scottish Ministers (s.52I) may apply for a treatment order (although in the latter case the person must be in custody at the time of application) and the court may make a treatment order *ex proprio motu* (s.52N).

The court can only make a treatment order when it is satisfied on the evidence (whether written or oral) of *two* medical practitioners (1) that the conditions for making an assessment order set out in s.52D(7) exist (namely, the person has a mental disorder which is amenable to treatment and if treatment were not given there would be a significant risk either to the person's health, safety or welfare or to another person's safety); (2) that the proposed hospital and the proposed medical practitioner are suitable for the purposes of giving the necessary treatment; (3) that if an order were made, the person could be admitted to the specified hospital before the expiry of seven days beginning with the day on which the order is made; and when the court is also satisfied that having regard to the offence and the alternative means of dealing with the person, it is appropriate to make such an order (s.52M(2)). The order authorises the detention of the person in a specified hospital for medical treatment (s.52M(6)).

Interim Compulsion Orders and Compulsion Orders

Sections 131 and 133 of the Mental Health (Care and Treatment) (Scotland) Act 2003 also amended the 1995 Act by substituting a new s.53 and inserting s.57A so as to make provision for respectively interim compulsion orders and compulsion orders. These orders are available to the court only in respect of persons who have been convicted of an offence (referred to as "the offender": s.53(1)). The court requires to be satisfied on the written or oral evidence of *two* medical practitioners that the offender has a mental disorder and that much the same conditions applicable to treatment orders are met before an interim compulsion order can be made (see s.53(2)–(5)). Additionally, the court must be satisfied that there are reasonable grounds for believing that the mental disorder is such that it would be appropriate to make either a compulsion order and a restriction order or a hospital direction (s.53(6)). An interim compulsion order may authorise detention in a state hospital but only if two medical practitioners satisfy the court that the offender requires to be detained under conditions of special security and that such conditions can only be provided in a state hospital (s.53(7)).

An interim compulsion order authorises the offender's confinement in a specified hospital for a period not exceeding 12 weeks beginning with the day on which the order is made for the purposes of giving the offender medical treatment (s.53(8)). Before the expiry of the specified period the offender's responsible medical officer must submit to the court making the order a report under s.53B setting out the medical officer's assessment of the offender's mental state, the type or types of mental disorder from which he is suffering and whether it is necessary to extend the duration of the order to allow further time for the assessment (s.53B(2)). The court may extend the period of the order but only if the total period of confinement does not exceed 12 months (s.53B(5)).

Compulsion orders can be made in respect of offenders under s.57A and may authorise the detention of the offender in a specified hospital (including a state hospital but only where the offender's treatment can only be provided in conditions of special security provided by a state hospital) for a period of six months beginning with the day on which the order is made but can alternatively impose requirements on an offender to attend a specified hospital for treatment as an outpatient on specified or directed dates or at specified or directed intervals, or to attend at a place for community care services, or to reside at a specified place or to do several other specified things (including obtaining approval for a change of address).

PART III

SOLEMN PROCEEDINGS

CHAPTER 8

THE INDICTMENT

Appeals in relation to extension of time for trial

8.1.—(1) A note of appeal under section 65(8) of the Act of 1995 (appeal to High Court against grant or refusal of extension of time) in respect of an appeal from a decision under section 65(3) of that Act (extension of periods for commencement of preliminary hearing or trial diet) shall be in Form 8.1-A.

(2) A note of appeal under section 65(8) of the Act of 1995 in respect of an appeal from a decision under section 65(5) of that Act (extension of 80, 110 or 140 days period of committal) shall be in Form 8.1-B.

(3) A note of appeal mentioned in paragraph (1) or (2) shall be served by the appellant on—

(a) the respondent;

(b) any co-accused; and

(c) the clerk of the court against the decision of which the appeal is taken.

(4) The appellant shall lodge with the Clerk of Justiciary—

(a) the note of appeal; and

(b) the execution of service in respect of the persons mentioned in paragraph (3).

(5) The clerk of the court against the decision of which the appeal is taken shall, as soon as practicable after being served with the note of appeal, transmit to the Clerk of Justiciary the original application and all the relative documents; and the Clerk of Justiciary shall, on receiving them, assign the appeal to the roll and intimate the date of the diet to the appellant and the respondent.

AMENDMENT

Rule 8.1 as amended by the Act of Adjournal (Criminal Procedure Rules Amendment) (Criminal Procedure (Amendment) (Scotland) Act) 2005 (SSI 2005/44), r.2(8) (subject to r.2(2)–(4)) (effective February 1, 2005).

Further provision as respects extension of twelve months period for commencement of trial on indictment

8.1A. [...]

AMENDMENT

Rule 8.1A inserted by the Act of Adjournal (Criminal Procedure Rules) (Amendment) 1999 (SI 1999/78: effective March 1, 1999).

Rule 8.1A repealed by the Act of Adjournal (Criminal Procedure Rules Amendment) (Criminal Procedure (Amendment) (Scotland) Act) 2005 (SSI 2005/44), r.2(9) (subject to r.2(2)–(4)) (effective February 1, 2005).

Fresh indictment as alternative to serving notice fixing new trial diet

8.1B. [...]

AMENDMENT

Rule 8.1B inserted by the Act of Adjournal (Criminal Procedure Rules) (Amendment) 1999 (SI 1999/78: effective March 1, 1999).

Rule 8.1B repealed by the Act of Adjournal (Criminal Procedure Rules Amendment) (Criminal Procedure (Amendment) (Scotland) Act) 2005 (SSI 2005/44), r.2(9) (subject to r.2(2)–(4)) (effective February 1, 2005).

Citation of accused and witnesses

8.2.—(1) Subject to paragraph (5), the notice to be affixed to the door of the relevant premises for the purposes of section 66(4)(b) of the Act of 1995 shall be in Form 8.2-A.

(2) Subject to paragraph (5), the notice for the purposes of section 66(6) of the Act of 1995 to be served on a person accused on indictment shall be in Form 8.2-B or, where the charge is of committing a sexual offence to which section 288C of that Act applies or, where it is known by the prosecutor that the offence is one to which section 288E of that Act (prohibition of personal conduct of defence where a child witness is under the age of 12) applies, Form 8.2-C.

(3) The form of postal citation of a witness under section 66(1) of the Act of 1995 shall be in Form 8.2-D; and the witness shall return Form 8.2-E to the procurator fiscal, or the accused person or his solicitor, as the case may be, in the pre-paid envelope provided, within 14 days after the date of citation.

(4) The form of personal citation of a witness under section 66(1) of the Act of 1995 shall be in Form 8.2-F.

(5) Where the accused is a body corporate,

(a) the notice to be affixed to the door of the relevant premises for the purposes of section 66(4)(b) of the Act of 1995 shall be in Form 8.2-G;

(b) the notice for the purposes of section 66(6) of the Act of 1995 shall be in Form 8.2-H

AMENDMENT

Rule 8.2 substituted by the Act of Adjournal (Criminal Procedure Rules Amendment) (Criminal Procedure (Amendment) (Scotland) Act) 2005 (SSI 2005/44), r.2(10) (subject to r.2(2)–(4)) (effective February 1, 2005).

Rule 8.2(2) as amended by the Act of Adjournal (Criminal Procedure Rules Amendment No.3) (Vulnerable Witnesses (Scotland) Act 2004) 2005 (SSI 2005/188), r.2, subject to the conditions in r.2(2) (effective April 1, 2005).

Notice of previous convictions

8.3. Any notice to be served on an accused under section 69(2) of the Act of 1995 (notice of previous convictions) shall be in Form 8.3.

GENERAL NOTE

Rule 8.1

The wording of this rule does not take account of the combined effect of the five judge decision in *Gardner v Lees*, 1996 S.L.T. 342; 1996 S.C.C.R. 168 and *Normand v Walker*, 1996 S.L.T. 418. It is now recognised that it is competent to apply for an extension of the 12 month time-limit in summary proceedings. An extension can also be granted retrospectively: see *McGowan v Friel*, High Court of Justiciary, February 1, 1996 (unreported) which was approved by a bench of five judges in *McDowall v Lees*, 1996 S.L.T. 871; 1996 S.C.C.R. 719. However, the change in the law effected by these decisions (and *McDonald v Gordon*, 1996 S.C.C.R. 740) is now superseded by s.73 of the Criminal Procedure and Investigation Act 1996 which amends the 1995 Act to restrict the freedom conferred by s.65 from further process when the 12 month period has expired to proceedings on indictment, thereby reinstating the effect of *MacDougall v Russell*, 1986 S.L.T. 403. So the wording of the rule is now apt.

Where a sheriff refuses to be addressed on an application by the Crown for an extension of the 12 month period, no appeal under s.65 is competent because there is no decision to grant or refuse the application, nor can the unsuccessful applicant competently petition the nobile officium of the High Court. A subsequent application for extension is accordingly competent (*McKnight v H.M. Advocate*, 1996 S.L.T. 834). It has also been held that since the circumstances of the granting of an arrest warrant are—for policy reasons of securing certainty in criminal proceedings—irrelevant to the application of the proviso to s.101(1) of the 1975 Act (now s.65(2) of the 1995 Act), an accused for whose apprehension a warrant has been mistakenly granted should seek review of the warrant by means of a bill of suspension as soon as he becomes aware that proceedings are being continued against him outwith the 12 month period in reliance on the warrant (*H.M. Advocate v Taylor*, 1996 S.L.T. 836; 1996 S.C.C.R. 510).

Rule 8.1A

The rule provides for an exception to the general principle that all significant stages in solemn proceedings should be conducted in the presence of the accused. Any extension granted in excess of the period applied for would be incompetent and render subsequent trial proceedings fundamentally null.

Rule 8.1B

If further witnesses are to be examined or further productions put in evidence at the trial beyond those listed in the schedule annexed to the original record copy of the indictment or in any s.67 notice (served before leave was given to serve a notice fixing a new trial diet) then the prosecutor will require to serve a further s.67 notice timeously.

The notice of previous convictions should be served on the accused along with his citation and the indictment so that he can timeously object to any previous convictions which do not relate to him or are otherwise incompetently libelled by giving written intimation under s.69(2). Intimation of his objection should be given at least five clear days before the first day of the sitting in which the trial diet is to be held (see s.69(3)).

CHAPTER 8A

ENGAGEMENT, DISMISSAL AND WITHDRAWAL OF SOLICITORS IN SOLEMN PROCEEDINGS

Notification

8A.1.—(1) The notification to the court in writing under section 72F(1) of the Act of 1995 that a solicitor has been engaged by the accused for the purposes of his defence in any part of proceedings on indictment shall be in Form 8A.1–A.

(2) The notification to the court in writinf under section 72F(2) of the Act of 1995 that a solicitor has been dismissed by the accused or has withdrawn from acting shall be in Form 8A.1–B.

Further pre-trial diet

8A.2.—(1) An order for a further pre-trial diet under section 72F(5) of the Act of 1995 may be signed by the clerk of court.

(2) An order mentioned in paragraph (1) shall be intimated by the clerk of court to all parties and to the governor of any institution in which the accused is detained.

AMENDMENT

Chapter 8A inserted by the Act of Adjournal (Criminal Procedure Rules Amendment No.4) (Criminal Procedure (Amendment) (Scotland) Act 2004) 2004 (SSI 2004/434), r.2 (effective October 4, 2004).

Rule 8A.2(1) as amended by the Act of Adjournal (Criminal Procedure Rules Amendment No.5) (Miscellaneous) 2004 (SSI 2004/481), r.2 (effective November 26, 2004).

GENERAL NOTE

Section 5 of the Criminal Procedure (Amendment) (Scotland) Act 2004 inserted s.72F into the 1995 Act. That provision applies to three types of case (s.72F(4)). First, where the accused is prohibited from conducting his defence personally because it is a sexual offence, he must engage a lawyer or the court will appoint one to act for him (see s.288C of the 1995 Act); secondly, in cases to which s.288E applies (*i.e.* certain cases involving child witnesses under 12 years of age); and, thirdly, in cases where the court has made an order under s.288F(2) of the 1995 Act (*i.e.* where there are vulnerable witnesses). Section 72F(1) provides that in any proceedings on indictment "it is the duty of a solicitor who is engaged by the accused for the purposes of his defence at any part of the proceedings to notify the court and the prosecutor of that fact forthwith". However, the solicitor is deemed to have complied with that duty if, before the indictment is served, he has notified the procurator fiscal of the district "in which the charge against the accused was then being investigated" that he has been engaged and has not notified the procurator fiscal that he has been sacked or has withdrawn from acting (s.72F(1A)). The notifications must be in writing: a telephone call will not suffice (though presumably an e-mail or a fax will).

Section 72F(2) provides, as a consequence of the foregoing, that where the solicitor withdraws or is sacked, it is his duty to inform the court and the prosecutor of that fact "forthwith in writing". When the court is so informed, the court comes under a duty to order a further pre-trial diet to be held so that legal representation can be inquired into and if necessary ordered (s.72F(3)).

CHAPTER 9

FIRST DIETS (SHERIFF COURT)

Minute giving notice of preliminary pleas or preliminary issues

9.1.—(1) Any notice given under section 71(2) of the Act of 1995 (notice of preliminary pleas or preliminary issues before first diet) shall be by minute in Form 9.1.

(2) That minute shall be lodged with the sheriff clerk and served on every other party by the minuter.

Procedure on lodging minute

9.2. On the lodging of a minute under rule 9.1 (minute giving notice of preliminary pleas or preliminary issues) with a certificate of execution of service, the sheriff clerk shall endorse on the minute the time and date on which it was received.

Orders for further diets under section 71 of the Act of 1995

9.3.—(1) An order for a further diet under section 71(2ZA) of the Act of 1995 (further diet to consider objection to the admissibility of evidence) may be signed by the sheriff clerk.

(2) Intimation of the terms of an order—

(a) mentioned in paragraph (1); or

(b) for an adjourned diet under section 71(5A) of the Act of 1995 (adjournment of first diet),

shall be given by the sheriff clerk to the governor of any institution in which the accused is detained.

Procedure at first diet

9.4.—(1) A first diet shall commence on the diet being called.

(2) A record of the proceedings at the first diet, including—

(a) a note of the decision made by the court in respect of any notice placed before it;

(b) any adjournment, and

(c) the plea stated under section 71(6) of the Act of 1995 (plea at first diet),

shall be kept in accordance with existing law and practice.

Applications for leave to appeal

9.5.—(1) An application for leave to appeal to the High Court under section 74(1) of the Act of 1995 (appeal against a decision of the sheriff at a first diet) shall be made by motion to the sheriff at that diet immediately following the making of the decision in question, and shall be granted or refused at that time.

(2) A decision under this rule shall be recorded in the minute of proceedings.

Note of appeal

9.6.—(1) An appeal under section 74(1) of the Act of 1995 against a decision of the sheriff at a first diet shall be made by lodging a note of appeal in Form 9.6.

(2) The note of appeal shall be lodged with the sheriff clerk not later than two days after the making of the decision in question.

Procedure on lodging note of appeal

9.7.—(1) On the lodging of a note of appeal with the sheriff clerk, he shall endorse on it a certificate that leave to appeal has been granted and the date and time of lodging.

(2) As soon as possible after the lodging of a note of appeal with the sheriff clerk, he shall—

(a) send a copy of the note of appeal to the other parties or their solicitors;

(b) request a report on the circumstances relating to the decision from the sheriff; and

(c) transmit the note of appeal to the Clerk of Justiciary with a certified copy of—

   (i) the indictment;

   (ii) the record of proceedings; and

   (iii) any other relevant document.

Report of sheriff

9.8.—(1) The sheriff, on receiving a request for a report under rule 9.7(2)(b) (report on circumstances relating to decision) shall, as soon as possible, send his report to the Clerk of Justiciary.

(2) The Clerk of Justiciary shall, on receiving the report of the sheriff—

(a) send a copy of the report to the parties or their solicitors;

(b) arrange for a hearing of the appeal as soon as possible; and

(c) cause to be copied any documents necessary for the appeal.

Intimation of order postponing trial diet

9.9.—(1) Where, in relation to an appeal under section 74(1) of the Act of 1995 (appeal in connection with first diet) in a case set down for trial in the sheriff court, the High Court makes an order under section 74(3) of that Act (postponement of trial diet), the Clerk of Justiciary shall send a copy of the order to—

(a) the sheriff clerk;

(b) all parties to the proceedings; and

(c) the governor of any institution in which any accused is detained.

(2) If, in relation to any case a trial diet has been postponed by virtue of an order mentioned in paragraph (1), any requirement to call that diet shall have effect only in relation to the date to which the diet has been postponed.

Orders of appeal court

9.10. The Clerk of Justiciary shall intimate to the sheriff clerk the decision of the High Court disposing of an appeal under section 74(1) of the Act of 1995 in relation to a first diet.

Abandonment of appeal

9.11.—(1) An appellant who has taken an appeal under section 74(1) of the Act of 1995 (appeal in connections with first diet) may abandon the appeal at any time before the hearing of the appeal.

(2) An abandonment of such an appeal shall be made by lodging a minute of abandonment in Form 9.11 with the Clerk of Justiciary.

(3) The Clerk of Justiciary, on receiving such a minute of abandonment, shall inform the sheriff clerk and the other parties or their solicitors.

(4) The sheriff, on the sheriff clerk being so informed, may proceed as accords with the case.

AMENDMENT

Chapter 9 substituted by the Act of Adjournal (Criminal Procedure Rules Amendment) (Criminal Procedure (Amendment) (Scotland) Act) 2005 (SSI 2005/44), r.2(11) (subject to r.2(2)–(4)) (effective February 1, 2005).

Paragraph 2(11) of the Act of Adjournal (Criminal Procedure Rules Amendment) (Criminal Procedure (Amendment) (Scotland) Act) 2005 replaced, as from February 1, 2005, the old ch.9 which had made provision for preliminary diets in the High Court and first diets in the sheriff court (but see the General Note at C1–31 for the applicability of the new procedure). The first diet was mandatory although preliminary diets were held only when a judge of the High Court was obliged, or in the exercise of his discretion considered it appropriate, to order that one be held.

Preliminary pleas and issues

Preliminary pleas are defined in s.79(2)(a) of the 1995 Act (as amended by s.13(1) of the Criminal Procedure (Amendment) (Scotland) Act 2004) as follows: (1) challenges to the competency or relevancy of the indictment; (2) objections to the validity of the accused's citation; and (3) pleas in bar of trial (such as insanity, tholed assize, nonage and oppression (by, for example, prejudicial pre-trial publicity or abuse of process by the prosecutor)).

Preliminary issues are defined in s.79(2)(b) as follows: (1) applications for separation or conjunction of charges or trials; (2) objections under ss.27(4A)(a), 255 or 255A of the 1995 Act (respectively challenges to the deemed admission that the offence was committed while on bail, that it was committed in any special capacity or that the age of any person specified in the indictment is true), or under s.9(6) of the Antisocial Behaviour etc. (Scotland) Act 2004 or under that section as applied by s.234AA(11) of the 1995 Act; (3) applications under s.278(2) of the 1995 Act (to have the court direct that the record of proceedings at judicial examination, or a part of that record, should not be read to the jury); (4) objections by either Crown or defence to the admissibility of any evidence; (5) assertions by either Crown or defence that there are documents the truth of the contents of which ought to be admitted, or that there is any other matter which in the applicant's view should be agreed; and (6) any other point raised by either Crown or defence as regards any matter which (not being mentioned in (1) to (5) *supra*) "could in his opinion be resolved with advantage before the trial".

Section 71(2) of the 1995 Act requires the sheriff at a first diet to "consider" any preliminary plea or issue of which notice has been given in terms of s.79(1). In *Wright v HM Advocate* [2006] HCJAC 66 (July 4, 2006, unreported) the sheriff had continued consideration of an objection to the admissibility of evidence of an identification parade to the trial diet. The High Court held that the sheriff was not required to determine or dispose of the issue at the first diet and was entitled to continue consideration of the issue to the trial diet to hear evidence before determining the issue.

Procedure at first diet

In addition to disposing of preliminary pleas and issues, the sheriff has certain other obligations. First, he must, where the accused is charged with a sexual offence listed in s.288C(2) (in respect of which an accused is prohibited from defending himself in person), ascertain whether the accused has engaged a solicitor for his defence at trial (s.71(A1)). Secondly, the sheriff must, so far as is reasonably practicable, ascertain whether the case is likely to proceed to trial on the date assigned as the trial diet and, in particular, ascertain the state of preparation of both Crown and defence with respect to their cases and the extent to which the parties have complied with their duties under s.257(1) of the 1995 Act to identify any facts which seem likely to be capable of agreement (s.71(1)(a) and (b)). Thirdly, the sheriff must ascertain which witnesses the Crown and defence will respectively require to attend at trial and, where the accused is on bail, review the bail conditions (so as, where appropriate, to vary them) (s.71(1C)). Fourthly, the sheriff must ascertain whether there is any objection to the admissibility of evidence which either the Crown or defence wishes to raise despite that party's not having given timeous notice of that preliminary issue and, if there is, the sheriff must decide whether to grant leave (which is granted on cause shown: s.79(1)) for the objection to be raised and, where the sheriff grants leave, dispose of the objection unless he considers it inappropriate to do so as the first diet (s.71(2YA)).

Rule 9.4 provides that a record of the proceedings shall be kept in accordance with "existing law and practice" and must include a record of the sheriff's decision on any notice under s.71(2) which has been placed before him. The effect of a failure to record all decisions on the various notices which might be argued at a first diet is not stated.

The accused must attend the first diet of which he has been given notice and if he fails to do so, the sheriff may grant warrant for his apprehension (s.71(4)). However, a first diet may proceed in the accused's absence (s.71(5)) but that is expressly not so in the case of an accused who is charged with a sexual offence listed in s.288C(2) and in respect of whom the court has not yet ascertained whether he has engaged a solicitor to represent him at trial (s.71(5A)). In such an eventuality, the sheriff must adjourn the diet and ordain the absent accused to appear.

After the business of the first diet is disposed of whether by decision or adjournment, the accused should then be called on to state how he pleads to the indictment (s.71(6)).

Objections to admissibility of evidence

As mentioned above, at the first diet the sheriff is also obliged to ascertain whether the parties have any objection to the admissibility of evidence of which no timeous notice has been given and if there is such an objection, he must decide whether to allow it to be raised late and then either dispose of the objection or, where that is inappropriate (because, for example, evidence requires to be led), appoint a further diet to be held before the trial diet for the purpose of disposing of the objection or direct the objection to be disposed of at the trial diet (s.71(2ZA)). (See *Wright, supra.*)

Appeals

Section 74(1) of the 1995 Act provides that, without prejudice to the accused's right of appeal against conviction and sentence and the Lord Advocate's right of appeal against disposal or his right to appeal by bill of advocation (see ss.106, 108 and 131), a party dissatisfied with the sheriff's decision at a first diet may appeal to the High Court by note of appeal in accordance with such procedure as is provided for by Act of Adjournal. Rule 9.6 provides that the note of appeal should be in Form 9.6 and must be lodged with the sheriff clerk not later than two days after the making of the decision (Rule 9.6(2)).

There is no automatic right to appeal. The accused and Crown require leave of the sheriff to appeal by note of appeal under s.74(1) although the Crown has an unfettered right to bring a bill of advocation. Thus, even where leave has been obtained by the Crown but the Crown has failed to exercise that right of appeal within the time limit, the Crown is entitled to present a bill of advocation (see *HM Advocate v Shepherd*, 1997 S.C.C.R. 246 at 249, *per* Lord Justice-Clerk Cullen).

Leave to appeal may be granted either on the party's motion or by the sheriff *ex proprio motu*. However, an appeal may not be taken, and leave should not therefore be given by the sheriff for appeal to be brought, against a decision to adjourn the first diet (for whatever reason) or to accelerate or postpone the trial diet (s.74(2)(a)).

Chapter 9A

Preliminary Hearings (High Court of Justiciary)

Notice of preliminary pleas and preliminary issues

9A.1.—(1) Any notice given under section 72(3) (notice of preliminary pleas) or section 72(6)(b)(i) (notice of preliminary issues) of the Act of 1995 shall be by minute in Form 9A.1.

(2) A minute under paragraph (1) shall be lodged with the Clerk of Justiciary and served on every other party by the minuter.

Applications to dispense with preliminary hearings

9A.2.—(1) An application to dispense with a preliminary hearing shall made in Form 9A.2.

(2) Prior to making an application under paragraph (1), the parties shall consult with the Clerk of Justiciary as to a suitable date for a trial diet.

(3) An application under paragraph (1) shall indicate whether or not a date for a trial diet has been agreed by the parties with the Clerk of Justiciary and shall give details of any applicable time limits under section 65 of the Act of 1995.

(4) On the lodging of an application under paragraph (1), the Clerk of Justiciary shall attach it to the record copy of the indictment and place it before a judge in chambers.

(5) The order made by the judge in chambers in respect of the application shall be—

(a) recorded by endorsation on the record copy of the indictment;

(b) signed by the Clerk of Justiciary;

(c) entered in the record of proceedings; and

(d) intimated by the Clerk of Justiciary to the applicants or their solicitors.

(6) The Clerk of Justiciary shall send to the governor of any institution in which any accused is detained a copy of any order of the court dispensing with a preliminary hearing.

Notice to appear where preliminary hearing deserted

9A.3. A notice referred to in section 72C(4) of the Act of 1995 (notice to appear at further preliminary hearing) shall be in Form 8.2-B or, where the charge is of committing a sexual offence to which section 288C of the Act of 1995 (prohibition of personal conduct of defence in cases of certain sexual offences) applies, Form 8.2-C.

Written record of state of preparation

9A.4.—(1) A written record referred to in section 72E of the Act of 1995 (written record of the state of preparation in certain cases) shall be in Form 9A.4 and shall contain the information indicated in that form.

(2) A written record under paragraph (1) may be lodged by sending a copy by facsimile or other electronic means followed by the lodging of the principal and the time and date of lodging shall be the date and time on which the copy was received by the Clerk of Justiciary.

(3) A written record under paragraph (1) which is lodged after 2pm on the last date for lodging under section 72E of that Act shall be deemed to have been lodged on the next day after that date.

Proceedings at preliminary hearing

9A.5.—(1) Any order under section 72(9)(a) (appointment of further diet) of the Act of 1995 shall be intimated by the Clerk of Justiciary to the parties or their solicitors.

(2) On the making of an order mentioned in paragraph (1), the Clerk of Justiciary shall send a copy of the order to the governor of any institution in which the accused is detained.

(3) On the appointment of a trial diet, the Clerk of Justiciary shall intimate the date of that diet to the governor of any institution in which the accused is detained.

Applications for leave to appeal

9A.6.—(1) An application for leave to appeal to the High Court under section 74(1) of the Act of 1995 against a decision of the High Court at a preliminary hearing shall be made by motion to the court at that hearing immediately following the making of the decision in question, and shall be granted or refused at that time.

(2) A decision made under this rule shall be recorded in the record of proceedings.

Note of appeal

9A.7.—(1) An appeal under section 74(1) of the Act of 1995 against a decision of the High Court at a preliminary hearing shall be made by lodging a note of appeal in Form 9A.7 with the Clerk of Justiciary.

(2) The appellant shall send a copy of a note of appeal under paragraph (1) to the other parties.

Abandonment of appeal

9A.8.—(1) An appellant who has taken an appeal under section 74(1) of the Act of 1995 (appeals against decision at a preliminary hearing) may abandon the appeal at any time before the hearing of the appeal.

(2) An abandonment of such appeal shall be made by lodging a minute of abandonment in Form 9A.8.

AMENDMENT

Chapter 9A inserted by the Act of Adjournal (Criminal Procedure Rules Amendment) (Criminal Procedure (Amendment) (Scotland) Act) 2005 (SSI 2005/44), r.2(11) (subject to r.2(2)–(4)) (effective February 1, 2005).

GENERAL NOTE

Lord Bonomy's Review of High Court practice (see *Improving Practice*, November 2002) was principally concerned with solving the problems created by the frequency with which High Court trials were adjourned (see P.W. Ferguson, "High Court Practice and Procedure", 2003 S.L.T. (News) 129–136). The Scottish Executive responded to Lord Bonomy's Report with a White Paper (*Modernising Justice in Scotland: The reform of the High Court of Justiciary*, para.16) by accepting his recommendation that there should be a mandatory pre-trial hearing in all High Court cases. That recommendation was implemented by the Criminal Procedure (Amendment) (Scotland) Act 2004 which amended the 1995 Act to introduce ss.72 and 72A into that statute.

A preliminary hearing must be held in all cases unless the High Court dispenses with such a hearing. Section 72B gives to the High Court the power, on an application to it jointly by the Crown and the defence, to dispense with the preliminary hearing and to appoint a trial diet where the court is satisfied of certain matters. These matters are: (1) that the state of the Crown and defence's preparations for trial is such that "the case is likely to be ready to proceed to trial on the date to be appointed for the trial diet" and (2) that there are no preliminary pleas, preliminary issues or other matters which require to be, or could with advantage be, disposed of before the trial diet (s.72B(1)). The joint application must be in Form 9A.2 which requires parties to state the expected length of the trial and specify which witnesses the parties shall require to be in attendance at the trial diet.

For the definition of preliminary pleas and preliminary issues, see the annotations to ch.9, *supra*.

Written Record of State of Preparation

Rule 9A.4 makes provision for an essential part of the new procedure. Both the Crown and the defence must submit to the court a written record of its state of preparation. Schedule 1 is to be completed by the prosecutor and Sch.2 is for the defence to complete. The High Court has issued Practice Note (No.1 of 2005), paras 7–10 of which are intended to guide practitioners as to what is expected of them by the court when complying with the obligation in s.72E to prepare a written record of preparation. It is imperative that the parties communicate with each other in sufficient time before the preliminary hearing with a view to preparing the joint written record. For preliminary hearings to be held in Glasgow, Form 9A.4 should be lodged with the Clerk of Justiciary in Glasgow. In all other cases the form should be lodged with the Justiciary Office in Edinburgh.

Appeals

A party desiring to bring under review a decision at a preliminary hearing must apply by motion to the judge at that hearing immediately following the making of the decision (r.9A.6(1)). In *HM Advocate v Fleming* [2005] HCJ 02 (October 28, 2005) Lord Brodie held that it was necessary for a party to apply for leave to appeal against his decision on a question relating to the recovery of documents even though his decision was not given at a preliminary hearing. The rationale of that conclusion was that while the diet at which the decision was made was not a preliminary hearing, the question was a preliminary issue (see para.22).

CHAPTER 9B

OBJECTIONS TO THE ADMISSIBILITY OF EVIDENCE RAISED AFTER FIRST DIET OR PRELIMINARY HEARING

Notice etc. of objections raised after first diet or preliminary hearing

9B.1.—(1) Any notice given under section 79A(2) of the Act of 1995(objections to the admissibility of evidence after first diet or preliminary hearing) shall be by minute in Form 9B.1 and shall be served on the other parties by the minuter.

(2) On the lodging of a minute under paragraph (1), the Clerk of Justiciary or the sheriff clerk, as the case may be, shall place the minute before a judge in chambers.

(3) On considering the minute in the absence of the parties or of any person acting on their behalf, the judge shall appoint—

(a) a further diet to be held before the trial diet for the purpose of hearing the parties on whether leave should be granted for the objection to be raised; or

(b) the question of whether leave should be granted under section 79A(2) of the Act of 1995 for the objection to be disposed of at the trial diet.

(4) The Clerk of Justiciary or the sheriff clerk, as the case may be, shall intimate the order under paragraph (3) to the parties and to the governor of any institution in which the accused is detained.

AMENDMENT

Chapter 9B inserted by the Act of Adjournal (Criminal Procedure Rules Amendment) (Criminal Procedure (Amendment) (Scotland) Act) 2005 (SSI 2005/44), r.2(11) (subject to r.2(2)–(4)) (effective February 1, 2005).

CHAPTER 10

PLEA OF GUILTY

Procedure for plea of guilty

10.1.—(1) A notice to appear at a diet of the appropriate court served on an accused under section 76(1) of the Act of 1995 (procedure where accused desires to plead guilty) shall—

(a) if an indictment has not already been served, be in Form 10.1-A;

(b) if an indictment has already been served, be in Form 10.1-B.

(2) In any case set down for trial in the High Court, any diet fixed by virtue of section 76(1) of the Act of 1995 may be called before the High Court sitting in Edinburgh whether or not—

(a) the case has already been set down for trial elsewhere, or

(b) any notice has already been served on the accused under section 66(6) of that Act (notice of first diet and trial diet or preliminary hearing).

(3) In the application of subsection (3) of section 76 of the Act of 1995, the court may postpone the trial diet under that section if, but only if—

(a) all the accused have been served with a notice in accordance with subsection (1) of that section;

(b) all the accused are present at the diet called by virtue of subsection (1) of that section; and

(c) a motion to postpone the trial diet is made to the court at that diet.

(4) Where the court grants that motion, the order granting it shall—

(a) be endorsed on the record copy of the indictment;

(b) be signed by the presiding judge;

(c) be entered in the record of proceedings; and

(d) [...]

(5) A copy of the order shall be sent by the clerk of court to the governor of any institution in which any accused is detained.

(6) Any requirement to call the diet in any case where such an order has been made shall have effect only in relation to the postponed trial diet.

AMENDMENT

Rule 10.1(2) as amended, and r.10.1(4)(d) repealed, by the Act of Adjournal (Criminal Procedure Rules Amendment) (Criminal Procedure (Amendment) (Scotland) Act) 2005 (SSI 2005/44), r.2(12) (subject to r.2(2)–(4)) (effective February 1, 2005).

GENERAL NOTE

Section 76 of the 1995 Act provides that an accused, who desires to plead guilty and to have his case disposed of "at once", can give written intimation of that desire to the Crown Agent. The written intimation must be given to the Crown Agent irrespective of whether the accused has been already indicted for trial in either the sheriff court or the High Court. An indictment (with a schedule of previous convictions where appropriate: s.69(4)) can then be served (if one has not already been served) without there being appended thereto any list of witnesses or productions, and it shall not be necessary for productions to be lodged in court. The accused will also be served with a notice to appear at a diet at which he can plead guilty, the diet being not less than four clear days after the date of the notice.

On receipt of a "section 76 letter" (such written intimation was known under the 1975 Act as a "section 102 letter"), the Crown can elect, if no indictment has by then been served, to indict in the High Court or the sheriff court. The election of the forum is sometimes influenced by prior negotiations with the Crown when consideration is being given by the accused's agents to submitting an offer to plead. Where, however, the accused thereafter pleads not guilty at a diet which had been fixed by reason of such a s.76 letter, or the accused otherwise reneges on the terms of his written intimation and offers a restricted plea, the diet is to be deserted *pro loco et tempore* and the court may postpone the trial diet. Any period of such postponement of the trial diet is not to count towards the statutory time-limit.

The Justiciary Office has announced (see 2000 S.L.T. (News) 147) that persons wishing to plead guilty in High Court cases may have these cases called and dealt with at the first day of a High Court sitting local to the case and the Crown Office has stated that ideally at least six weeks' notice should be given to the Crown and that the procurator fiscal will advise the accused's representatives whether particular petition cases are regarded as being of High Court potential. When submitting a letter under s.76, the procurator fiscal should be advised of the sitting of the High Court at which the accused wishes his case dealt with.

Rule 10.1(1)

It is essential that a notice is served on the accused as he is being called to a diet and his failure to appear when he is on bail will constitute an offence only if he has been given due notice of the time and place appointed for the diet (see s.27(1)(a) of the 1995 Act).

Rule 10.1(3)

Where an indictment has already been served on the accused and some but not all of the accused submit s.76 letters which lead the Crown to serve a notice upon the accused to appear at an earlier diet for the court to receive their pleas of guilty, the accused who have not submitted s.76 letters will not be present. Plainly they should not be prejudiced so far as the time-limits are concerned and the court is therefore prevented from postponing the trial diet unless all the accused have been served with a notice and are present at the diet called by virtue of that notice.

CHAPTER 11

NOTICES BY ACCUSED IN RELATION TO DEFENCE

Notices of special defence etc.

11.1.—(1) Where a notice under section 78(1) of the Act of 1995 (plea of special defence etc.) is to be served on a co-accused, that notice may be served on his solicitor.

Notices by accused of witnesses and productions

11.2. Any notice given by an accused under section 78(4) of the Act of 1995 (notice of witnesses and productions) shall be served on any co-accused or his solicitor.

AMENDMENT

Rule 11.2 as amended by Act of Adjournal (Criminal Procedure Rules Amendment) (Miscellaneous) (SI 1996/2147 (s.171)) (effective September 9, 1996).

GENERAL NOTE

Section 78(1) of the 1995 Act provides that in solemn proceedings it shall not be competent for the accused to state a special defence (which is deemed to include a defence of coercion or automatism (s.78(2)) or lead evidence calculated to exculpate himself by incriminating his co-accused, unless he lodges and intimates the plea or notice (under s.78(3)) to the Clerk of Justiciary, the Crown Agent and any co-accused not less than 10 clear days before the trial diet in the High Court and, if the trial is to take place in the sheriff court, to the sheriff clerk and the procurator fiscal at or before the first diet. A special defence can be received at a continued first diet without the necessity of the accused's showing cause under s.78(1)(b) of the 1995 Act because any diet includes a continuation of a diet (s.307(1)): see *O'Connell v H.M. Advocate*, 1996 S.C.C.R. 674. In *Trotter v. H.M. Advocate*, 2000 S.C.C.R. 968 the notice of a defence of coercion was not given in accordance with s.78(1) but was allegedly mentioned in chambers in the presence of the Crown and the sheriff. The sheriff withdrew the defence from the jury's consideration. The Appeal Court did not, however, require to consider the propriety of this decision as they held that the defence was not, in any event, open to the accused on the evidence.

Section 78(4) of the 1995 Act provides that in solemn proceedings it shall not be competent for the accused to examine any witnesses or put in evidence any productions which are not included in the lists lodged by the Crown appended to the indictment unless written notice of the names and addresses of these witnesses and of such productions have been given to the procurator fiscal at or before the first diet where the case is to be tried in the sheriff court or to the Crown Agent at least 10 days before the day on which the jury is sworn if the case is to be tried in the High Court, or unless the court on "cause shown" otherwise directs. A copy of any notice must be lodged with the appropriate court of trial.

Rule 11.2 therefore extends the right to receive notice of witnesses and productions to co-accused (or his solicitor) because a co-accused no doubt may be affected by the evidence which other accused persons propose to lead. Thus for example where an accused has given notice of his intention to incriminate a co-accused not less than 10 clear days before the trial diet in the High Court to the Crown and to the co-accused under s.78(1), or has given notice to the Crown and co-accused of a defence of coercion by a co-accused or automatism caused by a co-accused under s.78(2), there may be witnesses not on the Crown list upon whom the co-accused intends to rely.

Rule 11.2 does not however contain a time-limit. It might have been preferable for the same time-limits which are stipulated for in s.78(4) to be included in the rule. It is therefore open to an accused to withhold giving notice to the co-accused until immediately before the first Crown witness is sworn. Such a tactic may hamper a co-accused in the conduct of his defence in court. For that reason it is at least arguable that the draftsman intended that the time-limit in s.78(4) should be implied into r.11.2. In the event that no notice to a co-accused is given at all under r.11.2 it is open to question what the court will do. If the witness or production is intended to support a notice of incrimination of a co-accused, the co-accused cannot complain of prejudice by failure to serve a notice on him since he will have been made aware of the line of evidence at least 10 clear days before the trial diet (in High Court cases) by service of a notice of incrimination under s.78(1). If the witness or production relates to a special defence (*e.g.* self-defence or alibi) no prejudice at all could be founded on. However it may not be necessary for prejudice to be demonstrated to the court if r.11.2 is held to be mandatory (see *e.g.* Lord Justice Clerk's opinion in *Robertson v H.M. Advocate*, 1995 S.C.C.R. 152). It seems likely however that the High Court will require prejudice to be demonstrated before a breach of r.11.2 will be held to constitute a miscarriage of justice. In the course of a trial, a short adjournment might be considered all that is necessary to remedy the effects of failure to obtemper the rule.

Furthermore, it is noteworthy that since a notice of incrimination under s.78(1) requires to be given *only* where the line of evidence will have the *dual* effect of exculpating the accused by showing the co-accused committed the crime (*McQuade v H.M. Advocate*, 1996 S.C.C.R. 347), r.11.2 gives a co-accused some notice of another accused's intention to incriminate him albeit that the evidence will not wholly exculpate the incriminator, at least where evidence will be led from a witness not on the Crown list.

CHAPTER 12

Adjournment and Alteration of Diets in Solemn Proceedings

Adjournment

12.1.—(1) Where circumstances arise in which the court may adjourn a diet under section 75A(2) of the Act of 1995 (adjournment and alteration of diets), and the prosecutor proposes such an adjournment, he may for that purpose require the diet to be called on the date for which it was originally fixed at such time as he thinks appropriate.

(2) The presence of the accused in court when the diet was so called and adjourned shall be sufficient intimation to him of the adjourned diet.

(3) If the diet was so called and adjourned in the absence of the accused, the prosecutor shall forthwith serve on the accused an intimation of adjournment in Form 12.1.

(4) The calling and the adjournment of the diet including a record as to the presence or absence of the accused, as the case may be, shall be endorsed by the clerk of court on the record copy indictment and entered in the record of proceedings in accordance with existing law and practice.

(5) A copy of the order of the court adjourning the diet under section 75A(2) of the Act of 1995 shall be sent by the clerk of court to the governor of any institution in which the accused is detained.

Applications for alteration of diet

12.2.—(1) Subject to paragraph (2), an application under section 75A(5) of the Act of 1995 (application for alteration of diet) shall be made by minute in Form 12.2-A.

(2) Where all parties join in the application, the application shall be made by joint minute in Form 12.2-B.

(3) A minute under this rule shall be lodged—

    (a) in the case of proceedings in the High Court, with the Clerk of Justiciary,

    (b) in the case of proceedings in the sheriff court, with the sheriff clerk.

Orders fixing diet for hearing of application to alter diet

12.3. Where a minute referred to in rule 12.2 (applications for alteration of diet) has been lodged, the court shall, or, in a case in which all parties join in the application, may, make an order endorsed on the minute—

    (a) fixing a diet for a hearing of the application; and

    (b) for service of the minute with the date of the diet on all parties.

Calling of diet for hearing application

12.4. A diet fixed under rule 12.3 (orders fixing diet for hearing application to alter diet) shall be held in open court in the presence of all parties unless the court permits the hearing to proceed in the absence of the accused under section 75A(8) of the Act of 1995, and shall be commenced by the calling of the diet.

Joint applications without hearing

12.5—(1) Where, in the case of a joint application under subsection (5) of section 75A of the Act of 1995 (application for alteration of diet), the court proposes to proceed without hearing the parties by virtue of subsection (7) of that section (joint application for alteration of diet), the clerk of court shall on the lodging of the minute attach it to the record copy of the indictment and place it before a judge in chambers.

(2) The order made by the judge in chambers in respect of the joint application shall be—

    (a) recorded by endorsation on the record copy of the indictment;

    (b) signed by the clerk of court;

    (c) entered in the record of proceedings; and

    (d) intimated by the clerk of court to the applicants or their solicitors.

(3) The clerk of court shall send to the governor of any institution in which the accused is detained a copy of the following orders of the court—

    (a) an order under rule 12.3 (order fixing diet for hearing of application to alter diet);

    (b) an order under section 65(3) or (5) of the Act of 1995 (extension of time limits); and

(c) an order under section 75A(5) of the Act of 1995(discharging a diet and fixing a new diet).

Form of notice where trial diet does not take place

12.6. A notice referred to in section 81(5) of the Act of 1995 (notice to appear where trial diet has not taken place) shall be in Form 8.2-B or, where the charge is of committing a sexual offence to which section 288C of that Act (prohibition of personal conduct of defence in cases of certain sexual offences) applies, Form 8.2-C.

Floating diets in the High Court of Justiciary

12.7.—(1) A minute referred to in section 83A(2)(a) of the Act of 1995 (minute of continuation of floating trial diet) shall be in Form 12.7.

(2) The maximum number of days for which a floating diet may be continued from sitting day to sitting day shall be four days after the day originally appointed for the trial diet.

AMENDMENT

Chapter 12 substituted by the Act of Adjournal (Criminal Procedure Rules Amendment) (Criminal Procedure (Amendment) (Scotland) Act) 2005 (SSI 2005/44), r.2(13) (subject to r.2(2)–(4)) (effective February 1, 2005).

GENERAL NOTE

Chapter 12 in its original form was concerned with s.80 of the 1995 Act (which made provision for alteration and postponement of a trial diet). That provision was repealed by s.25 of, and para.26 to Sch.1 to the Criminal Procedure (Amendment) (Scotland) Act 2004 with effect from February 1, 2005. From that date s.75A was inserted into the 1995 Act by s.15 of the 2004 Act. Section 75A now regulates adjournment and alteration of diets. Under the reforms introduced by the 2004 Act, the old system of the Crown's indicting a trial for a sitting of the High Court has been abolished and indictments call the accused to a preliminary hearing on a fixed date. Once the case is considered ready for trial, the court fixes a trial diet which is either a fixed diet or a floating diet. In either event, a specific date is identified. Section 75A applies where any diet has been fixed in any proceedings on indictment (subs.(1)) and so applies to sheriff court as well as High Court cases.

Section 75A(2) provides, as the common law always has provided, that the court may, if it considers it appropriate to do so, adjourn the diet. However, adjournment of trial diets has to receive special treatment. First, the court (either a single judge of the High Court or the sheriff, as appropriate: s.75A(11)) may adjourn a trial diet "only if the indictment is not brought to trial at the diet" (s.75A(3)(a)). Trial diets commence when the jury is sworn (s.75A(12)(b)) and not on the calling of the diet (as is the rule for all other diets: s.75A(12)(a)). Secondly, a trial diet cannot be adjourned for more than 48 hours where the *only* reason for the adjournment is the failure of the accused to engage a solicitor for the purposes of conducting his defence at the trial (s.75A(3)(b)). This rule applies also to preliminary hearings.

High Court trial diets (but apparently not preliminary hearings, although s.72(9)(a) contains no restriction on venue for a continued hearing) may be adjourned to a diet to be held at a sitting of the court in another place (s.75A(4)). When determining an application to discharge a fixed diet and appoint another diet (which, except in the special case of trial diets, may be earlier or later than the diet originally fixed (see s.75A(5)(b))), the court must give parties an opportunity to be heard (s.75A(6)) unless parties are ultimately agreed in the application (s.75A(7)). The accused must attend any such hearing unless the court permits him to be absent (s.75A(8)).

Rule 12.1

Section 75A(2) allows adjournment of all fixed diets but note the special provisions in subs.(3) relating to both trial diets and diets (whether trial diets or preliminary hearings) which require to be adjourned only because of the accused's being unrepresented by a solicitor at these diets.

Rule 12.1(3) is on its face mandatory: "the prosecutor shall forthwith serve on an accused an intimation of adjournment". However, the Crown's failure to do so will not necessarily be fatal. In *Carruthers v HM Advocate*, 1994 J.C. 8; 1994 S.L.T. 900; 1993 S.C.C.R. 825 there was a failure to comply with r.41(4) of the 1988 Rules. That rule provided that "the prosecutor shall immediately serve on the accused an intimation of adjournment". Lord Justice-General Hope stated (1994 S.L.T. 900 at 902; 1993 S.C.C.R. 825 at 930): "The intention of the rule has to be seen against the background of s.77 of the 1975 Act. If one is concerned to find out whether a provision is directory or mandatory it is relevant to consider the purpose of the rule and its context, and to examine also the consequences if that rule is not observed. The proper view to take of the rule in this case is that its purpose is to provide notice to the accused of a competent adjournment. Failure to give that notice does not affect the competency of the adjournment as such. What itdoes do, or may do, is result in an absence of notice and possible prejudice to the accused . . . [W]here it cannot be suggested that there is any prejudice, the failure to observe the rule can have no adverse consequences, and it certainly cannot lead to the falling of the indictment."

Similarly, a failure to make the necessary endorsement on the record copy of the indictment, or to make the necessary entry in the record of proceedings, will not be fatal because there can never be any prejudice to the accused (*cf. R. v Soneji* [2005] 3 W.L.R. 303 and *R. v Knights* [2005] 3 W.L.R. 330).

Rule 12.4

A hearing on the minute in Form 12.2-A is itself a fixed diet under r.12.3(a) must be intimated to all parties (r.12.3(b)). The hearting must be in open court and in the presence of all parties unless the accused is excused attendance. No provision is made in s.75A for the hearing to be in open court (nor was any such requirement made in s.80(5) (now repealed)) but this rule makes that requirement. This contrasts with the chambers hearing which is all that is necessary when the parties are agreed on the adjournment and make a joint application under s.75A(7) and r.12.5.

Rule 12.5

Where the accused is in custody and there is a joint motion to adjourn, the prison governor must receive *copies* of the orders made on the original minute to adjourn (before it is agreed among the parties) and of the orders extending the time limits (where relevant) and fixing a new diet. This requirement is not simply to keep the governor informed of the next diet to which the accused must be brought from custody to appear (or to advise the governor of the continuing lawfulness of the accused's pre-trial incarceration) but presumably so that these copies can be transmitted to the accused for his information.

Rule 12.6

Section 81(2) provides (unlike the old position before amendment by the 2004 Act) that where a solemn trial diet is deserted *pro loco et tempore* the court may appoint a further trial diet for a later date. That will not always happen and in that event, s.81(4)(a) permits the prosecutor in the High Court, at any time within two months after the desertion of the diet, to give notice (under s.81(5)) to the accused on another copy of the (original) indictment to appear and answer the indictment at a further preliminary hearing (or, if the prosecutor so chooses, a first diet for further proceedings on the indictment to be taken in the lower court). Similarly, where the original indictment was due for trial in the sheriff court, the prosecutor can call upon the accused to appear at a further trial diet in that court not less than seven clear days after service of the notice or the prosecutor can elect to proceed against the accused in the High Court and in that event the notice should call the accused to appear at a preliminary hearing.

The prosecutor's power to give notice for the above purposes is not, however, limited to desertion of the trial diet. Under s.81(4)(b), where the indictment falls or is for any other reason not brought to trial and the diet has not been "continued, adjourned or postponed", the Crown may in its discretion proceed under s.81(5). In such a case, the Crown must give notice in the same fashion at any time within the period of two months after the date of the trial diet (see s.81(8)(b)).

CHAPTER 13

SUMMONING OF JURORS

List of jurors

13.1.—(1) A list of jurors shall—

(a) contain not less than 30 names;

(b) be prepared under the directions of the clerk of court before which the trial is to take place;

(c) be kept at the office of the sheriff clerk of the district in which the court of the trial diet is situated; and

(d) be headed "List of Assize for the sitting of the High Court of Justiciary (or the sheriff court of.at.) on the.of.".

(2) The clerk of the court before which the trial is to take place, in preparing a list of jurors for the trial diet, shall have regard, in determining the number of jurors to be listed, to the powers of altering the date of or adjourning any trial diet exercisable under the following provisions of the Act of 1995—

section 74(3) (postponement of trial diet in appeals in connection with first diets or preliminary hearings),

section 75A (adjournment and alteration of diets),

section 76(3) (postponement where not guilty plea accepted),

AMENDMENT

Rule 13.1 substituted by the Act of Adjournal (Criminal Procedure Rules Amendment) (Criminal Procedure (Amendment) (Scotland) Act) 2005 (SSI 2005/44), r.2(14) (subject to r.2(2)–(4)) (effective February 1, 2005).

Citation of jurors

13.2.—(1) The citation under section 85(4) of the Act of 1995 of a person summoned to serve as a juror shall be served on that person in Form 13.2-A.

(2) The execution of citation under section 85(4) of the Act of 1995 of persons summoned to serve as jurors shall be in Form 13.2-B.

GENERAL NOTE

Section 84(1) of the 1995 Act requires sheriffs principal to return such numbers of jurors as they think fit or such number of jurors in cases to be tried in the High Court as the Lord Justice Clerk or a Lord Commissioner of Justiciary directs. The clerk of court shall use only these lists for the trials for which they were required (s.84(7)). This rule provides that special regard should be had by the clerk of court in determining the number of jurors to be listed to the power of the court to postpone or adjourn trial diets. The accused is entitled to have a copy of the list of jurors supplied to him free of charge on application being made to the appropriate sheriff clerk (see s.85(1)).

Section 84 makes no provision as to the minimum number of potential jurors who should be included in what subs.(8) refers to as the "list of assize". Rule 13.1(a) supplies that want by requiring that there be no fewer than 30 names. However, by the time a jury is to be empanelled, there will almost always be a smaller number of available persons to serve on the jury. This can cause problems, both administrative and legal. "The system of jury trial is based on the constitutional principle that a person indicted for trial should be judged by a randomly chosen jury of his peers" (*B v HM Advocate* 2006 S.L.T. 143, para.21, *per* Lord Justice-Clerk Gill). For that reason, a miscarriage of justice was held to have occurred in *B* when an accused was tried by a jury chosen from a list of 22 names. The High Court stated, however, that it would be wrong to lay down the minimum number from which a jury should be balloted or whether and to what extent a gender imbalance within that number would be acceptable (para.26). In *B* out of a list of 60 names (comprising an equal number of males and females), only 7 men and 15 women constituted the eventual pool of potential jurors. A retrial was authorised.

CHAPTER 13A

WITNESSES

Citation of witnesses for precognition

13A.1 The form of citation of a witness for precognition under section 267A of the Act of 1995 shall be in Form 13A.1.

AMENDMENT

Chapter 13A inserted by the Act of Adjournal (Criminal Procedure Rules Amendment No.4)

(Criminal Procedure (Amendment) (Scotland) Act 2004) 2004 (SSI 2004/434), r.2 (effective October 4, 2004).

Rule 13A.1 as amended by the Act of Adjournal (Criminal Procedure Rules Amendment No.5) (Miscellaneous) 2004 (SSI 2004/481), r.2 (effective November 26, 2004).

Warrants for apprehension

13A.2.—(1) An application made in writing for a warrant for the apprehension of a witness under section 90A or 90D of the Act of 1995 shall be in Form 13A.2-A.

(2) On receipt of an application under paragraph (1), the Clerk of Justiciary or sheriff clerk, as the case may be, shall fix a diet for the hearing of the application and intimate the date of that hearing to the parties.

(3) A warrant for the apprehension of a witness under section 90A of the Act of 1995 shall be in Form 13A.2-B.

AMENDMENT

Rule 13A.2 inserted by the Act of Adjournal (Criminal Procedure Rules Amendment) (Criminal Procedure (Amendment) (Scotland) Act) 2005 (SSI 2005/44), r.2(15) (subject to r.2(2)–(4)) (effective February 1, 2005).

Review of orders

13A.3. An application for review under section 90D of the Act of 1995 of an order under section 90A(1)(a) or (b) of that Act shall be in Form 13A.3.

AMENDMENT

Rule 13A.3 inserted by the Act of Adjournal (Criminal Procedure Rules Amendment) (Criminal Procedure (Amendment) (Scotland) Act 2004) 2005 (SSI 2005/44), r.2(15) (subject to r.2(2)–(4)) (effective February 1, 2005).

Appeals

13A.4. An appeal under section 90E(1) of the Act of 1995 (appeal in respect of an order under section 90B(1) of the Act of 1995) shall be made by lodging a note of appeal in Form 13A.4 with the Clerk of Justiciary.

AMENDMENT

Rule 13A.4 inserted by the Act of Adjournal (Criminal Procedure Rules Amendment) (Criminal Procedure (Amendment) (Scotland) Act) 2005 (SSI 2005/44), r.2(15) (subject to r.2(2)–(4)) (effective February 1, 2005).

GENERAL NOTE

The common law power of the Crown to secure the attendance at trial of absconding witnesses in solemn proceedings (see Renton & Brown, *Criminal Procedure* (5th ed.), para.7–45) was swept away by s.90A(8) which provides: "It shall not be competent, in any proceedings on indictment, for a court to issue a warrant for the apprehension of a witness otherwise than in accordance with this section". Thus a petition to the sheriff for warrant to apprehend the witness and either to detain him in custody until the date of trial (*Stallworth v HM Advocate*, 1978 S.L.T. 93) or unless he can find sufficient caution for his appearance at trial (*Gerrard, Petitioner*, 1984 S.L.T. 108) is no longer competent. The power is now entirely statutory and introduces a greater degree of judicial control over the incarceration of witnesses.

Once a witness has been arrested on a warrant issued under s.90A(1), he must be brought before the court which issued it and, after the witness and both the prosecution and the defence have been afforded an opportunity to make submissions, the witness may be detained by order of the court until the conclusion of the diet at which he is to give evidence (e.g. the trial diet or preliminary hearing) or he may be released on bail or simply liberated (s.90B(1)). The court's power to find the witness in contempt is not affected by this new procedure (s.90B(3)). The court may order the detention of the witness (or grant his release on bail) only if it is satisfied of two matters under s.90B(2). First, the specific order must be necessary with a view to securing that the witness appears at the diet at which he is to give evidence. Secondly, it must be appropriate in all the circumstances that that specific order be made.

A warrant can only be granted under s.90A(1) where either the witness has been duly cited to appear and he "deliberately and obstructively fails to appear at the diet" (s.90A(2)) or the court is satisfied that the witness is being deliberately obstructive *and* is not likely to attend to give evidence at any diet in the proceedings without being compelled to do so (s.90A(3)). A witness who is proved (by production of an execution of service of citation in proper form) to have been duly cited for the purposes of s.90A(2) and fails to appear at the diet is presumed, in the absence of any evidence to the contrary, to have so failed deliberately and obstructively (s.90A(4)).

Rule 13A.1

The citation of a potential witness for precognition by the procurator fiscal must state the place and time of the proposed precognition since s.267A(3)(a) provides that a witness who, having been duly cited, fails without reasonable excuse (after having received at least 48 hours notice) to attend at the time and place mentioned in the citation shall be guilty of an offence (for which the maximum sentence is 21 days' imprisonment). The citation warns the witness of that fact.

Rule 13A.2

The usual situation in which a witness apprehension warrant becomes necessary is at the trial diet. However, it could arise earlier where, for example, the High Court at a preliminary hearing has ordered a further diet under s.72(9) to hear evidence on an objection to the admissibility of evidence. Usually the prosecutor will be the applicant. Usually the application will be made orally at the bar, as is expressly permitted by s.90A(5)(a). However, where the application is made for a witness who has not been cited and the contention is that he has deliberately and obstructively sought to evade citation—as was the position in *Stallworth v HM Advocate*, 1978 S.L.T. 93—it may be preferable to proceed by written application in Form 13A.2-A as that will allow (in para.2 of the application) specification of the circumstances from which the court is to be invited to infer both the witness's intention deliberately and obstructively to evade citation and thus the need to compel his attendance.

The statute does not prescribe the means of proof in cases where no citation has been effected. However, where the application is in writing, s.90A(5)(b) specifically provides that the court may dispose of the application in court or chambers and leaves it to the court to determine whether any inquiry or hearing (if any) is appropriate. The accused has no right to be present in chambers since the application for a warrant under s.90A(1) is not a part of the trial proceedings even if the trial has commenced.

A s.90A(1) warrant has implied in it warrant to officers of law (a term which is defined in s.307(1)), but is in practice restricted to police officers, although it may be noted that any person commissioned by the Commissioners of Customs and Excise (now HM Revenue and Customs) may also execute such a warrant) to arrest the witness, to bring him before the court (wherever practicable on the first day the court granting the warrant is sitting after the witness is taken into custody: s.90A(9)), to detain the witness *ad interim* and so far as necessary for the execution of the warrant, to break open shut and lockfast places (s.90A(6)).

Rule 13A.3

A drafting error in this rule has been carried through into para.2 of Form 13A.3. The orders which can be reviewed are those made under s.90B(1)(a) or (b), namely committal of the witness until conclusion of the diet and release of the witness on bail (with such conditions as the court considers necessary to secure the witness's attendance at the diet: s.90B(5)).

Section 90D(1) gives to the witness the right to apply to the court ordering detention to seek recall of the order so that he can be admitted to bail or liberated. The witness must show cause and the court must afford the parties an opportunity to be heard on the review. Section 90D(2)(a) allows the witness to seek review of the bail conditions if he can show cause, and s.90D(2)(b) allows the prosecutor or defence to seek review of the earlier bail order so that the court can be persuaded to recall bail and order detention or impose different bail conditions. It is incompetent for the court to entertain a review at the instance of the Crown or defence unless there is put before the court material information which was not available to the court when the order was originally made (s.90D(3)). The prosecution or defence can obtain issue of a warrant for arrest of the witness who is on bail when it seeks a review but only if the court is satisfied that the interests of justice require the witness's arrest (s.90D(5)(c)).

A review of a first detention order or a first bail order cannot be sought by the witness before the fifth day after the order was made and once a new order has been made, no subsequent review can be sought before the 15th day after that order was made (s.90D(4)).

Rule 13A.4

It is competent for the witness, the Crown and the accused to appeal to the High Court against an order for detention or the witness's liberation or his release on bail or the conditions on which bail is granted, as appropriate (s.90E(1) and (2)). The appeal should be intimated to the other parties and, where appropriate, the witness. The appeal may be disposed of in chambers or court after such inquiry and hearing of the parties as the court considers just. In light of the terms of s.90E(4), a single High Court judge will hear an appeal from an order made in the sheriff court; a quorum of at least two High Court judges should hear an appeal against a High Court order.

CHAPTER 14

PROCEDURE AT TRIAL IN SOLEMN PROCEEDINGS

Recording of not guilty plea

14.1. Where the accused pleads not guilty, the clerk of court shall make an entry in the record of proceedings for the purposes of section 88(1) of the Act of 1995 (recording plea of not guilty and balloting jury) that, in respect that the accused pleaded not guilty, the accused was remitted to an assize and that the jurors were balloted for and duly sworn to try the libel.

Balloting of jurors

14.2.—(1) The clerk of court shall cause the name and address of each juror to be written on a separate piece of paper, all the pieces being of the same size, and shall cause the pieces to be folded up, as nearly as may be in the same shape, and to be put into a box or glass and mixed, and the clerk shall draw out the pieces of paper one by one from the box or glass.

(2) Where any of the persons whose names shall be so drawn does not appear, or is challenged (with or without cause assigned) and is set aside or, before any evidence is led, is excused, then such further names shall be drawn until the number required for the trial is completed.

Form of oath or affirmation to jurors

14.3.—(1) Where the clerk of court administers the oath to the jury in terms of section 88(6) of the Act of 1995 (administration of oath in common form), he shall do so in accordance with the form in Form 14.3-A.

(2) In the case of any juror who elects to affirm, the clerk of court shall administer the affirmation in accordance with the form in Form 14.3-B.

(3) The oath or the affirmation administered in accordance with paragraph (1) or (2), as the case may be, shall be treated as having been administered for the purposes of section 88(6) of the Act of 1995.

Jurors chosen for one trial may continue to serve

14.4.—(1) Where the conditions in section 88(4) of the Act of 1995 (circumstances in which jurors for one trial may serve on another) are met, and subject to paragraph (2) of this rule, the clerk of court shall at the commencement of the first trial engross the names and addresses of the jurors in the record of proceedings; and in the record of proceedings of the subsequent trial it shall be sufficient to mention—

(a) that the jurors who served on the preceding trial also served on the assize of the accused then under trial; and

(b) that no objection was made to the contrary.

(2) The jurors referred to in paragraph (1) shall be sworn together in the presence of the accused in the subsequent trial.

Form of oath or affirmation to witnesses

14.5.—(1) Where the judge administers the oath to a witness, he shall do so in accordance with the form in Form 14.5-A.

(2) In the case of any witness who elects to affirm, the judge shall administer the affirmation in accordance with the form in Form 14.5-B.

(3) The oath or affirmation administered in accordance with paragraph (1) or (2), as the case may be, shall be treated as having been administered in common form.

Sheriff's notes of evidence

14.6. The sheriff who has presided at a trial on solemn procedure shall duly authenticate and preserve the notes of the evidence taken by him in the trial and, if called upon to do so by the High Court, shall produce them, or a certified copy of them, to the High Court.

Form of record of proceedings

14.7. Where the proceedings at a trial are recorded, the entry in the record of proceedings shall be signed by the clerk of court and shall be in the form in Form 14.7.

Interruption of trial for other proceedings

14.8.—(1) Where a trial is interrupted under section 102 of the Act of 1995 (interruption of trial for other proceedings), a minute of continuation of the diet of the interrupted trial shall be entered in the record of proceedings.

(2) Where a trial is interrupted under section 102 of the Act of 1995, the trial shall be continued to a time later on the same day or to such other time as may be specified in the minute of proceedings.

Interruption of proceedings for conviction or sentence

14.9.—(1) On conviction of an accused in solemn proceedings, the presiding judge may, without adjourning those proceedings, interrupt them by—

    (a) considering a conviction against that accused in other proceedings pending before that court for which he has not been sentenced; or

    (b) passing sentence on that accused in respect of the conviction in those other proceedings.

(2) Where the judge has interrupted any proceedings under paragraph (1), he may, in passing sentence on an accused person in respect of a conviction in those proceedings, at the same time pass sentence on that person in respect of any other conviction he has considered.

(3) No interruption of any proceedings under paragraph (1) shall cause the instance to fall in respect of any person accused in those proceedings or shall otherwise affect the validity of those proceedings.

Issue of extract convictions

14.10.—(1) Subject to the following paragraphs, no extract of a conviction shall be issued during the period of four weeks after the day on which the conviction took place.

(2) An extract of a conviction may be issued at any time where it is required as a warrant for the detention of the person convicted under any sentence which shall have been pronounced against him.

(3) In the event of—

    (a) an appeal under section 108 (Lord Advocate's appeal against sentence) or section 210F(3) (prosecutor's appeal against refusal to make an order for lifelong restriction),

    (b) an intimation of intention to appeal under section 109(1), or

    (c) a note of appeal under section 110 in respect of an appeal under section 106(1)(b) (appeal against sentence passed on conviction), of the Act of 1995 being lodged, no extract of a conviction shall be issued until such appeal, if it is proceeded with, is determined.

(4) Where an accused is convicted on indictment in the sheriff court of any crime or offence and an extract of that conviction is subsequently required in evidence, such extract shall be issued at any time by the clerk of the court having the custody of the record copy of the indictment although the plea of the accused may have been taken and the sentence on him pronounced in another court.

AMENDMENT

Rule 14.10(3)(a) as amended by the Act of Adjournal (Criminal Procedure Rules Amendment No.3) (Risk Assessment Orders and Orders for Lifelong Restriction) 2006 (SSI 2006/302), para.2(2) (effective June 20, 2006).

GENERAL NOTE

Sections 88 to 102 of the 1995 Act make detailed provision for the conduct of contested solemn proceedings at the trial stage from the recording of the plea of not guilty, the balloting of the jury, etc., right through to the receiving and recording of the verdict in open court in the presence of the accused.

It should be noted that the High Court has effectively held that it is incompetent to interfere with the principle of random selection of the jury by "vetting" prospective jurors on the list of assize, in order to determine their individual beliefs and possible prejudices: see *McDonald v HM Advocate*, 1997 S.L.T. 1237. This decision is in line with the English position that the court has no power to ensure that a multi-racial jury is empanelled: see *R. v Ford (Royston)* [1989] 1 Q.B. 868.

Rule 14.1

The minutes of proceedings should record the fact that the accused pled not guilty and that the jury were balloted and duly sworn to try the libel under rr.14.2 and 14.3, as these are essential steps in the trial process and accurate information about their having occurred is required in the event of an appeal against conviction. See also Chap.3.

Rule 14.2

Jurors can now only be challenged for cause (see s.86(2)) although the court is required to excuse a juror before he is sworn if the Crown and the accused agree (see s.86(1)) and in that event no reason need be given to the court. Any objection for cause must be stated to the court, before the juror is sworn to serve (see s.86(4)) and cannot be founded on any irregularity in the procedures for the preparation of the list of assize unless such irregularity is based on a criminal act by which jurors may be returned to serve in any case contrary to the 1995 Act or the Jurors (Scotland) Act 1825 (see s.84(10)).

Prospective jurors are cited to attend a sitting of the High Court (or the sheriff court) in terms of a warrant issued by the Clerk of Justiciary (or sheriff clerk, as appropriate) in terms of s.66(1) of the 1995 Act. Provision is made in s.1(2) of the Law Reform (Miscellaneous Provisions) (Scotland) Act 1980 for excusal as of right and, under s.1(3), for other prospective jurors to be excused in particular circumstances. Furthermore, any juror who cannot escape under these provisions can be excused by the clerk of court if the juror can show to the clerk's satisfaction that "there is good reason why he should be excused from attending in compliance with the citation" (s.1(5)). These provisions do not undermine the common law principle (expressed by Lord Justice-General Emslie in *M v HM Advocate*, 1974 S.L.T. (Notes) 25) that the jury ultimately balloted must be a random selection of the citizenry. Nor do these provisions provide a relevant ground of challenge under Art.6(1) of the European Convention that the jury is not an independent and impartial tribunal established by law: *Transco Plc v HM Advocate (No.2)*, 2004 S.L.T. 995.

Rule 14.4

Section 88(4) of the 1995 Act permits with the consent of the Crown and the accused, jurors who are chosen for one trial, which has been disposed of, to serve on the jury at other trials without again being selected by ballot. However r.14.4(2) reaffirms the requirement of s.92(1) that (subject to s.54(4) dealing with the plea of insanity in bar of trial, and where the accused misconducts himself) no part of a trial shall take place outwith the presence of the accused (see *Walker v Emslie* (1899) 3 Adam 102; *Bennett v HM Advocate*, 1980 S.L.T. (Notes) 73. See also notes to Chap. 12 for a qualification to this rule in respect of continuations of the diet).

A failure to put the appropriate form of oath or affirmation to the witness would not, it is submitted, invalidate the trial proceedings nor render the witnesses' evidence incompetent: see *McAvoy v HM Advocate*, 1992 S.L.T. 46 (*sub nom. McAvoy and Jackson v HM Advocate*, 1991 S.C.C.R. 123). If the witness is a child or arguably too young to be sworn, but the witness is sworn without the court first ascertaining the witness's age and satisfying itself that the witness is capable of understanding the nature of the oath—in accordance with the procedure desiderated in *Quinn v Lees*, 1994 S.C.C.R. 159—any evidence from the witness should be objected to timeously in order to preserve the accused's right of appeal in accordance with s.118(8) of the 1995 Act: *Jardine v Howdle*, 1997 S.C.C.R. 294 (applying s.192(3) in summary proceedings). However, it should be noted that *Jardine* is apparently inconsistent with *Kelly v Docherty*, 1991 S.L.T. 419 and that the court did not appear to consider the additional question of whether the alleged incompetency of the witness rendered the proceedings a fundamental nullity. It seems that no distinction was drawn between the competency of evidence (e.g. hearsay evidence is generally incompetent, but once admitted without objection it becomes competent evidence *in causa*) and the competency of witnesses.

Rule 14.6

No obligation is imposed on High Court judges to authenticate and preserve their notes of the evidence but it is the practice of the High Court for judges to keep detailed notes which can then be furnished to the High Court by way of a report in terms of s.113 or s.298(1) of the 1995 Act, and accordingly these detailed notes of evidence would be available in the (unlikely) event that the Criminal Appeal Court wished to inspect them.

Rule 14.7

Section 93(1) of the Criminal Procedure (Scotland) Act 1995 provides that the proceedings at the trial of any person who, if convicted, is entitled to appeal under Part VIII of the 1995 Act, shall be recorded by means of shorthand notes or by mechanical means. A breach of that provision, which can perhaps more easily occur now in the High Court because of the use of tape recording equipment, does not alone lead to the conviction being quashed: for a breach of s.93(1) to give rise to a miscarriage of justice the accused must also identify an issue on which it can be said that the trial judge misdirected the jury (*Carroll v HM Advocate*, 1999 S.L.T. 1185; 1999 S.C.C.R. 617).

Section 94 of the 1995 Act makes provision for the making and delivery of transcripts of evidence recorded under s.93(1). The Secretary of State (now Scottish Ministers) and the prosecutor are entitled to request such a transcript which the Clerk of Justiciary must then make available; and the same obligation applies where a request is made by any other person not being a person convicted at the trial although the third party must pay such charges as are fixed by the Treasury as a condition of obtaining the transcript (s.94(2)). Subsection (2A), inserted by s.65 of the Criminal Justice (Scotland) Act 2003, gives a convicted person the right to ask a High Court judge for a transcript where he has been granted leave to appeal and can show cause for his application; but in that case the convicted person must pay such charges as are fixed by the Treasury (just as third parties must do). Where the Crown Agent has received intimation of the High Court's decision on an application for leave to appeal (or a second sift application) under s.107(10)—whether the decision is to grant leave or to refuse it—the prosecutor is not entitled to a transcript as of right under subs.(2)(a) but must apply in writing to a High Court judge for a transcript and that request may be granted where the prosecutor shows cause for the transcript being made available (s.94(2B)). Cause will exist where the Crown proposes to try a co-accused separately because, for example, the evidence was insufficient in the absence of the first accused as a compellable witness or the co-accused had absconded prior to the first trial, and especially so where an essential witness has died after giving evidence at the first trial. It is necessary to apply to a High Court judge irrespective of whether the trial was in the sheriff court or High Court because it is the High Court which alone regulates appellate procedure.

Section 94(3) repeats the terms of s.275(3) of the Criminal Procedure (Scotland) Act 1975 (as inserted by s.47(1) of, and para.27 of Sch.5 to, the Prisoners and Criminal Proceedings (Scotland) Act 1993) and empowers the Secretary of State (now the Scottish Ministers) to make an order restricting the scope of s.94(2). The power was exercised in 1993 to make the Transcripts of Criminal Proceedings (Scotland) Order 1993 (SI 1993/2226) which, after amendment by the Transcripts of Criminal Proceedings (Scotland) Amendment Order 1995 (SI 1995/1751), provides that no transcript can be supplied unless the Clerk of Justiciary is satisfied that the person requesting the transcript (whether prosecutor, convicted person, any third party named in or immediately affected by an order made by the court in the proceedings, or any person authorised to act on behalf of such persons) intends to use it only for a specified purpose. This applies only to (a) trials where the court has made an order excluding persons from the court room because it is a trial for rape or a like offence (s.145(3) of the

1975 Act, now s.92(3) of the 1995 Act) or a trial relating to an offence or conduct contrary to decency or morality and a child witness is to give evidence (s.166(1) of the 1975 Act, now s.50(3) of the 1995 Act) and (b) trials where the court has made an order postponing publication of the proceedings under s.4(2) of the Contempt of Court Act 1981. The specified purposes which alone can be the justification for the supply of a transcript are (1) an appeal to the High Court (which does not include a reference by the Lord Advocate under s.123(1) of the 1995 Act or a reference by the Advocate General of a devolution issue under s.288A(1) of the 1995 Act); (2) a reference of a conviction and/or sentence to the High Court by the Secretary of State for Scotland under s.263(1) of the 1975 Act (which must now mean a reference by the Scottish Criminal Cases Review Commission under s.194B(1) of the 1995 Act, or any application or petition in relation thereto); (3) a petition for the exercise of Her Majesty's Prerogative of Mercy; (4) any proceedings before the European Court of Human Rights; and (5) any proceedings before the Court of Justice of the European Communities.

Rule 14.8

Section 102 of the 1995 Act allows for a jury trial to be interrupted in two distinct situations. First, where the jury is deliberating over its verdict and another trial has been called (it is unnecessary that the first witness has been sworn for this rule to apply), the presiding judge may receive the verdict in the preceding trial and pass sentence, or the presiding judge may give further directions in the preceding trial where the jury has sought a direction (although not where the presiding judge *ex proprio motu* decides to give further directions) or where any request by the jury has been made regarding any matter in the cause. For example the jury may request to examine a production and in such circumstances the procedure laid down in *Hamilton v HM Advocate*, 1980 J.C. 66 should be followed. Secondly, where a trial is "then proceeding", and an accused in a case where the diet has not yet been called intimates a desire to plead guilty or to plead in terms acceptable to the Crown, or where a case is remitted to the High Court for sentence under s.195, the presiding judge may interrupt the trial. Presumably the trial is "proceeding" immediately on the diet having been called. In either case the interruption is not to be deemed an irregularity, nor can the accused object to the proceedings (s.102(5)), although subs.(4) requires the trial diet to be called *de novo* after the interruption is concluded in order for the trial competently to be proceeded with anew. The interruption should accordingly be minuted so that there is a record of it and of the commencement of the trial in the event of an appeal against conviction.

Rule 14.9

This rule was first introduced by the Act of Adjournal (Sentencing Powers) 1978 (SI 1978/123) which was intended to assist court administration by curing the technical obstacles to an accused who is awaiting sentence in respect of another conviction being dealt with for both convictions simultaneously (see *Law and Nicol v HM Advocate*, 1973 S.L.T. (Notes) 14). The rule requires that there be a conviction in existence and accordingly does not permit the interruption of the proceedings to receive the plea and then proceed to sentence (*Watters v HM Advocate*, 1992 S.L.T. 149; 1992 S.C.C.R. 104. See also *MacDonald v HM Advocate*, 1994 S.L.T. 44 where a summary complaint in respect of which no conviction had been returned was tendered to but rejected by the sheriff at a deferred sentence diet).

CHAPTER 15

APPEALS FROM SOLEMN PROCEEDINGS

Register and lists of appeals

15.1.—(1) The Clerk of Justiciary shall keep a register, in such form as he thinks fit, of all cases in which he receives intimation of intention to appeal or, in the case of an appeal under section 106 (right of appeal), section 108 (Lord Advocate's appeal against sentence) or section 210F(3) (prosecutor's appeal against refusal to make an order for lifelong restriction) of the Act of 1995, a note of appeal under section 110 of that Act.

(2) The register kept under paragraph (1) shall be open for public inspection at such place and at such hours as the Clerk of Justiciary, subject to the approval of the Lord Justice General, considers convenient.

(3) The Clerk of Justiciary shall—

(a) prepare from time to time, a list of appeals to be dealt with by the High Court; and

(b) cause such list to be published in such manner as, subject to the approval of the Lord Justice General, he considers convenient for giving due notice to persons having an interest in the hearing of such appeals by the High Court.

(4) Subject to paragraph (5), the Clerk of Justiciary shall give the respective solicitors representing parties to an appeal so listed at least 14 days notice of the date fixed for the hearing of the appeal.

(5) In an appeal under sections 106(1)(b) to (e), 108(1) or 210F(3) of the Act of 1995, the period of notice mentioned in paragraph (4) shall be 42 days.

AMENDMENTS

Rule 15.1 as amended by Act of Adjournal (Criminal Appeals) 2003 (SSI 2003/387), art.3. Brought into force on September 1, 2003 in accordance with art.1.

Rule 15.1(1) and (5) as amended by Act of Adjournal (Criminal Procedure Rules Amendment No.3) (Risk Assessment Orders and Orders for Lifelong Restriction) 2006 (SSI 2006/302), para.2(3) (effective June 20, 2006).

Forms of appeal

15.2.—(1) Any intimation under section 109(1) of the Act of 1995 (written intimation of intention to appeal) shall be in Form 15.2-A.

(2) A note under section 110(1) of the Act of 1995 (written note of appeal) shall be in Form 15.2-B.

(3) An application under section 111(2) of the Act of 1995 (application to extend time) shall be made in Form 15.2-C.

(4) An application under section 112(1) of the Act of 1995 (application of appellant for bail) shall be made in Form 15.2-D.

(5) The following documents shall be signed by the appellant or by his counsel or solicitor—

(a) an intimation of intention to appeal under section 109(1) of the Act of 1995 except where the appellant is the Lord Advocate, or;

(b) an application under section 111(2) of the Act of 1995 (application to extend time).

(5A) The note of appeal shall be signed by—

(a) the counsel or solicitor advocate who has drafted it; or

(b) the appellant where the appellant has drafted it and intends to conduct the appeal himself.

(6) An appeal under section 19 of the Prisoners and Criminal Proceedings (Scotland) Act 1993 (appeals in respect of decisions relating to supervised release orders) shall be in Form 15.2-B.

AMENDMENT

Rule 15.2(5) as amended, and rule 15.2(5A) inserted, by Act of Adjournal (Criminal Appeals) 2002 (SSI 2002/387), art.3(2) (effective September 26, 2002).

Appeals against refusal of applications heard by single judge

15.3.—(1) Where an application has been dealt with by a single judge of the High Court by virtue of section 103(5) of the Act of 1995 (powers exercisable by single judge), the Clerk of Justiciary shall notify the decision to the applicant in Form 15.3-A.

(2) In the event of such judge refusing any such application, the Clerk of Justiciary on notifying such refusal to the applicant shall forward to him a form in Form 15.3-B to complete and return forthwith if he desires to have his application determined by the High Court as constituted for the hearing of appeals under Part VIII of the Act of 1995 (appeals from solemn proceedings).

Extension of time by Clerk of Justiciary

15.4. Where, under section 110(2) of the Act of 1995, the Clerk of Justiciary extends the period for lodging a note of appeal, the period of any such extension shall be recorded on the completed form of intimation of intention to appeal.

Intimation of appeal against sentence of death

15.5. The Clerk of Justiciary shall intimate an appeal against a conviction in respect of which sentence of death has been pronounced, and the determination in any such appeal, immediately on such intimation or determination, as the case may be, to—

(a) the Secretary of State for Scotland; and

(b) the governor of the prison in which the appellant is detained.

Procedural hearing

15.5A—(1) In any appeal against conviction or conviction and sentence, the Clerk of Justiciary may fix a procedural hearing for the purposes of determining whether the parties are ready to proceed to a hearing of the appeal.

(2) The procedural hearing shall be heard by a judge of the High Court and, where the appellant is an individual and is represented, may be held in his absence.

(3) The Clerk of Justiciary shall intimate to the parties in Form 15.5A-A the date of the procedural hearing fixed under paragraph (1), not later than twenty-one days before that date.

(4) Not later than seven days before the date of the procedural hearing, the appellant shall complete and lodge a notice in Form 15.5A-B with the Clerk of Justiciary and send a copy to the respondent. The said notice shall be signed by the counsel or solicitor advocate representing the appellant in the appeal, or by the appellant where the appellant intends to conduct the appeal himself.

(5) Where the appellant has lodged a notice in accordance with paragraph (4), the Clerk of Justiciary, having considered the terms of the said notice and any representations made to him by the respondent, may determine that it is unnecessary to proceed with the procedural hearing and, if he so determines, shall intimate this to the parties not less than forty-eight hours before the date of the procedural hearing.

(6) Not later than seven days after the last day of the appeal court sitting during which

(a) the procedural hearing at which it has been determined that the appeal is ready to proceed has been heard; or

(b) the procedural hearing was due to be heard but in respect of which the Clerk of Justiciary has made a determination in terms of paragraph (5),

the Clerk of Justiciary shall fix and intimate to the parties the date when the appeal is to be heard.

(7) Not later than seven days before the date of the appeal hearing, the appellant shall submit a list of the authorities upon which he intends to rely with references to the relevant passages and shall send a copy to the respondent.

AMENDMENT

Rule 15.5A inserted by Act of Adjournal (Criminal Appeals) 2002 (SSI 2002/387), art.3(2) (effective September 26, 2002).

Abandonment of appeals

15.6. A notice of abandonment under section 116(1) of the Act of 1995 (abandonment of appeal) shall be in Form 15.6.

Note of proceedings at trial

15.7. In an appeal under section 106(1) of the Act of 1995 (right of appeal), the High Court may require the judge who presided at the trial to produce any notes taken by him of the proceedings at the trial.

Clerk to give notice of date of hearing

15.8.—(1) Where the High Court fixes the date for the hearing of an appeal or of an application under section 111(2) of the Act of 1995 (application to extend time), the Clerk of Justiciary shall give notice to the Crown Agent and to the solicitor of the convicted person, or to the convicted person himself if he has no known solicitor; and the appellant or applicant shall, within seven days before the hearing, lodge three copies (typed or printed) of the appeal or application for the use of the court.

(2) Where the powers of the court are to be exercised by a single judge under section 103(5) of the Act of 1995 (powers exercisable by single judge), a copy of the application to be determined shall be lodged for the use of the judge.

(3) A notice by the Clerk of Justiciary to the Secretary of State for the purposes of section 117(4) of the Act of 1995 (notice that appellant or applicant be present at a diet) shall be in Form 15.8.

Continuation of hearings

15.9.—(1) The High Court, or any single judge exercising the powers of the High Court under section 103(5) of the Act of 1995 (powers exercisable by single judge), may continue the hearing of any appeal or application to a date, fixed or not fixed.

(2) Any judge of the High Court, or the person appointed by the court to take additional evidence, may fix any diet or proof necessary for that purpose.

Note to be kept of appeal

15.10.—(1) The Clerk of Justiciary shall, in all cases of appeal from a conviction obtained or sentence pronounced in the High Court, note on the margin of the record of the trial the fact of an appeal having been taken and the result of the appeal.

(2) In the case of an appeal taken against any conviction obtained or sentence pronounced in the sheriff court on indictment, the Clerk of Justiciary shall notify the clerk of that court of the result of the appeal; and it shall be the duty of the clerk of that court to enter on the margin of the record of the trial a note of such result.

Suspension of disqualification from driving pending appeal

15.11.—(1) Where a person who has been disqualified from holding or obtaining a driving licence following a conviction on indictment appeals against that disqualification to the High Court, any application to suspend that disqualification pending the hearing of the appeal shall be made—

  (a) if the sentencing court was the sheriff, by application to the sheriff; or

  (b) if the sentencing court was the High Court, or if an application to the sheriff under subparagraph (a) has been refused, by petition to the High Court.

(2) An application to the sheriff under paragraph (1)(a) shall be—

  (a) in Form 15.11-A, and

  (b) lodged with the sheriff clerk with a copy of the note of appeal endorsed with the receipt of the Clerk of Justiciary;

and the sheriff clerk shall record the order made by the sheriff on the application in the minute of proceedings.

(3) A petition to the High Court under paragraph (1)(b) shall be—

(a) in Form 15.11-B; and

(b) lodged with the Clerk of Justiciary.

Provisions supplemental to rule 15.11(3)

15.12.—(1) The petitioner or his solicitor shall, on lodging a petition under rule 15.11(3), send a copy of it to—

(a) the Crown Agent; and

(b) if the sentencing court was the sheriff, the clerk of that court.

(2) The High Court may order such further intimation (including intimation to the Lord Advocate) as it thinks fit, and may dispose of the application in open court or in chambers.

(3) An order made by a single judge under paragraph (2) shall not be subject to review.

(4) On an order being made on a petition under rule 15.11(3), the Clerk of Justiciary shall, if the sentencing court was the sheriff, send a certified copy of the order to the clerk of that court.

(5) Where the order referred to in paragraph (4) suspends a disqualification from driving, the Clerk of Justiciary shall also send a certified copy of the order to the Secretary of State with such further information as the Secretary of State may require.

(6) The Clerk of Justiciary shall, on determination of the appeal against a disqualification from driving—

(a) if the sentencing court was the sheriff, send the clerk of that court a certified copy of the order determining the appeal and the clerk of that court shall, if appropriate, make the appropriate endorsement on the appellant's driving licence and intimate the disqualification to the persons concerned; or

(b) if the appeal against the disqualification is refused, make the appropriate endorsement on the appellant's driving licence and intimate the disqualification to the persons concerned.

(7) Where leave to appeal has been refused under section 107 of the Act of 1995, "determination" in paragraph (6) of this rule means—

(a) the fifteenth day after the date of intimation to the appellant or his solicitor of refusal of leave under subsection (1)(b) of that section, unless the appellant applies to the High Court for leave to appeal; or

(b) the day two days after the date of intimation to the appellant or his solicitor of the refusal of leave by the High Court under subsection (5)(b) of that section.

Suspension of sentence under s.121A of the Act of 1995

15.12A.—(1) Where under section 109(1) of the Act of 1995 a person lodges intimation of intention to appeal, any application for suspension of a relevant sentence under section 121A of that Act shall be made by petition to the High Court in Form 15.12A-A.

(2) Where a convicted person or the prosecutor lodges a note of appeal in respect of an appeal under section 106(1)(b) to (e) or 108 of the Act of 1995, as the case may be, any application for suspension of a relevant sentence under section 121A of that Act shall be made by petition to the High Court in Form 15.12A-B.

(3) A petition to the High Court under paragraph (1) or (2) shall be lodged with the Clerk of Justiciary.

(4) The court shall grant or refuse any application under paragraph (1) or (2) within 7 days of the petition having been lodged as mentioned in paragraph (3).

(5) Where the court grants an application under paragraph (1) or (2) the Clerk of Justiciary shall, if the sentencing court was the sheriff, send a certified copy of the order to the clerk of that court.

(6) In any case where—

(a) intimation of intention to appeal is lodged under section 109(1) of the Act of 1995; and

(b) a relevant sentence is suspended under section 121A of that Act,

but no note of appeal is lodged under section 110 of that Act, the order suspending *ad interim* the relevant sentence shall be recalled with effect from the seventh day after the date on which the Clerk of Justiciary intimates that the appeal is deemed to have been abandoned.

(7) In the application of section 121A of the Act of 1995 (suspension of certain sentences pending appeal) to a case in which leave to appeal has been refused under section 107 of that Act, the word "determined" in subsection (1) of the said section 121A shall be construed as meaning—

(a) the fifteenth day after the date of intimation to the appellant or his solicitor and to the Crown Agent of refusal of leave under subsection (1)(b) of section 107 of that Act, unless the appellant applies to the High Court for leave to appeal; or

(b) the seventh day after the date of intimation to the appellant or his solicitor and to the Crown Agent of the refusal of leave by the High Court under subsection (5)(b) of section 107 of that Act.

AMENDMENT

Rule 15.12A inserted by Act of Adjournal (Criminal Procedure Rules Amendment No.4) (SI 1997/1834) (effective August 1, 1997).

Suspension of disqualification etc. under section 121 of the Act of 1995

15.13. In the application of section 121 of the Act of 1995 (suspension of disqualification, forfeiture, etc.) to a case in which leave to appeal has been refused under section 107 of the Act of 1995, the word "determined" in subsections (1) and (2) of section 121 of that Act shall be construed as meaning—

(a) the fifteenth day after the date of intimation to the appellant or his solicitor of refusal of leave under subsection (1)(b) of section 107 of that Act, unless the appellant applies to the High Court for leave to appeal; or

(b) the day seven days after the date of intimation to the appellant or his solicitor of the refusal of leave by the High Court under subsection (5)(b) of section 107 of that Act.

AMENDMENT

Rule 15.13 as amended by Act of Adjournal (Criminal Procedure Rules Amendment No.3) 1997 (SI 1997/1788) (effective August 11, 1997).

Remits in applications for leave to appeal

15.14. The judge of the High Court considering an application for leave to appeal under section 107 of the Act of 1995 may, before deciding to grant or refuse leave, remit the case to the judge who presided at the trial for a supplementary report to be produced to him as soon as is reasonably practicable on any matter with respect to the grounds of appeal.

AMENDMENT

Rule 15.14 inserted by Act of Adjournal (Criminal Procedure Rules Amendment) (Miscellaneous) (SI 1996/2747 (S.171)) (effective September 9, 1996).

Amended grounds of appeal

15.15—(1) On cause shown, the High Court may grant leave to an appellant to amend the grounds of appeal contained in the note of appeal.

(2) Where the High Court has granted leave to amend the grounds of appeal under paragraph (1), it may order—

(a) that the Clerk of Justiciary shall send a copy of the amended note of appeal to the judge who presided at the trial; and

(b) that as soon as is reasonably practicable after receiving a copy of the amended note of appeal, the judge who presided at the trial shall provide the Clerk of Justiciary with a written report on the amended grounds of appeal.

(3) Section 113(2) to (4) of the Act of 1995 (judge's report) shall apply to a report on the amended grounds of appeal ordered under paragraph (2) as it applies to a report under subsection (1) of that section.

(4) Where the High Court grants leave to amend under paragraph (1), section 107 of the Act of 1995 shall apply, unless the Court otherwise directs, for the purposes of obtaining leave to appeal for the amended grounds of appeal as it applied for the purposes of the original grounds of appeal and, for the references in subsection (2)(a) and (c) of that section to the note of appeal and the trial judge's report, there shall be substituted references to the amended grounds of appeal contained in the amended note of appeal and the trial judge's report, if any, on the amended grounds of appeal, respectively.

AMENDMENT

Rule 15.15 inserted Act of Adjournal (Criminal Appeals) 2002 (SSI 2002/387), art.3(2) (effective September 26, 2002).

Presentation of solemn sentence appeal in writing

15.16—(1) This rule applies to an appeal under sections 106(1)(b) to (e), 108(1) or 210F(3) of the Act of 1995 listed in terms of rule 15.1(3) (register and lists of appeals).

(2) In an appeal to which paragraph (1) applies, the appellant shall present his case in writing.

(3) The solicitor for the appellant or, if unrepresented, the appellant shall—

(a) not later than 21 days before the date assigned for the appeal court hearing, lodge a case and argument in Form 15.16;

(b) lodge with the case and argument all documents, or a copy thereof, referred to or founded upon in the case and argument and not already lodged; and

(c) at the same time as he lodges the case and argument referred to in sub-paragraph (a) and the supporting documents referred to in sub-paragraph (b), send a copy to the Crown or, where the Crown is the appellant, to the respondent.

(4) The case and argument referred to in paragraph (3) shall be signed by counsel or the solicitor advocate representing the appellant in the appeal, or by the appellant where the appellant intends to conduct the appeal himself.

(5) At the hearing of the appeal—

(a) the case and argument and supporting documents referred to in paragraph (3) shall constitute the submissions of the appellant;

(b) unless it otherwise directs, the Court will expect the appellant to rely upon the case and argument without reading it over to the Court; and

(c) the appellant may make supplementary comments to the case and argument; and shall answer any points raised by the Court.

(6) On cause shown, the Court may permit the appellant to introduce new information that has come to light in the period since the case and argument was lodged.

(7) Where the Court permits the introduction of new information, it may at its discretion permit the lodging of additional documents in support of the new information.

(8) A party who wishes to introduce new information and lodge additional documents shall send a copy of the information and documents to the Clerk of Justiciary as soon as the information and documents come into the appellant's possession.

(9) A party who has sent new information and documents to the Clerk of Justiciary shall make application at the bar to allow it to be introduced or lodged, as the case may be.

(10) Where the documents referred to in paragraph (3) are not lodged time-ously, the Deputy Principal Clerk of Justiciary shall refer the matter to the Lord Justice-General, whom failing the Lord Justice-Clerk, for such action as the Lord Justice-General or Lord Justice-Clerk, as the case may be, considers appropriate.

AMENDMENTS

Rule 15.16 inserted by Act of Adjournal (Criminal Appeals) 2003 (SSI 2003/387), art.3. Brought into force on September 1, 2003 in accordance with art.1.

Rule 15.16(1) as amended by Act of Adjournal (Criminal Procedure Rules Amendment No.3) (Risk Assessment Orders and Orders for Lifelong Restriction) 2006 (SSI 2006/302), para.2(4) (effective June 20, 2006).

GENERAL NOTE

The law in relation to an appeal against conviction and/or sentence in solemn proceedings is now radically altered from the state it existed in under the 1975 Act since an appeal on the ground of a miscarriage of justice can only be proceeded with now after the High Court has granted leave to appeal in terms of s.107 of the 1995 Act. Leave to appeal will only be granted in the first instance by a single judge of the High Court or, in the event of his refusing leave, by a quorum of two or three judges (depending on whether the appeal is against sentence alone or conviction (and sentence)), if the accused can satisfy the High Court that he has "arguable grounds of appeal". If the accused satisfies the court that there are arguable grounds then the appeal will be allowed to be proceeded with on these grounds *alone* (although the High Court can permit further grounds to be argued at the appeal hearing).

It is incompetent to apply to judges at a second sift in order to challenge the first sift judge's decision to limit the grounds of appeal on which the first sift judge has granted leave to appeal. The correct procedure, where leave is granted on restricted grounds, is to seek the Appeal Court's leave, under s.107(8) of the 1995 Act, to argue the grounds refused at the sift stage: see *Beggs, Petitioner*, 2005 S.L.T. 165 (para.9). The first sift judge must give reasons for his refusal of leave and these reasons must be "intelligible and deal with the issues of law that are raised in the grounds of appeal" but once that has been done there is no reason in principle for the second sift judges' not being able to express their reasons referentially by adopting those of the first sift judge: see *McSorley, Petitioner*, 2005 S.C.C.R. 508 (para.15). Where leave to appeal against sentence has been refused in respect of all the grounds advanced, it is incompetent to ask the Appeal Court to grant leave on cause shown even though the judges at the second sift have granted leave to appeal against conviction because such an appeal is "a quite different matter" (*McLeod v HM Advocate* [2005] HCJAC 128 (October 12, 2005), para.12).

In light of observations made by the court in *Ryan, Petitioner*, 2002 S.L.T. 275; 2002 S.C.C.R. 295 (para.7), a practice developed in Justiciary Office when leave to appeal had been refused at the first sift of advising solicitors who had intimated an appeal against the refusal of leave that the appeal would be withheld from the second sift for a stated period (in order to allow amplification of the written submissions on the grounds of appeal and quite often also to allow for the obtaining of counsel's opinion). This was nothing more than an informal administrative arrangement which only operated when the solicitor requested that the appeal be withheld from the second sift. If no such request were made and acceded to, the appeal could be considered by the second sift judges forthwith. There is no basis for solicitors believing that an appeal will not be considered at second sift before the 14-day period (under s.107(4)) for marking an appeal to the second sift expires: see *Strang v HM Advocate*, 2005 S.L.T. 1114 (paras 19–20).

It should be noted that where an application for leave to appeal has been refused by a single judge and the accused has failed within 14 days to apply to a quorum of the High Court, the High Court has no power in exercise of its *nobile officium* to waive or extend that time limit on an extra-statutory basis: see *Connolly, Petr*, 1997 S.L.T. 689; 1997 S.C.C.R. 295.

That decision was approved by a Bench of Five Judges in *Ryan, Petitioner*, 2002 S.L.T. 275 where *Connolly* was described as correctly decided although the court expressed concern that s.107(4) was inflexible in its operation because it applied even where an extension of time (which is available for other time limits governing related procedural steps on appeal) would occasion no prejudice to the Crown or any other party. Reconsideration of s.107(4) was therefore urged on the Scottish Parliament so as to avoid a situation where the consequence of failure, even by a day, to comply with the provision "would be out of all proportion to the culpability, if there was any, of a failure to comply with that time limit" (para.25, p.277L).

The remedy in such a situation would therefore appear to rest in the hands of the Scottish Criminal Cases Review Commission which is empowered by s.194B(1) of the 1995 Act to refer a convicted person's whole case to the High Court for determination as if it were an appeal, irrespective of whether an appeal against conviction had previously been heard and determined by the court, on the grounds that the Commission believes that a miscarriage of justice may have occurred *and* that it is in the interests of justice that the case should be referred (s.194C). However, given the limited resources of the Commission and the delay which being required to make application to the Commission would entail, this is at best an uneconomic way of avoiding the consequences of s.107(4) as it is presently framed. The provision has now been amended to give the court a discretion to allow the appeal to proceed.

Crown appeals against sentence

Where the Crown appeals against an unduly lenient sentence it can happen that the accused, though represented by counsel and agents, is absent at the hearing of the appeal when the appeal might be allowed and an increased sentence imposed. The High Court has held that "in principle, proceedings which may have that consequence ought not to take place outwith the presence of the respondent" (*Urquhart v Campbell*, 2006 S.C.C.R. 656, para.[4]). At present the court will therefore continue the appeal for the accused to have the opportunity to attend.

Rule 15.1

The Register of Appeals will be a record of all solemn cases in which an intention to appeal (though the appeal may subsequently be abandoned under s.116 of the 1995 Act) is given to the Justiciary Office in Edinburgh under s.109, or where a note of appeal against conviction and/or sentence is lodged by an accused after leave has been granted under s.107, or where the Lord Advocate has lodged a note of appeal against an unduly lenient sentence under s.108. The Clerk of Justiciary will thereafter prepare a criminal appeal roll detailing the appeals which have been granted leave to proceed and specifying the dates on which they are appointed to be heard.

Oddly, r.15.1 does not make provision for the recording of notes of appeal under r.31.7 against the decision of a solemn court to make a reference to the Court of Justice of the European Communities.

The additional r.15.1(4) and (5) provides that, except in appeals against sentence and the Lord Advocate's appeals against unduly lenient disposals (under s.106 and 108 respectively), there should be at least 14 days' notice given to the parties of the date of the proposed appeal hearing. The exception requiring 42 days' notice in sentence appeals is made necessary by the innovation in procedure effected by the Act of Adjournal (Criminal Appeals) 2003 (SSI 2003/387), para.3(b) which provides that these appeals shall be presented in writing.

Rule 15.2

Rule 15.2(1). Written intimation of an intention to appeal against conviction and/or sentence on indictment should be given within two weeks of the final determination of the proceedings (i.e. when sentence is passed in open court: s.109(4)).

Rule 15.2(2). A note of appeal by an accused person against conviction and/or sentence on indictment, should be lodged within six weeks of lodging intimation by way of Form 15.2-A but where the appeal is against sentence only, the note of appeal should be lodged within two weeks of sentence being passed in open court. Where the Lord Advocate appeals against an unduly lenient sentence (or a disposal which is either inappropriate or on unduly lenient terms), there is no requirement to lodge intimation of an intention to appeal as the Lord Advocate does not require leave to appeal. The Lord Advocate has "the right of direct access" to the Appeal Court: see *HM Advocate v McKay*, 1996 S.C.C.R. 410 at 416G–417A). The Lord Advocate's note of appeal must be lodged within four weeks of the passing of the sentence in open court. However, the period of six weeks applying to accused persons may be extended (before it expires) by the Clerk of Justiciary (see s.110(2)). The Clerk of Justiciary has no such power in relation to an appeal at the instance of the Lord Advocate.

Rule 15.2(3). A single judge of the High Court (see s.103(5)) may extend (i) the period of two weeks within which intimation of an intention to appeal should be given by the accused, and (ii) the periods of six weeks and two weeks within which the note of appeal should be lodged by the accused (see s.111(2)). This power is additional to the power of the Clerk of Justiciary under s.110(2) since the High Court can grant a retrospective extension of time.

Rule 15.2(4). A single judge of the High Court (see s.103(5)) may admit a convicted accused to bail pending the determination of his appeal against conviction and/or sentence or pending the Lord Advocate's appeal against an unduly lenient sentence, and an accused who is convicted on indictment should (if he has not yet lodged a note of appeal) apply stating the reasons for granting bail and what his grounds of appeal are (s.112(2)(a)). The scope for the allowance of bail pending an appeal is intended to be "especially limited" in cases where the convicted person has not yet lodged a note of appeal since s.112 of the 1995 Act provides that the High Court shall not admit such a convicted person to bail unless in exceptional circumstances" (see *Ogilvie, Petr*, 1998 S.L.T. 1339; 1998 S.C.C.R. 187). Furthermore, the mere fact that a convicted person has been granted leave to appeal is not in itself sufficient cause why bail should be granted although it is a factor which is relevant to the court's consideration of the merits of the application (*Ogilvie, supra*).

Rule 15.2(5). The Lord Advocate does not require to intimate an intention to appeal under s.108 (see note to r.15.2(2)) but Crown Counsel are required to sign the Lord Advocate's note of appeal.

Rule 15.2(5A). Contrary to previous practice, and in order to ensure so far as possible, that frivolous or futile grounds of appeal are not submitted on behalf of persons convicted in solemn proceedings, counsel or the solicitor advocate who drafts the note of appeal must now sign it. He shall then be expected to appear before the Appeal Court to present the appeal (see Practice Note (No.1 of 2002)).

The duties of counsel are made plain in *Smith (C.C.) v HM Advocate*, 2004 S.C.C.R. 521 which, though what was said was said in reference to the drafting of the case and argument (see r.15.16), applies equally to notes of appeal. An allegation of procedural irregularity in solemn proceedings should not be approached as a mere technicality. Proper inquiry must be made as to the factual basis of the allegation before the allegation is drafted or tendered to the court (para.16).

Rule 15.2(6). An accused in respect of whom a supervised release order has been made (i.e. the accused is a short-term prisoner serving a sentence of not less than 12 months but less than four years), may appeal to the High Court against the decision of the original court which made the order where he is dissatisfied with the court's decision on an application made either by himself or by his local authority supervisor to vary the order. The grounds should be fully set out in Form 15.2-D because the accused will not be allowed to found on any ground not contained in the note of appeal except with leave of the High Court on cause shown (s.19(2) of the Prisoners and Criminal Proceedings (Scotland) Act 1993).

Rule 15.3

Rule 15.3(1). Section 111(2) provides that the periods of two weeks (in s.109(1)) within which an appellant must lodge with Justiciary Office written intimation of his intention to appeal against conviction or conviction and sentence and of eight weeks (starting when intimation was lodged) within which an appellant must lodge with Justiciary Office a written note of appeal (as set out in s.110(1)(a)) may be extended at any time by the High Court. (The period of eight weeks may be extended by the Clerk of Justiciary *before* it expires: s.110(2)). Under s.103(5)(a) a single judge of the High Court may extend these periods as well as allow the appellant to be present at any proceedings in any cases where he is not entitled to be present without leave (s.103(5)(b)) and admit an appellant to bail (s.103(5)(c)).

The purpose of an application for extension under s.111(2) is to secure an indulgence from the court for non-compliance with the time limits. In terms of s.129(1) non-compliance with these limits "shall not prevent the further prosecution of an appeal if the High Court or a judge thereof considers it just and proper that the non-compliance is waived or, in the manner directed by the High Court or judge, remedied by amendment or otherwise". Thus, for example, an appellant may initially give written intimation of his intention to appeal against conviction but later desire to challenge sentence as well. In such a case the appellant may be allowed to amend his written intimation out of time to include a challenge to sentence.

However, there is no right to a second appeal. It is incompetent to seek extension of time within which to lodge a (further) note of appeal against conviction where the appellant has already had his appeal heard and determined (following which the Clerk of Justiciary will have given notice of final determination to various persons: s.120(4)). As Lord Osborne said in *Beck v HM Advocate*, 2006 S.L.T. 468 (para.6, p.470I–J): "The premise upon which s.111(2) operates is that there has not been an appeal, but that a convicted person desires that there should be . . . [Section] 111(2) was never intended by the legislators to afford to a person who has in fact appealed against conviction and has had that appeal determined upon certain grounds the opportunity again to initiate appeal proceedings, either upon these grounds, or upon some other grounds." (See Peter Ferguson, Q.C., "Late appeals", 2006 S.L.T. (News) 97.)

Rule 15.3(2). In terms of s.103(6), where a single judge has refused an application referred to in s.103(5), the appellant is entitled "to have the application determined by the High Court". Such procedure is not an appeal against, or review of, the single judge's decision but a rehearing of the application on its merits. Where the appellant does not desire a rehearing of his application, or fails within five days to return to the Justiciary Office a duly completed Form 15.3-B, the refusal of the application by the single judge becomes final (s.105(2)).

The High Court as constituted for the hearing of appeals under Pt 8 is a quorum of three judges for appeals against both conviction and sentence (s.103(2)) but two judges for appeals against sentence alone (s.102(3)). The single judge may sit as a member of the court and take part in determining the application (s.105(6)).

Rule 15.4

See note to r.15.2(2).

Rule 15.5

This provision is now redundant. The death sentence for all crimes was finally abolished by s.36 of the Crime and Disorder Act 1998. Section 36(3)–(5) applies also to Scotland (s.121(6)(b)). After the abolition of the death penalty for murder in 1965, the remaining crimes for which the capital sentence was prescribed were certain forms of treason and piracy. On conviction under s.1 of the Treason Act 1814 or s.2 of the Piracy Act 1837 the accused is now liable to imprisonment for life.

Rule 15.5A

Procedural hearings were introduced into Appeal Court practice in order to reduce the number of appeal continuations which were occasioned by the change of counsel, or motion to amend the note of appeal, or further preparations to be undertaken for the appeal hearing. Not later than seven days before the procedural hearing the appellant's counsel should complete Form 15.5A-B stating whether the appeal will be presented at the proposed appeal sitting dates. If no problem is identified the court can decide that a procedural hearing is unnecessary. If, however, the appeal is not ready to proceed, or if a motion to amend the grounds of appeal is likely to be made (see r.15.15), the court should be advised of this fact. The procedural hearing will enable the court to examine the reasons for the delay or determine whether leave to amend should be granted.

Rule 15.6

An accused person may abandon his appeal against conviction and/or sentence, or where he has appealed against both conviction and sentence, he may abandon his appeal against conviction and proceed against sentence alone, at any time by lodging a notice with the Clerk of Justiciary. The words "at any time" do not appear in s.116(1) but this omission has been held to be immaterial: "there is no time-limit on an abandonment" (*Hendry v HM Advocate* [2006] HCJAC 14; 2006 S.C.C.R. 178 (para.7, *per* Lord Justice-Clerk Gill)). The correct principle is not that stated in *Ferguson v HM Advocate*, 1980 J.C. 27, which prevailed for a quarter of a century and required the court's permission to be sought in order to abandon an appeal against sentence once the appeal had been called and was before the court, but that stated in *West v HM Advocate*, 1955 S.L.T. 425. An appeal can be abandoned orally at the bar of the court at any time prior to submissions in support of the appeal being presented to the Appeal Court. Once submissions are begun, the leave of the court is required before abandonment can be effected because the purpose of the court's having a discretion is to allow it to discourage the presentation of speculative appeals by use of the power to increase sentences under s.118(4)(b) (*Hendry* at paras 12–13) and, it may be added, to serve the public interest in doing justice where an inadequate sentence has been passed by the court of first instance. The date of lodging the notice is the time at which the appeal is deemed to have been dismissed by the Appeal Court.

Rule 15.7

High Court judges are not statutorily obliged to take or having taken, preserve notes of evidence at the trial. Sheriffs were obliged by s.146 of the 1975 Act to do so although this provision has not been preserved by the 1995 Act. The sheriff's duty is now imposed by r.14.6. Section 237 of the 1975 Act (as inserted by the Criminal Justice (Scotland) Act 1980) placed a duty on a High Court judge to produce any notes which he had taken at the trial when required to do so by the Appeal Court. The 1995 Act does not not repeat s.237 and this rule fills that gap.

Rule 15.9

Rule 15.9(1). Diets in appeal proceedings are not peremptory and the usual practice is for the hearing to be continued "to a date afterwards to be fixed".

Rule 15.9(2). Section 104(1)(b) of the 1995 Act empowers the Appeal Court to appoint a person other than a High Court judge to hear additional evidence. In *Marshall v MacDougall* 1986 J.C. 77; 1987 S.L.T. 123; 1986 S.C.C.R. 376, under an equivalent power for appeals in summary proceedings under the 1975 Act (s.452(d)), the Appeal Court appointed the sheriff principal rather than a High Court judge to hear additional evidence no doubt because it was a district court prosecution. Section 104(1)(d) of the 1995 Act gives the Appeal Court power to remit to any "fit person" to enquire and report in regard to any matter or circumstance affecting the appeal. This rule does not give such fit person any power to fix a diet of proof but presumably such a power would be regarded as necessarily inherent in a remit in order to allow the person to discharge his duty: *cf. Crossan v HM Advocate*, 1996 S.C.C.R. 279 at 292E and *X, Petr*, 1996 S.C.C.R. 436 at 439D. See also *Robertson v HM Advocate (No.2)*, 1996 S.C.C.R. 243.

Rule 15.11

Any disqualification shall not attach for four weeks from the date of the verdict against the accused or, where an intimation of intention to appeal or a note of appeal (by the accused or the Lord Advocate) has been lodged, until the appeal, if it is proceeded with, is determined.

Rule 15.12

Rule 15.12(1). The hearing can take place in open court unlike the sift procedures for appeals under s.107.

Rule 15.12(2). It is unclear why the Lord Advocate should require intimation when the Crown Agent should already have received a copy of the petition to the High Court.

Rule 15.12(3). Unlike the sift procedures for appeals, there is no appeal to a quorum of judges.

Rule 15.13

The rule takes account of the sift procedures under s.107 where either a single judge or a quorum of judges has refused leave to appeal. The accused has until the 15th day after intimation that the single judge has refused leave, in order to appeal to a quorum of judges against the refusal of leave to appeal by a single judge. The disqualification attaches seven days after intimation of the refusal of leave by a quorum of judges.

Rule 15.14

Parliament did not give express power to the judge who "sifts" solemn appeals against conviction to obtain a further report but since the 1995 Act envisages that an appeal can be granted leave on grounds which are not contained in the note of appeal (see s.107(7)), the power to remit to the trial judge is clearly necessary. It will also perhaps be of assistance where the trial judge has developed a practice of not commenting on grounds of appeal, unless questions of fact are raised, in breach of his duty under s.113(1) of the 1995 Act (see, e.g. *McPhelim v HM Advocate*, 1996 S.L.T. 992). It will also be of assistance where the sheriff's report is (at the stage of the "sift") immediately seen to be "conspicuous for its brevity" and lacking in an outline of the relevant matters giving rise to the appeal (as was the case in *McCutcheon v HM Advocate*, 2001 G.W.D. 18–694).

Rule 15.15

Section 110(4) of the 1995 Act provides: "Except by leave of the High Court on cause shown, it shall not be competent for an appellant to found any aspect of his appeal on a ground not contained in the note of appeal". In 2002 the Lord Justice-General and the Lord Justice-Clerk issued a consultation paper on appeals procedure and expressed concern that once an appeal had obtained the grant of leave on a specified ground in the note of appeal, there was the risk of abuse because leave could thereafter be sought to introduce a further ground which had not been before the sift judge. Thus, where leave of the High Court—it may be at a procedural hearing or when the appeal is called for a full hearing—is granted for an amendment of the note of appeal, the court *may* direct that the appeal be returned to the sift so that consideration can be given to whether the new ground raises an arguable point (r.15.15(4)). However, if the worth of an amendment is to be considered by the court, the court may be likely to consider whether the ground is arguable as well as whether there is any good reason for the ground not having been specified in the original note in accordance with the Practice Notice of March 29, 1985 (see C1–02).

Rule 15.16

This innovation in appeals procedure was introduced in September 2003 and is designed to reduce the time the Appeal Court expends on sentence appeals. Sentence appeals under s.106 and the Lord Advocate's appeals against unduly lenient disposals under s.108 shall be presented in writing. Thus, under r.15.1(5), notice of the appeal hearing is 42 days. Not later than 21 days before the hearing the case and argument must be lodged with Justiciary Office. That case and argument will constitute the submissions but "supplementary comments to the case" may be made (r.15.16(5)(c)). In *Houldsworth, Petitioner* [2006] HCJAC 34 (decided on March 14, 2006) a challenge to this new procedure as being incompatible with an accused's Art.6 right under the European Convention to a fair and public hearing of his appeal was rejected by the appeal court. The court explained that r.15.16(5)(c) "plainly provides that the appellant may make oral comments on the appeal supplementary to the case and argument required by the earlier parts of the rule. Thus an appellant is not deprived of the righ to make oral submissions by the provisions of the rule" (para.8, *per* Lord Osborne).

The case must be signed by counsel or the solicitor-advocate who is supporting the appeal. This is in line with the change effected in solemn conviction appeals (see Practice Note (No.1 of 2002), C1–24, *infra*). If new information has come to light since the case and argument were lodged, that will only be admitted if the court is satisfied that cause has been shown for doing so. What amounts to "cause" will likely depend on two factors: (1) why the information was not available when the case and argument were lodged and (2) whether the new information has a material bearing on the merits of the appeal. If the new information will almost certainly tip the balance in the appellant's favour, the Appeal Court will almost certainly allow it to be received at the hearing, even where there is no proper explanation for its lateness. That new information should be intimated to Justiciary Office immediately.

It should be noted, however, that this rule does not affect the general principle that sentence appeals should be determined on the basis of the information before the sentencing court because it is only on that basis that the actual sentence can be said to be a miscarriage of justice (Nicholson on *Sentencing* (2nd ed.), para.8–99), although that principle suffers exceptions (see *McLean v MacDougall*, 1989 S.C.C.R. 625). Similarly, this rule does not affect the power of the Appeal Court under s.106(3) of the 1995 Act to admit fresh evidence in a sentence appeal when the conditions of that subsection are satisfied (e.g. *Baikie v HM Advocate*, 2000 S.C.C.R. 119). The information referred to in the rule is new only because it is relied upon after the case was lodged.

PART IV

SUMMARY PROCEEDINGS

CHAPTER 16

COMPLAINTS

Form of complaints and related notices and forms

16.1.—(1) The form of complaint referred to in section 138(1) of the Act of 1995 shall be in Form 16.1-A.

(2) The form of citation of an accused referred to in section 140(2) and (2A) of the Act of 1995 shall be in Form 16.1-B.

(2A) The notice to be affixed to the door of the dwelling-house or place of business of an accused for the purposes of section 141(2A) of the Act of 1995 (citation of accused by affixing a notice) shall be in Form 16.1-BB

(3) The procurator fiscal shall send to the accused with the citation in Form 16.1-B—

(a) a reply form in Form 16.1-C for completion and return by him stating whether he pleads guilty or not guilty; and

(b) a means form in Form 16.1-D for completion and return by him.

(3A) The form of notice referred to in section 146(3A) of the Act of 1995 shall be in Form 16.1-BA.

(4) The form of notice of previous convictions to be served on an accused under section 166(2) of the Act of 1995 shall be in Form 16.1-E.

AMENDMENT

Rule 16.1(2) as amended, and rule 16.1(3A) inserted, by Act of Adjournal (Criminal Procedure

Rules Amendment No. 3) (Sexual Offences (Procedure and Evidence) (Scotland) Act 2002) 2002 (SSI 2002/454), r.2(8) (effective November 1, 2002).

Rule 16.1(2A) inserted by Act of Adjournal (Criminal Procedure Rules Amendment No.2) (Miscellaneous) 2003 (SSI 2003/468), r.2. Brought into force on October 27, 2003 in accordance with art.1.

Signature of prosecutor

16.2.—(1) The prosecutor shall sign the principal complaint and the citation to the accused.

(2) Any document sent with the citation to the accused including the copy complaint shall, for the purposes of such signature, be treated as part of the citation.

Effect of failure by prosecutor to comply with certain requirements

16.3. The validity of any proceedings against an accused shall not be affected by reason only of the failure of the prosecutor to comply in any respect with a requirement of rule 16.1(3) (reply and means forms).

Further procedural forms

16.4.—(1) The form of incidental application referred to in section 134 of the Act of 1995 (incidental applications) shall be in Form 16.4-A.

(2) The form of assignation of a diet shall be in Form 16.4-B.

(3) The form of minutes in the record of proceedings in summary proceedings shall be in Form 16.4-C.

Incidental applications out of hours

16.4A—(1) Where the prosecutor makes an incidental application in Form 16.4-A when the office of the prosecutor is closed, the application shall not require to be signed by the prosecutor but shall state the name of the prosecutor.

(2) The oath of a police officer shall be sufficient to authenticate the application as being an application by the prosecutor named on the application.

AMENDMENT

Rule 16.4A inserted by the Act of Adjournal (Criminal Procedure Rules Amendment No.2) (Miscellaneous) 2005 (SSI 2005/160), r.2 (effective March 31, 2005).

Form of certain warrants

16.5.—(1) The form of warrant referred to in section 135 of the Act of 1995 (warrants of apprehension and search)—

(a) to apprehend an accused shall be in Form 16.5-A;

(b) to search the person, dwelling house and repositories of the accused shall be in Form 16.5-B.

(2) The form of order adjourning a diet and granting warrant to detain an accused shall be in Form 16.5-C.

Citation of witnesses

16.6.—(1) The form of postal citation of a person to appear as a witness at a trial on a summary complaint shall be in Form 16.6-A; and the witness shall complete and return Form 16.6-B to the procurator fiscal, or the accused or his solicitor, as the case may be, in the pre-paid envelope provided within 14 days after the date of citation.

(2) The form of personal citation of a witness at a trial on a summary complaint shall be in Form 16.6-C.

(3) In the case of a postal citation in Form 16.6-A by the prosecutor under sec-

tion 141 of the Act of 1995, the citation may be signed by the prosecutor by use of an official stamp of his signature or by mechanical or electronic means.

Applications for alteration of diets

16.7.—(1) Where the prosecutor and the accused propose to make a joint application orally to the court under section 137(2) of the Act of 1995 (application for alteration of diet) for postponement of a diet that has been fixed, they may do so only at a diet which has been duly assigned and which has been called.

(2) An application by an accused under section 137(5) of the Act of 1995 (application to postpone or accelerate diet) shall be made in Form 16.7.

AMENDMENT

Rule 16.6(3) as inserted by Act of Adjournal (Criminal Procedure Rules Amendment) (Miscellaneous) (S.I. 1996 No. 2147 (s.171)) (effective September 9, 1996).

GENERAL NOTE

Section 307(1) provides that for the purposes of summary proceedings, the word "prosecutor" includes procurator fiscal, and any other person prosecuting in the public interest and complainer and any person duly authorised to represent or act for any public prosecutor. The procurator fiscal is the Lord Advocate's local representative and takes his instructions from the Lord Advocate as the public prosecutor. The procurator fiscal is not the "sheriff's advocate" (see *Green v Smith*, 1988 S.L.T. 175). All prosecutions in the summary courts are by way of complaint. Private prosecutions by individuals who can show title and interest in order to prosecute accused persons for crimes with or without the concurrence of the Lord Advocate, are initiated by way of a Bill for Criminal Letters and these prosecutions are pursued exclusively in the High Court (see *Dunbar v Johnstone* (1904) 4 Adam 505). Section 138(1) of the 1995 Act does, however, recognise that other persons can initiate proceedings by way of a summary complaint (e.g. local education authorities as in *Ross v Simpson*, 1995 S.L.T. 956, and customs officers) and they may be represented by a solicitor. They are not, however, public prosecutors in the true sense of the term but are prosecutors in the public interest under s.307(1).

Note should be made of the fact that it is observed in Renton and Brown, *Criminal Procedure* (5th ed.), para.13–11 that where the failure of a prosecutor to appear in court had been due to death, disability, or other unavoidable cause, the court has an inherent power to appoint a prosecutor *pro hac vice* to proceed with the prosecution, in order that the ends of justice may not be defeated. (See *Thomson v Scott*; *Walker v Emslie* (1899) 3 Adam 102; and *Hill v Finlayson* (1883) 5 Couper 284.) It is, however, to be doubted that the court has a power to appoint an ad hoc prosecutor at least in respect of procurators fiscal. Since no part of a criminal trial can take place in the absence of the prosecutor, and most summary prosecutions are instituted by the procurator fiscal as the Lord Advocate's local representative, it would appear that a more appropriate remedy would be adjournment or desertion of the diet *pro loco et tempore* by the court on its own motion. The instance would then be preserved by adjournment or the Crown would be entitled to raise proceedings *de novo* in order to meet the difficulty caused by the unforeseen occurrences of death, illness, or unavoidable absence (**cf.** *Platt v Lockhart*, 1988 S.L.T. 845 which concerned a sheriff's death during the adjournment of a part-heard trial; and *Annan, Complainer*, 1994 S.L.T. 157).

Rule 16.1

Rule 16.1(1). Form 16.1-A prescribes the form of summary complaint which should be employed in all prosecutions (see s.138(2)(b) of the 1995 Act). The styles of charge which should be used for common law and statutory offences are set out in Sch.5 to the 1995 Act, which incorporates for the purposes of summary complaints the other styles which are set out for indictment cases in Sch.2 to the 1995 Act. When a charge follows these styles it is most unlikely that the court will hold the charge to be irrelevant or lacking in fair notice (see *Anderson v Allan*, 1985 S.C.C.R. 399; see also *Coventry v Douglas*, 1944 S.C. 13; 1944 S.L.T. 129).

Rule 16.1(2). The citation is to proceed on an induciae of at least 48 hours unless in the special circumstances of the case the court fixes a shorter induciae (s.140(2)). The citation must be signed by the prosecutor in order to be valid (r.16.2(1)). Failure to state the date of the diet to which the accused is cited renders the citation *funditus* null and void: see *Beattie v McKinnon*, 1977 J.C. 64.

Rule 16.1(3). Failure to send the pleading and the means forms with the citation to the accused will not invalidate the proceedings (r.16.3).

Rule 16.1(4). Section 311(5) of the 1975 Act required in summary cases that the accused be served with a notice of penalties relevant to any statutory charge in the summary complaint but the 1995 Act (regrettably) makes no such requirement. However, the issue which arose in *Cowan v Guild*, 1991 S.C.C.R. 424, whether the accused was ever served with a notice, can still arise in respect of notices of previous convictions, an issue which is much more likely to surface where personal service has been effected. But if there is "substantial compliance" with a duty under s.166(2) to serve the notice on the accused with the complaint where he is cited to a diet or if he is in custody, before he is called on to plead, the court is entitled to take into account the previous convictions (*cf. Hutchison v Normand*, 1993 S.C.C.R. 1000 and *Normand v Buchanan*, 1996 S.C.C.R. 355 which were concerned with notices of penalty).

In any event, the court has a very wide power under s.159(1) of the 1995 Act, unless the court sees just cause to the contrary, to allow amendment of the complaint by deletion, alteration or addition so as inter alia to cure any error or defect in it or to meet any objection to it (such as relevancy or specification). There is only one restriction on the court's power to allow amendment: under s.159(2) the court cannot allow amendment where the effect of the amendment would be to change "the character of the offence charged" (*cf. MacArthur v MacNeill*, 1986 J.C. 182). Where a competent amendment appears to the court to prejudice the accused in any way "in his defence on the merits of the case" the court must grant such remedy to the accused by way of adjournment or otherwise as is just in the opinion of the court. It has been doubted that such other remedy includes refusal of the proposed amendment (*Brooks v HM Advocate*, unreported, January 19, 2007; [2007] HCJAC 9, para.[12]). If the amendment substitutes a different statutory offence which carries liability to an increased penalty (or a minimum penalty), that does not constitute a prejudice to the defence on the merits of the case (*Brooks*, para.[12]) nor can it amount to "just cause" under s.159(1) for refusing the amendment (*Brooks*, para.[13]; *cf. Cook v Jessop*, 1990 J.C. 286).

Rule 16.2

Rule 16.2(1). The prosecutor's signature is essential for the proceedings to be competent (*Lowe v Bee*, 1989 S.C.C.R. 476; see also *Milne v Normand*, 1994 S.L.T. 760; 1993 S.C.C.R. 1058 where, because a two page complaint was signed on the first page but not on the second page, the second page was treated *pro non scripto*).

Rule 16.2(2). The copy complaint need not be signed by the prosecutor.

Rule 16.4

Incidental applications can be made for a vast range of orders or warrants. One order of importance is where the Crown desires to postpone or accelerate a diet but the accused—or one of them—refuses to agree to a joint application to the court. The Crown may make an incidental application in these circumstances: see s.137(4).

Rule 16.6

The administrative burden imposed by the imperative requirement of r.16.2(1) is eased by allowing for a stamp or other mechanical or electronic means of reproducing the prosecutor's signature so far as the vast majority of citations are concerned.

Rule 16.7

In *White v Ruxton*, 1996 S.L.T. 556; 1996 S.C.C.R. 427, the court held that the authority for the fixing of a diet to hear a joint application to accelerate the diet in order that a later diet could be fixed on account of the absence on holiday of one of the co-accused, was contained in the joint minute signed by both parties under s.314(3) of the 1975 Act. It was, however, observed by the court that the better practice was to include authority in a minute in the record of proceedings.

CHAPTER 17

SUMMARY PRE-TRIAL PROCEDURE

Appeals against extension of period of detention

17.1.—(1) A note of appeal presented to the High Court under section 147(3) of the Act of 1995 (appeal against grant or refusal of extension of 40 days detention) shall be made in Form 17.1

(2) Such a note of appeal shall be served by the appellant on—

(a) the respondent; and

(b) the clerk of the court against the decision of which the appeal is taken.

(3) The appellant in such a note of appeal shall lodge with the Clerk of Justiciary—

(a) the note of appeal; and

(b) the certificate of execution of service in respect of the persons mentioned in paragraph (2).

(4) The clerk of the court against the decision of which the appeal is taken shall, as soon as practicable after being served with the note of appeal, transmit to the Clerk of Justiciary the original application and all the relative documents; and the Clerk of Justiciary shall, on receipt of those documents, assign the appeal to the roll and intimate the date of the diet to the appellant and the respondent.

(5) The Clerk of Justiciary shall intimate the result of the appeal to the court against the decision of which the appeal was taken and to the governor of the institution in which the appellant is detained.

GENERAL NOTE

An accused person is entitled to be liberated forthwith and to be thereafter free from all question or process for an offence charged against him on summary complaint if he has been detained on that charge for a total of more than 40 days after the bringing of the complaint in court unless his trial has been commenced within that period (s.147(1)). However, the sheriff can extend that period for such period as he thinks fit when a delay is caused by illness of the accused or the judge, the absence or illness of any witness or any other sufficient cause not attributable to the prosecutor's fault (s.147(2)). When an extension is granted or refused there is an automatic right of appeal (s.147(3)). The note of appeal should be served on *inter alia* the clerk of the lower court and be lodged with the Clerk of Justiciary. If the note is not lodged with the clerk of the lower court he cannot transmit the documents necessary for the appeal under r. 17.1(4) and Justiciary Office cannot assign the appeal to a roll for a hearing. No time-limits are specified and accordingly the onus is on the appellant—who is almost always the accused—to prosecute his appeal expeditiously.

CHAPTER 18

PROCEDURE AT TRIAL IN SUMMARY PROCEEDINGS

Accused to plead personally and to receive intimation of diets

18.1.—(1) Subject to paragraph (2), in any summary proceedings where a person accused in those proceedings is present in court, that person shall personally plead to the charge against him whether or not he is represented.

(2) Where the judge is satisfied that the accused is not capable for any reason of pleading personally to the charge against him, it shall be sufficient if the plea is tendered by a solicitor or by counsel on his behalf.

(3) Where an accused is not represented or not personally present and a court continues a diet without taking a plea from the accused, the prosecutor shall intimate the continuation and the date of the adjourned diet to the accused.

(4) Subject to section 150(2) of the Act of 1995 (adjournment to another diet), where an accused is not represented or not personally present, on the fixing of—

(a) a diet of trial,

(b) a diet after conviction, or

(c) any diet after a plea from the accused has been recorded,

the sheriff clerk or clerk of the district court shall intimate the diet to the accused.

(5) Where the accused pleads guilty to the charge or to any part of it, and his plea is accepted by the prosecutor, the plea shall be recorded and signed by the judge or clerk of court, and the court shall thereafter dispose of the case at the same or any adjourned diet.

(6) The plea referred to in paragraph (5) and any sentence may be combined, in which case one signature shall be sufficient to authenticate both.

Form of oath or affirmation to witnesses

18.2.—(1) Where the judge administers the oath to a witness in summary proceedings, he shall do so in accordance with the form in Form 14.5-A.

(2) In the case of any witness who elects to affirm, the judge shall administer the affirmation in accordance with the form in Form 14.5-B.

(3) The oath or the affirmation administered in accordance with paragraph (1) or (2), as the case may be, shall be treated as having been administered in common form.

Warrant to apprehend witness who fails to appear

18.3. The form of warrant to apprehend a witness who has failed to appear at a diet in summary proceedings in answer to a citation shall be in Form 18.3.

Record of proceedings to be written or printed

18.4.—(1) The record of proceedings in summary proceedings may be in writing or printed, or may be partly written and partly printed.

(2) All forms of minute of proceedings or orders of the court may be on the same sheet of paper as the complaint or on a separate sheet attached to it.

(3) Where the record of proceedings or minute of proceedings or orders of the Court referred to in paragraph (1) or (2) are for whatever reason unavailable to the Court, it shall be competent for the Court to proceed with a copy certified as a true copy by the clerk of court.

AMENDMENT

Rule 18.4(3) as amended by the Act of Adjournal (Criminal Procedure Rules Amendment) (S.I. 1997 No. 63).

Interruption of proceedings after conviction

18.5.—(1) On conviction of an accused in summary proceedings, the judge may, without adjourning those proceedings, interrupt them by—

(a) considering a conviction against that person in other proceedings pending before that court for which he has not been sentenced; or

(b) passing sentence on that person in respect of the conviction in those other proceedings.

(2) When the judge has interrupted any proceedings under paragraph (1), he may, in passing sentence on an accused person in respect of a conviction in those proceedings, at the same time pass sentence on that person in respect of any other conviction he has considered.

(3) No interruption of any proceedings under paragraph (1) shall cause the instance to fall in respect of any person accused in those proceedings or shall otherwise affect the validity of those proceedings.

Detention in precincts of court

18.6. An order under section 169(1) of the Act of 1995 (detention in precincts of court) shall be in Form 18.6.

GENERAL NOTE

By para. 2 of the Act of Adjournal (Criminal Procedure Rules Amendment) 1997 (S.I. 1997 No. 63), it appears that *per incuriam* the High Court has substituted a new r. 18.4(1). It seems that what was intended, but not achieved, was the insertion of a further rule (as r. 18.4(3)) allowing for certified copies to be used when the principals are unavailable for whatever reason.

Rule 18.1

The accused, unless he cannot do so because of any infirmity, must tender his plea even when he has legal representation. This is a fundamental requirement and breach of it renders the conviction null and void, although in appropriate circumstances the Appeal Court will authorise a fresh prosecution (see *McGowan v. Ritchie*, 1997 S.C.C.R. 322). There is, however, no obligation on the court to enquire if the accused has received the copy complaint or whether he has understood the charge or charges contained in it. If the Crown fails to intimate to the accused the date of the adjourned diet, the court will be entitled, in exercise of its own inherent discretionary power to regulate its own proceedings in the interests of justice, to refuse a further continuation without plea.

Rule 18.2

Form 14.5-A states that the witness is to raise his right hand and repeat the terms of the oath. The rule is directory only: see *McAvoy v. H.M. Advocate*, 1992 S.L.T. 46. If the witness is a child, but is sworn without the court first ascertaining his age and whether or not he understands the nature of the oath—as required by the procedure desiderated in *Quinn v. Lees*, 1994 S.C.C.R. 159—the witness's evidence must be objected to timeously in order to avoid losing a right of appeal under s.192(3) of the 1995 Act (*Jardine v. Howdle*, 1997 S.C.C.R. 294; but see notes to r. 14.5).

Rule 18.3

Form 18.3 requires the place and date of the granting of the warrant and also the signature of the sheriff (or justice of the peace) to be entered. Omission of these essentials will render the warrant bad and liable to suspension in the High Court. Equally, should the warrant be postdated *per incuriam* to, *e.g.* a year hence, it will be invalid.

Rule 18.4

The usual practice until the advent of computer technology was for the minutes, unless they became voluminous, to be written down the side of the principal complaint. Now minutes are more likely to be pre-printed and that may give rise to irregularities and inaccuracies in recording. Either party is entitled to insist that any objection taken to the competency or relevancy of the complaint or the proceedings, or to the competency or admissibility of evidence, be entered in the record of the proceedings: see s.157(2).

Rule 18.5

The sheriff may interrupt summary proceedings after he has convicted the accused in order to impose sentence in respect of another conviction irrespective of whether that conviction was in summary proceedings or on indictment so that he can simultaneously determine the appropriate disposal in respect of the original matter before him.

Rule 18.6

The power under s.169 of the 1995 Act is restricted to cases where a custodial sentence (not being a sentence imposed in default of payment of a fine) would be competent and the detention which the court orders does not extend beyond 8 p.m. The power should also not be exercised where its exercise would deprive the accused of a reasonable opportunity of getting home in the course of that day.

CHAPTER 19

APPEALS FROM SUMMARY PROCEEDINGS

Appeals relating to preliminary pleas

19.1.—(1) If—

(a) an accused states an objection to the competency or relevancy of a complaint or the proceedings; and

(b) that objection is repelled,

he may apply for leave to appeal against that decision under section 174(1) of the Act of 1995 (appeals relating to preliminary pleas) only after stating how he pleads to the charge or charges set out in the complaint.

(2) Subject to paragraph (1), the accused shall apply for leave to appeal against

any decision to which that paragraph applies; and the court which made the decision shall determine that application immediately following the decision in question.

(3) Where the court grants the application, the clerk of court shall enter in the minute of proceedings—

(a) details of the decision in question; and

(b) the granting of leave to appeal against it.

(4) An appeal to which this rule applies shall be made by note of appeal in Form 19.1-A.

(5) The note of appeal shall be lodged with the clerk of the court which granted leave to appeal not later than two days after the decision appealed against.

(6) The clerk of court shall, on the lodging of the note of appeal with him—

(a) send a copy to the respondent or his solicitor;

(b) request a report from the presiding judge; and

(c) transmit—

(i) the note of appeal,

(ii) two certified copies of the complaint and the minutes of proceedings, and

(iii) any other relevant documents,

to the Clerk of Justiciary.

(7) The presiding judge shall, as soon as possible after receiving a request for a report, send his report to the Clerk of Justiciary who shall send a copy to the appellant and respondent or their solicitors.

(8) The Clerk of Justiciary shall arrange for the High Court to hear the appeal as soon as possible, and shall cause to be copied any documents necessary for the High Court.

(9) Where the High Court makes any order postponing the trial diet under section 174(2) of the Act of 1995, or makes any such order and gives a direction under that section, the Clerk of Justiciary shall send a copy of that order and any direction to—

(a) the appropriate clerk of court;

(b) any accused who are not parties to the appeal or to their solicitors; and

(c) the governor of any institution in which any accused is detained.

(10) Any such appeal may be abandoned at any time prior to the hearing of the appeal.

(11) Where an appeal is abandoned, a minute of abandonment in Form 19.1-B shall be lodged with the Clerk of Justiciary.

(12) On the lodging of a minute of abandonment under paragraph (11), the Clerk of Justiciary shall inform the appropriate clerk of court and the respondent or his solicitor that the appeal has been abandoned.

Forms for appeals by stated case

19.2.—(1) An application under section 176(1) of the Act of 1995 (stated case: manner and time of appeal) shall be in Form 19.2-A.

(2) A stated case shall be in Form 19.2-B.

(3) The form of minutes of procedure in an appeal by stated case shall be in Form 19.2-C.

Forms for appeals against sentence only

19.3.—(1) A note of appeal under section 186(1) of the Act of 1995 (appeals against sentence only) shall be in Form 19.3-A.

(2) The form of minutes of procedure in an appeal under section 186(1) of the Act of 1995 shall be in Form 19.3-B.

Extension of time for appeals

19.4.—(1) An extension of time by the sheriff principal under section 186(5) (extension of time in appeal against sentence only), or section 194(2) (extension of time for stated case), of the Act of 1995 shall be in Form 19.4.

(2) Where, by virtue of subsection (8) of section 186 of the Act of 1995 (application of section 181 where appellant in appeal against sentence only fails to comply with a requirement), the court makes an order extending the period within which the note of appeal shall be lodged under subsection (2) of that section, the periods mentioned in subsections (2) and (4) of that section shall run from the date which is two days after the date on which the court makes that order and not from the date of the passing of the sentence.

Abandonment of appeals by stated case

19.5. A minute of abandonment of an appeal under section 184(1) of the Act of 1995 (abandonment of stated case before lodging it with the Clerk of Justiciary) shall be in Form 19.5.

Abandoning appeals against conviction only

19.6.—(1) This rule applies for the purpose of section 175(8) of the Act of 1995 (abandoning appeal against conviction and proceeding with appeal against sentence alone).

(2) An application to abandon an appeal under section 175(8) of the Act of 1995 shall be made by minute in Form 19.6 and intimated by the appellant to the respondent.

(3) Subject to paragraph (4), the minute shall be lodged with the clerk of the court which imposed the sentence being appealed against.

(4) Where, before the lodging of the minute, the stated case has been lodged with the Clerk of Justiciary, the minute shall be lodged with the Clerk of Justiciary who shall send a copy of the minute to the clerk of the court which imposed the sentence appealed against.

(5) Where, before the lodging of the minute, copies of the stated case and relative proceedings have been lodged with the Clerk of Justiciary, those copies shall be used for the purposes of the hearing of the appeal against sentence.

(6) On the lodging of the minute, section 186(3) to (9) of the Act of 1995 (provisions relating to appeal against sentence only) shall apply to the stated case as they apply to a note of appeal.

Abandonment of appeals against sentence only

19.7. A minute of abandonment under section 186(9) of the Act of 1995 (abandonment of appeal against sentence only) shall be in Form 19.7.

Intimation of abandonment

19.8. The Clerk of Justiciary or clerk of court, as the case may be, on the lodging with him of—

(a) a minute abandoning an appeal under section 184(1) of the Act of 1995 (abandonment of appeal by stated case before lodging of case with the Clerk of Justiciary), or

(b) a minute abandoning an appeal under section 186(9) of the Act of 1995 (abandonment of appeal against sentence only),

shall immediately notify the Crown Agent or the prosecutor, as the case may be, of the lodging of the minute; and the Clerk of Justiciary shall, where the minute is lodged with him, notify immediately the clerk of the appropriate court.

Applications for suspension of disqualification from driving in appeals

19.9.—(1) Where a person who has been disqualified from holding or obtaining a driving licence appeals against that disqualification under section 176(1) of the Act of 1995 by stated case, any application to suspend the disqualification shall be made with the application to the court to state a case for the opinion of the High Court.

(2) On an application being made under paragraph (1) to suspend a disqualification, the court shall grant or refuse to grant the application within seven days of it being made.

(3) Where the court refuses to grant the application and the appellant applies to the High Court to suspend the disqualification, any such application shall be made by note in Form 19.9.

(4) The note shall be lodged by the appellant or his solicitor with the Clerk of Justiciary.

(5) The appellant or his solicitor shall intimate the lodging of the note to the respondent and the clerk of the court which imposed the disqualification.

(6) The clerk shall, on receiving such intimation, forthwith send to the Clerk of Justiciary—

(a) a certified copy of the complaint; and

(b) a certified copy of the minute of proceedings.

(7) The High Court may order such further intimation (including intimation to the Lord Advocate) as it thinks fit, and may dispose of the application in open court or in chambers after such hearing as it thinks fit.

(8) On the High Court making an order on the note, the Clerk of Justiciary shall send a certified copy of the order to the clerk of the court which imposed the disqualification.

(9) Where the order suspends the disqualification, the Clerk of Justiciary shall also send a certified copy of the order to the Secretary of State with such further information as the Secretary of State may require.

(10) An order made by a single judge of the High Court under this rule shall not be subject to appeal or review.

Applications for suspension of disqualification from driving in bills of suspension

19.10.—(1) Where a person who has been disqualified from holding or obtaining a driving licence appeals against that disqualification by bill of suspension, an application to suspend the disqualification shall be made by requesting interim suspension of the disqualification in the prayer of the bill.

(2) Where the courts orders interim suspension, that order shall not have effect until—

(a) the bill has been served on the respondent; and

(b) the principal bill and first deliverance on the bill with an execution, or acceptance, of service—

(i) have been shown to the clerk of the sentencing court and he has endorsed a certificate of exhibition; and

(ii) they have been returned to the Clerk of Justiciary by the complainer or his solicitor.

(3) On certifying the bill under paragraph (2), the clerk of the court which imposed the disqualification shall send a certified copy of the complaint and the relative minute of proceedings to the Clerk of Justiciary.

(4) Paragraphs (2), (8), (9) and (10) of rule 19.9 (applications for suspension

of disqualification from driving in appeals) apply to this rule as they apply to that rule.

Suspension of sentence under s.193A of the Act of 1995

19.10A.—(1) Where a convicted person or the prosecutor appeals to the High Court under section 175 of the Act of 1995, any application to suspend a relevant sentence shall be made with—

(a) the application to the court to state a case for the opinion of the High Court; or

(b) the note of appeal, as the case may be.

(2) On an application being made under paragraph (1) to suspend a sentence the court shall grant or refuse to grant the application within seven days of its being made.

(3) In the application of section 193A of the Act of 1995 (suspension of certain sentences pending appeal) to a case in which leave to appeal has been refused under section 180 or 187 of that Act, the word "determined" in subsection (1) of the said section 193A shall be construed as meaning—

(a) the fifteenth day after the date of intimation to the appellant or his solicitor and to the Crown Agent of refusal of leave under subsection (1)(b) of section 180 or 187 of that Act, as the case may be, unless the appellant applies to the High Court for leave to appeal; or

(b) the seventh day after the date of intimation to the appellant or his solicitor and to the Crown Agent of the refusal of leave by the High Court under subsection (5)(b) of section 180 or subsection (4)(b) of section 187 of that Act, as the case may be.

AMENDMENT

Rule 19.10A inserted by Act of Adjournal (Criminal Procedure Rules Amendment No. 4) (SI 1997/1834) effective August 1, 1997).

Solicitor entering appearance etc.

19.11.—(1) Where an appellant in an appeal is represented by a solicitor who does not practise in Edinburgh, that solicitor may appoint a solicitor who practises in Edinburgh to carry out the duties of solicitor to the appellant in relation to that appeal.

(2) In paragraph (1), "appeal" includes any appeal whether by stated case, note of appeal, bill of suspension or advocation.

(3) The solicitor for the appellant or if unrepresented, the appellant, shall enter appearance and comply with the provisions of section 179(9) of the Act of 1995 (lodging of stated case with Clerk of Justiciary).

Duty to print stated case etc.

19.12.—(1) The solicitor for the appellant or, if unrepresented, the appellant shall—

(a) print the complaint, minutes of proceedings and stated case or bill of suspension;

(b) not later than twenty-one days before the hearing, return the process to the Clerk of Justiciary; and

(c) provide—

(i) the Clerk of Justiciary with four copies of the print; and

(ii) the respondent or his solicitor with three copies of the print.

(2) Where the solicitor for the appellant or the appellant, as the case may be, cannot comply with any of the requirements of paragraph (1), he shall, not later

than twenty-one days before the hearing, so inform the Clerk of Justiciary in writing with reasons.

(3) On being so informed, the Clerk of Justiciary may in his discretion postpone the hearing by dropping the appeal from the Justiciary Roll.

(4) Where the Clerk of Justiciary does not drop the appeal from the roll under paragraph (3), the court may, at the hearing, allow the appeal to be dropped from the roll or may dismiss the appeal.

AMENDMENT

Rule 19.12 as amended by the Act of Adjournal (Criminal Procedure Rules Amendment No.3) (Extradition etc.) 2004 (SSI 2004/346), r.2 (effective August 18, 2004).

Duty of solicitor in bill of suspension

19.13. A solicitor who requests a first deliverance in a bill of suspension shall comply with the requirements of rule 19.12(1) and (2) (printing of stated case) whether or not he is the nominated solicitor for the purposes of legal aid.

List of appeals

19.14.—(1) The Clerk of Justiciary shall, after consultation with the Lord Justice General or Lord Justice-Clerk, issue a list of appeals with the respective dates of hearing on the Justiciary Roll.

(2) Subject to paragraph (3) the Clerk of Justiciary shall give the respective solicitors representing parties to an appeal so listed at least 14 days notice of the date fixed for the hearing of the appeal.

(3) In an appeal under section 175(2)(b), (c) or (ca) or by virtue of section 175(4) of the Act of 1995, the period of notice mentioned in paragraph (2) shall be 42 days.

AMENDMENT

Rule 19.14 as amended by Act of Adjournal (Criminal Appeals) 2003 (SSI 2003/387), art.3. Brought into force on September 1, 2003 in accordance with art.1.

Diet for interim suspension

19.15. Where a bill of suspension contains a prayer for interim suspension of any order or for interim liberation—

    (a) the judge before whom the bill is laid for a first deliverance shall assign a diet at which counsel for each party may be heard on the crave for the interim order; and

    (b) the Clerk of Justiciary shall forthwith give notice of that diet to the parties.

Intimation of determination of appeal

19.16.—(1) The Clerk of Justiciary shall send to the clerk of the sentencing court a certified copy of the order made on determination of the appeal from summary proceedings.

(2) Where the appeal against a disqualification from driving is refused or abandoned, the clerk of the sentencing court shall—

    (a) make the appropriate endorsement on the driving licence of the appellant; and

    (b) intimate the disqualification to the appropriate driving licence and police authorities.

(3) In this rule, "appeal" includes any appeal whether by stated case, note of appeal, bill of suspension or advocation.

Suspension of disqualification etc. under section 193 of the Act of 1995

19.17. In the application of section 193 of the Act of 1995 (suspension of disqualification, forfeiture, etc.) to a case in which leave to appeal has been refused under section 180 or 187 of the Act of 1995, the word "determination" in subsection (1) of section 193 of that Act shall be construed as meaning—

(a) the fifteenth day after the date of intimation to the appellant or his solicitor of refusal of leave under subsection (1)(b) of section 180 or 187 of that Act, as the case may be, unless the appellant applies to the High Court for leave to appeal; or

(b) the day seven days after the date of intimation to the appellant or his solicitor of the refusal of leave by the High Court under subsection (5)(b) of section 180 or subsection (4)(b) of section 187 of that Act, as the case may be.

AMENDMENT

Rule 19.17 as amended by Act of Adjournal (Criminal Procedure Rules Amendment No. 3) (SI 1997/1788) (effective August 11, 1997).

Remits in applications for leave to appeal

19.18. The judge of the High Court considering an application for leave to appeal under section 180 (leave to appeal against conviction etc.), or section 187 (leave to appeal against sentence), of the Act of 1995 may, before deciding to grant or refuse leave, remit the case to the judge at first instance for a report or a supplementary report to be produced to him as soon as is reasonably practicable on any matter with respect to the grounds of appeal.

AMENDMENT

Rule 19.18 as inserted by Act of Adjournal (Criminal Procedure Rules Amendment) (Miscellaneous) (SI 1996/2747 (S.171)) (effective September 9 1996).

Presentation of summary sentence appeal in writing

19.19—(1) This rule applies to an appeal under section 175(2)(b), (c) or (ca) or by virtue of section 175(4) of the Act of 1995 listed in terms of rule 19.14 (list of appeals).

(2) In an appeal to which paragraph (1) applies the appellant shall present his case in writing.

(3) The solicitor for the appellant or, if unrepresented, the appellant shall—

(a) not later than 21 days before the date assigned for the appeal court hearing, lodge a case and argument in Form 19.18;

(b) lodge with the case and argument all documents, or a copy thereof, referred to or founded upon in the case and argument and not already lodged; and

(c) at the same time as he lodges the case and argument referred to in sub-paragraph (a) and the supporting documents referred to in sub-paragraph (b), send a copy to the Crown or, where the Crown is the appellant, to the respondent.

(4) The case and argument referred to in paragraph (3) shall be signed by counsel or the solicitor advocate representing the appellant in the appeal, or by the appellant where the appellant intends to conduct the appeal himself.

(5) At the hearing of the appeal—

(a) the case and argument and supporting documents referred to in paragraph (3) shall constitute the submissions of the appellant;

(b) unless it otherwise directs, the Court will expect the appellant to rely upon the case and argument without reading it over to the Court; and

(c) the appellant may make supplementary comments to the case and argument; and shall answer any points raised by the Court.

(6) On cause shown, the Court may permit the appellant to introduce new in-

formation that has come to light in the period since the case and argument was lodged.

(7) Where the Court permits the introduction of new information, it may at its discretion permit the lodging of additional documents in support of the new information.

(8) A party who wishes to introduce new information and lodge additional documents shall send a copy of the information and documents to the Clerk of Justiciary as soon as the information and documents come into the appellant's possession.

(9) A party who has sent new information and documents to the Clerk of Justiciary shall make application at the bar to allow it to be introduced or lodged, as the case may be.

(10) Where the documents referred to in paragraph (3) are not lodged time-ously, the Deputy Principal Clerk of Justiciary shall refer the matter to the Lord Justice-General, whom failing the Lord Justice-Clerk, for such action as the Lord Justice-General or Lord Justice-Clerk, as the case may be, considers appropriate.

AMENDMENTS

Rule 19.19 inserted by Act of Adjournal (Criminal Appeals) 2003 (SSI 2003/387), art.3. Brought into force on September 1, 2003 in accordance with art.1. Rule 19.19 as amended by Act of Adjournal (Criminal Procedure Rules Amendment No.2) (Miscellaneous) 2003 (SSI 2003/468), r.2. Brought into force on October 27, 2003 in accordance with art.1.

GENERAL NOTE

In many summary cases the appeal hearing proceeds in the absence of the appellant accused because he is neither in custody nor on bail pending the appeal. Where the accused has been admitted to bail he must attend the hearing (as it is a requirement of bail that he attend all lawful diets) and if he fails to do so the court will decline to entertain the appeal and will usually be persuaded to continue the appeal to a date to be afterwards fixed. However, in exceptional cases the court may be persuaded to hear the appeal in the accused's absence. In Crown appeals against unduly lenient sentences mat-ters are different since the accused is the respondent and he will not be on bail (and it is highly unlikely that he will be in custody). It has been held that in principle the court will not hear an appeal against sentence in the respondent accused's absence but will continue the appeal for the accused to be afforded the opportunity of attending. This is because it is wrong in principle to determine the Crown's appeal when the consequence of that decision could be to increase the sentence imposed on the accused (*Urquhart v Campbell*, 2006 S.C.C.R. 656, para.[4]).

Rule 19.1

An appeal is initiated by lodging a note of appeal with the clerk of the lower court and not with the Justiciary Office. The note must be lodged not later than two days after the decision of the lower court. If no note of appeal is lodged timeously the appeal is never, in fact, insisted in (there is therefore no need for a minute of abandonment in Form 19.1-B to be lodged) and, in the normal course of events, where a trial diet has been fixed already, the case will next call on the day fixed for the trial. Trial diets should, in the normal course, have been fixed because leave can only be applied for after the accused has pled not guilty. However, if leave to appeal is applied for and granted and *per incuriam* the accused has not already been asked to state how he intends to plead, the lower court will not have adjourned the diet to a trial diet and (unless a trial diet has previously been fixed when the accused stated his objection at the pleading diet), the instance will fall at midnight: see *Lafferty v Jessop*, 1989 S.L.T. 846; 1989 S.C.C.R. 451.

The lower court is not entitled to postpone determination of the motion for leave to appeal against its decision but must determine the application "immediately".

Once the appeal calls in the High Court it is necessary to obtain the leave of the High Court to abandon the appeal because the High Court may wish to hear argument on the appeal or (at least) an explanation as to why the appeal was marked in the first place.

Two recent decisions on what does and does not constitute relevancy and/or competency are worthy of notice because of their potentially far reaching implications. First, in *Rosselli v Vannet*, 1997 S.C.C.R. 655 the High Court observed that where in a summary prosecution the Crown's conduct at the intermediate diet was founded on as oppressive, it was open to the accused to raise the issue of oppression at the outset of the trial diet as it was not a matter of competency or relevancy and thus did not require to be stated before the accused was called on to plead (*cf. Normand v Rooney*, 1992 S.C.C.R. 336, to which the court in *Rosselli* made no reference). Secondly, in *McQueen v Hingston*, 1997 S.C.C.R. 765 it was held that where the accused required the Crown to prove by production of a non-statutory document the commencement of a period within which a statutory duty operated, failure to comply with such duty constituting an offence, the accused was bound to state objection to the relevancy and/or competency of the charge. The accused was not entitled to remain silent and submit that the Crown had failed to prove its case (see P.W. Ferguson, "Relevancy and Sufficiency", 1997 S.L.T. (News) 229).

Rule 19.2

Stated case appeals are a creation of statute. They are limited to questions of law which it is for the trial court to formulate with precision. An appellant must set forth "a full statement of all the matters which [he] desires to bring under review" in his application (under s.176(1)) to the lower court for that court to state a case. Where, however, the appellant wishes to amend any matter in his application, or add a new matter on which he seeks review, he is at liberty to do so by intimating that fact during the three-week period commencing with the issue of the draft stated case (s.179(1)). The case cannot be meaningfully stated unless the grounds of challenge are identified in advance of the issue of the final stated case.

Once the case has been finalised and transmitted to the Clerk of Justiciary in Edinburgh, it is incompetent for an appellant to present argument on matters not previously identified in the application for a stated case (as added to or amended under s.179(1)). However, the High Court has power under s.182(3) to grant leave, on cause being shown to the court's satisfaction, for the appellant to found any aspect of his appeal on a matter not contained in his application under s.176(1). Neither the 1995 Act nor the Criminal Procedure Rules provides a mechanism for seeking leave to amend the grounds of review.

The High Court has, therefore, provided guidance on what an appellant should do when he wishes leave to amend his appeal by stated case. In *Watt v Ralph*, unreported, January 12, 2007; [2007] HC-JAC 7 Lord Justice General Hamilton recently stated:

> "where a case has been stated and there subsequently arise matters upon which an appellant wishes to rely, he should promptly make an application to the court under s.182(3) for the relevant leave. That should be done in writing in a document headed 'Application under s.182(3) of the Criminal Procedure (Scotland) Act 1995' and setting out clearly and succinctly the basis upon which the application is made. The document should be lodged in court and intimated to the Crown sufficiently far in advance of the day on which leave is to be sought, so as to allow to the court and to the Crown time to give it mature consideration." (para.[9]).

The document should be lodged with the Justiciary Office and intimation should be given to the Crown Office in Edinburgh. This guidance applies also to new grounds of review in respect of sentences which are challenged by way of stated case.

It is competent for an appeal to be taken against the acquittal of the accused even though the Crown seeks to withdraw a concession in law which was the basis of the acquittal in the lower court (see *Brown v Farrel*, 1997 S.C.C.R. 356). There seems no reason in principle for that rule not to apply equally to a defence appeal. It must, however, be open to serious doubt whether an accused whose conviction proceeded on the basis that it was accepted—as so often happens in the lower court—that the case depended on issues of credibility and reliability, can thereafter appeal on the ground of a legal argument which was not advanced in the lower court either because it was not noticed or it was considered unsound (*cf. McGinty v HM Advocate*, 2000 J.C. 277 where an appellant was refused leave to revert to a ground of appeal which had been expressly abandoned at an earlier hearing).

Rule 19.6

Two different stages can have been reached when the appellant chooses to abandon his appeal. When the stated case has not been transmitted to the Justiciary Office, the appellant should lodge the minute with the clerk of the lower court but, once the stated case has been lodged with the Justiciary Office, the minute should be lodged with the Clerk of Justiciary who will then inform the clerk of the lower court.

Rule 19.9

Where an accused applies for a stated case he should also seek interim suspension of his driving disqualification and, if the court does not suspend the disqualification, the accused can apply to a judge of the High Court who shall normally hear the application in chambers though not necessarily with the attendance of counsel (*cf.* the situation where a bill of suspension contains a prayer for interim suspension: r.19.15). The judge's decision is final.

Rule 19.10

In bills of suspension the application is made direct to the High Court and no notice is given to the lower court which will therefore be unaware that the conviction and/or disqualification is being appealed. The interim suspension of the disqualification when granted must therefore (for administrative convenience) be postponed until the lower court has been informed that it has been suspended.

Rule 19.11

There is no obligation on agents outside Edinburgh to instruct correspondents in Edinburgh for appeals but they may do so.

Rule 19.12

While rr.19.11 and 19.16 refer to bills of advocation, r.19.12 does not include them although it is conceivable—but hardly likely nowadays—that an accused could bring an advocation during the course of a summary trial.

Rule 19.14

This rule was introduced in September 2003 and does for solemn sentence appeals (including Crown appeals) what is now provided for in summary appeals (see r.15.1(4) and (5), *supra*). In both such appeals the court must give at least 42 days' notice of the appeal hearing so as to allow for the appellant to comply with r.19.18.

Rule 19.17

Section 193(1) of the 1995 Act provides that where a disqualification, forfeiture or disability attaches as a result of conviction, the lower court can, if it thinks fit, suspend the disqualification, etc., pending the determination of any appeal. Where leave to appeal is required under either s.180 or s.187 of the 1995 Act, the single judge's decision to refuse leave will be intimated to the accused and, on the 15th day after the date of intimation, the disqualification, etc., will re-attach. Where, however, the accused applies to a quorum of judges—three judges are appropriate if conviction is being challenged but two judges are appropriate where sentence alone is appealed—the disqualification, etc., will attach seven days after the date of intimation of the refusal of leave to appeal.

Rule 19.18

The High Court when hearing appeals has an inherent power to call for a supplementary report. Presumably on the view that the single judge who "sifts" the appeals has no such inherent power and because (no doubt because it has become apparent in the months since the "sift" procedures have been operating) stated cases may disclose a ground of appeal which is not referred to in the application for a stated case, the single judge is now given a power to remit to the trial judge.

Rule 19.19

This rule is designed to ensure that sentence appeals by accused persons and the Crown do not occupy an undue amount of precious Appeal Court time. Such appeals should be presented in writing although the appellant *may* (at his or the court's discretion?) "make supplementary comments" (r.19.18(5)(c)). Information relied upon at the appeal hearing but not founded on in the case and argument may be admitted. See annotations to r.15.16, *supra*.

CHAPTER 19A

ADJOURNMENT BEFORE SENTENCE UNDER SECTION 201 OR DEFERRED SENTENCE UNDER SECTION 202 OF THE ACT OF 1995

Power of clerk of Justiciary to alter place where case to be heard

19A.1.—(1) Where the High Court has—

(a) adjourned a case under section 201 of the Act of 1995; or

(b) deferred sentence in a case under section 202 of the Act of 1995,

the Clerk of Justiciary may make an order altering the place where the case is to be heard, not later than two days before the case is to be called.

(2) The Clerk of Justiciary shall intimate an order made under paragraph (1) to—

(a) the parties to the proceedings; and

(b) the governor of any institution in which the accused is detained,

not later than two days before the case is to be called.

AMENDMENT

Chapter 19A inserted by Act of Adjournal (Criminal Procedure Rules Amendment No.2) (Miscellaneous) 2003 (SSI 2003/468), r.2. Brought into force on October 27, 2003 in accordance with art.1.

GENERAL NOTE

Section 201(1) of the 1995 Act provides that before sentence (or other disposal) the court may adjourn the diet for the purpose of enabling inquiries to be made or of determining the most suitable method of dealing with the accused's case. The case cannot be adjourned for any single period exceeding four weeks or, on cause shown, eight weeks (s.201(3)). If the accused is remanded in custody, he is entitled to appeal against the refusal of bail, or the conditions imposed in the bail order, within 24 hours of his remand, by note of appeal. This provision is to allow for the preparation of social enquiry reports, community service assessments, risk assessments and the like. Section 202, on the other hand, serves a different purpose (see *HM Advocate v Clegg*, 1991 S.L.T. 192). That provision is the sentence, or part of it, when deferral is ordered for the accused to be of good behaviour.

The rule is only necessary for, and therefore only applies to, High Court proceedings. So far as deferred sentences under s.202 are concerned, it is impossible to know where a High Court judge will be in 12 months' time and the same nowadays is true even for four-week adjournments. Thus, to avoid the need of calling the case before the "wrong" judge at the court previously announced (so as to adjourn it to a later date for the original judge to deal with it), Justiciary Office can now alter the place. This must be done not later than two days before the case is to be called; the same period of notice must be given to the accused. Failure to keep to the timetable when making the order could be fatal to the instance if the case then calls where it should not and is therefore not called where it is still bound to call.

CHAPTER 19B

CASES REFERRED BY THE SCOTTISH CRIMINAL CASES REVIEW COMMISSION
UNDER SECTION 194B OF THE ACT OF 1995

References in solemn proceedings

19B.1.—(1) This rule applies to a referral by the Scottish Criminal Cases Review Commission to the High Court in solemn proceedings under section 194B of the Act of 1995.

(2) Within eight weeks of the date of referral, the person who has been convicted shall lodge a note of appeal in Form 15.2-B with the Clerk of Justiciary and subsections (2) to (4) and (6) of section 110 of the Act of 1995 shall apply to the note.

(2A) On the lodging of a note of appeal under paragraph (2), the Clerk of Justiciary shall send a copy of the note to the Crown Agent.

(3) A note of appeal lodged under the preceding paragraph shall be treated as if leave to appeal in terms of section 107(1)(a) of the Act of 1995 has been granted.

AMENDMENT

Rule 19B.1 as amended by the Act of Adjournal (Criminal Procedure Rules Amendment No.3) (Extradition etc.) 2004 (SSI 2004/346), r.2 (effective August 18, 2004).

References in summary proceedings

19B.2.—(1) This rule applies to a referral by the Scottish Criminal Cases

Review Commission to the High Court in summary proceedings under section 194B of the Act of 1995.

(2) Where the Clerk of Justiciary receives a reference in summary proceedings, he shall—

(a) assign the referral to a procedural hearing; and

(b) as soon as possible thereafter, intimate the diet to every party and to the governor of any institution in which any accused is detained.

(3) At the procedural hearing the High Court may make directions as to the procedure to be followed in the determination of the referral.

AMENDMENT

Chapter 19B inserted by Act of Adjournal (Criminal Procedure Rules Amendment No.2) (Miscellaneous) 2003 (SSI 2003/468), r.2. Brought into force on October 27, 2003 in accordance with art.1.

GENERAL NOTE

Solemn cases

Section 194B of the 1995 Act provides, inter alia, that the Scottish Criminal Cases Review Commission may at any time, if they think fit (having regard to the grounds in s.194C), refer "the whole case" of a person convicted on indictment to the High Court and "the case shall be heard and determined, subject to any directions the High Court may make, as if it were an appeal under Part VIII" of the 1995 Act (which governs solemn appeals). The practice (whether there was a Secretary of State's reference (*Beattie v HM Advocate*, 1995 S.L.T. 275) or a Commission reference (*Boncza-Tomaszewski v HM Advocate*, 2000 J.C. 586)) has been for the accused to lodge a note of appeal containing all the grounds which he desires to argue: he was entitled to go beyond the specific grounds on which the Commission had stated that it referred the case and he was entitled to seek leave to amend his grounds. This was consistent with the deeming of the reference to be an appeal under the 1995 Act; and the Appeal Court would accordingly put the case out for a procedural hearing to give appropriate directions.

However, unlike s.110(1)(a), where the starting point for the eight-week period within which to lodge a note of appeal is prescribed, there was no definite starting point for references. Thus, r.19B.1(2) assimilates references to appeals by giving the date of referral as the commencement of the period. That period may be extended, within the eight weeks, by the Clerk of Justiciary (s.110(2)). However, it is only left to implication that the Appeal Court (or a single High Court judge: s.129(1) and (3)) may extend the eight-week period *after* it has expired (as is competent in "normal" appeals: s.111(2)) when he considers it "just and proper that the non-compliance is waived".

For the avoidance of doubt, r.19B.1(3) provides that there is no requirement for the note of appeal to pass the sifting process. Such would have been inconsistent with the purpose of the extra-judicial Commission's powers of reference.

Summary cases

Section 194B makes the same provision for summary convictions and sentences. However, while it is provided that the appeal is to be heard and determined as if it were an appeal under Part X of the 1995 Act (which provides the procedure to be followed for the statutory modes of appeal of stated case and note of appeal (where sentence alone is challenged)), it is necessary to avoid the consequences of that provision. Thus, the time limits for stated case procedure do not, because they cannot, apply. A procedural hearing is to be appointed so that the Appeal Court can determine what steps should be taken to advance the appeal and identify the grounds on which it is to be prosecuted. In *Crombie v Clark*, 2001 S.L.T. 635 the Appeal Court ordained the accused to lodge a bill of suspension (para.3) and this seems the likely direction to be given in all cases. The bill will then be the focus of the appeal and the Commission's statement of reasons for referring the case will simply be the background material (as Lord Prosser observed in *Crombie*, para.4).

CHAPTER 19C

RISK ASSESSMENT

Risk assessment orders

19C.1.—(1) A notice of intention to make a motion for a risk assessment order under section 210B(2) of the Act of 1995[8] shall be in Form 19C.1–A.

(2) A risk assessment order under section 210B(2) of the Act of 1995 shall be in Form 19C.1–B.

(3) An application under section 210B(5) of the Act of 1995 (application for extension of period of adjournment following order) shall be made by letter to the Clerk of Justiciary.

(4) On receipt of a letter under paragraph (3), the Clerk of Justiciary shall—

(a) send a copy of that letter to the prosecutor, the convicted person and the assessor; and

(b) fix a date and time for hearing the application which date and time shall be notified by the Clerk of Justiciary to the prosecutor; the convicted person and the governor of any institution in which the convicted person is detained.

(5) The Clerk of Justiciary shall notify the governor of any institution in which the convicted person is detained of any extension (or further extension) under section 210B(5) of the Act of 1995, of the period mentioned in section 210B(4) of the Act of 1995 (adjournment following risk assessment order).

Reports

19C.2. A report under section 210C or 210D of the Act of 1995 shall be in Form 19C.2.

Objections to reports

19C.3.—(1) A convicted person shall intimate any objection under section 210C(7) of Act of 1995 by lodging with the Clerk of Justiciary and serving on the prosecutor a notice of objection in Form 19C.3 within 14 days after receiving a copy of the report.

(2) On receipt of a notice of objection under paragraph (1), the Clerk of Justiciary shall fix a date and time for hearing the objection and shall intimate that date and time to the convicted person, the prosecutor and the governor if any institution in which the convicted person is detained.

(3) The convicted person and the prosecutor shall, not less than 7 days before the hearing mentioned in paragraph (2), lodge and serve on the other party lists of any witnesses and productions on which they propose to rely at the hearing.

AMENDMENT

Chapter 19C inserted by Act of Adjournal (Criminal Procedure Rules Amendment No.3) (Risk Assessment Orders and Orders for Lifelong Restriction) 2006 (SSI 2006/302), para.2(5) (effective June 20, 2006).

GENERAL NOTE

Section 1 of the Criminal Justice (Scotland) Act 2003 amends the 1995 Act to insert ss.210B–210G which make provision for risk assessment orders (RAOs) and lifelong restriction orders (LROs). The object of an RAO is to provide the court with sufficient information in the form of a risk assessment report prepared in an accredited manner by a psychologist (to be known as an "assessor": s.210B(5)) accredited by the Risk Management Authority, so as to be able to determine whether a LRO should be made when imposing sentence. The Risk Management Authority was established by s.3 of the 2003 Act (which came into force on June 27, 2003: see Criminal Justice (Scotland) Act 2003 (Commencement No.1) Order 2003 (SSI 2003/288)). The Authority has responsibility for preparing and issuing guidelines as to the assessment and minimisation of risk and for setting and publishing standards according to which measures taken in respect of such assessment and minimisation of risk are to be judged (2003 Act, s.5(1)). It is the duty of assessors to have regard to such guidelines and standards (2003 Act, s.5(2)). The scheme for accreditation to be administered by the Authority came into force on March 30, 2006 (see Risk Assessment and Minimisation (Accreditation Scheme) (Scotland) Order 2006 (SSI 2006/190)).

A LRO constitutes a sentence of imprisonment or detention for an indeterminate period (s.210F(2)) and may be appealed by note of appeal against sentence. Moreover, if the court refuses to make a LRO, the Crown is entitled to appeal against that refusal on the grounds that on balance of probabilities the risk criteria for making such an order were met (s.210F(3)). Thus, exceptionally in Scottish procedure, the Crown is in effect given a right to appeal on a question of fact. The Crown does not require leave to appeal. If a LRO is made there then arises an obligation on the Scottish Ministers to prepare a risk management plan (2003 Act, s.6(1)). The plan must be completed no later than nine months after sentence was imposed (2003 Act, s.8(1)) and must set out, inter alia, an assessment of the accused's risk to the public, the measures to be taken to minimise that risk and how such measures are to be coordinated (2003 Act, s.6(3)).

Rule 19C.1

The prosecution is not entitled to move for an RAO unless it has given notice of its intention to do so but the court may make an order *ex proprio motu* (s.210B(2)). In any event, the court is bound to make an order if it considers that the risk criteria set out in s.210E *may* be met, unless the court makes an interim hospital order or the accused is already subject to a LRO. An RAO can only be made by the High Court; it cannot be made in respect of a murder conviction; and it is necessary that the conviction before the High Court be for one or all of the following offences: (a) a sexual offence as defined in s.210A(10), (b) a violent offence as so defined, (c) an offence which endangers life (e.g. culpable and reckless conduct); or for (d) an offence the nature of which, or the circumstances of the commission of which, are such that it appears to the court that the accused has a "propensity to commit any such offence as is mentioned" in (a)–(c).

An RAO is an order for the accused to be taken to a place specified in the order so that there can be prepared a risk assessment report on the risk which the accused's being at liberty presents to the safety of the public at large; and the order provides for the accused to be remanded in custody there for so long as is necessary for that purpose (and thereafter detained there or elsewhere until the accused's sentencing diet) (s.210B(3)). On making the RAO the court must adjourn the case for no more than 90 days. However, the court may on one occasion, on cause shown, extend that period by not more than 90 days; and may, exceptionally, further extend the period for as long as the court considers appropriate for completion of the report if the reason for the report not having been completed is attributable to circumstances which were outwith the assessor's control (s.210B(5)). There is no right of appeal against an RAO or the refusal to make one (s.210B(6)).

Rule 19C.2

The assessor may take into account, for the purposes of assessing the accused's risk, not only the accused's previous convictions but also "any allegation that the [accused] has engaged in criminal behaviour (whether or not that behaviour resulted in prosecution and acquittal)". Where any allegation is taken into account, it must be specified in the risk assessment report, as must any additional evidence which supports the allegation and the assessor must explain the extent to which the allegation and the evidence have influenced him in forming his opinion as to the level of risk which the accused presents (s.210C(2) and (3)). The completed report must be sent by the assessor to the Clerk of Justiciary who must copy it to the Crown and the accused along with any documents available to, and referred to in the report by, the assessor (s.210C(4)). Upon receipt of the report the Clerk of Justiciary must fix a diet for sentence.

Rule 19C.3

An accused is entitled, while detained for the preparation of the risk assessment report, to instruct his own report (s.210C(5)). If he does, that report should be sent to the Clerk of Justiciary who will copy it, and any relevant documents, to the Crown. The accused may then be in a position to challenge the findings and/or opinion contained in the assessor's report. If he wishes to do so he must give notice. If objection is taken by the accused to the assessor's report, evidence may be led before the sentencing judge (s.210C(7)).

Risk criteria Whether or not objections are intimated and irrespective of whether a proof is held, the task of the sentencing judge is then to determine whether a LRO should be made. He must do so in light of the risk criteria which are that "the nature of, or the circumstances of the commission of, the offence of which the [accused] has been found guilty either in themselves or as part of a pattern of behaviour are such as to demonstrate that there is a likelihood that he, if at liberty, will seriously endanger the lives, or physical or psychological well-being, of members of the public at large" (s.210E). If in light of the RAO, any risk assessment prepared for the accused, any evidence led at a proof on the accused's objections or "any other information before it", the court is satisfied on balance of probabilities that the risk criteria are met, the court must make a LRO (s.210F(1)). Where the court does not make a LRO because it is not satisfied that the risk criteria are met, the court is thereby precluded from imposing an indeterminate sentence (s.210G(1)).

PART V

SENTENCING

CHAPTER 20

SENTENCING

Form of sentence of death
20.1. [...]

AMENDMENT

Repealed by the Act of Adjournal (Criminal Procedure Rules Amendment No. 3) 1999 (SI 1999/1387), para.2(4) (effective May 19, 1999).

Detention in police custody instead of imprisonment
20.2. An order under section 206(2) of the Act of 1995 (detention in police custody instead of imprisonment) shall be in Form 20.2.

Supervised release orders
20.3.—(1) An order under section 209 of the Act of 1995 (supervised release orders) shall be in Form 20.3-A.

(2) The citation of an offender to appear before a court under section 15(5) of the Prisoners and Criminal Proceedings (Scotland) Act 1993 (variation of supervised release order etc.) shall be in Form 20.3-B.

(3) The citation of an offender to appear before a court under section 18(1) of the Prisoners and Criminal Proceedings (Scotland) Act 1993 (breach of supervised release order) shall be in Form 20.3-C.

AMENDMENT

Rule 20.3 substituted by Act of Adjournal (Criminal Procedure Rules Amendment No.2) (Miscellaneous) 2003 (SSI 2003/468), r.2. Brought into force on October 27, 2003 in accordance with art.1.

Sexual offences to which Part 2 of the Sexual Offences Act 2003 applies
20.3A.—(1) A certificate under section 92(2) of the Sexual Offences Act 2003 (certificate that an accused has been convicted of, found not guilty by reason of insanity of, or found to be under a disability and to have done the act charged against him in respect of, an offence listed in Schedule 3 to that Act) shall be in Form 20.3A A.

(2) Subject to paragraph (3), when a certificate such as is mentioned in paragraph (1) is prepared, the accused shall be given a copy of it by the clerk of the court, together with a notice in Form 20.3A B.

(3) If the certificate is not prepared immediately after the statement in open court but is to be prepared subsequently, the clerk of the court shall forthwith give the accused the notice required by paragraph (2) and shall in due course send a copy of the certificate to the accused.

(3A) Where sentence has been deferred in respect of an accused who has been given a notice required by paragraph (2), the clerk of the court shall, when sentence is passed, give the accused a notice in Form 20.3A-C.

(4) The clerk of the court shall retain a copy of any notices given to the accused under paragraph (3) or (3A), as the case may be and shall record on those copies the fact that notice has been so given.

(5) The record made under paragraph (4) shall be sufficient evidence of the fact recorded; and a certificate of posting sufficient evidence of the sending of a copy under paragraph (3).

AMENDMENT

Rule 20.3A inserted by the Act of Adjournal (Criminal Procedure Rules Amendment No. 5) (SI 1997/2082) (effective September 1, 1997).

Rule 20.3A substituted by the Act of Adjournal (Criminal Procedure Rules Amendment No.2) (Sexual Offences Act 2003) 2004 (SSI 2004/206), r.2 (effective May 1, 2004).

Rule 20.3A(3A) inserted, and r.20.3A(4) as amended, by the Act of Adjournal (Criminal Procedure Rules Amendment No. 4) (Miscellaneous) 2006 (SSI 2006/436), r.2 (effective September 1, 2006).

Application of money found on offender towards fine

20.4.—(1) A direction under section 212(1) of the Act of 1995 that money found on an offender should not be applied towards payment of a fine shall be in Form 20.4-A.

(2) A notice for the purposes of section 212(7) of the Act of 1995 (notice to governor of prison as warrant to convey offender to court) shall be in Form 20.4-B.

Extension of time for payment of fine

20.5. An order under section 214(7) or 215(3) of the Act of 1995 (order allowing further time for payment of fine) shall be in Form 20.5.

Forms for enquiry for non-payment of fine

20.6.—(1) The citation of an offender issued under section 216(3)(a) of the Act of 1995 (citation to appear for enquiry before imprisonment in default of payment of fine) shall be in Form 20.6-A.

(2) The execution of a citation referred to in paragraph (1) which is served other than by post shall be in Form 20.6-B.

(3) The—

(a) execution of a citation referred to in paragraph (1) which is served by post,

(b) warrant for apprehension of an offender issued under section 216(3)(b) of the Act of 1995, and

(c) record of proceedings at an enquiry under section 216 of that Act, shall be in Form 20.6-C.

Supervision of payment of fine

20.7. A notice to be sent to an offender under section 217(7) of the Act of 1995 (appointment of different supervising officer to offender allowed time to pay fine) shall be in Form 20.7.

Forms of warrant for execution and charge for payment of fine or other financial penalty

20.8.—(1) In every extract of a sentence of a fine or other financial penalty, there shall be included a warrant for execution in the following terms: "and the Lords [*or* sheriff *or* justice(s)] grant(s) warrant for all lawful execution hereon".

(2) The charge for payment of a fine or other financial penalty to be used by a sheriff officer under section 90 of the Debtors (Scotland) Act 1987 (provisions relating to charges for payment) shall be in Form 20.8.

Transfer of fines

20.9.—(1) A transfer of fine order under section 222(1), and a notice of it required by section 223(1), of the Act of 1995 shall be in Form 20.9-A.

(2) A transfer of fine order made by virtue of section 222(5) of the Act of 1995, and a notice of it required by section 223(1), shall be in Form 20.9-B.

(3) Where a notice of a transfer of fine order is received by a court in Scotland, the clerk of that court shall serve by post a notice to the offender in Form 20.9-C.

Probation orders

20.10.—(1) A probation order shall be in Form 20.10-A.

(2) The citation of a probationer to appear before a court under section 232(1) (failure to comply with requirement of probation order), or section 233(1) (commission of further offence while on probation), of the Act of 1995 shall be in Form 20.10-B.

(3) The citation of a probationer under paragraph 5(1) of Schedule 6 to the Act of 1995 (amendment of probation order) shall be in Form 20.10-C.

AMENDMENT

Rule 20.10 as amended by Act of Adjournal (Criminal Procedure Rules Amendment No.2) (Miscellaneous) 2003 (SSI 2003/468), r.2. Brought into force on October 27, 2003 in accordance with art.1.

Form and notification of non-harassment order

20.10A.—(1) A non-harassment order made under section 234A of the Act of 1995 shall be in Form 20.10A.

(2) A non-harassment order mentioned in paragraph (1) above shall be intimated by the clerk of the court, by which it is made to any person, other than the offender, who is named in the order.

Variation or revocation of non-harassment order

20.10B.—(1) This rule applies to an application under section 234(6) of the Act of 1995 (application for variation or revocation of non-harassment order).

(2) In this rule—

"the offender" means the offender subject to the order to which the application relates; and

"the prosecutor" means the prosecutor at whose instance the order was made.

(3) The application shall—

(a) identify the proceedings in which the order was made;

(b) state the reasons for which the applicant seeks the variation or revocation of the order;

(c) be, as nearly as may be, in Form 20.10B.

(4) The applicant shall serve a copy of the application on—

(a) the clerk of the court which made the order;

(b) any person, other than the offender, who is named in the order; and

(c) where the applicant is—

(i) the offender, the prosecutor; and

(ii) the prosecutor, the offender,

but the application may proceed notwithstanding that, having taken reasonable steps to do so, the applicant has been unable to effect service of it on the offender or any person such as is mentioned in subparagraph (b) above.

(5) Where the offender is the applicant, the prosecutor shall, within fourteen days of the receipt of the copy of the application, notify the clerk of court in writing whether he intends to oppose the application.

(6) Where the prosecutor is the applicant, the offender shall, within fourteen days of receipt of the copy of the application, notify the clerk of court in writing whether he intends to oppose the application.

(7) Where a person notifies the clerk of court under paragraph (5) or (6) above that he does not intend to oppose the application, or fails to make any notification, the court shall proceed to dispose of the application and may do so in the absence of the applicant.

(8) Where a person notifies the clerk of court under paragraph (5) or (6) above

that he does intend to oppose the application, the clerk of court shall arrange a hearing before the court at which the prosecutor and the offender may appear or be represented.

(9) The clerk of court shall give notice in writing of the decision of the court on the application to—

(a) the applicant;

(b) any person served with a copy of the application under sub-paragraph (b) or (c) of paragraph (4) above.

Supervised attendance orders

20.11.—(1) A supervised attendance order made under section 235(1) of the Act of 1995 shall be in Form 20.11-A.

(2) A supervised attendance order made under section 236 of the Act of 1995 (supervised attendance orders in place of fines for 16 and 17 year olds) shall be in Form 20.11-B.

(3) The citation of an offender to appear before a court under paragraph 5(3) of Schedule 7 to the Act of 1995 (extension, variation and revocation etc. of supervised attendance orders) shall be in Form 20.11-C.

(4) The citation of an offender to appear before a court under paragraph 4(1) of Schedule 7 to the Act of 1995 (breach of requirement of or other provision relating to supervised attendance order) shall be in Form 20.11-D.

AMENDMENT

Rule 20.11 substituted by Act of Adjournal (Criminal Procedure Rules Amendment No.2) (Miscellaneous) 2003 (SSI 2003/468), r.2. Brought into force on October 27, 2003 in accordance with art.1.

Community service orders

20.12.—(1) A community service order made under section 238 of the Act of 1995 shall be in Form 20.12-A.

(2) The citation of an offender to appear before a court under section 239(4) (failure to comply with requirement of community service order), or section 240(3) (amendment or revocation of community service order), of the Act of 1995 shall be in Form 20.12-B.

Restriction of liberty orders

20.12A.—(1) A restriction of liberty order made under section 245A(1) of the Act of 1995 shall be in form 20.12A-A.

(2) An application under section 245E(1) (application to review a restriction of liberty order) of that Act shall be in form 20.12A-B.

(3) The citation of an offender under section 245E(3) (citation to appear before a court which proposes to vary or revoke a restriction of liberty order) of that Act shall be in form 20.12A-C.

(4) The citation of an offender under section 245F(1) (citation for failure to comply with requirement of restriction of liberty order) of that Act shall be in form 20.12A-D.

AMENDMENT

Rule 20.12A inserted by the Act of Adjournal (Criminal Procedure Rules Amendment) (Restriction of Liberty Orders) 1998 (SI 1998/1842) (effective August 17, 1998).

Drug treatment and testing orders

20.12B.—(1) A drug treatment and testing order made under section 234B of the Act of 1995 shall be in Form 20.12B-A.

(2) The citation of an offender to appear before a court under section 234E(2) of the Act of 1995 (variation or revocation of drug treatment and testing order) shall be in Form 20.12B-B.

(3) The citation of an offender to appear before a court under section 234G(1) of the Act of 1995 (breach of drug testing and treatment order) shall be in Form 20.12B-C.

AMENDMENT

Rule 20.12B inserted by the Act of Adjournal (Criminal Procedure Rules Amendment No. 4) (Drug Treatment and Testing Orders) 1999 (SSI 1999/191), para.2 (effective December 20, 1999).

Rule 20.12B substituted by Act of Adjournal (Criminal Procedure Rules Amendment No.2) (Miscellaneous) 2003 (SSI 2003/468), r.2. Brought into force on October 27, 2003 in accordance with art.1.

Community reparation orders

20.12C.—(1) A community reparation order under section 245K(1) of the Act of 1995 shall be in Form 20.12C-A.

(2) The citation of an offender to appear before a court under section 245N(2) of the Act of 1995 (failure to comply with a community reparation order) shall be in Form 20.12C-B.

(3) The citation of an offender to appear before a court under section 245P(3) of the Act of 1995 (extension, variation and revocation of a community reparation order) shall be in Form 20.12C-C.

AMENDMENT

Rule 20.12C inserted by the Act of Adjournal (Criminal Procedure Rules Amendment No.2) (Miscellaneous) 2005 (SSI 2005/160), r.2 (effective March 31, 2005).

Terms of compensation orders in record of proceedings

20.13. Entries shall be made in the record of proceedings by the clerk of court on the making of a compensation order, specifying the terms of the order and in particular—

(a) the name of the convicted person required to pay compensation;

(b) the amount of compensation required to be paid by such person;

(c) the name of the person entitled to the compensation payable; and

(d) where there is more than one person entitled to compensation, the amount of compensation each is entitled to and the priority, if any, among those persons for payment.

Legal disability of person entitled to compensation

20.14.—(1) The prosecutor, if he knows that any person entitled to payment of compensation under a compensation order is under any legal disability, shall so inform the court immediately it makes any such order in respect of any such person, and that information shall be entered by the clerk of court in the record of proceedings.

(2) Where payment of any sum is made under a compensation order to the clerk of court in respect of a person known to be under a legal disability, Part IV (except rule 36.17(1) (receipt sufficient discharge)) of Chapter 36 of the Ordinary Cause Rules 1993 in Schedule 1 to the Sheriff Courts (Scotland) Act 1907 (management of damages payable to persons under legal disability) shall apply to the administration of that sum as they apply to the administration of a sum of money paid into court in respect of damages for such a person.

Variation of compensation orders

20.15.—(1) The court may, at any time before a compensation order is fully complied with, and after such further inquiry as the court may order, vary the terms of the order as it thinks fit.

(2) A variation made under paragraph (1) may be made in chambers and in the absence of the parties or any of them.

GENERAL NOTE

Rule 22.15 shall apply in solemn proceedings which commenced after April 1, 2006, and in which there is a vulnerable witness within the meaning of s.271(1)(b) of the Criminal Procedure (Scotland) Act 1995, with proceedings being taken to have commenced when a report of the case has been received by the procurator fiscal (Acts of Adjournal (Criminal Procedure Rules Amendment) Animal Health and Welfare etc. (2007/238)).

Discharge or reduction of compensation order

20.16.—(1) An application to discharge a compensation order or to reduce the amount that remains to be paid under section 251(1) of the Act of 1995 (review of compensation order) shall be made in writing to the clerk of the court which made the order.

(2) The clerk of court shall, on any such application being made to him, serve a copy of the application on the prosecutor by post.

(3) The court to which the application is made may dispose of the application after such inquiry as it thinks fit.

Use of certified copy documents in certain proceedings

20.17.—(1) Subject to paragraph (2), in proceedings relating to—

(a) an order which imposed a fine,

(b) a supervised attendance order,

(c) a community service order,

(d) a probation order, or

(e) a community reparation order,

in a court other than the court which made the order, the principal indictment, complaint, record or minute of proceedings, or notice of previous convictions need not be before the court.

(2) The court to which paragraph (1) applies shall have before it a copy of the principal of each of such documents certified as a true copy by the clerk of the court which made the order.

AMENDMENT

Rule 20.17 as amended by the Act of Adjournal (Criminal Procedure Rules Amendment No.2) (Miscellaneous) 2005 (SSI 2005/160), r.2 (effective March 31, 2005).

Form of extract of sentence

20.18.—(1) An extract of a custodial sentence following a conviction on indictment, and warrant of detention and return of sentence, required for any purpose in connection with any case shall be in Form 20.18-A.

(2) An extract of a sentence of imprisonment, a fine or caution in summary proceedings under the Act of 1995 shall be in the appropriate form in Form 20.18-B.

(3) An extract issued in accordance with paragraph (1) or (2) shall be warrant and authority for execution.

Reduction of disqualification period for drink-drive offenders

20.19.—(1) In this rule—

"the Act of 1988" means the Road Traffic Offenders Act 1988;

"course organiser" has the meaning assigned in section 34C(2) of the Act of 1988;

"date specified" means the date specified in an order under section 34A of the Act of 1988;

"supervising court" has the meaning assigned in section 34C(2) of the Act of 1988.

(2) An application to the supervising court for a declaration under section 34B(6) of the Act of 1988 shall be—

(a) in Form 20.19-A;

(b) accompanied by a copy of the written notice required by section 34B(5) of the Act of 1988 intimating the course organiser's decision not to give a course completion certificate; and

(c) lodged with the clerk of court within 28 days after the date specified.

(3) An application to the supervising court for a declaration under section 34B(7) of the Act of 1988 shall be—

(a) in Form 20.19-B; and

(b) lodged with the clerk of court within 28 days after the date specified.

(4) On the lodging of an application under section 34B(6) or (7) of the Act of 1988—

(a) the sheriff or stipendiary magistrate, as the case may be, shall fix a date for hearing the application; and

(b) the clerk of court shall—

(i) notify the applicant of the date of hearing; and

(ii) serve a copy of the application, with notice of the hearing, on the course organiser and the procurator fiscal.

Antisocial behaviour orders

20.20. An antisocial behaviour order made under section 234AA of the Act of 1995 shall be in Form 20.20.

AMENDMENT

Rule 20.20 inserted by Act of Adjournal (Criminal Procedure Rules Amendment No.5) (Miscellaneous) 2004 (SSI 2004/481), r.2 (effective November 26, 2004).

Orders for lifelong restriction

20.21. An order for lifelong restriction under section 210F(1) of the Act of 1995 shall be in Form 20.21.

AMENDMENT

Rule 20.21 inserted by Act of Adjournal (Criminal Procedure Rules Amendment No.3) (Risk Assessment Orders and Orders for Lifelong Restriction) 2006 (SSI 2006/302), para.2(6) (effective June 20, 2006).

GENERAL NOTE

Chapter 20 is largely administrative in character in that it provides merely for the appropriate forms which are to be employed by clerks of court at the sentencing stage for different disposals and for consequential matters. Certain provisions should, however, be noted.

Rule 20.2

Section 206(2) provides that where a court of summary jurisdiction has power to impose imprisonment on an offender, it may sentence the offender to be detained in a police cell for a period not exceeding four days as an alternative to imprisonment since s.206(1) provides that no person shall be sentenced to imprisonment by a court of summary jurisdiction for a period of less than five days.

Rule 20.3A

Part I of the Sex Offenders Act 1997 requires persons who are convicted of certain sexual offences to notify their names and addresses to the police. Section 5 provides that where the court before whom an accused is convicted of a sexual offence states and certifies that the offender has been convicted of a sexual offence to which Pt I applies, the certificate granted by the court shall be evidence of that conviction (and therefore of the accused's liability to comply with the notification requirements). The relevant sexual offences are set out in Sch.1 to the 1997 Act (s.1(9)). It has been held that indecent exposure is a form of shameless indecency (which is listed as a relevant sexual offence in Sch.1) and so is an offence in respect of which the convicting court is entitled to grant a certificate (see *Lees, Petitioner*, 1998 S.C.C.R. 401).

Rule 20.8

Any sentence for any fine pronounced by a sheriff court or a district court may be enforced against the person or effects of any party against whom the sentence was awarded (a) in the district where the sentence or decree was pronounced or (b) in any other district (see s.211(3) of the 1995 Act). The word "or" is conjunctive and the provision does not set out mutually exclusive alternatives. The effect of the warrant which is added to the finding of the court imposing the fine is (under s.221(1)) to authorise the charging of the accused to pay the fine within the period specified in the charge and, in the event of his failure to make such payment within that period, the execution of an earnings arrestment and the poinding of articles belonging to him and, if necessary for the purpose of executing the poinding, the opening of shut and lockfast places. The warrant also has the separate effect of authorising an arrestment other than an arrestment of earnings in the hands of his employer.

Rule 20.10A

Section 234A of the 1995 Act was inserted by s.11 of the Protection from Harassment Act 1997 (c.40) which was brought into force on June 16, 1997. Section 234A(1) provides that where a person is convicted of an offence involving harassment of a person (whether on indictment or on summary complaint), the Crown may apply to the court to make a non-harassment order against the accused. The order shall require him to refrain from such conduct in relation to the victim as may be specified in the order for such period (which includes an indeterminate (i.e. life) period) as may be so specified, at the same time as passing any other sentence. The court can only make such an order if it is satisfied on a balance of probabilities that it is appropriate to do so (s.234A(8)). The order—including any variation or revocation of it (see r. 20.10B)—can be appealed as if it were a sentence.

The 1997 Act also gives civil courts the power to make a non-harassment order when an action of harassment is pursued by the victim (see s.8(5)(b)(ii)). It is essential before a non-harassment order can competently be made that the accused has been convicted of an offence which in itself involves at least two occasions of conduct which amounts to harassment (*McGlennan v McKinnon*, 1998 S.L.T. 494) but presumably the conduct does not require to be the same on each occasion. Section 8 creates an arguably new private law right to be "free from harassment" and provides that a person must not pursue a course of conduct which amounts to harassment of another and (a) is intended to amount to harassment *or* (b) occurs in circumstances where it would appear to a reasonable person that it would amount to harassment (see s.8(1)). Section 8(3) expressly includes speech as prohibited conduct and declares that harassment includes causing the victim alarm and distress. It is essential before a non-harassment order can competently be made that the prohibited conduct be established as having occurred on at least two occasions but presumably the conduct would not require to be the same on each occasion. Threatening words on one occasion and physical gestures on the other will suffice.

It should be noted that s.234A does not specifically require corroboration no doubt on the view that since the conviction will have proceeded on corroborated evidence, that provision would be redundant. However, it is conceivable that the accused could be convicted of breach of the peace involving two occasions, only one of which is corroborated: the uncorroborated incident would not be deleted from the libel as it would be narrative not requiring corroboration (see *Yates v HM Advocate*, 1977 S.L.T. (Notes) 42). It remains to be seen whether that conviction will be sufficient to bring s.234A into operation.

Breach of a non-harassment order is a criminal offence punishable on indictment by up to five years' imprisonment and/or an unlimited fine, or on summary complaint by up to six months' imprisonment and/or a fine not exceeding the statutory maximum (s.234A(4)). The Crown is permitted to appeal the refusal of its application for an order, although no rule prescribes the form which such an appeal should take. It is suggested that it would be perfectly appropriate, therefore, for the Crown to appeal by bill of advocation. However, it seems likely that where a non-harassment order is made on terms which the Crown consider to be unduly lenient, the Crown cannot appeal against the order under s.108 because, first, s.108 has not been amended to include specifically non-harassment orders (no doubt because they are not strictly speaking punishment) and, secondly, s.234A(3) treats variations and revocations as sentences for appeal purposes but excludes the right of the court when varying the order to increase the period for which it is to run.

Rule 20.10B

Section 234A(6) permits the prosecutor or the accused to apply to the court which made the non-harassment order to vary or revoke it though any variation cannot increase the period for which it was originally ordered to run. While an application for variation or revocation must be served on the victim, no provision is made for the victim to be present or represented at the hearing of the application (r.20.10B(8)). His or her only means of representation must therefore be through the prosecutor. The victim is, however, entitled to notice of the court's decision (r.20.10B(9)).

Rule 20.11

Section 235(2) of the 1995 Act provides that a supervised attendance order is an order which requires an offender (1) to attend a place of supervision (determined by the supervising officer appointed by the relevant local authority: s.235(8)) for such period between 10 and 50 hours (where the amount of the fine in question does not exceed level 1 of the standard scale) and (in all other cases) between 10 and 100 hours and (2) to carry out, during that period, such instructions as the supervising officer may give to the offender. Such an order can only competently be made under s.235 where (1) the offender is 16 years old or older; (2) having been convicted of an offence, the offender has had imposed on him a fine which (or any part or instalment of which) he has failed to pay; (3) the court, but for this section, would also have imposed on the offender a period of imprisonment in default of payment (whether immediately or at a future date) under s.219(1) of the 1995 Act; and (4) the court considers the order "more appropriate than the serving of or, as the case may be, the imposition of such a period of imprisonment" (s.235(4)). In short, supervised attendance orders are an alternative to custody for fine defaulters.

Schedule 7 to the 1995 Act makes further provision for supervised attendance orders (s.235(7)). Paragraph 4(2) specifies the course which the court may take in the event of the offender's failure, without reasonable excuse, to comply with any requirements imposed by the order or to notify his supervising officer of a change of address or in the offender's working times. The court may either: (a) revoke the order and imprison the offender for a maximum of (in the sheriff court) 30 days or (in the district court) 20 days; or (b) vary the number of hours specified in the order. An order, unless revoked, shall remain in force until the offender has carried out the instructions given under it for the number of hours specified in it (para.3(2)). These two courses are the only options open to the court. It is incompetent for the court to revoke the order and make a community service order (even though the offender consents to such community service order): *Crane, Petitioner* [2006] HCJAC 40 (para.14).

No right of appeal is conferred on an offender who wishes to challenge the court's order made on a finding of breach of a supervised order. Where the offender wishes to challenge the competency of the court's order, the offender should present a bill of suspension; where the appropriateness of the order is challenged or it is to be argued that the order is excessive, the competent mode of review is a petition to the *nobile officium*: see *Crane* at para.7.

Rule 20.12

Note that a community service order once made by the lower court cannot be competently suspended by the lower court pending determination of an appeal under s.193 (see *Magee, Petitioner*, 1996 S.L.T. 400).

Rule 20.12A

Sections 234A, 234E and 234F of the 1995 Act were inserted by s.5 of the Crime and Punishment (Scotland) Act 1997 (c.48). Section 245A empowers the court to make a restriction of liberty order in respect of any person aged 16 years or more where he is convicted of an offence (other than murder) if the court is of opinion that the making of such an order is the most appropriate method of disposal. Under s.245A(8) the order may restrict the accused's movements (during a period of up to 12 months (s.245A(3)) to such an extent as the court thinks fit and may include requiring the accused to be in certain places for certain periods in each day or week (for a period or periods not in total exceeding 12 hours per day) or requiring the accused not to be in these specified places for certain periods. Section 245E allows for such an order to be reviewed on the application (to the court which made the order) of either the accused or the person responsible for monitoring compliance with it by means of electronic "tagging". The court can change the order by extending or restricting its requirements, or extending its duration, or can revoke the order (s.245E(2)(a), (b)). Section 245F provides for breach of the requirements of the order being determined by the court which made the order. Where an accused is found to the court's satisfaction, to have failed to comply with any requirement of the order without reasonable excuse, the court can fine the accused without prejudice to the continuation of the order (s.245F(2)(a)). If the accused is fined (the fine being limited to level 3 on the standard scale), the court cannot vary or revoke the order. The fine is deemed to be a summary sentence for the purposes of an appeal to the High Court (s.245F(3)).

After the imposition of a compensation order it may come to the court's attention that the person to whom the compensation is payable (which is recorded in the record of proceedings when the compensation order is made: see r.20.13) has died or indeed was dead before the order was made. This rule would allow the court to take that factor into account since s.251(1) does not give the court power on the application of the accused, to discharge or reduce the compensation order. (See *Tudhope v Furphy*, 1982 S.C.C.R. 575.)

Rule 20.18

See s.198(3). In respect of r.20.18(3), see as an illustration, *Thorne v Stott*, 2000 J.C. 13 at 16E.

Rule 20.20

Section 232(2) of the 1995 Act provides that if it is proved to the satisfaction of the court—for which purpose the evidence of one witness shall be sufficient (s.232(3))—that a probationer has failed to comply with a requirement of his probation order, the court may do one or other of four things: (a) fine the probationer (except where compensation was the requirement which was breached); (b) "sentence the offender for the offence for which the order was made"; (c) vary the requirements of the probation order; or (d) make a community service order in tandem with the probation order. When the court finds that the accused has breached his probation order, the court must proceed to sentence the accused for the original offence in respect of which the probation order had been made and not for the failure to comply with the requirements of the probation order. Thus, the court is obliged by s.210(1) of the 1995 Act to have regard to any period of time spent by the probationer on remand awaiting trial or sentence for the original offence (*Wereszcznski v Procurator Fiscal, Dundee* [2006] HCJAC 58 (July 18, 2006, unreported), para.11).

PART VI

EVIDENCE

CHAPTER 21

UNCONTROVERSIAL EVIDENCE, HEARSAY AND PRIOR STATEMENTS

Notice of uncontroversial evidence

21.1.—(1) Where a party to criminal proceedings serves a copy of a statement and document on another party under section 258 of the Act of 1995 (uncontroversial evidence), he shall also serve with that statement and document a statement in Form 21.1-A.

(2) Where a document is annexed to a statement under section 258(2) of the Act of 1995 and is not described in the statement, a docquet in Form 21.1-B shall be endorsed on that document.

Notice of challenge of evidence as uncontroversial

21.2. A notice by a party under section 258(3) of the Act of 1995 (notice challenging fact in statement under section 258(2) of the Act of 1995) shall be in Form 21.2.

Application for direction that challenge be disregarded

21.2A. An application under section 258(4A) of the Act of 1995 (application for direction that challenge be disregarded) shall be in Form 21.2A.

AMENDMENT

Rule 21.2A inserted by the Act of Adjournal (Criminal Procedure Rules Amendment) (Criminal Procedure (Amendment) (Scotland) Act) 2005 (SSI 2005/44), r.2(16) (subject to r.2(2)–(4)) (effective February 1, 2005).

Notice of intention to have hearsay statement admitted

21.3. A notice under section 259(5) of the Act of 1995 (notice of intention to apply to have evidence of hearsay statement admitted) shall be in Form 21.3.

Authentication of certain prior statements of witnesses

21.4. A statement in a document which it is sought to be admitted in evidence under section 260(4) of the Act of 1995 (admissibility of certain prior statements of witnesses) shall be authenticated by a certificate in Form 21.4 endorsed on or attached to the first page of the statement or attached to the device on which the statement has been recorded.

AMENDMENT

Rule 21.4 as amended by the Act of Adjournal (Criminal Procedure Rules Amendment No.3) (Vulnerable Witnesses (Scotland) Act 2004) 2005 (SSI 2005/188), r.2, subject to the conditions in r.2(2) (effective April 1, 2005).

Form of application to introduce evidence relating to sexual offences

21.5. An application under section 275(1) of the Act of 1995 (exception to restrictions on evidence relating to sexual offences) shall be in Form 21.5.

AMENDMENT

Rule 21.5 inserted by Act of Adjournal (Criminal Procedure Rules Amendment No. 3) (Sexual Offences (Procedure and Evidence) (Scotland) Act 2002) 2002 (SSI 2002/454), r.2(9) (effective November 1, 2002).

Notice of intention to rely on presumption of identification

21.6—(1) A notice under section 281A(2)(a) of the Act of 1995 (notice of intention to rely on presumption of identification prior to trial) shall be in Form 21.6-A

(2) A notice under section 281A(2)(b) of the Act of 1995 (notice of intention to challenge facts in report of identification) shall be in Form 21.6-B.

AMENDMENT

Rule 21.6 inserted by the Act of Adjournal (Criminal Procedure Rules Amendment No.3) (Vulnerable Witnesses (Scotland) Act 2004) 2005 (SSI 2005/188), r.2, subject to the conditions in r.2(2) (effective April 1, 2005).

GENERAL NOTE

Ch.21 applies to both solemn and summary proceedings.

Rules 21.1 and 21.2

Section 258 of the 1995 Act provides that where either the Crown or the defence considers that any fact is unlikely to be disputed by any other party, he can prepare *and* sign a statement specifying the facts concerned or referring to the facts as set out in the document annexed to the statement, and serve a copy of the statement and the document (where appropriate) on every party not less than 14 days before the trial diet (see subss.(1) and (2)). The facts shall be deemed to have been conclusively proved unless a notice challenging any of the facts is served by any other party not more than seven days after the date of service of the statement and the document (see subs.(3)). It is irrelevant that the evidence is not capable of being led at the trial because the relevant witness or production is not specified in the lists annexed to the indictment.

Rule 21.3

Section 259 of the 1995 Act allows for hearsay evidence to be admitted in evidence in certain circumstances (see subss.(1) and (2)). Notice of intention to apply to the court to have hearsay evidence admitted should be given in writing before the trial diet and should specify the fact(s) and the witnesses and productions to be adduced in connection with such evidence (subs.(5)). Section 262(1) of the 1995 Act adheres to the common law rule and excludes a statement which is a precognition other than a precognition on oath. The most recent and authoritative discussion of the criteria by which the court must determine whether the statement if of the nature of a precognition is provided in *HM Advocate v McSween*, 2007 S.L.T. 645

It has been held that the court will not determine in advance of a trial whether use by the Crown of a statement by a deceased witness (against whom there was possibly some incriminating evidence) would violate the accused's right to a fair trial under Art.6(1) of the European Convention on Human Rights and that such a devolution issue had to be determined as and when the Crown sought to make use of the secondary evidence at the trial (*McKenna v HM Advocate*, 2000 J.C. 291).

Rule 21.4

Section 260(1) of the 1995 Act declares that a witness's prior statement shall be admissible if it is contained in a written document and if three conditions which are set out in subs.(2) are met—though precognitions on oath and evidence in earlier criminal or civil proceedings are excepted from these requirements and only require to be authenticated—and if it is sufficiently authenticated (see subs.(4)). The authentication should be by way of a certificate which is endorsed on or attached to the first page of the statement. (*Cf. Jamieson v HM Advocate (No.2)*, 1995 S.L.T. 666 which allowed at common law for a witness's adopting his earlier statement to the police even though he could not recall the details of it so long as he maintained that it was the truth.) Lord Osborne has questioned the precise purpose of ss.260 and 262 in the light of the ruling in *Jamieson (No.2)* (see *Hemming v HM Advocate*, 1997 S.C.C.R. 257 at 267). Section 262(1) provides that "statement" does not include a statement made in a precognition other than a precognition on oath.

CHAPTER 22

EVIDENCE OF VULNERABLE WITNESSES

Child witness notice

22.1. A notice under section 271A(2) of the Act of 1995 (child witness notice) shall be in Form 22.1 and shall be lodged with the clerk of court.

AMENDMENT

Chapter 22 substituted by Act of Adjournal (Criminal Procedure Rules Amendment No.3) (Vulnerable Witnesses (Scotland) Act 2004) 2005 (SSI 2005/188), r.2, subject to the conditions in r.2(2) (effective April 1, 2005).

Vulnerable witness application

22.1A. An application under section 271C(2) of the Act of 1995 (vulnerable witness application) shall be in Form 22.1A and shall be lodged with the clerk of court.

AMENDMENT

Rule 22.1A inserted by Act of Adjournal (Criminal Procedure Rules Amendment) (Vulnerable Witnesses (Scotland) Act 2004) 2006 (SSI 2006/76), para.2(4) (effective April 1, 2006). See para.2(2) and (3) for transitional provisions.

Procedure on lodging child witness notice or vulnerable witness application

22.2.—(1) On receipt of a notice under rule 22.1 (child witness notice) or application under rule 22.1A (vulnerable witness application) the clerk of court shall—

(a) endorse on the notice or application, as the case may be, the time and date on which it was received; and

(b) place the notice or application, as the case may be, before a judge in chambers.

(2) The party that lodges the child witness notice or vulnerable witness application, as the case may be, shall lodge a certificate of intimation with the clerk of court—

(a) within 7 days after lodging the notice or application, as the case may be; or

(b) at least 2 days before any first diet or preliminary hearing, whichever is the earlier.

AMENDMENT

Rule 22.2 substituted by Act of Adjournal (Criminal Procedure Rules Amendment) (Vulnerable Witnesses (Scotland) Act 2004) 2006 (SSI 2006/76), para.2(5) (effective April 1, 2006). See para.2(2) and (3) for transitional provisions.

Intimation of an order under section 271A

22.3.—(1) An order—
- (a) under section 271A(5)(a) of the Act of 1995 authorising the use of a special measure;
- (b) under section 271A(5)(b) of that Act authorising the giving of evidence without the benefit of any special measures;
- (c) appointing a child witness notice to be disposed of—
  - (i) under section 271A(5A)(a) of that Act, at a preliminary hearing; or
  - (ii) under section 271A(5A)(b) of that Act, at a first diet; or
- (d) under section 271A(5A)(c) or (7)(b)(ii) of that Act, appointing a diet to be held before the trial diet; or
- (e) under section 271A(9) of that Act (order in relation to special measures after hearing),

may be signed by the clerk of court.

(2) An order mentioned in paragraph (1) shall be intimated by the clerk of court to all parties, unless the party was present at the hearing at which the order was made, and in the case of an order under paragraph (1)(c) or (d), to the governor of any institution in which the accused is detained.

Intimation of an order under section 271C

22.3A.—(1) An order—
- (a) under section 271C(5)(a) of the Act of 1995 authorising the use of a special measure;
- (b) appointing a vulnerable witness application to be disposed of—
  - (i) under section 271C(5A)(a) of that Act, at a preliminary hearing; or
  - (ii) under section 271C(5A)(b) of that Act at a first diet;
- (c) under section 271C(5A)(c) of that Act, appointing a diet to be held before the trial diet; or
- (d) under section 271C(7) of that Act (order in relation to special measure after hearing),

may be signed by the clerk of court.

(2) An order mentioned in paragraph (1) shall be intimated by the clerk of court to all parties, unless the party was present at the hearing at which the order was made and, in the case of an order under paragraph (1)(b) or (c), to the governor of any institution in which the accused is detained.

AMENDMENT

Rule 22.3A inserted by Act of Adjournal (Criminal Procedure Rules Amendment) (Vulnerable Witnesses (Scotland) Act 2004) 2006 (SSI 2006/76), para.2(6) (effective April 1, 2006). See para.2(2) and (3) for transitional provisions.

Review of arrangements for vulnerable witnesses

22.4.—(1) An application under section 271D(1)(a) of the Act of 1995 (review of arrangements for vulnerable witnesses) may be made—

(a) orally; or

(b) in writing by minute in Form 22.4.

(2) A minute under paragraph (1)(b) shall be lodged with the clerk of the court and served on every other party by the minuter.

AMENDMENT

To be read with the transitional provisions contained in the Act of Adjournal (Criminal Procedure Rules Amendment) (Vulnerable Witnesses (Scotland) Act 2004) 2006 (SSI 2006/76), para.2(2) and (3) (effective April 1, 2006).

Procedure for review

22.5. On receipt of a minute under rule 22.4(1)(b) (minute for review of arrangements for vulnerable witnesses) or, on a review on the court's own motion, the court shall make an order endorsed on the minute or recorded in the minute of proceedings—

(a) fixing a diet for a hearing of the application or to hear parties; and

(b) for service of the minute or order with the date of the diet on all parties and to the governor of any institution in which the accused is detained.

AMENDMENT

To be read with the transitional provisions contained in the Act of Adjournal (Criminal Procedure Rules Amendment) (Vulnerable Witnesses (Scotland) Act 2004) 2006 (SSI 2006/76), para.2(2) and (3) (effective April 1, 2006).

Intimation of the order

22.6. Where an order under section 271D(2) of the Act of 1995 (order after review of arrangements for vulnerable witnesses) is made at a hearing fixed under rule 22.5 (procedure for review) it shall be intimated by the clerk of court to all parties unless the party was present at the hearing at which the order was made.

AMENDMENT

To be read with the transitional provisions contained in the Act of Adjournal (Criminal Procedure Rules Amendment) (Vulnerable Witnesses (Scotland) Act 2004) 2006 (SSI 2006/76), para.2(2) and (3) (effective April 1, 2006).

Notice of prohibition of personal conduct of defence

22.7. In proceedings to which section 288E of the Act of 1995 (prohibition of personal conduct of defence in certain cases involving child witnesses under the age of 12) applies, a notice in Form 22.7 shall be served on the accused by the prosecutor with any child witness notice, unless a notice in Form 8.2-C has already been served.

Application for prohibition of personal conduct of defence

22.8.—(1) An application under section 288F(2)(a) of the Act of 1995 (prohibition of personal conduct of defence) shall be made by minute in Form 22.8-A.

(2) The minute shall be lodged with the clerk of court and served on all parties by the minuter.

(3) On receipt of a minute under paragraph (1), or on the court's own motion, the court shall make an order endorsed on the minute or recorded in the minute of proceedings—

(a) fixing a diet for a hearing of the application or to hear parties; and

(b) for service of the minute or order with the date on all parties and to the governor of any institution in which the accused is detained.

(4) Where a party is not represented or personally present at a hearing under paragraph (3) when an order is made under section 288F of the Act of 1995 (order prohibiting personal conduct of defence) the clerk of court shall intimate the order to that party.

(5) On the making of an order under section 288F of the Act of 1995 in the absence of the accused, the prosecutor shall forthwith serve on the accused a notice in Form 22.8-B.

AMENDMENT

To be read with the transitional provisions contained in the Act of Adjournal (Criminal Procedure Rules Amendment) (Vulnerable Witnesses (Scotland) Act 2004) 2006 (SSI 2006/76), para.2(2) and (3) (effective April 1, 2006).

Transfer of cases

22.9. Where the sheriff makes an order under section 271J(4) or 271K(3) of the Act of 1995 (transfer of proceedings where evidence is by live television link or with the use of screens) transferring the proceedings to another sheriff court (the "receiving court") the sheriff clerk shall forthwith transmit the record copy of the indictment, the minute of proceedings, any productions and any relevant documents to the clerk of the receiving court.

AMENDMENT

To be read with the transitional provisions contained in the Act of Adjournal (Criminal Procedure Rules Amendment) (Vulnerable Witnesses (Scotland) Act 2004) 2006 (SSI 2006/76), para.2(2) and (3) (effective April 1, 2006).

Evidence in chief in form of prior statement

22.10. Where a witness is to give evidence in chief in the form of a prior statement the witness shall be called, and—

(a) the oath or affirmation administered under rule 14.5 (form of oath or affirmation); or

(b) be admonished to tell the truth,

before the evidence in the form of a prior statement is given.

AMENDMENT

To be read with the transitional provisions contained in the Act of Adjournal (Criminal Procedure Rules Amendment) (Vulnerable Witnesses (Scotland) Act 2004) 2006 (SSI 2006/76), para.2(2) and (3) (effective April 1, 2006).

Appointment of commissioner

22.11.—(1) On making an order under section 271A(5) or (9) of the Act of 1995 (order in relation to special measures) authorising the taking of evidence by a commissioner in accordance with section 271I of that Act, the High Court or the sheriff, as the case may be, shall appoint—

(a) a commissioner to take the evidence of the vulnerable witness; and

(b) a clerk to assist the commissioner in the carrying out of his duties,

and shall dispense with interrogatories.

(2) On the appointment of a commissioner under paragraph (1), the Clerk of Justiciary or sheriff clerk, as the case may be, shall send the order to the commissioner or his clerk with such other relative documents as the court may direct.

(3) On sending the order to the commissioner or his clerk under paragraph (2), the Clerk of Justiciary or sheriff clerk, as the case may be, shall note on the record copy of the indictment or in the minute of proceedings—

(a) the order and the documents sent;

(b) the names of the persons to whom the order and documents were sent;

(c) the date on which the order and documents were sent.

AMENDMENT

Rule 22.11 inserted by Act of Adjournal (Criminal Procedure Rules Amendment No. 6) (Vulnerable Witnesses (Scotland) Act 2004) (Evidence on Commission) 2005 (SSI 2005/574), r.2(3) (effective November 30, 2005).

To be read with the transitional provisions contained in the Act of Adjournal (Criminal Procedure Rules Amendment) (Vulnerable Witnesses (Scotland) Act 2004) 2006 (SSI 2006/76), para.2(2) and (3) (effective April 1, 2006).

The commission

22.12.—(1) The commissioner shall, on receiving the order and documents mentioned in rule 22.11(2) (appointment of commissioner), determine the place and date of the diet for the taking the evidence of the witness to whom the order of the court relates, and shall give reasonable notice of those matters to all parties.

(2) The commissioner may vary or revoke his determination or adjourn the taking of the evidence of the witness to such other place, at such other date and time, as he may determine.

(3) If, in the course of the examination of a witness under this rule, any question arises as to the admissibility of any evidence, the commissioner, unless a judge or sheriff of the relevant court, shall not determine any such question but shall allow the evidence subject to all questions of competency and relevancy.

Amendment

Rule 22.12 inserted by Act of Adjournal (Criminal Procedure Rules Amendment No. 6) (Vulnerable Witnesses (Scotland) Act 2004) (Evidence on Commission) 2005 (SSI 2005/574), r.2(3) (effective November 30, 2005).

To be read with the transitional provisions contained in the Act of Adjournal (Criminal Procedure Rules Amendment) (Vulnerable Witnesses (Scotland) Act 2004) 2006 (SSI 2006/76), para.2(2) and (3) (effective April 1, 2006).

Video recording of commission

22.13.—(1) On the carrying out of his commission in accordance with the terms of the order appointing him, or otherwise on concluding his commission, the commissioner or his clerk shall cause the tape or disc of the video recording of the commission to be sealed in an envelope or other similar container, which the commissioner shall sign and date, and on which the following information shall be endorsed—

    (a) the name of the accused;

    (b) the prosecution and court reference numbers; and

    (c) the time of commencement and of termination of the tape or disc;

which sealed envelope shall be returned, with the relative documents, to the Clerk of Justiciary or sheriff clerk, as the case may be.

(2) On the video recording and any documents being returned to him, the Clerk of Justiciary or sheriff clerk, as the case may be, shall—

    (a) note—

      (i) the documents returned;

      (ii) by whom the documents were returned; and

      (iii) the date on which the documents were returned;

      on the record copy of the indictment or in the minute of proceedings; and

    (b) intimate what he has noted to all parties.

(3) The seal on the envelope or container shall be broken only on the authority of the Clerk of Justiciary or sheriff clerk, as the case may be.

(4) The Clerk of Justiciary or sheriff clerk, as the case may be, shall only permit such access to the tape or disc for such period as may be required for the purposes of the authorisation and on expiry of that period, shall again cause the tape or disc of the video recording of the commission to be sealed, which the Clerk of Justiciary or sheriff clerk, as the case may be, shall sign, and on which the following information shall be endorsed—

    (a) the name of the accused;

(b) the date of the commission;

(c) the name of the commissioner;

(d) the prosecution and court reference numbers;

(e) the time of commencement and termination of the tape or disc;

(f) the time and date of sealing of the tape or disc.

AMENDMENT

Rule 22.13 inserted by Act of Adjournal (Criminal Procedure Rules Amendment No. 6) (Vulnerable Witnesses (Scotland) Act 2004) (Evidence on Commission) 2005 (SSI 2005/574), r.2(3) (effective November 30, 2005).

To be read with the transitional provisions contained in the Act of Adjournal (Criminal Procedure Rules Amendment) (Vulnerable Witnesses (Scotland) Act 2004) 2006 (SSI 2006/76), para.2(2) and (3) (effective April 1, 2006).

Custody of video recording and documents

22.14.—(1) The Clerk of Justiciary or sheriff clerk, as the case may be, shall keep the tape or disc of the video recording and documents referred to in rule 22.13(1) (video record of evidence on commission) in his custody.

(2) Where the tape or disc of the video recording of the evidence of a witness is in the custody of the Clerk of Justiciary or sheriff clerk, as the case may be, under this rule and where intimation has been given to that effect under rule 22.13(2)(b) to all the parties, the name and address of the witness and the tape or disc of the video recording of his or her evidence shall be treated as being within the knowledge of those parties; and no party shall be required, notwithstanding any enactment to the contrary, to include the tape or disc of the video recording of that witness's evidence in any list of productions.

AMENDMENT

Rule 22.14 inserted by Act of Adjournal (Criminal Procedure Rules Amendment No. 6) (Vulnerable Witnesses (Scotland) Act 2004) (Evidence on Commission) 2005 (SSI 2005/574), r.2(3) (effective November 30, 2005).

To be read with the transitional provisions contained in the Act of Adjournal (Criminal Procedure Rules Amendment) (Vulnerable Witnesses (Scotland) Act 2004) 2006 (SSI 2006/76), para.2(2) and (3) (effective April 1, 2006).

Applications for leave for accused to be present at commission

22.15.—(1) An application in writing under section 271I(3) of the Act of 1995 (application for leave for accused to be present in the room during commission) shall be in Form 22.15.

(2) The application shall be lodged with the clerk of court and served on every other party by the applicant.

(3) On receipt of an application under paragraph (2), the clerk of court shall place the application before a judge in chambers.

(4) On considering the application in the absence of parties, or of any person acting on their behalf, the judge shall—

(a) grant leave as requested; or

(b) fix a diet for a hearing of the application; and

(c) make an order for service of the application with the date on all parties and to the governor of any institution in which the accused is detained.

(5) Where an order under section 271I(3) of the Act of 1995 (leave for accused to be present in the room) is granted, it shall be intimated by the clerk of court to all parties unless the party was present at the hearing at which the order was made.

AMENDMENT

Rule 22.15 inserted by Act of Adjournal (Criminal Procedure Rules Amendment No. 6) (Vulnerable Witnesses (Scotland) Act 2004) (Evidence on Commission) 2005 (SSI 2005/574), r.2(3) (effective November 30, 2005).

The expression "vulnerable witness" is defined in s.271 of the 1995 Act as either (1) a witness who is under the age of 16 at the date of the commencement of the proceedings (i.e. when the indictment is served: see s.271(3))—and in such a case he is referred to as a child witness—or (2) a witness in respect of whose evidence there is a significant risk that his evidence will be diminished in quality by reason of either mental disorder within the meaning of s.328 of the Mental Health (Care and Treatment (Scotland) Act 2003 (asp 13) or "fear or distress in connection with giving evidence at the trial".

As a result of the bringing into force of the Act of Adjournal (Criminal Procedure Amendment No.6) (Vulnerable Witnesses (Scotland) Act 2004) (Evidence on Commission) 2005 on November 30, 2005, this chapter is enlarged with rr.22.11–22.15 being inserted to deal with the special measure for taking the evidence of child witnesses on commission. For the assistance of practitioners the High Court has also issued a Practice Note (No.3 of 2005) (effective from November 30, 2005) in which details of what the court will expect the child witness notice (see r.22.1) to contain are identified. The Practice Note should be read in conjunction with this chapter.

Vulnerable witnesses

As para.2 of the Practice Note No.3 of 2005 stated, the 2004 Act only applied to child witnesses in solemn proceedings commenced after April 1, 2005, but it was intended that the 2004 Act would be implemented in due course to apply to vulnerable witnesses in all criminal proceedings. The next stage of the reform programme was reached with the High Court's enactment of the Act of Adjournal (Criminal Procedure Rules Amendment) (Vulnerable Witnesses (Scotland) Act 2004) 2006 (SSI 2006/76) which came into force on April 1, 2006 (para.1(1)). The Act of Adjournal amends the Criminal Procedure Rules 1996 to apply certain of the rules of Ch.22 to vulnerable witnesses as defined by s.271(1)(b) of the 1995 Act (i.e. witnesses who are not children). The rules which now apply to vulnerable witnesses are: rr.22.4–22.6 and rr.22.8–22.14 (para.2(3)) and (with effect from March 26, 2007) r.22.15 (as a result of further amendment by Act of Adjournal (Criminal Procedure Rules Amendment) (Animal Health and Welfare etc.) 2007 (SSI 2007/238), para.2(2)) . Thus, for example, it is now permissible for the evidence of a vulnerable witness who is not a child witness to be taken on commission. This is a significant change in Scottish procedure which has hitherto proceeded on the understandable basis that the jury which is to try the charges should see and hear the witness in court as the witness gives his evidence. The extent to which this new procedure will be utilised must at this stage be unknown, but if it is permitted on a regular basis the disruption and expense which will be occasioned will be considerable. Much may, therefore, turn on the strictness with which the court considers applications for taking evidence on commission.

As in the reform in respect of child witnesses introduced in 2005, the 2006 Act of Adjournal does not apply to summary proceedings. It applies only to solemn proceedings which *commenced* after April 1, 2006 where there is a vulnerable witness. Paragraph 2(2) makes plain that proceedings are commenced for these purposes "when a report of a case has been received by the procurator fiscal". Thus, the new provisions for vulnerable witnesses will apply not only to crimes committed after April 1, 2006 but also to crimes committed before but not reported until after that date.

In order to be applicable to vulnerable witnesses generally, two new rules are inserted into Ch.22. Rule 22.1A provides for the request for a vulnerable witness order to be made by means of a vulnerable witness application in terms of Form 22.1A which is to be lodged with the appropriate clerk; and r.22.3A provides for intimation of an order under s.271C. Rule 22.2 is repealed and re-enacted so as to include reference to vulnerable witness applications.

With effect from April 1, 2007 rr.22.1-22.15 are now applied to summary proceedings in the sheriff court where a child witness is to give evidence (see Act of Adjournal (Criminal Procedure Rules Amendment No.2) (Vulnerable Witnesses (Scotland) Act 2004) 2007 (SSI 2007/237), para.2(2)). The proceedings must commence after April 1, 2007 and proceedings are taken to have commenced when a report of the case has been received by the procurator fiscal. In due course vulnerable witnesses within the meaning of s.271(1)(b) (non-child witnesses) will also be brought within the scope of ch.22 for the purposes of summary proceedings."

Summary proceedings

With effect from April 1, 2007, rr.22.1-22.15 are now applied to summary proceedings in the sheriff court where a child witness is to give evidence (see Act of Adjournal (Criminal Procedure

Rules Amendment No.2) (Vulnerable Witnesses (Scotland) Act 2004) 2007 (SSI 2007/237), para.2(2)). The proceedings must commence after April 1, 2007 and proceedings are taken to have commenced when a report of the case has been received by the procurator fiscal. In due course vulnerable witnesses within the meaning of s.271(1)(b) (non-child witnesses) will also be brought within the scope of ch.22 for the purposes of summary proceedings.

CHAPTER 23

LETTERS OF REQUEST

Applications for letters of request

23.1.—(1) An application to the court by the prosecutor or the defence under section 272(1)(a) of the Act of 1995 (evidence by letter of request) for the issue of a letter of request shall be made by petition—

(a) where the accused has appeared on petition under Part IV of the Act of 1995 (petition procedure) but an indictment has not been served on him, in Form 23.1-A presented to the High Court; or

(b) where an indictment or a complaint has been served on the accused, in Form 23.1-B presented to the appropriate court.

(2) A petition referred to in paragraph (1) shall—

(a) where it relates to proceedings in the High Court or to proceedings in respect of which the court where the trial is to take place is not yet known, be lodged with the Clerk of Justiciary, or

(b) where it relates to proceedings in the sheriff court, be lodged with the sheriff clerk,

and shall be accompanied by a proposed letter of request in Form 23.1-C.

(3) [...]

(4) Such an application made to the High Court may be disposed of by a single judge of that court.

(5) The High Court or the sheriff, as the case may be, shall—

(a) order intimation on the other party or parties to the proceedings;

(b) subject to paragraph (6), allow such time for lodging answers as appears appropriate; and

(c) fix a diet for hearing the petition and answers (if any).

(6) The High Court or the sheriff, as the case may be, may dispense with answers to the petition on cause shown.

AMENDMENT

Rule 23.1(3) repealed by the Act of Adjournal (Criminal Procedure Rules Amendment) (Miscellaneous) 2004 (SSI 2004/195), r.2 (effective April 26, 2004).

Powers of court in applications

23.2.—(1) The High Court or the sheriff, as the case may be, may, after considering the petition for the issue of a letter of request and any answers to it, grant the petition with or without modification or refuse it.

(2) On granting the petition, the High Court or the sheriff, as the case may be, shall—

(a) in relation to an application under section 272(1)(a) of the Act of 1995 (evidence by letter of request), allow interrogatories to be adjusted summarily;

(b) pronounce an order approving the terms—

(i) of the letter of request to be sent;

(ii) of any interrogatories and cross-interrogatories to be sent; and

(c) if English is not an official language of the body to which the letter of request is addressed, specify a period within which a translation of each of the letter, any interrogatories and cross-interrogatories, and any productions, are to be lodged.

Expenses

23.3.—(1) The solicitor for the petitioner or, if he is unrepresented, the petitioner shall be liable for the expenses of the petition for the issue of a letter of request.

(2) The High Court or the sheriff, as the case may be, may order the solicitor for the petitioner, or the petitioner, to consign into court such sum in respect of those expenses as may be specified, and on or before such date as may be specified, in the order.

(3) In the event of the sum so specified not being consigned into court on or before the date so specified, the petition shall be treated as having been abandoned.

Transmission of letters of request

23.4.—(1) On—

(a) the High Court or the sheriff, as the case may be, pronouncing an order under rule 23.2(2), or

(b) in a case where a translation requires to be lodged, on the lodging of the translation,

the Clerk of Justiciary or the sheriff clerk, as the case may be, shall send the letter of request and any documents to the Secretary of State for Foreign and Commonwealth Affairs for onward transmission to the body to which the letter of request is addressed.

(2) On sending the letter of request and any documents to the Secretary of State, the Clerk of Justiciary or sheriff clerk, as the case may be, shall note, on the petition, record copy of the indictment or in the minute of proceedings—

(a) the documents sent;

(b) to whom the documents were sent; and

(c) the date on which the documents were sent.

(3) On the relative documents being returned to him, the Clerk of Justiciary or sheriff clerk, as the case may be, shall—

(a) note—

(i) the documents returned,

(ii) by whom they were returned, and

(iii) the date on which they were returned,

on the application, the record copy of the indictment or in the minute of proceedings; and

(b) intimate what he has noted to all parties concerned.

Custody of documents

23.5.—(1) The Clerk of Justiciary or sheriff clerk, as the case may be, shall, subject to paragraph (2), keep the documents referred to in rule 23.4(3) in his custody.

(2) Where the petition for the issue of a letter of request was made to the High Court on the ground that the court in which the trial was to take place was not then known, the prosecutor shall, as soon as that court is known, inform the Clerk of Justiciary of that fact; and if that court is the sheriff court, the Clerk of Justiciary shall, as soon as is practicable, send to the sheriff clerk of that sheriff court the

record of the evidence of the witness obtained by a letter of request under section 272(1)(a) of the Act of 1995.

(3) Where the record of the evidence of a witness is in the custody of the Clerk of Justiciary or a sheriff clerk under this rule and where intimation has been given to that effect under rule 23.4(3) to all the parties concerned in the proceedings, the name and address of that witness and the record of his evidence shall be treated as being within the knowledge of those parties; and no party shall be required, notwithstanding any enactment to the contrary—

(a) to include the name of that witness in any list of witnesses; or

(b) to include the record of his evidence in any list of productions.

Prohibition of reference to evidence without leave

23.6.—(1) No reference shall be made either directly or indirectly in any proceedings to the evidence, or any part of the evidence, of a witness whose evidence has been taken by virtue of a letter of request under section 272(1)(a) of the Act of 1995 unless the party seeking to make such reference has made a motion to the court to that effect and that motion has been granted.

(2) The terms of any motion made under paragraph (1) and the grant or refusal of that motion by the court shall be noted by the clerk of court in the record or minute of proceedings.

(3) On any such motion in solemn proceedings being granted—

(a) the judge may direct copies of the evidence, to which he has granted leave for reference to be made, to be provided to the jury by the party making the motion; and

(b) the clerk of court shall read the record of that evidence to the jury and shall then record that he has done so in the record of proceedings.

GENERAL NOTE

Section 272 of the 1995 Act allows for the High Court or the sheriff court (but not the district court): (1) to issue a letter of request to a foreign court, *i.e.* outside the United Kingdom, Channel Islands or Isle of Man, for the taking of evidence from a witness resident there; and (2) to appoint a Commissioner to examine at any place within the United Kingdom, Channel Islands or Isle of Man a witness who cannot attend the trial diet because of illness or infirmity or who is not ordinarily resident here and is unlikely to be present here at the trial diet. No further elaboration is given in the 1995 Act of illness or infirmity but it is submitted that a psychiatric condition which would not render the witness's evidence valueless (*e.g.* agoraphobia) as well as physical illness is comprehended. A substantial degree of infirmity by reason of old age is sufficient (see *Lang, Petitioner*, 1991 S.L.T. 931). The evidence can be taken with or without interrogatories.

Chapter 23 deals with applications for letters of request to the foreign state to examine witnesses and to receive productions; Chap. 24 provides for applications to appoint commissioners to go abroad to examine witnesses and to receive productions.

In either case the court can *only* grant the application if it is satisfied on two matters: (i) that the evidence (which the Crown or defence must narrate as being what the witness is able to give) is "necessary for the proper adjudication of the trial"; and (ii) that there would be no unfairness to the other party in the taking of evidence in that way. The evidence need not be given on oath in order to be competent (s.272(4)). The taking of evidence by way of contemporaneous live television link in the course of the trial proceedings can also be sought by way of application for a letter of request (see s.273 of the 1995 Act).

Rule 23.1

Rule 23.1(1) and (2). The application is by way of petition which must contain averments as to the evidence which the petitioner maintains the witness will be able to give so that the court can be satisfied that the evidence is necessary for the proper adjudication of the trial and that there will be no unfairness (s.272(3)). It can be made in solemn or summary proceedings but must be made before the jury takes the oath or the first witness is sworn in summary proceedings. Except where in applications for the appointment of a commissioner, the court is satisfied by the petitioner that the circumstances justifying the application had not arisen or would not have merited such an application before the jury took the oath or the first witness was sworn (s.272(7)). The use of the word "or" in s.272(7) appears to be disjunctive. There may be cases where evidence which was known before the trial commenced takes on a different complexion once other witnesses have been examined.

Rule 23.1(3). Where in solemn proceedings (but not in summary proceedings) it is sought to take the evidence of a witness by contemporaneous live television link in the course of a trial, the Crown or the accused can apply for the issue of a letter of request which can only be granted if the court is satisfied that the witness's evidence (which should be narrated in the petition) is necessary for the proper adjudication of the trial and the granting of the application is in the interests of justice and, where the applicant is the Crown, there is no unfairness to the accused (s.273(3)).

Rule 23.1(5). The court must order intimation and if the other party does not receive notice the court is not entitled to grant the application. The court could never be satisfied that there would be no unfairness to the accused if he were not heard on the merits of the petition. Accordingly the petitioner should ensure that proof of intimation is available to the court. The hearing should take place in chambers but if a petition is unopposed the hearing can be dispensed with (s.272(2)).

Rule 23.2

The decision of the sheriff or a single judge of the High Court (see r.23.1(4)) is not susceptible of appeal and a petition to the *nobile officium* to review his decision is incompetent (see *Lang, Petitioner*, 1991 S.L.T. 931). However, the issue of fairness can still arise at the trial: see r.23.6 below.

Rule 23.5

Rule 23.5(3). Where the evidence of a witness or productions received at the examination are returned to the appropriate court, they need not be intimated on a list to the other side so long as intimation is given by the clerk of the court that the evidence or productions have been received. Rule 23.4(3) states that the clerk of the court "shall intimate" to the other parties the "documents returned" (though productions are not mentioned) and by whom and when they were returned. However, if the clerk by oversight fails to intimate when or by whom the documents were received by him, it is likely that the court would hold that there had been substantial compliance with the overall purpose of r.23.4(3) when taken together with r.23.5(3). In any event the court must first grant leave in the course of the trial for reference to be made to any part of the evidence or any production (see r.23.6 below).

Rule 23.6

The issue of fairness can be raised at the trial. The court must be requested by way of a motion to allow any part of the evidence or any production to be referred to. If no intimation is given under r.23.4(3) above to the other party then the court could not properly allow reference to be made to the evidence or productions. Equally the circumstances or the form in which the evidence was taken or the absence of cross-examination could arguably be prejudicial to the accused (or the Crown) and that would entitle the presiding judge to refuse to allow reference to the evidence. The judge's decision would however be capable of review on appeal on the ground of a miscarriage of justice in the event of conviction.

CHAPTER 23A

TELEVISION LINK EVIDENCE FROM ABROAD

Application for television link evidence from abroad

23A.1—(1) An application to the court by the prosecutor or the defence under section 273(2) of the Act of 1995 shall be by petition in Form 23A.1-A and shall be accompanied by a letter of request in Form 23A.1-B.

(2) Such an application made to the High Court may be disposed of by a single judge of that court.

(3) The High Court or the sheriff, as the case may be, shall—

(a) order intimation on the other party or parties to the proceedings;

(b) subject to paragraph (4), allow such time for lodging answers as appears appropriate; and

(c) fix a diet for hearing the petition and answers (if any).

(4) The High Court or the sheriff as the case may be, may dispense with answers to the petition on cause shown.

Powers of the court in applications

23A.2—(1) The High Court or the sheriff, as the case may be, may, after considering the petition and any answers to it, grant the petition with or without modification or refuse it.

(2) On granting the petition, the High Court or the sheriff, as the case may be, shall—

(a) pronounce an order approving the terms of the letter of request to be sent; and

(b) if English is not an official language of the body to which the letter is addressed, specify a period within which a translation of the letter is to be lodged.

Expenses

23A.3—(1) The solicitor for the petitioner or, if he is unrepresented, the petitioner shall be liable for the expenses of the petition for the issue of a letter of request.

(2) The High Court or the sheriff, as the case may be, may order the solicitor for the petitioner, or the petitioner, to consign into court such sum in respect of those expenses as may be specified, and on or before such date as may be specified, in the order.

(3) In the event of the sum so specified not being consigned into court on or before the date so specified, the petition shall be treated as having been abandoned.

Transmission of letters of request

23A.4—(1) On—

(a) the High Court or the sheriff, as the case may be, pronouncing an order under rule 23A.2(2), or

(b) in a case where a translation requires to be lodged, on the lodging of the translation,

the Clerk of Justiciary or the sheriff clerk, as the case may be, shall send the letter of request to the Lord Advocate for transmission to the body to which the letter of request is addressed.

(2) The Clerk of Justiciary or sheriff clerk, as the case may be, shall note, on the petition, record copy of the indictment or in the minute of proceedings, the date on which the letter of request was sent to the Lord Advocate for transmission and shall intimate that date to all parties concerned.

Procedural diet

23A.5—(1) On receipt of confirmation that the court, tribunal or other authority to which a letter of request was transmitted will provide assistance in facilitating the giving of evidence through a live television link, the Clerk of Justiciary or sheriff clerk, as the case may be, shall fix a procedural diet in accordance with paragraph (2) and shall intimate that diet to all parties concerned.

(2) The procedural diet shall be fixed for a date which is before the date on which the evidence is to be given by television link.

(3) The accused shall not require to be present at the procedural diet.

(4) At the procedural diet, the judge or sheriff, as the case may be, shall make inquiries as to whether or not arrangements are in place to facilitate the giving of evidence through a live television link.

AMENDMENT
Chapter 23A inserted by the Act of Adjournal (Criminal Procedure Rules Amendment) (Miscellaneous) 2004 (SSI 2004/195), r.2 (effective April 26, 2004).

CHAPTER 24

EVIDENCE ON COMMISSION

Applications to take evidence on commission

24.1.—(1) An application to the court by the prosecutor or the defence under section 272(1)(b) of the Act of 1995 for the appointment of a commissioner to examine a witness to whom that section applies, shall be made by petition—

(a) where the accused has appeared on petition under Part IV of the Act of 1995 (petition procedure) but an indictment has not been served on him, in Form 24.1-A presented to the High Court; or

(b) where an indictment or a complaint has been served on the accused, in Form 24.1-B presented to the appropriate court.

(2) A petition referred to in paragraph (1) shall—

(a) where it relates to proceedings in the High Court or to proceedings in respect of which the court where the trial is to take place is not yet known, be lodged with the Clerk of Justiciary; or

(b) where it relates to proceedings in the sheriff court, be lodged with the sheriff clerk.

(3) A petition in relation to section 272(1)(b)(i) of the Act of 1995 (examination of witness ill or infirm) shall be accompanied by an appropriate medical certificate duly certified on soul and conscience by a qualified medical practitioner.

(4) Such an application made to the High Court may be disposed of by a single judge of that court.

(5) The High Court or the sheriff, as the case may be, shall—

(a) order intimation on the other party or parties to the proceedings;

(b) subject to paragraph (6), allow such time for lodging answers as appears appropriate; and

(c) fix a diet for hearing the petition and answers (if any).

(6) The High Court or the sheriff, as the case may be, may dispense with answers to the petition on cause shown.

Appointment of commissioner

24.2.—(1) The High Court or the sheriff, as the case may be, may, after considering the petition for the taking of evidence on commission and any answers to it, grant the petition with or without modifications or refuse it.

(2) On making an order granting the petition, the High Court or the sheriff, as the case may be, shall appoint—

(a) a commissioner to examine the witness to whom the order applies, and

(b) a clerk to assist the commissioner in the carrying out of his duties,

and shall dispense with interrogatories.

(3) On the making of an order under paragraph (1), the Clerk of Justiciary or sheriff clerk, as the case may be, shall send the order to the commissioner or his clerk with the other relative documents.

(4) On sending the order to the commissioner or his clerk under paragraph (2), the Clerk of Justiciary or sheriff clerk, as the case may be, shall note on the petition, record copy of the indictment or in the minute of proceedings—

(a) the order and documents sent;

(b) to whom they were sent; and

(c) the date on which they were sent.

Expenses

24.3.—(1) The solicitor for the petitioner or, if he is unrepresented, the petitioner shall be liable for the expenses of the petition for the appointment of a commissioner to take the evidence of a witness on commission.

(2) The High Court or the sheriff, as the case may be, may order the solicitor for the petitioner, or the petitioner, to consign into court such sum in respect of those expenses as may be specified, and on or before such date as may be specified, in the order.

(3) In the event of the sum so specified not being consigned into court on or before the date so specified, the petition shall be treated as having been abandoned.

The commission

24.4.—(1) The commissioner shall, on receiving the order and documents mentioned in rule 24.2 (appointment of commissioner), determine the place and the date of the diet for the examination of the witness to whom the order of the court relates, and shall give reasonable notice of those matters to all the parties concerned.

(2) The commissioner may vary or revoke his determination or adjourn the examination of any witness to such other place, at such other date and time, as he may determine.

(3) If, in the course of the examination of a witness under this rule, any question arises as to the admissibility of any evidence, the commissioner shall not determine any such question but shall allow the evidence subject to all questions of competency and relevancy.

Commissioner's report

24.5.—(1) On the carrying out of his commission in accordance with the terms of the order appointing him, or otherwise on concluding his commission, the commissioner shall complete a written report of his commission, and he or his clerk shall return the report and relative documents to the Clerk of Justiciary or sheriff clerk, as the case may be.

(2) On the report and any documents being returned to him, the Clerk of Justiciary or sheriff clerk, as the case may be, shall—

(a) note—

(i) the documents returned,

(ii) by whom they were returned, and

(iii) the date on which they were returned,

on the application, the record copy of the indictment or in the minute of proceedings; and

(b) intimate what he has noted to all parties concerned.

Custody of documents

24.6.—(1) The Clerk of Justiciary or the sheriff clerk, as the case may be, shall, subject to paragraph (2), keep the documents referred to in rule 24.5(2) in his custody.

(2) In any case where the petition for the taking of evidence on commission was made to the High Court on the ground that the court in which the trial was to take place was not then known, the prosecutor shall, as soon as that court is

known, inform the Clerk of Justiciary of that fact; and if that court is the sheriff court, the Clerk of Justiciary shall, as soon as is practicable, send to the sheriff clerk of that sheriff court the record of the evidence of the witness or witnesses.

(3) Where the record of the evidence of a witness is in the custody of the Clerk of Justiciary or a sheriff clerk under this rule and where intimation has been given to that effect under rule 24.5(2) to all the parties concerned in the proceedings, the name and address of that witness and the record of his evidence shall be treated as being within the knowledge of those parties; and no party shall be required, notwithstanding any enactment to the contrary—

(a) to include the name of that witness in any list of witnesses; or

(b) to include the record of his evidence in any list of productions.

Prohibition of reference to evidence without leave

24.7.—(1) No reference shall be made either directly or indirectly in any proceedings to the evidence, or any part of the evidence, of a witness whose evidence has been taken on commission under this Chapter unless the party seeking to make such reference has made a motion to the court to that effect and that motion has been granted.

(2) The terms of any motion made under paragraph (1) and the grant or refusal of that motion by the court shall be noted by the clerk of court in the record or minute of proceedings.

(3) On any such motion in solemn proceedings being granted—

(a) the judge may direct copies of the evidence, to which he has granted leave for reference to be made, to be provided to the jury by the party making the motion; and

(b) the clerk of court shall read the record of that evidence to the jury and shall then record that he has done so in the record of proceedings.

GENERAL NOTE

Much of what was noted in relation to the procedure for applying for the issue of letters of request is applicable to this chapter and reference should therefore be made to the notes to Chap. 23 above.

Additionally however it should be noted that the petition seeking the taking of evidence on commission should be supported by a certificate from a qualified medical practitioner that the witness whose evidence is to be taken is ill or infirm in a particular respect. The certificate must be on soul and conscience (r. 24.1(3)). The court shall not authorise interrogatories (r. 24.2(3)) as the examination is to be left to the discretion of the parties. Any objection to the admissibility cannot be sustained by the commissioner who must allow the question or line of examination under reservation of all questions of relevancy and competency (r. 24.4(3)). However it should be noted that objections should nonetheless be timeously taken so that objection can competently be renewed before the trial judge.

CHAPTER 25

RECORD OF JUDICIAL EXAMINATION AS EVIDENCE IN SOLEMN PROCEEDINGS

Use of transcript of judicial examination

25.1.—(1) The record made under section 37 of the Act of 1995 (judicial examination: record of proceedings) shall be received in evidence in accordance with section 278(1) of that Act by means of the clerk of court, subject to paragraph (2) of this rule, reading the record of those proceedings to the jury.

(2) The clerk of court shall not read to the jury such part of the record as the court refuses to allow to be read to the jury on an application under section 278(2) of the Act of 1995.

(3) The presiding judge may direct that copies of such part of the record as has been read to the jury shall be made available to them together with copies of any written record of a confession allegedly made and received by the accused under section 36(3) of the Act of 1995 (written record of confession allegedly made received from prosecutor or constable).

CHAPTER 26

DOCUMENTARY EVIDENCE

Authentication of copies of documents

26.1.—(1) For the purposes of paragraph 1(1) of Schedule 8 to the Act of 1995 (production of copy documents), a copy, or a copy of a material part, of a document shall be authenticated—

- (a) by a person who is—
    - (i) the author of the original of it;
    - (ii) a person in, or who has been in, possession and control of the original of it or a copy of it; or
    - (iii) the authorised representative of the person in, or who has been in, possession and control of the original of it or a copy of it; and
- (b) by means of a signed certificate, certifying the copy as a true copy, which may be in Form 26.1-A—
    - (i) endorsed on the copy; or
    - (ii) attached to the copy.

(2) For the purposes of paragraph 4 of Schedule 8 to Act of 1995 (documents kept by businesses etc.), a document shall be certified by a docquet in Form 26.1-B—

- (a) endorsed on the document; or
- (b) attached to the document.

(3) For the purposes of paragraph 5(3) of Schedule 8 to the Act of 1995 (statements not contained in business documents), a certificate shall be in Form 26.1-C.

GENERAL NOTE

Schedule 8 to the 1995 Act makes provision for documentary evidence in all criminal proceedings. Paragraph 1 requires that unless the court otherwise directs, a document which purports to be authenticated in such manner and by such person as may be prescribed, *shall* be deemed to be a true copy and treated as if it were the actual copy whether or not the original is still in existence. It is immaterial whether the copy is a copy of a copy or even more removed from the original. Rule 26.1(1) even allows authentication by a person who at one time had possession of a copy of the original. Note that in *Lord Advocate's Reference No. 1 of 1992*, 1992 S.L.T. 1010 at 1016F the High Court observed that it was open to the court, when considering the exceptions to the hearsay rule which might be permitted, to take account of changing circumstances which might render the continued application of the rule against hearsay unacceptable.

Paragraph 4 is permissive and provides that (unless the court otherwise directs) a document may be taken to be a document kept by a business or by or on behalf of a holder of an office (whether paid or unpaid) if a docquet certifying that that is so is endorsed on or attached to the document. Form 26.1-B is the appropriate docquet style.

Paragraph 5 avoids the necessity of the attendance at court of a witness who is to speak to a negative. A certificate should be produced stating that a document which was created or received in the course of a business or undertaking or in pursuance of functions of an office-holder (whether paid or unpaid) and is or at any time was kept by a business or undertaking or by or on behalf of an office-holder, either does not contain a certain statement or that no such document contains a certain statement.

In *Lord Advocate's Reference No. 1 of 1996*, 1996 S.L.T. 740; 1996 S.C.C.R. 516 it has been held under reference to the statutory predecessor of Sched. 8 (namely Sched. 3 to the Prisoners and Criminal Proceedings (Scotland) Act 1993) that there are now two methods by which bank statements and

797

bank documents can be proved in criminal proceedings: either under Sched. 8 to the 1995 Act or under the (more strict) Bankers' Books Evidence Act 1879.

CHAPTER 27

ROUTINE EVIDENCE, SUFFICIENT EVIDENCE AND PROOF OF PREVIOUS CONVICTIONS

Notices in relation to use of autopsy and forensic science reports

27.1.—(1) Any notice given by an accused under subsection (1) or (2) of section 281 of the Act of 1995 (routine evidence: autopsy and forensic science reports) shall be in writing and shall be given to the prosecutor.

(2) For the purposes of the application of section 281(1) of the Act of 1995 to any summary proceedings, an autopsy report shall not be treated as having been lodged as a production by the prosecutor unless it has been lodged as a production not later than 14 days before the date of the trial diet.

(3) For the purposes of the application of subsection (2) of section 281 of the Act of 1995 to any summary proceedings, the prosecutor shall intimate his intention in accordance with that subsection by serving a copy of the autopsy or forensic science report lodged by him on the accused or his solicitor with a notice of his intention not later than 14 days before the date of the trial diet.

Form of certificates in relation to certain evidence

27.2. A certificate under any of the following provisions of the Act of 1995 shall be in Form 27.2:—

> section 283(1) (certificate as to time and place of video surveillance recordings),
> section 284(1) (certificate in relation to fingerprints),
> section 285(2) (certificate relating to previous convictions),
> section 285(4) (certificate relating to fingerprints),
> section 285(5) (certificate relating to fingerprints of previously convicted person).

Form of notice in relation to certain evidential certificates

27.3. A notice under any of the following provisions of the Act of 1995 shall be in Form 27.3:—

> section 282(3) (notice not accepting evidence as to controlled drugs or medicinal products),
> section 283(2) (notice not accepting evidence as to video surveillance),
> section 284(2) (notice not accepting evidence in relation to fingerprints),
> section 286(1) (notice denying extract conviction applies to accused).

Notices under section 16A(4) of the Criminal Law (Consolidation) (Scotland) Act 1995

27.4.—(1) A notice under section 16A(4) of the Criminal Law (Consolidation) (Scotland) Act 1995 (notice disputing that condition is satisfied and requiring prosecutor to prove such) shall be in Form 27.4.

(2) A notice by an accused under section 16A(4) of the Criminal Law (Consolidation) (Scotland) Act 1995 (notice disputing condition specified in section 16A(3)) may be served on the prosecutor by any of the methods of service in rule 2.3 (general provisions for service).

(3) At the same time as he serves a notice on the prosecutor under paragraph (2), the accused shall serve a copy of that notice on any co-accused or his solicitor.

(4) An accused shall serve a notice under paragraphs (2) or (3), no later than 21 days before the trial diet.

AMENDMENTS

Para. B1–59.3 as amended by the Act of Adjournal (Criminal Procedure Rules Amendment) 1997 (No. 63).

Subs. (4) as amended by Act of Adjournal (Criminal Procedure Rules Amendment No. 3) (S.I. 1997 No. 1788) (effective August 11, 1997).

Notice under section 16B(4) of Criminal Law (Consolidation) (Scotland) Act 1995

27.5.—(1) Any notice under section 16B(4) of the Criminal Law (Consolidation) (Scotland) Act 1995 (notice served on prosecutor by person accused of sexual offence disputing whether an act done by him abroad constituted an offence under the law in force in the country or territory in question) shall be in Form 27.5 and may be served on the prosecutor by any of the methods of service mentioned in rule 2.3.

(2) Any such notice shall be served not later than 21 days before the trial diet; and when he serves such a notice the accused shall serve a copy of it on any co-accused or on the solicitor of any co-accused.

AMENDMENT

Para. B1–59.4 inserted by Act of Adjournal (Criminal Procedure Rules Amendment No. 5) (S.I. 1997 No. 2082) (effective September 1, 1997).

GENERAL NOTE

Chapter 27 mainly provides for the appropriate forms of certificates and notices which require to be given. Rule 27.1 however merits notice. When the prosecutor in solemn or summary proceedings wishes to rely on the presumption in s.281(1) of the 1995 Act that the body examined at a post-mortem dissection was the deceased named in the charge, or wishes to rely on only one of two experts who prepared the autopsy report or the forensic science report as being sufficient evidence of the facts and conclusions contained in the report, he should give written notice to the accused. The accused then has to give a counter-notice not less than six days before the trial in order to prevent the prosecutor from relying on the presumption or calling only one expert. In summary proceedings r. 27.1(2) and (3) provide that the prosecutor must lodge the autopsy report or give the notice of his intention to rely on only one witness, not later than 14 days before the trial diet.

Rule 27.4 has been rendered necessary by the amendment of the Criminal Law (Consolidation) (Scotland) Act 1995 by s.6 of the Sexual Offences (Conspiracy and Incitement) Act 1996 (c. 29) which came into force on October 1, 1996. Section 16A provides that a person shall be guilty of conspiracy or incitement in respect of various sexual offences involving children (*i.e.* persons under 16 years) where these offences are intended to be committed abroad. Section 16A(4) allows for an essential condition of guilt to be taken as satisfied, unless notice is given by the accused that the condition is disputed (although the court is entitled to permit, if it thinks fit, the accused to require the Crown to prove the condition without prior service of a notice: s.16A(6)). The essential conditions are: either (a) where conspiracy is charged, the criminal purpose would involve at some stage either an act by him or by another party to the conspiracy, or the happening of some event, constituting an offence under the law of the place where the event was intended to take place; or (b) where incitement is libelled, what was in view would involve the commission of an offence under the law of that place. The Act also states that the conduct is an offence under that other country's law, howsoever the foreign law describes it so long as it is punishable under that law. Thus it is for Scots law as the *lex fori* to characterise the purpose of the conspiracy or the object of the incitement as an offence: to regard the foreign law as punishing the conduct the Scots court will ask whether the consequences of the conduct under the foreign law can be regarded as penal in nature.

PART VII

MISCELLANEOUS PROCEDURES

CHAPTER 28

IDENTIFICATION PARADES

Applications for identification parade

28.1.—(1) An application to the sheriff made by an accused under section 290 of the Act of 1995 (application by accused for identification parade) shall be made—

(a) to the sheriff in whose sheriffdom the proceedings in relation to which the order is sought have been commenced;

(b) by petition—

(i) where the accused has appeared on petition under Part IV of the Act of 1995 (petition procedure) but an indictment has not been served on him, in Form 28.1-A; or

(ii) where an indictment or a complaint has been served on the accused, in Form 28.1-B.

(2) On the petition referred to in paragraph (1) being lodged, the sheriff shall—

(a) order intimation of the petition to be made to the prosecutor;

(b) fix a diet for a hearing of the petition on the earliest practicable date; and

(c) after giving the prosecutor an opportunity to be heard at the hearing and allowing such further procedure as he thinks fit, make an order granting or refusing the petition.

(3) If—

(a) the prosecutor is not present at the hearing of the petition; and

(b) the sheriff makes an order granting the petition,

the sheriff clerk shall issue a certified copy of the order to the petitioner or his solicitor.

(4) The sheriff clerk shall record the order made by the sheriff under paragraph (2)(c) in the minute of proceedings, and shall keep the petition and relative documents in his custody.

GENERAL NOTE

When an identification parade involving the accused has not been held by the Crown, the accused is entitled to apply to the sheriff for an order that the prosecutor hold an identification parade in which the accused shall be one of those constituting the parade. The sheriff is only entitled to grant the order when the prosecutor has been requested by the accused to hold such a parade and the prosecutor has either refused to hold the parade or has unreasonably delayed in holding the parade, and the application is considered to be reasonable by the sheriff. Considerations which arose in cases where the Crown applied for a warrant to place accused persons, or suspects (see *Archibald v. Lees*, 1995 S.L.T. 231), on an identification parade such as whether there are "special circumstances" justifying the grant of the warrant (see, **e.g.** *McMurtrie v. Annan*, 1995 S.L.T. 642) do not apply when the accused seeks the warrant. Intimation of the petition craving the order on the prosecutor must be given to the prosecutor who is entitled to appear at the hearing of the petition and must be afforded an opportunity to be heard (see s.29(2)). For an example of a successful application, see *Wilson v. Tudhope*, 1985 S.C.C.R. 339.

In *Beattie v. Hingston*, 1999 S.L.T. 362, the sheriff had refused an accused's application for an identification parade to be held, on the basis that the accused had advanced no reasons for him to assess whether the application was reasonable. On a suspension brought by the accused the High Court remitted the application to be heard *de novo* by a different sheriff in respect that the sheriff had erred in his conclusion. The accused had explained that the parade was sought because (1) identification of the perpetrator was the main issue at the forthcoming trial, and (2) Crown witnesses had variously stated at precognition that they had identified the accused or had not or had been unsure. The High Court, however, expressed no opinion as to the sufficiency of the accused's reasons.

CHAPTER 29

PRECOGNITION ON OATH OF DEFENCE WITNESSES

Applications for warrant to cite for precognition

29.1.—(1) An application to the sheriff made by an accused under section 291(1) of the Act of 1995 (warrant to cite any person to appear for precognition on oath) shall be made—

(a) to the sheriff in whose sheriffdom the proceedings, in respect of which the accused seeks the precognition of that person, have been commenced;

(b) by petition—

(i) where the accused has appeared on petition under Part IV of the Act of 1995 (petition procedure) but an indictment has not been served on him, in Form 29.1-A; or

(ii) where an indictment or a complaint has been served on the accused, in Form 29.1-B.

(2) On a petition referred to in paragraph (1) being lodged, the sheriff shall—

(a) order intimation of the application to be made to the procurator fiscal; and

(b) fix a diet for a hearing of the application.

Orders for taking precognition

29.2. Where, after the hearing fixed under rule 29.1(2), the sheriff is satisfied that it is reasonable to require such precognition on oath in the circumstances, he shall—

(a) order the precognition to be taken;

(b) fix a diet for it to be taken; and

(c) grant warrant to cite the person from whom it is to be taken.

Citation to attend for precognition

29.3.—(1) Citation of a person to attend the diet fixed for taking his precognition on oath shall be in Form 29.3; and an execution of service shall be produced at the diet fixed under rule 29.1(2).

(2) Where a person fails to appear at a diet fixed for taking his precognition and the sheriff issues a warrant for his apprehension under section 291(2) of the Act of 1995, execution of that warrant—

(a) shall be made by an officer of law instructed by the accused or his solicitor; and

(b) may proceed on a copy of the petition and warrant duly certified by the sheriff clerk.

(3) The clerk shall immediately give notice of that person's failure to appear at the diet to the procurator fiscal.

Record of proceedings

29.4.—(1) Where a person appears before the sheriff to have his precognition taken on oath, the proceedings shall be recorded in shorthand by an official shorthand writer instructed by the accused or his solicitor.

(2) The shorthand writer shall extend his shorthand notes recording the proceedings, sign the transcript, and lodge it with the sheriff clerk.

(3) On the transcript being lodged, the sheriff clerk shall—

(a) send a copy to the solicitor for the accused or, it he is not represented, to the accused; and

(b) fix a diet for the person whose precognition has been taken on oath to attend before the sheriff to sign the precognition.

Fees of shorthand writer

29.5.—(1) The solicitor for the accused or, if he is not represented, the accused shall be liable for payment of—

(a) the fees of the shorthand writer, and

(b) the reasonable expenses of the person precognosed on oath;

and shall tender any such expenses in advance if required by that person to do so.

(2) Where the accused is not represented, the sheriff may, at the hearing of the application or at any time before the precognition is taken, order the accused to consign into court such sum as he may be required to pay under paragraph (1) in respect of fees and expenses on or before such date as the sheriff may specify in the order.

(3) If the sheriff orders the accused to consign a sum into court under paragraph (2) and that sum is not consigned by the date specified in the order, the petition shall be treated as abandoned.

GENERAL NOTE

Section 291(1) of the 1995 Act provides that the sheriff may grant warrant to cite any person (other than a co-accused) who is alleged to be a witness in relation to any offence of which the accused has been charged, to appear before him in chambers at such time or place as the sheriff specifies, for precognition on oath by the accused or his solicitor in relation to that offence (*cf. HM Advocate v Campbell*, 1996 S.C.C.R. 419). For an order to be granted the accused must satisfy the sheriff that it is reasonable to require such precognition on oath in the circumstances. For example, the Appeal Court has observed that where a partially dyslexic accused wishes himself to precognosce witnesses who are unwilling, in order to obtain a record of their evidence, his remedy is to apply for an order from the sheriff under s.291(1) which the sheriff should grant if he is satisfied that it is reasonable to require precognition on oath in the particular circumstances: see *Drummond, Petitioner*, 1998 S.L.T. 757 at 758, *per* Lord Justice General Rodger. As in the case of identification parades in Ch.28, the prosecutor is entitled to receive intimation of the application and is entitled to be heard at the hearing of the application.

Rule 29.1

It is incompetent to apply for an order for citation of a witness to submit to precognition on oath prior to full committal (see *Cirignaco, Petitioner*, 1985 S.C.C.R. 157). If intimation is not made by the accused of the application to the procurator fiscal then the sheriff is entitled—and no doubt would feel bound—to refuse the application.

Rule 29.3

The obligation on the sheriff clerk to give immediate notice of a witness's failure to appear at the diet to the procurator fiscal proceeds on the fact that failure to attend when duly cited and having been given at least 48 hours notice, exposes the witness to the risk of criminal prosecution under s.291(2) of the 1995 Act.

Rule 29.5

It is suggested that the tendering of reasonable witness expenses in advance, when so required, is a condition precedent of the sheriff's allowing the precognition on oath to proceed (irrespective of whether or not the sheriff makes an order in terms of r.29.5(2)). Accordingly, the failure to tender such expenses when they are sought will justify the witness in not attending for precognition and the witness will not incur any criminal liability by not attending.

The Appeal Court has observed that an unrepresented accused has no right to recover the expenses of the shorthand writer and the witnesses from the legal aid fund and accordingly, where such an accused has chosen not to seek legal aid, it has been held that he is not entitled to complain that precognition on oath is financially burdensome and that he should therefore be enabled to compel witnesses to submit to being precognosced by the accused himself in tape-recorded conditions (see *Drummond, Petitioner*, 1998 S.L.T. 759; 1998 S.C.C.R. 42).

CHAPTER 30

PROCEEDINGS FOR THE EXECUTION OF IRISH WARRANTS

[...]

AMENDMENT

Chapter 30 repealed by the Act of Adjournal (Criminal Procedure Rules Amendment No.3) (Extradition etc.) 2004 (SSI 2004/346), r.2 (effective August 18, 2004).

CHAPTER 31

REFERENCES TO THE EUROPEAN COURT OF JUSTICE

Interpretation of this Chapter

31.1.—(1) In this Chapter, unless the context otherwise requires—

"the European Court" means the Court of Justice of the European Communities;

"question" means a question or issue in respect of which the European Court has jurisdiction to give a preliminary ruling under the Community Treaties;

"reference" means a request to the European Court for a preliminary ruling on a question.

(2) [...]

AMENDMENT

Rule 31.1(1) as amended, and r.31.1(2) repealed, by the Act of Adjournal (Criminal Procedure Rules Amendment No. 4) (Miscellaneous) 2006 (SSI 2006/436), r.2 (effective September 1, 2006).

Notice of references in solemn proceedings

31.2.—(1) Where a question is to be raised in any proceedings on indictment (other than proceedings on appeal), notice of intention to do so shall be given to the court before which the preliminary hearing or first diet is to take place, as the case may be, and to the other parties not later than 14 days after service of the indictment.

(2) Where such a notice is given, a record of the notice shall be made on the record copy of the indictment or in the record of proceedings, as the case may be; and the court, in chambers, shall reserve consideration of the question to the preliminary hearing or first diet, as the case may be.

(3) [...]

(4) At the trial diet, the court, after hearing the parties, may determine the question or may decide that a preliminary ruling should be sought.

(5) Where the court determines the question, the accused shall then (if appropriate) be called on to plead to the indictment; and, without prejudice to any other power available to it, the court—

(a) may prorogate the time for lodging any special defence;

(b) may continue the diet to a specified time and place; and

(c) in a case where witnesses and jurors have not been cited to attend at the trial diet, shall continue the diet and order the citation of witnesses and jurors to attend the continued diet.

(6) No period during which the diet is continued under paragraph (5) shall—

(a) subject to paragraph (7), be longer than 21 days; or

(b) be taken into account for the purposes of determining whether any time limit has expired.

(7) The court may, on the application of the prosecutor or defence, extend any period during which the diet is continued for such longer period than 21 days as it thinks fit on special cause shown.

AMENDMENT

Rule 31.2(1) and (2) as amended, and r.31.2(3) repealed, by the Act of Adjournal (Criminal Procedure Rules Amendment No. 4) (Miscellaneous) 2006 (SSI 2006/436), r.2 (effective September 1, 2006).

Notice of references in summary proceedings

31.3.—(1) Where a question is to be raised in any summary proceedings (other than proceedings on appeal), notice of intention to do so shall be given before the accused is called on to plead to the complaint.

(2) Where such notice is given, a record of the notice shall be entered in the minute of proceedings and the court shall not then call on the accused to plead to the complaint.

(3) The court may hear parties on the question forthwith or may adjourn the case to a specified date for such hearing.

(4) After hearing parties, the court may determine the question or may decide that a preliminary ruling should be sought.

(5) Where the court determines the question, the accused shall then (where appropriate) be called on to plead to the complaint.

Proceedings on appeal etc.

31.4.—(1) Where a question is raised in the High Court in any proceedings on appeal or on a petition for the exercise of the *nobile officium*, the court shall proceed to make a reference.

(2) In paragraph (1), the reference to proceedings on appeal is a reference to proceedings on appeal under the Act of 1995 or on appeal by bill of suspension, bill of advocation or otherwise.

Preparation of case for reference

31.5.—(1) Where the court decides that a preliminary ruling should be sought, the court shall—

(a) give its reasons and cause those reasons to be recorded in the record or minute of proceedings, as the case may be; and

(b) continue the proceedings from time to time as necessary for the purposes of the reference.

(2) The reference—

(a) except in so far as the court may otherwise direct, shall be drafted in Form 31.5 and the court may give directions to the parties as to the manner in which and by whom the case is to be drafted and adjusted;

(b) shall thereafter if necessary, be further adjusted to take account of any adjustments required by the court; and

(c) after approval and the making of an appropriate order by the court, shall (after the expiry of the period for appeal) be transmitted by the clerk of court to the Registrar of the European Court with a certified copy of the record or minute of proceedings, as the case may be, and, where applicable, a certified copy of the relevant indictment or complaint.

(3) In preparing a reference, the parties shall have regard to guidance issued by the European Court.

AMENDMENT

Rule 31.5(3) substituted by the Act of Adjournal (Criminal Procedure Rules Amendment No. 4) (Miscellaneous) 2006 (SSI 2006/436), r.2 (effective September 1, 2006).

Procedure on receipt of preliminary ruling

31.6.—(1) Where a preliminary ruling has been given by the European Court on a question referred to it and the ruling has been received by the clerk of the court which made the reference, the ruling shall be laid by the clerk before the court.

(2) On the ruling being laid before the court, the court shall then give directions as to further procedure, which directions shall be intimated by the clerk, with a copy of the ruling, to each of the parties to the proceedings.

Appeals against references

31.7.—(1) Subject to paragraph (2), where an order making a reference is made, any party to the proceedings who is aggrieved by the order may, within 14 days after the date of the order, appeal against the order to the High Court sitting as a court of appeal.

(2) Paragraph (1) shall not apply to such an order made in proceedings in the High Court sitting as a court of appeal or in proceedings on petition to that court for the exercise of its *nobile officium*.

(3) Any appeal under this rule shall be taken by lodging with the clerk of the court which made the order a note of appeal in Form 31.7 and signed by the appellant or his solicitor; and a copy of the note shall be served by the appellant on every other party to the proceedings.

(4) The clerk of court shall record the lodging of the note in the record or minute of proceedings, as the case may be, and shall forthwith transmit the note to the Clerk of Justiciary with the record or minute of proceedings and a certified copy of the relevant indictment or complaint.

(5) In disposing of an appeal under this rule, the High Court (sitting as a court of appeal) may—

(a) sustain or dismiss the appeal, and in either case remit the proceedings to the court of first instance with instructions to proceed as accords; and

(b) give such directions for other procedure as it thinks fit.

(6) Unless the court making the order otherwise directs, a reference shall not be transmitted to the Registrar of the European Court before the time allowed by this rule for appealing against the order has expired or before the appeal has been disposed of or abandoned.

AMENDMENTS

Rules 31.1 and 31.7 as amended by the Act of Adjournal (Criminal Procedure Rules Amendment No. 2) 1999 (SI 1999/1282), para.2(2) (effective May 1, 1999).

Rule 31.5(2) as amended by the Act of Adjournal (Criminal Procedure Rules Amendment No. 2) 1999 (SI 1999/1282), para.2(3)(a) (effective May 1, 1999).

Rule 31.5(3) inserted by the Act of Adjournal (Criminal Procedure Rules Amendment No. 2) 1999 (SI 1999/1282), para.2(3)(b) (effective May 1, 1999).

Para. B1–67 as amended by Act of Adjournal (Criminal Procedure Rules Amendment) (Miscellaneous) (SI 1996/2147 (s.171)) (effective September 9, 1996).

GENERAL NOTE

Rules 63 to 67 and 112 to 118 of the 1988 Rules provided separately for solemn and summary proceedings in which references were made to the Court of Justice of the European Communities for a preliminary ruling on a question or issue of European law concerning the interpretation or validity of the Treaty provisions or an act of the Community institutions. The 1996 Rules bring these rules together under one chapter. A reference is a request for a preliminary ruling on a European legal question which *must* be made by the High Court when it sits as a Court of Appeal because there is no right of appeal from that court. Lower courts are not however compelled to make a reference but may do so (except in the case of a question or an issue arising under the European Coal and Steel Community Treaty (see Art. 41)) if they consider it appropriate.

A lower court is entitled to seek a preliminary ruling from the European Court of Justice if the lower court considers that a decision on the question raised before it is necessary to enable the court to give judgment (*Wither v Cowie*, 1991 S.L.T. 401 at 405F). National Courts have the widest discretion in seeking such a ruling (see *Rheinmuhlen-Dusseldorf v Einfuhr-Und Vorratsstelle fur Getreide und Futtermittel* (166/73) [1974] E.C.R. 33), although in *Wither v Cowie*, *supra*, Lord Justice-Clerk Ross referred only to the lower court's having "a wide discretion".

Where a sheriff, or justice of the peace or High Court judge sitting at first instance decides to make a reference to the European Court of Justice either at the suggestion of one of the parties or *ex proprio motu*—as the sheriff did in *Wither v Cowie*, *supra*—his decision can be appealed to the High Court of Justiciary sitting as a Court of Appeal. In such cases however the Appeal Court will not lightly interfere with the decision of the lower court to seek a preliminary ruling. In *Wither v Cowie*, *supra*, it was said that the Appeal Court "would not be justified in interfering with that exercise of the sheriff's discretion unless it felt that the sheriff's decision was plainly wrong" (1991 S.L.T. 401 at 406A) and Stephenson L.J.'s dictum in *Bulmer (H.P.) Ltd v J Bollinger S.A.* [1974] Ch. 401 was approved to the effect that the Appeal Court will only interfere when the lower court's decision "exceeds the generous ambit within which reasonable disagreement is possible and is, in fact, plainly wrong".

It has been argued that the provision of a right to appeal against the decision to make a reference is a fetter on the wide powers conferred on the national court by Art.177 of the Treaty of Rome. However, the Court of Justice has not regarded the application of national appeal procedures to decisions to refer as being incompatible with Art. 177 (see *Kledingverkoopbedrijf de Geus en Uitdenbogerd v Bosch* (13/61) [1962] E.C.R. 45 at 50; see also Anderson, *References to the European Court* (1995), paras 7–083 to 7–088).

It might also be questioned whether the fact that the power to make a reference is only available prior to the accused being called on to plead is itself an unlawful restriction on the powers conferred on the national courts by Art.177. However, the Court of Justice has held that national procedural rules which impinge on the power to refer a question for a preliminary ruling are not incompatible with Art.177 unless they either are less favourable than the rules governing domestic actions or render the rights conferred by Community law virtually impossible or extremely difficult to invoke (*Rheinmuhlen-Dusseldorf*, *supra*; *S.C.S. Peterbroeck van Campenhout & Cie. v Belgium* (C-312/93) [1996] All E.R. (E.C.) 242 at 257 (para. 12)).

Most European questions will involve a point of relevancy or competency and should be raised before the accused is called on to plead. For those cases which require the facts to be established before the question can be said to be raised, the accused or the Crown (at least in summary cases) can obtain his remedy on appeal when, if the High Court considers that a European question is raised, the court must make a reference (*cf.* the position envisaged in *Wither v Cowie*, 1991 S.L.T. 401 and the notes to rr.31.2 and 31.3).

For examples of decisions of the European Court of Justice on references for preliminary rulings, see *Walkingshaw v Marshall*, 1991 S.C.C.R. 397; *Wither v Cowie*, 1994 S.L.T. 363; and *Mehlich v Mackenzie*; *Gewiese v Mackenzie*, 1984 S.L.T. 449; 1984 S.C.C.R. 130.

Rule 31.1

The reference procedure most frequently invoked is that provided for in Art.234 of the EC Treaty (formerly Art.177 EEC) (see *Law of the European Union*, Vol.1, para.[308]). Prior to amendment of this chapter with effect from September 1, 2006, the preliminary ruling which a domestic court could seek was on a question or issue under Art.234, Art.150 of the Euratom Treaty or Art.41 of the ECSC Treaty. The change in definition of "question" in r.31.1(1) reflects the now enlarged jurisdictional competence of the Court of Justice. For example, the Treaty of Amsterdam introduced a new provision, Art.68, into the EC Treaty. That provision modifies the application of Art.234 EC (and in particular, by Art.68(2), provides that the Court of Justice does not have jurisdiction to rule on measures taken pursuant to Art.62(1) EC in relation to the maintenance of law and order and the safeguarding of internal security). Moreover, while the UK has not yet made a declaration of acceptance, Art.35 of the Treaty on European Union gives jurisdiction to the Court of Justice to provide preliminary rulings on inter alia the validity and interpretation of framework decisions and decisions under Title VI in respect of police and judicial cooperation in criminal matters.

Rule 31.2

While it is possible for the court *ex proprio motu* to seek a preliminary ruling on a question or issue under the Community Treaties (see *Rheinmuhlen-Dusseldorf*, at 38 (para.3)), it will normally be
the parties who wish a reference to be made. To take account of the introduction of preliminary hearings in the High Court and to acknowledge belatedly the creation of mandatory first diets in the sheriff
court, the notice which formerly had to be given by a party seeking a reference 14 days before the
trial diet is now amended (as from September 1, 2006) to be 14 days before the preliminary hearing or
first diet.

Rule 31.3

Notice of an intention to raise a question in summary proceedings need only be given at the pleading diet and can be determined there and then or at an adjourned diet. The court can also, as in solemn
cases, decide to reserve the question if it is the course least likely to lead to long delay. In that case the
court allows in effect a proof before answer, which was the course which the Appeal Court in *Wither
v Cowie*, 1991 S.L.T. 401 appeared to approve.

Rule 31.4

The Appeal Court has no discretion and must seek a preliminary ruling. There is no appeal against
the Appeal Court's decision to make a reference to the European Court of Justice: see r.31.7(2).
Indeed where an appeal against the lower court's decision to seek a preliminary ruling is taken under
r.31.7, it is arguable that since there is no appeal beyond the Appeal Court, the reference should be
made in all cases. (*Cf.* McCluskey, *Criminal Appeals*, para.5.17.)

Rule 31.5

The parties should prepare the draft reference which it is proposed that the court should make to
the Court of Justice and, where the referring court so directs (because, for example, the parties cannot
agree on the final terms of the reference), they should make further adjustments to the proposed reference before the court will sanction its terms.

The reference is made because the court considers that a preliminary ruling is necessary and accordingly the court has the duty to control the terms of the reference which must contain, inter alia,
(1) a statement of the facts which are essential to a full understanding of the legal significance of the
proceedings which give rise to the question and (2) an exposition of the national law in which the
question arises. Such details will usually appear in the opinion of the court on an appeal but that will
not suffice because, while the opinion will accompany the reference, it may not be translated into the
other official languages of the Community. In the case of references from inferior courts there will not
usually be a written decision or note from the sheriff or justice.

The reference after having been approved by the lower court, cannot be transmitted to the European
Court of Justice until after the expiry of the 14 day time-limit for appeal under r.31.7(1) (see r.31.7(6)).
However it should be noted that the High Court can in exercise of its *nobile officium* relieve a party
from the consequences of a failure to comply with that time-limit: see *HM Advocate, Petitioner*, 1990
S.L.T. 798; 1990 S.C.C.R. 195.

The Notes for Completion of Form 31.5 have been issued by the Court of Justice but have no binding or interpretative effect. They draw to practitioners' attention the fact that proceedings for a preliminary ruling under Art.234 are free of charge before the Court of Justice which will not award expenses to any party.

Rule 31.7

An appeal against the order making a reference is competent at the instance of any party to the
proceedings who is aggrieved by the order. A co-accused who is not involved in any charge raising a
question on which a preliminary ruling is sought, could therefore be prejudiced by the delay which
will be occasioned by a reference and might be well advised to appeal against the order. If his appeal
fails—as it is likely to do—he can then seek a separation of trials: see McCluskey, *Criminal Appeals*,
para.5.16.

CHAPTER 32

ANNOYING CREATURES

Interpretation of this Chapter

32.1. In this Chapter, "the Act of 1982" means the Civic Government
(Scotland) Act 1982.

Form of application to district court and service

32.2.—(1) An application to a district court under section 49(3) of the Act of 1982 (annoying creatures) shall be made in Form 32.2.

(2) On the lodging of any such application, the district court shall make an order for service of a copy of the application on any person mentioned in the application as having the creature so mentioned in his charge or keeping the creature, and fixing a date and time for the hearing of the application.

(3) A copy of the application and of the order made under paragraph (2) shall be served on any such person by recorded delivery at the normal place of residence or place of business of that person, and such service shall be treated as sufficient notice to that person of the terms of the application and the order for the purposes of paragraph (4).

(4) If any person upon whom service has been made in accordance with paragraph (3) fails to appear or be represented at the time and date of the hearing specified in the order without reasonable excuse, the court may proceed to hear and decide the application in his absence.

(5) Where the court makes an order in respect of any person under section 49(2) of the Act of 1982, the clerk of court shall, within seven days after the date on which the order was made, serve on that person, by recorded delivery at the normal place of residence or place of business of that person, a copy of the order and a notice setting out the terms of section 49(4) of the Act of 1982.

CHAPTER 33

LEGAL AID

Interpretation of this Chapter

33.1. In this Chapter, unless the context otherwise requires—

"the Act of 1986" means the Legal Aid (Scotland) Act 1986;

"assisted person" means a person who is in receipt of criminal legal aid in the proceedings in question;

"the Regulations" means the Criminal Legal Aid (Scotland) Regulations 1987.

Legal aid in High Court

33.2. Where an application for legal aid is made to the High Court under section 23 of the Act of 1986 (power of the court to grant legal aid), the court may—

(a) determine the application itself; or

(b) remit the application to the sheriff court for determination.

Discontinuance of entitlement to legal aid

33.3.—(1) Subject to paragraph (1A) below, where the court before which there are proceedings in which an assisted person is an accused or appellant is satisfied, after hearing that person—

(a) that he—

(i) has without reasonable cause failed to comply with a proper request made to him by the solicitor acting for him to supply any information relevant to the proceedings,

(ii) has delayed unreasonably in complying with any such request,

(iii) has without reasonable cause failed to attend at a diet of the court at which he has been required to attend or at a meeting with the counsel or solicitor acting for him under the Act of 1986 at which he has reasonably and properly been required to attend,

(iv) has conducted himself in connection with the proceedings in such a way as to make it appear to the court unreasonable that he should continue to receive criminal legal aid,

(v) has wilfully or deliberately given false information for the purpose of misleading the court in considering his financial circumstances under section 23(1) of the Act of 1986, or

(vi) has without reasonable cause failed to comply with a requirement of the Regulations, or

(b) that it is otherwise unreasonable for the solicitor to continue to act on behalf of the assisted person in the proceedings,

the court may direct that the assisted person shall cease to be entitled to criminal legal aid in connection with those proceedings.

(1A) Where the solicitor acting for the assisted person was appointed by the court under section 288D of the Act of 1995 (appointment of solicitors by court in proceedings in respect of sexual offence), paragraph (1) shall not apply.

(2) Where a direction is made under paragraph (1) of this rule in the course of proceedings to which section 22 of the Act of 1986 (automatic availability of criminal legal aid) applies, the accused shall not be entitled to criminal legal aid in relation to any later stages of the same proceedings before the court of first instance.

(3) Where a court issues a direction under paragraph (1), the clerk of court shall send notice of it to the Scottish Legal Aid Board.

(4) Where a court of first instance has made a direction under paragraph (1)(a), it shall instruct the clerk of court to report the terms of the finding made by the court to the Scottish Legal Aid Board for its consideration in any application for criminal legal aid in an appeal in connection with the proceedings in that court.

AMENDMENT

Rule 33.3(1) as amended, and (1A) inserted, by Act of Adjournal (Criminal Procedure Rules Amendment No.3) (Sexual Offences (Procedure and Evidence) (Scotland) Act 2002) 2002 (SSI 2002/454), r.2(10) (effective November 1, 2002).

Statements on oath

33.4. In considering any matter in regard to the entitlement of a person to criminal legal aid, the court may require that person to make a statement on oath for the purpose of ascertaining or verifying any fact material to his entitlement to criminal legal aid.

Intimation of determination of High Court

33.5. The Clerk of Justiciary shall intimate to the Scottish Legal Aid Board any decision of the High Court made under section 25(2A) of the Act of 1986 (determination by High Court that applicant should receive legal aid).

Intimation of appointment of solicitor by court in proceedings in respect of sexual offence

33.6. The clerk of court shall intimate to the Scottish Legal Aid Board any decision of the court to appoint a solicitor under section 288D(2) of the Act of 1995 (appointment of solicitors by court in proceedings in respect of sexual offence).

AMENDMENT

Rule 33.6 inserted by Act of Adjournal (Criminal Procedure Rules Amendment No.3) (Sexual Offences (Procedure and Evidence) (Scotland) Act 2002) 2002 (SSI 2002/454), r.2(11) (effective November 1, 2002).

GENERAL NOTE

Rule 33.3

Rule 33.3(1). It is incompetent for the court to make a direction that the assisted person shall cease to be entitled to criminal legal aid in connection with the proceedings unless the assisted person has been afforded an opportunity to be heard on that question: see *Lamont, Petitioner*, 1995 S.L.T. 566. It is competent for an assisted person who has had his entitlement to criminal legal aid terminated by the court without being heard, to petition the *nobile officium* of the High Court of Justiciary to quash that direction: see *Lamont, Petitioner, supra,* following *Hartley, Petitioner* (1968) 32 J.C.L. 191. Equally, it is incompetent for the court to refuse to hear an accused's legal representative and to insist in hearing the accused himself prior to revoking his legal aid certificate: such a decision to revoke legal aid can be reversed by the High Court in exercise of its *nobile officium* (see *Ness, Petitioner*, 1999 S.L.T. 214; 1998 S.C.C.R. 589).

In *Russell v Wilson*, 1994 S.C.C.R. 13 the sheriff, after the accused had pled guilty during a summary trial, adjourned the diet and remanded the accused in custody in order for investigations to be carried out into whether, as the sheriff strongly suspected, the accused had committed an offence under the Legal Aid (Scotland) Act 1986 in connection with his application for legal aid. The High Court suspended both the conviction and subsequent sentence on the ground that the adjournment was an extraneous and collateral matter with no legitimate bearing on any decision which the sheriff might have required to take and that the proceedings had accordingly come to an end at midnight on the day of the purported adjournment. The High Court also observed that it was unreasonable for the sheriff to remand the accused in custody simply on the basis of a suspicion.

Rule 33.3(2). Once the Court has made a direction that the assisted person should cease to be entitled to criminal legal aid, it is incompetent to petition the *nobile officium* to obtain an order restoring legal aid in relation to any later stages of the same proceedings before the court of first instance: see *McGettigan, Petitioner*, 1996 S.L.T. 76. However, where what is challenged before the High Court is the propriety of the order of the lower court revoking the legal aid certificate (which was not in issue in *McGettigan*), a petition to the *nobile officium* is competent (see *Anderson, Petr*, 1998 S.L.T. 101). Thus in *Reid, Petitioner*, 1998 S.C.C.R. 430 the High Court restored an accused's legal aid certificate because the sheriff at the trial diet had revoked the accused's certificate and backdated the revocation to the intermediate diet. While the High Court understood the sheriff's reasons for backdating the order revoking the certificate, backdating was not competent.

The principles on which the revocation of a legal aid certificate will be reviewed in a petition to the *nobile officium* are, with one possible exception, likely to be the same as for judicial review of administrative decisions (see *Council of Civil Service Unions v Minister for the Civil Service* [1985] A.C. 374). Thus taking into account an irrelevant consideration vitiates the decision to revoke a certificate (*Anderson*) and leaving out of account a relevant factor which favours not revoking a certificate would presumably also found a petition to the *nobile officium* (see Lord President Emslie's opinion in *Wordie Property Co. Ltd v Secretary of State for Scotland*, 1984 S.L.T. 345). Furthermore, r. 33.3(1) expressly requires that the accused be heard before the order to revoke the certificate is made and accordingly a breach of that requirement would also open up the order to review in the High Court (see, *e.g.*, *Brannigan, Petitioner*, 1999 S.L.T. 679; 1999 S.C.C.R. 274 where the sheriff granted warrant for the accused's arrest on the third occasion when she failed to appear for sentence and simultaneously directed that her legal aid certificate be withdrawn). However, it is doubtful whether the High Court would permit review on the grounds of *Wednesbury* unreasonableness (see *Associated Provincial Picture Houses v Wednesbury Corporation* [1948] 1 K.B. 223) since to do so would effectively subvert entirely the otherwise final nature of the decision which the rule has by implication entrusted exclusively to the lower court.

While the above propositions are not explicitly warranted by judicial authority, they do receive considerable support from two recent decisions of the Appeal Court. In *Ness, supra*, the High Court observed that cases involving the revocation of legal aid certificates raised "very real questions" about the factors which should be taken into account when a court decides to deprive an accused person of legal representation on charges which can result in his imprisonment. The reference to imprisonment is no doubt an oblique allusion to the decisions of the European Court of Human Rights in *Boner v United Kingdom*; *Maxwell v United Kingdom*, 1995 S.C.C.R. 1 and *Granger v United Kingdom*, Series A, No.174 (1990) 12 E.H.R.R. 469 and perhaps indicates that the scope for review might be broader since the European Court of Human Rights is likely to require that the sanction of the withdrawal of legal aid be a proportionate response to the accused's failures. The European Court's insistence on proportionality will, however, require a consideration of the likely length of the period of imprisonment and so it may be that at least for the usual type of summary trial where the maximum sentence is 3 or 6 months' imprisonment, the revocation of legal aid will be less open to being characterised as disproportionate.

The more significant decision is, however, *Shaw, Petr*, 1999 S.L.T. 215; 1998 S.C.C.R. 672 in which the Appeal Court stated that an accused's interest in having a fair trial was not merely a private interest but was an interest shared by the whole of society and that the availability of legal aid was of fundamental importance in helping the criminal justice system achieve its objective of securing a fair trial. The Appeal Court accordingly requires the court contemplating making an order revoking legal aid to bear these factors in mind and to make the order only where satisfied that by reason of some conduct on the accused's part falling within r.33.3(1), it would be unreasonable for the accused's solicitor to continue to act for the accused. The court should also be satisfied that such an order would be a reasonable or proportional response to the accused's conduct when measured against the potential effect of revocation on the accused's right to a fair trial. It was also observed that the power to revoke a legal aid certificate was not conferred on the court for use as a punishment of the accused.

CHAPTER 34

EXTRADITION

Interpretation of this Chapter

34.1. In this Chapter—

"the Act of 2003" means the Extradition Act 2003;

"arrested person" means a person who has been arrested under the Act of 2003; and

"required period" shall be construed in accordance with section 74(11) of the Act of 2003.

Arrest under provisional warrant

34.2.—(1) This rule applies where an arrested person is brought before the sheriff at Lothian and Borders under section 74(3) (person arrested under provisional warrant) of the Act of 2003.

(2) The sheriff—

(a) may fix a date for a review hearing to take place before the expiry of the required period; and

(b) shall fix a date for a review hearing to take place as soon as practicable after the expiry of the required period.

(3) At a review hearing under paragraph (2), the sheriff shall ascertain, so far as reasonably practicable, the state of preparation of the parties and may fix a further hearing to take place before the extradition hearing; and this paragraph may apply more than once.

Appeals

34.3.—(1) Subject to paragraph (3), an appeal under—

(a) section 26(1) of the Act of 2003 (appeal against extradition order under Part 1) shall be made by lodging a note of appeal in Form 34.3-A;

(b) section 28(1) of the Act of 2003 (appeal against discharge at extradition hearing under Part 1) shall be made by lodging a note of appeal in Form 34.3-B;

(c) section 103(1) (appeal where case sent to Scottish Ministers) or 108(1) (appeal against extradition order) of the Act of 2003 shall be made by lodging a note of appeal in Form 34.3-C;

(d) section 105(1) (appeal against discharge at extradition hearing) or section 110(1) (appeal against discharge by Scottish Ministers) of the Act of 2003 shall be made by lodging a note of appeal in Form 34.3-D, with the clerk.

(2) Notice of an appeal mentioned in paragraph (1) shall be given by serving a copy of the note of appeal—

(a) in the case of an appeal under section 26(1), 103(1) or 108(1) of the Act of 2003, on the Crown Agent, and

(b) in the case of an appeal under section 28(1), 105(1) or 110(1) of the Act of 2003, on the arrested person.

(3) No note of appeal under this rule shall be lodged without an execution of service.

(4) In this rule, "the clerk" means—

(a) in the case of an appeal under section 26(1), 28(1), 103(1) or 105(1) of the Act of 2003, the sheriff clerk, and

(b) in the case of an appeal under section 108(1) or 110(1) of the Act of 2003, the Clerk of Justiciary.

Hearing of appeals

34.4.—(1) The sheriff clerk shall, on the making of an appeal under section 26(1) (appeal against extradition order under Part 1), 28(1) (appeal against discharge at extradition hearing under Part 1), 103(1) (appeal where case sent to Scottish Ministers) or 105(1) (appeal against discharge at extradition hearing) of the Act of 2003—

(a) request a report from the presiding sheriff; and

(b) transmit—

(i) the note of appeal;

(ii) two certified copies of the minutes of proceedings; and

(iii) any other relevant documents,

to the Clerk of Justiciary who shall fix a diet for the hearing of the appeal.

(2) The Clerk of Justiciary shall, on the making of an appeal under section 108(1) (appeal against extradition order) or 110(1) (appeal against discharge by Scottish Ministers) of the Act of 2003, request a report from the Scottish Ministers and fix a diet for the hearing of the appeal.

(3) Within 14 days of the making of an appeal, the sheriff or, as the case may be, the Scottish Ministers shall comply with the request under paragraph (1)(a) or (2).

(4) The Clerk of Justiciary shall—

(a) intimate the date of any diet fixed under paragraph (1) or (2); and

(b) send a copy of the report received from the sheriff or, as the case may be, the Scottish Ministers, to the arrested person and the Crown Agent.

(5) Subject to section 31(4) of the Act of 2003 (extension of relevant period), the High Court shall begin to hear an appeal under section 26(1) or 28(1) of the Act of 2003 within 40 days after the date on which the arrested person—

(a) was arrested under section 5 of the Act of 2003, if he was arrested under that section;

(b) was arrested under the Part 1 warrant, if he was not arrested under that section.

(6) Subject to section 113(3) of the Act of 2003, the High Court shall begin to hear an appeal under section 103(1), 105(1), 108(1) or 110(1) of the Act of 2003 within 76 days after the date on which the note of appeal is lodged.

Applications for extension of time

34.5—(1) Subject to paragraph (2), an application seeking an extension of the relevant period under section 31(4) (extension of time limit for start of hearing) or section 113(4) (extension of time limit for start of hearing) of the Act of 2003 shall be lodged with the Clerk of Justiciary in Form 34.5, and the applicant shall serve a copy of the application on the other party in the appeal.

(2) At the diet fixed for the hearing of the appeal or an application mentioned in paragraph (1), the court may dispense with the requirements of paragraph (1).

Consent to extradition

34.6. Notice of consent to extradition shall be given—

(a) in the case of extradition to a category 1 territory, in Form 34.6-A; and

(b) in the case of extradition to a category 2 territory, in Form 34.6-B.

Post-extradition matters

34.7.—(1) A notice under section 54(4) (notice of request for consent to another offence being dealt with) of the Act of 2003 shall be in Form 34.7-A.

(2) A notice under section 56(4) (notice of request for consent extradition to another category 1 territory) of the Act of 2003 shall be in Form 34.7-B.

Part 3 warrants

34.8. Subject to section 142 of the Act of 2003, a Part 3 warrant issued by a sheriff shall be in the form set out in the Annex to Council Framework Decision 2002/584/JHA of 13 June 2002 on the European arrest warrant and the surrender procedures between Member States, with such variation as circumstances may require.

AMENDMENT

Chapter 34 substituted by the Act of Adjournal (Criminal Procedure Rules Amendment No.3) (Extradition etc.) 2004 (SSI 2004/346), r.2 (effective August 18, 2004).

GENERAL NOTE

Part 2 of the Extradition Act 2003 (which comprises ss.69–141) makes provision for extradition to what are termed "category 2" territories. These territories are states which, although they have an extradition treaty with the United Kingdom, are not party to the EU Council Framework Decision of June 13, 2002 on the European Arrest Warrant (see O.J. 2002 L 190). However, it is not a prerequisite for designation as a category 1 territory that the Framework Decision should apply to that state. The power to designate category 1 territories is not limited to member states of the European Union. The only restriction on designation is in s.1(3) of the 2003 Act, namely that a territory may not be designated for the purposes of Part I if a person found guilty in that territory of a criminal offence may be sentenced to death for the offence under the general criminal law of the territory (*Dabas v High Court of Justice in Madrid, Spain* [2007] 2 W.L.R. 254 at p.263 (para.24), per Lord Hope of Craighead).

It is worth noticing that the High Court in an appeal concerning an extradition request from the USA, stated:

"There is a strong public interest in the United Kingdom meeting its treaty obligations. There is also a strong public interest in the effective prosecution of trans-national crimes . . . It is important to the rule of law and to international comity that a person who is the subject of a proper request should be extradited to stand trial . . . There is also a strong public interest in honouring extradition treaties made with other states . . . It would only be in exceptional circumstances that the courts would be justified in not ordering extradition where that would otherwise be lawful." (*Calder v HM Advocate*; Calder v The Scottish Ministers [2006] HCJAC 71; 2006 S.C.C.R. 609, para.[17]).

Provisional warrants

Section 73 of the 2003 Act provides, so far as concerns Scotland (see s.73(10)), that the sheriff may issue a warrant for the arrest of a person who is either accused in a category 2 territory of the commission of an offence or alleged to be unlawfully at large after conviction of an offence by a court in a territory 2 country where the sheriff is satisfied on an application by the procurator fiscal that that person (a) is or is believed to be in the United Kingdom, or (b) is or is believed to be "on his way" to the United Kingdom (s.73(1) and (2)). Such a warrant is known as a "provisional warrant" (ss.73(3) and 216(12)) and may be issued if the sheriff has reasonable grounds for believing that (a) the offence of which the person is accused or has been convicted is an extradition offence, and (b) there is written evidence that would either justify the issue of a warrant for the person's arrest for the offence if committed in the sheriff's jurisdiction or justify his arrest for being unlawfully at large within the sheriff's jurisdiction (s.73(3) and (4)). (Where the category 2 territory has been designated for the purposes of s.73, information and not evidence will suffice: s.73(5)).

Rule 34.2

Where a person is arrested under a provisional warrant, he must be given a copy of the warrant as soon as practicable after his arrest (s.74(2)) and if that direction is not complied with and the arrested person applies to the sheriff to be discharged, the sheriff *may* order his discharge (s.74(5)). Further, the arrested person must be brought before the sheriff as soon as practicable after his arrest (s.74(3)) and if that is not done and the person applies to the sheriff to be discharged, the sheriff *must* order his discharge (s.74(6)). This latter requirement does not apply where either the person is granted bail following his arrest or the Scottish Ministers, having received a valid request for his extradition, decide under s.126 because of competing extradition requests, that the particular request is not to be proceeded with (s.74(4)).

Prior to the extradition hearing held under s.76, there must be at least one review hearing at which the sheriff must ascertain the state of preparation of the parties for the extradition hearing. The first review hearing should be fixed when the arrested person is first brought before the court. At that time the sheriff must also (i) inform the person that he is accused of the commission of an offence in the category 2 territory or that he is alleged to be unlawfully at large following conviction there; (ii) give the person the required information (defined in s.74(8)) about his option of consenting to extradition, whereby the procedure is expedited; and (iii) remand the person in custody or on bail (s.74(7)).

The "required period" referred to in r.34.2(2) is either (a) 45 days starting with the day on which the person was arrested, or (b) if the category 2 territory has been designated for the purposes of this provision, any longer period permitted by the designation order (s.74(10)).

CHAPTER 35

COMPUTER MISUSE ACT 1990

Notices in relation to relevance of external law

35.1. A notice under section 8(5) of the Computer Misuse Act 1990 (notice by defence that conditions not satisfied) shall be served on the prosecutor not later than 14 days before the trial diet.

CHAPTER 36

CRIME (INTERNATIONAL CO-OPERATION) ACT 2003

Interpretation of this Chapter

36.1. In this Chapter—

"Act of 2003" means the Crime (International Co-operation) Act 2003; and

"external court" means the court mentioned in section 30(1) or, as the case may be, section 31(1) of the Act of 2003; and.

"nominated court" means a court nominated under section 15(3), section 30(3) or section 31(4) of the Act of 2003.

Effecting citation or service of documents outside the United Kingdom

36.2.—(1) A notice under section 5(5)(b) of the Act of 2003 (notice to accompany citation being effected outside the United Kingdom) shall be in Form 36.2 and shall give the information specified in that form.

(2) Where citation is being effected outside the United Kingdom under section 5 or 6 of the Act of 2003, in the form of citation for—

"IF YOU DO NOT ATTEND COURT WITHOUT A LAWFUL EXCUSE

THE COURT MAY ORDER THAT YOU BE APPREHENDED AND PUNISHED."

or

"IF YOU FAIL TO ATTEND WITHOUT A LAWFUL EXCUSE THE COURT MAY ISSUE A WARRANT FOR YOUR ARREST."

or

"A warrant may be issued for your arrest",

there shall be substituted the following—

"As this citation is being effected outside the United Kingdom, no obligation under the law of Scotland to comply with the citation is imposed by virtue of its being so effected. Accordingly, failure to comply with the citation does not constitute contempt of court and is not a ground for issuing a warrant to secure your attendance or for imposing a penalty. But this citation may subsequently be effected against you in the United Kingdom, in which case, if you fail to attend without a lawful excuse, the court may issue a warrant for your arrest."

(3) Where a document is to be served on a person outside the United Kingdom under section 6 of the Act of 2003 (effecting citation etc. otherwise than by post), it shall be sent by the Clerk of Justiciary, sheriff clerk or clerk of the district court, as the case may be, to the Lord Advocate.

Proof of citation or service outside the United Kingdom

36.3. The service on any person of a citation or document under section 6 of the Act of 2003 (effecting citation etc. otherwise than by post) may be proved in any legal proceedings by a certificate given by or on behalf of the Lord Advocate.

Applications for requests for assistance

36.4. An application under section 7(1) of the Act of 2003 (application for request for assistance) shall—

(a) be in Form 36.4-A;

(b) be lodged with the Clerk of Justiciary or sheriff clerk, as the case may be; and

(c) state the particulars of the offence which it is alleged has been committed or the grounds on which it is suspected that an offence has been committed;

(d) state whether proceedings in respect of the offence have been instituted or the offence is being investigated; and

(e) include particulars of the assistance requested and a draft request in Form 36.4-B.

Hearing of applications for requests for assistance

36.5.—(1) Where the prosecutor presents an application under section 7(1) of the Act of 2003 (application for request for assistance) before either the first appearance of the accused on petition or the service of a summary complaint, the High Court or the sheriff, as the case may be, shall, without requiring intimation to any other party, proceed to consider the application.

(2) Where any party presents such an application following the first appearance of the accused on petition or the service of a summary complaint, the High Court or sheriff, as the case may be, may—

(a) before the lodging of an indictment, dispense on cause shown with intimation to any other party and proceed to consider the application; or

(b) fix a diet for hearing the application and order intimation of the diet and application to any other party.

(3) The High Court or sheriff, as the case may be, after considering such application—

(a) may allow summary adjustment of the statement of assistance required in the draft request;

(b) shall grant the application, with or without any modifications which it or he deems appropriate, or shall refuse it.

(4) On granting such application the High Court or sheriff, as the case may be, shall—

(a) approve and sign the draft request;

(b) if English is not an official language of the court or authority to which the request is addressed, specify a period within which a translation of the request and of any production is to be lodged.

Register of applications for requests for assistance

36.6.—(1) A register shall be kept by the Clerk of Justiciary and by the sheriff clerk of applications under section 7(1) of the Act of 2003 (application for request for assistance).

(2) Save as authorised by the court, the register mentioned in paragraph (1) shall not be open to inspection by any person.

Notification of requests for assistance

36.7. Where a court sends a request for assistance under section 8 of the Act of 2003 other than on an application by or on behalf of the Lord Advocate, the Clerk of Justiciary or sheriff clerk, as the case may be, shall forthwith notify the Lord Advocate of this and send with the notification a copy of the letter of request.

Citation for proceedings before a nominated court

36.8.—(1) The warrant to cite a person to proceedings before a nominated court shall be in Form 36.8-A.

(2) The form of postal citation of a person to proceedings before a nominated court shall be in Form 36.8-B; and the person shall complete and return Form 36.8-C to the procurator fiscal.

(3) The form of personal citation of a person to proceedings before a nominated court shall be in Form 36.8-D.

Proceedings before a nominated court

36.9.—(1) In proceedings before a nominated court—

(a) the procurator fiscal or Crown counsel shall participate in any hearing;

(b) the prosecutor of the requesting country mentioned in the request under section 13(1) of the Act of 2003 (request for assistance from overseas authorities) may participate in any hearing;

(c) where the request under section 13(1) of the Act of 2003 originates from current criminal proceedings any party to or persons with an interest in those proceedings may attend and, with the leave of the court, participate in any hearing;

(d) a judge or investigating magistrate in the current criminal proceedings may participate in any hearing;

(e) a lawyer or person with a right of audience from the requesting country who represents any party to the current criminal proceedings may participate in any hearing;

(f) a solicitor or counsel instructed by any party may participate in any hearing;

(g) any other person may, with the leave of the court, participate in any hearing;

(h) a shorthand writer may be present to record the proceedings; and

(i) the proceedings shall be in private.

(2) Where any person applies for leave to participate in any hearing the court shall, in determining such application, consider any relevant representations made by the court or authority making the request under section 13(1).

Provision of interpreters

36.10.—(1) This rule applies where a court has been nominated under section 30(3) (nomination to facilitate the giving of evidence by live television link) or section 31(4) (nomination to facilitate the giving of evidence by telephone) of the Act of 2003.

(2) Where it appears to the Clerk of Justiciary or sheriff clerk, as the case may be, that the witness is likely to give evidence in a language other than English, he shall make arrangements for an interpreter to be present at the proceedings to translate what is said into English.

(3) Where it appears to the Clerk of Justiciary or sheriff clerk, as the case may be, that the witness is likely to give evidence in a language other than that in which the proceedings of the external court will be conducted, he shall make arrangements for an interpreter to translate what is said into the language in which the proceedings of the external court will be conducted.

(4) Where the evidence in proceedings before a nominated court is either given in a language other than English or is not translated into English by an interpreter, the High Court or, as the case may be, the sheriff, shall continue the proceedings until such time as a translator can be present to provide a translation into English.

Court record of proceedings before a nominated court

36.11.—(1) Where a court receives evidence in proceedings by virtue of a nomination under section 15(3) (nomination to receive evidence), section 30(3) (nomination to facilitate the giving of evidence by live television link), or section 31(4) (nomination to facilitate the giving of evidence by telephone) of the Act of 2003, the Clerk of Justiciary or sheriff clerk, as the case may be, shall record in the minute of proceedings—

(a) particulars of the proceedings; and

(b) without prejudice to the generality of (a) above—

　(i) which persons were present;

　(ii) which of those persons was represented and by whom; and

　(iii) whether any of those persons was denied the opportunity of cross-examining a witness as to any part of his testimony.

(2) Save as authorised by the Lord Advocate or, with the leave of the court, the minute of proceedings mentioned in paragraph (1) above shall not be open to inspection by any person.

(3) The Clerk of Justiciary or sheriff clerk, as the case may be, shall send to the Lord Advocate and to the external authority a certified copy of the minute of proceedings.

(4) Where the court has been nominated under section 15(3) of the Act of 2003 the Clerk of Justiciary or sheriff clerk, as the case may be, shall comply with paragraph 6 of Schedule 1 to the Act of 2003 with regard to the forwarding of evidence received by the court.

AMENDMENT

Chapter 36 substituted by the Act of Adjournal (Criminal Procedure Rules Amendment) (Miscellaneous) 2004 (SSI 2004/195), r.2 (effective April 26, 2004).

Part 1 of the Crime (International Co-operation) Act 2003 deals with mutual assistance to be given by UK courts in respect of criminal proceedings and investigations. Sections 7–12 of Ch.2 of Part 1 provide for assistance in obtaining evidence from abroad. If it appears to any judge of the High Court of Justiciary or any sheriff, on an application made by (a) a prosecuting authority in England and Wales or Northern Ireland, (b) the Lord Advocate or a procurator fiscal, or (c) where proceedings have been instituted, the person charged in those proceedings (s.7(3)), that an offence has been committed (or that there are reasonable grounds for suspecting that that is so) *and* that proceedings in respect of that offence have been instituted (or that the offence is being investigated), the judge or sheriff may request assistance "in obtaining outside the United Kingdom any evidence specified in the request for use in the proceedings or investigation" (s.7(1) and (2)).

Section 13 makes provision for the reverse of s.7, namely assistance to overseas authorities in obtaining evidence within the United Kingdom. Where a request for assistance in obtaining evidence in Scotland is received by the Lord Advocate (who is the "territorial authority" in Scotland: s.28(9)) he may, if conditions specified in s.14 are met, arrange for the evidence to be obtained under s.15; or he may direct that a search warrant be applied for under or by virtue of s.18 (s.13(1)). Such a request for assistance may be made *only* by a court exercising criminal jurisdiction, or a prosecuting authority, in a foreign country; or any other foreign authority which appears to the Lord Advocate to have "the function of making such requests for assistance"; or the International Criminal Police Organisation; or any other body or person competent to make such a request under any provisions adopted under the Treaty on European Union (s.13(2) and (3)).

Nominated court

Under s.15(3) the Lord Advocate, upon receipt of such a request, may by a notice nominate a sheriff court to receive any evidence which relates to that request and appears to that court to be appropriate for the purpose of giving effect to the request. However, where it appears to the Lord Advocate that the request relates to an offence involving serious or complex fraud, he may give a direction under s.27 of the Criminal Law (Consolidation) (Scotland) Act 1995 (s.15(4)). Section 27 provides that the Lord Advocate may give a direction (which must be personally signed by the Lord Advocate: s.27(4)) when, for the purpose of investigating the affairs or any aspect of the affairs of any person (in the course of investigating a suspected offence which may involve serious or complex fraud), he is satisfied that there is good reason to do so (s.27(1) and (2)). The direction may also be made at the request of the Attorney-General of the Isle of Man, Jersey or Guernsey acting under legislation corresponding to Part IV of the 1995 Act (s.27(2)). The direction nominates a person who is then entitled to exercise the powers and functions conferred by Part IV (s.27(3)).

The sheriff's jurisdiction is to determine whether the evidence which he is asked to receive is evidence falling within the description in s.15(3). The High Court has stated: "The sheriff has no broader discretion to exercise than that .   .   . His sole concern is whether the evidence which he is asked to receive is within the proper scope of the request .   .   . the sheriff is concerned only with a process of evidence gathering. It is no part of his function to consider what may be made of the evidence by the requesting State. Nor is it part of his function to consider whether the evidence may lead the requesting State to request the extradition of the suspect. These are matters for the requesting State .   .   . Equally, it is no part of the sheriff's function to consider whether sending the evidence to the requesting State will affect the ability of the Scottish prosecuting authorities to prosecute the suspect in Scotland. That is a matter for the Lord Advocate in deciding whether in principle to give effect to the request by nominating a court to receive the evidence." (*Calder v Frame* [2006] HCJAC 62; 2006 S.L.T. 862; 2006 S.C.C.R. 487, para.[31]).

Evidence by television link or telephone for use in overseas proceedings

The last two rules in this chapter are required to give effect to two provisions of Ch.3 of Part 1 of the 2003 Act, namely the hearing of evidence through television links and by telephone. Under s.30(3), unless the Lord Advocate considers it inappropriate to do so, where he receives a request from an external authority (which is defined in s.30(2)) for "a person in the United Kingdom to give evidence through a live television link in criminal proceedings before a court in a country outside the United Kingdom", he *must* by written notice nominate a court in Scotland where that can be done. The nominated court must be either the High Court or the sheriff court. The notice need not be personally authorised by the Lord Advocate (see *HM Advocate v Copeland*, 1988 S.L.T. 249 and note to r.36.8 *infra*). Foreign proceedings include any proceedings on an appeal "before a court against a decision in administrative proceedings" (s.30(1)) and will by parity of reasoning also include evidence in the course of criminal appeals.

Section 31 replicates s.30 in respect of requests from an external authority to take evidence by telephone. The Lord Advocate must nominate a court unless he considers it inappropriate for the request to be acceded to. The request under s.31, unlike a request under s.30, must specify the external court, the name and address of the witness and state whether the witness is willing to give evidence by telephone in the proceedings before the external court (s.31(3)).

Rule 36.4

Applications under s.7 are for the issue of a request to a foreign state for assistance in obtaining evidence abroad. Such requests can be made either because proceedings have been raised or because a suspected offence is under investigation. Hence the requirement in r.36.4(d). The offences must have been committed in Scotland. Applications can be made to either the High Court or the sheriff court and are made by the Lord Advocate or the appropriate procurator fiscal.

Rule 36.5

For the purposes of intimation of an application for the issue of a request for foreign assistance, a distinction is drawn on the basis of the stage of the proceedings. Where neither petition nor summary complaint has been served, the court need not require intimation be given to the suspect. However, once the initiating document has been served the party making the application may seek dispensation from intimation to the suspect if he can show cause. Rule 36.5(2)(a) refers only to the period prior to the lodging of an indictment but that is inconsistent with the preceding reference to service of a summary complaint. Does it not make sense for the court also to be able to dispense with intimation on cause shown after service of a complaint?

Rule 36.8

The Lord Advocate may nominate an appropriate court to receive the evidence which the foreign authority seeks to obtain in Scotland. Such nomination must be given in writing (s.15(3)) but, unlike the direction under s.27 of the Criminal Law (Consolidation) (Scotland) Act 1995 (see above), does not require to be personally signed by the Lord Advocate (see *HM Advocate v Copeland*, 1988 S.L.T. 249; *Somerville v The Scottish Ministers*, [2006] CSIH 52; 2007 S.L.T. 96, para.[101]; and *Carltona Limited v Commissioners of Works* [1943] 2 All E.R. 560).

Rule 36.9

It is competent for the sheriff, at the hearing when he is to take his decision on the evidence which he is to receive, to proceed without intimation of the hearing having been given to the suspect. Rule 36.9 contains no requirement to notify (or even to consider notifying) the suspect of the hearing and the absence of any such requirement cannot amount to an absence of sufficient procedural safeguards such as to render the sheriff's decision unlawful under Art.8(1) of, and Art.1 of the First Protocol to, the European Convention on Human Rights (*Calder v Frame*, 2006 S.L.T. 862 at para.[33]).

Rule 36.10

Most external courts will not conduct their proceedings in English and it is also to be readily anticipated that witnesses will not speak English and may indeed speak neither English nor the language of the external court. Since the giving of the witness's evidence by either television link or telephone must be controlled by the judge of the nominated court (especially since any contempt by the witness in the presence of the nominated court is a contempt of that court: ss.30(4) and 31(5)), the nominated court must have available an interpreter to translate the witness's evidence into English for the benefit of the nominated court. Hence the direction in r.36.10(4). However, whatever the language in which the witness depones, it must be translated into the language of the external court if that witness's language is foreign to the external court. Wilfully false testimony before the nominated court is deemed perjury and liable to prosecution in Scotland (see ss.30(5) and 31(6)) even though the proceedings are foreign in nature and evidence given in pursuance of ss.30 and 31 is not to be treated for any purpose as evidence given in proceedings in Scotland (see ss.30(7) and 31(8)).

Rule 36.11

The proceedings before the nominated court are necessarily adjectival to the proceedings before the external criminal court. Accordingly, they are not a public matter as proceedings must be when the nominated court is exercising its domestic powers, although they may form part of public proceedings in the external court. Hence, the nominated court's proceedings are not held in public, the persons present and any legal representatives are to be named in the minute of proceedings (r.36.11(1)(b)) and the minute of proceedings are confidential and not to be inspected by anyone except where inspection is authorised by the Lord Advocate or the nominated court (r.36.11(2)). The direction to the appropriate clerk to transmit a certified copy of the minute of proceedings to the Lord

Advocate and the external authority which requested the witness's testimony (r.36.11(3)) is not of such a nature that a failure to comply with it would open the proceedings to challenge in the domestic courts. Parliament could not be taken to have intended such failure to invalidate the proceedings (see *R. v Soneji* [2006] 1 A.C. 340 and *R. v Ashton* [2007] 1 W.L.R. 181).

CHAPTER 37

PROCEEDINGS UNDER THE PROCEEDS OF CRIME (SCOTLAND) ACT 1995

Orders to make material available

37.1.—(1) An application by the procurator fiscal to the sheriff for an order under section 18(2) of the Proceeds of Crime (Scotland) Act 1995 (order to make material available in investigation into whether a person has benefited from commission of an offence shall be made by petition; and section 134 (incidental applications) of the Act of 1995 shall apply to any such application as it applies to an application referred to in that section.

(2) The sheriff may make the order sought in the petition under paragraph (1) before intimation of the petition to the person who appears to him to be in possession of the material to which the application relates.

(3) An application by the procurator fiscal for an order under section 18(5) of the Proceeds of Crime (Scotland) Act 1995 (order to allow constable to enter premises to obtain access to material) may be made in the petition applying for an order under section 18(2); and paragraph (2) of this rule shall apply to an order in respect of a person who appears to the sheriff to be entitled to grant entry to the premises in question as it applies to an order in respect of the person mentioned in that paragraph.

Discharge and variation of orders

37.2.—(1) A person, in respect of whom an order has been made under section 18(2) or (5) of the Proceeds of Crime (Scotland) Act 1995 (which relate to orders to make material available in investigating whether a person has benefited from commission of a offence), may apply to the sheriff for discharge or variation of the order in question.

(2) The sheriff may, after hearing the parties, grant or refuse to grant the discharge or variation sought.

Warrants to search premises

37.3. An application by the procurator fiscal to the sheriff under section 19(1) of the Proceeds of Crime (Scotland) Act 1995 (authority for search) shall be made by petition; and section 134 (incidental applications) of the Act of 1995 shall apply to any such application for a warrant as it applies to an application for a warrant referred to in that section.

Orders under sections 25 and 26

37.4. An application under section 25 (recall etc. of suspended forfeiture order) or 26 (return of property wrongly confiscated etc.) of the Proceeds of Crime (Scotland) Act 1995 by a person other than the accused to the court shall be made by petition in Form 37.4.

Appeals under section 27

37.5. An appeal under section 27 of the Proceeds of Crime (Scotland) Act 1995 (appeal against grant or refusal of application under section 25(1) or 26(1)) shall be in Form 37.5.

AMENDMENTS

Rules 37.1(1), 37.2(1) as amended by Act of Adjournal (Criminal Procedure Rules Amendment) (Miscellaneous) (SI 1996/2147 (S.171)) (effective September 9, 1996).

Rules 37.4 and 37.5 inserted by Act of Adjournal (Criminal Procedure Rules Amendment No.7) (SI 1997/2653) (effective November 21, 1997).

GENERAL NOTE

Section 18(1) of the Proceeds of Crime (Scotland) Act 1995 provides that the procurator fiscal may, for the purpose of an investigation into whether a person has benefited from the commisison of an offence described in s.1(2) of that Act and as to the amount of that benefit, apply to the sheriff for an order (a) to produce material to a constable for the constable to take away, or (b) to give a constable access to it within such period as the sheriff specifies in the order (s.18(2)). Section 18(5) of the 1990 Act provides that where the sheriff makes an order requiring access to be given to a constable he may also, on the application of the procurator fiscal, order any person who appears to him to be entitled to grant entry to the premises to allow a constable to enter the premises to obtain access to the material.

Section 19(1) of the 1995 Act provides that the procurator fiscal may, for the purpose of an investigation as aforesaid and as to the amount of that benefit, apply to the sheriff for a warrant authorising a constable to enter and search specified premises (see s.19(2)).

Section 18(1) and s.19(1) (see r.37.3) do not apply to offences of drug trafficking as that phrase is defined in s.49(2) and (3) of the Proceeds of Crime (Scotland) Act 1995 (see s.18(11))—which are provided for by equivalent legislation in s.31 of the Criminal Law (Consolidation) (Scotland) Act 1995—or into an offence under Part III of the Prevention of Terrorism (Temporary Provisions) Act 1989 which deals with financial assistance from terrorism (see s.1(2) of the Proceeds of Crime (Scotland) Act 1995), but otherwise they have application in respect of any offence which has been prosecuted on indictment or on summary complaint, if the offence is punishable by a fine of an amount greater than the amount corresponding to level 5 on the standard scale or by imprisonment for a period longer than three months or by both such fine and imprisonment.

Rules 37.1 and 37.3 apply the provisions of s.134 of the 1995 Act to such warrants which should in each case be applied for to the sheriff by way of petition. In view of the need to avoid giving warning to persons who are suspected of benefiting from drug trafficking the sheriff is entitled to grant the warrant before intimation has been given to the "suspects" of the procurator fiscal's application.

CHAPTER 37AA

PROCEEDINGS UNDER THE PROCEEDS OF CRIME ACT 2002

Interpretation of this Chapter

37AA.1 In this Chapter "the Act of 2002" means the Proceeds of Crime Act 2002.

CONFISCATION

Confiscation orders

37AA.2—(1) A request by the prosecutor under subsection (3) of section 92 of the Act of 2002 (making of order) may be made orally at the bar.

(2) A person who wishes to make representations to the court under subsection (8) of section 92 of the Act of 2002 shall do so—

(a) in writing to the Clerk of Court, unless the court otherwise directs; and

(b) by such date as the court directs.

(3) An application under—

(a) subsection (2) of section 111 (conviction or other disposal of accused); or

(b) subsection (2) of section 112 (accused neither convicted nor acquitted),

of the Act of 2002 may be made—

    (i) orally at the bar; or

    (ii) by minute.

Disposal of family home

37AA.3 An application by an administrator under subsection (2) of section 98 of the Act of 2002 (disposal of family home) to dispose of a right or interest in a person's family home shall be—

    (a) by petition; and

    (b) served on—

        (i) the person in respect of whose right or interest the application is made; and

        (ii) any other person likely to be affected by the application.

Application for postponement

37AA.4 An application by the accused or the prosecutor for postponement or extension under subsection (7) of section 99 of the Act of 2002 (postponement)—

    (a) may be made either—

        (i) orally at the bar; or

        (ii) in writing by minute; and

    (b) may be determined by the court without a hearing.

Statement of information

37AA.5—(1) This rule applies where the court ordains the prosecutor to give a statement of information or further statement of information, as the case may be, under any of the following provisions of the Act of 2002—

    (a) subsection (1) of section 101 (statement of information);

    (b) subsection (5) of that section; or

    (c) paragraph (b) of subsection (2) of section 110 (information).

(2) The prosecutor shall give a statement referred to in the foregoing paragraph within such period as the court determines.

(3) The prosecutor shall serve a copy of a statement given in terms of paragraph (1) on the accused.

(4) An accused who gives an indication under subsection (1) of section 102 of the Act of 2002 (accused's response to statement of information) shall do so in writing to the Clerk of Court.

Reconsideration of case, benefit or available amount

37AA.6—(1) This rule applies to an application by the prosecutor under any of the following provisions of the Act of 2002—

    (a) to consider new evidence under—

        (i) paragraph (c) of subsection (1) of section 104 (no order made: reconsideration of case);

        (ii) paragraph (b) of subsection (3) of section 105 (no order made: reconsideration of benefit); or

        (ii) paragraph (d) of subsection (1) of section 106 (order made: reconsideration of benefit); and

    (b) to make a new calculation of the available amount under paragraph (c) of subsection (1) of section 107 (order made: reconsideration of available amount).

(2) An application mentioned in the foregoing paragraph—

    (a) shall be made by minute; and

    (b) shall be served by the prosecutor on the accused and any other person likely to be affected by it.

Variation or discharge of confiscation order

37AA.7—(1) Any of the following applications made under any of the following provisions of the Act of 2002 shall be by minute—

(a) by the accused or the prosecutor under paragraph (b) of subsection (1) of section 108 (inadequacy of available amount: variation of order);

(b) by the prosecutor under paragraph (b) of subsection (1) of section 109 (inadequacy of available amount: discharge of order);

(c) by the accused under paragraph (e) of subsection (1) of section 113 (variation of order); or

(d) by the accused under—

    (i) paragraph (c) of subsection (1); or

    (ii) paragraph (d) of subsection (3),

of section 114 (discharge of order).

(2) A party who makes an application mentioned in the foregoing paragraph shall serve a copy on every person likely to be affected by it.

Time for payment

37AA.8—(1) An application by the accused under subsection (4) of section 116 of the Act of 2002 (time for payment) may be made—

(a) by minute; or

(b) orally at the bar.

(2) Where an accused makes an application by minute, he shall serve a copy on the prosecutor.

Hearings

37AA.9 Any request or application mentioned in the following rules shall be determined at a hearing, unless the court otherwise directs:

(a) 37AA.2 (confiscation orders);

(b) 37AA.3 (disposal of family home);

(c) 37AA.6 (reconsideration of case, benefit or available amount);

(d) 37AA.7 (variation or discharge of confiscation order),

(e) 37AA.8 (time for payment);

(f) 37AA.10 (application, discharge and variation).

AMENDMENT

Rule 37AA.9 as amended by Act of Adjournal (Criminal Procedure Rules Amendment No.2) (Miscellaneous) 2003 (SSI 2003/468), r.2. Brought into force on October 27, 2003 in accordance with art.1.

INVESTIGATIONS

Application, discharge and variation

37AA.10—(1) The following applications shall be by petition—

(a) by the appropriate person to the Sheriff under any of the following provisions of the Act of 2002—

    (i) subsection (1) of section 380 (production orders);

    (ii) subsection (1) of section 387 (search warrants);

    (iii) subsection (1) of section 397 (customer information orders);

    (iv) subsection (1) of section 404 (account monitoring orders),

    in relation to a confiscation investigation or money laundering investigation; and

(b) by the Lord Advocate, to the High Court of Justiciary under subsection (1) of section 391 of that Act (disclosure orders) for a disclosure order in relation to a confiscation investigation.

(2) An application under subsection (2) of section 382 of the Act of 2002 (order to grant entry)—

(a) may be included in a petition in respect of an application under paragraph (1)(a)(i) of this rule; or

(b) if made after the lodging of the petition, shall be by minute,

and paragraph (3) of this rule shall apply to such an application.

(3) An application under any of the following provisions of the Act of 2002 shall be by minute and shall be intimated to any person affected by it—

(a) subsection (4) of section 386 (production orders: supplementary) to discharge or vary a production order or an order to grant entry;

(b) subsection (4) of section 396 (disclosure orders: supplementary) to discharge or vary a disclosure order;

(c) subsection (4) of section 403 (customer information orders: supplementary) to discharge or vary a customer information order;

(d) subsection (4) of section 408 (account monitoring orders: supplementary) to discharge or vary an account monitoring order.

AMENDMENT

Chapter 37AA inserted by Act of Adjournal (Criminal Procedure Rules Amendment) (Proceeds of Crime Act 2002) 2003 (SSI 2003/120), r.2. Brought into force on February 24, 2003 (for proceedings under Chapter 3 of Part 8 of the Proceeds of Crime Act 2002) and on March 24, 2003 (for proceedings under Part 3 of that Act).

CHAPTER 37A

PROCEEDINGS UNDER SECTION 7 OF THE KNIVES ACT 1997

37A. An application to the sheriff under section 7(3) of the Knives Act 1997 (recovery order for delivery of property to applicant if it appears to court that he owns it) shall be made by petition in Form 37A.

AMENDMENT

Rule 37A inserted by Act of Adjournal (Criminal Procedure Rules Amendment No.6) (SI 1997/2081) (effective September 1, 1997).

CHAPTER 38

TRANSFER OF RIGHTS OF APPEAL OF DECEASED PERSONS

Applications for transfer under section 303A of the Act of 1995

38. Any application to the High Court under section 303A of the Act of 1995 for an order authorising a person (the "applicant") as executor, or as the case may be by reason of his having a legitimate interest, to institute or continue any appeal which could have been or has been instituted by a deceased person shall be made in Form 38 and shall be accompanied by a copy of the confirmation of the applicant as executor or evidence of his legitimate interest, as the case may be.

AMENDMENT

Rule 38 inserted by Act of Adjournal (Criminal Procedure Rules Amendment No.4) (SI 1997/1834) (effective August 1, 1997).

GENERAL NOTE

Section 20 of the Crime and Punishment (Scotland) Act 1997 (c.48) amended the 1995 Act by inserting a new provision (s.303A) in implementation of recommendation 16 of the Sutherland Committee's Report on Appeals Criteria and Miscarriages of Justice (Cmnd 3245 (1996), para.5.61) which itself was strongly influenced by the introduction in England in the Criminal Appeal Act 1995 of a similar right of appeal where the convicted person had died.

The convicted person's executor or anyone having a legitimate interest in the outcome of the appeal can not only continue with an appeal already commenced by the deceased before his death but also commence such an appeal (s.303A(1) and (4)). The deceased's representative requires the High Court's authority which must be sought within three months of the deceased's death or, where cause is shown, at such later time as the court allows (s.303A(2)). The transferred right relates not only to all statutory appeals relating to conviction and sentence but also to bills of suspension, bills of advocation and petititons to the *nobile officium* for review of "any conviction, penalty or other order made in respect of the deceased" (s.303A(6)).

In such appeals the deceased's representative or other person having a legitimate interest must stand in the deceased's shoes and accordingly where time has begun to run against the deceased, his representative only has the benefit of that portion of the time limit which remains unexpired at the date of the deceased's death (s.303A(5)).

Following the recommendation of the Sutherland Committee's Report (*supra*, para.5.50), the Scottish Criminal Cases Review Commission was created by s.25 of the Crime and Punishment (Scotland) Act 1997 (inserting Part XA into the Criminal Procedure (Scotland) Act 1995) and became operational on April 1, 1999. The transferred right shall apply also to appeals resulting from references by the Commission, but in such cases the executor or other interested person will require to apply to the court for an order under s.303A(1) within one month of the date of the deceased's death (s.303A(3)). The mother of a man convicted of lewd, indecent and libidinous practices was authorised to continue with her son's appeal against conviction when he died after having marked an appeal and obtained interim liberation. The appeal was successful: see *Cowan (Deceased) v H.M. Advocate*, May 3, 2001, Appeal Court (unreported).

In *R. v Whelan* [1997] Crim.L.R. 659, the Court of Appeal (Criminal Division) in England allowed a widow to continue with her deceased's husband's appeal against conviction for sexual offences because the couple had been close and she was doing what her husband had wished to be done to clear his name. In *R. v Bentley* [1998] T.L.R. 492 the Court of Appeal quashed a conviction for murder (in respect of which the accused had been hanged) on an appeal brought by the accused's niece following a reference to the Court of Appeal by the English Criminal Cases Review Commission. In *R. v Hanratty* (October 17, 2000) *The Times*, October 26, 2000, the Court of Appeal gave directions for the exhumation of the remains of a convicted murderer so that DNA samples could be obtained in order to assist in the determination of the murderer's appeal which was brought by the murderer's brother after a reference to the Court of Appeal by the Criminal Cases Review Commission.

CHAPTER 39

PROCEEDINGS UNDER CRIMINAL LAW (CONSOLIDATION) (SCOTLAND) ACT 1995

Orders to make material available

39.1.—(1) An application by the procurator fiscal to the sheriff for an order under section 31(2) of the Criminal Law (Consolidation) (Scotland) Act 1995 (order to make material available in investigation into drug trafficking) shall be made by petition; and section 134 of the Act of 1995 (incidental applications) shall apply to an application under section 31(2) as it applies to an application under section 31(2) as it applies to an application to which section 134 applies.

(2) The sheriff may make the order sought in the petition under paragraph (1) before intimation of the petition to the person who appears to him to be in possession of the material to which the application relates.

(3) An application by the procurator fiscal for an order under section 31(5) of the Criminal Law (Consolidation) (Scotland) Act 1995 (order allowing constable or person commissioned by Customs and Excise access to premises to obtain material) may be made in the petition applying for an order under section 31(2) of that Act; and paragraph (2) shall apply to an order in respect of a person who appears to the sheriff to be entitled to grant entry to the premises in question as it applies to an order in respect of the person mentioned in that paragraph.

Discharge and variation of orders

39.2.—(1) A person in respect of whom an order has been made under section 31(2) or (5) of the Criminal Law (Consolidation) (Scotland) Act 1995 may apply to the sheriff for discharge or variation of the order in question.

(2) The sheriff may, after hearing the parties, grant or refuse to grant the discharge or variation sought.

Warrants to search premises

39.3. An application by the procurator fiscal to the sheriff under section 32(1) of the Criminal Law (Consolidation) (Scotland) Act 1995 (authority for search) shall be made by petition; and section 134 of the Act of 1995 (incidental applications) shall apply to an application under section 32(1) as it applies to an application to which section 134 applies.

CHAPTER 40

DEVOLUTION ISSUES

Interpretation of this Chapter

40.1.—(1) In this Chapter—

"Advocate General" means the Advocate General for Scotland;

"devolution issue" means a devolution issue within the meaning of—

    (a) Schedule 6 to the Scotland Act 1998;

    (b) Schedule 10 to the Northern Ireland Act 1998; or

    (c) Schedule 8 to the Government of Wales Act 1998,

and any reference to Schedule 6, Schedule 10 or Schedule 8 is a reference to that Schedule to, respectively, the Scotland Act 1998, the Northern Ireland Act 1998 and the Government of Wales Act 1998;

"the Judicial Committee" means the Judicial Committee of the Privy Council;

"relevant authority" means the Advocate General and—

    (a) in the case of a devolution issue within the meaning of Schedule 6, the Lord Advocate;

    (b) in the case of a devolution issue within the meaning of Schedule 10, the Attorney General for Northern Ireland, and the First Minister and deputy First Minister acting jointly;

    (c) in the case of a devolution issue within the meaning of Schedule 8, the National Assembly for Wales.

(2) For the purposes of this Chapter, a trial shall be taken to commence—

(a) in proceedings on indictment, when the oath is administered to the jury;

(b) in summary proceedings, when the first witness is sworn.

(3) Rule 2.1 (service on the Crown) does not apply to any requirement to serve any document on or give any notice or intimation of any matter to the Lord Advocate in pursuance of this Chapter.

Raising devolution issues: proceedings on indictment

40.2.—(1) Where a party to proceedings on indictment proposes to raise a devolution issue he shall, not later than 7 days after the date of service of the indictment, give written notice of his intention to do so in Form 40.2A to the clerk of the court in which the trial is to take place; and a copy of the notice shall, at the same time, be served on the other parties to the proceedings and on the relevant authority.

(2) The copy notice served on the relevant authority under paragraph (1) shall be treated as intimation of the devolution issue arising in the proceedings as mentioned in paragraph 5 of Schedule 6 or, as the case may be, paragraph 23 of Schedule 10 or paragraph 14(1) of Schedule 8, unless the court determines that no devolution issue arises in the proceedings.

(3) Where a relevant authority wishes to become a party to the proceedings as mentioned in paragraph 6 of Schedule 6 or, as the case may be, paragraph 24 of Schedule 10 or paragraph 14(2) of Schedule 8, he shall, not later than 7 days after receipt of the notice served under paragraph (1), give notice in Form 40.2B to the clerk of the court in which the trial is to take place; and a copy of such notice shall be served on the Lord Advocate and every other party to the proceedings.

(3a) Where a relevant authority does not become a party to the proceedings at first instance the court may allow him to become a party to any subsequent appeal or reference to a higher court.

(4) A record of any notice given under paragraph (1) or (3) shall be made on the record copy of the indictment or in the record of the proceedings, as the case may be.

(5) This Rule is without prejudice to any right of or requirement upon any party to the proceedings to raise any matter, objection, preliminary plea or preliminary issue.

AMENDMENT

Rule 40.2(5) as amended by the Act of Adjournal (Criminal Procedure Rules Amendment) (Criminal Procedure (Amendment) (Scotland) Act 2004) 2005 (SSI 2005/44), r.2(17) (subject to r.2(2)–(4)) (effective February 1, 2005).

Raising devolution issues: summary proceedings

40.3.—(1) Where a party to summary proceedings proposes to raise a devolution issue he shall, before the accused or, where there is more than one accused, any accused is called upon to plead, give notice of his intention to raise the devolution issue in Form 40.3A to the clerk of court; and a copy of the notice shall, at the same time, be served on other parties to the proceedings and on the relevant authority.

(2) The copy notice served on the relevant authority under paragraph (1) shall be treated as intimation of the devolution issue arising in the proceedings as mentioned in paragraph 5 of Schedule 6 or, as the case may be, paragraph 23 of Schedule 10 or paragraph 14(1) of Schedule 8, unless the court determines that no devolution issue arises in the proceedings.

(3) Where notice is given under paragraph (1) the court, unless it determines that no devolution issue arises in the proceedings, shall adjourn the case under section 145 of the Act of 1995.

(4) Where a relevant authority wishes to become a party to the proceedings as mentioned in paragraph 6 of Schedule 6 or, as the case may be, paragraph 24 of Schedule 10 or paragraph 14(2) of Schedule 8, he shall, not later than 7 days after receipt of the notice served under paragraph (1), give notice to the clerk of court in Form 40.3B of his intention to do so: and he shall, at the same time, serve a copy of that notice on any other relevant authority and on every other party to the proceedings.

(5) Where a relevant authority does not become a party to the proceedings at first instance the court may allow him to become a party to any subsequent appeal or reference to a higher court.

Raising devolution issues: other criminal proceedings

40.4.—(1) This Rule applies to criminal proceedings which are not proceedings on indictment or summary proceedings.

(2) Where a party to proceedings to which this Rule applies proposes to raise a devolution issue he shall give notice of his intention to raise the devolution issue in Form 40.4A to the clerk of court; and a copy of the notice shall, at the same time, be served on the other parties to the proceedings and on the relevant authority.

(3) The copy notice served on the relevant authority under paragraph (2) shall be treated as intimation of the devolution issue arising in the proceedings as mentioned in paragraph 5 of Schedule 6 or, as the case may be, paragraph 23 of Schedule 10 or paragraph 14(1) of Schedule 8, unless the court determines that no devolution issue arises in the proceedings.

(4) Where a relevant authority wishes to become a party to the proceedings as mentioned in paragraph 6 of Schedule 6 or, as the case may be, paragraph 24 of Schedule 10 or paragraph 14(2) of Schedule 8, he shall, not later than 7 days after receipt of the notice served under paragraph (1), give notice to the clerk of court in Form 40.4B of his intention to do so: and he shall, at the same time, serve a copy of that notice on any other relevant authority and on every other party to the proceedings.

(5) Where a relevant authority does not become a party to the proceedings at first instance the court may allow him to become a party to any subsequent appeal or reference to a higher court.

Time for raising devolution issue

40.5.—(1) No party to criminal proceedings shall raise a devolution issue in those proceedings except as in accordance with Rule 40.2, 40.3 or 40.4, unless the court, on cause shown, otherwise determines.

(2) Where the court determines that a devolution issue may be raised as mentioned in paragraph (1), it shall make such orders as to the procedure to be followed as appear to it to be appropriate and, in particular, it shall make such orders—

(a) as are necessary to ensure that intimation of the devolution issue is given in writing to the relevant authority for the purposes of paragraph 5 of Schedule 6 or, as the case may be, paragraph 23 of Schedule 10 or paragraph 14(1) of Schedule 8; and

(b) as to the time in which any step is to be taken by any party in the proceedings.

Specification of the devolution issue

40.6. The notice given under paragraph (1) of Rule 40.2 or 40.3 or paragraph (2) of Rule 40.4 shall specify the facts and circumstances and contentions of law on the basis of which it is alleged that a devolution issue arises in the proceedings in sufficient detail to enable the court to determine, for the purposes of paragraph 2 of Schedule 6 or, as the case may be, of Schedule 10 or Schedule 8, whether a devolution issue arises in the proceedings.

Reference of devolution issue to the High Court

40.7.—(1) Where a court, other than a court consisting of two or more judges of the High Court of Justiciary, decides to refer a devolution issue to the High Court of Justiciary under paragraph 9 of Schedule 6 or, as the case may be, paragraph 27 of Schedule 10 or paragraph 17 of Schedule 8, the court shall—

(a) pronounce an order giving directions to the parties about the manner and time in which the reference is to be drafted;

(b) give its reasons for making the reference and cause those reasons to be recorded in the record or minutes of proceedings, as the case may be; and

(c) continue the proceedings from time to time as necessary for the purpose of the reference.

(2) The reference—

(a) shall then be adjusted at the sight of the court in such manner as the court may direct; and

(b) after approval and the making of an appropriate order by the court shall (after the expiry of any period for appeal) be transmitted by the clerk of court to the Clerk of Justiciary with a certified copy of the record or minutes of proceedings, as the case may be, and, where applicable, a certified copy of the relevant indictment or complaint.

(3) Where the court determines that a devolution issue may be raised during a trial, the court shall not refer the devolution issue to the High Court but shall determine the issue itself.

Orders pending determination of devolution issue

40.8.—(1) In any case where a devolution issue arises in criminal proceedings (including proceedings where there is a reference of a devolution issue to the High Court of Justiciary or the Judicial Committee), the court or, in the case of a reference or an appeal to the Judicial Committee, the High Court of Justiciary may make such orders as it considers just and equitable in the circumstances pending the determination of the devolution issue, including—

(a) postponing any diet, including a trial diet, fixed in the case;

(b) making such order as it considers appropriate in relation to bail;

(c) subject to paragraph (2), extending the period within which any step requires to be taken or event to have occurred.

(2) An order under paragraph (1)(c) extending a period which may be extended under section 65 or 147 of the Act of 1995 may be made only by a court which has power to do so under that section; and, for the purposes of that section, the fact that a devolution issue has been raised by the prosecutor shall not, without more, be treated as fault on the part of the prosecutor.

Reference of devolution issue to Judicial Committee

40.9.—(1) This Rule applies where—

(a) a court consisting if two or more judges of the High Court of Justiciary decides to refer a devolution issue to the Judicial Committee under paragraph 11 of Schedule 6 or, as the case may be, paragraph 29 of Schedule 10 or paragraph 19 of Schedule 8; or

(b) a court is required by a relevant authority to refer a devolution issue to the Judicial committee as mentioned in paragraph 33 of Schedule 6 or, as the case may be, paragraph 33 of Schedule 10 or paragraph 30(1) of Schedule 8.

(2) The court shall—

(a) pronounce an order giving directions to the parties about the manner and time in which the reference is to be drafted;

(b) give its reasons for making the reference and cause those reasons to be recorded in the record or minutes of proceedings, as the case may be; and

(c) continue the proceedings from time to time as necessary for the purpose of the reference.

(3) The reference shall include such matters as may be required by Rule 2.9 of the Judicial Committee (Devolution Issues) Rules 1999 and—

(a) shall be adjusted at the sight of the court in such manner as may be so directed; and

(b) after approval and the making of an appropriate order by the court, shall be transmitted by the clerk of court to the Registrar of the Judicial Committee with a certified copy of the record or minutes of proceedings, as the case may be, and, where applicable, a certified copy of the relevant indictment or complaint.

Procedure on receipt of determination of devolution issue

40.10.—(1) Where on a reference of a devolution issue the High Court of Justiciary or, as the case may be, the Judicial Committee has determined the issue and the determination has been received by the clerk of the court which made the reference, the determination shall be laid before the court.

(2) On the determination being laid before the court, the court shall then give directions as to further procedure, which directions shall be intimated by the clerk with a copy of the determination to each of the parties to the proceedings.

Procedure following disposal of appeal by Judicial Committee

40.11. The High Court of Justiciary shall, on the application of any party to the proceedings, fix a diet for the purpose of disposing of any matter in consequence of a judgment of the Judicial Committee on an appeal under paragraph 13(a) of Schedule 6 or, as the case may be, paragraph 31(a) of Schedule 10 or paragraph 21(a) of Schedule 8.

Orders mitigating the effect of certain decisions

40.12.—(1) In any proceedings where the court is considering making an order under—

(a) section 102 of the Scotland Act 1998;

(b) section 81 of the Northern Ireland Act 1998; or

(c) section 110 of the Government of Wales Act 1998,

(power of the court to vary or suspend the effect of certain decisions), the court shall order intimation of the fact to be made by the clerk of court to every person to whom intimation is required to be given by that section.

(2) Intimation as mentioned in paragraph (1) above shall—

(a) be made forthwith in Form 40.12 by first class recorded delivery post; and

(b) specify 7 days, or such other period as the court thinks fit, as the period within which a person may give notice of his intention to take part in the proceedings.

<small>AMENDMENTS</small>

Chapter 40 inserted by the Act of Adjournal (Devolution Issues Rules) 1999 (SI 1999/1346) (effective May 6, 1999).

Rules 40.12(3a), 40.3(5) and 40.4(5) inserted by the Act of Adjournal (Criminal Procedure Rules Amendment) (Miscellaneous) 2000 (SSI 2000/65), para.3 (effective April 7, 2000).

<small>GENERAL NOTE</small>

The Scotland Act 1998 (c.46) provides that the Lord Advocate (and the Solicitor General for Scotland) shall be members of the Scottish Executive: s.44(1)(c). Section 57(2) provides, *inter alia*, that a member of the Scottish Executive has no power to do any act so far as the act is incompatible with any of the "Convention rights" specified in s.1 of the Human Rights Act 1998 (c.42). These "Convention rights" are Arts 2 to 14 of the European Convention for the Protection of Human Rights and Fundamental Freedoms, Arts 1 to 3 of the First Protocol, and Arts 1 and 2 of the Sixth Protocol, as read with Arts 16 to 18 of the Convention. [These provisions are set out in Sch.1 to the Human Rights Act 1998.]

As a consequence of the Lord Advocate's powers being made subject to the requirement of compatibility with these "Convention rights" (although the Lord Advocate's decisions to prosecute or to hold a Fatal Accident Inquiry are not subject to this requirement of compatibility: see s.57(3); *cf. H.M. Advocate v Robb*, 2000 J.C. 127), and more generally as a result of the introduction of a novel jurisdiction in the Judicial Committee of the Privy Council (see ss.288A and 288B of the Criminal Procedure (Scotland) Act 1995) to determine "devolution issues" (as specified in the Scotland Act 1998, s.98 and Sch.6), it became necessary to provide a new procedure for the determination by the court of first instance and by the High Court of questions relating to the competence of the Lord Advocate's actings in criminal prosecutions. Chapter 40 was therefore inserted into the Criminal Procedure Rules 1996 with effect from May 6, 1999 by the Act of Adjournal (Devolution Issues Rules) 1999 (SI 1999/1346) which was made by the Lords Commissioners of Justiciary on May 4, 1999 (as to the *vires* of which, see *H.M. Advocate v Dickson*, 2000 J.C. 93 which was affirmed on appeal by a Bench of Five Judges, 2001 S.C.C.R. 397).

The procedure regulating the raising of devolution issues set out in Chapter 40 is of necessity somewhat novel because it requires to make provision for the involvement of a new United Kingdom Scottish law officer (the Advocate General for Scotland), rights of appeal to the Privy Council and references to the High Court and the Privy Council from inferior courts, as well as the more usual procedural requirements for the time at which, and the manner in which, devolution issues can be raised. Accordingly, the rules set out in Chapter 40 have been described as being to some extent freestanding (see *H.M. Advocate v Montgomery*, 2000 J.C. 111).

It should be noted, however, that this new procedure is not to be taken as being intended to be an alternative to simply invoking the Convention rights by reliance on the court's duty as a public authority under s.6 of the Human Rights Act 1998. After the coming into force of that statute on October 2, 2000, a practice started to develop of not raising a devolution issue (see, *e.g. H.M. Advocate v Bain*, 2002 S.L.T. 340; *Rimmer, Petitioner*, 2002 S.C.C.R. 1). That practice had the effect of depriving the Advocate General of notice of the human rights point being raised. Accordingly the Advocate General sought a ruling from the Hight Court on the appropriateness of that practice. In *Mills v H.M. Advocate (No.2)*, 2001 S.L.T. 1359 the High Court stated that s.6 of the Human Rights Act did not affect the operation of para.5 of Sch.6 to the Scotland Act and therefore, if an issue falling within the definition of 'devolution issue' in para.1 of Sch.6 were raised, there had to be intimation to the Advocate General in accordance with Sch.6.

Rule 40.1

Paragraph 1 of Part I of Sch.6 to the Scotland Act 1998 defines "devolution issues" as meaning:

(a) a question whether an Act of the Scottish Parliament or any provision of such an Act is within the legislative competence of the Parliament (since its legislation is also required to be compatible with the "Convention rights");

(b) a question whether any function is a function of the Scottish Executive (including the Lord Advocate);

(c) a question whether the purported or proposed exercise of a function by a member of the Scottish Executive is, or would be, within devolved competence;

(d) a question whether a purported or proposed exercise of a function by a member of the Scottish Executive is, or would be, incompatible with any of the "Convention rights" or E.C. law;

(e) a question whether a failure to act by a member of the Scottish Executive is incompatible with any of the "Convention rights" or E.C. law; and

(f) any other question about whether a function is exercisable within devolved competence or in or as regards Scotland and any other question arising by virtue of the Scotland Act 1998 about matters which are reserved to the exclusive competence of the United Kingdom Parliament.

It is specifically provided in para.2 of Sch.6 that a devolution issue shall not be taken to arise in any proceedings merely because of any contention of a party to the proceedings which "appears to the court … before which the proceedings take place to be frivolous or vexatious".

It has been (perhaps somewhat tentatively) suggested that the devolution jurisdiction which Sch.6 to the Scotland Act 1998 represents was "not generally meant for determining, and cannot completely determine, 'ordinary' human rights questions" (such 'ordinary' questions being issues such as whether the Lord Advocate's act in calling an indictment for trial, or seeking to adduce certain types of evidence, etc is in breach of the fair trial provision of Art.6(1) of the European Convention or whether the Lord Advocate's proceeding before a court which is not independent and impartial as required by Art.6(1) is a violation of the European Convention) (see A. Stewart, Q.C. "Devolution Issues and Human Rights", 2000 S.L.T. (News) 239 at p. 243; *cf.* I. Jamieson, "Relationship between the Scotland Act and the Human Rights Act", 2001 S.L.T. (News) 43). In the first devolution issue appeals to be heard by the Privy Council, while the appeals did not specifically raise this point for determination, considerable doubt was expressed as to whether a challenge to the Lord Advocate's insisting in an indictment (when it was complained that the accused would not be able to enjoy a fair trial because of allegedly prejudicial pre-trial publicity) raised a devolution issue within the meaning of Sch.6. Only Lord Hope of Craighead was satisfied that the appeal was competent and relevant as being an appeal against a decision of the High Court on a devolution issue. Lord Clyde considered that the challenge was a devolution issue and that the accused's application was "technically competent" but doubted whether the application was relevant, it being questionable whether the act complained of could be said to be incompatible with the particular Convention right founded upon. The other members of the Board reserved their opinion on this aspect of the appeal—which was raised by the Board prior to the hearing of the appeal—on the basis that the parties were agreed that the question was a devolution issue, no full argument was therefore heard on the point, the High Court had regarded the question as a devolution issue and, in any event, the appeals fell to be refused on their merits: see *Montgomery v H.M. Advocate*, 2001 S.L.T. 37 (publication of the reasons being postponed until the conclusion of the trial).

Thus the present position on whether a devolution issue arises is contained in Lord Hope's conclusion: "On these facts I would hold that the question which has been raised in this case is a devolution issue and that, as this appeal has been brought with the leave of the High Court of Justiciary, the Judicial Committee is bound to examine the question and to answer it. The act of the Crown in having a case called at the sitting of the High Court at which the trial is to take place is a proposed exercise of a function of the Lord Advocate within the meaning of paragraph 1(d) of Schedule 6 to the Scotland Act 1998 ... In my opinion it is sufficient, for the minute of notice to pass the test of relevancy as to whether a devolution issue has been raised, that a question has arisen whether the Lord Advocate's proposed act, or the proposed exercise of his function, is incompatible with the Convention right— whether his proposed act as a member of the Scottish Executive is inconsistent with the obligation to ensure a fair trial which is imposed on the State by the Convention. The fact that a negative answer may be given to that question—for example, on the ground that the measures which the court itself can take, in the particular circumstances of the case, will ensure that the criminal charges against the appellants will be determined by an independent and impartial tribunal—does not mean that it does not raise a devolution issue within the meaning of paragraph 1 of the Schedule." (2001 S.L.T. 37 at 50B–E). This approach is now recognised as correct by the Privy Council in the second appeal to reach that forum: see *Brown v Stott*, 2001 S.L.T. 59; 2000 J.C. 328; [2001] 2 W.L.R. 817.

Rule 40.2

Separate rules are prescribed for solemn, summary and other criminal proceedings so far as the manner in which a devolution issue should be raised. Rule 40.2 provides that not later than seven days after service of the indictment, the party seeking to challenge the Lord Advocate's act as being incompatible with the "Convention rights" must give notice by way of written minute to the clerk of court in which the trial is to take place of his intention to do so. The object of this restriction, which a bench of three judges of the High Court (sitting as a trial court) has held is a reasonable and proportionate requirement, is to secure the expeditious and orderly administration of criminal justice in which there is a plain public interest (*H.M. Advocate v Dickson*, 2000 J.C. 93 at 100H–I, *per* Lord Osborne).

Rule 40.5 provides that a devolution issue cannot be raised by any party to the proceedings (which includes the Lord Advocate but not the Advocate General) except according to that timetable "unless the court, on cause shown, otherwise determines". It has been held that the mere fact that there had been some failure by the accused or his representatives to raise the devolution issue in accordance with r.40.2(1) did not necessarily mean that cause had not been shown for allowing an issue to be raised late and that part of the cause for allowing a non-timeous issue to be raised might be the prima facie significance of the devolution issue, particularly for the proceedings as a whole (*H.M. Advocate v Montgomery*, 2000 J.C. 111 at 121C, *per* Lord Justice-General Rodger). It is not particularly helpful for the court simply to ask itself whether it is in the interests of justice to depart from the timetable requirements.

Rule 42.2(5) provides that the rule is without prejudice to any right of or requirement on any party to raise any matter or objection at a preliminary or first diet. While this rule obviously recognises that preliminary objections might exist apart from any devolution issue, no provision was made for defining the type of hearing which should take place for the determination of a devolution issue. In practice, most devolution issues will be capable of being formulated in terms of a common law plea (such as oppression, competency or relevancy) and will therefore be conveniently—or necessarily—raised at a preliminary or first diet and even if they are not focused in that way, the court will treat the devolution issue as such a preliminary matter and hear argument at a first or preliminary diet. At such a diet, of course, any appeal by the accused against the court's determination will, according to s.72, only be possible with leave of the court. Chapter 40 makes no provision for an appeal against the determination of the court. In *H.M. Advocate v Robb*, 2000 J.C. 127, Lord Penrose treated the diet as a preliminary diet and refused the accused leave to appeal. See also *H.M. Advocate v Workman*, 2000 J.C. 383.

It should be noted, however, that with effect from April 7, 2000 the Rules have been amended (by the insertion of r.40.2(3a)) to cater for the situation where the Advocate General has received intimation of a devolution minute and has chosen not to enter the proceedings at first instance but later wishes to become a party to an appeal or reference to a higher court. The Appeal Court or higher court has a discretion to allow the Advocate General to enter the process. It may be, however, that in exercising their discretion, the courts will require an explanation as to why the Advocate General did not join herself to the proceedings at first instance in order for the courts to be satisfied that the Advocate General should not be held, in effect, to have waived her right to oppose a devolution minute since she cannot be heard to argue that she is unaware of the relevant facts (*cf. Millar v Dickson*, 2000 J.C. 648 and on appeal to the Privy Council (notwithstanding the reversal of the decision): see *Millar v Dickson*, 2001 S.L.T. 988). The Advocate General was permitted to present submissions before the Privy Council in *Montgomery v H.M. Advocate*, 2001 S.L.T. 37 although she had not sought to be represented at the earlier stages of the proceedings prior to leave to appeal being granted by the Appeal Court in November 1999. In *Brown v Stott*, 2000 J.C. 328 the Appeal Court gave leave to the Advocate General to appear and be represented even though she had not intervened or been represented in the sheriff court (see p.332H).

It should, however, be noted that the Advocate General's functions are determined by the Scotland Act 1998. The present holder of the office has described her role and the occasions on which she has to date seen fit to intervene in proceedings on receiving intimation of devolution issues: see "Three Years On: The Role of the Advocate General for Scotland", 2002 S.L.T. (News) 139. In *Adams and Others v Lord Advocate* (July 31, 2002), Outer House, *The Times*, August 8, 2002, Lord Nimmo Smith discussed the Advocate General's role: "It is clear from the terms of the various provisions of the Scotland Act which allow the Advocate General to intervene at various stages that whether, and if so at what stage, to appear in legal proceedings is a decision which lies within her discretion. For this very reason, her decision not to intervene at all or at any particular stage should not, without good reason, be the subject of comment by the court. No doubt in considering how to exercise her discretion the Advocate General would have regard to the submissions proposed to be advanced by the Lord Advocate." (para.30)

Where a devolution issue has been departed from in the course of an appeal to the High Court, it is not competent to apply to the Privy Council for special leave to reopen the issue. The Privy Council's jurisdiction under Sch.6, para.13 is "entirely dependent upon there having first been a determination by two or more judges of the High Court of Justiciary of the devolution issue which [the appellant] wishes to argue before the Committee": *Follen v H.M. Advocate*, 2001 S.L.T. 774; 2001 S.C.C.R. 255 (para.9), *per* Lord Hope of Craighead.

Rule 40.3

The requirement of giving notice in summary proceedings is perhaps more exacting since written notice must be given when the accused is called upon to plead. However, where there is more than one accused and all accused are not called upon to plead at the same diet, the accused has until the last accused is called upon to plead to give notice of a devolution issue. A devolution issue can, however, be raised at a later stage in the proceedings—and indeed during the course of the trial or after adjournment of a part-heard summary trial—where the court is satisfied that cause has been shown for allowing the issue to be raised late. The same sheriff should hear the issue since devolution issues should be determined when they are raised (*Starrs and Chalmers v Ruxton*; *Ruxton v Starrs and Chalmers*, 2000 J.C. 208).

Rule 40.3(5)—inserted with effect from April 7, 2000—now confers on the High Court and Privy Council a discretion to allow the Advocate General to enter the proceedings even though she had chosen not to do so when the devolution minute was intimated to her.

Rule 40.4

Rule 40.4(1) does not identify the type of criminal proceedings to which this rule is intended to apply but it appears that, for example, a petition to the *nobile officium* by a third party who is a stranger to the proceedings and claims that a forfeiture order affects his interests (*e.g. Lloyd's & Scottish Finance Ltd v H.M. Advocate*, 1974 J.C. 24; 1974 S.L.T. 3) would fall within its terms, as would a petition for commission and diligence in the High Court where, for example, a haver opposed the call.

Where a finding of contempt is to be made in the course of criminal proceedings and a party proposes to raise a devolution issue relating to contempt of court, the High Court has stated that it will treat the matter, so far as possible, as though it fell within r.40.4 (Practice Note of May 6, 1999; see Cl.14, *infra*). This approach is consistent with the decision in *Express Newspapers plc, Petitioners*, 1999 S.L.T. 644; 1999 S.C.C.R. 262 where a Bench of Five Judges held that a petition and complaint for contempt of court was not solemn proceedings.

No time limit is stated for the raising of a devolution issue which should, however, be raised at the first opportunity. If it is not, the court may require to be satisfied that there is cause for the issue being raised at a later stage, since r.40.5(1) applies also to r.40.4. Once the point is taken and not rejected by the court as being unjustifiably late, the proceedings will require to be adjourned in order to allow the requisite intimation to be made to the Advocate General (and where appropriate, the Lord Advocate). For example, in *BBC, Petrs (No.1)*, 2000 J.C. 419 a devolution issue was raised by the petitioners under Art.10 of the European Convention on Human Rights (freedom of expression) in respect of the "Lockerbie trial" which the petitioners and various foreign and domestic commercial broadcasters wished to broadcast live from the Netherlands. The petition to the *nobile officium* was heard and refused by a single judge of the High Court and as it had been before a single judge, there was no power for the court to refer a devolution issue to the Privy Council or right of appeal. The petitioners accordingly sought review of the decision by means of a second petition to the *nobile officium* which they required to be put before three judges. The court reserved its opinion on the competency of a petition being used to "appeal" the decision taken in an earlier petition which was refused by a single judge (see *BBC, Petrs (No.2)* 2000 J.C. 521 at 523C–D, 525B and H).

Rule 40.4(5)—inserted with effect from April 7, 2000—now confers on the High Court and the Privy Council the discretion to allow the Advocate General to join herself as a party to the later stages of proceedings in which a devolution issue is raised, even though she declined to do so when intimation of the devolution minute was originally made to her.

Rule 40.6

If the court considers that the purported devolution issue is simply frivolous or vexatious, the court is obliged to hold that no devolution issue is raised. For that reason a party seeking to raise a devolution issue must give sufficient detail so that the court can conclude that the proposed issue is not precluded by para.2 of Sch.6 to the Scotland Act 1998. It has been stated by the Appeal Court that: "[I]t is not sufficient for a party simply to aver that a devolution issue has arisen. The court must consider whether, in light of the particular circumstances of each individual case, it has been demonstrated that a devolution issue does relevantly arise." (*BBC, Petrs (No.2)* 2000 J.C. 521 at 532G, *per* Lord Kirkwood). See also Lord Hope of Craighead's discussion of what constitutes a relevant devolution minute in *Montgomery v HM Advocate*, 2001 S.L.T. 37. In *Hoekstra v HM Advocate. (No.3)*, 2000 J.C. 599 the Appeal Court held that para.1 of Sch.6 to the Scotland Act 1998 contained an exhaustive list of what constituted devolution issues and, accordingly, rejected the argument that the Appeal Court was bound to refer to the Privy Council the appellants' purported devolution issue which sought to challenge the Appeal Court's earlier decision (in *Hoekstra v HM Advocate (No.2)*, 2000 J.C. 387) to set aside a prior interlocutor of the Appeal Court because the court was then inquorate as a result of the chairman of the Appeal Court's objective bias. The Privy Council subsequently refused special leave to appeal against that decision for the same reasons: see *Hoekstra v HM Advocate (No.5)*, 2001 S.L.T. 28; [2000] 3 W.L.R. 1817.

Rule 40.7

A district court justice, the sheriff or a single judge of the High Court is entitled to refer a devolution issue to the High Court for determination except when the issue is raised in the course of the trial. When the issue arises after the trial has commenced (i.e. either after the jury has been sworn or, in summary proceedings, after the first witness has been sworn: see r.40.1(2)), the court of first instance must determine the devolution issue itself. Notice must nonetheless be given to the Advocate General who is entitled to enter the proceedings. If the Advocate General intervenes and is unsuccessful in her representations on a devolution issue, and the accused is either convicted or acquitted, the Advocate General is entitled to refer a question to the High Court for its determination (see s.288A(1) and (2)) although the opinion of the High Court on the point referred shall not affect the acquittal or conviction of the accused (s.288A(6)).

Where the Appeal Court determines a devolution issue on a reference from an inferior court, an appeal lies to the Privy Council either with leave of the Appeal Court or, failing such leave, with special leave of the Privy Council (see para.13(a) of Sch.6 to the Scotland Act 1998).

The reference procedure is intended to provide the original court with a means of obtaining guidance so that it can decide the devolution issue raised before it. It is not intended as a free-standing device to allow parties to air purely academic or hypothetical issues and accordingly when the instance falls following a reference having been made, the reference procedure also comes to an end: *HM Advocate v Touati*, 2001 S.C.C.R. 392.

Rule 40.9

In terms of para.11 of Sch.6 to the Scotland Act 1998, the Appeal Court (i.e. a court comprising two or more judges of the High Court) may refer a devolution issue to the Privy Council (other than a question which has been referred to the Appeal Court by an inferior court prior to trial (see r.40.7, *supra* and para.9 of Sch.6)). Furthermore, by virtue of para.33 of Sch.6, both the Lord Advocate and the Advocate General are entitled to require *any* court to refer to the Privy Council any devolution issue which has arisen in proceedings before it to which the Lord Advocate or Advocate General is a party.

Rule 40.11

Where an appeal has been taken against the decision of the Appeal Court on a devolution issue (under para.13(a) of Sch.6), and the accused has been acquitted after trial or the accused's conviction has been quashed by the Appeal Court, the determination of the appeal by the Privy Council shall not affect any earlier acquittal or earlier quashing of any conviction in the proceedings (s.288B(2)). Subject to that qualification, the Appeal Court shall have the same powers in relation to the proceedings when remitted to it by the Privy Council as it would have if it were considering the proceedings otherwise than as a trial court (s.288B(3)).

It is for the High Court of Justiciary and not the Judicial Committee of the Privy Council, when an appeal to the Privy Council has been determined, to dispose of the case by the making of the appropriate order. Thus, in *Montgomery v HM Advocate*, 2001 S.L.T. 37 at 55L–56A, Lord Hope of Craighead rejected the suggestion that if the accused's appeals were successful, the Board should desert the diet *simpliciter*.

CHAPTER 41

HUMAN RIGHTS ACT 1998

Application and interpretation

41.1.—(1) This Chapter deals with various matters relating to the Human Rights Act 1998.

(2) In this Chapter—

"the 1998 Act" means the Human Rights Act 1998;

"declaration of incompatibility" has the meaning given by section 4 of the 1998 Act.

Evidence of judgments etc

41.2.—(1) Evidence of any judgment, decision, declaration or opinion of which account has to be taken by the court under section 2 of the 1998 Act shall be given by reference to any authoritative and complete report of the said judgment, decision, declaration or opinion and may be given in any manner.

(2) Evidence given in accordance with paragraph (1) shall be sufficient evidence of that judgment, decision, declaration or opinion.

Declaration of incompatibility

41.3.—(1) Where in any proceedings a party seeks a declaration of incompatibility or the court is considering whether to make such a declaration at its own instance—

(a) notice in Form 41.3-A shall be given as soon as reasonably practicable to such person as the Lord Justice General may from time to time direct—

(i) by the party seeking the declaration; or

(ii) by the clerk of court,

as the case may be, provided that there shall be no requirement to give such notice to a party or to the representative of a party; and

(b) where notice is given by the party seeking the declaration the party shall lodge a certificate of notification in process.

(2) Where any—

(a) Minister of the Crown (or person nominated by him);

(b) member of the Scottish Executive;

(c) Northern Ireland Minister;

(d) Northern Ireland department,

wishes to be joined as a party to proceedings in relation to which the Crown is entitled to receive notice under section 5 of the 1998 Act he or, as the case may be, it shall serve notice in Form 41.3-B to that effect on the Deputy Principal Clerk of Justiciary and shall serve a copy of the notice on all other parties to the proceedings.

AMENDMENT

Rule 41.3(1) substituted by the Act of Adjournal (Criminal Procedure Rules Amendment No. 4) (Miscellaneous) 2006 (SSI 2006/436), r.2 (effective September 1, 2006)

41.4. Within 14 days after the date of service of the notice under rule 41.3(2), the person serving the notice shall lodge a minute in the proceedings in Form 41.4 and shall serve a copy of that minute on all other parties to the proceedings.

41.5. The court may fix a diet for a hearing on the question of incompatibility as a separate hearing from any other hearing in the proceedings and may sist the proceedings if it considers it necessary to do so while the question of incompatibility is being determined.

AMENDMENTS

Chapter 41 inserted by the Act of Adjournal (Criminal Procedure Rules Amendment No.2) (Human Rights Act 1998) 2000 (SSI 2000/315) (effective October 2, 2000).

GENERAL NOTE

The Human Rights Act 1998 was brought into force on October 2, 2000. Subject to what is said below, the effect of the coming into force of that statute might have been though to be to eliminate any need to raise a devolution issue when an accused wishes to challenge the Crown's conduct in a prosecution since (in terms of s.6(3)(a)) all courts are public authorities for the purposes of the Human Rights Act 1998 (with the exception of claims for damages for judicial acts done in good faith, in respect of which damages may not be awarded otherwise than to compensate a person to the extent required by Art.5(5) of the European Convention on Human Rights: see s.9(3)) and are therefore bound to refrain from acting in a manner incompatible with the European Convention. The availability of the regime created by the Human Rights Act 1998 might therefore have been thought to rob of significance—except perhaps in the context of rights of appeal (see *Montgomery v HM Advocate*, 2001 S.L.T. 37 at 40K, *per* Lord Nicholls of Birkenhead)—any dispute over the scope of the devolution issues specified in Sch.6 to the Scotland Act 1998.

The purpose of this new chapter is necessarily very limited. This is because the duty of the court in its handling of all criminal business will be to ensure that it acts in a manner compatible with all of the Convention rights enumerated in s.1 of, and Sch.1 to, the Human Rights Act 1998. Accordingly, a human rights issue will be capable of arising at any stage in criminal proceedings prior to final determination in the Appeal Court and will not be dependent on demonstrating that the Lord Advocate or a procurator fiscal is acting incompatibly with a Convention right. Thus, no procedural rules for the raising of a human rights issue have been made in contradistinction to the provision made in Chap.40 of the Criminal Procedure Rules for the raising of devolution issues. Yet it may remain to be seen whether the use of the concept of waiver, which has been approved in devolution issues cases (see *Millar v Dickson*, 2000 J.C. 648 and *Clancy v Caird*, 2000 S.C. 441) will not also be considered appropriate to bar an accused from raising a challenge to certain procedural matters when he could have done so at an earlier stage in the proceedings.

Moreover, the related plea of acquiescence has also been approved by the High Court for use by the Crown in devolution issues cases (see *Lochridge v Miller*, 2002 S.L.T. 906; 2002 S.C.C.R. 628) and the Privy Council (see *Robertson v Frame*, 2006 S.L.T. 478; 2006 S.C.C.R. 151). Thus, once the trial proceedings are at an end without any complaint of a Convention breach having been stated, it will be necessary for any such complaint to be raised on appeal in a devolution issue minute without significant delay. If the point is not raised quickly the inference may be drawn that the accused has acquiesced in the breach and thereby lost his right to redress by suspension or advocation (or, indeed, any other remedy: see *Dickson v HM Advocate* [2006] HCJAC 74 (October 11, 2006, unreported), para.43.). However, especially where the Convention breach is said to have occurred prior to the commencement of the Scotland Act 1998 (where the retrospective application of Convention rights under the Human Rights Act 1998 will then be in issue (*cf. Dickson, supra*)), the plea will fail where "the circumstances do not disclose that the appellants during the relevant period had the requisite knowledge of the availability of the grounds of challenge to the validity of the . . . decisions which they [later] maintain to enable it to be inferred that they made an informed decision not to take the point" (*Dickson*, para.40).

Subject to the qualification which was expressed in *Mills v HM Advocate (No.2)*, 2001 S.L.T. 1359 (see B1–78.19 above), the Human Rights Act does not provide for a special procedure for raising human rights challenges but there is need for notice to be given by the *court* when it is considering whether or not to exercise its powers under s.4(2) or (4). These provisions provide respectively for the power of the court (which for these purposes is restricted to the High Court of Justiciary sitting otherwise than as a trial court, the Courts-Martial Appeal Court and the Judicial Committee of the Privy Council: s.4(5)) to make a "declaration of incompatibility" where the court determines that a provision of primary legislation or a provision of subordinate legislation made in the exercise of a power conferred by primary legislation is incompatible with a Convention right. In such cases it may be necessary for a government department (other than the Lord Advocate) to be afforded the opportunity of making submissions on the proposal to make a declaration of incompatibility.

The Appeal Court's powers of interpretation of potentially incompatible legislation are specified in s.3. So far as it is possible to do so, primary legislation and subordinate legislation (whenever enacted) must be read and given effect in a way which is compatible with the Convention rights (s.3(1)). Thus, when dealing with s.172 of the Road Traffic Act 1988, the Appeal Court in determining a devolution issue minute and having found that s.172 was incompatible with an accused's right to silence and privilege against self-incrimination, considered that it was obliged thereafter to consider whether that provision could be "read down" so as to be compatible with Art.6(1) (see *Brown v Stott*, 2000 J.C. 328 at 354E–355C, *per* Lord Justice-General Rodger). The duty to "read down" legislation does not, however, affect the validity, continuing operation or enforcement of any incompatible primary legislation or of any incompatible subordinate legislation which (disregarding any possibility of revocation) is prevented by primary legislation from being cured of its incompatibility (s.3(2)(b) and (c)). A declaration of incompatibility is declared by s.6(6) not to affect the validity, continuing operation or enforcement of the legislative provision in respect of which it is made and is also declared not to be binding on the parties to the proceedings in which it is made.

The approach to be adopted to whether a declaration of incompatibility should be made, or whether the statutory provision in question can be "read down" so as to be compatible with a Convention right has been considered in several cases. See *R. v Lambert* [2001] 3 W.L.R. 206 and *R. v A (No.2)* [2001] 2 W.L.R. 1546, both decided in the House of Lords; and *Wilson v First County Trust Ltd (No.2)* [2001] 3 W.L.R. 42 decided in the Court of Appeal (Civil Division). The interpretative obligation imposed on the courts by s.3, which has unsurprisingly been described as "the Humpty Dumpty rule of construction" (see Sir John Smith, Q.C. at [2001] Crim.L.R. 843) at best requires a strained construction and at worst frees the court to construe legislative provisions in terms in which Parliament on no reasonable view could ever have intended them to be understood.

The leading decision on the scope of the interpretative obligation in s.3 is *Ghaidan v Godin-Mendoza* [2004] 3 W.L.R. 113 in which the House of Lords recognised that s.3 was not confined to resolving ambiguities but was of an "unusual and far-reaching character" (para.30). There were bound to be cases in which "reading down" could not be possible (Lord Nicholls, para. 27) and these would arise where the Convention-compliant interpretation would go against the grain of the legislation (Lord Rodger, para.121). What is essential is that any modified meaning given under s.3 had to remain consistent with the fundamental features of the legislative scheme. If the modified meaning failed that test then the superior courts would be crossing the constitutional line between interpretation and statutory amendment. Certain Convention-compatible interpretations of legislation would not be possible because such alterations would involve consideration of issues which could only properly be decided upon by Parliament.

Rule 41.2

Section 2(1) of the Human Rights Act 1998 provides that a court determining a question which has arisen in connection with a Convention right must take into account any judgment, decision, declaration or advisory opinion of the European Court and various opinions or decisions of the European Commission—which ceased to function from and after November 1, 1998 by virtue of the merger of the Commission and Court in accordance with the Eleventh Protocol—and the Committee of Ministers. Section 2(2) provides that evidence of any such judgment, etc. is to be given in proceedings in such manner as may be provided by rules of court (s.2(3)). This rule implements that provision. It may seem odd that such provision should be seen as necessary but the necessity for rules about the form and manner of evidencing the judgments, etc. of the European Court and the other bodies follows from the fact that foreign (including international) court judgments are not self-proving and require to be proved. Equally, since the authenticity of foreign public registers may be called into question, the Parliamentary practice is to provide for a means of proving judgments entered in foreign court registers (see, e.g. Evidence (Foreign, Dominion, etc., Documents) Act 1933. s.1).

Rule 41.2(1) requires that to be admissible, the evidence of the judgment, etc. must be by reference to any "authoritative and complete" report. The same expression is used in the Practice Direction [2000] 4 All E.R. 288 issued by the President of the Family Division of the High Court in England in July, 2000. A précis of the decision in a legal publication will not suffice. The standard law reports cited as E.H.H.R. will be the norm for most practitioners although the official series of law reports will be preferable. The official series of reports of the European Court decisions, up to 1996, was called "Series A (Judgments and Decisions)". After 1996 the official series became "Reports of Judgments and Decisions". More recent reports of the European Court are referred to by the application number: transcripts of these reports are available from the European Court's website (*www.echr.coe.int*). The official series of reports of European Commission decisions is called "Decisions and Reports" (cited as "DR") and is published by the Council of Europe.

The doctrine of stare decisis and Strasbourg jurisprudence

What is the position where there is domestic judicial precedent of a superior court binding on an inferior court but that domestic authority is inconsistent with a European Court decision? Should the lower domestic courts disregard the binding domestic authority or the European decision? This difficulty arises from s.2 of the Human Rights Act 1998 which imposes what Lord Bingham of Cornhill has termed "the mandatory duty imposed on domestic courts . . . to take into account any judgment of the Strasbourg court and any opinion of the commission" (*Kay v Lambeth LBC* [2006] 2 W.L.R. 570 (para.28, p.583H). The House of Lords in *Kay* has provided the answer for England and Wales. The Court of Appeal in *Leeds City Council v Price* [2005] 1 W.L.R. 1825 had followed a House of Lords' decision but granted leave to appeal because of the obvious inconsistency of domestic and European decisions. That course was approved in *Kay*. Lord Bingham, with the express concurrence of the other six Law Lords (see paras 50, 62, 121, 177, 178 and 213), made the following points: first, adherence to precedent is a cornerstone of the English legal system (para.42); secondly, the need for certainty and the avoidance of conflicting decisions of lower courts on whether there is a "clear inconsistency" between the European and domestic authorities before disregarding domestic decisions are best achieved by adhering to domestic rules of precedent (para.43); thirdly, thus domestic courts should review Convention arguments and if they consider domestic precedents to be—or possibly to be—inconsistent with Strasbourg authority, they *may* express their views and give leave to appeal (para.43); and, fourthly, there is one "partial exception" to this approach: in an exceptional case, where the facts are of such an extreme character as existed in *D v East Berkshire Community NHS Trust* [2004] Q.B. 558, the lower court can depart from the superior court's decision and follow the Strasbourg authority (para.45).

The same approach would seem eminently sensible for Scotland. Where a sheriff or Lord Commissioner of Justiciary is confronted by a binding decision of a quorum of the High Court and it is arguably, or even clearly, incompatible with Strasbourg jurisprudence, the domestic court should follow the Scottish decision. If an appeal is taken the High Court can determine the present state of the law. Alternatively, as human rights issues are properly raised by way of devolution minutes, to which Ch.40 applies, the lower court may decide to refer the issue to the Appeal Court if that option remains open.

Rule 41.3(1)

Until amendment with effect from September 1, 2006 this rule required the court to give notice to persons specified by the Lord Justice General whenever the court was considering whether to make a declaration of incompatibility. Now the rule recognises that a party may seek the making of such a declaration and so requires that party to give notice to relevant persons. However, as the notice procedure is designed to alert vested governmental interests (such as the Advocate General for Scotland), there is no obligation on the court to give notice to the parties to the proceedings (or for the party seeking the declaration to give notice to other parties to the proceedings).

Rule 41.3(2)

Section 5(1) provides that where the Appeal Court is considering whether to make a declaration of incompatibility, the Crown is entitled to notice of that fact in accordance with rules of court. Section 5(2) provides that in any case to which subs.(1) applies, the persons or departments identified are entitled to be joined as a party to the proceedings if they give notice in accordance with the rules of court. Where the Ministers or departments wish to be joined as parties to the proceedings, it will be necessary for them to serve notice on the court and all other parties.

Paragraphs (a) and (b) draw the distinction, which is in terms of constitutional law correct, between members of the Scottish Executive (including the so-called Scottish "Cabinet") and Ministers of the Crown. Scottish Executive ministers are not Ministers of the Crown. The statutory functions of the Scottish Ministers are exercisable on behalf of Her Majesty (Scotland Act 1998, s.52(2)) but, as was recently observed, that does not mean that they are the Crown (see Lord Boyd of Duncansby Q.C., "Ministers and the Law", 2006 J.R. 179 at p.183).

According to the strict terms of s.5(1) the entitlement to notice arises only once the court is considering whether to make a declaration of incompatibility and thus the court has by that stage already in effect decided that the statutory provision cannot be "read down" so as to be compatible with the Convention rights scheduled to the 1998 Act. This procedural difficulty (which appears to have first surfaced in the course of a hearing of a purely private law civil appeal in the Court of Appeal (Civil Division) in *Wilson v First County Trust Ltd* [2001] 2 W.L.R. 302) has been addressed both by a committee of the House of Lords in a criminal appeal in *R v A (Joinder of appropriate minister)* [2001] 1 W.L.R. 789 and by the First Division in *Gunn v Newman*, March 21, 2001 (unreported) in a reclaiming motion arising out of a purely private law issue concerning the availability of civil jury trial and ss.9 and 11 of the Court of Session Act 1988.

In *Gunn*, following *R v A*, the First Division held that notice of the proposal to consider whether or not a statutory provision was incompatible, or could be "read down" and so avoid the necessity of making a declaration of incompatibility, should be given in advance of the hearing of the reclaiming motion so as to avoid the risk that the hearing would commence and then require to be adjourned so as to allow notice to be given to the appropriate ministers (as occurred in *Wilson v First County Trust Ltd*). Lord President Rodger stated: "[The purpose of intervention under s.5(2)] is not confined simply to arguing as to whether a court, which had in effect decided that a provision was incompatible with the Convention, should make a declaration in terms of s.4(1). That would be, at best, a most limited and unconstructive role. Rather, the minister has an opportunity to address the court on the objects and purposes of the legislation in question and on any other matters which may be relevant." (para.[9]). Thus notice was given under s.5(1) to the Lord Advocate as representing the Scottish Ministers who have the policy responsibility for Scots private law and to the Advocate-General as representing the UK Government who have responsibility for international relations including compliance with the European Convention.

Rule. 41.4

No time limit is set for compliance with the requirement of notice under r.41.3(2) but once notice has been given, a 14 day time limit is imposed for lodging a minute with the court and serving a copy of the minute on all other parties to the proceedings. It may be that failure to comply with that time limit will be fatal to the intervener's right to be heard.

Rule 41.5

This rule gives the court power to sist an appeal (including petition to the *nobile officium* or bill) or reference from an inferior court in which a declaration of incompatibility is being considered and also enables the court to hold a diet for a hearing on that issue as a separate hearing from any other hearing in the proceedings. It is an unusual provision and may be explained by the fact that the declaration of incompatibility will not affect the validity of the statutory provision or be binding on the parties to the proceedings (see s.4(6)) and so can conveniently be determined apart from the proceedings which have given rise to the declaration. However, the court's recently adopted approach to the timing of the notice to be given when the court is considering making a declaration (referred to above) suggests that hearings will not be held separately from the review proceedings and that a sist will be the only likely power exercised by the Appeal Court (and only when it appears necessary).

CHAPTER 42

CONVENTION RIGHTS (COMPLIANCE) (SCOTLAND) ACT 2001

Application and interpretation

42.1.—(1) This Chapter applies to punishment part hearings.

(2) In this Chapter—

"the 2001 Act" means the Convention Rights (Compliance) (Scotland) Act 2001;

"punishment part hearing" means a hearing in terms of paragraph 12 of Part 1 or paragraph 59 of Part 4 of the Schedule to the 2001 Act ;

"life prisoners" has the meaning given in paragraph 2 of Part 1 of the Schedule to the 2001 Act;

"procedural hearing" means a hearing, held in terms of rule 42.4, for the purpose of determining any matter raised in terms of rule 42.3.

Intimation

42.2.—(1) The Deputy Principal Clerk of Justiciary shall intimate the date, time and place of a punishment part hearing in Form 42.2.

Disputed or additional documents

42.3.—(1) If a life prisoner who has received intimation of a punishment part hearing in terms of rule 42.2(1) wishes to—

(a) dispute the terms of any document, or a part of any document, sent to him by the Scottish Ministers in terms of paragraph 9 of Part 1 or paragraph 56 of Part 4 of the Schedule to the 2001 Act; or

(b) lodge any other document,

he shall, not later than 21 days before the date of the punishment part hearing, give written intimation to the Deputy Principle Clerk of Justiciary.

(2) A life prisoner who gives intimation in terms of paragraph (1) of this rule shall, at the same time, specify the grounds upon which he seeks to—

(a) dispute the document or part of the document; or

(b) lodge any other document,

and shall lodge any document referred to in, or to which he intends to refer, in support of such grounds.

(3) None of the matters mentioned in paragraph (1) of this rule may be raised after the time specified in that paragraph.

Procedural hearing

42.4. Where a life prisoner gives intimation in terms of paragraph (1) of rule 42.3, there shall, 14 days before the date of the punishment part hearing, be a procedural hearing.

AMENDMENT

Chapter 42 inserted by the Act of Adjournal (Criminal Procedural Rules Amendment) (Convention Rights (Compliance) (Scotland) Act 2001) 2001 (SSI 2001/479 (effective December 21, 2001).

Rules 42.1, 42.3 and 42.4 as amended by Act of Adjournal (Criminal Procedure Rules Amendment) (Convention Rights (Compliance) (Scotland) Act 2001) 2002 (SSI 2002/137), r.2 (effective March 4, 2002).

GENERAL NOTE

The Convention Rights (Compliance) (Scotland) Act 2001 was passed to deal with, inter alia, the arguable incompatibility of the indeterminate life sentence for murder with the accused's rights under the European Convention to a review of the lawfulness of his detention after the punitive part of his sentence had elapsed. Judgments of the European Court had already considered the issue in respect of an accused convicted of murder when under-age and persons sentenced to a discretionary life term. In due course the European Court decided *Stafford v United Kingdom* [2002] 35 E.H.R.R. 1121 on May 25, 2002.

Consequently, s.2 of the 2001 Act, which came into force before the decision in *Stafford*, repealed s.205(4) of the 1995 Act (which permitted the trial judge to make a minimum recommendation) and amended the Prisoners and Criminal Proceedings (Scotland) Act 1993 so that in terms of s.2(2) the trial judge should make an order known as the "punishment part" which is the part of the life sentence for murder appropriate "to satisfy the requirements of retribution and deterrence (ignoring the period of confinement, if any, which may be necessary for the protection of the public)". Since there were existing life sentence prisoners convicted of murder before the coming into force of the 2001 Act, Part I of the Schedule to the 2001 Act made provision for persons who had been sentenced (before October 8, 2001) for murder committed when they were aged 18 or over.

In terms of para.12 of the Schedule, there must be a hearing at which the High Court shall make an order which is to be what the court considers would have been ordered as a punishment part had the relevant provisions been in force when the accused was sentenced for murder (para.13). For the purposes of the hearing the court will have available to it various documentary productions including the post-mortem report, the accused's previous convictions and the trial judge's report to the Parole Board (regarding the circumstances of the offence). These documents are to be sent to the accused before the hearing. Where the accused disputes the terms of any of these documents, or wishes to rely on another document, he must give notice of that fact to the court. At the same time he must state why he takes issue with the document or wishes to found on another document (which he must lodge with Justiciary Office). If he fails in any of these respects, within the timescale, he is precluded from raising his dispute or relying on the document at the punishment part hearing.

In *Flynn v HM Advocate*, 2004 S.C.C.R. 281 the Privy Council disapproved the High Court's decisions in *Stewart v HM Advocate*, 2002 S.L.T. 1307 and *McCreaddie v HM Advocate*, 2002 S.L.T. 1311 (which held as irrelevant to fixing the punishment part the views of the Preliminary Review Committee (PRC) of the Parole Board as to the appropriate review date for considering the accused's release) and decided that such views were relevant although not determinative. A bench of five judges subsequently overruled *Stewart* and *McCreaddie* in light of the Privy Council's judgments (see *Flynn v HM Advocate*, 2004 S.L.T. 1195 (para.15)) and held that (1) the PRC'S proposed review date was a relevant but not decisive factor in fixing the punishment part; (2) the weight to be given to it depended on the accused's prospects of release at that review date (para.19); and (3) in fixing the punishment part, the court had to start by considering what punishment part would have been set if it had been set at the date of the sentence (thus disregarding all subsequent events) and then look at subsequent events having a possible bearing on the accused's possible release and decide what weight, if any, should be given to them by way of adjustment of the punishment part (para.22).

It should also be noted that the Appeal Court has held that the *Practice Statement (Crime: Life Sentences)* [2002] 1 W.L.R. 1789 (which has been consolidated into the *Practice Direction (Criminal Proceedings: Consolidation)* [2002] 1 W.L.R. 2870 (paras 49.2–49.28)) setting out the normal "starting point" of 12 years and a "higher starting point" of 15–16 years for adult offenders, are guidelines which do not apply in Scotland although they may be useful for drawing attention to matters which may be relevant in the particular case (*Flynn v HM Advocate*, 2003 S.L.T. 954 (para.87); *Brown v HM Advocate*, HCJ, November 20, 2002 (unreported), para.7). In particular, it seems appropriate for the mitigating factors mentioned in paras 49.11, 49.17 and 49.18 and the aggravating factors set out in paras 49.13, 49.15, 49.16 and 49.20 to be taken into account, although the normal, higher and very serious offence tariffs are irrelevant in Scotland. (The relevant English guidance has been amended and is now to be found in *Practice Direction (Crime: Mandatory Life Sentences) (No.2)*[2004]1 W.L.R. 2551.)

The guidance as to sentencing is to be found for Scotland in the Appeal Court decisions: see *Flynn*; *Stewart* (para.18) and *Walker v HM Advocate*, 2003 S.L.T. 130 (para.8). In *Walker* the Appeal Court stated that "in the absence of significant mitigation most cases of murder would … attract a punishment part of 12 years or more, depending on the presence of one or more aggravating features".

CHAPTER 43

TERRORISM ACT 2000 AND ANTI-TERRORISM, CRIME AND SECURITY ACT 2001

Interpretation

43.1.—(1) In this Chapter—

"the Act of 2000" means the Terrorism Act 2000; and

"the Act of 2001" means the Anti-Terrorism, Crime and Security Act 2001.

Applications under the Act of 2000 or 2001

43.2.—(1) An application under any of the following provisions shall be made by petition:—

(a) paragraph 22(1) (production of material for the purposes of a terrorist investigation) of Schedule 5 to the Act of 2000;

(b) paragraph 30(1) (explanation of material seized or produced shall for the purposes of a terrorist investigation) of Schedule 5 to the Act of 2000;

(c) paragraph 2(b) (procedure for order requiring financial information) of Schedule 6 to the Act of 2000;

(d) paragraph 2(1) (account monitoring order) of Schedule 6A to the Act of 2000;

(e) paragraph 4(1) (discharge or variation of account monitoring order) of Schedule 6A to the Act of 2000.

(2) The sheriff may make the order sought in an application under paragraph 22(1) of Schedule 5 to the Act of 2000 before intimation of the application to the person who appears to him to be in possession of the material to which the application relates.

(3) The sheriff may make the order sought in an application under:—

(a) paragraph 2(b) of Schedule 6 to the Act of 2000;

(b) paragraph 2(1) of Schedule 6A to the Act of 2000; or

(c) paragraph 4(1)(a) of Schedule 6A to the Act of 2000,

before intimation of the application to the person who appears to him to be in possession of the information to which the application relates and the person who is the subject of that information.

(4) Notice under paragraph 5(3) of Schedule 1 to the Act of 2001 (release of cash where retention no longer justified) shall be given in writing.

NOTE

Chapter 43 inserted by the Act of Adjournal (Criminal Procedural Rules Amendment No.2) (Terrorism Act 2000 and Anti-Terrorism, Crime and Security Act 2001) 2001 (SSI 2001/486) (effective December 22, 2001).

Rule 43.2 as amended by Act of Adjournal (Criminal Procedure Rules Amendment No.2) (Anti-Terrorism, Crime and Security Act 2001) 2002 (SSI 2002/136), r.2 (effective March 4, 2002).

CHAPTER 44

INTERNATIONAL CRIMINAL COURT ACT 2001

Interpretation of this Chapter

44.1. In this Chapter, "the Act of 2001" means the International Criminal Court Act 2001.

Consent to surrender

44.2. Consent to surrender given under section 7 of the Act of 2001 (consent to surrender) shall be in writing in Form 44.2.

Waiver of right to review

44.3. Waiver given under section 13 of the Act of 2001 (waiver of the right to review) shall be in writing in Form 44.3.

AMENDMENT

Chapter 44 inserted by Act of Adjournal (Criminal Procedure Rules Amendment No.2) (Miscellaneous) 2003 (SSI 2003/468), r.2. Brought into force on October 27, 2003 in accordance with art.1.

GENERAL NOTE

Part 2 of the International Criminal Court Act 2001 (c.17) provides for the arrest and delivery of persons who either are the subject of investigation for an "ICC crime" (i.e. genocide, war crimes and crimes against humanity (s.1)) or have been convicted (with or without sentence having been imposed) of such a crime by the International Criminal Court. The Act is intended to provide an expeditious procedure which takes two forms.

Under s.2 the United Kingdom Government receives a request for the arrest and surrender of such persons and, after its transmission to the Scottish Ministers, if the request is accompanied by a warrant, the warrant must be endorsed for execution by the sheriff at Edinburgh (only Lothian and Borders has jurisdiction: s.26(c)) if the sheriff "is satisfied that the warrant appears to have been issued by the ICC" (s.2(3)). Where there is no arrest warrant, the sheriff must issue a warrant. Both warrants are termed "section 2 warrants" (s.2(5)).

In cases of urgency, the ICC may request the United Kingdom Government to secure the issue of an arrest warrant. There will not be time available for the ICC to supply the Government with the necessary documentation supporting a section 2 warrant request. Thus the Government may transmit the request to the Scottish Ministers "who shall instruct the procurator fiscal to apply for a warrant" to arrest the named individual. On that application being made, the sheriff "shall issue a warrant" (s.3(3)). Such warrants are termed "provisional warrants" (s.3(5)). Persons arrested on provisional warrants must be brought before the sheriff as soon as is practicable (s.4(1)) and must be remanded in custody pending the production of a section 2 warrant (s.4(3)). Where no section 2 warrant is produced the arrested person must be discharged but may subsequently be arrested under a section 2 warrant (s.4(7)).

Rule 44.2

Persons arrested under a section 2 warrant must be brought before the sheriff as soon as is practicable (s.5(1)) so that a delivery order can be made whereby they are delivered up to the ICC or, if they have been convicted, to the state which is to enforce the ICC's sentence. A person so arrested can consent to the delivery order (s.7) but such consent must be in a written form prescribed by Act of Adjournal and be signed in the presence of a sheriff (s.7(3)).

Rule 44.3

The Government may not instruct the execution of the delivery order under s.5 until "the end of the period of 15 days beginning with the date on which the order is made" (s.12(1)). This is to allow for review of the delivery order to be sought by bill of suspension (s.12(5)). However, the subject of the delivery order is entitled to waive his right to review of the delivery order under s.13. The waiver must be in writing in the prescribed form and signed in the presence of a sheriff (s.3(3)).

CHAPTER 45

FUR FARMING (PROHIBITION) (SCOTLAND) ACT 2002

Interpretation of this Chapter

45.1. In this Chapter, "the Act of 2002" means the Fur Farming (Prohibition) (Scotland) Act 2002.

Representations in forfeiture orders

45.2.—(1) This rule applies where the Court is deciding whether to make a forfeiture order in terms of section 2 of the Act of 2002 (forfeiture orders).

(2) A person who wishes to make representations to the court under subsection (7) of section 2 of the Act of 2002 shall do so—

(a) in writing to the Clerk of Court, unless the court otherwise directs; and

(b) by such date as the court directs.

AMENDMENT

Chapter 45 inserted by Act of Adjournal (Criminal Procedure Rules Amendment No.2) (Miscellaneous) 2003 (SSI 2003/468), r.2. Brought into force on October 27, 2003 in accordance with art.1.

GENERAL NOTE

Section 1(1) of the Fur Farming (Prohibition) (Scotland) Act 2002 makes it an offence for anyone to keep animals solely or principally for slaughter (whether by that person or another) for the value of the animals' fur or to breed progeny for such slaughter. This offence includes keeping or breeding animals for sale for subsequent slaughter (s.1(3)). It is also an offence for anyone to cause or permit an offence under s.1(1). The maximum penalty is a fine of £20,000. The offence is triable only summarily (s.1(6)).

In terms of s.2(1) a court in dealing with a person convicted of an offence under s.1(1) may make a forfeiture order (FO) in respect of any animals of any type to which the offence related if these animals are kept by the accused when the order is made or came into his keeping during the period (as defined in s.2(3)) beginning with the making of the FO and ending with the destruction or other disposal of the animals in pursuance of the order. A FO may also be made on conviction of an accused for causing or permitting the offence (s.2(2)). A FO is "an order for the forfeiture and destruction or other disposal of the animals to which the order applies (including any subsequent progeny of those animals)" (s.2(4)). It operates so as to deprive "any person of that person's rights in the animals" (s.2(5)). However, in deciding whether to make a FO the court must take into account any representations made to it by "any person who has an interest in any animals to which the order may apply" (s.2(7)). Persons with an interest in the animals are given a right to appeal to the High Court within seven days beginning with the date of the order (s.2(8)).

Thus it is imperative that any person with an interest in the animals should have notice of the proposed making of a FO so that he can make representations to the sheriff. Such persons are not given a right to appear although r.45.2(2) does not preclude the sheriff's allowing personal appearance or legal representation. Since legal representation or at least legal advice may be necessary (as there may be delicate legal rights in issue) the sheriff should allow a reasonable period within which any representations should be submitted or advice taken by persons whose rights or interests may be affected.

CHAPTER 46

PARENTAL DIRECTIONS UNDER THE SEXUAL OFFENCES ACT 2003

Young offenders: parental directions

46.1. Where a court makes a direction under section 89(1) of the Sexual Offences Act 2003 (young offenders: parental directions) in respect of an individual having parental responsibilities in relation to a young offender, the clerk of the court shall—

(a) intimate the making of the direction; and

(b) deliver or send by post a copy of the notice in Form 20.3A-B (notice of requirement to notify police under Part 2 of the Sexual Offences Act 2003),

to that individual and to the chief constable of the police force within the area of which the young offender resides.

Applications to vary, renew or discharge parental directions

46.2. An application under section 90(1) of the Sexual Offences Act 2003 (parental directions: variations, renewals and discharges) shall be made by petition in Form 46.2.

AMENDMENT

Chapter 46 inserted by Act of Adjournal (Criminal Procedure Rules Amendment No.2) (Sexual Offences Act 2003) 2004 (SSI 2004/206), r.2 (effective May 1, 2004).

GENERAL NOTE

Under s.89(2) of the Sexual Offences Act 2003, a young offender, in respect of whom a parental direction can be made, must be under 16 years of age (though in England he must be under 18 years). Where such a young offender is before the court in respect of a sexual offence the court may direct that the obligations in ss.83–86 (such as notification requirements) for sexual offenders should apply to the parent so that, for example, the parent must attend at the police station with the young offender when notifications obligations are complied with. The chief constable of the police force for the area within which the young offender resides has an interest to be informed of the direction as he is entitled to apply for variation, renewal or discharge of the parental directions (s.90(2)). Under s.90(4) the court, in adjudicating on a petition under r.46.2, must hear the party making the application and any other persons specified in s.90(2), if they wish to be heard, before making any order varying, renewing or discharging the direction as the court considers appropriate.

CHAPTER 47

PROTECTION OF CHILDREN (SCOTLAND) ACT 2003

References under the Protection of Children (Scotland) Act 2003

47.1. Where section 10(5) of the Protection of Children (Scotland) Act 2003 applies, the clerk of court shall forthwith—

(a) post a notice of reference in Form 47.1; and

(b) transmit, by facsimile or other electronic means, a copy of that notice, to the Scottish Ministers.

AMENDMENT

Chapter 47 inserted by Act of Adjournal (Criminal Procedure Rules Amendment No.5) (Miscellaneous) 2004 (SSI 2004/481), r.2 (effective November 26, 2004).

GENERAL NOTE

Section 10(1) of the Protection of Children (Scotland) Act 2003 provides that (subject to subs.(3) and (4)) on convicting an individual of an offence against a child where that offence is a relevant offence, the court *shall* "propose to refer the case of the individual to the Scottish Ministers"; and where the offence is not a relevant offence, the court *may* if it thinks fit propose such a reference. The reference procedure applies whenever the offence was committed (s.10(2)). However, where the accused is under 18 years of age when the offence was committed, the court is not obliged to propose making a reference but may do so *but only if* the court is satisfied that the individual is "likely to commit a further offence against a child" (s.10(3)). Furthermore, where the accused is over 18 years of age at the time of the offence, the court is directed not to propose making a reference "if it is satisfied that the individual is unlikely to commit a further offence against a child" (s.10(4)).

A "relevant offence" is defined in s.10(9)(a) as being those listed in para.1 of Sch.1 to the 2003 Act or if the accused falls within para.2 of that schedule. A person commits any other offence against a child (i.e. other than a relevant offence), in which event the court may propose making a reference, where "the person in relation to whom the offence was committed was a child" (s.10(9)(b)(ii)). Paragraph 1 lists contraventions of ss.12, 15, 22 and 33 of the Children and Young Persons (Scotland) Act 1937 and contraventions of ss.2, 3, 5, 6, 8, 9, 10, 12 and 13(5)(c) of the Criminal Law (Consolidation) (Scotland) Act 1995. Paragraph 2 provides that an accused falls within the scope of the paragraph if he (a) commits incest with a child; (b) procures unlawful sexual intercourse with a child; (c) trades in prostitution or engages in brothel-keeping in relation to a child; (d) procures the commission of a homosexual act in relation to a child; (e) commits any other offence which caused, or was intended to cause, bodily injury to a child; and (f) commits any other offence by engaging in lewd, libidinous practices or behaviour towards a child.

The purpose of a reference is to allow the Scottish Ministers to determine whether to add the individual's name to the list (which the Scottish Ministers keep under s.1(1) of the 2003 Act) of persons whom the Scottish Ministers "consider to be unsuitable to work with children".

The court may not make a reference unless (a) the time limit for applying to the High Court for leave to appeal against the proposed reference has expired without leave having been granted; or (b) if leave has been granted, the appeal has been either abandoned or dismissed (s.10(6)).

CHAPTER 48

PROTECTION OF CHILDREN AND PREVENTION OF SEXUAL OFFENCES
(SCOTLAND) ACT 2005

Interpretation

48.1. In this Chapter "sexual offences prevention order" means a sexual offences prevention order made where subsection (2) or (3) of section 104 of the Sexual Offences Act 2003 applies.

Sexual offences prevention orders

48.2. A sexual offences prevention order shall be in Form 48.2.

Variation, renewal or discharge of sexual offences prevention orders

48.3. An application for the variation, renewal or discharge of a sexual offences prevention order shall be made by petition in Form 48.3.

AMENDMENT

Chapter 48 inserted by Act of Adjournal (Criminal Procedure Rules Amendment No. 5) (Sexual Offences Prevention Orders) 2005 (SSI 2005/472), r.2(2) (effective October 7, 2005).

GENERAL NOTE

Sections 104–113 of the Sexual Offences Act 2003 (c.42) introduced the sexual offences prevention order (SOPO). The 2003 Act is principally concerned with English criminal law, and when it was passed it did not confer on Scottish courts the power given to English courts to make a SOPO. The Protection of Children and Prevention of Sexual Offences (Scotland) Act 2005 (asp 9) amends the 2003 Act to give Scottish courts that power. In terms s.107(1) of the 2003 Act a SOPO prohibits the accused from doing anything described in the order and has effect for a fixed period (which must be not less than five years) specified in the order "or until further order". Where an accused is convicted of an offence listed in paras 36–60 of Sch.3 to the 2003 Act the court may make a SOPO if it is satisfied that "it is necessary to make such an order, for the purpose of protecting the public or any particular members of the public from serious sexual harm from the [accused]" (s.104(1)). The phrase "protecting the public . . ." is defined in s.106(3) as meaning protecting the public in the UK or any particular members of that public from serious physical or psychological harm caused by the accused committing one or more of the scheduled offences.

Schedule 3 is out of date and was not amended by the Scottish Parliament in the 2005 Act to take account of changes in the common law. Thus, para.37 refers to clandestine injury to women although that crime is now comprehended in rape (para.36). Paragraph 42 also specifies "shameless indecency, if a person (other than the offender) involved in the offence was under 18". Shameless indecency is not a crime (see *Webster v Dominick*, 2003 S.L.T. 975). Paragraph 60 is also important. It lists "an offence in Scotland other than [paras 36–59] if the court, in imposing sentence or otherwise disposing of the case, determines for the purposes of this paragraph that there was a significant sexual aspect to the offender's behaviour in committing the offence". A SOPO can be made in respect of behaviour occurring before the commencement of the 2003 Act (s.106(4)).

Rule 48.2

The court may only include in a SOPO prohibitions which are necessary for the purpose of protecting the public or any particular members of the public from serious sexual harm from the accused (s.107(2)). Appeal against the making of a SOPO is by note of appeal. It is appealable as if it were an order referred to in s.106(1)(d) of the 1995 Act for solemn proceedings or, in summary proceedings, an order referred to in s.175(2)(c) (2003 Act, s.111(c) as amended by 2005 Act, s.17(2)). The Appeal Court may suspend a SOPO pending the disposal of the appeal (2003 Act, s.111(d)).

Rule 48.3

The only persons who may apply for variation, discharge or renewal are the accused and the prosecutor (2003 Act, s.112(1)(g) as inserted by 2005 Act, s.17(4)(f)). The appropriate court to apply to under this rule is either the High Court where the SOPO was made in that court or, where it was made in the sheriff court, the sheriff court for the area in which the accused is resident at the time of application and, in any other case, the sheriff court which originally made the order (2003 Act, s.112(1A) as inserted by 2005 Act, s.17(5)). The court must hear the applicant (and any other person if he wishes to be heard) before it determines whether to grant the application (s.108(4)).

A SOPO may be renewed or varied so as to impose additional prohibitions on the accused "only if it is necessary to do so for the purpose of protecting the public or any particular member of the public from serious sexual harm from the [accused] (and any renewed or varied order may contain only such prohibitions as are necessary for this purpose)" (2003 Act, s.108(5)). The accused is entitled to be given by the clerk of court, or sent to him by the clerk by registered post or recorded delivery service, a copy of the order and its renewal, variation or discharge (2003 Act, s.112(3)). There is no provision for an appeal against the court's decision to refuse a petition under r.48.3.

CHAPTER 49

FINANCIAL REPORTING ORDERS

Interpretation

49.1. In this Chapter "financial reporting order" means an order made under section 77(1) of the Serious Organised Crime and Police Act 2005.

Financial reporting orders

49.2. A financial reporting order shall be in Form 49.2.

Variation or revocation of financial reporting orders

49.3.—(1) An application for the variation or revocation of a financial reporting order shall be made by petition in Form 49.3.

(2) On a petition referred to in paragraph (1) being lodged, the court shall—

(a) order intimation of the application to be made to the person in respect of whom the financial reporting order was made or the person to whom reports are to be made under it, as the case may be;

(b) appoint a hearing on the application; and

(c) order intimation of the hearing to the persons referred to in sub-paragraph (a) and to the governor of any institution in which the person in respect of whom the financial reporting order was made is detained.

AMENDMENT

Chapter 49 inserted by Act of Adjournal (Criminal Procedure Rules Amendment No.2) (Financial Reporting Orders) 2006 (SSI 2006/205), para.2(2) (effective May 1, 2006).

GENERAL NOTE

Section 77 of the Serious Organised Crime Act 2005 (c.15) applies to Scotland (s.179(4)) and, taking account of Scottish procedure, makes separate provision for the making of financial reporting orders (FROs) along the lines provided in s.76 for FROs in England and Wales. Section 77(1) provides that a court sentencing or otherwise dealing with a person convicted of specific offences may also make an FRO in respect of him. However, an FRO may only be made where the court "is satisfied that the risk of the person's committing another [relevant offence] is sufficiently high to justify the making of a FRO" (s.77(2)). The relevant offences for subs.(1) and (2) are: common law fraud and any of the "lifestyle offences" specified in Sch.4 to the Proceeds of Crime Act 2002 (s.77(3)).

The effect of an FRO is set out in s.79. The person subject to it must make a report in respect of the period specified in the order starting with the date when the order comes into force (which is the date when it is made: s.77(5)) and for subsequent periods of specified lengths (s.79(2)); set out in the report in the manner specified in the order "such particulars of his financial affairs relating to the period in question as may be specified" (s.79(3)); he must include any specified documents with the report (s.79(4)); make each report within the specified number of days after the end of the specified period (s.79(5)); and make the report to the person specified in the FRO (s.79(6)). An FRO must, therefore, be highly detailed as to what is required (s.79(8)). The Scottish Ministers must make an order specifying the persons who are qualified to act as the persons to whom the report must be made (s.79(9)). This has been done. The list of persons from whom the court may select a specified person is specified as being either a chief constable of a Scottish police force or the Director of the Scottish Drug Enforcement Agency (see art.2 of the Serious Organised Crime and Police Act 2005 (Specified Persons for Financial Reporting Orders) (Scotland) Order 2006 (SSI 2006/170) which came into force on May 1, 2006 (para.1(1)).

An FRO may be made in the sheriff court or High Court. However, where it is made in the sheriff court, the duration of the order must not exceed five years (s.77(6)). If the order is made by the High Court, the order must be for a period not exceeding 20 years if the person is sentenced to life imprisonment (s.77(7)(a)) and otherwise must not exceed 15 years (s.77(7)(b)). Provision may in due course be made, by Act of Adjournal, for the maximum length of reporting periods to be specified in the orders (s.79(7)).

In terms of s.79(10) it is an offence for a person subject to an FRO, without reasonable excuse, to include false or misleading information in a report, or otherwise fail to comply with any requirement of s.79. The offence is prosecutable only on summary complaint but carries a maximum sentence of 12 months' imprisonment and a fine not exceeding level 5 on the standard scale.

Rule 49.1

An order can only be made in the sheriff court or the High Court and cannot be made unless (i) the person to be subject to it has been convicted of either fraud at common law or a lifestyle offence under Sch.4 to the Proceeds of Crime Act 2002; and (ii) the court is satisfied that there is a sufficiently high risk of his committing another offence (whether fraud or lifestyle offence) to justify making the order (s.77(1) and (2)). Convictions for theft, embezzlement, uttering and practical cheating are not qualifying offences.

Rule 49.3

Section 80 provides for variation and recall of an FRO. Application for recall or variation of an FRO may be made by either the person subject to it or the specified person to whom the reports during the reporting periods are to be made (s.80(1)). The application must be made by petition (r.49.3(1)) which must be presented to the court which made the order (s.80(2)).

CHAPTER 50

FOOTBALL BANNING ORDERS

Interpretation

50.1. In this Chapter—

"the 2006 Act" means the Police, Public Order and Criminal Justice Act 2006;

"football banning order" means an order made under section 51(2) of the 2006 Act;

"football banning orders authority" has the meaning given in section 69 of the 2006 Act.

Football banning orders

50.2. A football banning order shall be in Form 50.2.

Variation or termination of football banning orders

50.3.—(1) An application for the variation or termination of a football banning order shall be made by petition in Form 50.3.

(2) On a petition referred to in paragraph (1) being lodged, the court shall–

(a) order intimation of the application to–

(i) in the case of an application by the person subject to the order, the football banning orders authority; or

(ii) in any other case, to the person subject to the order;

(b) appoint a hearing on the application; and

(c) order intimation of the hearing to the persons referred to in sub-paragraph (a) and to the governor of any institution in which the person in respect of whom the football banning order was made is detained.

AMENDMENT

Chapter 50 inserted by the Act of Adjournal (Criminal Procedure Rules Amendment No. 4) (Miscellaneous) 2006 (SSI 2006/436), r.2 (effective September 1, 2006).

GENERAL NOTE

Football banning orders

A football banning order (FBO) under s.51(2) of the Police, Public Order and Criminal Justice Act 2006 (asp 10) can be made instead of, or in addition to, any sentence which the court passes on an accused for an offence which must involve the accused "engagingin violence or disorder" and relate to a football match (s.51(4)). The accused must also have been 16 or over at the time he committed the offence (s.51(1)). Further, an FBO can only be made where there are reasonable grounds to believe that making it would "help to prevent violence or disorder at or in connection with any football matches" (s.51(3)(b)). The index offence relates to a football match if it is committed (a) at a football match or while the accused is entering or leaving (or trying to enter or leave) the ground; or (b) on a journey to or from a football match; or (c) "otherwise, where it appears to the court from all the circumstances that the offence is motivated (wholly or partly) by a football match" (s.51(6)). A person may be regarded as having been on a journey to or from a football match whether or not he attended, or intended to attend, the match and "journey" includes breaks (including overnight breaks) (s.51(8)). References to a "football match" include any place, other than domestic premises, at which a football match is being televised (s.51(7)).

Declarations Section 51(5) provides that where the court does not make a FBO but the court is satisfied that the offence of which the accused was convicted involved the accused engaging in violence or disorder and related to a football match, the court *may* declare that that be the case. This provision is permissive; the court is not required to make this declaration but may consider it appropriate to make the declaration where reasonable grounds do not exist for believing that the making of a FBO would help to prevent violence or disorder at another match.

Violence or disorder The requirement that the accused's offence involved him in engaging in violence or disorder is a disjunctive condition. Either violence or disorder will suffice. Violence is defined as "violence against persons or intentional damage to property and includes (a) threatening violence and (b) doing anything which endangers the life of a person" (s.56(2)). Assault, breach of the peace by shouting menaces or even gesticulating in a manner to threaten violence (*cf. Dyer v Hutchison, Bell and Johnstone*, 2006 S.C.C.R. 377) are covered by this definition but apparently reckless vandalism is for some reason excluded.

Disorder is given an enormously detailed treatment but not an exhaustive definition. Section 56(3) provides that disorder includes (a) stirring up hatred against a group of persons based on their membership (or presumed membership, i.e. presumed by the accused) of a group defined by reference to characteristics specified in s.56(5). These are: colour, race, nationality (including citizenship), ethnic or national origins, membership of a religious group (within the meaning of s.74(7) of the Criminal Justice (Scotland) Act 2003 (asp 7)) or of a social or cultural group with a perceived religious affiliation, sexual orientation, transgender identity (which is defined in subs.(6)) and disability (which means physical or mental impairment of any kind). Transgender identity means any of the following: transvestism, transsexualism, intersexuality or having by virtue of the Gender Recognition Act 2004 (c.7) changed gender by gender reassignment surgery. Presumably sexual orientation, which is not further defined, means male homosexuality, lesbianism and bisexuality.

Appeals For the purposes of the appeal provisions under the 1995 Act, a FBO and a declaration under s.51(5) as well as an order varying a FBO under s.57 and an order terminating a FBO under s.58 are sentences (s.60(1)). Where the High Court quashes a FBO on appeal, that court may make a declaration under s.51(5) unless one of the grounds for quashing the order is that the lower court erred in holding that the index offence was one to which s.51(4) applied (i.e. the offence related to a football match and involved violence or disorder in which the accused engaged) (s.60(3)).

Offences Failure to comply with any condition imposed in a FBO is an offence (s.68(1)) which is triable only on summary complaint. The offence-creating provision makes no reference to any necessary mental element in the offence but it is provided that it is a defence for the accused to prove that he had a reasonable excuse for failing to comply with the requirement (s.68(2)). It is therefore a strict liability offence but subject to a defence which the accused must establish on balance of probabilities. The maximum penalties are six months' imprisonment or a fine not exceeding level 5, or both (s.68(3)).

Rule 50.2

Form 50.3 reflects the requirements in s.53 as to the content of a FBO. A FBO prohibits the accused from entering any premises for the purposes of attending any *regulated* football matches in the UK and requires him to report to a police station in connection with football matches outside the UK (s.53(1)). The order must require the accused (a) to report initially at a police station in Scotland specified in the FBO within five days beginning with the day on which the FBO was made and (b) where a relevant event as specified in Sch.5 to the 2006 Act occurs, to notify the football banning orders authority (i.e. the chief constable of Strathclyde Police: s.69(1)) of the prescribed information as defined in that schedule in relation to that event within seven days beginning with the day on which the event occurs (s.53(2)). All FBOs must require the accused to surrender his passport in connection with regulated football matches outside the UK unless it appears to the court that there are "exceptional circumstances" (s.53(3)). Additional requirements may be imposed in a FBO where the court "considers it would help to prevent violence or disorder at or in connection with any football match" (s.53(4)). Such additional requirements can include prohibiting the accused from entering any premises (including premises to be entered for the purposes of attending non-regulated football matches) (s.53(5)).

A copy of the FBO must be served on the accused and copies must also be sent as soon as reasonably practicable to both the chief constable of Strathclyde Police as the FBO authority and the named police station to which the accused must initially report and also, where the accused is in custody, to the relevant custodian (s.59(1)).

Duration A FBO must specify the period for which it is to have effect and that period must not exceed (a) 10 years where the order is made in tandem with a custodial sentence (whether detention or imprisonment: s.54(3)) or (b) 5 years where either no sentence is imposed or the sentence is non-custodial (s.53(6)–(7)). The period runs from the day on which the FBO is made (s.54(2)).

Regulated football matches This concept is central to FBOs and is defined in s.55. For football matches anywhere within the UK, regulated football matches involve at least one national or territorial team, or SPL club team or member of the Scottish Football League or other team which is a full or associate member of the Football League, the FA Premier League, Football Conference or League of Wales. Regulated matches outside the UK involve a national team appointed to represent Scotland, England or Wales by their respective football associations or a team representing a club.

Rule 50.3

A FBO may be varied by the court which made it where application for variation is made by (a) the accused, (b) the chief constable of the area where the accused resides or (c) the chief constable of an area either in which the police believe the accused already is present or to which the police believe the accused intends to come (s.57(1)). Variation is effected by omitting or imposing the requirement anent passport surrender (but the court can only omit that requirement where there are exceptional circumstances: s.57(2)); and by imposing, replacing or omitting any additional requirements.

Termination of a FBO may be ordered by the court which made the order (s.58(5)) where the accused applies to that court for that purpose but the accused may not seek termination unless the order has had effect for at least two-thirds of the period specified in the order (s.58(2)). In considering whether to order termination, the court is directed to have regard to (a) the accused's character; (b) his conduct since the order was made; (c) the nature of the offence which led to the making of the order; and (d) any other circumstances which the court thinks are relevant (s.58(3)). Where termination is refused, the accused may not re-apply for termination of that same order during a further period of six months beginning with the date of refusal (s.58(4)).

The same requirements for service of copies of orders varying or terminating a FBO apply as are applicable in respect of the original order (see r.50.2).

CHAPTER 51

ANIMAL HEALTH AND WELFARE

Interpretaion

51.1 In this Chapter–

"the 1981 Act"means the Animal Health Act 1981;

the 2006 Act"means the Animal Health and Welfare (Scotland) Act 2006;

"deprivation order"means an order made under section 28E of the 1981 Act, section 39 of the 2006 Act, or section 47 of the Animal Welfare Act 2006

"disqualification order"means an order made under section 28F of the 1981 Act or section 40 of the 2006 Act.

Deprivation Orders

51.2 A deprivation order shall be in Form 51.2.

Representations

51.3—(1) Where the court is considering making a deprivation order and it is practicable to do so–

(a) the court shall appoint a diet for parties to be heard; and

(b) the clerk of court shall intimate the diet to the owner of any animal to which the order would apply.

(2) A person who has received intimation under paragraph (1)(b) and wishes to make representations to the court under section 28E(9) of the 1981 Act, section 39(9) of the 2006 Act or section 47(9) of the Animal Welfare Act 2006 shall do so–

(a) in writing to the clerk of court, unless the court otherwise directs; and

(b) by such date as the court directs.

Forms of appeal by person with interest in animal

51.4 An application under section 28E(11) of the 1981 Act, section 43(2) of the 2006 Act or section 49(2) of the Animal Welfare Act 2006 (appeal) shall be in Form 51.4.

Disqualificaation Orders

51.5 A disqualification order shall be in Form 51.5.

Termination or variation of disqualification orders

51.6 An application for the termination or variation of a disqualification order shall be made by petition in Form 51.6.

GENERAL NOTE

The Animal Health and Welfare (Scotland) Act 2006 (asp 11) amends the Animal Health Act 1981 (c.22) and makes provision for various offences in relation to protected animals. These offences are termed "relevant offences" for the purposes of ss.39 and 40 of the 2006 Act (see s.39(10) and s.40(13)) and are: (i) causing unnecessary suffering to an animal (s.19); (ii) mutilation (by carrying out a prohibited act) (s.20); (iii) performing an operation without due care and humanity (s.21); (iv) administration of poison, etc (s.22); (v) organising and other activities in connection with animals fights (s.23); (vi) failing to take reasonable steps to ensure the needs of an animal are met to the extent required by good practice (s.24(1)); (vii) failing, without reasonable excuse, to comply with a care notice (s.25(7)); (viii) abandonment of an animal in circumstances likely to cause it unnecessary suffering (s.29); and (ix) breaching a disqualification order (s.40(11)).

The 2006 Act also makes provision for two orders which the court may make in the exercise of its discretion on the conviction of any person (including bodies corporate, unincorporated associations and Scottish partnerships: (s.45) of any of these nine relevant offences. The orders are deprivations orders and disqualification orders.

Deprivation orders

Where a person is convicted of a relevant offence (as defined in s.39(10)) the convicting court may make an order to be known as a "deprivation order" in addition to, or instead of, any other order or penalty which may be imposed in relation to a relevant offence (s.39(1) and (5)). A deprivation order is an order depriving a person of possession or ownership (or both) of an animal for the purpose of its destruction or sale or any other disposal. Such an order may include (1) a provision appointing a person who is to secure that the order is carried out and requiring any possessor of the animal in question to give it up to such appointed person; (2) a provision authorising an appointed person and any other person acting on the appointed person's behalf to enter (for the purposes of securing that the deprivation order is carried out) any premises where an animal to which the order applies is kept; and (3) any other provision "as the court considers appropriate in connection with the order" (s.39(6)).

It is further provided that, so far as (3) above is concerned, that power includes in particular the power to require reimbursement of any expenses reasonably incurred in carrying out the deprivation order and the power to give directions as to the retention of any proceeds arising from the disposal of the animal (s.39(7)). This power is necessary to cater for the accused who is unwilling to shoulder the costs of keeping his animals after his conviction (cf *Debidin v Chief Constable, Northern Constabulary*, 2002 S.L.T. (Sh. Ct.) 125 where the chief constable was left to bear the costs of kennelling 35 dogs under s.68 of the Civic Government (Scotland) Act 1982.

In respect of all but one of the relevant offences the court may not order destruction of the animal unless the court is satisfied, on evidence provided (orally or in writing) by a veterinary surgeon, that destruction would be "in the interests of the animal". The one exception is the offence under s.23 (animal fighting) (s.39(8)).

Disqualification orders Under s.40(1) of the 2006 Act, where a person is convicted of a relevant offence the court may make an order to be known as a "disqualification order" by which the court imposes on the convicted person one or more of the disqualifications listed in s.40(2). These disqualifications are from (1) owning or keeping animals (or both); (2) dealing in animals; (3) transporting animals; (4) working with or using animals; (5) riding or driving animals; (6) providing any service including care to animals such that the provision of the service requires taking possession of the animals; (7) taking possession of animals for any activity mentioned in (1)-(6); and (8) taking charge of animals for any, or any other, purpose.

The scope of the disqualification is wide and includes "disqualification from any participation in the activity" identified in the order (s.40(3)). The disqualification order can be made either in addition to, or instead of, any other order or penalty (s.40(6)); and it can be general or restricted to particular kinds of animals (s.40(7)). Where there is a restriction of that sort, the restriction may be expressed so as to allow the convicted person to own or possess a maximum number of the animals before the disqualification applies (s.40(8)). A disqualification order must prescribe its duration and may specify the period during which an application cannot be made under s.42(2) to terminate or vary the order (s.40(9)).

The court in making the order is empowered to suspend its operation (a) for such period as the court considers necessary for enabling arrangements to be made for the keep of the animals and (b) pending an appeal against the making of the order (s.40(10)).

Appeals   Where a deprivation order or a disqualification order is made against a person convicted of a relevant offence, the order is to be treated as a sentence for the purposes of any appeal under the Criminal Procedure (Scotland) Act 1995 (s.43(1)). Special provision required to be made for persons who have an interest in any animal where that person's interests are affected by the making of a deprivation order. In such cases the third party is given the same rights of appeal as the convicted person (s.43(2)).

Rule 51.3   Before the court can make a deprivation order, the court must give the owner of the animal in question an opportunity to make representations unless it is not practicable for the court to do so (s.39(9)). It is suggested that where there is a failure to obtemper this precondition the deprivation order is null and void but only to the extent that any such representations would have materially affected the court's decision to make an order (cf *Seal v Chief Constable of South Wales Police* [2007] UKHL 31).

Rule 51.4   Section 43(2) gives any person who has an interest in the animal in respect of which a deprivation order is made the same right of appeal as the convicted person. The third party may appeal to the High Court of Justiciary against the order "by the same procedure as applies [for convicted persons] in relation to a deprivation order". Thus, where a third party has not been given an opportunity to make representations before the deprivation order is made, he may appeal against the order. To make the right to make representations effectual it should not be material, for the purposes of exercising this right of appeal where the third party was not notified of the proposed order (see rule 51.3(1)), whether it was practicable at the time to give him notice.

The operation of a deprivation order is suspended until (a) any period for an appeal has expired; (b) the period for an appeal against conviction on which the order depends has expired; and (c) any appeal against the deprivation order (or the conviction) has been withdrawn or finally determined (s.43(4)). However, where an appeal is taken thereby suspending the operation of the order, the court which made the order may make an order to be known as an "interim order" containing such provision as the court considers appropriate in relation to the keeping of the animal for so long as the principal order remains suspended (s.43(5)). Where the order is suspended any person who sells or otherwise parts with an animal to which the order applies commits an offence (s.43(8)). The maximum penalty for this offence, which is a summary offence, is six months' imprisonment or a fine not exceeding level 5 on the standard scale, or both (s.46(2)).

Rule 51.6   A disqualification order may be terminated or varied under s.42(1). However, the court in making the order may provide that any application to vary or terminate it cannot be made before the expiry of a certain period (s.40(9)).

Act of Adjournal (Criminal Procedure Rules) 1996

APPENDIX

Form 2.2A

Rule 1.3

Rule 2.2A

Form of notice to accompany the indictment, lists of witnesses and productions and notice of compearance being served on a solicitor under section 66(6C) of the Criminal Procedure (Scotland) Act 1995

Prosecutor's reference ... (*specify*)

Your reference ... (*specify, if known*)

TAKE NOTICE that the attached indictment; list of witnesses; list of productions and notice under section 66(6) of the Criminal Procedure (Scotland) Act 1995 are served on you (*name of solicitor*), the solicitor for [A.B.] (*address*) [*or* Prisoner at the Prison of (*address*)]. By virtue of section 66(6C) of that Act, [A.B.] is taken to have been served with those documents.

Date: (*date*)

(*Signed*)

Prosecutor

(*Name, address, e-mail address and telephone number*)

AMENDMENT

Form 2.2A inserted by the Act of Adjournal (Criminal Procedure Rules Amendment) (Criminal Procedure (Amendment) (Scotland) Act) 2005 (SSI 2005/44), r.2(18) and Sch., Part 1 (subject to r.2(2)–(4)) (effective February 1, 2005).

Form 2.3A

Rule 2.3A

Form of notice to accompany anything being served on, given, notified or intimated to a solicitor under section 72G of the Criminal Procedure (Scotland) Act 1995

Prosecutor's reference . . . (*specify, if known*)

Your reference . . . (*specify, if known*)

TAKE NOTICE that the attached (*specify*) is served on [*or* given to *or* intimated to] you (*name of solicitor*), the solicitor for [A.B.] (*address*) [*or* Prisoner at the Prison of (*address*)] under section 72G of the Criminal Procedure (Scotland) Act 1995.

Date: (*date*)

(*Signed*)

Prosecutor

[*or* Officer of Law or Clerk of Court *or as the case may be*]

(*Name, address, e-mail address and telephone number*)

AMENDMENT

Form 2.3A inserted by the Act of Adjournal (Criminal Procedure Rules Amendment No.4) (Crim-

853

inal Procedure (Amendment) (Scotland) Act 2004) 2004 (SSI 2004/434), r.2 and Sch., Part 1 (effective October 4, 2004).

Form 2.6-A

Rule 2.6(1)

Form of execution of service of indictment and of citation of accused under section 66(2) of the Criminal Procedure (Scotland) Act 1995

EXECUTION OF SERVICE AND CITATION OF ACCUSED

I, *(name and designation)*, on *(date)* duly served on *(name and address of accused)* the indictment against him, with a notice to appear attached to it for the diet in the High Court of Justiciary [*or* Sheriff Court] at *(place)* on *(date)*.

This I did by *(state method of service)*.

(Signed)   *(Signed)*
Witness   Officer of Law

Form 2.6–AA

Rule 2.6(1A)

Form of execution of citation of accused by notice under section 66(4)(b) of the Criminal Procedure (Scotland) Act 1995

EXECUTION OF CITATION OF ACCUSED BY
AFFIXING A NOTICE

I, *(name and designation)*, on *(date)* lawfully cited *(name and address of accused)* to appear for the diet of the High Court of Justiciary [*or* Sheriff Court] at *(place)* on *(date)*.

This I did by affixing a notice in Form 8.2-AA of the Criminal Procedure Rules 1996 to the door of the relevant premises at *(address)*.

(Signed)   *(Signed)*

Witness   Constable

AMENDMENT

Form 2.6-AA inserted by Act of Adjournal (Criminal Procedure Rules Amendment No.2) (Miscellaneous) 2003 (SSI 2003/468), r.2(17) and Sch.3. Brought into force on October 27, 2003 in accordance with art.1.

Form 2.6-AA as amended by the Act of Adjournal (Criminal Procedure Rules Amendment) (Criminal Procedure (Amendment) (Scotland) Act) 2005 (SSI 2005/44), r.2(18) (subject to r.2(2)–(4)) (effective February 1, 2005).

Rule 2.6(2)

Form of execution of service of complaint on accused

EXECUTION OF SERVICE OF COMPLAINT

I, (*name and designation*), on (*date*) lawfully summoned (*name and address of accused as in complaint*) to appear before the Sheriff [*or* District] Court at (*address*) on (*date*) at (*time*) to answer to a complaint at the instance of the procurator fiscal charging him with (*state offence*).

This I did by delivering a copy of the complaint with a citation attached to it by (*state method of service*). [I also delivered to him with the copy of the complaint a notice specifying his previous conviction[s].]

(*Signed*)
Officer of Law

Form 2.6–BA

Rule 2.6(2A)

Form of execution of citation of accused by notice under section 141(2A) of the Criminal Procedure (Scotland) Act 1995

EXECUTION OF CITATION OF ACCUSED BY AFFIXING A NOTICE

I, (*name and designation*) on (*date*) lawfully cited (*name and address of accused as in complaint*) to appear before the Sheriff [*or* District] Court at (*address*) on (*date*) at (*time*) to answer to a complaint at the instance of the procurator fiscal charging him with (*state offence*).

This I did by affixing a notice in Form 16.1-BB of the Criminal Procedure Rules 1996 to the door of the relevant premises at (*address*).

(*Signed*)

Officer of Law

AMENDMENT

Form 2.6-BA inserted by Act of Adjournal (Criminal Procedure Rules Amendment No.2) (Miscellaneous) 2003 (SSI 2003/468), r.2(17) and Sch.3. Brought into force on October 27, 2003 in accordance with art.1.

Form 2.6-BA as amended by the Act of Adjournal (Criminal Procedure Rules Amendment) (Criminal Procedure (Amendment) (Scotland) Act) 2005 (SSI 2005/44), r.2(18) (subject to r.2(2)–(4)) (effective February 1, 2005).

Form 2.6-C

Rule 2.6(3)

Form of execution of personal service of citation of a witness at a trial on indictment

EXECUTION OF PERSONAL SERVICE OF CITATION OF WITNESS

I, (*name and designation*), on (*date*) duly served on (*name and address of witness*) a citation to attend the sitting of the High Court of Justiciary [*or* Sheriff Court] at (*place*) on (*date*), as witness in the case Her Majesty's Advocate v [C.D.] by delivering to him [*or* her] personally a citation in Form 8.2–E of the Criminal Procedure Rules 1996.

(*Signed*)
Officer of Law

Form 2.6-D

Rule 2.6(4)

Form of execution of personal service of citation of witness to appear at summary trial

EXECUTION OF PERSONAL SERVICE OF CITATION OF WITNESS

I, (*name and designation*), on (*date*) lawfully cited (*name and address of witness*) to appear before the Sheriff [*or* District] Court at (*address*) on (*date*) to give evidence for the prosecution [*or* defence] in the complaint at the instance of the procurator fiscal against (*name and address of accused*).

This I did by delivering to him [*or* her] personally a citation in Form 16.6–C of the Criminal Procedure Rules 1996.

(*Signed*)
Officer of Law

Form 2.6-EA

Rule 2.6(5)(a)

Form of execution of citation of offender under section 15(5) or 18(1) of the Prisoners and Criminal Proceedings (Scotland) Act 1993

EXECUTION OF CITATION

I, (*name and designation*), on (*date*) lawfully cited (*name and address of offender*) to appear before the High Court of Justiciary [*or* Sheriff [*or* District] Court at (*address*) on (*date*) at (*time*) for the purpose of answering the application attached [*or* the allegation set out in the written information attached].

This I did by posting on (*date*) a citation in Form 20.3-A [*or* Form 20.3-B] to the offender at the address shown above, by the recorded delivery service [*or* by (*specify method by which citation effected*)].

(Signed)

Clerk of Court
[*or* Officer of Law]

AMENDMENT

Form 2.6E substituted by Act of Adjournal (Criminal Procedure Rules Amendment No.2) (Miscellaneous) 2003 (SSI 2003/468), r.2(17) and Sch.1. Brought into force on October 27, 2003 in accordance with art.1.

Form 2.6-EB

Rule 2.6(5)(b)

Form of execution of citation of probationer under section 232 or 233 of or paragraph 5(1) of Schedule 6 to the Criminal Procedure (Scotland) Act 1995

EXECUTION OF CITATION

I, (*name and designation*), on (*date*) lawfully cited (*name and address of probationer*) to appear before the High Court of Justiciary [*or* Sheriff [*or* District] Court at (*address*) on (*date*) at (*time*) for the purpose of answering an allegation that he [*or* she] has failed to comply with a requirement of a probation order as set out in the attached written information [*or* has been convicted by a Court in Great Britain of an offence committed during the probation period and has been dealt with for that offence] [*or* for the purpose of answering a proposal that his or her probation order be amended by the court].

This I did by posting on (*date*) a citation in Form 20.10-B [*or* Form 20.10-C] to the probationer at the address shown above, by the recorded delivery service [*or* by (*specify method by which citation effected*)].

(Signed)

Clerk of Court
[*or* Officer of Law]

AMENDMENT

Form 2.6-EB inserted by Act of Adjournal (Criminal Procedure Rules Amendment No.2) (Miscellaneous) 2003 (SSI 2003/468), r.2(17) and Sch.1. Brought into force on October 27, 2003 in accordance with art.1.

Form 2.6-EC

Rule 2.6(5)(c)

Form of execution of citation of offender under paragraph 4(1) or 5(3) of Schedule 7 to the Criminal Procedure (Scotland) Act 1995

EXECUTION OF CITATION

I, (*name and designation*), on (*date*) lawfully cited (*name and address of offender*) to appear before the High Court of Justiciary [*or* Sheriff [*or* District] Court at (*address*) on (*date*) at (*time*) for the purpose of answering the application attached.

This I did by posting on (*date*) a citation in Form 20.11-C [*or* Form 20.11-D] to the offender at the address shown above, by the recorded delivery service [*or* by (*specify method by which citation effected*)].

(Signed)

Clerk of Court
[*or* Officer of Law]

AMENDMENT

Form 2.6-EC inserted by Act of Adjournal (Criminal Procedure Rules Amendment No.2) (Miscellaneous) 2003 (SSI 2003/468), r.2(17) and Sch.1. Brought into force on October 27, 2003 in accordance with art.1.

Form 2.6-ED

Rule 2.6(5)(d)

Form of execution of citation of offender under section 239(4) or 240(3) of the Criminal Procedure (Scotland) Act 1995

EXECUTION OF CITATION

I, (*name and designation*), on (*date*) lawfully cited (*name and address of offender*) to appear before the High Court of Justiciary [*or* Sheriff [*or* District] Court at (*address*) on (*date*) at (*time*) for the purpose of answering the application attached [*or* the allegation set out in the written information attached].

This I did by posting on (*date*) a citation in Form 20.12-B to the offender at the address shown above, by the recorded delivery service [*or* by (*specify method by which citation effected*)].

(Signed)

Clerk of Court
[*or* Officer of Law]

AMENDMENT

Form 2.6-ED inserted by Act of Adjournal (Criminal Procedure Rules Amendment No.2) (Miscellaneous) 2003 (SSI 2003/468), r.2(17) and Sch.1. Brought into force on October 27, 2003 in accordance with art.1.

Form 2.6-EE

Rule 2.6(5)(e)

Form of execution of citation of offender under section 245E(3) or 245F(1) of the Criminal Procedure (Scotland) Act 1995

EXECUTION OF CITATION

I, (*name and designation*), on (*date*) lawfully cited (*name and address of offender*) to appear before the High Court of Justiciary [*or* Sheriff [*or* District] Court at (*address*) on (*date*) at (*time*) for the purpose of answering the application attached [*or* the allegation set out in the written information attached].

This I did by posting on (*date*) a citation in Form 20.12A-C [*or* Form 20.12A-D] to the offender at the address shown above, by the recorded delivery service [*or* by (*specify method by which citation effected*)].

(Signed)

Clerk of Court
[*or* Officer of Law]

AMENDMENT

Form 2.6-EE inserted by Act of Adjournal (Criminal Procedure Rules Amendment No.2) (Miscellaneous) 2003 (SSI 2003/468), r.2(17) and Sch.1. Brought into force on October 27, 2003 in accordance with art.1.

Form 2.6-EF

Rule 2.6(5)(f)

Form of execution of citation of offender under section 234E(2) or 234G(1) of the Criminal Procedure (Scotland) Act 1995

EXECUTION OF CITATION

I, *(name and designation)*, on *(date)* lawfully cited *(name and address of offender)* to appear before the High Court of Justiciary [*or* Sheriff [*or* District] Court at *(address)* on *(date)* at *(time)* for the purpose of answering the application attached.

This I did by posting on *(date)* a citation in Form 20.12B-B [*or* Form 20.12B-C] to the offender at the address shown above, by the recorded delivery service [*or* by *(specify method by which citation effected)*].

(Signed)

Clerk of Court
[*or* Officer of Law]

AMENDMENT

Form 2.6-EF inserted by Act of Adjournal (Criminal Procedure Rules Amendment No.2) (Miscellaneous) 2003 (SSI 2003/468), r.2(17) and Sch.1. Brought into force on October 27, 2003 in accordance with art.1.

Form 2.6-EG

Rule 2.6(5)

Form of execution of citation under section 245N(2) or 245P(3) of the Criminal Procedure (Scotland) Act 1995

EXECUTION OF CITATION

I, *(name and designation)*, on *(date)* lawfully cited *(name and address of offender)* to appear before the Sheriff [*or* District] Court at *(address)* on *(date)* at *(time)* for the purpose of answering the allegation set out in the written information attached [*or* the application attached].

This I did by posting on *(date)* a citation in Form 20.12C-B [*or* Form 20.12C-C] to the offender at the address shown above, by the recorded delivery service [*or* by *(specify method by which citation effected)*].

(Signed)

Clerk of Court

[*or* Officer of Law]

AMENDMENT

Form 2.6EG inserted by Act of Adjournal (Criminal Procedure Rules Amendment No.2) (Miscellaneous) 2005 (SSI 2005/160), r.2 (effective March 31, 2005).

Form 2.6-F

Rule 2.6(6)

Form of execution of service under rule 2.3(1)

EXECUTION OF SERVICE

I, (*name and designation*), on (*date*) lawfully cited [*or* served on] (*name and address of person cited or served*) to appear before the High Court of Justiciary [*or* Sheriff [*or* District] Court] at (*address*) on (*date*) at (*time*) for the purpose of (*specify purpose*) [*or* the document a copy of which is attached to this execution [*or otherwise refer to or describe the document*]] [*or set out circumstances of the execution as may be required*].

This I did by (*state method of service*).

(*Signed*)
Officer of Law [*or as the case may be*]

Form 2.6-G

Rule 2.6(7)

Form of execution of service etc. of documents under section 66(6C) or section 72G of the Criminal Procedure (Scotland) Act 1995

EXECUTION OF SERVICE ON ACCUSED'S SOLICITOR IN SOLEMN PROCEEDINGS

I, (*name and designation*), on (*date*) duly served [*or* gave *or* notified *or* intimated *or specify*] the indictment, lists of witnesses and productions and notice of compearance [*or specify the document[s] being served etc.*] on [C.D.], the solicitor for the accused [A.B.].

This I did by (*state method of service*).

[(Signed)	(*Signed*)
Witness]	Prosecutor
	[*or* On behalf of Prosecutor *or* Clerk of Court *or specify*]

AMENDMENT

Form 2.6-G inserted by the Act of Adjournal (Criminal Procedure Rules Amendment) (Criminal Procedure (Amendment) (Scotland) Act) 2005 (SSI 2005/44), r.2(18) and Sch., Part 2 (subject to r.2(2)–(4)) (effective February 1, 2005).

Form 3.1–A

AMENDMENT

Form 3.1-A removed by Act of Adjournal (Criminal Procedure Rules Amendment No.2) (Miscellaneous) 2003 (SSI 2003/468), r.2(17). Brought into force on October 27, 2003 in accordance with art.1.

Form 3.1–B

AMENDMENT

Form 3.1-B removed by Act of Adjournal (Criminal Procedure Rules Amendment No.2) (Miscellaneous) 2003 (SSI 2003/468), r.2(17). Brought into force on October 27, 2003 in accordance with art.1.

Act of Adjournal (Criminal Procedure Rules) 1996

Form 5.2

Rule 5.2(1)

Form of record of proceedings at judicial examination

RECORD OF PROCEEDINGS AT JUDICIAL EXAMINATION

SHERIFF COURT:
DATE:
SHERIFF:
NAME OF ACCUSED APPEARING:
FOR THE PETITIONER: PROCURATOR FISCAL/DEPUTE
FOR THE ACCUSED: SOLICITOR (*address*)

The sheriff, under section 35(2) [*or* 35(6)] of the Criminal Procedure (Scotland) Act 1995 delays the examination until (*date*) at (*time*) in order to allow time for the attendance of the accused's solicitor (*name and address*); and grants warrant to imprison the said accused in the Prison of (*place*) until that date.

(*Signed*)
Sheriff

*The accused intimated that he did not desire to emit a declaration.
*The accused intimated that he desired to emit a declaration.

VERBATIM RECORDER: (*name and address*)
                            to whom the declaration *de fideli administratione officii* was administered.
                            Operation of tape recorder, for these proceedings was commenced at (*time*).

Thereafter the accused, having been judicially admonished, emitted a declaration which was recorded by the verbatim recorder for subsequent transcription.

Thereafter the prosecutor questioned the accused by virtue of section 36 of the Criminal Procedure (Scotland) Act 1995 and the proceedings were recorded by the verbatim recorder for subsequent transcription.

Operation of tape recorder for these proceedings was terminated at (*time*).

(*Signed*)
Sheriff Clerk

The sheriff, having [again] considered the foregoing petition under section 34 of the Criminal Procedure (Scotland) Act 1995, on the motion of the prosecutor, grants warrant to imprison the accused in the Prison of (*place*) for further examination [or until liberated in due course of law].

(*Signed*
Sheriff

*Delete whichever is not appropriate

Form 5.6-A

Rule 5.6(1)

Form of notice of opinion as to error in or incompleteness of transcript of judicial examination under section 38(1)(a) of the Criminal Procedure (Scotland) Act 1995

NOTICE OF OPINION AS TO ERROR IN OR INCOMPLETENESS OF TRANSCRIPT OF JUDICIAL EXAMINATION

To: (*name and address*)

Sheriff Court:

Name of accused:

Date of examination:

Date of service of transcript:

TAKE NOTICE that the Procurator Fiscal [*or* above accused] is of the opinion that the transcript of the proceedings at the above examination contains an error and [, or,] is incomplete in respect that:

(*here give full specification of all alleged points of error or incompleteness*).

(*Signed*)
Procurator Fiscal
[*or* Solicitor for accused]

(*Address and telephone number*)

Place and date:

Form 5.6-B

Rule 5.6(3)

Form of application for rectification of transcript of judicial examination under section 38(1)(b) of the Criminal Procedure (Scotland) Act 1995

APPLICATION FOR RECTIFICATION OF TRANSCRIPT OF JUDICIAL EXAMINATION

Sheriff Court:

Name of accused:

Date of examination:

Presiding sheriff:

Date of service of notice of opinion under section 38(1)(a)
of the Criminal Procedure (Scotland) Act 1995:

The Procurator Fiscal [*or* above accused] applies to the sheriff for rectification of the transcript of the proceedings relating to the above examination. Details of the alleged error and, or, incompleteness are specified in the notice of opinion a copy of which is attached to this application.

(*Signed*)
Procurator Fiscal
[*or* Solicitor for accused]

(*Address and telephone number*)

Place and date:

Form 5.6-C

Form of intimation of agreement for the purposes of section 38(1)(a) of the Criminal Procedure (Scotland) Act 1995

INTIMATION OF AGREEMENT WITH NOTICE OF OPINION

To: (*name and address*)

Sheriff Court:

Name of accused:

Date of examination:

Date of service of notice of opinion
under section 38(1)(a) of the
Criminal Procedure (Scotland) Act 1995:

The Procurator Fiscal [*or* above accused] agrees with the opinion expressed in the notice specified above.

A copy of this intimation has been sent to the sheriff clerk of the above court.

> (*Signed*)
> Procurator Fiscal
> [*or* Solicitor for accused]
>
> (*Address and telephone number*)

Place and date:

Form 5.8

Form of intimation by prosecutor of postponement of trial diet under section 37(7)(b) of the Criminal Procedure (Scotland) Act 1995

INTIMATION OF POSTPONEMENT OF TRIAL DIET

HER MAJESTY'S ADVOCATE against (*insert names of all accused*)

To: (*name and address*)

(1) On (*date*) the court, in exercise of its powers under section 37(7)(b) of the Criminal Procedure (Scotland) Act 1995, in your absence postponed the trial diet to the sitting commencing on (*date*);

(2) TAKE NOTICE THEREFORE that YOU ARE REQUIRED TO APPEAR at (*place*) Sheriff Court on (*date*) at (*time*) to answer to the indictment which has already been served upon you.

BY AUTHORITY OF HER MAJESTY'S ADVOCATE

> (*Signed*)
> Procurator Fiscal

Place and date:

Form 7.1

Form of written application for assessment order under sections 52B(1) and 52C(1) of the Criminal Procedure (Scotland) Act 1995

UNTO THE RIGHT HONOURABLE THE LORD JUSTICE GENERAL, LORD JUSTICE CLERK AND LORDS COMMISSIONERS OF JUSTICIARY

[*or* UNTO THE HONOURABLE THE SHERIFF OF (*name of sheriffdom*) AT (*place*)]

APPLICATION

under section 52B(1) [*or* 52C(1)] of the Criminal Procedure (Scotland) Act 1995

by

Her Majesty's Advocate

[*or* [A.B.] Procurator Fiscal] [*or* Scottish Ministers]

in respect of

[C.D.] (*address*) [*or* Prisoner in the Prison of (*place*)]

for

Assessment order

Prosecution reference ....

Court reference.........................

HUMBLY SHEWETH:

1. That [C.D.] has been indicted at the instance of Her Majesty's Advocate [*or* has been charged in the above court on a petition [*or* summary complaint] at the instance of the procurator fiscal] with a preliminary hearing [*or* trial diet] in the High Court of Justiciary sitting at (*place*) on (*date*) [*or* with a first diet on (*date*)] and [*or* with a trial diet on (*date*)] [in the sheriff court of (*place*)][*or* and has been convicted of (*state crime or offence*)].

[**2.** That [C.D.] is presently in custody at (*place*).]

3. That it appears [C.D.] has a mental disorder and that it is appropriate that an assessment order be made in respect of [C.D.] [, and a copy medical report is attached to this application.]

MAY IT THEREFORE, please your Lordship[s]—
[(a)] to fix a diet for the purpose of considering this application for an assessment order; [*or* and

(b) to make an assessment order authorising the measures under section 52D(6) of the Criminal Procedure (Scotland) Act 1995].

ACCORDING TO JUSTICE, etc.

(*Signed*)

For Her Majesty's Advocate

[*or* Procurator Fiscal (Depute)]

[*or* For Scottish Ministers].

AMENDMENT

Forms 7.1-A and 7.1-B substituted with Form 7.1 by the Act of Adjournal (Criminal Procedure Rules Amendment No. 4) (Mental Health (Care and Treatment) (Scotland) Act 2003) 2005 (SSI 2005/457), r.2(3) and Sch. (effective October 5, 2005).

Form 7.3

Rule 7.3(1)

Form of written application for treatment order under sections 52K(1) and 52L(1) of the Criminal Procedure (Scotland) Act 1995

UNTO THE RIGHT HONOURABLE THE LORD JUSTICE GENERAL, LORD JUSTICE CLERK AND LORDS COMMISSIONERS OF JUSTICIARY

[*or* UNTO THE HONOURABLE THE SHERIFF OF (*name of sheriffdom*) AT (*place*)]

APPLICATION

under section 52K(1) [*or* 52L(1)] of the Criminal Procedure (Scotland) Act 1995

by

Her Majesty's Advocate

[*or* [A.B.] Procurator Fiscal] [*or* Scottish Ministers]

in respect of

[C.D.] (*address*) [*or* Prisoner in the Prison of (*place*)]

for

Treatment order

Prosecution reference . . . .

Court reference . . . .

HUMBLY; SHEWETH:

1. That [C.D.] has been indicted at the instance of Her Majesty's Advocate [*or* has been charged in the above court on a petition [*or* summary complaint] at the instance of the procurator fiscal] [with a preliminary hearing [*or* trial diet] in the High Court of Justiciary sitting at (*place*) on (*date*)] [*or* with a first diet on (*date*)] and [*or* with a trial diet on (*date*)] [in the sheriff court of (*place*)][*or* and has been convicted of (*state crime or offence*)].

[**2.** That [C.D.] is presently in custody at (*place*).]

3. That it appears [C.D.] has a mental disorder and that it is appropriate that a treatment order be made in respect of [C.D.], [and a copy medical report is [*or* copy medical reports are] attached to this application].

MAY IT THEREFORE, please your Lordship[s]—
[(a)] to fix a diet for the purpose of considering this application for a treatment order; [*or* and

(b) to make a treatment order authorising the measures under section 52M(6) of the Criminal Procedure (Scotland) Act 1995].

ACCORDING TO JUSTICE, etc.

(*Signed*)

For Her Majesty's Advocate

[*or* Procurator Fiscal (Depute)]

[*or* For Scottish Ministers].

AMENDMENT

Form 7.3 inserted by the Act of Adjournal (Criminal Procedure Rules Amendment No. 4) (Mental Health (Care and Treatment) (Scotland) Act 2003) 2005 (SSI 2005/457), r.2(3) and Sch. (effective October 5, 2005).

Form 7.5

Rule 7.5

Form of order for diet of hearing and warrant to bring accused to court for hearing on variation of assessment order under section 52G(9) or review of treatment order under section 52Q of the Criminal Procedure (Scotland) Act 1995

(*Place and date*) The Lord Commissioner of Justiciary [*or* The Sheriff] appoints (*date*) at (*time*) within (*place*) as a diet for a hearing on a report for the variation of an assessment order [*or* report for review of a treatment order]; grants warrant to authorised officers of hospital [*or* officers of law] to bring (*name of accused*) before the court for that diet.

(*Signed*)

Clerk of Justiciary

[*or* Sheriff].

AMENDMENT

Form 7.5 inserted by the Act of Adjournal (Criminal Procedure Rules Amendment No. 4) (Mental Health (Care and Treatment) (Scotland) Act 2003) 2005 (SSI 2005/457), r.2(3) and Sch. (effective October 5, 2005).

Form 7.6

Rule 7.6(1)

Form of order for diet and warrant to bring offender to court for hearing on interim compulsion order

(*Place and date*) The Lord Commissioner of Justiciary [*or* The Sheriff] appoints (*date*) at (*time*) within (*place*) as a diet for a hearing on a report on an interim compulsion order; grants warrant to authorised officers of hospital [*or* officers of law] to bring (*name of offender*) before the court for that diet.

(*Signed*)

Clerk of Justiciary

[*or* Sheriff]

AMENDMENT

Form 7.6 inserted by the Act of Adjournal (Criminal Procedure Rules Amendment No. 4) (Mental Health (Care and Treatment) (Scotland) Act 2003) 2005 (SSI 2005/457), r.2(3) and Sch. (effective October 5, 2005).

Rule7.9

Form for order of diet and warrant

Form 7.9

Rule 7.9

Form of note of appeal under section 62 or 63 of the Criminal Procedure (Scotland) Act 1995

UNTO THE RIGHT HONOURABLE THE LORD JUSTICE GENERAL, THE LORD JUSTICE CLERK AND THE LORDS COMMISSIONERS OF JUSTICIARY

NOTE OF APPEAL

by

HER MAJESTY'S ADVOCATE

[*or* [A.B.] (*address*)

[*or* Prisoner in the Prison of (*place*)]]

HUMBLY SHEWETH:

1. That on (*date*) the High Court of Justiciary [*or* Sheriff] at (*place*) made the following finding [*or* order][*or* acquittal]:–

(*specify*)

2. That Her Majesty's Advocate [*or* [A.B.]] appeals to the High Court of Justiciary against that decision on the following grounds:–

(*specify*)

ACCORDING TO JUSTICE, ETC.

(*Signed*)

Prosecutor

[*or* Legal representative of [A.B.]]

(*Name, address, e-mail address and telephone number*)

(*Place and date*)

AMMENDMENT

Form 7.9 inserted by the Act of Adjournal (Criminal Procedure Rules Ammendment No. 3) (Miscellaneous) 2007 (SSI 2007/276), r.2(3) and Sch (effective May 2, 2007)

Form 8.1-A

Form of note of appeal against grant or refusal of extension of period of 11 or 12 months under section 65(8) of the Criminal Procedure (Scotland) Act 1995

UNTO THE RIGHT HONOURABLE THE LORD JUSTICE GENERAL, LORD JUSTICE CLERK AND LORDS COMMISSIONERS OF JUSTICIARY

NOTE OF APPEAL

under section 65(8) of the
Criminal Procedure (Scotland) Act 1995

by

[A.B.]

[whose domicile of citation has been specified as (*specify*)]

Appellant

against

[HER MAJESTY'S ADVOCATE]

Respondent

HUMBLY SHEWETH:

1. That at the sheriff court of the (*name of sheriffdom and place of court*) on (*date*) the appellant [, along with (*name(s) of co-accused*),] appeared on petition at the instance of the procurator fiscal of that court on [a] charge[s] of (*specify*).

2. That the appellant was committed for trial on (*date*) and was released on bail on (*date*).

3. That the appellant was indicted to a preliminary hearing within the High Court of Justiciary [*or* That the appellant was indicted to stand trial within the High Court of Justiciary] [*or* sheriff court] sitting at (*place*) on (*date*)].

4. That an application under section 65(3) of the Criminal Procedure (Scotland) Act 1995 was presented to the High Court of Justiciary [*or* sheriff court] on (*date*) by or on behalf of Her Majesty's Advocate and heard in the High Court of Justiciary [*or* sheriff court] at (*place*) on (*date*).

5. That Lord [*or* Sheriff] (*name*) extended [*or* refused to extend] the period of 11 [*or* 12] months which would have expired on (*date*) by (*number*) days.

6. That the grant [or refusal] of the extension is unreasonable in respect that (*here state briefly reasons for appeal*).

ACCORDING TO JUSTICE, etc.

(*Signed*)

Prosecutor

[*or* Legal representative of [A.B.]]

(*Name, address, e-mail address and telephone number*)

(*Place and date*)

AMENDMENT

Form 8.1-A substituted by the Act of Adjournal (Criminal Procedure Rules Amendment) (Criminal Procedure (Amendment) (Scotland) Act) 2005 (SSI 2005/44), r.2(18) and Sch., Part 3 (subject to r.2(2)–(4)) (effective February 1, 2005).

Form 8.1-B

Rule 8.1(2)

Form of note of appeal against grant or refusal of extension of 80, 110 or 140 days period of committal under section 65(8) of the Criminal Procedure (Scotland) Act 1995

UNTO THE RIGHT HONOURABLE THE LORD JUSTICE GENERAL, LORD JUSTICE CLERK AND LORDS COMMISSIONERS OF JUSTICIARY

NOTE OF APPEAL
under section 65(8) of the
Criminal Procedure (Scotland) Act 1995

by

[A.B.]
[presently a prisoner in the Prison of (place)]

Appellant

against

[HER MAJESTY'S ADVOCATE]

Respondent

HUMBLY SHEWETH:

1. That at the sheriff court of the (*name of sheriffdom and place of court*) on (*date*) the appellant [, along with (*name(s) of co-accused*),] appeared on petition at the instance of the procurator fiscal of that court on [a] charge(s) of (*specify*).

2. That the appellant was committed until liberated in due course of law on (*date*) and remains in custody.

3. That no indictment has been served on the appellant [*or* That the appellant was cited to a preliminary hearing within the High Court of Justiciary on (*date*) at (*place*).][A trial diet has been appointed by the court within the High Court of Justiciary sitting at (place) on (date)][*or* That the appellant was indicted to stand trial within the sheriff court] sitting at (*place*) on (*date*)].

4. That an application under section 65(5) of the Criminal Procedure (Scotland) Act 1995 was presented to the High Court of Justiciary [*or* sheriff court] sitting at (*place*) on (*date*) by or on behalf of Her Majesty's Advocate and was heard in that court on (*date*).

5. That Lord [*or* Sheriff] (*name*) extended [*or* refused to extend] the period of 80 [*or* 110 *or* 140] days which would have expired on (*date*) by (*number*) days.

6. That the grant [*or* refusal] of the extension is unreasonable in respect that (*here state briefly reasons for appeal*).

ACCORDING TO JUSTICE, etc.

(*Signed*)

Prosecutor
[*or* Legal representative of [A.B.]]

(*Name, address, e-mail address and telephone number*)

(*Place and date*)

AMENDMENT

Form 8.1-B substituted by the Act of Adjournal (Criminal Procedure Rules Amendment) (Criminal Procedure (Amendment) (Scotland) Act) 2005 (SSI 2005/44), r.2(18) and Sch., Part 3 (subject to r.2(2)–(4)) (effective February 1, 2005).

Form 8.2-A

Rule 8.2(1)

Form of notice of citation to be affixed to the door of the relevant premises under section 66(4)(b) of the Criminal Procedure (Scotland) Act 1995

IMPORTANT NOTICE

(CITATION)

Prosecution reference: . . . .

TO: (*name*) (*date of birth*) (*address*)

A CRIMINAL CASE IS BEING BROUGHT AGAINST YOU

A document has been prepared which sets out the criminal charges against you.

That document (the "indictment") may be collected by you with a list of the witnesses against you and a list of any productions to be put in evidence against you by the prosecutor from (*name and address of police station*).

YOU MUST APPEAR at (*place*) **High Court of Justiciary** (*address*) on (*date*) at (*time*) for a preliminary hearing [*or* at (*place*) **Sheriff Court** (*address*) on (*date*) at (*time*) for a first diet **and** on (*date*) at (*time*) for a trial diet] at which you will be required to answer the criminal charges against you in the indictment.

IF YOU DO NOT ATTEND THE COURT, A WARRANT MAY BE ISSUED FOR YOUR ARREST

This notice was affixed by me (*name and designation*) on (*date*).

(*Signed*)

Constable

(*Name*)

(*Signed*)

Witness

(*Name*)

AMENDMENT

Form 8.2-A substituted by the Act of Adjournal (Criminal Procedure Rules Amendment) (Criminal Procedure (Amendment) (Scotland) Act) 2005 (SSI 2005/44), r.2(18) and Sch., Part 4 (subject to r.2(2)–(4)) (effective February 1, 2005).

Form 8.2-B

Rule 8.2(2), 9A.3 and 12.7

Form of notice to appear under section 66(6) of the Criminal Procedure (Scotland) Act 1995

IMPORTANT NOTICE

(CITATION)

Prosecution reference: . . . .

TO: (*name*) (*date of birth*) (*address*)

A CRIMINAL CASE IS BEING BROUGHT AGAINST YOU

A document has been prepared which sets out the criminal charges against you.

That document (the "indictment") is attached to this notice.

YOU MUST APPEAR at (*place*) **High Court of Justiciary** (*address*) on (*date*) at (*time*) for a preliminary hearing [*or* at (*place*) **Sheriff Court** (*address*) on (*date*) at (*time*) for a first diet and on (date) at (time) for a trial diet] at which you will be required to answer the criminal charges against you in the indictment.

IF YOU DO NOT ATTEND THE COURT, A WARRANT MAY BE ISSUED FOR YOUR ARREST

(*Signed*)

Prosecutor

(*Name, address, e-mail address and telephone number*)

(*Place and date*)

AMENDMENT

Form 8.2-AA substituted by the Act of Adjournal (Criminal Procedure Rules Amendment) (Criminal Procedure (Amendment) (Scotland) Act) 2005 (SSI 2005/44), r.2(18) and Sch., Part 4 (subject to r.2(2)–(4)) (effective February 1, 2005).

Form 8.2-C

Rules 8.2(2), 9A.3 and 12.7

Form of notice to accused to appear under section 66(6) of the Criminal Procedure (Scotland) Act 1995 where the charge in the indictment is of committing a sexual offence to which section 288C, or an offence to which section 288E, of the Criminal Procedure (Scotland) Act 1995 applies.

IMPORTANT NOTICE

(CITATION)

Court Reference. . . . .

Prosecution Reference:. . . . .

TO: (*name*) (*date of birth*) (*address*)

A CRIMINAL CASE IS BEING BROUGHT AGAINST YOU

A document has been prepared which sets out the criminal charges against you.

That document (the "indictment") is attached to this notice.

YOU MUST APPEAR at (*place*) **High Court of Justiciary** (*address*) on (*date*) at (*time*) for a preliminary hearing [*or* at (*place*) **Sheriff Court** (*address*) on (*date*) at (*time*) for a first diet **and** on (*date*) at (*time*) for a trial diet] at which you will be required to answer the criminal charges against you in the indictment.

Because you are being charged with at least one sexual offence or a serious offence where a witness is under the age of twelve years old— ..

(1) if you are tried for the offence, your defence may be conducted only by a lawyer;

(2) it is therefore in your interests, if you have not already done so, to get the professional assistance of a solicitor;

(3) if you do not engage a solicitor for the purposes of your defence at the preliminary hearing or the trial, the court will do so.

IF YOU DO NOT ATTEND THE COURT, A WARRANT MAY BE ISSUED FOR YOUR ARREST

(*Signed*)

Prosecutor

(*Name, address, e-mail address and telephone number*)

(*Place and date*)

AMENDMENT

Form 8.2-B substituted by the Act of Adjournal (Criminal Procedure Rules Amendment) (Criminal Procedure (Amendment) (Scotland) Act) 2005 (SSI 2005/44), r.2(18) and Sch., Part 4 (subject to r.2(2)–(4)) (effective February 1, 2005).

Form 8.2-C substituted by the Act of Adjournal (Criminal Procedure Rules Amendment No.3) (Vulnerable Witnesses (Scotland) Act 2004) 2005 (SSI 2005/188), r.2, subject to the conditions in r.2(2) (effective April 1, 2005).

Rule 8.2(3)

Form of postal citation of witness to appear at trial on indictment

IMPORTANT NOTICE

(CITATION)

Prosecution reference (*if known*): . . . .

Defence reference (*if known*) . . . .

TO: (*name*) (*date of birth*) (*address*)

DATE OF CITATION: (*date*)

YOU ARE WITNESS FOR THE PROSECUTION [*OR* DEFENCE] IN THE CRIMINAL CASE AGAINST (*NAME*)

YOU MUST APPEAR at (*place*) **High Court of Justiciary** (*address*) on (*date*) at (*time*) [*or* at (*place*) **Sheriff Court** (*address*) on (*date*) at (*time*)].

IF YOU DO NOT ATTEND, THE COURT MAY GRANT A WARRANT FOR YOUR ARREST

Please complete, sign and return the enclosed response form to the Procurator Fiscal [*or* the accused *or* the solicitor for the accused] in the pre-paid envelope provided by (*date*).

(*Signed*)

Prosecutor

[*or* Accused *or* Solicitor for the Accused]

(*Name, address, e-mail address and telephone number*)

AMENDMENT

Forms 8.2-BA substituted by the Act of Adjournal (Criminal Procedure Rules Amendment) (Criminal Procedure (Amendment) (Scotland) Act) 2005 (SSI 2005/44), r.2(18) and Sch., Part 4 (subject to r.2(2)–(4)) (effective February 1, 2005).

Form 8.2-E

Form of response form to be completed and returned by witness cited to appear at a trial on indictment

WITNESS RESPONSE FORM

Prosecution reference (*if known*): . . . .

Defence reference (*if known*) . . . .

To: Procurator Fiscal [*or* (*name*) accused *or* solicitor for (*name*)] (*address and references to be completed by person serving the citation*)

From: (*name to be printed by person serving the citation*)

Date: (*specify*)

I, (*name and address of witness to be completed by person serving the citation*), have received the citation to appear as a witness for the prosecution [*or* defence] in the case of Her Majesty's Advocate against (*name of accused to be completed by person serving the citation*) on (*date to be inserted by person serving the citation*) at (*place to be inserted by person serving the citation*).

I shall attend on that date.

_____ (*Signed*) _____

Amendment

Form 8.2C substituted by the Act of Adjournal (Criminal Procedure Rules Amendment) (Criminal Procedure (Amendment) (Scotland) Act) 2005 (SSI 2005/44), r.2(18) and Sch., Part 4 (subject to r.2(2)–(4)) (effective February 1, 2005).

Form 8.2-F

Form of personal citation of witness to appear at a trial on indictment

IMPORTANT NOTICE

(CITATION)

Prosecution reference: . . . .

Defence reference: (*if known*) . . . .

TO: (*name*) (*date of birth*) (*address*)

DATE: (*date*)

YOU ARE WITNESS FOR THE PROSECUTION [OR DEFENCE] IN THE CRIMINAL CASE AGAINST (*NAME*)

YOU MUST APPEAR at (*place*) **High Court of Justiciary** (*address*) on (*date*) at (*time*) [*or* at (*place*) **Sheriff Court** (*address*) on (*date*) at (*time*)].

IF YOU DO NOT ATTEND, THE COURT MAY GRANT A WARRANT FOR YOUR ARREST

(*Signed*)

Officer of Law

(*Name, address, e-mail address and telephone number*)

AMENDMENT

Form 8.2-D substituted by the Act of Adjournal (Criminal Procedure Rules Amendment) (Criminal Procedure (Amendment) (Scotland) Act) 2005 (SSI 2005/44), r.2(18) and Sch., Part 4 (subject to r.2(2)–(4)) (effective February 1, 2005).

Form 8.2-G

Rule 8.2(1)

Form of notice of citation of body corporate to be affixed to the door of the relevant premises under section 66(4)(b) of the Criminal Procedure (Scotland) Act 1995

IMPORTANT NOTICE

(CITATION)

Prosecution reference: . . . .

TO: (*name of body corporate*) (*address*)

A CRIMINAL CASE IS BEING BROUGHT AGAINST (*NAME OF BODY CORPORATE*)

A document has been prepared which sets out the criminal charges against (*name of body corporate*).

That document (the "indictment") may be collected with a list of the witnesses and productions against (*name of body corporate*) from (*name and address of police station*).

(*NAME OF BODY CORPORATE*) **MUST BE REPRESENTED*** at (*place*) **High Court of Justiciary** (*address*) on (*date*) at (*time*) for a preliminary hearing [*or* at (*place*) **Sheriff Court** (*address*) on (*date*) at (*time*) for a first diet and on (*date*) at (*time*) for a trial diet] at which (*name of body corporate*) will be required to answer the criminal charges against it in the indictment.

[*Where the indictment is in respect of the High Court*: IF (*NAME OF BODY CORPORATE*) IS **NOT REPRESENTED AT THE PRELIMINARY HEARING—**

(a) THE HEARING MAY PROCEED; AND

(b) A TRIAL DIET MAY BE APPOINTED IN ITS ABSENCE]

IF (*NAME OF BODY CORPORATE*) IS NOT REPRESENTED AT THE TRIAL DIET, THE TRIAL MAY PROCEED IN ITS ABSENCE

This notice was affixed by me (*name and designation*) on (*date*).

(*Signed*)

Constable

(*Name*)

(*Signed*)

Witness

(*Name*)

*By a representative under section 70(4) of the Criminal Procedure (Scotland) Act 1995, by counsel (an advocate or solicitor advocate) or by a solicitor.

AMENDMENT

Form 8.2-E substituted by the Act of Adjournal (Criminal Procedure Rules Amendment) (Criminal Procedure (Amendment) (Scotland) Act) 2005 (SSI 2005/44), r.2(18) and Sch., Part 4 (subject to r.2(2)–(4)) (effective February 1, 2005).

Form 8.2-H

Rule 8.2(5)

Form of notice for body corporate to appear under section 66(6) of the Criminal Procedure (Scotland) Act 1995

IMPORTANT NOTICE

(CITATION)

Prosecution reference: . . . .

TO: (*name of body corporate*) (*address*)

A CRIMINAL CASE IS BEING BROUGHT AGAINST (*NAME OF BODY CORPORATE*)

A document has been prepared which sets out the criminal charges against (*name of body corporate*).

That document (the "indictment") is attached to this notice.

(*NAME OF BODY CORPORATE*) **MUST BE REPRESENTED*** at (*place*) **High Court of Justiciary** (*address*) on (*date*) at (*time*) for a preliminary hearing [*or* at (*place*) **Sheriff Court** (*address*) on (*date*) at (*time*) for a first diet and on (*date*) at (*time*) for a trial diet] at which (*name of body corporate*) will be required to answer the criminal charges against it in the indictment.

[*Where the indictment is in respect of the High Court*: **IF (*NAME OF BODY CORPORATE*) IS NOT REPRESENTED AT THE PRELIMINARY HEARING—**

(a) THE HEARING MAY PROCEED; AND

(b) A TRIAL DIET MAY BE APPOINTED IN ITS ABSENCE]

IF (*NAME OF BODY CORPORATE*) IS NOT REPRESENTED AT THE TRIAL DIET, THE TRIAL MAY PROCEED IN ITS ABSENCE.

(*Signed*)

Officer of Law

(*Name, address, e-mail address and telephone number*)

*By a representative under section 70(4) of the Criminal Procedure (Scotland) Act 1995, by counsel (an advocate or solicitor advocate) or by a solicitor.

AMENDMENT

Form 8.2-H inserted by the Act of Adjournal (Criminal Procedure Rules Amendment) (Criminal Procedure (Amendment) (Scotland) Act) 2005 (SSI 2005/44), r.2(18) and Sch., Part 4 (subject to r.2(2)–(4)) (effective February 1, 2005).

Rule 8.3

Form of notice of previous convictions in solemn proceedings

NOTICE OF PREVIOUS CONVICTIONS APPLYING TO (name of accused)

In the event of your being convicted of the charge(s) in the indictment to which this notice is attached, it is intended to place before the court the following previous conviction(s) applying to you.

Date	Place of Trial	Court	Offence	Sentence

(Signed)
Procurator Fiscal
Date:

[*To be inserted only where the notice is to include any details which the prosecutor proposes to provide under section 101(3A) of the Criminal Procedure (Scotland) Act 1995 (risk assessment order: details regarding offences):* In the event of your being convicted of the charge(s) in the indictment to which this notice is attached, it is intended to place before the court the following details regarding the offences in question: (*specify*)

(Signed)
Prosecutor]

AMENDMENT

Form 8.3 as amended by Act of Adjournal (Criminal Procedure Rules Amendment No.3) (Risk Assessment Orders and Orders for Lifelong Restriction) 2006 (SSI 2006/302), para.2(7) (effective June 20, 2006).

Rule 8A.1(1)

Form of notification of engagement as solicitor in solemn proceedings

NOTIFICATION

of

ENGAGEMENT AS SOLICITOR BY THE ACCUSED

in the case

against

[A.B.] (*address*)

[*or* Prisoner at the Prison of (*place*)]

Prosecutor's reference . . . (*specify, if known*)

My reference . . . (*specify*)

Date: (*date*)

TAKE NOTICE that I have been engaged by the accused, (*name*), (*date of birth*) for the purposes of his [*or* her] defence [*where appropriate, specify part of proceedings for which engaged*].

[The current intention is that the accused will be represented by [*name of counsel, if known*] at the (*specify diet*) on (*date*) at (*place*).]

(*Signed*)

Solicitor

(*Name, address, e-mail address and telephone number*)

AMENDMENT

Form 8A.1-A inserted by the Act of Adjournal (Criminal Procedure Rules Amendment No.4) (Criminal Procedure (Amendment) (Scotland) Act 2004) 2004 (SSI 2004/434), r.2 and Sch., Part 2 (effective October 4, 2004).

Rule 8A.1(2)

Form of notification of dismissal or withdrawal of solicitor for accused in solemn proceedings

NOTIFICATION

of

DISMISSAL OR WITHDRAWAL OF SOLICITOR

in the case

against

[A.B.] (*address*)

[*or* Prisoner at the Prison of (*place*)]

Prosecutor's reference . . . (*specify, if known*)

My reference . . . (*specify*)

Date: (*date*)

TAKE NOTICE that with effect from (*date*) I have been dismissed by [*or* have withdrawn from acting for] (*name of accused*) (*date of birth*).

A trial diet [*or specify any hearing(s) fixed*] has [*or* have] been fixed for (*date(s)*).

[*Insert any of the following statements which applies:–*

The accused is charged with an offence to which section 288C of the Criminal Procedure (Scotland) Act 1995 (certain sexual offences) applies.

The proceedings are proceedings to which section 288E of the Criminal Procedure (Scotland) Act 1995 (certain proceedings involving child witnesses under the age of 12) applies.

The accused is prohibited from conducting his defence by virtue of an order under section 288F of the Criminal Procedure (Scotland) Act 1995 (prohibition of personal defence in other cases involving vulnerable witnesses).]

(*Signed*)

Solicitor

(*Name, address, e-mail address and telephone number*)

AMENDMENT

Form 8A.1-B inserted by the Act of Adjournal (Criminal Procedure Rules Amendment No.4) (Criminal Procedure (Amendment) (Scotland) Act 2004) 2004 (SSI 2004/434), r.2 and Sch., Part 2 (effective October 4, 2004).

Act of Adjournal (Criminal Procedure Rules) 1996

Form 9.1

Rule 9.1(1)

Form of minute of notice under section 71(2) of the Criminal Procedure (Scotland) Act 1995

UNTO THE HONOURABLE SHERIFF OF (*name of sheriffdom*)

AT (*place*)

MINUTE

by

HER MAJESTY'S ADVOCATE

[*or* [A.B.] (*address*)

[*or* Prisoner in the Prison of (*place*)]]

HUMBLY SHEWETH:

1. That [A.B.] [, along with (*name(s) of co-accused*),] has been indicted at the instance of Her Majesty's Advocate for trial in the sheriff court at (*place*) on (*date*) with a first diet on (*date*).

2. That the minuter is raising the following preliminary plea[s] [*or* preliminary issue[s]]:- (*here specify the preliminary plea(s) and preliminary issue(s)*).

3. That a copy of this minute has been duly intimated to Her Majesty's Advocate [*or* A.B.] [and to the said (*name(s) of co-accused*)] conform to execution[s] attached to this minute.

MAY IT THEREFORE PLEASE YOUR LORDSHIP:

[(a)]to consider the above preliminary plea[s] [*and/or* issue[s]] at the first diet;

(b) to order that the following productions be made available at that diet].

IN RESPECT WHEREOF

(*Signed*)

Prosecutor

[*or* Legal representative of [A.B.]]

(*Name, address, e-mail address and telephone number*)

(*Place and date*)

AMENDMENT

Form 9.1 substituted by the Act of Adjournal (Criminal Procedure Rules Amendment) (Criminal Procedure (Amendment) (Scotland) Act) 2005 (SSI 2005/44), r.2(18) and Sch., Part 3 (subject to r.2(2)–(4)) (effective February 1, 2005).

Form 9.6

Rule 9.6(1)

Form of note of appeal under section 74(1) of the Criminal Procedure (Scotland) Act 1995 against a decision of the sheriff at a first diet

UNTO THE RIGHT HONOURABLE THE LORD JUSTICE GENERAL, LORD JUSTICE CLERK AND LORDS COMMISSIONERS OF JUSTICIARY

NOTE OF APPEAL

by

HER MAJESTY'S ADVOCATE

[[*or* A.B.] (*address*)

[*or* Prisoner in the Prison of (*place*)]]

HUMBLY SHEWETH:

1. That in the sheriff court sitting at (*place*) on (*date*) a first diet was held in the case of Her Majesty's Advocate against [A.B.] [and (*name(s) of co-accused*)].

2. That the diet appointed for trial on the indictment is (*diet*).

3. That the ground[s] of submission raised at the first diet was [*or* were] (*specify*).

4. That the decision of the court was (*specify*).

5. That the court granted leave to appeal to the High Court of Justiciary against that decision.

6. That Her Majesty's Advocate [*or* A.B.] appeals to the High Court of Justiciary against that decision on the following grounds (*specify*).

ACCORDING TO JUSTICE, etc.

(*Signed*)

Prosecutor

[*or* Legal representative of [A.B.]]

(*Name, address, e-mail address and telephone number*)

(*Place and date*)

AMENDMENT

Form 9.9 substituted with Form 9.6 by the Act of Adjournal (Criminal Procedure Rules Amendment) (Criminal Procedure (Amendment) (Scotland) Act) 2005 (SSI 2005/44), r.2(18) and Sch., Part 3 (subject to r.2(2)–(4)) (effective February 1, 2005).

Rule 9.11(2)

Form of minute of abandonment of appeal made under section 74(1) of the Criminal Procedure (Scotland) Act 1995 against a decision of the sheriff at a first diet

NOTICE OF ABANDONMENT OF APPEAL

Name of appellant:

Date of birth:

Prisoner in the Prison of (*place*) [*or as the case may be*]

Crime or offence to which appeal relates:

Court:

The above named appellant, having lodged a note of appeal under section 74(1) of the Criminal Procedure (Scotland) Act 1995, abandons, as from this date, that appeal against the decision at the first diet.

> (*Signed*)
>
> Prosecutor
>
> [*or* Legal representative of [A.B.]]
>
> (*Name, address, e-mail address and telephone number*)
>
> (*Place and date*)

AMENDMENT

Form 9.17 substituted with Form 9.11 by the Act of Adjournal (Criminal Procedure Rules Amendment) (Criminal Procedure (Amendment) (Scotland) Act) 2005 (SSI 2005/44), r.2(18) and Sch., Part 3 (subject to r.2(2)–(4)) (effective February 1, 2005).

Rule 9A.1(1)

Form of minute of notice under section 72(3) or (6)(b)(i) of the Criminal Procedure (Scotland) Act 1995

UNTO THE RIGHT HONOURABLE THE LORD JUSTICE GENERAL, LORD JUSTICE CLERK AND THE LORDS COMMISSIONERS OF JUSTICIARY

MINUTE

by

HER MAJESTY'S ADVOCATE

[*or* [A.B.] (*address*)

[or Prisoner in the Prison of (*place*)]]

HUMBLY SHEWETH:

1. That [A.B.][, along with (*name(s) of co-accused*),] has been indicted at the instance of Her Majesty's Advocate to a preliminary hearing in the High Court of Justiciary at (*place*) at (*time*) on (*date*).

2. That the minuter is raising the following preliminary plea[s] [*or* preliminary issue[s]]:– (*here specify the preliminary plea(s) or issue(s)*). ..

3. That a copy of this minute has been duly intimated to Her Majesty's Advocate [*or* the accused] [and to the said (*name(s) of co-accused*)] conform to execution[s] attached to this minute.

MAY IT THEREFORE PLEASE YOUR LORDSHIPS:

[(a)]to consider the above preliminary plea[s] [*and/or* preliminary issue[s]] at the preliminary hearing[;

(b) to order that the following productions be made available at that diet].

IN RESPECT WHEREOF

(*Signed*)

Prosecutor

[*or* Legal representative of [A.B.]]

(*Name, address, e-mail address and telephone number*)

(*Place and date*)

AMENDMENT

Form 9.12 substituted with Form 9A.1 by the Act of Adjournal (Criminal Procedure Rules Amendment) (Criminal Procedure (Amendment) (Scotland) Act) 2005 (SSI 2005/44), r.2(18) and Sch., Part 5 (subject to r.2(2)–(4)) (effective February 1, 2005).

Act of Adjournal (Criminal Procedure Rules) 1996

Form 9A.2

Rule 9A.2(1)

Form of application for dispensing with a preliminary hearing

UNTO THE RIGHT HONOURABLE THE LORD JUSTICE GENERAL, LORD JUSTICE CLERK AND
LORDS COMMISSIONERS OF JUSTICIARY

JOINT APPLICATION

by

HER MAJESTY'S ADVOCATE

and

[A.B.] (*address*)

[*or* Prisoner in the Prison of (*place*)]

HUMBLY SHEWETH:

1. That a preliminary hearing has been fixed in the case of Her Majesty's Advocate against (*name of accused*) at (*place*) on (*date*).

2. That the prosecutor and the accused are ready to proceed to trial as set out in the attached Joint Written Record in Form 9A.4.

3. That there are no preliminary pleas, preliminary issues or other matters which require to be, or could with advantage be, disposed of before the trial.

4. There are no persons to whom section 72(7) of the Criminal Procedure (Scotland) Act 1995 applies.

5. That the following witnesses are required by the prosecutor to attend the trial:-
(*specify*)

6. That the following witnesses are required by the accused to attend the trial:–
(*specify*)

7. That parties are ready and able to proceed to trial on (*date*) and that the expected length of the trial is (*specify*).

MAY IT THEREFORE PLEASE YOUR LORDSHIPS:

(1) to discharge the preliminary hearing fixed for (*date*);

(2) to appoint a trial diet.

IN RESPECT WHEREOF:

(*Signed*)

Prosecutor

(*Name, address, e-mail address and telephone number*)

(*Place and date*)

(*Signed*)

Legal representative of [A.B.]

(*Name, address, e-mail address and telephone number*)

(*Place and date*)

AMENDMENT

Form 9A.2 inserted by the Act of Adjournal (Criminal Procedure Rules Amendment) (Criminal Procedure (Amendment) (Scotland) Act) 2005 (SSI 2005/44), r.2(18) and Sch., Part 5 (subject to r.2(2)–(4)) (effective February 1, 2005).

Act of Adjournal (Criminal Procedure Rules) 1996

Form 9A.4

Rule 9A.4(1)

Form of written record of state of preparation

IN THE HIGH COURT OF JUSTICIARY

AT (*place*)

WRITTEN RECORD OF STATE OF PREPARATION

in the case of

HER MAJESTY'S ADVOCATE

against

[A.B.] (*address*)

[*or* Prisoner in the Prison of (*place*)]

Preliminary hearing: (*date*)

	Prosecutor	*Accused's legal representative*
Name:	(*name*)	(*name*)
Address:	(*address*)	(*address*)
E-mail address:		
Telephone number:		
Reference number:		

The prosecutor and the accused's legal representative record their state of preparation as set out in the Schedules.

(*Signed*)

Prosecutor

(*Date and place*)

(*Signed*)

Accused's legal representative

(*Date and place*)

SCHEDULE 1 (Prosecutor) *In this Schedule, unless otherwise stated, references to sections are to sections of the Criminal Procedure (Scotland) Act 1995* **Plea** **1.** Has a plea of guilty been accepted on behalf of Her Majesty's Advocate? If the answer to the preceding question is yes, the following questions are not applicable.	*delete as appropriate Yes/No*
Preliminary issues **2.** Has notice been given on behalf of Her Majesty's Advocate of a preliminary issue within the meaning of section 79(2)(b)? If the answer to the preceding question is yes, attach a copy of each notice.	Yes/No*
Objections to admissibility of evidence **3.** Is there any objection to the admissibility of any evidence you wish to raise on behalf of Her Majesty's Advocate despite not having given notice of a preliminary issue within the meaning of section 79(2)(b)? If the answer to the preceding question is yes, specify each objection to the admissibility of evidence and summarise the reasons for not having given notice under section 79(2)(b):–	Yes/No*

Other applications/notices **4.** Has any of the following been lodged with the court on behalf of Her Majesty's Advocate? - A child witness notice under section 271A(2) - A vulnerable witness application under section 271C(2) - An application under section 275(1) (application to admit evidence relating to the character and conduct of complainer) - An application under section 288F(2) (application for an order prohibiting the accused from conducting defence in person at trial) If the answer to the preceding question is yes, attach a copy of each application or notice. N.B. Sections 271A(2), 271C(2) and 288F(2) are not in force as at 1st February 2005. Until those provisions are in force, reference should be made here to any application under section 271 (evidence of vulnerable persons: special provisions).	Yes/No*
Other matters **5.** Are there any other matters which might be disposed of with advantage before the trial? For instance, are there any outstanding devolution minutes, section 67 notices or applications for recovery of documents? If the answer to the preceding question is yes, specify each matter which might be disposed of with advantage before the trial:–	Yes/No*

Agreements and admissions of evidence **6.** Have any facts and documents been the subject of a minute under section 256(2) (minute of admission or agreement)? If the answer to the preceding question is yes, attach a copy of each minute.	Yes/No*
Duty to seek agreement of evidence **7.** Specify any steps which have been taken under section 257 (duty to seek agreement of evidence):–	
Uncontroversial evidence **8.** Has either party served a statement under section 258(2) (statement of uncontroversial evidence) on the other party? If the answer to the preceding question is yes, (i) attach a copy of each statement (ii) specify any matters which are deemed to have been conclusively proved:– (iii) attach a copy of any notice of challenge under section 258(3) and (iv) attach a copy of any application under section 258(4A) (application for direction that a challenge in a notice under section 258(3) is to be disregarded)	Yes/No*

Witnesses **9.** Specify which of the witnesses included within the list of witnesses are required:– [*indicate which, if any, of these witnesses is a child witness:* ("*CW*") *or vulnerable witness:* ("*VW*")]	
Availability of witnesses **10.** Specify any dates on which any of the witnesses specified in paragraph 9 above would not be available to give evidence and indicate the reason (if known):–	
Preparation for trial **11.** Are you ready, if necessary, to proceed to trial? If your answer to the previous question is no, specify the reason(s) you are not ready to proceed to trial and the date by which you will be ready to proceed to trial.	Yes/No*

Estimated length of trial **12.** Specify how long you estimate that the trial, if any, will last.	
Name of counsel **13.** Specify the name of counsel and specify any dates on which it is known that he or she will not be available:–	
Equipment **14.** Will any of the following be required at the trial diet? - screens - display of video-tape evidence - playback of police interview audio-tape - document camera - CD/DVD evidence in computer format (parties must supply laptop PC or other means of display) - equipment for giving evidence by closed circuit television camera - other equipment If yes, specify:	Yes/No*
Interpreters **15.** Will an interpreter be required for the trial diet? If the answer is yes, please provide details:–	Yes/no*

SCHEDULE 2 (Legal Representative of [A.B.])	
In this Schedule, unless otherwise stated, references to sections are to sections of the Criminal Procedure (Scotland) Act 1995	*delete as appropriate
Plea **1.** Has the prosecutor accepted a plea of guilty? If the answer to the preceding question is yes, the following questions are not applicable.	Yes/No*
Section 196 **1A.** Is the accused aware of the terms of section 196?	Yes/No*
Preliminary pleas **1B.** Has notice been given on behalf of the accused of a preliminary plea within the meaning of section 79(2)(a)? If the answer to the preceding question is yes, attach a copy of each notice.	Yes/No*
Preliminary issues **2.** Has notice been given on behalf of the accused of a preliminary issue within the meaning of section 79(2)(b)? If the answer to the preceding question is yes, attach a copy of each notice.	Yes/No*
Objections to admissibility of evidence **3.** Is there any objection to the admissibility of any evidence which you wish to raise on behalf of the accused despite not having given notice of a preliminary issue within the meaning of section 79(2)(b)? If the answer to the preceding question is yes, specify each objection to the admissibility of evidence and summarise the reasons for not having given notice under section 79(2)(b):–	Yes/No*

Other applications/notices **4.** Has any of the following been lodged with the court on behalf of the accused? - A child witness notice under section 271A(2) - A vulnerable witness application under section 271C(2) - An application under section 275(1) (application to admit evidence relating to the character and conduct of complainer) - An application under section 288F(2) (application for an order prohibiting the accused from conducting defence in person at trial) If the answer to the preceding question is yes, attach a copy of each application or notice. N.B. Sections 271A(2), 271C(2) and 288F(2) are not in force as at 1st February 2005. Until those provisions are in force, reference should be made here to any application under section 271 (evidence of vulnerable persons: special provisions).	Yes/No*
Defence **4A.** Have any of the following been lodged with the court on behalf of the accused? - a plea of special defence or notice of intention to lead evidence calculated to exculpate the accused by incriminating a co-accused under section 78(1) - notice of witnesses or productions under section 78(4) If the answer to the preceding question is yes, attach a copy of each plea and notice.	Yes/No*
Other matters **5.** Are there any other matters which might be disposed of with advantage before the trial? For instance, are there any outstanding devolution minutes, section 67 notices or applications for recovery of documents? If the answer to the preceding question is yes, specify each matter which might be disposed of with advantage before the trial:–	Yes/No*

Agreements and admissions of evidence **6.** Have any facts and documents been the subject of a minute under section 256(2) (minute of admission or agreement)? If the answer to the preceding question is yes, attach a copy of each minute.	Yes/No*
Duty to seek agreement of evidence **7.** Specify any steps which have been taken under section 257 (duty to seek agreement of evidence):–	
Uncontroversial evidence **8.** Has either party served a statement under section 258(2) (statement of uncontroversial evidence) on the other party? If the answer to the preceding question is yes, (i) attach a copy of each statement (ii) specify any matters which are deemed to have been conclusively proved:– (iii) attach a copy of any notice of challenge under section 258(3) and (iv) attach a copy of any application under section 258(4A) (application for direction that a challenge in a notice under section 258(3) is to be disregarded)	Yes/No*

Witnesses **9.** Specify which of the witnesses included within the list of witnesses are required. [*indicate which, if any, of these witnesses is a child witness:* ("*CW*") *or vulnerable witness:* ("*VW*")]	
Availability of witnesses **10.** Specify any dates on which any of the witnesses specified in paragraph 9 above would not be available to give evidence and indicate the reason (if known):–	

Preparation for trial **11.** Are you ready, if necessary, to proceed to trial? If your answer to the previous question is no, specify the reason(s) you are not ready to proceed to trial and the date by which you will be ready to proceed to trial.	Yes/No*
Estimated length of trial **12.** Specify how long you estimate that the trial, if any, will last.	
Name of counsel **13.** Specify the name of counsel and specify any dates on which it is known that he or she will not be available:–	

Equipment	
14. Will any of the following be required at the trial diet?	Yes/No*
- screens	
- display of video-tape evidence	
- playback of police interview audio-tape	
- document camera	
- CD/DVD evidence in computer format (parties must supply laptop PC or other means of display)	
- equipment for giving evidence by closed circuit television camera	
- other equipment	
If yes, specify:	
Interpreters	
15. Will an interpreter be required for the trial diet?	Yes/No*
If the answer is yes, please provide details:–	

AMENDMENT

Form 9A.4 inserted by the Act of Adjournal (Criminal Procedure Rules Amendment) (Criminal Procedure (Amendment) (Scotland) Act) 2005 (SSI 2005/44), r.2(18) and Sch., Part 5 (subject to r.2(2)–(4)) (effective February 1, 2005).

Rule 9A.7

Form of note of appeal under section 74(1) of the Criminal Procedure (Scotland) Act 1995 against a decision of the High Court at a preliminary hearing

UNTO THE RIGHT HONOURABLE THE LORD JUSTICE GENERAL, LORD JUSTICE CLERK AND LORDS COMMISSIONERS OF JUSTICIARY

NOTE OF APPEAL

by

HER MAJESTY'S ADVOCATE

[*or* [A.B.] (*address*)

[*or* Prisoner in the Prison of (*place*)]]

HUMBLY SHEWETH:

1. That in the High Court sitting at (*place*) on (*date*) a preliminary hearing was held in the case of Her Majesty's Advocate against [A.B.] [and (*name(s) of co-accused*)].

2. That the trial has been appointed for (*date*).

3. That the ground[s] of submission raised at the preliminary hearing was [*or* were] (*specify*).

4. That the decision of the court was (*specify*).

5. That the court granted leave to appeal against that decision.

6. That [A.B.] appeals to the High Court of Justiciary against that decision on the following grounds:-

    (*specify*).

ACCORDING TO JUSTICE, etc.

(*Signed*)

Prosecutor

[*or* Accused's Legal Representative]

(*Name, address, e-mail address and telephone number*)

(*Place and date*)

AMENDMENT

Form 9A.7 inserted by the Act of Adjournal (Criminal Procedure Rules Amendment) (Criminal Procedure (Amendment) (Scotland) Act) 2005 (SSI 2005/44), r.2(18) and Sch., Part 5 (subject to r.2(2)–(4)) (effective February 1, 2005).

Rule 9A.8

Form of minute of abandonment of appeal made under section 74(1) of the Criminal Procedure (Scotland) Act 1995 against a decision of the court at a preliminary hearing

NOTICE OF ABANDONMENT OF APPEAL

Name of appellant:

[*If accused* Date of birth:

Prisoner in the Prison of (*place*) [*or as the case may be*]]

Crime or offence to which appeal relates:

Court:

The above appellant, having lodged a note of appeal under section 74(1) of the Criminal Procedure (Scotland) Act 1995, abandons, as from this date, that appeal against the decision at the first diet.

(*Signed*)

Prosecutor

·· [*or* Legal representative of [A.B.]]

(*Name, address, e-mail address and telephone number*)

(*Place and date*)

AMENDMENT

Form 9A.8 inserted by the Act of Adjournal (Criminal Procedure Rules Amendment) (Criminal Procedure (Amendment) (Scotland) Act) 2005 (SSI 2005/44), r.2(18) and Sch., Part 5 (subject to r.2(2)–(4)) (effective February 1, 2005).

Form 9B.1

Form of minute of notice under section 79A(2) of the Criminal Procedure (Scotland) Act 1995

UNTO THE RIGHT HONOURABLE THE LORD JUSTICE GENERAL, LORD JUSTICE CLERK AND THE LORDS COMMISSIONERS OF JUSTICIARY

[UNTO THE HONOURABLE THE SHERIFF OF (*name of sheriffdom*)
AT (*place*)]

MINUTE

by

HER MAJESTY'S ADVOCATE

[*or* [A.B.] (*address*)

[or Prisoner in the Prison of (*place*)]]

HUMBLY SHEWETH:

1. That [A.B.], [, along with (*name(s) of co-accused*),] has been indicted at the instance of Her Majesty's Advocate.

2. That a preliminary hearing [or first diet] took place at the High Court of Justiciary [*or* sheriff court] at (*place*) on (*date*).

3. That a trial diet is to take place at (*time*) on (*date*).

4. That the minuter intends to raise the following objections to the admissibility of evidence:–

   (*here specify objection(s)*).

5. That the minuter could not reasonably have raised that [or those]objection(s) at the preliminary hearing (or first diet) for the following reason(s):–

   (*here specify reason(s)*)

6. That a copy of this minute has been duly intimated conform to the execution(s) attached to this minute.

MAY IT THEREFORE PLEASE YOUR LORDSHIP(S):

   [(a)] to grant leave under section 79A(2) to raise the foregoing objection(s);

   (b) to appoint a diet to be held before the commencement of the trial for the purposes of disposing of this minute [and the objection(s)];

   (a) to appoint the question of whether leave should be granted under section 79A(2) of the Act of 1995 to be disposed of at the trial diet; or

   (b) to do otherwise as your Lordship(s) think(s) fit.

IN RESPECT WHEREOF

(*Signed*)

Prosecutor

[*or* Legal representative of [A.B.]]

(*Name, address, e-mail address and telephone number*)

(*Place and date*)

AMENDMENT

Form 9B.1 inserted by the Act of Adjournal (Criminal Procedure Rules Amendment) (Criminal Procedure (Amendment) (Scotland) Act) 2005 (SSI 2005/44), r.2(18) and Sch., Part 5 (subject to r.2(2)–(4)) (effective February 1, 2005).

Form 10.1-A

Rule 10.1(1)(a)

Form of notice of special diet where accused intends to plead guilty (where indictment not already served)

To: (*name and address of accused*)

TAKE NOTICE:

(1)   That the Crown Agent has received intimation that you intend to plead guilty to the charge(s) on which you have been committed for trial.

(2)   That YOU MUST THEREFORE APPEAR before the High Court of Justiciary at (*place*) [*or* (*place*) Sheriff Court (*address*)] on (*date*) at (*time*) to answer to the indictment to which this notice is attached.

(*Signed*)

For Her Majesty's Advocate
or Procurator Fiscal Depute

AMENDMENT

Form 10.1-A as amended by Act of Adjournal (Criminal Procedure Rules Amendment No.2) (Miscellaneous) 2003 (SSI 2003/468), r.2(17). Brought into force on October 27, 2003 in accordance with art.1.

Form 10.1-B

Rule 10.1(1)(b)

Form of notice of special diet where accused intends to plead guilty (where indictment already served)

To: (*name and address of accused*)

TAKE NOTICE:

(1)   That the Crown Agent has received intimation that you intend to plead guilty to the charge(s) contained in the indictment the trial of which is to take place at the High Court of Justiciary [*or* Sheriff Court] sitting at (*place*) on (*date*).

(2)   That YOU MUST THEREFORE APPEAR before the High Court of Justiciary at (*place*) [*or* (*place*) Sheriff Court (*address*)] on (*date*) at (*time*) to answer to the indictment which has already been served on you.

(*Signed*)

For Her Majesty's Advocate
or Procurator Fiscal Depute

AMENDMENT

Form 10.1-B as amended by Act of Adjournal (Criminal Procedure Rules Amendment No.2) (Miscellaneous) 2003 (SSI 2003/468), r.2(17). Brought into force on October 27, 2003 in accordance with art.1.

Form 12.1

Rule 12.1(3)

Form of intimation by prosecutor of adjournment of diet under section 75A of the Criminal Procedure (Scotland) Act 1995

HER MAJESTY'S ADVOCATE against (*here name all accused*)

To: (name and address of accused)

TAKE NOTICE:

(1)   That, the diet (*specify*) fixed for (*date*) was adjourned, in your absence, to (*date*);

(2)   That YOU ARE THEREFORE REQUIRED TO APPEAR at the High Court of Justiciary [*or* Sheriff Court] sitting at (*place*) on (*date*) at (*time*) to answer to the indictment which has already been served on you.

Served on the day of (*date*) by me by (*here state method of service*)

(*Signed*)

Prosecutor

(*Name, address, e-mail address and telephone number*)

(*Place and date*)

AMENDMENT

Form 12.1 substituted by the Act of Adjournal (Criminal Procedure Rules Amendment) (Criminal Procedure (Amendment) (Scotland) Act) 2005 (SSI 2005/44), r.2(18) and Sch., Part 6 (subject to r.2(2)–(4)) (effective February 1, 2005).

Form 12.2-A

Rule 12.2(1)

Form of minute for alteration of diet under section 75A of the Criminal Procedure (Scotland) Act 1995

UNTO THE RIGHT HONOURABLE THE LORD JUSTICE GENERAL, LORD JUSTICE-CLERK AND LORDS COMMISSIONERS OF JUSTICIARY

[*or* UNTO THE HONOURABLE THE SHERIFF
OF (*name of sheriffdom*) AT (*place*)]

MINUTE

by
Her Majesty's Advocate

[*or* [A.B.] (*address*)

[*or* Prisoner in the Prison of (*place*)]]

HUMBLY SHEWETH:

1. That [A.B.] [, along with (*name(s) of co-accused*),] has been indicted at the instance of Her Majesty's Advocate in the High Court of Justiciary [or in the sheriff court] at (*place*) and a diet of (*specify*) has been fixed for (*date*).

[2. (*Here narrate any hearings fixed previously and decisions of the court.*)]

2. That the minuter applies to the court for alteration of the diet for the following reasons:–

   (*here state reasons*).

3. The following statutory time-limits apply in this case:–

   (*specify relevant dates*).

MAY IT THEREFORE PLEASE YOUR LORDSHIP[S]:

(a) to fix a diet for hearing this application and to order intimation of this application and the diet to all the parties;

(b) thereafter, after hearing all the parties, to discharge the diet of (*specify*) and fix a new diet;

(c) or to do otherwise as to your Lordship[s] shall seem proper;

(d) to require the clerk of court to intimate the new diet to (*specify*).

IN RESPECT WHEREOF

(*Signed*)

Prosecutor

[*or* Legal representative of [A.B.]]

(*Name, address, e-mail address and telephone number*)

(*Place and date*)

AMENDMENT

Form 12.2-A substituted by the Act of Adjournal (Criminal Procedure Rules Amendment) (Criminal Procedure (Amendment) (Scotland) Act) 2005 (SSI 2005/44), r.2(18) and Sch., Part 6 (subject to r.2(2)–(4)) (effective February 1, 2005).

Form 12.2-B

Rule 12.2(2)

Form of joint minute for alteration of diet under section 75A of the Criminal Procedure (Scotland) Act 1995

UNTO THE RIGHT HONOURABLE THE LORD JUSTICE GENERAL, LORD JUSTICE-CLERK AND LORDS COMMISSIONERS OF JUSTICIARY

[*or* UNTO THE HONOURABLE THE SHERIFF
OF (*name of sheriffdom*) AT (*place*)]

JOINT MINUTE

By

(1) Her Majesty's Advocate and

(2) [A.B.] (*address*) [or Prisoner in the Prison of (*place*)]

MINUTERS

HUMBLY SHEWETH:

1. That [A.B.] has been indicted at the instance of Her Majesty's Advocate for trial in the High Court of Justiciary sitting [*or* in the sheriff court] at (*place*) and a diet of (*specify*) has been fixed for (*date*);

2. That the minuters apply to the court to discharge the diet for the following reasons:–

    (*here state reasons*).

3. That the following time limits under section 65 of the Criminal Procedure (Scotland) Act 1995 apply in this case:–

    (*here state time limits and relevant dates*)

MAY IT THEREFORE PLEASE YOUR LORDSHIP[S]:

    (a) to dispense with a hearing of this application;

    (b) to discharge the diet of (*specify*) and to fix a new diet;

    (c) or to do otherwise as to your Lordship[s] shall seem proper.

IN RESPECT WHEREOF

(*Signed*)

Prosecutor

(*Name, address, e-mail address and telephone number*)

(*Place and date*)

(*Signed*)

Legal representative of [A.B.]

(*Name, address, e-mail address and telephone number*)

(*Place and date*)

AMENDMENT

Form 12.2-B substituted by the Act of Adjournal (Criminal Procedure Rules Amendment) (Criminal Procedure (Amendment) (Scotland) Act) 2005 (SSI 2005/44), r.2(18) and Sch., Part 6 (subject to r.2(2)–(4)) (effective February 1, 2005).

Form 12.7

Rule 12.7

Form of minute of continuation of a floating trial diet in the High Court of Justiciary

Her Majesty's Advocate against [A.B.]

The court continued the trial diet appointed for [*date*] until [*date of next sitting day*].

(*Signed*)

Clerk

[The court further continued the trial diet appointed for [*date*] until [*date of next sitting day*].]

(*Signed*)

Clerk

[The court further continued the trial diet appointed for [*date*] until [*date of next sitting day*].]

(*Signed*)

Clerk

[The court further continued the trial diet appointed for [*date*] until [*date of next sitting day*].]

(*Signed*)

Clerk

AMENDMENT

Form 12.6 substituted with Form 12.7 by the Act of Adjournal (Criminal Procedure Rules Amendment) (Criminal Procedure (Amendment) (Scotland) Act) 2005 (SSI 2005/44), r.2(18) and Sch., Part 6 (subject to r.2(2)–(4)) (effective February 1, 2005).

Form 13.2-A

Rule 13.2(1)

Form of citation of person summoned to serve as a juror under section 85(4) of the Criminal Procedure (Scotland) Act 1995

CITATION TO SERVE AS JUROR

The High Court of Justiciary [*or* sheriff of (*name of sheriffdom*)] is to hold a sitting for the trial of persons accused on indictment at (*place*) on (*date*) with continuation of days:

YOU ARE HEREBY REQUIRED TO ATTEND at that place on that date as a person who may be called on to serve as a juror.

(*Signed*)
Clerk of Justiciary
[*or* Sheriff Clerk]

(*Place and date*)

Form 13.2-B

Rule 13.2(2)

Form of certificate of execution of service and citation of witness under section 85(4) of the Criminal Procedure (Scotland) Act 1995

EXECUTION OF CITATION OF JURORS

I, (*name and address*), on (*date*) duly served on each of the following persons:

(*here list names of jurors*)

a citation to attend the sitting of the High Court of Justiciary [*or* Sheriff Court] at (*place*) on (*date*), as jurors for that sitting by sending to or for each of them a notice of citation by first class recorded delivery post.

(*Signed*)
Sheriff Clerk

Form 13A.1–A

Rule 13A.1

Form of citation of witness for precognition under section 267A of the Criminal Procedure (Scotland) Act 1995

IMPORTANT NOTICE

(CITATION)

Prosecutor's reference . . . (*specify*)

TO: (*name*), (*date of birth*), (*address*)

DATE: (*date*)

You are a potential witness in a criminal case. The prosecutor requires to take a statement from you.

YOU MUST APPEAR at (*place*) at (*time*) so that the prosecutor can take a statement from you.

IT IS A CRIMINAL OFFENCE TO FAIL TO ATTEND AT THE PLACE AND TIME SET OUT ABOVE WITHOUT A REASONABLE EXCUSE

(*Signed*)

Prosecutor

(*Name, address, e-mail address and telephone number*)

AMENDMENT

Form 13A.1-A inserted by the Act of Adjournal (Criminal Procedure Rules Amendment No.4) (Criminal Procedure (Amendment) (Scotland) Act 2004) 2004 (SSI 2004/434), r.2 and Sch., Part 3 (effective October 4, 2004).

Form 13A.1-A as amended by the Act of Adjournal (Criminal Procedure Rules Amendment No.5) (Miscellaneous) 2004 (SSI 2004/481), r.2 (effective November 26, 2004).

Form 13A.2-A

Rule 13A.2(1)

Form of application for warrant for the apprehension of a witness under section 90A or 90D of the Criminal Procedure (Scotland) Act 1995

UNTO THE RIGHT HONOURABLE THE LORD JUSTICE GENERAL, LORD JUSTICE-CLERK AND LORDS COMMISSIONERS OF JUSTICIARY

[*or* UNTO THE HONOURABLE THE SHERIFF
OF (*name of sheriffdom*) AT (*place*)]

APPLICATION

for

WARRANT FOR THE APPREHENSION OF A WITNESS

by

Her Majesty's Advocate

[*or* [A.B.] (*address*)[or Prisoner in the Prison of (*place*)]]

HUMBLY SHEWETH:

1. That [A.B.] has been indicted at the instance of Her Majesty's Advocate in the High Court of Justiciary [*or* in the sheriff court] at (*place*).

2. (*Here state grounds for application*).

MAY IT THEREFORE PLEASE YOUR LORDSHIP[S]:

(a) to grant warrant for the apprehension of [C.D.] (*address*);or

(b) to fix a diet for the hearing of this application; or

(c) to do otherwise as to your Lordship[s] shall seem proper.

IN RESPECT WHEREOF

(*Signed*)

Prosecutor

[*or* Legal representative of [A.B.]]

(*Name, address, e-mail address and telephone number*)

(*Place and date*)

AMENDMENT

Form 13A.2-A inserted by the Act of Adjournal (Criminal Procedure Rules Amendment) (Criminal Procedure (Amendment) (Scotland) Act) 2005 (SSI 2005/44), r.2(18) and Sch., Part 7 (subject to r.2(2)–(4)) (effective February 1, 2005).

Rule 13A.2(3)

Form of warrant for the apprehension of a witness under section 90A of the Criminal Procedure (Scotland) Act 1995

(*Place and date*). The High Court of Justiciary [*or* Sheriff] at (*place*) grants a warrant under section 90A(1) of the Criminal Procedure (Scotland) Act 1995 in the case of Her Majesty's Advocate against [A.B.] for the apprehension of [C.D.] (*address*) ("the witness").

By virtue of section 90A(6) of that Act, this warrant implies warrant to officers of law-

    (a) to search for and apprehend the witness;

    (b) to bring the witness before the court;

    (c) in the meantime, to detain the witness in a police station, police cell or other convenient place; and

    (d) so far as necessary for the execution of the warrant, to break open shut and lockfast places.

(*Signed*)

Sheriff [*or*, in the High Court, Clerk of Court]

(*Name, address, e-mail address and telephone number*)

Note to officers of law: contact the clerk of court on apprehension of the witness.

AMENDMENT

Form 13A.2-B inserted by the Act of Adjournal (Criminal Procedure Rules Amendment) (Criminal Procedure (Amendment) (Scotland) Act) 2005 (SSI 2005/44), r.2(18) and Sch., Part 7 (subject to r.2(2)–(4)) (effective February 1, 2005).

Form 13A.3

Rule 13A.3

Form of application for review under section 90D(1) of the Criminal Procedure (Scotland) Act 1995

UNTO THE RIGHT HONOURABLE THE LORD JUSTICE GENERAL, LORD JUSTICE-CLERK AND LORDS COMMISSIONERS OF JUSTICIARY

[*or* UNTO THE HONOURABLE THE SHERIFF
OF (*name of sheriffdom*) AT (*place*)]

APPLICATION

under section 90D of the Criminal Procedure (Scotland) Act 1995

for

REVIEW OF AN ORDER

By

[C.D.](*address*)

HUMBLY SHEWETH:

1. That [C.D.] is a witness in the case of Her Majesty's Advocate against [A.B.].

2. That an order under section 90A(1)(a) [*or* 90A(1)(b)] of the Criminal Procedure (Scotland) Act 1995 was made against [C.D.] on (*date*).

3. (*Here state the grounds for the application*).

MAY IT THEREFORE PLEASE YOUR LORDSHIP(S) TO:

(*specify*)

IN RESPECT WHEREOF

(*Signed*)

Legal representative of [C.D.]

(*Name, address, e-mail address and telephone number*)

AMENDMENT

Form 13A.3 inserted by the Act of Adjournal (Criminal Procedure Rules Amendment) (Criminal Procedure (Amendment) (Scotland) Act) 2005 (SSI 2005/44), r.2(18) and Sch., Part 7 (subject to r.2(2)–(4)) (effective February 1, 2005).

Rule 13A.4

Form of note of appeal under section 90E(1) of the Criminal Procedure (Scotland) Act 1995

UNTO THE RIGHT HONOURABLE THE LORD JUSTICE GENERAL, LORD JUSTICE CLERK AND LORDS COMMISSIONERS OF JUSTICIARY

NOTE OF APPEAL

by

HER MAJESTY'S ADVOCATE

[*or* [A.B.] (*address*)

[*or* Prisoner in the Prison of (*place*)]

[*or* [C.D.] (*address*)]]

HUMBLY SHEWETH:

1. That on (*date*) the High Court of Justiciary [*or* Sheriff] at (*place*) made the following order under section 90B of the Criminal Procedure (Scotland) Act 1995:–

    (*specify*)

2. That Her Majesty's Advocate [*or* A.B. *or* C.D.] appeals to the High Court of Justiciary against that decision on the following grounds:-

    (*specify*).

ACCORDING TO JUSTICE, etc.

(*Signed*)

Prosecutor

[*or* Accused's Legal Representative *or* specify*]

(*Name, address, e-mail address and telephone number*)

(*Place and date*)

AMENDMENT

Form 13A.4 inserted by the Act of Adjournal (Criminal Procedure Rules Amendment) (Criminal Procedure (Amendment) (Scotland) Act) 2005 (SSI 2005/44), r.2(18) and Sch., Part 7 (subject to r.2(2)–(4)) (effective February 1, 2005).

Form 14.3-A

Form of oath for jurors

The jurors to raise their right hands and the clerk of court to ask *them*: "Do you swear by Almighty God that you will well and truly try the accused and give a true verdict according to the evidence?"

The jurors to reply: "I do".

Form 14.3-B

Form of affirmation for juror

The juror to repeat after the clerk of court: "I, (*name*), do solemnly, sincerely and truly declare and affirm that I will well and truly try the accused and give a true verdict according to the evidence".

Form 14.5-A

Form of oath for witnesses

The witness to raise his right hand and repeat after the judge: "I swear by Almighty God that I will tell the truth, the whole truth and nothing but the truth".

Form 14.5-B

Form of affirmation for witnesses

The witness to repeat after the judge: "I solemnly, sincerely and truly declare and affirm that I will tell the truth, the whole truth and nothing but the truth".

Form 14.7

Form of minute of recording of proceedings

The court directed that the whole proceedings in this case [*or* in all the cases] set down for trial at this sitting be recorded by means of (*specify means*) and appointed (*name, designation and address*) to do so.

Form 15.2-A

Rule 15.2(1)

Form of intimation of intention to appeal under section 109(1) of the Criminal Procedure (Scotland) Act 1995

IN THE HIGH COURT OF JUSTICIARY

INTIMATION OF INTENTION TO APPEAL

under section 109(1) of the Criminal Procedure (Scotland) Act 1995

To: Clerk of Justiciary

Name of convicted person:

Date of birth:

Prisoner in the Prison of:

Date of final determination of the proceedings:

Crime or offence to which the appeal relates:

Court and name of judge:

Sentence:

Intimation is hereby given that the above named convicted person intends to appeal to the High Court of Justiciary against the foregoing *conviction/sentence/conviction and sentence.

> (*Signed by the convicted person, his counsel or solicitor*)
> [Counsel [*or* Solicitor] for appellant]
>
> (*Address and telephone number of solicitor*)

Date:

* *Delete whatever is not applicable.*

NOTE: THE PARTY LODGING THIS FORM MUST, IMMEDIATELY AFTER IT IS LODGED, INTIMATE IT TO:

THE CROWN AGENT, THE CROWN OFFICE, 25 CHAMBERS STREET, EDINBURGH, EH1 1LA

AMENDMENT

Form 15.2-A as amended by Act of Adjournal (Criminal Procedure Rules Amendment No.2) (Miscellaneous) 2003 (SSI 2003/468), r.2(17). Brought into force on October 27, 2003 in accordance with art.1.

Act of Adjournal (Criminal Procedure Rules) 1996

Form 15.2-B

Form of note of appeal under section 110(1) of the Criminal Procedure (Scotland) Act 1995 or section 19 of the Prisoners and Criminal Proceedings (Scotland) Act 1993

IN THE HIGH COURT OF JUSTICIARY

NOTE OF APPEAL

under section 110 of the
Criminal Procedure (Scotland)
Act 1995
[*or* section 19 of the Prisoners and Criminal
Proceedings (Scotland) Act 1993]

To: Clerk of Justiciary

Name of convicted person:

Date of birth:

Prisoner in the Prison of:

Date of final determination of the proceedings:

Crime or offence to which the appeal relates:

Court and name of judge:

Sentence:

The above named convicted person appeals against conviction [*or as the case may be*] on the following grounds:—[*here give full statement of all grounds of appeal*].

> (*Signed by the convicted person, his counsel or solicitor*)
> [Counsel [*or* Solicitor] for appellant]
>
> (*Address and telephone number of solicitor*)

(*Date*)

NOTE: THE PARTY LODGING THIS FORM MUST, IMMEDIATELY AFTER IT IS LODGED, INTIMATE IT TO:

THE CROWN AGENT, THE CROWN OFFICE, 25 CHAMBERS STREET, EDINBURGH, EH1 1LA

AMENDMENT

Form 15.2-B as amended by Act of Adjournal (Criminal Procedure Rules Amendment No.2) (Miscellaneous) 2003 (SSI 2003/468), r.2(17). Brought into force on October 27, 2003 in accordance with art.1.

Form 15.2-C

Form of application for extension of time under section 111(2) of the Criminal Procedure (Scotland) Act 1995

UNTO THE RIGHT HONOURABLE THE LORD JUSTICE GENERAL, LORD JUSTICE-CLERK and LORDS COMMISSIONERS OF JUSTICIARY

APPLICATION FOR EXTENSION OF TIME

under section 111(2) of the
Criminal Procedure (Scotland) Act 1995

Name of convicted person:

Date of birth:

Prisoner in the Prison of:

Date of final determination of the proceedings:

Crime or offence to which the appeal relates:

Court and name of judge:

Sentence:

Application is hereby made for extension of time within which to:—
    *intimate an intention to appeal against conviction
    *intimate an intention to appeal against conviction and sentence
    *lodge a note of appeal against sentence
    *lodge a note of appeal against conviction
    *lodge a note of appeal against conviction and sentence

for the following reasons:—
    [*here fully state the reasons for the failure to lodge timeously the intimation of intention to appeal or note of appeal as the case may be*].

                (*Signed by the convicted person, his counsel or solicitor*)
                [Counsel [*or* Solicitor] for applicant]

                (*Address and telephone number of solicitor*)

(*Date*)

* *Delete whatever is not applicable.*

Form 15.2-D

Form of petition to High Court of Justiciary for bail pending appeal

UNTO THE RIGHT HONOURABLE THE LORD JUSTICE GENERAL, LORD JUSTICE-CLERK and LORDS COMMISSIONERS OF JUSTICIARY

PETITION

of

[A.B.] presently a prisoner in the
Prison of (*place*)

PETITIONER

HUMBLY SHEWETH:

1. That on (*date*) the petitioner was convicted in the High Court of Justiciary [*or* sheriff court] at (*place*) of (*state crime or offence*) and sentenced to (*state sentence*).

2. That on (*date*) the petitioner lodged an intimation of intention to appeal [*or* a note of appeal] to the High Court of Justiciary under the Criminal Procedure (Scotland) Act 1995.

3. That (*state the relevant facts in support of grant of bail and, where the petitioner has not lodged a note of appeal, the grounds of appeal*).

4. That the said crime [*or* offence] is bailable.

MAY IT THEREFORE please your Lordships to remit this petition and relative documents to the sheriff at (*place*) with a direction to admit the petitioner to bail under section 112(1) of the Criminal Procedure (Scotland) Act 1995 so far as detained under said sentence upon his formal acceptance and, or, fulfilment of such conditions as your Lordships shall fix.

ACCORDING TO JUSTICE, etc.

(*Signed by the convicted person, his counsel or solicitor*)
[Counsel [*or* Solicitor] for petitioner]

(*Address and telephone number of solicitor*)

(*Date*)

NOTE: THE PARTY LODGING THIS FORM MUST, IMMEDIATELY AFTER IT IS LODGED, INTIMATE IT TO:

THE CROWN AGENT, THE CROWN OFFICE, 25 CHAMBERS STREET, EDINBURGH, EH1 1LA

AMENDMENT

Form 15.2-D as amended by Act of Adjournal (Criminal Procedure Rules Amendment No.2) (Miscellaneous) 2003 (SSI 2003/468), r.2(17). Brought into force on October 27, 2003 in accordance with art.1.

Form 15.3-A

Form of notification of decision of single judge under section 103(5) of the Criminal Procedure (Scotland) Act 1995

NOTIFICATION TO APPLICANT OF A DECISION OF A JUDGE
under section 103(5) of the Criminal Procedure (Scotland) Act 1995

To: (*name and address*)

I hereby give notice that a judge of the High Court of Justiciary having considered your application for:—

* * extension of time within which an intimation of intention to appeal against *conviction/ conviction and sentence may be lodged,
* * extension of time within which a note of appeal against *conviction/conviction and sentence/sentence may be lodged,
* * permission to you to be present at the hearing of any proceedings in relation to your appeal *and/or application,
* * admission to bail,
* * refused/granted the application.

If you wish to have the above mentioned application(s) which *has/have been refused, determined by the High Court of Justiciary constituted as provided in the Criminal Procedure (Scotland) Act 1995 you are required to fill up the enclosed Form 15.3–B and return it to me within five days of its receipt by you, otherwise the decision of the single judge will be final.

(*Signed*)
Clerk of Justiciary

Date:

* Delete whatever is not applicable.

Form 15.3-B

Rule 15.3(2)

Form of application for determination by High Court under section 103(6) of the Criminal Procedure (Scotland) Act 1995

APPLICATION

for

DETERMINATION BY THE HIGH COURT OF JUSTICIARY
OF APPLICATION(S) REFUSED BY A SINGLE JUDGE

under section 103(6) of the Criminal Procedure (Scotland) Act 1995

To: Clerk of Justiciary

I, (*name in full*), having received your notification that my application(s) for:—
* extension of time within which an intimation of intention to appeal against *conviction/ conviction and sentence may be lodged,
* extension of time within which a note of appeal against *conviction/conviction and sentence/sentence may be lodged,
* permission to me to be present at the hearing of any proceedings in relation to my appeal *and/or application,
* admission to bail,

*has/have been refused, HEREBY GIVE NOTICE that I desire that the said application(s) be considered and determined by the High Court of Justiciary constituted as provided in section 103(6) of the Criminal Procedure (Scotland) Act 1995.

(*Signed*)
Applicant

Date:

Note:—If the applicant desires to be present at the hearing by the court in relation to the application(s), the following should completed and signed:—
I, (*name in full*), *being/not being legally represented, desire to be present at the hearing of my application(s) above mentioned.

(*Signed*)
Applicant

Date:

Delete whatever is not applicable.

NOTE: THE PARTY LODGING THIS FORM MUST, IMMEDIATELY AFTER IT IS LODGED, INTIMATE IT TO:

THE CROWN AGENT, THE CROWN OFFICE, 25 CHAMBERS STREET, EDINBURGH, EH1 1LA

AMENDMENT

Form 15.3-B as amended by Act of Adjournal (Criminal Procedure Rules Amendment No.2) (Miscellaneous) 2003 (SSI 2003/468), r.2(17). Brought into force on October 27, 2003 in accordance with art.1.

Form 15.5A-A

Rule 15.5A(3)

HIGH COURT OF JUSTICIARY, EDINBURGH

NOTICE OF INTIMATION OF PROCEDURAL HEARING

TO:

APPEAL: v HMA

The above appeal has been set down for a procedural hearing on at 10.00am.

It is intended to allocate this appeal to a date between and

Form 15.5A–B is attached to this Notice and in terms of Rule 15.5A(4) of the Act of Adjournal (Criminal Appeals) 2002 the completed form should be lodged with the Clerk of Justiciary *not less* than 7 days before the procedural hearing.

In terms of Rule 15.5A(5), if the Clerk of Justiciary determines that the appeal is ready to proceed, you will receive a letter of confirmation from this office within 48 hours before the procedural hearing confirming that no appearance is required. Thereafter you will be advised of the date for the Appeal Court hearing. However should you not lodge the form, lodge it partially completed, or advise that the Appeal is not ready to proceed, you will require to instruct counsel for the procedural hearing.

Justiciary Office

Form 15.5A-B

Rule 15.5A(4)

HIGH COURT OF JUSTICIARY, EDINBURGH

PROCEDURAL HEARING

This notice should be completed and lodged with the Justiciary Office not later than 7 days before the procedural hearing

	Case Ref No: /	
	Solicitor Ref. No:	
	Solicitor Contact No:	
Name of Appellant		
Date of Final Determination		
Court of First Instance	*Judge*	
Date of Procedural Hearing		
Proposed appeal sitting dates		
1. Is appeal ready to proceed?	Yes	No
2. Who is the nominated counsel?		
3. When is the nominated counsel available during the appeal sitting dates?		
4. What is the estimate of court time required to deal with the appeal?		
5. (a) If the appeal is *not* ready to proceed, what are the reasons and what is the current position? (b) How much time is required to carry out the necessary work?		
(counsel or solicitor advocate or appellant)		

AMENDMENT

Forms 15.5A–A and 15.5A–B inserted by Act of Adjournal (Criminal Appeals) 2002 (SSI 2002/387), art.3 (effective August 26, 2002).

Form of notice of abandonment of appeal

ABANDONMENT OF APPEAL

under section 116(1) of the
Criminal Procedure (Scotland) Act 1995

Name of convicted person:

Date of birth:

Prisoner in the Prison of:

Crime or offence to which the appeal relates:

Court:

Sentence:

I, (*name in full*), abandon as from this date my appeal against:—
    *conviction.
    *conviction but proceed with my appeal against sentence.
    *conviction and sentence.
    *sentence.

               (*Signed*)
               Appellant

To:—   The Clerk of Justiciary
          Parliament Square
          Edinburgh
          EH1 1RF

* *Delete whatever is not applicable.*

Form 15.8

Form of notice to Secretary of State for the purposes of section 117(4) of the Criminal Procedure (Scotland) Act 1995

IN THE HIGH COURT OF JUSTICIARY

NOTICE TO SECRETARY OF STATE

of

INTIMATION OF DIET
for the purposes of section 117(4) of the
Criminal Procedure (Scotland) Act 1995

To: Governor of H M Prison mentioned below for the Secretary of State for Scotland

Name of *appellant/applicant:

Date of birth:

Prisoner in the Prison of:

In respect of the—
     *appeal
     *continued appeal
     *petition for bail
     *appeal under section (*specify*) of the Criminal Procedure (Scotland) Act 1995
by the above-named *appellant/applicant:

TAKE NOTICE that the court has fixed (*day*) of (*month*) at 10.30 a.m. as a diet for hearing the above *appeal/petition.

> (*Signed*)
> Clerk of Justiciary

Date:

* *Delete whatever is not applicable.*

Form of application to sheriff for suspension of order for disqualification pending appeal

APPLICATION

for

SUSPENSION
OF ORDER FOR DISQUALIFICATION
FROM DRIVING PENDING APPEAL

by

[A.B.] (*address*)

[*or* Prisoner in the Prison of (*place*)]

APPELLANT

under

Section 41(2) of the Road Traffic Offenders Act 1988

HUMBLY SHEWETH:

1. That on (*date*) the appellant was convicted in the sheriff court at (*place*) and was, *inter alia*, ordered to be disqualified for a period of (*specify*) under section 34 of the Road Traffic Offenders Act 1988.

2. That on (*date*) the appellant lodged with the Clerk of Justiciary a note of appeal under section 110 of the Criminal Procedure (Scotland) Act 1995. A copy of that note is attached to this application and is endorsed as having been received by the Clerk of Justiciary.

3. That the appellant has served a copy of this application on the Procurator Fiscal at (*place*).

MAY IT THEREFORE please your Lordship under section 41(2) of the Road Traffic Offenders Act 1988 to suspend the disqualification on such terms as your Lordship thinks fit.

IN RESPECT WHEREOF

(*Signed*)
[Solicitor for Appellant]

(*Address and telephone number of solicitor*)

(*Place and date*)

Form 15.11-B

Rule 15.11(3)(a)

Form of petition to High Court of Justiciary for suspension of order for disqualification from driving pending appeal

UNTO THE RIGHT HONOURABLE THE LORD JUSTICE GENERAL, LORD JUSTICE-CLERK and LORDS COMMISSIONERS OF JUSTICIARY

PETITION

of

[A.B.] (*address*)
[*or* Prisoner in the Prison of (*place*)]

PETITIONER

under

Section 41(2) of the Road Traffic Offenders Act 1988

HUMBLY SHEWETH:

1. That on (*date*) the petitioner was convicted in the High Court of Justiciary [*or* sheriff court] at (*place*) and was, *inter alia*, ordered to be disqualified for a period of (*specify*) under section 34 of the Road Traffic Offenders Act 1988.

2. That on (*date*) the petitioner lodged with the Clerk of Justiciary a note of appeal under section 110 of the Criminal Procedure (Scotland) Act 1995.

[3. That an application for suspension of the disqualification made under section 39(2) of the Road Traffic Offenders Act 1988 was refused by the sheriff on (*date*) and that the petitioner has served a copy of this petition on the sheriff clerk of the sheriff court at (*place*).]

[4.] That the petitioner has served a copy of this petition on the Crown Agent.

    MAY IT THEREFORE please your Lordships under section 41(2) of the Road Traffic Offenders Act 1988 to suspend the disqualification on such terms as your Lordships think fit.

ACCORDING TO JUSTICE, etc.

(*Signed*)
[Solicitor for petitioner]

(*Address and telephone number of solicitor*)

Form 15.12A-A

Form of petition to High Court of Justiciary for suspension of sentence where intimation of intention to appeal lodged

UNTO THE RIGHT HONOURABLE THE LORD JUSTICE GENERAL, LORD JUSTICE-CLERK and LORDS COMMISSIONERS OF JUSTICIARY

PETITION

of

[A.B.] (*address*)
[*or* Prisoner in the Prison of (*place*)]

PETITIONER

under

section 121A of the Criminal Procedure (Scotland) Act 1995

HUMBLY SHEWETH:

1. That on (*date*) the petitioner was convicted in the High Court of Justiciary [*or* sheriff court] at (*place*) of (*specify offence*) and was sentenced to (*specify relevant sentence*).

2. That on (*date*) the petitioner lodged with the Clerk of Justiciary an intimation of intention to appeal under section 109(1) of the Criminal Procedure (Scotland) Act 1995.

3. That (state facts relevant to application).

4. That the applicant has served a copy of this application on the Crown Agent.

MAY IT THEREFORE please your Lordships under section 121A of the Criminal Procedure (Scotland) Act 1995 to suspend *ad interim* the sentence.

ACCORDING TO JUSTICE, etc.

(*Signed*)
[Solicitor for petitioner]

(*Address and telephone number of solicitor*)

NOTE
[1]Inserted by Act of Adjournal (Criminal Procedure Rules Amendment No. 4) (S.I. 1997 No. 1834) (effective August 1, 1997).

Rule 15.12A(2)

Form of petition to High Court of Justiciary for suspension of sentence pending appeal

*UNTO THE RIGHT HONOURABLE THE LORD JUSTICE GENERAL, LORD
JUSTICE-CLERK and LORDS COMMISSIONERS OF JUSTICIARY*

PETITION

of

[A.B.] (*address*)
[*or* Prisoner in the Prison of (*place*)]
or Her Majesty's Advocate]

PETITIONER

under

section 121A of the Criminal Procedure (Scotland) Act 1995

HUMBLY SHEWETH:

1. That on (*date*) the petitioner [*or* [A.B.] (*address*) *or* Prisoner in the Place of (*place*) was convicted in the High Court of Justiciary [*or* sheriff court] at (*place*) of (*specify offence*) and was sentenced to (*specify relevant sentence*).

2. That on (*date*) the petitioner lodged with the Clerk of Justiciary [a note of appeal under section 110 of the Criminal Procedure (Scotland) Act 1995 in respect of an appeal under section 106(1)(b) to (e) of that Act] [*or* an appeal under section 108 of the Criminal Procedure (Scotland) Act 1995].

3. That the petitioner has served a copy of this petition on the Crown Agent [*or* [A.B.]].

MAY IT THEREFORE please your Lordships under section 121A of the Criminal Procedure (Scotland) Act 1995 to suspend *ad interim* the sentence.

ACCORDING TO JUSTICE, etc.

(*Signed*)
[Solicitor for petitioner]
[Advocate Depute [*or* Procurator Fiscal]
On behalf of Her Majesty's Advocate]

(*Address and telephone number of solicitor*)

NOTE
¹Inserted by Act of Adjournal (Criminal Procedure Rules Amendment No. 4) (S.I. 1997 No. 1834) (effective August 1, 1997).

Rule 15.16

HIGH COURT OF JUSTICIARY, EDINBURGH

APPEAL: -v- HMA

CASE REF:

Provide the following details

1. The specification of the charges of which the appellant was convicted, subject to any amendments and deletions:

2. The sentence or sentences imposed:

3. The grounds of appeal that have passed the sift:

4. An articulate statement of reasons in support of each ground of appeal:

5. A list of authorities relied upon, if any:

6. A schedule of the documents founded upon, if any:

(Signed)
Counsel, solicitor advocate or appellant

(Date)

AMENDMENT

    Form 15.16 inserted by Act of Adjournal (Criminal Appeals) 2003 (SSI 2003/387), Sch.1. Brought into force on September 1, 2003 in accordance with art.1.

Form 16.1-A

Rule 16.1(1)

Form of complaint under section 138(1) of the Criminal Procedure (Scotland) Act 1995

IN THE SHERIFF [*or* DISTRICT] COURT

AT (*place*)

THE COMPLAINT OF THE PROCURATOR FISCAL

AGAINST

(*name and address sufficient to distinguish person*)
[*or* at present in custody]

Date of birth:

The charge against you is that on (*date*) in [*or* at] you did (*set forth charge as nearly as may be in the form set out in Schedule 5 to the Criminal Procedure (Scotland) Act 1995*).

(*Signed*)
Procurator Fiscal
[*or* Complainer *or* Solicitor for Complainer]

Act of Adjournal (Criminal Procedure Rules) 1996

Form 16.1-B

Form of citation of accused in summary proceedings

CITATION OF ACCUSED PERSON

PF REF ....
(This number must be quoted on all correspondence)

A COPY COMPLAINT IS ENCLOSED
FROM THE PROCURATOR FISCAL   ....

YOUR CASE WILL BE HEARD ON   ....

IN THE SHERIFF COURT HOUSE   at ....
                                     .... am [*or* pm]

PROCURATOR FISCAL DEPUTE   ....

WHAT MUST I DO?

You must answer the complaint on or before the date the case is to be heard.

HOW DO I ANSWER THE COMPLAINT?

There are 3 methods—
(1) Attend court personally.
(2) Arrange for your lawyer or some other person to attend.
(3) Write to the court (REPLY FORM and envelope attached).

WHAT IF I AM CHARGED WITH A SEXUAL OFFENCE?

If you are tried for a sexual offence, your defence may be conducted only by a lawyer. It is therefore in your interests, if you have not already done so, to get the professional assistance of a solicitor. If you do not engage a solicitor for the purposes of your defence at the trial, the court will do so.

WHAT WILL HAPPEN IF I DO NOTHING?

A warrant may be issued for your arrest.

WHAT ABOUT MY FINANCIAL CIRCUMSTANCES?

YOU DO NOT HAVE TO GIVE ANY INFORMATION ABOUT THESE: but if you are pleading guilty and you wish the court to consider your financial circumstances you should give as much information as you can on the enclosed form (INFORMATION ABOUT YOUR MEANS).

CAN I GET LEGAL AID?

In certain circumstances Legal Aid is granted. If you want to know more, apply to the clerk of court in the sheriff court where your case will be heard.

NAME AND ADDRESS OF ACCUSED   ....
                                  ....
                                  ....

DATE OF BIRTH   ....

Check that your name, address and date of birth are shown correctly.

AMENDMENT

Form 16.1–B as amended by Act of Adjournal (Criminal Procedure Rules Amendment No. 3) (Sexual Offences (Procedure and Evidence) (Scotland) Act 2002) 2002 (SSI 2002/454), r.2(12) (effective November 1, 2002).

Form 16.1-BA

Form of notice to accompany complaint under section 146(3A) of the Criminal Procedure (Scotland) Act 1995 where the accused is charged with a sexual offence to which section 288C of that Act applies

To: (*name and address of accused*)

TAKE NOTICE THAT:

(1) if you are tried for the offence, your defence at trial may be conducted only by a lawyer,

(2) it is therefore in your interests, if you have not already done so, to get the professional assistance of a solicitor, and

(3) if you do not engage a solicitor for the purposes of your defence at trial, the court will do so.

(*Signed*)

For Procurator Fiscal Depute

AMENDMENT

Form 16.1–BA inserted by Act of Adjournal (Criminal Procedure Rules Amendment No. 3) (Sexual Offences (Procedure and Evidence) (Scotland) Act 2002) 2002 (SSI 2002/454), r.2(12), Sch.2 (effective November 1, 2002).

Form 16.1-BB

Rule 16.1(2A)

Form of notice of citation to be affixed to the door of the accused's dwelling-house or place of business under section 141(2A) of the Criminal Procedure (Scotland) Act 1995

PROCURATOR FISCAL AT (PLACE)

Against

(*name of accused*), residing at (*address*)

To: (*name of accused*)

TAKE NOTICE THAT by virtue of the affixing of this notice you are cited in respect of the above.

You may collect a copy of the complaint and your citation in Form 16.1-B of the Criminal Procedure Rules 1996 [and a notice specifying your previous convictions] from (*name of police station*) Police Station at (*address*).

Your case will be heard at the Sheriff [*or* District] Court at (*address*) on (*date*) at (*time*). You must answer the complaint on or before that date. Form 16.1-B explains how to answer the complaint.

IF YOU DO NOT ANSWER THE COMPLAINT, THE COURT MAY ISSUE A WARRANT FOR YOUR ARREST

This notice was affixed by me (*name and designation*) on: (*date*)

(*Signed*)

Officer of Law

AMENDMENT

Form 16.1-BB inserted by Act of Adjournal (Criminal Procedure Rules Amendment No.2) (Miscellaneous) 2003 (SSI 2003/468), r.2(17) and Sch.3. Brought into force on October 27, 2003 in accordance with art.1.

Act of Adjournal (Criminal Procedure Rules) 1996

Form 16.1-C

Form of reply to complaint

REPLY FORM

PF REF...........................
COURT DATE ....
SHERIFF COURT AT ....

PLEASE COMPLETE WHICHEVER SECTION APPLIES

---

1.   PLEADING NOT GUILTY

I PLEAD NOT GUILTY. Please send me a note of the date of trial.

Signed .... Date ....

PLEASE NOW RETURN THIS FORM IN THE ENVELOPE PROVIDED

---

2. PLEADING GUILTY

I PLEAD GUILTY TO THE CHARGE(S)

except ....

....

Signed.. Date..

PLEASE CONTINUE TO COMPLETE THIS FORM

MOTORING OFFENCES

If you are pleading guilty to a motoring offence PLEASE SEND YOUR DRIVING LICENCE (PAPER LICENCE OR PHOTOCARD LICENCE BUT NOT HGV LICENCE) WITH THIS FORM.
WHEN SENDING A PHOTOCARD LICENCE PLEASE SEND BOTH PARTS – THE PHOTOCARD AND THE COUNTERPART.

NAME AND ADDRESS
OF ACCUSED

DATE OF BIRTH ....

Check that your name, address and date of birth are shown correctly.

Please correct anything that is wrong.

ONLY COMPLETE THIS PAGE IF PLEADING GUILTY

PREVIOUS CONVICTIONS

If previous convictions are attached to your complaint please tick the appropriate box.

I ADMIT THE PREVIOUS CONVICTIONS ☐

I DO NOT ADMIT THE PREVIOUS CONVICTIONS ☐

I ADMIT THE PREVIOUS CONVICTIONS EXCEPT THOSE
LISTED BELOW ☐

....

....

NOTE   If convictions are listed and you do not complete this section, the court will take it that you admit all of them.

CAN I SEND A WRITTEN EXPLANATION?

YES. If you want to, use the space below and continue on a separate sheet if required.

....
....
....
....
....
....
....

PLEASE CHECK YOU HAVE SIGNED THE FORM AT THE PROPER PLACE AND RETURN IT IN THE ENVELOPE PROVIDED.

FOR OFFICIAL USE ONLY

D.L.   Documents Returned

Other Documents

AMENDMENT

Form 16.1-C as amended by the Act of Adjournal (Criminal Procedure Rules Amendment) (Miscellaneous) 2004 (SSI 2004/195), r.2 (effective April 26, 2004).

Form 16.1-D

Rule 16.1(3)(b)

Means Form

INFORMATION ABOUT YOUR MEANS

You are not required by law to return this form completed but it can help you and the court.

If you are found guilty and are fined the information you give here will help the court to set an amount which you can reasonably afford and to give you the time you need to pay.

The information you give on this form will not be used for any other purpose.

PF REF.........................

If you decide to plead guilty by letter please complete this and the reply form and send them to the court.

If you decide to appear in court you may hand the form in when you appear.

If the information you have given below changes a great deal between now and the court hearing you should tell the clerk of court – he will give you another form to fill in.

PERSONAL DETAILS (Please use BLOCK CAPITALS and tick the appropriate box where required).

1. Your full name ....

2. Your address ....

3. Are you   Married   Single   Separated   Divorced   Widowed

4. Are you the head of your household?   Yes   No

5. How many children under 16 do you support ....

6. Is there anyone else financially dependent on you?   Yes   No
    (a)   If YES what is their relationship to you ....

YOUR JOB

---

7. Are you   Employed   Unemployed   Self-employed   Other
    (a) If OTHER, please give details here...
    (b) If EMPLOYED, please give your job here..

YOUR WEEKLY INCOME   YOUR WEEKLY EXPENSES

You may not receive your money or pay your bills weekly. Even so please try to work out what the weekly figures would be.

	£			£
8.(a) Your usual weekly take-home pay including overtime (if self-employed give your usual earnings)	__	9.(a)	Housing (rent, rates, mortgage) (If you pay board and lodgings give the amount)	__
(b) Usual total weekly take-home pay of other household earners	__	(b)	Fuel (electricity, coal, gas, etc.)	__
(c) Total Social Security payments received in your household each week	__	(c)	Food	__
(d) Total pensions received in your household each week	__	(d)	Travel	__
		(e)	Weekly cost of supporting anyone else (see questions 5 and 6)	__
(e) Any other form of income (eg student grant, etc), per week	__	(f)	Other big weekly payments (such as hire purchase agreements or repayment of rent arrears)	__
Usual total WEEKLY household income	__		Usual total WEEKLY expenses	__

GENERAL DETAILS

10.   If the court decides to fine you how much do you think you could afford to pay each week?

       £ ....

11.   Please give any further information about your finances which you would like the court to know here. (You can continue over the page if you need.)

SIGNATURE BOX

12.   I declare that the information I have given in this form is true and complete.

Signed .... Date ....

Form 16.1-E

Form of notice of previous convictions in summary proceedings

NOTICE OF PREVIOUS CONVICTIONS APPLYING TO (*name of accused*)

In the event of your being convicted of the charge(s) in the complaint to which this notice is attached, it is intended to place before the court the following previous conviction(s) applying to you.

Date	Place of Trial	Court	Offence	Sentence

(*Signed*)
Procurator Fiscal

Date:

Form 16.4-A

Form of incidental application in summary proceedings

UNTO THE HONOURABLE THE SHERIFF OF (*name of sheriffdom*)
AT (*place of court*)

PETITION

of

[A.B.] (*address*)
[*or* Prisoner in the Prison of   (*place*)]

under

section 134 of the Criminal Procedure (Scotland) Act 1995

PETITIONER

HUMBLY SHEWETH:

(*Here set out in numbered paragraphs the reasons for the order sought and the statutory process*)

MAY IT THEREFORE please your Lordship to (*set out orders sought*).

ACCORDING TO JUSTICE, etc.

(*Signed*)
[Solicitor for petitioner]
(*Address and telephone number of solicitor*)

Form 16.4-B

Form of assignation of a diet in summary proceedings

(*Place and date*). The court assigns (*date*) at (*time*) within the Sheriff Court House, (*address*), as a diet in this case.

(*Signed*)
Clerk of Court

Form 16.4-C

Form of minutes in minute of proceedings

(Place and date). *(Name of judge)*, Sheriff [*or* District Judge].

Plea of guilty.—Compeared the accused and, in answer to the complaint, pled guilty.

Sentence.—Sentence: Twenty-one days' imprisonment.

(Signed)
Clerk of Court

Where different pleas tendered.—Compeared the accused and, in answer to the complaint, [C.D.] pled guilty and [E.F.] pled guilty to the third charge.

Sentence where more than one accused and different pleas.—Sentence: [C.D.] Twenty-one days' imprisonment. [E.F.] seven days' imprisonment.

(Signed)
Clerk of Court

Plea and sentence combined.—Compeared the accused and. in answer to the complaint, pled guilty *(or state to what extent plea tendered)*, and was sentenced to   days' imprisonment *(or* was fined £   and in default of payment   days' imprisonment) *(or as the case may be)*.

(Signed)
Clerk of Court

Plea of not guilty.—Compeared the accused who, in answer to the complaint, pled not guilty.

Adjournment.—The court adjourned the diet for trial to *(date)* at *(time)*, and ordained the accused then to appear.

[*or* The court adjourned the diet for trial to *(date)* at *(time)*, and ordered the accused to be imprisoned until that date.]

[*or* The court adjourned the diet for trial to *(date)* at *(time)*, and ordered the accused to appear personally at that diet under a penalty of £   in default.]

(Signed)
Clerk of Court

Application to introduce evidence relating to sexual offences.—

The application was heard by *(Name of judge)*, Sheriff [*or* District Judge], at [*place*] on [*date*]: *(narrate terms of application)*

Finding.—The court decided: *(narrate decision and reasons)*

Conditions and directions.—the court imposed the following conditions and directions: *(narrate conditions and directions)*.

(Signed)
Clerk of Court

Trial.—(Place and date), *(Name of judge)*, Sheriff [*or* District Judge]. Compeared the accused [*or* the accused failed to appear after being duly cited *or* after receiving due intimation of this diet].

Finding.—The court found the accused guilty as libelled [*or* as first (*or* last) alternatively libelled, *or state to what extent found guilty*] [*or* not guilty], [*or* found the charge not proven], [*or* found [C.D.] guilty as libelled and [E.F.] guilty as second libelled (*or as the case may be*)].

(Signed)
Clerk of Court

Sentence. Imprisonment.—   day's imprisonment.

[*or Fine, time allowed.—Fined* £   , [*or* £   each],   days allowed for payment].

Fine, imprisonment imposed for future default.—Fine £   , [*or* £   each].   days allowed for payment. For the reason stated below   days imprisonment [*or* days imprisonment each] imposed in default of payment within the time allowed:—

(here state reason)

[*or Fine, no time to pay.—Fined* £   , [*or* £   each], and in default of payment   days' imprisonment. For the reason stated below, no time allowed for payment:—]

(here state reason)

Caution.—To find £   caution for good behaviour,   days allowed for finding such caution.

Fine imposed on parent in lieu of child.—The court found the accused [C.D.] guilty as libelled and fined him [£   ], and, in respect that [E.F.] has conduced to the commission of the said offence by habitually neglecting to exercise due care of the said [C.D.], ordered the fine to be paid by the said [E.F.], and in default of payment sentenced the said [E.F.] to   days' imprisonment.

Sentence deferred.—Sentence deferred till *(date)* at *(time)*, when accused ordained to appear.

Admonition.—Admonished and dismissed.

Desertion of diet.—The court, on the motion of the prosecutor, deserted the diet *pro loco et tempore.*

(Signed)
Clerk of Court

AMENDMENT

Form 16.4–C as amended by Act of Adjournal (Criminal Procedure Rules Amendment No. 3) (Sexual Offences (Procedure and Evidence) (Scotland) Act 2002) 2002 (SSI 2002/454), r.2(12) (effective November 1, 2002).

Form 16.5-A

Rule 16.5(1)(a)

Form of warrant to apprehend an accused person referred to in section 135 of the Criminal Procedure (Scotland) Act 1995

(*Place and date*). The court grants warrant to apprehend the said accused.

(*Signed*)
Sheriff

Form 16.5-B

Rule 16.5(1)(b)

Form of warrant to search referred to in section 135 of the Criminal Procedure (Scotland) Act 1995

(*Place and date*). The court grants warrants to search the person, dwelling-house, and repositories of the accused, and any place where he may be found, and to take possession of the property mentioned or referred to in the complaint, and all articles and documents likely to afford evidence of his guilt or of guilty participation.

(*Signed*)
Sheriff

Form 16.5-C

Rule 16.5(2)

Form of warrant to detain accused in prison or adjourning the case against him

(*Place and date*). The court, on the motion of the prosecutor [*or* accused (*or as the case may be*)], continued the case against the accused until (*date*), and meantime grants warrant to detain the accused in prison until that time [; the accused meantime being liberated on bail conform to separate order attached].

Form 16.6-A

Form of postal citation of witness to appear in summary proceedings

IN THE SHERIFF [*or* DISTRICT] COURT

AT (*place*)

CITATION

To: (*name and address of witness*)

Date of citation: (*day after the date of posting*)

YOU ARE HEREBY CITED to appear on (*date*) at (*time*) in the Sheriff [*or* District] Court House at (*address*) to give evidence for the prosecution [*or* defence] in the complaint by the procurator fiscal against (*name of accused person(s)*).

Please return the enclosed form to the procurator fiscal [*or* the accused person *or* the solicitor for the accused] in the pre-paid envelope provided within 14 days after the date of citation stated at the top of this citation.

IF YOU DO NOT ATTEND COURT WITHOUT A LAWFUL EXCUSE THE COURT MAY ORDER THAT YOU BE APPREHENDED AND PUNISHED.

(*Signed*)
Prosecutor
[*or* Solicitor for accused]

Form 16.6-B

Rule 16.6(1)

Form of reply slip to be completed and returned by witness cited to appear at trial on summary complaint

To: Procurator Fiscal [*or accused or his solicitor*] (*address to be completed by person serving the citation*)

From: (*name to be printed by person serving the citation*)

Date:

I, (*name and address of witness to be completed by person serving the citation*), acknowledge that I have received the citation to appear as a witness for the prosecution [*or* defence] on the complaint by the procurator fiscal against (*name of accused person(s) to be completed by person serving the citation*) on (*date to be inserted by person serving citation*) at (*place to be inserted by person serving the citation*).

I shall attend on that date.

(*Signed*)

Form 16.6-C

Form of personal citation of witness to appear at trial on summary complaint

IN THE SHERIFF [*or* DISTRICT] COURT

AT (*place*)

CITATION

To: (*name and address of witness*)
Date: (*date of citation*)

You are hereby cited to appear on (*date*) at (*time*) in the Sheriff [*or* District] Court House at (*address*) to give evidence for the prosecution [*or* defence] in the complaint by the procurator fiscal against (*name of accused person(s)*).

IF YOU DO NOT ATTEND COURT WITHOUT A LAWFUL EXCUSE THE COURT MAY ORDER THAT YOU BE APPREHENDED AND PUNISHED.

> (*Signed*)
> [Officer of Law]
> (*Designation*)

Form of petition to postpone or accelerate diet in summary proceedings

IN THE SHERIFF [*or* DISTRICT] COURT

AT (*place*)

PETITION

of

[A.B.] (*address*)]
[*or* Prisoner in the Prison of (*place*)]

under section 137(5) of the Criminal Procedure (Scotland) Act 1995

PETITIONER

HUMBLY SHEWETH:

1. That the petitioner [, along with (*name(s) of co-accused*),] has been charged in the above court on a summary complaint at the instance of the procurator fiscal with the offence of (*specify*).

2. That a diet in the proceedings has been fixed for (*date*).

3. That (*narrate circumstances on which application is based*).

4. That the petitioner has intimated to [(*name(s) of any co-accused*) and] the procurator fiscal that he desired a postponement [*or* an acceleration] of the said trial diet.

5. That the procurator fiscal refuses [*and*][*or* (*names(s) of co-accused*) refuse*] to make a joint application to the court for that purpose.

THE PETITIONER THEREFORE craves the court:
   (a)   to appoint intimation of this petition to be made to (*name(s) of co-accused*) [and] [*or* the Procurator Fiscal]
   (b)   to appoint parties to be heard on this petition; and
   (c)   thereafter, in terms of section 137(5) of the Criminal Procedure (Scotland) Act 1995, to discharge the said diet and to fix in lieu of that diet a later [*or* earlier] diet.

ACCORDING TO JUSTICE, etc

(*Signed*)
[Solicitor for petitioner]

(*Address and telephone number of solicitor*)

Form 17.1

Rule 17.1(1)

Form of note of appeal against grant or refusal of extension of 40 days period under section 147(3) of the Criminal Procedure (Scotland) Act 1995

UNTO THE RIGHT HONOURABLE THE LORD JUSTICE GENERAL, LORD JUSTICE-CLERK AND LORDS COMMISSIONERS OF JUSTICIARY

NOTE OF APPEAL

by

[A.B.], prisoner in the Prison of (*place*)

under section 147(3) of the Criminal Procedure (Scotland) Act 1995

APPELLANT

HUMBLY SHEWETH:

1. That at the sheriff [*or* district] court at (*place*) on (*date*) the appellant [, along with (*names of any co-accused*),] appeared on a complaint at the instance of the procurator fiscal on charges of (*specify*).

2. That he pled not guilty and trial was fixed for (*date*) and the appellant was remanded in custody.

3. That an application in terms of section 147(3) of the Criminal Procedure (Scotland) Act 1995 was presented to the sheriff at (*place*) on (*date*) [*in district court cases add:*—he having concurrent territorial jurisdiction with the Lay Justices [*or* Stipendiary Magistrate(s)] of said district court]. The application was heard by Sheriff (*name of judge*) in the said sheriff court on (*date*).

4. That Sheriff (*name of judge*) extended the period of 40 days which would have expired on (*date*) by (*number*) days from that date.

5. That the granting of that extension is unreasonable in respect that (*here state shortly reasons for appeal*).

ACCORDING TO JUSTICE, etc.

(*Signed*)
[Solicitor for appellant]

(*Address and telephone number of solicitor*)

Form 18.3

Rule 18.3

Form of warrant to apprehend witness who has failed to answer a citation

(*Place and date*). The court, in respect that [E.F.], a witness in the cause, has failed to appear after being duly cited, adjourns the diet till (*date*) at (*time*), and ordains the accused and witnesses to appear personally at the said diet, and grants warrant to apprehend [E.F.] and to detain him in any prison or in police cells until the said diet, or bring him before a justice for the purpose of fixing security for his appearance at all diets of the court.

(*Signed*)
Sheriff

Form 18.6

Rule 18.6

Form of order of detention in precincts of court under section 169(1) of the Criminal Procedure (Scotland) Act 1995

The court ordered the accused [*or* offender] to be detained within the precincts of the court [*or* the police station at (*place*)] until (*state time*) of this day.

(*Signed*)
Clerk of Court

Form 19.1-A

Rule 19.1(4)

Form of note of appeal against decision relating to a preliminary plea

IN THE COURT OF JUSTICIARY

NOTE OF APPEAL

under section 174(1) of the Criminal Procedure
(Scotland) Act 1995

by

[A.B.] (*address*)
[*or* Prisoner in the Prison of (*place*)]

APPELLANT

against

[The Procurator Fiscal]

RESPONDENT

To the Sheriff Clerk [*or* Clerk to the District Court] at (*place of court*)

Date of decision appealed against:

Date of trial:

The appellant appeals to the High Court of Justiciary in respect that:—

(1) (*State whether objection taken to competency or relevancy of the complaint or the proceedings or denial issued that the appellant was the person charged by the police with the offence and specify the terms of the objection or denial*).
(2) (*State the decision which it is desired to bring under review by the High Court*).
(3) (*State the grounds of appeal*).

(*Signed*)
[Solicitor for Appellant]

(*Address and telephone number of solicitor*)

Place and date:

Form of minute of abandonment of appeal

IN THE HIGH COURT OF JUSTICIARY

MINUTE OF ABANDONMENT

of

appeal under section 174(1) of the
Criminal Procedure (Scotland) Act 1995

To: Clerk of Justiciary

Name of appellant:

Name of respondent:

Date of decision appealed against:

Date of appeal hearing:

The above-named appellant abandons his [*or* her *or* its] appeal.

(*Signed*)
[Solicitor for Appellant]

(*Address and telephone number of solicitor*)
[*or* Procurator Fiscal]

Place and date:

Form 19.2-A

Form of application for stated case

IN THE SHERIFF [*or* DISTRICT] COURT
AT (*place of court*)

APPLICATION FOR STATED CASE

under section 176(1) of the
Criminal Procedure (Scotland) Act 1995
by
[C.D.] [*or* [A.B.], Procurator Fiscal, (*place*)]

in

The Procurator Fiscal

against

[C.D.] (*address*)
[*or* Prisoner in the Prison of (*place*)]

1. [C.D.] [*or* The Procurator Fiscal] craves the court to state a case for the opinion of the High Court of Justiciary in the above proceedings in which the date of final determination was (*date*).

2. The matter[s] which it is desired to bring under review is [*or* are]:—

(*here specify*)

[3. The appeal is also against sentence.]

[4. The said [C.D.] [*or* Procurator Fiscal] also craves the court to (*here insert any application for bail, for interim suspension of an order for disqualification imposed under the Road Traffic Acts for interim suspension of sentence under section 193A of the Criminal Procedure (Scotland) Act 1995, or for any other interim order under section 177(1) of the Criminal Procedure (Scotland) Act 1995).*]

(*Signed*)
[Solicitor for [C.D.]]

(*Address and telephone number of solicitor*)
[*or* Procurator Fiscal]

(*Place and date*)

AMENDMENT

Form 19.2-A as amended by the Act of Adjournal (Criminal Procedure Rules Amendment No.4) (SI 1997/1834) (effective August 1, 1997).

Form 19.2-B

Form of stated case

IN THE SHERIFF [*or* DISTRICT] COURT
AT (*place*)

CASE
for the Opinion of the High Court of Justiciary at Edinburgh
stated by (*name of judge*)

in

[A.B.] (*address*) [*or* Prisoner in the Prison of (*place*)]
[*or* The Procurator Fiscal at (*place*)]

APPELLANT

against
[C.D.] (*address or as the case may be*)

RESPONDENT

The appellant [*or* respondent] was charged with (*here summarise the relevant charges*).

(*Here state concisely the relevant procedural history of the proceedings.*)

(*Here state the decision and disposal.*)

I [*or* We] found the following facts admitted or proved:—

(*Here set out in numbered paragraphs the facts admitted or proved.*)

(*Where the appeal is against a decision on a submission of no case to answer, identify and summarise the Crown evidence and inferences drawn.*)

(*Here state the reasons for the decision with reference to the evidence on which the facts were found admitted or proved, objections to the admission or rejection of evidence, the grounds of the decision, and any other matters necessary to be stated for the information of the superior court.*)

The question[s] submitted for the opinion of the court is [*or* are]:—

(*here state the question or questions in numbered paragraphs for the opinion of the court*).

This case is stated by me [*or* us]
(*Signature of the judge(s)*)
(*Name of judge(s)*)

(*Append any additional material required by section 179(7) of the Criminal Procedure (Scotland) Act 1995.*)

(*Initials of the judge(s)*)

Form of minutes of procedure in appeal by stated case

(*Date*)	Application for stated case lodged.
	Clerk of Court
(*Date*)	(*Name of judge.*) The court refused [*or* granted] bail conform to separate order attached.
	Clerk of Court
(*Date*)	(*Name of judge.*) The court refused to suspend [*or ad interim* suspended] the order for disqualification under section 41(2) of the Road Traffic Offenders Act 1988.
	Clerk of Court
(*Date*)	(*Name of judge.*) The court refused to suspend [*or ad interim* suspended] the appellant's sentence under section 193A of the Criminal Procedure (Scotland) Act 1995.
	Clerk of Court
(*Date*)	Draft stated case issued to appellant['s solicitor] and duplicate of it issued to respondent['s solicitor]. Last date for receipt of adjustment is (*date*).
	Clerk of Court
(*Date*)	Adjustments for appellant [*or* respondent] received.
	Clerk of Court
(*Date*)	Adjustments for appellant [*or* respondent] received.
	Clerk of Court
(*Date*)	Intimation by appellant [*or* respondent] that no adjustments proposed.
	Clerk of Court
(*Date*)	Intimation by appellant [*or* respondent] that no adjustments proposed.
	Clerk of Court
(*Date*)	Appeal deemed to be abandoned under section 179(3) of the Criminal Procedure (Scotland) Act 1995, and so intimated to appellant['s solicitor] and to respondent['s solicitor].
	Clerk of Court
(*Date*)	Hearing on adjustments and any intended alteration to the draft case to be held on (*date and time*). Appellant['s solicitor] and Respondent['s solicitor] informed.
	Clerk of Court

(*Place and date.*) (*Name(s) of judge(s)*)

Appeared: (*specify*)

Parties heard on the adjustments and on intended alterations to the draft case.

Case adjusted.

The following adjustments rejected by judge:— (*here specify*)

The following alterations proposed by judge not accepted by the appellant [*or* respondent]:—
(*here specify*)

Clerk of Court

(*Date*)	Case signed and sent to appellant['s solicitor] and duplicate sent to respondent['s solicitor]. Complaint, proceedings and all relevant documents transmitted to Clerk of Justiciary.
	Clerk of Court

NOTE

[1]As amended by Act of Adjournal (Criminal Procedure Rules Amendment No. 4) (S.I. 1997 No. 1834) (effective August 1, 1997).

Form of note of appeal against sentence under section 186(1) of the Criminal Procedure (Scotland) Act 1995

IN THE SHERIFF [*or* DISTRICT] COURT AT (*place*)

NOTE OF APPEAL
against sentence

by

[A.B.] (*address*)
[or presently prisoner in the Prison of (*place*)]

APPELLANT

against

The Procurator Fiscal

RESPONDENT

1. The appellant appeals to the High Court of Justiciary against the sentence of (*specify*) passed in the above court on (*date*).

2. The ground[s] of appeal is [*or* are]:—

(*here set out the grounds(s)*).

[3. The appellant also craves the court to (*here insert any application for bail, for interim suspension of any order for disqualification imposed under the Road Traffic Acts for interim suspension of sentence under section 193A of the Criminal Procedure (Scotland) Act 1995, or for any other interim order under section 177(1) by virtue of section 188(10) of the Criminal Procedure (Scotland) Act 1995*).]

(*Signed*)
[Solicitor for appellant]

(*Address and telephone number of solicitor*)

(*Place and date*)

NOTE
[1]As amended by Act of Adjournal (Criminal Procedure Rules Amendment No. 4) (S.I. 1997 No. 1834) (effective August 1, 1997).

Rule 19.3(2)

Form of minutes of procedure in note of appeal against sentence alone under section 186(1) of the Criminal Procedure (Scotland) Act 1995

(Date)	Note of appeal lodged.	
		Clerk of Court
Eo die	Copy note of appeal sent to procurator fiscal.	
		Clerk of Court
Eo die	Copies of note of appeal, complaint, minutes of proceedings and relevant documents sent to *(name of judge)* for report. Proceedings to be sent to Clerk of Justiciary no later than *(date)*.	
		Clerk of Court
(Date)	*(Name of judge.)* The court refused bail [or granted bail] conform to separate order attached.	
		Clerk of Court
(Date)	*(Name of judge.)* The court refused to suspend [or ad interim suspended] the order for disqualification in terms of section 41(2) of the Road Traffic Offenders Act 1988.	
		Clerk of Court
(Date)	Report received.	
		Clerk of Court
(Date)	Copy report sent to [A.B.] [or [C.D.]] and the Procurator Fiscal.	
		Clerk of Court
Eo die	Note of appeal, report and certified copy of the complaint, minutes of proceedings and relevant documents sent to Clerk of Justiciary.	
		Clerk of Court

Rule 19.4

Form of extension of time by sheriff principal

IN THE SHERIFF [*or* DISTRICT] COURT AT (*place*)

[A.B.] v [Procurator Fiscal]

(*Place of date.*) I, (*name*), Sheriff Principal of the Sheriffdom of (*name of sheriffdom*) by virtue of the powers vested in me by section 186(5) [*or* 194(2)] of the Criminal Procedure (Scotland) Act 1995, and in respect that (*name of judge*) is temporarily absent from duty, extend the period specified in section (*specify relevant section*) of that Act so that it will now expire on (*date*).

(*Signed*)

B–138

Form of minute abandoning appeal under section 184(1) of the Criminal Procedure (Scotland) Act 1995

IN THE SHERIFF [*or* DISTRICT] COURT AT (*place*)

MINUTE OF ABANDONMENT

in the

APPEAL BY STATED CASE

by

[A.B.] (*address*)
[*or* presently a prisoner in the Prison of (*place*)]

APPELLANT

against

[The Procurator Fiscal (*or as the case may be*)]

RESPONDENT

The appellant abandons his [*or* her *or* its] appeal as from this date against conviction [*or* conviction and sentence] [*or* the acquittal of the respondent] [*or* the sentence passed on the respondent].

Intimation of the foregoing abandonment has been made to the respondent.

(*Signed*)
[Solicitor for appellant]

(*Address and telephone number of solicitor*)

(*Place and date*)

Form 19.6

Form of minute abandoning appeal under section 175(8) of the Criminal Procedure (Scotland) Act 1995

IN THE HIGH COURT OF JUSTICIARY

MINUTE OF ABANDONMENT

in the

APPEAL BY STATED CASE

by

[A.B.] (*address*)
[*or* presently a prisoner in the Prison of (*place*)]

APPELLANT

against

The Procurator Fiscal

RESPONDENT

The appellant abandons his [*or* her *or* its] appeal as from this date against conviction but proceeds with the appeal against sentence.

Intimation of the foregoing abandonment has been made to the respondent.

(*Signed*)
[Solicitor for appellant]

(*Address and telephone number of solicitor*)

(*Place and date*)

Form of minute of abandonment of appeal against sentence alone under section 186(9) of the Criminal Procedure (Scotland) Act 1995

MINUTE OF ABANDONMENT

of

APPEAL AGAINST SENTENCE

under section 186(9) of the Criminal Procedure (Scotland) Act 1995

Name of appellant:

Date of birth:

Prisoner in the Prison of:

Crime or offence to which appeal relates:

Sheriff/District Court at:

Sentence:

The above named appellant having lodged a note of appeal abandons as from this date the appeal against sentence under section 186(9) of the Criminal Procedure (Scotland) Act 1995.

Intimation of the foregoing abandonment has been made to the respondent.

(*Signed*)
[Solicitor for appellant]

(*Address and telephone number of solicitor*)

(*Place and date*)

Form of application to High Court for suspension of disqualification from driving

UNTO THE RIGHT HONOURABLE THE LORD JUSTICE GENERAL, LORD JUSTICE-CLERK AND LORDS COMMISSIONERS OF JUSTICIARY

NOTE OF APPLICATION

for

SUSPENSION OF DISQUALIFICATION

under section 41 (2) of the Road Traffic Offenders Act 1988

in

SUMMARY COMPLAINT

in causa

The Procurator Fiscal

COMPLAINER AND RESPONDENT

against

[C.D.] (*address*)

APPLICANT AND APPELLANT

HUMBLY SHEWETH:

1. That the applicant and appellant, having been convicted on a complaint brought under the Criminal Procedure (Scotland) Act 1995 at the instance of the complainer and respondent of (*specify charge*), was on (*date*) in the sheriff [*or* district] court at (*place*) fined [*or* sentenced to (*specify*)] and ordered to be disqualified for a period of (*state period of disqualification*) in terms of section [34] of the Road Traffic Offenders Act 1988.

2. That on (*date*) the applicant and appellant applied to the said court to state a case for the opinion of the High Court of Justiciary under section 176 of the Act of 1995.

3. That the applicant and appellant thereafter requested the court to suspend the period of disqualification under section 39(2) of the Road Traffic Offenders Act 1988.

4. That the court, on (*date*), refused to suspend the disqualification.

5. That the applicant and appellant has served a copy of this note on the clerk of the said court and on the respondent.

MAY IT THEREFORE please your Lordships under section 41(2) of the Road Traffic Offenders Act 1988 to suspend the said disqualification on such terms as your Lordships think fit.

ACCORDING TO JUSTICE, etc.

[Solicitor for applicant and appellant]

(*Address and telephone number of solicitor*)

Rule 19.18

HIGH COURT OF JUSTICIARY, EDINBURGH

APPEAL: -v- **PF** *(specify place)*

CASE REF:

Provide the following details

1. The specification of the place and date of conviction and of the charges of which the appellant was convicted, subject to any amendments and deletions:

2. The sentence or sentences imposed:

3. The grounds of appeal that have passed the sift:

4. An articulate statement of reasons in support of each ground of appeal:

5. A list of authorities relied upon, if any:

6. A schedule of the documents founded upon, if any:

> *(Signed)*
> Counsel, solicitor advocate or appellant

(Date)

* Delete as appropriate

AMENDMENT

    Form 19.18 inserted by Act of Adjournal (Criminal Appeals) 2003 (SSI 2003/387), Sch.1. Brought into force on September 1, 2003 in accordance with art.1.

Form 19C.1–A

Rule 19C.1(1)

Form of notice of intention to apply for a risk assessment order under section 210B of the Criminal Procedure (Scotland) Act 1995

Prosecution reference..............

Court reference.....................

IMPORTANT NOTICE

The prosecutor in the case against you in the High Court of Justiciary intends to make a motion for a **RISK ASSESSMENT ORDER** within the meaning of section 210B of the Criminal Procedure (Scotland) Act 1995.

A risk assessment order is an order–

(a)   for you to be taken to a place specified in the order, so that there may be prepared there–

(i)   by a person accredited for the purposes of section 210B of the Criminal Procedure (Scotland) Act 1995 by the Risk Management Authority; and

(i)   in such manner as may be so accredited,

a risk assessment report (that is to say, a report as to what risk your being at liberty presents to the safety of the public at large); and

(b)   providing for you to be remanded in custody there for so long as is necessary for those purposes and thereafter there or elsewhere until such diet as is fixed for sentence.

(*Signed*)

Prosecutor

(*Name, address, e-mail address and telephone number*)

(*Place and date*)

AMENDMENT

Form 19C.1-A inserted by Act of Adjournal (Criminal Procedure Rules Amendment No.3) (Risk Assessment Orders and Orders for Lifelong Restriction) 2006 (SSI 2006/302), para.2(7) and Sch., Part 1 (effective June 20, 2006).

Rule 19C.1(2)

Form of risk assessment order under section 210B of the Criminal Procedure (Scotland) Act 1995

Prosecution reference..............

Court reference.....................

RISK ASSESSMENT ORDER

under section 210B of the Criminal Procedure (Scotland) Act 1995

HIGH COURT OF JUSTICIARY sitting at [*place*]

DATE:

OFFENDER:

Address:

Date of birth:

THE COURT having convicted the offender of (*specify offence or offences*), being an offence [*or* offences] to which section 210B(1) of the Criminal Procedure (Scotland) Act 1995 applies:

AND considering that the risk criteria set out in section 210E of that Act may be met;

ORDERS–

1. That the offender be taken to [*place*] so that there may be prepared there–

   (a) by a person accredited for the purposes of section 210B of that Act; and

   (b) in such manner as may be so accredited;

a risk assessment report (that is to say, a report as to what risk his being at liberty presents to the safety of the public at large); and

2. That the offender be remanded in custody there for so long as is necessary for those purposes and thereafter there or elsewhere until such diet as is fixed for sentence; and

ADJOURNS the case against the offender until (*specify date not exceeding 90 days after date of order*) or such earlier date as may be fixed for the offender to be brought before the court following receipt of the risk assessment order.

(*Signed*)

Clerk of Court

AMENDMENT

Form 19C.1-B inserted by Act of Adjournal (Criminal Procedure Rules Amendment No.3) (Risk Assessment Orders and Orders for Lifelong Restriction) 2006 (SSI 2006/302), para.2(7) and Sch., Part 1 (effective June 20, 2006).

Rule 19C.2

Form of risk assessment report under section 210C of the Criminal Procedure (Scotland) Act 1995

RISK ASSESSMENT REPORT

under section 210C of the Criminal Procedure (Scotland) Act 1995

Prosecution reference..............

Court reference....................

CONVICTED PERSON: (*name*)

DATE OF BIRTH: (*place*)

REMANDED AT: (*place*)

CASE ADJOURNED TO: (*date*)

HIGH COURT OF JUSTICIARY SITTING AT: (*place*)

REPORT INSTRUCTED BY: (*name and designation*)

Under section 210C [*or* 210D] of the Criminal Procedure (Scotland) Act 1995, I, (*name*) report to the High Court of Justiciary as follows:–

[*here state terms of report*]

IN WITNESS WHEREOF

(*Signed*)

Assessor

(*Name, qualifications (including details of accreditation by the Risk Management Authority, address, e-mail address and telephone number*)

(*Place and date*)

AMENDMENT

Form 19C.1-B inserted by Act of Adjournal (Criminal Procedure Rules Amendment No.3) (Risk Assessment Orders and Orders for Lifelong Restriction) 2006 (SSI 2006/302), para.2(7) and Sch., Part 1 (effective June 20, 2006).

Form 19C.3

Rule 19C.3(1)

Form of notice of objection to risk assessment report under section 210C(7) of the Criminal Procedure (Scotland) Act 1995

NOTICE OF OBJECTION

by

[A.B.], (address)

[or, Prisoner in the Prison of (*place*) [*or* Patient at (*specify hospital*)]]

Prosecution reference..............

Court reference.....................

I, [A.B.] object to the content or findings of the risk assessment report dated (*date*) by (*name of assessor*).

The grounds of my objection are as follows:–

(*Here state the grounds of objection in numbered paragraphs*)

[Legal representative of] [A.B.]]

(*Name, address, e-mail address and telephone number*)

(*Place and date*)

AMENDMENT

Form 19C.3 inserted by Act of Adjournal (Criminal Procedure Rules Amendment No.3) (Risk Assessment Orders and Orders for Lifelong Restriction) 2006 (SSI 2006/302), para.2(7) and Sch., Part 1 (effective June 20, 2006).

Form 20.1

Rule 20.1(1)

Form of sentence of death

[Repealed by the Act of Adjournal (Criminal Procedure Rules Amendment No.3) 1999 (S.I.1999 No. 1387) para. 2(5) (effective May 19,1999).]

Form 20.2

Rule 20.2

Form of order of detention in police custody instead of imprisonment under section 206(2) of the Criminal Procedure (Scotland) Act 1995

The court ordered the offender to be detained in the custody of the police at (*place*) for (*number of days not exceeding four*).

(*Signed*)

Clerk of Court

Form 20.3-A

Rule 20.3

Form of supervised release order under section 209 of the Criminal Procedure (Scotland) Act 1995

SUPERVISED RELEASE ORDER

under section 209 of the Criminal Procedure (Scotland) Act 1995

Court:

Date:

Offender:

Address:

Date of birth:

Offence(s) of which convicted:

Date of offence(s):

THE COURT, having sentenced the offender to imprisonment for a term of (*state period*) being less than four years:

AND being of the opinion that this order is necessary to protect the public from serious harm from the offender on his release:

AND having explained to the offender the effect of the order and the possible consequences for the offender of any breach of it including any failure to comply with requirements mentioned below:

ORDERS that the offender shall, during a period of (*insert period being a period not exceeding 12 months and not extending beyond the date by which the entire term of imprisonment will elapse*) after the date of his release, be under the supervision either of a relevant officer of a local authority or of a probation officer appointed for or assigned to a petty sessions area designated by the Scottish Ministers under section 14(4) or 15(1) of the Prisoners and Criminal Proceedings (Scotland) Act 1993 and shall be subject to—

    (a) the following standard requirements specified by virtue of section 209(4)(a) of the Criminal Procedure (Scotland) Act 1995:—

        (i) to report to the supervising officer in a manner and at intervals specified by that officer; and

        (ii) to notify that officer without delay of any change of address;

    (b) such reasonable requirements as may, by virtue of section 209(3)(b) of the Criminal Procedure (Scotland) Act 1995, be specified by the supervising officer; and

    (c) (*insert any requirements which the court may wish to specify, e.g., as to counselling on drug or alcohol abuse, staying away from victims, etc.*).

(*Signed*)
Clerk of Court

Copy to: Offender
           Scottish Ministers

AMENDMENT

    Form 20.3 as amended by the Act of Adjournal (Criminal Procedure Rules Amendment No.2) (Miscellaneous) 2000 (SSI 2000/65), para.2 (effective April 7, 2000).

    Form 20.3 as amended by Act of Adjournal (Criminal Procedure Rules Amendment No.2) (Miscellaneous) 2003 (SSI 2003/468), r.2(17). Brought into force on October 27, 2003 in accordance with art.1.

Form 20.3-B

Rule 20.3(2)

Form of citation of offender under section 15(5) of the Prisoners and Criminal Proceedings (Scotland) Act 1993

IN THE HIGH COURT OF JUSTICARY

[*or* IN THE SHERIFF [*or* DISTRICT] COURT]

AT (*place*)

CITATION

To: (*name and address of offender*)

Date: (*date*)

YOU ARE HEREBY CITED to appear on (*date*) at (*time*) in the High Court of Justiciary [*or* Sheriff [*or* District] Court] at (*address*) because an application has been made to the court by your supervising officer [*or* by a relevant officer of the local authority] [*or* by an officer of the local probation board] for the amendment, variation or cancellation of a requirement specified in your supervised release order. A copy of that application is attached. [*or* The application has been made because (*specify reasons for the application*)].

IF YOU FAIL TO ATTEND COURT WITHOUT A LAWFUL EXCUSE THE COURT MAY ISSUE A WARRANT FOR YOUR ARREST.

(*Signed*)

Clerk of Court

AMENDMENT

Form 20.3-B inserted by Act of Adjournal (Criminal Procedure Rules Amendment No.2) (Miscellaneous) 2003 (SSI 2003/468), r.2(17) and Sch.3. Brought into force on October 27, 2003 in accordance with art.1.

Form 20.3-C

Rule 20.3(3)

Form of citation of offender under section 18(1) of the Prisoners and Criminal Proceedings (Scotland) Act 1993

IN THE HIGH COURT OF JUSTICARY

[*or* IN THE SHERIFF [*or* DISTRICT] COURT]

AT (*place*)

CITATION

To: (*name and address of offender*)

Date: (*date*)

YOU ARE HEREBY CITED to appear on (*date*) at (*time*) in the High Court of Justiciary [*or* Sheriff [*or* District] Court] at (*address*) because it has been reported to the court that you have failed to comply with a requirement specified in the supervised release order made in respect of you on (*date*) as alleged in the written information attached [*or* by (*specify the failure alleged*)].

IF YOU FAIL TO ATTEND COURT WITHOUT A LAWFUL EXCUSE THE COURT MAY ISSUE A WARRANT FOR YOUR ARREST

(*Signed*)

Clerk of Court

AMENDMENT

Form 20.3-C inserted by Act of Adjournal (Criminal Procedure Rules Amendment No.2) (Miscellaneous) 2003 (SSI 2003/468), r.2(17) and Sch.3. Brought into force on October 27, 2003 in accordance with art.1.

Form 20.3A-A

Form of a certificate under section 92(2) of Sexual Offences Act 2003 of conviction or of finding

CERTIFICATE UNDER SECTION 92(2) OF THE SEXUAL OFFENCES ACT 2003
OF CONVICTION [*or* FINDING]

. . . . Court Date . . . .

Case No. . . . .

Name:	
Address:	
Date of birth:	
Date of [conviction] [*or* finding]:	
Date of sentence if different:	
Offence(s) and sentence(s):	

I hereby certify, under section 92(2) of the Sexual Offences Act 2003, that the above named accused was on the above date convicted of [or found not guilty by reason of insanity of] [or found to be under a disability and to have done the act[s] charged against him in respect of] the above offence[s]; that the offence is a sexual offence [or offences are sexual offences] to which Part 2 of that Act applies; and that the court so stated in open court on that date.

. . . .
CLERK OF COURT

AMENDMENT

Inserted by Act of Adjournal (Criminal Procedure Rules Amendment No.5) 1997 (SI 1997/2082) (effective September 1, 1997).

Form 20.3A-A substituted by the Act of Adjournal (Criminal Procedure Rules Amendment No.2) (Sexual Offences Act 2003) 2004 (SSI 2004/206), r.2 and Sch.1 (effective May 1, 2004).

Rule 20.3A(2)

Form of notice of requirement to notify police

PART 2

Form 20.3A-B

Rule 20.3A(2)

Form of notice of requirement to notify police under Part 2 of the Sexual Offences Act 2003

NOTICE OF REQUIREMENT TO NOTIFY POLICE

(This notice contains a summary of the notification requirements you must comply with. It is not a complete statement of the law. If you need further explanation or advice you should consult a solicitor.)

Case No. ....

You have been convicted of [*or* found not guilty by reason of insanity of] [*or* found to be under a disability and to have done the act charged against you in respect of] a sexual offence covered by the Sexual Offences Act 2003. The details are set out in the certificate of conviction [*or* finding] which is attached to this notice [*or* will be sent to you].

This means that you are now required by law to:

- **Notify the police** within the next 3 days (or, if you are in custody, within 3 days after your release) of your name and any other names you use or have used, your date of birth, your home address (*i.e.* your sole or main residence in the UK or, if you have no such residence, the address or location of any place in the UK where you can regularly be found and, if there is more than one place, your choice of one of these places), and your national insurance number.

- **Notify the police** of any change to your name or home address, or that you have been released from custody, within 3 days after the date of the change, or your release.

- **Notify the police** of any address in the UK where you reside or stay for 7 days or longer. This means either 7 days at a time or a total of 7 days in any 12 month period.

- **Notify the police** of your details every 12 months even if there is no change to those details.

- **Notify the police** 7 days in advance of the date of leaving the United Kingdom of any plans to travel abroad for a period of 3 days or longer.

- **Notify the police** whether you have a passport and in relation to each passport you have, specify the issuing authority, the number, the dates of issue and expiry and the name and date of birth given as being those of the passport holder. Should you lose or cease to have a passport that has been notified or receive a passport that has not been notified, you must notify the police of this within 3 days of the change in circumstances.

- **Notify the police** whether you hold any bank accounts or accounts with credit card providers, in you own name, or jointly with another person, or in the name of an unincorporated business operated by you, or by you jointly with another person and whether you hold any debit cards or credit cards in connection with these accounts. You must provide detailed information in respect of each account including the names of any business in which the account or card is held, the names and addresses of each bank or credit card provider where each account is maintained, the account numbers and sort codes for each account, the number, validation and expiry dates of each card. Where such an account is opened or card is obtained which has not been notified, or any account or card which has been notified is closed or expired or no longer held, or information in relation to an account or card becomes inaccurate or incomplete you must notify the police within 3 days of the date the account was opened, closed, or the information changed

Please note: if you are already subject to the notification requirements because of a previous conviction, or finding for a relevant offence then it is not necessary to make another initial notification. However, you will have to comply with all other notification requirements (including the requirement to notify the police within 3 days of any release from custody or detention)

You must give this notice by going to a designated police station at the police area at which your home is situated and giving it in person. If you do not know the designated police station in the police area your home is situated in, or which police stations are in that area, then ask at any police station.

These requirements apply to you from [*date of conviction or finding*] and shall continue to apply for 5 years [*or* for 7 years] [*or* for 10 years] [*or* for the duration of your probation order] [*or* indefinitely].

If you fail to comply with these requirements without reasonable excuse, or give the police false information, you could be fined, or sent to prison for up to 5 years, or both.

AMENDMENT

Form 20.3A-B substituted by the Act of Adjournal (Criminal Procedure Rules Amendment No.3) (Miscellaneous) 2007 (SSI 2007/276), r.2(3) and Sch (effective May 2, 2007).

Form 20.3A-C

Form of notice of duration of notification period under Part 2 of the Sexual Offences Act 2003

Case No. ....

You were given notice of the notification requirements which you must comply with under Part 2 of the Sexual Offences Act 2003 on [*date notice given*]. Those requirements apply to you from [*date of conviction or finding*] and shall continue to apply for 5 years [*or* for 7 years] [*or* for 10 years] [*or* for the duration of your probation order] [*or* indefinitely].

AMENDMENT

Form 20.3A-C inserted by the Act of Adjournal (Criminal Procedure Rules Amendment No. 4) (Miscellaneous) 2006 (SSI 2006/436), r.2 and Sch. Pt 1 (effective September 1, 2006).

Form 20.4-A

Rule 20.4(1)

Form of direction as to money found on offender under section 212(1) of the Criminal Procedure (Scotland) Act 1995

The court directed that the money found on the person (*name of offender*) should not be applied to payment of the fine of £   imposed on him on (*date*).

(*Signed*)
Judge

Act of Adjournal (Criminal Procedure Rules) 1996

Form 20.4-B

Rule 20.4(2)

Form of notice to governor of prison under section 212(7) of the Criminal Procedure (Scotland) Act 1995

To the Governor of the Prison of (*place*).

TAKE NOTICE that the attendance of (*name*), presently in your custody, is required at (*place and address of court*) on (*date*) at (*time*).

(*Signed*)
Judge

(*Place and date*)

Form 20.5

Rule 20.5

Form of order for further time for payment of fine under section 214(7) or 215(3) of the Criminal Procedure (Scotland) Act 1995

The court, having considered the application of the offender for extension of time for payment of the fine of £   , allowed payment to be made within   days from this date.

(*Signed*)
Clerk of Court

Form 20.6-A

Rule 20.6(1)

Form of citation to appear for enquiry under section 216(3)(a) of the Criminal Procedure (Scotland) Act 1995

Court

To: (*name and address*)	No.
	Date
	Fine
	Class of offence
	Rate of payment

Citation to attend for enquiry

Balance
outstanding £

On (*date*)

At (*time*)

In respect that you were fined as shown above, that you are in default of payment and that the outstanding balance of the fine is as shown above, you are ordained to appear personally at the time and date shown above in the Sheriff [*or* District] Court at (*place and address*) for an enquiry under section 216 of the Criminal Procedure (Scotland) Act 1995.

(*Place and date*)   (*Signed*)
                                       Clerk of Court

NOTES

(1) If you fail to appear personally at the enquiry court, the court may issue a warrant for your arrest.
(2) If you pay the whole outstanding balance of the fine before the enquiry court, it will not be necessary for you to appear.

Form 20.6-B

Rule 20.6(2)

Form of execution of citation otherwise than by post of offender for enquiry for non-payment of fine

I, (*name and designation*), on (*date*), did lawfully cite (*name and address of offender in the citation*) to appear in person before the Sheriff [*or* District] Court at (*place and address*) on (*date*) at (*time*) for an enquiry under section 216 of the Criminal Procedure (Scotland) Act 1995. This I did by handing the citation to (*name*) personally [*or if not served personally, state other method of service*].

(*Signed*)
Officer of Law

Form 20.6-C

Execution of citation by post, warrant to apprehend and record of proceedings at enquiry under section 216 of the Criminal Procedure (Scotland) Act 1995

(*Name and address of offender*)	No.
	Date
	Fine
	Class of offence
	Rate of payment

To attend for enquiry   Balance
                                         outstanding £

on (*date*)

at (*time*)

Today I lawfully cited the above named offender to appear in person before the Sheriff [*or* District] Court, on the date and time shown above for an enquiry under section 216 of the Criminal Procedure (Scotland) Act 1995.

This I did by posting a copy of the citation to the offender addressed as shown above, by the recorded delivery service.

(*Signed*)
Clerk of Court

(*Place and date*)

(*Place and date.*) In respect that the above named offender has failed to pay the outstanding balance of the fine as shown above within the time allowed and has failed to appear in person for enquiry after being duly cited, the court grants warrant for the apprehension of the said offender for the purposes of his [*or* her] appearance before the court for enquiry under section 216 of the Criminal Procedure (Scotland) Act 1995.

(*Signed*)
Judge

(*Place and date*)   Judge:

Compeared the offender for enquiry. After enquiry, the court in relation to the fine referred to above—
(1)   allowed payment of the fine to be made within   days from   ;
(2)   allowed payment of the fine to be made by instalments of £   per week
commencing on   19   ;
(3) imposed as an alternative to the fine   days' imprisonment to commence forthwith.

(*Signed*)
Clerk of Court

Form 20.7

Rule 20.7

Form of notice of fines supervision order under section 217(7) of the Criminal Procedure (Scotland) Act 1995

Court:
To: (*name and address of offender*)

In respect that a fine of £   was imposed on you by the court at (*place*) on (*date*) and that fine [*or* balance of £   ] remains unpaid, the court today has placed you under the supervision of (*name of supervising officer*) who will assist you and advise you on the payment of the fine for so long as the fine remains unpaid or until the further order of court.

Payment of the fine is now to be made by weekly instalments of £   per week, the first instalment being due within   days from this date.

(*Place and date*)   (Signed)
                                             Clerk of Court

Copy to: Chief Social Work Officer
           (*Address*)

Form 20.8

Rule 20.8(2)

Form of charge for payment of a fine or other financial penalty

CHARGE FOR PAYMENT OF FINE OR OTHER FINANCIAL PENALTY

instructed by the sheriff clerk (*address*) [*or* Clerk to the District Court (*address*)]

To: (*name and address of person fined or subject to the financial penalty*)

On (*date*) a fine [*or* financial penalty] (*give details and total amount of fine or other financial penalty*) was imposed on you in the High Court of Justiciary [*or* Sheriff Court *or* District Court] at (*place*)]

The court authorised recovery of the fine [*or specify other financial penalty*] on (*date*) and an extract conviction was issued in respect of the outstanding balance of £

I, (*name and address*), Messenger-at-Arms [*or* sheriff officer], by virtue of the extract conviction, in Her Majesty's name and authority and in the name and authority of the Lords Commissioners of Justiciary [*or* sheriff *or* justice] at (*place*), charge you to pay the total sum due within [14] days after the date of this charge to the sheriff clerk [*or* clerk to the District Court] (*address*).

If you do not pay this sum within [14] days you are liable to have further action taken against you.

This charge is served on you today by me by (*state method of service*) and is witnessed by (*name and address of witness*).

Dated the   day of

(*Signed*)   (*Signed*)

                                    Messenger-at-Arms
Witness   [or Sheriff Officer]

Form 20.9-A

Form of notice of transfer of fine order under section 222(1) of the Criminal Procedure (Scotland) Act 1995

IN THE SHERIFF [*or* DISTRICT] COURT

AT (*place*)

(*Name of offender*)

Date of birth:

was on (*date*) convicted of (*crime or offence*) and was sentenced to pay a fine of £ , the fine to be paid by (*date*) [*or* by weekly (*or otherwise*) instalments of £ , the first instalment to be paid on (*date*)]; and that fine [*or* the balance of that fine as shown in the statement below] is still unpaid and (*state period*) of imprisonment has been fixed in the event of a future default in payment of the sum in question.

And as it appears that (*name of offender*) is now residing at (*address*) a transfer of fine order is hereby made under section 222(2) of the Criminal Procedure (Scotland) Act 1995, transferring to the (*specify the court*) at (*place*) and to the clerk of that court in respect of that fine all the functions referred to in section 222 of that Act.

(*Signed*)
Clerk of Court

Date:

STATEMENT REFERRED TO

Fine	£	
Instalment(s) paid to date of transfer	£	
Balance due		
In instalments of	£	

Form of notice of further transfer of fine order by virtue of section 222(5) of the Criminal Procedure (Scotland) Act 1995

IN THE SHERIFF [*or* DISTRICT] COURT

AT (*place*)

(*Name of offender*)

Date of birth:

was on (*date*) at (*name of court*) convicted of (*offence*) and was sentenced to pay a fine of £   , the fine to be paid by (*date*) [*or* by weekly (*or otherwise*) instalments of £   , the first instalment to be paid on (*date*)];

By virtue of a Transfer of Fine Order dated (*insert date*) the functions of the sheriff [*or* district] court were transferred to (*specify the court*) at (*place*). The clerk of that court has sent a notice stating that (*name of offender*) is not residing within its jurisdiction.

The fine or the balance of the fine as shown in the statement below is still unpaid and (*state period*) of imprisonment has been fixed in the event of a future default in payment of the sum in question.

And as it appears that (*name of offender*) is now residing at (*address*) outwith the jurisdiction of this court, a further transfer of fine order is hereby made under section 222(1) of the Criminal Procedure (Scotland) Act 1995, transferring to the (*specify the court*) at (*place*) and to the clerk of that court in respect of the fine all the functions referred to in section 222 of that Act.

(*Signed*)
Clerk of Court

Date:

STATEMENT REFERRED TO

Fine	£
Instalment(s) paid to date of transfer	£
Balance due	_____
In instalments of	£

Form 20.9-C

Form of notice to offender of transfer of fine order under section 222(1) of the Criminal Procedure (Scotland) Act 1995

IN THE SHERIFF [*or* DISTRICT] COURT

AT (*place*)

TO: (*name and address of offender*)

On (*date*), you were convicted by the (*specify the court*) at (*place*) and were sentenced to pay a fine of £   , to be paid by (*date*) [*or* by weekly (*or otherwise*) instalments of £   , the first instalment to be paid on (*date*)]. The fine has not been [fully] paid and (*state period*) of imprisonment has been fixed in the event of a future default in payment of the sum in question.

NOTICE IS HEREBY GIVEN TO YOU that in consequence of a transfer of fine order made by the (*specify the court*) at (*place*) on (*date*), the enforcement of the fine [*or* the balance of the fine] due by you as shown in the statement below, has become a matter for this court.

Payment of that fine [*or* the balance of that fine] due by you should therefore be made within the time [*or* times] ordered, either by post or personally to me (*clerk of court and address*).

If you cannot pay forthwith [*or* by (*date*)], you should at once make an application for further time to be granted. Such an application should be made either in person to this court or by letter addressed to me stating fully why you are unable to pay the sum due.

(*Signed*)
Clerk of Court

(*Address*)

Date:

NOTE: Any communication sent by post must be properly stamped.
Cash should not be sent in an unregistered envelope.

STATEMENT REFERRED TO

Fine	£
Instalment(s) paid to date of transfer	£
Balance due	_____
In instalments of	£

Form 20.10-A

Rule 20.10(1)

Form of probation order made under section 228 of the Criminal Procedure (Scotland) Act 1995

PROBATION ORDER

under section 228 of the Criminal Procedure (Scotland) Act 1995

COURT:
DATE:
OFFENDER:
Address:
Date of birth:

THE COURT, having convicted the offender, and being of the opinion that, having regard to the circumstances, including the nature of the offence and the character of the offender, it is expedient to make a probation order containing the undernoted requirements;

AND the court having explained to the offender the effect of the probation order (including the requirements set out below), and that if he or she fails to comply with the probation order, he may be brought before the court by his supervising officer for a breach of probation and may be fined or sentenced or dealt with for the original offence, and that, if he or she commits another offence during the period of the probation order, he or she may be dealt with for that offence;

AND the offender having expressed his or her willingness to comply with the requirements of the probation order;

ORDERS that for a period of (*specify period*) from the date of this order the offender who resides [*or* is to reside] in the local authority area of (*specify*) shall be under the supervision of an officer of that local authority allocated for the purpose [*or* allocated for the purpose as required by the court] at (*place*) in the said local authority area; that the offender shall be notified in writing by the clerk of court of the name and official address of the officer who is to supervise him or her and be similarly notified if at any time such supervision is to be undertaken by another officer of the local authority allocated for the purpose; and that the offender shall comply with the following requirements, namely—
    (1) to be of good behaviour;
    (2) to conform to the directions of the supervising officer;
    (3) to inform the supervising officer at once if he or she changes his residence or place of employment;
    (4) (*here insert any additional requirements*).

(*Signed*)
Clerk of Court

Date:

Note: (*Name of supervising officer*) of (*name of local authority*) has been allocated as supervising officer in this case.

I confirm that I understand the conditions of the probation order.

Signature of offender:

Signature of supervising officer:

Form 20.10-B

Rule 20.10(2)

Form of citation of probationer under section 232(1) or 233(1) of the Criminal Procedure (Scotland) Act 1995

IN THE HIGH COURT OF JUSTICIARY

[*or* IN THE SHERIFF [*or* DISTRICT] COURT]

AT (*place*)

CITATION

To: (*name and address of probationer*)

Date of citation: (*date of citation or, if citation by post, the day after the date of posting*)

YOU ARE HEREBY CITED to appear on (*date*) at (*time*) in the High Court of Justiciary [*or* Sheriff [*or* District] Court] at (*address*) because it has been reported to the court that you have failed to comply with a requirement of your probation order as alleged in the written information attached [*or* by (*specify the failure alleged*)] [*or* committed an offence while on probation, namely, (*specify*)].

IF YOU DO NOT ATTEND COURT WITHOUT A LAWFUL EXCUSE THE COURT MAY ORDER THAT YOU BE APPREHENDED AND PUNISHED

(*Signed*)
Clerk of Court

AMENDMENT

Form 20.10-B as amended by Act of Adjournal (Criminal Procedure Rules Amendment No.2) (Miscellaneous) 2003 (SSI 2003/468), r.2(17). Brought into force on October 27, 2003 in accordance with art.1.

Form 20.10-C

Form of citation of probationer under paragraph 5(1) of Schedule 6 to the Criminal Procedure (Scotland) Act 1995

IN THE HIGH COURT OF JUSTICIARY

[*or* IN THE SHERIFF [*or* DISTRICT] COURT]

AT (*place*)

CITATION

To: (*name and address of probationer*)

Date: (*date*)

YOU ARE HEREBY CITED to appear on (*date*) at (*time*) in the High Court of Justiciary [*or* Sheriff [*or* District] Court] at (*address*) because the court proposes to amend the probation order made in respect of you on (*date*) as indicated in the information attached [*or* (*specify the proposed amendment*)].

IF YOU FAIL TO ATTEND COURT WITHOUT A LAWFUL EXCUSE THE COURT MAY ISSUE A WARRANT FOR YOUR ARREST

(*Signed*)

Clerk of Court

AMENDMENT

Form 20.10-C inserted by Act of Adjournal (Criminal Procedure Rules Amendment No.2) (Miscellaneous) 2003 (SSI 2003/468), r.2(17) and Sch.3. Brought into force on October 27, 2003 in accordance with art.1.

Form 20.10A

Form of non-harassment order made under section 234A of the Criminal Procedure (Scotland) Act 1995

NON HARASSMENT ORDER

Under section 234A of the Criminal Procedure (Scotland) Act 1995

COURT:
DATE:
OFFENDER:
Address:
Date of birth:

THE COURT, having convicted the offender of *(specify offence or offences)*, being [an offence] [offences] involving harassment, within the meaning of section 8 of the Protection from Harassment Act 1997 of a person;

AND being satisfied, on the balance of probabilities, that it is appropriate to make an order to protect that person from further harassment;

ORDERS that [for a period of *(specify period)* from the date of this order] [until further order] the offender shall *(specify conduct from which offender is to refrain)*.

(Signed)

CLERK OF COURT

Form of application under section 234A(6) of the Criminal Procedure (Scotland) Act 1995

UNTO THE RIGHT HONOURABLE THE LORD JUSTICE GENERAL, LORD
JUSTICE-CLERK AND LORDS COMMISSIONERS OF JUSTICIARY

[*or* UNTO THE HONOURABLE THE SHERIFF
OF (*name of sheriffdom*) AT (*place*)]

[*or* UNTO THE JUSTICES in the DISTRICT COURT
OF (*name of district*) AT (*place*)]

APPLICATION

by

Her Majesty's Advocate [*or*
[A.B.] (*address*) [*or* Prisoner in the Prison of (*place*)]

APPLICANT

HUMBLY SHEWETH:

1. That a non-harassment order was made against [A.B.] on (*date*) in the High Court of Justiciary sitting [*or* in the sheriff court *or* in the district court] at (*place*) on (*date*) in terms of the non-harassment order annexed hereto,

2. That the applicant applies to the court in terms of section 234A(6) of the Act of 1995 to revoke [*or* vary] the non-harassment order for the following reasons:—

(*here state reasons*).

MAY IT THEREFORE PLEASE YOUR LORDSHIP[S] [OR THE COURT]:
    (a) to [revoke the non-harassment order] [vary the non-harassment order by (*here state terms of variation of order sought*)].
    (b) or to do otherwise as to your Lordship[s] [OR to the court] shall seem proper.

IN RESPECT WHEREOF

(*Signed*)
Advocate Depute [*or* Procurator Fiscal]
On behalf of Her Majesty's Advocate [*or*]
[Solicitor for [A.B.]
(*Address and telephone number of solicitor*)].

NOTE
    You must notify the clerk of Court within 14 days of the receipt of this application whether or not you intend to oppose it. Failure so to notify will result in the court disposing of the matter in your absence.

Act of Adjournal (Criminal Procedure Rules) 1996

Form 20.11-A

Rule 20.11(1)

Form of supervised attendance order under section 235(1) of the Criminal Procedure (Scotland) Act 1995

SUPERVISED ATTENDANCE ORDER

under section 235(1) of the Criminal Procedure (Scotland) Act 1995

COURT:
DATE:
OFFENDER:
Address:
Date of birth:

(1) THE COURT, being satisfied that the requirements of paragraphs (a), (b) and (c) of section 235(3) of the Criminal Procedure (Scotland) Act 1995 have been met;

AND having explained to the offender the purpose and effect of this order (including the requirements set out below), and that if the offender fails to comply with this order the offender may be brought before the court which may revoke this order and impose a period of imprisonment or may vary the number of hours specified in this order, and that the court has power to review this order on the application either of the offender or of an officer of the local authority in whose area the offender for the time being resides;

AND the offender having expressed his or her willingness to comply with this order;

IN RESPECT that the offender [resides] [*or* is to reside] in the District of (*specify district of local authority*) in the area of (*specify the local authority*), REQUIRES the said Council to appoint or assign an officer to discharge the functions assigned to him or her by virtue of section 235 of, and Schedule 7 to, the Criminal Procedure (Scotland) Act 1995 in respect of the offender and to notify the offender forthwith of the particulars of the officer;

ORDERS that the offender shall—
    (a) attend a place of supervision notified to him or her by the officer for (*specify number of hours*) hours during the period of 12 months from this date or until the stated hours of attendance have been completed, whichever is the shorter, and while at that place of supervision carry out such instructions as may be given to him or her by the officer; and
    (b) report to the officer and notify the officer without delay of any change of residence or of any change in the times, if any, at which the offender usually works.

(2) IF for any reason the offender fails to carry out the instructions given under this order for the number of hours specified at (1)(a) above within the period of 12 months from the date of this order:—
    (a) this order will remain in force until the offender has carried out the said instruction for the number of hours specified in this order;
    (b) the offender's obligations stated above will continue; and
    (c) the officer shall bring the circumstances to the attention of the court.

(*Signed*)
Clerk of Court

Copy: Offender
       Chief Social Work Officer
       [Clerk of appropriate court]

Form of supervised attendance order under section 236 of the Criminal Procedure (Scotland) Act 1995

SUPERVISED ATTENDANCE ORDER

under section 236 of the Criminal Procedure (Scotland) Act 1995

COURT:
DATE:
OFFENDER:
Address:
Date of birth:

(1) THE COURT, being satisfied that the offender is likely to pay the fine of £
imposed by the court [*or* is unlikely to pay the fine of £   imposed by the court];

AND having explained to the offender the purpose and effect of this order (including the requirements set out below), and that if the offender fails to comply with this order the offender may be brought before the court which may revoke this order and impose a period of imprisonment or may vary the number of hours specified in this order, and that the court has power to review this order on the application either of the offender or of an officer of the local authority in whose area the offender for the time being resides;

AND the offender having expressed his [*or* her] willingness to comply with this order;

IN RESPECT that the offender [resides] [*or* is to reside] in the District of (*specify district of local authority*) in the area of (*specify the local authority*), REQUIRES the said Council to appoint or assign an officer to discharge the functions assigned to him or her by virtue of Schedule 7 to the Criminal Procedure (Scotland) Act 1995 in respect of the offender and to notify the offender forthwith of the particulars of the officer;

ORDERS that the offender shall [in default of payment of the said fine within 28 days of (*date*)]—
  (a) attend a place of supervision notified to him or her by the officer for (*specify number of hours*) hours during the period of 12 months from this date or until the stated hours of attendance have been completed, whichever is the shorter, and while at that place of supervision carry out such instructions as may be given to him or her by the officer; and
  (b) report to the officer and notify the officer without delay of any change of residence or of any change in the times, if any, at which the offender usually works.

(2) IF for any reason the offender fails to carry out the instructions given under this order for the number of hours specified at (1)(a) above within the period of 12 months from the date of this order:—
  (a) this order will remain in force until the offender has carried out the said instruction for the number of hours specified in this order;
  (b) the offender's obligations stated above will continue; and
  (c) the officer shall bring the circumstances to the attention of the court.

(*Signed*)
Clerk of Court

Copy: Offender
       Chief Social Work Officer
       [Clerk of appropriate court]

Form 20.11-C

Rule 20.11(3)

Form of citation under paragraph 5(3) of Schedule 7 to the Criminal Procedure (Scotland) Act 1995

IN THE HIGH COURT OF JUSTICIARY

[*or* IN THE SHERIFF [*or* DISTRICT] COURT]

AT (*place*)

CITATION

To: (*name and address of offender*)

Date: (*date*)

YOU ARE HEREBY CITED to appear on (*date*) at (*time*) in the High Court of Justicary [*or* Sheriff [*or* District] Court] at (*address*) because an application has been made by your supervising officer for the extension, variation or revocation of the supervised attendance order made in respect of you on (*date*). A copy of that application is attached [*or* (*specify nature of the application*)].

IF YOU FAIL TO ATTEND COURT WITHOUT A LAWFUL EXCUSE THE COURT MAY ISSUE A WARRANT FOR YOUR ARREST

(*Signed*)

Clerk of Court

AMENDMENT

Form 20.11-C inserted by Act of Adjournal (Criminal Procedure Rules Amendment No.2) (Miscellaneous) 2003 (SSI 2003/468), r.2(17) and Sch.3. Brought into force on October 27, 2003 in accordance with art.1.

Form 20.11-D

Rule 20.11(4)

Form of citation under paragraph 4(1) of Schedule 7 to the Criminal Procedure (Scotland) Act 1995

IN THE HIGH COURT OF JUSTICIARY

[*or* IN THE SHERIFF [*or* DISTRICT] COURT]

AT (*place*)

CITATION

To: (*name and address of offender*)

Date: (*date*)

YOU ARE HEREBY CITED to appear on (*date*) at (*time*) in the High Court of Justicary [*or* Sheriff [*or* District] Court] at (*address*) because it has been reported to the court that you have failed to comply with a requirement of the supervised attendance order made in respect of you on (*date*) as alleged in the written information attached [*or* by (*specify the failure alleged*)].

IF YOU FAIL TO ATTEND COURT WITHOUT A LAWFUL EXCUSE THE COURT MAY ISSUE A WARRANT FOR YOUR ARREST

(*Signed*)

Clerk of Court

AMENDMENT

Form 20.11-D inserted by Act of Adjournal (Criminal Procedure Rules Amendment No.2) (Miscellaneous) 2003 (SSI 2003/468), r.2(17) and Sch.3. Brought into force on October 27, 2003 in accordance with art.1.

Form 20.12-A

Rule 20.12(1)

Form of community service order under section 238 of the Criminal Procedure (Scotland) Act 1995

COMMUNITY SERVICE ORDER

under section 238 of the Criminal Procedure (Scotland) Act 1995

COURT:
DATE:
OFFENDER:
Address:
Date of birth:
Offence(s):

(1) THE COURT, being satisfied that the offender has committed the offence with which he or she is charged [*or* in view of the conviction of the offender], and being of the opinion that, having regard to the circumstances, including the nature of the offence and the character of the offender, it is expedient to make a community service order containing the undernoted requirements:

AND having explained to the offender the effect of the community service order (including the requirements set out below), and that if he or she fails to comply with the community service order, he or she may be brought before the court by his or her supervising officer for a breach of the community service order and may be fined or sentenced or dealt with for the original defence, and that, if he or she commits another offence during the period of the community service order, he or she may be dealt with for that offence:

IN RESPECT that the offender who resides [*or* is to reside] in the District of (*specify district of local authority*) in the area of (*specify the local authority*) has been convicted of the said offence(s) REQUIRES the said Council to appoint or assign an officer to discharge the functions assigned by sections 239 to 245 of the Criminal Procedure (Scotland) Act 1995 in respect of the offender and to notify the offender forthwith of the particulars of the officer:

ORDERS that the offender shall, during the period of twelve months from this date or until the performance of the hours of unpaid work specified at (2) below, whichever is shorter—
    (a) report to the local authority officer appointed or assigned to him or her and notify the said officer without delay of any change of address or of any change in the times, if any, at which the offender usually works; and
    (b) perform for (*specify number of hours*) hours such unpaid work at times as the local authority officer may instruct.

(2) If for any reason the offender fails to perform the unpaid work specified in paragraph (1)(a) above during the period of twelve months from the date of the order—
    (a) the order shall remain in force beyond the twelve month period;
    (b) the offender's obligation under paragraph (1) above will continue, and;
    (c) the local authority officer appointed under the order shall take whatever action is appropriate to bring the circumstances to the attention of the court.

(*Signed*)
Clerk of Court

Copy to: Offender
             Chief Social Worker

Act of Adjournal (Criminal Procedure Rules) 1996

Form 20.12-B

Rule 20.12(2)

Form of citation of offender under section 239(4) or 240(3) of the Criminal Procedure (Scotland) Act 1995

IN THE HIGH COURT OF JUSTICIARY

[*or* IN THE SHERIFF [*or* DISTRICT] COURT]

AT (*place*)

CITATION

To: (*name and address of offender*)

Date: (*date*)

YOU ARE HEREBY CITED to appear on (*date*) at (*time*) in the High Court of Justiciary [*or* Sheriff [*or* District] Court] at (*address*) because it has been reported to the court that you have failed to comply with a requirement of the community service order made in respect of you on (*date*) as alleged in the written information attached [*or* by (*specify the failure alleged*)] [*or* because an application has been made by the local authority officer for the amendment or revocation of the community service order made in respect of you on (*date*)]. A copy of the application is attached [*or* (*specify nature of proposed amendment or nature of application*)].

IF YOU FAIL TO ATTEND COURT WITHOUT A LAWFUL EXCUSE THE COURT MAY ISSUE A WARRANT FOR YOUR ARREST

(*Signed*)

Clerk of Court

AMENDMENT

Form 20.12-B substituted by Act of Adjournal (Criminal Procedure Rules Amendment No.2) (Miscellaneous) 2003 (SSI 2003/468), r.2(17) and Sch.2. Brought into force on October 27, 2003 in accordance with art.1.

Act of Adjournal (Criminal Procedure Rules) 1996

Form 20.12A-A

RESTRICTION OF LIBERTY ORDER

under section 245A(l) of the Criminal Procedure (Scotland) Act 1995

COURT:
DATE:
OFFENDER'S NAME, ADDRESS AND DATE OF BIRTH:
OFFENDER'S TELEPHONE NUMBER (*if available*):
(*If a phone number is not available, specify how the
number is to be provided.*)
OFFENCE FOR WHICH CONVICTED:

THE COURT, having convicted (*name of offender*) of (*specify offence*) and being satisfied that the most appropriate method of disposal is to make an order under subsection (1) of section 245A of the Criminal Procedure (Scotland) Act 1995;

AND having complied with any requirement imposed on it by subsection (6) of, and provided the offender with the explanation required by subsection (4) of, that section and obtained from him his agreement that he will comply with the requirements of the proposed order;

ORDERS that for (*specify, as respects a day* [*or week*], *a period in that day* [*or week*]) the offender shall be in (*specify a place*) [*or that at* (*specify a time*) [*or during* (*specify a period*)] the offender shall not be in (*specify a place*)].

[ORDERS that the offender shall continuously [or (*specify*)] wear or carry a device for the purposes of enabling the remote monitoring of his compliance with this order to be carried out.]

[ORDERS that the offender shall not tamper with or intentionally damage the device or knowingly allow it to be tampered with or intentionally damaged.]

(*Signed*)
Clerk of Court.
Date:

Note: (*Name and address of monitor*) has been designated by the court, under section 245B(2) of the Criminal Procedure (Scotland) Act 1995, as the person responsible for monitoring the offender's compliance with this order.

I confirm that I understand the requirements of this order and will comply with them.

(*Signed*)
Offender

AMENDMENT

Inserted by the Act of Adjournal (Criminal Procedure Rules Amendment) (Restriction of Liberty Orders) 1998 (SI 1998/1842).

Form 20.12A-A as amended by Act of Adjournal (Criminal Procedure Rules Amendment No.2) (Miscellaneous) 2003 (SSI 2003/468), r.2(17). Brought into force on October 27, 2003 in accordance with art.1.

Form 20.12A-A as amended by the Act of Adjournal (Criminal Procedure Rules Amendment No.4) (Criminal Procedure (Amendment) (Scotland) Act 2004) 2004 (SSI 2004/434), r.2 (effective October 4, 2004).

Form 20.12A-B

Rule 20.12A(2)

Form of application under section 245E(1) of the Criminal Procedure (Scotland) Act 1995

UNTO THE RIGHT HONOURABLE THE LORD JUSTICE GENERAL, LORD JUSTICE-CLERK AND LORDS COMMISSIONERS OF JUSTICIARY

[*or* Unto The Honourable The Sheriff of (*name of sheriffdom*)
At (*place*)]
[*or* Unto The Stipendiary Magistrates In The District Court Of (*name of district*) At (*place*)]
Application
by
(*name of offender*) (*address*) [*or* Prisoner
in the Prison of (*place*)]

[**or** *name and address of applicant with responsibility for monitoring offender's compliance with restriction of liberty order*]

APPLICANT
HUMBLY SHEWETH
1. That a restriction of liberty order, a copy of which is annexed to this application, was made in respect of (*name of offender*) on (*date*) in the High Court of Justiciary sitting [*or* in the sheriff court *or* in the district court] at (*place*).
2. That the applicant applies to the court in terms of subsection (1) of section 245E of the Criminal Procedure (Scotland) Act 1995 to revoke [*or* vary] the order for the following reason—

(*statement of reason*)

MAY IT THEREFORE PLEASE YOUR LORDSHIP[S] [*OR* THE COURT]:
   (a) to [revoke the restriction of liberty order] [vary the restriction of liberty order by (*statement of variation sought in terms of subsection (2)(a) of the said section 245E*)],
   (b) to do otherwise as to your Lordship[s] [*or* to the court] shall seem proper.

IN RESPECT WHEREOF
(*Signed*)

Offender
[*or* Solicitor for offender]
[*or* applicant with responsibility
for monitoring compliance]
(*Where a solicitor signs, the
address and telephone number
of the solicitor*).

AMENDMENT

Inserted by the Act of Adjournal (Criminal Procedure Rules Amendment) (Restriction of Liberty Orders) 1998 (SI 1998/1842).

Form 20.12A-B as amended by Act of Adjournal (Criminal Procedure Rules Amendment No.2) (Miscellaneous) 2003 (SSI 2003/468), r.2(17). Brought into force on October 27, 2003 in accordance with art.1.

Form 20.12A-C

Rule 20.12A(3)

Form of citation of offender under section 245E(3) of the Criminal Procedure (Scotland) Act 1995

IN THE HIGH COURT OF JUSTICIARY

[*or* IN THE SHERIFF [*or* DISTRICT] COURT]

AT (*place*)

CITATION

To: (*name and address of offender*)

Date of citation: (*date of citation or, if citation by post, the day after the date of posting*)

YOU ARE HEREBY CITED to appear on (*date*) at (*time*) in the High Court of Justiciary [*or* Sheriff [*or* District] Court] at (*address*) because it appears to the court to be in the interests of justice that the restriction of liberty order made in respect of you on (*date*) should be varied or revoked.

IF YOU FAIL TO ATTEND COURT WITHOUT A LAWFUL EXCUSE THE COURT MAY ISSUE A WARRANT FOR YOUR ARREST.

(*Signed*)

Clerk of Court.

AMENDMENT

Inserted by the Act of Adjournal (Criminal Procedure Rules Amendment) (Restriction of Liberty Orders) 1998 (SI 1998/1842).

Form 20.12A-C as amended by Act of Adjournal (Criminal Procedure Rules Amendment No.2) (Miscellaneous) 2003 (SSI 2003/468), r.2(17). Brought into force on October 27, 2003 in accordance with art.1.

Form 20.12A-D

Form of citation of offender under section 245F(1) of the Criminal Procedure (Scotland) Act 1995

IN THE HIGH COURT OF JUSTICIARY

[*or* IN THE SHERIFF [*or* DISTRICT] COURT]

AT (*place*)

CITATION

To: (*name and address of offender*)

Date of citation: (*date of citation or, if citation by post. the day after the date of posting*)

YOU ARE HEREBY CITED to appear on (*date*) at (*time*) in the High Court of Justiciary [*or* Sheriff [*or* District] Court] at (*address*) because it has been reported to the court that you have failed to comply with a requirement of your restriction of liberty order by (*specify the failure alleged*).

IF YOU FAIL TO ATTEND COURT WITHOUT A LAWFUL EXCUSE THE COURT MAY ISSUE A WARRANT FOR YOUR ARREST.

(*Signed*)

Clerk of Court

AMENDMENT

Inserted by the Act of Adjournal (Criminal Procedure Rules Amendment) (Restriction of Liberty Orders) 1998 (SI 1998/1842).

Form 20.12A-D as amended by Act of Adjournal (Criminal Procedure Rules Amendment No.2) (Miscellaneous) 2003 (SSI 2003/468), r.2(17). Brought into force on October 27, 2003 in accordance with art.1.

Act of Adjournal (Criminal Procedure Rules) 1996

Form 20.12B-A

Rule 20.12B

Form of drug treatment and testing order made under section 234B of the Criminal Procedure (Scotland) Act 1995

DRUG TREATMENT AND TESTING ORDER

under section 234B of the Criminal Procedure (Scotland) Act 1995

COURT:

DATE:

OFFENDER:

Address:

Date of birth:

THE COURT, having convicted the offender and being of the opinion that having regard to the circumstances, including the nature of the offence and the character of the offender, it is expedient to make a drug treatment and testing order containing the undernoted requirements;

AND the Court having explained to the offender the effect of the order (including the requirements set out below) and the consequences of failure to comply with the order or with any requirement thereof;

AND the offender having expressed willingness to comply with the requirements of the order;

REQUIRES, in respect that in terms of this order the offender is to reside in the local authority area of (*specify*), the said Council to appoint or assign an officer (the "supervising officer") to discharge the functions assigned by sections 234C and 234F of the Criminal Procedure (Scotland) Act 1995 in respect of the offender and to notify the offender forthwith of the particulars of the supervising officer, of any change in the particulars of the supervising officer and of any change of appointed or assigned supervising officer;

ORDERS that the offender shall, for a period of (*specify period*) from the date of the order, reside in the local authority area of (*specify*) under the supervision of the supervising officer at (*place*) in the said local authority area; and that he shall throughout that period comply with the following requirements, namely—
- (i) to submit to treatment (*specify whether as a resident or as a non-resident*) by or under the direction of (*name of treatment provider*) (the "treatment provider") at (*name of institution*) with a view to the reduction or elimination of dependency on or propensity to misuse drugs;
- (ii) to conform to the directions of the supervising officer and of the treatment provider;
- (iii) to inform the supervising officer immediately of any change of address;
- (iv) to provide for the purpose of ascertaining whether he has any drug in his body such samples, of such description, at such times, in such circumstances, as the treatment provider may determine;
- (v) to keep in touch with the supervising officer as instructed from time to time by that officer;
- (vi) to attend each review hearing;
- (vii) (*any additional requirement*).

ORDERS that the treatment provider shall communicate to the supervising officer the results of the tests carried out on the samples provided by the offender in pursuance of this order;

ORDERS that the supervising officer shall report in writing on the offender's progress under this order to the court conducting the review hearing; and that he shall include in each such report the results of the tests communicated to him by the treatment provider and the views of the treatment provider as to the treatment and testing of the offender;

FURTHER ORDERS that this Order shall be reviewed periodically at intervals of not less than one month at a hearing held for the purpose by (*specify the appropriate court*), the first such review to be heard on (*date*).

Signed

Clerk of Court

Date:

Note: (*name of supervising officer*) of (*name of local authority*) has been allocated as supervising officer in this case.

I confirm that I understand the conditions of this drug treatment and testing order.

Signature of offender:
Signature of supervising officer:

NOTE
[1]Inserted by the Act of Adjournal (Criminal Procedure Rules Amendment No. 4) (Drug Treatment and Testing Orders) 1999 (S.S.I. 1999 No.191) para.2(3) and Sched.I (effective December 20, 1999).

AMENDMENT
Form 20.12B as amended by Act of Adjournal (Criminal Procedure Rules Amendment No.2) (Miscellaneous) 2003 (SSI 2003/468), r.2(17). Brought into force on October 27, 2003 in accordance with art.1.

Form 20.12B-B

Rule 20.12B(2)

Form of citation of offender under section 234E(2) of the Criminal Procedure (Scotland) Act 1995

IN THE HIGH COURT OF JUSTICIARY

[*or* IN THE SHERIFF [*or* DISTRICT] COURT]

AT (*place*)

CITATION

To: (*name and address of offender*)

Date: (*date*)

YOU ARE HEREBY CITED to appear on (*date*) at (*time*) in the High Court of Justiciary [*or* Sheriff [*or* District] Court] at (*address*) because an application has been made by your supervising officer for the variation or revocation of the drug treatment and testing order made in respect of you on (*date*). A copy of that application is attached [*or* (*specify nature of the application*)].

IF YOU FAIL TO ATTEND COURT WITHOUT A LAWFUL EXCUSE THE COURT MAY ISSUE A WARRANT FOR YOUR ARREST

(*Signed*)

Clerk of Court

AMENDMENT
Form 20.12B-B inserted by Act of Adjournal (Criminal Procedure Rules Amendment No.2)

(Miscellaneous) 2003 (SSI 2003/468), r.2(17) and Sch.3. Brought into force on October 27, 2003 in accordance with art.1.

Form 20.12B-C

Rule 20.12B(3)

Form of citation under section 234G(1) of the Criminal Procedure (Scotland) Act 1995

IN THE HIGH COURT OF JUSTICIARY

[*or* IN THE SHERIFF [*or* DISTRICT] COURT]

AT (*place*)

CITATION

To: (*name and address of offender*)

Date: (*date*)

YOU ARE HEREBY CITED to appear on (*date*) at (*time*) in the High Court of Justicary [*or* Sheriff [*or* District] Court] at (*address*) because it has been reported to the court that you have failed to comply with a requirement of the drug treatment and testing order made in respect of you on (*date*) as alleged in the written information attached [*or* by (*specify the failure alleged*)].

IF YOU FAIL TO ATTEND COURT WITHOUT A LAWFUL EXCUSE THE COURT MAY ISSUE A WARRANT FOR YOUR ARREST.

(*Signed*)

Clerk of Court

AMENDMENT

Form 20.12B-C inserted by Act of Adjournal (Criminal Procedure Rules Amendment No.2) (Miscellaneous) 2003 (SSI 2003/468), r.2(17) and Sch.3. Brought into force on October 27, 2003 in accordance with art.1.

Rule 20.12C(1)

Form of community reparation order under section 245K(1) of the Criminal Procedure (Scotland) Act 1995

COMMUNITY REPARATION ORDER

under section 245K(1) of the Criminal Procedure (Scotland) Act 1995

COURT:

DATE:

OFFENDER:

Address:

Date of birth:

(1) THE COURT, being satisfied that the requirements of paragraphs (a), (b), (c) and (d) of section 245K(2) of the Criminal Procedure (Scotland) Act 1995 have been met;

AND the court having explained to the offender the purpose and effect of this order (including the requirements set out below), and that if the offender fails to comply with this order or any direction given under it without reasonable excuse the offender may be brought before the court which may revoke this order and deal with the offender in any manner in which he or she could have been dealt with for the original offence, and that the court has the power to review this order on the application either of the offender or of the supervising officer of the local authority specified in this order and extend the period of the order beyond the maximum of 12 months, vary the number of hours specified in the order, or revoke the order;

IN RESPECT that the court now specifies (*specify the local authority*) as the specified local authority, REQUIRES the said Council to appoint a supervising officer for the purposes of section 245K(4)(a) of the Criminal Procedure (Scotland) Act 1995 and to notify the offender forthwith of the particulars of the officer;

ORDERS that the offender shall—

    (a) undertake prescribed activities determined by the supervising officer for (*specify number of hours*) during a period of 12 months beginning with the day on which this order is made or until the stated hours have been completed whichever is the shorter;

    (b) comply with any determination made by the supervising officer on the times and localities at which the offender should undertake those activities; and

    (c) comply with any directions given during that period by the supervising officer to undertake those prescribed activities.

(2) IF for any reason the offender fails to comply with a direction given by a supervising officer by virtue of this order within a period of 12 months from the day on which the order was made:—

    (a) this order will remain in force until the offender has complied with the direction; and

    (b) the officer shall bring the circumstances to the attention of the court.

(*Signed*)

Clerk of Court

Copy: Offender

Chief Social Work Officer

[Clerk of the appropriate court]

AMENDMENT

Form 20.12C-A inserted by the Act of Adjournal (Criminal Procedure Rules Amendment No.2) (Miscellaneous) 2005 (SSI 2005/160), r.2 (effective March 31, 2005).

Form 20.12C-B

Rule 20.12C(2)

Form of citation under section 245N(2)(b) of the Criminal Procedure (Scotland) Act 1995

IN THE SHERIFF [*or* DISTRICT] COURT

AT (*place*)

CITATION

To: (*name and address of offender*)

Date: (*date*)

YOU ARE HEREBY CITED to appear on (*date*) at (*time*) in the Sheriff [*or* District] Court at (*address*) because it has been reported to the court that you have failed to comply with the community reparation order made in respect of you on (*date*) or with a direction given under it as alleged in the written information attached [*or* by (*specify the failure alleged*)].

IF YOU FAIL TO ATTEND COURT WITHOUT A LAWFUL EXCUSE THE COURT MAY ISSUE A WARRANT FOR YOUR ARREST

(*Signed*)

Clerk of Court

AMENDMENT

Form 20.12C-B inserted by the Act of Adjournal (Criminal Procedure Rules Amendment No.2) (Miscellaneous) 2005 (SSI 2005/160), r.2 (effective March 31, 2005).

Act of Adjournal (Criminal Procedure Rules) 1996

Form 20.12C-C

Rule 20.12C(3)

Form of citation under section 245P(3) of the Criminal Procedure (Scotland) Act 1995

IN THE SHERIFF [*or* DISTRICT] COURT

AT (*place*)

CITATION

To: (*name and address of offender*)

Date: (*date*)

YOU ARE HEREBY CITED to appear on (*date*) at (*time*) in the Sheriff [*or* District] Court at (*address*) because an application has been made by your supervising officer for the extension, variation or revocation of the community reparation order made in respect of you on (*date*). A copy of that application is attached [*or* (*specify the nature of the application*)].

IF YOU FAIL TO ATTEND COURT WITHOUT A LAWFUL EXCUSE THE COURT MAY ISSUE A WARRANT FOR YOUR ARREST

(*Signed*)

Clerk of Court

AMENDMENT

Form 20.12C-C inserted by the Act of Adjournal (Criminal Procedure Rules Amendment No.2) (Miscellaneous) 2005 (SSI 2005/160), r.2 (effective March 31, 2005).

Form 20.18-A

Form of extract of custodial sentence following conviction on indictment, warrant of detention and return of sentence

PROCEEDINGS ON INDICTMENT

under the Criminal Procedure (Scotland) Act 1995

EXTRACT SENTENCE, WARRANT OF DETENTION AND RETURN OF SENTENCE

Court		Judge	
Accused		Date of Sentence	
Address (where known)		Method of conviction	
		Jury trial	Sec.76
		Plea	Sec.195
Date of Birth	Marital Status	Occupation	

Offence(s) for which sentenced

Sentence:

The court sentenced the accused to be imprisoned/detained as from this date for the period specified below and thereafter to be set at liberty.

Period of imprisonment/detention:

Total period: To date from:

Warrant:

In respect of the foregoing sentence, the court ordained the accused to be conveyed by officers of law to the Prison of

thereafter to be dealt with in due course of law.

Officers
to prove conviction

Previous record
(as per list attached)

Extracted by me (*name*)   (*Signed*)
                                             Clerk of Justiciary
                                             [*or* Sheriff Clerk]

Form 20.18-B

Rule 20.18(2)

Form of extract of sentence imposed in summary proceedings

In the Sheriff [*or* District] Court of   at (*place*)

Name of accused:
Date of conviction:
Offence of which convicted:

[*Imprisonment*] Sentence, Imprisonment   months [*or* days].
In respect of which sentence, warrant is hereby granted to officers of law to convey the accused to the prison of (*place*) and for the detention of the accused therein for   days from the date of imprisonment.

[*Fine or imprisonment immediate*] Sentence, £   fine or   months' [*or* days'] imprisonment. In respect of which sentence warrant is hereby granted to officers of law to convey the accused to the prison of (*place*) and for the detention of the accused therein until the said fine is paid, but not exceeding   months [*or* days] from the date of imprisonment.

[*Fine or imprisonment time allowed and expired*] Sentence, £   fine (payable within   days) or   months' [*or* days'] imprisonment.
In respect of which sentence, the period allowed for payment of the said fine having expired and the said fine not having been paid, warrant is hereby granted to officers of law to convey the accused to the prison of (*place*) and for the detention of the accused therein until the fine is paid, but not exceeding   months [*or* days] from the date of imprisonment.

[*Fine and surrender of accused for imprisonment*] Sentence, £   fine payable within   months [*or* days] or   months' [*or* days'] imprisonment.

In respect of which sentence the accused, having surrendered himself to the court and stated that he prefers immediate imprisonment to waiting for the expiry of the time allowed, warrant is hereby granted to officers of law to convey the accused to the prison of (*place*) and for the detention of the accused therein until such fine is paid, but not exceeding   days from the date of imprisonment.

[*Caution*] Sentence, £   caution for good behaviour for six months (from date of conviction) or   months' [*or* days'] imprisonment.
In respect of which sentence warrant is hereby granted to officers of law to convey the accused to the prison of (*place*) and for the detention of the accused therein until the said caution is found, but not exceeding   days from the date of imprisonment.

[*Fine and caution*] Sentence, £   fine or   months' [*or* days'] imprisonment and £   caution for good behaviour for   months (from payment of the fine or from the expiry of the period of imprisonment for non-payment) or   months' [*or* days'] imprisonment further.
In respect of which sentence warrant is hereby granted to officers of law to convey the accused to the prison of (*place*) and for the detention of the accused therein until the said fine is paid and the said caution is found, the detention for non-payment of the said fine not exceeding   months [*or* days] from the date of imprisonment, and the detention for failure to find the said caution not exceeding   months [*or* days] further from payment of the fine or from expiry of the term of imprisonment for non-payment thereof.

[*Imprisonment and caution*] Sentence, imprisonment   months [*or* days] and £   caution for good behaviour for   months thereafter, or   months' [*or* days'] imprisonment.
In respect of which sentence warrant is hereby granted to officers of law to convey the accused to the prison of (*place*) and for the detention of the accused therein for   months [*or* days] from the date of imprisonment and for his further detention thereafter until the said caution is found, but not exceeding   months [*or* days] further.

(*Signed*)
Clerk of Court

Act of Adjournal (Criminal Procedure Rules) 1996

Form 20.19-A

Rule 20.19(2)(a)

Form of application under section 34B(6) of the Road Traffic Offenders Act 1988

UNTO THE HONOURABLE THE SHERIFF OF (*name of sheriffdom*)
[*or* UNTO THE STIPENDIARY MAGISTRATE OF
THE CITY OF GLASGOW DISTRICT]
AT (*place*)

APPLICATION

under

section 34B(6) of the Road Traffic Offenders Act 1988

by

[A.B.] (*address*)

APPLICANT

HUMBLY SHEWETH:

1. That the applicant is (*name of applicant*), and resides at (*address*).

2. That the sheriff [*or* stipendiary magistrate] on (*date of order*) made an order under section 34A of the Road Traffic Offenders Act 1988 (hereinafter referred to as "the Act of 1988") that the period of disqualification imposed on the applicant under section 34 of the Act of 1988 shall be reduced, if, by the date specified in the order, the applicant has completed satisfactorily an approved course as specified in the order.

3. That the course organiser of the course specified in the order was (*name and address of course organiser*).

4. That the date specified in the order for satisfactory completion by the applicant of the course was (*insert date specified*).

5. That the course organiser has given to the applicant the written notice required by section 34B(5) of the Act of 1988, by means of the notice dated (*date of notice*) which is lodged with this application, that he has decided not to give a course completion certificate to the applicant.

6. That the course organiser's decision not to give a course completion certificate is contrary to section 34B(4) of the Act of 1988 because (*state grounds of application*).

MAY IT THEREFORE please Your Lordship [*or* Your Honour]:
   (1)   to fix a date for hearing this application;
   (2)   to order the clerk of court to serve this application, with notice of the hearing, on the course organiser and the procurator fiscal; and thereafter
   (3)   to declare that the course organiser's decision not to give a course completion certificate is contrary to section 34B(4) of the Act of 1988.

IN RESPECT WHEREOF
(*Signed*)
Applicant
[*or* Solicitor for applicant]

(*Address and telephone number of solicitor*)

(*Date*)

Form of application under section 34B(7) of the Road Traffic Offenders Act 1988

UNTO THE HONOURABLE THE SHERIFF OF (*name of sheriffdom*)
[*or* UNTO THE STIPENDIARY MAGISTRATE OF
THE CITY OF GLASGOW DISTRICT]
AT (*place*)

APPLICATION

under

section 34B(7) of the Road Traffic Offenders Act 1998

by

[A.B.] (*address*)

APPLICANT

HUMBLY SHEWETH:

1. That the applicant is (*name of applicant*), and resides at (*address*).

2. That the sheriff [*or* stipendiary magistrate] on (*date of order*) made an order under section 34A of the Road Traffic Offenders Act 1988 (hereinafter referred to as "the Act of 1988") that the period of disqualification imposed on the applicant under section 34 of the Act of 1988 shall be reduced, if, by the date specified in the order, the applicant has completed satisfactorily an approved course as specified in the order.

3. That the course organiser of the course specified in the order was (*name and address of course organiser*).

4. That the date specified in the order for satisfactory completion by the applicant of the course was (*insert date specified*).

5. That the course organiser has not given to the applicant either a course completion certificate under section 34B(1) and (4) of the Act of 1988 or the written notice required by section 34B(5) of the Act of 1988 that he has decided not to give a course completion certificate, and that accordingly the course organiser is in default.

MAY IT THEREFORE please Your Lordship [*or* Your Honour]:
   (1) to fix a date for hearing this application;
   (2) to order the clerk of court to serve this application, with notice of the hearing, on the course organiser and the procurator fiscal; and thereafter
   (3) to declare that the course organiser is in default.

IN RESPECT WHEREOF

(*Signed*)
Applicant
[*or* Solicitor for applicant]

(*Address and telephone number of solicitor*)

(*Date*)

Rule 20.20

Form of antisocial behaviour order under section 234AA of the Criminal Procedure (Scotland) Act 1995

ANTISOCIAL BEHAVIOUR ORDER

under section 234AA of the Criminal Procedure (Scotland) Act 1995

COURT:

DATE:

OFFENDER:

Address:

Date of Birth:

THE COURT, being satisfied under section 234AA(2)(d) that the making of an antisocial behaviour order is necessary;

AND the court having explained to the offender the effect of this order (including the requirements set out below) and that if he or she, without reasonable excuse, does anything that the order to which he or she is subject prohibits him or her from doing, shall be guilty of an offence, and that the court has the power to revoke or vary the order on the application of the offender subject to the order;

ORDERS that the offender shall for (*specify period*) from the date of this order be prohibited from (*specify prohibitions imposed*)

(i)

(ii)

(iii)

(*Signed*)

Clerk of Court

Copy: Offender

      Local Authority

AMENDMENT

Form 20.20 inserted by the Act of Adjournal (Criminal Procedure Rules Amendment No.5) (Miscellaneous) 2004 (SSI 2004/481), r.2 and Sch., Part 1 (effective November 26, 2004).

Form 20.21

Rule 20.21

Form of order for lifelong restriction under section 210F of the Criminal Procedure (Scotland) Act 1995

ORDER FOR LIFELONG RESTRICTION

Prosecution reference..............
Court reference....................

HIGH COURT OF JUSTICIARY sitting at [*place*]

DATE:

OFFENDER:

Address:

Date of birth:

THE COURT, being satisfied that the risk criteria were met, makes this ORDER FOR LIFELONG RESTRICTION under section 210F of the Criminal Procedure (Scotland) Act 1995.

[ORDAINS the accused to be conveyed to and detained in the Prison of (*place*) [*or* (*specify hospital*)]]; and

GRANTS warrant to officers of law to convey the accused from the Bar to said prison [*or* hospital], therein to be detained.

(*Signed*)

Clerk of Court

AMENDMENT

Form 20.21 inserted by Act of Adjournal (Criminal Procedure Rules Amendment No.3) (Risk Assessment Orders and Orders for Lifelong Restriction) 2006 (SSI 2006/302), para.2(7) and Sch., Part 2 (effective June 20, 2006).

Form of statement of uncontroversial evidence under section 258 of the Criminal Procedure (Scotland) Act 1995

IN THE HIGH COURT OF JUSTICIARY
[*or* IN THE SHERIFF [*or* DISTRICT] COURT]

AT (*place*)

STATEMENT OF UNCONTROVERSIAL EVIDENCE

by

[A.B.] (*address*)
[*or* Prisoner in the Prison of (*place*)]

in

HER MAJESTY'S ADVOCATE [*or* THE PROCURATOR FISCAL, (*place*)]

against

(*Insert name(s) of accused*)

TAKE NOTICE:

1. That the fact[s] listed below has [*or* have] been identified by me [*or* us] as uncontroversial and capable of being agreed in advance of trial under section 258 of the Criminal Procedure (Scotland) Act 1995.

[*Or* (1) That the fact[s] set out in the [following] document(s) annexed to this statement has (*or* have] been identified as uncontroversial and capable of being agreed in advance of trial under section 258 of the Criminal Procedure (Scotland) Act 1995:—

2. That a failure to challenge [any of] the foregoing fact[s] within seven days of the date of service of this notice will result in the unchallenged fact being treated by the court as having been conclusively proved unless the court makes a direction under subsection (6) of section 258 of the above-mentioned Act.

Served on (*date*) by me [*or* as the case may be] by (*state method of service*).

(*Signed*)
Procurator Fiscal
[*or* Accused]
[*or* Solicitor for [A.B.]

(*Address and telephone number of solicitor*)]

Form 21.1-B

Form of docquet to be endorsed on document annexed to, but not described in, statement of uncontroversial evidence

I, (*insert name and address of party serving the notice*), hereby certify that this document is a document referred to in the foregoing statement of uncontroversial facts.

(*Signed*)

(*Date*)

Form 21.2

Rule 21.2

Form of notice of challenge under section 258(3) of the Criminal Procedure (Scotland) Act 1995

NOTICE OF CHALLENGE OF FACT[S]
specified [*or* referred to] in statement under
section 258(2) of the Criminal Procedure (Scotland) Act 1995

by

[A.B.] (*address*)
[*or* Prisoner in the Prison of (*place*)]

in

HER MAJESTY'S ADVOCATE [*or* THE PROCURATOR FISCAL, (*place*)]

against

(*Insert name(s) of accused*)

NOTICE IS HEREBY GIVEN that the following document[s] [*or* fact[s]] specified [*or* referred to] in the statement of uncontroversial evidence under section 258(2) of the Criminal Procedure (Scotland) Act 1995 served on (*date*) is [*or* are] challenged by me:—

(*here state or refer to the statement(s), document(s) or fact(s) challenged*).

(*Signed*)
Accused
[*or* Solicitor for accused *or* Procurator Fiscal]

(*Address and telephone number of solicitor*)

(*Date*)

Rule 21.2A

Form of application under section 258(4A) of the Criminal Procedure (Scotland) Act 1995

UNTO THE RIGHT HONOURABLE THE LORD JUSTICE GENERAL, LORD JUSTICE-CLERK AND LORDS COMMISSIONERS OF JUSTICIARY

[*or* UNTO THE HONOURABLE THE SHERIFF
OF (*name of sheriffdom*) AT (*place*)]

APPLICATION

under section 258(4A) of the Criminal Procedure (Scotland) Act 1995

by

HER MAJESTY'S ADVOCATE

[*or* [A.B.] (*address*)

[or Prisoner in the Prison of (*place*)]

APPLICANT

HUMBLY SHEWETH:

1. That [A.B.][along with (*name(s) of co-accused*),] has been indicted at the instance of Her Majesty's Advocate with a preliminary hearing in the High Court of Justiciary sitting at (*place*) on (*date*) [*or* with a first diet on (*date*) at the sheriff court of (*place*)].

2. That on (*date*) the Applicant served the attached statement of uncontroversial evidence under section 258(2) of the Criminal Procedure (Scotland) Act 1995 ("the 1995 Act").

3. That on (*date*) Her Majesty's Advocate [or A.B.] served the attached notice of challenge under section 258(3) of the 1995 Act in respect a fact [*or* fact[s]] specified or referred to in that statement.

4. That the following challenge[s] in the notice of challenge is [*or* are] unjustified for the following reason[s]:–

   (*here specify challenges and reasons*)

MAY IT THEREFORE PLEASE YOUR LORDSHIP[S]:

  (a) to direct that the challenge[s] be disregarded for the purposes of section 258(4) of the Criminal Procedure (Scotland) Act 1995; or

  (b) to do otherwise as your Lordships[s] think[s] fit.

IN RESPECT WHEREOF

(*Signed*)

Prosecutor

[*or* Legal representative of [A.B.]]

(*Name, address, e-mail address and telephone number*)

(*Place and date*)

AMENDMENT

Form 21.2A inserted by the Act of Adjournal (Criminal Procedure Rules Amendment) (Criminal Procedure (Amendment) (Scotland) Act) 2005 (SSI 2005/44), r.2(18) and Sch., Part 8 (subject to r.2(2)–(4)) (effective February 1, 2005).

Form 21.3

Rule 21.3

Form of notice under section 259(5) of the Criminal Procedure (Scotland) Act 1995

IN THE HIGH COURT OF JUSTICIARY
[*or* IN THE SHERIFF [*or* DISTRICT] COURT]
AT (*place*)

NOTICE

under

Section 259(5) of the Criminal Procedure (Scotland) Act 1995

by

[A.B.]

in

HER MAJESTY'S ADVOCATE [*or* THE PROCURATOR FISCAL, (*place*)]

against

(*Insert name(s) of accused*)

TAKE NOTICE:

1. That [A.B.] intends to apply to the court to have evidence of a statement by (*name and address of person not giving oral evidence*) admitted in evidence under section 259 of the Criminal Procedure (Scotland) Act 1995 and that evidence of that statement will be given—
    * orally to the court by (*name and address of witness who will give evidence of the statement of that person*). A copy of an affidavit stating what the witness will say is attached.
    * in the form of a document, a copy of which is attached.
    * in the form of a document, a copy of which is attached, made by (*insert name, designation and address of maker of document*).

2. That there is evidence that the statement referred to in paragraph 1 above was made and that the person who will give evidence about it has direct personal knowledge of the making of the statement as appears from the affidavit of that person attached to this notice [*or* that the statement is contained in the document, the copy of which is attached to this notice].

3. That the reason why this evidence is not to be given personally by (*name*) is that:—
    * He/She is dead. An extract death certificate (*or specify other means of proof*) is attached.
    * He/She is unfit by reason of *his/her bodily condition to give evidence in any other competent manner. A copy of a report to this effect by a certified medical practitioner is attached.
    * He/She is unfit by reason of *his/her mental condition to give evidence in any other competent manner. A copy of a report to this effect by a certified medical practitioner is attached.
    * He/She is outwith the United Kingdom and is at (*address*) and it is not reasonably practicable to secure *his/her attendance at trial because (*state steps which have been taken to secure attendance*). The evidence may not be obtained in any other competent manner because (*state why the evidence may not be obtained in any other competent manner*).
    * He/She cannot be found and the following steps which are all reasonable steps which, in the circumstances, could have been taken to find *him/her have been taken (*state steps which have been taken*).

4. That I, (*insert name and address of party serving the notice*), procurator fiscal [*or* solicitor acting on behalf of (*specify*)] certify that, the information given above is accurate in every respect to the best of my knowledge.

Served on (*date*) by me [*or as the case may be*] by (*state method of service*).

(*Signed*)

(*Capacity in which signing*)

(*Date of service if not by post*)

* *Delete whatever is not applicable.*

Form 21.4

Rule 21.4

Form of certificate of authentication of a prior statement for the purposes of section 260(4) of the Criminal Procedure (Scotland) Act 1995

Prosecution reference. . . . .

Court reference. . . . .

I, (*insert name and designation of person authenticating*), HEREBY CERTIFY THAT this document [*or* the attached document], comprising [this and] the following (*insert number*) pages [*or* (*insert number*) hours, (*insert number*) minutes and (*insert number*) seconds of recorded time] is a full and accurate record of evidence given by (*insert name and designation of person who gave the prior statement and brief details of the nature, place and date of the proceedings during which the statement was made*).

(*Signed*)

(*Date*)

AMENDMENT

Form 21.4 substituted by the Act of Adjournal (Criminal Procedure Rules Amendment No.3) (Vulnerable Witnesses (Scotland) Act 2004) 2005 (SSI 2005/188), r.2, subject to the conditions in r.2(2) (effective April 1, 2005).

Rule 21.5

Form of application under section 275(1) of the Criminal Procedure (Scotland) Act 1995

IN THE HIGH COURT OF JUSTICIARY
[*or* IN THE SHERIFF [*or* DISTRICT] [COURT]

AT (*place*)

APPLICATION UNDER SECTION 275(1) OF THE CRIMINAL PROCEDURE
(SCOTLAND) ACT 1995

by

[A.B.] *address*

[*or* Prisoner in the Prison of (*place*)]

in

HER MAJESTY'S ADVOCATE [*or* THE PROCURATOR FISCAL, (*place*)]

against

(*Insert name(s) of accused*)

TAKE NOTICE:

That [A.B.] makes an application to the court for the purposes of section 275(1) of the Criminal Procedure (Scotland) Act 1995 as follows:—

1. the following evidence is sought to be admitted or elicited:

2. the nature of the proposed questioning is as follows:

3. the issues to which the evidence is considered to be relevant are as follows:

4. the reasons why the evidence is considered to be relevant are as follows:

5. the inferences which the applicant proposes to submit to the court that it should draw from the evidence are as follows:

(*Signed*)

AMENDMENT

Form 21.5 inserted by Act of Adjournal (Criminal Procedure Rules Amendment No. 3) (Sexual Offences (Procedure and Evidence) (Scotland) Act 2002) 2002 (SSI 2002/454), r.2(12), Sch.3 (effective November 1, 2002).

Form 21.5 as amended by Act of Adjournal (Criminal Procedure Rules Amendment No.3) (Risk Assessment Orders and Orders for Lifelong Restriction) 2006 (SSI 2006/302), para.2(7) (effective June 20, 2006).

Form 21.6-A

Rule 21.6(1)

Form of notice of intention to rely on presumption as to identification under section 281A of the Criminal Procedure (Scotland) Act 1995

IN THE HIGH COURT OF JUSTICIARY

[*or* IN THE SHERIFF COURT

AT (*place*)]

NOTICE OF INTENTION TO RELY ON PRESUMPTION AS TO IDENTIFICATION

by

HER MAJESTY'S ADVOCATE [*or* THE PROCURATOR FISCAL, (*place*)]

in the case against

(*insert name(s) of accused*)

Prosecution reference. . . . .

Court reference. . . . .

To: (*name and address of accused*)

TAKE NOTICE:

(1) That a report stating the fact[s] of an identification of (*insert name of accused identified*) in an identification parade or other identification procedure by a witness, and the name of that witness, has been lodged under section 281A of the Criminal Procedure (Scotland) Act 1995 by the prosecutor as a production in advance of trial.

(2) That the prosecutor intends to rely on a presumption that the person named in the report as having been identified by the witness is the person of the same name who appears in answer to the indictment [*or* complaint].

(3) That if you do not challenge [any of] the fact[s] in the report within seven days after the date of service of this notice it shall be presumed under section 281A of the above-mentioned Act that the person named in the report as having been identified by the witness is the person who appears in answer to the indictment [*or* complaint].

Served on (*date*) by me by (*state method of service*).

(*Signed*)

Prosecutor

(*Name, address, e-mail address and telephone number*)

(*Place and date*)

AMENDMENT

Form 21.6-A inserted by the Act of Adjournal (Criminal Procedure Rules Amendment No.3) (Vulnerable Witnesses (Scotland) Act 2004) 2005 (SSI 2005/188), r.2, subject to the conditions in r.2(2) (effective April 1, 2005).

Form 21.6-B

Rule 21.6(2)

Form of notice of challenge under section 281A(2) of the Criminal Procedure (Scotland) Act 1995

NOTICE OF INTENTION TO CHALLENGE FACTS STATED IN REPORT OF IDENTIFICATION

by

[A.B.] (*address*)

[*or* Prisoner in the Prison of (*place*)]

in

HER MAJESTY'S ADVOCATE [*or* THE PROCURATOR FISCAL, (*place*)]

against

(*insert name(s) of accused*)

Prosecution reference. . . . .

Court reference. . . . .

NOTICE IS HEREBY GIVEN under section 281A(2) of the Criminal Procedure (Scotland) Act 1995 that [A.B.] intends to challenge the following fact[s] stated in the report of an identification prior to trial lodged by the prosecutor as production number [*insert production number*] served on (*date*):–

(*here state or refer to the fact(s) challenged*)

(*Signed*)

Accused

[*or* Legal representative for accused]

(*Name, address and e-mail address and telephone number of solicitor*).

AMENDMENT

Form 21.6-B inserted by the Act of Adjournal (Criminal Procedure Rules Amendment No.3) (Vulnerable Witnesses (Scotland) Act 2004) 2005 (SSI 2005/188), r.2, subject to the conditions in r.2(2) (effective April 1, 2005).

Form of child witness notice under section 271A(2) of the Criminal Procedure (Scotland) Act 1995

FORM 22.1

Rule 22.1

Form of child witness notice under section 271A(2) of the Criminal Procedure (Scotland) Act 1995

UNTO THE RIGHT HONOURABLE THE LORD JUSTICE GENERAL, LORD JUSTICE-CLERK AND LORDS COMMISSIONERS OF JUSTICIARY

[*or* UNTO THE HONOURABLE THE SHERIFF OF (*name of sheriffdom*)s AT (*place*)]

CHILD WITNESS NOTICE

by

HER MAJESTY'S ADVOCATE [*or* THE PROCURATOR FISCAL, (*place*)]

[*or* [A.B.] (*address*)

[*or* Prisoner in the Prison of (*place*)]]

Prosecution reference. . . . .

Court reference. . . . .

HUMBLY SHEWETH:

1. That [A.B.], (*date of birth*) [, along with (*name(s) of co-accused*)] has been indicted on (*date of indictment*) at the instance of Her Majesty's Advocate with a preliminary hearing [*or* a trial diet] in the High Court of Justiciary sitting at (*place*) on (*date*) [*or* with a first diet on (*date*) and a trial diet on (*date*) in the sheriff court of (*place*)] [*or* has been charged on the above court on a summary complaint at the instance of the procurator fiscal with a trial diet on (*date*) in the sheriff court of (*place*)].

[*or, where the child witness notice is lodged for the purposes of proceedings under section 210C(7) of the Criminal Procedure (Scotland) Act 1995 (objection to risk assessment report etc.*):

1. That on (*date*) the High Court of Justiciary sitting at (*place*) made a risk assessment order [*or* an interim compulsion order] in respect of [A.B.].]

2. That [A.B.] is charged with (*specify charge*)[, which is an offence to which section 288C [*or* section 288E] of the Criminal Procedure (Scotland) Act 1995 applies][*or* and an order has been made under section 288F(2) of the Criminal Procedure (Scotland) Act 1995].

[*or, where the child witness notice is lodged for the purposes proceedings under section 210C(7) of the Criminal Procedure (Scotland) Act 1995 (objection to risk assessment report etc.*):

2. That [A.B.] was convicted of (*specify*), which is an offence to which section 288C [or section 288E] of the Criminal Procedure (Scotland) Act 1995 applies [*or* and an order has been made under section 288F(2) of the Criminal Procedure (Scotland) Act 1995]

3. That the applicant has cited [*or* intends to cite][C.D.], (*date of birth*) as a witness who is to [*or* [A.B.] may] give evidence at, or for the purposes of, the trial.

[*or*, proceedings under section 210C(7) of the Criminal Procedure (Scotland) Act 1995]

4. That [C.D.] [*or* [A.B.]] is a child witness under section 271(1)(a) of the Criminal Procedure (Scotland) Act 1995 [and was under the age of twelve on the date of commencement of proceedings].

5. The following special measure[s] is [*or* are] considered the most appropriate for the purpose of taking the evidence of [C.D.][*or* the applicant]:-

(*here specify any special measure(s) sought*)

[and that the special measure(s) of (*here specify special measure(s), other than the standard special measure(s) sought*) is [*or* are] not a standard special measure under section 271A(14) of the Act of 1995.

The reason[s] this [*or* these] special measure[s], other than the standard special measure[s], is [*or* are] considered the most appropriate is [*or* are] as follows:-

(*here specify reason(s) for the special measure(s), other than the standard special measure(s) sought*)].

6. [*or* Authorisation of the use of no special measures is considered the most appropriate for the taking of evidence of

[C.D.] [*or* the applicant] for the following reasons:-

(*here specify the reasons for no special measures being sought*).]

7. That [C.D.] [*or* [A.B.]] and the parent[s] of [*or* person[s] with parental responsibility for] [C.D.] [*or* [A.B.]] under section 271E(4) of the Act of 1995 have expressed the following view[s]:-

(*here set out the view(s) expressed, how and when they were obtained*).

8. [That other information considered relevant to this application is as follows:-

(*here set out any other information relevant to the child witness notice*).]

9. That the applicant has intimated a copy of the Notice on [A.B.] [*or* the legal representative of [A.B.]][*or* on the Crown Agent] [*or* the Procurator Fiscal].

MAY IT THEREFORE PLEASE YOUR LORDSHIP[S]-

(a) to authorise the special measure[s] sought; and [*or*

(b) to authorise the giving of evidence without the benefit of special measures];

(c) or to do otherwise as to your Lordship[s] shall seem proper;

(d) to require the clerk of court to intimate the order to (*specify*).

ACCORDING TO JUSTICE, etc.

(*Signed*)

[A.B.]

[*or* Legal representative of A.B.]

[*or* Prosecutor]

(*Address, e-mail address and telephone number of agent*).

AMENDMENT

Form 22.1 substituted by Act of Adjournal (Criminal Procedure Rules Amendment No.3) (Vulnerable Witnesses (Scotland) Act 2004) 2005 (SSI 2005/188), r.2, subject to the conditions in r.2(2) (effective April 1, 2005).

Form 22.1 as amended by Act of Adjournal (Criminal Procedure Rules Amendment No.3) (Risk Assessment Orders and Orders for Lifelong Restriction) 2006 (SSI 2006/302), para.2(7) (effective June 20, 2006).

Form 22.1 as amended by Act of Adjournal (Criminal Procedure Rules Ammendment No.2) Vulnerable Witnesses (Scotland) Act 2004) 2007, r.2(3).

Form 22.1A

Rule 22.1A

Form of vulnerable witness application under section 271C(2) of the Criminal Procedure (Scotland) Act 1995

UNTO THE RIGHT HONOURABLE THE LORD JUSTICE GENERAL, LORD JUSTICE CLERK AND LORDS COMMISSIONERS OF JUSTICIARY

[*or* UNTO THE HONOURABLE THE SHERIFF OF (*name of sheriffdom*) AT (*place*)]

VULNERABLE WITNESS APPLICATION

by

HER MAJESTY'S ADVOCATE [*or* THE PROCURATOR FISCAL, (*place*)]

[*or* [A.B.] (*address*)

[*or* Prisoner in the Prison of (*place*)]]

Prosecution reference.....................

Court reference............................

HUMBLY SHEWETH:

1.   That [A.B.], (*date of birth*) [, along with (*name(s) of co-accused*)] has been indicted on (*date of indictment*) at the instance of Her Majesty's Advocate with a preliminary hearing [*or* a trial diet] in the High Court of Justiciary sitting at (*place*) on (*date*) [*or* with a first diet on (*date*) and a trial diet on (*date*) in the sheriff court of (*place*)].

2.   That [A.B.] is charged with (*specify charge*)[, which is an offence to which section 288C of the Criminal Procedure (Scotland) Act 1995 applies][*or* an order has been made under section 288F(2) of the Criminal Procedure (Scotland) Act 1995].

3.   That the applicant has cited [*or* intends to cite][C.D.], (*date of birth*) as a witness who is to [*or* [A.B.] may] give evidence at, or for the purposes of, the trial.

4.   That [C.D.] [*or* [A.B.]] is likely to be a vulnerable witness under section 271(1)(b) of the Criminal Procedure (Scotland) Act 1995 for the following reasons:–

(*here specify reasons witness is considered likely to be a vulnerable witness*).

5.   The following special measure[s] is [*or* are] considered the most appropriate for the purpose of taking the evidence of [C.D.] [*or* the applicant]:–

(*here specify all special measures sought*)

The reason[s] this [*or* these] special measure[s] is [*or* are] considered the most appropriate is [*or* are] as follows:–

(here specify reason(s) for the special measure(s) including any information known on the possible effect on the witness if required to give evidence without the benefit of any special measures).

6.   That [C.D.] [*or* [A.B.]] has expressed the following view[s]:–

(here set out the view(s) expressed, how and when they were obtained).

7.   [That other information considered relevant to this application is as follows:–

(here set out any other information relevant to the vulnerable witness application)]

8.   That the applicant has intimated a copy of this Application on [A.B.] [*or* the legal representative of [A.B.]][*or* on the Crown Agent] [*or* the Procurator Fiscal].

MAY IT THEREFORE PLEASE YOUR LORDSHIP[S]–

(a)   to authorise the special measure[s] sought; and

(b)   to do otherwise as to your Lordship[s] shall seem proper;

(c)   to require the clerk of court to intimate the order to *(specify)*.

ACCORDING TO JUSTICE, etc.

(Signed)

[A.B.]

[*or* Legal representative of [A.B.]]

[*or* Prosecutor]

(Address, e-mail address and telephone number of agent).

AMENDMENT

Form 22.1A inserted by Act of Adjournal (Criminal Procedure Rules Amendment) (Vulnerable Witnesses (Scotland) Act 2004) 2006 (SSI 2006/76), para.2(7) and Sch., Pt 1 (effective April 1, 2006).

Rule 22.4

Form of application for review of arrangements for taking eveidence under section 271(D) of the Criminal Procedure (Scotland) Act 1995

FORM 22.4   Form of application for review of arrangements for taking evidence under section 271D of the Criminal Procedure (Scotland) Act 1995

Rule 22.4   UNTO THE RIGHT HONOURABLE THE LORD JUSTICE GENERAL, LORD JUSTICE CLERK AND LORDS COMMISSIONERS OF JUSTICIARY

[*or* UNTO THE HONOURABLE SHERIFF OF (*name of sheriffdom*) AT (*place*)]

MINUTE

by

HER MAJESTY'S ADVOCATE [*or* THE PROCURATOR FISCAL, (*place*)]

[*or* [A.B.] (*address*)

[*or* Prisoner in Prison of (*place*)]]

in

HER MAJESTY'S ADVOCATE [*or* THE PROCURATOR FISCAL, (*place*)]

against

[A.B.] (*address*)

[*or* Prisoner in Prison of (*place*)]

Prosecution reference. . . . .

Court reference. . . . .

HUMBLY SHEWETH:

1. That [A.B.][, along with (*names of co-accused*)] has been indicted at the instance of Her Majesty's Advocate [*or* has been charged on a summary complaint at the instance of the procurator fiscal].

[*or*, 1. That [A.B.] was convicted of (*specify*) on (*date*)].

2. That the Minuter has cited [*or* intends to cite] [C.D.] as a witness who is to [*or* [A.B.] may] give evidence at, or for the purposes of, the trial. [*or*, proceedings under section 210C(7) of the Criminal Procedure (Scotland) Act 1995] That [C.D.] [*or*

[A.B.]] is a vulnerable witness under section 271(1) of the Criminal Procedure (Scotland) Act 1995.

3. That the current arrangements for taking the evidence of [C.D.][*or* [A.B.]] are (*here specify current arrangements*).

4. That the current arrangements should be reviewed as (*here specify reason(s) for review*).

5. That an order should be made to (*here specify the order sought*).

6. That [C.D.] [*or* [A.B.]] and the parent[s] of [*or* person[s] with parental responsibility for] [C.D.] [*or* [A.B.]] under section 271E(4) of the Act of 1995 have expressed the following view[s]:-

(*here set out the view(s) expressed, how and when they were obtained*).

7. That a copy of this Minute has been duly intimated conform to the execution[s] attached to this Minute.

MAY IT THEREFORE PLEASE YOUR LORDSHIP[S] -

(a) to fix a diet for hearing this application and to order intimation of this application and the diet to all parties;

(b) thereafter, after hearing all the parties, to make an order (specify);

(c) or to do otherwise as to your Lordship[s] shall seem proper;

(d) to require the clerk of court to intimate the order to (specify).

IN RESPECT WHEREOF

(*Signed*)

[Prosecutor]

[*or* [A.B.]]

[*or* Legal representative of [A.B.]]

(*Name, address, e-mail address, telephone number of agent*)

(*Place and date*).

AMENDMENT

Form 22.4 inserted by Act of Adjournal (Criminal Procedure Rules Amendment No.3) (Vulnerable Witnesses (Scotland) Act 2004) 2005 (SSI 2005/188), r.2, subject to the conditions in r.2(2) (effective April 1, 2005).

Form 22.4 as amended by Act of Adjournal (Criminal Procedure Rules Amendment No.3) (Risk Assessment Orders and Orders for Lifelong Restriction) 2006 (SSI 2006/302), para.2(7) (effective June 20, 2006).

Form 22.4 as amended by Act of Adjournal (Criminal Procedure Rules Ammendment No.2) Vulnerable Witnesses (Scotland) Act 2004) 2007, r.2(3).

Form 22.7

Rule 22.7

Form of notice of prohibition of personal conduct of defence in certain cases involving child witnesses under the age of twelve under section 288E of the Criminal Procedure (Scotland) Act 1995

IMPORTANT NOTICE

HER MAJESTY'S ADVOCATE [*or* THE PROCURATOR FISCAL, (*place*)]

against

[A.B.] (*address*)

[*or* Prisoner in the Prison of (*place*)]

Prosecution reference. . . . .

Court reference. . . . .

To: (*name*), (*date of birth*), (*address*)

You have been charged with [*or* convicted of] at least one serious offence in which a child witness under the age of twelve is to give evidence at or for the purposes of the trial or other proceedings before the Court, therefore—

(1) if you are tried for the offence *or* there are proceedings under section 210C(7) of the Criminal Procedure (Scotland) Act 1995, your defence may be conducted only by a lawyer;

(2) it is in your interests, if you have not already done so, to get the professional assistance of a solicitor;

(3) if you do not engage a solicitor for the purpose of your defence at the preliminary hearing [*or* first diet] or the trial [*or* proceedings under section 210C(7) of the Criminal Procedure (Scotland) Act 1995], the court will do so.

(*Signed*)

Prosecutor

(*Name, address, e-mail address, and telephone number*)

(*Place and date*)

AMENDMENT

Form 22.7 inserted by Act of Adjournal (Criminal Procedure Rules Amendment No.3) (Vulnerable Witnesses (Scotland) Act 2004) 2005 (SSI 2005/188), r.2, subject to the conditions in r.2(2) (effective April 1, 2005).

Form 22.7 as amended by Act of Adjournal (Criminal Procedure Rules Amendment No.3) (Risk Assessment Orders and Orders for Lifelong Restriction) 2006 (SSI 2006/302), para.2(7) (effective June 20, 2006).

Rule 22.8(1)

Form of minute seeking prohibition of the personal conduct of defence by the accused under section 288F of the Criminal Procedure (Scotland) Act 1995

UNTO THE RIGHT HONOURABLE THE LORD JUSTICE GENERAL, LORD JUSTICE CLERK AND LORDS COMMISSIONERS OF JUSTICIARY

[*or* UNTO THE HONOURABLE THE SHERIFF OF (*name of sheriffdom*) AT (*place*)]

MINUTE

by

HER MAJESTY'S ADVOCATE [*or* THE PROCURATOR FISCAL, (*place*)]

in

HER MAJESTY'S ADVOCATE [*or* THE PROCURATOR FISCAL (*place*)]

against

[A.B.] (*address*)

[*or* Prisoner in the Prison of (*place*)]

Prosecution reference. . . . .
Court reference. . . . .

HUMBLY SHEWETH:

1. That [A.B] [, along with (*name(s) of co-accused*)] has been indicted at the instance of Her Majesty's Advocate in the High Court of Justiciary [*or* in the sheriff court] at (*place*) and a diet of (*specify*) has been fixed for (*date*).
[*Or*: 1. That on (*date*) the High Court of Justiciary sitting at (*place*) made a risk assessment order [*or* an interim compulsion order] in respect of [A.B.].]

2. That [C.D.] is a witness who is to [*or* [A.B.] may] give evidence at, or for the purposes of, the trial [*or*, in any proceedings under section 210C(7) of the Criminal Procedure (Scotland) Act 1995]. That [C.D.] [*or* [A.B.]] is a vulnerable witness under section 271(1) of the Criminal Procedure (Scotland) Act 1995 as (*here state the reasons the witness is a vulnerable witness*).

3. That the Minuter applies for an order prohibiting [A.B.] from conducting his [*or* her] defence in person at the trial [*or*, in any proceedings under section 210C(7) of the Criminal Procedure (Scotland) Act 1995] and in any victim statement proof relating to any offence to which the trial relates for the following reasons:–
(*here state reasons*).

4. That the offence in the indictment is not one to which sections 288C or 288E of the Criminal Procedure (Scotland) Act 1995 applies.

5. That a copy of this Minute has been duly intimated conform to the execution[s] attached to this Minute.

MAY IT THEREFORE PLEASE YOUR LORDSHIP[S] -

(a) to fix a diet for hearing this application and to order intimation of this application and the diet to all the parties;
(b) thereafter, on being satisfied in terms of section 288F(3) of the Criminal Procedure (Scotland) Act 1995, to make an order prohibiting [A.B.] from conducting his [*or* her] defence in person at the trial and in any victim statement proof [*or*, any proceedings under section 210C(7) of the Criminal Procedure (Scotland) Act 1995.];
(c) or to do otherwise as to your Lordship[s] shall seem proper;

to require the clerk of court to intimate the order to (*specify*).

IN RESPECT WHEREOF

(*Signed*)

Prosecutor

(*Name, address, e-mail address, telephone number*)

(*Place and date*)

AMENDMENT

Form 22.8-A inserted by Act of Adjournal (Criminal Procedure Rules Amendment No.3) (Vulnerable Witnesses (Scotland) Act 2004) 2005 (SSI 2005/188), r.2, subject to the conditions in r.2(2) (effective April 1, 2005).

Form 22.8-A as amended by Act of Adjournal (Criminal Procedure Rules Amendment No.3) (Risk Assessment Orders and Orders for Lifelong Restriction) 2006 (SSI 2006/302), para.2(7) (effective June 20, 2006).

Form 22.8-B

Rule 22.8(5)

Form of notice to accused where an order granted prohibiting the personal conduct of defence by the accused under section 288F of the Criminal Procedure (Scotland) Act 1995

Prosecution reference. . . . .
Court reference. . . . .

To: (*name and address of accused*)

You have been charged with an offence where a witness, who is to give evidence at, or for the purposes of, the trial, is [*or* you are] a vulnerable witness under section 271(1) of the Criminal Procedure (Scotland) Act 1995.

[*Or*: You have intimated under section 210C(7) of the Criminal Procedure (Scotland) Act 1995 your objection to a report as to the risk your being at liberty presents to the safety of the public at large where a witness is [*or* you are] a vulnerable witness under section 271(1) of that Act]

On (*date*) at the High Court of Justiciary [*or* in the sheriff court] at (*place*) an order was made under section 288F(2) of that Act prohibiting you from personally conducting your defence to this charge [*or* in those proceedings.].

TAKE NOTICE THAT—

(1) if you are tried for the offence [*or* if there are proceedings under section 210C(7) of that Act], your defence may be conducted only by a lawyer;

(2) it is therefore in your interests, if you have not already done so, to get the professional assistance of a solicitor;

(3) if you do not engage a solicitor for the purposes of your defence at the preliminary hearing [*or* first diet] or the trial or proceedings under section 210C(7) of the Criminal Procedure (Scotland) Act 1995 , the court will do so.

(*Signed*)

Prosecutor

(*Name, address, e-mail address and telephone number*)

(*Place and date*)

AMENDMENT

Form 22.8-B inserted by Act of Adjournal (Criminal Procedure Rules Amendment No.3) (Vulnerable Witnesses (Scotland) Act 2004) 2005 (SSI 2005/188), r.2, subject to the conditions in r.2(2) (effective April 1, 2005).

Form 22.8-B as amended by Act of Adjournal (Criminal Procedure Rules Amendment No.3) (Risk Assessment Orders and Orders for Lifelong Restriction) 2006 (SSI 2006/302), para.2(7) (effective June 20, 2006).

Rule 22.15

Form of application for leave for accused to be present during a commission under section 271I(3) of the Criminal Procedure (Scotland) Act 1995

FORM 22.15   Form of application for leave for accused to be present during a commission under section 271I(3) of the Criminal Procedure (Scotland) Act 1995

Rule 22.15   UNTO THE RIGHT HONOURABLE THE LORD JUSTICE GENERAL, LORD JUSTICE CLERK AND LORDS COMMISSIONERS OF JUSTICIARY

[*or* UNTO THE HONOURABLE THE SHERIFF OF (*name of sheriffdom*) AT (*place*)]

APPLICATION FOR LEAVE TO BE PRESENT AT COMMISSION

under section 271I(3) of the Criminal Procedure (Scotland) Act 1995

by

[A.B.] (*address*)

[*or* Prisoner in the Prison of (*place*)]

Prosecution reference. . . . .

Court reference. . . . .

HUMBLY SHEWETH:

1. That [A.B.], (*date of birth*) [, along with (*name(s) of co-accused*)] has been indicted on (*date of indictment*) at the instance of Her Majesty's Advocate in the High Court of Justiciary [*or* in the sheriff court of (*place*)] [*or* has been charged in the above court on a summary complaint at the instance of the procurator fiscal] and a diet of (*specify*) has been fixed for (*date*).

2. That on (*date*) an order was made to allow the evidence of [C.D.] to be taken on commission as [C.D.] is a vulnerable witness under section 271(1) of the Criminal Procedure (Scotland) Act 1995.

3. That [A.B.] seeks leave of the court to be present in the room during the proceedings before the commissioner.

4. That [A.B.] can show special cause for leave to be granted as follows:–

(*here state reasons that show special cause*).

5. That a copy of this application has been duly intimated conform to the execution[s] attached to this application.

MAY IT THEREFORE, please your Lordship[s]—

(a) to grant leave under section 271I(3) of the Act of 1995 for [A.B.] to be present in the room during the commission proceedings; [or

(b) to fix a diet for hearing this application and to order intimation of the diet to all parties;]

(c) to do otherwise as to your Lordship[s] shall seem proper;

(d) to require the clerk of court to intimate the order to (*specify*).

IN RESPECT WHEREOF

(*Signed*)

[A.B.]

[*or* Legal representative of [A.B.]]

(*Address, e-mail address and telephone number of agent*).

(*Place and date*)

AMENDMENT

Form 22.15 inserted by the Act of Adjournal (Criminal Procedure Rules Amendment No. 6) (Vulnerable Witnesses (Scotland) Act 2004) (Evidence on Commission) 2005 (SSI 2005/574), r.2(4) and Sch. (effective November 30, 2005).

Form 22.15 as amended by Act of Adjournal (Criminal Procedure Rules Ammendment No.2) Vulnerable Witnesses (Scotland) Act 2004) 2007, r.2(3).

Act of Adjournal (Criminal Procedure Rules) 1996

Form 23.1-A

Form of petition for issue of letter of request in High Court before indictment served

UNTO THE RIGHT HONOURABLE THE LORD JUSTICE GENERAL, LORD JUSTICE-CLERK AND LORDS COMMISSIONERS OF JUSTICIARY

PETITION

of

HER MAJESTY'S ADVOCATE

[*or* [A.B.] (*address*)
[*or* Prisoner in the Prison of (*place*)]]

PETITIONER

HUMBLY SHEWETH:

1. That the petitioner [*or* [C.D.]] [. along with (*name(s) of co-accused*),] on (*date*) in the sheriff court at (*place*) was committed to prison till liberated in due course of law on a petition at the instance of the Procurator Fiscal [*or* the petitioner] in that court charging the petitioner [*or* [C.D.]] with the crime of (*specify*).

2. That no indictment has been served on the petitioner [*or* [C.D.]] in respect of the said crime and that accordingly the court in which any trial of the petitioner [*or* [C.D.]] in respect of the crime for which he stands committed is not yet known.

3. That (*name of witness*) residing at (*address*) is a witness whose evidence the petitioner intends to adduce in the course of the trial.

4. That the evidence to the effect specified in the schedule attached to this petition which it is averred that the said witness is able to give is necessary for the proper adjudication of the trial.

5. That there would be no unfairness to the prosecutor [*or as the case may be*] if such evidence were to be received in the form of the record of an examination conducted by virtue of section 272(1)(a) of the Criminal Procedure (Scotland) Act 1995.

6. That (*name of court*) is a court or tribunal exercising jurisdiction in the country or territory of (*specify*) in which the said witness resides being a country or territory outside the United Kingdom, Channel Islands or Isle of Man.

7. That English is [not] the official language or one of the official languages of the said country or territory.

MAY IT THEREFORE please your Lordships:

    (1) to appoint intimation of this petition and schedule to be made to (*specify*);

    (2) to appoint parties to be heard on the petition on the earliest practicable date hereafter; and

    (3) thereafter, on being duly satisfied in terms of section 272(3) of the Criminal Procedure (Scotland) Act 1995, to issue a letter of request to (*state judge or tribunal within whose jurisdiction the witness is resident*) to take the evidence of the said witness; and to do further or otherwise as to your Lordships shall seem proper.

ACCORDING TO JUSTICE, etc.

(*Signed*)
[Solicitor for petitioner]

(*Address and telephone number of solicitor*)

Act of Adjournal (Criminal Procedure Rules) 1996

Form 23.1-B

Rule 23.1(1)(b)

Form of petition for issue of letter of request where indictment served or in summary proceedings

UNTO THE RIGHT HONOURABLE THE LORD JUSTICE GENERAL, LORD JUSTICE-CLERK AND LORDS COMMISSIONERS OF JUSTICIARY
[*or* UNTO THE HONOURABLE THE SHERIFF OF (*name of sheriffdom*)
AT (*place*)]

PETITION

of

HER MAJESTY'S ADVOCATE [*or* THE PROCURATOR FISCAL, (*place*)]
[*or* [A.B.] (*address*)
[*or* Prisoner in the Prison of (*place*))]

PETITIONER

HUMBLY SHEWETH:

1. That the petitioner [*or* [C.D.]] [, along with (*name(s) of co-accused*),] has been indicted [*or* charged] in your Lordships' [*or* Lordship's] court at the instance of Her Majesty's Advocate [*or* the petitioner] with the crime of (*specify*) [*or* on a summary complaint at the instance of the procurator fiscal [*or* the petitioner] with the crime [*or* offence] of (*specify*)].

2. That the trial of the petitioner [*or* [C.D.]] is to take place in your Lordships' [*or* Lordship's] court [sitting at (*place*)] on (*date*).

3. That (*name of witness*) residing at (*address*) in the country or territory of (*specify*) is a witness whose evidence the petitioner intends to adduce in the course of the trial.

4. That the evidence to the effect specified in the schedule attached to this petition, which it is averred that the said witness is able to give, is necessary for the proper adjudication of the trial.

5. That there would be no unfairness to the prosecutor [*or as the case may be*] if such evidence were to be received in the form of the record of an examination conducted by virtue of section 272(1)(a) of the Criminal Procedure (Scotland) Act 1995.

6. That (*name of court*) is a court or tribunal exercising jurisdiction in the said country or territory of (*specify*) being a country or territory outside the United Kingdom, Channel Islands or Isle of Man.

7. That English is [not] the official language or one of the official languages of the said country or territory.

MAY IT THEREFORE please your Lordship[s]:

(1) to appoint intimation of this petition and schedule to be made to (*specify*);

(2) to appoint parties to be heard thereon on the earliest practicable date hereafter; and

(3) thereafter, on being duly satisfied in terms of section 272(3) of the Criminal Procedure (Scotland) Act 1995, to issue a letter of request to (*state judge or tribunal within whose jurisdiction the witness is resident*) to take the evidence of the said witness; and to do further or otherwise as to your Lordship[s] shall seem proper.

ACCORDING TO JUSTICE, etc.

(*Signed*)
[Solicitor for petitioner]

(*Address and telephone number of solicitor*)

Act of Adjournal (Criminal Procedure Rules) 1996

Form 23.1-C

Form of letter of request

LETTER OF REQUEST

(*Items to be included in all letters of request*)

1. Sender ....(*identity and address*)
....
....

2. Central authority of the requested ....(*identity and address*)
State ....

3. Person to whom the executed ....(*identity and address*)
request is to be returned ....
....

4. The undersigned applicant has the ....(*identity and address*)
honour to submit the following ....
request: ....
(a) Requesting judicial authority
(b) To the competent authority ....(*the requested State*)
....
....

5. Names and addresses of the ....
parties and their representatives: ....
(a) Prosecutor ....
(b) Accused
....
....
....

6. Nature and purpose of the ....
proceedings and summary of the ....
facts ....

7. Evidence to be obtained or other ....
judicial act to be performed ....
....

(*Items to be completed where applicable*)

8. Identity and address of any ....
person to be examined ....
....

9. Questions to be put to the .... (*or see attached list*) ....
persons to be examined or ....
statement of the subject-matter ....
about which they are to be
examined

10. Documents or other property to be inspected

(specify whether it is to be produced, copied, valued, etc.).....................................
....
....
....
....

11. Any requirement that the evidence be given on oath or affirmation and any special form to be used

(in the event that the evidence cannot be taken in the manner requested, specify whether it is to be taken in such manner as provided by local law for the formal taking of evidence) ...
....
....

12. Special methods or procedure to be followed

....
....
....

13. Request for notification of time and place for the execution of the request and identity and address of any person to be notified

....
....
....

14. Request for attendance or participation of judicial personnel of the requesting authority at the execution of the letter of request

....
....
....

15. Specification of privilege or duty to refuse to give evidence under the law of the State of origin

....
....
....

16. The fees and costs incurred will be borne by

............................*(identity and address)*
....
....

(Items to be included in all letters of request)

17. Date of request

....
....
....

18. Signature and seal of the requesting authority

....
....
....

Form 23A.1-A

Rule 23A.1

Form of petition for issue of letter of request under section 273(2) of the Criminal Procedure (Scotland) Act 1995

J

UNTO THE RIGHT HONOURABLE THE LORD JUSTICE GENERAL, LORD JUSTICE-CLERK AND LORDS COMMISSIONERS OF JUSTICIARY

[*or* UNTO THE HONOURABLE THE SHERIFF OF (*name of sheriffdom*) AT (*place*)]

PETITION

of

HER MAJESTY'S ADVOCATE
[*or* [A.B.] (*address*)
[*or* Prisoner in the Prison of (*place*)]]

PETITIONER

HUMBLY SHEWETH:

1. That the petitioner [*or* [C.D.]] [, along with (*name(s) of co-accused*),] has appeared on petition [*or* been indicted] [*or* charged] in your Lordships' [*or* Lordship's] court at the instance of Her Majesty's Advocate [*or* the procurator fiscal at (*place*)][or the petitioner] with the crime of (*specify*).

2. That no indictment has been served on the petitioner [*or* [C.D.]] in respect of the said crime and that accordingly the court in which any trial of the petitioner [*or* C.D.]] in respect of the said crime for which he stands committed is not yet known. [*or* That the trial of the petitioner [*or* [C.D.]] is to take place in your Lordships' [*or* Lordship's] court [sitting at (*place*)] on (*date*).]

3. That (*name of witness*) residing at (*address*) in the country or territory of (*specify*) is a witness whose evidence the petitioner intends to adduce in the course of the trial. He seeks to adduce that evidence through a live television link in that country or territory under section 273 of the Criminal Procedure (Scotland) Act 1995.

4. That the evidence to the effect specified in the schedule attached to this petition, which it is averred that the said witness is able to give, is necessary for the proper adjudication of the trial.

5. That (*name of court*) is a court or tribunal exercising jurisdiction in the said country or territory of (*specify*) being a country or territory outside the United Kingdom.

6. That English is [not] the official language or one of the official languages of the said country or territory.

7. That the law of the said country or territory provides for evidence to be taken by live television link [in accordance with the following procedure:- (*specify, if known*)].

[8. That there would be no unfairness to the accused if such evidence were to be given through a live television link.]

ACCORDING TO JUSTICE, etc.

(*Signed*)
[Solicitor for petitioner]

(*Address and telephone number of solicitor*)

AMENDMENT

Form 23.1-D substituted with Form 23A.1-A by the Act of Adjournal (Criminal Procedure Rules Amendment) (Miscellaneous) 2004 (SSI 2004/195), r.2 and Sch.1 (effective April 26, 2004).

Form 23A.1-B

Rule 23A.1

Form of letter of request for evidence to be obtained by television link

IN THE HIGH COURT OF JUSTICIARY

[*or* IN THE SHERIFF COURT OF (*name of sheriffdom*)
AT (*place*)]

LETTER OF REQUEST

in the Indictment [*or*
Petition *or* Complaint]

at the instance of
THE RIGHT HONOURABLE [A.B.],
HER MAJESTY'S ADVOCATE
[*or* PROCURATOR FISCAL]
for the Public Interest

against

[C.D.] (*address*)
[*or* Prisoner in the Prison of (*place*)]

The Honourable Lord (*name*), one of the Lords Commissioners of Justiciary, [*or* (*name*), Sheriff of (*name of sheriffdom*) at (*place*)] presents his compliments to (*here specify the court, tribunal or authority to which the request is addressed*) and has the honour of informing it of the following facts:

1. The High Court of Justiciary, of which the Honourable Lord (*name*) is one of the judges, is the supreme criminal court in Scotland and exercises a jurisdiction as a trial court [*or* The Sheriff Court of which Sheriff (*name*) is one of the judges, is a criminal court in Scotland which exercises jurisdiction as a trial court and in pre-trial procedures in all prosecutions for crime].

2. (*Specify briefly the applicant's part in the proceedings including, where appropriate, his relationship to the investigating agency.*)

3. Criminal proceedings have been instituted before the High Court of Justiciary at the instance of the Right Honourable [A.B.]. Her Majesty's Advocate, [*or*, before the Sheriff Court of (*name sheriffdom*) at (*place*), at the instance of [A.B.], Procurator Fiscal,] against [C.D.] (*specify the nationality of the accused*) who is presently charged that (*here narrate the charge on the indictment, petition or complaint*). [*In a case where the accused has appeared on petition but has not yet been indicted, insert the following if it is known in which court the case will be indicted:—* It is expected that in due course the trial of [C.D.] will take place in the High Court of Justiciary [*or* the Sheriff Court of (*name of sheriffdom*) at (*place*).*]

4. The crime of (*specify the nomen juris of the crime charged or under investigation*) is a criminal offence at common law in Scotland and is not contained in any statute. It consists of (*summarise the essential elements of the crime*) [*or* It is a criminal offence under (*narrate statutory provision and its terms and add any explanation beyond the bare words of the statute thought necessary in order to enable the foreign court, tribunal or authority to understand clearly the elements of the crime*)]. The penalties for conviction are (*specify*).

5. It has been shown to the Honourable Lord (*name*) on application by Her Majesty's Advocate [*or* [C.D.]] [*or* It has been shown to the Sheriff of (*name of sheriffdom*) at (*place*) on application by the procurator fiscal [*or* [C.D.]]], a copy of which is annexed to this request, that it is necessary for the proper adjudication of the trial that the evidence of (*name and address of witness*) be given through a live television link.   .

6. The Criminal Procedure (Scotland) Act 1995 empowers the High Court of Justiciary [*or* the Sheriff Court] to request your assistance in facilitating the giving of that evidence by (*name of witness*) who resides within your jurisdiction through a live television link.

7. [*Here specify arrangements to be made and name, address and telephone number of clerk of court with whom arrangements are to be made.*]

[8.] In thanking (*specify the court, tribunal or authority to which the request is addressed*) in advance for its co-operation in this case, the Honourable Lord (*name*) [*or* Sheriff (*name*)] avails himself [*or* herself] of this opportunity to renew the assurance of his [*or* her] high consideration.

> (*Signed*)
> Lord Commissioner of Justiciary
> [*or* Sheriff of (*name of sheriffdom*) at (*place*)]

Dated this (*date*).

AMENDMENT

Form 23.1-E substituted with Form 23A.1-B by the Act of Adjournal (Criminal Procedure Rules Amendment) (Miscellaneous) 2004 (SSI 2004/195), r.2 and Sch.1 (effective April 26, 2004).

Form of petition for appointment of commissioner to examine a witness in High Court before indictment served

UNTO THE RIGHT HONOURABLE THE LORD JUSTICE GENERAL, LORD JUSTICE-CLERK AND LORDS COMMISSIONERS OF JUSTICIARY

PETITION

of

HER MAJESTY'S ADVOCATE
[*or* [A.B.] (*address*)
[*or* Prisoner in the Prison of (*place*)]]

PETITIONER

HUMBLY SHEWETH:

1. That the petitioner [*or* [C.D.]] [, along with (*name(s) of co-accused*),] on (*date*) in the sheriff court at (*place*) was committed to prison till liberated in due course of law on a petition at the instance of the procurator fiscal [*or* the petitioner] in the said court charging the petitioner with the crime of (*specify*).

2. That no indictment has been served on the petitioner [*or* [C.D.]] in respect of the said crime and that accordingly the court in which any trial of the petitioner [*or* [C.D.]] in respect of the crime for which he stands committed is not yet known.

3. That (*name of witness*) residing at (*address*) is a witness whose evidence the petitioner intends to adduce in the course of the trial. The witness is unable to attend the trial diet by reason of being ill [*or* infirm] as appears from the medical certificate produced with this petition [*or* the witness is not ordinarily resident, and is, at the time of the trial diet, unlikely to be present, in the United Kingdom, Channel Islands or Isle of Man].

4. That the evidence to the effect specified in the schedule attached to this petition, which it is averred that the said witness is able to give, is necessary for the proper adjudication of the trial.

5. That there would be no unfairness to the prosecutor [*or as the case may be*] if such evidence were to be received in the form of the record of an examination conducted by virtue of section 272(1)(b) of the Criminal Procedure (Scotland) Act 1995.

MAY IT THEREFORE please your Lordships—

   (1)   to appoint intimation of this petition and schedule to be made to (*specify*);

   (2)   to appoint parties to be heard on the petition on the earliest practicable date hereafter; and

   (3)   thereafter, on being duly satisfied in terms of section 272(3) of the Criminal Procedure (Scotland) Act 1995, to appoint (*name of proposed commissioner*) or such other person as your Lordships shall think fit to be a commissioner to take evidence of the said witness within the United Kingdom, Channel Islands or Isle of Man and to report to your Lordships *quam primum*; and to do further or otherwise as to your Lordships shall seem proper.

ACCORDING TO JUSTICE, etc.

(*Signed*)
[Solicitor for petitioner]

(*Address and telephone number of solicitor*)

Form 24.1-B

Rule 24.1(1)(b)

Form of petition for appointment of commissioner to examine a witness where indictment served or in summary proceedings

UNTO THE RIGHT HONOURABLE THE LORD JUSTICE GENERAL, LORD JUSTICE-CLERK AND LORDS COMMISSIONERS OF JUSTICIARY

[*or* UNTO THE HONOURABLE THE SHERIFF OF (*name of sheriffdom*) AT (*place*)]

PETITION

of

HER MAJESTY'S ADVOCATE [*or* THE PROCURATOR FISCAL, (*place*)]

[*or* [A.B.] (*address*)
[*or* Prisoner in the Prison of (*place*)]]

PETITIONER

HUMBLY SHEWETH:

1. That the petitioner [*or* [C.D.]] [, along with (*name(s) of co-accused*),] has been indicted [*or* charged] in your Lordships' [*or* Lordship's] Court at the instance of Her Majesty's Advocate [*or* the petitioner] with the crime of (*specify*) [*or* on a summary complaint at the instance of the procurator fiscal [*or* the petitioner] with the crime [*or* offence] of (*specify*)].

2. That the trial of the petitioner [*or* [C.D.]] is to take place in your Lordships' [*or* Lordship's] court [sitting at (*place*)] on (*date*).

3. That (*name of witness*) residing at (*address*) is a witness whose evidence the petitioner intends to adduce in the course of the trial. The witness is unable to attend the trial diet by reason of being ill [*or* infirm] as appears from the medical certificate produced with this petition [*or* the witness is not ordinarily resident, and is, at the time of the trial diet, unlikely to be present, in the United Kingdom, Channel Islands or Isle of Man].

4. That the evidence to the effect specified in the schedule attached to this petition, which it is averred that the witness is able to give, is necessary for the proper adjudication of the trial.

5. That there would be no unfairness to the prosecutor [*or as the case may be*] if such evidence were to be received in the form of the record of an examination conducted by virtue of section 272(1)(b) of the Criminal Procedure (Scotland) Act 1995.

MAY IT THEREFORE please your Lordship[s]—

    (1) to appoint intimation of this petition and schedule to be made to (*specify*);

    (2) to appoint parties to be heard on the petition on the earliest practicable date hereafter; and

    (3) thereafter, on being duly satisfied in terms of section 272(3) of the Criminal Procedure (Scotland) Act 1995, to appoint (*name of proposed commissioner*) or such other person as your Lordship[s] shall think fit to be a commissioner to take the evidence of the said witness within the United Kingdom, Channel Islands or Isle of Man and to report to your Lordship[s] *quam primum*; and to do further or otherwise as to your Lordship[s] shall seem proper.

ACCORDING TO JUSTICE, etc.

(*Signed*)
[Solicitor for petitioner]

(*Address and telephone number of solicitor*)

Form 26.1-A

Rule 26.1(1)(b)

Form of certificate of authentication of document

I, (*insert name, address and title of office held*), being
    the author
    [*or* the person in [*or* who was on (*date*) in] possession and control]
    [*or* the authorised representative of (*name and address*) who [*or* which] is in [*or* who [*or*
    which] was on (*date*) in] possession and control]
of
    the original(s)
    [*or* a copy [*or* copies] of the original(s)]
    [*or* a copy [*or* copies] of a material part [*or* material parts] of the original(s)]
of the copy document [*or* documents listed and described below] on which this certificate is
endorsed [*or* to which this certificate is attached]
hereby certify that
    it is a true copy
    [*or* they are true copies]
of [*or* part(s) of]
    the original(s)
    [*or* the copy [*or* copies] of the original(s)]
    [*or* the copy [*or* copies] of the material part [*or* material parts] of the original(s)]
[of] which
    I am the author
    [*or* is [*or* are] [*or* was] [*or* were] in my possession and control]
    [*or* is [*or* are] [*or* was] [*or* were] in the possession and control of (*name and address*) of
    whom [*or* which] I am the authorised representative.]

> (*Signed*)
> (*Add authorised capacity in which certificate
> signed*)

Date: (*insert date*)

[*List and describe documents*]

Form 26.1-B

Rule 26.1(2)

Form of docquet certifying a document as one kept by a business or undertaking

I, (*insert name and title of office held*), hereby certify that this document [*or* the documents listed
and described below and to which this certificate is attached] is [*or* are] [*or* was] [*or* were] a
document [*or* documents] kept by a business [*or* undertaking] [*or* by or on behalf of the holder
of a paid [*or* unpaid] office], namely (*insert name and address of business, undertaking or office*).

> (*Signed*)
> (*Add authorised capacity in which certificate
> signed*)

Date: (*insert date*)

[*List and describe documents*]

NOTE
[1] As amended by S.I. 1996 No. 2147.

Form 26.1-C

Rule 26.1(3)

Form of certificate that statement not contained in business document

I, (*insert name and title of office held*), being a person authorised to give evidence on behalf of (*insert name and address of business or undertaking, or body of which the signatory is an officeholder*), hereby state that (*name and describe document*) being a document [*or that no document within the category of documents of* (*name and describe category*) *being documents*] in respect of which the conditions (*specified in paragraph 2(1)(a) and (b) of Schedule 8 to the Criminal Procedure (Scotland) Act 1995*) are satisfied does not contain [*or, where no documents within a category of documents satisfying those conditions contains such a statement, contains*] (*specify the relevant statement as to the particular matter not contained in the documents*).

(*Signed*)
(*Add authorised capacity in which certificate signed*)

Date: (*insert date*)

NOTE
¹As amended by Act of Adjournal (Criminal Procedure Rules Amendment No. 3) (S.I. 1997 No. 1788) (effective August 11, 1997).

Form 27.2

Rule 27.2

Form of certificate under section 283(1), 284(1) or 285(2), (4) or (5) of the Criminal Procedure (Scotland) Act 1995

I, (*insert name, designation and capacity in which the certificate is given*), being a person who may sign a certificate under section 283(1) [*or* 284(1) *or* 285(2), (4) or (5)] of the Criminal Procedure (Scotland) Act 1995,

HEREBY CERTIFY THAT (*here insert the matter which is being certified and specify enactment in respect of which the evidence is given*).

[If a notice is not served by you, under section 283(2) [*or* 284(2)] not more than seven days after the date of service of this certificate, the evidence contained in this certificate shall be sufficient evidence of the facts contained in the certificate.]

(*Signed*)

(*Date*)

Form 27.3

Form of notice in relation to certain evidential certificates

IN THE HIGH COURT OF JUSTICIARY
[*or* IN THE SHERIFF [*or* DISTRICT] COURT]

AT (*place*)

NOTICE

by

[A.B.] (*address*) [*or* Prisoner in the Prison of (*place*)]

under section (*specify*)

of the Criminal Procedure (Scotland) Act 1995

To: (*name of person to whom notice sent*)

I HEREBY GIVE NOTICE under section (*specify*) that I [*or* [A.B.]] do [*or* does] not accept the evidence contained in the certificate under section (*specify*).

(*Signed*)
[A.B.]
[*or* Solicitor for [A.B.]]

(*Address and telephone number of Solicitor*)

Form 27.4

Form of notice under section 16A(4) of the Criminal Law (Consolidation) (Scotland) Act 1995

IN THE HIGH COURT OF JUSTICIARY [*or* IN THE SHERIFF COURT]

AT (*place*)

NOTICE

by

[A.B.] (*address*) [or Prisoner in the Prison of (*place*)]

under

Section 16A(4) of the Criminal Law (Consolidation) (Scotland) Act 1995

To: (*name of prosecutor, or co-accused*)

I HEREBY GIVE NOTICE that under section 16A(4) of the Criminal Law (Consolidation) (Scotland) Act 1995 that on the facts as alleged with respect to the relevant conduct, the condition in section 16A(3)(r) [*or* (b)] of the Criminal Law (Consolidation) (Scotland) Act 1995 is not satisfied for the following reasons:—

(*here set out reasons for regarding condition as unsatisfied*)

I HEREBY REQUIRE (*insert name and designation of prosecutor*) to prove that the said condition is satisfied.

(*Signed*)
[A.B.]
[*or* Solicitor for [A.B.]]
(*Address and telephone number of Solicitor*)

NOTE
[1]As added by the Act of Adjournal (Criminal Procedure Rules Amendment) 1997 (No. 63).

Form 27.5

Form of notice under section 16B(4) of the Criminal Law (Consolidation) (Scotland) Act 1995

[IN THE HIGH COURT OF JUSTICIARY]

[IN THE SHERIFF COURT]

AT (*place*)

NOTICE

by

[A.B.] (*address*) [*or* prisoner in the Prison of (*place*)]

under

Section 16B(4) of the Criminal Law (Consolidation) (Scotland) Act 1995

To: (*name of prosecutor or co-accused*)

I HEREBY GIVE NOTICE under subsection (4) of section 16B of the Criminal Law (Consolidation) (Scotland) Act 1995 that on the facts as alleged with respect to the act described

in the charge against me, the condition in subsection (1)(a) of that section is not satisfied for the following reason[s]:—

(*here set out reason[s] for regarding condition as unsatisfied*)

I HEREBY REQUIRE (*insert name and designation of prosecutor*) to prove that the said condition is satisfied.

> (*Signed*)
> [A.B.]
> [or Solicitor for [A.B.]]
> (*Address and telephone number of Solicitor*)

Form of petition for order to hold identification parade in solemn proceedings before serving of indictment under section 290(1) of the Criminal Procedure (Scotland) Act 1995

UNTO THE HONOURABLE THE SHERIFF OF (*name of sheriffdom*)

AT (*place*)

PETITION

of

[A.B.] (*address*)
[*or* Prisoner in the Prison of (*place*)]

PETITIONER

HUMBLY SHEWETH:

1. That the petitioner [, along with (*name(s) of co-accused*),] has been charged in your Lordship's court at (*place*) on a petition at the instance of the procurator fiscal with the offence of (*specify*).

2. That the trial of the petitioner is to take place in your Lordship's court [*or* the High Court of Justiciary sitting at (*place*)] on (*date*).

3. That an identification parade in which the petitioner was one of those constituting the parade has not been held.

4. That the petitioner has requested the prosecutor to hold such a parade but he has refused to hold, or has unreasonably delayed holding, such a parade.

5. That it is reasonable in the circumstances in relation to the alleged crime [*or* offence] that such an identification parade should be held (*specify circumstances*).

MAY IT THEREFORE please your Lordship—

(1) to appoint intimation of this petition to be made to the procurator fiscal;

(2) to appoint parties to be heard thereon on the earliest practicable date hereafter; and

(3) thereafter, on being duly satisfied in terms of section 290(2) of the Criminal Procedure (Scotland) Act 1995, to order the prosecutor to hold an identification parade in which the petitioner shall be one of those constituting the parade, in relation to the offence referred to above with which the petitioner has been charged.

ACCORDING TO JUSTICE, etc.

(*Signed*)
[Solicitor for petitioner]

(*Address and telephone number of solicitor*)

Form 28.1-B

Rule 28.1(1)(b)(ii)

Form of petition for order to hold identification parade where indictment served or in summary proceedings under section 290(1) of the Criminal Procedure (Scotland) Act 1995

UNTO THE HONOURABLE THE SHERIFF OF (*name of sheriffdom*)

AT (*place*)

PETITION

of

[A.B.] (*address*)
[*or* Prisoner in the Prison of (*place*)]

PETITIONER

HUMBLY SHEWETH:

1. That the petitioner [, along with (*name(s) of co-accused*),] has been indicted [*or* charged] in your Lordship's court [*or* the High Court of Justiciary sitting at (*place*)] [*or* the District Court at (*place*)] at the instance of Her Majesty's Advocate [*or* the procurator fiscal] with the crime [*or* offence] of (*specify*).

2. That the trial of the petitioner is to take place in your Lordship's court [*or* the High Court of Justiciary sitting at (*place*)] [*or* the District Court at (*place*)] on (*date*).

3. That an identification parade in which the petitioner was one of those constituting the parade has not been held.

4. That the petitioner has requested the prosecutor to hold such a parade but he has refused to hold, or has unreasonably delayed holding, such a parade.

5. That it is reasonable in the circumstances in relation to the alleged crime [*or* offence] that such an identification parade should be held (*specify circumstances*).

MAY IT THEREFORE please your Lordship—

(1) to appoint intimation of this petition to be made to Her Majesty's Advocate [*or* the procurator fiscal];

(2) to appoint parties to be heard thereon on the earliest practicable date hereafter; and

(3) thereafter, on being duly satisfied in terms of section 290(2) of the Criminal Procedure (Scotland) Act 1995, to order the prosecutor to hold an identification parade in which the petitioner shall be one of those constituting the parade, in relation to the offence referred to above with which the petitioner has been charged.

ACCORDING TO JUSTICE, etc.

(*Signed*)
[Solicitor for petitioner]

(*Address and telephone number of solicitor*)

Form 29.1-A

Rule 29.1(1)(b)(i)

Form of petition to take precognition on oath before service of indictment under section 291(1) of the Criminal Procedure (Scotland) Act 1995

UNTO THE HONOURABLE THE SHERIFF OF (*name of sheriffdom*)

AT (*place*)

PETITION

of

[A.B.] (*address*)
[*or* Prisoner in the Prison of (*place*)]

PETITIONER

HUMBLY SHEWETH:

1. That the petitioner [, along with (*name(s) of co-accused*),] has been charged in your Lordship's court at (*place*) on a petition at the instance of the procurator fiscal with the crime [*or* offence] of (*specify*).

2. That the trial of the petitioner is to take place in your Lordship's court [*or* the High Court of Justiciary sitting at (*place*)] on (*date*).

3. That the petitioner believes that [C.D.] residing at (*address*) is a witness in relation to the said crime [*or* offence]. That [C.D.] is not a witness to whom section 291(6) of the Criminal Procedure (Scotland) Act 1995 applies [*or* that as [C.D.] is a witness under section 291(6) of the Criminal Procedure (Scotland) Act 1995 warrant is sought to cite the witness to attend for precognition on oath by the solicitor for the accused only].

4. That (*narrate all steps taken to obtain precognition from the witness and, or, the circumstances justifying the taking of the precognition on oath*).

5. That the petitioner [*or* the solicitor for the petitioner] is unable to complete his [*or* her] investigation [on behalf of the petitioner] without precognosing [C.D.].

MAY IT THEREFORE please your Lordship—

(1) to appoint intimation of this petition to be made to the procurator fiscal;

(2) to appoint parties to be heard thereon on the earliest practicable date hereafter; and

(3) thereafter, on being duly satisfied in terms of section 291(1) of the Criminal Procedure (Scotland) Act 1995, that it is reasonable to require such precognition on oath, to grant warrant to cite [C.D.] to attend for precognition on oath before your Lordship on the earliest practicable date thereafter; and to do further or otherwise as to your Lordship shall seem proper.

ACCORDING TO JUSTICE, etc.

(*Signed*)
[Solicitor for petitioner]

(*Address and telephone number of solicitor*)

AMENDMENT

Form 29.1-A as amended by the Act of Adjournal (Criminal Procedure Rules Amendment No.3) (Vulnerable Witnesses (Scotland) Act 2004) 2005 (SSI 2005/188), r.2, subject to the conditions in r.2(2) (effective April 1, 2005).

Form of petition to take precognition on oath where indictment served or in summary proceedings under section 291(1) of the Criminal Procedure (Scotland) Act 1995

UNTO THE HONOURABLE THE SHERIFF OF (*name of sheriffdom*)

AT (*place*)

PETITION

of

[A.B.] (*address*)
[*or* Prisoner in the Prison of (*place*)]

PETITIONER

HUMBLY SHEWETH:

1. That the petitioner [, along with (*name(s) of co-accused*),] has been indicted [*or* charged] in your Lordship's court [*or* the High Court of Justiciary sitting at (*place*)] [*or* the District Court at (*place*)] at the instance of Her Majesty's Advocate [*or* the procurator fiscal] with the crime [*or* offence] of (*specify*).

2. That the trial of the petitioner is to take place in your Lordship's court [*or* the High Court of Justiciary sitting at (*place*)] [*or* the District Court at (*place*)] on (*date*).

3. That the petitioner believes that [C.D.] residing at (*address*) is a witness in relation to the said crime [*or* offence] [*or* is witness no. (*slate number*) on the list of witnesses attached to the indictment]. That [C.D.] is not a witness to whom section 291(6) of the Criminal Procedure (Scotland) Act 1995 applies [or as [C.D.] is a witness under section 291(6) of the Criminal Procedure (Scotland) Act 1995 warrant is sought to cite the witness to attend for precognition on oath by the solicitor for the accused only].

4. That (*narrate all steps taken to obtain a precognition from the witness and, or, the circumstances justifying the taking of the precognition on oath*).

5. That the petitioner [*or* the solicitor for the petitioner] is unable to complete his [*or* her] investigation [on behalf of the petitioner] without precognosing [C.D.].

MAY IT THEREFORE please your Lordship—

(1) to appoint intimation of this petition to be made to Her Majesty's Advocate [*or* the procurator fiscal];

(2) to appoint parties to be heard thereupon on the earliest practicable date hereafter; and

(3) thereafter, on being duly satisfied in terms of section 291(1) of the Criminal Procedure (Scotland) Act 1995 that it is reasonable to require such precognition on oath, to grant warrant to cite [C.D.] to attend for precognition on oath before your Lordship on the earliest practicable date thereafter; and to do further or otherwise as to your Lordship shall seem proper.

ACCORDING TO JUSTICE, etc.

(*Signed*)
[Solicitor for petitioner]

(*Address and telephone number of solicitor*)

Form 29.1-B as amended by the Act of Adjournal (Criminal Procedure Rules Amendment No.3) (Vulnerable Witnesses (Scotland) Act 2004) 2005 (SSI 2005/188), r.2, subject to the conditions in r.2(2) (effective April 1, 2005).

Form 29.3

Rule 29.3(1)

Form of citation of person to attend a diet for taking his precognition on oath

IN THE SHERIFF COURT AT (*place*)

CITATION

To: (*name and address of witness*)

Date of citation: (*date of citation or, if citation by post, the day after the date of posting*)

YOU ARE HEREBY CITED to appear on (*date*) at (*time*) in the Sheriff Court House at (*address*) in chambers to be precognosed on oath for the accused, (*name*), in relation to the offence with which he has been charged.

IF YOU DO NOT ATTEND COURT WITHOUT A REASONABLE EXCUSE THE COURT MAY ORDER THAT YOU BE APPREHENDED AND PUNISHED.

(*Signed*)
Officer of Law
[*or* Solicitor for accused]

Form 30.2-A

AMENDMENT

Form 30.2-A repealed by the Act of Adjournal (Criminal Procedure Rules Amendment No.3) (Extradition etc.) 2004 (SSI 2004/346), r.2 (effective August 18, 2004).

Form 30.2-B

AMENDMENT

Form 30.2-B repealed by the Act of Adjournal (Criminal Procedure Rules Amendment No.3) (Extradition etc.) 2004 (SSI 2004/346), r.2 (effective August 18, 2004).

Form 30.5

•
AMENDMENT

Form 30.5 repealed by the Act of Adjournal (Criminal Procedure Rules Amendment No.3) (Extradition etc.) 2004 (SSI 2004/346), r.2 (effective August 18, 2004).

Form of reference to the European Court

THE HIGH COURT OF JUSTICIARY
[*or* SHERIFF [*or* DISTRICT] COURT] IN SCOTLAND

HER MAJESTY'S ADVOCATE [*or* THE PROCURATOR FISCAL]

against

[C.D.] (*address*)

[*or* Prisoner in the Prison of (*place*)]

[*Here set out a clear and succinct statement of the case giving rise to the request for the ruling of the European Court in order to enable the European Court to consider and understand the issues of Community law raised and to enable governments of Member States and other interested parties to submit observations. The statement of the case should include:*

(a) *particulars of the parties;*
(b) *the history of the dispute between the parties;*
(c) *the history of the proceedings;*
(d) *the relevant facts as agreed by the parties or found by the court or, failing such agreement or finding. the contentions of the parties on such facts;*
(e) *the nature of the issues of law and fact between the parties;*
(f) *the Scots law so far as is relevant;* ..
(g) *the Treaty provisions or other acts, instruments or rules of Community law concerned; and*
(h) *an explanation of why the reference is being made.*]

The preliminary ruling of the Court of Justice of the European Communities is accordingly requested on the following questions:
1, 2, etc. [*Here set out the questions on which the ruling is sought. identifying the Treaty provisions or other acts, instruments or rules of Community law concerned.*]

Dated the   day of   19 .

Form 31.7

Form of appeal to High Court from the making of a reference to the European Court of Justice

NOTE OF APPEAL

by

[C.D.]

APPELLANT

in

HER MAJESTY'S ADVOCATE [*or* THE PROCURATOR FISCAL, (*place*)]

against

[C.D.] (*address*)
[*or* Prisoner in the Prison of (*place*)]

1. The appellant appeals to the High Court of Justiciary sitting as a court of appeal against the order of (*name of judge*) in the High Court of Justiciary sitting at (*place*) [*or* the sheriff [*or* district] court at (*place*)] on (*date*).

2. The appellant appeals against the order on the following grounds:—

(*here set out the grounds of appeal*).

IN RESPECT WHEREOF

(*Signed*)
[Solicitor for appellant]

(*Address and telephone number of solicitor*)

(*Date*)

Form 32.2

Rule 32.2(1)

Form of application under section 49 of the Civic Government (Scotland) Act 1982

IN THE DISTRICT COURT OF (*place*)

APPLICATION

under

section 49(2) and (3) Civic Government (Scotland) Act 1982

by

[A.B.] (*address*)

COMPLAINER

against

[C.D.] (*address*)

RESPONDENT

HUMBLY SHEWETH:

1. That the complainer is resident at (*address*).

2. That the respondent occupies premises at (*specify address or place*) being in the vicinity of (*specify complainer's address*).

3. That at those premises [C.D.] keeps (*here identify the creature and describe the circumstances in which the creature is kept*).

4. (*Here describe in detail in one or more paragraphs the circumstances in which it is alleged the creature is causing annoyance.*)

MAY IT THEREFORE please the court to order service of a copy of this application on the said [C.D.]; to fix a date for the hearing of this application no earlier than 14 days after such service; and thereafter to make an order on [C.D.] to take within such period as may be specified in the order such steps (short of destruction of the creature) as may be so specified to prevent the continuation of the annoyance.

IN RESPECT WHEREOF

(*Signed*)
[Solicitor for complainer]

(*Address and telephone number of solicitor*)

Form 34.3-A

Rule 34.3(1)(a)

Form of note of appeal under section 26(1) of the Extradition Act 2003

IN THE HIGH COURT OF JUSTICIARY

NOTE OF APPEAL

under section 26(1) of the Extradition Act 2003

by

[A.B.] (*address*)

1.   [A.B.] (*address*) ("the appellant") was arrested at (*place*) on (*date*) under section 5 of the Extradition Act 2003 [*or* under a warrant issued under Part 1 of the Extradition Act 2003].

2.   On (*date*) the sheriff of Lothian and Borders at (*place*) ordered the appellant's extradition to (*country*) being a category 1 territory within the meaning of section 1 of the Extradition Act 2003.

3.   The Appellant appeals to the High Court of Justiciary under section 26(1) of the Extradition Act 2003 on the grounds set out in the following paragraphs.

(*Here state in brief specific numbered propositions the grounds on which it is proposed to submit that the appeal should be allowed.*)

> (*Signed*)
>
> Appellant's legal representative
>
> (*Address*)
>
> (*Telephone number*)
>
> (*E-mail address*)

AMENDMENT

Form 34.3-A inserted by by the Act of Adjournal (Criminal Procedure Rules Amendment No.3) (Extradition etc.) 2004 (SSI 2004/346), r.2 and Sch. (effective August 18, 2004).

Form 34.3-B

Form of note of appeal under section 28(1) of the Extradition Act 2003

IN THE HIGH COURT OF JUSTICIARY

NOTE OF APPEAL

under section 28(1) of the Extradition Act 2003

by

HER MAJESTY'S ADVOCATE

on behalf of (*authority which issued the warrant under Part 1 of the Act of 2003*)

1. [A.B.] (*address*) ("the arrested person") was arrested at (*place*) on (*date*) under section 5 of the Extradition Act 2003 [*or* under Part 1 warrant within the meaning of section 2 of the Extradition Act 2003].

2. On (*date*) the sheriff of Lothian and Borders at (*place*) ordered the discharge of the arrested person.

3. Her Majesty's Advocate appeals to the High Court of Justiciary under section 28(1) of the Extradition Act 2003 on the grounds set out in the following paragraphs.

(*Here state in brief specific numbered propositions the grounds on which it is proposed to submit that the appeal should be allowed.*)

> (*Signed*)
>
> On behalf of Her Majesty's Advocate
>
> (*Address*)
>
> (*Telephone number*)
>
> (*E-mail address*)

AMENDMENT

Form 34.3-B inserted by the Act of Adjournal (Criminal Procedure Rules Amendment No.3) (Extradition etc.) 2004 (SSI 2004/346), r.2 and Sch. (effective August 18, 2004).

Form 34.3-C

Rule 34.3(1)(c)

Form of notice of appeal under section 103(1) or 108(1) of the Extradition Act 2003

IN THE HIGH COURT OF JUSTICIARY

NOTE OF APPEAL

under section 103(1) [*or* 108(1)] of the Extradition Act 2003

by

[A.B.] (*address*)

1. [A.B.] (*address*) ("the appellant") was arrested at (*place*) on (*date*) under a warrant issued by the sheriff of Lothian and Borders under section 71(2) of the Extradition Act 2003 [*or* under a provisional warrant issued by the sheriff of (*name of sheriffdom*) under section 73 of the Extradition Act 2003].

2. On (*date*) the sheriff of Lothian and Borders at (*place*) sent the appellant's case to the Scottish Ministers for their decision whether the appellant was to be extradited. [On (*date*) the Scottish Ministers ordered the extradition of the appellant].

3. The appellant appeals to the High Court of Justiciary under section 103(1) [*or* 108(1)] of the Extradition Act 2003 on the grounds set out in the following paragraphs.

(*Here state in brief specific numbered propositions the grounds on which it is proposed to submit that the appeal should be allowed.*)

> (*Signed*)
>
> Appellant's legal representative
>
> (*Address*)
>
> (*Telephone number*)
>
> (*E-mail address*)

AMENDMENT

Form 34.3-C inserted by the Act of Adjournal (Criminal Procedure Rules Amendment No.3) (Extradition etc.) 2004 (SSI 2004/346), r.2 and Sch. (effective August 18, 2004).

Rule 34.3(1)(d)

Form of note of appeal under section 105(1) or 110(1) of the Extradition Act 2003

IN THE HIGH COURT OF JUSTICIARY

NOTE OF APPEAL

under section 105(1) [*or* 110(1)] of the Extradition Act 2003

by

HER MAJESTY'S ADVOCATE

on behalf of (*specify category 2 territory*)

1.   [A.B.] (*address*) ("the arrested person") was arrested at (*place*) on (*date*) under a warrant issued by the sheriff of Lothian and Borders under section 71(2) of the Extradition Act 2003 [*or* under a provisional warrant issued by the sheriff of (*name of sheriffdom*) under section 73(3) of the Extradition Act 2003].

2.   On (*date*) the sheriff of Lothian and Borders at (*place*) ordered the discharge of the arrested person. [*or* That on (*date*) the sheriff of Lothian and Borders sent the arrested person's case to the Scottish Ministers for their decision whether the arrested person was to be extradited. That on (*date*) the Scottish Ministers ordered the discharge of the arrested person].

3.   Her Majesty's Advocate appeals on behalf of (*specify category 2 territory*) to the High Court of Justiciary under section 105(1) [*or* 110(1)] of the Extradition Act 2003 on the grounds set out in the following paragraphs.

(*Here state in brief specific numbered propositions the grounds on which it is proposed to submit that the appeal should be allowed.*)

> (*Signed*)
>
> On behalf of Her Majesty's Advocate
>
> (*Address*)
>
> (*Telephone number*)
>
> (*E-mail address*)

AMENDMENT

Form 34.3-D inserted by the Act of Adjournal (Criminal Procedure Rules Amendment No.3) (Extradition etc.) 2004 (SSI 2004/346), r.2 and Sch. (effective August 18, 2004).

Form 34.5

Rule 34.5

Form of application seeking extension of time under section 31(4) or 113(4) of the Extradition Act 2003

UNTO THE RIGHT HONOURABLE THE LORD JUSTICE GENERAL, LORD JUSTICE CLERK AND LORDS COMMISSIONERS OF JUSTICIARY

APPLICATION FOR EXTENSION OF TIME

under section 31(4) [*or* 113(4)] of the Extradition Act 2003

by

HER MAJESTY'S ADVOCATE

[or [A.B.], (*address*)]

Name of arrested person: (*name*)

Date of Birth: (*date*)

Address: (*address*)

The time within which the High Court must begin.to hear the appeal by (*specify*) under section 26(1) [*or* 28(1) *or* 103(1) *or* 105(1) *or* 108(1) *or* 110(1)] of the Extradition Act 2003 expires on (*date*).

Application is hereby made under section 31(4) [*or* 113(4)] of that Act for extension of the period within which the High Court must begin to hear that appeal for the following reasons:-

(*Here state in brief specific numbered propositions the reasons why it would be in the interests of justice for the application to be granted.*)

(Signed)

On behalf of Her Majesty's Advocate

[*or* On behalf of the arrested person]

(*Address*)

(*Telephone number*)

(*E-mail address*)

AMENDMENT

Form 34.5 substituted by the Act of Adjournal (Criminal Procedure Rules Amendment No.3) (Extradition etc.) 2004 (SSI 2004/346), r.2 and Sch. (effective August 18, 2004).

Rule 34.6(a)

Form of notice of consent to extradition to category 1 territory

NOTICE OF CONSENT TO EXTRADITION

by

(A.B.) (*date of birth*)

On (*date*) I was arrested under section 5 of the Extradition Act 2003 [*or* under a Part 1 warrant within the meaning of section 2 of the Extradition Act 2003] with a view to my extradition to (*specify category 1 territory*).

I understand that by consenting to my extradition I am to be taken as having waived any right not to be dealt with in (*specify category 1 territory*) for an offence committed before my extradition.

I understand that by consenting to my extradition, I waive any right—

    (a) to make representations at an extradition hearing before a sheriff, or

    (b) to appeal against the decision of the sheriff.

I understand that this written consent to my extradition is irrevocable.

I consent to my extradition.

(*Signed*)

(A.B.)

This notice of consent was signed by the above-mentioned person in my presence on (*date*) at (*place*).

(*Signed*)

Sheriff of Lothian and Borders

AMENDMENT

    Form 34.6 substituted by the Act of Adjournal (Criminal Procedure Rules Amendment No.3) (Extradition etc.) 2004 (SSI 2004/346), r.2 and Sch. (effective August 18, 2004).

Rule 34.6(b)

Form of notice of consent to extradition to category 2 territory

NOTICE OF CONSENT TO EXTRADITION

by

(A.B.) (*date of birth*)

On (*date*) I was arrested under a warrant issued under section 71(2) of the Extradition Act 2003 [*or* under a provisional warrant under 73(3) of the Extradition Act 2003] with a view to my extradition to (*specify category 2 territory*).

I understand that by consenting to my extradition I am to be taken as having waived any right not to be dealt with in (*specify category 2 territory*) for an offence committed before my extradition.

I understand that by consenting to my extradition, I waive any right—

   (a) to make representations at an extradition hearing before a sheriff, or

   (b) to appeal against the decision of the sheriff or the Scottish Ministers.

I understand that by consenting to my extradition I lose any protection afforded by section 95 of the Extradition Act 2003.

I understand that this written consent to my extradition is irrevocable.

I consent to my extradition.

(*Signed*)

(A.B.)

This notice of consent was signed by the above-mentioned person in my presence on (*date*) at (*place*).

(*Signed*)

Sheriff of Lothian and Borders

AMENDMENT

   Form 34.6-B inserted by the Act of Adjournal (Criminal Procedure Rules Amendment No.3) (Extradition etc.) 2004 (SSI 2004/346), r.2 and Sch. (effective August 18, 2004).

Rule 34.7(1)

Form of notice of request under section 54(1) of the Extradition Act 2003

To: (*name of extradited person*) (*date of birth*) (*address*)

Date: (*date*)

TAKE NOTICE:

1. That on (*date*) the sheriff of Lothian and Borders at (*place*) received a request from (*specify judicial authority of the category 1 territory*) for consent to deal with you in relation to the offence of (*specify*) in addition to the offence for which you were extradited to (*category 1 territory*).

2. That the request for consent was received by the Crown Agent on (*date*).

3. That the request for consent was certified by the Crown Agent under section 54(2) of the Extradition Act 2003 on (*date*).

4. That the certified request is attached to this notice.

5. That a consent hearing has been fixed for (*time and date*) at (*place*). At that hearing the sheriff will consider whether consent should be given to your being dealt with in (*category 1 territory*) in relation to the offence of (*specify*) in addition to the offence for which you were extradited. You may therefore wish to appear or be represented at that hearing.

You should seek legal advice about the implications of this notice.

(*Signed*)

Sheriff

AMENDMENT

Form 34.7-A inserted by the Act of Adjournal (Criminal Procedure Rules Amendment No.3) (Extradition etc.) 2004 (SSI 2004/346), r.2 and Sch. (effective August 18, 2004).

Form 34.7-B

Rule 34.7(2)

Form of notice of request under section 56(1) of the Extradition Act 2003

To: (*name of extradited person*) (*date of birth*) (*address*)

Date: (*date*)

TAKE NOTICE:

1.   That on (*date*) the sheriff of Lothian and Borders at (*place*) received a request from (*specify judicial authority of the category 1 territory*) for your extradition to (*category 1 territory*).

2.   That the request for consent was received by the Crown Agent on (*date*).

3.   That the request for consent was certified by the Crown Agent under section 56(2) of the Extradition Act 2003 on (*date*).

4.   That the certified request is attached to this notice.

5.   That a consent hearing has been fixed for (*time and date*) at (*place*). At that hearing the sheriff will consider whether consent should be given to your being extradited to (*category 1 territory*). You may therefore wish to appear or be represented at that hearing.

You should seek legal advice about the implications of this notice.

(*Signed*)

_____
                              Sheriff

AMENDMENT

Form 34.7-B inserted by the Act of Adjournal (Criminal Procedure Rules Amendment No.3) (Extradition etc.) 2004 (SSI 2004/346), r.2 and Sch. (effective August 18, 2004).

Rule 36.2

Form of notice to accompany a citation being effected or document being served outside the United Kingdom

To: (*name*)

Date: (*date*)

TAKE NOTICE:

(1) That the enclosed citation [or *specify*] is being served on you in respect of criminal proceedings against you [*or* in which you have been cited as a witness *or specify*] in Scotland, United Kingdom.

(2) The citation seeks your appearance on (*date*) at (*time*) in the High Court of Justiciary [*or* Sheriff [*or* District] Court] at (*address*), Scotland, United Kingdom.

(3) If you are not going to be able to attend you should contact us immediately.

(4) You can obtain further information from us about your rights.

[(5) The citation [*or* document] is accompanied by a translation as required under section 5(4) of the Crime (International Co-operation) Act 2003.]

(Signed)

Advocate Depute [*or* Procurator Fiscal *or* Clerk of Court]

(address including telephone and fax number)

AMENDMENT

Form 36.2 inserted by the Act of Adjournal (Criminal Procedure Rules Amendment) (Miscellaneous) 2004 (SSI 2004/195), r.2 and Sch.2 (effective April 26, 2004).

Form 36.4-A

Form of application for request for assistance under section 7(1) of the Crime (International Co-operation) Act 2003

UNTO THE RIGHT HONOURABLE THE LORD JUSTICE GENERAL, LORD JUSTICE-CLERK AND LORDS COMMISSIONERS OF JUSTICIARY

[or UNTO THE HONOURABLE THE SHERIFF OF *(name of sheriffdom)*

AT (place)]

PETITION

of

THE RIGHT HONOURABLE [A.B.],

HER MAJESTY'S ADVOCATE

[*or* THE PROCURATOR FISCAL]

for the Public Interest [*or* [C.D.]

Accused Person]

PETITIONER

HUMBLY SHEWETH:

1. That [C.D.] born on *(specify accused's date of birth)*, was on *(date)* in the sheriff court at (place) fully committed on a petition at the instance of the petitioner [*or as the case may be*] charging [C.D.] with *(specify the nomen juris of the charge)* as more particularly specified in the copy petition annexed to this petition. [*Insert the following if it is known in which court the case will be indicted*: It is expected that in due course the trial of [C.D.] will take place in the High Court of Justiciary [*or* the sheriff court of (name of sheriffdom)] sitting at *(place)*.]

[*or* 1. That there are reasonable grounds for suspecting that an offence has been committed, namely, (specify nomen juris of or otherwise describe the offence or specify the statute and section contravened) in respect that on (specify the date of the offence) at (specify locus of the offence) it is alleged that (specify the modus of the offence). Police officers (or Officers of Customs and Excise] acting on the instructions of the petitioner are investigating the alleged offence.]

2. That in order that justice may be done in the case against [C.D.] [*or* in order that the investigation may be completed], it is necessary that evidence be obtained from *(specify country to which the request is being sent)*. The precise evidence required is *(specify)*.

3. That section 7 of the Crime (International Co-operation) Act 2003 provides that where on an application made by the Lord Advocate or a procurator fiscal or, where proceedings have been instituted, by the person charged in those proceedings, it appears to a judge or a sheriff (a) that an offence has been committed or that there are reasonable grounds for suspecting that an offence has been committed or (b) that proceedings in respect of the offence have been instituted or that the offence is being investigated, the judge or sheriff may issue a request for assistance in obtaining outside the United Kingdom such evidence as is specified in the request for use in the proceedings or investigation.

MAY IT THEREFORE please your Lordship[s] to issue a request to (*specify the court, tribunal or authority to whom it is desired to have the request addressed*) to obtain the evidence specified herein; and to do further or otherwise as to your Lordship[s] shall seem proper.

ACCORDING TO JUSTICE, etc.

(*Signed*)

[Solicitor for petitioner]

(Address and telephone number of solicitor)

AMENDMENT

Form 36.4-A inserted by the Act of Adjournal (Criminal Procedure Rules Amendment) (Miscellaneous) 2004 (SSI 2004/195), r.2 and Sch.2 (effective April 26, 2004).

Form 36.4-B

Rule 36.4

Request for assistance under section 7 of the Crime (International Co-operation) Act 2003

IN THE HIGH COURT OF JUSTICIARY

[or IN THE SHERIFF COURT OF (name of sheriffdom) AT (place)]

REQUEST FOR ASSISTANCE

in the Indictment [*or*

Petition *or* Complaint]

at the instance of

THE RIGHT HONOURABLE [A.B.],

HER MAJESTY'S ADVOCATE

[*or* THE PROCURATOR FISCAL]

for the Public Interest

against

[C.D.] (*address*)

[or REQUEST FOR ASSISTANCE

in the investigation into

(here specify the crime under investigation e.g. Murder of [E.F.])

The Honourable Lord (*name*), one of the Lords Commissioners of Justiciary, [or (*name*), Sheriff of (*name of sheriffdom*) at (*place*)] presents his compliments to (*here specify the court, tribunal or authority to which the request is addressed*) and has the honour of informing it of the following facts:

1. The High Court of Justiciary, of which the Honourable Lord (*name*) is one of the judges, is the supreme criminal court in Scotland and exercises a jurisdiction as a trial court [*or* The Sheriff Court of which Sheriff (name) is one of the judges, is a criminal court in Scotland which exercises jurisdiction as a trial court and in pre-trial procedures in all prosecutions for crime].

2. (Specify briefly the applicant's part in the proceedings including, where appropriate, his relationship to the investigating agency.)

3. Criminal proceedings have been instituted before the High Court of Justiciary at the instance of the Right Honourable [A.B.], Her Majesty's Advocate, [*or*, before the Sheriff Court of (*name of sheriffdom*) at (*place*), at the instance of [A.B.], Procurator Fiscal,] against [C.D.] (*specify the nationality of the accused*) who is presently charged that (*here narrate the charge on the indictment, petition or complaint*). [*In a case where the accused has appeared on petition but has not yet been indicted, insert the following if it is known in which court the case will be indicted:-*

It is expected that in due course the trial of [C.D.] will take place in the High Court of Justiciary [*or*, the Sheriff Court of (*name of sheriffdom*)] at (*place*).]

[or 3. There are reasonable grounds for suspecting that an offence has been committed, namely (specify the nomen juris of or otherwise describe the offence or specify the statute and section contravened) in respect that on (specify the date of the offence). Police officers [*or* Officers of Customs and Excise] acting on the instructions of the procurator fiscal are investigating the alleged offence.]

4. The crime of (*specify the nomen juris of the crime charged or under investigation*) is a criminal offence at common law in Scotland and is not contained in any statute. It consists of (*summarise the essential elements of the crime*) [*or* It is a criminal offence under (*narrate statutory provision and its terms and add any explanation beyond the bare words of the statute thought necessary in order to enable the foreign court, tribunal or authority to understand clearly the elements of the crime*)]. The penalties for conviction are (*specify*).

[*Where relevant, insert*:- [5. A person may be convicted of an attempt at a crime where he has taken an overt step in pursuance of his criminal intention and has passed from the stage of preparation to the stage of perpetration but has not completed the crime. Paragraph 10 of Schedule 3 to the Criminal Procedure (Scotland) Act 1995 provides:-

" (1) Under an indictment or, as the case may be, a complaint which charges a completed offence, the accused may be lawfully convicted of an attempt to commit an offence.

(2) Under an indictment or complaint charging an attempt, the accused may be convicted of such attempt although the evidence is sufficient to prove the completion of the offence said to have been attempted.

(3) Under an indictment or complaint which charges an offence involving personal injury inflicted by the accused, resulting in death or serious injury to the person, the accused may be lawfully convicted of the assault or other injurious act, and may also be lawfully convicted of the aggravation that the assault or other injurious act was committed with intent to commit such offence."]

[*Where relevant, insert*:- The Law of Scotland makes no distinction between commission and accession, and by the common law of Scotland anyone who gives assistance to or otherwise acts in previous concert with the principal or who is guilty of concert, assistance or participation in the crime is liable to be convicted of the crime.]

[6.] It has been shown to the Honourable Lord (*name*) on application by Her Majesty's Advocate [*or* [C.D.]] [*or*, it has been shown to the Sheriff of (*name of sheriffdom*) at (*place*) on application by the procurator fiscal [*or* [C.D.]]], a copy of which is annexed to this request, that in order that justice may be done in the proceedings [*or*, in order that the investigation may be completed] it is necessary that evidence be obtained from (*specify country to which the request is being sent*).

[7.] The circumstances giving rise to this request are as follows: - (narrate fully such evidence as is known which has relevance to the request so that the foreign court, tribunal or authority will have a clear understanding of the subject-matter of the case and the need for the evidence they are requested to obtain).

[8.] The Crime (International Co-operation) Act 2003 empowers the High Court of Justiciary [*or* the Sheriff Court*] to seek from and to give to courts, tribunals and other authorities exercising criminal jurisdiction in countries or territories outside the United Kingdom reciprocal assistance in the obtaining of evidence and it is requested in the present case that (*specify the court, tribunal or authority to which the request is addressed*) give assistance in the obtaining of the evidence herein specified. In particular, it is requested that (*specify the assistance requested, whether that is by the interview of witnesses, recovery of documents or other articles, search of premises, issue of extracts or otherwise. If witnesses are to be interviewed, identify them clearly and state nationality if known. If relevant, state any privilege which the witness might be able to claim and provide for the witness to claim that privilege under interview but to be required to answer the question nevertheless, leaving the application of that privilege and the admissibility of the answers given for the determination of the trial court. Specify the subject-matter of the questions to be put or formulate questions as appropriate; also specify any special procedures desired to be followed (for example, "It is desired that, where competent, a witness be interviewed on oath"). Where it is sought to recover documents or other articles specify precisely what is sought and identify the holder of the documents and other articles. State any request for parties or their agents or counsel to be present at the execution of the request and state any other request made. Schedules may be used.)*

[9.] [*Here narrate any time limit to which the case is subject and, if appropriate, insert*: In view of the foregoing it is respectfully requested that this request be treated as urgent.]

[10.] Any evidence provided in response to this letter of request will not, without the consent of the appropriate authority in (*name the country*), be used for any purpose other than the said proceedings [*or* the said investigation and any criminal proceedings arising out of it].

[11.] In thanking (*specify the court, tribunal or authority to which the request is addressed*) in advance for its co-operation in this case, the Honourable Lord (*name*) [*or* Sheriff (*name*)] avails himself [*or* herself] of this opportunity to renew the assurance of his [*or* her] high consideration.

(Signed)

Lord Commissioner of Justiciary

[or Sheriff of (name of sheriffdom) at (place)]

Dated this (*date*).

AMENDMENT

Form 36.4-B inserted by the Act of Adjournal (Criminal Procedure Rules Amendment) (Miscellaneous) 2004 (SSI 2004/195), r.2 and Sch.2 (effective April 26, 2004).

Form 36.8-A

Rule 36.8

Form of warrant to cite a person to proceedings before a nominated court

WARRANT FOR CITATION

Whereas the High Court of Justiciary [*or* Sheriffdom of (*sheriffdom*) at (*place*)] has been nominated by the Lord Advocate to receive evidence under section 15 of the Crime (International Co-operation) Act 2003 [*or* nominated under section 30(3) of the Crime (International Co-operation) Act 2003 to facilitate the giving of evidence by live television link] [*or* nominated under section 31(4) to facilitate the giving of evidence by telephone], the court grants warrant for the citation of witnesses to proceedings to take place at (*time*) on (*date*) at (*place*).

AMENDMENT

Form 36.8-A inserted by the Act of Adjournal (Criminal Procedure Rules Amendment) (Miscellaneous) 2004 (SSI 2004/195), r.2 and Sch.2 (effective April 26, 2004).

Act of Adjournal (Criminal Procedure Rules) 1996

Form 36.8-B

Form of postal citation to proceedings before a nominated court

IN THE HIGH COURT OF JUSTICIARY

[*or* IN THE SHERIFF COURT]

AT (*place*)

CITATION

To: (name and address)

Date of citation: (day after date of posting)

YOU ARE HEREBY CITED to appear on (*date*) at (*time*) in the High Court of Justiciary [*or* Sheriff Court] at (*address*) to give evidence in connection with proceedings against (*name of accused*) before (*name of external court*) [*or* in connection with an investigation by (*name of external authority*)].

[*You will be required to give your evidence through a live television link to (*name of external authority*) [*or* by telephone to (*name of external authority*)].

Please return the enclosed form to the Procurator Fiscal in the pre-paid envelope provided within 14 days after the date of citation stated at the top of this citation.

IF YOU FAIL TO ATTEND WITHOUT A LAWFUL EXCUSE THE COURT MAY ISSUE A WARRANT FOR YOUR ARREST.

*delete if inapplicable

AMENDMENT

Form 36.8-B inserted by the Act of Adjournal (Criminal Procedure Rules Amendment) (Miscellaneous) 2004 (SSI 2004/195), r.2 and Sch.2 (effective April 26, 2004).

Act of Adjournal (Criminal Procedure Rules) 1996

Form 36.8-C

Form of reply slip to be completed and returned by person cited to appear before a nominated court

To: Procurator Fiscal

(address to be inserted by person effecting citation)

From: (name to be inserted by person effecting citation)

Date: (*date*)

I, (name and address of person cited to be inserted by person effecting citation), acknowledge that I have received the citation to appear to give evidence on (date to be inserted by person effecting citation) at (time to be inserted by person effecting citation) in the High Court of Justiciary [*or* Sheriff Court] at (address to be inserted by person effecting citation).

I shall attend on that date.

(Signed)

AMENDMENT

Form 36.8-C inserted by the Act of Adjournal (Criminal Procedure Rules Amendment) (Miscellaneous) 2004 (SSI 2004/195), r.2 and Sch.2 (effective April 26, 2004).

Form 36.8-D

Form of personal citation for proceedings before a nominated court

IN THE HIGH COURT OF JUSTICIARY

[*or* IN THE SHERIFF COURT]

AT (*place*)

CITATION

To: (name and address)

Date of citation: (*date of citation*)

YOU ARE HEREBY CITED to appear on (*date*) at (*time*) in the High Court of Justiciary [*or* Sheriff Court] at (*address*) to give evidence in connection with proceedings against (*name of accused*) before (*name of external court*) [*or* in connection with an investigation by (*name of external authority*)].

[*You will be required to give your evidence through a live television link to (*name of external court or authority*) [*or* by telephone to (*name of external court or authority*)].

IF YOU FAIL TO ATTEND WITHOUT A LAWFUL EXCUSE THE COURT MAY ISSUE A WARRANT FOR YOUR ARREST.

*delete if inapplicable

(Signed)

Officer of Law

AMENDMENT

Form 36.8-D inserted by the Act of Adjournal (Criminal Procedure Rules Amendment) (Miscellaneous) 2004 (SSI 2004/195), r.2 and Sch.2 (effective April 26, 2004).

Form 37.4

Rule 37.4

Form of petition under section 25 or 26 of the Proceeds of Crime (Scotland) Act 1995

UNTO THE RIGHT HONOURABLE THE LORD JUSTICE GENERAL, THE LORD JUSTICE-CLERK and LORDS COMMISSIONERS OF JUSTICIARY

[*or* UNTO THE HONOURABLE THE SHERIFF OF (*name of sheriffdom*)

AT (*place*)]

PETITION

of

[A.B.] (*address*)

PETITIONER

HUMBLY SHEWETH:

1. That the Petitioner is (*name*) and resides at (*address*).

2. That on (*date*) the court in the case of Her Majesty's Advocate [*or* Procurator Fiscal] against (*name and address*) made an order under section 21 of the Proceeds of Crime (Scotland) Act 1995 forfeiting (*specify property and, for heritable property in Scotland, state conveyancing description (unless already stated in suspended forfeiture order) and date and county of recording of a certified copy of the suspended forfeiture order in the General Register of Sasines or, as the case may be, the Title Number under which a certified copy of the suspended forfeiture order was registered in the Land Register of Scotland*).

3. That (*state the relevant facts in support of grant of order*).

MAY IT THEREFORE please your Lordship(s):

    (1)   to appoint intimation of this petition to be made to (*specify*):

    (2)   to appoint parties to be heard thereon on the earliest practicable date thereafter; and

    (3)   thereafter, on being duly satisfied in terms of section 25(1)(a) [or section 26(1)(a)] of the Proceeds of Crime (Scotland) Act 1995, to make an order under section 25 [or section 26] of that Act; and to do further or otherwise as to your Lordship(s) shall seem proper.

ACCORDING TO JUSTICE, etc.

(*Signed*)
Petitioner
[*or* Solicitor for Petitioner]

(*Address and telephone number of Solicitor*)

Rule 37.5

Form of note of appeal under section 27 of the Proceeds of Crime (Scotland) Act 1995

IN THE HIGH COURT OF JUSTICIARY

[*or* IN THE SHERIFF COURT]

AT

(*place*)

NOTE OF APPEAL

under the Proceeds of Crime (Scotland) Act 1995

by

[A.B.] (*address*)

APPELLANT

against

[C.D.] (*address*)

. RESPONDENT

1. The appellant appeals to the High Court of Justiciary against the refusal of an application under section 25(1) [*or* the granting of an application under section 26(1)] of the Proceeds of Crime (Scotland) Act 1995 in the above court on (*date*).

2. The ground(s) of appeal is (are):

(*here set out the ground(s)*)

(*Signed*)
Appellant
[*or* Solicitor for appellant]

(*Address and telephone number of solicitor*)

(*Place and date*)

Form 37A

Rule 37A

Form of petition to sheriff under section 7(3) of the Knives Act 1997

UNTO THE HONOURABLE THE SHERIFF OF (*name of sheriffdom*)

AT (*place*)

PETITION

of

[A.B.] (*address*)

PETITIONER

HUMBLY SHEWETH:

1. That the petitioner is (*name*) and resides at (*address*).

2. That on (*date*) the court in the case (*Procurator Fiscal*) against (*name and address*), accused, made an Order in terms of section 6 of the Knives Act 1997 forfeiting (*specify property forfeited*).

3. That (*state facts relevant to application*).

MAY IT THEREFORE please your Lordship:

(1) to appoint intimation of this petition to be made to (*specify*).

(2) to appoint parties to be heard thereon on the earliest practicable date thereafter; and

(3) thereafter, on being duly satisfied, to make an order in terms of section 7(3) of the Knives Act 1997; and to do further or otherwise as Your Lordship shall deem proper.

ACCORDING TO JUSTICE, etc.

(*Signed*)
[Solicitor for petitioner]

(*Address and telephone number of solicitor*)

NOTE
[1]Inserted by Act of Adjournal (Criminal Procedure Rules Amendment No. 6) (S.I. 1997 No. 2081) (effective September 1, 1997).

Rule 38

Form of application to High Court for transfer of rights of appeal of deceased person

UNTO THE RIGHT HONOURABLE THE LORD JUSTICE GENERAL, LORD
JUSTICE CLERK and LORDS COMMISSIONERS OF JUSTICIARY

APPLICATION

for

TRANSFER OF RIGHTS OF APPEAL OF DECEASED PERSON

by

[A.B.] (*address*)

APPLICANT

under

section 303A of the Criminal Procedure (Scotland) Act 1995

HUMBLY SHEWETH:—

1. That on (*date*) [C.D.] (*address*) was convicted in the High Court of Justiciary [*or* sheriff court
or district court] at (*place*) of (*specify offence*) and sentenced to (*specify sentence*).

2. That [C.D.] did not institute any appeal in relation to that conviction or sentence [*or state
details of any appeal instituted by* [C.D.]].

3. That [C.D.] died on (*date*) at (*place*).

4. That the applicant is executor of [C.D.] conform to attached copy confirmation [*or* has a
legitimate interest (*specify nature of interest and attach supporting documents*)].

5. That the applicant has served a copy of this application on the Crown Agent.

MAY IT THEREFORE please your Lordships under section 303A of the Criminal Procedure
(Scotland) Act 1995 to authorise the applicant to institute any appeal in relation to that
conviction which [C.D.] could have instituted [*or* to continue the appeal instituted by
[C.D.]].

ACCORDING TO JUSTICE, etc.

(*Signed*)
[Solicitor for applicant]

(*Address and telephone number of solicitor*)

AMENDMENT

Form 38 inserted by Act of Adjournal (Criminal Procedure Rules Amendment No.4) (SI 1997/
1834) (effective August 1, 1997).

Form 40.2A

Rule 40.2(1)

Form of minute of notice of intention to raise a devolution issue

UNTO THE RIGHT HONOURABLE THE LORD JUSTICE GENERAL, LORD
JUSTICE-CLERK AND LORDS COMMISSIONERS OF JUSTICIARY

[UNTO THE HONOURABLE THE SHERIFF OF (*name of sheriffdom*)
AT (*place*)]

MINUTE

by

[A.B.] (*address*)
[*or* Prisoner in the Prison of (*place*)]

HUMBLY SHEWETH:

1. That [*name of accused*] has been indicted at the instance of Her Majesty's Advocate for preliminary hearing in the High Court of Justiciary sitting at (*place*) on (*date*) [*or* sheriff court at (*place*) on (*date*) with a first diet on (*date*)].

2. That [A.B.] intends to raise a devolution issue within the meaning of Schedule 6 to the Scotland Act 1998/Schedule 10 to the Northern Ireland Act 1998/Schedule 8 to the Government of Wales Act 1998 on the following grounds (*here specify the facts and circumstances and contentions of law which are alleged to give rise to the devolution issue*).

3. That a copy of this minute has been duly intimated to Her Majesty's Advocate [and to (*name(s) of co-accused*)] and to the relevant authority within the meaning of Rule 40.1 conform to execution[s] attached to this minute.

MAY IT THEREFORE PLEASE YOUR LORDSHIP[S]:

to order that there be a diet and to assign a date for that diet:

IN RESPECT WHEREOF

[Solicitor for minuter]

(*Address and telephone number of solicitor*)

(*Place and date*)

AMENDMENT

Form 40.2A inserted by the Act of Adjournal (Devolution Issues Rules) 1999 (SI 1999/1346) (effective May 6, 1999).

Form 40.2A as amended by the Act of Adjournal (Criminal Procedure Rules Amendment) (Criminal Procedure (Amendment) (Scotland) Act) 2005 (SSI 2005/44), r.2(18) (subject to r.2(2)–(4)) (effective February 1, 2005).

Form of notice of intervention by relevant authority

UNTO THE RIGHT HONOURABLE THE LORD JUSTICE GENERAL, LORD
JUSTICE-CLERK AND LORDS COMMISSIONERS OF JUSTICIARY

[UNTO THE HONOURABLE THE SHERIFF OF (*name of sheriffdom*)
AT (*place*)]

NOTICE

by

[C.D.] (*address*)

HUMBLY SHEWETH:

1. That [*name of accused*] has been indicted at the instance of Her Majesty's Advocate for
preliminary hearing in the High Court of Justiciary sitting at (*place*) on (*date*) [*or* sheriff court at
(*place*) on (*date*) with a first diet on (*date*)].

2. That [C.D.] (*here specify the name and title of the relevant authority and the fact of the
intimation of the devolution issue*) intends to take part in the proceedings so far as they relate to
the devolution issue.

3. That a copy of this notice has been duly intimated to Her Majesty's Advocate [and to said
(*name(s) of accused*)] and to any other relevant authority within the meaning of Rule 40.1
conform to execution[s] attached to this minute.

IN RESPECT WHEREOF

[Solicitor for the relevant authority]

(*Address and telephone number of solicitor*)

(*Place and date*)

AMENDMENT

Form 40.2B inserted by the Act of Adjournal (Devolution Issues Rules) 1999 (SI 1999/1346) (effective May 6, 1999).

Form 40.2B as amended by the Act of Adjournal (Criminal Procedure Rules Amendment) (Criminal Procedure (Amendment) (Scotland) Act) 2005 (SSI 2005/44), r.2(18) (subject to r.2(2)–(4)) (effective February 1, 2005).

Form 40.3A

Rule 40.3(1)

Form of minute of notice of intention to raise a devolution issue

UNTO THE HONOURABLE THE SHERIFF OF (*name of sheriffdom*)
AT (*place*)

[or UNTO THE JUSTICES in the DISTRICT COURT IF (*name of district*)
AT (*place*)]

MINUTE

by

[E.F.] (*address*)

[*or* Prisoner in the Prison of (*place*)]

HUMBLY SHEWETH:

1. That [*name of accused*] has been charged at the instance of [G.H.] procurator fiscal at (*place*) with the crime [*or* offence] of (*specify*) and a diet is fixed for (*specify date*).

2. That [E.F.] intends to raise a devolution issue within the meaning of Schedule 6 to the Scotland Act 1998/Schedule 10 to the Northern Ireland Act 1998/Schedule 8 to the Government of Wales Act 1998 on the following grounds (*here specify the facts and circumstances and contentions of law which are alleged to give rise to the devolution issue*).

3. That a copy of this minute has been duly intimated to the said G.H., procurator fiscal [and to said (*name(s) of co-accused*)] and to the relevant authority within the meaning of Rule 40.1 conform to execution[s] attached to this minute.

MAY IT THEREFORE PLEASE YOUR LORDSHIP [or THE COURT]:

to order that there be a diet and to determine the devolution issue and to assign a date for that diet;

IN RESPECT WHEREOF

[Solicitor for minuter]

(*Address and telephone number of solicitor*)

(*Place and date*)

AMENDMENT

Form 40.3A inserted by the Act of Adjournal (Devolution Issues Rules) 1999 (SI 1999/1346) (effective May 6, 1999).

Form 40.3B

Rule 40.3(3)

Form of notice of intervention by relevant authority

UNTO THE HONOURABLE THE SHERIFF OF (*name* of *sheriffdom*)

AT (*place*)

[or UNTO THE JUSTICES in the DISTRICT COURT OF (*name of district*) AT (*place*)]

NOTICE

by

[J.K.] (*address*)

HUMBLY SHEWETH:

1. That [*name of accused*] has been charged at the instance of [G.H.], procurator fiscal at (*place*) with the crime [*or* offence] of (*specify*) and a diet has been fixed for (*specify date*).

2. That [J.K.] (*here specify the name and title of the relevant authority and the fact of the intimation of the devolution issue*) intends to take part in the proceedings so far as they relate to the devolution issue.

3. That a copy of this notice has been duly intimated to the said G.H., procurator fiscal [and to said (*name(s) of accused*)] and to any other relevant authority within the meaning of Rule 40.1 conform to execution[s] attached to this minute.

IN RESPECT WHEREOF

[Solicitor for the relevant authority]

(*Address and telephone number of solicitor*)

(*Place and date*)

AMENDMENT

Form 40.3B inserted by the Act of Adjournal (Devolution Issues Rules) 1999 (SI 1999/1346) (effective May 6, 1999).

Rule 40.4(2)

Form of minute of notice of intention to raise a devolution issue

UNTO THE RIGHT HONOURABLE THE LORD JUSTICE GENERAL, LORD
JUSTICE-CLERK AND LORDS COMMISSIONERS OF JUSTICIARY

[or UNTO THE HONOURABLE THE SHERIFF OF (*name of sheriffdom*)
AT (*place*)]

[or UNTO THE JUSTICES in the DISTRICT COURT OF (*name of district*) AT (*place*)]

MINUTE

by

[L.M.] (*address*)

[*or* Prisoner in the Prison of (*place*)]

HUMBLY SHEWETH:

1. That (*here specify the nature of the proceedings, the names of the parties and the date of the diet fixed*).

2. That [L.M.] intends to raise a devolution issue within the meaning of Schedule 6 to the Scotland Act 1998/Schedule 10 to the Northern Ireland Act 1998/Schedule 8 to the Government of Wales Act 1998 on the following grounds (*here specify the facts and circumstances and contentions of law which are alleged to give rise to the devolution issue*).

3. That a copy of this minute has been duly intimated to Her Majesty's Advocate [*and to* (*name(s) of any other parties to the proceedings*)] and to the relevant authority within the meaning of Rule 40.1 conform to execution[s] attached to this minute.

MAY IT THEREFORE PLEASE YOUR LORDSHIP[S] [OR THE COURT]:

to order that there be a diet and to assign a date for that diet:

IN RESPECT WHEREOF

[Solicitor for minuter]

(*Address and telephone number of solicitor*)

(*Place and date*)

Form 40.4B

Rule 40.4(4)

Form of notice of intervention by relevant authority

UNTO THE RIGHT HONOURABLE THE LORD JUSTICE GENERAL, LORD JUS-
TICE-CLERK AND LORDS COMMISSIONERS OF JUSTICIARY

[UNTO THE HONOURABLE THE SHERIFF OF *(name of sheriffdom)*

AT *(place)*]

[or UNTO THE JUSTICES in the DISTRICT COURT OF *(name of district)* AT *(place)*]

NOTICE

by

[N.O.] *(address)*

HUMBLY SHEWETH:

1. That *(here specify the nature of the proceedings, the names of the parties and the date of any diet fixed)*.

2. That [N.O.] *(here specify the name and title of the relevant authority and the fact of the intimation of the devolution issue)* intends to take part in the proceedings so far as they relate to the devolution issue.

3. That a copy of this notice has been duly intimated to Her Majesty's Advocate [and to said *(name(s) of other parties)*] and to any other relevant authority within the meaning of Rule 40.1 conform to execution[s] attached to this minute.

IN RESPECT WHEREOF

[Solicitor for the relevant authority]

(Address and telephone number of solicitor)

(Place and date)

NOTE

[1]Inserted by the Act of Adjournal (Devolution Issues Rules) 1999 (S.I. 1999 No. 1346) (effective May 6, 1999).

Form 40.12

Rule 40.12

Form of intimation to a relevant authority that the court is considering making an order under [section 102 of the Scotland Act 1998/section 81 of the Northern Ireland Act 1988/section 110 of the Government of Wales Act 1998]

To: (*name and address of relevant authority*)

1. You are given notice that in criminal proceedings in the [High Court of Justiciary/Sheriff/ District Court at (*place*)], at the instance of (*name and title of prosecutor*) against (*name of accused*) the court has decided [that an Act/provision of an Act of the Scottish Parliament is not within the legislative competence of the Parliament] [a member of the Scottish Executive does not have the power to make, confirm or approve a provision of subordinate legislation he has purported to make, confirm or approve]. A copy of the relevant decision is enclosed.

2. The court is considering whether to make an order [removing or limiting the retrospective effect of the decision/suspending the effect of the decision to allow the defect to be corrected].

3. If you wish to take part as a party to the proceedings so far as they relate to the making of the order mentioned in paragraph 2 you must lodge with (*title and address of clerk of court*) a notice in writing stating that you intend to take part as a party in the proceedings. The notice must be lodged within 7 days of (*insert date on which intimation was given*).

Date (*insert date*)

(*Signed*)

Clerk of Court

NOTE
[1]Inserted by the Act of Adjournal (Devolution Issues Rules) 1999 (S.I. 1999 No. 1346) (effective May 6, 1999).

Form 41.3–A

Rule 41.3(1)

Form of notice to Crown under section 5(1) of the 1998 Act

IN THE HIGH COURT OF JUSTICIARY

AT (*place*)

IN

HER MAJESTY'S ADVOCATE

against

[C.D.] (*address* or *Prisoner in the Prison of (place)*)

Date: (*date of posting or other method of service*)

To: (*specify Minister or other person on whom notice is to be served*)

TAKE NOTICE
That the court is considering whether or not to [*or:* That (*specify party*) is seeking that the court] make a declaration under section (*specify section 4(2), in relation to primary legislation or section 4(4) in relation to subordinate legislation*) of the Human Rights Act 1998 that (*specify the primary or subordinate legislation which is the subject of the proposed declaration*) is incompatible with (*specify the Convention right*) for the following reasons:

(*set out the reasons in summary*).

You may apply to become a party to the proceedings. If you wish to do so you should notify the Deputy Principal Clerk of Justiciary in Form 41.3–B.

(*Signed*)

Deputy Principal Clerk of Justiciary [*or* Solicitor [*or* Agent] for (*specify*)]

AMENDMENT

   Form 41.3-A as amended by the Act of Adjournal (Criminal Procedure Rules Amendment No. 4) (Miscellaneous) 2006 (SSI 2006/436), r.2 (effective September 1, 2006).

Form 41.3–B

Rule 41.3(2)

Form of notice to court under section 5(2) of the 1998 Act

IN THE HIGH COURT OF JUSTICIARY

in

HER MAJESTY'S ADVOCATE

against

[C.D.] (address or Prisoner in the Prison of {place})

To the Deputy Principal Clerk of Justiciary

The (*specify Minister or other person*) intends to join as a party to these proceedings.

(Signed)

Solicitor for (specify Minister of other person)

(Address)

NOTE
¹Inserted by the Act of Adjournal (Criminal Procedure Rules Amendment No.2) (Human Rights 1998) 2000 (S.S.I. 2000 No. 315) (effective October 2, 2000).

Form 41.4

Rule 41.4

Form of minute under Rule 41.4

IN THE HIGH COURT OF JUSTICIARY

MINUTE

By

[A.B.] (*designation and address*)

in

HER MAJESTY'S ADVOCATE

against

[C.D.] (*address* or *Prisoner in the Prison of (place)*)

1. The Minuter lodged a Notice under section 5(2) of the Human Rights Act 1998 on (*date*).

2. The position of the Minuter as to the proposed declaration of incompatibility is as follows:–

(*here specify the position of the Minuter including where appropriate a summary of any facts on which the Minuter proposes to rely, of any propositions of law which the Minuter proposes to advance and of any argument which the Minuter proposes to make.*)

(Signed)

Solicitor for (specify Minister or other person)

AMENDMENT

Form 41.4 substituted by the Act of Adjournal (Criminal Procedure Rules Amendment No. 4) (Miscellaneous) 2006 (SSI 2006/436), r.2 and Sch. Pt 2 (effective September 1, 2006).

Form 42.2

Rule 42

HIGH COURT OF JUSTICIARY

CONVENTION RIGHTS (COMPLIANCE) (SCOTLAND) ACT 2001

To:

CROWN AGENT;

SOLICITOR FOR LIFE PRISONER (*if no solicitor, to the life prisoner*);

THE GOVERNOR, HM Prison, Edinburgh;

THE GOVERNOR, HM Prison, (*enter name of prison in which life prisoner is detained*);

In the case of a life prisoner who is detained in a hospital—

THE MEDICAL DIRECTOR, (*enter name of hospital in which life prisoner is detained*) Hospital; and

SCOTTISH EXECUTIVE HEALTH DEPARTMENT (*for the attention of Ms R Toal*);

SCOTTISH EXECUTIVE JUSTICE DEPARTMENT;

SCOTTISH PRISON SERVICE HEADQUARTERS (*for the attention of Craig Oliver & Michael Godley*)

FIXING OF PUNISHMENT PART OF MANDATORY LIFE SENTENCE

Name of Life Prisoner:

Prisoner in the Prison of (*enter name of prison in which life prisoner is detained*)

In the case of a life prisoner who is detained in a hospital—

Restricted patient (who is a life prisoner) in (*enter name of hospital in which life prisoner is detained*) Hospital

TAKE NOTICE that the Court has fixed

the   day of   at 10 o'clock as a diet for the hearing of the above at   High Court.

JUSTICIARY OFFICE
LAWNMARKET
EDINBURGH
EH1 2NS

Clerk of Justiciary

Date

AMENDMENT

Form 42.2 inserted by Act of Adjournal (Criminal Procedure Rules Amendment) (Convention Rights (Compliance) (Scotland) Act 2001) 2001 (SSI 2001/479) (effective December 21, 2001) and substituted by Act of Adjournal (Criminal Procedure Rules Amendment) (Convention Rights (Compliance) (Scotland) Act 2001) 2002 (SSI 2002/137), r.2 (effective March 4, 2002).

Form 44.2

Rule 44.2

Form of notice of consent to surrender under section 7 of the International Criminal Court Act 2001

(a) Whereas on the (*enter day*) day of (*enter month*) 20 , I was arrested in pursuance of a warrant under section 2 of the International Criminal Court Act 2001 with a view to a delivery order being made providing for me to be delivered up into the custody of the International Criminal Court.

or

(b) Whereas on the (*enter day*) day of (*enter month*) 20 , I was convicted by the International Criminal Court and on the (*enter day*) day of (*enter month*) 20 , I was arrested in pursuance of a warrant under section 2 of the International Criminal Court Act 2001 with a view to a delivery order being made providing for me to be delivered up into the custody of [the International Criminal Court] [the state of enforcement (*insert name of the state of enforcement*)].

And whereas I understand that, unless I consent to my delivery, I shall have the right:

(a) to make representations at delivery proceedings as to the matters of which the competent court is to be satisfied before making a delivery order, and

(b) to make an application to the competent court at the time of the delivery proceedings for the determination of whether I was lawfully arrested in pursuance of the warrant and whether my rights have been respected, and

(c) if a delivery order is made, to seek a review of the delivery order, and

(d) not to have the delivery order executed against me until after the end of the period of 15 days beginning with the date on which the order is made.

I therefore give notice of my consent to surrender to be delivered up into the custody of the International Criminal Court or into the custody of the state of enforcement (*insert name of the state of enforcement*), whichever is appropriate. I understand that by consenting to my surrender I waive my right to seek a review of the delivery order under section 12 of the International Criminal Court Act 2001 and I consent to the Secretary of State giving directions for the execution of the delivery order before the period of 15 days has expired.

(Signed by the person to be delivered)

(*Print and sign name*)

or where it is inappropriate to act for themselves under section 7(2)(b) of the International Criminal Court Act 2001.

(Signed on their behalf)

(*Print and sign name*)

This notification was signed by the above-mentioned person in my presence on the (*enter day*) day of (*enter month*) 20 .

(Sheriff)

AMENDMENT

Form 44.2 inserted by Act of Adjournal (Criminal Procedure Rules Amendment No.2) (Miscellaneous) 2003 (SSI 2003/468), r.2(17) and Sch.3. Brought into force on October 27, 2003 in accordance with art.1.

Form of notice of waiver of the right to review under section 13 of the International Criminal Court Act 2001

(a) Whereas on the (*enter day*) day of (*enter month*) 20 , a competent court made a delivery order providing for me to be delivered up into the custody of the International Criminal Court.

or

(b) Whereas on the (*enter day*) day of (*enter month*) 20 , a competent court made a delivery order providing for me to be delivered up into the custody of the state of enforcement (*insert name of the state of enforcement*).

And whereas I understand that, unless I waive my right to seek a review of the delivery order I have the right:
(a) for the delivery order to be reviewed, and
(b) not to have the delivery order executed against me until after the end of the period of 15 days beginning with the date on which the order is made.

I therefore give notice that I waive my right to seek a review of the delivery order and I consent to the Secretary of State giving directions for the execution of the delivery order before the period of 15 days has expired.

(Signed by the person to be delivered)

(*Print and sign name*)

or where it is inappropriate to act for themselves under section 13(2)(b) of the International Criminal Court Act 2001.

(Signed on their behalf)

(*Print and sign name*)

This notification was signed by the above-mentioned person in my presence on the (*enter day*) day of (*enter month*) 20 .

(Sheriff)

AMENDMENT

Form 44.3 inserted by Act of Adjournal (Criminal Procedure Rules Amendment No.2) (Miscellaneous) 2003 (SSI 2003/468), r.2(17) and Sch.3. Brought into force on October 27, 2003 in accordance with art.1.

Form 46.2

Rule 46.2

Form of petition under section 90(1) of the Sexual Offences Act 2003

UNTO THE RIGHT HONOURABLE THE LORD JUSTICE GENERAL, THE LORD JUSTICE CLERK, and LORDS COMMISSIONERS OF JUSTICIARY

[*or* UNTO THE HONOURABLE THE SHERIFF OF (*name of sheriffdom*)

[*or* UNTO THE JUSTICES in the DISTRICT COURT OF (*name of district*)

AT (*place*)

PETITION

of

[A.B.] (*address*)

PETITIONER

HUMBLY SHEWETH:

1. That the petitioner is (*name*) and resides at (*address*).

2. That on (*date*) the court in the case of Her Majesty's Advocate [*or* Procurator Fiscal] against [C.D.], residing at (*specify address*) made a direction under section 89(1) of the Sexual Offences Act 2003 directing that any obligations imposed on young offender [C.D.] under sections 83 to 86 of the Sexual Offences Act 2003 were to be treated instead as obligations on [E.F.] as an individual having parental responsibilities in relation to [C.D.].

3. That the petitioner under section 90(1) of the Act of 2003, seeks to renew [*or* discharge] [*or* vary] the direction for the following reasons:–

(*here state reasons*)

MAY IT THEREFORE PLEASE YOUR LORDSHIP[S] [*or* THE COURT]:

(1) to appoint intimation of this petition to be made to (*specify*);

(2) to appoint parties to be heard thereon on the earliest practicable date thereafter; and

(3) thereafter, on being duly satisfied, to make an order under section 90(1) to renew [*or* discharge] [*or* vary] the parental direction [by] (*here state the terms of the variation of direction sought*) and to do further and otherwise as to your Lordship[s] [*or* to the court] shall seem proper.

ACCORDING TO JUSTICE, etc.

(*Signed*)

Advocate Depute [*or* Procurator Fiscal]

On behalf of Her Majesty's Advocate [*or*]

[Solicitor for [A.B.]]
(*address and telephone number of solicitor*)

AMENDMENT

Form 46.2 inserted by the Act of Adjournal (Criminal Procedure Rules Amendment No.2) (Sexual Offences Act 2003) 2004 (SSI 2004/206), r.2 and Sch.2 (effective May 1, 2004).

Form 47.1

Rule 47.1

Form of notice of reference under section 10(5) of the Protection of Children (Scotland) Act 2003

Reference number: (*specify*)

To: The Scottish Ministers

TAKE NOTICE that the case of the individual named below is referred to you by the court under section 10(5) of the Protection of Children (Scotland) Act 2003.

That is because–

* the individual named below has been convicted of an offence against a child;
* on convicting that individual, the court proposed to refer the case of that individual to you, the Scottish Ministers; and
* either–
  (a) the period during which an appeal against that proposed reference might have been brought has expired without an appeal being brought; or
  (b) an appeal against the proposed reference was brought within that period but the appeal has now been dismissed or abandoned.

Name of individual: (*name and any known aliases*)

Address: (*specify last known address*)

Date of birth: (*date*)

Court: (*specify*)

Date of conviction: (*date*)

Offence(s): (*specify*)

Date of offence(s): (*date*)

(*Signed*)

Depute Clerk of Justiciary [*or* Sheriff Clerk Depute]

Date: (*date*)

Telephone number: (*specify*)

E-mail address: (*specify*)

AMENDMENT

Form 47.1 inserted by the Act of Adjournal (Criminal Procedure Rules Amendment No.5) (Miscellaneous) 2004 (SSI 2004/481), r.2 and Sch., Part 2 (effective November 26, 2004).

Act of Adjournal (Criminal Procedure Rules) 1996

Rule 48.2

Form of sexual offences prevention order

SEXUAL OFFENCES PREVENTION ORDER

COURT:

DATE:

OFFENDER:

Address:

Date of birth:

THE COURT, dealing with the offender in respect of an offence listed at paragraphs 36–60 of Schedule 3 to the Sexual Offences Act 2003, [*or*, dealing with the offender in respect of a finding that he is not guilty of an offence listed in Schedule 3 to the Sexual Offences Act 2003 by reason of insanity] [*or*, dealing with the offender in respect of a finding that the offender is under a disability and has done the act charged against him in respect of an offence listed in Schedule 3 to the Sexual Offences Act 2003], namely the offence(s) of (*specify*);

AND being satisfied that it is necessary for the purposes of protecting the public or any particular member of the public from serious sexual harm from the offender;

ORDERS that the offender shall for (*specify period of not less than 5 years*) from the date of this order be prohibited from (*specify in numbered paragraphs the prohibitions imposed*).

Signed

Clerk of Court

AMENDMENT

Form 48.2 inserted by the Act of Adjournal (Criminal Procedure Rules Amendment No. 5) (Sexual Offences Prevention Orders) 2005 (SSI 2005/472), r.2(3) and Sch. (effective October 7, 2005).

Rule 48.3

Form of petition for variation, renewal or discharge of a sexual offences prevention order

UNTO THE RIGHT HONOURABLE THE LORD JUSTICE GENERAL, THE LORD JUSTICE CLERK, and LORDS COMMISSIONERS OF JUSTICIARY

[*or* UNTO THE HONOURABLE THE SHERIFF OF (*name of sheriffdom*)]

AT (*place*)

PETITION

of

HER MAJESTY'S ADVOCATE

[*or* [A.B.] (*address*)

[*or* Prisoner at the Prison of (*place*)]

PETITIONER

HUMBLY SHEWETH:

1. That there is annexed to this petition a copy of the sexual offences prevention order which was made by the sheriff at (*place*) [*or* by the High Court sitting at (*place*)] on (*date*).

[**2.** That the sexual offences prevention order has been varied or renewed as follows:– (*specify details of any previous variation or renewal*).]

2. That the petitioner seeks to renew [*or* discharge] [*or* vary] the sexual offences prevention order for the following reasons:– (*here state reasons*).

MAY IT THEREFORE PLEASE YOUR LORDSHIP[S]:

    (1) to appoint intimation of this petition to be made to [A.B.] [*or* Her Majesty's Advocate];

    (2) to appoint parties to be heard thereon on the earliest practicable date thereafter; and

    (3) thereafter, on being duly satisfied, to make an order renewing [*or* discharging] [*or* varying] the sexual offences prevention order [by] (*here state the terms of the variation of direction sought*) and to do further and otherwise as to your Lordship[s] [*or* to the court] shall seem proper.

ACCORDING TO JUSTICE, etc.

(*Signed*)

Prosecutor [*or*]

[Solicitor for [A.B.]]

(*address, e-mail address and telephone number of solicitor*)

AMENDMENT

    Form 48.3 inserted by the Act of Adjournal (Criminal Procedure Rules Amendment No. 5) (Sexual Offences Prevention Orders) 2005 (SSI 2005/472), r.2(3) and Sch. (effective October 7, 2005).

Rule 49.2

Form of financial reporting order

FINANCIAL REPORTING ORDER

COURT:

DATE:

OFFENDER:

Address:

Date of birth:

THE COURT, sentencing or otherwise dealing with the offender in respect of an offence mentioned in section 77(3) of the Serious Organised Crime and Police Act 2005, namely the offence(s) of (*specify*);

AND being satisfied that the risk of the offender committing another offence mentioned in section 77(3) of that Act is sufficiently high to justify the making of a financial reporting order;

ORDERS that during a period of (*specify length of period*) from the date of this order the offender shall make reports to (*specify person*) in respect of the period of (*specify length of period*) beginning with the date of this order and subsequent period(s) of (*specify length(s) of period(s)*), each period beginning immediately after the end of the previous one; and that each report shall be made within (*specify number*) days after the end of the period in question; and that each report shall set out (*specify particulars of financial affairs to be provided and the manner in which they are to be provided*); [and that (*specify documents*) shall be included with each report].

Signed

Clerk of Court

Amendment

Form 49.2 inserted by Act of Adjournal (Criminal Procedure Rules Amendment No.2) (Financial Reporting Orders) 2006 (SSI 2006/205), para.2(3) and Sch. (effective May 1, 2006).

Rule 49.3

Form of petition for variation or revocation of financial reporting order

UNTO THE RIGHT HONOURABLE THE LORD JUSTICE GENERAL, THE LORD JUSTICE CLERK, and THE LORDS COMMISSIONERS OF JUSTICIARY

[*or* UNTO THE HONOURABLE THE SHERIFF OF (*name of sheriffdom*)]

AT (*place*)

PETITION

of

[A.B] (*address*)

[*or* Prisoner at the Prison of (*place*)]

PETITIONER

HUMBLY SHEWETH:

1. That there is annexed to this petition a copy of the financial reporting order which was made by the sheriff at (*place*) [*or* by the High Court sitting at (*place*)] on (*date*).

[2. That the financial reporting order has been varied as follows:– (*specify details of any previous variation*)].

3. That the petitioner seeks to vary [*or* revoke] the financial reporting order for the following reasons:– (*here state reasons*).

MAY IT THEREFORE PLEASE YOUR LORDSHIP[S]:

(1)   to appoint intimation of this petition to be made to (*specify person*);

(2)   to appoint parties to be heard thereon on the earliest practicable date thereafter;

(3)   to appoint intimation of the hearing to be made to (*specify persons*); and

(4)   thereafter, on being duly satisfied, to make an order varying [*or* revoking] the financial reporting order [by] (*here state the terms of the variation sought*) and to do further and otherwise as to your Lordship[s] [*or* to the court] shall seem proper.

ACCORDING TO JUSTICE, etc.

(Signed)

Petitioner

[*or*

[Solicitor for Petitioner]

(address, e-mail address and telephone number of solicitor)

AMENDMENT

Form 49.3 inserted by Act of Adjournal (Criminal Procedure Rules Amendment No.2) (Financial Reporting Orders) 2006 (SSI 2006/205), para.2(3) and Sch. (effective May 1, 2006).

Form 50.2

Rule 50.1

Form of football banning order

FOOTBALL BANNING ORDER

COURT:

DATE:

OFFENDER:

Address:

Date of birth:

THE COURT, sentencing or otherwise dealing with the offender in respect of an offence to which section 51(4) of the Police, Public Order and Criminal Justice (Scotland) Act 2006 ("the 2006 Act") applies;

AND being satisfied that there are reasonable grounds to believe that making the football banning order would help to prevent violence or disorder at or in connection with any football matches;

AND having explained to the offender the effect of this order (including the requirements set out below);

ORDERS that the offender shall report at the police station at [*state address of police station*] within 5 days beginning with the day on which this order is made;

AND ORDERS that during a period of (*specify length of period*) from the date of this order the offender shall—

1. be prohibited from entering any premises for the purposes of attending any regulated football matches in the United Kingdom;

2. report at a police station in accordance with Chapter 1 of Part 2 of the 2006 Act in connection with regulated football matches outside the United Kingdom;

3. where a relevant event as specified in Schedule 5 to the 2006 Act occurs, notify the football banning orders authority of the prescribed information as defined in that Schedule in relation to that event within 7 days beginning with the day on which the event occurs;

[4. surrender his [*or* her] passport in accordance with Chapter 1 of Part 2 of the 2006 Act in connection with regulated football matches outside the United Kingdom;]

[5. (*set out in numbered paragraphs any additional requirements imposed by the court*)]

Signed

Clerk of Court

AMENDMENT

Form 50.2 inserted by the Act of Adjournal (Criminal Procedure Rules Amendment No. 4) (Miscellaneous) 2006 (SSI 2006/436), r.2 and Sch. Pt 3 (effective September 1, 2006).

Rule 50.3

Form of petition for variation or termination of football banning order

UNTO THE RIGHT HONOURABLE THE LORD JUSTICE GENERAL, THE LORD JUSTICE CLERK, and THE LORDS COMMISSIONERS OF JUSTICIARY

[*or* UNTO THE HONOURABLE THE SHERIFF OF (*name of sheriffdom*)]

AT (*place*)

PETITION

of

[A.B] (*address*)

PETITIONER

HUMBLY SHEWETH:

1.   That there is annexed to this petition a copy of the football banning order which was made by the sheriff at (*place*) [*or* by the High Court sitting at (*place*)] on (*date*).

[2.   That the football banning order has been varied as follows:- (*specify details of any previous variation*).]

3.   That the petitioner seeks to vary [*or* terminate] the football banning order for the following reasons:– (*here state reasons*).

MAY IT THEREFORE PLEASE YOUR LORDSHIP[S]:

(1)   to appoint intimation of this petition to be made to (*specify person*);

(2)   to appoint parties to be heard thereon on the earliest practicable date thereafter;

(3)   to appoint intimation of the hearing to be made to (*specify persons*); and

(4)   thereafter, on being duly satisfied, to make an order varying [*or* terminating] the football banning order [by] (*here state the terms of the variation sought*) and to do further and otherwise as to your Lordship[s] [*or* to the court] shall seem proper.

ACCORDING TO JUSTICE, etc.

(*Signed*)

Petitioner

[*or*

[Solicitor for Petitioner]

(*address, e-mail address and telephone number of solicitor*)

AMENDMENT

Form 50.3 inserted by the Act of Adjournal (Criminal Procedure Rules Amendment No. 4) (Miscellaneous) 2006 (SSI 2006/436), r.2 and Sch. Pt 3 (effective September 1, 2006).

Depriciation order

FORM 51.2   Form of deprivation order

Rule 51.2   DEPRIVATION ORDER

COURT:

DATE:

OFFENDER:

Address:

Date of birth:

Owner of animal[s] to which offence relates if not offender:

THE COURT, sentencing the offender in respect of an offence mentioned in section 28E(1) of the

Animal Health Act 1981 [*or* section 39(10) of the Animal Health and Welfare (Scotland) Act

2006] [*or* section 47(1) of the Animal Welfare Act 2006] namely the offence[s] of (*specify*);

[AND being satisfied on the evidence of (*specify name*) veterinary surgeon that destruction would

be in the best interests of [some of] the animal[s] to which this order applies;]

ORDERS that the offender shall be deprived of the possession and/or ownership of the animal[s]

in relation to which the offence was committed;

AND for

[(a) the destruction of (*specify animals identified in report of veterinary surgeon to be destroyed*);]

[and]

[(b) the sale of (*specify animals to be sold*);][and]

[(c) the disposal of (*specify animals to be disposed of*) by (*specify means of disposal*);]

[AND that any dependent offspring of an animal to which this order applies shall be (*specify*

provision to be made for dependent offspring);]

[APPOINTS (*specify person appointed*) as the officer responsible for securing that this order is

carried out;

REQUIRES any person possessing an animal to which this order applies to give the animal up to

the officer appointed;

PROVIDES that the officer appointed and any person acting on the officer's behalf is authorised to enter, for the purposes of securing that the order is carried out, any premises where an animal to which the order applies is kept;]

[AND (*specify any other provision considered appropriate in connection with the order*)].

Signed

Clerk of Court

Copy: Offender, Officer appointed, Owner of animal[s] if not offender

[This Order is not operational until any period for an appeal against the order or conviction

has expired or any such appeal has been withdrawn or finally determined.]

AMENDMENT

Form 51.2 inserted by the Act of Adjournal (Criminal Procedure Rules Amendment) Animal Health and Welfare etc.) 2007 (SSI 2007/238), r.2(4).

Rule 51

Forms of appeal under section 23E(II) of the Animal Health Act 1981, section 43(2) of the Animal Heath and Welfare (Scotland) Act 2006 or section 49(2) of the Animal Welfare Act 2006

FORM 51.4   Form of appeal under section 28E(11) of the Animal Health Act
                 1981, section 43(2) of the Animal Health and Welfare (Scotland)
                 Act 2006 or section 49(2) of the Animal Welfare Act 2006

Rule 51.4   IN THE HIGH COURT OF JUSTICIARY
                        [*or* IN THE SHERIFF [*or* DISTRICT] COURT AT (*place*)]
                                    NOTE OF APPEAL
                                 against deprivation orde
                         under section 28E(11) of the Animal Health Act 1981
                    [*or* section 43(2) of the Animal Health and Welfare (Scotland) Act
                                            2006]
                       [*or* section 49(2) of the Animal Welfare Act 2006]

                                            by

                                   [A.B.] (*address*)

                                       APPELLANT
                                        Against

                                  The Procurator Fiscal

                                     RESPONDENT

To: Clerk of Justiciary
Name of convicted person:
Date of birth:
[Prisoner in the Prison of:]
Date of final determination of the proceedings:
Offence to which appeal relates:
Court and name of judge:

1. A deprivation order has been made against the above named
convicted person.

2. The appellant has an interest in an animal to which the deprivation order applies as follows:–

(*specify interest in animal(s) to which order applies*).

3. The appellant appeals against the deprivation order on the following grounds:– (*here give full*

statement of all grounds of appeal).

(*Signed*)

[Solicitor for the appellant]
(*Address and telephone number of solicitor*)

(*Place and date*)

AMENDMENT

Form 51.4 inserted by the Act of Adjournal (Criminal Procedure Rules Amendment) Animal Health and Welfare etc.) 2007 (SSI 2007/238), r.2(4).

Disqualification orders

FORM 51.5   Form of disqualification order

Rule 51.5   DISQUALIFICATION ORDER

COURT:

DATE:

OFFENDER:

Address:

Date of birth:

THE COURT, sentencing the offender in respect of an offence mentioned in section 28F(1) of the

Animal Health Act 1981 [*or* section 40(13) of the Animal Health and Welfare (Scotland) Act

2006], namely the offence[s] of (*specify*);

ORDERS that the offender shall be disqualified from (*specify in numbered paragraphs the activities that the offender is disqualified from; the kind of animals the order applies to and if the order is to apply to animals over a specified maximum number*);

[during a period of (*specify length of period*) from the date of this order [*or* the date that this suspended order becomes operational]];

[AND that during a period of (*specify length of period*) from the date of this order [*or* the date this suspended order becomes operational] the offender may not apply for this order to be terminated or varied;]

[BUT the operation of this order shall be suspended for a period of (*specify period of suspension*)].

Signed

Clerk of Court

Copy: Offender

AMENDMENT

Form 51.5 inserted by the Act of Adjournal (Criminal Procedure Rules Amendment) Animal Health and Welfare etc.) 2007 (SSI 2007/238), r.2(4).

Form 51.6

Rule 51

Termination or variation of disqualification orders

FORM 51.6   Form of petition for termination or variation of disqualification order

Rule 51.6   UNTO THE RIGHT HONOURABLE THE LORD JUSTICE GENERAL,
                        THE LORD JUSTICE
                CLERK and THE LORDS COMMISSIONERS OF JUSTICIARY

                [*or* UNTO THE HONOURABLE THE SHERIFF

                OF (*name of sheriffdom*)]

                [*or* UNTO THE JUSTICES in the DISTRICT COURT OF (*name of district*)]
                AT (*place*)

                PETITION

                Of

                [A.B.] (*address*)

                [*or* Prisoner at the Prison of (*place*)]

                PETITIONER

        HUMBLY SHEWETH

        1. That there is annexed to this petition a copy of the disqualification order which was made by the court [*or* the sheriff] [*or* the High Court sitting] at (*place*) on (*date*).

        2. That no previous petition to terminate [*or* vary] the disqualification order has been made [*or* That a previous petition to terminate [*or* vary] the disqualification order was determined on (*date*)].

[3. That the disqualification order has been varied on (*date*) as follows:– (*specify details of any previous variation*).]

4. That the petitioner seeks to terminate [*or* vary] the disqualification order for the following reasons:– (*here state reasons*).

MAY IT THEREFORE PLEASE YOUR LORDSHIP[S] [*or* THE COURT]:

(1) to appoint intimation of this petition to be made to Her Majesty's Advocate;

(2) to appoint parties to be heard thereon on the earliest practicable date thereafter; and

(3) thereafter, on being duly satisfied, to make an order terminating [*or* varying] the disqualification order [by (*here state the terms of variation sought*)] and to do further and otherwise as to your Lordship[s] [*or* the court] shall seem proper.

ACCORDING TO JUSTICE, etc.

(*Signed*)

Solicitor for [A.B.]

(*address, e-mail address and telephone number of solicitor*)

AMENDMENT

Form 51.6inserted by the Act of Adjournal (Criminal Procedure Rules Amendment) Animal Health and Welfare etc.) 2007 (SSI 2007/238), r.2(4).

ANNEX: NOTES FOR COMPLETION OF FORM 31.5

[...]

AMENDMENT

Annex repealed by the Act of Adjournal (Criminal Procedure Rules Amendment No. 4) (Miscellaneous) 2006 (SSI 2006/436), r.2 (effective September 1, 2006).

Paragraph 3   SCHEDULE 3

ACTS OF ADJOURNAL REVOKED

Statutory Instrument Year and Number	*Title of Act of Adjournal*	*Extent of Revocation*
1988/110	Act of Adjournal (Consolidation) 1988	The whole Act of Adjournal
1989/48	Act of Adjournal (Consolidation Amendment) (Reference to European Court) 1989	The whole Act of Adjournal
1989/1020	Act of Adjournal (Consolidation Amendment No.2) (Forms of Warrant for Execution and Charge for Payment of Fine or Other Financial Penalty) 1989	The whole Act of Adjournal
1990/718	Act of Adjournal (Consolidation Amendment No.2) (Drug Trafficking) 1990	The whole Act of Adjournal
1990/2106	Act of Adjournal (Consolidation Amendment No.2) (Miscellaneous) 1990	The whole Act of Adjournal
1991/19	Act of Adjournal (Consolidation Amendment) (Extradition Rules and Backing of Irish Warrants) 1991	The whole Act of Adjournal
1991/847	Act of Adjournal (Consolidation Amendment No.1) 1991	The whole Act of Adjournal
1991/1916	Act of Adjournal (Consolidation Amendment No.2) (Evidence of Children) 1991	The whole Act of Adjournal
1991/2676	Act of Adjournal (Consolidation Amendment No.3) 1991	The whole Act of Adjournal
1991/2677	Act of Adjournal (Consolidation Amendment No.4) (Supervised Attendance Orders) 1991	The whole Act of Adjournal
1992/1489	Act of Adjournal (Consolidation Amendment) (Criminal Justice International Co-operation Act 1990) 1992	The whole Act of Adjournal
1993/1955	Act of Adjournal (Consolidation Amendment) (Courses for Drink-drive Offenders) 1993	The whole Act of Adjournal
1993/2391	Act of Adjournal (Consolidation Amendment No.2) (Miscellaneous) 1993	The whole Act of Adjournal
1994/1769	Act of Adjournal (Consolidation Amendment) (Miscellaneous) 1994	The whole Act of Adjournal
1995/1875	Act of Adjournal (Consolidation Amendment) (Supervised Release Orders) 1995	The whole Act of Adjournal

S. 138 - Form of Summary Complaint

S. 140 - Citation of Witnesses

S. 141 - Manner of Citation

S. 150 - Failure of accused to appear at diet where cited to appear.

S. 155 - Failure of Witnesses to Attend Court when cited

S. 156 - Detention of Witness who has failed to appear

S4-11A - Jurisdiction + powers of Sheriff Court

S5 - Powers of Sheriff in Summary Court

S.7(8) - List of offences excluded from District Court

S144-146 - The First / Pleading Diet

S144(4) - Competency + Relevancy - Objection to.

S.255 - Special Capacity

S.145 - Opportunity to Adjourn case without plea being given

S.145A - Where the Accused is not Present

S.144(2)(a) - Not Guilty plea in letter to P.F. before first diet

S.23(6) - Application for Bail

S.24(6) - Deposit of Money can be made a condition of bail

S.24(5) - Standard conditions of Bail - accused undertakes to abide by

S.24(4) - Special Conditions of Bail

S.25 - Bail - Address - fixed address to reside required

S.32 - Bail Appeals

S.147 - 40 day rule - Custody - in Summary cases

S.146 - Plea Not Guilty

S.196 - Advantages to Early Plea of Guilty

S.144(3)(b) - Guilty plea by letter - Accused not Present

Webcast 3

S.144(4)+(5) - Competency + Relevancy

Schedules 2,3+5 - Styles of Addresses & / given statutory approval different to see an argument on Relevancy (P.654-661)

Relevancy - Does the complaint properly set out the offence?

Schedule 3 (Sects 1+12) - The proper ways to aver the contravention of a statutory provision

Relevancy - Charge has to set out (i) time (ii) place/locus + (iii) method/mode by which crime has committed.

Fair notice - Obligation y Crown to give accused

Schedule 3 Sect 4(1) :- Latitude as to Time - Relevancy

Schedule 3 Sect 4(2) :- Relevancy - Latitude - Place

Place y Essence - Must be accurately specified

Mode - Complaint must set out facts + circumstances y crime $\quad$ charged crime P. 394

Competency

(1) **Jurisdiction** :- Court does not have jurisdiction to try case
   (a) Territorial Jurisdiction
   (b) Gravity y Crime - Exceeds powers y Court
   (c) Material Interest - Judge/Sheriff

(2) Title/Interest y Prosecutor

(3) Time Limits - Statutory Offences - RTA (6 months)

(4) Offences Created by Statute Triable Summarily
   S. 136 (6 months), S. 147 (40 days - custody)

(5) Summary Court - Eg. Murder, Rape

(6) Prosecution is based on Scottish Legislation which is Ultra Vires

Competency - Prosecutor - Court - Time Limits

Pleas In Bar y Trial

(A) **Non-age** - Accused is under 8

(B) **Insanity:** That the accused is insane at the time of the trial, unable to plead, or unable to give instructions to his defence

(C) **Res Judicata** - 2 ways :-
   (i) Has already been a judgement holding a Complaint on the same form as the present one to be irrelevant
   (ii) Charge libelled has already been made against the accused + been brought to a conclusion.

(D) **Socii Criminis:** That the accused is now charged with an offence in respect y which he has given evidence as a previous trial y another accused with whom he has associated at the instance y the crown

13

(E) Personal Bar :- Where the ~~accused~~ Crown by its previous actings is personally barred from insisting on a prosecution

(i) Where ~~from~~ previously deserted the case simpliciter against accused

(ii) Crown ~~ch~~ decided to deal - by way of warning rather than prose

(iii) Where publicly Crown has intimated there are to be no further proceedings against accused. [2]

(F) Entrapment :- Where accused can demonstrate ~~to he h~~ he has committed crime at instigation / persuasion of police

(G) Oppression :- Where to ~~continue with trial~~ allow case to proceed would be oppressive and + unfair, the court maintains inherent power to intervene to prevent injustice. Very Rare - only where there - prejudice so grave as ~~too~~ to be incapable of being removed by an appropriate direction by a trial judge to a jury or other appropriate action to get fair trial Sugden v HMA). "

(H) Oppression - delay at Common law - Summary Procedure - no judge - result of delay. could be expected to reach fair verdict in all the circumstances

(I) Oppression - Suspect interviewed by authorities on oath

(J) Prejudicial Publicity - Pre-trial publicity - caused prejudice so grave - no judge can put ~~it~~ from his mind + so research a fair verdict.

Separation of Charges + Trials

Motion for Separation of charges or accused - discretion of court

Separation of Charges :- material risk of real prejudice to accused if charges are tried together

Granted - Indictment - murder + breach of peace - no connection

Not granted - Connection in time + circumstance between the charges - made it proper to put on one indictment eg. alleged murder by shooting + contravention of Firearms Act

Test - real prejudice Summary courts unlikely to ~~be~~ be granted

Separation of Accused - Granted - No connection - them + their crimes

* Devolution Issue - Right of Appeal to H of L sitting as Privy Council

Devolution matter - If raised court will appoint diet for consideration

Preliminary Matter - Relevancy, Competency + Plea in Bar of Trial Raised before Plea Guilty / Not guilty tendered

Dietry Debate - First diet continued to another date

Preliminary Pleas - Raised at earliest opportunity. eg. Insanity

Right of Appeal - S.174 · Only if Sheriff grants leave of appeal
    - 2 days

Competency - Upheld - Should end matters - subject to Crown's
    right to re-raise matters in a competent fashion if possible

Relevancy - Upheld - Court - wide powers of Amendment

Amendment - S.159 - Must not alter the character of
    the offence charged (MacArthur v MacNeill)

Powery Amendment - Can be exercised at any time prior to
    the determination of the case, - Even after evidence has been
    led. S.159(1)(c)

Fundamental Nullity - P.392 Conviction will be quashed. If was not
    + never was a crime. eg. No locus specified in a crime of theft

※ _____ Webcast 4 - The Intermediate Diet. S.148

S.148(b) - Plea of guilty can be tendered - Intermediate diet - S.196

Purpose of Intermediate Diet - See S.148(1)

(1) To ascertain state of preparation of the parties
(ii) Does accused still adhere to plea of guilty
(iii) Whether the parties have fulfilled their obligations under
    S.257(1) to secure agreement as to evidence not in dispute

Postpone trial diet - S.148(2) + if further intermediate d.

Sexual Offences (Procedure + Evidence)(Scot) Act 2002
    introduced S.143 (3A)+ (3B) to Act. - In cases of a Sexual
    nature at an intermediate diet the court can consider
    · application either party - S.275 - permission - questions of a
    complainer - otherwise not allowed.

Sects 274-275   Restrictions on Procedure + Evidence Sexual cases

S.274 - Restrictions on questions in sexual offences
    designed to show complainer etc.

Summary + Solemn cases - applies to both

Crown + Defence - Applies to both

(1) Accused cannot now cross-examine complainer. — Accused must be legally represented throughout trial.

(2) Pre-trial notice of a defence of consent — Accused must give this.

(3) Necessary for defence to give evidence notice + to secure the court's approval

S.275(3) Applications for Exceptions to the Restrictions in s.274 — what applications must cover.

S.275A — Disclosure of an accused's previous convictions

Preparation For Trial

Crown must prove 2 things (1) Crime was committed
  (2) The accused committed it. — Defence must introduce a doubt.

Secs 260 + 263 — Prior Statements.
Precognition — No evidential value
Prior Statement — May have evidential value.
Police Report — Summary of incident, names + addresses of witnesses + their part in incident, action by police, apprehension, statements g/c
Labels — Documentary productions or articles
Alibi — S.149. Must give prior notice to Crown — Summary procedure.
Sexual Offences — Defence of Consent — Notice to Crown — S.149A

Defence — Can apply to crown for list of crown witnesses, take their precognitions, if won't co-operate fiscal will give at least note of evidence he expects them to give.
  Then speak to client — May accept guilt.
  Defence witness — Spoken to + obtain docs to support case
  Witnesses should be given to fiscal + court + cited

Police powers

Exercise (proper or not) very important to admissability / inadmissability of evidence
S.135 — Warrant of Apprehension + Search
Warrant of apprehension — can search for + apprehend
See secs 135 (3) + (4)
Warrant to Search — Power to search person of accused, his dwelling house + the place where he is found + to seize

...tems or documents which may afford his guilt.

Warrant to Search Suspect - May enable police to put on ID parade, take fingerprints, dental impressions - anything not too invasive

Warrant - signed by proper person

Surveillance - Regulation of Investigatory Powers Act 2000 (Scot)
 - authorisation - obtained usually senior police officer

Detention - Secs 13, 14, 15

S 13 - Initial form of detention
- Police officer can use reasonable force to require person to remain with him while he identifies person + obtains an explanation of any circumstances which have given rise to suspicion in PC's mind that an offence has been committed or is being committed.

S 14 - power to detain a person + to question him where a constable has reasonable grounds for suspecting that a person has committed an offence, punishable by imprisonment.

S 14(2) - can be detained for period not exceeding 6 hours. After 6 hours - Detainee has to be arrested, detained under some other enactment; or released from detention.

S 14(1)(a) + (b) - Why powers of detention are given.

Arrest

When Arrested - Must be told immediately the nature of the charge + subsequently any arrest must be justified by reference to that charge - ECHR Art. 5

S 17 - Right to contact a solicitor + to a private interview.

S 135(3): Right to be brought to court as ASAP.

Arrest Without Warrant - If PC has seen a crime being committed or in commission, or to prevent commission of a crime.
- Also could be justified - gravity of offence or likelihood of offender absconding

S 13(7): Detention → Arrest without warrant

S 21 - Arrest without warrant - Offences Against Children under the age of 17.

Release

S.22 - Arrested person released upon written undertaking signed by him - agrees to attend specified court. specified

* Webcast 5 - The TRIAL

S.150 - Failure of an Accused to Appear

S.151 - Illness / Absence of a Judge

Desertion of the Diet

S.152 - Prosecutor cannot proceed - make motion to desert diet for time being (pro loco et tempore). If refused + prosecutor cannot proceed - Court must (shall) desert diet simpliciter Crown cannot re-raise proceedings without appeal.

Adjournment of Trial Diet S.146 + S.137(2)

S.146(7) - Adjournment "for the" "proper conduct of the case".

S.137(2) - Joint application to adjourn case - unless unnecessary delay — 1 or both parties

Common law power to adjourn - where in the interests of justice

Proceeding to Trial

S.153 - Accused must be present throughout trial unless removed for misconduct.

Fiscal calls crown witnesses, defence cross-examines, crown re-examine.

Evidence - Hearsay Evidence S.259-262

General Rule - Hearsay Evidence - not allowed

Exceptions (1) - De Recenti - When a statement is made by a complainer shortly after an offence has been committed against them.

(2) Res Gestae - Made during the occurrence of offence

(3) Made by accused person - Made by a party + so not hearsay

PRIOR STATEMENTS

S.259 (Prior Statements) Purpose - To ensure evidence has not lost to a party because eg. death of a witness etc - S.259(2)

Conditions for admission of earlier statement include notice - party intends to proceed by having earlier statement - S.259(5)

S.260 - After asking witness questions in witness box - prior statement of witness can then asked if he wants to adopt prior statement as his evidence.

S.263 - Where prior statement can be used to undermine evidence witness gives in witness box

S.261 - Permits accused to rely on earlier statement of another accused provided notice is given

268-9 Additional Evidence / Evidence in Replication

S.268 - Both parties can lead additional evidence - before prosecutor addresses judge (closing speech)

S.269 - Evidence in Replication can be led by crown.

S.157 - No record of proceeding except etc

Witnesses . S.263

Incrimination - A witness need not answer any question which would incriminate him in for a crime for which he has not been dealt or granted immunity. If so warned judge would tend to advise him of this.

Boyes v McLeod - future proceedings. incriminatory stats. forewarned

Spouses   S.264

Spouses - Competent but not compellable

Spouse - Competent witness for accused, co-accused + crown - but not compellable except where accused is charged with an offence against him/her

Matrimonial Communications - Spouse cannot be compelled to disclose

Accused as a Witness - S.266   S.266(c)

Competent Witness - Himself or (with his consent) for co-accused

Number of co-accused - Case against 1 quits - he then becomes a
    Compellable witness for both Crown + defence S.266(1)(c)

S.271   **Children / Vulnerable Witnesses**

Judge must satisfy himself child, has sufficient intelligence to understands obligation to tell the truth.

Child under 12 - Simply admonished to tell the truth
Child over 14 - Sworn as an adult
Lord J. General (1990) suggested measures - decrease stress - child witness
In deciding what measures - appropriate - judge is to have regard to
- See S.271(2)(a) eg. whether solemn or summary, practicality
Child - Defined as under 18 - see S.271(12)(1)
Provisions only apply in High Court + Sheriff Court

            Agreed / Documentary / Uncontroversial / Routine Evidence
- Evidence court doesn't have to hear
  S.256/257 - Certain evidence can be agreed by parties

Joint Minutes Admissions - Document - Records facts agreed
Good practise to consult client first
S.279, Sched. 8, S.279A - provision - use of Copy Documents
Uncontroversial Evidence - S.258
Routine Evidence - S.280-281

S.159-160 Sched 3, Pr. 7-19 **No Case to Answer Submission** ✗

Made after the close of the Crown case - insufficient
evidence in law which is believed would enable judge to
convict the accused of any charge in the complaint, or of any
other charge which the accused could be competently convicted
in which respect of that complaint
S.159 Entitles Crown to seek amend charge + (2) to support that
alternative charge if the evidence is sufficient to support
alternative eg evidence may not support charge of theft, but
still support a conviction of reset

Judge must take the crown case at its highest + e. making the assumption that all the witnesses are to be believed
If successful charge(s) fall.

Conviction + Sentence

S.164 Court may convict of the charge, party the charge or competent alternative (Schedule 3)

Previous Convictions S.166, 266 + 270

Court should not see previous convictions until read verdict
Exceptions S 266 + 270
S.275A Sexual Offences

Webcast 4 (cont) Police Powers

Identification Parade

Early identification - more valuable

S.290 - Accused person can request Identification parade. However if identification made the witness's credibility + reliability may simply be enhanced

Police - Normally held instance of police.
Police - Issued with a form of procedure as parade which requires them to conform to comply with the rules.

Rules: Composition of parade :- Suspect plus a minimum of 5 stand-ins — should be of a similar age, height, dress + general appearance as subject. - generally conducted behind 1 way glass. Suspect can take up any position. PC conducting parade should not be involved in investigation. Witnesses brought 1 by 1 from adjoining room - walk/talk/ do anything. - "person in your statement may/may not be here. If they are tell to their number". If yes - name asked If no. - "does anyone here resemble person in statement", + again no. asked.
Duties of Solicitor - To observe + ensure that the parade is conducted in accordance with the rules. P.TO

* Identification at parades - good evidence - can substitute for failure to identify by a witness at the later trial. (Muldoon v Herron, Neeson v HMA 1984)

Webcast 6 - Sentence

Restrictions of Sentence   Secs 204 + 207

In certain circumstances the court is prevented from imposing a custodial sentence in the case of a young offender (custodial sentence ie. imprisonment or detention)

S.204(1)- Where a person is not legally represented + has not received a custodial sentence in the past- shall not impose custodial sentence unless

S. 204 (2)- Person over 21 shall not get custodial sentence unless no other method is appropriate

S.207- Person under 21

Social Enquiry Report - Must be obtained where S.204-207 apply

S.201- Court will defer sentence or adjourn case for SER

Community Service Assessment - Attached to SER where community service is canvassed

S.201- Period of Adjournment for SER must not exceed 4 weeks or on cause shown 8 weeks

Custodial Sentences   - Sect 5

Common law Offence- 3 months maximum sheriff can impose

Unless 2nd or subsequent Offence- Violence or Dishonesty or Aggravated by breach of bail conditions - 6 months maximum

Statutory Offences - Summary- Can impose longer sentences

Appearance same day- Different Complaints - Sheriff's powers are applied to each complaint separately + he can impose consecutive sentences (eg 3+3 or 6+3)

Concurrent - Defence can plead this

Admonition + Absolute Discharge

Admonition - Often a 1st Offender for a minor offence may receive a warning in this way. Is nevertheless a conviction.

Absolute Discharge - Offender discharged absolutely without conviction

Deferred Sentence secs 202

§202 - No time limit + court can discuss the conditions

Fines   secs 211-218

§211(7) - In fixing the level of the fine the court must take into account the means of the offender.

§.214 - Must allow 7 days for payment of fine

§214(2) - Unless circumstances given in this sec.

§.217 - Fine supervision Order if non-payment

§.216 - Enquiry as to reasons for non-payment

Caution - S.227

Offender can be ordered to make payment of sum of money to be forfeited by court if he be not of good behaviour during period selected by court

Probation S.228-234

Probation Order - between 6 months - 3 years - Offender expected to be of good behaviour + supervised by said worker

Other requirements to be Complied - eg. seek counselling or to attend treatment for eg. drug/alcohol addiction

§.228(5) - **Failure to Comply** - or Committed Further Offence - can be brought back + dealt with as if Probation Order never made in first place

Community Service   Secos 228-245

Unpaid work in community under supervision
Summary Conviction - between 80-240 hours
Direct Alternative to Custodial Sentence
Could be painting, cleaning etc

The Court has to be satisfied -(1) Offender consents to order
(2) Place available for him
(3) He is a suitable person to perform the work.

S.240(1) - Failure to Perform - Sanction - Offender brought
back to court + dealt with as if order hadn't been made

Webcast 7 - Appeals - Secos 173-194
Ordinary Case

(1) Judge in lower Court prepares a Report or "Stated case"
(2) Report Submitted to High Court J. sitting as an Appeal Court
    - together with whole papers of case - where
(3) Appeal heard in due course by 2/3 judges (S.273).
(4) Appeal presented by counsel/solicitor advocate. Defended- Advocate Pepur
(5) Sifting process to reduce no. of appeals.
(6) Some allowed to proceed - Some refused (Sect. 180 + 187)
(7) Grounds of Appeal - very full statement required..
(8) Grounds of Appeal - must be stated with sufficient specification

Particular Methods of Appeal
Note of Appeal   Secos 175-186

Sentence Alone - Appropriate appeal whether by person
        Convicted or prosecutor

Prosecutor may Appeal against Sentence - eg. if too lenient, or
        inappropriate or any of reasons specified in S.175(4)
S.186 - Procedure - Note of appeal must be lodged in that
    week. Must state the ground. eg. sentence excessive

Inferior judge writes a report

Appeal Court - Can affirm sentence or quash it + substitute
   different sentence whether more or less severe.

Stated Case Secs. 175-184

Used by an accused to challenge conviction + sentence, or
by prosecutor on a point of law against acquittal or
sentence.

Alleged Miscarriage of Justice (S.175(5) - sole ground of review

Miscarriage of Justice - Said to have occurred when a prosecution
results in a substantial failure to do justice to the accused
person in a matter either of conviction or sentence
   (Winning v Jeans)

Appeal by Stated Case - Can review e.g. sufficiency of evidence
to some mistake, irregularity or unfairness in proceeding
to the wrongful inclusion / exclusion of evidence.

Procedure secs 176-179

'Stated Case' - Refers to Report Prepared by Sheriff

S.176 - Application or appeal must be made - 1 week of decision
   unless period extended.

Stated Case - Include - (1) Brief history of case, (2) an account of
decision found proved upon or upon which he has proceeded
(3) narration of any law upon which his decision depended
(4) a note giving reasoning he applied.

S.179 Days sent to parties to appeal. — Who can represent
amendment adjustment
If proposed adjustment hearing in lower court will take place
Papers sent to High Court - Sifting Process etc

S.183 - In disposing of the Appeal the High Court may
      (see S.183)

(Appeals) Bill of Suspension / Advocation

Suspension - Restricted to criminal cases whereby an
illegal warrant conviction or judgement issued by an
inferior judge may be set aside by the High Court.
- Not open to a prosecutor

Prosecutor - has remedy of Advocation

Grounds of Appeal Include :-
(1) Lack of jurisdiction
(2) Oppression by the judge or prosecutor
(3) Fundamental Nullity
(4) Incompetent Sentence

Sects 34-40   Webcast 8 Solemn Procedure S.64-102

S.3. Jurisdiction + Powers - Solemn Procedure
High Court Exclusive Jurisdiction - Murder, Rape, Treason, Breach
of Duty by Magistrates
High Court - Unrestricted powers of sentence except by
Statute creating the particular offence eg. Misuse of
Drugs Act, Firearms Act
High Court - Common law crimes - Could pass life sentence - murder

Sheriff Court - Solemn Procedure - 5 Years maximum - common law crimes

S.195 Inadequate Sentencing Powers - A sheriff can remit a
case for sentence to a single judge of the High
Court of J. if he considers any sentence he can impose is
inadequate.
                                    for sentence
Case Remitted to High Court - Whole papers sent to H.C. Sheriff
prepares a report detailing the case to date + his reasons for
remitting case. Copy given to judge + the parties.

xtended Sentence (Sheriff) - S.210A + AA - A sheriff can pass an extended sentence where a person is convicted of a sexual or violent offence (or a form of abduction) + court considers - usual period of licence is inadequate to protect public from serious harm.

Sentence passed - custodial sentence (usual way) + extended period when the offender is ~~in custody in the usual way~~ released into community but subject to close supervision + a return to custody for the term of the extended sentence should he re-offend. At present - power of Sheriff - extend sentence - limited to 3 years

Criminal Procedure Route - Solemn Cases

(1) Fiscal prepares a petition - includes a warrant for the arrest of a person sometimes still known as the panel. but equally the accused.

(2) Accused brought before Court for Judicial Exam.

(3) Case continued for further exam. (usually 8 days later) or accused committed to prison until liberated in due course of law (entitled to apply for bail): in due course indictment served.

(4) Trial fixed - Sheriff Court or High Court

(5) Trial takes place before judge + jury.

(6) Verdict - jury

(7) Appeal can be taken

S.34   The Petition
       presented

In name of PF. ~~Sent~~ to Sheriff:-

(1) Name + address of accused
(2) A Criminal charges to be laid against him
(3) Craves or requests court to grant the necessary warrants
(a) Arrest individual.
(b) Search his premises+ person + place in which he is found
(c) Cite witnesses for precognition to produce writs or other articles of evidence
(d) To commit accused after exam. to further exam. or until liberated in due course of law

Custody Statement - Accompanies Petition - Sets out grounds by which person is bound

Judicial Examination — seeks P.35-38

(1) Accused entitled to make a plea or declaration

(2) Prosecutor may intimate to court he wishes to examine the accused.

(3) S.36 - Prosecutor entitled to ask questions of accused directed generally towards any defence accused may have. May not carry out a cross-exam.

(4) S.36(5) : Prosecutor restricted - May not carry out a cross-exam.

(5) Declaration & & exam - recorded on tape - transcript produced

Generally happens

Accused identified - Solicitor intimates he has "No plea, no declaration" but has a request for bail."

If no Prosecutor no exam - (1) Discussion regarding bail,
(2) Discussion whether accused to be committed for further exam. or committed until liberated in due course of law (S.40)

Bail - First Appearance - Court obliged to consider bail
Subsequent Appearance - Only consider bail on written bail ~~Court~~ application

Time S.65 (Limits)

Tried on Indictment - Must begin within 12 months of date accused first appears on petition - Otherwise proceedings fall + no further proceedings competent on those charges

High Court - Preliminary Hearing must start within 11 months of first appearance on petition

These periods do not apply where warrant has been issued against an accused for failing to appear in the case

Time Limits Applying to Those in Custody

80 Days - An accused person is entitled to bail if he is detained for longer than 80 days from full committal without having an indictment served on him.

110 days - In High C. an accused may not be detained for more than 110 days without a preliminary hearing having commenced.

140 days - In High C. his trial must have commenced within 140 days.

110 days - In Sheriff C. trial must commence within 110 days of full committal.

Result of failure to Keep to Time Limits - Accused is entitled to bail.

No High C. Preliminary Hearing - 11 month + 110 day requirement don't apply.

On Cause Shown - These periods may all be extended by High C. judge or sheriff "on cause shown". Have even been extended retrospectively.

The Indictment s. 66-70

Following full committal Fiscal will carry out precognition of witnesses + assemble a report known as Precognition for consideration of Crown Counsel at Crown Office.

Fiscal recommendations - charges to be presented + venue.

Accused solicitor - Receives provisional list of witnesses

* Crown - general obligation to disclose case to defence of its case

Indictment Name of Lord Adv. - Comprises charges - List of doc productions (labels) + witnesses Crown intends to call to prove case - Often Notice of Uncontroversial Evidence

Previous Convictions - Notice of - attached to Indictment

Served on Accused. In H. Court - appended notice of preliminary hearing. Sheriff C- first diet + trial diet

The Preliminary Hearing

Now mandatory in H. Cases - although can be dispensed with in a minority of cases. Allows court to deal with :-

(1) Preliminary pleas to Relevancy + Competency

(2) Preliminary issues eg. vulnerable witnesses applications, applications to lead evidence in cases of a sexual nature

(3) Case Informed - (a) State of preparation of parties - parties must co-operate + prepare - "written record" - dealing eg. preparation. witnesses essential for trial + evidence which can be agreed.

· (b) Declaration - accused - informed of benefits of guilty plea

First Diet secs 71 + 72

Sheriff Court - Relevancy + Competency can be decided. State of preparation of parties assessed - which witnesses are essential + Sheriff - review conditions of bail.

Rights of Appeal

S.74 - Rights of Appeal from prelim. hearings or 1st diet - only if leave to appeal granted by Sheriff / Judge

Guilty Pleas - S.76

Special Defences) Defence Witnesses / Productions S.78

Solemn cases - range of special defences which need to be intimated is expanded.
Special Ds include alibi, self-defence, insanity automatism, incrimination (both of a 3rd party + of accused), co-ercion + now consent in sexual cases

Only special defence, where defence believe it is must necessarily lead to be acquittal of accused (Mc Brade v HMA) - Lohinson to need to intimate a special defence

S.89 - Copies of special defence given to jury at beginning of trial

S.85 78 - Defence must lodge list of witnesses + also notice of intention to crossack hole character complainer

Guilty Plea

S76 - Accused can intimate to crown or solemn case by letter desire to plead guilty

If crown accepts restricted indocement can be served (without witnesses or producations) + containing only the charges to which he wishes to plead guilty

Advice - "S 76 diet" - fixed - H.C. or S.C for the plea to be taken + sentence imposed.

Webcast 9

Mental Health - S.52

S.61 - Requirements to medical evidence

S.58 Hospital Order Guardianship

S.55, 56, 57
Public Repress Prosecution - Serious harm